SOMETHING ABOUT THE AUTHOR®

Something about
the Author *was named
an "Outstanding
Reference Source,"
the highest honor given
by the American
Library Association
Reference and Adult
Services Division.*

ISSN 0276-816X

SOMETHING ABOUT THE AUTHOR®

**Facts and Pictures about Authors
and Illustrators of Books for Young People**

volume 237

GALE
CENGAGE Learning®

Detroit • New York • San Francisco • New Haven, Conn • Waterville, Maine • London

Something about the Author, Volume 237

Project Editor: Lisa Kumar

Permissions: Sheila Spencer

Imaging and Multimedia: Sheila Spencer, John Watkins

Composition and Electronic Capture: Amy Darga

Manufacturing: Rhonda Dover

Product Manager: Mary Onorato

For product information and technology assistance, contact us at **Gale Customer Support, 1-800-877-4253.** For permission to use material from this text or product, submit all requests online at **www.cengage.com/permissions.** Further permissions questions can be emailed to **permissionrequest@cengage.com**

Since this page cannot legibly accommodate all copyright notices, the acknowledgments constitute an extension of the copyright notice.

While every effort has been made to ensure the reliability of the information presented in this publication, Gale, a part of Cengage Learning, does not guarantee the accuracy of the data contained herein. Gale accepts no payment for listing; and inclusion in the publication of any organization, agency, institution, publication, service, or individual does not imply endorsement of the editors or publisher. Errors brought to the attention of the publisher and verified to the satisfaction of the publisher will be corrected in future editions.

EDITORIAL DATA PRIVACY POLICY: Does this publication contain information about you as an individual? If so, for more information about our editorial data privacy policies, please see our Privacy Statement at www.gale.cengage.com.

Gale, Cengage Learning
27500 Drake Rd.
Farmington Hills, MI, 48331-3535

LIBRARY OF CONGRESS CATALOG CARD NUMBER 62-52046

ISBN-13: 978-1-4144-8093-0
ISBN-10: 1-4144-8093-8

ISSN 0276-816X

This title is also available as an e-book.
ISBN-13: 978-1-4144-8239-2
ISBN-10: 1-4144-8239-6
Contact your Gale, Cengage Learning sales representative for ordering information.

Printed in Mexico
1 2 3 4 5 6 7 16 15 14 13 12

Contents

Authors in Forthcoming Volumes vii

Introduction ix

SATA Product Advisory Board xi

Illustrations Index 187

Author Index 223

A

Abramson, Andra Serlin 1

B

Badoe, Adwoa 2

Baker, E.D. 4

Barker, Claire 1969- 6

Bartoletti, Susan Campbell 1958- 6

Bladek, John 1963(?)- 14

Bleiman, Andrew 14

Bow, Erin 1972- 16

Brennan, Caitlin
    See Tarr, Judith 140

Bristow, David 17

Bristow, David L.
    See Bristow, David 17

Bryan, Kathleen
    See Tarr, Judith 140

C

Clark, Karen Henry 19

Costa Bates, Janet 1959- 19

Crowley, James 1969- 20

Cummings, Priscilla 1951- 21

D

de Quidt, Jeremy 26

Donovan, Jane Monroe 27

Downing, Erin 1976- 28

E

Eagland, Jane 30

Ehlert, Lois 1934- 31

Ehlert, Lois Jane
    See Ehlert, Lois 31

F

Fixmer, Elizabeth 39

Friar, Joanne 40

Friar, Joanne H.
    See Friar, Joanne 40

G

Geisert, Arthur 1941- 43

Geisert, Arthur Frederick
    See Geisert, Arthur 43

Gonzalez, Thomas 1959- 49

H

Hamilton, Emma Walton 1962- 50

Hills, Tad 53

Hudson, Cheryl Willis 1948- 56

J

Jones, Tim 60

Julian, Russell 1975- 60

K

Kate, Lauren 1981- 62

Keeter, Susan 63

Keplinger, Kody 1991- 65

Kramer, Andrew 66

Kulling, Monica 1952- 66

L

Lackey, Mercedes 1950- 71

le Vann, Kate 78

Light, Steve 79

Logan, Laura 81

Lynn, Sarah 82

M

Mair, J. Samia 83

Mair, Julie Samia
   See Mair, J. Samia 83

Maltbie, P.I. 84

Maltbie, Priscilla
   See Maltbie, P.I. 84

Mariz, Rae 1981- 86

McBride, Lish 87

McCurdy, Michael 1942- 88

McCurdy, Michael Charles
   See McCurdy, Michael 88

Mehling, Carl 1969(?)- 96

Moore, Sean L. 1976- 97

Murphy, Stuart J. 1942- 98

N

Noteboom, Erin
   See Bow, Erin 16

P

Perkins, Mitali 1963- 105

Pham, LeUyen 1973- 109

Price, Charlie 114

Q

Quimby, Laura 117

R

Rees, Douglas 1947- 118

Ries, Lori 122

Roth, Stephanie
   See Sisson, Stephanie Roth 129

Ryan, Rob 1962- 125

S

Scheerger, Sarah Lynn
   See Lynn, Sarah 82

Schneider, Katy 127

Serlin, Andra
   See Abramson, Andra Serlin 1

Sexton, Brenda 1957- 129

Sisson, Stephanie Roth 129

Soderberg, Erin Kate
   See Downing, Erin 28

Souders, Taryn 1977- 133

Stiefvater, Maggie 1981- 133

Sturman, Jennifer 137

T

Tanner, Lian 1951- 139

Tarr, Judith 1955- 140

Thake, Richard 1938- 145

Titcomb, Gordon 146

Toffler-Corrie, Laura 146

Tuttle, Cameron 147

V

Venuti, Kristin Clark 149

W

Wagner, Hilary 150

Walsh, Pat 1954- 151

Watson, Geoff 1978- 153

Watson, Stephanie 1979- 154

Wells, Rosemary 1943- 155

Wesselhoeft, Conrad 1953- 166

Wheeler, Lisa 1963- 168

Willis, Jeanne 1959- 174

Y

Young, Karen Romano 1959- 182

Z

Zappitello, Beth 186

Authors in Forthcoming Volumes

Below are some of the authors and illustrators that will be featured in upcoming volumes of *SATA*. These include new entries on the swiftly rising stars of the field, as well as completely revised and updated entries (indicated with *) on some of the most notable and best-loved creators of books for children.

*Bob Barner ▮ Based in San Francisco, Barner has illustrated numerous picture books, including many which he has written himself. His first two books, *Elephant Facts* and the fanciful and award-winning *The Elephants' Visit*, were sparked by his interest in pachyderms, and he has continued to share his curiosity about dinosaurs, bugs, penguins, bears, dogs, and fish in his mixed-media illustrations which combine pen-and-ink, watercolor, and cut- and torn-paper collage. He also takes on a more unusual topic in *The Day of the Dead/El día de los muertos,* a bilingual picture book that focuses on a well-known Latin-American holiday.

Cassandra Clare ▮ With her debut novel, *City of Bones,* Clare introduces a complex cast of characters and a vibrant, supernatural otherworld that has proved popular not only with readers but with reviewers as well. The works in her "Mortal Instruments" urban fantasy series and its steampunk prequels, the "Infernal Devices" novels, have found their way onto numerous bestseller lists and earned a host of honors from the American Library Association and the International Reading Association, among other organizations.

Hillary Duff ▮ Duff became a household name and a worldwide phenomenon thanks to her starring role in the wildly popular Disney television series *Lizzie McGuire*. With her wholesome blonde looks and exuberant personality, she stepped into the part of the likable middle-schooler with ease and parlayed that success into a thriving film and television career before making her mark as a singer. In 2010 she expanded her creative efforts to writing, producing the teen paranormal romance *Elixir.*

Christ Grabenstein ▮ Grabenstein first gained fame in the literary world with his "John Ceepak" mystery series, which follows the adventures of police officer John Ceepak, a veteran of the Iraq war who lives his life by a strict moral code. In 2008 he expanded his reading audience to younger readers with *The Crossroads,* a ghost story that earned him both an Anthony award and an Agatha award. Fans of *The Crossroads* have continued to be pulled into the author's ghostly fantasy in sequels that include *The Hanging Hill* and *The Smoky Corridor.*

Mark Peter Hughes ▮ Hughes entertains preteens and young adults in his engaging novels *I Am the Wallpaper* and *A Crack in the Sky,* as well as his companion novels *Lemonade Mouth* and *Lemonade Mouth Puckers Up.* Praised for creating realistic teen char-acters with relatable worries, fears, and foibles, his novels also tap into adolescent ambitions regarding fitting in, being heard and acknowledged, and making a difference.

*Peter Mandel ▮ In addition to his work as an award-winning travel writer, where his exploits include slashing through jungles, hiking the length of a suburban strip mall, and taking a taxicab from Washington, DC, to Manhattan, Mandel shares his witty take on life with younger readers in children's books that include *Red Cat, White Cat, Say Hey: A Song of Willie Mays*, and *Jackhammer Sam.* As a journalist, his travel pieces have appeared in well-known periodicals ranging from the *Washington Post* and *Chicago Tribune* to magazines such as *Reader's Digest* and *National Geographic Kids.*

*Rick Riordan ▮ Known to adult readers as the award-winning author of the "Tres Navarre" mystery novels, Riordan has also earned fans through his "Percy Jackson and the Olympians" series of young-adult novels. In addition to these books, which focus on a hyperactive middle schooler who is also the son of the Greek god Poseidon, the author serves up similar adventures in his five-novel "Heroes of Olympus" series, and he turns to Egyptian mythology in *The Red Pyramid,* the first novel in his "Kane Family Chronicles" saga for middle-grade readers.

*Howard Schwartz ▮ Known for his focus on Jewish traditions, Schwartz has produced award-winning fiction, nonfiction, and poetry, as well as editing several anthologies, in his long career writing for both children and adults. Many of his works retell ancient folktales, reflecting his belief in the importance of passing cultural traditions from one generation to the next. He often finds inspiration in biblical, midrashic, and kabbalistic lore, producing dreamy and mysterious stories grounded in Jewish mythology and history.

Michele Torrey ▮ Trained as a microbiologist, Torrey worked as a laboratory scientist for many years before producing her first book for children. Tapping her long-held interest in history, her middle-grade historical novels *Bottles of Eight and Pieces of Rum* and *Sisters unto Death* were published in the late 1990s. She has continued to share her love of adventure in *To the Edge of the World* and her "Chronicles of Courage" series, while melding her scientific expertise with storytelling in her engaging "Doyle and Fossey Science Detectives" books.

*Gita Wolf ▮ Born and raised in India, author and publisher Wolf has written educational titles as well as picture books that feature illustrations featuring traditional art from her native country. In her works for children, which include *The Very Hungry Lion, The Flight of the Mermaid, The Tree Girl,* and *The Night Life of Trees,* as well as *Monkey Photo* and *The Churki-Burki Book of Rhyme,* she approaches traditional stories from a contemporary perspective: her protagonists are often resourceful girls who combat the odds to make positive changes in the world around them.

Introduction

Something about the Author (*SATA*) is an ongoing reference series that examines the lives and works of authors and illustrators of books for children. *SATA* includes not only well-known writers and artists but also less prominent individuals whose works are just coming to be recognized. This series is often the only readily available information source on emerging authors and illustrators. You'll find *SATA* informative and entertaining, whether you are a student, a librarian, an English teacher, a parent, or simply an adult who enjoys children's literature.

What's Inside *SATA*

SATA provides detailed information about authors and illustrators who span the full time range of children's literature, from early figures like John Newbery and L. Frank Baum to contemporary figures like Judy Blume and Richard Peck. Authors in the series represent primarily English-speaking countries, particularly the United States, Canada, and the United Kingdom. Also included, however, are authors from around the world whose works are available in English translation. The writings represented in *SATA* include those created intentionally for children and young adults as well as those written for a general audience and known to interest younger readers. These writings cover the entire spectrum of children's literature, including picture books, humor, folk and fairy tales, animal stories, mystery and adventure, science fiction and fantasy, historical fiction, poetry and nonsense verse, drama, biography, and nonfiction. Obituaries are also included in *SATA* and are intended not only as death notices but also as concise overviews of people's lives and work. Additionally, each edition features newly revised and updated entries for a selection of *SATA* listees who remain of interest to today's readers and who have been active enough to require extensive revisions of their earlier biographies.

Autobiography Feature

Beginning with Volume 103, many volumes of *SATA* feature one or more specially commissioned autobiographical essays. These unique essays, averaging about ten thousand words in length and illustrated with an abundance of personal photos, present an entertaining and informative first-person perspective on the lives and careers of prominent authors and illustrators profiled in *SATA*.

Two Convenient Indexes

In response to suggestions from librarians, *SATA* indexes no longer appear in every volume but are included in alternate (odd-numbered) volumes of the series, beginning with Volume 57.

SATA continues to include two indexes that cumulate with each alternate volume: the Illustrations Index, arranged by the name of the illustrator, gives the number of the volume and page where the illustrator's work appears in the current volume as well as all preceding volumes in the series; the Author Index gives the number of the volume in which a person's biographical sketch, autobiographical essay, or obituary appears in the current volume as well as all preceding volumes in the series.

These indexes also include references to authors and illustrators who appear in *Gale's Yesterday's Authors of Books for Children, Children's Literature Review,* and *Something about the Author Autobiography Series.*

Easy-to-Use Entry Format

Whether you're already familiar with the *SATA* series or just getting acquainted, you will want to be aware of the kind of information that an entry provides. In every *SATA* entry the editors attempt to give as complete a picture of the person's life and work as possible. A typical entry in *SATA* includes the following clearly labeled information sections:

PERSONAL: date and place of birth and death, parents' names and occupations, name of spouse, date of marriage, names of children, educational institutions attended, degrees received, religious and political affiliations, hobbies and other interests.

ADDRESSES: complete home, office, electronic mail, and agent addresses, whenever available.

CAREER: name of employer, position, and dates for each career post; art exhibitions; military service; memberships and offices held in professional and civic organizations.

MEMBER: professional, civic, and other association memberships and any official posts held.

AWARDS, HONORS: literary and professional awards received.

WRITINGS: title-by-title chronological bibliography of books written and/or illustrated, listed by genre when known; lists of other notable publications, such as plays, screenplays, and periodical contributions.

ADAPTATIONS: a list of films, television programs, plays, CD-ROMs, recordings, and other media presentations that have been adapted from the author's work.

WORK IN PROGRESS: description of projects in progress.

SIDELIGHTS: a biographical portrait of the author or illustrator's development, either directly from the biographee—and often written specifically for the *SATA* entry—or gathered from diaries, letters, interviews, or other published sources.

BIOGRAPHICAL AND CRITICAL SOURCES: cites sources quoted in "Sidelights" along with references for further reading.

EXTENSIVE ILLUSTRATIONS: photographs, movie stills, book illustrations, and other interesting visual materials supplement the text.

How a *SATA* Entry Is Compiled

SATA editors examine a wide variety of published sources to gather information for an entry. Biographical and bibliographic sources are consulted, as are book reviews, feature articles, published interviews, and material sometimes obtained from the biographee's family, publishers, agent, or other associates. Whenever possible, the author or illustrator is sent a copy of the entry to check for accuracy and completeness.

Entries that have not been verified by the biographees or their representatives are marked with an asterisk (*).

Contact the Editor

We encourage our readers to examine the entire *SATA* series. Please write and tell us if we can make *SATA* even more helpful to you. Give your comments and suggestions to the editor:

Editor
Something about the Author
Gale, Cengage Learning
27500 Drake Rd.
Farmington Hills MI 48331-3535

Toll-free: 800-877-GALE
Fax: 248-699-8070

Something about the Author Product Advisory Board

The editors of *Something about the Author* are dedicated to maintaining a high standard of excellence by publishing comprehensive, accurate, and highly readable entries on a wide array of writers for children and young adults. In addition to the quality of the content, the editors take pride in the graphic design of the series, which is intended to be orderly yet inviting, allowing readers to utilize the pages of *SATA* easily and with efficiency. Despite the longevity of the *SATA* print series, and the success of its format, we are mindful that the vitality of a literary reference product is dependent on its ability to serve its users over time. As literature, and attitudes about literature, constantly evolve, so do the reference needs of students, teachers, scholars, journalists, researchers, and book club members. To be certain that we continue to keep pace with the expectations of our customers, the editors of *SATA* listen carefully to their comments regarding the value, utility, and quality of the series. Librarians, who have firsthand knowledge of the needs of library users, are a valuable resource for us. The *Something about the Author* Product Advisory Board, made up of school, public, and academic librarians, is a forum to promote focused feedback about *SATA* on a regular basis. The nine-member advisory board includes the following individuals, whom the editors wish to thank for sharing their expertise:

something ABOUT the AUThOR

ABRAMSON, Andra Serlin
(Andra Serlin)

Personal

Married; children: one daughter. *Education:* New York University, B.F.A. (film/television studies), 1992; University of Scranton, M.S. (reading education), 2002.

Addresses

Home—Gaithersburg, MD. *Office*—FlirtyGirl Productions, 1739 Lombard St., Philadelphia, PA 19146.

Career

Author and editor. Dial Books for Young Readers, New York, NY, associate editor, 1995-98; Highlights for Children (magazine), associate editor, 1999-2001; Running Press, Philadelphia, PA, senior editor, 2003-06; Flirty Girl Productions (book and Web packager), Philadelphia, cofounder, beginning 2006. Presenter at schools.

Writings

FOR CHILDREN

(As Andra Serlin) *Super Sheep Saves the Day* (interactive board book), illustrated by Paul Nicholls and Richard Codor, Running Press Kids (Philadelphia, PA), 2004.

Escape from the Towers, Crabtree Pub. Co. (New York, NY), 2009.
Take Me out to the Ballgame: A Trip to a Major League Baseball Game, Applesauce Press, 2009.
(With Jason Brougham and Carl Mehling) *Inside Dinosaurs,* Sterling Innovation (New York, NY), 2010.
(With Mordecai-Mark Mac Low) *Inside Stars,* Sterling Innovation (New York, NY), 2011.

Also author of *Building Your Family Tree* (interactive gift book).

"UP CLOSE" NONFICTION SERIES

Fighter Planes up Close, Sterling (New York, NY), 2007.
Fire Engines up Close, Sterling (New York, NY), 2007.
Heavy Equipment up Close, Sterling (New York, NY), 2007.
Submarines up Close, Sterling (New York, NY), 2007.
Race Cars up Close, Sterling (New York, NY), 2008.
Ships up Close, Sterling (New York, NY), 2008.

Sidelights

Andra Serlin Abramson began her editorial career in children's publishing and now writes books for children and preteens. Series nonfiction by Abramson include contributions to the "Up Close" and "Inside" series, well-respected resources for report-writers in the upper-elementary grades, as well as the sports-related *Take Me out to the Ballgame: A Trip to a Major League*

Baseball Game. Her books are noted for pairing numerous illustrations with an information-packed text that is designed to attract even reluctant readers. Abramson enjoys writing about contemporary topics that focus on technology and science. In *Escape from the Towers* she also turns to current history, using a countdown approach that pairs photographs and diagrams with a text featuring first-hand descriptions written by witnesses to the terrorist attacks on the World Trade Center on September 11, 2001.

Abramson's contributions to the "Up Close" series focus on transportation, making her books especially popular among preteen boys. Characteristic of the series, *Fighter Planes up Close* features interactive elements, such as fold-out components and photographs that allow readers to learn how a military fighter jet is engineered, constructed, and operated. Tractors, cultivators, excavators, bulldozers, and even a machine used to move equipment on space-shuttle missions: all these and more are described in *Heavy Equipment up Close,* from their specific use and design to their power plant and operation. Readers pick up speed in *Race Cars up Close,* as they get a peek into Formula One and NASCAR racers, from their evolving design and engineering to the fuel and tires that help such vehicles attain record-breaking raceway speeds.

Recommending the "Up Close" books for their large-scale illustrations, Eldon Younce predicted in *School Library Journal* that Abramson's contributions "will be immensely popular" among the series' intended readership. *Heavy Equipment up Close* "is tailor-made for children known to gaze longingly at construction sites," asserted *Booklist* contributor Jennifer Mattson, the critic also citing the book's "terrific mix of fun technical vocabulary . . . and trivia ripe for sharing."

Inside Dinosaurs finds Abramson teaming up with noted paleontologist Carl Mehling and anthropological illustrator Jason Brougham, both of whom are on staff at New York City's American Museum of Natural History. *Inside Dinosaurs* "is sure to fascinate future paleontologists" who will enjoy its mix of "riveting details and awesome art," according to *School Library Journal* contributor Heather Acerro, while in *Science Scope* David Gillam cited the book's fold-out illustrations, charts and graphs, and a fact-filled text that presents "an inside look at the tools of science." "Middle-level readers will return to [*Inside Dinosaurs*] . . . again and again for more details," Gillam predicted, and a *Kirkus Reviews* writer recommended the book as a "pleasantly specific overview" of both "dinosaurs' distinctive physical characteristics" and the discoveries of "paleontologists in both field and lab."

Biographical and Critical Sources

PERIODICALS

Booklist, April 1, 2008, Jennifer Mattson, review of *Heavy Equipment up Close,* p. 72.

Kirkus Reviews, September 1, 2010, review of *Inside Dinosaurs.*

School Library Journal, April, 2008, Eldon Younce, reviews of *Fighter Planes up Close, Heavy Equipment up Close, Fire Engines up Close,* and *Submarines up Close,* all p. 127; December, 2010, Heather Acerro, review of *Inside Dinosaurs,* p. 133.

Science Scope, David Gillam, review of *Inside Dinosaurs,* p. 68.

ONLINE

Andra Abramson Home Page, http://www.andraabramson. com (January 2, 2012).

FlirtyGirl Productions Web site, http://www.flirtygirl.com/ (January 2, 2012).*

* * *

BADOE, Adwoa

Personal

Born in Ghana; married Fulé Badoe (a performer and educator). *Education:* Kwame Nkrumah University of Science and Technology, medical degree, 1988. *Hobbies and other interests:* History, writing, dancing, dining out.

Addresses

Home—Guelph, Ontario, Canada. *E-mail*—adwoa@ afroculture.com.

Career

Author, storyteller, educator, and dancer. Afroculture, Guelph, Ontario, Canada, co-owner and artistic director, 2002—. Performer at Toronto Storytelling Festival, Montreal Storytelling Festival, and Eden Mills Writers Festival, among others.

Member

Women of the World, Canadian Society of Children's Authors, Illustrators and Performers, Ghana Medical Association, Guelph Arts Council.

Awards, Honors

Word of Mouth grant, Ontario Arts Council; Ghanaian Women's Courage Award, Endless Possibilities and Hope Development Organization, 2005; Ghanaian Canadian Achievement Award for Arts and Culture, *Ghanaian News,* 2006; YMCA/YWCA Woman of Distinction Award, 2007; designated "Storykeeper," Storytellers of Canada Conference, 2007.

Writings

Crabs for Dinner, illustrated by Belinda Ageda, Sister Vision (Toronto, Ontario, Canada), 1995.

The Queen's New Shoes, illustrated by Belinda Ageda, Women's Press (Toronto, Ontario, Canada), 1998.

The Pot of Wisdom: Ananse Stories, illustrated by Baba Wagué Diakité, Douglas & McIntyre (Toronto, Ontario, Canada), 2001.

Nana's Cold Days, illustrated by Bushra Junaid, Groundwood Books/Douglas & McIntyre (Toronto, Ontario, Canada), 2002.

The Taste of Words: A Guide to Vibrant Storytelling, [Guelph, Ontario, Canada], 2009.

Between Sisters (novel), Groundwood Books/House of Anansi Press (Toronto, Ontario, Canada), 2010.

Also author of *Street Girls: The Project, Memuna's Baby, A Wedding Story, Radio Rescue, Kobby's Trolley, Mr. Bempong's House, Papa Jonah, The Chief's Telephone,* and *The Runaway Bicycle,* all published by Smartline (Accra, Ghana).

Writer, choreographer, and director of *The River Bride* (dance and drum spoken-word performance); author (with Kwame Badoe) of *The Dance of the Elifons* (audiotape for children).

Sidelights

A native of Ghana who now lives in Canada, Adwoa Badoe is the author of *Nana's Cold Days,* which looks at the immigrant experience, and *Between Sisters,* a young-adult novel set in the author's homeland. Badoe, who trained as a physician in Ghana, is a tireless promoter of African cultural arts and now works as a storyteller, dance instructor, and performer in her adopted country. Among the many honors she has received is the Ghanaian Women's Courage Award, given in recognition of her contributions to art and literature.

After releasing the picture books *Crabs for Dinner* and *The Queen's New Shoes,* Badoe garnered strong reviews for her third work, *The Pot of Wisdom: Ananse Stories,* a collection of trickster tales. Inspired by stories that the author heard while growing up in Ghana, *The Pot of Wisdom* offers ten tales featuring the folkloric spider, including "Why Ananse Lives on the Ceiling," "Ananse the Even-Handed Judge," and the title story. "Ananse is like any human being—imperfect and fragile—and readers may recognize their own shortcomings in these tales," Evette Signarowski commented in *Resource Links,* and *Horn Book* reviewer Margaret A. Bush remarked that the "well-paced stories offer readers and storytellers enjoyable glimpses into Ananse's triumphs and humiliations." Although many of the stories will be familiar to readers, a critic in *Kirkus Reviews* observed that "the author's distinctive voice and variations give them fresh life," and Jeffrey Canton, writing in *Quill & Quire,* similarly noted that Badoe "has certainly infused these retellings with her own particular spicy storytelling voice."

An African woman finds it difficult to adjust to life in an unfamiliar setting in *Nana's Cold Days,* a picture book by Badoe. After stepping off the airplane that has brought her from Africa to North America, Nana immediately complains of the wintry conditions and takes to her bed, refusing to come out from beneath the warmth of her blankets. Although her relatives try to entice her with food and music, Nana will not leave her comfortable surroundings until a doctor proposes that breathing in cold air will help her recover from her croup. "Nana's stubborn reaction and her family's efforts to rouse her are amusingly and gently presented," Gwyneth Evans stated in *Quill & Quire,* and a *Publishers Weekly* contributor maintained that Badoe infuses [her] tale with a spicy sampling of African culture, describing 'hi-life music from Africa' and traditional palaver sauce and plantains."

Between Sisters focuses on Gloria Bampo, an uneducated sixteen year old who lives with her unemployed father and ailing mother in Accra. After failing her school exams, Gloria begins working as a nanny for a distant relative, Christine, a doctor who takes the teen under her wing and teaches her to read. As Gloria's economic situation improves, she begins testing the limits of her newfound freedom, which includes gaining attention from a host of suitors. Badeo "vividly evokes the contemporary setting of middle-class Ghana," Hazel Rochman stated in *Booklist,* and Betty Carter com-

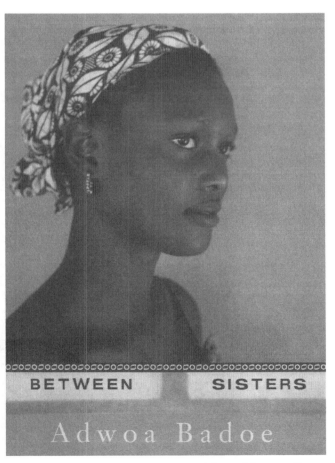

Cover of Adwoa Badoe's poignant young-adult novel **Between Sisters,** *which is set in the author's native Ghana.* (Groundwood Books, 2010. Cover photograph by Mimi Mollica/Corbis. Reproduced by permission of Groundwood Books.)

mented in *Horn Book* that the novel "is as particular to the well-detailed West African setting as it is universal in subject and theme." According to a contributor in *Kirkus Reviews,* "Badoe's sharp and engaging prose unfolds the story with spryness, deftly navigating readers through heady social issues."

Biographical and Critical Sources

PERIODICALS

Booklist, December 1, 2001, GraceAnne A. DeCandido, review of *The Pot of Wisdom: Ananse Stories,* p. 641; October 1, 2010, Hazel Rochman, review of *Between Sisters,* p. 82.

Canadian Review of Materials, September 3, 2010, Ruth Latta, review of *Between Sisters.*

Horn Book, January-February, 2002, Margaret A. Bush, review of *The Pot of Wisdom,* p. 87; November-December, 2010, Betty Carter, review of *Between Sisters,* p. 84.

Kirkus Reviews, August 15, 2001, review of *The Pot of Wisdom*; August 15, 2010, review of *Between Sisters.*

Publishers Weekly, December 24, 2001, review of *The Pot of Wisdom,* p. 67; September 23, 2002, review of *Nana's Cold Days,* p. 71.

Quill & Quire, January, 2002, Jeffrey Canton, review of *The Pot of Wisdom*; October, 2002, Gwyneth Evans, review of *Nana's Cold Days.*

Resource Links, December, 2001, Evette Signarowski, review of *The Pot of Wisdom,* p. 13.

School Library Journal, October, 2001, Grace Oliff, review of *The Pot of Wisdom,* p. 134; April, 2003, Anna Dewind Walls, review of *Nana's Cold Days,* p. 114; October, 2010, Naphtali L. Faris, review of *Between Sisters,* p. 106.

Voice of Youth Advocates, July, 2011, Elaine Gass Hirsch, review of *Between Sisters.*

ONLINE

Adwoa Badoe Home Page, http://www.afroculture.com (December 15, 2011).

Adwoa Badoe Web log, http://adwoabadoe.blogspot.com (December 15, 2011).*

*   *   *

BAKER, E.D.

Personal

Born in Buffalo, NY; children: three. *Education:* Allegheny College, B.A. (psychology); Johns Hopkins University, M.A.T.

Addresses

Home—Churchville, MD. *E-mail*—edbakerbooks@gmail.com.

Career

Writer and horse breeder. Worked variously as an elementary school teacher, parrot caretaker, and member of Red Cross disaster team.

Awards, Honors

Book Sense Children's Pick, Lone Star Reading List inclusion, Texas Library Association, and Sunshine State Young Readers Award listee, all 2002, all for *The Frog Princess.*

Writings

Wings: A Fairy Tale, Bloomsbury (New York, NY), 2008, published as *Fairy Wings,* 2012.

The Wide-Awake Princess, Bloomsbury (New York, NY), 2010.

"TALES OF THE FROG PRINCESS" NOVEL SERIES

The Frog Princess, Bloomsbury (New York, NY), 2002.

Dragon's Breath, Bloomsbury (New York, NY), 2003.

Once upon a Curse, Bloomsbury (New York, NY), 2004.

No Place for Magic, Bloomsbury (New York, NY), 2006.

Tales of the Frog Princess (contains *The Frog Princess, Dragon's Breath,* and *Once upon a Curse*), Bloomsbury (New York, NY), 2007.

The Salamander Spell, Bloomsbury (New York, NY), 2007.

The Dragon Princess, Bloomsbury (New York, NY), 2008.

Dragon Kiss, Bloomsbury (New York, NY), 2009.

A Prince among Frogs, Bloomsbury (New York, NY), 2010.

Adaptations

Several of Baker's novels were adapted as audiobooks. *The Frog Princess* was the basis of the animated film *The Princess and the Frog,* Walt Disney Pictures, 2009.

Sidelights

In her "Tales of the Frog Princess" novels for middle-grade readers, E.D. Baker employs fairy-tale conventions in new and surprising ways. Featuring curses, good and evil witches, and humans who turn into frogs and back again, the humorous series details the adventures of smart, resourceful Princess Emeralda ("Emma" for short) and Prince Eadric, the brave and good, if sometimes undisciplined, young man Emma loves. When she began writing her fantasy tales, Baker wanted to create a strong heroine "who could take care of herself and not have to rely on a prince to solve her problems," as the author stated on her home page. "Remembering the old story of the frog prince, I thought that it would be fun to write about how a princess could solve the problem if she were a frog as well."

When readers meet her in *The Frog Princess,* Emma is fourteen years old and depressed about the arranged marriage that awaits her. Encountering a talking frog one day, she agrees to kiss it in order to lift a curse and enable the frog to become Eadric once again. Instead of turning the frog into a prince, however, her kiss turns the princess into a frog. Because the witch who cast the spell is the only one who can undo it and restore the young royals to human form, Emma and Eadric go on a journey to find her. Along the way they have many comic problems—including Emma's difficulty adjusting to her frog form—and eventually become attracted to each other. In *The Frog Princess* "Baker reworks the traditional story into high-spirited romantic comedy," noted a *Kirkus Reviews* contributor, while a *Publishers Weekly* critic praised the novel for its "peppy dialogue" and "comical scenes."

The sequel, *Dragon's Breath,* finds Emma learning witchcraft, hoping to help her aunt Grassina—a good and powerful witch who protects the family's realm—reverse a spell that turned the woman's lover, Haywood, into an otter. Dragon's breath is one of the ingredients required. Meanwhile, Emma is having a problem: her sneezes cause her and Eadric to annoyingly shapeshift between human and frog. *Dragon's Breath* is "as tasty as its prequel," remarked John Peters in *School Library Journal,* the critic adding that Brown's novel has "several ingenious twists." A *Kirkus Reviews* critic dubbed the same story "a rollicking sequel" that "does not disappoint."

In *Once upon a Curse* Emma is almost sixteen years old. However, she dreads her upcoming birthday because a family curse will cause her to turn ugly and wicked when she reaches that age. Joined by Eadric and a friendly bat, the teen travels back through time in an attempt to break the spell, and on their trip the trio meets many bizarre characters. Emma and Eadric are married in *No Place for Magic,* although their wedding is not without complications when the groom's younger brother, Bardston, is kidnapped by trolls and Eadric's mother forbids her future daughter-in-law from using magic to rescue the lad. *Booklist* critic Todd Morning applauded the "humorous, lighthearted spirit" in *No Place for Magic* and Tim Wadham observed in *School Library Journal* that readers "will get a kick out of the hip 'Shrek' vibe that Baker creates in this updated fairy tale."

The Salamander Spell, a prequel to *The Frog Princess,* centers on the adventures of Aunt Grassina when, as a teenager, she first discovers her magic powers. After a spell transforms Grassina's mother, the Green Witch, into a cruel hag, tragedy strikes the kingdom of Greater Greensward. Bullied by her older sister, Princess Chartreuse, Grassina flees to a swampy island where she meets Haywood, a young wizard who helps the teen develop her wondrous gifts. *The Salamander Spell* "satisfyingly explains much of the history behind the other books" in Baker's series, Kathleen Meulen observed in *School Library Journal.*

In *The Dragon Princess* Baker introduces Millie, the daughter of Emma and Eadric, who turns into a fire-breathing dragon every time she loses her temper. With the help of three friends, Millie ventures into the Frozen North in the hope that an audience with the powerful Blue Witch will help her rectify the problem. *Dragon Kiss* concerns Audun, a dragon who wishes to become human so he can court Millie. To prove his worth, Audun must complete a series of arduous tasks while battling a nefarious sorcerer. In *A Prince among Frogs* Millie and Audun's nuptials are interrupted by a host of evil creatures that threaten Greater Greensward.

In addition to her "Tales of the Frog Princess" series, Baker entertains older readers with the fantasy novels *Wings: A Fairy Tale* and *The Wide-Awake Princess. Wings* focuses on Tamisin Warner, a high-school student who has always felt different than her peers due to with her sparkling freckles and ability to see goblins on Halloween. When Tamisin suddenly sprouts wings, her parents disclose that the teen was adopted, and when she meets Jak, another halfling, he escorts her to the fairy world. There she finds herself at the center of a conflict waged by Jak's goblin uncle against Tamisin's birth mother, Titania, the fairy queen. Carolyn Phelan, reviewing writing *Wings* in *Booklist,* praised Baker's portrayal of Tamisin, "whose identity lies at the heart of the story."

In *The Wide-Awake Princess* Baker offers a "clever twist on a selection of fairy tales [ranging] from 'Sleeping Beauty' to 'Rapunzel,'" in the words of a *Kirkus Reviews* contributor. When Princess Annie is born, a fairy's spell renders her impervious to magic. Her older sister, Gwen, has no such luck, however, and when Gwen pricks her finger, all the inhabitants of the castle fall asleep save for Annie. Joining forces with Liam, a loyal footman, Annie treks into the forest to locate the requisite Prince Charming, and during her journey she encounters Hansel and Gretel, Rapunzel, and several other familiar characters. Calling *The Wide-Awake Princess* "humorous at times," Karen Alexander observed in *School Library Journal* that Baker's "fractured fairy tale will be enjoyed by readers who like adventure with a touch of romance."

Biographical and Critical Sources

PERIODICALS

Booklist, December 15, 2006, Todd Morning, review of *No Place for Magic,* p. 48; September 15, 2007, Kathleen Isaacs, review of *The Salamander Spell,* p. 61; May 15, 2008, Carolyn Phelan, review of *Wings: A Fairy Tale,* p. 60.

Kirkus Reviews, October 15, 2002, review of *The Frog Princess,* p. 1526; November 1, 2003, review of *Dragon's Breath,* p. 1309; September 1, 2006, review of *No Place for Magic,* p. 900; April 15, 2008, review of *Wings*; April 15, 2010, review of *The Wide-Awake Princess.*

Publishers Weekly, November 18, 2002, review of *The Frog Princess,* p. 61.

School Library Journal, December, 2003, John Peters, review of *Dragon's Breath,* p. 144; January, 2005, Miriam Lang Budin, review of *Once upon a Curse,* p. 122; November, 2006, Tim Wadham, review of *No Place for Magic,* p. 129; December, 2007, Kathleen Meulen, review of *The Salamander Spell,* p. 118; November, 2008, Kathleen Isaacs, review of *Wings,* p. 114; January, 2010, Miriam Lang Budin, review of *Dragon Kiss,* p. 68; June, 2010, Karen Alexander, review of *The Wide-Awake Princess,* p. 94.

Voice of Youth Advocates, December, 2008, Beth E. Andersen, review of *The Dragon Princess,* p. 446.

ONLINE

E.D. Baker Home Page, http://www.edbakerbooks.com (December 15, 2011).

E.D. Baker Web log, http://edbakerbooks.blogspot.com (December 15, 2011).

Tales of E.D. Baker Web site, http://www.talesofedbaker. com/ (December 15, 2011).

*   *   *

BARKER, Claire 1969-

Personal

Born 1969, in Plymouth, England; married; husband's name Julien; children: Daisy, Maya. *Education:* University of Bath, B.A. (English literature; with honors), 1992; studied art at North Devon College (now Petroc College). *Hobbies and other interests:* Walking.

Addresses

Home—South Molton, North Devon, England. *Agent*—Elizabeth Roy Literary Agency, White Cottage, Greatford, Stamford, Linconshire PE9 4PR, England. *E-mail*—toboggan@btinternet.com.

Career

Writer and fine-art painter. Presenter at schools.

Member

Association of Illustrators.

Writings

SELF-ILLUSTRATED

Magical Mail, Sterling Pub. (New York, NY), 2010.

ILLUSTRATOR

Sue Graves, *What a Frog!,* Franklin Watts (London, England), 2007.

Biographical and Critical Sources

PERIODICALS

Booklist, December 1, 2010, Abby Nolan, review of *Magical Mail,* p. 59.

Kirkus Reviews, September 1, 2010, review of *Magical Mail.*

School Library Journal, January, 2011, Kathy Kirchoefer, review of *Magical Mail,* p. 99.

ONLINE

Claire Barker Home Page, http://www.clairebarkerpaintings.com (October 2, 2011).

Magical Mail Web site, http://www.magicalmailclaire barker.com/ (October 2, 2011).

North Devon Gazette Online, http://www.northdevon gazette.co.uk/ (November 5, 2010), Tom Leaning, "Magical Debut for North Devon Author."*

*   *   *

BARTOLETTI, Susan Campbell 1958-

Personal

Born November 18, 1958, in Harrisburg, PA; married Joseph Bartoletti (a history teacher); children: Brandy, Joe. *Education:* Attended Keystone College; Marywood College, B.A. (English and secondary education), 1979, then graduate study; University of Scranton, M.A. (English), 1982; State University of New York at Binghamton, Ph.D., 2001.

Addresses

Home—PA. *Agent*—Ginger Knowlton, Curtis Brown, Ltd., 10 Astor Place, New York, NY 10003. *E-mail*—scbartoletti@gmail.com.

Career

Writer and educator. North Pocono Middle School, Moscow, PA, English teacher, 1979-97; Hollins University, Roanoke, VA, visiting associate professor of creative writing in graduate program in children's literature, 1999-2005. Northeast Education Intermediate Unit 19, Archbald, PA, instructor, 1984-88; Keystone College, La Plume, PA, adjunct faculty, 1984-86; University of Scranton, Scranton, PA, adjunct faculty, 1997-98; Spalding University, Louisville, KY, member of graduate faculty, 2003—; Pennsylvania State University, University Park, member of graduate faculty, 2010. Marywood University, Scranton, distinguished scholar/ artist, 2002. Chair of Judging Committee, National Book Award for Young People's Literature, 2003; chair of advisory board, Pennsylvania Center for the Book, 2003-10; judge, "Letters about Literature" contest,

Susan Campbell Bartoletti (Photograph copyright © by Stephanie Klein-Davis. Reproduced by permission.)

2003—. Judge, Society of Children's Book Writers and Illustrators nonfiction category, 2010. Member, Highlights Foundation Board of Trustees, beginning 2004.

Member

Society of Children's Book Writers and Illustrators, Children's Literature Council (board member, 2001-04).

Awards, Honors

Highlights for Children fiction contest winner, 1993, for "No Man's Land"; Jane Addams Children's Book Award, American Library Association (ALA) Notable Book designation, ALA Best Book for Young Adults designation, Golden Kite Honor Book for Nonfiction selection, Society of Children's Book Writers and Illustrators, Carolyn W. Field Award, Pennsylvania Library Association, *Booklist,* Editor's Choice Award, Notable Children's Trade Book in the Field of Social Studies, National Council for the Social Studies/Children's Book Council (NCSS/CBC), Orbis Pictus Recommended Title, National Council of Teachers of English (NCTE), Lamplighter Award, and Parents Gold Choice Award, all c. 1997, all for *Growing up in Coal Country;* Best Books of 1999, *School Library Journal,* ALA Best Book for Young Adults designation, Notable Book designation, *Smithsonian* magazine, Books for the Teen Age designation, New York Public Library, Jane Addams Children's Book Honor Award, Carolyn W. Field Honor Award, Orbis Pictus Recommended Title, Notable Children's Trade Book in the Field of Social Studies, NCSS/CBC, and Jefferson Cup Recommended Title, all 1999, all for *Kids on Strike!;* Notable Children's Trade Book in the Field of Social Studies, 1999, for *No Man's Land;* Books for the Teen Age designation, New York Public Library, 2000, for *A Coal Miner's Bride;* named Outstanding Pennsylvania Author of the Year, Pennsylvania Library Association, 2001; Excellence in Research Award, State University of New York at Binghamton; Robert F. Sibert Award, ALA/Bound to Stay Bound Books, 2002, and Carolyn W. Field Award, 2003, both for *Black Potatoes;* Orbis Pictus Honor Book designation, Sydney Taylor Notable Book designation, Newbery Honor Book designation, Carolyn W. Field Award, and Robert F. Sibert Honor Book designation, all 2006, all for *Hitler Youth; Washington Post*/Children's Book Guild Nonfiction Award, 2009; Notable Book for a Global Society and Teachers Choice Award, both International Reading Association, ALA Best Book for Young Adults designation, Notable Book in the Language Arts, NCTE, and Carolyn W. Field Award, 2009, all for *The Boy Who Dared;* Best of the Best selection, Chicago Public Library, Notable Book designation, ALA, Excellence in Young Adult Nonfiction finalist, ALA, and Cooperative Children's Book Center Choices selection, all 2011, all for *They Called Themselves the K.K.K.*

Writings

NONFICTION

Growing up in Coal Country, Houghton Mifflin (Boston, MA), 1996.

Kids on Strike!, Houghton Mifflin (Boston, MA), 1999.

Black Potatoes: The Story of the Great Irish Famine, 1845-1850, Houghton Mifflin (Boston, MA), 2001.

Hitler Youth: Growing up in Hitler's Shadow, Scholastic (New York, NY), 2005.

They Called Themselves the K.K.K.: The Birth of an American Terrorist Group, Houghton Mifflin Harcourt (Boston, MA), 2010.

JUVENILE FICTION

No Man's Land: A Young Soldier's Story, Blue Sky Press (New York, NY), 1999.

A Coal Miner's Bride: The Diary of Anetka Kaminska, Scholastic (New York, NY), 2000.

The Journal of Finn Reardon, a Newsie, Scholastic (New York, NY), 2003.

The Boy Who Dared, Scholastic (New York, NY), 2008.

PICTURE BOOKS

Silver at Night, illustrated by David Ray, Crown Books (New York, NY), 1994.

Dancing with Dziadziu, illustrated by Annika Nelson, Harcourt (San Diego, CA), 1997.

The Christmas Promise, illustrated by David Christiana, Blue Sky Press (New York, NY), 2001.

Nobody's Noisier than a Cat, illustrated by Beppe Giacobbe, Hyperion (New York, NY), 2003.

The Flag Maker, illustrated by Claire A. Nivola, Houghton Mifflin (Boston, MA), 2004.

Nobody's Diggier than a Dog, illustrated by Beppe Giacobbe, Hyperion (New York, NY), 2005.

Naamah and the Ark at Night, illustrated by Holly Meade, Candlewick Press (Somerville, MA), 2011.

Sidelights

Susan Campbell Bartoletti is a writer whose strength lies in looking back rather than ahead. Bartoletti pens novels, works of nonfiction, and picture books that inspire and nudge young readers to look into history and see themselves in its reflection. In her award-winning works, which include *Kids on Strike!, Hitler Youth: Growing up in Hitler's Shadow,* and *The Boy Who Dared,* she focuses on what she terms the "gaps" in history: the everyday lives of individuals, especially children, during tumultuous historical eras.

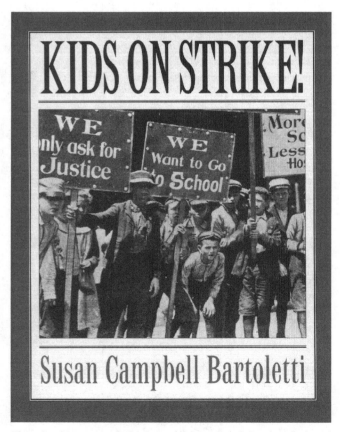

The role of young people in the social struggles of the nineteenth and twentieth centuries is the focus of Bartoletti's Kids on Strike! (Houghton Mifflin Company, 1999. Photograph © Corbis/Bettman.)

Often using her native Pennsylvania as the setting for her early books, Bartoletti has made a specialty of labor history, more specifically of tales from the coal mines that warren the underworld of Pennsylvania. With the nonfiction books *Growing up in Coal Country* and *Kids on Strike!* she delves into the world of child labor in the anthracite coal, while her fictional *A Coal Miner's Bride: The Diary of Anetka Kaminska* reveals the hardships and political turmoil present in a coal-mining community through the eyes of a young immigrant girl. In her debut picture book, *Silver at Night,* Bartoletti moves close to home to tell a fictionalized account of her husband's grandfather, who emigrated from Italy and spent nearly half a century in the mines of Pennsylvania.

The versatile Bartoletti has gone further afield in both fiction and nonfiction: to the U.S. Civil War for *No Man's Land: A Young Soldier's Story,* to Ireland for *Black Potatoes: The Story of the Great Irish Famine, 1845-1850;* and to Nazi Germany for *The Boy Who Dared.* "I let my instinct tell me whether the story is fiction or nonfiction, picture book or novel," Bartoletti noted in the *Meet Authors and Illustrators* Web site. Regardless of the genre, Bartoletti's message remains the same. "Many books show kids as disenfranchised victims," she related in an interview for *Authors and Artists for Young Adults* (*AAYA*). "But that is not the whole story. In the coal mines, in the Civil War, there were many who fought for their rights. They weren't powerless. They did not always need adults to lead the way. And it's important that kids get that message. For their future, they need to see that other kids have power and can be powerful."

Born in Harrisburg, Pennsylvania, Bartoletti and her family moved several times after the death of her father in 1959. She grew up in the countryside outside of Scranton, enjoying the freedom of open land with few urban restrictions placed on her. "I loved to read and draw as a kid," the author told *AAYA.* "Those were my main passions." Ironically, for a writer who would later make her mark mining the ore of the past, history was not Bartoletti's favorite subject in school. "I guess it serves me right that later I not only chose to write history, but I also married a history teacher," she noted in her interview.

A good student, Bartoletti also had an independent mind, and as a sixteen-year-old high-school junior she decided to skip senior year and enter college. "I majored in art in college," she explained. "I got good grades in my art classes, but I could see the difference in talent between me and some of the others." Meanwhile she was earning high praise from her composition instructor, with her essays were read aloud as models. "So I switched majors," Bartoletti recalled. "I became an English major. It was meant to be."

Bartoletti landed a job teaching eighth-grade English as soon as she graduated from college. "I didn't think I was going to like teaching in a junior high where I got

my first job," Bartoletti once stated. "I figured I would rather teach older kids. But I grew to love teaching. I stayed for eighteen years."

Bartoletti blended her enjoyment of writing with her teaching, and she began selling short fiction to various magazines, including *Highlights for Children*. When one of her stories, "No Man's Land," won a fiction contest in that magazine, Bartoletti began to think seriously about writing book-length fiction. Although she would later adapt her award-winning short story into a juvenile novel, she chose the picture-book format for her first longer work. She also chose a subject that had animated many dinner conversations with her husband's grandfather.

"Although *Silver at Night* is fiction, the story was inspired by my husband's family, who were immigrant coal miners," Bartoletti explained. "His grandfather, Massimino Santarelli, came to the United States from Italy when he was nine years old, and he quit school at age eleven to work in the coal industry." This grandfather was full of stories about working in the mines, and his wife, Pearl, also had tales of being a miner's wife.

Silver at Night tells the story of Massimino as he leaves his country to make his fortune in the New World. He departs from his village and his one true love, promising that some day he will be a rich man with "gold in the morning and silver at night." In his new country, Massimino works in the coal mines by day and at night he counts the silver coins he has earned, while also longing for his lost love. "First-time author Bartoletti throngs the simple story with an avalanche of fulsome imagery," noted a reviewer for *Publishers Weekly*.

Writing *Silver at Night* inspired Bartoletti's interest in the anthracite coal industry. As she read about the mining industry, she discovered one of the historical "gaps" she has tried to fill with her own words. "As I began to read more and more about coal mining," the author recalled, "I found that most books concentrated on what it was like to be a wealthy and powerful coal operator, or what the hardships were of being a miner. However, few told what it was like to be a child in that industry, and fewer still what it was like to be a female then." Bartoletti began reading newspapers of the period, as well as magazines, autobiographies, diaries, and interview transcripts of oral histories. She also examined collections of photographs and even began collecting her own oral-history interviews. These first-hand accounts of life in the coal fields excited her and showed her the way to new books.

In 1998 Bartoletti left her job as an eighth-grade English teacher to commit herself to writing full time and to earning her doctorate in English. One of her first projects was the reworking of her prize-winning short story, "No Man's Land," about a makeshift baseball game between young Rebel and Yankee soldiers under a private truce during the U.S. Civil War. In the novel

Cover of Bartoletti's nineteenth-century historical novel No Man's Land, *which focuses on a boy's experiences during the U.S. Civil War.* (Illustration copyright © 1999 by David Shannon. Reproduced by permission of Scholastic Inc.)

No Man's Land, she tells the story of fourteen-year-old Thrasher McGee, who lies about his age in order to join the Confederate Army. Searching for heroic adventures, Thrasher at first finds mostly boredom waiting for the battle. Arriving too late for one battle, he and his comrades are assigned the gory job of burying the dead. Echoing the original short story, the novel also details the friendly relations that develop between Yankee and Rebel troops until they are forced to fight each other once again. In the final climactic battle, Thrasher loses an arm and what little illusions he has left about the glory of war. "Bartoletti compellingly and carefully crafts her characters," noted a writer for *Publishers Weekly,* "especially the boys-turned-soldiers Thrasher, Baylor Frable and Trim LaFaye." The same reviewer concluded that Bartoletti "spins a history as fresh as the day it happened." Rochman also praised the novel, calling attention to Bartoletti's "careful historical research."

In *Growing up in Coal Country* Bartoletti presents "a concise, thoroughly researched account of working and living conditions in Pennsylvania coal towns," observed *Horn Book* critic Anne Deifendeifer. Bartoletti begins by describing the various jobs existing in a coal camp, from those performed by young boys to those of adult

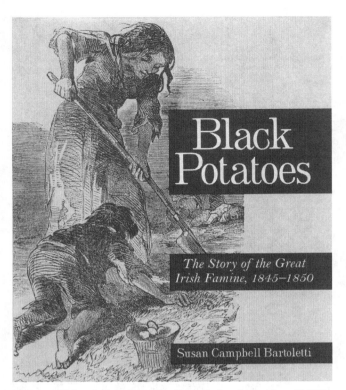

The tragedy that decimated an island population during the mid-1800s is the focus of Bartoletti's **Black Potatoes: The Story of the Great Irish Famine.** (Houghton Mifflin Company, 2001. Illustrations from "London Illustrated News," 22 December 1849. Reproduced by permission of Houghton Mifflin Company. All rights reserved.)

miners. In the second half of the book she details life in the company town, drawing on first-person source material that "provides a refreshing . . . frame of reference," as Deifendeifer noted. Full of anecdotes and personal histories, *Growing up in Coal Country* is also well illustrated with "compelling black-and-white photographs of children at work in the coal mines of northeastern Pennsylvania about 100 years ago," according to *Booklist* contributor Hazel Rochman. These contemporary images were captured by well-known photographer Lewis Hine, who was hired by the National Child Labor Committee to document child labor in early twentieth-century America. Rochman also drew attention to the "heartfelt memories of long hours, hard labor, and extremely dangerous working conditions, as well as lighter accounts" included in Bartoletti's book. "As with most fine juvenile nonfiction," the critic concluded, "this will also have great appeal for adults." *Growing up in Coal Country* won numerous awards, including a Golden Kite Honor Book award for nonfiction, and has attracted a readership that bridges the generations.

An extension of Bartoletti's coal-industry research, *Kids on Strike!* examines child labor from 1836 to the early twentieth century as revealed in the stories of young people who rebelled against unfair working conditions. Examining strikes from the New York bootblack action of 1899 to the Pennsylvania anthracite coals strikes of 1900 and 1902 and the mill workers' strike in Lawrence, Massachusetts in 1913, the author focuses on the roles children played in such labor disputes. "Bartoletti has a gift for collecting stories with telling details," noted a contributor to *Publishers Weekly.* "Her dense but highly readable prose brings individual children and the struggles in which they engaged vividly to life." The same reviewer called *Kids on Strike!* "accessible and engrossing," and "tangible proof for would-be activists that children have made and continue to make a difference." Writing in *Booklist,* Hazel Rochman concluded that, "along with unforgettable photos by Lewis Hine and others on nearly every page, Bartoletti dramatizes the politics with individual stories of hardship and struggle." "As memorable as their inspiring stories are," commented a reviewer for *Horn Book* of the tales included in the author's chronicles, "they represent just a few of the children who worked and battled for better lives."

Another work of nonfiction, *Black Potatoes: The Story of the Great Irish Famine, 1845-1850,* had its basis as Bartoletti's doctoral dissertation. Researching the records and transcripts of oral-history interviews in Dublin, she put together a presentation of the famine with a folklore basis, focusing again on personal stories, historical records and documents, and photographic illustrations to bring history alive for young readers. According to *Booklist* critic Rochman, "Bartoletti humanizes the big events by bringing the reader up close to the lives of ordinary people." *Black Potatoes* is "a powerful and important book," Maureen Griffin concluded in her *Kliatt* review.

Bartoletti chronicles the evolution of the Ku Klux Klan during the era of Reconstruction in *They Called Themselves the K.K.K.: The Birth of an American Terrorist Group.* The author draws from slave narratives, diaries, letters, newspapers, and Congressional testimony to trace the origins of the white supremacist organization, "writ[ing] in admirably clear, accessible language about one of the most complex periods in U.S. history," in the words of *Booklist* contributor Gillian Engberg. In a *Kirkus Reviews* interview with Clay Moore, Bartoletti noted that this book "is as much about the character of our nation as it is about the individuals who make up our country. After our country tore itself apart, we had to figure out how to mend and how to reconstruct our nation. It was a time of great tension and of great risk— and yet, a time of great opportunity." Barbara Bader, reviewing *They Called Themselves the K.K.K.* in *Horn Book,* stated that "Bartoletti tackles a tough, grim subject with firmness and sensitivity," and *Voice of Youth Advocates* contributor Mary Ann Darby maintained that the author "is richly deserving of her reputation as an exemplary historian."

In *Hitler Youth,* a Newbery Honor Book selection, Bartoletti looks at the horrors of Nazi Germany through the experiences of twelve individuals who were members of the Hitler Youth. The organization, which was man-

datory for many German children and adolescents during World War II, trained young people to be followers of Nazi leader Adoph Hitler. "Hitler recognized the natural energy, enthusiasm, and loyalty that young people possess," Bartoletti told *Booklist* interviewer Hazel Rochman. "He understood that they could be a powerful political force. Once properly indoctrinated, they could provide him with a limitless supply of leaders and followers." Using oral histories, diaries, and interviews, she traces the development of the movement, which involved millions of youth, focusing on the period from 1933 to 1945. "Bartoletti lets many of the subjects' words, emotions, and deeds speak for them-

selves," remarked *School Library Journal* contributor Andrew Medlar, "bringing them together clearly to tell this story unlike anyone else has." A *Publishers Weekly* reviewer stated that *Hitler Youth* "will allow readers to comprehend the circumstances that led to the formation of Hitler's youngest zealots."

Also set in Nazi Germany, *The Boy Who Dared* offers a fictionalized version of the life of Helmuth Hübener, a German teenager who was executed for his opposition to the Third Reich. Originally a member of the Hitler Youth, Hübener, a Mormon, grows disillusioned with the Nazi party, and by distributing pamphlets that criti-

***Bartoletti brings to life a tragic era in U.S. history in* They Called Themselves the KKK.** (Illustration from Frank Leslie's Illustrated Newspaper, October 7, 1871; Library of Congress. Reprinted by permission of Houghton Mifflin Harcourt Publishing Company. All rights reserved.)

cize the regime he causes his arrest. Bartoletti tells Hübener's story through a series of flashbacks as the teen sits in his jail cell, and she "does an excellent job of conveying the political climate surrounding Hitler's ascent to power," according to a *Publishers Weekly* reviewer. "The teen's perspective makes this a particularly gripping way to personalize the history," Rochman observed, and *School Library Journal* critic Rita Soltan maintained that in *The Boy Who Dared* Bartoletti demonstrates that "the courage and convictions of a minority should be motivation to speak the truth rather than remain silent."

Returning to fiction with *A Coal Miner's Bride,* Bartoletti takes a "vivid and compelling look at the lives of Pennsylvania's immigrant coal miners and their families at the turn of the [twentieth] century," according to Valerie Diamond in *School Library Journal.* "I wrote about a spirited thirteen-year-old-girl," Bartoletti noted in *Book Links,* "whose father has arranged a marriage for her to . . . a man she does not know in Lattimer, Pennsylvania." Anetka thus immigrates to America in 1896 and keeps a diary of her experiences in her new country. As a miner's wife and the stepmother to three children, she recorded the hardships of her new life. When her husband is killed soon after the marriage, Anetka must take in boarders in order to support her small stepdaughters. She soon falls in love with a labor organizer, Leon Nasevich, and things come to a crisis during the Lattimer Massacre in which nineteen miners were killed during a march on September 10, 1987. "Bartoletti paints an accessible and evocative picture of life in a harsh era," Diamond concluded. Reviewing *A Coal Miner's Bride* in *Booklist,* Rochman commended this "dramatic" history, but found problems with the "format," wondering when the busy Anetka could find time to write in her diary. Rochman went on to note, however, that Bartoletti's historical note at the end "authenticates the account of the immigration, the labor struggle, the massacre, and the role of strong women."

Another work of historical fiction, *The Journal of Finn Reardon, a Newsie* introduces a young Irish teen who hawks newspapers on the streets of New York City. Set in 1899, the work follows the members of the impoverished Reardon family and their efforts to improve their dire financial circumstances. While aspiring journalist Finn works alongside fellow newsies Racetrack and Mush, his parents take on odd jobs to provide for their children. When Finn's father becomes gravely ill from exposure to dangerous lead-based chemicals while painting houses, Finn becomes the family breadwinner. "From the journal, readers get an idea of unscrupulous landlords, of the lack of basics (no bathrooms or running water in the apartments), and the constant insecurity of working people," noted *Kliatt* reviewer Claire Rosser. *School Library Journal* contributor Carol A. Edwards stated of *The Journal of Finn Reardon, a Newsie* that "the family's Irish background helps the story to become much more than a recitation of historical facts."

Turning to younger readers, Bartoletti tells the story of Gabriella, who dances for the last time with her beloved elderly grandmother, Babci, in the picture book *Dancing with Dziadziu.* "Far from sad," wrote a contributor for *Publishers Weekly,* "the story is largely a celebration of Babci's life as a Polish immigrant." The same reviewer described this picture book as a "mellifluously written tale" featuring a "motif of rebirth" established with the family's early Easter celebration before the death of Babci. Reviewing the picture book in *Booklist,* Karen Morgan noted that "in direct and uncomplicated language and through a series of flashbacks, Bartoletti captures the spirit of love and caring across generations." Further picture books from Bartoletti include *The Christmas Promise,* about a Great Depression-era father and daughter in search of a home, and the humorous *Nobody's Diggier than a Dog.*

The flag that inspired Francis Scott Key to compose "The Star-Spangled Banner" is the subject of *The Flag Maker.* Bartoletti tells her picture-book story from the point of view of Caroline Pickersgill, whose mother, Mary, constructs the huge flag that flies over Fort McHenry during the War of 1812. "As a recounting both of the making of the flag and its role in the defense of Fort McHenry, the tale is impeccably told, with

David Christiana creates the evocative art that brings to life Bartoletti's meaningful holiday story in **The Christmas Promise.** (Illustration copyright © 2001 by David Christiana. Reproduced by permission of Scholastic Inc.)

short lines that add tension and speed the action along," wrote Martha V. Parravano in *Horn Book. Booklist* critic Jennifer Mattson also offered a positive assessment of *The Flag Maker*, writing that "Bartoletti writes feelingly of the talismanic comfort [the flag] . . . provides when Caroline glimpses it from afar during the British attack."

In *Naamah and the Ark at Night* Bartoletti presents an interpretation of a well-known Biblical tale from an unusual perspective: that of Noah's wife. On a dark night after the great flood the animals restlessly pace about the ark, and Naamah attempts to reassure them with a gentle song. Bartoletti's lyrical verse is based on the ghazal, an ancient poetic form that employs couplets that end with an identical word preceded by a rhyming word. "It's a story of quiet confidence and comfort," a *Publishers Weekly* critic remarked, and a *Kirkus Reviews* critic stated that the narrative in *Naamah and the Ark at Night* "has a lovely, soothing effect, with the repeated ending words and a lilting cadence that effectively suggests a comforting lullaby."

"I like working with primary sources because they connect us in a way that individualizes history," Bartoletti told *Booklist* interviewer Rochman. "To write the 'truth,' a writer must research to the edges. Otherwise, she stays in the middle. That creates one-sided, voiceless stories with stereotypical characters—stories that are not fleshed-out reality, stories without depth and complexity."

"Story comes first for me," Bartoletti concluded in her *AAYA* interview. "I need to look at history in a way that makes sense, and one way of making sense is by following story, which is not always about chronology. . . . I choose a character or characters and I think that if I develop them honestly and truly, then readership will follow. But in the end, it is up to the individual reader to decide if I have succeeded. With these stories of hard times from another era, my primary goal is not just to let kids of today see how easy they have it. Rather my hope is that I can give kids hope and courage with these stories."

Biographical and Critical Sources

BOOKS

Authors and Artists for Young Adults, Volume 44, Gale (Detroit, MI), 2002.

PERIODICALS

Book Links, August-September, 2000, Susan Campbell Bartoletti, "Exploring the Gaps in History," pp. 16-21.
Booklist, December 1, 1996, Hazel Rochman, review of *Growing up in Coal Country,* p. 652; March 15, 1997, Karen Morgan, review of *Dancing with Dziadziu,* p.

1238; April 1, 1999, Hazel Rochman, review of *No Man's Land: A Young Soldier's Story,* p. 1424; December 1, 1999, Hazel Rochman, review of *Kids on Strike!,* p. 691; April 1, 2000, Hazel Rochman, review of *A Coal Miner's Bride: The Diary of Anetka Kaminska,* p. 1473; September 15, 2001, GraceAnne A. DeCandido, review of *The Christmas Promise,* p. 234; October 15, 2001, Hazel Rochman, review of *Black Potatoes: The Story of the Great Irish Famine,* p. 394; November 1, 2003, Abby Nolan, review of *Nothing's Nosier than a Cat,* p. 103; March 1, 2004, Jennifer Mattson, review of *The Flag Maker,* p. 1206; January 1, 2005, Jennifer Mattson, review of *Nothing's Diggier than a Dog,* p. 867; April 15, 2005, Hazel Rochman, review of *Hitler Youth: Growing up in Hitler's Shadow,* p. 1454; January 1, 2006, Hazel Rochman, interview with Bartoletti, p. 80; February 15, 2008, Hazel Rochman, review of *The Boy Who Dared,* p. 81; August 1, 2010, Gillian Engberg, review of *They Called Themselves the K.K.K.: The Birth of an American Terrorist Group,* p. 48.
Horn Book, March-April, 1997, Anne Deifendeifer, review of *Growing up in Coal Country,* pp. 210-211; January-February, 2000, review of *Kids on Strike!,* p. 91; January-February, 2002, Margaret A. Bush, review of *Black Potatoes,* p. 91; May-June, 2004, Martha V. Parravano, review of *The Flag Maker,* p. 343; May-June, 2005, Roger Sutton, review of *Hitler Youth,* pp. 345-346; September-October, 2010, Barbara Bader, review of *They Called Themselves the K.K.K.,* p. 106; July-August, 2011, Joanna Rudge Long, review of *Naamah and the Ark at Night,* p. 123.
Kirkus Reviews, September 15, 2003, review of *Nothing's Nosier than a Cat,* p. 1171; April 1, 2004, review of *The Flag Maker,* p. 324; January 15, 2005, review of *Nothing's Diggier than a Dog,* p. 116; April 1, 2005, review of *Hitler Youth,* p. 412; July 15, 2011, review of *Naamah and the Ark at Night.*
Kliatt, July, 2003, Claire Rosser, review of *The Journal of Finn Reardon, a Newsie,* p. 8; September 15, 2003, Daniel J. Levinson, review of *Kids on Strike!,* p. 41; November, 2005, Maureen Griffin, review of *Black Potatoes,* p. 33.
Publishers Weekly, November 14, 1994, review of *Silver at Night,* p. 67; February 10, 1997, review of *Dancing with Dziadziu,* p. 83; May 31, 1999, review of *No Man's Land,* p. 94; November 29, 1999, review of *Kids on Strike!,* p. 72; September 24, 2001, review of *The Christmas Promise,* p. 53; May 3, 2004, review of *The Flag Maker,* p. 195; February 7, 2005, review of *Nothing's Diggier than a Dog,* p. 58; May 23, 2005, review of *Hitler Youth,* pp. 79-80; February 11, 2008, review of *The Boy Who Dared,* p. 70; July 26, 2010, review of *They Called Themselves the K.K.K.,* p. 77; June 27, 2011, review of *Naamah and the Ark at Night,* p. 155.
School Library Journal, August, 2000, Valerie Diamond, review of *A Coal Miner's Bride,* p. 177; October, 2001, review of *The Christmas Promise,* p. 62; November, 2001, Mary R. Hoffmann, review of *Black Potatoes,* p. 168; October, 2003, Carol A. Edwards, review of *The Journal of Finn Reardon, a Newsie,* p.

158; December, 2003, Grace Oliff, review of *Nothing's Nosier than a Cat,* p. 103; April, 2004, Dona Ratterree, review of *The Flag Maker,* p. 102; February, 2005, Sally R. Dow, review of *Nothing's Diggier than a Dog,* p. 94; June, 2005, Andrew Medlar, review of *Hitler Youth,* p. 174; May, 2008, Rita Soltan, review of *The Boy Who Dared,* p. 119; August, 2010, Gerry Larson, review of *They Called Themselves the K.K.K.,* p. 117.

Voice of Youth Advocates, October, 2010, Mary Ann Darby, review of *They Called Themselves the K.K.K,* p. 375.

ONLINE

Children's Literature Web site, http://www.childrenslit. com/ (June 30, 2001), "Susan Campbell Bartoletti."

Cynsations Web log, http://cynthialeitichsmith.blogspot. com/ (August 26, 2010), "Guest Post: Susan Campbell Bartoletti on Writing Nonfiction and *They Called Themselves the K.K.K.*"

Kirkus Reviews Web log, http://www.kirkusreviews.com/ blog/young-adult/ (December 1, 2010), Clay Moore, "Behind the KKK," interview with Bartoletti.

Susan Campbell Bartoletti Home Page, http://www.scbarto letti.com (December 15, 2011).*

*   *   *

BLADEK, John 1963(?)-

Personal

Born c. 1963. *Education:* Washington State University, B.A., M.A. (English, history, and education); University of Washington, Ph.D. (American history).

Addresses

Home—Spokane Valley, WA. *Agent*—Jamie Weiss Chilton, Andrea Brown Literary, jamie@andreabrownlit. com. *E-mail*—bladekj@aol.com.

Career

Author and educator. Teacher of history and English; University of Washington, former manager of history writing lab. Works as a tutor.

Member

Society of Children's Book Writers and Illustrators (N. Idaho/E. Washington chapter).

Writings

Roll up the Streets, Kane Miller (Tulsa, OK), 2010.

Contributor to academic journals, including *Virginia Magazine of History and Biography,* and to anthologies, including *Encyclopedia of the American Civil War,* ed-

ited by David S. Heidler and Jeanne T. Heidler, ABC-Clio, 2001, and *Online Study Guide for America: A Concise History,* edited by James A. Henretta and others, Bedford/St. Martin's Press, 2002.

Sidelights

"Like most children's authors," John Bladek told *SATA,* "I enjoy the glamorous life: sitting in front of a computer trying to explain how sarcastic, insecure twelve year olds are humanity's only hope against worldwide zombification by corndog and the tyranny of life-like dolls.

"I earned a Ph.D. just to force people to call me 'Doctor'. I spend my spare time contemplating the great questions of our age, like what's that smell? Why does it smell so bad? Is it coming from me? And, huh?

"These deep thoughts take up much of my time, except when I'm distracted by bright lights or shiny objects.

"I also love to share my work with kids and to visit their schools to talk about writing and terrible smells, which is way better than math homework (and is also big on standardized tests)."

Biographical and Critical Sources

PERIODICALS

Kirkus Reviews, September 1, 2010, review of *Roll up the Streets.*

ONLINE

John Bladek Web log, http://johnbladek.blogspot.com (December 15, 2011).

*   *   *

BLEIMAN, Andrew

Personal

Married; wife's name Lillian. *Education:* University of Pennsylvania, B.A., 2002; Northwestern University, M.B.A., 2011.

Addresses

Home—Chicago, IL.

Career

Marketing and new media strategist, animal activist, and author. MBI, Inc., associate program manager, 2002-05; Nature Technologies, marketing director,

2005-06; Dieselpoint, Chicago, IL, marketing strategist, 2006-08; Bradford Group, Niles, IL, senior program manager, 2008-10; Trunk Club, Chicago, director of marketing, 2011—. Co-founder of ZooBorns.com. Member of board at Lincoln Park Auxiliary Zoo and Shedd Aquarium.

Member
Big Brothers and Big Sisters.

Writings

ZooBorns!: Zoo Babies from around the World, photographs by Chris Eastland, Beach Lane Books (New York, NY), 2010.

ZooBorns: The Newest, Cutest Animals from the World's Zoos and Aquariums, photographs by Chris Eastland, Simon & Schuster (New York, NY), 2010.

ZooBorns Cats!: The Newest, Cutest Kittens and Cubs from the World's Zoos, photographs by Chris Eastland, Simon & Schuster (New York, NY), 2011.

Sidelights
A lifelong animal lover, Andrew Bleiman is the co-founder of ZooBorns.com, a Web site devoted to news of animal births at zoos and aquariums across the globe. Bleiman has parlayed the success of his Web site into books that offer profiles of dozens of the cuddly creatures, including *ZooBorns!: Zoo Babies from around the World,* a work aimed at young readers, and *ZooBorns: The Newest, Cutest Animals from the World's*

Andrew Bleiman captures the wonder of the earth's wildlifes in ZooBorns!, *a book produced by his ZooBorn Foundation.* (Beach Lane Books, 2010. Photograph by Audubon Nature Institute.)

Zoos and Aquariums, a companion volume suitable for all ages. Both books feature photographs by Chris Eastland, who also collaborates on the Web site.

ZooBorns! showcases a diverse group of animals, from a baby fennec fox housed in South Korea's Everland Zoo to a newborn beluga whale living at the Shedd Aquarium in Chicago, Bleiman's adopted home town. Each creature is introduced with a brief biography that is accompanied by a full-page color picture, and a section at book's end presents information about the animal's conservation status. "Agonizingly adorable photographs . . . steal the spotlight," noted a critic in *Publishers Weekly* in describing Bleiman and Eastland's collaboration, and Cynde Suite remarked in *School Library Journal* that the "text and extras" in *ZooBorns!* "provide good factual material to satisfy curious readers." Discussing a third collaboration between author and photographer, *ZooBorns Cats!: The Newest, Cutest Kittens and Cubs from the World's Zoos,* Karen M. Bensing stated in *Library Journal* that the creators "draw attention to the increasing number of the world's wild felines on the brink of extinction."

Bleiman hopes that his books and Web site will help increase awareness regarding the plight of endangered species, as well as highlighting the steps being saved to help them. "We aim to educate while we entertain," he told *Zooillogix* online interviewer Scott Butki. "You visit [ZooBorns.com] because you want to see an orphan sea otter pup going for its first swim at the aquarium. You leave knowing that the Monterey Bay Aquarium's Sea Otter Research and Conservation program has rehabilitated over 500 wild otters since its inception."

Biographical and Critical Sources

PERIODICALS

Kirkus Reviews, September 1, 2010, review of *ZooBorns!: Zoo Babies from around the World,* p. 58.

Library Journal, December 1, 2011, Karen M. Bensing, review of *ZooBorns Cats!: The Newest, Cutest Kittens and Cubs from the World's Zoos,,* p. 139.

Publishers Weekly, September 27, 2010, review of *ZooBorns!,* p. 58.

School Library Journal, October, 2010, Cynde Suite, review of *ZooBorns!,* p. 98.

ONLINE

Blogcritics.org, http://blogcritics.org/ (April 26, 2011), Scott Butki, interview with Bleiman.

ZooBorns Web site, http://www.zooborns.com/ (January 1, 2012).

Zooillogix Web log, http://scienceblogs.com/zooillogix/ (January 1, 2012).*

BOW, Erin 1972-
(Erin Noteboom)

Personal

Born April 1, 1972, in Des Moines, IA; immigrated to Canada; married James Bow (a writer); children: Vivian, Eleanor. *Education:* B.S. (physics).

Addresses

Home—Kitchener, Ontario, Canada. *Agent*—Emily van Beek, Folio Literary Management, Film Center Bldg., 630 9th Ave., Ste. 1101, New York, NY 10036. *E-mail*—erin.n.bow@googlemail.com.

Career

Author, editor, and poet. Writer-in-residence at schools and libraries. Worked briefly at European Centre for Nuclear Research (CERN), Geneva, Switzerland.

Awards, Honors

Acorn-Plantos Award for Peoples Poetry, and Canadian Children's Book Centre Literary Award, both 2001, both for *Ghost Maps;* TD Canadian Children's Literature Award, and Best Fiction for Young Adults designation, American Library Association, both 2011, both for *Plain Kate.*

Writings

Plain Kate (young-adult novel), Arthur A. Levine Books (New York, NY), 2010, published as *Wood Angel,* Chicken House (Frome, England), 2011.

FOR ADULTS

(As Erin Noteboom) *Ghost Maps: Poems for Carl Hruska* (poetry), Wolsak & Wynn (Toronto, Ontario, Canada), 2001.
(As Erin Noteboom) *Seal up the Thunder* (poetry), Wolsak & Wynn (Toronto, Ontario, Canada), 2005.
(As Erin Noteboom) *The Moongoose Diaries* (memoir), Wolsak & Wynn (Toronto, Ontario, Canada), 2007.

Member of editorial board of *New Quarterly.*

Sidelights

In *Plain Kate,* her critically acclaimed debut novel, Erin Bow offers readers "a compelling story of dark magic," in the words of *Quill & Quire* reviewer Jean Mills. The tale, which received the 2011 TD Canadian Children's Literature Award, concerns a lonely woodcarver's daughter and the odd bargain she strikes with a traveling stranger; it has also been published in the United Kingdom under the title *Wood Angel.* Praising the author's use of "familiar folktale elements," *Booklist* contributor Lynn Rutan declared that, with *Plain Kate,* "Bow establishes herself as a novelist to watch."

Growing up in Omaha, Nebraska, Bow developed a love of reading, and as a teen her favorite books included Peter S. Beagle's *The Last Unicorn* and Richard Adams' *Watership Down.* An outstanding student, she served as captain of her high school's debate team and also founded the math club; at university she would study particle physics. After graduation, Bow worked for a time at CERN, the European Centre for Nuclear Research located near Geneva, Switzerland, before pursuing her interest in writing.

Plain Kate was inspired, in part, by a volume of Russian fairy tales that Bow once read. "I love fairy tales, and I thought I knew them, but the Russian ones blew me away," the author remarked to Sarah Rachel Egelman in *Teenreads.com.* "They are like dark chocolate—very dark chocolate. They're full of white nights and strange transformations, villains that read as tragic heroes, and doomed heroes that still stand tall. *Plain Kate* ended up with a setting that's more Eastern European than anything, but that book of Russian tales cast the spell under which I wrote it."

Cover of Erin Bow's middle-grade novel **Plain Kate,** *featuring cover art by Julia Kolesova.* (Cover art by Julia Kolesova. Reproduced by permission of Scholastic, Inc.)

Bow's novel centers on the title character, a gifted woodcarver who learned the craft from her late father. After his death, Kate is forced to move into his tiny market stall with her only companion, a cat named Taggle. Kate's skill worries her superstitious neighbors, who wonder if her gifts are magical, and they blame her for a series of events that trouble the region. Fearing she will be burned as a witch, Kate realizes that she must leave the village, and she gains the means to do this from a wanderer named Linay. In exchange for Kate's shadow, Linday will give her supplies and fulfill a single wish; realizing that the girl will need a friend on her journey, Linay grants Taggle the power of speech. Upon leaving her village, Kate joins a band of gypsy-like Roamers, and she also discovers that Linay plans to use her shadow for evil purposes.

Calling *Plain Kate* an "outstanding novel," *New York Times Book Review* contributor Sherie Posesorski observed that Bow "demonstrates a mature, haunting artistry." The critic added that "the plot unfolds with the swiftness and dramatic urgency of an adventure tale, yet each event has a measured gravity," while "ambiguity and complexity shade the characterizations and the story line." Amanda Craig, writing in the London *Times,* described *Plain Kate* as "gorgeously well written, unafraid of plumbing joy and sorrow, and with a story that you can't bear to stop reading." *School Library Journal* reviewer Beth L. Meister also praised the novel, stating that Bow's "careful and evocative writing reflects her work as a published poet."

Biographical and Critical Sources

PERIODICALS

Booklist, October 15, 2010, Lynn Rutan, review of *Plain Kate,* p. 61.

Horn Book, September-October, 2010, Anita L. Burkam, review of *Plain Kate,* p. 72.

Kirkus Reviews, September 1, 2010, review of *Plain Kate.*

New York Times Book Review, January 16, 2011, Sherie Posesorski, review of *Plain Kate,* p. 12.

Publishers Weekly, August 16, 2010, review of *Plain Kate,* p. 54.

Quill & Quire, September, 2010, Jean Mills, review of *Plain Kate.*

School Library Journal, October, 2010, Beth L. Meister, review of *Plain Kate,* p. 108.

Times (London, England), March 19, 2011, Amanda Craig, review of *Wood Angel,* p. 12.

Voice of Youth Advocates, December, 2010, Diane Colson, review of *Plain Kate,* p. 466.

ONLINE

Erin Bow Home Page, http://erinbow.com (December 15, 2011).

Erin Bow Web log, http://erinbow.livejournal.com (December 15, 2011).

Quill & Quire Online, http://www.quillandquire.com/ (May 1, 2008), Dory Cerny, "The Fantastic Bows."

Teenreads.com, http://www.teenreads.com/ (September, 2010), Sarah Rachel Egelman, interview with Bow.*

* * *

BRENNAN, Caitlin
See TARR, Judith

* * *

BRISTOW, David
(David L. Bristow)

Personal

Married; wife's name Danette. *Education:* Degree (psychology).

Addresses

Home—Lincoln, NE. *Office*—Nebraska State Historical Society, P.O. Box 82554, 1500 R St., Lincoln, NE 68501. *E-mail*—bristow@windstream.net.

Career

Author, editor, and researcher. Nebraska State Historical Society, Lincoln, associate director for research and publications; *Nebraska Life* magazine, former managing editor; *Nebraska History* magazine, editor; freelance writer and editor. Also worked in the mental-health field.

Awards, Honors

Notable Social Studies Trade Books for Young People designation, National Council for the Social Studies/ Children's Book Council, and Nebraska Book Award for Youth Nonfiction, Nebraska Center for the Book, both 2010, both for *Sky Sailors.*

Writings

(As David L. Bristow) *A Dirty, Wicked Town: Tales of Nineteenth-century Omaha,* Caxton Press (Caldwell, ID), 2000.

Sky Sailors: True Stories of the Balloon Era, Farrar, Straus & Giroux (New York, NY), 2010.

Sidelights

In *Sky Sailors: True Stories of the Balloon Era*, a non-fiction work for middle-grade readers, David Bristow explores the history of early aviation, focusing on the development of hot-air and helium balloons. The inspiration for the work came to Bristow while he was researching his first book—a history of Omaha, Nebraska—and discovered a story about an ill-fated 1875 balloon flight. "That got me interested in the subject of early ballooning," the author recalled on his home page. "Back before airplanes it was the only way to fly, and the early 'aeronauts,' as they called themselves, often pursued their aerial adventures with a great disregard for safety."

Sky Sailors covers the period from 1783, when brothers Joseph and Étienne Montgolfier constructed the first balloon designed for manned flight, to the early twentieth century. Among the individuals Bristow profiles are John Steiner, a U.S. aeronaut who attempted to balloon over Lake Erie in 1857; Salomon Andrée, a Swedish explorer who died while leading an balloon expedition to the North Pole; and Dolly Shepherd, a daring British parachutist and aerial performer. "The writing is crisp and lively," remarked *School Library Journal* critic Jody Kopple, and Michael Cart predicted in *Booklist* that *Sky Sailors* "is sure to inspire readers to search for more stories like these."

Biographical and Critical Sources

PERIODICALS

Booklist, September 15, 2010, Michael Cart, review of *Sky Sailors: True Stories of the Balloon Era,* p. 58.
Bulletin of the Center for Children's Books, November, 2010, Elizabeth Bush, review of *Sky Sailors,* p. 122.
Horn Book, January-February, 2011, Jonathan Hunt, review of *Sky Sailors,* p. 108.
Kirkus Reviews, September 1, 2010, review of *Sky Sailors.*
School Library Journal, November, 2010, Jody Kopple, review of *Sky Sailors,* p. 136.

ONLINE

David Bristow Home Page, http://www.davidbristow.com (December 15, 2011).*

*   *   *

BRISTOW, David L.
See BRISTOW, David

*   *   *

BRYAN, Kathleen
See TARR, Judith

C

CLARK, Karen Henry

Personal

Married; children: one daughter. *Education:* Degree (education); University of Tulsa, M.A. (English). *Hobbies and other interests:* Walking.

Addresses

Home—Saint Paul, MN.

Career

Educator and writer. Worked as a teacher.

Writings

Sweet Moon Baby: An Adoption Tale, illustrated by Patrice Barton, Knopf (New York, NY), 2010.

Biographical and Critical Sources

PERIODICALS

Kirkus Reviews, October 15, 2010, review of *Sweet Moon Baby: An Adoption Tale.*
Publishers Weekly, October 18, 2010, review of *Sweet Moon Baby,* p. 48.
School Library Journal, January, 2011, Deborah Vose, review of *Sweet Moon Baby,* p. 70.

ONLINE

Mymcbooks Web log, http://mymcbooks.wordpress.com/ (October 28, 2011), Ella Johnson, interview with Clark.*

*   *   *

COSTA BATES, Janet 1959-

Personal

Born 1959; married; children: two sons. *Education:* College degree.

Addresses

Home—Boston, MA. *Agent*—Jill Corcoran, Herman Agency, 350 Central Park W., New York, NY 10025.

Career

Author and counselor. Boston College, Boston, MA, career counselor.

Awards, Honors

Highlights for Children fiction contest award, 2004; *Pockets* magazine Fiction Contest award, 2006; New Voices Award Honor selection, 2011, for *Seaside Dream.*

Writings

Seaside Dream, illustrated by Lambert Davis, Lee & Low (New York, NY), 2010.

Contributor to periodicals, including *Highlights for Children* and *Pockets.*

Sidelights

Janet Costa Bates loved to write while growing up, but it was not until her own two children were born that she began to focus her talent on writing for young readers. Just as Costa Bates's family helped inspire her writing, they also helped inspire the story in her first published children's book. Illustrated by Lambert Davis, *Seaside Dream* is a multigenerational tale about a girl and her immigrant grandmother and the elderly woman's wish to share special days with her family.

In *Seaside Dream* Costa Bates welcomes readers into a close-knit family with its roots in Cape Verde. Cora's grandmother is about to turn seventy, and everyone is coming to celebrate at the woman's seaside home. After an afternoon of delicious *Crioulo* cooking, gift giving, and festivities, Cora and Grandma take a moonlit walk along the beach, and the older woman expresses her

deep regret that she and her sister Aura did not keep in touch after she left Aura behind in Cape Verde many years before. In a dream she has later that night, the little girl finds a way to give Grandma a very special gift that demonstrates her own compassionate nature and also shows her acceptance of her cultural heritage.

Praising the "realistic acrylic paintings" that Davis contributes to Costa Bates's tale, Gay Lynn Van Vleck added that *Seaside Dream* features "tidbits of Cape Verdean culture" that make the story useful for "multicultural" story hours. A *Kirkus Reviews* writer recommended the picture book due to its "distinctive take on universal aspects of immigration," while a contributor to *Children's Bookwatch* described *Seaside Dreams* as "a wonderful book about strong connections and honoring one's family traditions and past." Writing that Costa Bates sprinkles her text with Cape Verdean dialect and expressions, a *Publishers Weekly* reviewer added that "the strength of Cora and her grandmother's relationship emanates from nearly every page."

Biographical and Critical Sources

PERIODICALS

Children's Bookwatch, January, 2011, review of *Seaside Dream.*
Kirkus Reviews, September 1, 2010, review of *Seaside Dream.*

Janet Costa Bates's multigenerational story in **Seaside Dream** *is captured in artwork by Lambert Davis.* (Illustrations copyright © 2010 by Lambert Davis. Reproduced by permission of Lee & Low Books.)

Publishers Weekly, September 13, 2010, review of *Seaside Dream,* p. 45.
School Library Journal, November, 2010, Gay Lynn Van Week, review of *Seaside Dream,* p. 65.

ONLINE

Authors Now Web site, http://www.authorsnow.com/ (December 12, 2011), "Janet Costa Bates."
Janet Costa Bates Home Page, http://janetcostabates.com (December 12, 2011).

*   *   *

CROWLEY, James 1969-

Personal

Born 1969. *Education:* Attended St. Edward's University.

Addresses

Home—Austin, TX.

Career

Writer and filmmaker. Director of films, including *Slappy the Clown* 1999; and *The Journeyman,* 2001. Location manager of films, including *The People Next Door,* 1996; *SubUrbia,* 1996; *Home Fries,* 1998; *The White River Kids,* 1999; *Bullfighter,* 2000; *The Rookie,* 2002, *Hidalgo,* 2004; *The Chronicles of Narnia: The Lion, the Witch, and the Wardrobe,* 2005; *The Chronicles of Narnia: Prince Caspian,* 2008; and *Bernie,* 2011. Coproducer of *Fool's Gold,* 1997; production supervisor of *The Wendell Baker Story,* 2005.

Awards, Honors

Audience Award, South by Southwest Film Festival, 2001, for *The Journeyman.*

Writings

Starfish (young-adult novel), illustrated by Jim Madsen, Disney-Hyperion (New York, NY), 2010.

SCREENPLAYS

(And director) *Slappy the Clown* (short), Harbinger Pictures, 1999.
(And director) *The Journeyman,* Harbinger Pictures, 2001.

Sidelights

James Crowley, a film-industry veteran who has scouted locations for *The Chronicles of Narnia: The Lion, the Witch, and the Wardrobe* and other popular films, is

also the author of *Starfish,* a work of historical fiction geared for teen readers. Crowley's debut novel concerns a pair of orphaned siblings who flee from the boarding school they attend on the Blackfeet Indian reservation. The tale was inspired by Crowley's experiences working on the film *Hidalgo,* during which he got to known members of the Blackfeet Nation. "Some were . . . older guys who had actually attended the [old reservation] boarding schools," the author told *Austin American-Statesman* contributor Matt Odam. "So that kind of opened my eyes. We all know about reservations and the history of it, but sometimes when you're standing there looking at it, it obviously has a lot more impact."

Set in Montana in the early 1900s, *Starfish* focuses on Lionel, a quiet Blackfeet youth, and Lionel's older sister, Beatrice. Infuriated by the treatment she receives at the Chalk Bluff boarding school, Beatrice refuses to cut her hair or given up her native language, despite de-

Illustrated by James Madsen, James Crowley's young-adult novel **Starfish** *find a Native-American girl vowing to retain her tribal culture.* (Illustration copyright © 2010 by Dorling-Kindersley/Getty Images, Jim Madsen and Norbet Piechotta. Reprinted by permission of Disney Book Group. All rights reserved.)

mands that she do so. After Lionel's discovery of a frozen corpse leads to an incident with the authorities, the siblings steal a horse and go into hiding in the mountains, getting assistance from their grandfather and an African-American fugitive while attempting to outwit the soldiers tracking them.

According to Cynthia Gray in her *Voice of Youth Advocates* review of *Starfish,* "readers will be fascinated with the skills and knowledge Beatrice has held on to . . . and how well Lionel learns from her." *ALAN* online critic Adrienne Kisner also praised the work, remarking that "Lionel is a sympathetic character [that] . . . readers will root for," while "Beatrice is a warrior woman . . . and an inspiring heroine." Kathleen Isaacs, writing in *Booklist,* maintained that Crowley's filmmaking background served him well in writing *Starfish*: The book's "pacing is solid, and both setting and action are clearly described and easy to picture," noted the critic.

Biographical and Critical Sources

PERIODICALS

Austin American-Statesman, March 24, 2011, Matthew Odam, "Austinite Takes Break from Work on the Set to Pen Novel."
Booklist, June 1, 2010, Kathleen Isaacs, review of *Starfish,* p. 78.
Kirkus Reviews, October 15, 2010, review of *Starfish.*
Voice of Youth Advocates, December, 2010, Cynthia Grady, review of *Starfish,* p. 450.

ONLINE

ALAN Online, http://www.alan-ya.org/ (November, 2010), Adrienne Kisner, review of *Starfish.*
James Crowley Home Page, http://www.jamesjcrowley. com (January 1, 2012).*

*　　　*　　　*

CUMMINGS, Priscilla 1951-

Personal

Born April 13, 1951, in Ludlow, MA; daughter of Robert (a farmer and chemistry/physics teacher) and Brenda (a homemaker) Cummings; married John W. Frece (a U.S. government administrator), September 17, 1983; children: William Frece, Hannah Frece. *Education:* University of New Hampshire, B.A. (English literature), 1973. *Hobbies and other interests:* Reading, playing piano, taking walks.

Addresses

Home—Annapolis, MD. *E-mail*—priscummings@gmail. com.

Priscilla Cummings (Photograph reproduced by permission.)

Career

Journalist and author. *Holyoke Transcript-Telegram,* Holyoke, MA, newspaper reporter, 1973-75; *Hartford Courant,* Hartford, CT, newspaper reporter, 1975-76; *Richmond News Leader,* Richmond, VA, newspaper reporter, 1976-82; magazine editor and writer, 1982-85; writer of children's books, beginning 1986.

Member

Society of Children's Book Writers and Illustrators, Children's Book Guild of Washington, DC.

Awards, Honors

Journalism awards from United Press International (UPI) News Editors of New England, National Federation of Press Women, and Virginia Press Association; Virginia Journalist of the Year, UPI, 1980; Arthur J. Blaney Award, 1982; Pick of the List selection, American Booksellers Association, 1997, and Maryland Black-Eyed Susan Book List inclusion, 1999-2000, both for *Autumn Journey;* International Literacy Award, Metro-Washington Association for Childhood Education, 2001, for "Chadwick the Crab" books; Notable Children's Book selection, American Library Association (ALA), 2002, for *A Face First;* Children's Choice designation, International Reading Association/Children's Book Council (IRA/CBC), and New York Public Library Books for the Teen Age designation, both 2005, and Best Books for Young Adults designa-

tion, ALA, 2006, all for *Red Kayak;* Children's Choice designation, IRA/CBC, 2010, for *Blindsided;* books named to various state reading lists.

Writings

PICTURE BOOKS

Oswald and the Timberdoodles, illustrated by A.R. Cohen, Tidewater Publishers (Centreville, MD), 1990.

Sid and Sal's Famous Channel Marker Diner, illustrated by A.R. Cohen, Tidewater Publishers (Centreville, MD), 1991.

Toulouse: The Story of a Canada Goose, illustrated by A.R. Cohen, Tidewater Publishers (Centreville, MD), 1995.

Chesapeake ABC, illustrated by David Aiken, Tidewater Publishers (Centreville, MD), 2000.

Chesapeake 1 2 3, illustrated by David Aiken, Tidewater Publishers (Centreville, MD), 2002.

Chesapeake Rainbow, illustrated by David Aiken, Tidewater Publishers (Centreville, MD), 2004.

Santa Claws: The Christmas Crab, illustrated by Marcy Dunn Ramsey, Tidewater Publishers (Centreville, MD), 2006.

Beetle Boddiker, illustrated by Marcy Dunn Ramsey, Tidewater Publishers (Centreville, MD), 2008.

Beddy Bye in the Bay, illustrated by Marcy Dunn Ramsey, Schiffer Publishing (Atglen, PA), 2010.

"CHADWICK THE CRAB" PICTURE-BOOK SERIES; ILLUSTRATED BY A.R. COHEN

Chadwick the Crab, Tidewater Publishers (Centreville, MD), 1986.

Chadwick and the Garplegrungen, Tidewater Publishers (Centreville, MD), 1987.

The Chadwick Coloring Book, Tidewater Publishers (Centreville, MD), 1988.

Chadwick's Wedding, Tidewater Publishers (Centreville, MD), 1989.

Chadwick Forever, Tidewater Publishers (Centreville, MD), 1993.

Meet Chadwick and His Friends, Tidewater Publishers (Centreville, MD), 1999.

NOVELS

Autumn Journey, Dutton (New York, NY), 1997.

A Face First, Dutton (New York, NY), 2001.

Saving Grace, Dutton (New York, NY), 2003.

Red Kayak, Dutton (New York, NY), 2004.

What Mr. Mattero Did, Dutton (New York, NY), 2005.

Blindsided, Dutton (New York, NY), 2010.

Author's novels have been translated into Korean and German.

Sidelights

A former journalist, Priscilla Cummings is the author of novels for middle-grade readers and young adults, among them such award-winning titles as *Autumn Journey, Red Kayak,* and *Blindsided.* "Each of these stories was inspired by something in real life that moved me emotionally," Cummings stated in an essay on her home page. "When I talk about this with students, I explain how many of the skills I learned as a newspaper reporter helped me transform the spark of an idea into an entire book."

Although many of Cummings' books are set on the Chesapeake Bay, she grew up on a dairy farm in western Massachusetts. "Even as a little girl, I enjoyed writing about animals," she recalled on the Children's Book Guild Web site. She enjoyed writing so much, in fact, that she once had more than twenty pen pals from around the world. Cummings followed her dreams and became a newspaper reporter, then moved to magazine writing and editing.

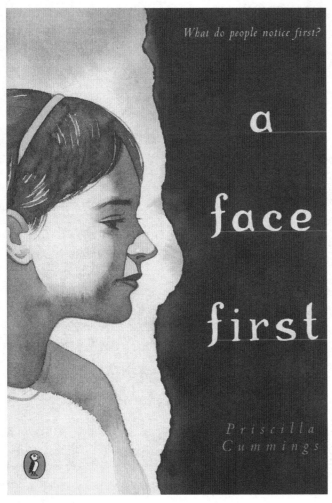

Cover of Cummings' middle-grade novel **A Face First,** *featuring artwork by Goro Sasaki.* (Puffin Books. Cover illustration copyright © by Goro Sasaki/ Bernstein & Andriulli, Inc. Reproduced by permission.)

When she relocated to Maryland, Cummings' curiosity about the region's native blue crabs inspired her to begin the "Chadwick the Crab" series. Along with the "Chadwick" books, Cummings has written several picture books set near the Chesapeake Bay, and others featuring different animal characters. Her first story for young readers, published in 1986 as the picture book *Chadwick the Crab,* introduces a blue crab who calls the Chesapeake Bay home. Chadwick and his other animal friends return in several other stories in which they introduce children to the importance of preserving the marine environment from pollution. The author's stories about the crab's adventures have proved particularly popular in the Maryland region, with the "Chadwick the Crab" series selling over 300,000 copies.

Cummings has more recently added a new dimension to her literary career by writing for older readers, and her novels include *Autumn Journey* and *A Face First.* In an interview with *Washington Post* contributor Holly Smith, she confided that this transition was not easy. "I'm embarrassed to say this, but parts of *Autumn Journey* were written almost ten years before the book was published." Despite this slow start, however, the author persisted and the middle-grade novel was finally released in 1997; Cummings' second novel, *A Face First,* was released four years later. "Some authors write children's books with lovable characters and straightforward text," Smith claimed, in describing Cummings' efforts. "Others create complex novels that connect with tough-to-reach adolescents. A few can do both. Priscilla Cummings is one of them."

Praised for presenting "true strength of character and respect for both family and the natural world" by *School Library Journal* contributor Susan Oliver, *Autumn Journey* follows the story of eleven-year-old Will Newcomb after his father loses his job and the family must leave their Maryland home and move in with relatives. Despite the extra chores, the fifth grader enjoys living on his grandfather's farm, but his parents' constant fighting disturbs him. When his grandfather suffers a heart attack, Will fears that his family will fall apart, a concern that intensifies after his father temporarily disappears. A Canada goose Will shoots but cannot bring himself to kill ultimately teaches the boy about perseverance, as he nurses the wounded creature back to health. Writing in *Kirkus Reviews,* a critic found *Autumn Journey* to be "less a tale of unmitigated woe than a beautifully told, uplifting story about the power and strength of family."

A Face First deals with a different type of tragedy in its focus on twelve-year-old Kelley, who suffers severe burns to her face, hands, and leg during a car accident. As her memory of the events preceding the accident returns, Kelley realizes that her mother's carelessness caused the crash and begins to blame the woman for her disfigurement. Forced to wear protective coverings—including a plastic pressure face mask to help her skin heal—the sixth grader retreats into her own private world and rejects efforts by family and friends to com-

fort her. However, with the support of other burn victims, Kelley begins to realize that she is not alone in her suffering and she starts working to accept the changes in her life. Critics noted Cummings' extensive knowledge of medical treatment for burn victims, remarking that it is evidenced in *A Face First* through the author's descriptive passages of Kelley's experience in the hospital. However, according to *School Library Journal* critic Cindy Darling, the author "really shines in showing the careful balance of push, pull, and nurturing that must be maintained by the dedicated medical staff." In *Booklist* Carolyn Phelan remarked that the story's "knowledgeable but compassionate tone rings true," going on to call *A Face First* "a thoughtful read that will encourage empathy."

Another novel for middle-grade readers, *Saving Grace* is set during the Great Depression, when eleven-year-old Grace is placed in a charity shelter until her family can afford to take care of her and her siblings. That Christmas, Grace is taken in by a wealthy family, and when the Hammonds announce that they may want to adopt her, Grace must decide whether to go back to her family and hope for better times or to stay where she is. "The realistic historical detail is an integral part of the family drama," wrote Hazel Rochman in her *Booklist* review. A *Kirkus Reviews* contributor also noted Cummings' attention to the time period, writing that her "vivid rendition of the Depression era" in *Saving Grace* "makes this a valuable addition to the genre."

Red Kayak, a work for older readers, centers on Brady Parks, a working-class teen who befriends the DiAngelos, a well-to-do family spending the summer in Brady's tight-knit Chesapeake Bay community. When some of Brady's friends play a prank that results in the death of the DiAngelos' three-year-old son, the teen feels responsible; while he does not want to betray his friends, he also wants to do what is right. "Cummings has created a multifaceted story that is as much about the families and life in the Chesapeake as it is about a prank gone awry," wrote Vicki Reutter in *School Library Journal,* while a *Kirkus Reviews* contributor described *Red Kayak* as a "well-written, sometimes gripping story." As Anne O'Malley noted in her *Booklist* review, "Brady's ultimate decision is both anguished and well reasoned, making for a realistic conclusion."

Also written for teens, *What Mr. Mattero Did* tells the story of three seventh graders who accuse their school music teacher of sexual abuse. Mr. Mattero's own daughter, Melody, is in eighth grade; the story is told partly from her perspective and details what the baseless accusation does to her family. The narrative is also expanded through the viewpoint of Claire, one of the accusers. Knowing the truth of what happened—that Mr. Mattero is innocent—Claire begins to question her own actions, as well as those of her friends. Jennifer Hubert, reviewing the novel for *Booklist,* considered *What Mr. Mattero Did* to be "an age-appropriate introduction to a difficult topic," and a *Publishers Weekly* re-

viewer predicted that, "riveting and timely, this shocking slice-of-life drama is sure to keep pages turning." Jeffrey Hastings wrote in *School Library Journal* that in *What Mr. Mattero Did* "Cummings has crafted an engrossing and thought-provoking tale involving sensitive, real-life issues."

Blindsided centers on Natalie O'Reilly, a fourteen year old with an uncertain future. For several years, Natalie's vision has been deteriorating, the result of a congenital disease. After enduring several surgeries, the teen faces the prospect of losing her sight completely, and her concerned parents enroll her in the Baltimore Center for the Blind, where she can learn essential life skills. Distraught and angry, Natalie struggles to adjust to her new environment, hoping for a miracle that never comes, until a devastating event forces the teen to draw on her hidden strengths. With the help of some new-found friends at her school, Natalie begins to learn Braille, takes self-defense classes, and adapts to life with a cane.

Cover of Cummings' young-adult novel **Blindsided,** *in which a girl must come to terms with her failing eyesight.* (Cover image courtesy of Getty Images, Inc. Used by permission of Dutton Children's Books, a division of Penguin Young Readers Group, a member of Penguin Group (USA) Inc., 345 Hudson Street, New York, NY 10014. All rights reserved.)

Alison Follos, writing in *School Library Journal,* commented that *Blindsided* "probes the overlooked gifts of physical normalcy and brings awareness to the tremendous barriers the blind face—visible and otherwise." "The young characters' courage is unforgettable, and so are the heartbreaking details," Rochman observed, and a *Kirkus Reviews* contributor stated that "Natalie's classmates . . . provide distinct and multidimensional voices that powerfully introduce life with vision loss."

Cummings once told *SATA:* "When children at school ask me what advice I have for them, as future authors, I tell them they should be reading at every opportunity: books, magazines, newspapers. I tell them to write—not just stories, but poems, letters, journal entries, essays—whatever. And I tell them this: they should be learning to watch and listen.

"As a newspaper reporter for ten years, I learned that standing back to watch and listen often gave me as much compelling information as asking a question or demanding an answer. As an author, I have discovered that standing back to watch and listen gives me many of the valuable details that bring a character to life and drive a story forward.

"When I was on the burn unit of a local hospital researching my novel, *A Face First,* I stood back to become the eyes and ears of my character, Kelley, a twelve-year-old burn victim, slowly recovering in a hospital bed. Outside the window, I saw how 'the traffic never stopped.' In the book, I wrote: 'At two, three, four o'clock in the morning, headlights came and went steadily in the darkness. Like a pulse, Kelley couldn't help but think. Life outside the hospital went on: People got in their cars, buckled themselves in, and went places, even if it was just to pick up shirts at the cleaners or get a gallon of milk at the 7-Eleven or order a meatball sub at Jerry's.'

"Inside the hospital, I listened to a burn patient cry as he struggled to eat a canned pear, and heard the sounds of a Medivac helicopter landing outside the window to deliver another patient into the emergency room entrance below. Both of these details also become part of Kelley's story.

"Standing back to watch, and listen, for the telling detail has been just as important to me as watching for the right ideas, and listening to my heart and mind for the story to emerge."

Biographical and Critical Sources

PERIODICALS

Baltimore Sun, March 8, 2006, Nia-Malika Henderson, "Making a Splash among Schools, Libraries, Teens" (profile of Cummings).
Booklist, February 1, 2001, Carolyn Phelan, review of *A Face First,* p. 1052; May 15, 2003, Hazel Rochman, review of *Saving Grace,* p. 1665; September 1, 2004, Anne O'Malley, review of *Red Kayak,* p. 106; July, 2005, Jennifer Hubert, review of *What Mr. Mattero Did,* p. 1915; June 1, 2010, Hazel Rochman, review of *Blindsided,* p. 50.
Bulletin for the Center of Children's Books, February, 2001, review of *A Face First,* p. 220; October, 2004, Deborah Stevenson, review of *Red Kayak,* p. 66.
Kirkus Reviews, June 1, 1997, review of *Autumn Journey,* p. 871; June 1, 2003, review of *Saving Grace,* p. 801; September 1, 2004, review of *Red Kayak,* p. 862; July 15, 2005, review of *What Mr. Mattero Did,* p. 788; June 15, 2010, review of *Blindsided.*
Kliatt, September, 2004, review of *Red Kayak,* p. 6.
Publishers Weekly, August 11, 1997, Claire Rosser, review of *Autumn Journey,* p. 402; January 22, 2001, review of *A Face First,* p. 325; August 29, 2005, review of *What Mr. Mattero Did,* p. 57.
School Library Journal, February, 1987, Hayden E. Atwood, review of *Chadwick the Crab,* p. 66; October, 1997, Susan Oliver, review of *Autumn Journey,* p. 132; February, 2001, Cindy Darling, review of *A Face First,* p. 117; June, 2003, review of *Saving Grace,* p. 137; September, 2004, Vicki Reutter, review of *Red Kayak,* p. 202; August, 2005, Jeffrey Hastings, review of *What Mr. Mattero Did,* p. 126; July, 2010, Alison Follos, review of *Blindsided,* p. 85.
Voice of Youth Advocates, February, 2001, Mary E. Heslin, review of *A Face First,* p. 421; October, 2003, review of *Saving Grace,* p. 302; August, 2005, Rollie Welch, review of *What Mr. Mattero Did,* p. 214; October, 2010, Cheryl Clark, review of *Blindsided,* p. 344.
Washington Post, July 5, 2001, Holly Smith, "Maturing with Her Audience."

ONLINE

Authors Unleashed Web log, http://authorsunleashed. blogspot.com/ (September 1, 2010), Jen Wardrip, interview with Cummings.
Children's Book Guild Web site, http://www.childrensbook guild.org/ (December 15, 2011), "Pricilla Cummings."
Priscilla Cummings Home Page, http://www.priscillacummings.com (December 15, 2011).*

D

de QUIDT, Jeremy

Personal

Born in England; married; children: Jack, two other children.

Addresses

Home—Somerset, England. *E-mail*—jerevydeq@gmail.com.

Career

Story teller and author. Writer-in-residence and visitor at schools.

Awards, Honors

Branford Boase Award shortlist, 2009, Waterstone's Children's Book of the Year Award shortlist, 2010, and Southern Schools Book Award shortlist, 2011, all for *The Toymaker.*

Writings

The Toymaker, illustrated by Gary Blythe, Oxford University Press (Oxford, England), 2008, David Fickling Books (New York, NY), 2010.
The Feathered Man, David Fickling Books (London, England), 2012.

Author's work has been translated into German.

Sidelights

Jeremy de Quidt is a British storyteller whose first novel, *The Toymaker,* was inspired by his work with school students. In 2005 de Quidt was a guest storyteller at Wells Central School when the seeds of the novel's plot first took shape. As he completed each chapter of the tale, he shared it with a group of interested students at the school, and their ideas about characters and plot guided the course of the fantasy novel. Compared by London *Guardian* contributor Philip Ardagh to the work of Philip Pullman, *The Toymaker* combines classic storybook elements—"the orphan, the circus, the well-to-do gent with villainous aims, and slavering wolves"—and combines them with what Pullman described as "the tantalising mysteries of the automaton . . . to create an intriguing and atmospheric plot."

Illustrated by Gary Blythe, *The Toymaker* is a horrific fantasy that is set in the 1700s in a Germanic city that is home to the ruling duke. After being introduced to Menschenmacher, the toymaker of the city, readers are directed to a traveling circus that comes to the region. Meanwhile, Doctor Leiter lusts for power over the region, and his influence is strengthened with the help of his hulking, superhuman manservant, Valter. When Leiter learns of the boasts of elderly circus conjurer Gustav, he is determined to discover the man's secret, and at Gustav's death he suspects (rightly) that the secret has passed (in cryptic form) to the conjurer's grandson and servant, Mathias. Determined to avoid the relentless Leiter, Mathias flees from the city, aided by a serving maid named Katta. In the forbidding countryside, the boy is aided in his effort to discover the secret's meaning by a rag-tag group of questionable companions that includes a suave highwayman named König and a charcoal-burner's son.

"With its choreographed fights, damaged bodies, flowing blood, and cliff-hanging chapter endings, [*The Toymaker*] . . . will appeal to readers who like nonstop action," assured Margaret A. Chang in her *School Library Journal* review of de Quidt's fiction debut. In *Kirkus Reviews* a critic sensed something more in the novel, calling *The Toymaker* "a disturbing dark fantasy" that is characterized by a "taut pace, elegant craftsmanship and shattering originality." For *Booklist* contributor Andrew Medlar, de Quidt's "stylized adventure" can be classed with the novels of Charles Dickens and Victor Hugo, its

mix of "intrigue and exhilaration," a "wild cast," and "a bloody, mysterious, and darkly thrilling quest" propelling the story to its "unexpected end."

De Quidt has followed *The Toymaker* with a second novel, *The Feathered Man,* which is also set in a German town and features a young boy faced with a grim task. Klaus works as an apprentice for the local tooth-puller, and when his master discovers a diamond hidden in the tooth of a corpse, the boy is a witness. Klaus eventually winds up with the gem in his possession, and it is then that he realizes that its value is something other than commercial. Otherwise, why would he be pursued by a sinister physician, a Jesuit priest, and a strangely garbed man who is said to have traveled from the Aztec empire, all who seem intent upon gain possession of the glasslike stone?

Biographical and Critical Sources

PERIODICALS

Booklist, July 1, 2010, Andrew Medlar, review of *The Toymaker,* p. 63.
Bulletin of the Center for Children's Books, September, 2010, Kate Quealy-Gainer, review of *The Toymaker,* p. 13.
Guardian (London, England), August 30, 2008, Philip Ardagh, review of *The Toymaker,* p. 14.
Horn Book, September-October, 2010, Joanna Rudge Long, review of *The Toymaker,* p. 75.
Kirkus Reviews, July 1, 2010, review of *The Toymaker.*
Publishers Weekly, August 9, 2010, review of *The Toymaker,* p. 53.
School Library Journal, October, 2011, Margaret A. Chang, review of *The Toymaker,* p. 112.

ONLINE

Jeremy de Quidt/DFB Storyblog, http://www.davidfickling books.co.uk/blog/ (December 24, 2011), "Jeremy de Quidt."*

*   *   *

DONOVAN, Jane Monroe

Personal

Married; husband's name Bruce; children: Ryan, Joey.

Addresses

Home—Pinckney, MI.

Career

Painter and children's book illustrator.

Awards, Honors

National Parenting Publications Honor Award, 2003, and Children's Choices selection, International Reading Association (IRA)/Children's Book Council, 2004, both for *My Momma Likes to Say;* Children's Book Award, IRA, 2005, and Eric Hoffer Award, 2006, both for *Winter's Gift;* Best Children's Book of the Year listee, Bank Street College of Education, 2007, for *My Grandma Likes to Say;* Children's Read-Aloud Book Award, University of Mississippi Center for Excellence in Literacy Instruction, 2010, for *My Daddy Likes to Say;* inclusion in several state reading association lists.

Writings

SELF-ILLUSTRATED

Winter's Gift, Sleeping Bear Press (Chelsea, MI), 2004.
Small, Medium, and Large, Sleeping Bear Press (Ann Arbor, MI), 2010.

ILLUSTRATOR

Carol Crane, *Sunny Numbers: A Florida Counting Book,* Sleeping Bear Press (Chelsea, MI), 2001.
Denise Brennan-Nelson, *My Momma Likes to Say,* Sleeping Bear Press (Chelsea, MI), 2003.
Denise Brennan-Nelson, *My Teacher Likes to Say,* Sleeping Bear Press (Chelsea, MI), 2004.
Anna Sewell, *Black Beauty's Early Days in the Meadow,* Sleeping Bear Press (Chelsea, MI), 2006.
Denise Brennan-Nelson, *My Grandma Likes to Say,* Sleeping Bear Press (Chelsea, MI), 2007.
Denise Brennan-Nelson, *My Daddy Likes to Say,* Sleeping Bear Press (Chelsea, MI), 2009.

Sidelights

A self-taught artist based in Michigan, Jane Monroe Donovan has created illustrations for picture books that include *My Momma Likes to Say* by Denise Brennan-Nelson. In her story, Brennan-Nelson offers a humorous look at American idioms and proverbs, focusing on a child's literal-minded interpretations of such well-worn clichés as "Money doesn't grow on trees" and "Cat got your tongue?" For the familiar saying "Don't let the bed bugs bite," Donovan's painting "shows three adorable creatures happily snoozing alongside the boy narrator," according to *School Library Journal* reviewer Bina Williams. In a companion volume, *My Daddy Likes to Say,* Brennan-Nelson presents another set of misinterpreted maxims, including "cool as a cucumber" and "wild goose chase." "Donovan's pictures add humorous charm" to this second book, as Maura Bresnahan noted in *School Library Journal.*

Donovan's love of both animals and the natural world informs her work as an illustrator. *Black Beauty's Early Days in the Meadow* is based on the original text of

Jane Monroe Donovan tells a humorous story in her self-illustrated picture book **Small, Medium, and Large.** (Sleeping Bear Press, 2010. Illustration copyright © 2010 by Jane Monroe Donovan. Reproduced by permission of The Gale Group.)

Anna Sewell's 1877 classic about a kind-hearted horse. Here Donovan's "expansive artwork captures the essence of spring," a contributor remarked in a *Children's Bookwatch* review of the updated story.

In *Winter's Gift,* Donovan's first self-illustrated title, she depicts the unlikely relationship between a broken-hearted farmer and a stranded horse. While *Small, Medium, and Large* follows a young girl's adventures with her three new Christmas gifts: a cat, a dog, and a miniature horse. In *School Library Journal,* Eva Mitnick applauded the "super-sweet yet cozy story" in *Small, Medium, and Large,* and a contributor in *Kirkus Reviews* praised the accompanying artwork, particularly the way Donovan brings to life her story's "snow-speckled outdoor scenes."

Biographical and Critical Sources

PERIODICALS

Booklist, July, 2003, Ilene Cooper, review of *My Momma Likes to Say,* p. 1893.
Children's Bookwatch, February, 2007, review of *Black Beauty's Early Days in the Meadow*; January, 2011, review of *Small, Medium, and Large.*
Kirkus Reviews, September 1, 2010, review of *Small, Medium, and Large.*
School Library Journal, September, 2003, Bina Williams, review of *My Momma Likes to Say,* p. 195; August, 2007, Linda Ludke, review of *My Grandma Likes to Say,* p. 77; June, 2009, Maura Bresnahan, review of *My Daddy Likes to Say,* p. 104; October, 2010, Eva Mitnick, review of *Small, Medium, and Large,* p. 71.

ONLINE

Sleeping Bear Press Web site, http://www.sleepingbear press.com/ (January 1, 2012), "Jane Monroe Donovan."*

* * *

DOWNING, Erin 1976-
(Erin Kate Soderberg)

Personal

Born October, 1976, in Duluth, MN; married Greg Downing; children: three. *Education:* University of Minnesota, B.A. (English literature); New York University, M.B.A. *Hobbies and other interests:* Traveling, walking, baking, swimming.

Addresses

Home—Minneapolis, MN. *Agent*—Michael Bourret, Dystel & Goderich Literary Management, 1 Union Square W., Ste. 904, New York, NY 10003; mbourret@ dystel.com. *E-mail*—erin@erindowning.com.

Career

Author. Worked as children's book editor and marketer in New York, NY, c. 1997; Nickelodeon, worked in marketing and business development until 2010.

Writings

PICTURE BOOKS; UNDER NAME ERIN SODERBERG

Dinosaur Dig, illustrated by Duendes del Sur, Scholastic (New York, NY), 2000.
Count to 100 with the NBA!, Scholastic (New York, NY), 2001.
Spooky Sports Day ("Scooby-Doo! Picture Clue" series), illustrated by Duendes del Sur, Scholastic (New York, NY), 2002.

CHAPTER BOOKS; UNDER NAME ERIN SODERBERG

Monkey See, Monkey Zoo ("Animal Tale" series), illustrated by Guy Francis, Bloomsbury (New York, NY), 2010.
The Quirks, Bloomsbury (New York, NY), 2012.

MIDDLE-GRADE NOVELS

Juicy Gossip, Scholastic (New York, NY), 2009.

YOUNG-ADULT NOVELS

Dancing Queen, Simon Pulse (New York, NY), 2006.
Prom Crashers, Simon Pulse (New York, NY), 2007.
Drive Me Crazy, Simon Pulse (New York, NY), 2009.

Kiss It, Simon Pulse (New York, NY), 2010.
A Funny Thing about Love, Simon Pulse (New York, NY), 2011.

Sidelights

A former book editor with a New York City publisher, Erin Downing now writes for both teens and younger children. Downing's early picture books, published under her maiden name, Erin Soderberg, weave together simple concepts and boy-friendly themes, as in *Count to 100 with the NBA!* and *Dinosaur Dig,* while her more-recent novels appeal to older girls with titles such as *Prom Crashers, Dancing Queen, Juicy Gossip,* and *Kiss It.* As an author, Downing creates stories that have been praised for being accessible and helping to inspire an interest in reading.

Recalling her start as a writer, Downing wrote on her home page that "I was a book editor first and swore I wasn't one of those editors who was secretly slaving away as an editorial assistant to get my big break as an author. But as soon as I left my job as an editor, I missed it. I missed working with authors to shape their characters, I missed futzing with plot to find and develop a hidden scene, I missed the fun that comes with making a book out of well, nothing at all, other than your own inner crazy. So that's when I started writing my own stories, and I've been hooked ever since."

Geared for preteens, *Juicy Gossip* focuses on seventh grader Jenna Sampson, who is proud of her role as editor of her school's newspaper. Jenna likes fitting in with the norm, and she cringes when her parents force her to work at their new hippy-dippy juice bar at the shopping mall where her friends are sure to see her. However, as a waitress working in the thick of gossip central, her new job might not be so bad, especially when the newspaper needs an added jolt to expand its readership. Olivia gets an internship at a British television station in *Dancing Queen,* where her confidence on the dance floor clinches her summer romance with a handsome pop singer, while love at first sight may be foiled for Emily and Ethan in *Prom Crashers.* Downing also appeals to preteen readers in *Drive Me Crazy,* in which three best friends set out on a week-long road trip to rural Wisconsin, where Kate plans to rekindle last year's summer romance. When a tagalong cousin hitches a ride, he begins to wear on Kate's nerves, but his sarcastic comments ultimately prompt the teen to view her trip—and her romantic future—in a new light.

Downing courts a more-mature teen readership in *Kiss It,* which focuses on teen sexuality. Eighteen-year-old Chastity Bryan lives in a small town, but she has never been afraid of stirring up gossip. Chastity enjoys sex, but her brief relationship with the now-besotted Hunter Johnson has left her cold. When family troubles come to light and a good friend winds up pregnant, Chaz balances her worries with the quest for a new sexual relationship. And who better to be with than dishy stranger Sebastian, who seems to share her cavalier attitude toward sex without love? Unfortunately, life has a way of teaching lessons in underhanded ways, as both Chaz and Sebastian discover. Chastity's first-person narration in *Kiss It* features "tongue-in cheek observations [that] are funny and smart," noted Johanna Lewis in her *School Library Journal* review of the novel, and the high schooler's "running commentary on small-town life sets a playful mood" in Downing's teen-focused relationship novel.

While Downing enjoys writing for teen girls, she has not abandoned younger readers. In *Monkey See, Monkey Zoo* she contributes to the "Animal Tales" chapter-book series in a story about a mischievous, tiara-wearing monkey named Willa. Life at the zoo is humdrum, except when groups of school children visit. One day Willa hears a young boy talking about his busy day, and she too wants to experience life in the bigger world. When the child leaves his school backpack behind, the monkey takes it as a sign that this is her chance to escape. Willa shoulders the backpack and determines to return it to its young owner. She sets out into the Human City, where her day of adventure is captured in humorous illustrations by Guy Francis. Willa's "story snaps right along with one close call after another," noted *School Library Journal* contributor Amy Holland, and a *Kirkus Reviews* writer noted of *Monkey See, Monkey Zoo* that Downing's "sly references to human behavior are particularly witty."

Biographical and Critical Sources

PERIODICALS

Bulletin of the Center for Children's Books, September, 2010, Karen Coats, review of *Kiss It,* p. 14.
Kirkus Reviews, September 1, 2010, review of *Monkey See, Monkey Zoo.*
School Library Journal, July, 2010, Johanna Lewis, review of *Kiss It,* p. 86; September, 2010, Amy Holland, review of *Monkey See, Monkey Zoo,* p. 134.

ONLINE

Erin Downing Home Page, http://www.erindowning.com (December 15, 2011).

E-F

EAGLAND, Jane

Personal

Born in Essex, England. *Education:* Bachelor's degree; Lancaster University, M.A. (creative writing). *Hobbies and other interests:* Gardening.

Addresses

Home—Lancashire, England. *Agent*—Lindsey Fraser, Fraser Ross Associates, 6 Wellington Pl., Edinburgh EH6 7EQ, Scotland.

Career

Writer and tutor. Worked as an English teacher at secondary schools until c. 2001; Alston Hall (adult learning center), Preston, Lancashire, England, currently teacher of creative writing.

Member

National Association of Writers in English, Scattered Authors Society.

Writings

Second Best, illustrated by Terry Milne, Andersen Press (London, England), 2005.
Wildthorn, Young Picador (London, England), 2009, Houghton Mifflin (Boston, MA), 2010.
Whisper My Name, Macmillan Children's Books (London, England), 2010.

Contributor of short story to anthology *Square Cuts,* 2006.

Sidelights

Making her home in the north of England, Jane Eagland worked as a grammar-school teacher for many years, until, at age fifty, she decided that it was time to indulge her lifelong interest in writing. Eagland's first published work, a story for young children called *Second Best,* has been followed by several novels geared for older readers and set in Victorian England, among them *Wildthorn* and *Whisper My Name.*

Inspired by a true story about a French woman who, in the nineteenth century, was mistakenly committed to an insane asylum for fifteen years, *Wildthorn* is set in 1870 and focuses on seventeen-year-old Louisa Cosgrove. Bright and independent-minded, Louisa is misunderstood by her aloof mother, and her stubborn assertion that she plans to follow her late father's path and become a medical doctor convinces her family to commit her to an asylum for the mentally unstable. Registered under a false name that she continually denies is hers, Louisa has no hope that her whereabouts will be discovered, and she endeavors to retain her sanity as she endures the misguided efforts of Victorian psychologists to effect a "cure". Through Louisa's narrative, which alternates between present and past, readers are allowed a view of the young woman's childhood, which included a jealous brother, her penchant for boy's playthings in favor of more feminine pursuits, and her growing romantic attachment for her beautiful cousin Grace.

"Eagland casts just the right amount of doubt about Louisa's sanity," noted Courtney Jones in her *Booklist* review of *Wildthorn,* and Wendy Scalfaro wrote in *School Library Journal* that the author tweaks reader expectations by including "an unusual twist on the conventional romantic denouement" expected in most gothic-style historical romances. "The anguish of a girl being forced to behave conventionally and being accused of moral insanity when she does not is conveyed in clear, dramatic prose," asserted Amanda Craig in her review of *Wildthorn* for the London *Times,* and *Voice of Youth Advocates* contributor Amy Wyckoff praised the novel as "a dark tale featuring a vibrant protagonist who refuses to let others squelch her passion." "I think part of my motivation in writing *Wildthorn* was to give voice to all those poor lost people down the years who couldn't speak for themselves . . . ," Eagland explained

Cover of Jane Eagland's historical novel Wildthorn, *a story of adventure and injustice set in Victorian England.* (Copyright © 2009 by Jane Eagland. Reprinted by permission of Houghton Mifflin Harcourt Publishing Company. All rights reserved.)

on her home page. "The asylum is a dark place and what Louisa experiences there is frightening. But despite the secret that threatens to undermine her confidence, she has courage . . . [enough] to face up to the truth about herself and at the same time tries to unravel the mystery that lies behind her imprisonment." In a nod to Eagland's motivation, a *Kirkus Reviews* writer commented that *Wildthorn* reveals "a shameful history of mental health care and women's incarceration," while a *Publishers Weekly* contributor commended the author for portraying "the atrocities and filth of the [nineteenth-century] asylum with shocking vividness."

Praised by London *Daily Mail* contributor Sally Morris as an "atmospheric, dramatic novel led by a suitably feisty heroine," Eagland's *Whisper My Name* is also set in the Victorian era. The year now is 1885, and an older teen named Meriel becomes haunted by a medium named Sophie Casson. Inspired by the author's research into the spiritualism craze of the era, *Whisper My Name* also mixes in elements of colonial India, contemporary English theatre, and the sometimes macabre innovations that are characteristic of Victorian science.

Biographical and Critical Sources

PERIODICALS

Booklist, September 15, 2010, Courtney Jones, review of *Wildthorn,* p. 73.

Bookseller, November 21, 2008, Caroline Horn, review of *Wildthorn,* p. 28.

Bulletin of the Center for Children's Books, October, 2010, Karen Coats, review of *Wildthorn,* p. 72.

Daily Mail (London, England), August 20, 2010, Sally Morris, review of *Whisper My Name,* p. 58.

Kirkus Reviews, September 1, 2010, review of *Wildthorn.*

Publishers Weekly, September 6, 2010, review of *Wildthorn,* p. 42.

School Library Journal, November, 2011, Wendy Scalfaro, review of *Wildthorn,* p. 112.

Times (London, England), April 22, 3009, Amanda Craig, review of *Wildthorn,* p. 12.

Voice of Youth Advocates, December, 2010, Amy Wyckoff, review of *Wildthorn,* p. 451.

ONLINE

Jane Eagland Home Page, http://www.janeeagland.co.uk (December 27, 2011).*

*   *   *

EHLERT, Lois 1934-
(Lois Jane Ehlert)

Personal

Born November 9, 1934, in Beaver Dam, WI; daughter of Harry and Gladys Ehlert; married John Reiss, 1967 (separated, 1977). *Education:* Layton School of Art, degree, 1957; University of Wisconsin, B.F.A., 1959.

Addresses

Home—Milwaukee, WI.

Career

Writer and illustrator. Layton School of Art Junior School, Milwaukee, WI, teacher; John Higgs Studio, Milwaukee, layout and production assistant; Jacobs-Keelan Studio, Milwaukee, layout and design illustrator; freelance illustrator and designer, beginning 1962. Designer of toys and games for children, basic art books, and banners, posters, and brochures. Moppet Players (children's theater), set designer. *Exhibitions:* Work included in Creativity on Paper Show, New York, NY, 1964; Society of Illustrators shows, 1971, 1989, 1990; International Children's Book Exhibit, Bologna, Italy, 1979; and solo exhibit at Milwaukee Art Museum, 2003.

Member

American Institute of Graphic Arts.

Awards, Honors

Three gold medals for outstanding graphic art, best-of-show citation, and fourteen merit awards, all Art Directors Club of Milwaukee, 1961-69; five awards of excellence, five merit awards, one gold medal, and one bronze medal, all Society of Communicating Arts of Milwaukee, 1970-72, 1976; Graphic Arts awards, Printing Industries of America, 1980-81, for Manpower posters; Paul Revere Award for Graphic Excellence, Hal Leonard Publishing Corp., 1983; National Endowment for the Arts/Wisconsin Arts Board grant, 1984; Design Award, Appleton Paper Co., 1985; Wisconsin Arts Board grants, 1985, 1987; Award of Excellence citations, Art Museum Association of America, 1985, 1986, 1987; Best Children's Book citations, New York Public Library, 1987, for *Growing Vegetable Soup,* and 1989, for *Planting a Rainbow;* Pick of the Lists citations, American Booksellers, 1988, for *Planting a Rainbow,* 1989, for *Color Zoo* and *Eating the Alphabet;* Caldecott Honor Book citation, American Library Association (ALA), 1989, for *Color Zoo;* Museum of Science and Industry Children's Science Books listee, 1989, and *Parents' Choice* Award for paperback, 1990, both for *Growing Vegetable Soup; Planting a Rainbow* included on John Burroughs List of Nature Books for Young Readers, 1989; Notable Children's Book citation, ALA, 1989, and *Boston Globe/Horn Book* Award Honor selection, 1990, both for *Chicka Chicka Boom Boom* by Bill Martin, Jr., and John Archambault; Wisconsin Library Association citation, 1989; Outstanding Science Trade Book for Children citation, National Science Teachers Association (NSTA), 1989, for *Planting a Rainbow,* 1990, for *Color Farm;* John Cotton Dana Award, Wisconsin Summer Reading Program, 1990; Parents' Choice Honor Book award for best story book, 1990, for both *Chicka Chicka Boom Boom* and *Fish Eyes;* Ten Best Illustrated Books inclusion, *New York Times,* and Certificate of Merit, Graphics Arts Awards, both 1990, both for *Fish Eyes;* Certificate of Excellence, *Parenting,* and NSTA Outstanding Science Trade Book designation, both 1991, and Elizabeth Burr Award, Wisconsin Library Association, *Boston Globe/Horn Book* Nonfiction Honor Book designation, and California Children's Media Award for Nonfiction, all 1992, all for *Red Leaf, Yellow Leaf;* Gold Award, Dimensional Illustrators Awards Show, 1991, for *Color Zoo;* first place award for Juvenile Trade Specialty, New York Book Show, and Reading Magic Award, *Parenting* magazine, both 1992, both for *Circus;* New York Public Library Best Children's Books inclusion, and Notable Book selection, ALA, both 1992, both for *Moon Rope; Boston Globe/Horn Book* Nonfiction Honor designation, 1992, and NSTA Outstanding Science Trade Book selection, 1993, both for *Feathers for Lunch;* D.H.L., University of Wisconsin, Milwaukee, 1994; Best Children's Books designation, Printing Industry of America, 1994, for *Nuts to You!;* Gold Seal Award, Oppenheim Toy Portfolio, 1996, for *Eating the Alphabet;* New York Show Award, 1996, for *Snowballs;* Best Books designation, *Book Links,* Reading Magic Award, *Parenting*

magazine, and *Booklist* Editors' Choice designation, all 1997, all for *Hands;* named to Wisconsin Writers Wall of Fame, Milwaukee Public Library, 1999; named Wisconsin Notable Author, Wisconsin Library Association; Bill Martin, Jr., Picture Book Award nomination, and Oppenheim Toy Portfolio Gold Award, both 2004, both for *Chicka Chicka 1, 2, 3;* Choices selection, Cooperative Children's Book Council (CCBC), and Notable Children's Book citation, ALA, both 2005, and *Boston Globe/Horn Book* Award, 2006, all for *Leaf Man;* Best Children's Books of the Year selection, Bank Street College of Education, Children's Choices selection, IRA/CBC, and Choices selection, CCBC, all 2009, all for *Boo to You!;* Choices selection, CCBC, 2010, for *Lots of Spots.*

Writings

SELF-ILLUSTRATED

Growing Vegetable Soup, Harcourt (San Diego, CA), 1987, reprinted, Red Wagon (San Diego, CA), 2004.

Planting a Rainbow, Harcourt (San Diego, CA), 1988, reprinted, Red Wagon (San Diego, CA), 2003.

Color Zoo, HarperCollins (New York, NY), 1989.

Eating the Alphabet: Fruits and Vegetables from A to Z, Harcourt (San Diego, CA), 1989.

Color Farm, HarperCollins (New York, NY), 1990.

Feathers for Lunch, Harcourt (San Diego, CA), 1990.

Fish Eyes: A Book You Can Count On, Harcourt (San Diego, CA), 1990.

Red Leaf, Yellow Leaf, Harcourt (San Diego, CA), 1991.

Circus, HarperCollins (New York, NY), 1992.

Moon Rope: A Peruvian Folktale, Spanish translation by Amy Prince, Harcourt (San Diego, CA), 1992.

Nuts to You!, Harcourt (San Diego, CA), 1993.

Mole's Hill: A Woodland Tale, Harcourt (San Diego, CA), 1994.

Snowballs, Harcourt (San Diego, CA), 1995.

Under My Nose (autobiography), photographs by Carlo Ontal, Richard C. Owen (Katonah, NY), 1996.

Hands, Harcourt (San Diego, CA), 1997.

Cuckoo: A Mexican Folktale, Spanish translation by Gloria de Aragon Andujar, Harcourt (San Diego, CA), 1997.

Top Cat, Harcourt (San Diego, CA), 1998.

Market Day: A Story Told with Folk Art, Harcourt (San Diego, CA), 2000.

Waiting for Wings, Harcourt (San Diego, CA), 2001.

In My World, Harcourt (San Diego, CA), 2002.

Pie in the Sky, Harcourt (Orlando, FL), 2004.

Leaf Man, Harcourt (Orlando, FL), 2005.

Wag a Tail, Harcourt (Orlando, FL), 2007.

Oodles of Animals, Harcourt (Orlando, FL), 2008.

Boo to You!, Beach Lane Books (New York, NY), 2009.

Lots of Spots, Beach Lane Books (New York, NY), 2010.

Rrralph, Beach Lane Books (New York, NY), 2011.

ILLUSTRATOR

Patricia M. Zens, *I Like Orange,* F. Watts (New York, NY), 1961.

Edward Lear, *Limericks,* World Publishing (Chicago, IL), 1965.

Mary L. O'Neill, *What Is That Sound!,* Atheneum (New York, NY), 1966.

Mannis Charosh, *Mathematical Games for One or Two,* Crowell (New York, NY), 1972.

Andrea Di Noto, *The Great Flower Pie,* Bradbury (New York, NY), 1973.

Vicki Silvers, *Sing a Song of Sound,* Scroll Press, 1973.

Nina Sazer, *What Do You Think I Saw?: A Nonsense Number Book,* Pantheon (New York, NY), 1976.

Diane Wolkstein, *The Visit,* Knopf (New York, NY), 1977.

Jane J. Srivastava, *Number Families,* Crowell (New York, NY), 1979.

Richard L. Allington, *Shapes and Sizes,* Raintree Publishers, 1979.

Bill Martin, Jr., and John Archambault, *Chicka Chicka Boom Boom,* Simon & Schuster (New York, NY), 1989, twentieth-anniversary edition, 2009.

Gene Baer, *Thump, Thump, Rat-a-tat-tat,* Harper (New York, NY), 1989.

Bill Martin, Jr., and John Archambault, *Words,* Little Simon (New York, NY), 1993.

Sarah Weeks, *Crocodile Smile: Ten Songs of the Earth as the Animals See It,* Harper Collins (New York, NY), 1994.

Bill Martin, Jr., and John Archambault, *Chicka Chicka Sticka Sticka: An ABC Sticker Book,* Little Simon (New York, NY), 1995.

Stuart J. Murphy, Jr., *A Pair of Socks,* HarperCollins (New York, NY), 1996.

Ann Turner, *Angel Hide and Seek,* HarperCollins (New York, NY), 1998.

Bill Martin, Jr., and Michael Sampson, *Chicka Chicka, 1, 2, 3,* Simon & Schuster (New York, NY), 2004.

Bill Martin, Jr., *Ten Little Caterpillars,* Beach Lane Books (New York, NY), 2011.

Rose Fyleman, *Mice,* Beach Lane Books (New York, NY), 2012.

Also illustrator and designer of "Scribbler's" products for Western Publishing.

Cover of Lois Ehlert's classic self-illustrated picture book, **Planting a Rainbow.** (Copyright © 1988 by Lois Ehlert. Reproduced by permission of Houghton Mifflin Harcourt Publishing Company. This material may note be reproduced in any form or by any means without the prior written permission of the publisher.)

A selection of Ehlert's papers are housed in the Kerlan Collection at the University of Minnesota.

Adaptations

Chicka Chicka Boom Boom was adapted for video, Weston Woods, 2000.

Sidelights

Known for creating vibrant collage artwork that features bold colors and clear, crisp shapes, Lois Ehlert has entertained and educated children since beginning her career in the early 1960s. Initially providing illustrations for the books of others, Ehlert began writing original texts to accompany her artwork in the mid-1980s, focusing on subjects such as birds, flowers, weather, work, retellings of folktales, and the alphabet. Ehlert has received a host of honors for her work, among them a Caldecott Honor Book designation and a *Boston Globe/Horn Book* Award. "I think of my books as little love notes, records of things I care about," the artist stated in her *Boston Globe/Horn Book* Award acceptance speech. "The words and pictures move from page to page, hand in hand. I hope to convey to young readers the same sense of excitement, wonder, and surprise I still have about the world around me."

In **Nuts to You!** *Ehlert pairs a whimsical nature story with her colorful collage art.* (Copyright © 1993 by Lois Ehlert. Reproduced by permission of Houghton Mifflin Harcourt Publishing Company. This material may not be reproduced in any form or by any means without the prior written permission of the publisher.)

As a child, Ehlert received both the encouragement and the environment to develop an interest in art. Her mother, who liked to sew, supplied her with scraps of cloth, and her father gave her wood from his woodworking projects. "Fabric was interesting to me because of its tactile sense and the vibrant colors," Ehlert recalled to Edie Boatman for the Milwaukee *Journal Sentinel.* "When I was young, construction paper was wimpy in color. I always made things out of stuff other people would throw away. Part of it was economic. I've always seen more of a pattern in design—my eyes are different from other people's. I seem to see colors that other people don't see." Ehlert's parents also provided her with a place to work by setting up a card table in a small room in their house; she still uses this table, modifying it as needed. Throughout high school she continued to work on projects that helped her to develop her talent and she eventually earned a scholarship to study at the Layton School of Art.

After graduating from art school in 1957, Ehlert did graphic design work and illustrated some children's books. She did not enjoy working on picture books at this point in her career, however, mainly because she could not approve the final color selections for her illustrations when her books went to the printer. Although she stopped working on picture books and concentrated on graphic design projects, friends eventually convinced her to go back to book illustration. "I began to see an emphasis on graphics in picture books," she noted in an essay for *Horn Book,* "and I thought that the time might be right for my work. I could see that there was a lot more care being taken in the production of children's books."

After providing artwork for many children's books as a freelance graphic designer, Ehlert created *Growing Vegetable Soup,* combing pictures and words to show the steps involved in cultivating a vegetable garden. In *Planting a Rainbow* her text and art tells the story of a mother and a child who created a flower garden. Noting that both of these books show Ehlert's passion for using bold colors, Andrea Barnet wrote in the *New York Times Book Review* that the artist's "colors are tropical, electric and hot—the grape purples and sizzling pinks children tend to choose when they paint. Often she pairs complementary hues . . . to startling effect, giving her illustrations a vibrant op-art feel, a visual shimmer that makes them jump off the page."

After achieving success with *Growing Vegetable Soup,* Ehlert took a class at the University of Wisconsin and found new ways to design books by incorporating such eye-catching techniques as die-cut holes in the pages and using different combinations of light and dark colors in the illustrations. She made use of such methods in *Color Zoo,* a book that introduces children to a wide range of colors and geometrical figures through the use of different-shaped holes cut in sturdy paper and placed on top of a design. Each new cutout shape—circle, square, triangle—is decorated with the features of different animals, cluing readers to think of the whole fig-

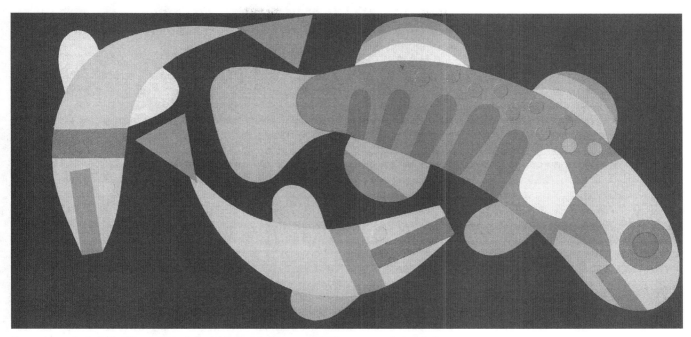

Set against a dark field, Ehlert's artwork for **Fish Eyes** *helps young children master their 1-2-3's.* (Copyright © 1990 by Lois Ehlert. Reproduced by permission of Houghton Mifflin Harcourt Publishing Company. This material may not be reproduced in any form or by any means without the prior written permission of the publisher.)

ure as a tiger, then a mouse, and then a fox. Ehlert repeats this routine with two more sets of shapes and ends *Color Zoo* with a summary of all of the shapes and colors used in the book. She reprised this technique in creating *Color Farm,* another award-winning title in which she "uses an array of brilliant graphics with carefully planned die-cuts to introduce geometric shapes," according to *Horn Book* reviewer Mary M. Burns.

For the self-illustrated *Feathers for Lunch* Ehlert uses colored paper to create a series of collages chronicling the story of a hungry cat that chases after a dozen birds at mealtime. However, a bell worn around the cat's neck alerts the birds of its presence. Ehlert's artwork is accompanied by a rhyming text, a list of all the birds presented, and printed representations of each of the birds' calls. In order to create a book that is both educational and attractive, she presents the birds in natural settings with flowers that are harmonious with the birds' colorful plummage. Since she wanted to make sure that her collages of the birds were the right colors and sizes, Ehlert checked them against the skins of birds kept at the Field Museum in Chicago.

In *Fish Eyes: A Book You Can Count On* Ehlert uses the patterns and shapes of sea creatures in order to teach kids about arithmetic. Holes cut in the book's pages encourage youngsters to interact while they learn about numbers by counting fish. Ehlert also puts black type on blue pages, hoping that children will find the subtle, hidden text. As she explained in *Horn Book,* "I purposely didn't want that design element to be dominant because I already had a dominant theme. So I worked on my layout, and then I stood in front of a full-length mirror to see how close I had to come to the

mirror before I could read that second line. I wanted the type to be a surprise to a child discovering it. I try to work on a lot of different levels in every book. Some things are more successful than others." Ehlert's efforts in this particular case were rewarded by Andrea Barnet, who wrote in the *New York Times Book Review* that *Fish Eyes* has "enough novelty to hold a child's interest, and enough complexity to sustain repeated readings."

Other animals are introduced by Ehlert in *Circus, Nuts to You!, Top Cat,* and *Waiting for Wings.* Hugo the elephant, Fritz the wonder bear, and Samu, the fiercest tiger in the world, are just part of the amazing menagerie presented in *Circus,* which exhibits "a most joyous use of the graphic-art style which Lois Ehlert continues to expand and refine," according to *Horn Book* critic Margaret A. Bush. With *Nuts to You!* a cheeky squirrel gets braver and braver as it approaches an open apartment window and finally scampers inside. *Horn Book* reviewer Ellen Fader dubbed this book "imaginatively designed," calling special attention to the title page and verso which are camouflaged to look like tree bark. A *Publishers Weekly* reviewer called *Nuts to You!* a "work of extraordinary visual splendor with an effectively simple, active plot."

In *Top Cat* Ehlert features a feline who rules the roost until a striped kitten makes an appearance. At first angry and spitting at the youngster, Top Cat finally figures out that the kitten is here to stay and ultimately makes the best of the situation by becoming a teacher and mentor to the younger pet. "Children and other feline fans will quickly warm to this spunky story of rivalry and acceptance," predicted a contributor for *Publishers*

Weekly, and in *Booklist* Linda Perkins wrote that the "distinctive collages" in *Top Cat* "portray a remarkable range of expression and movement and are sure to tickle funny bones."

A butterfly takes center stage in *Waiting for Wings,* "a marvelous presentation of the butterfly life cycle," according to a reviewer for *Horn Book,* and one that will "engage children curious about a seemingly magical process." In this work the author/artist accompanies her usual cut-paper illustrations with simple rhymes set out in large black letters. "Ehlert again spreads her creative wings to deliver this inventively designed picture book," noted a contributor to *Publishers Weekly.* Tracing the metamorphosis of the caterpillar into the graceful flying insect readers will recognize as a butterfly, Ehlert creates a "beautifully woven blend of information," according to Lisa Gangemi Kropp, writing in *School Library Journal,* and an "original and vivid introduction," as *Booklist* reviewer Carolyn Phelan observed.

For the illustrations in both *Red Leaf, Yellow Leaf* and *Snowballs* Ehlert constructs her characteristic collages not only out of layered colored paper, but also from found objects such as ribbons, seeds, bottle caps, twigs, and pieces of string and cloth. "Only an artist as gifted as Ehlert could take so well-worn a topic as building a snowman and make it as fresh as—well, new-fallen snow," remarked a *Publishers Weekly* reviewer. The same critic dubbed *Snowballs* a "joyful and inventive book." In *Cuckoo* Ehlert retells a folktale about the evolution of the vain cuckoo. "Sombreros off to this innovative artist for yet another eye-catching work," wrote a contributor for *Publishers Weekly.* Phelan, reviewing

Cuckoo for *Booklist,* called the book an "exhilarating adaptation" with "arresting artwork, some of [Ehlert's] best to date."

Ehlert finds inspiration in native and folk cultures when crafting the illustrations in several of her books. For the bilingual *Moon Rope: A Peruvian Folktale* she draws on the designs found in ancient Peruvian textiles, jewelry, ceramics, and even architecture, while *Mole's Hill: A Woodland Tale* gains inspiration from the beadwork designs of Native Americans. In *Moon Rope* Fox talks Mole into climbing with him up a braided grass rope—a rope he has hooked to the moon. As Fox climbs, he keeps his eyes upward, but timid Mole keeps looking back to Earth until he falls, thus explaining his preference for life in solitary tunnels. A critic for *Kirkus Reviews* felt that *Moon Rope* "may be [Ehlert's] handsomest book yet," and appraised the work as "altogether outstanding."

Mole's Hill, a Seneca Indian tale, is a "whimsical story of overcoming the might of an adversary through ingenuity," according to a reviewer for *Publishers Weekly.* The same reviewer also applauded Ehlert's illustrations, in which she "achieves dazzling effects with simple geometric shapes and strong, pure hues." Fox and Mole are at it once again in this story, in which Fox is so frustrated at having to walk around Mole's hill that he sends Raccoon and Skunk to tell her to move out. However, Mole uses her cleverness to defeat Fox, enlarging the hill and planting seeds to create such a pretty spot that Fox cannot bring himself to destroy it. In a *Horn Book* review, Margaret A. Bush also praised Ehlert's illustrations in *Mole's Hill,* which depict the flowers and

Ehlert employs folk-art forms and colors in her collage art for her picture-book story in **Market Day.** (Copyright © 2000 by Lois Ehlert. Reproduced by permission of Houghton Mifflin Harcourt Publishing Company. This material may not be reproduced in any form or by any means without the prior written permission of the publisher.)

trees of Wisconsin woodlands "as primitive abstractions in folk art style." Bush concluded that the book is "vivid and spare . . . a feast for the eye."

With *Hands* Ehlert celebrates such crafts as gardening and art through the use of photo-collage. The easy text is told from the point of view of a child who watches his father creating things in his workshop and his mother sewing wonderful creations. *Booklist* contributor Stephanie Zvirin wrote that *Hands* "is full of lovely surprises," resulting in a "thoughtfully designed book [that is] wonderful for lap sharing." A tribute to Ehlert's own parents, both of whom enjoyed working with their hands and who encouraged Ehlert in her art career, *Hands* grew out of an earlier project "to create a portrait of someone without using photographs" of that person, as the author/illustrator told Connie Goddard in a *Publishers Weekly* interview. Here Ehlert uses mementos such as pigskin work gloves, screws, and a folding ruler to call up the sense of her subject. Approaching the realm of the toy book, *Hands* employs die-cut pages, including one with the image of a tin box with screwdrivers inside. More tools of the trade pop up throughout this innovative book. A *Publishers Weekly* critic noted that Ehlert "works visual magic" in this "inventive effort that deserves nothing less than a big hand."

Ehlert links many of her favorite things together via abstract imagery to create the artwork for *In My World.* Here her "precise, die-cut figures . . . create stunning visuals that tell a story and make sense on both sides of the page," Kay Weisman maintained in *Booklist.* The picture book superimposes familiar shapes, such as birds, fish, and butterflies, die-cut over designs in Ehlert's signature bright colors. According to Joanna Rudge Long in *Horn Book,* "the vibrant colors and lively three-dimensional effects may well inspire children . . . to experiment with overlaying patterns and colors."

Pie in the Sky also contains elements of the natural world. The narrator does not quite believe it when Dad calls the tree in the backyard a "pie tree." In observing the tree over the passing seasons, however, the narrator vews all the animals that live in it, as well as the large cherries the tree bears in the summer. "Throughout, an economy of words and the narrator's chipper tone keep Ehlert's vision on track," wrote a critic for *Publishers Weekly,* while Phelan characterized the text in *Pie in the Sky* as "short and well suited to reading aloud." *School Library Journal* contributor Corrina Austin wrote that "each spread is an amazing work of art on its own," and concluded that "children will clamor for *Pie in the Sky.*" As *Horn Book* reviewer Susan P. Bloom quipped, "In luscious primary colors, collagist Ehlert struts her stuff."

"Whenever I see a beautiful leaf, I have to pick it up. I can't help myself; it's something I've done all my life," Ehlert explained in an interview for the Harcourt Pub-

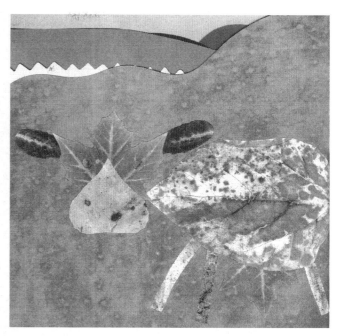

Featuring collage illustrations composed of a variety of pressed leaves, Ehlert tells a blustery fall story in **Leaf Man.** (Copyright © 2005 by Lois Ehlert. Reproduced by permission of Houghton Mifflin Harcourt Publishing Company. This material may not be reproduced in any form or by any means without the prior written permission of the publisher.)

lisher Web site. That habit became the inspiration for *Leaf Man,* an "eye-popping book," according to Ilene Cooper in *Booklist.* The story traces the paths blowing leaves can take while windborne in the fall, and Ehlert's illustrations are comprised of leaf collages. "When I began thinking about making *Leaf Man,* I carried a plastic bag with me, picking up treasures wherever I went," the artist explained, noting that she collected leaves from such diverse spots as Kansas City, Ithaca, New York, and Washington, DC, as well as from her own neighborhood. "Ehlert combines vivid collage artwork, effulgent colors, and an inventive design to create an eye-catching picture book," wrote Joy Fleishhacker in *School Library Journal.* A *Publishers Weekly* critic commented that "Ehlert sparks her foliage flight of fancy with her snazzy leaf collages," while a *Kirkus Reviews* contributor deemed *Leaf Man* "excellent to read aloud and to look at many times over." As *Horn Book* reviewer Joanna Rudge Long commented, "both craft and visualization are sure to inspire emulation."

Told in rhyming couplets, *Wag a Tail* follows the most-recent graduates of the Bow Wow School as they spend a day cavorting around a farmer's market and a dog park with their owners. When one of the pups forgets his lessons, however, his bewhiskered pals step in and remind him of his obedience training. "Ehlert's distinctive collage style works to great advantage in this strikingly simple story," a writer in *Kirkus Reviews* stated, and a *Publishers Weekly* critic maintained that "there's a lot to see in Ehlert's crisply textured compositions . . ., challenging young readers to dive right into her visual storytelling." Julie Roach, reviewing *Wag a Tail*

In Lots of Spots *Ehlert once again uses her creative talent to craft a world of imagination.* (Illustration copyright © 2010 by Lois Ehlert. Reprinted with the permission of Beach Lane Books, an imprint of Simon & Schuster Children's Publishing Division.)

in *School Library Journal,* commented that "this well-designed package pays tribute to dogs and life in the city."

Worried that an annoying feline could ruin their harvest feast, two mice carefully arrange their decorations in Ehlert's *Boo to You!*, creating a spooky scene that fools the predator. According to Daniel Kraus in *Booklist,* the artist's "use of paper, fruit, seeds, and string is labyrinthine enough to have young children tracing their routes," and Laura Lutz remarked in *School Library Journal* that the illustrations for *Boo to You!* "evoke the textures, shapes, and colors of autumn that pop against the red backgrounds, teal paper, and green vegetables."

In *Rrralph* a "talking" dog responds to questions from his owner, describing the ground beneath his feet as "rough rough" and identifying the top of his doghouse as a "roof roof." The canine's "'words' and his owner's narrative . . . are intrinsic to the virtuoso graphic design that is Ehlert's hallmark," Joanna Rudge Long stated in *Horn Book.* The book's illustrations incorporate both textured paper and found objects, including a zipper that serves as the dog's teeth and a metal pop-top that doubles as his nose, "giv[ing] him a playful, slightly rakish look that's not soon forgotten," according to a critic in *Publishers Weekly.* "Bold and bright, filled with kid-pleasing riddles and collage illustrations," according to a *Kirkus Reviews* writer, *Rrralph* "is a perfect offering for new readers and storytime."

Ehlert offers brief verse profiles of a variety of creatures, from butterflies to skunks to lobsters, in *Oodles of Animals,* another title featuring her signature collage artwork. Using just pinking shears, a hole punch, and nine geometric shapes, she "fashions . . . a menagerie guaranteed to spark readers' imaginations," in the words of *School Library Journal* contributor Martha Simpson.

Booklist reviewer Jennifer Mattson also applauded Ehlert's illustrations for *Oodles of Animals,* predicting that young readers "will marvel at her ability to cull animal essences from the simplest forms," and a *Publishers Weekly* contributor stated that the collages "strike a playful balance between boldness of color and simplicity of shape."

Biological adaptation is the focus of *Lots of Spots,* which examines the ways animals develop unique markings that are useful for camouflage or identification. Here "Ehlert's signature paper collage art reflects keen observation of each of the dozens of creatures depicted," Susan Dove Lempke commented in *Horn Book,* and a *Kirkus Reviews* writer stated that the "eye-catching, colorful, textured images provide plenty of visual interest." Noting that *Lots of Spots* includes descriptions of some fifty creatures, from iguanas to chickadees to badgers, Andrew Medlar maintained in *Booklist* that young readers "will enjoy . . . identifying the multitude of brilliantly hued animals that make up this visual zoo."

Biographical and Critical Sources

BOOKS

Authors of Books for Young People, 3rd edition, Scarecrow Press (Metuchen, NJ), 1990.

Children's Book Illustration and Design, edited by Julie Cummins, Library of Applied Design (New York, NY), 1992.

Children's Books and Their Creators, edited by Anita Silvey, Houghton (Boston, MA), 1995.

Children's Literature Review, Volume 28, Gale (Detroit, MI), 1992.

Cummings, Pat, *Talking with Artists,* Bradbury (New York, NY), 1991.

Ehlert, Lois, *Under My Nose,* photographs by Carlo Ontal, Richard C. Owen (Katonah, NY), 1996.

PERIODICALS

Booklist, April 1, 1997, Carolyn Phelan, review of *Cuckoo: A Mexican Folktale,* p. 1330; November 15, 1997, Stephanie Zvirin, review of *Hands,* p. 558; August, 1998, Linda Perkins, review of *Top Cat,* p. 2014; March 2, 2001, Carolyn Phelan, review of *Waiting for Wings,* p. 1276; December 1, 2001, Stephanie Zvirin, review of *Waiting for Wings,* p. 658; May 1, 2002, Kay Weisman, review of *In My World,* p. 1520; February 15, 2004, Carolyn Phelan, review of *Pie in the Sky,* p. 1062; June 1, 2005, Ilene Cooper, review of *Leaf Man,* p. 1796; January 1, 2007, Abby Nolan, review of *Wag a Tail,* p. 113; July 1, 2008, Jennifer Mattson, review of *Oodles of Animals,* p. 73; May 15, 2009, Daniel Kraus, review of *Boo to You!,* p. 43; April 15, 2010, Andrew Medlar, review of *Lots of Spots,* p. 52; February 15, 2011, Carolyn Phelan, review of *Rrralph,* p. 69.

Horn Book, January-February, 1991, Mary M. Burns, review of *Color Farm,* p. 55; November-December, 1991, Lois Ehlert, "The Artist at Work: Card Tables and Collage," p. 695; March-April, 1992, Margaret A. Bush, review of *Circus,* p. 189; May-June, 1993, Ellen Fader, review of *Nuts to You!,* p. 315; July-August, 1994, Margaret A. Bush, review of *Mole's Hill,* p. 461; March-April, 2001, review of *Waiting for Wings,* p. 346; July-August, 2002, Joanna Rudge Long, review of *In My World,* p. 446; July-August, Susan P. Bloom, review of *Pie in the Sky,* p. 436; September-October, 2005, Joanna Rudge Long, review of *Leaf Man,* p. 563; January-February, 2007, Lois Ehlert, transcript of *Boston Globe/Horn Book* Award acceptance speech, p. 19; July-August, 2010, Susan Dove Lempke, review of *Lots of Spots,* p. 129; May-June, 2011, Joanna Rudge Long, review of *Rrralph,* p. 74.

Journal Sentinel (Milwaukee, WI), March 7, 2003, Edie Boatman, "Getting Personal with Lois Ehlert."

Kirkus Reviews, August 1, 1991, review of *Red Leaf, Yellow Leaf,* p. 1019; September 1, 1992, review of *Moon Rope: A Peruvian Folktale,* p. 1128; February 15, 2004, review of *Pie in the Sky,* p. 176; September 1, 2004, review of *Hands,* p. 864; August 1, 2005, review of *Leaf Man,* p. 847; March 15, 2007, review of *Wag a Tail*; April 15, 2008, review of *Oodles of Animals*; July 15, 2009, review of *Boo to You!*; June 15, 2010, review of *Lots of Spots*; April 1, 2011, review of *Rrralph.*

New York Times Book Review, May 20, 1990, Andrea Barnet, review of *Fish Eyes: A Book You Can Count On,* p. 40.

Publishers Weekly, February 12, 1992, Connie Goddard, interview with Ehlert, pp. 18-19; August 17, 1992, review of *Moon Rope,* p. 499; February 15, 1993, review of *Nuts to You!,* pp. 372-373; February 21, 1994, review of *Mole's Hill,* p. 252; October 16, 1995, review of *Snowballs,* p. 60; January 20, 1997, review of *Cuckoo,* p. 401; June 30, 1997, review of *Hands,* p. 76; August 3, 1998, review of *Top Cat,* p. 84; April 2, 2001, review of *Waiting for Wings,* p. 63; February 18, 2002, review of *In My World,* p. 94; March 29, 2004, review of *Pie in the Sky,* p. 61; July 11, 2005, review of *Leaf Man,* p. 91; April 23, 2007, review of *Wag a Tail,* p. 49; May 12, 2008, review of *Oodles of Animals,* p. 53; June 28, 2010, review of *Lots of Spots,* p. 126; March 21, 2011, review of *Rrralph,* p. 72; May 30, 2011, review of *Ten Little Caterpillars,* p. 67.

School Library Journal, April, 2001, Lisa Gangemi Kropp, review of *Waiting for Wings,* p. 129; May, 2002, Rachel Fox, review of *In My World,* p. 112; February, 2003, Lee Bock, review of *Mole's Hill,* p. 96; April, 2004, Corrina Austin, review of *Pie in the Sky,* p. 109; November, 2005, Joy Fleishhacker, review of *Leaf Man,* p. 89; March, 2007, Julie Roach, review of *Wag a Tail,* p. 160; May, 2008, Martha Simpson, review of *Oodles of Animals,* p. 96; August, 2009, Laura Lutz, review of *Boo to You!,* p. 74; August, 2010, Lindsay Persohn, review of *Lots of Spots,* p. 74.

Teacher Librarian, June, 2000, Shirley Lewis, review of *Market Day: A Story Told with Folk Art,* p. 50.

ONLINE

Harcourt Publisher Web site, http://www.harcourtbooks. com/ (June 22, 2006), interview with Ehlert.

Reading Rockets Web site, http://www.readingrockets.org/ (January 1, 2012), interview with Ehlert.*

*   *   *

EHLERT, Lois Jane
See EHLERT, Lois

*   *   *

FIXMER, Elizabeth

Personal

Born in MN; daughter of Robert (an international textbook consultant) and Audrey (an English teacher) Fixmer. *Education:* University of Illinois, Chicago, B.S. (sociology), 1996; University of Wisconsin, Madison, M.S. (social work), 1978; graduate study at Vermont College, 2006; Hamline University, M.F.A., 2008.

Addresses

Home—Fort Atkinson, WI. *Agent*—BookStop Literary Agency, 67 Meadow View Rd., Orinda, CA 94563. *E-mail*—elizabeth@elizabethfixmer.com.

Career

Writer. Worked as a psychotherapist in Denver, CO, 1984-2001.

Member

American Library Association, Society of Children's Book Writers and Illustrators.

Writings

Saint Training (novel), Zonderkidz (Grand Rapids, MI), 2010.

Sidelights

A former child psychotherapist, Elizabeth Fixmer examines a tumultuous period in U.S. history in her debut novel *Saint Training,* a semi-autobiographical work aimed at a middle-grade audience. Set in 1967, the work focuses on Mary Clare O'Brian, a sixth grader whose large Roman-Catholic family faces a host of problems. Already struggling to pay the bills, Mary Clare's parents are expecting their tenth child, and the added financial stress that will result causes the girl's mother to question her faith. Meanwhile, as war rages

in Vietnam, her older brother must make a fateful decision when he receives his draft notice. To help her family, the opinionated and determined Mary Clare decides to strive for sainthood, hoping God will take pity on the O'Brian clan, and she enters a correspondence with the Mother Superior of the convent she intends to join.

Saint Training "is by turns heartbreaking and hilarious," Kelly Roth stated in *School Library Journal,* and *Booklist* critic Ilene Cooper commented that Fixmer "gives readers a strong sense of what was happening during this turbulent time." Although some critics felt that the author addresses too many issues in their novel, including the rise of feminism and the effects of Vatican II, most praised the story's well-drawn characters, especially headstrong Mary Clare. A *Publishers Weekly* contributor, for instance, observed that in *Saint Training* Fixmer's heroine gains "insight into the complex choices faced by those she loves, as well as her own character and calling."

Fixmer maintains that her work as a mental-health professional opened the door to her literary career. "It was during those years of working with children and families that I discovered my love for writing," she told Chris Welch in Wisconsin's *Daily Jefferson County Union.* "The more I read of young adult and middle-grade novels, the more I realized they were such a great tool for kids in terms of being able to talk about things for which they did not have words for their thoughts or feelings or values."

Biographical and Critical Sources

PERIODICALS

Booklist, November 15, 2010, Ilene Cooper, review of *Saint Training,* p. 40.
Kirkus Reviews, September 1, 2010, review of *Saint Training.*
Publishers Weekly, September 6, 2010, review of *Saint Training,* p. 40.
School Library Journal, November, 2010, Kelly Roth, review of *Saint Training,* p. 112.

ONLINE

Cynsations Web log, http://cynthialeitichsmith.blogspot.com/ (December 9, 2010), Cynthia Leitich Smith, interview with Fixmer.
Daily Jefferson County (WI) Union Online, http://dailyunion.com/ (August 6, 2010), Chris Welch, "*Saint Training* Pens New Vocation for Fort's Fixmer."
Elizabeth Fixmer Home Page, http://www.elizabethfixmer.com (December 15, 2011).
Elizabeth Fixmer Web log, http://elizabethfixmer.livejournal.com (December 15, 2011).

FRIAR, Joanne
(Joanne H. Friar)

Personal

Married; children: four. *Education:* University of Massachusetts—Dartmouth, B.F.A., 1974.

Addresses

Home and office—Somerset MA. *Agent*—Christina A. Tugeau, 3009 Margaret Jones Ln., Williamsburg VA 23185; chris@ctugeau.com. *E-mail*—jhfriar@comcast.net.

Career

Illustrator. New Bedford High School, New Bedford, MA, former art teacher; children's book illustrator, beginning 1991.

Member

Society of Children's Book Writers and Illustrators, Picture Book Artists Association, Freelance Artists Network.

Awards, Honors

Notable Social Studies Trade Books for Young People selection, National Council for the Social Studies/Children's Book Council (NCSS/CBC), 2001, for *Margaret Knight* by Marlene Targ Brill; John Burroughs List of Nature Books for Young Readers inclusion, and Outstanding Science Trade Books for Students K-12 selection, National Science Teachers Association/CBC, both 2002, both for *The Shape of Betts Meadow* by Meghan Nuttall Sayres.

Illustrator

(As Joanne H. Friar) Linnea Mulder, *Sarah and Puffle: A Story for Children about Diabetes,* Magination Press (New York, NY), 1992.
Cathy Grant Helmso, *Jump the Broom,* Richard C. Owen Publishers (Katonah, NY), 1997.
Marlene Targ Brill, *Margaret Knight: Girl Inventor,* Millbrook Press (Brookfield, CT), 2001.
Ann Purmell, *Apple Cider Making Days,* Millbrook Press (Brookfield, CT), 2002.
Meghan Nuttall Sayres, *The Shape of Betts Meadow: A Wetlands Story,* Millbrook Press (Brookfield, CT), 2002.
Cathy Grant Helmso, *The Freedom Quilt,* Richard C. Owen Publishers (Katonah, NY), 2003.
C.H. Colman, *The Bald Eagle's View of American History,* Charlesbridge (Watertown, MA), 2006.
Brian J. Heinz, *Nathan of Yesteryear and Michael of Today,* Millbrook Press (Minneapolis, MN), 2007.
Jacqueline Farmer, *O Christmas Tree: Its History and Holiday Traditions,* Charlesbridge (Watertown, MA), 2010.

Contributor of illustrations to educational texts.

Sidelights

An award-winning artist who works in water color and colored pencil, Joanne Friar has provided the artwork for such children's books as *Margaret Knight: Girl Inventor,* a biography by Marlene Targ Brill, and *O Christmas Tree: Its History and Holiday Traditions,* a seasonal tale by Jacqueline Farmer. A graduate of the University of Massachusetts—Dartmouth, Friar taught high-school art for several years before pursuing a career as an illustrator. "Ever since I can remember I always loved to draw," she told Deborah Allard in the Fall River, Massachusetts, *Herald News.* "Now, I have a career doing something I really love."

In *Margaret Knight* Brill explores the life of the nineteenth-century factory worker who patented a design for the flat-bottomed paper bag and also devised an important safety device that reduced significantly reduced injuries in textile mills. Friar's "softly colored paintings enhance information given in the text," observed *School Library Journal* reviewer Carolyn Janssen, and Connie Fletcher noted in *Booklist* that the art-

Joanne Friar creates the detailed images that bring to life Jacqueline Farmer's holiday tale in **Oh Christmas Tree.** (Illustration copyright © 2010 by Joanne Friar. Used with permission by Charlesbridge Publishing Inc., 85 Main Street, Watertown, MA 02472, www.charlesbridge.com. All rights reserved.)

ist's "colored pencil drawings are realistic, if somewhat cheerful, as they depict factory life." *The Shape of Betts Meadow: A Wetlands Story,* featuring a text by Meghan Nuttall Sayres, centers on the efforts of a Washington State physician to restore a dry meadow to its natural state. According to *Booklist* critic Todd Morning, Friar's illustrations for this story artfully "show the gradual return of birds, fish, frogs, and large mammals."

In her fictional celebration of family unity, Ann Purmell explores a fall tradition in *Apple Cider Making Days,* another book featuring artwork by Friar. Purmell's story follows two children, Alex and Abigail, who join their relatives in harvesting, processing, and selling apple cider at their grandfather's orchard. "The comfortable, colorful art brings little ones up close to the process," Helen Rosenberg observed in *Booklist,* while a contributor remarked in *Kirkus Reviews* that "Friar's . . . drawings perfectly fit the topic." "Details are rich and the colors are just right for autumn apple-picking days," the critic added. According to *School Library Journal* critic Deanna Romriell, Friar's "pleasant watercolor illustrations" are also a highlight of C.H. Colman's *The Bald Eagle's View of American History,* a tribute to American's national emblem.

Friar drew praise from Shelle Rosenfeld in *Booklist* for the "intricately detailed watercolor and pencil art" she crafted for *Nathan of Yesteryear and Michael of Today,* a story by Brian J. Heinz that compares and contrasts the world of a modern boy with that of his great-grandfather. Farmer's *O Christmas Tree* explains not only the origins of a familiar holiday tradition but also the agricultural methods used to grow different types of trees. Here "Friar's gouache illustrations have plenty of detail," Maya Alpert commented in *School Library Journal,* and Carolyn Phelan stated in *Booklist* that the paintings in *O Christmas Tree* "brighten the presentation and provide visual information that complements the text."

Biographical and Critical Sources

PERIODICALS

Booklist, September 15, 2001, Connie Fletcher, review of *Margaret Knight: Girl Inventor,* p. 217; June 1, 2002, Todd Morning, review of *The Shape of Betts Meadow: A Wetlands Story,* p. 1728; December 1, 2002, Helen Rosenberg, review of *Apple Cider Making Days,* p. 676; October 15, 2006, Shelle Rosenfeld, review of *Nathan of Yesteryear and Michael of Today,* p. 42; September 1, 2010, Carolyn Phelan, review of *O Christmas Tree: Its History and Holiday Traditions,* p. 89.
Horn Book, November-December, 2010, Martha V. Parravano, review of *O Christmas Tree,* p. 62.
Kirkus Reviews, October 15, 2002, review of *Apple Cider Making Days,* p. 1536; September 1, 2010, review of *O Christmas Tree.*
School Library Journal, December, 2001, Carolyn Janssen, review of *Margaret Knight,* p. 118; April, 2002, Kathy Piehl, review of *The Shape of Betts Meadow,* p. 141; January, 2007, Deanna Romriell, review of *The Bald Eagle's View of American History,* p. 114; October, 2010, Mara Alpert, review of *O Christmas Tree,* p. 71.

ONLINE

Christina A. Tugeau, Agent, Web site, http://www.catugeau. com/ (December 15, 2011), "Joanne Friar."
Herald News Online (Fall River, MA), http://www. heraldnews.com/ (February 3, 2011), Deborah Allard, "Illustrated Lady: Joanne Friar Doesn't Need a Lot of Space to Illustrate Her Talents."
Joanne Friar Web log, http://www.joannefriar.blogspot. com (December 15, 2011).*

* * *

FRIAR, Joanne H.
See FRIAR, Joanne

G-H

GEISERT, Arthur 1941-
(Arthur Frederick Geisert)

Personal

Born September 20, 1941, in Dallas, TX; son of Leonard (an engineer) and Doris (a homemaker) Geisert; married Bonnie Meier (a teacher), June 1, 1963 (divorced); children: Noah. *Education:* Concordia University (Seward, NE), B.S., 1963; University of California, Davis, M.A., 1965; additional study at Chouinard Art Institute, Otis Art Institute, and Art Institute of Chicago. *Politics:* Republican. *Religion:* Lutheran.

Addresses

Home and office—Bernard, IL. *E-mail*—geisert@galenalink.net.

Career

Printmaker, artist, and educator. Art teacher at Concordia College, River Forest, IL, Concordia College, Seward, NE, and Clark College, Dubuque, IA, beginning 1965. Invitational lecturer at colleges, universities, and institutions, including University of Wisconsin, Madison, University of Minnesota, Minneapolis, and Smithsonian Institute. *Exhibitions:* Has exhibited artwork at Dubuque Museum of Art, Dubuque, IA, 2004-05, 2007-10, and Figge Art Museum, Davenport, IA, 2010, and at shows of Society of American Graphic Artists, New York, NY, 1986, 1991, 1993, and Society of Illustrators Museum of American Illustration, New York, NY, 1991, 1992, 1996. Dubuque Museum of Art serves as the repository for hundreds of Geisert's original copper plates.

Member

Los Angeles Printmaking Society, Boston Printmakers, Art Institute of Chicago, Print Center (Philadelphia, PA).

Arthur Geisert (Photograph reproduced by permission.)

Awards, Honors

Named Illinois Arts Council fellow, 1986; Best Illustrated Children's Books selection, *New York Times,* 1986, for *Pigs from A to Z;* Reading Magic Award, *Parenting,* 1991, for *Oink;* Honor Book selection, *Parents Choice,* Ten Recommended Picture Books selection, *Time* magazine, and Honor Book designation, *Boston Globe/Horn Book,* all 1995, all for *Haystack;* Best

Illustrated Children's Books selection, *New York Times,* 1996, for *Roman Numerals I to MM,* 2011, for *Ice;* honorary doctorate, Concordia University, 2002.

Writings

SELF-ILLUSTRATED

Pa's Balloon and Other Pig Tales, Houghton (Boston, MA), 1984.
Pigs from A to Z, Houghton (Boston, MA), 1986.
The Ark, Houghton (Boston, MA), 1988.
Oink, Houghton (Boston, MA), 1991.
Pigs from 1 to 10, Houghton (Boston, MA), 1992.
Oink Oink, Houghton (Boston, MA), 1993.
After the Flood, Houghton (Boston, MA), 1994.
Roman Numerals I to MM: Numerabilia romana uno ad duo mila, Houghton (Boston, MA), 1996.
The Etcher's Studio, Houghton (Boston, MA), 1997.
The Ark, Houghton (Boston, MA), 1999.
Nursery Crimes, Houghton (Boston, MA), 2001.
The Giant Ball of String, Houghton (Boston, MA), 2002.
Mystery, Houghton (Boston, MA), 2003.
Pigaroons, Houghton (Boston, MA), 2004.
Lights Out, Houghton (Boston, MA), 2005.
Oops, Houghton (Boston, MA), 2006.
Hogwash, Houghton Mifflin (Boston, MA), 2008.
Country Road ABC: An Illustrated Journey through America's Farmland, Houghton Mifflin Harcourt (Boston, MA), 2010.
Ice, Enchanted Lion Books (New York, NY), 2011.
The Big Seed, Enchanted Lion Books (New York, NY), 2012.

ILLUSTRATOR

Barbara Bader, *Aesop and Company: With Scenes from His Legendary Life,* Houghton (Boston, MA), 1991.
Bonnie Geisert, *Haystack,* Houghton (Boston, MA), 1995.
Bonnie Geisert, *Prairie Town,* Houghton (Boston, MA), 1998.
Bonnie Geisert, *River Town,* Houghton (Boston, MA), 1999.
Bonnie Geisert, *Mountain Town,* Houghton (Boston, MA), 2000.
Bonnie Geisert, *Desert Town,* Houghton (Boston, MA), 2001.
Bonnie Geisert, *Prairie Summer,* Houghton (Boston, MA), 2002.

OTHER

Contributor to numerous books, including *Paradis Perdu,* Atelier Contraste Fribourg, 1991; *Children's Book Illustration and Design,* edited by Julie Cummins, P.B.C. International, 1992; *World Book Encyclopedia,* 1993; and *The Very Best of Children's Book Illustration,* compiled by Society of Illustrators, North Light Books, 1993.

Geisert's books have been published in Japan, Korea, France, Spain, and Germany.

Sidelights

Arthur Geisert combines wonderfully detailed colored etchings with wry humor to produce award-winning children's books, including *Haystack, Roman Numerals I to MM: Numerabilia romana uno ad duo mila,* and *Ice.* "The fine lines and small scale of Geisert's . . . art work perfectly to give an effect that is intimate, energetic, and delightful," Kathie Meizner remarked in *School Library Journal.* A resident of the Midwest, Geisert has become somewhat of an expert on pigs, and many of his nearly wordless picture books feature the porcine critters, who typically find themselves dealing with cumulative scenarios that would make Rube Goldberg proud. Describing *Oops,* an action-packed tale that begins with a glass of spilled milk and ends with a demolished house, *Booklist* critic Randall Enos stated that Geisert presents "a comfortable pig family and a complex (and outrageous) chain of events."

Trained as a teacher of primary grades and of art, Geisert soon discovered that his real passion lay in the studio, not in the classroom. Taking up residence in rural Galena, Illinois, Geisert, his wife Bonnie, and their child lived for many years a "dirt poor" existence, as he later wrote in *Something about the Author Autobiography Series* (*SAAS*). While his wife taught at a local school, Geisert worked selling etchings and building two homes for the family. As he explained in *SAAS,* his early etching subjects focused on "Noah's Ark, with a lot of detailed cutaway pieces, pigs, views of Galena, and humorous prints." Beginning with a small business loan of 800 dollars, Geisert was able to develop a lucrative business in prints. For many years he also submitted proposals to publishers of children's books. Over the years he managed to collect a drawer full of rejections for his troubles.

In the end, publishers came to Geisert. An editor at Houghton Mifflin, after seeing his etchings in an art exhibition, took a look at his portfolio and the happy result was Geisert's first picture book, *Pa's Balloon and Other Pig Tales.* "It was illustrated with etchings," Geisert explained in *SAAS,* "a rarely used technique in children's books, and the color was done with manual color separations."

Relatively long for a picture book, *Pa's Balloon and Other Pig Tales* "has the look of a short novel," according to Karen Stang Hanley writing in *Booklist.* Geisert's debut contains three stories about a pig family: a disastrous picnic, a balloon race, and a journey to the North Pole. All are "narrated with childlike economy by a plucky piglet," Hanley noted. Writing in *Horn Book,* Karen Jameyson commented that while the stories themselves are slight, the illustrations "distinguish the book," utilizing "an array of perspectives to record the activ-

***Geisert introduces young readers to the math system utilized by Julius Caesar in* Roman Numerals I to MM.**

ity." A *Publishers Weekly* reviewer concluded that "Geisert's first book is sure to leave children wanting more from him."

Characteristically, Geisert illustrates his puzzle alphabet book *Pigs from A to Z* with original etchings. A minimal text details a story line about building a tree house that reflects the author/illustrator's boyhood carpentry efforts as well as his adult construction of houses. Denise M. Wilms noted in *Booklist* that *Pigs from A to Z* presents an "intriguing venture for curious, ambitious browsers," and *Horn Book* critic Jameyson concluded that "the graphically pleasing and very clever book may fascinate even those well beyond the picture-book age."

A suspension bridge Geisert was busy building on his property ended up playing an integral part in *Pigs from 1 to 10,* in which numerals from zero to nine are hidden in each double-page, black-and-white etching. The story chronicles the saga of a pig family searching for a lost land, and Geisert's etched illustrations show the piglets building elaborate machinery that will allow them to explore from mountaintop to mountaintop. "Few will be able to resist the game," concluded Nancy Vasilakis in her *Horn Book* review of *Pigs from 1 to 10.*

Animals figure in most of Geisert's graphic productions, and with *The Ark* there is a definite plethora of beasts. "A dignified, somber retelling of the flood story"

was how Ellen D. Warwick described the book in her *School Library Journal* review. *Horn Book* reviewer Elizabeth S. Watson noted of the same book that "children will love finding the beasts who have wandered from their proper spaces," while "parents and religious educators will welcome Geisert's handsome rendition of the story." Geisert continues this episode in *After the Flood,* which describes what happens after the waters recede and the animals leave Noah's Ark. "A glowing, impelling, visually stimulating panorama of hope and affirmation of life," is how Mary M. Burns described *The Ark* in *Horn Book.*

Geisert never strays far from his beloved pigs, and many of his other books employ playful porkers. Chief among these, *Oink, Oops,* and *Ice* employ a minimal text. "*Oink* . . . was a silly one-word (oink, oink, oink, etc.) book," Geisert reported in *SAAS.* "Earlier versions done on a single etching-plate date back fifteen years. *Oink* was the culmination of an idea that I had worked at, on and off, for years. I used our neighbor's pigs for models. It was a popular little book which received several awards and was translated into Spanish, German, Korean, and Japanese." As the sound that a pig makes is rendered the same in several languages, *Oink* was not much of a translation effort. A contributor to *Publishers Weekly* noted that the book's "droll illustrations exude an understated hilarity," and a *Kirkus Reviews* critic dubbed Geisert's wordless sequel, *Oink Oink,* an equally "joyful adventure."

Lights Out follows the construction efforts of a young pig as he finds a way to make the transition from light to dark more gradual while also obeying his parents' rule about turning out his bedroom light at eight o'clock. "The meticulously rendered illustrations carefully track the ingenious work of this junior Rube Goldberg," Kitty Flynn noted in *Horn Book,* and a writer in *Kirkus Reviews* described *Lights Out* as "imaginatively, ingeniously inventive." In *School Library Journal* Kathie Meizner praised Geisert's small-scale drawings for the book, writing that they "give an effect that is intimate, energetic, and delightful."

Pigs also pop up on the pages of *Nursery Crimes,* a story about two pigs on the track of turkey-shaped topiaries that Phelan dubbed a "quirky, imaginative, dressed-animal tale." *The Giant Ball of String* finds two communities competing for a giant ball of string when the unusually large object is dislodged from its place of prominence in the mining town of Rumpus Ridge and floats down the river to neighboring Cornwall. Praising the silly tale, which is peopled—in typical Geisert fashion—with pigs and features a host of interesting mechanical contraptions, a *Kirkus Reviews* writer cited the author/illustrator's "clear, deadpan prose and carefully detailed illustrations." Calling *The Giant Ball of String* an "offbeat tale of how cooperation and resourcefulness can overcome deceit," a *Publishers Weekly* writer also praised the book's "poker-face text." An "inventive, engaging" story, in the opinion of a *Kirkus Reviews* contributor, *Mystery* tells the story of a young piglet whose

Pilfering from a neighboring town inhabited by pirate descendants soon threaten to disrupt an annual ice festival in Geisert's picture book **Pigaroons.**

trip to the museum with her grandfather reveals a patchwork art theft that will pull in gleeful readers. In *School Library Journal* Susan Scheps praised the book's "clever concept and illustrations" and "well-crafted colored etchings," while a *Publishers Weekly* reviewer deemed the museum setting of *Mystery* to be "the perfect canvas" for Geisert's "gentle humor" and "fondness for both art and pigs."

Hogwash, another of Geisert's wordless picture books, focuses on an elaborate bath-and-laundry system that produces well-scrubbed piglets. After a day of playing in mud and paint, dozens of little piggies are shepherded by their mothers to a marvelous contraption—powered by wind and water—that soaps, washes, rinses, and dries the lot of them. Geisert's meticulous illustrations "invite readers to trace the mechanical connections in this tantalizing, quirkily dignified, and joyous world," Sarah Ellis commented in *Horn Book.* Julie Cummins, writing in *Booklist,* maintained of *Hogwash* that "only Geisert could take a one-word title and create such an engaging scenario," and a contributor in *Publishers Weekly* remarked: "The pigs appear delighted with the whole process. Readers will be, too."

Ice chronicles the zany quest of a group of island-dwelling pigs. With their water supply running low, the pigs set off aboard a balloon-powered airship for the frozen north, where they attach a rope to an iceberg and proceed to tow it home. In *Booklist* Ian Chipman applauded the "odd little world of Geisert's meticulously etched and colored artwork," and a writer in *Kirkus Reviews* noted that the pictures "certainly conjure a fully realized piggy world—an island at home with itself, floating way out there in the ocean." A critic in *Publishers Weekly* stated that the depiction of the airship, "a charming marriage of sailing and balloon technology, is a standout among Geisert's many contraptions."

Geisert departs from his porcine-related tales to create *Country Road ABC: An Illustrated Journey through America's Farmland,* which is a tribute to the land and people in and around his Iowa home. "I wanted a picture of what farming is like in northeast Iowa right now," he told *Quad-City Times* reporter David Burke. "It's not romanticized, no sentimentality." To this end, Geisert introduces young readers to such farm-related terms as "ammonia fertilizer," "disking," a method of preparing the soil for planting, and "z-brace," a construction method used to sturdy barn doors. According to *Horn Book* critic Lolly Robinson, Geisert's "fine intaglio line with delicate watercolor is ideally suited to both detail and wide vistas," and Wendy Lukehart maintained in *School Library Journal* that young readers "will return to the illustrations to revel in Geisert's detailed etchings of farmers working and relaxing." A contributor in *Kirkus Reviews* also praised *Country Road ABC,* lauding the "accurate, realistic and fascinating alphabetical farmland journey."

During part of his career Geisert collaborated with former wife, Bonnie Geisert, on several books that fo-

Geisert treats young children to a rural take on basic vocabulary in his self-illustrated **Country Road ABC.** (Illustration copyright © 2010 by Arthur Geisert. Reprinted by permission of Houghton Mifflin Harcourt Publishing Company.)

cus on life in the rural Midwest. In *Haystack* they create a "quiet tribute to a bygone era," according to a *Publishers Weekly* critic, while in *Prairie Town, River Town, Mountain Town,* and *Desert Town,* they "explore the changing rhythms of a community throughout the year," according to a critic for *Publishers Weekly.* A *Publishers Weekly* critic wrote that "the Geiserts draw readers into a fully realized world that just might resemble their own hometown—or give them new appreciation for a town's inner workings," while *Booklist* critic GraceAnne A. DeCandido called the books "an absolutely engaging series." Similar in theme to the "Town" books is *Prairie Summer,* an elementary-grade novel in which Geisert's line drawings bring to life Bonnie Geisert's story about a 1950s farming family living in South Dakota.

In *The Etcher's Studio* Geisert expresses his feelings about his art while also telling the story of a boy who helps his grandfather prepare his etchings for sale. In the process, the story explains how etchings are made. According to a *Publishers Weekly* critic, "Geisert's portrait of an involving intergenerational relationship is warm and welcome," while Lolly Robinson wrote in *Horn Book* that the author/illustrator succeeds in "vividly portraying both the romance and the hard work of creating a work of art through a painstaking technical process." As Geisert wrote in *SAAS,* "For me there is no more beautiful way of putting line on paper than by etching."

Biographical and Critical Sources

BOOKS

Silvey, Anita, editor, *Children's Books and Their Creators,* Houghton Mifflin (Boston, MA), 1995.

Something about the Author Autobiography Series, Volume 23, Gale (Detroit, MI), 1997.

PERIODICALS

Booklist, August, 1984, Karen Stang Hanley, review of *Pa's Balloon and Other Pig Tales,* p. 1625; November 15, 1986, Denise M. Wilms, review of *Pigs from A to Z,* p. 509; September 15, 1995, Leone McDermott, review of *Haystack,* p. 161; May 1, 1996, Carolyn Phelan, review of *Roman Numerals I to MM: Numerabilia romana uno ad duo mila,* p. 1509; April 1, 1997, Carolyn Phelan, review of *The Etcher's Studio;* April, 1998, Kay Weisman, review of *Prairie Town,* p. 1326; July, 1999, Ellen Mandel, review of *River Town,* p. 1948; March 15, 2000, Susan Dove Lempke, review of *Mountain Town,* p. 1386; April 1, 2001, GraceAnne A. DeCandido, review of *Desert Town,* p. 1474; November 15, 2001, Carolyn Phelan, review of *Nursery Crimes,* p. 572; March 1, 2002, John Peters, review of *Prairie Summer,* p. 1136; September 15, 2002, Michael Cart, review of *The Giant Ball of String,* p. 232; July, 2003, Carolyn Phelan, review of *Mystery,* p. 1896; September 15, 2004, Gillian Engberg, review of *Pigaroons,* p. 249; November 1, 2005, Jennifer Mattson, review of *Lights Out,* p. 40; September 1, 2006, Randall Enos, review of *Oops,* p. 135; January 1, 2008, Julie Cummins, review of *Hogwash,* p. 94; April 15, 2010, review of *Country Road ABC: An Illustrated Journey through America's Farmland,* p. 49; April 15, 2011, Ian Chipman, review of *Ice,* p. 59.

Horn Book, August, 1984, Karen Jameyson, review of *Pa's Balloon and Other Pig Tales,* p. 457; January-February, 1986, Karen Jameyson, review of *Pigs from A to Z,* p. 43; January-February, 1989, Elizabeth S. Watson, review of *The Ark,* pp. 52-53; September-October, 1992, Nancy Vasilakis, review of *Pigs from 1 to 10,* p. 575; July-August, 1994, Mary M. Burns, review of *After the Flood,* pp. 440-441; May-June, 1997, Lolly Robinson, review of *The Etcher's Studio,* p. 306; May-June, 1998, Joanna Rudge Long, review of *Prairie Town,* p. 332; March, 2001, review of *Desert Town,* p. 229; November-December, 2005, Kitty Flynn, review of *Lights Out,* p. 705; March-April, 2008, Sarah Ellis, review of *Hogwash,* p. 203; May-June, 2010, Lolly Robinson, review of *Country Road ABC,* p. 67.

Kirkus Reviews, February 1, 1993, review of *Oink Oink,* p. 146; July 1, 2002, review of *The Giant Ball of String,* p. 954; September 1, 2003, review of *Mystery,* p. 1123; September 1, 2004, review of *Pigaroons,* p. 865; September 1, 2005, review of *Lights Out,* p. 973; September 1, 2006, review of *Oops,* p. 903; February 1, 2008, review of *Hogwash;* April 15, 2010, review of *Country Road ABC;* March 15, 2010, review of *Ice.*

New York Times Book Review, July 14, 1991, review of *Oink,* p. 25; January 31, 1993, review of *Oink Oink,* p. 22; March 27, 1994, review of *After the Flood,* p. 21; January 28, 1996, review of *Roman Numerals i to MM,* p. 27; May 17, 1998, Anne Scott MacLeod, review of *Prairie Town,* p. 23.

Geisert's early books for children include his self-illustrated biblical-based story **After the Flood.** (Copyright © 2004 by Arthur Geisert. Reprinted by permission of Houghton Mifflin Harcourt Publishing Company. All rights reserved.)

Publishers Weekly, June 22, 1984, review of *Pa's Balloon and Other Pig Tales,* p. 100; March 29, 1991, review of *Oink,* p. 92; August 28, 1995, review of *Haystack,* p. 112; March 3, 1997, review of *The Etcher's Studio,* p. 74; March 23, 1998, review of *Prairie Town,* p. 98; April 19, 1999, review of *River Town,* p. 72; October 25, 1999, review of *The Ark,* p. 75; September 10, 2001, review of *Nursery Crimes,* p. 91; October 8, 2001, review of *Roman Numerals I to MM,* p. 67; March 4, 2002, review of *Prairie Summer,* p. 80; July 22, 2002, review of *The Giant Ball of String,* p. 177; September 15, 2003, review of *Mystery,* p. 64; February 18, 2008, review of *Hogwash,* p. 153; April 5, 2010, review of *Country Road ABC,* p. 60; February 21, 2011, review of *Ice,* p. 130.

School Library Journal, October, 1988, Ellen D. Warwick, review of *The Ark,* p. 120; September, 1995, Lee Bock, review of *Haystack,* p. 193; September, 1996, Jennifer Fleming, review of *Roman Numerals I to MM;* April, 1997, Barbara Elleman, review of *The Etcher's Studio,* p. 102; April, 1998, Eunice Weech, review of *Prairie Town,* p. 116; May, 1999, Lee Bock, review of *River Town,* p. 105; March, 2001, Nina Lindsay, review of *Desert Town,* p. 208; May, 2002, Carolyn Janssen, review of *Prairie Summer,* p. 114; September, 2002, Lisa Dennis, review of *The Giant Ball of String,* p. 192; October, 2003, Susan Scheps, review of *Mystery,* p. 125; December, 2004, Jane Barrer, review of *Pigaroons,* p. 108; December, 2005, Kathie Meizner, review of *Lights Out,* p. 112; October, 2006, Robin Gibson, review of *Oops,* p. 110; April, 2010, Wendy Lukehart, review of *Country Road ABC,* p. 124.

ONLINE

Patricia Newman Web site, http://www.patriciamnewman.com/ (January, 2007), Patricia Newman, "Who Wrote That?: Featuring Arthur Geisert."

Quad-City Times Online, http://qctimes.com/ (February 17, 2010), David Burke, "Artist Finds Inspiration in Town of 98 People."

School Library Journal Online, http://blog.schoollibrary journal.com/afuse8production/ (March 23, 2011), Elizabeth Bird, review of *Ice.**

*   *   *

GEISERT, Arthur Frederick
See GEISERT, Arthur

GONZALEZ, Thomas 1959-

Personal

Born August 8, 1959, in Havana, Cuba; immigrated to United States, 1970; married; children: one daughter. *Education:* Atlanta College of Art, degree, 1983.

Addresses

Office—11950 Jones Bridge Rd., Ste. 115-157, Alpharetta, GA 30005-8911. *Agent*—Dwyer & O'Grady, Inc., P.O. Box 790, Cedar Key, FL 32625-0790. *E-mail*—etgonzalez@att.net.

Career

Artist and designer. Coca-Cola Company, Atlanta, GA, designer and creative development manager, 1984-2007; Beck Compression, Atlanta, creative director, 2008-10; freelance designer and illustrator, beginning 2010.

Awards, Honors

Numerous advertising and design related awards, including a gold and two silver ADDY Awards, two *Print* magazine awards, two Show South Awards, and a bronze International Brand Packaging Award; Parents' Choice Gold Award, 2009, for *Fourteen Cows for America.*

Illustrator

Carmen Agra Deedy and Wilson Kimeli Naiyomah, *Fourteen Cows for America,* Peachtree Publishers (Atlanta, GA), 2009.

Carmen T. Bernier-Grand, *Sonia Sotomayor: Supreme Court Justice,* Marshall Cavendish (New York, NY), 2010.

Jo S. Kittinger, *The House on Dirty-third Street,* Peachtree Publishers (Atlanta, GA), 2012.

Author's work has been translated into Spanish.

Sidelights

Artist Thomas Gonzalez provided the illustrations for *Fourteen Cows for America,* a "moving tale of compassion and generosity," in the words of a *Publishers Weekly* critic. Gonzalez, who was born in Cuba, moved to the United States with his family when he was a teen and settled in Atlanta, Georgia. He eventually graduated from the Atlanta College of Art and spent more than twenty years as a designer and creative director for the Coca-Cola Company before pursuing a career as a freelance illustrator.

Based on a true story, *Fourteen Cows for America* was coauthored by Carmen Agra Deedy and Wilson Kimeli Naiyomah, a Kenyan who witnessed the terrorist attack on New York City while visiting the United States on September 11, 2001. Returning to his Maasai village, Naiyomah relates the destruction of the World Trade Center to the members of his tribe, all who react with sorrow and disbelief. In a gesture of healing, the Maasai bless fourteen cows—a sacred possession to these nomadic cattle herders—and offer them to a visiting U.S. ambassador, who accepts them on behalf of the American people.

Gonzalez's artwork for *Fourteen Cows for America* was lauded by critics. "The colors of Kenya explode off the page: rich blues, flaming oranges, fire-engine reds, and chocolate browns," Rebecca Dash observed in her *School Library Journal* review. According to a contributor in *Kirkus Reviews,* "Gonzalez's saturated paintings . . . radiate a warmth that is matched only by the Maasai's generosity," and Mary Anne Hannibal maintained in *Childhood Education* that the artist "captures both the landscape and the people as his illustrations enhance Carmen's telling of this true story and remarkable example of global friendship." In the *New York Times Book Review* Nicholas D. Kristof described Gonzalez's artwork for *Fourteen Cows for America* as "beautifully evocative." "Over and over in the scenes," he stated, "two spears or two sticks or even two giraffe necks appear in the background, [providing] a subtle echo of the twin towers."

Biographical and Critical Sources

PERIODICALS

Booklist, July 1, 2009, Hazel Rochman, review of *Fourteen Cows for America,* p. 57.

Childhood Education, winter, 2009, Mary Anne Hannibal, review of *Fourteen Cows for America,* p. 118.

Children's Bookwatch, August, 2009, review of *Fourteen Cows for America.*

Kirkus Reviews, July 1, 2009, review of *Fourteen Cows for America.*

New York Times Book Review, November 8, 2009, Nicholas D. Kristof, review of *Fourteen Cows for America,* p. 15.

Publishers Weekly, August 3, 2009, review of *Fourteen Cows for America,* p. 45.

Reading Teacher, November, 2010, Linda J. Armstrong, review of *Fourteen Cows for America,* p. C4.

School Library Journal, August, 2009, Rebecca Dash, review of *Fourteen Cows for America,* p. 89.

Wall Street Journal, July 31, 2009, Meghan Cox Gurdon, review of *Fourteen Cows for America.*

ONLINE

Dwyer & O'Grady Web site, http://www.dwyerogrady. com/ (December 15, 2011), "Thomas Gonzalez."

Fourteen Cows for America Web site, http://14cowsfor america.com/ (December 15, 2011).

Thomas Gonzalez Home Page, http://www.tomprints.com (December 15, 2011).*

HAMILTON, Emma Walton 1962-

Personal

Born November 27, 1962, in London, England; daughter of Julie Andrews (an actor, vocalist, and author) and Tony Walton (an illustrator); married Steve Hamilton (an actor and producer); children: Sam, Hope. *Education:* Brown University, B.A. (theatre).

Addresses

Home—Sag Harbor, NY.

Career

Author, editor, and educator. HarperCollins Publishers, New York, NY, then Little, Brown Books for Young Readers, editorial director of Julie Andrews Collection (imprint), beginning 2000; freelance editor, beginning 2006; Beech Tree Books, editorial director, beginning 2008. Bay Street Theatre, Sag Harbor, NY, co-founder and director of education and programs for young audiences, 1992-2008. Ensemble Studio Theatre Institute, New York, NY, former member of faculty; Stony Brook Southampton, Southampton, NY, member of M.F.A. faculty, executive director of Young American Writers Project, and conference director. Former stage, film, and television actor; voiceover artist for audio books; creator and host of *Children's Book Hub* Web site. Speaker at schools and conferences; advocate on behalf of literacy causes.

Member

International Reading Association, Author's Guild, Society of Children's Book Writers and Illustrators, Dramatists Guild, Screen Actors Guild, Actor's Equity Association, American Federation of Television and Radio Artists, Association of Songwriters, Composers, and Publishers.

Awards, Honors

Parent's Choice Gold Medal, *ForeWord* magazine Best Book Honorable Mention, IPPY Book Award silver medal, and Living Now Book Award silver medal, all 2009, all for *Raising Bookworms;* (with Julie Andrews) Grammy Award for Best Spoken-word Album for Children, 2011, for *Julie Andrews' Collection of Poems, Songs, and Lullabies.*

Writings

(With mother, Julie Andrews Edwards) *Simeon's Gift,* illustrated by Gennady Spirin, HarperCollins (New York, NY), 2003.

(With Julie Andrews Edwards) *Dragon: Hound of Honor,* HarperCollins (New York, NY), 2004.

(With Julie Andrews Edwards) *The Great American Mousical,* illustrated by father, Tony Walton, HarperCollins (New York, NY), 2006.

(With Julie Andrews Edwards) *Thanks to You: Wisdom from Mother and Child,* HarperCollins (New York, NY), 2007.

(Selector, with Julie Andrews) *Julie Andrews' Collection of Poems, Songs, and Lullabies,* paintings by James McMullan, Little, Brown Books for Young Readers (New York, NY), 2009.

Raising Bookworms: Getting Kids Reading for Pleasure and Empowerment, Beech Tree Books (Sag Harbor, NY), 2009.

(With Julie Andrews Edwards) *Little Bo in Italy: The Continued Adventures of Bonnie Boadicea,* illustrated by Henry Cole, HarperCollins Children's Books (New York, NY), 2010.

(With Julie Andrews) *The Very Fairy Princess,* illustrated by Christine Davenier, Little, Brown (New York, NY), 2010.

(With Julie Andrews) *The Very Fairy Princess Takes the Stage,* illustrated by Christine Davenier, Little, Brown (New York, NY), 2011.

(With Julie Andrews Edwards) *Little Bo in London,* illustrated by Henry Cole, HarperCollins (New York, NY), 2012.

(With Julie Andrews) *The Very Fairy Princess: Here Comes the Flower Girl,* illustrated by Christine Davenier, Little, Brown (New York, NY), 2012.

"DUMPY THE DUMP TRUCK" SERIES; WITH JULIE ANDREWS EDWARDS

Dumpy the Dump Truck, illustrated by Tony Walton, Hyperion (New York, NY), 2000.

Dumpy at School, illustrated by Tony Walton, Hyperion (New York, NY), 2000.

Emma Walton Hamilton collaborates with her mother, actress Julie Andrews, on Dumpy the Dump Truck, *and the illustrations by her father, Tony Walton, make it a family affair.* (Illustration copyright © 2000 by Tony Walton. Reprinted by permission of Disney Book Group. All rights reserved.)

Dumpy and His Pals, illustrated by Tony Walton, Hyperion (New York, NY), 2001.

Dumpy Saves Christmas, illustrated by Tony Walton, Hyperion (New York, NY), 2001.

Dumpy's Friends on the Farm, illustrated by Tony Walton, Hyperion (New York, NY), 2001.

Dumpy and the Big Storm, illustrated by Tony Walton, Hyperion (New York, NY), 2002.

Dumpy and the Firefighters, illustrated by Tony Walton, HarperCollins (New York, NY), 2003.

Dumpy's Happy Holiday, illustrated by Tony Walton, HarperCollins (New York, NY), 2004.

Dumpy's Apple Shop, illustrated by Tony Walton and Cassandra Boyd, HarperCollins (New York, NY), 2004.

Dumpy to the Rescue!, illustrated by Tony Walton and Cassandra Boyd, HarperCollins (New York, NY), 2004.

Dumpy's Extra-Busy Day, illustrated by Tony Walton, HarperCollins (New York, NY), 2006.

Dumpy's Valentine, illustrated by Tony Walton, HarperCollins (New York, NY), 2006.

Sidelights

Emma Walton Hamilton is the coauthor, with her mother, well-known actor and singer Julie Andrews, of children's books such as *Dumpy the Dump Truck, Simeon's Gift, The Great American Mousical,* and *The Very Fairy Princess.* Ranging from preschool picture books to middle-grade readers, these volumes are published through HarperCollins' Julie Andrews Collection, an imprint for which Hamilton is editorial director. Discussing the mother-daughter collaboration with Sally Lodge in *Publishers Weekly,* Hamilton explained: "We want our books to embrace themes of integrity, creativity and the gifts of nature." Until the death of her husband in 2010, the series credited Julie Andrews under her married name, Julie Andrews Edwards.

Augmenting her work writing for children, Hamilton has also published *Raising Bookworms: Getting Kids Reading for Pleasure and Empowerment,* an award-winning guide for parents hoping to convince children to opt for the imaginative world of books over media such as video games and television. Noting that the book is designed for browsing, Daniel Kraus added in *Booklist* that *Raising Bookworms* "is a great tool for parents hoping to instill in their child a love of the printed word."

The mother-daughter team of Hamilton and Andrews began writing picture books after being inspired by Hamilton's truck-crazy young son, Sam. When Andrews' publishers asked her if she had any story ideas that would appeal to young children, she and Hamilton came up with the idea of a story starring a dump truck, and the "Dumpy" series was born. The first title in the "Dumpy" series, *Dumpy the Dump Truck,* describes how young Charlie and his grandfather decide to fix up the old farm dump truck rather than getting rid of it. After they give Dumpy new seat coverings and a new coat of paint, the truck becomes one of the most reliable vehicles on the farm. The story "may well leave readers with the idea that some things are meant to last," wrote a *Publishers Weekly* contributor. The series continues in *Dumpy Goes to School,* as the helpful vehicle contributes to the construction of a playground and also helps Charlie deal with school anxiety. In *Dumpy and the Big Storm* Charlie's seaside village loses power in a storm and it is up to Dumpy and other local trucks to shine their headlights out on the ocean to assist boats at sea while the lighthouse is dark. Kathy Broderick, writing in *Booklist,* noted that the traits Dumpy models include "cooperation, assisting those in need, remaining calm in an urgent situation, [and] friendship."

In both *Little Bo in Italy: The Continued Adventures of Bonnie Boadicea* and *Little Bo in London* Hamilton joins her mother in continuing the story of a curious young kitten in search of her litter mates. Andrews began Little Bo's story in *Little Bo: The Story of Bonnie Boadicea* and *Little Bo in France,* both illustrated by Henry Cole. The kitten's travels continue in *Little Bo in Italy,* which finds her joining human friend Billy in his work as a cabin boy aboard the yacht of the friendly Lord and Lady Goodlad, while the United Kingdom is the backdrop for the kitten's quest in *Little Bo in London.* Noting that Cole's illustrations give the series the look of "an old-fashioned classic," Andrew Medlar added in *Booklist* that *Little Bo in Italy* carries reader interest with its use of dialogue, a "simple, progressive plot," and a "manageable conflict."

Hamilton and Andrews introduce another engaging character in *The Very Fairy Princess.* Illustrated by Christine Davenier, the story introduces narrator Geraldine, a redheaded girl who is firmly convinced that she is actually a fairy princess. Although Gerry is careful to dress like a fairy princess and tries hard to perfect her prin-

The mother-daughter team of Hamilton and Andrews team up with artist Christine Davenier in creating the book series that includes **The Very Fairy Princess Takes the Stage.** (Illustration copyright © 2011 by Christine Davenier. Reproduced by permission of Little, Brown and Company. All rights reserved.)

Hamilton and Andrews treat readers to quite the show in their engaging story for The Great American Mousical, *and the antics come to life in Tony Walton's line art.* (Illustration © 2006 by Tony Walton. Used by permission of HarperCollins Children's Books, a division of HarperCollins Publishers.)

cess talents, she also realizes that it is okay to sometimes relax and just be a little girl. In true princess style, Gerry loves her ballet class, and *The Very Fairy Princess Takes the Stage* finds her excited about an upcoming dance recital. Although she is mistakenly cast in a non-princess role (a court jester), and her costume is not pink and frilly, Gerry finds that her abilities as a fairy princess are needed to help the production come off without a hitch. Citing the book's fanciful title, Diane Foote noted in *Booklist* that "it's refreshing to find a very real little girl as the protagonist," and "princesses who just want to have fun will find plenty of that here." In *Publishers Weekly* a critic praised Davenier's "luminous" water color illustrations, adding that "Andrews and Hamilton's narrative voice . . . [is] self-assured" and "fun."

Along with their series stories, Andrews and Hamilton have also written several stand-alone picture books and middle-grade readers, as well as editing the *Julie Andrews' Collection of Poems, Songs, and Lullabies,* an anthology featuring paintings by James McMullan. *Simeon's Gift* is the tale of the minstrel Simeon who decides to prove his love to a noblewoman by traveling and learning the music of the world. Their middle-grade novel *Dragon: Hound of Honor* also uses a medieval setting, this time to retell the legend of the dog of Montargis, an heroic canine that helps to solve the murder

of its master. "Readers who like their costume dramas heavily embroidered with high sentiment . . . will enjoy this fare," predicted a contributor to *Publishers Weekly*. Writing in *School Library Journal*, Anna M. Nelson deemed *Dragon* "a well-done historical novel with an exciting mystery," while GraceAnne A. DeCandido maintained in *Booklist* that the coauthors' use of "lavish details" provides readers with "a good sense of the times."

A miniature Broadway theater is the setting for *The Great American Mousical,* which finds a group of mice struggling to keep their model theater from being destroyed. Hamilton and Andrews, both veterans of the stage, infuse their text with theatrical terms and Broadway settings, while Hamilton's father, Tony Walton, contributes engaging illustrations. Kay Weisman, writing in *Booklist,* dubbed the book "an affectionate spoof of New York theater life" and predicted that the coauthors' "hilarious tale will appeal to would-be thespians everywhere." A *Publishers Weekly* critic concluded of *The Great American Mousical* that, although "the players here may be small in stature, . . . the story is big of heart."

Biographical and Critical Sources

PERIODICALS

Booklist, December 1, 2002, Kathy Broderick, review of *Dumpy and the Big Storm,* p. 673; September 1, 2004, GraceAnne A. DeCandido, review of *Dragon: Hound of Honor,* p. 120; January 1, 2006, Kay Weisman, review of *The Great American Mousical,* p. 99; December 1, 2008, Daniel Kraus, review of *Raising Bookworms: Getting Kids Reading for Pleasure and Empowerment,* p. 8; April 15, 2010, Diane Foote, review of *The Very Fairy Princess,* p. 54; February 1, 2011, Andrew Medlar, review of *Little Bo in Italy: The Continued Adventures of Bonnie Boadicea,* p. 78.

Kirkus Reviews, November 1, 2003, review of *Simeon's Gift,* p. 1310; February 1, 2006, review of *The Great American Mousical,* p. 130.

Publishers Weekly, September 25, 2000, review of *Dumpy the Dump Truck,* p. 115; July 21, 2003, Sally Lodge, "New Hats in the Ring," p. 85; October 27, 2003, review of *Simeon's Gift,* p. 68; May 31, 2004, review of *Dragon,* p. 75; January 9, 2006, review of *The Great American Mousical,* p. 54; October 5, 2009, review of *From the Playroom to the Coffee Table,* p. 51; April 9, 2010, review of *The Very Fairy Princess,* p. 50.

School Library Journal, April, 2001, Martha Link, reviews of *Dumpy the Dump Truck* and *Dumpy at School,* both p. 106; November, 2003, Rosalyn Pierini, review of *Simeon's Gift,* p. 91; June, 2004, Gloria Koster, reviews of *Dumpy to the Rescue* and *Dumpy's Apple Shop,* both p. 108; September, 2004, Anna M. Nelson, review of *Dragon,* p. 204; February, 2006, Eva Mitnick, review of *The Great American Mousical,* p. 96;

October, 2009, Marilyn Raniguchi, review of *Julie Andrews' Collection of Poems, Songs, and Lullabies,* p. 109.

ONLINE

Emma Walton Hamilton Home Page, http://www.emma waltonhamilton.com (December 29, 2011).
Julie Andrews Collection Web site, http://www.julie andrewscollection.com/ (February 23, 2007).*

* * *

HILLS, Tad

Personal

Married Lee Wade (an art director); children: Elinor, Charlie. *Education:* Skidmore College, degree (art), 1986.

Addresses

Home—Brooklyn, NY. *E-mail*—tadhills@gmail.com.

Career

Author and illustrator of children's books. Worked variously as an actor, a designer of marionettes and jewelry, and in interior renovation.

Awards, Honors

100 Titles for Reading and Sharing selection, New York Public Library, and Best of the Best Books designation, Chicago Public Library, both 2006, Children's Choice designation, International Reading Association/ Children's Book Council (IRA/CBC), Notable Children's Book designation, American Library Association, and Cardozo Award for Children's Literature, all 2007, all for *Duck and Goose;* Children's Choice designation, IRA/CBC, 2008, for *Duck, Duck, Goose;* Parents' Choice Silver Award, and Irma Simonton Black and James H. Black Award for Excellence in Children's Literature, Bank Street College of Education, both 2011, both for *How Rocket Learned to Read.*

Writings

SELF-ILLUSTRATED

My Fuzzy Friends: Cuddle up with These Soft and Furry Animals!, Little Simon (New York, NY), 1999.
Knock, Knock! Who's There?: My First Book of Knock-Knock Jokes, Little Simon (New York, NY), 2000.
My Fuzzy Farm Babies, Little Simon (New York, NY), 2001.
My Fuzzy Safari Babies, Little Simon (New York, NY), 2001.

The Twelve Days of Christmas: A Carol and Count Book, Little Simon (New York, NY), 2003.
How Rocket Learned to Read, Schwartz & Wade (New York, NY), 2010.

SELF-ILLUSTRATED; "DUCK AND GOOSE" SERIES

Duck and Goose, Schwartz & Wade (New York, NY), 2006.
Duck, Duck, Goose, Schwartz & Wade (New York, NY), 2007.
Duck and Goose 1 2 3, Schwartz & Wade (New York, NY), 2008.
What's Up, Duck?: A Book of Opposites, Schwartz & Wade (New York, NY), 2008.
Duck and Goose Find a Pumpkin, Schwartz & Wade (New York, NY), 2009.
Duck and Goose, How Are You Feeling?, Schwartz & Wade (New York, NY), 2009.
Duck and Goose, It's Time for Christmas!, Schwartz & Wade (New York, NY), 2010.
Duck and Goose, Here Comes the Easter Bunny!, Schwartz & Wade (New York, NY), 2012.

ILLUSTRATOR

Lilian Moore, *Poems Have Roots: New Poems,* Atheneum (New York, NY), 1997.
Jeannine Atkins, *A Name on the Quilt: A Story of Remembrance,* Atheneum (New York, NY), 1999.
Gerald Hausman, *Tom Cringle: Battle on the High Seas* (chapter book), Simon & Schuster (New York, NY), 2000.
Gerald Hauman, *Tom Cringle: The Pirate and the Patriot* (chapter book), Simon & Schuster (New York, NY), 2001.
Wendi J. Silvano, *Hey Diddle Riddle,* Little Simon (New York, NY), 2003.
April Stevens, *Waking up Wendell,* Schwartz & Wade (New York, NY), 2007.

Adaptations

How Rocket Learned to Read was adapted as a digital book, Random House Digital, 2011.

Sidelights

Children's writer and illustrator Tad Hills is best known for his series of picture books featuring Duck and Goose, an engaging pair of feathered friends. In such works as *Duck, Duck, Goose* and *Duck and Goose Find a Pumpkin,* Hills has earned critical acclaim for his appealing characters, vibrant illustrations, and quiet but humorous narratives.

One of Hills' early titles, *Knock Knock! Who's There?: My First Book of Knock-Knock Jokes,* provides plenty of jokes for beginning readers to share, as well as colorful illustrations of animal characters. "This is a great choice for individual sharing or story time," wrote Hen-

Tad Hills entertains readers in his artwork for April Stevens' picture-book story in **Waking up Wendell.** (Illustration copyright © 2007 by Tad Hills. Used by permission of Schwartz & Wade Books, an imprint of Random House Children's Books, a division of Random House, Inc.)

nie Vaandrager in *School Library Journal.* Another early picture book, *The Twelve Days of Christmas: A Carol and Count Flap Book,* enhances the text of the traditional holiday song with hidden pictures depicting lively animal characters. Susan Patron, reviewing the Yuletide offering for *School Library Journal,* considered *The Twelve Days of Christmas* to be "original, clever, amusing, and interactive."

With *Duck and Goose* Hills introduces readers to two friendly rivals, both who lay claim to a seemingly abandoned egg. Duck and Goose each want to incubate the egg on their own, but after spending time sitting on the egg together, the two begin to think of themselves as a team. Only after an observant bluebird points out what readers have known from the beginning—that the "egg" is actually a toy ball—do Duck and Goose decide to share and play together. Hills' "feathered heroes enact a dialogue familiar to anyone who has negotiated with siblings or playground rivals," wrote a *Publishers Weekly* critic, while a *Kirkus Reviews* contributor explained that the feathered friends' "gradual shift from adversaries to partners to playmates is indicated artfully by effective but subtle changes in book design and text." While Lisa S. Schindler found the story entertaining for

young readers, "it's the bright colorful artwork that will attract youngsters' attention," she wrote in her *School Library Journal* review. Hills' "cartoony illustrations are aimed at child viewers . . . and extract every drop of humor from the situation," asserted *Horn Book* reviewer Martha V. Parravano, and Jennifer Mattson wrote in *Booklist* that the author/illustrator's "whimsically rendered" protagonists "will instantly endear themselves to children."

Duck and Goose reappear in *Duck, Duck, Goose,* which finds the duo's friendship changing after a young duck named Thistle befriends Duck. Because Thistle seems to be good at everything he tries, Goose worries that his own friendship with Duck may be threatened, so he pretends to be unimpressed. Fortunately, by story's end, Duck and Goose have overcome their differences of opinion, and manage to remain friends. "The charming illustrations portray this tale of friendship perfectly," maintained a contributor in *Kirkus Reviews.* Rachael Vilmar, writing in *School Library Journal,* also praised the artwork in *Duck, Duck, Goose,* stating that Hills' illustrations "of a hazy, sunlit landscape and endearing animals make this a book worth lingering over with a good pal."

The search for the perfect decoration is at the heart of *Duck and Goose Find a Pumpkin*. After spotting their friend Thistle's pumpkin, the playful friends want one for their own, but their search takes them to the unlikeliest of spots, including a hollow log and a pile of leaves. Fortunately, Thistle steps in and suggests the ideal place to locate the longed-for object. "This appealing story is told in simple, well-chosen words," observed Mary Jean Smith in *School Library Journal*. Another seasonal tale, *Duck and Goose, It's Time for Christmas!*, centers on Duck's efforts to keep his friend focused on decorating their tree, rather than playing in the snow. Here Hill serves up "cheery holiday fare for pre-readers," according to *School Library Journal* critic Mara Alpert.

Hills received the prestigious Irma Black Award for *How Rocket Learned to Read*, a work inspired by the author/illustrator's Wheaten terrier. "Since the award is determined by writers, teachers, librarians, and children—people who know and care so much about kids' books—I feel especially honored," Hills remarked to *School Library Journal* interviewer Rocco Staino. In the work, a rambunctious canine finds himself the unwilling pupil of a tiny, yellow bird that is determined to teach him the alphabet. After Rocket's instructor finally captures his attention by spinning an exciting tale, the pup begins practicing the letters and spelling out words on his own, even when his new friend flies away for the winter. "Hills' gentle, sweet tale is a paean to the joy of reading," a *Kirkus Reviews* critic stated in appraising *How Rocket Learned to Read*. According to Marianne Saccardi in *School Library Journal*, "Youngsters will find this addition to Hills's cast of adorable animal characters simply irresistible."

In addition to his self-illustrated titles, Hills has provided the artwork for texts by other authors. His "illustrations are quiet and hieratic," wrote GraceAnne A. DeCandido in a *Booklist* review of the artist's contribution to Jeannine Atkins' *A Name on the Quilt: A Story of Remembrance*. Of the same title, a *Publishers Weekly* critic noted that "Hills contributes a very homespun touch" to the text borders with his illustrations. Roger Leslie, writing in *Booklist*, considered Hills' illustrations for Gerald Hausman's "Tom Cringle" chapter books to be "rough-and-ready" and appealing to the middle-grade boys for whom the seagoing adventure series is geared.

Waking up Wendell a tale by April Stevens, depicts the early-morning activities in a raucous neighborhood. Here "Hills' . . . witty watercolors depict action and facial expressions with equal ease, and they target both children's and adults' sensibilities," according to a reviewer in *Publishers Weekly*. Donna Cardon observed in *School Library Journal* that Hill's illustrations for Stevens' story "enliven the text and add extra humor."

One of Hills' biggest influences as a children's book author and illustrator has been his own children. "Spending time with my kids helps me remember what

A young pup shares his lessons with young readers in Hills' self-illustrated picture book **How Rocket Learned to Read.** (Illustration copyright © 2010 by Tad Hills. Reproduced by permission of Random House Children's Books, a division of Random House, Inc.)

it's like to be a child," he remarked in an essay on the Random House Web site. "I try to capture that innocence and enthusiastic vision of the world in my books. I want kids to see themselves in my characters."

Biographical and Critical Sources

PERIODICALS

Booklist, January 1, 1999, GraceAnne A. DeCandido, review of *A Name on the Quilt: A Story of Remembrance*, p. 885; September 15, 2001, Roger Leslie, review of *Tom Cringle: The Pirate and the Patriot*, p. 222; January 1, 2006 Jennifer Mattson, review of *Duck and Goose*, p. 114; March 1, 2007, Ilene Cooper, review of *Duck, Duck, Goose*, p. 88; April 1, 2008, Jennifer Mattson, review of *What's up Duck?: A Book of Opposites*, p. 53; September 15, 2009, Ilene Cooper, review of *Duck and Goose Find a Pumpkin*, p. 64; May 15, 2010, Abby Nolan, review of *How Rocket Learned to Read*, p. 43.

Horn Book, January-February, 2006, Martha V. Parravano, review of *Duck and Goose*, p. 69.

Kirkus Reviews, December 15, 2005, review of *Duck and Goose*, p. 1322; November 15, 2006, review of *Duck, Duck, Goose*, p. 1174; August 1, 2007, review of *Waking up Wendell*; June 15, 2010, review of *How Rocket Learned to Read*.

Publishers Weekly, January 11, 1999, review of *A Name on the Quilt*, p. 72; December 12, 2005, review of *Duck and Goose*, p. 64; November 27, 2006, review of *Duck, Duck, Goose*, p. 49; September 3, 2007, review of *Waking up Wendell*, p. 58; February 18, 2008, Diane Roback, "About Our Cover Artist" (profile of Hills), p. 1.

School Library Journal, August, 2000, Hennie Vaandrager, review of *Knock, Knock! Who's There?: My First Book of Knock-Knock Jokes,* p. 156; November, 2000, William McLoughlin, review of *Tom Cringle: Battle on the High Seas,* p. 154; October, 2001, Patricia B. McGee, review of *Tom Cringle,* p. 160; October, 2003, Susan Patron, review of *The Twelve Days of Christmas: A Carol-and-Count Flap Book,* p. 64; January, 2006, Lisa S. Schindler, review of *Duck and Goose,* p. 103; January, 2007, Rachael Vilmar, review of *Duck, Duck, Goose,* p. 97; September, 2007, Donna Cardon, review of *Waking up Wendell,* p. 176; March, 2009, Marge Loch-Wouters, review of *Duck and Goose, How Are You Feeling?,* p. 116; August, 2009, Mary Jean Smith, review of *Duck and Goose Find a Pumpkin,* p. 77; July, 2010, Marianne Saccardi, review of *How Rocket Learned to Read,* p. 61; October, 2010, Mara Alpert, review of *Duck and Goose, It's Time for Christmas,* p. 72.

ONLINE

BookPage.com, http://bookpage.com/ (September 8, 2010), "Meet Tad Hills."
Children's Book Review, http://www.thechildrensbook review.com/ (September 8, 2010), Bianca Schulze, "Bestselling Author Tad Hills Encourages You to Read to Your Kids."
Patricia Newman Web site, http://www.patriciamnewman. com/meet.html (May, 2007), "Who Wrote That? Featuring Tad Hills."
Random House Web site, http://www.randomhouse.com/ (December 15, 2011), "Tad Hills."
School Library Journal Web site, http://www.schoollibrary journal.com/ (May 19, 2011), Rocco Staino, "Tad Hills on Winning the 2011 Irma Black Award."
Tad Hills Home Page, http://www.tadhills.com (December 15, 2011).*

* * *

HUDSON, Cheryl Willis 1948-

Personal

Born April 7, 1948, in Portsmouth, VA; daughter of Hayes Elijah III (an insurance executive) and Lillian (an educator) Willis; married Wade Hudson (president of Just Us Books), June 24, 1972; children: Katura, Stephan. *Education:* Oberlin College, B.A.; postgraduate work at Northeastern University. *Religion:* Baptist.

Addresses

Office—Just Us Books, 356 Glenwood Ave., East Orange, NJ 07017. *E-mail*—cheryl_hudson@justusbooks. com.

Career

Writer/designer and publisher. Houghton Mifflin, Boston, MA, art editor; Macmillan Publishing, New York, NY, design manager; Arete Publishing Company, Prince-ton, NJ, assistant art director; freelance art director, graphic designer, and design consultant; Just Us Books, Orange, NJ, co-founder and publisher, beginning 1988. Former member of advisory board of Small Press Center; member of advisory board of Langston Hughes Library, Children's Defense Fund, and Alex Haley Farm. Presenter/facilitator at conferences, seminars, workshops, schools, and libraries.

Member

Author's Guild, PEN American Center, Society of Children's Book Writers and Illustrators.

Awards, Honors

Stephen Crane Award; inducted into International Literary Hall of Fame for Writers of African Descent, 2003; National Black Writers Conference award; Phillis Wheatley Award, Harlem Book Fair; Orbis Pictus Recommended selection, 2007, for *Construction Zone.*

Writings

Afro-Bets ABC Book, Just Us Books (East Orange, NJ), 1987.
Afro-Bets 123 Book, Just Us Books (East Orange, NJ), 1987.
(With Bernette G. Ford) *Bright Eyes, Brown Skin,* Just Us Books (East Orange, NJ), 1990.
Good Morning Baby, illustrated by George Ford, Scholastic (New York, NY), 1992.
Good Night Baby, illustrated by George Ford, Scholastic (New York, NY), 1992.
(Compiler) *Hold Christmas in Your Heart: African-American Songs, Poems, and Stories for the Holidays,* Scholastic (New York, NY), 1995.
(Compiler, with husband Wade Hudson) *How Sweet the Sound: African-American Songs for Children,* illustrated by Floyd Cooper, Scholastic (New York, NY), 1995.
Let's Count Baby, illustrated by George Ford, Scholastic (New York, NY), 1995.
Animal Sounds for Baby, illustrated by George Ford, Scholastic (New York, NY), 1995.
(Editor, with Wade Hudson) *Kids Book of Wisdom: Quotes from the African-American Tradition,* illustrated by Anna Rich, Just Us Books (East Orange, NJ), 1996.
(Editor, with Wade Hudson) *In Praise of Our Fathers and Our Mothers: A Black Family Treasury by Outstanding Authors and Artists,* Just Us Books (East Orange, NJ), 1997.
(Adapter) *Many Colors of Mother Goose,* illustrated by Ken Brown, Mark Corcoran, and Cathy Johnson, Just Us Books (East Orange, NJ), 1997.
The Harlem Renaissance: Profiles in Creativity, Newbridge (New York, NY), 2002.
Hands Can, photographs by John-Francis Bourke, Candlewick (Cambridge, MA), 2003.
What Do You Know?: Snow!, illustrated by Sylvia Walker, Scholastic (New York, NY), 2004.

Construction Zone, photographs by Richard Sobol, Candlewick Press (Cambridge, MA), 2006.

Hands Can, photographs by John-Francis Bourke, Candlewick Press (Cambridge, MA), 2007.

Clothes I Love to Wear, illustrated by Laura Freeman, Turnaround (New York, NY), 2008.

From Where I Stand: In the City, illustrated by Nancy Devard, Turnaround (New York, NY), 2008.

My Friend Maya Loves to Dance, illustrated by Eric Velasquez, Abrams Books for Young Readers (New York, NY), 2010.

Designer and art director for graphic-novel series *Pink Flamingos,* Simon & Schuster.

Sidelights

Cheryl Willis Hudson and her husband, Wade Hudson are the founders of Just Us Books, an award-winning publisher that specializes in children's books and learning materials that reflect the diversity of African-American culture and history. As a writer, Hudson has crafted stories published by her own company, such as *Bright Eyes, Brown Skin.* Tapping the resources of mainstream publishers, she has gained an even wider distribution for her multicultural picture books *Good Night Baby, Construction Zone, Hands Can,* and *My Friend Maya Loves to Dance,* the last illustrated by noted artist Eric Velasquez. As Hudson once told *SATA,* she "strongly believes that African-American children have a right to see themselves portrayed positively and accurately in the literature of this society."

Bright Eyes, Brown Skin exemplifies the Hudsons' goal of reinforcing the self-esteem of young African Americans. In the work, which Cheryl coauthored with Bernette G. Ford, four African-American children exuding self-confidence are happily at play in school. The illustrations show the children drawing, dancing, and playing games, and the text, in the words of Anna DeWind in *School Library Journal,* is a "poem extolling the beauty" of these exuberant young people. Kathleen Horning, writing in *Booklist,* concluded that *Bright Eyes, Brown Skin* may be a "favorite in preschool story hours," and a *Publishers Weekly* reviewer wrote that the Hudsons' book answers the "great" need for books which provide images of happy, confident black children.

Designed for toddlers, Hudson's *Good Morning Baby, Let's Coung Baby,* and *Good Night Baby* also feature African-American children. *Good Morning Baby* follows a little girl as she goes through her daily morning routine of waking, dressing, eating breakfast, and leaving the house with her father. In *Good Night Baby* a little boy gets ready for bed with a bath and a story. The text of both books, with few words, emphasizes the beauty of the babies, as do the realistic illustrations which take up most of each page. A *Publishers Weekly* critic remarked that these books serve as "a gratifying addition" to "multicultural literature" for babies and toddlers.

Hudson sometimes ranges from fictional texts in her books for children, producing collective biographies of African-American inventors and explorers as well as anthologies of music and poetry. In *How Sweet the Sound: African-American Songs for Children* she in-

***George Ford creates the colorful illustrations for Cheryl Willis Hudson's family-centered concept book* Let's Count Baby.** (Illustration copyright © 1995 by George Ford. Reprinted by permission of Scholastic Inc.)

Hudson joined her husband, Wade Hudson, in compiling the anthology **In Praise of Our Fathers and Mothers,** *which includes illustrations by George Ford as well as dozens of other talented artists, writers, and poets.* (Illustration copyright © 1997 by George Ford. Reproduced by permission.)

cludes traditional spirituals, protest songs, street cries, and popular soul tunes, all accompanied by information about the composers. *Hold Christmas in Your Heart: African-American Songs, Poems, and Stories for the Holidays* is a compilation that celebrates the holiday season. In this work Hudson includes selections from Langston Hughes, Gwendolyn Brooks, Lucille Clifton, and Paul Dunbar, as well as two of her own short verses. Coedited with her husband, Hudson's *In Praise of Our Fathers and Our Mothers: A Black Family Treasury by Outstanding Authors and Artists* brings together some four dozen works—poems, paintings, interviews, memoirs, and illustrations from various writers and artists—that celebrate the African-American family. According to *Horn Book* reviewer Rudine Sims Bishop, the couple's "shared values are . . . woven through these works, including an emphasis on creating and surrounding oneself with beauty; a high regard for education; the necessity to maintain a life of the spirit; and the need for familial and cultural continuity." "This is a black family album, which will appeal to readers across generations and across cultural boundaries as well," the critic added.

In *Hands Can* Hudson shows preschoolers engaged in such activities as clapping, waving, and tying shoes. The author's "rhythmic, rhyming text bounces along in a satisfying way," noted *Booklist* contributor Carolyn Phelan. Martha Topol, reviewing *Hands Can* for *School*

Library Journal, called the work an "inviting offering" that gives young readers "an almost sensory experience" while learning "how their hands help them to explore" their environment.

Praised by *School Library Journal* contributor Mary N. Oluonye as "a simple, sweet story about music, dance, and friendship," *My Friend Maya Loves to Dance* finds a little girl describing her good friend Maya, whose costumed dance performances capture a wide range of cultures and music—from jazz and reggae to swaying gospel and classical ballet—and are a joy to those around her. In *Kirkus Reviews* a contributor described Hudson's brief rhyming text as "a poetic love note" from one friend to another, the narrator eventually discovered to be especially appreciative of Maya's talents because she herself is in a wheelchair. Carolyn Phelan asserted in her *Booklist* review of *My Friend Maya Loves to Dance* that Velasquez's colorful oil paintings "are at their best when interpreting various styles of music" by integrating images of well-known musicians into Maya's exuberant performances, and *School Librarian* contributor Margaret Pemberton cited the artwork's "sophisticated feel."

"My career as a writer, designer, and publisher basically took off during my childhood when I doodled with pencils and markers in the margins of my schoolwork," Hudson told *SATA.* "I graduated to helping to create bulletin boards for my mother's classroom and by the time I finished college I knew that I wanted a career making children's books. I'm still doodling now but it's officially known as art and editorial direction. In my school visits, I encourage students to follow their passions, instincts, and their talents. With some guidance and discipline those three things can lead them to a rewarding career that they can love."

Biographical and Critical Sources

BOOKS

African-American Women Writers of New Jersey 1863-2000, edited by Sibyl E. Moses, Rutgers University Press (Rutgers, NJ), 2003.
Contemporary Black Biography, Volume 15, Gale (Detroit, MI), 1997.

PERIODICALS

Booklist, December 1, 1990, Kathleen Horning, review of *Bright Eyes, Brown Skin,* p. 756; September 15, 1995, Mary Harris Veeder, *Hold Christmas in Your Heart: African-American Songs, Poems, and Stories for the Holidays,* p. 170; April, 1997, Hazel Rochman, review of *In Praise of Our Fathers and Our Mothers: A Black Family Treasury by Outstanding Authors and Artists,* p. 1321; February 15, 2001, Henrietta M. Smith, review of *Let's Count, Baby,* p. 1160; October 1, 2003,

Hudson teams up with noted illustrator Eric Velasquez to create her picture book **My Friend Maya Loves to Dance.** (Abrams Books for Young Readers, 2010. Illustration copyright © 2010 Eric Velasquez. Reproduced by permission.)

Carolyn Phelan, review of *Hands Can,* p. 327; September 1, 2006, Shelle Rosenfeld, review of *Construction Zone,* p. 131; April 1, 2010, Carolyn Phelan, review of *My Friend Maya Loves to Dance,* p. 47.

Horn Book, March-April, 1997, Rudine Sims Bishop, review of *In Praise of Our Fathers and Our Mothers,* pp. 217-218.

Kirkus Reviews, May 1, 2006, review of *Construction Zone*; March 15, 2010, review of *My Friend Maya Loves to Dance.*

Publishers Weekly, November 16, 1990, review of *Bright Eyes, Brown Skin,* p. 55; November 9, 1992, reviews of *Good Morning Baby* and *Good Night Baby,* both p. 81; September 18, 1995, review of *Hold Christmas in Your Heart,* p. 98; May 14, 2007, review of *Hands Can,* p. 57.

School Librarian, autumn, 2010, Margaret Pemberton, review of *My Friend Maya Loves to Dance,* p. 155.

School Library Journal, January, 1991, Anna DeWind, review of *Bright Eyes, Brown Skin,* p. 76; December, 2003, Martha Topol, review of *Hands Can,* pp. 116-117; February, 2005, Catherine Callegari, review of *What Do You Know? Snow!,* p. 97; June, 2006, Carolyn Janssen, review of *Construction Zone,* p. 136; June, 2010, Mary N. Oluonye, review of *My Friend Maya Loves to Dance,* p. 74.

Virginian Pilot, June 3, 2007, Cherise M. Williams, "Norcom Grad Revisits Her Story for Children."

ONLINE

Cheryl Willis Hudson Home Page, http://cherylwhudson.weebly.com (December 26, 2011).

Just Us Books Web site, http://www.justusbooks.com/ (May 23, 2005), "Cheryl Hudson."

J-K

JONES, Tim

Personal
Male. *Education:* Attended Rhode Island School of Design.

Addresses
Home—Somerville, MA. *E-mail*—tim@timjonesillustration.com.

Career
Illustrator, beginning 1992.

Illustrator
Ann Braybrooks, *Pooh's Best Friend,* Disney Press (New York, NY), 1998.
Wild Critters, Epicenter Press (Kenmore, WA), 2007.
(With Mike Johnson) Roberto Orci and Alex Kurtzman, *Star Trek: Countdown,* IDW Pub. (San Diego, CA), 2009.

Contributor to books, including *Foundation Flash Cartoon Animation,* Friends of Ed/Springer-Verlag, 2007.

"I SEE I LEARN" SERIES BY STUART J. MURPHY

Emma's Friendwich, Charlesbridge (Watertown, MA), 2010.
Freda Plans a Picnic, Charlesbridge (Watertown, MA), 2010.
Good Job, Ajay!, Charlesbridge (Watertown, MA), 2010.
Percy Plays It Safe, Charlesbridge (Watertown, MA), 2010.
Freda Is Found, Charlesbridge (Watertown, MA), 2011.
Write on, Carlos!, Charlesbridge (Watertown, MA), 2011.
Freda Stops a Bully, Charlesbridge (Watertown, MA), 2012.

Works featuring Jones' illustrations have been translated into Spanish.

Biographical and Critical Sources

PERIODICALS

Booklist, September 1, 2010, Gillian Engberg, review of *Emma's Friendwich,* p. 112.
Kirkus Reviews, June 15, 2010, review of *Emma's Friendwich.*
School Library Journal, August, 2010, Margaret R. Tassia, review of *Emma's Friendwich,* p. 81; July, 2011, Melissa Smith, review of *Freda Is Found,* p. 73.

ONLINE

Tim Jones Home Page, http://www.timjonesillustration.com (December 12, 2011).*

* * *

JULIAN, Russell 1975-

Personal
Born 1975, in Derbyshire, England; partner's name Arianna; children: two. *Education:* Attended Anglia Ruskin University. *Hobbies and other interests:* Gardening, reading.

Addresses
Home—London, England. *Agent*—Jodie Marsh, United Agents, 12-26 Lexington St., London W1F 0LE, England; jmarsh@unitedagents.co.uk.

Career
Writer and illustrator.

Awards, Honors
Booktrust Early Years Award shortlist, 2005, for *It's a George Thing!* by David Bedford.

Writings

SELF-ILLUSTRATED

Lost Calf (also see below), Egmont (London, England), 2004.

Hungry Pig (also see below), Egmont (London, England), 2004.

Busy Dog (also see below), Egmont (London, England), 2004.

Happy Cockerel (also see below), Egmont (London, England), 2004.

My First Farm Books (contains *Lost Calf, Hungry Pig, Busy Dog,* and *Happy Cockerel*), Egmont (London, England), 2005.

Farmyard Friends, Egmont (London, England), 2005.

ILLUSTRATOR

Simon Puttock, *Horsey,* Egmont (London, England), 2004.

Melissa Balfour, *The Magic Footprints,* Crabtree Publishing (New York, NY), 2005.

Beth Webb, *The Junkyard Dragon,* Lion Children's Books (Oxford, England), 2007.

Simon Puttock, *Goat and Donkey in Strawberry Sunglasses,* Good Books (Intercourse, PA), 2007.

Simon Puttock, *Goat and Donkey in the Great Outdoors,* Good Books (Intercourse, PA), 2007.

Simon Puttock, *Goat and Donkey in the Noise Downstairs,* Oxford University Press (Oxford, England), 2008.

David Bedford, *It's a George Thing!,* Egmont (London, England), 2008.

Trudy Harris, *Splitting The Herd: A Corral of Odds and Evens,* Millbrook Press (Minneapolis, MN), 2008.

(With Estelle Corke) Su Box, *The Christmas Star,* Lion Children's Books (Oxford, England), 2008.

(With Estelle Corke) Su Box, *The Christmas Cat,* Lion Children's Books (Oxford, England), 2008.

Victoria Tebbs, *What Can You See? on Christmas Night,* Lion Children's Books (Oxford, England), 2009.

Claire Freedman, *Tappity-Tap! What Was That?,* Scholastic (London, England), 2009.

Ann Bonwill, *Pocket's Christmas Wish,* Oxford University Press (Oxford, England), 2009, Barron's (Hauppauge, NY), 2010.

Carrie Weston, *Crocodiles Need Kisses Too,* Scholastic (London, England), 2010.

Claire Freedman, *George's Dragon,* Scholastic (London, England), 2011.

David Bedford, *Bouncy Bouncy Bedtime,* Egmont (London, England), 2011.

Sidelights

British children's book illustrator Russell Julian has earned a strong critical reception for the colorful and charming paintings he creates to grace the pages of such works as Simon Puttock's *Goat and Donkey in Strawberry Sunglasses* and Ann Bonwill's *Pocket's Christmas Wish.* Reviewing another of his illustration projects, *Horsey,* Puttock's fantasy about a pair of stuffed toys that embarks on a series of nighttime escapades, London *Guardian* critic Julia Eccleshare called Julian's pictures "a delight," adding that the characters' "feelings are conveyed in their richly expressive faces."

In their picture-book careers, Julian and Puttock have collaborated on several books centering on the friendship between a distractible goat and his sensible donkey pal. In *Goat and Donkey in Strawberry Sunglasses* Goat volunteers to go shopping for his all-too-busy friend, but he makes several odd purchases when he has difficulty reading Donkey's handwriting on the grocery list. "Inventive designs and fruity colors in vibrant tones . . . make this a pleasure to look at," as Ilene Cooper remarked in *Booklist.* "Featuring electric hues and amusing particulars," a contributor in *Publishers Weekly* similarly observed, "Julian's playful pictures" in *Goat and Donkey in Strawberry Sunglasses* "capture the bond between these fast friends."

An unusual vacation is at the heart of *Goat and Donkey in the Great Outdoors,* another Julian-Puttock collaboration. Although Goat decides that he needs a getaway to the country, he eventually realizes that he could have just as much fun at home, splashing in his pool and camping with Donkey in their backyard tent. "Julian's warm oil paintings capture the sunny dispositions of the characters," Linda Ludke remarked in *School Library Journal,* and a *Kirkus Reviews* critic maintained that "the soft finish and richly colored palette of Julian's illustrations add gentle warmth" to Puttock's story.

Splitting the Herd: A Corral of Odds and Evens, a work by Trudy Harris, offers young readers a lesson in basic arithmetic. Harris's tale follows the misadventures of Cowboy Kirby and Miss Emma, neighboring ranchers who simply cannot keep their two herds separated. "Julian's illustrations are bright, with cattle faces as friendly and expressive as the humans'," a *Kirkus Reviews* contributor in a review of *Splitting the Herd,* and a *Children's Bookwatch* critic remarked that pictures of "sneaky cows" skuttling between ranches "provide lots of extra giggles." In Bonwill's *Pocket's Christmas Wish,* a cuddly bunny discovers the true spirit of the holiday. Here Julian "depict[s] snowy outdoor scenes in muted cream and lavender tones," as Eva Mitnick reported in *School Library Journal.*

In addition to his illustration work, Julian also has several original, self-illustrated children's books to his credit, including *Lost Calf, Hungry Pig,* and *Happy Cockerel.* These works follow a group of farm animals, and each contains a sound chip that mimics the titular creature's sound. According to a critic in *Publishers Weekly,* "Julian's humorous depiction of the barnyard denizens playfully exaggerates a porcine snout or the prideful posture of a papa rooster."

Biographical and Critical Sources

PERIODICALS

Booklist, May 15, 2007, Ilene Cooper, review of *Goat and Donkey in Strawberry Sunglasses,* p. 51.

Children's Bookwatch, January, 2010, review of *Splitting the Herd: A Corral of Odds and Evens.*

Guardian (London, England), July 10, 2004, Julia Eccleshare, review of *Horsey,* p. 33.

Kirkus Reviews, May 15, 2007, review of *Goat and Donkey in the Great Outdoors*; July 15, 2008, review of *Splitting the Herd.*

Publishers Weekly, January 24, 2005, reviews of *Happy Cockerel, Lost Calf, Hungry Pig,* and *Busy Dog,* all p. 245; June 4, 2007, review of *Goat and Donkey in Strawberry Sunglasses,* p. 48.

School Library Journal, June, 2007, Linda Ludke, review of *Goat and Donkey in Strawberry Sunglasses,* p. 120; October, 2008, Marge Loch-Wouters, review of *Splitting the Herd,* p. 132; October, 2010, Eva Mitnick, review of *Pocket's Christmas Wish,* p. 69.

ONLINE

Oxford University Press Web site, http://www.oup.com/ (January 1, 2012), "Russell Julian."

United Artists Web site, http://unitedagents.co.uk/ (January 1, 2012), "Russell Julian."*

*   *   *

KATE, Lauren 1981-

Personal

Born 1981, in Dayton, OH; married.

Addresses

Home—Los Angeles, CA. *E-mail*—laurenkatebooks@gmail.com.

Career

Novelist.

Writings

The Betrayal of Natalie Hargrove, Razorbill (New York, NY), 2009.

"FALLEN" PARANORMAL NOVEL SERIES

Fallen, Delacorte Press (New York, NY), 2009.
Torment, Delacorte Press (New York, NY), 2010.
Passion, Delacorte Press (New York, NY), 2011.
Fallen in Love (short stories), Delacorte Press (New York, NY), 2011.
Rapture, Delacorte Press (New York, NY), 2012.

Author's work has been translated into several languages, including French, German, Italian, Russian, and Spanish.

Adaptations

Author's novels have also been adapted as audiobooks, produced by Listening Library.

Sidelights

Although she now makes her home in southern California, Lauren Kate sets her fiction in locales that she remembers from her past. Her memories of attending high school in Plano, Texas, provided the details that bring to life the setting of her first novel, *The Betrayal of Natalie Hargrove,* while her college years spent in Atlanta, Georgia, gave her the understanding of the Civil-War South that grounds her "Fallen" series of paranormal novels for young adults.

With a setting inspired by her childhood hometown, *The Betrayal of Natalie Hargrove* introduces a beautiful young woman who is determined that her position at the top of the social pecking order will be reflected in her election as Palmetto Princess during the upcoming school prom. Natalie's current status has been achieved through sheer determination: she has successfully erased

Cover of Lauren Kate's young-adult novel Torment, *featuring artwork by Fernanda Brussi Goncalves.* (Jacket cover copyright © 2011 by Ember. Used by permission of Ember, an imprint of Random House Children's Books, a division of Random House, Inc.)

all evidence of her family's questionable past, and she is determined to use the same ruthlessness to achieve this new goal. When hunky football-star boyfriend Mike seems less than enthusiastic about fighting for the corresponding spot as Palmetto Prince, Natalie decides that it is time for Plan B: convince Mike's competition to opt out of the contest. Plan B ends in tragedy, however, but Natalie does not let that deter her, and her "acid perspective drives Kate's deliciously twisted story," according to a *Publishers Weekly* critic. The author "revels in her duplicitous South Carolina setting," asserted Daniel Kraus in his *Booklist* review of *The Betrayal of Natalie Hargrove,* as well as her creation of "the bitchy, bratty Natalie."

Kate's "Fallen" novels include *Fallen, Torment, Passion,* and *Rapture,* as well as *Fallen in Love,* a short-story collection that fills in the characters' backstory. Inspired by the legends of fallen angels, the first novel introduces Lucinda Price, a high-school senior who seems to be having terrible luck. After almost-boyfriend Trevor is killed in an accident that seems to be her fault, Luce is forcibly enrolled at Sword & Cross boarding school. Although she feels haunted by shadows, her current heartache ends when she meets two handsome fellow students: the outgoing and affectionate Cam and the taciturn Daniel Grigori. It is Daniel who quickly steals Luce's heart, and despite being drawn to him he urges her to steer clear because a relationship with him could result in her death. The beginning of *Fallen* "is gripping and foreshadows the supernatural elements to come," asserted Kris Hickey in a *School Library Journal* review of the novel, and in *Booklist* Ian Chipman noted that Kate's depictions of Daniel and his fellow fallen angels give them "a similarly ideal blend of brooding mystery and sexy rebellion" as the vampires in Stephenie Meyer's "Twilight" novels.

Luce returns in *Torment,* as she and Daniel must take separate paths in order to save her from the group of immortal Outcasts who now seek her demise. While living at Shoreline, a boarding school for nephilim (children born to angel and human parents), Luce makes new friends while her relationship with Daniel grows ever more tense. She has known Daniel throughout the past centuries, but her memories are murky and Luce whether he is telling her everything she needs to know to piece together her history. In *Passion* Luce hopes to break the cycle of death and sacrifice that has marked her long relationship with Daniel, but to do that she must return to the biblical era in which they first met. "In *Torment,* we find a much more independent Luce than we saw in *Fallen,*" asserted *Voice of Youth Advocates* contributors Cheryl Clark and Erica Alexander, and Kate's "novel is compellingly readable." "Interest is piqued with the hint of a love triangle," noted *School Library Journal* critic Patricia N. McClune of the same novel, "and the suspense is ratcheted up in the heart-pounding" conclusion.

Biographical and Critical Sources

PERIODICALS

Booklist, September 15, 2009, Daniel Kraus, review of *The Betrayal of Natalie Hargrove,* p. 66; December 1, 2009, Ian Chipman, review of *Fallen,* p. 35.
Kirkus Reviews, November 1, 2009, review of *Fallen;* September 1, 2010, review of *Torment.*
Magpies, March, 2010, Tehani Wessely, review of *Fallen,* p. 40.
Publishers Weekly, November 16, 2009, review of *The Betrayal of Natalie Hargrove,* p. 55; November 23, 2009, review of *Fallen,* p. 57; September 6, 2010, review of *Torment,* p. 41.
School Library Journal, January, 2010, Kris Hickey, review of *Fallen,* p. 104; September, 2010, Patricia N. McClune, review of *Torment,* p. 156.
Voice of Youth Advocates, December, 2010, Cheryl Clark, review of *Torment,* p. 472.

ONLINE

Lauren Kate Home Page, http://laurenkatebooks.net (December 12, 2011).
Random House Web site, http://www.randomhouse.com/ (December 2, 2011), "Lauren Kate."*

*   *   *

KEETER, Susan

Personal

Married Seth Tucker; children: Sara, Emma. *Education:* Syracuse University, B.F.A. (illustration). *Religion:* Episcopalian.

Addresses

Home—Syracuse, NY. *Agent*—MB Artists, 775 6th Ave., Ste. No. 6, New York, NY 10001. *E-mail*—keeters@ upstate.edu.

Career

Illustrator and fine artist. *Exhibitions:* Work exhibited in numerous juried and one-person exhibitions.

Awards, Honors

Best Picture Book Award, Society of School Librarians International, 2000, for *The Piano* by William Miller.

Illustrator

Lila Jukes, *I'm a Girl!,* Cool Kids Press (Boca Raton, FL), 1995.
Henry Billings and Melissa Billings, compilers, *Young People's Stories of Truthfulness,* Young People's Press (San Diego, CA), 1995.

William Miller, *The Piano,* Lee & Low Books (New York, NY), 2000.

Patricia C. McKissack, *Tippy Lemmey,* Aladdin (New York, NY), 2003.

Alice Faye Duncan, *Honey Baby Sugar Child,* Simon & Schuster Books for Young Readers (New York, NY), 2005.

Glennette Tilley Turner, *An Apple for Harriet Tubman,* Albert Whitman (Morton Grove, IL), 2006.

Mary K. LeClair and Justin D. White, *Three Nineteenth-Century Women Doctors: Elizabeth Blackwell, Mary Walker, Sarah Loguen Fraser,* Hofmann (Syracuse, NY), 2007.

Alexandra Jessup Altman, *Waiting for Benjamin: A Story about Autism,* Albert Whitman (Morton Grove, IL), 2008.

Ann Malaspina, *Phillis Sings out Freedom: The Story of George Washington and Phillis Wheatley,* Albert Whitman (Chicago, IL), 2010.

Adaptations

An Apple for Harriet Tubman was adapted for video, Nutmeg Media, 2007.

Sidelights

A fine-art painter whose work has been shown in juried group exhibitions and one-person shows, Susan Keeter has also gained a reputation for her work in picture-book illustration. Effective in library story hours, Keeter's oil paintings have appeared in such picture books as *The Piano* by William Miller and *An Apple for Harriet Tubman* by Glennette Tilley Turner. She also demonstrates her talent for drawing in her black-and-white spot art for Patricia C. McKissack's chapter book *Tippy Lemmey.* Miller's music-minded "characters are brought to life . . . in the expressive artwork" for *The Piano,* asserted *School Library Journal* contributor Marlene Gawron in appraising Keeter's work as an illustrator, and a *Publishers Weekly* reviewer cited the artist's ability to enrich the same story by visually "captur[ing] . . . the deepening bond between . . . unlikely friends."

Describing *An Apple for Harriet Tubman* as "an excellent introduction" to an inspirational woman, Mary Hazelton heaped special praise on Keeter's art for the

Susan Keeter's evocative paintings are a feature of Ann Malaspina's biographical picture book **Phillis Sings out Freedom.** (Illustration copyright © 2010 by Susan Keeter. Reproduced by permission of Albert Whitman & Company.)

book in her _School Library Journal_ review. The artist's "paintings offer an opulent backdrop" to Turner's story, Hazelton asserted, citing their "thick brushstrokes and careful use of light." Another illustration project by Keeter that focuses on a former slave and writer, Ann Malaspina's _Phillis Sings out Freedom: The Story of George Washington and Phillis Wheatley,_ benefits from paintings that "are full of period details that help to clarify" the Revolutionary era in which Wheatley lived, according to _Booklist_ critic Kay Weisman. Also featuring Keeter's oil paintings, _Honey Baby Sugar Child_ "enfolds" a rhyming text by Alice Fay Duncan within what _Booklist_ critic Jennifer Mattson described as "joyful images" that create a visual "cocoon of burnt-sugar warmth and sweetness."

Biographical and Critical Sources

PERIODICALS

Booklist, February 1, 1996, Ilene Cooper, review of _I'm a Girl!,_ p. 938; July, 2000, Gillian Engberg, review of _The Piano,_ p. 2042; January 1, 2003, Shelle Rosenfeld, review of _Tippy Lemmey,_ p. 892; February 1, 2005, Jennifer Mattson, review of _Honey Baby Sugar Child,_ p. 976; August 1, 2006, Hazel Rochman, review of _An Apple for Harriet Tubman,_ p. 81; July 1, 2008, Bina Williams, review of _Waiting for Benjamin: A Story about Autism,_ p. 75; September 1, 2010, Kay Weisman, review of _Phillis Sings out Freedom: The Story of George Washington and Phillis Wheatley,_ p. 91.

Black Issues Book Review, July, 2000, Khafre Abif, review of _The Piano,_ p. 74.

Horn Book, March-April, 2003, Roger Sutton, review of _Tippy Lemmey,_ p. 213.

Kirkus Reviews, December 15, 2002, review of _Tippy Lemmey,_ p. 1853; September 1, 2006, review of _An Apple for Harriet Tubman,_ p. 913.

School Library Journal, July, 2000, Marlene Gawron, review of _The Piano,_ p. 84; March, 2005, Mary N. Oluonye, review of _Honey Baby Sugar Child,_ p. 170; October, 2006, Mary Hazelton, review of _An Apple for Harriet Tubman,_ p. 143; July, 2008, Wendy Smith-D'Arezzo, review of _Waiting for Benjamin,_ p. 66; October, 2010, Lucinda Snyder Whitehurst, review of _Phillis Sings out Freedom,_ p. 101.

ONLINE

MB Artists Web site, http://www.mbartists.com/ (December 25, 2011). "Susan Keeter."*

*   *   *

KEPLINGER, Kody 1991-

Personal

Born 1991, in KY. _Education:_ Attended Ithaca College. _Hobbies and other interests:_ Watching television and movies, going to the theatre.

Addresses

Home—New York, NY. _Agent_—Joanna Volpe, Nancy Coffey Literary, Joanna@nancycoffeliterary.com. _E-mail_—kodykeplinger@gmail.com.

Career

Author.

Writings

The DUFF: Designated Ugly Fat Friend, Poppy (New York, NY), 2010.
Shut Out, Poppy (New York, NY), 2011.

Adaptations

Film rights to _The DUFF_ were optioned to Vast Entertainment.

Sidelights

Kody Keplinger draws on her own feelings of not fitting in with her high-school friends in her first novel, _The DUFF: Designated Ugly Fat Friend._ Although she

Cover of Kody Keplinger's debut young-adult novel The DUFF, _which focuses on the dynamics of female friendships._ (Little, Brown & Company, 2010. Jacket cover photograph by Adri Berger/Getty Images. Reproduce by permission of Hachette Book Group.)

started writing her story during her senior year of high-school as a humorous response to a hurtful comment by a fellow student, Keplinger ultimately got the last word when her novel was published two years later.

In *The DUFF* Keplinger tells the story of seventeen-year-old Bianca Piper, whose social life alternates from hanging out with her two best friends and trading put-downs with notorious player Wesley Rush. When Wesley tells Bianca that her girlfriends like to have her tag along because she is their "DUFF", he hits his mark, although the girl has never harbored illusions about her looks or popularity. In the hope of worming his way toward intimacies with Bianca's friends, Wesley starts to hit on Bianca, and family upheavals and loneliness ultimately propel her into a secret romance with the conniving young man. Over time, the preconception of both teens are shown to be less than accurate in a novel that captures the hushed intimacy of "spontaneous notes passed between friends during class," according to *Voice of Youth Advocates* contributor Suzanne Osman. According to *School Library Journal* critic Kathleen E. Gruver, *The DUFF* "is a fun read and surprisingly feminist in a number of ways," because "Keplinger makes good points about female body image and female friendship." A *Kirkus Reviews* writer praised the debut novelist by citing the author's "snarky teen speak, true-to-life characterizations and rollicking sense of humor," and in *Publishers Weekly* a critic described the narrator of *The DUFF* as "strong, witty, and confident."

Keplinger steps into more risky territory in *Shut Out*, a contemporary retelling of Aristophanes' drama *Lysistrata,* which focuses on the power of women when withdrawing their sexual favors from men. Like *The DUFF*, *Shut Out* is set in high school and finds seventeen-year-old Lissa tired of having her time with football-playing boyfriend Randy curtailed by his participation in his team's ongoing feud with the school's soccer team. Marshaling other girlfriends of Hamilton High athletes, Lissa starts a strike, proclaiming that there will be no more sex until the inter-school sports rivalry ends. Noting that an R-rated Greek play seems "an unlikely choice for the basis of a contemporary teen novel," Stacey Hayman added in *Voice of Youth Advocates* that *Shut Out* pivots on a questionable assumption: that high-school girls "are all sexually active." Although Keplinger's plot device allows teen girls to get together and share "their own experiences with sexuality," a *Kirkus Reviews* writer maintained that the novel "reinforces as many stereotypes as it overturns." Voicing a slightly differing view, a *Publishers Weekly* critic ranked *Shut Out* as a "teen sex . . . comedy" that benefits from "some honest, sensitive, and surprising conversations about sex and relationships."

Biographical and Critical Sources

PERIODICALS

Kirkus Reviews, September 1, 2010, review of *The DUFF: Designated Ugly Fat Friend;* August 15, 2011, review of *Shut Out.*

Publishers Weekly, August 16, 2010, review of *The DUFF,* p. 55; August 15, 2011, review of *Shut Out,* p. 74.

School Library Journal, November, 2010, Kathleen E. Gruver, review of *The DUFF,* p. 118.

Voice of Youth Advocates, October, 2010, Suzanne Osman, review of *The DUFF,* p. 351; October, 2011, Stacey Hayman, review of *Shut Out,* p. 385.

ONLINE

Kody Keplinger Home Page, http://kodykeplinger.com (December 2, 2011).

Kody Keplinger Web log, http://kodymekellkeplinger. blogspot.com (December 2, 2011).

*　　*　　*

KRAMER, Andrew

Personal

Married; wife's name Jennifer (an attorney and author); children: Mitchell, Patrick, Jessica, Jeffrey. *Hobbies and other interests:* Playing hockey.

Addresses

Home—Marietta, GA. *E-mail*—akramer9@hotmail.com.

Career

Author. Works for a software company.

Writings

Pajama Pirates, illustrated by Leslie Lammle, HarperCollins (New York, NY), 2001.

Biographical and Critical Sources

PERIODICALS

Kirkus Reviews, August 15, 2010, review of *Pajama Pirates.*

Publishers Weekly, August 23, 2010, review of *Pajama Pirates,* p. 47.

School Library Journal, September, 2010, Julie Roach, review of *Pajama Pirates,* p. 128.

ONLINE

Andrew Kramer Home Page, http://www.pajamapirates. com/ (December 15, 2011).*

*　　*　　*

KULLING, Monica 1952-

Personal

Born January 12, 1952, in Vancouver, British Columbia, Canada; daughter of Walter (a store owner) and Anita Margot (a homemaker and artist) Kulling. *Educa-*

Monica Kulling (Reproduced by permission.)

tion: University of Victoria, B.A. *Hobbies and other interests:* Photography, walking her dogs, baking, collecting toys, movies, reading.

Addresses

Home and office—Toronto, Ontario, Canada. *E-mail*—kulling@bell.net.

Career

Writer. Researcher and developer of anthologies for Scholastic Canada, 1983-87, Ginn Publishing Canada, 1987-90, Houghton Mifflin Canada, 1990-92, and Prentice-Hall, beginning 1992.

Member

Writers' Union of Canada.

Awards, Honors

Best Bets selection, Ontario Library Association, 2009, Silver Birch Express Award nomination, 2011, Red Cedar Book Award nomination, 2011-12, and Information Book Award finalist, Vancouver Children's Literature Roundtable, all for *It's a Snap!;* Information Book Award finalist, Vancouver Children's Literature Roundtable, for *All Aboard!*

Writings

FICTION

Little Peanut at the Zoo, Valley Zoo (Edmonton, Ontario, Canada), 1983.
I Hate You, Marmalade!, illustrated by Alex Ayliffe, Viking (New York, NY), 1992.
Waiting for Amos, illustrated by Vicky Lowe, ABC Books (London, England), 1992, Simon & Schuster (New York, NY), 1993.
(Adaptor) Louisa May Alcott, *Little Women,* Random House (New York, NY), 1994.
(Adaptor) Victor Hugo, *Les Misérables,* Random House, 1995.
(Adaptor) Mark Twain, *The Adventures of Tom Sawyer,* Random House (New York, NY), 1995.
(Adaptor) Charles Dickens, *Great Expectations,* Random House (New York, NY), 1996.
Marmee's Surprise: A Little Women Story, Random House (New York, NY), 1996.
Edgar Badger's Balloon Day, illustrated by Carol O'Malia, Mondo (Greenville, NY), 1997.
Edgar Badger's Fix-It Day, illustrated by Neecy Twinem, Mondo (Greenvale, NY), 1997.
Fairy Tale: A True Story (movie novelization), Random House (New York, NY), 1997.
(Adaptor) Louise May Alcott, *Marmee's Surprise: A Little Women Story,* illustrated by Diane Paterson, Random House (New York, NY), 1997.
(Adaptor) Robert Louis Stevenson, *The Body Snatcher,* Random House (New York, NY), 1998.
Edgar Badger's Butterfly Day, illustrated by Neecy Twinem, Mondo (Greenvale, NY), 1999.
Edgar Badger's Fishing Day, illustrated by Neecy Twinem, Mondo (Greenvale, NY), 1999.
Queen in Disguise ("Star Wars: Episode One" series), illustrated by John Alvin, Random House (New York, NY), 2000.
Go, Stitch, Go! (movie tie-in), illustrated by Denise Shimabukuro and the Disney Storybook Artists, Random House (New York, NY), 2002.
(With Nan Walker) *The Messiest Room on the Planet,* illustrated by Jerry Smath, Kane Press (New York, NY), 2009.
Merci Mister Dash!, illustrated by Esperança Melo, Tundra Books of Northern New York (Plattsburgh, NY), 2011.

Also contributor of short stories to magazines, including *Ladybug.*

POETRY

Go-Cart Getaway, Nelson (Toronto, Ontario, Canada), 1993.
(Editor) *Bubblegum, Books, and Bugs: Poems for You and Me,* Scholastic Canada (Markham, Ontario, Canada), 2005.
(Editor) *Say It out Loud: Poems to Play With,* Scholastic Canada (Markham, Ontario, Canada), 2005.

(Editor) *An Early Worm Got out of Bed and Other Poems to Read out Loud,* Scholastic Education (Markham, Ontario, Canada), 2007.

(Editor) *I Swallowed a Gnat!: Poems to Munch On,* Scholastic Education (Markham, Ontario, Canada), 2007.

Contributor of poetry to periodicals, including *Cricket* and *Hopscotch for Girls,* and to anthologies, including *Friend to Friend,* Houghton Mifflin, 1992, *Imagine Poetry,* Prentice-Hall, 1993, and *There Will Always Be Sky,* Nelson, 1993.

NONFICTION

Sea of Ice: The Wreck of the Endurance, illustrated by John Edens, Random House (New York, NY), 1999.

Life in the Wild: Alligators, illustrated by Marty Roper, Golden Books (New York, NY), 2000.

Life in the Wild: Elephants, illustrated by Michael Maydak, Golden Books (New York, NY), 2000.

Horses, illustrated by Betina Ogden, Random House (New York, NY), 2001.

Life in the Wild: Bears, illustrated by Jean Cassels, Random House (New York, NY), 2004.

BIOGRAPHY

Vanished! The Mysterious Disappearance of Amelia Earhart, illustrated by Cornelius Van Wright and Ying-Hwa Hu, Random House (New York, NY), 1996.

Eleanor Everywhere: The Life of Eleanor Roosevelt, illustrated by Cliff Spohn, Random House (New York, NY), 1999.

The Great Houdini: World Famous Magician and Escape Artist, illustrated by Anne Reas, Random House (New York, NY), 1999.

Escape North!: The Story of Harriet Tubman, illustrated by Teresa Flavin, Random House (New York, NY), 2000.

Eat My Dust!: Henry Ford's First Race, illustrated by Richard Walz, Random House (New York, NY), 2004.

Listen Up!: Alexander Graham Bell's Talking Machine, illustrated by Richard Walz, Random House (New York, NY), 2007.

It's a Snap!: George Eastman's First Photograph, illustrated by Bill Slavin, Tundra Books of Northern New York (Plattsburgh, NY), 2009.

All Aboard! Elijah McCoy's Steam Engine, illustrated by Bill Slavin, Tundra Books of Northern New York (Plattsburgh, NY), 2010.

In the Bag!: Margaret Knight Wraps It Up, illustrated by David Parkins, Tundra Books of Northern New York (Plattsburgh, NY), 2011.

Francis Scott Key's Star-Spangled Banner, illustrated by Richard Walz, Random House (New York, NY), 2012.

Sidelights

Monica Kulling's books for young readers include the award-winning biographies *It's a Snap!: George Eastman's First Photograph* and *All Aboard! Elijah Mc-*

Coy's Steam Engine as well as picture books and works of poetry. Kulling notes that her fictional efforts have proven valuable to her biographical works. "You write your way into your subject's life by imagining life as they lived it," she stated on the Canadian Children's Book Centre Web site.

Kulling started writing for children while she was still a student at the University of Victoria in her native British Columbia, Canada. Although those first efforts were never published, she enjoyed writing for children so much that she eventually made it her career. Beginning as a reader at a Toronto publishing company, Kulling graduated to copyeditor, editor, and finally to writer, which she considers her most valuable work experience. "I learned how to write for different age groups," she once told *SATA,* "and to write 'to order.' The experience taught me discipline—you sit down to write every day whether you feel 'inspired' or not."

Among Kulling's first picture books for children were *I Hate You, Marmalade!* and *Waiting for Amos,* the latter which was inspired by the "Frog and Toad" books of author and illustrator Arnold Lobel. "The best picture books are poems," Kulling once explained to *SATA.* "The text evokes a world of feeling and meaning in a few well-chosen words." *I Hate You, Marmalade!* is the story of a fat orange tabby cat who moves in with a family and starts taking over, much to the dismay of the young boy of the house. Kulling calls Marmalade "a cat with definite personality," and the cantankerous feline is based on one of her own cats. *School Library Journal* reviewer Valerie F. Patterson noted that the author "gives a wry observation of the way cats first establish superiority and then offer loyalty." A case of mistaken

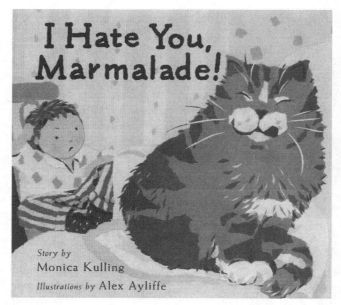

Cover of Kulling's early picture book I Hate You, Marmalade!, *featuring illustrations by Alex Ayliffe.* (Illustration copyright © 1992 by Alex Ayliffe. Used by permission of Viking Penguin, a division of Penguin Young Readers Group, a member of Penguin Group (USA) Inc., 345 Hudson Street, New York, NY 10014. All rights reserved.)

identity is at the heart of *Waiting for Amos,* another humorous tale. A contributor in *Publishers Weekly* remarked of this story that "Kulling's gentle narrative will comfort little ones while offering a subtle message about comradeship."

In *Merci Mister Dash!* Kulling introduces a gentle canine with style and class. A mixed breed, Mr. Dash enjoys a reputation as an impeccable dresser, and he enchants the customers who enter the shop belonging to his owner, Madame Croissant. The dapper pooch has one problem, though: every Sunday morning, Madame Croissant's rambunctious granddaughter, Daphne, comes to visit, upsetting his carefully ordered life. When Daphne's play turns reckless and dangerous one afternoon, Mr. Dash must set aside his feelings to come to her rescue. "The ironic contrast between unruly child and peace-loving dog is great entertainment," Chelsea Donaldson observed in *Quill & Quire.* A critic in *Kirkus Reviews* applauded the "well-paced portrait of patience and toleration" in *Merci Mister Dash!,* and Reesa Cohen noted in the *Canadian Review of Materials* that "Kulling's skill for telling a charming story is evident here."

In addition to her picture books, Kulling has written a number of adaptations of classic novels, among them Louisa May Alcott's *Little Women* and *Great Expectations* by Charles Dickens. "Besides being satisfying work for me, writing the adaptations has taught me how to structure a novel," she noted. "After completing three adaptations, I wrote my first novel for middle-grade readers. I had begun novels in the past but always found myself lost in the process and dropped the work by the time chapter four rolled around. Adaptation work taught me the importance of a chapter-by-chapter outline. Knowing roughly where your story is going is some insurance that you will actually finish it. You don't find yourself staring at a blank page with a blank chapter in mind."

Kulling has earned plaudits for her carefully researched biographies for young readers. One of the most influential first ladies of the United States is the subject of *Eleanor Everywhere: The Life of Eleanor Roosevelt,* an illustrated chapter book. Kulling "packs in a lot of information about Eleanor Roosevelt's life without condescension," Hazel Rochman observed of this work in *Booklist.* In *Escape North!: The Story of Harriet Tubman* Kulling examines the life of the African-American hero, a former slave who served as a conductor on the Underground Railroad as well as a suffragette and Civil War spy. Rochman also offered praise for this work, noting that in *Escape North!* Kulling's "telling is direct and dramatic."

Eat My Dust!: Henry Ford's First Race is based on a true story about a 1901 competition that helped finance the fledgling Ford Motor Company. Kulling's tale offers so much excitement that children "won't want to stop reading until Ford crosses the finish line," in the words

Kulling takes readers back to the nineteenth century in her picture book **All Aboard!,** *featuring artwork by Bill Slavin.* (Illustration copyright © 2010 by Bill Slavin. Used with permission of Tundra Books.)

of *Booklist* contributor Stephanie Zvirin. In *It's a Snap!* the author explores the early history of photography through the eyes of George Eastman, the pioneering figure who invented the dry plate, the film roll, and the Kodak camera. "The book will entertain and inform readers," Michele Sealander wrote in her *School Library Journal* review of *It's a Snap!* and *Quill & Quire* reviewer Laurie McNeill remarked that "Kulling's prose is crisp and accessible."

All Aboard! focuses on Elijah McCoy, an acclaimed African-American inventor. The son of slaves who escaped to Canada via the Underground Railroad, McCoy studied mechanical engineering in Scotland before returning to the United States, where he found work as a railroad fireman and developed a number of improvements for steam engine lubricators. As Aileen Wortley stated in the *Canadian Review of Materials, All Aboard!* "is an intriguing and readable introduction to Elijah McCoy that whets the appetite for more, but it also touches on other thought-provoking themes such as slavery, the Underground Railroad, racial discrimination, railroad history, everyday inventions and belief in one's own ideals."

"I love writing full-time, even though it can be very hard at times," Kulling once admitted to *SATA.* "There are days when I have to make myself sit in front of that computer and write, even though I don't know what

I'm writing and I've just received a couple of rejection letters. Then there are other days when writing is like sailing on a clear day with a wind at your back and you can't think of anything you'd rather be doing. Writing is only partly driven by inspiration. For the most part, writing is a discipline and on days when the going is tough a writer needs to keep to her schedule and not be lured away from the work at hand by any whim. A writer writes and that's all there is to it. So I tell myself," Kulling added, "on days when there isn't a breeze on the waters and it's a hard slog."

Asked if she had any advice for budding authors, Kulling told an Open Book Toronto Web site interviewer, "Make sure that you have a real passion for writing. If you don't, try something else because the business of writing is always tough. If you do, keep on writing and learning about the craft. There are many excellent books on writers and how they work. Over the years, I've been encouraged and inspired by the working habits of other writers. If you have the passion, you just need to persevere."

Biographical and Critical Sources

PERIODICALS

Booklist, March 15, 1999, Stephanie Zvirin, review of *Life in the Wild: Bears,* p. 1337; April 15, 1999, Hazel Rochman, review of *Eleanor Everywhere: The Life of Eleanor Roosevelt,* p. 1526; February 15, 2001, Hazel Rochman, review of *Escape North!: The Story of Harriet Tubman,* p. 1153; August, 2004, Stephanie Zvirin, review of *Eat My Dust!: Henry Ford's First Race,* p. 1943.

Canadian Review of Materials, May 21, Aileen Wortley, review of *All Aboard!: Elijah McCoy's Steam Engine*; January 21, 2011, Reesa Cohen, review of *Merci Mister Dash!*

Kirkus Reviews, July 15, 2009, review of *It's a Snap!: George Eastman's First Photograph*; June 15, 2010, review of *All Aboard!*; March 1, 2011, review of *Merci Mister Dash!*

Publishers Weekly, October 12, 1992, review of *I Hate You, Marmalade!,* p. 77; March 8, 1993, review of *Waiting for Amos,* p. 76.

Quill & Quire, September, 2009, review of *It's a Snap!*; April, 2011, review of *Merci Mister Dash!*

School Library Journal, February, 1993, Valerie F. Patterson, review of *I Hate You, Marmalade!,* p. 74; August, 2009, S. McClendon, review of, *The Messiest Room on the Planet,* p. 79; September, 2009, Michele Sealander, review of *It's a Snap!,* p. 144; August, 2010, Linda L. Walkins, review of *All Aboard!,* p. 90.

ONLINE

Canadian Children's Book Centre Web site, http://www.bookcentre.ca/ (December 15, 2011), "Monica Kulling."

Monica Kulling Home Page, http://www.monicakulling.com (December 15, 2011).

Open Book Toronto Web site, http://www.openbooktoronto.com/ (September 4, 2009), "Ten Questions with Monica Kulling and Bill Slavin."*

L

LACKEY, Mercedes 1950-

Personal

Born June 24, 1950, in Chicago, IL; daughter of Edward George and Joyce Ritche; married Anthony Lackey, June 10, 1972 (marriage ended); married Larry Dixon (an artist and writer), 1992. *Education:* Purdue University, B.S., 1972. *Politics:* "Esoteric." *Religion:* "Nontraditional." *Hobbies and other interests:* SCUBA diving, costuming, needlework, beadwork.

Addresses

Home—Tulsa, OK. *Agent*—Russell Galen, Scovil Galen Ghosh Literary Agency, 276 5th Ave., Ste. 708, New York NY 10001; russellgalen@sgglit.com.

Career

Writer, novelist, editor, wildlife rehabilitator, and recording artist. Artist's model, South Bend, IN, 1975-81; Associates Data Processing, South Bend, computer programmer, 1979-82; CAIRS (survey and data processing firm), South Bend, surveyor, layout designer, and analyst, 1981-82; American Airlines, Tulsa, OK, computer programmer, beginning 1982. Licensed wildlife rehabilitator, working at rescuing and rehabilitating birds of prey. Has worked as a lab technician and a short-order cook.

Member

Science Fiction Writers of America.

Awards, Honors

Five Pegasus awards; Best Books for Young Adults citation, American Library Association, 1987, for *Arrows of the Queen;* Lambda Literary Award, 1991, for *Magic's Price;* Book of the Year selection, Science Fiction Book Club, 1991, for *The Elvenbane.*

Writings

FICTION

(With C.J. Cherryh) *Reap the Whirlwind,* Baen (Riverdale, NY), 1989.

By the Sword, DAW Books (New York, NY), 1991.

The Last Herald Mage, Penguin (New York, NY), 1992.

(With Ellen Guon) *Wing Commander: Freedom Flight* (science fiction), Baen (Riverdale, NY), 1992.

(With Anne McCaffrey) *The Ship Who Searched* (second book in the "Brainship" series created by Anne Mc-Caffrey), Baen (Riverdale, NY), 1992.

(With Ellen Guon) *Freedom Flight* ("Wing Commander" series; based on Wing Commander computer game), 1992.

(With Piers Anthony) *If I Pay Thee Not in Gold,* Baen (Riverdale, NY), 1993.

(With Marion Zimmer Bradley) *Rediscovery: A Novel of Darkover,* DAW Books (New York, NY), 1993.

Sacred Ground (fantasy and suspense novel), Tor Books (New York, NY), 1994.

(With others) *Sword of Knowledge,* Baen (Riverdale, NY), 1995.

(With Andre Norton and Marion Zimmer Bradley) *Tiger Burning Bright,* Morrow (New York, NY), 1995.

Firebird ("Fairy Tales" series), Tor Books (New York, NY), 1996.

Lammas Night, Baen (Riverdale, NY), 1996.

The River's Gift (novella), Roc (New York, NY), 1999.

The Black Swan ("Fairy Tales" series), DAW Books (New York, NY), 1999.

(Editor, with Martin H. Greenberg, and contributor) *Flights of Fantasy* (short fiction), DAW Books (New York, NY), 1999.

Werehunter (short stories), Baen (Riverdale, NY), 1999.

Brightly Burning (novel), DAW Books (New York, NY), 2000.

(With Catherine Asaro and Rachel Lee) *Charmed Destinies* (novellas; contains "Counting Crows" by Lackey), 2003.

(With Eric Flint and Dave Freer) *The Wizard of Karres,* Baen (Riverdale, NY), 2004.

(With Tanith Lee and C.E. Murphy) *Winter Moon* (stories; includes "Moontide" by Lackey), Luna (New York, NY), 2005.

Gwenhwyfar: The White Spirit, DAW Books (New York, NY), 2009.

(With Michelle Sagara and Cameron Haley) *Harvest Moon* (novellas), Luna (New York, NY), 2010.

Trio of Sorcery, Tor (New York, NY), 2010.

(With Cody Martin) *Reboots* (novellas; includes "Just the Right Bullets" by Lackey), Tor (New York, NY), 2010.

(Editor and contributor) *Finding the Way and Other Tales of Valdemar,* DAW Books (New York, NY), 2010.

Contributor of stories to numerous anthologies, including *Horse Fantastic,* edited by Martin Greenberg, DAW Books; *Tales of the Witchworld,* edited by Andre Norton, DAW Books; *Catsfantastic,* edited by Norton, DAW Books; *Magic in Ithkar,* edited by Robert Adams and Norton; and *Stars: Original Stories Based on the Songs of Janis Ian,* edited by Janis Ian and Mike Resnick, DAW Books, 2003. Contributor of stories to periodicals, including *Fantasy Book* and *American Fantasy.*

Author's works have been translated into six languages.

"HERALDS OF VALDEMAR" NOVEL SERIES

Arrow's Flight, DAW Books (New York, NY), 1987.
Arrows of the Queen, DAW Books (New York, NY), 1987.
Arrow's Fall, DAW Books (New York, NY), 1988.

"VALDEMAR: VOWS AND HONOR" NOVEL SERIES

The Oathbound, DAW Books (New York, NY), 1988.
Oathbreakers, DAW Books (New York, NY), 1989.
Oathblood, DAW Books (New York, NY), 1998.
Take a Thief (crossover to *Arrows of the Queen*), DAW Books (New York, NY), 2001.
Exile's Honor, DAW Books (New York, NY), 2002.
Exile's Valor, 2003.

"VALDEMAR: LAST HERALD MAGIC" NOVEL SERIES

Magic's Pawn, DAW Books (New York, NY), 1989.
Magic's Promise, DAW Books (New York, NY), 1990.
Magic's Price, DAW Books (New York, NY), 1990.

"VALDEMAR: MAGE WINDS" NOVEL SERIES

Winds of Fate, DAW Books (New York, NY), 1991.
Winds of Change, DAW Books (New York, NY), 1992.
Winds of Fury, DAW Books (New York, NY), 1993.

"VALDEMAR: MAGE STORMS" NOVEL SERIES

Storm Warning, DAW Books (New York, NY), 1994.
Storm Rising, DAW Books (New York, NY), 1995.
Storm Breaking, DAW Books (New York, NY), 1996.

"VALDEMAR: MAGE WARS" NOVEL SERIES; WITH LARRY DIXON

The Black Gryphon, DAW Books (New York, NY), 1994.
The White Gryphon, DAW Books (New York, NY), 1995.
The Silver Gryphon, DAW Books (New York, NY), 1996.

"VALDEMAR: OWL MAGE" NOVEL SERIES; WITH LARRY DIXON

Owlflight, DAW Books (New York, NY), 1997.
Owlsight, DAW Books (New York, NY), 1998.
Owlknight, DAW Books (New York, NY), 1999.

VALDEMAR SHORT-STORY COLLECTIONS; EDITOR AND CONTRIBUTOR

Sword of Ice and Other Tales of Valdemar, DAW Books (New York, NY), 1997.
Sun in Glory and Other Tales of Valdemar, DAW Books (New York, NY), 2003.
Crossroads and Other Tales of Valdemar, DAW Books (New York, NY), 2005.
Moving Targets and Other Tales of Valdemar, DAW Books (New York, NY), 2008.
Changing the World and Other Tales of Valdemar, DAW Books (New York, NY), 2009.

"BEDLAM'S BARD" NOVEL SERIES

(With Ellen Guon) *Knight of Ghosts and Shadows* (also see below), Baen (Riverdale, NY), 1990.
(With Ellen Guon) *Summoned to Tourney* (also see below), Baen (Riverdale, NY), 1992.
(With Ellen Guon) *Bedlam's Bard* (omnibus; contains *Knight of Ghosts and Shadows* and *Summoned to Tourney*), Baen (Riverdale, NY), 1992.
(With Rosemary Edghill) *Beyond the World's End,* Baen (Riverdale, NY), 2001, also published as *Leagues Beyond.*
Spirits White as Lightning, Baen (Riverdale, NY), 2001.
(With Rosemary Edghill) *Mad Maudlin,* Baen (Riverdale, NY), 2003.
(Editor, with Rosemary Edghill) *Bedlam's Edge,* Baen (Riverdale, NY), 2005.
(With Rosemary Edghill) *Music to My Sorrow,* Baen (Riverdale, NY), 2005.

"DIANA TREGARDE" NOVEL SERIES

Children of the Night, Tor Books (New York, NY), 1990, reprinted, Tor (New York, NY), 2005.
Jinx High, Tor Books (New York, NY), 1991.
Burning Water, Tor Books (New York, NY), 1993.

"HALFBLOOD" NOVEL SERIES

(With Andre Norton) *The Elvenbane,* Tor Books (New York, NY), 1991.

(With Andre Norton) *Elvenblood,* Tor Books (New York, NY), 1995.

(With Andre Norton) *Elvenborn,* Tor Books (New York, NY), 2002.

"BARDIC VOICES" NOVEL SERIES

The Lark and the Wren (also see below), Baen (Riverdale, NY), 1992.

The Robin and the Kestrel (also see below), Baen (Riverdale, NY), 1993.

(With Joshua Sherman) *A Cast of Corbies,* Baen (Riverdale, NY), 1994.

The Eagle and the Nightingales (also see below), Baen (Riverdale, NY), 1995.

Four and Twenty Blackbirds, Baen (Riverdale, NY), 1997.

The Free Bards (contains *The Lark and the Wren, The Robin and the Kestrel,* and *The Eagle and the Nightingales*), Simon & Schuster (New York, NY), 1997.

"BARD'S TALE" NOVEL SERIES

(With Josepha Sherman) *Castle of Deception,* Baen (Riverdale, NY), 1992.

(With Ru Emerson) *Fortress of Frost and Fire,* Baen (Riverdale, NY), 1993.

(With Mark Shepherd) *Prison of Souls,* Baen (Riverdale, NY), 1993.

"SERRATED EDGE" NOVEL SERIES

(With husband Larry Dixon) *Born to Run* (also see below), Baen (Riverdale, NY), 1992.

(With Mark Shepherd) *Wheels of Fire* (also see below), Baen (Riverdale, NY), 1992.

(With Holly Lisle) *When the Bough Breaks* (also see below), Baen (Riverdale, NY), 1993.

(With Larry Dixon) *Chrome Circle* (also see below), Baen (Riverdale, NY), 1994.

(With Larry Dixon) *The Chrome Borne* (omnibus; contains *Born to Run* and *Chrome Circle*), Baen (Riverdale, NY), 1999.

(With Holly Lisle and Mark Shepherd) *Otherworld* (omnibus; contains *When the Bough Breaks* and *Wheels of Fire*), 1999.

(With Josepha Sherman) *Stoned Souls,* Baen (Riverdale, NY), 2005.

"ELEMENTAL MASTERS" NOVEL SERIES

The Fire Rose, Baen (Riverdale, NY), 1995.

The Serpent's Shadow, DAW Books (New York, NY), 2001.

The Gates of Sleep, DAW Books (New York, NY), 2002.

Phoenix and Ashes, DAW Books (New York, NY), 2004.

The Wizard of London, DAW Books (New York, NY), 2005.

Reserved for the Cat, DAW Books (New York, NY), 2007.

Unnatural Issue, DAW Books (New York, NY), 2011.

"HEIRS OF ALEXANDRIA" NOVEL SERIES

(With Eric Flint and Dave Freer) *The Shadow of the Lion,* Baen Books (Riverdale, NY), 2002.

This Rough Magic, Baen Books (Riverdale, NY), 2003.

(With Eric Flint and Dave Freer) *Much Fall of Blood,* Baen Books (Riverdale, NY), 2010.

"DRAGON JOUSTERS" NOVEL SERIES

Joust, DAW Books (New York, NY), 2003.

Alta, DAW Books (New York, NY), 2004.

Sanctuary, DAW Books (New York, NY), 2005.

Aerie, DAW Books (New York, NY), 2006.

"OBSIDIAN MOUNTAIN" NOVEL TRILOGY; WITH JAMES MALLORY

The Outstretched Shadow, Tor (New York, NY), 2003.

To Light a Candle, Tor (New York, NY), 2004.

When Darkness Falls, Tor (New York, NY), 2006.

"DOUBLED EDGE" NOVEL SERIES; WITH ROBERTA GELLIS

This Scepter'd Isle, Baen Books (Riverdale, NY), 2004.

Ill Met by Moonlight, Baen Books (Riverdale, NY), 2005.

By Slanderous Tongues, Baen Books (Riverdale, NY), 2007.

And Less than Kind, Baen Books (Riverdale, NY), 2008.

"FIVE HUNDRED KINGDOMS" NOVEL SERIES

The Fairy Godmother, Luna (New York, NY), 2004.

One Good Knight, Luna Books (New York, NY), 2006.

Fortune's Fool, Luna Books (New York, NY), 2007.

The Snow Queen, Luna (New York, NY), 2008.

The Sleeping Beauty, Luna (New York, NY), 2010.

Beauty and the Werewolf, Luna (New York, NY), 2011.

"ENDURING FLAME" NOVEL SERIES; WITH JAMES MALLORY

The Phoenix Unchained, Tor (New York, NY), 2007.

The Phoenix Endangered, Tor (New York, NY), 2008.

The Phoenix Transformed, Tor (New York, NY), 2009.

"COLLEGIUM CHRONICLES" NOVEL SERIES

Foundation, DAW Books (New York, NY), 2008.

Intrigues, DAW Books (New York, NY), 2010.

Changes, DAW Books (New York, NY), 2011.

"SHADOW GRAIL" NOVEL SERIES

(With Rosemary Edghill) *The Legacies,* Tor (New York, NY), 2010.

(With Rosemary Edghill) *Conspiracies,* Tor (New York, NY), 2011.

"SECRET WORLDS CHRONICLES" NOVEL SERIES

(With Steve Libbey, Cody Martin, and Dennis Lee) *Invasion,* Baen (New York, NY), 2011.

(With Steve Libbey, Cody Martin, and Dennis Lee) *World Divided,* Baen (New York, NY), 2012.

SOUND RECORDINGS

Heralds, Harpers, and Havoc, Firebird Arts (Portland, OR), 1987.

Mercedes Lackey—Live!, Firebird Arts (Portland, OR), 1989.

Leslie Fish—Live!, Firebird Arts (Portland, OR), 1989.

Magic, Moondust, and Melancholy, Firebird Arts (Portland, OR), 1989.

Oathbound: Mercedes Lackey Vows and Honor, Firebird Arts (Portland, OR), 1990, adaptation released as *Oathbreakers,* 1991.

Freedom, Flight, and Fantasy, Firebird Arts (Portland, OR), 1992.

(With D.F. Sanders) *Shadow Stalker,* Firebird Arts (Portland, OR), 1994.

Author of lyrics for nearly fifty songs recorded for Off-Centaur (recording company specializing in science-fiction folk music).

OTHER

(Editor, with Leah Wilson, and contributor) *Mapping the World of Harry Potter: Science-Fiction and Fantasy Writers Explore the Best-Selling Fantasy Series of All Time,* BenBella Books (Dallas, TX), 2006.

Contributor to books, including *The Valdemar Companion: A Guide to Mercedes Lackey's World of Valdemar,* edited by John Helfers and Denise Little, DAW Books (New York, NY), 2001.

Adaptations

Many of Lackey's novels have been adapted as audio-books.

Sidelights

Beginning with her 1987 novel *Arrows of the Queen,* Mercedes Lackey has established a reputation as a popular, prolific, and versatile author of fantasy fiction. Lackey's works, particularly those set in the world of Valdemar, are especially enjoyed by teens due to their themes of personal growth, responsibility, and social consciousness. Her involving tales have earned plaudits for their intriguing plots, fantastic creatures, psychic and magical abilities, and complex, believable characters. "I'm a storyteller; that's what I see as 'my job,'" Lackey commented on her home page. "My stories come out of my characters; how those characters would react to the given situation."

Born in Chicago, Illinois, Lackey discovered science fiction and fantasy at a young age and spent much of her childhood reading. Educated at Purdue University, she worked variously as an artist's model, computer programmer, and analyst before turning to fiction in the early 1980s. "I began writing out of boredom," Lackey stated on her home page. "I continue out of addiction."

Lackey often blends musical lyrics into her works, and indeed she has written and recorded over fifty songs with a recording company that specializes in science fiction folk music, commonly known as filk. Commenting on her use of song lyrics, Lackey once observed: "One of the reasons I write song lyrics is because I see songs as a kind of 'story pill'—they reduce a story to the barest essentials or encapsulate a particular crucial moment in time. I frequently will write a lyric when I am attempting to get to the heart of a crucial scene; I find that when I have done so, the scene has become absolutely clear in my mind, and I can write exactly what I wanted to say. Another reason is because of the kind of novels I am writing: that is, fantasy, set in an other-world semi-medieval atmosphere. Music is very important to medieval peoples; bards are the chief news-bringers. When I write the 'folk music' of these peoples, I am enriching my whole world, whether I actually use the song in the text or not."

Lackey's fantasy land of Valdemar is the setting of such works as *Arrows of the Queen* and *Winds of Fury.* This land is peopled by several intelligent species, including humans and a variety of bird known as Gryphons. *Winds of Fury* tells about the need to reinstate the power of magic in Valdemar, and Lackey's story places the heir of the throne, Elspeth, in direct conflict with a political schemer, Ancar of Hardorn, and an evil and manipulative mage named Mornilithe Falconsbane. *The Black Gryphon,* set in ancient times long before the founding of Valdemar, recounts the legendary mage wars and the friendship between Skandragon, the title character, and the Healer Amberdrake. The popularity of the Valdemar cycle has prompted Lackey to announce "that she will keep writing Valdemar stories as long as people want them," reported a *Voice of Youth Advocates* critic in a review of *Winds of Fury.*

In a stand-alone addition to the Valdemar books, *Brightly Burning,* Lackey presents an "action-packed story," according to *Booklist* critic Sally Estes, in which Valdemar must face war with the Karse. Young Lan Chitward almost destroys himself with his fire-starting powers before he is marked as a future Herald destined to aid Valdemar in its fight against the powerful Karse. As Estes concluded in her *Booklist* review, "Splendidly maintaining the world of so much of her fiction, Lackey adds yet more substance to the characters and their relationships." Supplying more critical praise for *Brightly Burning, Library Journal* critic Jackie Cassada wrote that "Lackey combines the intensity of a young man's agonized coming of age with a tale of love, honor, and sacrifice."

Several of Lackey's "Valdemar" tales have been written in collaboration with her husband, Larry Dixon. In *Owlflight, Owlsight,* and *Owlknight* the central character is Darian Firkin, who is introduced as a thirteen year old. Known to have magical talent, Darian is apprenticed to a bumbling wizard until a surprise attack interrupts his training. Most of the villagers are enslaved, but he escapes into the forest. Although Darian is at first "whiny", "sullen", and "lacking self-esteem," according to *Booklist* critic Sally Estes in a review of *Owlflight,* by the end of the first book, he has come of age as a "courageous, caring man" who has earned his own psychically-bonded bird.

In *Owlsight* Lackey's story is divided between Darian and his love, Keisha. Keisha has healing powers and, like Darian, her gifts are undeveloped. As a *Publishers Weekly* writer noted, "her empathic abilities often overwhelm her and so thwart her desire to help others," while Darian "learns to see the current of magic through all things." In *Owlknight* Darian has become a knight as well as a master mage, and he works hard to wield his influence for good within Valdemar and its neighbors. Keisha and Darian encounter many threats in this tale, and Valdemar is shown to be "an immensely well-developed world," according to another *Publishers Weekly* writer.

Lackey's "Vows and Honor" series, also set in the Valdemar universe, includes such titles as *Take a Thief* and *Exile's Honor.* The former centers on Skif, an orphaned pickpocket who first appeared in *Arrows of the Queen.* After an encounter with one of Valdemar's magical horses, Skif is chosen to serve the queen as a Herald. "For fans of the series, this will be a must read," Sherry S. Hoy noted in *Kliatt.*

In *Exile's Honor* and its sequel, *Exile's Valor,* Lackey tells the story of Alberich, a precognitive soldier from the land of Karse who becomes a valuable asset to Selenay, the new and inexperienced queen of Valdemar. Writing in *Booklist,* Roland Green called *Exile's Honor* "a treat for established Valdemar fans," and a *Publishers Weekly* critic maintained of *Exile's Valor* that fans of the series "will appreciate learning more of favorite characters." Five years after the release of *Exile's Valor,* Lackey returned to the world of Valdemar for her "Collegium Chronicles," which explore the early history of the kingdom. In *Foundation,* an orphan named Magpie is plucked from the mines and begins training at the Heralds' Collegium during a time of great unrest. According to *Booklist* contributor Frieda Murray, the "outstanding characters" to be discovered in *Foundation,* "especially Mags, will greatly please Valdemar fans."

Lackey's "Diana Tregarde," "Serrated Edge," and "Doubled Edge" novels are set in the same magical universe. *This Scepter'd Isle,* the initial work in the "Doubled Edge" series, was co-written with Roberta Gellis. Set during the reign of King Henry VIII of England, the novel concerns the efforts of the Bright

Court elves, which are battling the evil Unseleighe Sidhe to ensure that one of Henry's red-haired children will eventually assume the throne. According to a *Publishers Weekly* contributor, readers "will enjoy the interplay between elven intervention and historical fact." The saga continues in *Ill Met by Moonlight, By Slanderous Tongues,* and *And Less than Kind,* as elves from the Dark Court and the Bright Court further involve themselves in court intrigue. The authors "blend the best of high fantasy with a grand dose of English history," a *Publishers Weekly* critic observed in a review of *By Slanderous Tongues.*

Lackey opens her "Elemental Masters" series with *The Fire Rose,* which describes an alchemist's experiments with lycanthropy. A second work, *The Serpent's Shadow,* set in early twentieth-century London, focuses on Dr. Maya Witherspoon, the offspring of a British doctor and a Brahmin lady. Raised in India, Maya is familiar with the magic of that land, and when she comes to England she must use all the knowledge at her disposal to conquer the evil Kali, the Hindu goddess of destruction, has unleashed on the land with the help of her aunt. Green, reviewing *The Fire Rose* in *Booklist,* found that Lackey employs "her characteristic carefulness, narrative gifts, and attention to detail" to create an "altogether superior fantasy." In *Library Journal* Cassada stated that Lackey tries on a new genre with a historical fantasy which is an "intriguing and compelling recreation of England in the waning days of its imperial glory."

In *The Gates of Sleep,* another title from Lackey's "Elemental Masters" series, the author retells the story of Sleeping Beauty, sifting magic into the historical setting of pre-World War I Great Britain. "This is a wonderful example of a new look at an old theme," a critic stated in *Publishers Weekly.* In *Phoenix and Ashes,* a twist on the Cinderella legend, Lackey chronicles the story of Eleanor, a nascent Fire Master who is enslaved by her Earth Master stepmother, Alison, and horrid stepsisters. Eleanor secretly practices to perfect her magic before the upcoming family ball, where she hopes to convince Reggie Fenyx, a former pilot and Air Master who believes he has lost his powers, that she is his one true love.

Two students attending a school for magic are marked for death by an Elemental Master in *The Wizard of London,* the fifth installment in Lackey's well-received series. "Interestingly drawn characters hold our attention to the end," Murray commented in a review of the novel. Inspired in part by "Puss in Boots," *Reserved for the Cat* centers on Ninette Dupond, a dancer who impersonates a famed ballerina at the suggestion of a feline gifted with Elemental powers. "This is Lackey at her best," a writer in *Publishers Weekly* remarked, "mixing whimsy and magic with a fast-paced plot," and Murray dubbed *Reserved for the Cat* a "clever fairy-tale adventure." Set in England just before World War I, *Unnatural Issue* focuses on a disturbed Elemental Earth

Master who attempts to revive his dead wife's spirit in the body of his daughter. "Historical fantasy and gothic romance combine beautifully in this fantasy adventure," observed Cassada in a review of *Unnatural Issue.*

Lackey inaugurated Harlequin Books's Luna imprint with her romantic fantasy novel *The Fairy Godmother.* All the residents of the land of Five Hundred Kingdoms are bound to Tradition and preordained to live their lives as though they were in fairy tales. When Elena finds that she cannot fulfill her Cinderella-like role because Prince Alexander is too young, she is apprenticed to a local fairy godmother. When she loses her temper with Prince Alexander and transforms him into a donkey, she sees no other choice but to take him home with her and help him remake his life. The story "will enchant readers with this delightful twist on traditional fairy tales," commented *Booklist* contributor Diana Tixier Herald. "Original, fascinating, and full of marvelous potential, the Five Hundred Kingdoms is a setting that simply begs for future stories," remarked Kristin Ramsdell in *Library Journal.*

Lackey continues the "Five Hundred Kingdoms" series with *One Good Knight* and *Fortune's Fool,* featuring Princess Ekaterina, a daughter of the Sea King who can employ magic to rise from the water and live on land. Sent on a secret mission by her father, Ekaterina falls in love with the musical son of the king of Drylands. Soon the two are courting, but this affair is interrupted when the malevolent Jinn captures Princess Ekaterina. Writing for *Library Journal,* Cassada called *Fortune's Fool* a "classic fairy tale with a pair of proactive, resourceful heroes."

Lackey has also collaborated with James Mallory on several trilogies. Their first, the "Obsidian Mountain" sequence, is a high-fantasy series that follows Kellen Tavadon, son of the master magician of Armethalieh, as she sets off to discover the secrets of another, older sort of magic: wild magic. This search takes Kellen into unexpected realms filled with demons, unicorns, and swordplay. A *Publishers Weekly* contributor called the series conclusion, *When Darkness Falls,* "intelligent storytelling with an unmistakable flavor of Andre Norton at her best."

Lackey's "Enduring Flame" series, again coauthored with Mallory, is set a millennia after the events of the "Obsidian Mountain" trilogy. Armethalieh is no longer ruled by magicians or mages. In fact, the former high magic has been long forgotten until Tiercel Rolfort stumbles upon it and sets off on a quest to reestablish the old ways. Cassada praised the "lavishly detailed stage peopled with intriguing and well-developed characters" that Lackey sets forth in *The Phoenix Unchained.* Tiercel's adventures continue in *The Phoenix Endangered,* as the protagonist, accompanied by a unicorn and a dragon, does battle with the powers of the Dark. Cassada applauded the book's "solidly developed characters, appealing magical companions, and an in-

triguing tale." *Booklist* reviewer Murray termed the same work "good stuff to relax with." The "Obsidian Mountain" trilogy concludes with *The Phoenix Transformed.*

Lackey and Edghill's "Shadow Grail" series follows the goings-on at Oakhurst Academy, an elite boarding school for orphans endowed with magical powers. In series opener *The Legacies* teenaged Spirit White discovers that several of her classmates have mysteriously vanished, prompting an investigation that reveals a menacing presence on the campus. "This dark mirror of the standard magic-school story makes an intriguing premise," a contributor observed in a *Kirkus Reviews* appraisal of *The Legacies,* and Corinne Henning-Sachs reported in *School Library Journal* that Lackey and Edghill "do a nice job with the metaphor of magical gifts as means of self-actualization." In *Conspiracies,* a follow-up, Spirit and her friends once again find themselves in danger from an evil cabal.

Many of Lackey's non-series titles combine contemporary themes and characters with medieval settings—or, sometimes, fantastic characters with modern settings. *When the Bough Breaks* is an example of the latter; it features an elfish race-car driver, a fifth-grade human teacher, and a sexually abused girl who has developed multiple personalities. Reviewer Elaine M. McGuire stated in *Voice of Youth Advocates* that the book's opening is "full of today's realities" and it "succeeds in masterfully blending the real and unreal."

Born to Run follows a similar pattern in dealing with the weighty topics of child pornography, teenage prostitution, and a teenaged mage who is fascinated by fast cars and rock music. Calling it "part morality tale" and "part fast-action adventure," Diane G. Yates in *Voice of Youth Advocates* wrote that Lackey's "improbable mixture is tied together well." *Summoned to Tourney* takes place in San Francisco and involves psychically summoned creatures called Nightflyers who are capable of eating souls, while *Wheels of Fire,* set mostly in Oklahoma, concerns parental abduction of children, fanatical religious cults, religious and political intolerance, racism, violence, and abuse.

With over one hundred published works to her credit, Lackey shows no sign of slowing down. "I love what I'm doing; it's an extraordinary thing, to be able to do what you love for a living," the author remarked in *The Valdemar Companion: A Guide to Mercedes Lackey's World of Valdemar.* "I have absolutely no plans to stop, ever. I just hope that people continue wanting to read what I have to write for as long as I'm able to write it!"

Biographical and Critical Sources

BOOKS

Helfers, John, and Denise Little, editors, *The Valdemar Companion: A Guide to Mercedes Lackey's World of Valdemar,* DAW Books (New York, NY), 2001.

St. James Guide to Fantasy Writers, St. James Press (Detroit, MI), 1996.

St. James Guide to Young-Adult Writers, 2nd edition, St. James Press (Detroit MI), 1999.

PERIODICALS

Booklist, March 15, 1992, Roland Green, review of *Born to Run,* p. 1344; September 15, 1992, Roland Green, review of *Winds of Change,* p. 130; February 15, 1993, Roland Green, review of *Rediscovery: A Novel of Darkover,* p. 1011; December 15, 1994, Roland Green, review of *The Eagle and the Nightingales,* p. 740; October 15, 1996, Roland Green, review of *Storm Breaking,* p. 408; January 1, 1997, Roland Green, review of *Firebird,* p. 826; September 15, 1997, Sally Estes, review of *Owlflight,* p. 216; November 1, 1997, Roland Green, review of *Four and Twenty Blackbirds,* p. 457; September 15, 1998, Diana Tixier Herald, review of *Sacred Ground,* p. 213; October 15, 1998, Roland Green, review of *Owlsight,* p. 407; May 15, 1999, Roland Green, review of *The Black Swan,* p. 1681; September 1, 1999, Ray Olson, review of *The River's Gift,* p. 75; April, 15, 2000, Sally Estes, review of *Brightly Burning,* p. 1534; January 1, 2001, Roland Green, review of *Beyond the World's End,* p. 928; February 15, 2001, Roland Green, review of *The Serpent's Shadow,* p. 1122; November 15, 2001, Roland Green, review of *Spirits White as Lightning,* p. 560; March 15, 2002, Roland Green, review of *The Shadow of the Lion,* p. 1219; September 15, 2002, Roland Green, review of *Exile's Honor,* p. 212; October 1, 2002, Roland Green, review of *Elvenborn,* p. 309; September 15, 2003, Paula Ludtke, review of *The Outstretched Shadow,* p. 218; October 15, 2003, Frieda Murray, review of *Exile's Valor,* p. 399; January 1, 2004, Diana Tixier Herald, review of *The Fairy Godmother,* p. 837; February 15, 2004, Frieda Murray, review of *This Scepter'd Isle,* p. 1048; August, 2004, Regina Schroeder, review of *The Wizard of Karres,* p. 1913; March 15, 2005, Frieda Murray, review of *Ill Met by Moonlight,* p. 1275; May 1, 2005, Sally Estes, review of *Sanctuary,* p. 1576; October 15, 2005, Frieda Murray, review of *The Wizard of London,* p. 37; December 1, 2005, Frieda Murray, review of *Music to My Sorrow,* p. 31; February 15, 2007, Frieda Murray, review of *By Slanderous Tongues,* p. 45; November 1, 2007, Frieda Murray, review of *Reserved for the Cat,* p. 33; September 15, 2008, Frieda Murray, review of *The Phoenix Endangered,* p. 32; October 15, 2008, Frieda Murray, review of *Foundation,* p. 29; October 15, 2009, Krista Hutley, review of *Gwenhwyfar: The White Spirit,* p. 31.

Kirkus Reviews, October 15, 2001, review of *Spirits White as Lightning,* p. 1461; February 1, 2002, review of *The Shadow of the Lion,* p. 149; June 15, 2011, review of *Conspiracies.*

Kliatt, March 2003, Sherry S. Hoy, review of *Take a Thief,* p. 35.

Library Journal, June 15, 1988, Jackie Cassada, review of *The Oathbound,* p. 71; June 15, 1989, Jackie Cassada, review of *Magic's Pawn,* p. 83; October 15, 1991,

Jackie Cassada, review of *Winds of Fate,* p. 126; September 15, 1992, Jackie Cassada, review of *Winds of Change,* p. 97; March 15, 1993, Jackie Cassada, review of *Rediscovery,* p. 111; August, 1994, Jackie Cassada, reviews of *Storm Warning* and *Chrome Circle,* p. 139; June 15, 1995, Jackie Cassada, review of *Elvenblood,* p. 98; August, 1995, Jackie Cassada, review of *Storm Rising,* p. 122; October 15, 1996, Susan Hamburger, review of *Storm Breaking,* p. 93; October 15, 1997, Susan Hamburger, review of *Owlflight,* p. 98; April 15, 1998, Jackie Cassada, review of *Oathblood,* p. 119; May 15, 1999, Jackie Cassada, review of *The Black Swan,* p. 131; October 15, 1999, Jackie Cassada, review of *Owlknight,* p. 110; January 1, 2001, Jackie Cassada, review of *Beyond the World's End,* p. 163; February 15, 2001, Jackie Cassada, review of *The Serpent's Shadow,* p. 205; February 15, 2004, Kristin Ramsdell, review of *The Fairy Godmother,* p. 112, and Jackie Cassada, review of *The Scepter'd Isle,* p. 167; October 15, 2004, Jackie Cassada, review of *Beyond the World's End,* p. 57; March 15, 2007, Jackie Cassada, review of *Fortune's Fool,* p. 64; September 15, 2007, Jackie Cassada, review of *The Phoenix Unchained,* p. 52; October 15, 2007, Jackie Cassada, review of *Reserved for the Cat,* p. 56; August 1, 2008, Jackie Cassada, review of *The Phoenix Endangered,* p. 75; October 15, 2008, Jackie Cassada, review of *Foundation,* p. 60; January 1, 2009, Lisa Anderson, review of *The Phoenix Endangered,* p. 46; October 15, 2009, Jackie Cassada, review of *Gwenhwyfar,* p. 68; October 15, 2010, Jackie Cassada, review of *Trio of Sorcery,* p. 73; December, 2010, Jackie Cassada, review of *Finding the Way and Other Tales of Valdemar,* p. 106; June 15, 2011, Jackie Cassada, review of *Unnatural Issue,* p. 82.

Publishers Weekly, August 30, 1991, review of *Winds of Fate,* p. 72; September 20, 1991, review of *The Elvenbane,* p. 124; August 17, 1992, review of *Winds of Change,* p. 492; March 15, 1993, review of *Rediscovery,* p. 74; July 18, 1994, review of *Storm Warning,* p. 239; March 27, 1995, review of *The White Gryphon,* p. 77; May 22, 1995, review of *Elvenblood,* p. 52; August 21, 1995, review of *Storm Rising,* p. 51; October 7, 1996, review of *Storm Breaking,* p. 66; November 18, 1996, review of *Firebird,* p. 66; November 24, 1997, review of *Four and Twenty Blackbirds,* p. 57; September 28, 1998, review of *Owlsight,* p. 78; September 27, 1999, reviews of *The River's Gift* and *Owlknight,* both p. 79; April 17, 2000, review of *Brightly Burning,* p. 59; December 18, 2000, review of *Beyond the World's End,* p. 59; March 11, 2002, review of *The Gates of Sleep,* p. 55; February 17, 2003, review of *Joust,* p. 62; July 21, 2003, review of *Mad Maudlin,* p. 179; August 11, 2003, review of *The Outstretched Shadow,* p. 262; October 27, 2003, review of *Exile's Valor,* p. 48; November 17, 2003, review of *This Rough Magic,* p. 50; December 15, 2003, review of *The Fairy Godmother,* p. 58; January 26, 2004, review of *This Scepter'd Isle,* p. 236; February 16, 2004, review of *Alta,* p. 157; October 18, 2004, review of *To Light a Candle,* p. 52; April 18, 2005, review of *Sanctuary,* p. 48; May 29, 2006, review of *When Darkness Falls,* p. 41; January 1, 2007, review

of *By Slanderous Tongues,* p. 35; January 15, 2007, review of *Fortune's Fool,* p. 36; October 1, 2007, review of *Reserved for the Cat,* p. 42; July 14, 2008, review of *The Phoenix Endangered,* p. 49; May 10, 2010, review of *The Sleeping Beauty,* p. 32.

Reference & Research Book News, May 1, 2006, review of *Mapping the World of Harry Potter: Science Fiction and Fantasy Writers Explore the Best-Selling Fantasy Series of All Time.*

School Library Journal, May, 1992, Barbara Hawkins, review of *Winds of Fate,* p. 152; July, 1992, Judy Sokoll, review of "Bardic Voices" series, p. 97; September, 1994, review of *A Cast of Corbies,* p. 259; October, 1994, Katherine Fitch, review of *Sacred Ground,* p. 158; August, 1996, Beth Devers, review of *The Silver Gryphon,* p. 185; May, 1997, Bobbi Thomas Skaggs, review of *Firebird,* p. 164; January, 2000, Marsha Masone, review of *The Black Swan,* p. 158; November, 2004, Christine C. Menefee, review of *The Wizard of Karres,* p. 176; August, 2010, Corinne Henning-Sachs, review of *Legacies,* p. 105.

Voice of Youth Advocates, April, 1992, review of "Bardic Voices" series, pp. 44-45; August, 1992, Diane G. Yates, review of *Born to Run,* p. 176; October, 1992, review of *Summoned to Tourney,* p. 240; June, 2011, MaryAnn Darby, review of *Finding the Way and Other Tales of Valdemar,* p. 186.

ONLINE

Locus Online, http://www.locusmag.com/ (November 10, 2010), "Mercedes Lackey: Making Fun."

Mercedes Lackey Home Page, http://www.mercedeslackey.com (January 1, 2012).*

*   *   *

le VANN, Kate

Personal

Born in Doncaster, England; married; children: daughters. *Education:* Manchester University, degree (law). *Hobbies and other interests:* Watching television.

Addresses

Home—London, England. *E-mail*—katelevann@me.com.

Career

Author. *Modern Review* (magazine), London, England, former assistant; freelance journalist.

Writings

Tessa in Love, Piccadilly Press (London, England), 2005.
Things I Know about Love, Piccadilly Press (London, England), 2006, Egmont USA (New York, NY), 2010.

Two Friends, One Summer, Piccadilly Press (London, England), 2007.
Rain, Piccadilly Press (London, England), 2008.
The Worst of Me, Piccadilly Press (London, England), 2010.

ADULT NOVELS

Trailers, Viking (London, England), 1999.
Bad Timing, Viking (London, England), 2000.

Contributor to periodicals, including *The Big Issue, CosmoGirl!, Company,* and *Vogue.*

Sidelights

British author Kate le Vann began her writing career in adult fiction, detailing the ups and downs of her twenty-something heroines in the novels *Trailers* and *Bad Timing.* Le Vann first demonstrated her talent for creating realistic, likeable teen characters facing interesting romantic dilemmas in *Tessa in Love,* the story of a sixteen year old whose growing self-confidence is challenged by a relationship setback. The author has always

Cover of Kate le Vann's entertaining young-adult novel **Things I Know about Love.** (Egmont USA, 2010. Jacket photograph by iStockphoto.com. Reproduced by permission of Egmont USA.)

enjoyed reading love stories and also gave relationship advice as a teen magazine columnist; not surprisingly, romance continues to figure prominently in her novels, which include *Things I Know about Love, Two Friends, One Summer,* and *The Worst of Me.*

For Livia Stowe, the seventeen-year-old narrator of *Things I Know about Love,* the last few years have been difficult: she has been battling leukemia since age thirteen and has not enjoyed the typical teen life of hanging out with good friends and dating. With her cancer now in remission, Livia plans to make up for lost time during a trip to visit her older brother, a student at Princeton University. She starts a private blog (the novel's text) to record her experiences, the most important being her search for romance. As readers follow her entries, Livia finds love in a surprising place, and her story is eventually recorded in stereo as fellow teen Brit Adam falls in love with Livia and chronicles his growing affection for her as well as their shared tragedy. "This romantic account of first love will be treasured by teen girls," predicted *School Library Journal* contributor Susan Riley, and a *Kirkus Reviews* writer called le Vann's narrator "a friendly, observant person." In *Booklist* Kristen McKulski recommended *Things I Know about Love* as a "satisfying beach read" for romance-minded teens, adding that the author's "winsome, often humorous" diary-like text results in a "swiftly paced novel."

A longtime friendship is threatened during a trip to France in le Vann's teen novel *Two Friends, One Summer,* as Rachel and Samantha travel to France for a summer abroad. While boarding with two very different French families, one urban and one rural, the two teens find that their rock-solid friendship is on its way to becoming a casualty, especially when a handsome boy enters the mix. A summer also changes life for the title character in *Rain,* as the teen discovers much that has been hidden about her parents' past during a summer spent with her London-based grandmother. Characteristic of le Vann's penchant for romance, a young man named Harry also appears on the scene, and her shifting feelings toward him allow Rain to understand how her own mother could have become pregnant at age sixteen.

Cassidy is one year away from graduating from secondary school when readers meet her in *The Worst of Me,* and even she has to admit that it is not shaping up to be a year of fun. Not only has her boyfriend broken off their relationship and her girl friends cooled toward her, but Cassidy's single mom is totally head-over-heels in love with a new boyfriend who is now moving in. When she meets Joshua, a college-bound teen who has recently transferred from a prep school, Cassidy feels welcomed into his crowd, but when his strong anti-Muslim views become clear she wonders whether it is right to continue the relationship. Noting that le Vann sets *The Worst of Me* "against a background of religious controversy and racial tensions," Peter Hollindale added

in *School Librarian* that the author succeeds in crafting a "readable and psychologically astute" story that will hold the attention of the author's fans through to its "memorable climax of gothic melodrama."

Biographical and Critical Sources

PERIODICALS

Booklist, July 1, 2010, Kristen McKulski, review of *Things I Know about Love,* p. 51.
Bulletin of the Center for Children's Books, July-August, 2010, Karen Coats, review of *Things I Know about Love,* p. 489.
Kirkus Reviews, May 15, 2010, review of *Things I Know about Love.*
School Librarian, summer, 2010, Peter Hollindale, review of *The Worst of Me,* p. 116.
School Library Journal, July, 2010, Susan Riley, review of *Things I Know about Love,* p. 92.
Times (London, England), March 6, 1999, Lottie Moggach, review of *Trailers,* p. 17.

ONLINE

Kate le Vann Home Page, http://www.katelevann.com (December 12, 2011).*

*   *   *

LIGHT, Steve

Personal

Born March 19, in NJ; married; wife's name Christine (a teacher). *Education:* Pratt Institute, degree (illustration), 1992.

Addresses

Home—New York, NY. *E-mail*—steve@stevelightart.com.

Career

Illustrator, sculptor, and educator. Teacher of art to young children, beginning c. 2002; Storytime with Steve Light, founder. *Exhibitions:* Work exhibited at Society of Illustrators Book Show, New York, NY.

Writings

SELF-ILLUSTRATED

(Reteller) *Puss in Boots,* Harry N. Abrams (New York, NY), 2002.

Steve Light (Reproduced by permission.)

I Am Happy: A Touch-and-Feel Book of Feelings, Candlewick Press (Cambridge, MA), 2003.
The Shoemaker Extraordinaire, Harry N. Abrams (New York, NY), 2003.
Trucks Go, Chronicle Books (San Francisco, CA), 2008
The Christmas Giant, Candlewick Press (Somerville, MA), 2010.
Trains Go, Chronicle Books (San Francisco, CA), 2012.
Zephyr Takes Flight, Candlewick Press (Somerville, MA), 2012.

Also author of interactive picture books *Hello Kitty: Hello Playtime! Tricycle*, *Hello Kitty: Hello Playtime! Rocking Horse,* and *Uncle Sam: A Press-out-and-Play Book.* Contributor of illustrations to periodicals, including *New York Times Book Review.*

Sidelights

For Steve Light, a childhood aptitude for drawing led to studies at New York's prestigious Pratt Institute, where he earned a degree in illustration and eventually found his calling teaching art to very young children. Light also uses his art to tell stories, which he shares in picture books such as *Puss in Boots*, *The Shoemaker Extraordinaire*, and *The Christmas Giant*. In addition, he creates three-dimensional storyboxes that capture narratives through their tiny, carved figures and colorful backdrops. In his board books *Trucks Go* and *Trains Go* Light appeals to the chubby-fingered toddler set, and here his "brilliant watercolors" set against white pages "lend a terrific sense of movement" to his rhyming text, according to a *Kirkus Reviews* writer.

Light's first picture book retells seventeenth-century French author Charles Perrault's classic story "Puss in Boots," capturing the tale in a colorful mix of collage and line art. Dressed in a pair of tall boots, the bravado puss tricks his way to an audience with the king and eventually wins a princess bride for his lowborn master, a miller's youngest son. In her *School Library Journal* review of the book, Marianne Saccardi noted Light's

visual debut to French rococo, with its curly, sinuous lines, and wrote that his "bright, busy, cheery spreads . . . suit his light-hearted retelling" of Perrault's tale. "This collage adaptation of the old tale is alive with texture," asserted a *Kirkus Reviews* writer, adding that Light's "playful and rich"images are "fresh and full of energy," while a *Publishers Weekly* critic dubbed *Puss in Boots* "a noteworthy debut" exhibiting the storyteller's "wry touch."

Light mixes paper and textiles in his collage art for *The Shoemaker Extraordinaire,* an original story with folktale-like themes. Hans Crispin is a traveling shoemaker whose shoes impart special gifts to all who wear them. When Hans comes to one town, the local cobbler attempts to eliminate the competition by convincing the peripatetic Hans that a local giant desires his cobbler services. Hans must think quickly when he realizes that the giant actually desires a shoemaker as his main course for dinner, and his story plays out in what *Booklist* contributor GraceAnne A. DeCandido described as "a giggle-inducing story [that] shines in marvelous collages," many printed using the textured soles of actual shoes. Light's "formal" story stands in interesting "contrast to the art's extravagant forms and colors," concluded a *Kirkus Reviews* writer, giving *The Shoemaker Extraordinaire* "high marks for energy."

Light uses ink and pastel in his artwork for *The Christmas Giant,* a holiday story in which his supersized title character has a far-more pleasing personality. For the large-of-scale Humphrey, his size allows him to help rather than frighten, and his job at the North Pole is to help make all the wrapping paper for Santa's gifts. This year he also has a second task: to grow and harvest the special tree that will decorate Christmas town. Humphrey is helped by Leetree, his tiny elf coworker, who will handle the small details, like planting the seed and trimming tiny buds. When their special tree is lost during delivery, the giant and the elf do not despair: they draw on their different creative talents to craft a suitable paper substitute, making *The Christmas Giant* a story about "friendship, persistence, and resourcefulness," according to *School Library Journal* critic Linda Israelson. Light's "charming" pastel-toned pen-and-ink illustrations feature what a *Kirkus Reviews* writer characterized as a "clever use of multiple panels to show the various creative processes," and his choice of "warm, muted tones [is] perfectly suited to the quiet mood of the tale," according to *Booklist* critic Karen Cruze. In *Horn Book* Katrina Hedeen cited the "expressive characters" in *The Christmas Giant,* adding that "Light's colorful illustrations . . . do most of the storytelling."

Biographical and Critical Sources

PERIODICALS

Booklist, March 15, 2003, GraceAnne A. DeCandido, review of *The Shoemaker Extraordinaire*, p. 1333; October 15, 2010, Karen Cruze, review of *The Christmas Giant*, p. 54.

Horn Book, November-December, 2010, Katrina Hedeen, review of *The Christmas Giant,* p. 65.

Kirkus Reviews, February 1, 2002, review of *Puss in Boots,* p. 183; January 15, 2003, review of *The Shoemaker Extraordinaire,* p. 143; December 15, 2008, review of *Trucks Go*; September 1, 2010, review of *The Christmas Giant.*

Publishers Weekly, March 4, 2002, review of *Puss in Boots,* p. 78; February 10, 2003, review of *The Shoemaker Extraordinaire,* p. 186.

School Library Journal, April, 2002, Marianne Saccardi, review of *Puss in Boots,* p. 137; July, 2003, Anna DeWind Walls, review of *The Shoemaker Extraordinaire,* p. 100; October, 2010, Linda Israelson, review of *The Christmas Giant,* p. 74.

ONLINE

Happy Birthday Author Web site, http://www.happybirthdayauthor.com/ (December 5, 2010), interview with Light.

Steve Light Home Page, http://www.stevelightart.com (December 12, 2011).

Steve Light Web log, http://stevelightart.wordpress.com (December 12, 2011).

*   *   *

LOGAN, Laura

Personal

Married; children: one son, one daughter.

Addresses

Home—Dripping Springs, TX. *Agent*—Chris Tugeau, C.A. Tugeau Artist's Agent, chris@catugeau.com. *E-mail*—laura@lauralogan.com.

Career

Illustrator.

Member

Society of Children's Book Writers and Illustrators (Austin, TX, chapter).

Illustrator

Jan Jugran, *I Love You, Teddy,* Innovative Kids, 2007.

Alison Feigh, *I Can Play It Safe,* Free Spirit Pub. (Minneapolis, MN), 2008.

Jesus Loves Me, CandyCane Press (Nashville, TN), 2008.

Alison Feigh, *On Those Runaway Days,* Free Spirit Pub. (Minneapolis, MN), 2008.

Max Lucado, *God's Great Big Love for Me,* Thomas Nelson (Nashville, TN), 2008.

Jan Jugran, *Nobody Ever Feels Orange,* Piggy Toes Press (Atlanta, GA), 2008.

Megan E. Bryant and Judith Bryant, *The Easter Bunny's Workshop,* Running Press Kids (Philadelphia, PA), 2008.

Eileen Spinelli, *Two to Cuddle,* CandyCane Press (Nashville, TN), 2009.

Lidia Bastianich and Eva Mitnick, *Nonna Tell Me a Story: Lidia's Christmas Kitchen,* Running Press Kids (Philadelphia, PA), 2010.

Lynn Plourde, *Springtime with Bunny,* Sterling Children's Books (New York, NY), 2012.

Contributor to periodicals, including *High Five* and *BabyBug.* Contributor to anthologies, including *The Bill Martin Jr. Big Book of Poetry,* edited by Bill Martin, Simon & Schuster, 2008.

Sidelights

Working in a media mix that can include colored pencil, water color and gouache, and digitals, Texas-based artist Laura Logan has created engaging illustrations for children's stories and poems by writers such as Eileen Spinelli, Max Lucado, and Lidia Bastianich. Logan's artwork for Alison Feigh's picture book *On Those Runaway Days* is of special value: it helps Feigh, a child-safety expert, teach small children to trust their instincts and avoid situations that do not feel safe, even when adults are present. As a *Children's Bookwatch* critic noted of the work, the artist's "simple, color illustrations add a comforting touch" to Feigh's text, making *On Those Runaway Days* a "highly recommended" story for parent and group read alouds.

In *Nonna Tell Me a Story: Lidia's Christmas Kitchen* well-known Italian-American cook and restaurant owner Lidia Matticchio Bastianich shares the hustle and bustle of an Italian family Christmas. Bastianich recalls childhood memories of cooking alongside her grandmother, Nonna Rosa, and the central place food had in her family's holiday traditions. A freshly cut juniper tree and handmade decorations also feature in the activities of the young Lidia and her brothers, and she later recounts them to her own grandchildren in the multigenerational tale. A "warmhearted autobiographical story," according to a *Kirkus Reviews* writer, *Nonna Tell Me a Story* brings to life an old-fashioned celebration complete with sixteen cookie recipes, stories, and crafts. Logan's "pleasant illustrations" featuring Lidia and her close-knit Italian family "add to the amiable overall effect," the critic added. "The soft-toned illustrations" for *Nonna Tell Me a Story* ". . . are as cozy as all get-out," asserted *Booklist* contributor Julie Cummins, while Eva Mitnick recommended the picture book in *School Library Journal* for its "cheerful depiction of the making and sharing of holiday traditions."

Biographical and Critical Sources

PERIODICALS

Booklist, December 1, 2010, Julie Cummins, review of *Nonna Tell Me a Story: Lidia's Christmas Kitchen,* p. 66.

Children's Bookwatch, May, 2008, review of *On Those Runaway Days.*
Kirkus Reviews, September 1, 2010, review of *Nonna Tell Me a Story.*
School Library Journal, October, 2010, Eva Mitnick, review of *Nonna Tell Me a Story,* p. 69.

ONLINE

Laura Logan Home Page, http://www.lauralogan.com (December 13, 2011).

*   *   *

LYNN, Sarah
(Sarah Lynn Scheerger)

Personal

Married; children: sons. *Education:* University of California, Los Angeles, B.S. (psychology); University of Southern California, M.A. (social work).

Addresses

Home—Ventura County, CA.

Career

Clinical social worker and author. Worked variously in group homes and as a child-care conselor; Ventura County Behavioral Health, former psychiatric social worker; Ventura County SELPA, school counselor; social worker in private practice in Thousand Oaks, CA. California Lutheran University, instructor in M.F.T. program.

Member

Author's Guild.

Writings

Tip-Tap Pop, illustrated by Valeria Docampo, Marshall Cavendish (Tarrytown, NY), 2010.

Also author of *Frankie and the Pig Squish* (digital picture book), illustrated by Laura-Susan Thomas, www.istorytimeapp.com.

Biographical and Critical Sources

PERIODICALS

Kirkus Reviews, September 1, 2010, review of *Tip-Tap Pop.*
School Library Journal, September, 2010, Tanya Boudreau, review of *Tip-Tap Pop,* p. 130.

ONLINE

Cynsations Web log, http://cynthialeitichsmith.blogspot.com/ (January, 2011), Cynthia Leitich Smith, interview with Lynn.
Sarah Lynn Home Page, http://www.sarahlynnbooks.com (January 3, 2011).

M-P

MAIR, J. Samia
(Julie Samia Mair)

Personal

Born in PA; married; children: twin daughters. *Education:* Smith College, B.A. (cum laude); University of Pennsylvania, J.D. (cum laude); Johns Hopkins University, M.P.H. and certificates in Humanitarian Assistance, Health and Human Rights, and Injury Control. *Religion:* Islam (Muslim).

Addresses

Home—Baltimore, MD. *E-mail*—jsamiamair@gmail.com.

Career

Writer and educator. Called to the bar in Maryland and Washington, DC; practicing attorney for five years; Philadelphia District Attorney's Office, Philadelpha, PA, appeals prosecutor for three years; Johns Hopkins Bloomberg School of Public Health, Baltimor, MD, member of faculty for six years.

Member

National Writers Union, Islamic Writers Alliance, Muslimah Writers Alliance, National Association of Muslim Lawyers.

Awards, Honors

(With others) Community Service Award, D.C. Prisoners' Legal Services Project, 2004.

Writings

(Editor) Ali Shehata and Heather el Khiyari, *Demystifying Islam,* Elysium River Press, 2009.

Amira's Totally Chocolate World, Kube Publishing (Seattle, WA), 2010.
The Perfect Gift, illustrated by Craig Howarth, Kube Publishing (Seattle, WA), 2010.

Contributor of articles to periodicals, including *Annual Review of Public Health, Baltimore Examiner* online, *Hiba, Islamic Ink, Journal of Law, Medicine & Ethics,* and *Sisters.* Short fiction and poetry anthologized in *Between Love, Hope, and Fear,* An-Najm, 2007; and *Many Voices, One Faith II,* Islamic Writers Alliance, 2009.

Sidelights

Based in Baltimore, Maryland, J. Samia Mair writes in several genres, from essays, articles, and reviews to fictional short stories and poetry. A former attorney and educator, Mair began writing for children after starting her own family. A Muslim by conversion, she focuses stories such as *Amira's Totally Chocolate World* and *The Perfect Gift* on children of her chosen faith. In line with her writing for adults, Mair's tales also promote religious tolerance by opening a windows onto Islamic culture and traditions for children of other faiths.

Both *Amira's Totally Chocolate World* and *The Perfect Gift* take place during Eid, the first on Eid ul-Fitr, the holiday marking the end of the Islamic holy month of Ramadan, and the second on Eid ul-Adha, a day of prayer and celebration that is fixed by the lunar calendar and has its origins in Abraham's willingness to sacrifice his son, Ishmael. In the first story, Amira loves chocolate, and her bedtime prayers always include the wish that God transform everything in her world into chocolate. When her wish is granted on Eid, Amira is thrilled at first, but soon she begins to realize that the world was much more beautiful when it was multicolored rather than chocolate brown.

Another Eid story, *The Perfect Gift,* finds little Sarah unhappy because she has not been able to find the perfect gift to present to her mother on Eid ul-Adha. Her brother and sister have found wonderful gifts, which

J. Samia Mair shares her Muslim culture in her picture book The Perfect Gift, *which features artwork by Craig Howarth.* (Illustration copyright © 2010 by J. Samia Mair. Reproduced by permission of Kube Publishing.)

are wrapped and ready, but Sarah has no money for such things. While she tries to console herself during a walk in a nearby wood, the little girl spots a tiny burst of color peeking up from under the brown leaves underfoot. Carefully marked and left in its woodland home, this first flower of spring provides the perfect gift for Mother as well as reminding Sarah that God watches all things. In *School Library Journal* Fawzia Gilani-Williams praised *The Perfect Gift* as a "realistic picture book" in which Craig Howarth's softly toned "watercolor illustrations effectively portray a contemporary Muslim family." A *Children's Bookwatch* critic also praised Mair's story and dubbed *The Perfect Gift* "a beautiful multicultural book."

Biographical and Critical Sources

PERIODICALS

Children's Bookwatch, August, 2010, review of *The Perfect Gift.*
Kirkus Reviews, September 1, 2010, review of *The Perfect Gift.*

School Library Journal, January, 2011, Fawzia Gilani-Williams, review of *The Perfect Gift,* p. 80.

ONLINE

Islamic Writers Alliance Web site, http://www.islamicwriter salliance.net/ (October 3, 2011), "Julie Samia Mair."*

*   *   *

MAIR, Julie Samia
See MAIR, J. Samia

*   *   *

MALTBIE, P.I.
(Priscilla Maltbie)

Personal

Born in CA. *Education:* B.A. (English).

Addresses

Home—Long Beach, CA.

Career

Writer. Orange County Department of Education, Orange County, CA, author of educational video scripts.

Awards, Honors

Best Children's Book Medal, Cat Writer's Association, 2005, for *Picasso and Minou.*

Writings

Picasso and Minou, illustrated by Pau Estrada, Charlesbridge (Watertown, MA), 2005.
Claude Monet: The Painter Who Stopped the Trains, illustrated by Jos. A. Smith, Abrams Books for Young Readers (New York, NY), 2010.
Bambino and Mr. Twain, illustrated by Daniel Miyares, Charlesbridge (Watertown, MA), 2012.

Contributor of articles and short fiction to periodicals, including Long Beach, CA, *Press-Telegram.* Contributing editor to *New Mobility.*

Sidelights

P.I. Maltbie lives in California, where she has worked as a freelance writer since graduating from college. While she began her career writing articles focusing on issues related to people with health issues and disabilities, Maltbie has more recently found a new writing niche: telling children's stories about whimsical episodes in the lives of famous people. Featuring engaging illustrations, her picture books include *Picasso and Minou* and *Claude Monet: The Painter Who Stopped the Trains* as well as *Bambino and Mr. Twain,* the last a story about the relationship between nineteenth-century American author Samuel Clements (better known as Mark Twain) and the beloved cat that filled his world following his wife's death. "I'm focusing on non-fiction, and true life stories, as I find actual experiences are filled with more drama and twists and turns than I could ever imagine," Maltbie told Bonnie O'Brian in an interview for *California Readers Online.* "I particularly love the 'aha' moments when my subject finds the solution to a problem, or takes the road that leads him/her to success."

In *Picasso and Minou,* illustrated by Pau Estrada, Maltbie takes readers to 1900s Paris, where a young Pablo Picasso is channeling his grief over a friend's death by

P.I. Maltbie opens a window onto the life of a noted impressionist in **Claude Monet,** *a picture book featuring artwork by Jos. A. Smith.* (Illustration copyright © 2010 by Jos. A. Smith. Reproduced by permission of Harry N. Abrams.)

painting in blue oils. Nobody wants Picasso's blue paintings, however, and soon the impoverished painter must let his Siamese cat, Minou, go free in the hopes that the animal can scavenge enough to food to survive. What Minou finds on the streets is far more magical, however, and it ultimately inspires joy in the morose painter. "In her debut children's book, Maltbie playfully imagines the impact that the famed artist's cat has on his work," observed a *Publishers Weekly* writer, recommending *Picasso and Minou* to "aspiring artists and budding animal lovers." The author "balances the gloom" of Picasso's situation "with a sweet friendship story that ends successfully," noted Gillian Engberg in her *Booklist* review of the same picture book, while in *School Library Journal* Wendy Lukehart asserted that, as captured in Estrada's "skillful renderings" of Picasso and his world, Maltbie's tale "offers a historically accurate explanation regarding the Blue Period as well as an engaging story."

A noted French artist of the late nineteenth century is Maltbie's subject in *Claude Monet*, which comes to life in colorful impressionist-styled paintings by Jos. A. Smith. In the story, Monet has become known for his impressionistic style of painting, but critics complain that the loosely painted style is only suited to landscapes and seascapes. Noting his son's interest in locomotives, the painter determines to prove the art critics wrong, and he spends three months with his easel set up at a Paris train station, capturing the coming and going of the massive steam-powered engines. "Maltbie ground her imagined scenes in actual incidents," creating "another engaging and perceptive historical reconstruction," according to John Peters in *Booklist,* while *School Library Journal* critic Allison Tran dubbed *Claude Monet* "a lively telling" that is also "an accessible option for biography reports." Smith's "Impressionist-inspired watercolors complement the text," Tran added, and a *Kirkus Reviews* writer asserted that the "detailed and carefully worked" illustrations for *Claude Monet* "are well integrated" into Maltbie's "admirable" story.

Biographical and Critical Sources

PERIODICALS

Booklist, February 15, 2005, Gillian Engberg, review of *Picasso and Minou,* p. 1085; November 1, 2010, John Peters, review of *Claude Monet: The Painter Who Stopped the Trains,* p. 56.

Publishers Weekly, January 10, 2005, review of *Picasso and Minou,* p. 56; August 9, 2010, review of *Claude Monet,* p. 48.

School Arts, September, 2005, Ken Marantz, review of *Picasso and Minou,* p. 58.

School Librarian, spring, 2011, Derek Lomas, review of *Claude Monet,* p. 42.

School Library Journal, April, 2005, Wendy Lukehart, review of *Picasso and Minou,* p. 106; October, 2010, Allison Tran, review of *Claude Monet,* p. 101.

ONLINE

California Readers Online, http://www.californiareaders.org/ (December 15, 2011), Bonnie O'Brian, interview with Maltbie.

Children's Book Review Web log, http://www.thechildrensbookreview.com/weblog/ (September, 2010), review of *Claude Monet.*

Looking Glass Review Online, http://lookingglassreview.com/ (December 12, 2011), review of *Claude Monet.**

*   *   *

MALTBIE, Priscilla
See MALTBIE, P.I.

*   *   *

MARIZ, Rae 1981-

Personal

Born 1981, immigrated to Sweden, c. 2003. *Education:* Attended art school in Portland, OR. *Hobbies and other interests:* Video games, crafts, languages.

Addresses

Home—Stockholm, Sweden.

Career

Translator and writer. Formerly worked at Seattle Public Library, Seattle, WA. Swedish-to-English translator for film production and publishing companies.

Writings

The Unidentified, Balzer & Bray (New York, NY), 2010.

Sidelights

Rae Mariz is an American now living in Sweden, where she works as a translator for publishers and film-production companies. Mariz was inspired to write her first novel, *The Unidentified,* after reading M.T. Anderson's future-world satire *Feed,* in which citizens are plugged into the media and programmed to become useful consumers at birth. "I didn't set out to write a novel," Mariz admitted on her home page, noting that learning to tell a story was a job in itself. "I wrote it to see if I could." "I was inspired by the challenge," she added. "Building up a world with words" to create *The Unidentified* "was a really fun way to work through ideas and share stuff I think is interesting."

For fifteen-year-old Katey "Kid" Dade, Mariz's heroine in *The Unidentified*, life in the near future means getting an education at corporate-run Game Centers. Converted shopping malls, these Game Centers keep children interested by encouraging cell phones and other social media; meanwhile their whereabouts are constantly tracked via GPS and video cameras for the edification of market researchers. Students move up through each level of the Game by becoming more proficient consumers, and the highest achievers have mastered the art of self-branding. While it all seems normal to Kid, the teen eventually discovers the existence of a rogue group called the Unidentified, who live off the grid and think up ways to disrupt the Game's status quo. As the group's antics become more popular, they are pulled into the Game's consumer dynamic, leaving Kid to find another way to take control of her own destiny.

Calling the future world of *The Unidentified* "a startlingly plausible dystopian society," Jessica Miller added in her *School Library Journal* review that "teens will immediately be able to see the connections to today's technology-dependent society," while a *Kirkus Reviews* writer described Mariz's fictional setting as "frighten-

ingly real" and "sadly jaded." A *Publishers Weekly* compared the debut novel to futuristic fiction by Scott Westerfeld and Cory Doctorow and cited the story's "all-too-logical extrapolation of today's trends. It also benefits from "an optimistic, antiestablishment undercurrent," the critic added, while *Voice of Youth Advocates* contributor Erin Wyatt asserted that in *The Unidentified* "Mariz creates a chilling look at a future that seems uncomfortably probably in [her] . . . engaging, thought-provoking read."

Biographical and Critical Sources

PERIODICALS

Booklist, September 15, 2010, Heather Booth, review of *The Unidentified,* p. 64.
Bulletin of the Center for Children's Books, November, 2010, April Spisak, review of *The Unidentified,* p. 139.
Kirkus Reviews, September 1, 2010, review of *The Unidentified.*
Publishers Weekly, September 20, 2010, review of *The Unidentified,* p. 67.
School Library Journal, October, 2010, Jessica Miller, review of *The Unidentified,* p. 122.
Voice of Youth Advocates, December, 2010, Erin Wyatt, review of *The Unidentified,* p. 473.

ONLINE

Rae Mariz Home Page, http://raemariz.com (December 29, 2011).*

* * *

Cover of Rae Mariz's futuristic teen novel The Unidentified, *in which a young woman fights a corrupt educational system.* (Balzer + Bray, 2010. Jacket photograph by Louis Fox/Getty Images. Reproduced by permission of Getty Images.)

McBRIDE, Lish

Personal

Married; children: one. *Education:* University of New Orleans, M.F.A. (fiction). *Hobbies and other interests:* Reading.

Addresses

Home—Seattle, WA. *Agent*—Jason Anthony, Lippincott Massie McQuilkin Literary Agents, 27 W. 20th St., Ste. 305, New York, NY 10011. *E-mail*—LishMcBride@gmail.com.

Career

Author. Presenter at conferences.

Awards, Honors

William C. Morris Young-Adult Debut Novel Award finalist, 2010, and Scandiuzzi Children's Book Award for Middle Grades and Young Adults, Washington State

Book Awards, and Top-Ten Fiction for Young Adults selection, both 2011, and Best Books for Young Adults selection, American Library Association, Best Children's Book of the Year selection, Bank Street College of Education, and Capitol Choices Noteworthy Titles for Children and Teens selection, all for *Hold Me Closer, Necromancer.*

Writings

Hold Me Closer, Necromancer, Henry Holt (New York, NY), 2010.

Sidelights

Lish McBride wrote the first draft of her first novel, *Hold Me Closer, Necromancer,* while completing her master's degree in fiction at the University of New Orleans. A native of the Pacific Northwest, McBride has since returned to western Washington State and now lives in Seattle, where her imaginative fantasy is set.

Life after high school has not exactly been stellar for Samhairn Corvus LaCroix, the main character in *Hold Me Closer, Necromancer.* Since dropping out of college, Sam now divides his time between hanging out with friends and working a dead-end job flipping burgers at a local fast-food restaurant. Things pick up, but in a bad way, when he winds up on the radar of Douglas, a violent man who makes his living bringing dead things back to life. Douglas sees in Sam something that Sam does not yet understand about himself: he too has the necromancer's power, and he tries to convince Sam to join with him. When arranging to have the teen beaten up by thugs and receiving talking disembodied heads does not work, Douglas gets more creative. Meanwhile Sam depends on his new friendship with a ten-year-old, brainiac Catholic-school student to save him.

Citing *Hold Me Closer, Necromancer* for relating its "sardonic and outrageous" storyline with "a pace that smashes through any curtain of disbelief," Francisca Goldsmith added in her *Booklist* review that McBride's "fine writing" and "tight plotting" also add to the novel's appeal. In *School Library Journal* Hayden Bass dubbed the story a "sometimes goofy, sometimes gory debut" that will likely appeal to fans of offbeat horror films such as *Sean of the Dead.* Spring Lea Henry noted in *Voice of Youth Advocates* that McBride's unlikely hero is made likeable through a "snappy, first-person account" that is "lush with all the jaded sarcasm of a down-on-his-luck college dropout," but without the "whiny angst." "A title this good has a lot to live up to," asserted a *Kirkus Reviews* critic, "and [in *Hold Me Closer, Necromancer*] . . . McBride proves she's largely up to the task."

Biographical and Critical Sources

PERIODICALS

Booklist, November 15, 2010, Francisca Goldsmith, review of *Hold Me Closer, Necromancer,* p. 36.

Bulletin of the Center for Children's Books, December, 2010, Claire Gross, review of *Hold Me Closer, Necromancer,* p. 197.
Kirkus Reviews, September 1, 2010, review of *Hold Me Closer, Necromancer.*
Publishers Weekly, September 13, 2010, review of *Hold Me Closer, Necromancer,* p. 47.
School Library Journal, January, 2011, Hayden Bass, review of *Hold Me Closer, Necromancer,* p. 111.
Voice of Youth Advocates, February, 2011, Spring Lea Henry, review of *Hold Me Closer, Necromancer,* p. 574.

ONLINE

Lish McBride Home Page, http://www.lishmcbride.com (December 13, 2011).
Seattlest Web site, http://seattlest.com/ (October 15, 2010), interview with McBride.*

*   *   *

McCURDY, Michael 1942-
(Michael Charles McCurdy)

Personal

Born February 17, 1942 in New York, NY; son of Charles Errett (an artist) and Beatrice McCurdy; married Deborah Lamb (a social worker), September 7, 1968; children: Heather, Mark. *Education:* Attended School of the Museum of Fine Arts, Boston, MA, 1960-66; Tufts University, B.F.A., 1964, M.F.A., 1971. *Politics:* Democrat. *Religion:* Episcopalian. *Hobbies and other interests:* Playing piano, reading history and biography, hiking.

Addresses

Home—Great Barrington, MA. *Agent*—Susan Cohen, Writers House, 21 W. 26th St., New York, NY 10010.

Career

Artist and illustrator. Printer, director, and publisher, Penmaen Press, Lincoln and Great Barrington, MA, 1968-85. School of the Museum of Fine Arts, Boston, MA, instructor in drawing, 1966-67; Impressions Workshop, Boston, designer and printer, 1970; Concord Academy, Concord, MA, instructor in printmaking, 1972-75; Wellesley College, Wellesley, MA, instructor in fine printing, 1976. *Exhibitions:* Work included in numerous exhibitions, including at Boston Athenaeum, Boston, MA, 1976; Berkshire Museum, Pittsfield, MA, 1988; University of Missouri Library, 1988; Simon's Rock of Bard College, Great Barrington, MA, 1988; Chartwell's Bookstore, New York, NY, 1990; Welles Gallery, Lenox, MA, 1991; Elizabeth Stone Gallery, Birmingham, MI, 1992; Stockwood Gallery, Lenox, MA, 1993; Gallery 30, Gettysburg, PA, 1995; and St. Botolph Club, Boston, 2001.

Member

Society of Printers (director of publications, 1978), Albany Print Club, St. Botolph Club (Boston, MA).

Awards, Honors

Bronze Medal, International Book Show (Leipzig, Germany), 1983, for *Toward the Light;* Best Illustrated Children's Book Award, *New York Times,* 1986, for *The Owl-Scatterer,* and 1996, for *The Seasons Sewn: A Year in Patchwork;* Notable Children's Trade Book in the Field of Social Studies citation, National Council for the Social Studies/Children's Book Council, 1988, for *Hannah's Farm: The Seasons on an Early American Homestead;* named Literary Light, Boston Public Library, 2002; awards from New England Book Show and American Institute of Graphic Arts.

Writings

SELF-ILLUSTRATED

The Devils Who Learned to Be Good, Joy Street Books (Boston, MA), 1987.
Hannah's Farm: The Seasons on an Early American Homestead, Holiday House (New York, NY), 1988.
(Reteller) *The Old Man and the Fiddle,* Putnam (New York, NY), 1992.
(Editor) Frederick Douglass, *Escape from Slavery: The Boyhood of Frederick Douglass in His Own Words* (nonfiction), Knopf (New York, NY), 1994.
Trapped by the Ice!: Shackleton's Amazing Antarctic Adventure, Walker (New York, NY), 1997.
The Sailors Alphabet, Houghton Mifflin (Boston, MA), 1998.
An Algonquian Year: The Year according to the Full Moon, Houghton Mifflin (Boston, MA), 2000.
So Said Ben, Creative Editions (Mankato, MN), 2007.
Walden Then and Now: An Alphabetical Tour of Henry Thoreau's Pond, Charlesbridge (Watertown, MA), 2010.

Author's Penmaen Press archive is housed at the Thomas Dodd Center, University of Connecticut—Storrs; other works are archived at the Boston Public Library, Boston, MA.

ILLUSTRATOR

Isaac Asimov, *Please Explain,* Houghton Mifflin (Boston, MA), 1973.
Linda Grant de Pauw, *Founding Mothers: Women in America in the Revolutionary Era* (nonfiction), Houghton Mifflin (Boston, MA), 1975.
B.A. King, *The Very Best Christmas Tree,* David R. Godine (Boston, MA), 1984, published as *A Yankee Christmas,* Yankee Books (Emmaus, PA), 1992.
Howard Norman, *The Owl-Scatterer,* Atlantic Monthly Press (Boston, MA), 1986.

B.A. King, *The Christmas Junk Box,* David R. Godine (Boston, MA), 1987.
Howard Norman, reteller, *How Glooskap Outwits the Ice Giants, and Other Tales of the Maritime Indians,* Little, Brown (Boston, MA), 1989.
Louisa May Alcott, *An Old-Fashioned Thanksgiving,* Holiday House (New York, NY), 1989.
Mary Pope Osborne, *American Tall Tales,* Knopf (New York, NY), 1991.
X.J. Kennedy, *The Beasts of Bethlehem* (poetry), Margaret K. McElderry Books (New York, NY), 1992.
Diana Appelbaum, *Giants in the Land* (nonfiction), Houghton Mifflin (Boston, MA), 1993.
Amelia Stewart Knight, *The Way West: Journal of a Pioneer Woman,* adapted by Lillian Schlissel, Simon & Schuster (New York, NY), 1993.
Donald Hall, *Lucy's Christmas,* Harcourt (San Diego, CA), 1994.
Donald Hall, *Lucy's Summer,* Harcourt (San Diego, CA), 1995.
Neil Philip, editor, *Singing America: Poems That Define a Nation,* Viking (New York, NY), 1995.
Abraham Lincoln, *The Gettysburg Address,* Houghton Mifflin (Boston, MA), 1995.
Neil Philip, compiler, *American Fairy Tales: From Rip Van Winkle to the Rootabaga Stories,* Hyperion (New York, NY), 1996.
Ann Whitford Paul, *The Seasons Sewn: A Year in Patchwork,* Harcourt (San Diego, CA), 1996.
Laura Simms, *The Bone Man: A Native American Modoc Tale,* Hyperion (New York, NY), 1997.
Esther Forbes, *Johnny Tremain,* Houghton Mifflin (Boston, MA), 1998.
Edgar Rice Burroughs, *Tarzan,* retold by Robert D. San Souci, Hyperion (New York, NY), 1999.
Jan Wahl, *Christmas Present,* Creative Education (Mankato, MN), 1999.
L. Frank Baum, *The Wonderful Wizard of Oz* (Kansas Centennial edition), University Press of Kansas (Lawrence, KS), 1999.
Verla Kay, *Iron Horses,* Putnam (New York, NY), 1999.
Peter and Connie Roop, *Take Command, Captain Farragut!,* Atheneum (New York, NY), 2002.
Dennis Brindell Fradin, *The Signers: The Fifty-six Stories behind the Declaration of Independence,* Walker (New York, NY), 2002.
Steve Goodman, *The Train They Call the City of New Orleans,* Putnam (New York, NY), 2003.
(And author of introduction and notes) Edgar Allan Poe, *Tales of Terror,* Alfred A. Knopf (New York, NY), 2005.
Dennis Brindell Fradin, *The Founders: The Thirty-nine Stories behind the U.S. Constitution,* Walker (New York, NY), 2005.

Contributor of illustrations to *An Illustrated Treasury of African-American Read Aloud Stories,* edited by Susan Kantor, Black Dog & Leventhal Publishers (New York, NY), 2003.

FOR ADULTS; SELF-ILLUSTRATED

(With George Selleck) *Dove at the Windows: Last Letters of Four Quaker Martyrs,* Penmaen Press (Lincoln, MA), 1973.

(Compiler and editor, with Michael Peich) *The First Ten: A Penmaen Press Bibliography,* Penmaen Press (Lincoln, MA), 1978.

Toward the Light: Wood Engravings by Michael McCurdy, Porcupine's Quill (Erin, Ontario, Canada), 1982.

The Illustrated Harvard: Harvard University in Wood Engravings and Words, Globe Pequot Press (Chester, CT), 1986.

McCurdy's World: Prints and Drawings by Michael McCurdy, Capra Press (Santa Barbara, CA), 1992.

FOR ADULTS; ILLUSTRATOR

Edward Everett Hale, *The Brick Moon,* Imprint Society (Barre, MA), 1971.

Joseph Seccombe, *A Discourse Utter'd in Part at Amauskeeg Falls in the Fishing Season,* Barre Publishers (Barre, MA), 1971.

Everett S. Allen, *This Quiet Place,* Little, Brown (Boston, MA), 1971.

The Narrative of Alvar Nunez Cabeza de Vaca, Imprint Society (Barre, MA), 1972.

Sarah Kemble Knight, *The Journal of Madam Knight,* David R. Godine (Boston, MA), 1972.

William Ferguson, *Light of Paradise* (poetry), Penmaen Press (Lincoln, MA), 1973.

X.J. Kennedy, *Celebrations after the Death of John Brennan* (poetry), Penmaen Press (Lincoln, MA), 1974.

George E. Gifford, Jr., *Cecil County Maryland 1608-1850,* privately printed, 1974.

Richard Eberhart, *Poems to Poets,* Penmaen Press (Lincoln, MA), 1976.

Leo Connellan, *Crossing America,* Penmaen Press (Lincoln, MA), 1976.

Henry David Thoreau, *Clear Sky, Pure Light,* Penmaen Press (Lincoln, MA), 1978.

Pardee Lowe, Jr., translator, *King Harald and the Icelanders,* Penmaen Press (Lincoln, MA), 1979.

Osmond Beckwith, *Vernon: An Anecdotal Novel,* Breaking Point (New York, NY), 1981.

John Gilgun, *Everything That Has Been Shall Be Again: The Reincarnation Fables of John Gilgun,* Bieler Press (St. Paul, MN), 1981.

X.J. Kennedy, editor, *Tygers of Wrath: Poems of Hate, Anger, and Invective,* University of Georgia Press (Athens, GA), 1981.

John Muir, *A Thousand-Mile Walk to the Gulf,* Houghton Mifflin (Boston, MA), 1981.

Vicente Aleixandre, *Mundo a solas/World Alone* (bilingual edition), translations by Lewis Hyde and David Unger, Penmaen Press (Lincoln, MA), 1982.

Margaret Atwood, *Encounters with the Element Man,* W.B. Ewert (Concord, NH), 1982.

Philip Dacey, *Gerard Manley Hopkins Meets Walt Whitman in Heaven, and Other Poems,* Penmaen Press (Lincoln, MA), 1982.

May Sarton, *A Winter Garland: New Poems,* W.B. Ewert (Concord, NH), 1982.

Susan Efird, *The Eye of Heaven: A Narrative Poem,* Abattoir Editions/University of Nebraska at Omaha (Omaha, NE), 1982.

Sandor Csoori, *Memory of Snow,* translation by Nicholas Kolumban, Penmaen Press (Lincoln, MA), 1983.

William Edgar Stafford, *Listening Deep: Poems,* Penmaen Press (Lincoln, MA), 1984.

Weldon Kees, *Two Prose Sketches,* Aralia Press (West Chester, PA), 1984.

Chet Raymo, *The Soul of the Night: An Astronomical Pilgrimage,* Prentice-Hall (Englewood Cliffs, NJ), 1985.

Jean Giono, *The Man Who Planted Trees,* Chelsea Green Publishing (Chelsea, VT), 1985.

Henry David Thoreau, *The Winged Life: The Poetic Voice of Henry David Thoreau,* edited with commentaries by Robert Bly, Yolla Bolly Press (Covelo, CA), 1986, Harper (New York, NY), 1992.

Mary W. Freeman, *The Revolt of Mother,* Redpath Press (Minneapolis, MN), 1987.

Somerset Maugham, *The Three Fat Women of Antibes,* Redpath Press (Minneapolis, MN), 1987.

Charles Dickens, *A Christmas Carol: Bah! Humbug!,* Redpath Press (Minneapolis, MN), 1987.

John Muir, *My First Summer on the Sierra,* Yolla Bolly Press (Covelo, CA), 1988, Sierra Club Books (San Francisco, CA), 1989.

John Muir, *The Yosemite,* Sierra Club Books (San Francisco, CA), 1988.

John Muir, *Travels in Alaska,* Sierra Club Books (San Francisco, CA), 1988.

Eva A. Wilbur-Cruz, *A Beautiful, Cruel Country,* University of Arizona Press (Tucson, AZ), 1988.

Scott E. Hastings, Jr., *Goodbye Highland Yankee,* Chelsea Green Publishing (Chelsea, VT), 1988.

Villy Sorenson, *Downfall of the Gods,* University of Nebraska Press (Lincoln, NE), 1988.

David Lee, *Day's Work,* Copper Canyon (Port Townsend, WA), 1990.

Nathan Smith, *Sermon to the Birds,* Oxzimoron Press (Great Barrington, MA), 1990.

David Peterson, *Racks: The Natural History of Antlers and the Animals That Wear Them,* Capra Press (Santa Barbara, CA), 1991.

Noel Perrin, *Last Person Rural,* David R. Godine, (Boston, MA), 1991.

Richard Nunley, editor, *The Berkshire Reader: Writings from New England's Secluded Paradise,* Berkshire House (Stockbridge, MA), 1992.

David Mamet, *American Buffalo,* Arion Press (San Francisco, CA), 1992.

(With Julia Granda and Barbieo B. Gizzi) R. Wilbur, *Under One Roof: A Gathering of Poems,* Mad River Press (Eureka, CA), 1992.

John Muir, *The Cruise of the Corwin,* Sierra Club Books (San Francisco, CA), 1993.

Clarissa Pinkola Estes, *The Gift of Story,* Ballantine Books (New York, NY), 1993.

Edward Abbey, *Earth Apples,* St. Martin's Press (New York, NY), 1994.

Ralph L. Voss and Michael L. Keene, editors, *The Heath Guide to College Writing,* 2nd edition, D.C. Heath (Boston, MA), 1994.

Harry Crews, *A Childhood: The Biography of a Place,* University of Georgia Press (Athens, GA), 1995.

David Mamet, *Passover,* St. Martin's Press (New York, NY), 1995.

Bruce Smith, *The Distance,* Press of Appletree Alley (Lewisburg, PA), 1996.

Rabindranath Tagore, *The Post Office,* translation by Krishna Dutta and Andrew Robinson, St. Martin's Press (New York, NY), 1996.

Neil Philip, editor, *War and the Pity of War,* Clarion Books (New York, NY), 1998.

W.D. Wetherell, *One River More: A Celebration of Rivers and Fly Fishing,* Lyons Press (New York, NY), 1998.

Iris Murdoch, *Something Special,* Norton (New York, NY), 2000.

Daniel Perron, *Tales of Adam,* Context Books (New York, NY), 2003.

David Henry Thoreau, *Walden: 150th Anniversary Edition,* Shambhala Press (Boston, MA), 2004.

(X.J. Kennedy and Dorothy M. Kennedy, selectors) James Hayford, *Knee-deep in Blazing Snow: Growing Up in Vermont: Poems,* Wordsong (Honesdale, PA), 2005.

Ted Kooser, *Out of That Moment: Twenty-one Years of Valentines, 1986-2006,* Brooding Heron Press (Waldron Island, WA), 2006.

Sidelights

With his illustrations gracing the pages of hundreds of books for children and adults, Michael McCurdy has become one of the most respected book illustrators at work in the United States. His distinctive wood engraving artwork and drawings illustrate both adult and children's books, celebrating themes from country life to U.S. history to the natural world. In an industrial age, when mass production dominates the publishing industry, McCurdy's efforts to preserve the art of engraving and craft books by hand have provided book lovers with numerous treasures. While his wood engravings enhance the beauty of books produced by mainstream publishers, his own small publishing house, Penmaen Press, has produced exquisitely illustrated and bound editions of contemporary works. McCurdy "somehow manages to make each book an artistic achievement," noted *Horn Book* contributor Robert D. Hale. The artist/publisher once commented that his "preoccupation is with the entire book": from writing the text and engraving the illustrations to setting the type and binding.

The artist explained his attraction to wood engraving in *Toward the Light: Wood Engravings by Michael McCurdy.* "The wood engraving is an honest medium," he wrote. "It's straightforward and there is no room for error, no room for cover-up. A cut is made, and it stays. . . . I've always had a feeling that this is another reason wood engraving is not enormously popular as a technique among artists. It can't hide one's weaker moments."

Born in New York City in 1942, McCurdy was brought up in New Rochelle, New York, and Marblehead, Massachusetts. His grandparents and father were artists, and McCurdy himself first became interested in wood engraving as a student at the School of the Museum of Fine Arts in Boston. For a year during attendance at that school, he roomed with another future illustrator, David McPhail.

Two years after graduating from Tufts University in 1966, McCurdy was awarded a traveling scholarship from the Museum School. The country was at this time involved in the Vietnam War, and he became a conscientious objector rather than serve in the military. For two years he worked as an orderly at a Boston hospital, then joined his wife for a six-month tour of Europe and the then-Soviet Union before returning to the United States and establishing the Penmaen Press. McCurdy also had teaching positions at several schools on the East Coast, including the Museum of Fine Arts in Boston, Concord Academy, and Wellesley College. Throughout this time, he began illustrating books for children and for adults and completed his M.F.A. at Tufts University.

In an *American Artist* article, Eunice Agar noted that McCurdy laid the groundwork for his career as a student in the Boston area. He crafted his first book, illustrating two chapters from the Book of Genesis, during that time. Also, while a student of poet X.J. Kennedy at Tufts University, McCurdy realized his interest in contemporary literature. After working as an art instructor at the Concord Academy and Wellesley College, he began to devote himself full time to engraving, bookmaking, and his press. As Agar wrote, McCurdy "took the name for his press from Gerard Manley Hopkins's poem, 'Penmaen Pool.' Penmaen is a town in Wales and also the Welsh word for land's end."

While McCurdy did not publish books specifically for children at Penmaen, the quality of his work there characterizes the fiction and nonfiction children's books he would craft for other publishers. One example is *Founding Mothers: Women in America in the Revolutionary Era*, which was released by Boston-based Houghton Mifflin. Written by Linda Grant de Pauw and with wood engravings by McCurdy, this work, according to a reviewer for *Horn Book,* "stands as a prototype of what can be done to make nonfiction appealing." The text, which tells of the lives of the women of the Revolutionary War generation, is enhanced by McCurdy's engravings, which are "expertly drafted" and "stand as introduction to the bold, heavy typeface." Working in the adult genre, McCurdy has contributed wood engravings to special-edition poetry and essay collections, to the work of nineteenth-century naturalist and philosopher Henry David Thoreau and naturalist John Muir, and to texts by writers such as film director David Mamet.

Based on a traditional Russian story, *The Devils Who Learned to Be Good* exemplifies McCurdy's work as a writer and illustrator of children's fiction. After serving

With his dynamic scratchboard illustrations, Michael McCurdy creates a picture-book variation of a nineteenth-century sea chantey in The Sailor's Alphabet, *which presents a picture of shipping during the 1800s.*

in the army for thirty-five years, an old soldier returns home with nothing but two loaves of bread. He gives one loaf to a beggar, who rewards him with a magic deck of playing cards that never lets its owner lose a game. He offers the second loaf to another beggar, who gives the soldier a flour sack that will envelop anything the bearer wishes to control. The soldier uses his two magic objects to roust devils from the tsar's palace; they play cards with the soldier, lose all their pilfered gold and silver to him, learn to be good, and ultimately practice community service throughout the countryside (despite some occasional lapses into deviltry). *New York Times Book Review* contributor Barbara Thompson praised McCurdy's "witty retelling" and "striking" engravings in the book, while a *Publishers Weekly* critic noted the artist's ability to "capture the somber intensity of the countryside." "With its lively pace and ingenious central character and an ending as logical as it is unexpected," Mary M. Burns concluded in *Horn Book* that *The Devils Who Learned to Be Good* "will become a staple in the storyteller's repertoire."

In *Hannah's Farm: The Seasons on an Early American Homestead* McCurdy presents a "series of nostalgic pictures recreating life in pre-industrial New England," according to a *Kirkus Reviews* writer. Quiet, bucolic activities such as cutting wood for winter, harvesting, and decorating a Christmas tree are depicted. A writer for the *New York Times Book Review* praised McCurdy's "handsome woodcuts" for this story, and a contributor for *Booklist* dubbed the art in *Hannah's Farm* "striking."

McCurdy also mines U.S. history in *Escape from Slavery: The Boyhood of Frederick Douglass in His Own Words,* a book for which Coretta Scott King wrote the foreword, while in *Trapped by the Ice!: Shackleton's Amazing Antarctic Adventure* the artist used full-color acrylic paintings for the first time. Writing in the *New York Times Book Review* about *Trapped by the Ice!,* Rebecca Pepper Sinkler noted that McCurdy's text and artwork "capture . . . not only the elemental fears but the daily grubbiness of adventure." Appraising *Escape*

from Slavery, *Horn Book* critic Lois F. Anderson complimented McCurdy for successfully preserving "the spirit and integrity of Douglass's story," adding that the book's ten scratchboard illustrations "capture Douglass's indignation and suffering and yet contain a glimmer of optimism on the young boy's face." *Booklist* contributor Hazel Rochman added that "McCurdy has done a splendid job of bringing the narrative of the life of Frederick Douglass to middle-grade readers."

In *So Said Ben* McCurdy shares thirteen proverbs originally published in Benjamin Franklin's *Poor Richard's Almanack.* Along with McCurdy's signature art, the book features his introductory foreword as well as a biography of Benjamin Franklin. "Traditional American values come across loud and clear" in this book, asserted *School Library Journal* critic Jayne Damron, the critic adding that McCurdy's art here is "reminiscent of early printing processes."

"Beautifully designed, from jacket art to trim size to the choice of ivory-toned paper" is how *Horn Book* critic Mary M. Burns described McCurdy's presentation of *The Gettysburg Address.* Complementing U.S. President Abraham Lincoln's famous speech in this work are a series of dramatic scratchboard illustrations depicting Lincoln and his audience as well as other Civil War-era scenes. Wendy Lukeheart, writing in *School Library Journal,* remarked that McCurdy's illustrations for this work "provide the dark serious tone and high drama appropriate for the subject."

In *Take Command, Captain Farragut!* McCurdy works with Peter and Connie Roop to visualize the true story of the second-youngest midshipman ever commissioned by the U.S. Navy. David Farragut became a midshipman at age nine, almost fifty years before he distinguished himself in the U.S. Civil War. In *Booklist* Carolyn Phelan remarked favorably upon the "period look" of the book's illustrations. Working with noted historian Dennis Brindell Fradin, McCurdy has also illustrated *The Signers: The Fifty-six Stories behind the Declaration of Independence* and *The Founders: The Thirty-nine Stories behind the U.S. Constitution.* Reviewing *The Signers,* Heather E. Miller noted in *School Library Journal* that McCurdy's scratchboard illustrations "reinforce the historical tone of the text," and Wilborn Hampton wrote in the *New York Times Book Review* that the book's "fine woodcuts not only put a face to the name but illustrate a key event in each life." In *The Founders* "Fradin and McCurdy have produced another compelling collective biography," asserted GraceAnne A. DeCandido in her *Booklist* review, and a *Kirkus Reviews* writer maintained that the book's "excellent black-and-white scratchboard illustrations are a perfect complement to the text."

McCurdy adapted a nineteenth-century sea chantey in *The Sailor's Alphabet,* an abecedarian that a *New York Times Book Review* critic described as "as rich in emotion as it is in detail." Kathleen Karr, writing in the *Washington Post Book World,* had further praise for *The Sailor's Alphabet,* noting that McCurdy illustrates this alphabet story seen through the eyes of a young cabin boy with "tremendous good humor and charm." Another A-to-Z offering, *Walden Then and Now: An Alphabetical Tour of Henry Thoreau's Pond,* prompted Frances E. Millhouser to describe McCurdy's art as "elegiac," adding that the author/artist enhances the book with a text explaining the "differences between a New England life in the 1840s and 1850s and today."

Among his many illustration projects, McCurdy can count many well-known children's writers among his credits. For B.A. King's *The Very Best Christmas Tree,* he contributed "detailed" wood engravings that "add charm" to the holiday story, according to Elizabeth M. Simmons in *School Library Journal.* McCurdy has illustrated several other works celebrating holidays and special times of the year. In illustrating the words of Louisa May Alcott in *An Old-Fashioned Thanksgiving,* for example, he created "arresting" colored woodcut

McCurdy's self-illustrated picture book **Walden Then and Now** *takes readers on an A-to-Z tour of the world of nineteenth-century American thinker Henry Thoreau.* (Illustration copyright © 2010 by Michael McCurdy. Reproduced by permission of Charlesbridge Publishing, Inc.)

artwork, as Cynthia Bishop commented in *School Library Journal.* Another work containing McCurdy's well-received scratchboard illustrations is *The Seasons Sewn: A Year in Patchwork* by Ann Whitford Paul. Here his "well-composed pictures, reminiscent of the work of Currier and Ives," take the form of quilt squares depicting early-American frontier life, according to *Booklist* critic Carolyn Phelan. Noel Perrin, writing in the *New York Times Book Review,* deemed *The Seasons Sewn* to be "one of [McCurdy's] masterpieces."

Working again with Kennedy, McCurdy provided artwork for a poetic version of the Christmas story titled *The Beasts of Bethlehem,* which finds nineteen animals in the manger at the time of Jesus' birth. In *Booklist,* Kathryn Broderick noted that the volume's combination of "outstanding verse and visuals . . . results in a truly stunning interpretation," while a *Horn Book* critic wrote that the artist's "highly accomplished scratchboard and colored-pencil drawings . . . serve to broaden the appeal of this special collection." Donald Hall's *Lucy's Christmas* and *Lucy's Summer,* both set in early twentieth-century New Hampshire, recall the childhood of Hall's mother, Lucy Wells. Kay Weisman, reviewing *Lucy's Summer* for *Booklist,* remarked that McCurdy's pictures "are suited to the nostalgic flavor of the text and feature many period details," and Jane Marino noted in *School Library Journal* that the "cozy, comfortable artwork" in *Lucy's Christmas* "is filled with light and color."

Other creative collaborations include working with Neil Philip on two collections of verse and stories about America. In *Singing America: Poems That Define a Nation* "the strength and clarity of McCurdy's woodcuts intensify" the idea that the country can be defined by certain poetry, according to Renee Steinberg in *School Library Journal.* McCurdy's artwork accompanies verses from writers such as Walt Whitman and Woody Guthrie in this collection, and *Booklist* critic Hazel Rochman maintained that his woodcuts "extend the energy and individuality of the[se] words." In *American Fairy Tales: From Rip Van Winkle to the Rootabaga Stories* Philips collects a dozen stories that represent the collective voice of America. In *Booklist* Karen Morgan wrote that McCurdy's images here "give the stories a sense of the past yet still allow plenty of room for fantasy," while *Horn Book* critic Mary M. Burns concluded that the "forceful" woodcuts in *American Fairy Tales* "capture the brash spirit of a newly minted country."

Working with Mary Pope Osborne, McCurdy illustrated American stories of a different sort in *American Tall Tales,* a "strikingly handsome" book, according to Luann Toth in *School Library Journal.* Here tales about Pecos Bill, Paul Bunyan, and Johnny Appleseed are captured in "intricate wood engravings" that are tinted with watercolor [to] equal their tall task," as Toth further commented. Liz Rosenberg, writing for *Parents,* dubbed the engraved images "just right," and Rochman

McCurdy's illustration projects include creating the art for Diana Appelbaum's historical story in **Giants in the Land.** (Illustration copyright © 1993 by Michael McCurdy. Reprinted by permission of Houghton Mifflin Harcourt Publishing Company. All rights reserved.)

wrote that McCurdy's "handsome color woodcuts are full of the exaggerated action and comedy of the stories."

McCurdy covers Native-American tales in several of his illustration projects. *The Bone Man: A Native American Modoc Tale* by Laura Simms is a coming-of-age story about Nulwee, a young Modoc boy who must live up to his grandmother's prediction of his future heroism. *How Glooskap Outwits the Ice Giants, and Other Tales of the Maritime Indians* is a retelling of Maritime Indian tales by Howard Norman that benefits from "vigorous woodcut illustrations," according to Denise Anton Wright in *School Library Journal. An Algonquian Year: The Year according to the Full Moon* traces the moon cycles observed by the Algonquian tribes who lived, during precolonial times, in what would one day become New England and southern Canada. "A beautiful book," exclaimed Sean George in his *School Library Journal* review of *An Algonquian Year,* while Linda Perkins wrote in *Booklist* that McCurdy's work "portrays the Algonquians with great dignity." A *Kirkus Reviews* contributor pointed out the "hieratic power" of the same book's scratchboard illustrations, and a re-

viewer for *Publishers Weekly* commented that "the clean, elegant lines of McCurdy's informative prose echo the bold cross-hatching and linear detail of his artwork."

More factual history is served up in Diana Applebaum's *Giants in the Land,* which tells of the destruction of the giant evergreens of New England. Writing in *Booklist,* Rochman asserted of this work that McCurdy's illustrations "capture the sweep and detail of the landscape" as well as "the anguish of the tree felling." The Native American perspective on the construction of the transcontinental railroad is portrayed in Verla Kay's *Iron Horses,* a book in which "excellent" illustrations by McCurdy "offer vivid images that add to the drama," as Steven Engelfried commented in *School Library Journal.* A contributor for *Publishers Weekly* also had positive words for McCurdy's scratchboard-and-watercolor art for Kay's text, noting that its "stark beauty has the feeling of old-fashioned woodcuts." A *Horn Book* reviewer deemed the illustrations for *Iron Horses* to be "eloquent."

Biographical and Critical Sources

BOOKS

McCurdy, Michael, *Toward the Light: Wood Engravings by Michael McCurdy,* Porcupine's Quill (Erin, Ontario, Canada), 1982.

PERIODICALS

American Artist, August, 1984, Eunice Agar, "Michael McCurdy's Penmaen Press," pp. 42-46, 86-87.

Booklist, October 1, 1989, review of *Hannah's Farm: The Seasons on an Early American Homestead,* p. 360; March 15, 1992, Hazel Rochman, review of *American Tall Tales,* p. 1352; September 15, 1992, Kathryn Broderick, review of *The Beast of Bethlehem,* p. 146; October 1, 1993, Hazel Rochman, review of *Giants in the Land,* p. 341; November 15, 1993, Carolyn Phelan, review of *The Way West: Journal of a Pioneer Woman,* p. 618; February 15, 1994, Hazel Rochman, review of *Escape from Slavery: The Boyhood of Frederick Douglass in His Own Words,* p. 1076; August, 1994, Carolyn Phelan, review of *Lucy's Christmas,* p. 2051; April 15, 1995, Kay Weisman, review of *Lucy's Summer,* pp. 1505-1506; June 1, 1995, Hazel Rochman, review of *Singing America: Poems That Define a Nation,* p. 1746; October 15, 1995, Carolyn Phelan, review of *The Gettysburg Address,* p. 400; April 1, 1996, Carolyn Phelan, review of *The Seasons Sewn: A Year in Patchwork,* p. 1358; December 15, 1996; Karen Morgan, review of *American Fairy Tales: From Rip Van Winkle to the Rootabaga Stories,* p. 721; September 15, 1997, Susan Dove Lempke, review of *Trapped by the Ice!: Shackleton's Amazing Antarctic Adventure,* pp. 232-233; November 1, 1997, Karen Morgan, re-

view of *The Bone Man: A Native American Modoc Tale,* p. 469; April 15, 1998, review of *The Sailor's Alphabet,* p. 1443; June 1, 1999, Hazel Rochman, review of *Iron Horses,* p. 1842; November 1, 2000, Linda Perkins, review of *An Algonquian Year: The Year according to the Full Moon,* p. 533; April 15, 2002, Carolyn Phelan, review of *Take Command, Captain Farragut!,* p. 1400; December 1, 2002, Carolyn Phelan, review of *The Signers: The Fifty-six Stories behind the Declaration of Independence,* pp. 658-659.

Bulletin of Center for Children's Books, January, 1988, Betsy Hearne, review of *The Devils Who Learned to Be Good,* p. 96; September, 1997, Deborah Stevenson, review of *Trapped by the Ice!,* pp. 18-19; August, 2005, review of *Tales of Terror,* p. 2016; October 15, 2005, GraceAnne A. DeCandido, review of *The Founders: The Thirty-nine Stories behind the U.S. Constitution,* p. 45; January 1, 2006, Gillian Engberg, review of *Knee Deep in Blazing Snow: Growing up in Vermont,* p. 89; December 1, 2007, John Peters, review of *So Said Ben,* p. 38; September 1, 2010, Hazel Rochman, review of *Walden Then and Now: An Alphabetical Tour of Henry Thoreau's Pond,* p. 91.

Childhood Education, summer, 1994, Charles J. Blume, review of *Escape from Slavery,* p. 250.

Horn Book, February, 1976, review of *Founding Mothers: Women in America in the Revolutionary Era;* November-December, 1984, review of *The Very Best Christmas Tree,* pp. 744; January-February, 1988, Mary M. Burns, review of *The Devils Who Learned to Be Good,* p. 77; July, 1992, Carolyn Phelan, review of *The Old Man and the Fiddle,* p. 1944; November-December, 1992, review of *The Beast of Bethlehem,* pp. 771-771; September-October, 1993, Margaret A. Bush, review of *The Way West,* p. 624; January-February, 1994, Ellen Fader, review of *Giants in the Land,* pp. 83-84; September-October, 1994, Lois F. Anderson, review of *Escape from Slavery,* p. 607; November-December, 1994, Elizabeth S. Watson, review of *Lucy's Christmas,* p. 711; May-June, 1995, Nancy Vasilakis, review of *Lucy's Summer,* pp. 324-325; November-December, 1995, Mary M. Burns, review of *The Gettysburg Address,* p. 756-757; January-February, 1996, Robert D. Hale, "Musings," pp. 115-116; January-February, 1997, review of *American Fairy Tales,* pp. 66-67; January-February, 1998, Susan P. Bloom, review of *The Bone Man,* p. 84; July, 1999, review of *Iron Horses,* p. 456.

Kirkus Reviews, September 1, 1987, review of *The Devils Who Learned to Be Good,* p. 1323; October 1, 1988, review of *Hannah's Farm,* p. 1471; June 15, 1992, review of *The Old Man and the Fiddle,* p. 781; June 15, 2000, review of *An Algonquian Year,* p. 889; November 1, 2002, review of *The Signers,* p. 1611; July 15, 2005, review of *The Founders*; June 15, 2010, review of *Walden Then and Now.*

New York Times Book Review, November 2, 1986, review of *The Owl-Scatterer,* p. 38; November 15, 1987, Tom Miller, review of *A Beautiful, Cruel Country,* p. 27; December 13, 1987, Barbara Thompson, review of *The Devils Who Learned to Be Good,* p. 37; February 26, 1989, review of *Hannah's Farm,* p. 22; November

10, 1996, Noel Perrin, review of *The Seasons Sewn,* p. 48; February 15, 1998, Rebecca Pepper Sinkler, review of *Trapped by the Ice!,* p. 25; July 19, 1998, Susan Bolotin, review of *The Sailor's Alphabet,* p. 25; June 15, 2000, review of *An Algonquian Year;* November 12, 2000, Stephen Amidon, review of *Something Special,* p. 26; September 29, 2002, Wilborn Hampton, review of *The Signers,* p. 26.

Parents, July, 1992, Liz Rosenberg, review of *American Tall Tales,* p. 154.

Publishers Weekly, April 25, 1986, review of *The Illustrated Harvard,* p. 62; November 13, 1987, review of *The Devils Who Learned to Be Good,* p. 70; December, 1991, review of *American Tall Tales,* p. 62; June 8, 1992, review of *The Old Man and the Fiddle,* p. 62; September 7, 1992, review of *The Beasts of Bethlehem,* p. 69; August 2, 1993, review of *Giants in the Land,* pp. 81-82; November 1, 1993, review of *The Way West,* p. 79; February 7, 1994, review of *Escape from Slavery,* p. 89; September 19, 1994, review of *Lucy's Christmas,* p. 31; April 10, 1995, review of *Lucy's Summer,* p. 62; August 7, 1995, review of *The Gettysburg Address,* p. 459; July 7, 1997, review of *Trapped by the Ice!,* p. 68; March 30, 1998, review of *Sailor's Alphabet,* p. 80; June 21, 1999, review of *Iron Horses,* p. 67, June 21, 1999, review of *Iron Horses,* p. 67; June 21, 1999, review of *Tarzan,* p. 68; July 26, 1999, review of *The Way West,* p. 93; September 27, 1999, review of *Christmas Present,* p. 62; March 27, 2000, review of *Giants in the Land,* p. 83; September 25, 2000, review of *An Algonquian Year,* p. 117; May 20, 2002, review of *Take Command, Captain Farragut!,* p. 70; June 9, 2003, review of *The Train They Call the City of New Orleans,* p. 51.

School Library Journal, March, 1985, Elizabeth M. Simmons, review of *The Very Best Christmas Tree,* p. 154; November, 1986, Constance A. Mellon, review of *The Owl-Scatterer,* p. 81; February, 1989, Shirley Wilton, review of *Hannah's Farm,* p. 74; October, 1989, Cynthia Bishop, review of *An Old Fashioned Thanksgiving,* pp. 110-112; January, 1990, Denise Anton Wright, review of *How Glooskap Outwits the Ice Giants, and Other Tales of the Maritime Indians,* p. 97; December, 1991, Luann Toth, review of *American Tall Tales,* pp. 125-126; August, 1992, Patricia Dooley, review of *The Old Man and the Fiddle,* p. 143; September, 1993, Martha Rosen, review of *The Way West,* pp. 243-244; November, 1993, Steve Matthews, review of *Giants in the Land,* p. 96; October, 1994, Jane Marino, review of *Lucy's Christmas,* p. 40; July, 1995, Corinne Camarata, review of *Lucy's Summer,* p. 62; September, 1995, Wendy Lukehart, review of *The Gettysburg Address,* p. 195, Renee Steinberg, review of *Singing America,* p. 228; May, 1996, Darcy Schild, review of *The Seasons Sewn,* p. 125; November, 1997, Barbara Elleman, review of *The Bone Man,* p. 112; September, 1998, Herman Sutter, review of *War and the Pity of War,* p. 224; July, 1999, Steven Engelfried, review of *Iron Horses,* p. 74; September, 1999, Sue Sherif, review of *Tarzan,* pp. 203-204; December, 2000, Sean George, review of *An Algonquian Year,* p. 134; April, 2002, Carolyn Janssen, review of *Take Command, Captain Farragut!,* p. 140; November, 2002, Heather E. Miller, review of *The Signers,* p. 186.

Washington Post Book World, March 1, 1998, Kathleen Karr, review of *The Sailor's Alphabet,* p. 11; October, 2003, review of *The Signers;* September, 2005, Linda Beck, review of *The Founders,* p. 222; November, 2005, Kirsten Cutler, review of *Knee Deep in Blazing Snow,* p. 162; January, 2008, Jayne Damron, review of *So Said Ben,* p. 106; September, 2010, Frances E. Millhouser, review of *Walden Then and Now,* p. 175.

ONLINE

Michael McCurdy Home Page, http://www.michaelmccurdy.com (December 29, 2011).*

*   *   *

McCURDY, Michael Charles
See McCURDY, Michael

*   *   *

MEHLING, Carl 1969(?)-

Personal

Born c. 1969, in New York, NY; married Fiona Brady (a promotions coordinator), June 26, 1999. *Education:* University of California Santa Cruz, B.A. (paleontology and art), 1993. *Hobbies and other interests:* Fossil hunting, foraging for native foods.

Addresses

Home—Bronx, NY. *Office*—American Museum of Natural History, Central Park W. at 79th St., New York, NY 10024-5192. *E-mail*—cosm@amnh.org.

Career

Scientist, author, and editor. American Museum of Natural History, New York, NY, volunteer, 1990-95, assistant, now senior scientific assistant and manager of fossil amphibian, reptile, and bird collection, beginning 1995.

Writings

Would a Dinosaur Eat My Teacher?, Kidsbooks, Inc. (New York, NY), 2001.

(With Andra Serlin Abramson and Jason Brougham) *Inside Dinosaurs,* illustrated by Brougham, Sterling Innovation (New York, NY), 2010.

General editor of reference books, including *Fossils,* Thunder Bay Press (San Diego, CA), 2007, and *Encyclopedia of Dinosaurs,* Transatlantic Press, 2009. Contributor to periodicals, including *American Paleontologist, The Mosasaur,* and *Natural History.*

EDITOR; "DISCOVERING DINOSAURS" SERIES

Armored Dinosaurs, Windmill Press, 2010.
Giant Plant-eating Dinosaurs, Windmill Press, 2010.
Horned, Spiked, and Crested Dinosaurs, Windmill Press, 2010.

Sidelights

Paleontologist Carl Mehling poses an intriguing question in *Would a Dinosaur Eat My Teacher?,* a provocatively titled picture book that he wrote for young dinosaur fans. A member of the staff at New York City's American Museum of Natural History since 1995, Mehling credits the museum with inspiring his career; while earning his degree at the University of California at Santa Cruz he returned to the east coast as a museum volunteer each summer. Now he leads tours and oversees part of the museum's fossil holdings, which includes the world's largest collection of dinosaur fossils. "I'm interested in all aspects of paleontology, especially the fringe areas that normally get little attention . . . ," explained Mehling on the museum's Web site. "I'll also happily collect anything fossil, anywhere in the rock record."

Apart from *Would a Dinosaur Eat My Teacher?,* Mehling has written several technical papers during his long career, as well as working with other writers on informational books in which he can share his fascination for paleontology with both children and adults. In editing the "Discovering Dinosaurs" books, he helps introduce three different dinosaur "types": *Armored Dinosaurs, Horned, Spiked and Crested Dinosaurs,* and *Giant Plant-eating Dinosaurs. Inside Dinosaurs,* a book Mehling coauthored with Andra Serlin Abramson and museum illustrator Jason Brougham, "is sure to fascinate future paleontologists" with its collection of "riveting details and awesome art," according to *School Library Journal* contributor Heather Acerro, while in *Science Scope* David Gillam noted the inclusion of foldout illustrations, helpful charts and graphs, and a fact-filled text that provides children with "an inside look at the tools of science." "Middle-level readers will return to [*Inside Dinosaurs*] . . . again and again for more details," Gillam predicted.

Biographical and Critical Sources

PERIODICALS

Natural History, May, 2005, Carl Mehling, "The Past Recaptured, Again," p. 78; September, 2005, profile of Mehling, p. 61.
Popular Mechanics, May, 2011, Erin McCarthy, "This Is My Job," p. 156.
School Library Journal, August, 2010, Patricia Manning, reviews of *Armored Dinosaurs, Giant Plant-eating Dinosaurs,* and *Horned, Spiked, and Crested Dinosaurs,* all p. 121; December, 2010, Heather Acerro, review of *Inside Dinosaurs,* p. 133.

Science Scope, April-May, 2011, David Gillam, review of *Inside Dinosaurs,* p. 68.

ONLINE

American Museum of Natural History Web site, http://research.amnh.org/ (December 13, 2011), "Carl Mehling."

*   *   *

MOORE, Sean L. 1976-

Personal

Born 1976, in Toronto, Ontario, Canada. *Education:* Sheridan College, B.A. (classical animation), 1998.

Addresses

Home—Vancouver, British Columbia, Canada. *E-mail*—seanlmoore@shaw.ca.

Career

Illustrator/author and character designer. Creative productions include *Mission Hill, Atomic Betty, Being Ian, Something Else, Class of the Titans,* and *Kid vs. Kat. Exhibitions:* Work exhibited at Cummer Museum of Art & Gardens, Jacksonville, FL.

Awards, Honors

Distinguished Achievement Award finalist, Association of Educational Publishers, 2009; Chocolate Lily Award nomination in picture-book category, 2011, for *Where Are You Bear?* by Frieda Wishinsky.

Writings

SELF-ILLUSTRATED

Always Run up the Stairs, Simply Read Books (Vancouver, British Columbia, Canada), 2003.
Veggies Smeggies, Simply Read Books (Vancouver, British Columbia, Canada), 2006.
(Self-illustrated) *Yellow Blues,* Raincoast Books (Berkeley, CA), 2008.
Doggy Bag, Benjamin Brown Books (Vancouver, British Columbia, Canada), 2009.

Contributor to periodicals, including *Chirp.*

ILLUSTRATOR

Frieda Wishinsky, *Where Are You, Bear?: A Canadian Alphabet Adventure,* Owlkids (Toronto, Ontario, Canada), 2010.

Contributor to periodicals, including *ChickaDee* and *Chirp.*

Sidelights

Born and raised in Toronto but now living in Vancouver, Canadian illustrator and character designer Sean L. Moore has found his brightly colored, animation-style art to be a good fit with children's picture books. Inspired by his fascination for Jim Henson's Muppet characters while growing up, Moore earned a degree in classical animation at Sheridan College, then worked as a character designer for animated television programs. In addition to creating original self-illustrated stories such as *Veggies Smeggies, Yellow Blues,* and *Doggie Bag,* Moore has also created the artwork for Frieda Wishinsky's *Where Are You, Bear?: A Canadian Alphabet Adventure.*

In *Yellow Blues* Moore introduces a little girl named Jane, who dreams of splashing around in puddles in a pair of bright yellow boots. Because her parents do not take the hint and treat their daughter to a trip to the shoe store, Jane comes down with a case of the "yellow blues" and her problem ultimately resolves itself in Moore's rhyming text. Praising Moore as "an accomplished artist," Carol L. Mackay added in *Quill & Quire* that the animation-style images in *Yellow Blues* "have style and visual appeal," and *Canadian Review of Materials* critic Devon Greyson wrote that the author/illustrator's "animation background shines in his spunky main character and whimsical bits of action hidden in the pictures."

Sean L. Moore's illustration projects include creating the art for Frieda Wishinsky's Where Are You Bear: A Canadian Alphabet Adventure.
(Illustration copyright © 2010 by Sean L. Moore. Reproduced by permission of Owl Kids, Inc.)

With a text by Wishinsky, *Where Are You, Bear?* focuses on a little girl who is unable to find her favorite stuffed bear in time to bring him along on a family road trip across Canada. When Bear realizes that he has been left behind, he sets out to find her in a saga that is told A-to-Z style. The story's "bright, cartoonish characters, with their oversized heads and eyes . . . will appeal to the target audience," predicted *Quill & Quire* critic Joanne Findon, while John Dryden cited Moore's "whimsical and folksy" artwork in his *Canadian Review of Materials* review of *Where Are You, Bear?* For *School Library Journal* contributor Sarah Townsend, Moore's "flat, stylized cartoon illustrations will keep young readers engaged," and a *Kirkus Reviews* writer cited the "bright, blocky cartoon illustrations" in *Where Are You, Bear?* as a factor in making the picture book "an absolute must in the Great White North and the [U.S.] border states."

"Always find time to draw for yourself, even if you think you've landed the best gig in the world," Moore advised budding illustrators in an interview with Randall Sly for the *Character Design* Web log. "I firmly believe if you're not drawing or writing everyday for yourself, you're not drawing or writing enough. Even it's utter nonsense, put it down on a post-it."

Biographical and Critical Sources

PERIODICALS

Canadian Review of Materials, June 13, 2008, Devon Greyson, review of *Yellow Blues;* November 19, 2010, John Dryden, review of *Where Are You, Bear?: A Canadian Alphabet Adventure.*
Kirkus Reviews, September 1, 2010, review of *Where Are You, Bear?*
Quill & Quire, June, 2008, Carol L. MacKay, review of *Yellow Blues;* September, 2010, Joanne Findon, review of *Where Are You, Bear?*
School Library Journal, October, 2010, Sarah Townsend, review of *Where Are You, Bear?,* p. 104.

ONLINE

Character Design Web log, http://characterdesignlinks. blogspot.com/ (June, 2009), Randall Sly, interview with Moore.
Sean L. Moore Web log http://www.freshsmoores.blogspot. com (December 29, 2011).*

*　　*　　*

MURPHY, Stuart J. 1942-

Personal

Born 1942, in Rockville, CT; married Nancy Kolanko; children: Randall, Kristin. *Education:* Rhode Island

Stuart J. Murphy (Photograph by Dennis O'Reilly. Courtesy of Stuart J Murphy.)

School of Design, B.F.A., 1964; graduate, Harvard Business School management program. *Hobbies and other interests:* Sketching, Italian language.

Addresses

Home—Boston, MA; Tuscany, Italy. *E-mail*—stuart@ stuartjmurphy.com.

Career

Education research consultant and author of children's books. *The Art Gallery* (magazine), art director, 1964-67; Ginn & Company (educational publishers), designer and art director, 1967-80; Ligature, Inc. (educational research and development firm), co-founder and president, 1980-92; freelance writer, consultant, and lecturer, beginning 1992. Member of board of trustees, Rhode Island School of Design; member of committees on museum education for Art Institute of Chicago and Harvard University Graduate School of Education arts advisory council; member of board of governors, Northwestern University Library Council.

Awards, Honors

Xerox Social Service Leave, 1973; Mary Alexander Award, Chicago Book Clinic, 1992; W.A. Dwiggins Award, Bookbuilder of Boston, 1993; Top-Ten Nonfiction Series for Young Children listee, *Booklist*, 1999, for "MathStart" series; Bank Street College of Education Best Children's Book of the Year designation, 2003, for *Slugger's Car Wash* illustrated by Barne Saltzberg; Oppenheim Toy Portfolio Gold Seal, and *Science Books and Film* Best Book designation, both 2004, both for *Less than Zero* illustrated by Frank Remkiewicz.

Writings

"MATHSTART" SERIES

The Best Bug Parade, illustrated by Holly Keller, HarperCollins (New York, NY), 1996.

Give Me Half!, illustrated by G. Brian Karas, HarperCollins (New York, NY), 1996.

Ready, Set, Hop!, illustrated by Jon Buller, HarperCollins (New York, NY), 1996.

A Pair of Socks, illustrated by Lois Elhert, HarperCollins (New York, NY), 1996.

Get up and Go!, illustrated by Diane Greenseid, HarperCollins (New York, NY), 1996.

Too Many Kangaroo Things to Do!, illustrated by Kevin O'Malley, HarperCollins (New York, NY), 1996.

The Best Vacation Ever, illustrated by Nadine Bernard Westcott, HarperCollins (New York, NY), 1997.

Divide and Ride, illustrated by George Ulrich, HarperCollins (New York, NY), 1997.

Every Buddy Counts, illustrated by Fiona Dunbar, HarperCollins (New York, NY), 1997.

Betcha!, illustrated by S.D. Schindler, HarperCollins (New York, NY), 1997.

Elevator Magic, illustrated by G. Brian Karas, HarperCollins (New York, NY), 1997.

Just Enough Carrots, illustrated by Frank Remkiewicz, HarperCollins (New York, NY), 1997.

Lemonade for Sale, illustrated by Tricia Tusa, HarperCollins (New York, NY), 1998.

Circus Shapes, illustrated by Edward Miller, HarperCollins (New York, NY), 1998.

A Fair Bear Share, illustrated by John Speirs, HarperCollins (New York, NY), 1998.

The Greatest Gymnast of All, HarperCollins (New York, NY), 1998.

Animals on Board, HarperCollins (New York, NY), 1998.

The Penny Pot, HarperCollins (New York, NY), 1998.

Henry the Fourth, illustrated by Scott Nash, HarperCollins (New York, NY), 1999.

Jump, Kangaroo, Jump!, illustrated by Kevin O'Malley, HarperCollins (New York, NY), 1999.

Super Sand Castle Saturday, illustrated by Julia Gorton, HarperCollins (New York, NY), 1999.

Rabbit's Pajama Party, HarperCollins (New York, NY), 1999.

Spunky Monkeys on Parade, HarperCollins (New York, NY), 1999.

Room for Ripley, HarperCollins (New York, NY), 1999.

Beep Beep, Vroom Vroom, HarperCollins (New York, NY), 2000.

Pepper's Journal, HarperCollins (New York, NY), 2000.

Dave's Down-to-Earth Rock Shop, HarperCollins (New York, NY), 2000.

Game Time, HarperCollins (New York, NY), 2000.

Let's Fly a Kite, HarperCollins (New York, NY), 2000.

Monster Musical Chairs, HarperCollins (New York, NY), 2000.

Captain Invincible and the Space Shapes, illustrated by Remy Simard, HarperCollins (New York, NY), 2001.

Dinosaur Deals, illustrated by Kevin O'Malley, HarperCollins (New York, NY), 2001.

Missing Mittens, illustrated by G. Brian Karas, HarperCollins (New York, NY), 2001.

Probably Pistachio, illustrated by Marsha Winborn, HarperCollins (New York, NY), 2001.

Seaweed Soup, HarperCollins (New York, NY), 2001.

The Shark Swimathon, HarperCollins (New York, NY), 2001.

Bigger, Better, Best!, illustrated by Marsha Winborn, HarperCollins (New York, NY), 2002.

Bug Dance, illustrated by Christopher Santoro, HarperCollins (New York, NY), 2002.

One—Two—Three—Sassafrass!, illustrated by John Wallace, HarperCollins (New York, NY), 2002.

Racing Around, illustrated by Mike Reed, HarperCollins (New York, NY), 2002.

Safari Park, illustrated by Steve Björkman, HarperCollins (New York, NY), 2002.

Sluggers' Car Wash, illustrated by Barney Saltzberg, HarperCollins (New York, NY), 2002.

Three Little Firefighters, illustrated by Bernice Lum, HarperCollins (New York, NY), 2003.

Coyotes All Around, illustrated by Steve Björkman, HarperCollins (New York, NY), 2003.

Double the Ducks, illustrated by Valerie Petrone, HarperCollins (New York, NY), 2003.

The Grizzly Gazette, illustrated by Steve Björkman, HarperCollins (New York, NY), 2003.

Less than Zero, illustrated by Frank Remkiewicz, HarperCollins (New York, NY), 2003.

The Sundae Scoop, illustrated by Cynthia Jabar, HarperCollins (New York, NY), 2003.

100 Days of Cool, illustrated by John Bendall-Brunello, HarperCollins (New York, NY), 2004.

Earth Day-Hooray!, illustrated by Renee Andriani, HarperCollins (New York, NY), 2004.

A House for Birdie, illustrated by Edward Miller, HarperCollins (New York, NY), 2004.

Mighty Maddie, illustrated by Bernice Lum, HarperCollins (New York, NY), 2004.

Tally O'Malley, illustrated by Cynthia Jabar, HarperCollins (New York, NY), 2004.

Treasure Map, illustrated by Tricia Tusa, HarperCollins (New York, NY), 2004.

Same Old Horse, illustrated by Steve Björkman, HarperCollins (New York, NY), 2005.

Hamster Champs, illustrated by Pedro Martin, HarperCollins (New York, NY), 2005.

It's about Time!, illustrated by John Speirs, HarperCollins (New York, NY), 2005.

Leaping Lizards, illustrated by JoAnn Adinolfi, HarperCollins (New York, NY), 2005.

More or Less, illustrated by David T. Wenzel, HarperCollins (New York, NY), 2005.

Polly's Pen Pal, illustrated by Rémy Simard, HarperCollins (New York, NY), 2005.

Jack the Builder, illustrated by Michael Rex, HarperCollins (New York, NY), 2006.

Mall Mania, illustrated by Renee Andriani, HarperCollins (New York, NY), 2006.

Rodeo Time, illustrated by David T. Wenzel, HarperCollins (New York, NY), 2006.

"I SEE I LEARN" SERIES; ILLUSTRATED BY TIM JONES

Emma's Friendwich, Charlesbridge (Watertown, MA), 2010.

Freda Plans a Picnic, Charlesbridge (Watertown, MA), 2010.

Good Job, Ajay!, Charlesbridge (Watertown, MA), 2010.

Percy Plays It Safe, Charlesbridge (Watertown, MA), 2010.

Camille's Team, Charlesbridge (Watertown, MA), 2011.

Freda Is Found, Charlesbridge (Watertown, MA), 2011.

Percy Gets Upset, Charlesbridge (Watertown, MA), 2011.

Write on, Carlos!, Charlesbridge (Watertown, MA), 2011.

Freda Stops a Bully, Charlesbridge (Watertown, MA), 2012.

Happy, Healthy Ajay, Charlesbridge (Watertown, MA), 2012.

Left, Right, Emma!, Charlesbridge (Watertown, MA), 2012.

Percy Listens Up, Charlesbridge (Watertown, MA), 2012.

OTHER

Also author of *Elementary Mathematics*, Silver Burdett Ginn, *Integrated Mathematics 1-3*, McDougal Littel, and *The Fat Firm*, McGraw Hill.

A number of Murphy's works have been published in Spanish.

Sidelights

Stuart J. Murphy is an education consultant whose "MathStart" books have helped kick-start a new approach to teaching math skills. Including dozens of titles, the series presents math concepts such as comparing, counting, matching, sequencing, fractions, adding, and subtracting, among dozens of others, all in the context of an entertaining story. Additionally, Murphy is the creator of the "I See I Learn" series, which focuses on children's social, emotional, and cognitive skills as well as their physical health and safety. Both series incorporate visual cues, such as diagrams, icons, and illustrations, to reinforce their lessons. "I think that most people understand things best when they can see them," Murphy once told *SATA*. "It's often better to draw a map then to try and explain where you're going to meet someone. Family trees help to show how people are related to one another. And graphs are usually the easiest way to demonstrate comparisons between two or more things."

Murphy served a long apprenticeship before inaugurating his popular math series. Graduating from the Rhode Island School of Design in 1964, he served as art director for the magazine *The Art Gallery* for three years before joining textbook publisher Ginn & Company as a designer. In 1971 he became art director for Ginn, a position he held until 1980. In that year Murphy co-founded Ligature, Inc., an educational research and development firm that worked with publishers to conceptualize and prepare high quality books for U.S. schools. During these years he worked on social-studies projects as well as math books.

Combining his background in the visual arts with his work in educational publishing and research, Murphy now began working on the books that would become

"MathStart." He took as his starting point two principles: first, that many kids are visual learners, and second, that people do not study math the same way they experience it. That is to say that while they study mathematics in terms of word problems or operations symbols and numbers, they experience it directly by telling time, quantifying things, keeping score, and hundreds of other real-life situations. Murphy put these two principles together and came up with the concept for his narrative and visual approach to teaching math. When he pitched the idea to HarperCollins, they contracted an initial three, then twenty-four books in the series, ultimately expanding it to sixty-three.

Written on three levels from preschool through second grade and up, "MathStart" deals with beginning math concepts such as counting, comparing, and ordering in Level 1; in Level 2 basic math skills such as adding and subtracting are introduced; and in Level 3 multiplying and dividing are demonstrated. As Ian Elliot noted in *Teaching K-8,* "It's easy to see why Murphy is so successful in getting young children turned on to math." Elliot pointed out the "lively but simple story lines," "delightful illustrations," and "visual representations of the math that's involved."

The first three books in the series were some four years in the making, and covered each of the three levels in the "MathStart" program. *The Best Bug Parade* is aimed at Level 1, while *Give Me Half!* is geared for Level 2 and *Ready, Set, Hop!* for Level 3. *The Best Bug Parade* deals with size comparisons, with a red ladybug parade marshal as a constant referent, while a sibling squabble over pizza is the story line in *Give Me Half!* and two frogs debate their estimated length of leaping distance in *Ready, Set, Hop!* Reviewing the first title in *School Library Journal,* Diane Nunn noted that concepts such as long/short and big/bigger/biggest "are presented by an assortment of cheery insects marching through a colorful environment of flowers and grass," and concluded that "teachers and parents will all find this a useful book, and youngsters will be attracted to the lively il-

Murphy's humorous story in **100 Days of Cool** *comes to life in cartoon art by John Bendall-Brunello.* (Illustration copyright © 2004 by John Bendall-Brunello. Reproduced by permission HarperCollins Children's Books, a division of HarperCollins Publishers.)

lustrations." Reviewing *Give Me Half!*, Carolyn Phelan noted in *Booklist* that Murphy's is "one of the few math concept books with realistic dialogue, authentic emotions, and genuine humor."

While the initial "MathStart" books did not impress all reviewers, critical reception improved as the series continued. Reviewing the next three books in the series—*A Pair of Socks, Get up and Go,* and *Too Many Kangaroo Things to Do*—for *School Library Journal,* Marsha McGrath noted that each "focuses on a simple math concept: matching, time lines, or multiplication." McGrath went on to comment that "Bright hues of acrylic paint and collage are used in the cartoon illustrations," while the end pages provide "helpful hints about using the books to teach additional concepts." In *Booklist* Phelan noted that Murphy's *A Pair of Socks* might be the only picture book story "told from the point of view of a sock." "Short, snappy rhymes and Elhert's brilliantly colored collage illustrations combine to make this tale from the MathStart series an entertaining book," the critic added.

Reviewing *Every Buddy Counts, The Best Vacation Ever,* and *Divide and Ride* for *School Library Journal,* Christine A. Moesch pointed out that their subject matter—counting, collecting data, and dividing—presents students with an "entertaining approach to progressive levels of math concepts." *Booklist* reviewer Hazel Rochman, reviewing the same three books, remarked that "these stories use everyday situations and lively line-and-watercolor illustrations to teach math concepts at various levels of difficulty." Citing *Divide and Ride* as "the most sophisticated in math and story," Rochman predicted that kids "of all ages will be drawn into the story" of how eleven children at the carnival need to divide up into twos and threes and fours for various rides.

Rochman also applauded Murphy's *Betcha!*, calling it "a real winner that will entertain kids with the buddy story and the causal dialogue and with Schindler's bright, active pictures of two boys having fun in the city." Commenting on how the boys in *Betcha!* play at estimating the number of people on the bus as they ride to the city and the number of jellybeans in a window display, a writer for *Kirkus Reviews* noted that all the while readers are introduced to concepts and techniques such as "rounding off and how to count a small number and apply that to the great, uncounted whole through the use of multiplication, fractions, and simple geometry." The same reviewer concluded that "Murphy's success is in beveling the sharp, unforgiving reputation of math and in showing how numbers can be toyed with."

As the "Math Starts" series progresses, Murphy introduces broader math concepts to readers. *Treasure Map,* for example, explores a basic understanding of mapping in a story about a group of kids who find a map leading to a time capsule and must work together to follow the map to its treasure. In *Earth Day-Hooray!* the Save-the-Planet Club hosts a can drive to make money recycling so they can plant flowers in a local park. As Murphy teaches about conservationism and teamwork, he also teaches about sorting and place value. A *Kirkus Reviews* critic declared this book a "marvelous addition to the series," making special note of the "excellent activity suggestions." Kay Weisman wrote in *Booklist* that *Earth Day-Hooray!* would be a "good choice for jazzing up a routine math lesson or as a springboard for Earth Day activities."

Traditional counting concepts provide the basis of both *100 Days of Cool* and *Sluggers' Car Wash. 100 Days of Cool* finds a class of students trying to meet the challenge of staying "cool" for one hundred days. As they come to school in sunglasses, sequins, dyed hair, and other looks, they also decorate their bikes and form volunteer groups. As the days pass, Murphy reinforced counting ideas with a number line and comments from kids about fractions. In *Booklist,* Rochman praised the "lively classroom scenario" and noted that the "play and socializing dramatize the math."

In *Sluggers' Car Wash* a baseball team earns money for new team shirts by holding a car wash. One player, CJ, is in charge of the money, but his teammates make sure he gets as soaked as the rest of them at day's end. As CJ takes customers' money and makes change, readers learn counting and keeping track of sums as the team approaches their goal. Phelan was impressed by the variety of concepts presented in this simple story, commenting in *Booklist,* that learning to make change is a confusing task for many adults. A reviewer for *Kirkus Reviews* also noted that "lots of math/money games can be spun off from this story."

Double the Ducks and *The Sundae Scoop* offer light-hearted stories for young readers ready to tackle the basics of subtraction, multiplication, and combinations. In *Double the Ducks* a young farm boy must feed his five ducks with three bags of food, four bundles of hay, and only two hands. When he discovers that his ducks have invited friends, he realizes he must now feed twice as many ducks. Rochman commented in *Booklist* that this story makes "preschoolers' first steps into addition and multiplication more fun," while a *Kirkus Reviews* writer concluded that "readers will delight in all the fun they're having on the farm while they're learning some new math." *The Sundae Scoop* is about a picnic where a group of kids are making sundaes. The assembled ingredients enable them to make eight kinds of sundaes, but after the sprinkles are spilled, the caramel is tipped, and the chocolate ice cream melts the number of possibilities decreases. "Murphy easily folds the math concepts into a lively story that will capture young readers," wrote Helen Rosenberg in *Booklist,* while a *Kirkus Reviews* critic remarked that the author "plays the concept like a slide trombone," increasing and decreasing the number of sundae possibilities for the picnic.

Captain Invincible and the Space Shapes uses an outer-space setting for a story about three-dimensional shapes.

Murphy teams up with artist Tricia Tusa in the pages of the picture book **Lemonade for Sale.**

Captain Invincible and his dog, Comet, use various objects from their spaceship to solve problems they encounter on their journey through space. According to Shelley Townsend-Hudson in *Booklist,* "The story gives the math lesson an out-of-this-world appeal." Wanda Meyers-Hines concluded in *School Library Journal* that the "reinforcement strategies and activities are very good," and deemed *Captain Invincible and the Space Shapes* a "good choice as a read-aloud or for independent reading."

Murphy offers a primer on angles in *Hamster Champs.* When three hamsters want to play outside their cage, they make a bargain with a pesky housecat: in exchange for some uninterrupted free time, they will steer a toy car over a series of ramps fit for a daredevil. Writing in *Booklist,* Shelle Rosenfeld maintained that "plenty of good-natured banter between the hamsters and the cat helps make the concept clear." In *More or Less* a youngster learns about comparing numbers by guessing people's ages at his school fair. The questioning process

used by the protagonist "leads children into the world of logical, educated guesses," as Ilene Cooper stated in *Booklist.* Similar in nature, *Mighty Maddie* concerns a girl who learns to compare weights while cleaning her room. According to *School Library Journal* reviewer Erlene Bishop Killeen, this work "has uses beyond the math concept, and offers messages about family life, self-image, and responsibility."

Addition is the focus of *Mall Mania.* Wonderful gifts await the 100th person to enter Parkside Mall, and members of a local chess club are on hand to count the individuals who enter the building. As in his other works, Murphy supports the "math lesson by making it seem a part of daily life," commented Hazel Rochman in *Booklist.* In *Rodeo Time* a pair of siblings help their bull-riding uncle stay on schedule during a busy competition. "Math concepts are neatly integrated into the story," Elaine Lesh Morgan observed in her *School Library Journal* review.

Tim Jones created the artwork for Murphy's upbeat story in Emma's **Friendwich.** (Illustration copyright © 2010 by Tim Jones Illustration. Used with permission by Charlesbridge Publishing Inc., 85 Main Street, Watertown, MA 02472, www. charlesbridge.com. All rights reserved.)

The "MathStart" series also has works geared for the very youngest learners, and those titles have earned general praise from reviewers, teachers, and students alike. Reviewing *Circus Shapes, A Fair Bear Share,* and *Lemonade for Sale,* a *Publishers Weekly* contributor praised Murphy's "disarmingly chipper stories" anda writer for *Kirkus Reviews* described *Lemonade for Sale* as a "lively entry" demonstrating the use of bar graphs. The same reviewer called the series "a winning way to make some basic concepts and techniques less intimidating." Reviewing *Henry the Fourth* and *Jump, Kangaroo, Jump!,* *Booklist* critic John Peters wrote that the former has "the more complex story line," but that both follow "a winning formula." Writing in *School Library Journal,* Jane Claes reviewed a further addition to the series, *Super Sand Castle Saturday.* Here "Murphy does a good job of imparting the math lesson while delivering a natural story," Claes noted.

Murphy expounded on his methodology and writing technique in a *Booklist* interview. Noting that "most people don't see math as part of their daily lives," he explained that the driving force behind his "MathStart" series is "to draw kids into a story based on their own experiences sorting socks, rushing to get ready for school, fighting for a fair share of a pizza." His books begin with a concept, and he then searches his mind for a story to fit. "For example, I wanted to do a book on division. I was looking for a model in the daily experiences of children, but I kept coming up with things that were more like fractions. Then I remembered going to the carnival with my kids." At the carnival, Murphy and his children always had the problem of how they were going to divide up to go on rides, and by employing this in his story *Divide and Ride* he provided a very realistic approach to the concept of division.

A trained artist, Murphy also oversees the early versions of artwork for his "Math Starts" books, supplying roughs for the artists to work from. His end-of-the-book suggestions for further reading and extended activities come from his own experiences and are also added to

and checked by teachers in the field. Finally, each title is tested in the field with children's workshops at schools. Murphy remarked that kids in these workshops "end up having so much fun giggling and participating and explaining their work that I almost have to remind them that this is math."

"The 'MathStart' series is designed to help children become more fluent in the language of mathematics, be more comfortable with match concepts, and make math part of their system of communication," Murphy once remarked in *SATA.* "By presenting math concepts in stories, supporting those stories with high-quality illustrations and carefully constructed math diagrams, and providing easy-to-accomplish activities that extend the learning of the story at the end of each book, children will realize that math can be easy—and fun!"

Murphy has expanded his teaching technique into basic skill-building with his "I See I Learn" series, which is "modeled on real-life situations" and reinforces essential skills "such as how to make friends, build confidence, play safely, work together, manage emotions, and make plans," as he noted on his home page. "These skills are important for school readiness and for living happy, healthy, productive lives." Among the "I See I Learn" books are *Emma's Friendwich,* in which a youngster who has just moved into a new house makes friends with her neighbors by sharing her toys. "As in the MathStart titles, Murphy folds his educational points into a warm stand-alone story," *Booklist* reviewer Gillian Engberg noted in reviewing this "I See I Learn" installment.

A group of children learn to pool their talents to successfully construct a sandcastle in *Camille's Team,* and here "Murphy explicates the steps to good cooperation with insets and diagrams and includes some thought-provoking follow-up questions," according to a *Kirkus Reviews* writer. In *Freda Is Found* a girl becomes separated from her classmates while on a field trip. After locating a responsible adult and relaying important information, including the names of her school and teacher, Freda is safely reunited with her friends. A youngster diligently works on his penmanship in *Write on, Carlos!,* another book in Murphy's skill-building series. Discussing both "I See I Learn" books in *Kirkus Reviews,* a critic judged them to be "solid series additions that teach useful skills and the power of practice."

Good Job, Ajay!, a story about building confidence, centers on a boy's efforts to improve his ball-throwing skills. "Key words are bolded within the text, while the concepts are illustrated using insets and diagrams," a *Kirkus Reviews* contributor noted, adding that these qualities enhance all the books in Murphy's "I See I Learn" series.

Biographical and Critical Sources

PERIODICALS

Booklist, May 1, 1996, Carolyn Phelan, review of *Give Me Half!,* p. 1510; October 1, 1996, Carolyn Phelan, re-

view of *A Pair of Socks,* p. 355; February 1, 1997, Hazel Rochman, review of *The Best Vacation Ever,* p. 943; April 1, 1997, interview with Murphy, p. 1347; October 1, 1997, Hazel Rochman, review of *Betcha!,* p. 336; April 15, 1999, John Peters, reviews of *Henry the Fourth* and *Jump, Kangaroo, Jump!,* both p. 1534; November 15, 2001, Shelley Townsend-Hudson, review of *Captain Invincible and the Space Shapes,* p. 578; January 1, 2003, Helen Rosenberg, review of *The Sundae Scoop,* p. 899; February 1, 2003, Carolyn Phelan, review of *Sluggers' Car Wash,* p. 999; March 15, 2003, Hazel Rochman, review of *Double the Ducks,* p. 1328; January 1, 2004, Kay Weisman, review of *Earth Day-Hooray!,* p. 868; April 1, 2004, Hazel Rochman, review of *100 Days of Cool,* p. 1367; September 1, 2004, Lauren Peterson, review of *Treasure Map,* p. 127; February 15, 2005, Ilene Cooper, review of *More or Less,* p. 1081; March 1, 2005, Carolyn Phelan, review of *It's about Time!,* p. 1200; October 15, 2005, Shelle Rosenfeld, review of *Hamster Champs,* p. 51; January 1, 2006, Hazel Rochman, review of *Jack the Builder,* p. 105; February 1, 2006, Hazel Rochman, review of *Mall Mania,* p. 52; March 1, 2006, Todd Morning, review of *Rodeo Time,* p. 96; September 1, 2010, Gillian Engberg, review of *Emma's Friendwich,* p. 112; May 15, 2011, Diane Foote, review of *Camille's Team,* p. 50; March 15, 2011, Stuart J. Murphy, "See and Learn," p. S12.

Bulletin of the Center for Children's Books, May, 1996, Elizabeth Bush, review of *The Best Bug Parade,* p. 310.

Kirkus Reviews, September 15, 1997, review of *Betcha!,* p. 1460; November 15, 1998, review of *Lemonade for Sale,* p. 1711; July 15, 2002, review of *Sluggers' Car Wash,* p. 355; November 15, 2002, review of *The Sundae Scoop,* p. 1700; December 1, 2002, review of *Double the Ducks,* p. 1770; January 1, 2004, review of *100 Days of Cool,* p. 39; January 15, 2004, review of *Earth Day-Hooray!,* p. 87; August 1, 2004, review of *Treasure Map,* p. 746; June 15, 2010, reviews of *Emma's Friendwich, Good Job, Ajay!, Freda Plans a Picnic,* and *Percy Plays It Safe;* January 15, 2011, reviews of *Percy Gets Upset* and *Camille's Team;* June 15, 2011, reviews of *Freda Is Found* and *Write On, Carlos!*

Publishers Weekly, January 19, 1998, review of *Circus Shapes,* pp. 379-380.

School Library Journal, June, 1996, Diane Nunn, review of *The Best Bug Parade,* pp. 106-107; June, 1996, JoAnn Rees, review of *Ready, Set, Hop!,* pp. 117-118; December, 1996, Marsha McGrath, review of *A Pair of Socks,* p. 116; March, 1997, Christine A. Moesch, review of *The Best Vacation Ever,* pp. 179-180; July, 1999, Jane Claes, review of *Super Sand Castle Saturday,* p. 88; October, 2001, Wanda Meyers-Hines, review of *Captain Invincible and the Space Shapes,* p. 144; March, 2004, Gloria Koster, review of *100 Days of Cool,* p. 198; October, 2004, Erlene Bishop Killeen, review of *A House for Birdie* and *Mighty Maddie,* both p. 146; July, 2005, Erlene Bishop Killeen, reviews of *It's about Time!, More or Less,* and *Polly's Pen Pal,* all p. 79; March, 2006, Erlene Bishop Killeen, reviews of *Hamster Champs, Leaping Liz-*

ards, and *Same Old Horse,* all p. 211; October, 2006, Elaine Lesh Morgan, review of *Rodeo Time,* p. 142; August, 2010, Margaret R. Tassia, reviews of *Emma's Friendwich, Freda Plans a Picnic, Good Job, Ajay!,* and *Percy Plays It Safe,* all p. 81.

Teaching K-8, January, 1998, Ian Elliot, "Murphy's Magical MathStart," pp. 43-44.

ONLINE

MathStart Web site, http://www.mathstart.net/ (January 1, 2012).

Stuart J. Murphy Home Page, http://stuartjmurphy.com (January 1, 2012).*

*   *   *

NOTEBOOM, Erin
See BOW, Erin

*   *   *

PERKINS, Mitali 1963-

Personal

Born April 30, 1963, in Calcutta, West Bengal, India; immigrated to United States; daughter of Sailendra Nath (a civil engineer and port director) and Madhusree (a teacher) Bose; married Robert K. Perkins (a Presbyterian minister), August 16, 1986; children: twin sons. *Education:* Stanford University, B.A. (political science), 1984; University of California, Berkeley, M.P.P., 1987. *Religion:* Christian. *Hobbies and other interests:* Tennis, travel, hiking.

Addresses

Home—Newton, MA. *Agent*—Laura Rennert, Andrea Brown Literary Agency; laura@andrearownlit.com. *E-mail*—mitaliperk@yahoo.com.

Career

Writer and educator. World Vision International, technical writer, 1988-91; freelance writer and social media consultant. Pepperdine University, Malibu, CA, visiting professor in international relations; Chiang Mai International School, Thailand, teacher of literature and writing, 1996-98; Saint Mary's College of California, Moraga, instructor, 2011. Presenter at schools.

Member

PEN, Society of Children's Book Writers and Illustrators, Boston Author's Club, readergirlz.

Awards, Honors

Bank Street College Best Book for Children designation, New York Public Library Book for the Teen Age designation, and Texas/TAYSHAS Best Book for Young

Adults designation, all 2004, and American Library Association (ALA) Popular Paperback for Young Adults designation, 2008, all for *Monsoon Summer;* ALA Book for Reluctant Readers designation, and Lamplighter Award, Christian Schools Association, both 2007, both for *The Not-so-Star-Spangled Life of Sunita Sen;* Boston Author's Club Honor Book Award, ALA Amelia Bloomer Project citation, and Lupine Honor Book Award (ME), all 2008, all for *Rickshaw Girl;* Notable Book for a Global Society selection, International Reading Association, Amelia Bloomer Project citation, and Massachusetts Book Award shortlist, all 2009, all for *Secret Keeper.*

Writings

FOR CHILDREN

The Sunita Experiment, Joy Street Books (Boston, MA), 1993, published as *The Not-so-Star-Spangled Life of Sunita Sen,* 2005.
Monsoon Summer, Delacorte Press (New York, NY), 2004.
Rickshaw Girl, illustrated by Jamie Hogan, Charlesbridge (Watertown, MA), 2007.
Secret Keeper, Delacorte Press (New York, NY), 2009.
Bamboo People, Charlesbridge (Watertown, MA), 2010.

"FIRST DAUGHTER" NOVEL SERIES

Extreme American Makeover, Dutton (New York, NY), 2007.
White House Rules, Dutton (New York, NY), 2008.

OTHER

Islam and Christianity, Congregational Ministries/Presbyterian Church U.S.A. (Louisville, KY), 2003.
Ambassador Families: Equipping Your Kids to Engage Popular Culture, Brazos Press (Grand Rapids, MI), 2005.

Contributor of articles to periodicals, including *Campus Life* and *Horn Book.* Member of editorial advisory board, *Kahani* magazine.

Sidelights

Mitali Perkins is the author of young-adult novels that focus on young women coming to terms with their mixed racial and cultural identity. She addresses this topic in her first novel, *The Sunita Experiment*—also published as *The Not-so-Star-Spangled Life of Sunita Sen*—as well as in her other books for teen readers, such as *Monsoon Summer, Secret Keeper,* and the books in her "First Daughter" series. In *Rickshaw Girl,* a picture book, Perkins turns to younger readers, while her nonfiction book *Ambassador Families: Equipping Your Kids to Engage Popular Culture* shares her lifelong experiences alongside parents working to help their children adjust to a new culture.

Perkins was born in Calcutta, India, and her name means "friendly" in Bangla. As a child, she and her family moved frequently due to her father's work as a civil engineer; she spent time in Ghana, Cameroon, England, and Mexico before settling in northern California in time to attend middle school. Perkins' experiences learning to accept the United States as her new home helped inspire *The Sunita Experiment.* Praised as a "gentle coming of age story" by *Voice of Youth Advocates* contributor Mary L. Adams, the novel recounts the year thirteen-year-old Sunni's Indian grandparents come to visit her family in California. Sunni leads a typical American life, complete with sports tryouts, boy trouble, and battles with her parents over clothing and makeup. These battles take a new turn after her tradition-minded grandparents arrive, as the teen gradually realizes that the subtle influence of her Indian heritage sets her apart from her Caucasian friends and classmates. Perkins' "personal experience shows," Karen Ray observed of the novel in the *New York Times Book Review,* the critic concluding that *The Sunita Experiment* contains "genuine insights."

Critics praise the warm humor of Perkins' narrative, which enlivens the troubles Sunni experiences without negating them. The teen's narration is dotted with the exaggerated expressions that typify teen speak, and her "exasperation is real but funny," according to *Bulletin of the Center for Children's Books* contributor Roger Sutton. The transformation of Sunni's mother from blue-jean-clad chemistry instructor to dutiful, sari-draped daughter adds depth to what Sutton dubbed "a perky, upbeat story." Other critics focused on Sunni's altered relationships with her friends, her family, and herself as she begins to perceive herself as both Indian and American. "Perkins refrains from lecturing," wrote Adams, "letting the reader and Sunita work out answers to simple and difficult problems." A *Kirkus Reviews* critic also noted the author's light touch, writing that, "gentle and palatable, the lessons are offered with compassion and easily absorbed insights."

In *Monsoon Summer* Perkins focuses on Jasmine Gardner, a fifteen-year-old half-Indian teen who goes by the name Jazz. When her family leaves California for Pune, India, in the midst of her budding love affair with best friend Steve, Jazz is understandably frustrated. When she arrives in India and begins to help her family in their work setting up a birth clinic in the midst of the rainy season, she finds her sporty all-American persona slipping away in favor of that of a compassionate young woman. Her efforts to help a new friend avoid an arranged marriage also builds the teen's sense of self, as well as her confidence, and the "romance [she] develops even over such a long distance is . . . appealing," in the opinion of *Kliatt* contributor Claire Rosser. Noting that the novel successfully introduces readers to "India's culture and its problems," a *Publishers Weekly* critic added that in *Monsoon Summer* Perkins "sensitively traces an American girl's emotional growth." In *Booklist* Gillian Engberg cited the teen narrator for her "smart, funny, self-deprecating voice," and added that

the novel's focus extends beyond cultural differences. The author's "warm, romantic story . . . shows how the deepest private discoveries often come from very public risks," the critic concluded.

In *Rickshaw Girl,* featuring illustrations by Jamie Hogan, Perkins takes readers to Bangladesh to tell a story about challenging traditions. Ten-year-old Naima is known throughout her rural village for her skill at painting the decorative patterns called *alpanas,* but it is her younger sister's turn to get her basic education, Naima must go to work to help support her family. Because of her village's traditional culture, she must disguise herself as a boy in order to help her father in his job as a rickshaw driver. Although her scheme backfires, the girl ultimately finds a way to allow her to paint and earn money as well. Noting the "lively" nature of Perkins' tale, Rochman wrote that *Rickshaw Girl* "tells a realistic story with surprises that continue until the end." A *Kirkus Reviews* writer also praised the chapter book for presenting "a child-eye's view of Bangladesh that makes a strong and accessible statement about heritage, tradition and the changing role of women." In *Horn Book,* Norah Piehl viewed *Rickshaw*

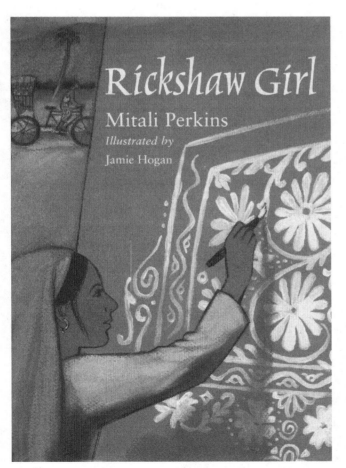

Cover of Mitali Perkins' well-received middle-grade novel **Rickshaw Girl,** *featuring artwork by Jamie Hogan.* (Illustration copyright © 2007 by Jamie Hogan. Used with permission by Charlesbridge Publishing Inc., 85 Main Street, Watertown, MA 02472, www.charlesbridge.com. All rights reserved.)

Girl in a different light, writing that Perkins ties her "vibrant plot to the economic model of microfinance— probably a first for an early chapter book!"

Readers are drawn into the culture of a family living in 1970s India in the young-adult novel *Secret Keeper,* which a *Publishers Weekly* critic described as "a moving portrait about a rebellious teen who relies on ingenuity rather than charm to prove her worth." Sixteen-year-old Asha Gupta and seventeen-year-old sister Reet face a family upheaval when their engineer father moves to the United States to find work. Together with their mother, the sisters must move from Delhi to the Calcutta home of their uncle and his extended family, where they suddenly find themselves in a patriarchal household ruled by tradition. While their mother grows increasingly depressed, Reet becomes the prize in her uncle's search for a suitor of financial means. Since Asha had promised her father that she would look out for her sister, she views her uncle's actions as disloyal, and when the first suitor arrives she vows to derail the courtship. Asha records her observations and feelings in her diary, which comprises the text of Perkins' novel, and through this "secret keeper" she also records her growing affection for Jay, an artistic teen who lives nearby. In *School Library Journal* Monika Schroeder praised *Secret Keeper,* citing its "well-developed characters, funny dialogue, and the authentic depiction of spunky Asha's longing for romance and female self-determination." The experiences of Perkins' heroine "will enlighten and inspire young women, and encourage them to value their own freedom," according to a *Kirkus Reviews* writer, while in *Booklist* Hazel Rochman wrote that the sisters' close relationship and "their mutual sacrifices are both heartbreaking and hopeful."

Perkins focuses on a male protagonist in her novel *Bamboo People,* which finds fifteen-year-old Chiko facing compulsory military service as a resident of Burma (now Myanmar). Soon the bookish teen—whose father is in prison and accused of dissenting with the government—finds himself involved in the government's ethnic war against the Karenni. Wounded, he is discovered by Tu Reh, a Karenni teen who has vowed revenge on the Burmese army since they destroyed his family's home and livelihood as bamboo growers. Recommending *Bamboo People* as a good choice for sparking conversation, Michael Cart noted in *Booklist* that Perkins' novel explores "the realities of warfare rooted in long-standing antagonisms and unreasoning hatred." A "culturally rich coming-of-age novel," according to *School Library Journal* critic Gerry Larson, *Bamboo People* shares a story rich "with authenticity, insight, and compassion," and the story's "universal themes . . . will inspire readers to ponder humanitarian issues." In *Horn Book* Roger Sutton observed that the "differing perspectives" of Chiko and Tu Reh, "as well as their commonalities, make the drama as moral as it is physical," and a *Publishers Weekly* critic deemed *Bamboo People* "a graceful exploration of the redemptive power of love, family and friendship under untenable circumstances."

Cover of Perkins' highly acclaimed young-adult novel Bamboo People, *featuring cover art by Carol Chu.* (Illustration copyright © 201 by Carol Chu. Used with permission by Charlesbridge Publishing Inc., 85 Main Street, Watertown, MA 02472, www.charlesbridge.com. All rights reserved.)

In Perkins' "First Daughter" series readers meet sixteen-year-old Sameera Righton. Adopted from Pakistan at age three, Sameera was raised in a household where politics rules. In *Extreme American Makeover* her father is running for president of the United States, and this puts the teen in the public eye. Members of her father's campaign staff push for her to acquire an all-American look, and soon the teen undergoes a total image reconstruction: wardrobe, hairstyle, posture, Web presence, and all. For Sameera, honesty is most important, however, and she manages to support her father's P.R. presence while also being true to her political viewpoint with the help of a group of South Asian students at her new school. In *White House Rules* readers follow Sameera as she morphs into "daughter of the president," and experiences life in Washington, DC, as a resident of the White House. In *Publishers Weekly* a critic observed that Perkins' teen narrator is "intelligent, witty and prepossessed," adding that *Extreme American Makeover* provides a "lighthearted . . . peek at the behind-the-scenes finessing that goes on in modern politics." "Both the public and private worlds depicted" in the "First Daughter" books "will grab readers," added *Booklist* contributor Hazel Rochman, and in *School Li-*

brary Journal Kathleen E. Gruver wrote that the series successfully conveys "a sense of the demands made on those who are constantly in the public eye."

Even though her academic studies have taken her into the realm of international public policy and a part-time teaching career, reading and writing have continued to be important to Perkins. As a writer, she also visits schools and libraries, talking about her experiences crossing cultures and the power of fiction. In an interview with Laura Atkins for *Paper Tigers* online, she discussed how writing reflects her lifelong goals. "I've always longed to help the poor and the displaced, and to inspire others to do the same . . . ," Perkins explained. "You'll find 'development' themes interwoven into many of my stories." However, she added, "When I write, I don't ask myself: 'Now I'm going to teach THIS political science lesson. . . . Hmm . . . how can I stuff it into a story?'" "I focus on character, place, plot, like most writers. But heartfelt convictions are part of who I am," she admitted, "so they are bound to come out through my writing. At least, I hope so!" "I write . . . to bring some of the excellent values that saturate good children's books from the past into the fiction I publish today," Perkins also once explained to *SATA*. "Books were the ticket as this young immigrant New Yorker journeyed to the four corners, perched on a sixth-story fire escape. I write so that I can help others to fly."

Biographical and Critical Sources

PERIODICALS

Booklist, May 1, 1993, review of *The Sunita Experiment,* p. 1582; June 1, 2004, Gillian Engberg, review of *Monsoon Summer,* p. 1720; November 1, 2006, Hazel Rochman, review of *Rickshaw Girl,* p. 54; May 15, 2007, Hazel Rochman, review of *Extreme American Makeover,* p. 41; February 1, 2008, Ilene Cooper, review of *White House Rules,* p. 40; December 15, 2008, Hazel Rochman, review of *Secret Keeper,* p. 41; May 15, 2010, Michael Cart, review of *Bamboo People,* p. 38.

Bulletin of the Center for Children's Books, September, 1993, Roger Sutton, review of *The Sunita Experiment,* p. 21; May, 2007, Hope Morrison, review of *Rickshaw Girl,* p. 380.

Horn Book, November-December, 2004, Jennifer M. Brabander, review of *Monsoon Summer,* p. 715; May-June, 2007, Norah Piehl, review of *Rickshaw Girl,* p. 288; July-August, 2010, Roger Sutton, review of *Bamboo People,* p. 119.

Kirkus Reviews, May 15, 1993, review of *The Sunita Experiment,* p. 67; July 15, 2004, review of *Monsoon Summer,* p. 692; December 1, 2006, review of *Rickshaw Girl,* p. 1225; May 1, 2007, review of *Extreme American Makeover;* December 15, 2008, review of *Secret Keeper;* June 15, 2010, review of *Bamboo People.*

Kliatt, July, 1994, review of *The Sunita Experiment,* p. 11; July, 2004, Claire Rosser, review of *Monsoon Summer,* p. 12; January, 2008, Claire Rosser, review of *White House Rules,* p. 12.

Los Angeles Times Book Review, June 20, 1993, review of *The Sunita Experiment,* p. 3.

New York Times Book Review, June 27, 1993, Karen Ray, review of *The Sunita Experiment,* p. 21.

Publishers Weekly, May 24, 1993, review of *The Sunita Experiment,* p. 88; August 23, 2004, review of *Monsoon Summer,* p. 55; June 25, 2007, review of *Extreme American Makeover,* p. 61; November 17, 2008, review of *Secret Keeper,* p. 58; June 14, 2010, review of *Bamboo People,* p. 53.

School Library Journal, June, 1993, review of *The Sunita Experiment,* p. 132; September, 2004, Kathleen Isaacs, review of *Monsoon Summer,* p. 215; April, 2007, Susan Hepler, review of *Rickshaw Girl,* p. 115; June, 2007, Kathleen E. Gruver, review of *Extreme American Makeover,* p. 157; February, 2008, Catherine Ensley, review of *White House Rules,* p. 126; March, 2009, Monika Schroeder, review of *Secret Keeper,* p. 150; November, 2010, Gerry Larson, review of *Bamboo People,* p. 124.

Voice of Youth Advocates, October, 1993, Mary L. Adams, review of *The Sunita Experiment,* p. 218; August, 1997, review of *The Sunita Experiment,* p. 173; August, 2007, Ava Donaldson, review of *Extreme American Makeover,* p. 248.

ONLINE

Cynsations Web log, http://cynthialeitichsmith.blogspot.com/ (June 5, 2008), Cynthia Leitich Smith, interview with Perkins.

Mitali Perkins Home Page, http://www.mitaliperkins.com (December 26, 2011).

Mitali Perkins Web log, http://www.mitaliblog.com (December 26, 2011).

Paper Tigers Web site, http://www.papertigers.org/ (July 1, 2005), Laura Atkins, interview with Perkins.*

*   *   *

PHAM, LeUyen 1973-

Personal

First name pronounced "Le-Win"; born September 7, 1973, in Saigon, Vietnam; daughter of Phong T. and LeHuong Pham; immigrated to United States; married Alexandre Puvilland (an artist), October 29, 2005; children: Leo, Adrien. *Ethnicity:* "Vietnamese." *Education:* Attended University of California, Los Angeles, 1991-93; Art Center College of Design (Pasadena CA), B.A., 1996.

Addresses

Agent—Linda Pratt, Wernick & Pratt Agency, linda@wernickpratt.com. *E-mail*—Uyen@leuyenpham.com.

Career

Children's book author and illustrator. Dreamworks Feature Animation, Glendale, CA, layout artist, 1996-99; Art Center College of Design, Pasadena, CA, instructor, 2000; Academy of Art University, San Francisco, CA, instructor; LeUyen Pham Illustration, San Francisco, freelance artist, 1999—. *Exhibitions:* Work exhibited at New York Society of Illustrators Original Art Show, 2005; and New York Society of Illustrators Spectrum Exhibition, 2005.

Member

Society of Illustrators.

Awards, Honors

American Booksellers Association Pick of the List designation, and Oppenheim Toy Portfolio Gold Award, both 2000, both for *Can You Do This, Old Badger?* by Eve Bunting; Best Children's Books of the Year designation, *Child* magazine, 2002, for *Whose Shoes?* by Anna Grossnickle Hines, and 2005, for *Big Sister, Little Sister;* 100 Titles for Reading and Sharing designation, and Oppenheim Toy Portfolio Gold Award, both 2004, both for *Twenty-one Elephants* by Phil Bildner; Society of Illustrators, Los Angeles, Bronze Medal in Children's Book Category; Texas 2x2 Reading List inclusion, 2004, for *Sing-along Song* by JoAnn Early Macken.

Writings

SELF-ILLUSTRATED

Big Sister, Little Sister, Hyperion Books for Children (New York, NY), 2005.

All the Things I Love about You, Balzer & Bray (New York, NY), 2010.

ILLUSTRATOR

Adrienne Moore Bond, *Sugarcane House, and Other Stories about Mr. Fat,* Harcourt Brace (San Diego, CA), 1997.

Eve Bunting, *Can You Do This, Old Badger?,* Harcourt (San Diego, CA), 1999.

Anna Grossnickle Hines, *Whose Shoes?,* Harcourt (San Diego, CA), 2001.

Eve Bunting, *Little Badger, Terror of the Seven Seas,* Harcourt (San Diego, CA), 2001.

Anna Grossnickle Hines, *Which Hat Is That?,* Harcourt (San Diego, CA), 2002.

Eve Bunting, *Little Badger's Just-about Birthday,* Harcourt (San Diego, CA), 2002.

Dori Chaconas, *One Little Mouse,* Viking (New York, NY), 2002.

Charlene Costanzo, *A Perfect Name,* Dial Books for Young Readers (New York, NY), 2002.

Karma Wilson, *Sweet Briar Goes to School,* Dial Books for Young Readers (New York, NY), 2003.

Kathryn Lasky, *Before I Was Your Mother,* Harcourt (San Diego, CA), 2003.

Kathi Appelt, *Piggies in a Polka,* Harcourt (San Diego, CA), 2003.

Esme Raji Codell, *Sing a Song of Tuna Fish: Hard-to-Swallow Stories from Fifth Grade,* Hyperion Books for Children (New York, NY), 2004.

Phil Bildner, *Twenty-one Elephants,* Simon & Schuster Books for Young Readers (New York, NY), 2004.

JoAnn Early Macken, *Sing-along Song,* Viking (New York, NY), 2004.

Esme Raji Codell, *Hanukkah, Shmanukkah!,* Hyperion Books for Children (New York, NY), 2005.

Karma Wilson, *Sweet Briar Goes to Camp,* Dial Books for Young Readers (New York, NY), 2005.

Jabari Asim, *Whose Toes Are Those?,* Little, Brown (New York, NY), 2006.

Bobbi Katz, *Once around the Sun,* Harcourt (Orlando, FL), 2006.

Jean Van Leeuwen, *Benny and Beautiful Baby Delilah,* Dial Books for Young Readers (New York, NY), 2006.

Jabari Asim, *Whose Knees Are These?,* Little, Brown (New York, NY), 2006.

Charlotte Zolotow, *A Father like That,* HarperCollins (New York, NY), 2007.

Kelly S. DiPucchio, *Grace for President,* Hyperion Books for Children (New York, NY), 2007.

Bruce Coville, reteller, *William Shakespeare's The Winter's Tale,* Dial Books for Young Readers (New York, NY), 2007.

Archbishop Desmond Tutu, with Douglas Carlton, *God's Dream,* Candlewick Books (Cambridge, MA), 2008.

(With husband Alex Puvilland) A.B. Sina, *Jordan Mechner's Prince of Persia* (graphic novel), First Second (New York, NY), 2008.

Charlotte Herman, *My Chocolate Year: A Novel with Twelve Recipes,* Simon & Schuster (New York, NY), 2008.

Laurel Snyder, *Any Which Wall,* Random House Children's Books (New York, NY), 2009.

Doug Wood, *Aunt Mary's Rose,* Candlewick Press (Cambridge, MA), 2010.

Amy Krouse Rosenthal, *Bedtime for Mommy,* Bloomsbury (New York, NY), 2010.

Jabari Asim, *Boy of Mine,* LB Kids (New York, NY), 2010.

Jabari Asim, *Girl of Mine,* LB Kids (New York, NY), 2010.

(With Alex Puvilland) Jordan Mechner, *Solomon's Thieves, Book One* (graphic novel), First Second (New York, NY), 2010.

Karen Beaumont, *Shoe-la-la!,* Scholastic Press (New York, NY), 2011.

Jennifer LaRue Huget, *The Best Birthday Party Ever,* Schwartz & Wade (New York, NY), 2011.

Marilyn Singer, *A Stick Is an Excellent Thing: Poems Celebrating Outdoor Play,* Clarion Books (New York, NY), 2012.

Books featuring Pham's art have been translated into several other languages, including French.

ILLUSTRATOR; "AKIMBO" SERIES BY ALEXANDER McCALL SMITH

Akimbo and the Lions, Bloomsbury Children's Books (New York, NY), 2005.

Akimbo and the Elephants, Bloomsbury Children's Books (New York, NY), 2005.

Akimbo and the Crocodile Man, Bloomsbury Children's Books (New York, NY), 2006.

Akimbo and the Snakes, Bloomsbury Children's Books (New York, NY), 2006.

Akimbo and the Baboons, Bloomsbury Children's Books (New York, NY), 2008.

ILLUSTRATOR; "ALVIN HO" CHAPTER-BOOK SERIES BY LENORE LOOK

Allergic to Girls, School, and Other Scary Things, Schwartz & Wade (New York, NY), 2008.

Allergic to Camping, Hiking, and Other Natural Disasters, Schwartz & Wade (New York, NY), 2009.

Allergic to Birthday Parties, Science Projects, and Other Man-Made Catastrophes, Schwartz & Wade (New York, NY), 2010.

Allergic to Dead Bodies, Funerals, and Other Fatal Circumstances, Schwartz & Wade (New York, NY), 2011.

LeUyen Pham's illustration projects include creating the colorful art for Kelly PiPucchio's picture book **Race for President.** (Illustration copyright © 2008 by LeUyen Pham. Reprinted by permission of Disney Book Group. All rights reserved.)

ILLUSTRATOR; "FRECKLEFACE STRAWBERRY" SERIES BY JULIANNE MOORE

Freckleface Strawberry, Bloomsbury Children's Books (New York, NY), 2007.
Freckleface Strawberry and the Dodgeball Bully, Bloomsbury (New York, NY), 2009.
Freckleface Strawberry: Best Friends Forever, Bloomsbury Children's Books (New York, NY), 2011.

Sidelights

Vietnamese-born children's book author and illustrator LeUyen Pham has produced picture-book illustrations for texts by a number of writers, among them Alexander McCall Smith, Eve Bunting, Jean Van Leeuwen, Amy Krouse Rosenthal, Marilyn Singer, and Karma Wilson. Earning her first illustration credit with the publication of Adrienne Moore Bond's *Sugarcane House, and Other Stories about Mr. Fat* in 1997, Pham has gone on to earn additional respect from critics for her original self-illustrated picture books *Big Sister, Little Sister* and *All the Things I Love about You.*

Big Sister, Little Sister is told through the eyes of a little girl who compares her life to that of her older sister. While big sister wears lipstick and is orderly, little sister is always a little messy, and she is only allowed to wear lipstick at playtime. To accompany her story, Pham created full-page illustrations featuring striking inked brush-and-pen renderings. *Big Sister, Little Sister* "has beautifully captured the touch-and-go affection that is a verity of sibling life," commented a *Publishers Weekly* reviewer, the critic going on to praise the author/illustrator's "bold, accomplished brush strokes." Writing in *School Library Journal,* Linda Ludke noted that, "with warmth and good humor, the ups and downs of sisterly love are perfectly conveyed" in Pham's art, while a *Kirkus Reviews* critic deemed *Big Sister, Little Sister* "a frothy fun tale that at its heart shows the depth and breadth of these relationships as something to be cherished."

Pham focuses on another special relationship in *All the Things I Love about You,* which was inspired by her own experiences as a mother to two young children. Here her evocative ink-and-wash illustrations are paired with a text that details a mother's affection for her infant son, from the way he plays with his breakfast to the way he wiggles out of his pajamas and calls for his mother each night. "Children will giggle, and mothers and grandmas will enjoy sharing" Pham's "reassuring message," predicted Patricia Austin in her *Booklist* review of *All the Things I Love about You,* and the book's art prompted Rachel G. Payne to note in *School Library Journal* that the author/illustrator shows herself to be "a master at conveying . . . facial expressions and delightful comic details." A "made-for-snuggling" bedtime story, according to a *Publishers Weekly* critic, *All the Things I Love about You* shows Pham to be "among the most natural and gifted illustrators working today."

Douglas Wood teams up with Pham to tell a story about the strength of family tradition in **Aunt Mary's Rose.** (Illustration copyright © 2010 by LeUyen Pham. Reproduced by permission of Candlewick Press, Somerville, MA.)

Similar praise has been given to Pham in her work illustrating stories by other writers. The half-tone art she creates for McCall Smith's series of books about an African boy living with his ranger father were called "evocative" by a *Publishers Weekly* contributor in a review of *Akimbo and the Elephants,* and a *Kirkus Reviews* critic wrote that Pham's illustrations for a new edition of Charlotte Zolotow's *A Father like That* "flow across each . . . spread and beautifully capture the spirit of the text." Rosenthal's *Bedtime for Mommy* takes a more lighthearted tack, reversing the role of mother and child such that Mommy's attempts to stall before bedtime are captured in Pham's art. Noting the story's comic-book-speech-bubble style, Patricia Austin added in *Booklist* that "uncluttered watercolor paintings" and a "switcheroo" story make *Bedtime for Mommy* "a perfect bedtime choice," while a *Kirkus Reviews* writer asserted that "Pham's ink-and-watercolor vignettes . . . milk the situation for all its worth."

Also featuring Pham's art, *God's Dream,* a picture book by Nobel Peace Prize-winner Archbishop Desmond Tutu, was commended by a *Publishers Weekly* critic who noted that the artist "nimbly sidesteps triteness through her velvety, saturated palette and the unassuming sweetness" of Tutu's multicultural cast of young characters. *Once around the Sun,* a picture book by Bobbi Katz, benefits from "large, color illustrations [by Pham that] are perfect for engaging youngsters in discussion" about the seasons, according to *School Library Journal* contributor Teresa Pfeifer.

Bobbi Katz's nature-themed story for Once around the Sun *comes to life in Pham's colorful illustrations.* (Illustration copyright © 2006 by LeUyen Pham. Reproduced by permission of Houghton Mifflin Harcourt Publishing Company. This material may not be reproduced in any form or by any means without the prior written permission of the publisher.)

With a text by Lenore Look, the "Alvin Ho" chapter books star a Chinese-American second grader who, while timid at school, on vacations, and every other social situation, transforms into a feisty superhero when he is at home in a safe environment. In a review of *Allergic to Girls, School, and Other Scary Things*, Jennifer Mattson wrote in *Booklist* that "many children will sympathize" with Look's young hero, and "Pham's thickly brushed artwork matches the [story's] quirky characterizations stroke for stroke." Continuing the adventures of the super-shy second grader in *Allergic to Camping, Hiking, and Other Natural Disasters*, a *Kirkus Reviews* stated that the artist's "simple but vibrant line drawings leap off the page."

In *Jordan Mechner's Prince of Persia* Pham teams up with her husband, fellow artist Alex Puvilland, to illustrate a graphic novel based on a popular video game, producing a book that *School Library Journal* critic Andrea Lipinski praised for its "vibrant colors and stirring images." The couple's second graphic-novel project, Mechner's *Solomon's Thieves,* takes readers to fourteenth-century France and follows Martin, a Templar knight, and fellows Bernard and Dominic. Their long trip back from the Crusades ends in betrayal by king and pope and a plot to break the power of the Knights Templar by robbing them of their wealth. The first volume in a planned trilogy, the graphic novel depicts "a believably harsh medieval world" in which Pham and Puvilland's "action sequences feel particularly cinematic," according to *School Library Journal* contributor Alana Joli Abbott. In *Booklist* Ian Chipman

wrote that *Solomon's Thieves* shows the artists to be "in top form, balancing grainy, hatched textures and clean spaces" to create "a vibrant sense of kineticism."

Pham once told *SATA:* "When I first considered doing children's books, I was told, flat out by every art instructor I met, that one could 'never make a living at it.' Children's books has long been considered a field that one does for the pure love of, and not to find one's fortune, much less to make a simple living at.

"I have never been one to listen to such things, and I set about trying to prove everyone wrong. Besides which, I simply could not imagine doing anything else with my life.

"I think it was that single idea, the belief that I really had no other choice in my life other than to write and illustrate books, that has kept me motivated and going for all this time. And truth be told, it *is* an extremely difficult field to be in, and one has to be quite prolific to stick around for very long. I might even wager to guess that my ability to ebb with the tide, to change my style from book to book to match the different mood of every story, has kept me adrift in this business, and has made it extremely challenging and enormously engaging in the process.

"It's interesting that in the field of illustration, one is encouraged to 'find one's voice,' as if style is simply an ever-present constant. I supposed there's merit to thinking that one can become a rather reliable illustrator in this way, that there are no surprises to the work, and what you ask for is what you get each time. For myself, I never found this thought very appealing, and what's more, it's always seemed a bit derogatory to the text, as though the words themselves are as predictable as the artist's consistent work.

"Each time I receive a manuscript, I can't help but look for the uniqueness of the story, the voice that I haven't heard anywhere else that attracts and holds my imagination. If I find a story like that, my goal is to find a visual translation for it that is just as unique, just as attractive, to do the thing justice. So begins my journey—of finding a new style to translate the story.

"From book to book, I've made it a goal to try to be different than the book before, in everything from the medium to the rendering to the storytelling. Admittedly, this hasn't always been an easy task. It means feeling extremely insecure each time I start a new book, wondering if this style is working at all, if the graphic imagery is actually beneficial, or if it's taking away from the story. And of course, there is the matter of convincing the editor that this direction is the right direction. Somehow, I've been lucky enough to work with people who seem to really trust my instincts and have let me express and change fluidly from book to book.

"Has this changing style been the reason for having done so many books in my short career? Heaven only knows there's no key to success. At least, I haven't

found it yet. And all these years later, when I think back at my girlish stubbornness at sticking it out in this field, I can't help but laugh. Because somewhere, along the way, among the many, many books illustrated, and many stories, to tell, I discovered that what I was looking for wasn't a way to make a living—I was simply looking for a way to love living. Ain't it grand?"

Biographical and Critical Sources

PERIODICALS

Booklist, March 15, 2003, Ilene Cooper, review of *Before I Was Your Mother,* p. 1332; July, 2004, Ilene Cooper, review of *Sing-along Song,* p. 1848; October 1, 2004, Karin Snelson, review of *Twenty-one Elephants,* p. 332; June 1, 2005, Jennifer Mattson, review of *Big Sister, Little Sister,* p. 1823; September 1, 2005, Kay Weisman, review of *Hanukkah, Shmanukkah!,* p. 131; September 1, 2005, Shelle Rosenfeld, review of *Akimbo and the Elephants,* p. 135; February 1, 2006, Ilene Cooper, review of *Benny and Beautiful Baby Delilah,* p. 59; April 15, 2006, Hazel Rochman, review of *Once around the Sun,* p. 49; May 15, 2007, Julie Cummins, review of *A Father like That,* p. 50; February 15, 2008, Ilene Cooper, review of *Grace for President,* p. 84; July 1, 2008, Jennifer Mattson, review of *Allergic to Girls, School, and Other Scary Things,* p. 61; August 1, 2008, Hazel Rochman, review of *God's Dream,* p. 76; September 1, 2008, Ian Chipman, review of *Jordan Mechner's Prince of Persia,* p. 98; May 15, 2009, Courtney Jones, review of *Any Which Wall,* p. 54; February 15, 2010, Patricia Austin, review of *Bedtime for Mommy,* and Julie Cummins, review of *Aunt Mary's Rose,* both p. 79; April 15, 2010, Ian Chipman, review of *Solomon's Thieves,* p. 57; November 1, 2010, Patricia Austin, review of *All the Things I Love about You,* p. 72; April 15, 2011, Diane Foote, review of *The Best Birthday Party Ever,* p. 58.

Books, December 11, 2005, review of *Hanukkah, Shmanukkah!,* p. 2.

Bulletin of the Center for Children's Books, March, 2005, Karen Coats, review of *Sing a Song of Tuna Fish: Hard-to-Swallow Stories from Fifth Grade,* p. 285; September, 2005, Timnah Card, review of *Big Sister, Little Sister,* p. 36; May, 2006, Deborah Stevenson, review of *Benny and Beautiful Baby Delilah,* p. 426; July-August, 2006, Deborah Stevenson, review of *Once around the Sun,* p. 504.

Children's Bookwatch, May, 2004, review of *Piggies in a Polka,* p. 2.

Horn Book, July-August, 2008, Jennifer M. Brabander, review of *Allergic to Girls, School, and Other Scary Things,* p. 453; September-October, 2009, Jennifer M. Brabander, review of *Allergic to Camping, Hiking, and Other Natural Disasters,* p. 567; September-October, 2010, Jennifer M. Brabander, review of *Allergic to Birthday Parties, Science Projects, and Other Man-made Catastrophes,* p. 82.

Kirkus Reviews, March 1, 2003, review of *Before I Was Your Mother,* p. 257; July 15, 2003, review of *Piggies in a Polka,* p. 961; May 1, 2004, JoAnn Macken, review of *Sing-along Song,* p. 444; October 1, 2004, review of *Twenty-one Elephants,* p. 956; June 15, 2005, review of *Big Sister, Little Sister,* p. 689; November 1, 2005, review of *Hanukkah, Shmanukkah!,* p. 1191; March 15, 2006, review of *Once around the Sun,* p. 293; May 1, 2007, review of *A Father like That;* September 15, 2007, review of *William Shakespeare's The Winter's Tale;* July 15, 2008, review of *Jordan Mechner's Prince of Persia;* August 15, 2008, review of *God's Dream;* April 15, 2009, review of *Any Which Wall;* May 15, 2009, review of *Allergic to Girls, School, and Other Scary Things;* February 15, 2010, review of *Aunt Mary's Rose;* March 15, 2010, review of *Bedtime for Mommy;* November 15, 2010, review of *All the Things I Love about You;* December 15, 2010, review of *Shoe-la-la!*

Kliatt, September, 2008, George Galuschak, review of *Prince of Persia,* p. 34.

Library Media Connection, August-September, 2005, Quinby Frank, review of *Big Sister, Little Sister,* p. 71; March, 2006, Pamela Ott, review of *Akimbo and the Elephants,* p. 64.

Publishers Weekly, January 27, 2003, review of *Before I Was Your Mother,* p. 257; August 25, 2003, review of *Piggies in a Polka,* p. 63; August 22, 2005, review of *Big Sister, Little Sister,* p. 64; September 5, 2005, review of *Akimbo and the Elephants,* p. 63; September 26, 2005, review of *Hanukkah, Shmanukkah!,* p. 85; April 3, 2006, review of *Akimbo and the Crocodile Man,* p. 76; July 31, 2006, review of *Sing a Song of Tuna Fish,* p. 77; January 14, 2008, review of *Grace for President,* p. 57; February 18, 2008, review of *My Chocolate Year,* p. 153; July 7, 2008, reviews of *God's Dream,* p. 57, and *Allergic to Girls, School, and Other Scary Things,* p. 58; July 28, 2008, review of *Jordan Mechner's Prince of Persia,* p. 58; March 22, 2010, review of *Bedtime for Mommy,* p. 67; October 25, 2010, review of *All the Things I Love about You,* p. 48; November 8, 2010, review of *Shoe-la-la!,* p. 60.

School Library Journal, May, 2003, Catherine Threadgill, review of *Before I Was Your Mother,* p. 122; September, 2003, Grace Oliff, review of *Piggies in a Polka,* p. 166; June, 2004, Marianne Saccardi, review of *Sing-along Song,* p. 114; November, 2004, Susan Lissim, review of *Twenty-one Elephants,* p. 90; September, 2005, Linda Ludke, review of *Big Sister, Little Sister,* p. 184; March, 2006, Martha Topol, review of *Benny and Beautiful Baby Delilah,* p. 204; May, 2006, Teresa Pfeifer, review of *Once around the Sun,* p. 114; June, 2006, Amelia Jenkins, review of *Whose Knees Are These?,* p. 104; February, 2008, Cheryl Ashton, review of *My Chocolate Year,* p. 116; August, 2008, review of *Allergic to Girls, School, and Other Scary Things,* p. 96; September, 2008, Andrea Lipinski, review of *Jordan Mechner's Prince of Persia,* p. 219; February, 2009, Linda L. Walkins, review of *God's Dream,* p. 95; March, 2009, Kim Dare, review of *Samantha Hansen Has Rocks in Her Head,* p. 156; June, 2009, Nicole Waskie, review of *Allergic to Camping, Hiking, and Other Natural Disasters,* p. 66, and Eva

Mitnick, review of *Any Which Wall,* p. 138; October, 2009, Mary Elam, review of *Freckleface Strawberry and the Dodgeball Bully,* p. 99; March, 2010, Carolyn Janssen, review of *Bedtime for Mommy,* p. 130; April, 2010, Susan Scheps, review of *Aunt Mary's Rose,* p. 149; July, 2010, Alana Joli Abbot, review of *Solomon's Thieves,* p. 110; December, 2010, Rachel G. Payne, review of *All the Things I Love about You,* p. 88; February, 2011, Kathleen Finn, review of *She-la-la!,* p. 75; April, 2011, Ieva Bates, review of *The Best Birthday Party Ever,* p. 146.

Washington Post Book World, December 11, 2005, Lori Smith, review of *Hanukkah, Shmanukkah,* p. 10.

ONLINE

LeUyen Pham Home Page, http://www.leuyenpham.com (May 20, 2009).

Web Esteem Web site, http://art.webesteem.pl/ (December 27, 2006), "LeUyen Pham."

* * *

PRICE, Charlie

Personal

Married Joanie Pechanec (a psychotherapist); children: Jessica Rose. *Education:* Stanford University, B.A.; San Francisco State University, M.S. *Hobbies and other interests:* Reading, guitar playing, fly fishing, movies, basketball.

Addresses

Home—CA. *Agent*—Adams Literary, 7845 Colony Rd., C4, No. 215, Charlotte, NC 28226. *E-mail*—charlesbprice@sbcglobal.net.

Career

Writer and consultant. Worked variously as a therapist, program director, and clinical supervisor in psychiatric hospitals, and a teacher and academic dean in several private schools. Business consultant; presenter at schools and workshops.

Member

Society of Children's Book Writers and Illustrators, Mystery Writers of America.

Awards, Honors

Quick Pick for Young-Adults selection, and Best Book for Young Adults selection, both American Library Association (ALA), both 2006, both for *Dead Connection;* ALA Quick Pick for Young-Adult Readers selection, and Edgar Allen Poe Award for Best Young-Adult Mystery, Mystery Writers of America, both 2011, both for *The Interrogation of Gabriel James;* nominations for several state awards.

Charlie Price (Reproduced by permission.)

Writings

Dead Connection, Roaring Brook Press (New Milford, CT), 2006, published as *Hear the Dead Cry,* Corgi (London, England), 2010.

Lizard People, Roaring Brook Press (New York, NY), 2007.

The Interrogation of Gabriel James, Farrar, Straus & Giroux (New York, NY), 2010.

Desert Angel, Farrar, Straus & Giroux (New York, NY), 2011.

Dead Girl Moon, Farrar, Straus & Giroux (New York, NY), 2012.

Sidelights

Charlie Price worked for thirty years as an educator and mental-health professional before beginning his second career as a novelist. After growing up in Colorado and Montana, Price attended Stanford University in California, and he lived for a time in New York City, Italy, and Mexico before returning to California where he now makes his home. "I grew to deeply admire the courage of those who lived and worked with mental illness on a daily basis," he explained on his home page, discussing his work in the medical field. It was through his experiences with troubled young people, as well as events within his own community, that Price came to write his first novel, *Dead Connection.* His success as a writer

for teens has led Price to continue producing teen fiction in addition to his work as a business consultant and coach.

"*Dead Connection* was written as an adult novel and edited to become Young Adult," Price explained to *SATA.* "I never write 'down'; We're all in this together. I try to write stories that are thrilling and real. I hear feedback equally from teen and adult readers. Since the subject matter is intense and the style mature, my novels have become 'crossover' books. All of them have both strong adolescent and strong adult characters. Many of these characters are based on young people I encountered in schools and hospitals.

"In my work as a counselor, my clients and students came from all walks of life. In wealthy homes, in professional homes, in average homes, and in poor homes, there can be horrible daily dramas that often remain secret until later, grown up, a family member enters therapy or winds up in our legal system. Every family—*every* family—has members at some level (mother, father, sister, brother, aunt, uncle, grandparent, cousin) with problems of addiction, domestic abuse, and/or mental illness. Feelings of shame and fears of stigma or legal intervention prevent most families from talking about the affected persons or sharing those problems with outsiders. Literary characters that mirror those kinds of issues are safer, easier to discuss, in less-guarded arenas where we might encounter fresh or useful ideas."

Dead Connection is the story of Murray, a high-school outcast who finds solace in hanging around the town's cemetery. He is so lonely that he beings conversing with some of the headstones as if they were friends and winds up actually talking to the spirits of dead children and adolescents. Soon Murray becomes involved in helping newly deceased classmate Nikki to expose her killer and the location of her corpse while a plethora of secondary characters add their voices to the plot. Christine M. Heppermann, writing in *Horn Book,* wrote of the adolescent cast in Price's debut that the author "ably fleshes out his characters and adds a distinctive member to the ranks" in Murray. "Readers will find themselves rooting for these characters," wrote a contributor to *Publishers Weekly,* and in *School Library Journal* Francisca Goldsmith predicted that *Dead Connection* "will be an easy sell to mystery readers, and will have lots of appeal to those familiar with that genre only through television or movies."

In *Lizard People* a teen's efforts to cope with a parent's mental illness gradually unleash his own demons. At age seventeen, Ben Mander is his mother's sole caretaker now that his father has abandoned the family, and Mother refuses to care for herself by taking the medication that will deal with her schizophrenia. Haunted by delusions that she is being attacked by a race of Lizard People, the woman is admitted to a local psychiatric hospital, where Ben now visits regularly. A friendship with Marco, whose mom is also at the hospital, makes things easier to bear until Marco's talk of a future world where the Lizard People live prompts Ben to question what is actually real in his own life. "Price writes honestly and with compassion" in his exploration of what it means to have a parent suffering from a mental illness," according to Wendy Smith-D'Arezzo in *School Library Journal,* and his story "moves quickly and contains enough mystery" to sustain reader interest. Noting the novel's "wild, manic pacing," a *Kirkus Reviews* writer wrote that *Lizard People* propels teen readers toward an "unsettling conclusion" that is also thought provoking. "Price's graphic depiction of . . . a future without mental illness is a powerful metaphor . . . that brings real hope to readers," asserted Frances Bradburn in her *Booklist* review of *Lizard People,* while *Horn Book* contributor Caitlin J. Berry stated that the novel "tantalizingly blurs the boundaries between madness and lucidity."

Price sets *The Interrogation of Gabriel James* in the Montana town where he once attended high school and where Gabe James now finds himself a witness to a double murder. As he sits in an interrogation room, answering questions from Billings' deputy sheriff, Gabe is uncertain how much he himself is responsible for the brutal crimes. If he had not tried to help the girl dealing with her bizarre home life, would any of this have happened? He realizes that the arson, the hate crimes that focused on the town's Native-American population, and a rash of stolen pets may all be connected. As the interrogation continues, more questions are raised: did a homeless man's attempt to kill himself have anything to do with the town's illegal drug trade? And would Gabe not agree that his behavior in following the dead man's sister seems to qualify as stalking? Gabe attempts to sort through the various threads "in true plucky teen fashion," according to *Booklist* critic Ian Chipman, the reviewer praising *The Interrogation of Gabriel James* as both "well-structured and well-paced." "Suspense and mystery dominate this exciting double-layer story," asserted a *Kirkus Reviews* writer, and a *Publishers Weekly* critic predicted that Price's mix of a "fast pace, dark mood, and well-plotted story line should have readers hooked."

Desert Angel, a thriller set in the California desert, focuses on fourteen-year-old Angel as she attempts to evade the man who killed and buried her mother in the sand not far from their camouflaged trailer. Scotty, the most recent in her mom's long trail of abusive boyfriends, intends to kill Angel next, using his considerable tracking skill. Angel flees until she encounters a caring Mexican-American community whose members put themselves at risk in their willingness to help. As the teen wrestles with the morality of accepting others' help when she knows it will put them in danger, she also becomes more resolute in her determination to avenge her mother's death. Focusing on this intolerable bind, *Desert Angel* distills into what *Voice of Youth Advocates* contributor Mirta Espinola described as an "in-

triguing story of suspense topped off with despair, heart-ache, mistrust, and murder." The "suspense never lets up" in Price's fast-paced read," wrote a *Kirkus Reviews* contributor, and "the small, decaying towns, the Salton Sea and the desert heat provide a vivid backdrop for the unfolding drama." "Both the best and the worst of humanity shine through in this gripping novel," asserted a *Publishers Weekly* contributor, and Espinola dubbed *Desert Angel* "a riveting and suspenseful tale."

Biographical and Critical Sources

PERIODICALS

Booklist, May 1, 2006, Ilene Cooper, review of *Dead Connection,* p. 47; July 1, 2007, Frances Bradburn, review of *Lizard People,* p. 49; July 1, 2010, Ian Chipman, review of *The Interrogation of Gabriel James,* p. 52; November 1, 2011, Daniel Kraus, review of *Desert Angel,* p. 70.

Horn Book, July-August, 2006, Christine M. Heppermann, review of *Dead Connection,* p. 449; November-December, 2007, Caitlin J. Berry, review of *Lizard People,* p. 685.

Kirkus Reviews, May 1, 2006, review of *Dead Connection,* p. 465; July 15, 2007, review of *Lizard People;* June 15, 2010, review of *The Interrogation of Gabriel James;* August 15, 2011, review of *Desert Angel.*

Publishers Weekly, March 20, 2006, review of *Dead Connection,* p. 56; August 27, 2007, review of *Lizard People,* p. 91; July 26, 2010, review of *The Interrogation of Gabriel James,* p. 77; August 22, 2001, review of *Desert Angel,* p. 67.

School Library Journal, April, 2006, Francisca Goldsmith, review of *Dead Connection,* p. 147; September, 2007, Wendy Smith-D'Arezzo, review of *Lizard People,* p. 206; September, 2010, Jessie Spalding, review of *The Interrogation of Gabriel James,* p. 162.

Voice of Youth Advocates, October, 2010, Ed Goldberg, review of *The Interrogation of Gabriel James,* p. 356; October, 2011, Mirta Espinola, review of *Desert Angel,* p. 392.

ONLINE

Adams Literary Web site, http://www.adamsliterary.com/ (March 2, 2007), "Charlie Price."

Charlie Price Home Page, http://www.charlieprice.info (December 15, 2011).

Q-R

QUIMBY, Laura

Personal
Born in MD; married Steven Muchow. *Education:* Towson State University, B.A. (English literature). *Hobbies and other interests:* Yoga, traveling, watching movies, cooking.

Addresses
Home—Fallston, MD. *E-mail*—laura@lauraquimby.com.

Career
Author. Formerly worked in marketing, advertising, and book production; freelance writer, beginning 2005.

Member
Society of Children's Book Writers and Illustrators.

Writings

The Carnival of Lost Souls, Amulet Books (New York, NY), 2010.

Sidelights
Writing was an integral part of Laura Quimby's work in advertising and marketing, and after several years circling around the idea, she took a chance and set about fulfilling her dream of writing a novel for young readers. In *The Carnival of Lost Souls* she achieved her goal, producing just the sort of off-beat fantasy that she enjoyed reading as a child. "I was inspired to write the story after I read an autobiography about Harry Houdini and was inspired by how hard he worked to create magic tricks," Quimby noted in an interview with Janet Fox on the *Through the Wardrobe* Web log. "Magic is often portrayed as easy and effortless, literally magic, and I loved the idea that magic was man made and tough."

For Jack Carr, the young hero in *The Carnival of Lost Souls*, his love of magic—particularly the work of early-twentieth-century escape artist Harry Houdini—has been the one constant while growing up in a succession

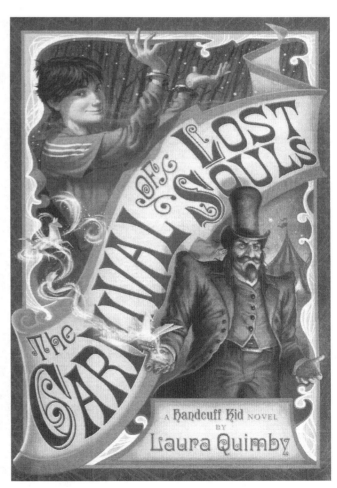

Cover of Laura Quimby's unusual middle-grade novel Carnival of Lost Souls, *featuring artwork by Brandon Dorman.* (Jacket art by Brandon Dorman. Reproduced by permission of Amulet Books, an imprint of Harry N. Abrams Books.)

of foster homes. When he finds himself living with quirky old Professor Hawthorne, Jack feels an instant affinity for the man. The boy's instinct prove sadly wrong, however, when the professor uses Jack as his own replacement, trading the boy for the soul he lost years before in a wager with an evil magician called the Amazing Mussini. Brought to Mussini's home in a purgatory-like place called the Forest of the Dead, Jack is forced to become part of the stage show Mussini performs for the guilty and haunted spirits trapped there. Knowing that he must either escape or be used up by the evil of the place, Jack joins with Mussini's other young assistants, hoping that Houdini's tricks prove to be real life-savers rather than mere illusions.

Calling Quimby's Forest of the Dead "a unique world" full of a strange mix of lifeless humans and otherworldly creatures, Clare A. Dombrowski added in *School Library Journal* that *The Carnival of Lost Souls* sustains both "tension and danger throughout the story." The novel plays out in "a nicely paced, clever mix of ghost story and sideshow spectacle," noted Ian Chipman in his review of Quimby's story for *Booklist,* while a *Publishers Weekly* critic cited *The Carnival of Lost Souls* as an "homage to Houdini filtered through the lens of traditional fantasy tropes" and featuring "fun characters to follow."

Biographical and Critical Sources

PERIODICALS

Booklist, October 15, 2010, Ian Chipman, review of *The Carnival of Lost Souls,* p. 63.
Bulletin of the Center for Children's Books, November, 2010, April Spisak, review of *The Carnival of Lost Souls,* p. 144.
Kirkus Reviews, September 1, 2010, review of *The Carnival of Lost Souls.*
Publishers Weekly, October 11, 2010, review of *The Carnival of Lost Souls,* p. 45.
School Library Journal, December, 2010, Clare A. Dombrowski, review of *The Carnival of Lost Souls,* p. 123.

ONLINE

Laura Quimby Home Page, http://www.lauraquimby.com (December 13, 2011).
Laura Quimby Web log, http://lauraquimby.blogspot.com (December 13, 2011).
Through the Wardrobe Web log, http://kidswriterjfox. blogspot.com/ (October 17, 2010), Janet Fox, interview with Quimby.

*　　*　　*

REES, Douglas 1947-

Personal

Born October 19, 1947, in Riverside, CA; son of Norman (a career sergeant) and Agnes (a nurse) Rees; mar-

Douglas Rees (Photograph by Glen Kaltenbrun. Courtesy of Douglas Rees.)

ried Bonnie Rostonovich (marriage ended 1977); remarried; second wife's name JoAnn (a librarian); children: Philip Rostonovich. *Politics:* "Liberal." *Religion:* High-church Episcopalian.

Addresses

Home—Sunnyvale, CA. *E-mail*—zeppelinpilot@yahoo. com.

Career

Author and librarian. San Jose Public Library, San Jose, CA, part-time librarian.

Awards, Honors

Notable Book designation, American Library Association (ALA), and New York Public Library Best Book for the Teen Age designation, both 1999, both for *Lightning Time;* Best Children's Book of the Year nomination, Bay Area Book Reviewers, 1999, for *Lightning Time,* and 2003, for *Vampire High;* Quick Pick for Reluctant Readers citation, ALA, 2004, for *Vampire High;* Book Sense Children's Pick, American Bookseller's Association, 2008, for *Uncle Pirate.*

Writings

NOVELS

Lightning Time, Dorling Kindersley (New York, NY), 1997.

Vampire High, Delacorte (New York, NY), 2003.

Smoking Mirror: An Encounter with Paul Gauguin, Watson-Guptill (New York, NY), 2005.

The Janus Gate: An Encounter with John Singer Sargent, Watson-Guptill (New York, NY), 2006.

Vampire High: Sophomore Year, Delacorte (New York, NY), 2009.

Author's work has been translated into French and German.

JUVENILE FICTION

Grandy Thaxter's Helper, illustrated by S.D. Schindler, Atheneum (New York, NY), 2004.

Uncle Pirate, illustrated by Tony Auth, Margaret K. McElderry Books (New York, NY), 2008.

Jeannette Claus Saves Christmas, illustrated by Olivier Latyk, Margaret K. McElderry Books (New York, NY), 2010.

Uncle Pirate to the Rescue, illustrated by Tony Auth, Margaret K. McElderry Books (New York, NY), 2010.

Adaptations

Uncle Pirate was adapted as a stage musical, produced in New York, NY, 2009-10.

Sidelights

Douglas Rees is the author of several award-winning books for children and teens, including *Vampire High* and *Uncle Pirate.* Interestingly, although Rees had long dreamed of becoming a writer, his first story was not published until he was fifty years old. Asked why it took so long to realize his dream, Rees explained on his home page: "When I was forty-seven I realized that all the ideas I'd had for books and plays were going to stay ideas unless I wrote them. But the larger answer is that it takes a long time for some people to get strong enough to become writers."

Rees's first book, the young-adult historical novel *Lightning Time,* focuses the exploits of notorious abolitionist John Brown, who attacked a U.S. military arsenal at Harpers Ferry, Virginia, and helped spark the U.S. Civil War. Narrator Theodore is fourteen years old when he meets the charismatic Brown, and he is drawn into Brown's idealistic cause. Theodore's decision to leave his family to follow the revolutionary is a difficult one for the teen, but his convictions strengthen throughout the course of the novel. "Theodore makes a sympathetic narrator," noted Carolyn Phelan in her *Booklist* review of *Lightning Time,* while Elizabeth S. Watson wrote in *Horn Book* that Rees's "fine historical novel . . . explores the complexities of the abolitionist cause."

After *Lightning Time* Rees decided to explore the horror genre in *Vampire High.* "I drew deeply on my early teen years to write it; more deeply than I knew at the time," he told *Cynsations* online interview Cynthia Leitich Smith. "Certainly I was aware of basing the story on my one year in Massachusetts, when I went to a brand-new high school in Chicopee. What I didn't realize until a year ago, was that I also was using the material laid down by my three years in Germany as an Air Force brat. Vlad Dracul is really just my old high school transmuted into a series of palaces." Vlad Dracul High School is an elite magnet school attended almost entirely by vampires. When fifteen-year-old Cody Elliott transfers there, it is only a matter of time before he figures out who—or what—his classmates are. Unlike the other non-blood-sucking teens attending Vlad Dracul, Cody sets out to challenge the school's standards and social hierarchy, determined to be treated like the other students, regardless of his non-vampire status.

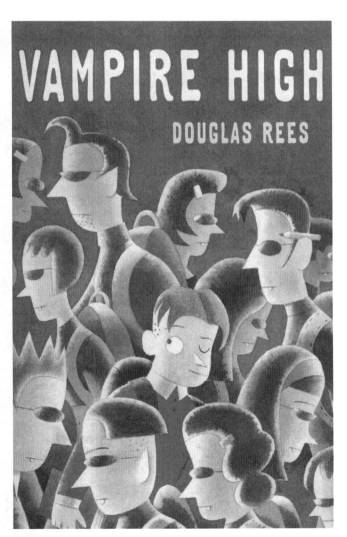

When Cody transfers to a new high school the only course requirement is water polo in Rees's amusing teen novel Vampire High, *featuring cover art by Greg Clarke.* (Jacket cover copyright © 2003 by Laurel-Leaf. Used by permission of Laurel-Leaf, an imprint of Random House Children's Books, a division of Random House, Inc.)

"There's barely a false note in this rollicking tale of horror, humor, and light romance," concluded *Booklist* reviewer Frances Bradburn in an appraisal of *Vampire High*. A *Publishers Weekly* critic commented on Rees's "bold, almost hyperbolic humor," while Lauren Adams wrote in *Horn Book* that the tale is "a light, engaging parable with a reader-pleasing happy ending." *Vampire High* includes "amusing twists on the fantasy tropes about vampires," according to a *Kirkus Reviews* contributor, and Paula Rohrlick noted in *Kliatt* that "snappy dialogue and the age-old appeal of the vampire make this comedy a winner."

Cody makes a return appearance in *Vampire High: Sophomore Year*. Although the likeable protagonist manages to fit in with his gruesome classmates, Cody's tough-talking artist cousin, Turk, rankles the student body when she proposes building a studio in a desolate part of town with a violent and secret history. In the words of a *Kirkus Reviews* critic, the "exciting, nonstop plot and electrifying climax" in *Vampire High: Sophomore Year* "lead to an over-the-top resolution guaranteed to produce satisfied readers." "Rees's fast-paced

Cody's adventures continue in Rees' novel Vampire High: Sophomore Year, *featuring cover art by John Ritter.* (Cover copyright © 2010 by Delacorte Press. Used by permission of Delacorte Press, an imprint of Random House Children's Books, a division of Random House, Inc.)

and action-packed story line tackles important teen issues like identity, belonging, friendship, and acceptance," Donna Rosenblum noted in *School Library Journal.*

A number of Rees's books introduce historical information to readers, among them *Smoking Mirror: An Encounter with Paul Gauguin* and *The Janus Gate: An Encounter with John Singer Sargent.* Part of the "Art Encounters" series, these books tell fictional stories that capture moments in the lives of famous artists. Paul Gauguin is the featured artist in *Smoking Mirror,* which follows fifteen-year-old Joe Sloan as he runs away to Tahiti. There, Joe meets Gauguin and they form a friendship based on mutual need and admiration. The novel gives readers "an intimate peek at Gauguin's creative process," according to a *Kirkus Reviews* contributor. Ken Marantz, writing in *School Arts,* also commented on the "suspenseful story," while *Booklist* reviewer Gillian Engberg praised Rees for his ability to "weave . . . biographical facts about a famous artist into a compelling novel."

The Janus Gate features portrait painter John Singer Sargent in a fictional supernatural thriller in which the artist must decide whether or not to help the girls who are the subjects of one of his paintings, "The Daughters of Edward Darley Boit." "Rees provides plenty of detail and insight into Sargent's creative process as he paints this dark portrait of the" siblings, Roxanne Myers Spencer reported in *School Library Journal,* and *Kliatt* reviewer Claire Rosser predicted that "everyone familiar with this painting will enjoy Rees's ghostly tale, and will certainly look at Sargent's work differently."

Rees combines two folktale motifs in his picture book *Grandy Thaxter's Helper.* Set against an early American backdrop—a new setting for the traditional tale—the book tells how Grandy Thaxter outwits Death by explaining that she can only go with him if she gets all her chores done. Since it will surely go faster if Death helps, she enlists him in her tasks and by the end of the day the bony spectre is far too tired to take Grandy Thaxter away. After two more increasingly exhausting tries, Death announces that he will come back when she is no longer so busy. "*Grandy Thaxter's Helper* will be a welcome story-time visitor," suggested Kitty Flynn in her *Horn Book* review of Rees's picture book. "For pure entertainment value, this book is hard to beat," agreed a critic for *Publishers Weekly.* "What makes this rendition of a classic theme interesting, slyly funny, and informative is its Colonial setting," explained Marge Loch-Wouters in *School Library Journal,* the critic pointing out that each chore of Grandy Thaxter's, such as making soap or mush, introduces young children to details from America's past.

Santa's daughter takes control of the reins when her jolly pappy falls ill in *Jeannette Claus Saves Christmas,* a "fun holiday read-aloud with a resourceful young heroine," in the words of *School Library Journal* critic

An appointment with Death is postponed when an elderly woman works the grim reaper to exhaustion in Rees's picture book **Granny Thaxter's Helper,** *featuring artwork by S.D. Schindler.* (Illustration copyright © 2004 S.D. Schindler. Reprinted with the permission of Atheneum Books for Young Readers, an imprint of Simon & Schuster Children's Publishing Division.)

Mara Alpert. Forewarned that Dasher, Dancer, Prancer & Company will flee if given the chance, Jeannette finds herself stranded on a housetop when the reindeer harnesses loosen. When the youngster spots some stray cats and dogs, however, she devises a clever solution to her problem. "With its unlikely antagonists and plucky heroine," Daniel Kraus wrote in *Booklist, Jeannette Claus Saves Christmas* ". . . has the potential to be a fan favorite."

In *Uncle Pirate,* a humorous adventure tale, a youngster attends Jolly Roger Elementary, an unruly school filled with bullies. The lucky lad soon gets help from his long-lost relative, a real-life buccaneer who transforms the educational environment using decidedly nontraditional methods. According to *School Library Journal* critic Laura Butler, Rees's "quick-paced jaunt will amuse children," and a critic in *Kirkus Reviews* predicted that *Uncle Pirate* will appeal to "any young land-lubber who likes a good yarn and believes everyone de-

serves a chance." In a sequel, *Uncle Pirate to the Rescue,* Rees's title character sets off to rescue his former crew, who have been imprisoned on a tropical island by the evil brother of the school's principal. "Adventure, villains and overall mollymockery make this great armchair traveling for the pirate-loving middle-grade reader," a contributor observed in *Kirkus Reviews.*

In his *Cynsations* interview, Rees offered advice to young writers. "Recognize that your conscious mind is the servant of your unconscious. I really believe that, by the time your conscious mind 'has an idea,' your unconscious has already done most of the work. But the thing is, the unconscious mind doesn't deal in words. It deals in pictures and feelings. It's up to the conscious mind to translate it into a form that a reader can absorb consciously, through reading. Now there's one problem with that: these two parts of the self don't readily communicate. You have to find the way to facilitate that."

Biographical and Critical Sources

PERIODICALS

Booklist, January 1, 1998, Carolyn Phelan, review of *Lightning Time,* p. 794; August, 2003, Frances Bradburn, review of *Vampire High,* p. 1973; March 15, 2005, Gillian Engberg, review of *Smoking Mirror: An Encounter with Paul Gauguin,* p. 1285; November 15, 2010, Daniel Kraus, review of *Jeannette Claus Saves Christmas,* p. 50.

Bulletin of the Center for Children's Books, January, 1998, review of *Lightning Time,* p. 173; October, 2004, Timnah Card, review of *Grandy Thaxter's Helper,* p. 97.

Horn Book, January-February, 1998, Elizabeth S. Watson, review of *Lighting Time,* p. 80; September-October, 2003, Lauren Adams, review of *Vampire High,* p. 617; November-December, 2004, Kitty Flynn, review of *Grandy Thaxter's Helper,* p. 700; November-December, 2010, Kitty Flynn, review of *Jeannette Claus Saves Christmas,* p. 67.

Kirkus Reviews, September 1, 2003, review of *Vampire High,* p. 1129; September 15, 2004, review of *Grandy Thaxter's Helper,* p. 919; January 1, 2005, review of *Smoking Mirror,* p. 56; May 1, 2008, review of *Uncle Pirate*; March 15, 2010, review of *Uncle Pirate to the Rescue*; June 15, 2010, review of *Vampire High: Sophomore Year*; September 1, 2010, review of *Jeannette Claus Saves Christmas.*

Kliatt, September, 2003, Paula Rohrlick, review of *Vampire High,* p. 11; July, 2006, Claire Rosser, review of *The Janus Gate: An Encounter with John Singer Sargent,* p. 13.

Library Media Connection, March, 2004, review of *Vampire High,* p. 65.

New York Times, March 13, 2005, Beth Gutcheon, review of *Grandy Thaxter's Helper.*

Public Libraries, September-October, 2005, Dominique McCafferty, interview with Rees, pp. 266-268.

Publishers Weekly, April 12, 1999, review of *Lightning Time,* p. 78; August 4, 2003, review of *Vampire High,* p. 81; September 20, 2004, review of *Grandy Thaxter's Helper,* p. 61.

School Arts, February, 2005, Ken Marantz, review of *Smoking Mirror,* p. 55.

School Library Journal, December, 1997, Peggy Morgan, review of *Lightning Time,* p. 129; November, 2003, Lynn Evarts, review of *Vampire High,* p. 146; November, 2004, Marge Loch-Wouters, review of *Grandy Thaxter's Helper,* p. 116; March, 2005, Heather E. Miller, review of *Smoking Mirror,* p. 217; September, 2006, Roxanne Myers Spencer, review of *The Janus Gate,* p. 216; February, 2009, Laura Butler, review of *Uncle Pirate,* p. 84; March, 2010, Wendy E. Dunn, review of *Uncle Pirate to the Rescue,* p. 166; July, 2010, Donna Rosenblum, review of *Vampire High,* p. 96; October, 2010, Mara Alpert, review of *Jeannette Claus Saves Christmas,* p. 76.

Voice of Youth Advocates, April, 1998, review of *Lightning Time,* p. 47; February, 2004, Jennifer Bromann, review of *Vampire High,* p. 506.

ONLINE

Cynsations Web log, http://cynthialeitichsmith.blogspot.com/ (March 15, 2006), Cynthia Leitich Smith, interview with Rees.

Douglas Rees Home Page, http://otterlimits.org/doug (December 15, 2011).

Douglas Rees Web log, http://dougrees.wordpress.com (December 15, 2011).

TRT Book Club Web log, http://trtbookclub.blogspot.com/ (August 3, 2010), Jen Wardrip, "Visit with Douglas Rees."*

*   *   *

RIES, Lori

Personal

Born in Syracuse, NY; married David Ries; children: three.

Addresses

Home and office—Tigard, OR. *E-mail*—readermail@LoriRies.net.

Career

Children's writer. Presenter at conferences, workshops, and schools.

Member

Author's Guild, Society of Children's Book Writers and Illustrators.

Awards, Honors

Bank Street College Best Books selection, and Oregon Book Award finalist, both 2006, both for *Aggie and Ben;* Bank Street College Best Books selection, and Friends Medallion Special Award, both 2007, both for *Fix It, Sam!;* Oregon Book Award finalist, and Bank Street College Best Books selection, both 2009, both for *Punk Wig;* CYBIL Award finalist, Bank Street College Best Books selection, and Maryland Blue Crab Young Readers Award, all 2010, all for *Good Dog, Aggie!;* Chicago Public Library Best of the Best selection, and Oregon Spirit Award Honor Book selection, both 2011, both for *Aggie the Brave;* CYBIL Award finalist, 2011, for *Aggie Gets Lost.*

Writings

Super Sam!, illustrated by Sue Ramá, Charlesbridge (Watertown, MA), 2004.

Mrs. Fickle's Pickles, illustrated by Nancy Cote, Boyds Mills (Honesdale, PA), 2006.

Aggie and Ben: Three Stories, illustrated by Frank W. Dormer, Charlesbridge (Watertown, MA), 2006.

Fix It, Sam, illustrated by Sue Ramá, Charlesbridge (Watertown, MA), 2007.

Punk Wig, illustrated by Erin Eitter-Kono, Boyds Mills (Honesdale, PA), 2008.

Good Dog, Aggie!, illustrated by Frank W. Dormer, Charlesbridge (Watertown, MA), 2009.

Aggie the Brave, illustrated by Frank W. Dormer, Charlesbridge (Watertown, MA), 2010.

Aggie Gets Lost, illustrated by Frank Dormer, Charlesbridge (Watertown, MA), 2011.

Author's work has been translated into Spanish.

Sidelights

While growing up, children's author and literacy advocate Lori Ries loved to read. She wrote her first tale, "Jo-Jo the Raccoon," at the age of ten, and continued making up stories with her mother's encouragement. In high school, after a short-story writing assignment, Ries was taken aside by her English teacher and told: "Lori, this isn't a short story, this is a preface to a novel, and if you work hard enough you could become a great writer." Ries always enjoyed keeping a personal journal, but it was not until she had children of her own that she began to consider writing as a career. She enrolled with the Institute of Children's Literature, and started attending workshops provided by the Highlights

Cover of Lori Ries' picture book* Super Sam!, *featuring colorful cartoon illustrations by Sue Ramá. (Illustration © 2004 by Sue Ramá. Reproduced by permission of Charlesbridge Publishing, Inc., 85 Main Street, Watertown, MA 02472, www.charlesbridge.com. All rights reserved.)

Foundation. "I think that having kids, being around kids, being a stay-at-home mom let me know kids," Ries explained in an interview in Oregon's *Tigard Times*.

It was being around children that sparked the idea for Ries' first book, *Super Sam!* While attending the Highlights Chautauqua Writer's Workshop, she spotted a little boy playing very earnestly, and she watched him for awhile, appreciating how he was in his own world. When she identified his mother, the two women chatted, and soon Ries met Sam, who, his mother told her, posed as a super hero at home. That tale ultimately found its way into print as Ries' first picture book.

Home from preschool, the titular hero of *Super Sam!* borrows baby brother Petey's blanket for use as the cape that transforms him into a super hero. The boy piles up pillows to prepare for leaping over tall buildings, hefts toys over his head to show his strength, and performs other feats of daring. When Sam accidentally steps on Petey's finger, however, he realizes that his super powers cannot solve the problem—but his cape can. Given back the baby blanket, Petey's tears soon end. "Ries tells the story in short sentences, using only fifty-three words," noted a *Kirkus Reviews* contributor, and a *Publishers Weekly* critic maintained that in her brief text the author "expresses everything there is to say" about the relationship between young siblings. Gay Lynn Van Vleck, writing in *School Library Journal,* dubbed *Super Sam!* "a cozy tale of brotherly affection."

Sam and Petey return in *Fix It, Sam.* When the siblings attempt to build a tent from a blanket and chairs, it keeps sagging in the middle. Although Petey has absolute faith that Sam will come up with a solution, it is Petey who eventually solves the problem: when he sits in the middle of the tent, his head holds up the blanket. "Little sibs will easily grasp the story," wrote Shelle Rosenfeld in *Booklist,* while *School Library Journal* contributor Catherine Callegari recommended *Fix It, Sam* as a picture book that "works as a read-aloud and a beginning reader."

In *Aggie and Ben: Three Stories* Ries introduces beginning readers to narrator Ben and his new puppy, Aggie, and their adventures are brought to life in Frank W. Dormer's illustrations. In the first story, Ben brings Aggie home from the pet shop. The second tale shows Ben trying to act like a puppy, although his play-acting stops short of drinking from the toilet bowl. In the third tale, Ben and Aggie keep each other safe from fears in the dark. "This unassuming tale will prove a welcome addition to any collection for emerging readers," wrote Jill Heritage Maza in her review of the book for *School Library Journal,* and a *Publishers Weekly* critic called *Aggie and Ben* "an impressive and original effort" that "bodes well for a sequel." Betty Carter, writing in *Horn Book,* explained that, while "kids can't be dogs, . . . Ben and Aggie let them know they can be readers."

Also featuring Dormer's art, *Good Dog, Aggie!*, *Aggie the Brave,* and *Aggie Gets Lost* continue the adventures

Ries teams up with artist Frank W. Dormer to introduce two engaging young characters in a series of beginning readers that includes Aggie and Ben. (Illustration copyright © 2006 by Frank W. Dormer. Used with permission by Charlesbridge Publishing Inc., 85 Main Street, Watertown, MA 02472, www.charlesbridge.com. All rights reserved.)

of Ben and his loyal pup. In *Good Dog, Aggie!* dog-training lessons are underway, although Aggie struggles with "sit" and "stay." The three chapters in *Aggie the Brave* follow the pup as she faces a scary visit to the local veterinarian, and *Aggie Gets Lost* finds Ben teary-eyed when his loyal puppy runs away. Praising Dormer's cartoon illustrations for *Good Dog, Aggie!* as "quirky" and "delightful," Gloria Koster added in *School Library Journal* that Ries' humorous chapter book would be a good choice "for independent reading," and a *Kirkus Reviews* writer dubbed the story's canine hero "one lovable pup." The three-chapter story in *Aggie the Brave* "cheerfully and tenderly persuad[es] . . . new readers to keep turning the page," asserted Alyson Low in her *School Library Journal* appraisal, while *Horn Book* critic Betty Carter noted of the series that "Ries displays a keen understanding of kids."

Mrs. Fickle's Pickles is a simple verse story that shows Mrs. Fickle making pickles by growing them from seed to cucumber and then pickling them in jars where they eventually win the blue ribbon at the county fair. "The simplicity of this breezy rural story will invite repeat readings," wrote a *Kirkus Reviews* contributor of Ries' country-themed picture book.

Ries wrote *Punk Wig* in response to her concern over a friend's journey with bone cancer. The woman's worries over how to tell her child that she will lose all her hair was heart-wrenching, the author once explained to *SATA*. "*Punk Wig* is a humorous story with serious undertones that opens communications for kids whose lives are turned upside down by cancer," explained the author. "In the story, a boy is a support to his mother throughout her chemotherapy treatments. When she loses her hair, they both go to Harriet's hair for some serious wig play. In the book, the seasons pass, and the ending holds a celebration when all the 'alien blobs' (cancer) have gone away." *Punk Wig* "features a family who gets through a tough time with flying colors," noted Abby Nolan in her *Booklist* review of Ries' story, and Carolyn Lehman wrote in *School Library Journal* that the book's "reassuring" story is "quick moving, positive, and funny at times."

"I don't know why a lot of people write, but I write because I really love it," Ries told the *Tigard Times* interviewer. "Books embrace children," she added, "and I like that."

Biographical and Critical Sources

PERIODICALS

Booklist, January 1, 2007, Shelle Rosenfeld, review of *Fix It, Sam,* p. 116; March 1, 2008, Abby Nolan, review of *Punk Wig,* p. 74.
Bulletin of the Center for Children's Books, May, 2007, Karen Coats, review of *Fix It, Sam,* p. 382.
Horn Book, September-October, 2006, Betty Carter, review of *Aggie and Ben: Three Stories,* p. 595; January-February, 2007, review of *Aggie and Ben,* p. 13; September-October, 2010, Betty Carter, review of *Aggie the Brave,* p. 92.
Kirkus Reviews, June 1, 2004, review of *Super Sam!,* p. 540; October 15, 2006, review of *Mrs. Fickle's Pickles,* p. 1078.
Publishers Weekly, July 5, 2004, review of *Super Sam!,* p. 54; July 31, 2006, review of *Aggie and Ben,* p. 74; December 15, 2007, review of *Punk Wig*; January 1, 2009, review of *Good Dog, Aggie*; June 15, 2010, review of *Aggie the Brave*; June 15, 2011, review of *Aggie Gets Lost.*
School Library Journal, September, 2004, Gay Lynn Van Vleck, review of *Super Sam!,* p. 177; July, 2006, Jill Heritage Maza, review of *Aggie and Ben,* p. 86; February, 2007, Catherine Callegari, review of *Fix It, Sam,* p. 94; April, 2008, Carolyn Lehman, review of *Punk Wig,* p. 120; May, 2009, Gloria Koster, review of *Good Dog, Aggie,* p. 87; August, 2010, Alyson Low, review of *Aggie the Brave,* p. 84.

ONLINE

Lori Ries Home Page, http://loriries.net (December 29, 2011).

Tigard Times Online, http://www.tigardtimes.com/ (January 18, 2007), interview with Ries.*

*   *   *

ROTH, Stephanie
See SISSON, Stephanie Roth

*   *   *

RYAN, Rob 1962-

Personal

Born November 5, 1962, in Cyprus; father an RAF officer; married; children: two. *Education:* Attended Nottingham Trent Polytechnic; Royal College of Art, M.A. (printmaking), 1987.

Addresses

Home—London, England.

Career

Illustrator and visual artist. Designer of greeting cards for Trocaire (nonprofit organization); images appear on peper products and ceramics. *Exhibitions:* Work exhibited widely, including at Air Gallery, London, England, and at Royal Academy of Arts, London.

Writings

SELF-ILLUSTRATED

This Is for You, Sceptre (London, England), 2007.
A Sky Full of Kindness, Sceptre (London, England), 2011.

OTHER

(Illustrator) Carol Ann Duffy, *The Gift,* Barefoot Books (Cambridge, MA), 2010.
(Author of preface) Laura Heyenga, compiler, *Paper Cutting: Contemporary Artists, Timeless Craft,* Chronicle Books (San Francisco, CA), 2011.

Contributor of illustrations to periodicals, including *Elle, Stylist,* and *Vogue.*

Sidelights

Rob Ryan is a visual artist whose intricate and romantic-styled cut-paper work has appeared in magazines, on album covers, and in the cover of several novels for adults. Because his father was in the military, Ryan and his family frequently moved while he was growing up, and he focused on his drawing as a way to keep consis-

tency in his world. Although he first intended to be a painter, he turned to silk screening and then to paper cutting because of its simplicity and ability to incorporate text elements. In creating his detailed papercut art, Ryan starts with a pencil drawing, carves out the background with a scalpel, and then sprays the intricate, final doily-like result with color. In addition to illustrating stories by others, he has also created the original picture books *This Is for You* and *A Sky Full of Kindness*.

In *This Is for You* Ryan shares an original fairy tale that focuses on a young man's loneliness and his search for true love. Equally inspiring in tone, *A Sky full of Kindness* focuses on love, but this time it is the unrequited love of a parent for a child, as two birds worry that they will not be prepared to care for the chicks about to hatch from their nest. Praising *This Is for You* in *New Statesman*, Hermione Buckland-Hoby described the work as a "whimsical, visual fairytale for not-so-grown-up grown-ups" that is told "through exquisitely detailed pictures."

As an illustrator, Ryan captures the nuances of *The Gift*, a children's story by Scottish-born U.K. poet laureate Carol Ann Duffy. In Duffy's tale, a little girl finds herself in an enchanting woodland, where she soon meets an elderly stranger. She continues to return to this magical spot at various points throughout her life, and as an elderly woman she ultimately comes to meet another little girl, becoming the elderly stranger who passes the magic of the place on to another generation as she approaches her death. Ryan's creation of "intricate floral details in a folk-art style capture the girl's artistic spirit," according to *School Library Journal* reviewer Julie R. Ranelli, while Phelan praised the artist for capturing the essence of a "lovely, idyllic life story [that] has magic and beauty at its core." In *School Librarian* Elizabeth Baskeyfield cited the "bewitching" nature of Ryan's story, praising *The Gift* as "a captivating, timeless" tale that is brought to life in "clever and intricate paper cut illustrations," and a *Publishers Weekly* critic asserted that the art adds "an airy feeling of light and plenty" to Duffy's thought-provoking verse.

Biographical and Critical Sources

PERIODICALS

Booklist, November 1, 2010, Carolyn Phelan, review of *The Gift*, p. 68.

Guardian (London, England), October 19, 2010, Huma Qureshi, profile of Ryan.

New Statesman, October 8, 2007, Hermione Buckland-Hoby, review of *This Is for You*.

Publishers Weekly, October 11, 2010, review of *The Gift*, p. 44.

School Library Journal, January, 2011, Julie R. Ranelli, review of *The Gift*, p. 74.

School Librarian, spring, 2011, Elizabeth Baskeyfield, review of *The Gift*, p. 34.

ONLINE

Independent Online, http://www.independent.co.uk/ (April 12, 2008), Clare Dwyer Hogg, interview with Ryan; (April 10, 2010) Charlotte Philby, interview with Ryan.

Just Children's Books Web site, http://www.justchildrensbooks.com/ (March 1, 2011), video interview with Ryan.

Rob Ryan Home Page, http://www.misterrob.co.uk (December 29, 2011).*

S

SCHEERGER, Sarah Lynn
See LYNN, Sarah

*   *   *

SCHNEIDER, Katy

Personal

Born in NY; married David Gloman (a painter); children: Olive, Mae, Ellis. *Education:* Yale University, B.A. (painting; cum laude), 1986; attended Skowhegan School of Painting and Sculpture, 1989; Indiana University, M.F.A., 1989.

Addresses

Home—Northampton, MA. *E-mail*—katyschneider@ comcast.net.

Career

Illustrator and fine-art painter. Smith College, Northampton, MA, lecturer in art, beginning 1990. Visiting artist at Hampshire College, Amherst, MA, 1996, and Boston University, 1999-2000. *Exhibitions:* Works exhibited in numerous group shows, and in solo shows at Hudson D. Walker Gallery, Provincetown, MA, 1987; Meekins Library Gallery, Williamsburg, MA, 1990, Northampton Center for the Arts, Northampton, MA, 1991, 1996; Springfield Technical and Community College, Springfield, MA, 1993; Amherst College, Amherst, MA, 1993; Hampshire College, Amherst, 1994; Bromfield Gallery, Boston, MA, 1995; Pepper Gallery, Boston, 1997-1999, 2002, 2004, 2006-07; Wright State University, Dayton, OH, 2000; and Riot, New York, NY, 2006.

Awards, Honors

Numerous awards from juried art shows; Williamsburg, MA, Arts Lottery grant, 1991; New England Foundation for the Arts regional fellowship, 1996; Massachu-

setts Cultural Council grant, 2000; Blanche Colman Award, 2000; Thomas B. Clarke Prize, National Academy of Design, 2002; John Guggenheim Memorial fellowship, 2004; Best Book Award, Oppenheim Toy Portfolio, 2004, for *Painting the Wind* by Patricia MacLachlan and Emily MacLachlan Charest; Irma S. and James H. Black Book Award, Bank Street College of Education, 2006, for *Once I Ate a Pie* by MacLachlan and Charest.

Illustrator

Patricia MacLachlan and Emily MacLachlan, *Painting the Wind,* Joanna Cotler Books (New York, NY), 2003.

Patricia MacLachlan and Emily MacLachlan, Charest, *Once I Ate a Pie,* Joanna Cotler Books (New York, NY), 2006.

Patricia MacLachlan and Emily MacLachlan Charest, *I Didn't Do It,* Katherine Tegen Books (New York, NY), 2010.

Sidelights

Katy Schneider is a fine-art painter whose evocative images of home and family have been featured in juried shows and in galleries throughout New England. A resident of Northampton, Massachusetts, where she teaches art at Smith College, Schneider is also known to a wider audience through her work in picture-book illustration. Her paintings are a feature of several picture books by well-known author Patricia MacLachlan and MacLachlan's daughter, Emily MacLachlan Charest, among them *Painting the Wind, Once I Ate a Pie,* and *I Didn't Do It.*

Praised by a *Publishers Weekly* contributor as an "elegantly conceived picture book," *Painting the Wind* showcases Schneider's technical abilities as it focuses on four artists who visit an island community on a painting holiday. The story is narrated by a young boy who

is also a painter, and he describes how each artist—portrait artists as well as painters who specialize in flowers, landscapes, and still lifes—translates the island sights onto canvas differently. Complementing the work in *Booklist,* Julie Cummins noted that the artist "evokes warm, strong sensory impressions" through paintings featuring "thick brushwork, texture, and a vibrant color palette." Debut illustrator "Schneider's masterful paintings are light-splashed gems," announced Lee Bock in his review of *Painting the Wind* for *School Library Journal.* A *Kirkus Reviews* writer dubbed the same book "atmospheric" and predicted that *Painting the Wind* "will broaden children's understanding of how and why art is made."

Schneider's talent for painting animals has been noted by several critics, and she has ample opportunity to showcase this talent in the companion picture books *Once I Ate a Pie* and *I Didn't Do It.* In each book Charest and MacLachlan present fourteen free-verse poems that use first-person narratives to capture the thoughts of several dogs, each a different breed and some actually admitting to bad behavior or other doggy antics. Set against a white backdrop, Schneider's fourteen accompanying portraits accentuate "the postures and personalities of the pups" and produce what Judith Constantinides described in *School Library Journal* as "an entertaining visit with some very appealing canines." The artist's skill in depicting various breeds with accuracy "indicate[s] thorough knowledge of canine behavior," asserted a *Kirkus Reviews* critic, the writer adding that *Once I Ate a Pie* entrances viewers with its mix of "expressive [doggy] eyes and playful postures." In *Booklist* Abby Nolan wrote that Schneider's art for *Once I Ate a Pie* distills "the mischief and movement young dog lovers find so irresistible," while in *School Library Journal* Linda Ludke wrote of *I Didn't Do It* that the book's "striking" illustrations "capture the impulsive and impetuous nature" of their doggy subjects and serve up "an irresistible treat for animal lovers."

Katy Schneider's lighthearted illustrations bring to life **I Didn't Do It,** *a picture book by Patricia MacLachlan and daughter Emily MacLachlan Charest.* (Illustration copyright © 2010 by Katy Schneider. Reproduced by permission of Katherine Tegan Books, an imprint of HarperCollins Children's Books, a division of HarperCollins Publishers.)

Biographical and Critical Sources

PERIODICALS

Booklist, August, 2003, Julie Cummins, review of *Painting the Wind,* p. 1980; May 1, 2006, Abby Nolan, review of *Once I Ate a Pie,* p. 87.
Kirkus Reviews, April 15, 2003, review of *Painting the Wind*; May 1, 2006, review of *Once I Ate a Pie,* p. 462.
Publishers Weekly, February 10, 2003, review of *Painting the Wind,* p. 185; August 9, 2010, review of *I Didn't Do It,* p. 50.
School Library Journal, May, 2003, Lee Bock, review of *Painting the Wind,* p. 125; May, 2006, Judith Constantinides, review of *Once I Ate a Pie,* p. 114; October, 2010, Linda Ludke, review of *I Didn't Do It,* p. 90.

ONLINE

Katy Schneider Home Page, http://www.katyschneider.com/ (December 15, 2011).
Smith College Web site, http://www.smith.edu/ (December 15, 2011), "Katy Schneider."*

*   *   *

SERLIN, Andra
See ABRAMSON, Andra Serlin

*   *   *

SEXTON, Brenda 1957-

Personal
Born 1957. *Education:* Temple University, B.A. (art).

Addresses
Home—Marina del Rey, CA. *E-mail*—brenda@brendasexton.com.

Career
Illustrator and author. Creator of artwork for greeting card and household objects.

Member
Society of Children's Book Writers and Illustrators.

Awards, Honors
Portfolio Award, Society of Children's Book Writers and Illustrators; Parent's Choice award; N.S.S. Louie Award finalist.

Writings

HOW-TO BOOKS

(With Jannie Ho) *Easy to Draw Animals,* Picture Window Books (Mankato, MN), 2011.
(With Mattia Cerato) *Easy to Draw Vehicles,* Picture Window Books (Mankato, MN), 2011.
(With Matt Bruning) *You Can Draw Pets,* Picture Window Books (Mankato, MN), 2011.
You Can Draw Planes, Trains, and Other Vehicles, Picture Window Books (Mankato, MN), 2011.
(With Mattia Cerato) *Easy to Draw Mythical Creatures,* Picture Window Books (Mankato, MN), 2012.
You Can Draw Fairies and Princesses, Picture Window Books (Mankato, MN), 2012.

ILLUSTRATOR

S. Simeon, *The Little Golden Bible Storybook,* Golden Books (New York, NY), 2005.
Busy Bath, Scholastic (New York, NY), 2006.
If You're Happy and You Know It, Scholastic (New York, NY), 2006.
The Itsy Bitsy Spider, Scholastic (New York, NY), 2007.
David LaRochelle, *1 + 1 = 5, and Other Unlikely Additions,* Sterling (New York, NY), 2010.

Also creator of digital books *Where's Mr. Dog?, Where's Mr. Cat?, Where's That Pig?, Zoom,* and *Mr. Square Can Wiggle!,* utales.com.

Books featuring Sexton's art have been translated into Spanish.

Biographical and Critical Sources

PERIODICALS

Booklist, September 15, 2010, Hazel Rochman, review of *1 + 1 = 5, and Other Unlikely Additions,* p. 62.
School Library Journal, September, 2010, Grace Oliff, review of *1 + 1 = 5, and Other Unlikely Additions,* p. 129.

ONLINE

Brenda Sexton Home Page, http://www.newshoesdesign.com (December 15, 2011).*

*   *   *

SISSON, Stephanie Roth
(Stephanie Roth)

Personal
Born in Frankfurt, Germany; married Fred Sisson; children: Tristam. *Hobbies and other interests:* Yoga, travel, trivia, history, cooking, music, decorating, gardening.

Addresses

Home—Shell Beach, CA. *Agent*—Abigail Samoun, Red Fox Literary, 129 Morro Ave., Shell Beach, CA 93449. *E-mail*—Stephanitely@charter.net.

Career

Illustrator.

Member

Society of Children's Book Writers and Illustrators, Children Book Council.

Awards, Honors

Best Children's Books of the Year selection, Bank Street College of Education, 2004, for *Meow Means Mischief* by Ann Whitehead Nagda; Best of the Best selection, Chicago Public Library, 2010, for *Princess Posey and the First Grade Parade* by Stephanie Greene.

Illustrator

(As Stephanie Roth) Robert TallTree, *The Legend of Spinoza: The Bear Who Speaks from the Heart,* Universal Tradewinds (St. Paul, MN), 1995.

(As Stephanie Roth) Mike Nappa and Amy Nappa, *Imagine That!: 365 Wacky Ways to Build a Creative Christian Family,* Augsburg Fortress (Minneapolis, MN), 1995.

(As Stephanie Roth) Barbara Oehlerg, *Making It Better: Activities for Children Living in a Stressful World,* Redleaf Press (St. Paul, MN), 1996.

(As Stephanie Roth) Rhoda Redleaf, *Open the Door: Let's Explore More,* Redleaf Press (St. Paul, MN), 1996.

(As Stephanie Roth) Connie Jo Smith, Charlotte Mitchell Hendricks, and Becky S. Bennett, *Growing, Growing Strong: A Whole Health Curriculum for Young Children,* Redleaf Press (St. Paul, MN), 1997.

(As Stephanie Roth) Susan Blackaby, *River Home,* McGraw-Hill (New York, NY), 1997.

(As Stephanie Roth) Debbie Hewitt and Sandra Heidemann, *The Optimistic Classroom: Creative Ways to Give Children Hope,* Redleaf Press (St. Paul, MN), 1998.

(As Stephanie Roth) Harriet Brown, *The Babysitter's Handbook: The Care and Keeping of Kids,* Pleasant Company (Middleton, WI), 1999.

(As Stephanie Roth) C. Anne Scott, *Lizard Meets Ivana the Terrible,* Holt (New York, NY), 1999.

(As Stephanie Roth) Margaret Holtschlag and Carol Trojanowski, *Clothespin Crafts,* Random House (New York, NY), 1999.

(As Stephanie Roth) Penny Warner, *Slumber Parties: Twenty-five Fun-filled Party Themes,* Meadowbrook Press (Minnetonka, MN), 2000.

(As Stephanie Roth) Uma Krishnaswami, *Yoga Class,* Lee & Low Books (New York, NY), 2000.

(As Stephanie Roth) Ann Pelo and Fran Davidson, *That's Not Fair!: A Teacher's Guide to Activism with Young Children,* Redleaf Press (St. Paul, MN), 2000.

(As Stephanie Roth) Ann Whitehead Nagda, *Dear Whiskers,* Holiday House (New York, NY), 2000.

(As Stephanie Roth) Gail Herman, *Bad Luck Brad,* Kane Press (New York, NY), 2002.

(As Stephanie Roth) Virginia Dooley, *I Need Glasses: My Visit to the Optometrist,* Mondo Publishing (New York, NY), 2002.

(As Stephanie Roth) Marjorie Blain Parker, *Ice Cream Everywhere!,* Scholastic (New York, NY), 2002.

(As Stephanie Roth) Ann Whitehead Nagda, *Meow Means Mischief,* Holiday House (New York, NY), 2003.

(As Stephanie Roth) Marilyn Singer, *Block Party Today!,* Knopf (New York, NY), 2004.

(As Stephanie Roth) Corinne Demas, *Two Christmas Mice,* Holiday House (New York, NY), 2005.

(As Stephanie Roth) Ann Whitehead Nagda, *Tarantula Power!,* Holiday House (New York, NY), 2007.

(As Stephanie Roth) Ann Whitehead Nagda, *The Perfect Cat-Sitter,* Holiday House (New York, NY), 2007.

Robin Pulver, *Thank You, Miss Doover,* Holiday House (New York, NY), 2010.

"GORDIE BARR" SERIES BY COLLEEN O'SHAUGHNESSY MCKENNA; AS STEPHANIE ROTH

Third Grade Stinks!, Holiday House (New York, NY), 2001.

Third Grade Ghouls!, Holiday House (New York, NY), 2001.

Doggone . . . Third Grade!, Holiday House (New York, NY), 2002.

Third Grade Wedding Bells?, Holiday House (New York, NY), 2006.

"BITTY TWINS" SERIES BY JENNIFER HIRSCH; AS STEPHANIE ROTH

The Bitty Twins at Night, Pleasant Company (Middleton, WI), 2002.

The Bitty Twins Have Fun, Pleasant Company (Middleton, WI), 2002.

The Bitty Twins' Christmas Surprise, Pleasant Company (Middleton, WI), 2003.

The Bitty Twins Snowy Day Coloring Book, Pleasant Company (Middleton, WI), 2003.

The Bitty Twins in the Woods, Pleasant Company (Middleton, WI), 2003.

The Bitty Twins at the Park, Pleasant Company (Middleton, WI), 2003.

The Bitty Twins' Christmas Cookies, Pleasant Company (Middleton, WI), 2004.

The Bitty Twins at Play, Pleasant Company (Middleton, WI), 2004.

The Bitty Twins' Parade, Pleasant Company (Middleton, WI), 2005.

The Bitty Twins' Royal Rules, Pleasant Company (Middleton, WI), 2005.

The Bitty Twins' Play Story, Pleasant Company (Middleton, WI), 2005.

Meet the Bitty Twins, Pleasant Company (Middleton, WI), 2006.

The Bitty Twins Go to School, Pleasant Company (Middleton, WI), 2006.

The Bitty Twins' Halloween, Pleasant Company (Middleton, WI), 2006.

The Bitty Twins Play, Pleasant Company (Middleton, WI), 2006.

The Bitty Twins' Christmas Coloring Book, Pleasant Company (Middleton, WI), 2006.

The Bitty Twins' Bedtime Story, Pleasant Company (Middleton, WI), 2007.

The Bitty Twins' Picnic, Pleasant Company (Middleton, WI), 2007.

The Bitty Twins Learn to Share, Pleasant Company (Middleton, WI), 2008.

The Bitty Twins' Tea Party, Pleasant Company (Middleton, WI), 2008.

The Bitty Twins' Bedtime Rhyme, Pleasant Company (Middleton, WI), 2009.

"PRINCESS POSEY" CHAPTER-BOOK SERIES

Stephanie Greene, *Princess Posey and the First Grade Parade,* G.P. Putnam's Sons (New York, NY), 2010.

Princess Posey and the Next Door Dog, G.P. Putnam's Sons (New York, NY), 2011.

Princess Posey and the Perfect Present, G.P. Putnam's Sons (New York, NY), 2011.

Princess Posey and the Monster Stew, G.P. Putnam's Sons (New York, NY), 2012.

Princess Posey and the Tiny Treasure, G.P. Putnam's Sons (New York, NY), 2012.

Sidelights

Stephanie Roth Sisson is a prolific illustrator whose works include Stephanie Greene's "Princess Posey" books as well as *Block Party Today!* by Marilyn Singer, *Tarantula Power!* by Ann Whitehead Nagda, and picture-book series by Jennifer Hirsch and Colleen O'Shaughnessy McKenna. Born in Germany, Sisson began drawing "as soon as I could hold a pencil," as she noted on her home page, often sketching illustrations for the stories her grandfather read to her. She made her literary debut in 1995, providing the artwork for Robert TallTree's *The Legend of Spinoza: The Bear Who Speaks from the Heart.* Since that time, Sisson has created art for dozens of other stories, working under the name Stephanie Roth until the late 2000s.

Sisson's pencil and acrylic illustrations bring to life Colleen O'Shaughnessy McKenna's "Gordie Barr" series of humorous chapter books about a creative but anxious youngster. In *Third Grade Stinks!* Gordie learns that his favorite teacher, Mrs. Tingle, has assigned him the worst possible locker partner: Lucy, the class show-off. Determined to rid himself of the pompous girl, Gordie decides to place Limburger cheese in his locker, hoping that the foul odor will drive Lucy away. Sisson's pictures for the book drew praise from *School Library Journal* critic Teri Markson, who wrote that "friendly black-and-white illustrations complement the

text." Gordie returns in *Third Grade Ghouls!,* a Halloween tale. As the holiday approaches, Gordie worries about finding the perfect costume and turns to his best friend, Lamont, for help. When Lamont's suggestion only leads to humiliation, Gordie brags to the school bully that he will return with something frightening. Further complicating matters, at the school parade Gordie volunteers to care for a first-grader who vomits at the sight of a scary outfit. According to a contributor in *Kirkus Reviews,* Sisson's "sweet occasional pencil sketches for *Third Grade Ghouls!* will make the book "attractive to the early reader."

In *Doggone . . . Third Grade!* Gordie and his friends prepare for the class talent show, and when he learns that his classmates plan to display a variety of artistic and musical skills, he announces that his dog, Scratch, will perform a clever math trick. Unfortunately, the training-deprived Scratch does not even roll over and there is only one week left before the curtain rises. "The appealing pencil sketches add to the story's humor," noted Marilyn Ackerman in a *School Library Journal* review of *Doggone . . . Third Grade!* and a *Kirkus Reviews* critic remarked that Sisson's "delightful and emotional black-and-white illustrations . . . add a lot" to the story. Gordie becomes jealous of his teacher's fiancée and schemes to prevent the marriage in *Third Grade Wedding Bells?,* and here Sisson's illustra-

Stephanie Roth Sisson's illustration projects include creating the art for Stephanie Greene's chapter book **Princess Posey and the First Grade Parade.** (Illustration copyright © 2010 by Stephanie Roth Sisson. Used by permission of GP Putnam's Sons, a division of Penguin Young Readers Group, a member of Penguin Group (USA) Inc., 345 Hudson Street, New York NY 10014. All rights reserved.)

tions show the action "from Gordie's awkward, nervy viewpoint," as Hazel Rochman commented in *Booklist*.

Sisson has also enjoyed an enduring collaboration with Nagda that begin with *Dear Whiskers*. As part of her classroom's pen-pal project, which involves writing from the perspective of a mouse, fourth-grader Jenny is teamed with second-grader Sameera, a new student from Saudi Arabia who speaks very little English. Sisson's "expressive illustrations capture the tone and characterization" of Nagda's tale, Carolyn Phelan reported in her *Booklist* review of the multicultural story. In a companion volume, *Meow Means Mischief*, Rana struggles to adjust to a new school just as her grandparents arrive from India for an extended visit. After the youngster adopts a troublesome stray cat, her classmates stop by and offer friendly advice. According to Jean Gaffney, writing in *School Library Journal*, Sisson's drawings for this story "capture typical school activities and reflect the diversity of the characters."

In Nagda's *The Perfect Cat-sitter* Rana's friend, Susan, agrees to care for the house pet while Rana travels to India. Although Susan believes she will have no problems keeping everything under control, the cat immediately runs away, which causes the ultra-responsible Susan to doubt her abilities. "Soft black-and-white illustrations capture Susan's emotions throughout her escapades," noted *Booklist* critic Suzanne Harold. A fourth grader is the focus of *Tarantula Power!* as Kevin stops his obnoxious science partner from bullying a younger student with the help of the class spider. A contributor in *Kirkus Reviews* remarked that Sisson's pictures for *Tarantula Power!* "help move the story along," and June Wolfe wrote in *School Library Journal* that Sisson's "illustrations match the action and give the book appeal for reluctant readers."

Sisson's artwork has also graced Singer's text for *Block Party Today!*, which celebrates a sun-splashed get-together in a multiethnic neighborhood in Brooklyn, New York. "Warm, relaxed watercolors depict the 'big fun' of the day," noted *Booklist* reviewer Jennifer Mattson, and a *Kirkus Reviews* critic stated that the story's "airy" images capture "a diverse cast of characters dancing, drumming, and lounging in lawn chairs." Elissa Schappell, writing in the *New York Times Book Review*, complimented the artist's "playful palette," adding that "Sisson's illustrations catch the bustle and camaraderie as Lola's neighbors stream across and sometimes off the margins of the page—some on roller skates and skateboards, others bringing corn bread and bongos."

In *Two Christmas Mice*, a picture book by Corinne Demas, a pair of snowbound neighbors spends Christmas Eve sharing holiday decorations with each other. Here "Sisson's paintings employ well-chosen details with a humorous touch," wrote a contributor in *Kirkus Reviews*, while Gillian Engberg noted in *Booklist* that the "pencil-and-paint illustrations" for *Two Christmas Mice* "create delightfully expressive mouse characters and communicate the sense of warmth in detailed scenes."

Like the "Georgie Barr" stories, many of Sisson's illustration projects focus on youngsters at school. Such is the case with Robin Pulver's *Thank You, Miss Doover*, which focuses on a boy's experiences with a very patient teacher. When Miss Doover shows her class how to write a thank-you note, young Jack gets off to a slow start, attempting to thank his stuffy great aunt for a gift of stationary. Working through several revisions, he finally expresses his appreciation clearly, although as readers soon learn, his use for the gift is likely not what his great aunt intended. Remarking on the "clever pictures" Sisson crafts to resemble a child's homework assignment, Mary Jean Smith added in *School Library Journal* that *Thank You, Miss Doover* treats readers to "a fine, funny writing lesson," and Michael Cart asserted in *Booklist* that the "cartoon-like illustrations . . . capture and expand the wit of" Pulver's humorous text.

School is also the setting for the "Princess Posey" chapter-books, which pair Sisson's pencil drawings with texts by Stephanie Greene. In *Princess Posey and the First-Grade Parade* readers meet Posey, a likeable little girl who overcomes her worries over starting elementary school by putting on her bright pink tutu and transforming herself into a confident princess. Posey's birthday gift for a favorite teacher seems to come up short in *Princess Posey and the Perfect Present*, until thinking like a princess allows the child to put things in perspective. An extra-big helping of confidence is needed in *Princess Posey and the Next-Door Dog*, as a new neighbor's pet presents Posey with the opportunity to overcome her fear and make a special new friend. "Sisson's charming, expressive black-and-white illustrations" help make *Princess Posey and the First-Grade Parade* "just right" for novice readers, according to a *Kirkus Reviews* writer, while Jennifer M. Brabander wrote in *Horn Book* that the "generously illustrated" chapter book "will be warmly received by youngsters looking for something comfortable and familiar."

Biographical and Critical Sources

PERIODICALS

Booklist, November 15, 2000, Carolyn Phelan, review of *Dear Whiskers*, p. 642; July, 2002, Hazel Rochman, review of *Doggone . . . Third Grade!*, p. 1848; October 1, 2003, Kay Weisman, review of *Meow Means Mischief*, p. 321; May 15, 2004, Jennifer Mattson, review of *Block Party Today!*, p. 1627; October 15, 2005, Gillian Engberg, review of *Two Christmas Mice*, p. 56; May 1, 2006, Hazel Rochman, review of *Third Grade Wedding Bells?*, p. 82; July 1, 2007, Carolyn Phelan, review of *Tarantula Power!*, p. 63; December 1, 2007, Suzanne Harold, review of *The Perfect Cat-sitter*, p. 42; July 1, 2010, Carolyn Phelan, review of *Princess Posey and the First Grade Parade*, p. 67; November 15, 2010, Michael Cart, review of *Thank*

You, Miss Doover, p. 51; March 1, 2011, Carolyn Phelan, review of *Princess Posey and the Perfect Present,* p. 58.

Horn Book, July-August, 2006, Susan Dove Lempke, review of *Third Grade Wedding Bells?,* p. 447; July-August, 2010, Jennifer M. Brabander, review of *Princess Posey and the First Grade Parade,* p. 106; March-April, 2011, Jennifer M. Brabander, review of *Princess Posey and the Perfect Present,* p. 116.

Kirkus Reviews, December 1, 2001, review of *Third Grade Ghouls,* p. 1687; May 15, 2002, review of *Doggone . . . Third Grade!,* p. 736; April 15, 2004, review of *Block Party Today!,* p. 401; November 1, 2005, review of *Two Christmas Mice,* p. 1192; April 15, 2007, review of *Tarantula Power!;* April 15, 2010, review of *Princess Posey and the First Grade Parade.*

New York Times Book Review, July 11, 2004, Elissa Schappell review of *Block Party Today!,* p. 18.

Publishers Weekly, September 26, 2005, review of *Two Christmas Mice,* p. 87; May 3, 2010, review of *Princess Posey and the First Grade Parade,* p. 50.

School Library Journal, November, 2001, Teri Markson, review of *Third Grade Stinks!,* p. 129; July, 2002, Marilyn Ackerman, review of *Doggone . . . Third Grade!,* p. 95; October, 2003, Jean Gaffney, review of *Meow Means Mischief,* p. 132; May, 2004, Genevieve Gallagher, review of *Block Party Today!,* p. 124; April, 2006, Diane Eddington, review of *Third Grade Wedding Bells?,* p. 112; June, 2007, June Wolfe, review of *Tarantula Power!,* p. 117; April, 2008, Jennifer Cogan, review of *The Perfect Cat-sitter,* p. 118; June, 2010, Elizabeth Swistock, review of *Princess Posey and the First Grade Parade,* p. 72; October, 2010, Mary Jean Smith, review of *Thank You, Miss Doover,* p. 92.

ONLINE

Stephanie Roth Sisson Home Page, http://www.stephanitely.com (December 12, 2011).

Stephanie Roth Sisson Web Log, http://www.stephscribbles.blogspot.com (December 12, 2011).*

* * *

SODERBERG, Erin Kate
See DOWNING, Erin

* * *

SOUDERS, Taryn 1977-

Personal

Born 1977, in Dallas, TX; married; children: three. *Education:* University of North Texas, B.S. (elementary education).

Addresses

Home—Winter Park, FL. *E-mail*—Contact@fractionsarefun.com.

Career

Educator and author. Formerly taught math. Presenter at schools.

Writings

Whole-y Cow!: Fractions Are Fun, illustrated by Tatjana Mai-Wyss, Sleeping Bear Press (Ann Arbor, MI), 2010.

Sidelights

"My goal is to help students who struggle with Math Anxiety by introducing math in fun ways," Taryn Souders told *SATA.* "I dealt with Math Anxiety for many years as a child until I had a math teacher who made math fun and easy for me. After becoming a math teacher myself, I decided to write books portraying math in humorous settings. Now I present around the country doing author visits as well as workshops showing other teachers how to use children's literature to reduce Math Anxiety in the classroom."

Biographical and Critical Sources

PERIODICALS

Kirkus Reviews, August 15, 2010, review of *Whole-y Cow!: Fractions Are Fun.*

School Library Journal, November, 2010, Loreli E. Stochaj, review of *Whole-y Cow!,* p. 94.

ONLINE

Sleeping Bear Press Web site, http://www.sleepingbearpress.com/ (December 15, 2011), "Taryn Souters."

Taryn Souders Home Page, http://www.fractionsarefun.com/ (December 15, 2011).

* * *

STIEFVATER, Maggie 1981-

Personal

Born November 18, 1981; married; husband's name Edward; children: one son, one daughter. *Education:* University of Mary Washington, B.A. (history), 2002. *Religion:* Christian. *Hobbies and other interests:* Young-adult fiction, playing music, reading, British and Celtic history and mythology.

Addresses

Home—Montross, VA. *E-mail*—StiefvaterReaderMail@gmail.com.

Career

Author, artist, and musician. Has taught workshops on illustration. Creator of animated short films. Performer with bands, including Ballynoola, 2000, and Kate Hummel, 2007-11; Sergeant of Mary Washington College Eagle Pipes and Drums, 1999-2002. *Exhibitions:* Work included in shows at American Academy of Equine Art; Uniquely Fredericksburg, Fredericksburg, VA; Master of Foxhounds Association centennial traveling art exhibition, Cross Gate Gallery, Lexington, KY, 2007; and Colored Pencil Society of America International Exhibition, 2007.

Awards, Honors

Best Books for Young Adults and Popular Paperbacks for Young Adults designations, both American Library Association (ALA), both 2010, both for *Lament;* Best Books for Young Adults and Quick Pick for Reluctant Readers designations, both ALA, Children's Choice Award finalist, Children's Book Council, and Midwest Booksellers' Choice Award for Children's Literature, all 2010, all for *Shiver;* numerous state reading association awards.

Writings

"BOOKS OF FAERIE" NOVEL SERIES

Lament: The Faerie Queen's Deception, Flux (Woodbury, MN), 2008.
Ballad: A Gathering of Faerie, Flux (Woodbury, MN), 2009.

"WOLVES OF MERCY FALLS" NOVEL SERIES

Shiver, Scholastic Press (New York, NY), 2009.
Linger, Scholastic Press (New York, NY), 2010.
Forever, Scholastic Press (New York, NY), 2011.

OTHER

The Scorpio Races, Scholastic Press (New York, NY), 2011.

Contributor to *Kiss Me Deadly: Thirteen Tales of Paranormal Love,* edited by Trisha Telep, Running Press (Philadelphia PA), 2010; and *Demons: Encounters with the Devil and His Minions, Fallen Angels, and the Possessed,* edited by John Skipp, Black Dog & Leventhal (New York, NY), 2011. Contributor of short fiction to *Merry Sisters of Fate* Web log. Contributor to periodicals, including the *New York Times.*

Author's work has been translated into over thirty languages, including Brazilian, Bulgarian, Finnish, French, German, Japanese, Spanish, and Turkish.

Adaptations

Shiver and *Linger* were released as audiobooks.

Sidelights

Maggie Stiefvater's fantasy novels have earned praise for their fully realized characters, rich prose, and gripping narratives. In works such as *Lament: The Faerie Queen's Deception, Shiver,* and *The Scorpio Races,* Stiefvater blends romance, adventure, and mythology, offering readers compelling supernatural love stories. As the author stated in a *YA Reads* online interview, "I believe in that . . . *something more.* Something outside of ordinary. It's not that I believe in werewolves or faeries per se, but I do believe in . . . something more. And writing about them lets me write about that feeling of wonder and curiosity."

A self-described "Navy brat," Stiefvater grew up in Virginia, Florida, and California, among other places, and as her family moved frequently she developed an early love of both reading and music. As her tastes evolved, she found herself drawn to contemporary fantasy tales such as *The Girl with the Silver Eyes* by Willo Davis Roberts, *The Castle in the Attic* by Elizabeth Winthrop, *The Indian in the Cupboard* by Lynne Reid Banks, and the works of Diana Wynne Jones. After majoring in his-

A sixteen year old who can see faeries falls in love with the faerie assassin sent to kill her in **Lament: The Faerie Queen's Deception,** *Maggie Stiefvater's debut novel.* (Copyright © by Llewellyn Publications. All rights reserved. Reproduced by permission.)

tory at the University of Mary Washington, Stiefvater earned a living as a landscape and equestrian artist and musician before finding success in the literary world.

Set in Virginia, *Lament* concerns sixteen-year-old Deirdre Monaghan, a talented harpist who finds herself at the heart of an otherworldly conflict. While competing at a music festival, Deirdre meets the mysterious Luke Dillon, a flautist who joins her onstage during her number; their gorgeous duet stuns the crowd and earns the grand prize. As the days pass, Deirdre becomes infatuated with Luke, whose disturbing presence prompts Deirdre's grandmother to give the teen an unusual gift: an antique iron ring. While wearing the ring Deirdre begins spotting strange creatures and develops telekinetic powers; she also learns that she is a "cloverhand", one who can see and attract faeries, charming but soulless tricksters who enjoy toying with humans yet are repulsed by iron. She grows suspicious of Luke when she learns from her grandmother that he has appeared to their family before, when Deirdre's mother and Aunt Delia were children. Ultimately, she is led to Thomas Rhymer, a human imprisoned by the queen of the Faeries who tells Deirdre that her powers threaten the queen's reign.

Booklist reviewer Diana Tixier Herald described *Lament* as "beautiful and out-of-the-ordinary," further praising "its authentic depiction of Celtic Faerie lore and dangerous forbidden love in a contemporary American setting." Cara Chancellor, writing in *Kliatt*, predicted that Stiefvater's story "will delight nearly all audiences with its skillful blend of magic and ordinary life." According to a *Publishers Weekly* contributor, the author is "unafraid of taking plot developments to their logical outcomes, even when they mar the characters' happiness," and *Voice of Youth Advocates* critic Caitlin Augusta applauded Deirdre's narrative voice, calling it "intimate and immediate."

Ballad, a sequel of sorts, focuses on James Morgan, a gifted bagpiper and a loyal friend to Deirdre. During his first week at the prestigious Thornking-Ash School of Music, James is drawn to the woods by a haunting melody and spies a wondrous, antlered figure, just as fellow student Deirdre begins seeing the faerie on campus. Nuala, a beguiling creature whose life is at risk, promises to make James the greatest piper who ever lived, and when he refuses her offer Nuala invades his dreams and becomes his muse. Ultimately James falls in love with her, and they make a deal with the king of the Dead to save her life. Torn between his love for Nuala and his love for Deirdre, James is ultimately faced with a heartbreaking decision. "The book's backdrop, so firmly rooted in Celtic myth, is scary, mysterious, magical, and horrifying," Herald stated in her *Booklist* review of *Ballad.*

Stiefvater turns her attention to another mythological creature—the werewolf—in *Shiver,* the first book in her "Wolves of Mercy Falls" series and a novel described as "sensuous, intense, riveting, and so very satisfying"

by *Voice of Youth Advocates* contributor Bonnie Kunzel. Attacked by wolves as a child, high-school junior Grace is now obsessed with animals, especially the yellow-eyed wolf that once saved her life and now roams alone in the woods near Grace's home in Mercy Falls, Minnesota. When schoolmate Jack Culpeper becomes the victim of another wolf attack, a hunting party pursues the vicious pack. When Grace finds a yellow-eyed boy, Sam, at her back door, naked and bleeding, she realizes that her wolf has taken human form. Sam's ability to transform is controlled by the seasons: summers find him human while he lives as a wolf the rest of the year and will ultimately revert to wolven form. Despite being bitten, Grace does not transform, and their research leads them to believe that a high fever can halt the slow mutation from human to wolf.

Shiver was praised as "a lyrical tale of alienated werewolves and first love" by a *Publishers Weekly* contributor, and it offers "a paranormal romance that is beautiful and moving," according to *School Library Journal* critic Donna Rosenblum. In *Booklist,* Ian Chipman complimented Stiefvater's "elegant writing," adding that

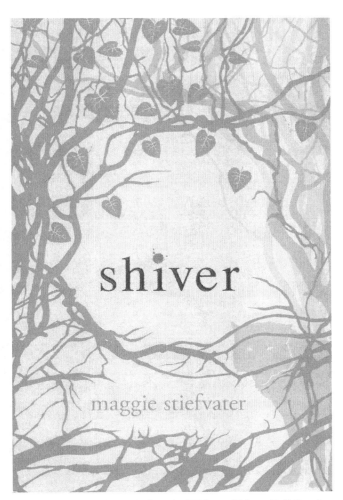

Shiver, *the first work in Stiefvater's "Wolves of Mercy Falls" series, concerns a pair of star-crossed lovers, one human, the other a wolf in* **human form.** (Cover art by Christopher Stengel. Reprinted by permission of Scholastic, Inc.)

Cover of Stiefvater's young-adult novel **Forever,** *the third novel in her "Wolves of Mercy Falls" series.* (Illustration copyright © 2011 by Yuta Onoda. Reproduced by permission of Scholastic, Inc.)

she "is especially intuitive about the animal world," and Shelly Shaffer observed in the *Journal of Adolescent & Adult Literacy* that the "compelling story will keep readers guessing until the final page."

In *Linger,* the second installment of Stiefvater's "Wolves of Mercy Falls" series, a now fully human Sam assumes the role as caretaker of the pack, even as Grace begins suffering from headaches and fever. When Grace's parents discover Sam in her bedroom one night, they try to prevent the teens from seeing one another. Meanwhile, recently arrived pack member Cole devises a new theory to explain the transformations, and his theory may help Grace when she becomes violently ill and is taken to the hospital. "Stiefvater's slow-perk style of crafting suspense builds to a satisfying boil in the final pages" of *Linger,* observed *School Library Journal* critic Amy Pickett, and a *Publishers Weekly* critic reported that the novel "sets the stage for an explosive third installment" in the "Wolves of Mercy Falls" saga.

Stiefvater's werewolf series concludes in *Forever,* "an intelligent paranormal romance that surreptitiously folds in serious adolescent issues, including teens' relation-ships with their parents, suicidal ideation, morphing bodies and young love," according to *Los Angeles Times* reporter Susan Carpenter. After transforming from human to wolf, Grace disappears into the woods and Sam is now a suspect in her mysterious disappearance. After a local girl is killed in a rogue wolf attack, an army of sharpshooters hunts down the remaining wolves of Mercy Falls. "Stiefvater's emotional prose is rich without being melodramatic," Cindy Welch noted in *Booklist,* and Lauren Newman wrote in *School Library Journal* that Sam and Grace's "plight is palpable and heart-wrenching." Carpenter praised the story's themes of romance, writing that "how the two couples work together to combat the wolf hunt, and their own werewolf-ism, is the magic of Stiefvater, who wraps up this captivating series in a manner that is sure to satisfy fans."

Stiefvater turns to Celtic mythology in *The Scorpio Races,* a "beautifully told coming-of-age story," according to *Voice of Youth Advocates* critic Blake Norby. Set on the island of Thisby, the work centers on Sean Kendrick and Kate "Puck" Connolly, orphans who lost their parents to a breed of man-eating water horse that is ridden in local competitions. Sean, a champion rider, is able to soothe the wild creature while Puck hopes to save her destitute family by riding her land mare to victory. According to *Booklist* contributor Karen Cruze, in *The Scorpio Races* "Stiefvater has created a thrilling backdrop for the love story that blooms between Sean and Puck," and Martha V. Parravano maintained in *Horn Book* that the author "masterfully combines an intimate voice . . . with a wealth of horse detail" set within "a plot full of danger, intrigue, and romance." "If *The Scorpio Races* sounds like nothing you've ever read, that's because it is," Jennifer Hubert Swan remarked in the *New York Times Book Review,* adding that "Stiefvater has successfully plumbed lesser-known myths and written a complex literary thriller that pumps new blood into a genre suffering from post-*Twilight* burnout."

Biographical and Critical Sources

PERIODICALS

Booklist, December 1, 2008, Diana Tixier Herald, review of *Lament: The Faerie Queen's Deception,* p. 50; August 1, 2009, Ian Chipman, review of *Shiver,* p. 61; October 1, 2009, Diana Tixier Herald, review of *Ballad: A Gathering of Faerie,* p. 33; June 1, 2010, Cindy Welch, review of *Linger,* p. 58; September 1, 2011, Karen Cruze, review of *The Scorpio Races,* p. 102; September 15, 2011, Cindy Welch, review of *Forever,* p. 74.
Bulletin of the Center for Children's Books, January, 2010, Karen Coats, review of *Ballad,* p. 220.
Financial Times, January 9, 2010, James Lovegrove, review of *Shiver,* p. 16; July 10, 2010, Suzi Feay, review of *Linger,* p. 17.
Horn Book, July-August, 2010, Tanya D. Auger, review of *Linger,* p. 123; November-December, 2011, Martha V. Parravano, review of *The Scorpio Races,* p. 114.

Journal of Adolescent & Adult Literacy, May, 2010, Shelly Shaffer, review of *Shiver,* p. 692; February, 2011, Ashley Huskey, review of *Linger,* p. 384.

Kliatt, November, 2008, Cara Chancellor, review of *Lament,* p. 30.

Los Angeles Times, July 17, 2011, Susan Carpenter, review of *Forever.*

New York Times Book Review, November 13, 2011, Jennifer Hubert Swan, review of *The Scorpio Races,* p. 40.

Publishers Weekly, October 13, 2008, review of *Lament,* p. 55; August 3, 2009, review of *Shiver,* p. 46; June 14, 2010, review of *Linger,* p. 54; August 22, 2011, review of *The Scorpio Races,* p. 67.

School Library Journal, October, 2009, Donna Rosenblum, review of *Shiver,* p. 138; August, 2010, Amy Pickett, review of *Linger,* p. 114; September, 2011, Lauren Newman, review of *Forever,* p. 174.

Voice of Youth Advocates, December, 2008, Caitlin Augusta, review of *Lament,* p. 458; December, 2009, Bonnie Kunzel, review of *Shiver,* p. 424; April, 2010, Caitlin Augusta, review of *Ballad,* p. 75; August, 2010, Bonnie Kunzel, review of *Linger,* p. 275; October, 2011, Blake Norby, review of *The Scorpio Races,* p. 411.

ONLINE

BookPage.com, http://bookpage.com/ (June 1, 2011), Emily Masters, interview with Stiefvater.

Maggie Stiefvater Home Page, http://www.maggiestiefvater.com (May 1, 2011).

Maggie Stiefvater Web log, http://m-stiefvater.livejournal.com (May 1, 2011).

Open Book Society Web site, http://openbooksociety.com/ (November 14, 2009), Karin Perry, interview with Stiefvater.

Publishers Weekly Online, http://www.publishersweekly.com/ (October 6, 2011), Sue Corbett, "Q & A with Maggie Stiefvater."

Seventeen Online, http://www.seventeen.com/ (December 15, 2011), Laura Rosenfeld, interview with Stiefvater.

YA Reads Web log, http://www.yareads.com/ (September 29, 2009), interview with Stiefvater.*

*   *   *

STURMAN, Jennifer

Personal

Born in Cleveland, OH. *Education:* Harvard College, A.B. (history and literature; magna cum laude), 1991; Harvard University, M.B.A., 1995.

Addresses

Home—New York, NY. *E-mail*—jen@jennifersturman.com.

Career

Novelist and business executive. Goldman, Sachs & Co., New York, NY, financial analyst, 1991-93; McKinsey & Co., New York, NY, management consultant, 1995-99; Time Warner Books, New York, NY, corporate strategist, 2002-08; management consultant.

Awards, Honors

Romantic Times Award for Best Chick Lit Novel nomination, 2004, for *The Pact.*

Writings

"RACHEL BENJAMIN" ADULT MYSTERY SERIES

The Pact, Red Dress Ink (Don Mills, Ontario, Canada), 2004.

The Jinx, Red Dress Ink (Don Mills, Ontario, Canada), 2005.

The Key, Red Dress Ink (Don Mills, Ontario, Canada), 2007.

The Hunt, Red Dress Ink (Don Mills, Ontario, Canada), 2007.

YOUNG-ADULT NOVELS

And Then Everything Unraveled, Point (New York, NY), 2009.

And Then I Found out the Truth, Point (New York, NY), 2010.

Sidelights

Jennifer Sturman entertains twenty-something mystery fans with her "Rachel Benjamin" mystery novels, which includes *The Pact, The Jinx, The Key,* and *The Hunt.* Featuring an investment banker with a high-fashion wardrobe and a knack for solving mysteries, *The Pact* finds Rachel tracking down a murderer after an friend's fiancée winds up floating face down in a swimming pool the night before her wedding. A suspicious Wall Street deal has Rachel concerned about her job in *The Hunt,* continuing a series that *Booklist* critic John Charles cited for its "irresistible mix of a neatly constructed mystery, . . . entertaining characters, and writing seasoned with a tart sense of humor."

Sturman's "Rachel Benjamin" novels were inspired by her own experience working on Wall Street. Raised in Ohio, she attended Harvard College, where she studied literature and history and then went on to earn an M.B.A. She has worked as a financial analyst, management consultant, and corporate strategist in addition to developing her career as a fiction writer.

Sturman shifts her focus to younger readers in her companion novels *And Then Everything Unraveled* and *And Then I Found out the Truth,* both which find a sixteen

Cover of Jennifer Sturman's young-adult mystery **And Then I Found out the Truth**, *featuring cover art by McFaul.* (Jacket art copyright © 2010 by McFaul. Reproduced by permission of Scholastic, Inc.)

year old facing a mystery involving her own family. When readers first meet her in *And Then Everything Unraveled*, California high-school junior Delia Truesdale is enjoying a summer at the beach while her widowed mom, T.K. Truesdale, is off sailing somewhere in South America on business. When news comes that T.K.'s ship has disappeared, the wealthy woman is certified as lost at sea and her will specifies that Delia must life with her aunts in New York City until she comes of age. Delia refuses to believe that her mom is dead, however, especially after she receives several strange phone messages. While attempting to make the best of living with two aunts whom she scarcely knows, the teen gleans some clues from T.K.'s business papers and hires an Ecuadorian psychic and a P.I. to start her search for the woman. Two new friends are there to help her, but things become complicated when it becomes clear that her mom's business partner has something to hide and her own boyfriend's family may be involved in the mystery. Reviewing *And Then Everything Unraveled* in *Booklist*, Gillian Engberg predicted that the story's "gentle romance, and likeable Delia will grab readers," while Brandy Danner wrote in *School Li-*

brary Journal that "all of the major characters have strong, distinct voices, and their actions are realistic and consistent." *And Then Everything Unraveled* "treats readers to intrigue and taut dialogue," as well as paving the way for a sequel," concluded a *Publishers Weekly* contributor.

When readers rejoin Delia in *And Then I Found out the Truth* the teen is still determined to locate her mom, especially now that she knows T.K. is still alive. Meanwhile, she is also still learning to navigate New York City with the help of bohemian Aunt Charley and society maven Aunt Patience, both who live in different worlds. Current heartthrob Quinn seems to return her affections, but Delia is still not sure that his father is uninvolved in the unfolding mystery. With passport in hand, the teen books a trip to Buenos Aires, where Argentinean petrochemical interests may hold the key to her mother's whereabouts. "Fans of the first book will find all the same rewards here," asserted Engberg in her review of *And Then I Found out the Truth,* and a *Kirkus Reviews* writer praised Sturman's ability to create a secondary cast of "wacky-yet-loyal friends and family" in her "tightly written" teen mystery.

Biographical and Critical Sources

PERIODICALS

Booklist, November 1, 2004, John Charles, review of *The Pact,* p. 469; November 1, 2004, John Charles, review of *The Pact,* p. 469; December 15, 2005, John Charles, review of *The Jinx,* p. 29; December 1, 2006, John Charles, review of *The Key,* p. 24; November 15, 2007, John Charles, review of *The Hunt,* p. 23; July 1, 2009, Gillian Engberg, review of *And Then Everything Unraveled,* p. 52; May 1, 2010, Gillian Engberg, review of *And Then I Found out the Truth,* p. 55.

Kirkus Reviews, June 1, 2009, review of *And Then Everything Unraveled*; June 15, 2010, review of *And Then I Found out the Truth.*

Publishers Weekly, October 25, 2004, review of *The Pact,* p. 30; October 23, 2006, review of *The Key,* p. 35; July 13, 2009, review of *And Then Everything Unraveled,* p. 59.

School Library Journal, August, 2009, Brandy Danner, review of *And Then Everything Unraveled,* p. 115; July, 2010, Betsy Fraser, review of *And Then I Found out the Truth,* p. 97.

ONLINE

Authors Unleashed Web log, http://authorsunleashed.blogspot.com/ (August 22, 2009), interview with Sturman.

Jennifer Sturman Home Page, http://jennifersturman.com (December 29, 2011).

T

TANNER, Lian 1951-

Personal

Born 1951, in Tasmania, Australia. *Education:* Attended university (earth science); attended drama school. *Hobbies and other interests:* Gardening, reading, walking on the beach.

Addresses

Home—Tasmania, Australia. *Agent*—Jill Grinberg, Grinberg Literary Management, 244 5th Ave., 11th Fl., New York, NY 10001.

Career

Children's author and playwright. Worked as a teacher in Papua New Guinea; stage actor with touring company for three years; former freelance journalist.

Awards, Honors

Aurealis Award for Children's Fiction, 2010, for *Museum of Thieves.*

Writings

Rats!, Lothian Books (South Melbourne, Victoria, Australia), 2004.

Author of stage plays, including *Heroes.*

"KEEPERS" NOVEL TRILOGY

Museum of Thieves, illustrations by Sebastian Ciaffaglione, Delacorte Press (New York, NY), 2010.
City of Lies, Delacorte Press (New York, NY), 2011.

Author's work has been translated into several languages, including Bahasa, Bulgarian, Chinese, German, Portuguese, Thai, and Turkish.

Adaptations

Museum of Thieves was adapted for audiobook, read by Claudia Black, Listening Library, 2010.

Sidelights

Lian Tanner worked at a variety of jobs before she decided to become an author. A former actress in her native Australia, Tanner wrote several stage plays, then authored an elementary-grade story, *Rats!,* before embarking on her "Keepers" novel trilogy. Awarded the 2010 Aurealis Award for Children's Fiction for its first installment, *Museum of Thieves,* the "Keepers" sequence also includes *City of Lies;* it has been translated into several languages in addition to making its way from Australia to fans in North America.

In *Museum of Thieves* readers meet Goldie Roth, a preteen with an adventurous spirit. Unfortunately for Goldie, she lives in Jewel, a city where only obedience is rewarded. In fact, all the children of Jewel are bound by a silver chain until they attain age twelve, and they receive mandatory training in obedience and conformity. Each year, on Separation Day, those who have turned twelve are released from their chains and allowed to walk the streets. When an explosion occurs, sparking chaos and fear, Goldie's Separation Day is canceled, and so the girl runs away despite the risk such flight entails. Making her way to the Museum of Dunt, Goldie meets a boy named Toadspit, as well as the museum's four keepers, who inform her that her parents have been imprisoned as punishment for their daughter's rash actions. As she is taught to become a keeper as well, Goldie's quick mind helps her navigate the museum's shifting rooms and hallways, where terrible threats to Jewel have been banished and are now hidden. Her talents as a thief and dissembler also have a part to play in Jewel's future, a part that the power-hungry leader Fugleman wishes to prevent. When he sends his minions after Goldie, their presence at the museum threatens to unleash the captive terrors on the city.

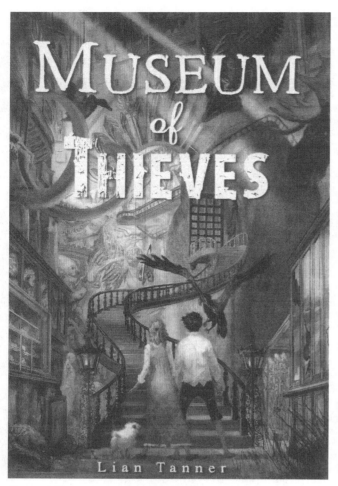

Cover of Lian Tanner's debut middle-grade adventure Museum of Thieves, *featuring artwork by Jon Foster.* (Jacket cover copyright © 2010 by Delacorte Press. Used by permission of Delacorte Press, an imprint of Random House Children's Books, a division of Random House, Inc.)

Praising "the strong characters" in *Museum of Thieves,* Ilene Cooper added in *Booklist* that Tanner's debut novel "will be popular with fans of [books by] Diana Wynne Jones." In *School Library Journal* Beth L. Meister praised the imaginative fantasy as "a fun read and an intriguing start to a new series," and a *Kirkus Reviews* writer dubbed it "a strong fantasy adventure" featuring "an intriguing setting, interesting characters, a riveting plot, and an engaging narrative style."

When readers rejoin Goldie in *City of Lies,* she has become an apprentice keeper of the Museum of Dent. Her love for her parents, newly released from prison, comes first, however, and she has recently abandoned her duties from the museum to care for them. Then Toadspit's sister Bonnie is kidnaped, and Goldie must help her friend track the girl down. The kidnappers' trail leads to the city of Spoke, and Toadspit is abducted during their journey there. Once in Spoke Goldie is faced with a new dilemma: every word she utters is not what she means, and nobody is able to speak the truth. Even her talent for lying is put to the test as she is joined by several unusual friends in her search for her friends and

also discovers a secret that may endanger the museum she has vowed to protect. In *Booklist* Cooper wrote that the history of Spoke "is neatly delivered" in *City of Lies,* and Goldie's latest adventures "are exhilarating."

Biographical and Critical Sources

PERIODICALS

Booklist, October 1, 2010, Ilene Cooper, review of *Museum of Thieves,* p. 91; November 1, 2011, Ilene Cooper, review of *City of Lies,* p. 71.
Bulletin of the Center for Children's Books, October, 2010, April Spisak, review of *Museum of Thieves,* p. 97.
Horn Book, November-December, 2010, Jonathan Hunt, review of *Museum of Thieves,* p. 106.
Kirkus Reviews, September 1, 2010, review of *Museum of Thieves;* August 1, 2011, review of *City of Lies.*
School Library Journal, October, 2010, Beth L. Meister, review of *Museum of Thieves,* p. 127.

ONLINE

Children's Book Review Web site, http://www.thechildrensbookreview.com (September 19, 2010), Bianca Schulze, interview with Tanner.
Lian Tanner Home Page, http://liantanner.com.au (December 29, 2011).*

*   *   *

TARR, Judith 1955-
(Caitlin Brennan, Kathleen Bryan)

Personal

Born January 30, 1955, in Augusta, ME; daughter of Earle A., Jr. (a waterworks manager and real estate salesman) and Regina (a teacher) Tarr. *Education:* Mount Holyoke College, A.B. (Latin and English), 1976; Newnham College, Cambridge, M.A. (classics), 1979; Yale University, M.Phil., 1983, Ph.D. (medieval studies), 1988.

Addresses

Home—Dancing Horse Farm, P.O. Box 429, Vail, AZ 85641. *Agent*—Russell Galen, Scout Chichak Galen, 381 Park Ave. S., Ste. 1112, New York, NY 10016.

Career

Writer and educator. Edward Little High School, Auburn, ME, Latin teacher, 1979-81; writer, beginning 1985. Wesleyan University, Middletown, CT, visiting lecturer in liberal studies and visiting writer, 1989-92, visiting assistant professor of classics, 1990-93. Dancing Horse Farm (riding camp), Vail, AZ, breeder of Lipizzan horses. Writing coach and mentor.

Member

Lipizzan Association of North America, United States Lipizzan Registry, Science Fiction Writers of America.

Awards, Honors

Crawford Memorial Award, 1987; Mary Lyon Award, Mount Holyoke College, 1989.

Writings

A Wind in Cairo, Bantam (New York, NY), 1989.
Ars Magica, Bantam (New York, NY), 1989.
Alamut, Doubleday (New York, NY), 1989.
The Dagger and the Cross: A Novel of the Crusades, Doubleday (New York, NY), 1991.
(With Harry Turtledove and others) *Blood Vengeance* (science fiction), Baen (New York, NY), 1993.
(With Harry Turtledove and others) *Blood Feuds* (science fiction), Baen (New York, NY), 1993.
His Majesty's Elephant, Jane Yolen Books (San Diego, CA), 1993.
Lord of the Two Lands, Tor (New York, NY), 1993.
Throne of Isis, Forge (New York, NY), 1994.
The Eagle's Daughter, Forge (New York, NY), 1995.
Pillar of Fire, Forge (New York, NY), 1995.
King and Goddess, Forge (New York, NY), 1996.
Queen of Swords, Forge (New York, NY), 1997.
The Shepherd Kings, Forge (New York, NY), 1999.
(With Harry Turtledove) *Household Gods,* Tor (New York, NY), 1999.
Kingdom of the Grail, Roc (New York, NY), 2000.
Pride of Kings, Roc (New York, NY), 2001.
Devil's Bargain, Roc (New York, NY), 2002.
House of War (sequel to *Devil's Bargain*), Roc (New York, NY), 2003.
Queen of the Amazons, Tor (New York, NY), 2004.
Rite of Conquest, Roc (New York, NY), 2004.
King's Blood, Roc (New York, NY), 2005.
Bring down the Sun, Tor (New York, NY), 2008.

Work represented in anthologies, including *Moonsinger's Friends,* edited by Susan Schwartz, Bluejay Books (New York, NY), 1985; *Four from the Witch World,* edited by Andre Norton, Tor (New York, NY), 1989; *Alternate Kennedys,* edited by Mike Resnick, Tor, 1992; *Sisters in Fantasy I,* edited by Schwartz, Roc (New York, NY), 1995; *Return to Avalon,* edited by Jennifer Roberson, DAW (New York, NY), 1996; *Alternate Generals II,* edited by Harry Turtledove, 2002; and *Emerald Magic,* edited by Andrew Greeley, 2004. Contributor to *Isaac Asimov's Science Fiction Magazine*

"HOUND AND THE FALCON" FANTASY NOVELS

The Isle of Glass, Bluejay Books (New York, NY), 1985.
The Golden Horn, Bluejay Books (New York, NY), 1985.
The Hounds of God, Bluejay Books (New York, NY), 1986.

The Hound and the Falcon (omnibus), Orb (New York, NY), 1993.

"AVARYAN RISING" FANTASY NOVELS

The Hall of the Mountain King (also see below), Bluejay Books (New York, NY), 1986.
The Lady of Han-Gilen (also see below), Bluejay Books (New York, NY), 1986.
A Fall of Princes (also see below), Bluejay Books (New York, NY), 1987.
Avaryan Rising (includes *The Hall of the Mountain King, The Lady of Han-Gilen,* and *A Fall of Princes*), Doubleday (New York, NY), 1988.
Arrows of the Sun (also see below), Tor (New York, NY), 1993.
Spear of Heaven (also see below), Tor (New York, NY), 1994.
Tides of Darkness (also see below), Tor (New York, NY), 2002.
Avaryan Resplendent (contains *Arrows of the Sun, Spear of Heaven,* and *Tides of Darkness*), Tor (New York, NY), 2003.

"EPONA SEQUENCE" PREHISTORICAL NOVEL TRILOGY

White Mare's Daughter, Forge (New York, NY), 1998.
Lady of Horses, Forge (New York, NY), 2000.
Daughter of Lir, Forge (New York, NY), 2001.

"WHITE MAGIC" FANTASY NOVELS; UNDER PEN NAME CAITLIN BRENNAN

The Mountain's Call, Luna, 2004.
Son of Unmaking, Luna, 2005.
Shattered Dance, Luna, 2006.

"WAR OF THE ROSES" FANTASY NOVELS; UNDER PEN NAME KATHLEEN BRYAN

The Serpent and the Rose, Tor (New York, NY), 2007.
The Golden Rose, Tor (New York, NY), 2008.
The Last Paladin, Tor (New York, NY), 2009.

Sidelights

A prolific author of fantasy fiction, Judith Tarr grounds her novels in the past; a trained historian, she draws on her academic background in adding depth and realism to her works. The three volumes of Tarr's "Hound and the Falcon" series transport readers back to late-twelfth and early-thirteenth-century Europe as well as the Middle East, while her novels *Lord of the Two Lands* and *Bring down the Sun* are set in and around the age of Alexander the Great in the fourth century B.C. In *Pillar of Fire* Tarr turns to Egypt, telling an alternative version of the fate of the ancient pharaoh Akhenaten, while the companion novels *Devil's Bargain* and *House of War* draw fans into the battle for the holy land that

consumed the life of Richard the Lionhearted. In addition to writing under her own name, Tarr has also produced fiction under several pseudonyms, her "War of the Roses" novels as Kathleen Bryan, and her "White Magic" books as Caitlin Brennan. When not writing, Tarr breeds and trains Lipizzans at her Arizona ranch, Dancing Horse Farm.

Tarr began her fiction-writing career with her "Hound and the Falcon" fantasy series, consisting of *The Isle of Glass, The Golden Horn,* and *The Hounds of God.* The series traces the adventures of Alfred, an immortal of unknown origins who was abandoned at birth, as many unwanted children were in ancient and medieval times. Alfred was raised in a monastery as an oblate, and because of his ancestry he suffers a conflict involving "his spiritual needs as a monk, his magical ability, and his physical reality as a non-human," according to Phyllis J. Day in *Fantasy Review.* In *The Isle of Glass* Alfred is sent on an important mission to crusader King Richard I of England. *The Golden Horn* finds him and his immortal lover Thea in the city of Constantinople, which is besieged by Crusaders, while *The Hounds of God* places Alfred as chancellor of the kingdom of Rhiyana, where the few surviving immortals are under attack by the Inquisition. Many critics reacted positively to Tarr's mix of history, romance, and fantasy, and the popular trilogy has been more-recently republished in a single volume, *The Hound and the Falcon.* "Tarr provides loving detail to each characterization, subplot, image, and interaction—her craft is exceptional," Day concluded of the novels.

In *The Lady of Han-Gilen,* part of Tarr's "Avaryan Rising" series, Elian recalls the ancient Greek legend of Atalanta: she is beautiful, intelligent, and determined not to marry until she finds someone she cannot best. Her chosen mate turns out to be a childhood friend named Mirain, who is a demigod. "Proving herself an able warrior as well as a royal hellion with prophetic gifts," as Anne Raymer explained in *Voice of Youth Advocates,* "Elian wins more than the admiration of her child love." Subsequent volumes in the series chronicle the future of the kingdom that Mirain and Elian establish. *Spear of Heaven,* which describes the path of one of their descendants, "owes more to adventure novels such as [Rudyard Kipling's] *Kim* and . . . [James Hilton's] *Lost Horizons,*" stated Faren Miller in *Locus,* the critic adding that the novel reads like "an exotic hybrid of *Lost Horizons* and [Shakespeare's] *The Taming of the Shrew.*" Praising Tarr's "elegant" prose in *The Lady of Han-Gilen,* a *Publishers Weekly* reviewer observed that the author "beautifully conveys splendid regal settings, realistic politics, convincing cultural details—and cultural clashes."

In *White Mare's Daughter* Tarr creates a world populated by peaceful, goddess-worshiping nomads who come in conflict with a tribe of warrior horsemen which deny freedom to their women. *Library Journal* reviewer Laurel Bliss stated that the book "showcases Tarr's

ability to create fascinating, passionate characters and to bring their unique cultures to life." This same world is revisited by the author in *Daughter of Lir.* The city of Lir, which has been founded by the goddess-worshipers, must now combat invaders armed with chariots. Determined to build her own chariot army, Rhian, the chosen one of the White Mare, must ally forces with her brother, Prince Emry, to save her people. "Lir's matriarchal utopia will please feminist and romantics alike," maintained a *Publishers Weekly* reviewer in appraising the fantasy sequel.

Tarr places actual historical characters in fantastic contexts in several of her novels. The title character of *His Majesty's Elephant,* for example, is Abul Abbas, an elephant given by Haroun al-Rashid, the caliph of Baghdad, to Frankish Emperor Charlemagne in the early ninth century. Tarr adds a subplot about a magical talisman that arrives with Abul Abbas. When a sorcerer wishes to use it to cast a spell that will kill the emperor, Charlemagne's youngest daughter Rowan and a British slave named Kerrec confront him. "Tarr has written a

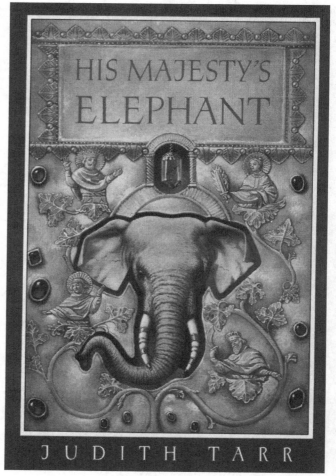

Cover of Judith Tarr's imaginative novel **His Majesty's Elephant,** *featuring artwork by Bryan Leister.* (Illustration copyright © 1993 by Brian Leister. Reproduced by permission of Houghton Mifflin Harcourt Publishing Company. This material may not be reproduced in any form or by any means without the prior written permission of the publisher.)

marvelous fantasy tale," asserted Renee Troselius in her *Book Report* appraisal of *His Majesty's Elephant,* the critic adding that "Rowan is a strong-willed character that readers will care about."

Also mixing fact and fantasy, *The Eagle's Daughter* is set in the tenth century as a chaotic Roman empire fragments into eastern and western halves. Praising the work as a "fully realized novel," a *Booklist* critic added that Tarr recreates successfully the complex politics of an ancient empire at the cusp of the modern world.

"Tarr's ability to give equal weight to both history and myth provides her historical fantasies with both realism and wonder," commented *Library Journal* contributor Jackie Cassada in her review of *Kingdom of the Grail,* a story set amid the Camelot legend. Like her "Hound and the Falcon" series, the author's novel *Pride of Kings* is an historical fantasy set in the twelfth century. When King Richard the Lionheart leaves for Palestine on a crusade, he assigns his brother John to watch over his kingdom. John is tempted by the power he now controls and he attempts to claim his brother's kingdom as his own. "Gracefully and convincingly told," according to Jackie Cassada in *Library Journal, Pride of Kings* inspired a *Publishers Weekly* critic to comment that "the fantastic may be subsidiary to fact . . . but it lends an eerily beautiful, sometimes frightening undercurrent to this engrossing, thoroughly satisfying novel."

Tarr returns to the time of the Crusades in both *Devil's Bargain* and *House of War,* which again focus on Richard the Lionheart and his effort to regain Christendom. Eventually taking control of the city of Jerusalem in *House of War,* Richard is forced to return to England and end the predations of his ambitious brother Henry. Into this story Tarr weaves the tale of Signed, illegitimate half-sister to the king and a woman capable of second sight, as she wrestles with internal demons while also attempting to keep a sorcerer from capturing the king's earthly essence. Reviewing *House of War,* Whitney Scott dubbed the work a "beautifully researched, masterfully written historical fantasy," the critic citing the novel's "compelling mixture of magic, myth, and history" in her *Booklist* review.

Another mix of fantasy and fact, *Bring down the Sun* focuses on the reign of King Philip of Macedon, father to the man who history would immortalize as Alexander the Great. In her story, Tarry focuses on Polyxena, a priestess who gains the king's favor and, wed under her new name Myrtale, eventually becomes mother to Alexander. "Much of the delight" of the story's mix of fantasy and "meticulously researched history" "lies in Tarr's realization of the past as a living, palpable present," asserted Whitney Scott in her *Booklist* review of *Bring down the Sun,* and a *Publishers Weekly* critic praised the author's ability to meld a romantic tale with "a strong narrative about a fascinating woman."

Alexander's relationship with heroic female warrior Hippolyta is the focus of *Queen of the Amazons.* When the queen gives birth to her first child, the infant is found to have no soul. Named Etta, the girl is made heiress to Hippolyta's kingdom although many in her tribe of Amazons are angered. The queen realizes that she must remain alive until the child can be made wholly human, and when news of the powerful Persian king Alexander arrives, his legend takes control of the young girl. Although Etta receives a soul, it is not as her mother would wish it in a novel that *Library Journal* contributor Jackie Cassada dubbed "essential for fans of historical fiction." "Tarr's gift for combining . . . magical fantasy with fully drawn, compelling characters acting within the framework of history again bears fruit," asserted Scott in *Booklist,* while a *Publishers Weekly* contributor praised *Queen of the Amazons* as a "stirring historical fantasy" and a novel in which "fluid plotting and carefull research will keep readers intrigued."

The rein of William the Conqueror becomes Tarr's focus in a series of novels that begins with *Rite of Conquest* and follows the end of Saxon rule over England. Born in Norman France as the illegitimate son of a duke and a mystic, William gains renown through his mix of bravery and brutality in battle. When he meets Matilda, a woman of noble birth who can help him harness his temper through magic, William's fate as the conqueror of Britain is set. William's son, William the Red, now has the throne in *King's Blood,* but when he decides to forswear the magic that built Norman Britain the kingdom falls into decline. Younger brother Henry and Edith, a Scottish princess, may be able to harness the magical power to restore the health of the island kingdom, but first they must win the king's consent. The strength of *Rite of Conquest* "derives as much from the solidly grounded, multifaceted backdrop [Tarr] . . . weaves as from the magical elements . . . she injects into her scenarios," asserted Scott, while a *Publishers Weekly* critic wrote that "break-neck pacing and compelling historical detail help the reader suspend disbelief" in Tarr's fanciful take on British history. Calling *King's Blood* a "gripping alternate history," Scott continued to express her admiration for the sister's ability to "satisfy her present fans and garner new ones," and a *Kirkus Reviews* writer described the same novel as "a fast and entertaining read" in which "Tarr's all-too-human characters are not easily forgotten."

Tarr's novels *Lord of the Two Lands, Throne of Isis,* and *Pillar of Fire* are set in ancient Egypt and describe, respectively, the country's conquest by Alexander the Great, the reign of Cleopatra and her romance with the Roman soldier Marc Anthony, and the career of the pharaoh Akhenaten and the prophet Moses. Egypt's infamous Queen Hatshepsut is the focus of *King and Goddess,* and here Tarr captures the spirit of this powerful queen and the unusual events that marked her years as ruler of the ancient kingdom. *Booklist* reviewer Whitney Scott called the novel "meticulously researched" and noted that Tarr's "artistry again brings [an ancient world] to life for twentieth century readers."

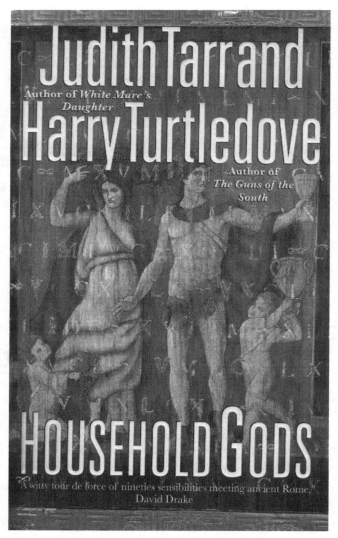

Cover of Household Gods, *a collaborative novel by Tarr and Harry Turtledove that features cover art by Cynthia von Buhler.* (Jacket cover by Cynthia von Buhler. Reproduced by permission of St. Martin's Press, LLC.)

Tarr returns to the kingdom of Egypt in *The Shepherd Kings*, and here readers discover a world cast into despair by foreign invaders. The hopes of the Egyptians rest on a slave girl named Iry who feels destined to rid her land of the barbarians and free Egypt. A *Booklist* contributor called *The Shepherd Kings* a "dramatically imagined chapter in ancient Egyptian history."

In addition to her novels, Tarr has occasionally worked in collaboration with other authors and has contributed many stories to fantasy and alternate-history anthologies. She joins forces with noted fantasy writer Harry Turtledove in *Household Gods,* an adaptation of the *Wizard of Oz* that invites readers into the life of Nicole Gunter-Perrin. A frustrated single mom, Nicole awakens one morning to find herself inhabiting the body of a second-century Roman woman. She quickly discovers that life in the ancient world is much more difficult than she imagined. Jackie Cassada noted in *Library Journal* that the story in *Household Gods* "emphasizes the human qualities that transcend the limitations of history."

"Fantasy is more than an illogical escape, or a conglomeration of elements from Tolkien, C.S. Lewis, and the *Dungeons and Dragons Monster Manual*," Tarr once commented. "Good fantasy requires a knowledge of history, a feeling for language—one's own and, preferably, a number of others (I have classical and medieval Latin, classical Greek, Old and Middle English, medieval and modern French, some German, and some Provençal)—and an affinity for plain old hard work. The training and techniques required to earn a Ph.D. adapt themselves very well indeed to the exigencies of creating and populating a world. If nothing else, I have learned where to look for what I need, what to look for, and what to do with it when I have it—not to mention the ability to produce work of consistent and, I can hope, high quality, on command and against a deadline.

"I write what I write . . . because I *like* writing fantasy. The challenge of historical fantasy is to adhere as closely as possible to actual historical events, while incorporating elements of fantasy: magical beings and powers, imaginary kingdoms, and straightforward alternate history. In high fantasy, the challenge becomes at once simpler and more complex. The need for scrupulous historical research is less, but in its place comes the task of creating lands, people, languages, histories, cultures, and all the manifold aspects of a living world. Not only must I create them, I must create them as a whole, connected logically and plausibly, with characters drawn to the best of my ability. It is not easy. There are few shortcuts. The result is never as close to perfection as it might be, but the sheer, exhilarating fun of it is well worth the effort."

Biographical and Critical Sources

BOOKS

St. James Guide to Fantasy Writers, St. James Press (Detroit, MI), 1996.
St. James Guide to Science-Fiction Writers, 4th edition, St. James Press (Detroit, MI), 1996.

PERIODICALS

Booklist, February 15, 1993, Denise Perry Donavin, review of *Lord of the Two Lands,* pp. 1036-1037; September 15, 1993, Roland Green, review of *Arrows of the Sun,* p. 132; January 1, 1994, Julie Corsaro, review of *His Majesty's Elephant,* p. 817; April 15, 1994, Whitney Scott, review of *Throne of Isis,* p. 1516; November 15, 1994, Roland Green, review of *Spear of Heaven,* p. 582; March 15, 1995, Brad Hooper, review of *The Eagle's Daughter,* p. 1310; June 1, 1995, Whitney Scott, review of *Pillar of Fire,* p. 1732; August, 1996, review of *King and Goddess,* p. 1891; January, 1997, review of *Queen of Swords,* p. 822; June 1, 1998, Whitney Scott, review of *White Mare's Daughter,* p. 1729; July, 1999, reviews of

Household Gods, p. 1896, and *The Shepherd Kings,* p. 1925; June 1, 2000, Diana Tixier Herald, review of *Lady of Horses,* p. 1862; August, 2000, Roland Green, review of *Kingdom of the Grail,* p. 2126; August, 2001, Whitney Scott, review of *Pride of Kings,* p. 2102; October 1, 2002, Whitney Scott, review of *Devil's Bargain,* p. 309; November 1, 2002, Roland Green, review of *Tides of Darkness,* p. 481; October 1, 2003, Whitney Scott, review of *House of War,* p. 308; March 1, 2004, Whitney Scott, review of *Queen of the Amazons,* p. 1147; September 15, 2004, Whitney Scott, review of *Rite of Conquest,* p. 215; October 15, 2005, Whitney Scott, review of *King's Blood,* p. 37; June 1, 2008, Whitney Scott, review of *Bring down the Sun,* p. 57.

Book Report, May-June, 1994, Renee Troselius, review of *His Majesty's Elephant,* pp. 46-47.

Fantasy Review, January, 1986, Phyllis J. Day, review of "Hound and the Falcon" series, p. 26.

Horn Book, January-February, 1994, Ann A. Flowers, review of *His Majesty's Elephant,* pp. 76-77.

Kirkus Reviews, June 15, 1996, review of *King and Goddess,* p. 853; December 15, 1996, review of *Queen of Swords,* p. 1764; June 1, 1998, review of *White Mare's Daughter,* p. 775; May 1, 1999, review of *The Shepherd Kings,* p. 667; July 1, 1999, review of *Household Gods,* p. 1000; September 1, 2005, review of *King's Blood,* p. 948.

Kliatt, July, 1996, review of *Throne of Isis,* p. 56; September, 1997, review of *Pillar of Fire,* p. 54; November, 1997, review of *The Eagle's Daughter,* p. 38; January, 2002, Liz LaValley, review of *Pride of Kings,* pp. 20-21; March, 2003, Liz LaValley, review of *Devil's Bargain,* pp. 36-37; May, 2003, Ginger Armstrong, review of *Daughter of Lir,* p. 28.

Library Journal, March 15, 1986, Jackie Cassada, review of *The Hounds of God,* p. 81; May 15, 1988, Jackie Cassada, review of *A Fall of Princes,* p. 96; December, 1989, Jackie Cassada, review of *Alamut,* p. 176; February 15, 1991, Jackie Cassada, review of *The Dagger and Cross,* p. 224; April 1, 1994, Mary Ann Parker, review of *Throne of Isis,* pp. 134-135; October 15, 1994, Jackie Cassada, review of *Deals with the Devil,* p. 90; November 15, 1994, Jackie Cassada, review of *Spear of Heaven,* p. 89; June 15, 1995, Cynthia Johnson, review of *Pillar of Fire,* p. 96; February 1, 1997, review of *Queen of Swords,* p. 108; June 1, 1998, review of *White Mare's Daughter,* p. 161; August, 1999, reviews of *The Shepherd Kings,* p. 143, and *Household Gods,* p. 147; August, 2000, Jackie Cassada, review of *Kingdom of the Grail,* p. 167; June 15, 2001, Laurel Bliss, review of *Daughter of Lir,* p. 106; September 15, 2001, Jackie Cassada, review of *Pride of Kings,* p. 115; October 15, 2002, Jackie Cassada, review of *Devil's Bargain,* p. 97; November 15, 2002, Jackie Cassada, review of *Tides of Darkness,* p. 106; March 15, 2004, Jackie Cassada, review of *Queen of the Amazons,* p. 110; September 15, 2004, Jackie Cassada, review of *Rite of Conquest,* p. 52; October 15, 2005, Jackie Cassada, review of *King's Blood,* p. 51.

Publishers Weekly, April 10, 1987, Sybil Steinberg, review of *The Lady of Han-Gilen,* pp. 85-86; April 1, 1988, Sybil Steinberg, review of *A Fall of Princes,* p. 78; July 28, 1989, Penny Kaganoff, review of *Ars Magica,* p. 215; February 1, 1993, review of *Lord of the Two Lands,* pp. 76-77; August 30, 1993, review of *Arrows of the Sun,* p. 80; November 1, 1993, review of *His Majesty's Elephant,* p. 81; March 21, 1994, review of *Throne of Isis,* p. 56; October 17, 1994, review of *Spear of Heaven,* p. 68; March 20, 1995, review of *The Eagle's Daughter,* p. 44; May 22, 1995, review of *Pillar of Fire,* p. 50; July 8, 1996, review of *King and Goddess,* p. 74; January 6, 1997, review of *Queen of Swords,* p. 66; April 27, 1998, review of *White Mare's Daughter,* p. 45; May 31, 1999, review of *The Shepherd Kings,* p. 67; August 23, 1999, review of *Household Gods,* p. 54; September 4, 2000, review of *Lady of Horses,* p. 91; June 18, 2001, review of *Daughter of Lir,* p. 61; August 13, 2001, review of *Pride of Kings,* p. 291; October 14, 2002, review of *Tides of Darkness,* p. 69; February 23, 2004, review of *Queen of the Amazons,* p. 56; September 20, 2004, review of *Rite of Conquest,* p. 50; August 15, 2005, review of *King's Blood,* p. 38; April 7, 2008, review of *Bring down the Sun,* p. 46.

School Library Journal, February, 2000, Christine C. Menefee, review of *Household Gods,* p. 143.

Science Fiction Chronicle, August, 1999, review of *Household Gods,* p. 40.

ONLINE

Judith Tarr Home Page, http://www.sff.net/ (January 8, 2011).*

* * *

THAKE, Richard 1938-

Personal

Born 1938, in Ontario, Canada; married; wife's name Barb; children: three. *Hobbies and other interests:* Model aircraft.

Addresses

Home—Newcastle, Ontario, Canada.

Career

Children' author. Formerly worked in advertising as associate creative director. Richard Thake INK, Inc., Newcastle, Ontario, Canada, advertising consultancy.

Writings

Sir Seth Thistlethwaite and the Soothsayer's Shoes, illustrated by Vince Chui, Owlkids (Berkley, CA), 2010.

Sir Seth Thistlethwaite and the Kingdom of the Caves, illustrated by Vince Chui, Owlkids (Berkley, CA), 2011.

Biographical and Critical Sources

PERIODICALS

Kirkus Reviews, August 15, 2010, review of *Sir Seth Thistlethwaite and the Soothsayer's Shoes.*
Publishers Weekly, August 23, 2010, review of *Sir Seth Thistlethwaite and the Soothsayer's Shoes,* p. 49.
School Library Journal, November, 2010, Amy Holland, review of *Sir Seth Thistlethwaite and the Soothsayer's Shoes,* p. 85.

ONLINE

Open Book Ontario Web site, http://www.openbookontario. com/ (December 3, 2010), interview with Thake.*

*   *   *

TITCOMB, Gordon

Personal

Has children. *Hobbies and other interests:* Antiques, aviation.

Addresses

Home—Winsted, CT. *E-mail*—tunesmith53@yahoo. com.

Career

Studio musician and writer. Performer on pedal steel, mandolin, guitar, dobro, and five-string banjo. Composer; Omnimusic, staff writer. Performer with numerous artists; soloist performing at Grand Ole Opry, Ryman Auditorium, Carnegie Hall, Lincoln Center, and others. Teacher of music.

Member

Association Society of Composers, Authors, and Publishers.

Writings

The Last Train, illustrated by Wendell Minor, Roaring Brook Press (New York, NY), 2010.

Author of song lyrics.

Adaptations

The Last Train was adapted for audiobook, with musical performance by Titcomb, Live Oak Media, 2010.

Biographical and Critical Sources

PERIODICALS

Booklist, September 15, 2010, Karen Cruze, review of *The Last Train,* p. 69.
Kirkus Reviews, September 1, 2010, review of *The Last Train.*
New York Times Book Review, December 19, 2010, Abby Mcganney Nolan, review of *The Last Train.*
Publishers Weekly, August 15, 2010, review of *The Last Train,* p. 50.
School Library Journal, October, 2010, Wendy Lukehart, review of *The Last Train,* p. 94.

ONLINE

Gordon Titcomb Home Page, http://www.gordontitcomb. com (December 29, 2011).*

*   *   *

TOFFLER-CORRIE, Laura

Personal

Born in New York, NY; married Tom Corrie; children: Hannah, Rachel (twins). *Education:* New York University, M.S. (school psychology), M.F.A. (dramatic writing).

Addresses

Home—South Salem, NY. *Agent*—Elana Roth, Johnson Literary Agency, elana@johnsonliterary.com.

Career

Freelance writer. Silvermine Arts Center, New Canaan, CT, teacher of writing for children, 2012.

Writings

The Life and Opinions of Amy Finawitz, Roaring Brook Press (New York, NY), 2010.

Sidelights

Laura Toffler-Corrie grew up on Long Island and remembers visiting the nearby island of Manhattan frequently as a child, where the diversity and energy of New York City was contagious. These memories, as well as her experiences as an older teen juggling friends, school, and dating, inspired her debut middle-grade novel, *The Life and Opinions of Amy Finawitz.*

A New York City native, Amy is none too happy when readers first meet her in *The Life and Opinions of Amy Finawitz.* Her long-time best friend Callie has moved with her family to rural Kansas, leaving the self-absorbed and introspective eighth grader without a much-needed confidante. The drama in Amy's life soon ratchets up another notch when her brother drops out of college and announces to their academic-minded parents that he plans to become an actor. Fortunately, a

reading assignment involving the journal of a nineteenth-century immigrant helps Amy to put her own situation into a more realistic perspective. Although the preteen is less than enthusiastic about writing an essay on the journal of Jewish teenager Anna Slonovich, her mother makes things worse by suggesting that she work on the project with Miss Sophia, an elderly neighbor, and the woman's nephew, Beryl, an Hasidic Jew. Touring the city with Sophia and Beryl in search of landmarks from Anna's time, Amy eventually learns that the city she thought she knew so well is a very different place when viewed from others' perspective. A budding romance, as well as a long-hidden secret from Anna's past, draw the preteen into a surprising mystery in Toffler-Corrie's fiction debut.

While noting Amy's adolescent tendency to be self-absorbed, a *Publishers Weekly* contributor added that the letters to Callie that serve as the narrative of *The Life and Opinions of Amy Finawitz* are "genuinely funny." In *School Library Journal* Susan Riley praised Toffler-Corrie's prose style as "authentic" and deemed the novel "a strong first effort." "An eighth graders voice progresses from forced to funny in this medley of Judaisms," asserted a *Kirkus Reviews* writer, the critic going on to write that the author "portrays both Beryl's Orthodox Judaism . . . and Amy's hippie-flaky Judaism . . . with value and sweetness."

Biographical and Critical Sources

PERIODICALS

Kirkus Reviews, July 1, 2010, review of *The Life and Opinions of Amy Finawitz.*
Publishers Weekly, July 26, 2010, review of *The Life and Opinions of Amy Finawitz,* p. 76.
School Library Journal, November, 2010, Susan Riley, review of *The Life and Opinions of Amy Finawitz,* p. 130.

ONLINE

Johnson Literary Agency Web site, http://www.johnson literary.com/ (December 29, 2011).
Laura Toffler-Corrie Home Page, http://www.lauratoffler -corrie.com (December 29, 2011).*

*   *   *

TUTTLE, Cameron

Personal
Female.

Addresses
Home—San Francisco, CA.

Career
Writer.

Writings

The Paranoid's Pocket Guide, Chronicle Books (San Francisco, CA), 1997, Fine Communications (New York, NY), 2004.
The Bad Girl's Guide to the Open Road, Chronicle Books (San Francisco, CA), 1999.
The Bad Girl's Guide to Getting What You Want, Chronicle Books (San Francisco, CA), 2000.
The Bad Girl's Guide to the Party Life, Chronicle Books (San Francisco, CA), 2002.
The Bad Girl's Guide to Getting Personal, Chronicle Books (San Francisco, CA), 2004.
Paisley Hanover Acts Out, Dial Books for Young Readers (New York, NY), 2008.
Paisley Hanover Kisses and Tells, Dial Books for Young Readers (New York, NY), 2010.

Sidelights
Writer Cameron Tuttle is the originator of the "Bad Girl Guide Books" series, irreverent volumes on various subjects that range from travel to dating to getting ahead

Cover of Cameron Tuttle's middle-grade novel **Paisley Hanover Kisses and Tells,** *featuring artwork by Michael Frost.* (Cover photograph copyright © 2010 by Michael Frost. Used by permission of Dial Books for Young Readers, a division of Penguin Young Readers Group, a member of Penguin Group (USA) Inc., 345 Hudson Street, New York, NY 10014. All rights reserved.)

in the world. The books have been translated into more than a dozen foreign languages, and each provides readers with space for notes or thoughts that help to keep the books personal and worthy of a place on the bookshelf. Illustrated with color photographs, these books serve to keep a girl's life in order. Titles include *The Paranoid's Pocket Guide, The Bad Girl's Guide to the Open Road, The Bad Girl's Guide to Getting What You Want, The Bad Girl's Guide to the Party Life, The Bad Girl's Guide to Getting Personal,* and her young-adult novels *Paisley Hanover Acts Out* and *Paisley Hanover Kisses and Tells.*

In *The Paranoid's Pocket Guide* Tuttle offers readers a sane approach to paranoia. Fear can be crippling, particularly when it seems to touch on every aspect of one's life. Fortunately, in her book Tuttle suggests how to channel or work through readers' anxiety in order to stop the irrational paranoia that occasionally becomes debilitating. This includes allowing fear but also giving it a focus and direction. For instance, rather than allowing a long list of worries to scroll through one's mind, pick a single instance and focus solely on that one worry. Tuttle believes that while worry is inevitable, it can be dealt with on one's own terms and not allowed to become crippling. In an interview with Michael R. Lewisfor the *New York Times* online, Tuttle explained simply that "paranoia is proof that one is aware."

With *Paisley Hanover Acts Out,* Tuttle expands her readership to young adults, introducing a high-school sophomore who thinks her life is ruined when someone switches her schedule and she is moved from the yearbook to drama class. Paisley knows that she will never be trendy or highly popular at Pleasant Hill High School, which is why former friend Jen abandoned her in favor of the most stylish clique at school. She fits in with the yearbook crowd, but she doubts she has much in common with the overly artsy and peculiar individuals she now finds in drama class. Resigned to her fate, Paisley starts to pay attention to what is going on around her, and she soon comes to realize that Jen's new crowd is cruel and seems anxious to abuse anyone who comes across their path, particularly those who are weaker or shy. The more she thinks about the situation, the more Paisley struggles between her longing to fit in and her understanding that there is more to life than being cool. She ultimately writes a column about the subject for the school paper, hiding behind the name Miss UnPleasant. The result is a raucous school-wide debate and a wave of teens decide to be labeled as "Un" cool.

Heather E. Miller, reviewing the novel for *School Library Journal,* praised Tuttle's ear for youthful dialogue, stating of *Paisley Hanover Acts Out* that "the characters are fully developed and multifaceted, with even the most unpleasant popular teens having moments of humanity." A contributor for *Kirkus Reviews* also enjoyed the author's debut, writing that "Paisley is a feisty and compelling heroine to whom female readers will respond."

Paisley returns in *Paisley Hanover Kisses and Tells,* as the battle line is drawn between the Uns and the Pops. When the vice principal prevents her Miss UnPleasant column from continuing in the school newspaper, Paisley sees her sophomore year going from bad to worse. She takes a time-out from feeling sorry for herself when she learns that former-friend Jen is the subject of a compromising photo that is being texted around school. As she attempts to salvage Jen's social standing, Paisley finds herself teaming up with former rival Candy Esposito, while romance may be blooming with Eric . . . or maybe with Clint. Citing Tuttle's use of "snappy catchphrases" in her dialogue-heavy text, Melissa Rabey noted in *School Library Journal* that *Paisley Hanover Kisses and Tells* features a heroine who has an "ability to inspire others . . . thanks to her larger-than-life-personality and way with words." A *Kirkus Reviews* writer dubbed the same book a "spunky sequel" and concluded that, "jam-packed with snarky observations and razor-sharp" wit, Tuttle's *Paisley Hanover Kisses and Tells* treats readers to "teen chick lit with a brain."

Biographical and Critical Sources

PERIODICALS

Kirkus Reviews, September 15, 2008, review of *Paisley Hanover Acts Out*; June 15, 2010, review of *Paisley Hanover Kisses and Tells.*
New York Times Magazine, July 13, 1997, Michael R. Lewis, interview with Tuttle.
Publishers Weekly, August 14, 2000, review of *Paisley Hanover Acts Out,* p. 277.
School Library Journal, January 1, 2009, Heather E. Miller, review of *Paisley Hanover Acts Out,* p. 120; September, 2010, Melissa Rabey, review of *Paisley Hanover Kisses and Tells,* p. 166.

ONLINE

Cameron Tuttle Home Page, http://web.me.com/cameron tuttle (December 29, 2011).
Paisley Hanover Web site, http://www.paisleyhanover.com/ (December 29, 2011).*

V-W

VENUTI, Kristin Clark

Personal

Born in NV; daughter of Thomas L. Clark (an educator); married; children. *Education:* Attended University of Las Vegas. *Hobbies and other interests:* Tae Kwon Do.

Addresses

Home—Saratoga, CA. *Agent*—Adams Literary, 7845 Colony Rd., C4, No. 215, Charlotte, NC 28226; info@ adamsliterary.com.

Career

Author and journalist. Producer of children's theatre. Formerly taught Tae Kwon Do.

Member

Society of Children's Book Writers and Illustrators.

Writings

"BELLWEATHER" NOVEL SERIES

Leaving the Bellweathers, Egmont USA (New York, NY), 2009.
The Butler Gets a Break Egmont USA (New York, NY), 2010.

Sidelights

California author Kristin Clark Venuti began her writing career as a journalist, tracking down local human-interest stories and penning articles that drew on her knowledge of the martial arts. She also wrote several short stories for adult readers before realizing that her sly humor and penchant for whimsy would be a good fit with children's literature. Venuti combines what *Booklist* critic Shelle Rosenfeld described as "an eccentric cast, absurdities, and droll details" and couches them in the "formal narrative and interspersed diary entries" that make up her first novel, *Leaving the Bellweathers.*

Geared for middle-grade readers, *Leaving the Bellweathers* takes readers to the small town of Eel-Smack-by-the-Bay, where a couple and their five children inhabit a local lighthouse. Venuti's story mixes the purported tell-all of professional butler Tristan Benway with a chronicle of the quirky Bellweather family: curmudgeonly inventor Professor Bellweather, his wife Lillian, and their children Spider, Ninda, and ten-year-old triplets Brick, Spike, and Sassy. Benway resolutely suffers his appointment with the family because he is bound by a 200-year-old oath of service made to the late Nigel Benway after Tristan's distant forebear was saved by Nigel from drowning. Flash forward to the present as Benway now counts down the days to the end of his required service, planning to revenge himself on the antic family by crafting a no-holds-barred memoir which he hopes will fund his retirement. With only weeks to go, the butler suddenly becomes the focus of the children's unbridled appreciation, and this flood of good feelings—along with waves of characteristic chaos—prompts him to rethink his plans for the future.

Noting that Venuti's "lighthearted" story "promises to amuse with every turn," *School Library Journal* contributor Robyn Gioia added that the characters in *Leaving the Bellweathers* "are pleasantly nutty, with each distinctive voice adding to the mayhem." While a *Kirkus Reviews* writer remarked that "character development is secondary to silliness," Chelsey Philpot asserted in *Horn Book* that Venuti's "madcap debut novel" features a narrative mix that "makes the episodic text spark with humor," ultimately resolving in a "comforting" conclusion that makes way for a sequel.

Cover of Kristin Clark Venuti's quirky young-adult novel Leaving the Bellweathers, *featuring artwork by Lizzy Bromley.* (Jacket art copyright © 2009 by Lizzy Bromley. Reproduced by permission of Egmont USA.)

Fans of the antic Bellweather clan will rejoice as Benway retains his post in *The Butler Gets a Break.* Although the children attempt to keep their energy in check, mishaps continue in the form of a misguided art project that trips up the butler and places him in the safety of a nearby hospital. While Benway's broken leg heals, the family must tackle butler-type duties as best they can, and the children attempt to limit the injured man's worries by creating a fictional paragon of butlery who they claim is caring for the family in his absence. As Benway records, with increasing jealousy, the purported exploits of his heroic replacement, the actual chaos building within the Bellweather household is captured in Venuti's third-person counter-narrative. "The comically dysfunctional family is back for another outing," announced a *Kirkus Reviews* writer in appraising *The Butler Gets a Break,* while in *Booklist* Shelle Rosenfeld cited the story as a "sometimes touching sequel" that benefits from Benway's characteristic "delightfully archaic prose." Describing Venuti's second novel as a "wacky romp," Helen Foster James added in *School Library Journal* that *The Butler Gets a Break* treats fans to "a humorous, edgy read that feels like a blend of Roald Dahl and Lemony Snicket."

Biographical and Critical Sources

PERIODICALS

Booklist, September 15, 2009, Shelle Rosenfeld, review of *Leaving the Bellweathers,* p. 61; November 1, 2010, Shelle Rosenfeld, review of *The Butler Gets a Break,* p. 62.

Horn Book, November-December, 2009, Chelsey Philpot, review of *Leaving the Bellweathers,* p. 688.

Kirkus Reviews, August 15, 2009, review of *Leaving the Bellweathers*; September 1, 2010, review of *The Butler Gets a Break.*

School Library Journal, September, 2009, Robyn Gioia, review of *Leaving the Bellweathers,* p. 175; November, 2010, Helen Foster James, review of *The Butler Gets a Break,* p. 132.

ONLINE

Adams Literary Web site, http://www.adamsliterary.com/ (October 9, 2011).

Kristin Clark Venuti Home Page, http://www.leavingthe bellweathers.com (December 19, 2011).

*   *   *

WAGNER, Hilary

Personal

Married; husband's name Eric; children: Vincent, Nomi. *Education:* University of Kansas, B.F.A. (painting and art history).

Addresses

Home—Metropolitan Chicago, IL. *Agent*—Marietta Zacker, Nancy Gallt Literary Agency, 273 Charlton Ave., South Orange, NJ 07079. *E-mail*—h.wagner@ nightshadecity.com.

Career

Author, fine-art painter, and corporate recruiter. Sterling Engineering, Elmhurst, IL, technical recruiter, 2000-02; TAC WorldWide, Chicago, IL, senior technical recruiter, 2004-07; Geneca, Oakbrook Terrace, IL, senior corporate recruiter and vendor manager, 2007-10; Genesis10, senior technical recruiter, beginning 2010. Founder, Project Middle-Grade Mayhem (Web log). Presenter at schools.

Awards, Honors

Best Book selection, Center for Children's Books, Crystal Kite Award finalist, Society of Children's Book Writers and Illustrators, and Westchester Fiction Award, all 2011, all for *Nightshade City.*

Writings

Goblin Shark Rising, Holiday House (New York, NY), 2012.

Author of fiction for National Geographic School Publishing.

"NIGHTSHADE CHRONICLES" MIDDLE-GRADE NOVELS

Nightshade City, illustrated by Omar Rayyan, Holiday House (New York, NY), 2010.
The White Assassin, Holiday House (New York, NY), 2011.

Sidelights

Hilary Wagner casts her "Nightshade Chronicles" stories with perhaps the most unusual heroes in middle-grade fantasy: escaped lab rats who have been bred to achieve human-like intelligence. Set beneath a large city, the novels focus on orphaned rat brothers Victor and Vincent Nightshade and their friend Clover (also a rat), who join a rag-tag band of rodent rebels in a valiant effort to overthrow the evil rat dictators of the subterranean rat kingdom known as the Catacombs. Featuring colorful illustrations by Omar Rayyan, Wagner's novels include *Nightshade City* and *The White Assassin,* both of which have been compared by critics to Brian Jacques' popular "Redwall" stories.

As readers venture between the covers of *Nightshade City,* they enter the Catacombs, where a terrible battle has left the once-peaceful kingdom under the control of the ruthless High Minister Killdeer and his sharp-toothed enforcer Billycan, an albino whose natural rodent aggressions were enhanced in the lab through special injections. Outside the Catacombs, Juniper Belancort, a wise older rat, and his rebel band have established a democratic society they call Nightshade City. Jupiter is preparing for the time when his group becomes strong enough to effect Killdeer's downfall, and the arrival of Vincent, Victor, and Clover (Juniper's niece) signals that moment.

In her third-person narrative for *Nightshade City,* Wagner crafts what *Booklist* critic Andrew Medlar characterized as an archetypal "battle between good and evil" that interweaves "themes of . . . loyalty, spirituality, freedom, unrequited love, and coming-of-age." Praising the novel as "an atmospheric and action-filled tale," *School Library Journal* contributor Beth L. Meister cited the story's "balance of strong male and female protagonists," while a *Publishers Weekly* critic praised Wagner's ability to enrich "her sprawling cast with compelling villains and heroes." "A good story well told," according to a *Kirkus Reviews* writer, *Nightshade City* ends on an affirming note as "moments of darkness and violence are ultimately overpowered by hope and redemption."

The villainous Billycan scuttles, ratlike, back into the fray in *The White Assassin,* and in the three years since the action of *Nightshade City* he has been busy. Now the leader of an army of vicious swamp rats, he plans for the moment when he can avenge himself on Juniper

and his band. When the swamp-rat army gains the help of an informant, the future of Nightshade City looks dim, but everything changes when Billycan is captured and a game-changing truth is revealed. Announcing that the second "Nightshade Chronicles" novel "doesn't disappoint," a *Kirkus Reviews* contributor praised *The White Assassin* for addressing weighty issues such as honor, integrity, and responsibility. Wagner's talent for "worldbuilding carries readers through these heavy themes with ease," the critic added.

Biographical and Critical Sources

PERIODICALS

Booklist, September 15, 2010, Andrew Medlar, review of *Nightshade City,* p. 67.
Bulletin of the Center for Children's Books, December, 2010, April Spisak, review of *Nightshade City,* p. 210.
Kirkus Reviews, September 1, 2010, review of *Nightshade City;* September 1, 2011, review of *The White Assassin.*
Publishers Weekly, October 25, 2010, review of *Nightshade City,* p. 49.
School Library Journal, January, 2011, Beth L. Meister, review of *Nightshade City,* p. 118.
Voice of Youth Advocates, December, 2010, Laura Woodruff, review of *Nightshade City,* p. 477.

ONLINE

Chicago Pop Artist Hilary Wagner Web site, http://www.chicagopopart.com (December 19, 2011).
Hilary Wagner Home Page, http://www.nightshadecity.com (December 9, 2011).
Hilary Wagner Web log, http://hilarywagner.blogspot.com (December 9, 2011).

*   *   *

WALSH, Pat 1954-

Personal

Born 1954, in Kent, England; married; children: two. *Education:* College degree (archaeology).

Addresses

Home—Bedfordshire, England.

Career

Archaeologist and author.

Awards, Honors

Carnegie Medal longlist, Branford Boase Award longlist, London *Times*/Chicken House Prize shortlist, and Waterstone's Children's Prize shortlist, all c. 2010,

Salford Children's Book Award shortlist, 2011, Calderdale Children's Book of the Year shortlist, 2012, and several U.S. state award nominations, all for *The Crowfield Curse*.

Writings

The Crowfield Curse, Chicken House (New York, NY), 2010.
The Crowfield Demon, Chicken House (London, England), 2011, Chicken House (New York, NY), 2012.

Adaptations

The Crowfield Curse and *The Crowfield Demon* were adapted as audiobooks.

Sidelights

Pat Walsh went on her first dig as a twelve year old, and this experience encouraged her to train and work as an archaeologist. Inspired by her work exploring the remains of the ancient cultures discovered throughout her native United Kingdom, Walsh began writing as a way to bring such cultures to life, and she taps her talent for storytelling and her interest in fantasy in her first novel, *The Crowfield Curse*.

Set in England during the harsh winter of 1347, *The Crowfield Curse* takes readers to Crowfield Abbey, which shares a boundary with an ancient forest. Fourteen-year-old orphan Will Paynel works as a servant to the abbey's monks, where his tasks take him out into the forest, a haunted place. One day Will comes upon a long-tailed hob-goblin that has been caught in an animal trap. In return for releasing it, the hob tells the boy a long-held secret: somewhere near the abbey can be found the grave of an angel. This secret is also known to two travelers—an itinerant musician and his servant—who arrive shortly thereafter and begin asking revealing questions. As others soon appear and further questions are raised, Will realizes that some have come for good and some for ill, and that it may be up to him to resolve the angel's death and uphold the powers of good.

Will returns in *The Crowfield Demon,* as spring comes to the abby and its surrounds. Just as the stone building has slowly started to fail under the stress of time and wear, a growing evil has also caused the neighboring fey to flee from the area. Will is put to work repairing the tile floor of a small chapel, and when he discovers a hidden box dating from a time before Christianity, he unwittingly unleashes a terrible demon that has been trapped there for many lifetimes.

Praising Walsh's first novel in the London *Times,* Amanda Craig wrote that *The Crowfield Curse* evokes "a strong feeling of nature, place and character," and "the rhythm of monastic life, the austerity, the charity and the kindliness of individuals are beautifully evoked." "Walsh expertly mixes the fantastical with the humdrum necessities of medieval life," asserted *Booklist* contributor Ilene Cooper, and in *School Library Journal* Kathy Kirchoefer deemed *The Crowfield Curse* a "suspenseful and spooky story [that] will thrill readers." In *School Librarian* Rachel Bowler recommended Walsh's prose style as "compelling and at times very moving," concluding that the characters in *The Crowfield Curse* "are well drawn throughout and the air of menace which pervades the narrative is well sustained."

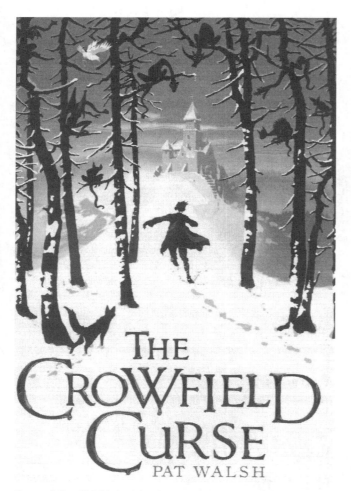

Cover of Pat Walsh's imaginative mystery **The Crowfield Curse,** *the first novel in a trilogy and featuring artwork by David Frankland.* (Jacket art copyright © 2010 by David Frankland. Reproduced by permission of Scholastic, Inc.)

Biographical and Critical Sources

PERIODICALS

Booklist, October 15, 2010, Ilene Cooper, review of *The Crowfield Curse,* p. 63.
Bulletin of the Center for Children's Books, October, 2010, Kate Quealy-Gainer, review of *The Crowfield Curse,* p. 101.

Guardian (London, England), January 30, 2010, Mary Hoffman, review of *The Crowfield Curse,* p. 14.

Kirkus Reviews, September 1, 2010, review of *The Crowfield Curse.*

School Librarian, spring, 2010, Rachel Bowler, review of *The Crowfield Curse,* p. 40.

School Library Journal, September, 2010, Kathy Kirchoefer, review of *The Crowfield Curse,* p. 166.

Times (London, England), January 2, 2010, Amanda Craig, review of *The Crowfield Curse,* p. 12.

ONLINE

Pat Walsh Home Page, http://www.pat-walsh.com (December 29, 2011).*

*   *   *

WATSON, Geoff 1978-

Personal

Born 1978, in PA. *Education:* Harvard University, B.A. (history; magna cum laude), 2000. *Hobbies and other interests:* Movies.

Addresses

Home—Glendale, CA. *Agent*—Meredith Kaffel, Sterling Lord Literary Literistic, 65 Bleecker St., New York, NY 10012; meredith@sll.com.

Career

Screenwriter and author. ICM, Los Angeles, CA, mailroom staffer; worked for writers Joel Silver and Charles Shyer. Presenter at schools. Coach of children's lacrosse.

Awards, Honors

Disney fellowship finalist, 2009, for *Ice Heist.*

Writings

Edison's Gold, Egmont USA (New York, NY), 2010.

Author of screenplays, including *Ice Heist,* 2009, and (with sister Adele Griffin) *The Alchemy Papers,* 2007, and *E-Male,* 2010.

Sidelights

When screenwriter Geoff Watson teamed up with his sister, young-adult novelist Adele Griffin, to write film screenplays he had little idea that one of their efforts would actually become the basis for his first published young-adult novel. In *Edison's Gold* Watson introduces a modern seventh grader whose interest in his famous great-great-great grandfather inspires him to seek the solution to a family mystery. In addition to possibly helping his parents, his search ultimately leads him on a rip-roaring adventure.

Sharing the same name as his famous forebear, Thomas Edison IV is preparing to move with his family from Yonkers, New York, to Kansas when readers first meet him in *Edison's Gold.* The move is precipitated by his father's job loss, and nobody wants to leave, least of all Tom. When he uncovers information that may help solve the rumor that nineteenth-century inventor Thomas Edison discovered how to change base metal into gold, the teen sees even more reason to stay in Yonkers. Teaming up with friends Noodle and Colby to uncover the truth, he discovers the existence of a secret society while perfecting his sleuthing skills, all the time trying to stay a step ahead of a descendent of Edison's competitor in the race to harness electricity: Nikola Tesla.

Watson's "action-packed novel will fit the bill for readers craving adventure stories," predicted Carolyn Phelan in her *Booklist* review of *Edison's Gold,* the critic also praising the story's "clever" young hero. Noting that

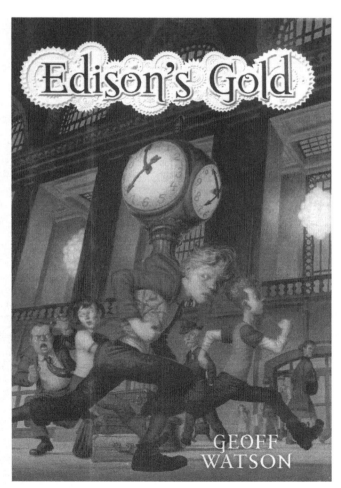

Cover of Geoff Watson's middle-grade adventure Edison's Gold, *a mystery based in history that features cover art by Peter Ferguson.* (Cover illustration copyright © 2010 by Peter Ferguson. Reproduced by permission of Egmont USA.)

the novel introduces a cast of real-life characters that range from Henry Ford and Babe Ruth to U.S. president Franklin D. Roosevelt, Shannon Seglin added in *School Library Journal* that the "fast-paced adventure filled mystery" is one "that middle schoolers will like." "Part treasure hunt, part mystery and part quest adventure, this is all fun," concluded a *Kirkus Reviews* writer in describing *Edison's Gold,* and a *Publishers Weekly* critic dubbed Watson's novel a "spirited debut."

Biographical and Critical Sources

PERIODICALS

Booklist, November 1, 2010, Carolyn Phelan, review of *Edison's Gold,* p. 67.

Bulletin of the Center for Children's Books, February, 2011, Elizabeth Bush, review of *Edison's Gold,* p. 304.

Kirkus Reviews, September 1, 2010, review of *Edison's Gold.*

Publishers Weekly, September 27, 2010, review of *Edison's Gold,* p. 60.

School Library Journal, January, 2011, Shannon Seglin, review of *Edison's Gold,* p. 119.

ONLINE

Geoff Watson Home Page, http://geoffwatsonbooks.com (December 29, 2011).

Script Online, http://www.scriptmag.com/ (September 28, 2010), Jenna Milly, interview with Watson.*

*   *   *

WATSON, Stephanie 1979-

Personal

Born April 21, 1979, in Minneapolis, MN; children: a daughter. *Education:* Attended Sarah Lawrence College. *Hobbies and other interests:* Drawing, painting, crafting, dance, theater, guitar.

Addresses

Home—St. Paul, MN. *Agent*—David Black Literary Agency, 156 5th Ave., New York, NY 10010. *E-mail*—sw@stephanie-watson.com.

Career

Freelance writer and author of children's literature. Presenter at schools.

Writings

Elvis & Olive, Scholastic Press (New York, NY), 2008.

Elvis & Olive: Super Detectives, Scholastic Press (New York, NY), 2010.

The Wee Hours, Disney Hyperion (New York, NY), 2013.

Sidelights

Stephanie Watson, a Minnesota-based writer, entertains upper-elementary-grade readers with her engaging stories in both *Elvis & Olive* and its sequel, *Elvis & Olive: Super Detectives.* Despite being a lifelong fan of children's literature and retaining many vivid memories of her own childhood, Watson admitted to an interviewer for *Kidsreads.com* that she initially approached writing for children with some trepidation. "I really wasn't sure if I could do it," she admitted, "so when I started writing *Elvis & Olive* I kept the process a secret. I didn't tell anyone . . . for over a year. And in the funny way that creativity works, the plot soon became about secrets."

Elvis & Olive explores the unlikely friendship of two preteens: shy, artistic Natalie and raucous, loyal Annie. When Annie suggests that the two form a spying club, they take on suitable aliases—Olive and Elvis respectively—and begin collecting their neighbors' secrets, writing them out on index cards and pinning these to the walls of their special club house beneath Annie's porch. While many of these secrets are simple, innocent oddities, such as an elderly neighbor's whimsical sculpting hobby, others are somewhat more sinister. Matters come to a head when the girls, in the throes of a spat, begin revealing each other's secrets.

Kim Dare wrote in *School Library Journal* of *Elvis & Olive* that readers "will enjoy the twists and turns the story takes as the two try to undo the damage," and *Booklist* critic Kathleen Isaacs called the chapter book "a solid exploration of friendship and self-confidence themes . . . important to middle-grade girls." A contributor to *Kirkus Reviews* concluded that Watson's first novel treats readers to "a satisfying friendship story with drama and humor in fine balance."

Natalie and Annie return in *Elvis & Olive: Super Detectives,* as the ten year olds turn their penchant for secrets into a positive endeavor—and also fulfill their school's community service requirement—by starting the E & O Detective Agency. A lost dog searching for its home, a songwriter seeking a word that seems just out of reach, and a neighbor perplexed by the loss of a favorite sandal: these are just some of the clients that detective-minded alter-egos Elvis and Olive take on in their new enterprise. As Natalie and Annie hone their detecting skills on such cases, they also realize that their knack for asking the right questions may help them in solving their personal dilemmas as well.

In *Elvis & Olive: Super Detectives* readers can cheer on the girls as they "uncover hidden inner strengths" as well as "leadership skills, and realizations about their personal mysteries," noted *School Library Journal* con-

Elvis & Olive: Super Detectives, *a chapter book by Stephanie Watson,* *features cover art by Shane Rebenshied.* (Jacket art copyright © 2010 by Shane Rebenshied. Reproduced by permission of Scholastic, Inc.)

tributor Krista Welz, and a *Kirkus Reviews* reviewer praised Watson's "lightly poetic prose" for imbuing her "fresh and affecting" chapter book with "an overall sense of goodwill."

Biographical and Critical Sources

PERIODICALS

Booklist, April 1, 2008, Kathleen Isaacs, review of *Elvis & Olive,* p. 46.

Kirkus Reviews, April 1, 2008, review of *Elvis & Olive;* June 15, 2010, review of *Elvis & Olive: Super Detectives.*

School Library Journal, April 1, 2008, Kim Dare, review of *Elvis & Olive,* p. 152; August, 2010, Krista Welz, review of *Elvis & Olive: Super Detectives,* p. 116.

ONLINE

Kidsreads.com, http://www.kidsreads.com/ (January 29, 2009), interview with Watson.

Stephanie Watson Home Page, http://www.stephanie-watson.com (December 15, 2011).

WELLS, Rosemary 1943-

Personal

Born January 29, 1943, in New York, NY; married Thomas Moore Wells (an architect), 1963 (deceased); children: Victoria, Marguerite. *Education:* Attended Boston Museum School and a small private junior college (now defunct) in New York State. *Religion:* "Nominal Episcopalian."

Addresses

Home—Briarcliff Manor, NY.

Career

Author and illustrator of children's books. Allyn & Bacon, Inc., Boston, MA, art editor; Macmillan Publishing Co., Inc., New York, NY, art designer; freelance author and illustrator, 1968—. Worked as shoe and small-goods buyer in New York, NY; founder, with Susan Jeffers, of book design studio in New York, NY, c. early 1970s. Speaker for national literacy campaign "Twenty Minutes a Day," beginning 1994; founder of "Read to Your Bunny" campaign (part of Prescription for Reading program), 1998. *Exhibitions:* Work included in American Institute of Graphic Arts Children's Book shows.

Awards, Honors

Honor Book citation, *Book World* Spring Children's Book Festival, 1972, for *The Fog Comes on Little Pig Feet;* American Library Association (ALA) Notable Children's Book citations, 1973, for both *Noisy Nora* and *Benjamin and Tulip,* 1982, for *Morris's Disappearing Bag,* 1985, for *Max's Breakfast,* 1986, *Max's Christmas,* 1989, for *Max's Chocolate Chicken,* 1991, for *Max's Dragon Shirt,* and 2007, for *Red Moon at Sharpsburg;* Children's Book Showcase Award, Children's Book Council, 1974, for *Noisy Nora;* Citation of Merit, Society of Illustrators, 1974, and Art Book for Children citation, Brooklyn Museum/Brooklyn Public Library, 1975, 1976, 1977, all for *Benjamin and Tulip;* Pick-of-the-List citations, American Bookseller Association (ABA), 1975, for *Abdul,* 1978, for *Stanley and Rhoda,* 1981, for both *Timothy Goes to School* and *Good Night, Fred,* 1982, for *A Lion for Lewis,* 1988, for *Forest of Dreams,* 1989, for *Max's Chocolate Chicken;* Irma Simonton Black Award, Bank Street College of Education, 1975, for *Morris's Disappearing Bag;* Children's Books of the Year citations, Child Study Association, 1977, for *Don't Spill It Again, James,* 1982, for *Morris's Disappearing Bag;* International Reading Association (IRA) Children's Choice citation, 1981, for *Timothy Goes to School,* 1982, for *A Lion for Lewis,* 1983, for *Peabody,* 1989, for *Max's Chocolate Chicken;* Edgar Allan Poe Award runner-up, Mystery Writers of America, 1981, for *When No One Was Looking,* 1988, for *Through the Hidden Door;* New Jersey Institute of Technology Award, 1983, for both *A Lion for Lewis* and *Peabody;* Best Illustrated Books designation, *New York*

Times, 1985, for *Hazel's Amazing Mother;* Washington Irving Children's Book Choice Award, Westchester Library Association, 1986, for *Peabody,* 1988, for *Max's Christmas,* 1992, for *Max's Chocolate Chicken;* Golden Sower Award, 1986, for *Peabody;* New Jersey Institute of Technology Award, 1987, for *Max's Christmas;* Virginia Young Readers Award, and New York Public Library Books for the Teen Age citation, both 1987, both for *The Man in the Woods;* Best Books for Young Adults citation, ALA, 1988, for *Through the Hidden Door;* Golden Kite Award, Society of Children's Books Writers and Illustrators, 1988, and Teacher's Choices listee, IRA, both for *Forest of Dreams; Boston Globe/Horn Book* Award, and Parents' Choice Foundation Award, both 1989, both for *Shy Charles;* David McCord Children's Literature citation, 1991, for body of work; Missouri Building Blocks Picture Book Award nominations, Missouri Library Association, 1998, for both *Bunny Cakes* and *McDuff Moves In;* Oppenheim Toy Portfolio Platinum Award, 1999, for both *Old MacDonald* and *The Itsy-Bitsy Spider; Riverbank Review* Children's Book of Distinction Award, and Notable Children's Book in the Language Arts designation, National Council of Teachers of English/Children's Literature Assembly, both 1999, both for *Mary on Horseback.*

Writings

SELF-ILLUSTRATED

John and the Rarey, Funk & Wagnalls, 1969.
Michael and the Mitten Test, Bradbury (New York, NY), 1969.
The First Child, Hawthorn, 1970.
Martha's Birthday, Bradbury (New York, NY), 1970.
Miranda's Pilgrims, Bradbury (New York, NY), 1970.
Unfortunately Harriet, Dial (New York, NY), 1972.
Benjamin and Tulip, Dial (New York, NY), 1973.
Noisy Nora, Dial (New York, NY), 1973, revised with new illustrations, 1997.
Abdul, Dial (New York, NY), 1975.
Morris's Disappearing Bag: A Christmas Story, Dial (New York, NY), 1975.
Don't Spill It Again, James, Dial (New York, NY), 1977.
Stanley and Rhoda, Dial (New York, NY), 1978.
Good Night, Fred, Dial (New York, NY), 1981.
Timothy Goes to School, Dial (New York, NY), 1981.
A Lion for Lewis, Dial (New York, NY), 1982.
Peabody, Dial (New York, NY), 1983.
Hazel's Amazing Mother, Dial (New York, NY), 1985.
Shy Charles, Dial (New York, NY), 1988.
Fritz and the Mess Fairy, Dial (New York, NY), 1991.
(With Maria Tallchief) *Tallchief: America's Prima Ballerina* (nonfiction), Viking (New York, NY), 1999.
Emily's First 100 Days of School, Hyperion (New York, NY), 2000.
Timothy's Lost and Found Day, Viking (New York, NY), 2000.
Timothy Goes to School, Viking (New York, NY), 2000.

Felix Feels Better, Candlewick Press (Cambridge, MA), 2001.
Practice Makes Perfect, Hyperion Books for Children (New York, NY), 2002.
Timothy's Tales from Hilltop School, Viking (New York, NY), 2002.
Make New Friends, Volo (New York, NY), 2002.
Leave Well Enough Alone, Dial (New York, NY), 2002.
Bubble-Gum Radar, Hyperion Books for Children (New York, NY), 2002.
When I Grow Up, Hyperion Books for Children (New York, NY), 2003.
Only You, Viking (New York, NY), 2003.
Felix and the Worrier, Candlewick Press (Cambridge, MA), 2003.
Emily's World of Wonders, Hyperion Books for Children (New York, NY), 2003.
My Kindergarten, Hyperion (New York, NY), 2004.
Twinkle, Twinkle, Little Star, Scholastic (New York, NY), 2006.
Carry Me!, Scholastic (New York, NY), 2006.
My Shining Star: Raising a Child Who Is Ready to Learn, Scholastic (New York, NY), 2006.
Otto Runs for President, Scholastic (New York, NY), 2008.
Hands Off, Harry! ("Kindergators" series), Katherine Tegen Books (New York, NY), 2011.
Miracle Melts Down ("Kindergators" series), Katherine Tegen Books (New York, NY), 2012.

Contributor to books, including *So I Shall Tell You a Story: The Magic World of Beatrix Potter,* edited by Judy Taylor, Warne, 1993, and *Stories and Fun for the Very Young,* Candlewick Press, 1998.

FOR CHILDREN

Forest of Dreams, illustrated by Susan Jeffers, Dial (New York, NY), 1988.
Waiting for the Evening Star, illustrated by Susan Jeffers, Dial (New York, NY), 1993.
Night Sounds, Morning Colors, illustrated by David McPhail, Dial (New York, NY), 1994.
Lucy Comes to Stay, illustrated by Mark Graham, Dial (New York, NY), 1994.
The Language of Doves, illustrated by Greg Shed, Dial (New York, NY), 1996.
Mary on Horseback: Three Mountain Stories (middle-grade nonfiction), illustrated by Peter McCarty, Dial (New York, NY), 1998.
Streets of Gold (nonfiction; based on Mary Antin's memoir *The Promised Land*), illustrated by Dan Andreasen, Dial (New York, NY), 1999.
(With husband, Tom Wells) *The House in the Mail,* illustrated by Dan Andreasen, Dial (New York, NY), 1999.
Wingwalker, illustrated by Brian Selznick, Hyperion Books for Children (New York, NY), 2002.
Adding It Up, illustrated by Michale Koelsch, Viking (New York, NY), 2002.
Ready to Read, illustrated by Michale Koelsch, Viking (New York, NY), 2002.
The Small World of Binky Braverman, illustrated by Richard Egielski, Viking (New York, NY), 2003.

The Miraculous Tale of the Two Maries, illustrated by Petra Mathers, Viking (New York, NY), 2006.

The Gulps, illustrated by Marc Brown, Little, Brown (New York, NY), 2007.

Lincoln and His Boys, illustrated by P.J. Lynch, Candlewick Press (Somerville, MA), 2009.

(With Dino Fernandez) *My Havana: Memories of a Cuban Boyhood,* illustrated by Peter Ferguson, Candlewick Press (Somerville, MA), 2010.

On the Blue Comet, illustrated by Bagram Ibatoulline, Candlewick Press (Somerville, MA), 2010.

Love Waves, Candlewick Press (Somerville, MA), 2011.

"MAX AND RUBY" SERIES; SELF-ILLUSTRATED

Max's First Word, Dial (New York, NY), 1979.

Max's New Suit, Dial (New York, NY), 1979.

Max's Ride, Dial (New York, NY), 1979.

Max's Toys: A Counting Book, Dial (New York, NY), 1979.

Max's Bath, Dial (New York, NY), 1985.

Max's Bedtime, Dial (New York, NY), 1985.

Max's Breakfast, Dial (New York, NY), 1985.

Max's Birthday, Dial (New York, NY), 1985.

Max's Christmas, Dial (New York, NY), 1986.

Hooray for Max, Dial (New York, NY), 1986.

Max's Chocolate Chicken, Dial (New York, NY), 1989.

Max's Dragon Shirt, Dial (New York, NY), 1991.

Max and Ruby's First Greek Myth: Pandora's Box, Dial (New York, NY), 1993.

Max and Ruby's Midas: Another Greek Myth, Dial (New York, NY), 1995.

Bunny Cakes, Dial (New York, NY), 1997.

Bunny Money, Dial (New York, NY), 1997.

Max Cleans Up, Viking (New York, NY), 2000.

Goodnight Max, Viking (New York, NY), 2000.

Bunny Party, Viking (New York, NY), 2001.

Max's Snowsuit, Grosset & Dunlap (New York, NY), 2001.

Play with Max and Ruby, Grosset & Dunlap (New York, NY), 2002.

Ruby's Beauty Shop, Viking (New York, NY), 2003.

Max's Christmas Stocking, Viking (New York, NY), 2003.

Max Drives Away, Viking (New York, NY), 2003.

Ruby's Tea for Two, Viking (New York, NY), 2003.

Bunny Mail, Viking (New York, NY), 2004.

Max's Halloween, Viking (New York, NY), 2004.

Max's ABC, Viking (New York, NY), 2006.

Max Counts His Chickens, Viking (New York, NY), 2007.

Max's Bunny Business, Viking (New York, NY), 2008.

Baby Max and Ruby: Clean-up Time, Viking (New York, NY), 2009.

Baby Max and Ruby: Red Boots, Viking (New York, NY), 2009.

Max and Ruby's Bedtime Book, Viking (New York, NY), 2010.

"VOYAGE TO THE BUNNY PLANET" SERIES; SELF-ILLUSTRATED

Voyage to the Bunny Planet, Dial (New York, NY), 1992, reprinted, Viking (New York, NY), 2008.

First Tomato, Dial (New York, NY), 1992.

The Island Light, Dial (New York, NY), 1992.

Moss Pillows, Dial (New York, NY), 1992.

"EDWARD THE UNREADY" SERIES; SELF-ILLUSTRATED

Edward Unready for School, Dial (New York, NY), 1995.

Edward's Overwhelming Overnight, Dial (New York, NY), 1995.

Edward in Deep Water, Dial (New York, NY), 1995.

"MCDUFF" SERIES; ILLUSTRATED BY SUSAN JEFFERS

McDuff Moves In, Hyperion (New York, NY), 1997.

McDuff Comes Home, Hyperion (New York, NY), 1997.

McDuff and the Baby, Hyperion (New York, NY), 1997.

McDuff's New Friend, Hyperion (New York, NY), 1998.

McDuff, Hyperion (New York, NY), 1998.

McDuff's Birthday, Hyperion (New York, NY), 2000.

The McDuff Stories, Hyperion (New York, NY), 2000.

McDuff Goes to School, Hyperion (New York, NY), 2001.

McDuff Saves the Day, Hyperion (New York, NY), 2002.

McDuff Steps Out, Hyperion (New York, NY), 2004.

McDuff's Favorite Things, Hyperion (New York, NY), 2004.

McDuff's Hide-and-Seek, Hyperion (New York, NY), 2004.

McDuff's Wild Romp, Hyperion (New York, NY), 2005.

"BUNNY READS BACK" SERIES; SELF-ILLUSTRATED

Read to Your Bunny, Scholastic (New York, NY), 1998.

Old MacDonald, Scholastic (New York, NY), 1998.

The Bear Went over the Mountain, Scholastic (New York, NY), 1998.

Bingo, Scholastic (New York, NY), 1998.

The Itsy-Bitsy Spider, Scholastic (New York, NY), 1998.

"YOKO AND FRIENDS SCHOOL DAYS" SERIES; SELF-ILLUSTRATED, UNLESS OTHERWISE NOTED

Yoko, Hyperion (New York, NY), 1998.

Mama, Don't Go!, Hyperion (New York, NY), 2001.

The School Play, Hyperion (New York, NY), 2001.

The Halloween Parade, Hyperion (New York, NY), 2001.

Doris's Dinosaur, Hyperion (New York, NY), 2001.

Yoko's Paper Cranes, Hyperion (New York, NY), 2001.

The World around Us, illustrated by Lisa Koelsch, Hyperion (New York, NY), 2001.

Be My Valentine, illustrated by John Nez, Hyperion (New York, NY), 2001.

Read Me a Story, Hyperion (New York, NY), 2001.

The Germ Busters, illustrated by Jody Wheeler, Hyperion (New York, NY), 2002.

Yoko's World of Kindness: Golden Rules for a Happy Classroom, interior illustrated by John Nez and Jody Wheeler, Hyperion (New York, NY), 2005.

Yoko Writes Her Name, Japanese calligraphy by Masako Inkyo, Hyperion (New York, NY), 2008.

Yoko's Show-and-Tell, Japanese calligraphy by Masako Inkyo, Hyperion (New York, NY), 2010.

Yoko Learns to Read, Disney-Hyperion Books (New York, NY), 2012.

FICTION; FOR YOUNG ADULTS

The Fog Comes on Little Pig Feet, Dial (New York, NY), 1972.
None of the Above, Dial (New York, NY), 1974.
Leave Well Enough Alone, Dial (New York, NY), 1977.
When No One Was Looking, Dial (New York, NY), 1980, reprinted, Puffin (New York, NY), 2000.
The Man in the Woods, Dial (New York, NY), 1984.
Through the Hidden Door, Dial (New York, NY), 1987.
Red Moon at Sharpsburg, Viking (New York, NY), 2007.

RETELLER

The Little Lame Prince (based on the book by Dinash Mulock Craik), Dial (New York, NY), 1990.
Lassie Come-Home (based on the book by Eric Knight), illustrated by Susan Jeffers, Holt (New York, NY), 1995.
Jack and the Beanstalk, illustrated by Norman Messenger, Dorling Kindersley (New York, NY), 1997.
The Fisherman and His Wife: A Brand-New Version, illustrated by Eleanor Hubbard, Dial (New York, NY), 1998.
Hitty: Her First Hundred Years, with New Adventures (based on the book by Rachel Field), illustrated by Susan Jeffers, Simon & Schuster (New York, NY), 1999.

ILLUSTRATOR

W.S. Gilbert, *"A Song to Sing, O!"* (from *The Yeoman of the Guard*), Macmillan (New York, NY), 1968.
W.S. Gilbert, *"The Duke of Plaza Toro"* (from *The Gondoliers*), Macmillan (New York, NY), 1969.
Paula Fox, *Hungry Fred,* Bradbury, 1969.
(With Susan Jeffers), Charlotte Pomerantz, *Why You Look like You Whereas I Tend to Look like Me,* Young Scott Books, 1969.
Robert W. Service, *The Shooting of Dan McGrew* [and] *The Cremation of Sam McGhee,* Young Scott Books, 1969.
Rudyard Kipling, *The Cat That Walked by Himself,* Hawthorn, 1970.
Winifred Rosen, *Marvin's Manhole,* Dial (New York, NY), 1970.
Marjorie Weinman Sharmat, *A Hot Thirsty Day,* Macmillan, 1971.
Ellen Conford, *Impossible, Possum,* Little, Brown (Boston, MA), 1971.
Beryl Epstein and Dorrit Davis, *Two Sisters and Some Hornets,* Holiday House (New York, NY), 1972.
Virginia A. Tashjian, editor, *With a Deep-Sea Smile: Story Hour Stretches for Large or Small Groups,* Little, Brown (Boston, MA), 1974.
Lore G. Segal, *Tell Me a Trudy,* Farrar, Straus (New York, NY), 1977.

Jostein Gaarder, *The Christmas Mystery,* translated by Elizabeth Rokkan, Farrar, Straus (New York, NY), 1996.
Iona Opie, editor, *My Very First Mother Goose,* Candlewick Press (Cambridge, MA), 1996.
Iona Opie, editor, *Humpty Dumpty and Other Rhymes,* Candlewick Press (Cambridge, MA), 1997.
Iona Opie, editor, *Little Boy Blue and Other Rhymes,* Candlewick Press (Cambridge, MA), 1997.
Iona Opie, editor, *Pussycat, Pussycat and Other Rhymes,* Candlewick Press (Cambridge, MA), 1997.
Iona Opie, editor, *Wee Willie Winkie and Other Rhymes,* Candlewick Press (Cambridge, MA), 1997.
(Watercolorist) E.B. White, *Stuart Little: Collector's Edition,* HarperCollins (New York, NY), 1999.
(Watercolorist) E.B. White, *Charlotte's Web: Collector's Edition,* HarperCollins (New York, NY), 1999.
Iona Opie, editor, *Here Comes Mother Goose,* Candlewick Press (Cambridge, MA), 1999.
(Watercolorist) Garth Williams, *Benjamin's Treasure* (excerpt from *The Adventures of Benjamin Pink*), Candlewick Press (Cambridge, MA), 2001.
Oscar Hammerstein and Richard Rogers, *Getting to Know You!: Rogers and Hammerstein Favorites,* HarperCollins (New York, NY), 2002.
(Watercolorist) Mary Stolz, *Emmett's Pig,* HarperCollins (New York, NY), 2003.
Frank Loesser, *I Love You! A Bushel and a Peck,* HarperCollins (New York, NY), 2005.
Iona Opie, editor, *Mother Goose's Little Treasures,* Candlewick Press (Cambridge, MA), 2007.

OTHER

(With Joanna Hurley) *Cooking for Nitwits,* photographs by Barbara Olcott, Dutton (New York, NY), 1989.

Contributor to *Worlds of Childhood: The Art and Craft of Writing for Children,* edited by William Zinsser, Houghton Mifflin, 1990.

Author's work has been translated into Spanish.

Adaptations

Morris's Disappearing Bag and *Max's Christmas* were adapted for film by Weston Woods, 1982 and 1988 respectively. *Timothy Goes to School* was adapted as a filmstrip by Weston Woods, 1982. *Max's Christmas* was released as a filmstrip and on video by Weston Woods, 1987. *Timothy Goes to School* was adapted for television, 2000. The "Max and Ruby" characters appeared in sticker-book adaptations published by Grosset & Dunlap; the "Max and Ruby" books were adapted for an animated television series produced by Nickelodeon. Several of Wells' books were adapted for audiobooks, among them *On the Blue Comet,* Brilliance Audio, 2010. Several of Wells' characters have been licensed as stuffed toys.

Sidelights

Rosemary Wells is a popular and talented artist and writer whose credits include a wealth of humorous picture books as well as several perceptive young-adult

novels. Acclaimed for her originality, versatility, wry humor, and sensitivity toward both children and the human condition, Wells is also praised for her characterizations and her beloved picture-book characters include sibling bunnies Max and Ruby and little kitten Yoko. As an illustrator, she has provided the artwork for texts by such authors as Paula Fox, Rudyard Kipling, and Ellen Conford as well as illustrating librettos by Gilbert and Sullivan and verse anthologies by Iona Opie. "I believe that all stories and plays and paintings and songs and dances come from a palpable but unseen space in the cosmos . . . ," Wells once noted in *Worlds of Childhood: The Art and Craft of Writing for Children.* "According to how gifted we are, we are all given a large or small key to this treasury of wonders. I have been blessed with a small key to the world of the young."

In her picture books, Wells takes a lighthearted but heartfelt approach to universal childhood experiences: many of her stories find anthropomorphic animal characters caught up in childhood dilemmas or comic predicaments involving sibling rivalry or distracted parents. Noted for accurately reflecting the feelings of children while emphasizing the child as an individual, Wells is also acknowledged for giving young readers and listeners the chance to laugh at themselves. As Janet Zarem observed in the *New York Times Book Review,* "Her respect and compassion for children's needs, feelings and dilemmas are boundless: for fear . . ., for embarrassment . . ., for anger . . ., for reassurance . . . and always for feeling cherished and for possessing a natural talent or ability worth acknowledging."

Rosemary Wells introduces an engaging young kitten in her charmingly illustrated picture book Yoko. (Illustration copyright © 1998 by LeUyen Pham. Reprinted by permission of Disney Book Group. All rights reserved.)

Wells' young-adult novels deal with ethical dilemmas such as betrayal, the pressures of competition, and the search for truth. Refusing to provide easy answers, she lets her characters tap their inner strength while establishing their identities and independence in a confusing world. Wells frequently creates a story-within-a-story and often concludes her books—some of which are written in verse—with unconventional endings. "Just as there are universal emotions and predicaments common to young childhood, so there are for teenagers as well," she remarked in *Worlds of Childhood.* "In some ways, to be fourteen now is no different than it was for me or my mother. That part of writing for teenagers is familiar to me, and having those fragile and unstoppable joys and fears in my grasp is where I start."

As an artist, Wells favors line and water color, and she is often praised for creating deceptively simple drawings that are filled with nuance and expression. "In a few lines and pale colors," noted Jennifer Farley Smith in the *Christian Science Monitor,* "Wells can speak volumes to her young audience." In *Booklist* Hazel Rochman also praised Wells' artwork, adding that the author/illustrator "has that rare ability to tell a funny story for very young children with domestic scenes of rising excitement and heartfelt emotion, and with not one word too many."

Born in New York City, Wells grew up in a home that was, as she recalled in an essay for *Something about the Author Autobiography Series* (*SAAS*), "always filled with books, dogs, nineteenth-century music, and other things my parents held in great esteem." Most of her childhood was spent on the New Jersey coast, where her maternal grandmother had a home overlooking the ocean. The author's parents—her father was a playwright and her mother was a ballet dancer—and her grandmother encouraged her early artistic endeavors. Wells' grandmother, to whom she was very close, was widely read and had been a great beauty in New York society. She often read to Rosemary from works by authors such as Longfellow, Kipling, and Poe. As Wells recalled on her home page, "Both my parents flooded me with books and stories. My grandmother took me on special trips to the theater and museums in New York."

At age thirteen Wells attended an upscale boarding school for girls, but she "reacted badly," as she later admitted in *SAAS:* "The school was a jail to me although the other girls seemed to be having a grand time." Wells found the regimentation, scrutiny, and constant supervision to be oppressive; in addition, "there was no privacy, no time to draw." Miserable, she was eventually released from this torture. Back at home, Wells entered Red Bank High School, where she was an admittedly poor student. Enrolling at a small private junior college in upstate New York, she decided to shed "the high-school stigma of 'not being popular.'" At junior college she became a top student and made two lifelong friends. However, she soon got sidetracked by romance after meeting Tom Wells, a Dartmouth student. She left school after one year and moved to Boston.

In Boston, the nineteen-year-old Wells entered the Boston Museum School, where she studied anatomy, perspective, life drawing, and printing. In 1963, she and Tom Wells married, and she left school to enter the job market. On the strength of her portfolio, Wells landed a job as art editor with Boston-based publishers Allyn & Bacon. "I was assigned an American history book for Catholic high-school seniors," as she wrote in *SAAS*. "It was 1,300 pages long and I had to send away for all the prints and photos that would illustrate it. The book was wonderful. The Sisters of the Sacred Heart, who were involved in the editorial end, were splendid women. There was a party when it was published and I felt like a success at something for the first time in my life."

Two years later, Tom was accepted at the Columbia University School of Architecture and the couple moved to New York City. While working as an art designer for Macmillan, Wells created a small illustrated dummy of a Gilbert & Sullivan song taken from their light opera *The Yeomen of the Guard* and sent it to the company's editor in chief. This became her first published book, *"A Song to Sing, O!"*, and it was followed by W.S. Gilbert's *"The Duke of Plaza Toro,"* a picture book based on a Gilbert & Sullivan song from *The Gondoliers.*

After illustrating well-received volumes by Paula Fox and Robert W. Service, Wells created her first original picture book, *John and the Rarey.* Published in 1969, the work features a little boy who does not want to be an airplane pilot like his father. What John does want is a pet: he finds a fantastic, blue-eyed creature that takes him into the sky on its back. A reviewer in *Publishers Weekly* called Wells "a fresh new talent in children's books" and praised *John and the Rarey* as a "witty story," while *Horn Book* critic Sidney D. Long wrote that her story would "appeal to all children who have been faced with a frustrating family situation."

Throughout her career Wells has continued to illustrate the work of other authors while adding to her growing list of solo picture books. Inspired by the antics of her own two children, in 1979 she produced the first four books in her ongoing "Max and Ruby" series: *Max's First Word* and *Max's Toys: A Counting Book.* Described by *Children's Books and Their Creators* contributor Maeve Visser Knoth as "the first funny board books for very young children," the "Max and Ruby" volumes use story, information, and humor to introduce preschoolers to topics such as prepositions, getting dressed, and the importance of individuality. Max is a white bunny; Ruby is an older sister who thinks she knows what is best for Max and tries to control him. Through it all, Max remains easygoing and undaunted, innocently outsmarting Ruby and always getting the last word. Paired with Wells' minimal but lively text, the books' pictures are enlivened by vivid primary colors and feature an uncluttered page layout.

Writing in *Booklist,* Judith Goldberger praised the "Max and Ruby" series for "driv[ing] . . . a real wedge into the existing block of unnotable, overcute, didactic baby-toddler tomes." Wells has continued the adventures of the brother-and-sister rabbit duo for new generations of pre-readers in books such as *Bunny Money, Ruby's Beauty Shop,* and *Max and Ruby's Bedtime Book.* Reviewing *Ruby's Beauty Shop,* in which Ruby and friend Louie make Max their guinea pig in a game of beauty parlor that goes awry, a *Kirkus Reviews* critic noted that "Wells has an unerring ability to hit just the right note to tickle small-fry funny bones." "Each story portrays a typical preschool trauma resolved with humor and understanding," Trev Jones asserted in *School Library Journal,* while in *Booklist* Hazel Rochman wrote of *Max and Ruby's Bedtime Book* that Wells' "detailed pictures" help lead readers to a "snuggly conclusion." In her *Bulletin of the Center for Children's Books* review Zena Sutherland dubbed each book in the series "equally delectable," adding that they should be as useful for very young children as they are appealing."

Max's Christmas breaks with Wells' board-book tradition by presenting a full-length picture-book treatment of the escapades of Max and Ruby. A bunny with an inquiring mind, Max has lots of unanswered questions about Santa Claus that Ruby answers curtly, prompting her little brother to take matters into his own hands. Calling Max "that epitome of the small child in rabbit guise," Judith Glover added in *School Library Journal* that Wells "has an extraordinary talent for capturing a welter of thoughts and emotions with the placement of an eye or a turn of a smile." *Horn Book* critic Karen Jameyson concluded that, despite the longer format of *Max's Christmas,* "an uncanny perceptive simplicity, both in line and in word, is still Wells's most effective tool."

Several other books about Max and Ruby adhere to the picture-book format. In *Bunny Cakes* the siblings have separate ideas for creating treats: Ruby wants to make an angel surprise cake while Max wants to present his grandmother with an earthworm cake decorated with red-hot marshmallow squirters. Max—who is too young to read and write—thinks of a way to communicate his shopping list to the grocer, and Grandma is thrilled when she receives two cakes. Pat Mathews, a reviewer for the *Bulletin of the Center for Children's Books,* claimed that "in this take on written communication kidstyle, pudgy Max is at his winsome best."

Bunny Money finds the pair shopping to buy a birthday present for Grandma. The siblings' money goes fast—most of it is spent on Max, and Wells shows the gradual reduction of the contents of Ruby's wallet at the bottom of each page—but a compromise is soon reached: Grandma drives the pair home wearing musical earrings from Ruby and plastic vampire teeth from Max. A *Kirkus Reviews* critic called *Bunny Money* "a great adjunct to primary-grade math lessons," while Mathews concluded that Wells' "combination of gentle comedy, shrinking assets, and those expressive bunny eyes" will attract "old and new Max and Ruby fans."

Wells' original self-illustrated picture books include Max Cleans Up, *part of her popular "Max and Ruby" series.* (Copyright © 2000 by Rosemary Wells. Reproduced by permission of Rosemary Sandberg, Ltd., and Puffin Books, a division of Penguin Putnam Books for Young Readers.)

Max Counts His Chickens is a counting book of sorts. Here the siblings hunt for ten marshmallow chicks on Easter morning, but Ruby's incredible success at ferreting out the hiding places leaves Max wanting. "Wells's artwork creates a warm, comfortable atmosphere in which counting to ten is a simple pleasure," a *Kirkus Reviews* critic observed, and Julie Cummins applauded the "perfect pairing of concept and story" in *Max Counts His Chickens*, noting that Wells' illustrations include "clever details that spill out across the Easter-egg-colored picture borders."

Ruby and her brother engage in a heated competition in *Max's Bunny Business*. When the big-sister bunny teams up with her best friend to open a lemonade stand, they refuse to let Max join the fun but he outwits them by creating a more profitable endeavor. "As always, Wells' Easter-bright artwork tells a dramatic story of sibling rivalry," Rochman stated in *Booklist*.

In addition to penning stories involving the irrepressible Max and Ruby, Wells has also created several other popular series. Her "Voyage to the Bunny Planet" books feature little bunnies that have bad days and imagine themselves transported to the Bunny Planet, where good times restore their equilibrium. The "Edward the Unready" series follows a little bear that is unenthusiastic about going to school or staying overnight at a friend's house, preferring to be at home among familiar surroundings.

Other series feature Yoko, a little Asian kitten, and Felix, a young guinea pig. In *Yoko Writes Her Name*, the tiny feline, who is learning Japanese, grows anxious after two of her meddling classmates tease her about her penmanship, while *Yoko's Show-and-Tell* finds the kitten shares a special Japanese doll with her schoolmates. A critic in *Kirkus Reviews* observed that the work "teaches

a subtle lesson on acceptance and maturity with great clarity," and in *School Library Journal* Piper Nyman described *Yoko Writes Her Name* as "a carefully crafted picture book with Asian-inspired illustrations that delight the eye just as the gentle story soothes the soul."

In *Felix Feels Better,* the title character is nursed back to health by Mom after overindulging in his favorite chocolate candy, and in *Felix and the Worrier* the protagonist discovers the courage to confront his fears, symbolized by an impish creature that invades Felix's dreams. Kay Weisman, writing in *Booklist,* noted of *Felix Feels Better* that "Wells' watercolor-and-ink illustrations will charm and comfort young listeners," and *Horn Book* reviewer Kitty Flynn maintained that the author/illustrator's message "will come across loud and clear to young worrywarts."

In the "McDuff" series, a West Highland white terrier—based on Wells' own pet—escapes from a dogcatcher's truck and is adopted by a young couple. Written for three-to-six-year-old readers, the series takes up McDuff's problems and adventures, like getting lost while chasing a rabbit and dealing with a new baby in the house. In *McDuff Goes to School* the energetic terrier must attend obedience classes after he upsets his new canine companion's French owners. "Wells injects a warm humor into this brief story," a critic for *Kirkus Reviews* noted. A near-disastrous outing on the Fourth of July is the subject of *McDuff Saves the Day.* Here Wells' "cozy, old-fashioned story is simple enough to be understood by younger preschoolers, [and] with enough humor from McDuff's antics to entertain" readers of all ages, maintained a *Kirkus Reviews* contributor.

The first volume in Wells' self-illustrated "Kindergators" series, *Hands Off, Harry!* introduces a classroom of ten young alligators who are members of Miss Harmony's kindergarten class. Young Harry likes to attract attention through his constant fidgeting, and after he knocks several students off their stools, gets paint and glue on others' clothes, and breaks one boy's eyeglasses, the class must find a way to educate Harry in appropriate social boundaries. The alligator friends return in *Miracle Melts Down,* as one young gator learns about table manners with the help of her true-blue school friends. Calling Wells' artwork for *Hands Off, Harry!* "spot on," Gillian Engberg added in *Booklist* that "her illustrations . . . perfectly capture young children's body language and emotions." The "Kindergators" series will be useful for classroom use, noted a *Kirkus Reviews* writer, citing the author's inclusion of "some valuable lessons in problem solving and expressing oneself," and a *Publishers Weekly* critic noted the "inventiveness and sense of community" exhibited by Wells' young alligator characters.

Stand-alone picture books by Wells include *Wingwalker* and *The House in the Mail,* the latter a collaboration with her architect husband. *Wingwalker,* which takes place during the Great Depression of the 1930s, finds a young Oklahoma boy and his family trying to make ends meet during the sustained drought that caused the Dust Bowl. The story was praised by a *Kirkus Reviews* critic who noted that "Wells' prose is spare but has both richness and freshness of simile and image." *The House in the Mail* takes readers back to an even earlier decade, when houses could be ordered in kits from the Sears, Roebuck catalogue. The story is narrated by twelve-year-old Emily, whose father summons friends to help assemble his modern home. Complete with a refrigerator, running water, a washing machine, and other conveniences, the new six-room bungalow is put together piece by piece, and the story is illustrated in scrap-book style by Dan Andreasen. Noting that "anecdotes and snatches of conversation flesh out the era," a *Publishers Weekly* contributor praised *The House in the Mail* as a story that "speaks . . . to the strong bond among the members of Emily's family." "This remarkable picture book . . . is like discovering a slice of American life in a family scrapbook," added Connie Fletcher in *Booklist.*

Wells has also enjoyed successful literary collaborations with other artists. In *The Small World of Binky Braverman,* a work illustrated by Richard Egielski, narrator Stanley "Binky" Braverman recalls the events of 1938, when a host of magical playmates helped ease his feelings of homesickness during a summer-long stay with relatives. "The watercolor illustrations complement Wells's imaginative text," Shawn Brommer wrote in *School Library Journal.* Based on French folklore, *The Miraculous Tale of the Two Maries* centers on a pair of girls who drown at sea but are given the chance to perform good deeds in the afterlife. "It's certainly an oddball tale, but it has its own logic and whimsical devout-

A little guinea pig is a cute stand-in for young toddlers in Wells' self-illustrated **Felix and the Worrier.** (Copyright © 2003 by Rosemary Wells. Reproduced by permission of the publisher, Candlewick Press, Inc., Somerville, MA.)

ness," noted *Horn Book* critic Roger Sutton, who also complimented the artwork of Petra Mathers. In *The Gulps* a family of junk-food junkies gets whipped into shape after its members find themselves stranded in the countryside during their summer vacation. "Wells' message, though couched in silliness and humor, is still obvious," *Booklist* critic Shelle Rosenfeld maintained, and Gloria Koster remarked in *School Library Journal* that illustrator Marc Brown's "busily patterned cartoons in confectionery colors with cotton-candy clouds humorously depict the rotund characters in this tongue-in-cheek tale."

In addition to being a prolific author of picture books, Wells has written several well-respected novels for teen readers. The award-winning *When No One Was Looking* is a mystery that focuses on a highly competitive teen tennis player who is placed under suspicion when her arch rival conveniently drowns just before a face-off match. *The Fog Comes on Little Pig Feet*, which is based on Wells' boarding-school experience, takes the form of a diary written by thirteen-year-old Rachel Sakasian. A Brooklyn girl who wants to become a concert pianist, Rachel longs to attend New York City's Music and Art High School, but her parents instead enroll her at North Place, an elite boarding school. When she becomes friends with upper-classman Carlisle Duggett, who is rumored to be mentally unbalanced, Rachel finds herself covering for her new friend when the girl leaves school to live in Greenwich Village. After she learns that Carlisle has tried to commit suicide, Rachel is torn between protecting her friend and telling the truth. In a *School Library Journal* review, Alice Miller Bregman predicted that "teens will devour this fast-paced, adequately written entertainment." A contributor to *Best Sellers* applauded the novel's "priceless vignettes," concluding that Wells "brilliantly demonstrates [that] her writing abilities are an easy match for her already famous artistic talents."

None of the Above outlines five years in the life of Marcia, a teen who favors pink angora sweaters, reading movie magazines, and watching television. When her father remarries, Marcia feels out of place with her sophisticated stepmother and ambitious stepsister. In reaction, she decides to turn herself around: she switches to college prep classes and succeeds, although reluctantly, in school. However, she also becomes involved with Raymond, a good-looking though hoodish classmate. Calling Marcia an "unusual and oddly affecting heroine," *School Library Journal* critic Joni Brodart claimed that Wells "captures the girl's confusion in this timely, realistic, and moving novel which should reach a large audience." Writing in the *Bulletin of the Center for Children's Books*, Zena Sutherland noted that the story's "characterization is strong and consistent, and the complexities of relationships within the family are beautifully developed. Wells is particularly adept at dialogue."

Illustrated by Bagram Ibatoulline, Wells' fanciful novel *On the Blue Comet* takes place in Cairo, Illinois, a small town on the banks of the Mississippi River where

Wells treats train fans to an exciting story in On the Blue Comet, *a story featuring artwork by Bagram Ibatoulline.* (Illustration copyright © 2010 by Bagram Ibatoulline. Reproduced by permission of Candlewick Press, Somerville, MA.)

eleven-year-old Oscar Ogilvie, Jr., has watched the stock-market crash of 1929 devastate his family. When Mr. Ogilvie leaves town in search of a paying job, Oscar moves in with Aunt Carmen and her daughter Willa Sue. The boy is miserable, not only because he misses his dad but because his precious model trains had to be sold to keep the family financially afloat. After meeting a stranger in town, Oscar witnesses a bank robbery and escapes magically, via train, to California, where his father is now living. Oddly enough, when the two meet, Oscar is ten years older and his father is ten years younger, making them both the same age. After hobnobbing with several famous movie stars of the 1930s, as well as with film director Alfred Hitchcock, Oscar makes another time-travel train trip, winding up in New York City several years younger than when his travels first started. Wells "blends just enough hyperbolic elements to give the story the feel of a tall tale," noted *School Library Journal* critic Connie Tyrrell Burns in her review of *On the Blue Comet*, and Ibatoulline's "intricately detailed illustrations. . . . perfectly capture the nostalgic, wistful tone of the narrative." In *Kirkus Reviews* a writer dubbed Wells' fantasy a "warm, cleverly crafted adventure" enriched by "abundant historical

and literary allusions," while *New York Times Book Review* contributor Abby Mcganney Nolan asserted that *On the Blue Comet* "is packed with inventive plotting, engaging descriptions and sharp dialogue."

Inspired by her interest in history, Wells has produced several biographies of historical and contemporary women. *Mary on Horseback: Three Mountain Stories,* a book for middle graders, profiles Mary Breckinridge, founder of the Frontier Nursing Service in the Appalachian Mountains. Wells reveals the hardships and triumphs experienced by the valiant nurse from the perspectives of three young people whom Mary helped. Noting the "historical accuracy and elegance" of the story, a reviewer in *Publishers Weekly* stated that Wells' "well-honed first-person narratives add up to an outstanding biography." *Booklist* reviewer Helen Rosenberg predicted that "these beautifully written stories will remain with the reader long after the book is closed; Wells has given much deserved honor to a true heroine," while *School Library Journal* critic Peggy Morgan dubbed *Mary on Horseback* "a gem."

In *Streets of Gold* Wells presents a picture-book biography of Mary Antin, a Jewish girl who immigrated to the United States from tsarist Russia in the early twentieth century. A year after her arrival, Antin wrote an epic poem about U.S. President George Washington that was published in a Boston newspaper. A reviewer in *Publishers Weekly* claimed that, "among a profusion of books about turn-of-the-[twentieth-]century Russian-Jewish emigrants, Wells's . . . story about Mary Antin stands out for its exceptional economy and tenderness." Wells has also produced a well-received biography of Native American ballet dancer Maria Tallchief, collaborating with the noted artist on this project.

Wells examines life in Virginia's Shenandoah Valley during the U.S. Civil War in *Red Moon at Sharpsburg.* The novel centers on India Moody, a young woman who must fend for herself after the death of her father, a wagon driver for the Confederacy. The intelligent and sensitive India finds a companion in her neighbor, a scientist who tutors her after the local schools close, and she later risks her life by harboring a wounded Union soldier. A "powerful novel," *Red Moon at Sharpsburg* "is unflinching in its depiction of war and the devastation it causes," Shannon Seglin commented in *School Library Journal,* and Claire Rosser stated in *Kliatt* that "India's character is a marvelous combination of vulnerability, strength and intelligence."

In *Lincoln and His Boys,* a fictional work based on an essay by Abraham Lincoln's son, Willie Lincoln, Wells looks at three events from the life of the sixteenth U.S. president, all as reflected in the relationship between Lincoln and his sons, Willie and Tad. "Lincoln is shown to be a caring and fun-loving parent," Francisca Goldsmith observed in *Booklist,* and *School Library Journal* reviewer Janet S. Thompson acknowledged that viewing Lincoln "from his children's viewpoint" in *Lincoln and His Boys* "brings both the family and the times to life."

Wells mines history in writing her family-centered story for* Lincoln and His Boys, *a story featuring artwork by P.J. Lynch. (Illustration copyright © 2008 by P.J. Lynch. Reproduced by permission of Candlewick Press, Somerville, MA.)

Biographical and Critical Sources

BOOKS

Children's Books and Their Creators, edited by Anita Silvey, Houghton Mifflin (Boston, MA), 1995.
Children's Literature Review, Gale (Detroit, MI), Volume 16, 1989, Volume 69, 2001.
St. James Guide to Children's Writers, Gale (Detroit, MI), 1999.
St. James Guide to Young-Adult Writers, Gale (Detroit, MI), 1999.
Something about the Author Autobiography Series, Volume 1, Gale (Detroit, MI), 1986.
Worlds of Childhood: The Art and Craft of Writing for Children, edited by William Zinsser, Houghton Mifflin (Boston, MA), 1990.

PERIODICALS

Best Sellers, July 15, 1972, review of *The Fog Comes on Little Pig Feet,* p. 200.
Booklist, October 15, 1978, Judith Goldberger, reviews of *Max's First Word, Max's New Suit, Max's Ride,* and *Max's Toys: A Counting Book,* all p. 359; January 1, 1997, Hazel Rochman, review of *Bunny Cakes,* p.

857; September 1, 1998, Helen Rosenberg, review of *Mary on Horseback: Three Mountain Stories,* p. 113; February 1, 2001, Kathy Broderick, review of *Max Cleans Up,* p. 1059; February 15, 2001, Shelley Townsend Hudson, review of *Benjamin's Treasure,* p. 1142; May 1, 2001, Hazel Rochman, review of *Felix Feels Better,* p. 1693; November 1, 2001, Hazel Rochman, review of *Language of Doves,* p. 475; December 15, 2001, Stephanie Zvirin, review of *Felix Feels Better,* p. 728; March 1, 2002, Connie Fletcher, review of *The House in the Mail,* p. 1137; July, 2002, Shelle Rosenfeld, review of *McDuff Saves the Day,* p. 1861; August, 2002, Hazel Rochman, review of *Ruby's Beauty Shop,* p. 1977; November 1, 2003, Kay Weisman, review of *Felix and the Worrier,* p. 507; October 1, 2003, Gillian Engberg, review of *The Small World of Binky Braverman,* p. 329; August, 2004, Hazel Rochman, review of *My Kindergarten,* p. 1949; January 1, 2007, Julie Cummins, review of *Max Counts His Chickens,* p. 93; March 1, 2007, Shelle Rosenfeld, review of *The Gulps,* p. 90; March 1, 2008, Hazel Rochman, review of *Max's Bunny Business,* p. 73; January 1, 2009, Francisca Goldsmith, review of *Lincoln and His Boys,* p. 82; April 15, 2010, Ilene Cooper, review of *Yoko's Show-and-Tell,* p. 54; July 1, 2010, Daniel Kraus, review of *On the Blue Comet,* p. 61, and Hazel Rochman, review of *Max and Ruby's Bedtime Book,* p. 66; May 1, 2011, Gillian Engberg, review of *Hands Off, Harry!,* p. 93.

Bulletin of the Center for Children's Books, April, 1975, Zena Sutherland, review of *None of the Above,* p. 139; April, 1985, Zena Sutherland, review of *Max's Bath,* p. 157; November, 1993, Betsy Hearne, review of *Max and Ruby's First Greek Myth: Pandora's Box,* p. 106; March, 1997, Pat Mathews, review of *Bunny Cakes,* p. 261; October, 1997, Pat Mathews, review of *Bunny Money,* p. 71.

Childhood Education, winter, 2000, Susan A. Miller, review of *Goodnight Max,* p. 110.

Christian Science Monitor, March 6, 1974, Jennifer Farley Smith, "Animals Are Enduring Heroes," p. F2.

Horn Book, August, 1969, Sidney D. Long, review of *John and the Rarey,* pp. 399-400; March-April 1987, Rosemary Wells, "The Artist at Work: The Writer at Work," pp. 163-170; June, 1987, Roger Sutton, review of *None of the Above,* pp. 368-371; July-August, 2002, Christine M. Heppermann, review of *Wingwalker,* p. 474; January-February, 2004, Kitty Flynn, review of *Felix and the Worrier,* p. 74; March-April, 2006, Roger Sutton, review of *The Miraculous Tale of the Two Maries,* p. 177; May-June, 2006, Joanna Rudge Long, review of *Max's ABC,* p. 307; May-June, 2008, Susan Dove Lempke, review of *Max's Bunny Business,* p. 301; July-August, 2008, Jennifer M. Brabander, review of *Otto Runs for President,* p. 435; September-October, 2010, Martha V. Parravano, review of *Max and Ruby's Bedtime Book,* p. 66, Jennifer M. Brabander, review of *Yoko's Show-and-Tell,* p. 67, and Betty Carter, review of *On the Blue Comet,* p. 98.

Kirkus Reviews, September 1, 1993, review of *Max and Ruby's First Greek Myth,* p. 1154; July 15, 1997, review of *Bunny Money,* p. 1119; August 1, 2001, review of *McDuff Goes to School,* p. 1222; April 15, 2002, review of *Wingwalker,* p. 581; May 15, 2002, review of *McDuff Saves the Day,* p. 743; June 15, 2002, review of *Timothy's Tales from Hilltop School,* p. 890; July 15, 2002, review of *Ruby's Beauty Shop,* p. 1047; August 15, 2003, reviews of *Felix and the Worrier,* p. 1080, and *The Small World of Binky Braverman,* p. 1081; December 15, 2004, review of *I Love You! A Bushel and a Peck,* p. 1204; December 15, 2006, review of *Max Counts His Chickens,* p. 1274; August 1, 2007, review of *Mother Goose's Little Treasures;* June 15, 2008, review of *Yoko Writes Her Name;* June 15, 2010, review of *Yoko's Show and Tell;* July 1, 2010, review of *My Havana: Memories of a Cuban Boyhood;* August 1, 2010, reviews of *On the Blue Comet* and *Max and Ruby's Bedtime Book;* June 1, 2011, review of *Hands Off, Harry!*

Kliatt, March, 2007, Claire Rosser, review of *Red Moon at Sharpsburg,* p. 20.

New York Times, April 20, 2003, Suzanne MacNeille, "He's Not Just a Bunny. He's My Brother," p. 55.

New York Times Book Review, November 24, 1974, Dale Carlson, review of *None of the Above,* p. 8; September 19, 2004, Janet Zarem, review of *My Kindergarten,* p. 16; December 19, 2010, Abby Mcganney Nolan, review of *On the Blue Comet,* p. 14.

Publishers Weekly, April 21, 1969, review of *John and the Rarey,* p. 64; November 15, 1970, review of *Miranda's Pilgrims,* p. 1245; August 5, 1974, Jean F. Mercier, review of *None of the Above,* p. 58; October 9, 1978, review of *Stanley and Rhoda,* p. 76; February 29, 1980, Jean F. Mercier, interview with Wells, pp. 72-73; September 14, 1998, review of *Mary on Horseback,* p. 70; October 19, 1998, review of *Yoko,* p. 78; April 19, 1999, review of *Streets of Gold,* p. 73; June 4, 2001, review of *Felix Feels Better,* p. 79; January 14, 2002, review of *The House in the Mail,* p. 60; March 25, 2002, review of *Wingwalker,* p. 65; May 27, 2002, review of *Happy Anniversary, Charlotte and Wilbur,* p. 61; May 12, 2003, review of *Only You,* p. 65; August 18, 2003, review of *The Small World of Binky Braverman,* p. 78; September 1, 2003, review of *Felix and the Worrier,* p. 91; September 8, 2003, review of *Back to School,* p 78; November 14, 2005, review of *Carry Me!,* p. 67; April 9, 2007, review of *Red Moon at Sharpsburg,* p. 54; August 20, 2007, review of *Mother Goose's Little Treasures,* p. 67; June 2, 2008, review of *Otto Runs for President,* p. 45; July 19, 2010, review of *My Havana,* p. 127; September 20, 2010, review of *On the Blue Comet,* p. 66; May 2, 2011, review of *Hands Off, Harry!,* p. 53.

School Library Journal, May, 1972, Alice Miller Bregman, review of *The Fog Comes on Little Pig Feet,* p. 89; November, 1974, Joni Brodart, review of *None of the Above,* p. 69; March, 1985, Trev Jones, review of *Max's Bath,* pp. 159-160; October, 1986, Judith Glover, review of *Max's Christmas,* p. 112; July, 1997, Christy Norris, review of *McDuff Comes Home,* p. 78; October, 1998, Peggy Morgan, review of *Mary on Horseback,* p. 130; December, 2000, Christina F. Renaud, review of *Max Cleans Up,* p. 127; Novem-

ber, 2001, Rosalyn Pierini, review of *Yoko's Paper Cranes,* p. 138; December, 2001, Lisa Gangemi Kropp, review of *The World around Us,* p. 129; January, 2002, Marilyn Taniguchi, review of *Mama, Don't Go!,* p. 112; March, 2002, Rita Soltan, review of *Adding It Up,* p. 223; May, 2002, Heide Piehler, review of *Wingwalker,* p. 162; July, 2002, Janie Schomberg, review of *The Germ Busters,* p. 100; July, 2002, Shara Alpern, review of *Be My Valentine,* p. 100; August, 2002, Maryann H. Owen, review of *McDuff Saves the Day,* p. 172; October, 2002, Laurie von Mehren, review of *Timothy's Tales from Hilltop School,* p. 134; October, 2002, Shara Alpern, review of *Ruby's Beauty Shop,* p. 134; December, 2002, Anne Knickerbocker, review of *Read Me a Story,* p. 112; May, 2003, Heather E. Miller, review of *Only You,* p. 132; November, 2003, Shawn Brommer, review of *The Small World of Binky Braverman,* p. 118; August, 2004, Lisa Gangemi Kropp, review of *My Kindergarten,* p. 103; February, 2005, Bina Williams, review of *I Love You! A Bushel and a Peck,* p. 123; April, 2005, Bina Williams, review of *McDuff's Wild Romp,* p. 115; June 1, 2005, Shelle Rosenfeld, review of *McDuff's Wild Romp,* p. 1826; January, 2006, Maryann H. Owen, review of *Carry Me!,* p. 115; March, 2006, Catherine Callegari, review of *The Miraculous Tale of the Two Maries,* p. 204; May, 2006, Jacki Kellum, review of *Max's ABC,* p. 106; March, 2007, Gloria Koster, review of *The Gulps,* p. 190, and Shannon Seglin, review of *Red Moon at Sharpsburg,* p. 220; August, 2008, Piper Nyman, review of *Yoko Writes Her Name,* p. 105; January, 2009, Janet S. Thompson, review of *Lincoln and His Boys,* p. 122; July, 2010, Kristine M. Casper, review of *Yoko's Show-and-Tell,* p. 71; September, 2010, Connie Tyrrell Burns, review of *On the Blue Comet,* p. 167; June, 2011, Meg Smith, review of *Max and Ruby's Bedtime Book,* p. 98; July, 2011, Gay Lynn Van Vleck, review of *Hands Off, Harry!,* p. 81.

ONLINE

Children's Literature Comprehensive Database, http://www.childrenslit.com/ (November 15, 2009), "A Conversation with Rosemary Wells."

Reading Rockets Web site, http://www.readingrockets.org/ (November 15, 2009), "Meet Rosemary Wells" (transcript of video interview).

Rosemary Wells Home Page, http://www.rosemarywells.com (December 29, 2011).

Scholastic Web site, http://www2.scholastic.com/ (November 15, 2009), autobiographical essay by Wells.

OTHER

A Visit with Rosemary Wells (film), Penguin USA, 1994.*

*   *   *

WESSELHOEFT, Conrad 1953-

Personal

Born 1953, in Seattle, WA; married; wife's name Lyn (deceased, 2006); children: Claire, Kit and Jen (twins).

Conrad Wesselhoeft (Photograph by Bronwyn Edwards. Reproduced by permission.)

Education: Lewis & Clark College, B.A. (English), 1976; Ohio State University, M.A. (journalism), 1988. *Hobbies and other interests:* Playing guitar.

Addresses

Home—Seattle, WA. *Agent*—Erin Murphy Literary Agency, Inc., 2700 Woodlands Village, No. 300-458, Flagstaff, AZ 86001-7127; erin@emliterary.com. *E-mail*—cwesselhoeft@comcast.net.

Career

Journalist, technical editor, marketing writer, and novelist. Worked variously as a tugboat hand in Singapore and a Peace Corps volunteer teaching English in Western Samoa (Polynesia); member of editorial staff of five newspapers, including *New York Times;* Cisco Systems, former senior editor; World Vision, former senior writer; Community News Group, executive editor, 1996-97; freelance writer and editor, beginning 2008.

Awards, Honors

Best Fiction for Young Adults inclusion, American Library Association, 2011, for *Adios, Nirvana.*

Writings

Adios, Nirvana, Houghton Mifflin Harcourt (Boston, MA), 2010.

Author's work has been translated into German.

Sidelights

Conrad Wesselhoeft cites American writers John Steinbeck, Jack Kerouac, Willa Cather, Ernest Hemingway, Larry McMurtry, and Scott O'Dell among his literary mentors, and his resumé as a young man reflected the quest for life experience that might be credited to such reading. After a year of college, Wesselhoeft left school to work on the crew of a tugboat sailing from Singapore to other Asian ports, and after earning his bachelor's degree he joined the Peace Corps to teach English in Western Samoa. His skill as a writer ultimately combined with his curiosity and led him into journalism, where he worked for newspapers such as the *New York Times* before returning to his native Seattle. Wesselhoeft's first novel, *Adios, Nirvana,* is set in that city, incorporating its landmarks and focusing on its vibrant urban culture. While the complex story the author tells in *Adios, Nirvana* was born from several intersecting experiences, the teen characters in the novel were inspired by his son, Kit, whose adolescent world was shaped by close friends and a shared passion for music.

Framed as a first-person narrative, *Adios, Nirvana* introduces Jonathan, a talented teen guitarist and high-school junior who also has a gift for lyrical poetry. Since the death of his twin brother Telly, in a tragic accident, Jonathan has been unable to sleep, and he functions by consuming super doses of caffeinated drinks and NoDoz. Without Telly to confide in, Jonathan turns to alcohol as well as to his literary idols, and he soon becomes consumed by the need to put his thoughts down on paper. After his grade-point average at Taft High School plummets from stellar to no-show, Jonathan's friends and an understanding school principal refuse to let the teen go under. A perceptive English teacher also helps refocus the young man's pain, allowing him to bolster his grade point by helping a dying World-War II veteran complete his life story. The older man's "story of loss resonates with and amplifies Jonathan's own survivor's guilt," observed Suzanne Gordon in *School Library Journal,* and the teen's ultimate turn-around is the high point in Wesselhoeft's "brash, hip story."

In *Adios, Nirvana* the author "offers a psychologically complex debut that will intrigue heavy-metal aficionados and drama junkies alike," predicted *Booklist* contributor Frances Bradburn, the critic adding that Wesselhoeft's intended rock-band readership is infrequently the target of young-adult fiction. While a *Publishers Weekly* critic praised the novelist's "ability to deliver genuine emotion" in his "moving" teen drama, *Voice of Youth Advocates* contributor Sharon Blumberg made special note of the book's literary sophistication. In *Adios, Nirvana* Wesselhoeft serves up "a wonderful blend of contemporary, historical, and literary fiction," Blumberg asserted, and "his . . . figurative language makes each page dance with images of raw realism."

Discussing the growing resilience of Jonathan, the main character in *Adios, Nirvana,* Wesselhoeft noted on his Web log: "I'm reminded of what Winston Churchill said to the students at Harrow School in the darkest hour of World War II—what Churchill called [England's] . . . 'finest hour.' It's the message echoed by old Agnes the Oracle, and it's what I hope readers will take away: 'Never give up. Never give up. Never, never, never, never—in nothing, great or small, large or petty—never give up.'"

"Scott O'Dell was my friend and mentor," Wesselhoeft noted in an essay on his Web log that he also shared with *SATA.* "That's a tall statement considering that I met him only once. But that day changed my life.

"I was a young staffer at *The New York Times,* harboring a secret ambition: to write novels. But how? Writing a novel seemed far out of my depth. However, writing a feature story about a novelist might be a stroke in the right direction. So I set up an interview, hopped a train at Grand Central, and headed north to Westchester County, New York.

Cover of Wesselhoeft's young-adult novel **Adios, Nirvana,** *in which a teen turns to music to deal with personal tragedy.* (Houghton Mifflin Harcourt Publishing Company. Photograph by Bronwyn Edwards reproduced by permission of Bronwyn Edwards. All rights reserved.)

"Who was Scott O'Dell? Probably the most acclaimed young-adult author of his generation. He had written nearly two dozen books, including the classic *Island of the Blue Dolphins,* and garnered a barrel of prizes: the Newbery Medal; three Newbery Honor awards; and the Hans Christian Andersen Award for a body of work.

"Scott greeted me at the station. Now 85, he looked time-chiseled and fit, with a shock of white hair, barrel chest, and deep tan. We climbed into his big car, and he peeled for his home on Long Pond. He seemed to enjoy speed.

"The interview was supposed to last about two hours, but it filled the morning and lapped into the afternoon. We broke for a late lunch.

"'Enough about me,' he said, over seafood chowder. 'What about you? What do you want to do with your life?'

"I stammered out the true contents of my gut: 'I want to write novels.'

"'Well, then, write them.'

"'But I don't have time. I don't know how.'

"He planted a hand on the table and leaned close. His blue eyes sparked. 'Now listen—listen!'

"I did listen. Here's what Scott O'Dell taught me:

"Writing is about starting. Start simply, even if it amounts to no more than 15 minutes a day. Open an empty notebook and on page one write: 'I want to write a book about. . . .' Then write: 'I want the main character to be. . . .' It's okay to write in fragments. It's okay to use weak verbs. Just write. Spill all of your ideas into that notebook. On about day five, or seventeen, or fifty-five, something will happen. A light will turn on. You will see the way.

"Writing is about finishing. He liked to quote Anthony Trollope, the [nineteenth-century] English novelist: 'The most important thing a writer should have is a piece of sticking plaster with which to fasten his pants to a chair.'

"Writing is about reading. Soak up all the great books you can. He loved Willa Cather's spare, lyrical prose style, singling out her novel *Death Comes for the Archbishop.*

"Writing is humble. Let your forebears guide you. He followed Hemingway's advice: Stop your day's work at a point where you know what is going to happen next. That way, you'll never get stuck.

"Writing for young readers has a special reward. Scott told me that before he discovered young audiences, he had only a tentative commitment to the craft of writing.

Now it was strong. 'The only reason I write,' he said, 'is to say something. I've forsaken adults because they're not going to change, though they may try awfully hard. But children can and do change.'

Before driving me back to the train station, Scott took me out on his deck and pointed to a grove of trees across Long Pond. During the Revolutionary War, a teenage girl had sought refuge from the Redcoats in a cave hidden by the grove. For years, she had drawn on her wits and fortitude to survive. After learning this bit of local history, Scott had crafted one of his best novels, *Sarah Bishop.*

"His message was simple. Good stories are everywhere. You don't have to look far. Open your eyes.

"We corresponded for a few years, and he kindly critiqued my awkward early efforts at YA fiction. Years later, I read that he had been working on his last novel, *My Name is Not Angelica,* in his hospital bed, just days before his death at age ninety-one.

"Scott taught me many things about writing, but one stands out. Writing is about perseverance. Never give up."

Biographical and Critical Sources

PERIODICALS

Booklist, September 15, 2010, Frances Bradburn, review of *Adios, Nirvana,* p. 64.
Bulletin of the Center for Children's Books, November, 2010, Deborah Stevenson, review of *Adios, Nirvana,* p. 155.
Kirkus Reviews, September 1, 2010, review of *Adios, Nirvana.*
Publishers Weekly, September 27, 2010, review of *Adios, Nirvana,* p. 63.
School Library Journal, November, 2010, Suzanne Gordon, review of *Adios, Nirvana,* p. 133.
Voice of Youth Advocates, December, 2010, Sharon Blumberg, review of *Adios, Nirvana,* p. 464.
West Seattle Herald, September 9, 2010, Steve Shay, "New Book 'Adios, Nirvana' Set in West Seattle."

ONLINE

Conrad Wesselhoeft Web log, http://adiosnirvana.com (December 19, 2011).
Novel Novice Web site, http://novelnovice.com/ (December 20, 2010), interview with Wesselhoeft.
Wordstock Web site, http://wordstockfestival.com/ (December 13, 2010), interview with Wesselhoeft.

*   *   *

WHEELER, Lisa 1963-

Personal

Born 1963; married Glen Wheeler; children: two daughters, one son.

Addresses

Home—MI. *E-mail*—lisa@lisawheelerbooks.com.

Career

Writer.

Awards, Honors

Notable Children's Books designation, American Library Association (ALA), Parents' Choice Award, and Society of School Librarians International Book Award Honor designation, all for *Mammoths on the Move;* 100 Titles for Reading and Sharing inclusion, New York Public Library, and Choices designation, Cooperative Children's Book Center (CCBC), both 2004, both for *Seadogs;* Theodor Seuss Geisel Award Honor Book designation, Notable Children's Books designation, ALA, Charlotte Zolotow Award highly commended title, and Choices designation, CCBC, all 2008, all for *Jazz Baby;* numerous honors from state reading associations.

Writings

FOR CHILDREN

Wool Gathering: A Sheep Family Reunion, illustrated by Frank Ansley, Atheneum (New York, NY), 2001.
Turk and Runt, illustration by Frank Ansley, Atheneum (New York, NY), 2002.
Sixteen Cows, illustration by Kurt Cyrus, Harcourt (San Diego, CA), 2002.
Sailor Moo: Cow at Sea, illustrated by Ponder Goembel, Atheneum (New York, NY), 2002.
Porcupining: A Prickly Love Story, illustrated by Janie Bynum, Little, Brown (Boston, MA), 2002.
Old Cricket, illustrated by Ponder Goembel, Atheneum (New York, NY), 2003.
Avalanche Annie: A Not-so Tall Tale, illustrated by Kurt Cyrus, Harcourt (San Diego, CA), 2003.
One Dark Night, illustrated by Ivan Bates, Harcourt (San Diego, CA), 2003.
Seadogs: An Epic Ocean Operetta, illustrations by Mark Siegel, Atheneum (New York, NY), 2004.
Farmer Dale's Red Pickup Truck, illustrated by Ivan Bates, Harcourt (Orlando, FL), 2004.
Te Amo, Bebé, Little One, illustrated by Mariel Suárez, Little, Brown (New York, NY), 2004.
Uncles and Antlers, illustrated by Brian Floca, Atheneum (New York, NY), 2004.
Bubble Gum, Bubble Gum, illustrated by Laura Huliska-Beith, Little, Brown (New York, NY), 2004.
Mammoths on the Move, illustrated by Kurt Cyrus, Harcourt (Orlando, FL), 2006.
Hokey Pokey: Another Prickly Love Story, illustrated by Janie Bynum, Little, Brown (New York, NY), 2006.
Castaway Cats, illustrated by Ponder Goembel, Atheneum (New York, NY), 2006.
Where, oh Where, Is Santa Claus?, illustrated by Ivan Bates, Harcourt (Orlando, FL), 2007.

The Christmas Boot, illustrated by Michael Glenn Monroe, Mitten Press (Ann Arbor, MI), 2007.
Dino-Hockey, Carolrhoda (Minneapolis, MN), 2007.
Jazz Baby, illustrated by R. Gregory Christie, Harcourt (Orlando, FL), 2007.
Boogie Knights, illustrated by Mark Siegel, Atheneum (New York, NY), 2008.
Dino-Soccer, illustrated by Barry Gott, Carolrhoda (Minneapolis, MN), 2009.
Dino-Baseball, illustrated by Barry Gott, Carolrhoda (Minneapolis, MN), 2010.
Ugly Pie, illustrated by Heather Solomon, Harcourt (Boston, MA), 2010.
Dino-Basketball, illustrated by Barry Gott, Carolrhoda Books (Minneapolis, MN), 2011.
Spinster Goose: Twisted Rhymes for Naughty Children, illustrated by Sophie Blackall, Atheneum (New York, NY), 2011.

Contributor to periodicals, including *Humpty Dumpty, Children's Playmate, Children's Writers and Illustrator's Market,* and *U.S. Kids.*

"FITCH AND CHIP" READER SERIES

When Pigs Fly, illustrated by Frank Ansley, Atheneum (New York, NY), 2003.
New Pig in Town, illustrated by Frank Ansley, Atheneum (New York, NY), 2003.
Who's Afraid of Granny Wolf?, illustrated by Frank Ansley, Atheneum (New York, NY), 2004.
Invasion of the Pig Sisters, illustrated by Frank Ansley, Atheneum (New York, NY), 2005.

Sidelights

Described by *Booklist* reviewer Karin Snelson as a "rollicking rhymer," Michigan-based author Lisa Wheeler has written a host of humorous tales, many of which feature puns and other wordplay. Among Wheeler's critically acclaimed works are *Mammoths on the Move, Jazz Baby,* and *Ugly Pie.* Asked what she likes best about writing for children, the author told *Suite101* online interviewer Jillian Bost: "I get to play with words! Writing for adults does not allow the freedom for combinations like ooey-gooey or icky-sticky. It doesn't let me use alliteration, onomatopoeia, or rhyme. Adults might not like a wolf who speaks or a mouse who wears clothing. Writing for kids allows me to do all-of-the-above and more."

Growing up in Pittsburgh, Pennsylvania, Wheeler was a bookish child, and when she moved to Michigan during her early teens, the shy new student relied on reading to compensate for loneliness. After dedicating many years to raising her three children, Wheeler made the decision to write children's books in the mid-1990s, and the result was *Wool Gathering: A Sheep Family Reunion.* "Writing books for children is definitely a dream come true," the author stated on her home page. "I am doing exactly what I am supposed to be doing with my life."

Lisa Wheeler's bilingual picture book Te Amo, Bebé, Little One *features brightly tinted cartoon art by Maribel Suárez.*

Animal characters, a favorite of smaller children, often take top billing in Wheeler's stories. Both *Porcupining: A Prickly Love Story* and *Hokey Pokey: Another Prickly Love Story* capture the excitement of a burgeoning romance between a porcupine and a hedgehog, resulting in what a *Publishers Weekly* critic described as two stories "with plenty of giggle opportunities." Designed as a Thanksgiving storybook, *Turk and Runt* focuses on a young turkey whose proud parents see their strong young son's potential as a dancer or athlete. Turk's less-burly brother, Runt, agrees that Turk's good looks will make him the first to be picked; not for a sports team, however, but for the main course on a Thanksgiving dinner table. When Turk does indeed get marked for the kill, Runt saves his comely but clueless sibling in a book that *Booklist* reviewer Ilene Cooper dubbed "funny from beginning to end."

Wheeler again turns to farmyard favorites in *Sailor Moo: Cow at Sea,* telling the story of a delusional bovine in rhyming verse. Standing near a sea of wheat,

Moo dreams of the salty spray of the ocean. When her wish comes true and she ends up aboard a cattle barge-turned-pirate ship, pirate captain Red Angus finds in Moo his "dairy queen." Praising the illustrations by Ponder Goembel, a *Publishers Weekly* reviewer noted that *Sailor Moo* is chock full of "silly cow puns," and John Peters predicted in a *Booklist* review that Wheeler's bouncy story will make young listeners "stampede into story time . . . and that's no bull."

Other collaborations between Wheeler and Goembel include *Old Cricket* and *Castaway Cats. Old Cricket* finds a creaky, crabby insect faking a host of aches and pains in order to avoid having to help his wife out around the house. Sent into town to see the doctor, Old Cricket manages to wheedle his way out of helping neighbors Uncle Ant and Cousin Katydid, even though he is given food by these insect friends. Finally, when he has to hurry to avoid a hungry crow, Old Cricket realizes that he really does need Doc Hopper's help, and when he returns home he is more enthusiastic about helping those

around him. *Old Cricket,* a trickster tale, was praised as "smartly paced and skillfully drawn" by a *Publishers Weekly* reviewer, while in *Kirkus Reviews* a contributor wrote that Wheeler's "sidesplitting animal story" is "a natural for reading aloud" due to its alliterative, repetitive refrain.

Ranked as "another winner" by the author/illustrator team by *School Library Journal* critic Kara Schaff Dean, *Castaway Cats* finds eight cats and seven kitties cast adrift in the ocean after their ship goes down. When they wash up on the beach of a deserted island, the cats must overcome their natural tendencies to be loners in order to work together to build a boat to carry them all home. "Wheeler's neatly honed verse is a pleasure to read aloud," wrote *Horn Book* critic Joanna Rudge Long. Praising the story's rhyming text and quirky cast of soggy felines, as well as Goembel's "fantastic" ink-and-acrylic illustrations, Schaff concluded that *Castaway Cats* treats readers to an "animated, witty" tale, and in *Booklist* Julie Cummins deemed it "a categorically clever yarn" in which Wheeler's wordplay contributes "even more fun."

In a more fantastic vein, *Avalanche Annie: A Not-so-Tall Tale* features a Native-American heroine who is only four-foot three inches tall. Living in a nonexistent region called Michisota, Annie Halfpint refuses to let herself be limited by her short stature, and when her home in Yoohoo Valley is threatened by an avalanche from nearby Mount Himalachia, Annie saves the day. Snelson had special praise for Wheeler's "small but mighty heroine" as well as for the author's ability to mimic the made-up language and exaggeration of actual American tall tales, such as the story of Paul Bunyan and Babe the Blue Ox. Recommending *Avalanche Annie*, the *Booklist* critic also cited the story's "mellifluous metered verse."

Wheeler's "snappy rhyming text" in *Jazz Baby* "celebrates an extended family's joyous gyrations" while listening to their favorite music, according to a contributor to *Kirkus Reviews*. Brought to life in what *Booklist* critic Janice Del Negro described as "stylish, retro" gouache paintings by R. Gregory Christie, Wheeler's high-energy story "scans like a musical dream," the critic added. Backing up their musical grandparents, Brother taps his foot, Sister snaps her fingers, and the baby of the family shows that he also has a case of jazz fever through his jubilant clap in a text that listeners can participate in. *Jazz Baby* is no bedtime tale, cautioned a *Publishers Weekly* critic, the reviewer writing that young listeners are "likely to clamor for repeats of [Wheeler's] . . . buoyant musical jaunt." In *Horn Book* Susan Dove Lempke deemed the upbeat picture book "a rousing celebration of music and family."

Wheeler threads a ghostly element into her story for *Boogie Knights,* which focuses on a party at a haunted castle. Goblins, ghosts of knights and deceased royals,

Wheeler's folktale adaptation in **Old Crow** *comes to life in detailed artwork by Ponder Goembel.* (Illustration copyright © 2003 by Ponder Goembel. Reprinted with the permission of Aladdin Paperbacks, an imprint of Simon & Schuster Children's Publishing Division.)

werewolves, zombies, wizards, demons, and even mummies gather at the Madcap Monster Ball to dance away the night, their festivities captured in Mark Siegel's tinted charcoal drawings. Wheeler's "freewheeling rhyme scheme and [Siegel's] judicious use of color amp up the party atmosphere," wrote a *Publishers Weekly* critic in reviewing *Boogie Knights,* and *School Library Journal* critic Joy Fleishhacker maintained that the author's "rhythmic text is filled with taut rhymes, alliteration, and vivid images." In *Kirkus Reviews,* a contributor dubbed the picture book "a pitch-perfect Halloween-time poem."

In *Dino-Hockey* and *Dino-Soccer* Wheeler creates an enticing mix for young boys who are fans of both team sports and dinosaurs. In her characteristic humorous rhyming text for *Dino-Hockey,* she describes a rough-and-tumble game between the Meat-Eaters and the Veggisaurs as several prehistoric creatures battle with hockey sticks rather than tooth and claw. Noting the book's "slapstick humor," Gillian Engberg added in her *Booklist* review of *Dino-Hockey* that Wheeler's decision to divide her dinosaur teams into "herbivores and carnivores . . . sneaks in a science lesson." In *School Library Journal,* Julie Roach wrote that Barry Gott's computer-generated illustrations "accentuate funny details" of the fast-paced plot, while Wheeler's "clever rhyming couplets keep the game lively and slip in facts about dinosaurs." "It's prehistoric pandemonium on ice" in which the text "captures the slapshot-quick pace," quipped a *Kirkus Reviews* contributor in a review of *Dino-Hockey.*

The carnivorous Rib-Eye Reds take the field against the Green Sox, a team of herbivores, in *Dino-Baseball,* Wheeler's third sports-related tale featuring prehistoric creatures. The toothy fans that stream into Jurassic Park are treated to a hotly contested game winding up to a wild finish, all captured in the author's humorous verse narrative. "Wheeler's sturdy, concise couplets provide a nicely percussive play-by-play," maintained a *Publishers Weekly* contributor. In *Dino-Basketball* the Meat tip off against the Grass Clippers for hoops supremacy. Here "the commentary is fast paced and exciting," Tanya Boudreau remarked in *School Library Journal,* and a *Kirkus Reviews* contributor wrote that the "rhyming verse" in *Dino-Baseball* "mimics both the play-by-play announcement and the action of a basketball game, making readers feel a part of the excitement."

One of Wheeler's most unusual picture-book offerings, *Seadogs: An Epic Opera,* was inspired by the light operas composed by nineteenth-century British composers Gilbert & Sullivan. In the picture book an operetta about a band of pirates is staged using an all-dog cast. After the curtain rises, song and rhyme relate a saga starring Old Seadog and Brave Beagle, who set sail on the *Beauty* but are attacked by a pirate ship's "mongrel hoard" led by the wily Captain Fifi. A treasure map and a comely canine stowaway also figure in the rollicking tale, which "contains a good deal of whimsical humor,"

Wheeler gives Mother Goose tales a twist in **Spinster Goose,** *a picture book featuring artwork by Sophie Blackall.* (Illustration copyright © 2011 by Sophie Blackall. Reprinted with the permission of Atheneum Books for Young Readers, an imprint of Simon & Schuster Children's Publishing Division.)

according to *School Library Journal* reviewer Marilyn Taniguchi. In *Booklist* Francisca Goldsmith described *Seadogs* as "a delightful book to share with pre-readers," while a *Kirkus Reviews* critic wrote: "Chock full of . . . wonderfully clever turns of phrase," Wheeler's book is "a genuine howl."

A hungry bruin goes searching for a tasty treat in Wheeler's *Ugly Pie,* a "homespun story about finding value in items thought of as waste," observed a contributor *Kirkus Reviews.* When Ol' Bear wakes up with a craving for Ugly Pie, he takes a stroll through the countryside to visit his neighbors, none of whom have the delicacy he desires. Ol' Bear does not leave empty-handed, however, as each of his friends donates leftovers—sour green apples, wrinkled raisins, bumpy walnuts—that he can use to create his own dessert. According to a critic in *Publishers Weekly,* "Wheeler's . . . rural dialect text . . . is fun to read," and *Horn Book* reviewer Lempke stated that young readers will "like the gentle humor, the repetition, . . . and the folksy tone" of *Ugly Pie.*

Wheeler offers an unusual take on some favorite childhood verses in *Spinster Goose: Twisted Rhymes for Naughty Children,* a "semi-subversive collection," in the opinion of *Horn Book* critic Roger Sutton. In these tales, Mother Goose sends insubordinate youngsters to a most unappealing reform school headed by her no-nonsense sister, Spinster Goose, where misbehaviors lead to some unorthodox punishments. "Delectably satiric nursery rhymes play with naughtiness and punish-

ment," a contributor in *Kirkus Reviews* noted. Thom Barthelmess, writing in *Booklist,* called the work "irresistibly sinister," and *School Library Journal* critic Barbara Elleman believed that *Spinster Goose* "will appeal most to those who like their giggles with a bit of a spin."

In a *Cynsations* online interview with Cynthia Leitich Smith, Wheeler gave advice to budding writers. "If you study your craft, read everything that is out there, [and] write the books only you can write, good things will happen," she asserted. "Yes, it is hard to break into print. We all pay our dues. Some work longer than others. But I have to believe that the cream rises to the top. If I didn't believe that, I couldn't keep doing this."

Biographical and Critical Sources

PERIODICALS

Booklist, Ilene Cooper, review of *Wool Gathering: A Sheep Family Reunion,* p. 480; May 21, 2002, John Peters, review of *Sailor Moo: Cow at Sea,* p. 1529; September 1, 2002, Ilene Cooper, review of *Turk and Runt,* p. 141; May 15, 2003, Lauren Peterson, review of *Old Cricket,* p. 1674; July, 2003, GraceAnne A. DeCandido, review of *New Pig in Town,* p. 1903; October 15, 2003, Karin Snelson, review of *Avalanche Annie: A Not-so-Tall Tale,* p. 420; February 1, 2004, Francisca Goldsmith review of *Seadogs: An Epic Ocean Operetta,* p. 986; August, 2004, Hazel Rochman, review of *Te Amo, Bebé, Little One,* p. 339; November 1, 2004, Karin Snelson, review of *Farmer Dale's Red Pickup Truck,* p. 494; May 1, 2006, Carolyn Phelan, review of *Mammoths on the Move,* p. 87; August 1, 2006, Julie Cummins, review of *Castaway Cats,* p. 94; September 1, 2007, Gillian Engberg, review of *Dino-Hockey,* p. 137; October 15, 2007, Janice Del Negro, review of *Jazz Baby,* p. 51; October 15, 2008, Randall Enos, review of *Boogie Nights,* p. 40; September 1, 2009, Daniel Kraus, review of *Dino-Soccer,* p. 110; March 1, 2010, Gillian Engberg, review of *Dino-Baseball,* p. 78; July 1, 2010, Julie Cummins, review of *Ugly Pie,* p. 68; February 15, 2011, Thom Barthelmess, review of *Spinster Goose: Twisted Rhymes for Naughty Children,* p. 67.

Horn Book, March-April, 2004, Lolly Robinson, review of *Seadogs,* p. 176; July-August, 2006, Joanna Rudge Long, review of *Castaway Cats,* p. 432; January-February, 2008, Susan Dove Lempke, review of *Jazz Baby,* p. 80; July-August, 2010, Susan Dove Lempke, review of *Ugly Pie,* p. 96; May-June, 2011, Roger Sutton, review of *Spinster Goose,* p. 114.

Kirkus Reviews, September 15, 2001, review of *Wool Gathering,* p. 1371; March 1, 2002, review of *Sixteen Cows,* p. 348; June 15, 2002, review of *Sailor Moo,* p. 890; September 1, 2002, review of *Turk and Runt,* p. 1323; December 15, 2002, review of *Porcupining,* p. 1859; April 15, 2003, review of *Old Cricket,* p. 613; September 1, 2003, review of *New Pig in Town,* p.

1132; October 1, 2003, review of *Avalanche Annie,* p. 1233; January 1, 2004, review of *Seadogs,* p. 43; March 1, 2004, review of *Bubble Gum, Bubble Gum,* p. 231; March 15, 2004, review of *Te Amo, Bebé, Little One,* p. 279; August 15, 2004, review of *Farmer Dale's Red Pickup Truck,* p. 814; November 1, 2004, review of *Uncles and Antlers,* p. 1055; March 15, 2006, review of *Mammoths on the Move,* p. 303; September 1, 2007, review of *Hokey Pokey: Another Prickly Love Story,* p. 1281; May 1, 2006, review of *Castaway Cats,* p. 470; September 1, 2007, review of *Dino-Hockey;* October 15, 2007, review of *Jazz Baby;* July 15, 2008, review of *Boogie Knights;* June 15, 2010, review of *Ugly Pie;* February 15, 2011, reviews of *Dino-Basketball* and *Spinster Goose.*

Publishers Weekly, October 8, 2001, review of *Wool Gathering,* p. 62; March 25, 2002, review of *Sixteen Cows,* p. 63; June 3, 2002, review of *Sailor Moo,* p. 87; December 2, 2002, review of *Porcupining,* p. 52; January 6, 2003, review of *One Dark Night,* p. 481; April 7, 2003, review of *Old Cricket,* p. 65; September 15, 2003, reviews of *When Pigs Fly* and *New Pig in Town,* both p. 65; February 9, 2004, review of *Seadogs,* p. 81; December 5, 2005, review of *Hokey Pokey,* p. 54; October 22, 2007, review of *Where, Oh Where, Is Santa Claus?,* p. 55; November 19, 2007, review of *Jazz Baby,* p. 56; June 23, 2008, review of *Boogie Knights,* p. 53; April 5, 2010, review of *Dino-Baseball,* p. 60; July 12, 2010, review of *Ugly Pie,* p. 44; January 10, 2011, review of *Spinster Goose,* p. 49.

School Library Journal, October, 2001, Linda Ludke, review of *Wool Gathering,* p. 147; April, 2002, Helen Foster James, review of *Sixteen Cows,* p. 128; August, 2002, Judith Constantinides, review of *Sailor Moo,* p. 172; October, 2002, Melinda Piehler, review of *Turk and Runt,* p. 134; January, 2003, Carol Ann Wilson, review of *Porcupining,* p. 115; May, 2003, Kathy Piehl, review of *Old Cricket,* p. 132; December, 2003, Faith Brautigam, review of *Avalanche Annie,* p. 130; March, 2004, Marilyn Taniguchi, review of *Seadogs,* p. 186; May, 2004, Sheilah Kosco, review of *Te Amo, Bebé, Little One,* and Andrea Tarr, review of *Bubble Gum, Bubble Gum,* both p. 126; August, 2004, Corrina Austin, review of *Who's Afraid of Granny Wolf?,* p. 103; December, 2004, Carolyn Janssen, review of *Farmer Dale's Red Pickup Truck,* p. 124; January, 2006, Sally R. Dow, review of *Hokey Pokey,* p. 115; June, 2006, Kara Schaff Dean, review of *Castaway Cats,* p. 128, and Steven Engelfried, review of *Mammoths on the Move,* p. 141; December, 2007, Julie Roach, review of *Dino-Hockey,* p. 102; January, 2008, Susan Scheps, review of *Jazz Baby,* p. 100; August, 2008, Joy Fleishhacker, review of *Boogie Knights,* p. 105; August, 2009, Linda L. Walkins, review of *Dino-Soccer,* p. 86; April, 2010, Marge Loch-Wouters, review of *Dino-Baseball,* p. 142; July, 2010, Judith Constantinides, review of *Ugly Pie,* p. 71; March, 2011, Tanya Boudreau, review of *Dino-Basketball,* p. 139, and Barbara Elleman, review of *Spinster Goose,* p. 146.

ONLINE

Cynsations Web site, http://cynthialeitichsmith.blogspot. com/ (February 28, 2006), Cynthia Leitich Smith, interview with Wheeler.

Debbi Michiko Florence Web site, http://www.debbi michikoflorence.com/ (May 5, 2009), interview with Wheeler.

Lisa Wheeler Home Page, http://www.lisawheelerbooks. com (December 15, 2011).

Suite101 Web site, http://www.suite101.com/ (September 2, 2010), Jillian Bost, interview with Wheeler.*

* * *

WILLIS, Jeanne 1959-

Personal

Born November 5, 1959, in St. Albans, Hertfordshire, England; daughter of David Alfred (a language teacher) and Dorothy Hilda Celia (a teacher of domestic science) Willis; married Ian James Wilcock (an animator), May 26, 1989; children: one son, one daughter. *Education:* Watford College of Art, diploma (advertising writing), 1979.

Addresses

Home—London, England. *Agent*—Catherine Clarke, Felicity Bryan Associates Literary Agency, 2A N. Parade Ave., Oxford OX2 6LX, England.

Career

Children's book author. Doyle, Dane, Berenbach, London, England, advertising copywriter, 1979-81; Young & Rubicam Ltd., London, senior writer, group head, and member of board of directors, c. 1980s; freelance writer and author of television scripts. Presenter at schools.

Member

British Herpetological Association.

Awards, Honors

Top-Ten Picture Books designation, *Redbook,* 1987, for *The Monster Bed;* Whitbread Award nomination, 2003, for *Naked without a Hat;* Smarties Silver Medal, 2004, for *Tadpole's Promise;* Carnegie Medal longlist inclusion, 2005, for *Dumb Creatures;* several advertising-industry awards.

Writings

The Tale of Georgie Grub, illustrated by Margaret Chamberlain, Andersen Press (London, England), 1981, Holt (New York, NY), 1982, reprinted, Andersen Press, 2012.

The Tale of Fearsome Fritz, illustrated by Margaret Chamberlain, Andersen Press (London, England), 1982, Holt (New York, NY), 1983.

The Tale of Mucky Mabel, illustrated by Margaret Chamberlain, Andersen Press (London, England), 1984.

The Monster Bed, illustrated by Susan Varley, Andersen Press (London, England), 1986, Lothrop, (New York, NY), 1987, reprinted, Andersen Press, 2007.

The Long Blue Blazer, illustrated by Susan Varley, Andersen Press (London, England), 1987, Dutton (New York, NY), 1988.

Toffee Pockets (poems), illustrated by George Buchanan, Bodley Head (London, England), 1992.

In Search of the Hidden Giant, illustrated by Ruth Brown, Andersen Press (London, England), 1993, published as *In Search of the Giant,* Dutton (New York, NY), 1994.

The Lion's Roar, illustrated by Derek Collin, Ginn (London, England), 1994.

The Rascally Cake, illustrated by Korky Paul, Andersen Press (London, England), 1994, reprinted, 2009.

Two Sea Songs, Ginn (London, England), 1994.

The Monster Storm, illustrated by Susan Varley, Lothrop (New York, NY), 1995.

Dolly Dot, Ginn (London, England), 1995.

Flower Pots and Forget-Me-Nots, Ginn (London, England), 1995.

Wilbur and Orville Take Off, illustrated by Roger Wade Walker, Macdonald Young (Hemel Hempstead, England), 1995.

The Princess and the Parlour Maid, illustrated by Pauline Hazelwood, Macdonald Young (Hemel Hempstead, England), 1995.

Tom's Lady of the Lamp, illustrated by Amy Burch, Macdonald Young (Hemel Hempstead, England), 1995.

The Pet Person, illustrated by Tony Ross, Dial (New York, NY), 1996.

The Pink Hare, illustrated by Ken Brown, Andersen Press (London, England), 1996.

What Do You Want to Be, Brian?, illustrated by Mary Rees, Andersen Press (London, England), 1996.

Sloth's Shoes, illustrated by Tony Ross, Andersen Press (London, England), 1997, Kane/Miller (Brooklyn, NY), 1998.

The Wind in the Wallows (poetry), illustrated by Tony Ross, Andersen Press (London, England), 1998.

The Boy Who Lost His Belly Button, illustrated by Tony Ross, Andersen Press (London, England), 1999, Dorling Kindersley (New York, NY), 2000.

Tinkerbill, illustrated by Paul Cox, Collins (London, England), 1999.

Susan Laughs, illustrated by Tony Ross, Andersen Press (London, England), 1999, Holt (New York, NY), 2000.

Take Turns, Penguin!, illustrated by Mark Birchall, Carolrhoda (Minneapolis, MN), 2000.

Parrot Goes to Playschool, illustrated by Mark Birchall, Andersen Press (London, England), 2000, published as *Be Quiet, Parrot!,* Carolrhoda (Minneapolis, MN), 2000.

What Did I Look like When I Was a Baby?, illustrated by Tony Ross, Putnam (New York, NY), 2000.

The Hard Man of the Swings (young-adult novel), Faber & Faber (London, England), 2000, published as *The Truth or Something,* Henry Holt (New York, NY), 2002.

Do Little Mermaids Wet Their Beds?, illustrated by Penelope Jossen, Albert Whitman (Morton Grove, IL), 2001.

No Biting, Panther!, illustrated by Mark Birchall, Carolrhoda (Minneapolis, MN), 2001.

Be Gentle, Python!, illustrated by Mark Birchall, Carolrhoda (Minneapolis, MN), 2001.

No Biting, Puma!, illustrated by Mark Birchall, Carolrhoda Books (Minneapolis, MN), 2001.

The Boy Who Thought He Was a Teddy Bear: A Fairy Tale, illustrated by Susan Varley, Peachtree (Atlanta, GA), 2002.

Don't Let Go!, illustrated by Tony Ross, Andersen Press (London, England), 2002, G.P. Putnam's Sons (New York, NY), 2003.

Rocket Science, Faber Children's Books (London, England), 2002.

Sleepover!: The Best Ever Party Kit, illustrated by Lydia Monks, Candlewick Press (Cambridge, MA), 2002.

I Want to Be a Cowgirl, illustrated by Tony Ross, Henry Holt (New York, NY), 2002.

The Beast of Crowsfoot Cottage ("Shock Shop" series), Macmillan Children's Books (London, England), 2003.

Naked without a Hat (young-adult novel), Faber & Faber (London, England), 2003, Delacorte (New York, NY), 2004.

Adventures of Jimmy Scar, Andersen Press (London, England), 2003.

New Shoes, Andersen Press (London, England), 2003.

When Stephanie Smiled, illustrated by Penelope Jossen, Andersen Press (London, England), 2003.

Zitz, Glitz, and Body Blitz, illustrated by Lydia Monks, Walker Books (London, England), 2004.

Shhh!, illustrated by Tony Ross, Hyperion Books for Children (New York, NY), 2004.

I Hate School, illustrated by Tony Ross, Atheneum Books for Young Readers (New York, NY), 2004.

Bits, Boobs, and Blobs, illustrated by Lydia Monks, Walker Books (London, England), 2004.

Snogs, Sex, and Soulmates, illustrated by Lydia Monks, Walker Books (London, England), 2004.

Manky Monkey illustrated by Tony Ross, Andersen Press (London, England), 2004.

The Magic Potty Show with Trubble and Trixie, illustrated by Edward Eaves, Pan MacMillan (London, England), 2004.

Misery Moo, illustrated by Tony Ross, Henry Holt (New York, NY), 2005.

Tadpole's Promise, illustrated by Tony Ross, Atheneum Books for Young Readers (New York, NY), 2005.

Operation Itchy, illustrated by Penny Dann, Candlewick Press (Cambridge, MA), 2005.

Never Too Little to Love, illustrated by Jan Fearnley, Candlewick Press (Cambridge, MA), 2005.

Secret Fairy Talent Show ("Secret Fairy" series), illustrated by Penny Dann, Orchard Books (London, England), 2005.

Dumb Creatures, illustrated by Nicola Slater, Macmillan Children's Books (London, England), 2005.

Daft Bat, illustrated by Tony Ross, Andersen Press (London, England), 2006, Sterling Publishing (New York, NY), 2008.

The Really Rude Rhino, illustrated by Tony Ross, Andersen Press (London, England), 2006.

Dozy Mare, illustrated by Tony Ross, Andersen Press (London, England), 2006.

Mayfly Day, illustrated by Tony Ross, Andersen Press (London, England), 2006.

Gorilla! Gorilla!, illustrated by Tony Ross, Atheneum Books for Young Readers (New York, NY), 2006.

Rat Heaven, Macmillan Children's Books (London, England), 2006.

Deliah Darling Is in the Library, illustrated by Rosie Reeve, Puffin (London, England), 2006, published as *Delilah D. at the Library,* Clarion Books (New York, NY), 2007.

Who's in the Loo?, illustrated by Adrian Reynolds, Andersen Press (London, England), 2006, published as *Who's in the Bathroom?,* Simon & Schuster Books for Young Readers (New York, NY), 2007.

Grill Pan Eddy, illustrated by Tony Ross, Andersen Press (London, England), 2007.

Killer Gorilla, illustrated by Tony Ross, Andersen Press (London, England), 2007.

Little Big Mouth, illustrated by Lydia Monks, Walker Books (London, England), 2007.

Deliah Darling Is in the Classroom, illustrated by Rosie Reeve, Puffin (London, England), 2007.

Grandad and John, illustrated by Jessica Meserve, Walker Books (London, England), 2007.

Cottonwool Colin, illustrated by Tony Ross, Andersen Press (London, England), 2007, published as *Cottonball Colin,* Eerdmans (Grand Rapids, MI), 2008.

Shamanka, Walker Books (London, England), 2007, Candlewick Press (Somerville, MA), 2009.

Princess Candytuft, illustrated by Penny Dann, Orchard (London, England), 2007.

Mommy, Do You Love Me?, illustrated by Jan Feanley, Candlewick Press (Cambridge, MA), 2008.

Dear Father Christmas, illustrated by Rosie Reeve, Puffin (London, England), 2009.

Big Bad Bun, illustrated by Tony Ross, Walker Books (London, England), 2009.

Flabby Cat and Slobby Dog, illustrated by Tony Ross, Carolrhoda Books (Minneapolis, MN), 2009.

The Bog Baby, illustrated by Gwen Millward, Schwartz & Wade (New York, NY), 2009.

Old Dog, illustrated by Tony Ross, Andersen Press (London, England), 2009.

The Nanny Goat's Kid, illustrated by Tony Ross, Andersen Press (London, England), 2010.

Caterpillar Dreams, illustrated by Tony Ross, Andersen Press (London, England), 2010.

That's Not Funny!, illustrated by Adrian Reynolds, Lerner (Minneapolis, MN), 2010.

Bottoms Up, illustrated by Adam Stower, Puffin (London, England), 2010.

I'm Sure I Saw a Dinosaur, illustrated by Adrian Reynolds, Lerner (Minneapolis, MN), 2011.

We're Going to a Party!, illustrated by Tony Ross, Andersen Press (London, England), 2011.

Sticky Ends, illustrated by Tony Ross, Andersen Press (London, England), 2011.

The Wheels on the Bus: A Read-along Sing-along Trip to the Zoo, illustrated by Adam Stower, Puffin (London, England), 2012.

The Goffins: Puppets and Plays (middle-grade novel), illustrated by Nick Maland, Walker Children's Books (London, England), 2012.

Penguin Pandemonium, illustrated by Ed Vere, HarperCollins (New York, NY), 2012.

Wild Child, photographs by Lorna Freytag, Walker Children's Books (London, England), 2012.

Author of educational CD-ROM scripts for Dorling Kindersley; writer for television series, including *Marvelous Millie,* 1999; *The Ark,* 2002; *Dr. Xargle,* HTV/Cinar; *Maisy,* Polygram; *Dog and Duck,* United Films; and *The Slow Norris,* HTV/United.

"DR. XARGLE" SERIES; ILLUSTRATED BY TONY ROSS; FOR YOUNG READERS

Dr. Xargle's Book of Earthlets, Andersen Press (London, England), 1988, published as *Earthlets, as Explained by Professor Xargle,* Dutton (New York, NY), 1989, reprinted, 2011.

Dr. Xargle's Book of Earth Hounds, Andersen Press (London, England), 1989, published as *Earth Hounds, as Explained by Professor Xargle,* Dutton (New York, NY), 1990, reprinted, 2011.

Dr. Xargle's Book of Earth Tiggers, Andersen Press (London, England), 1990, published as *Earth Tigerlets, as Explained by Professor Xargle,* Dutton (New York, NY), 1991, reprinted, 2011.

Dr. Xargle's Book of Earth Mobiles, Andersen Press (London, England), 1991, published as *Earth Mobiles, as Explained by Professor Xargle,* Dutton (New York, NY), 1992.

Dr. Xargle's Book of Earth Weather, Andersen Press (London, England), 1992, published as *Earth Weather, as Explained by Professor Xargle,* Dutton (New York, NY), 1993.

Dr. Xargle's Book of Earth Relations, Andersen Press (London, England), 1993, published as *Relativity, as Explained by Professor Xargle,* Dutton (New York, NY), 1994.

"CRAZY JOBS" SERIES; ILLUSTRATED BY PAUL KORKY; FOR YOUNG READERS

Annie the Gorilla Nanny, Orchard Books (London, England), 2005.

Gabby the Vampire Cabby, Orchard Books (London, England), 2005.

Jeff, the Witch's Chef, Orchard Books (London, England), 2005.

Lillibet, the Monster Vet, Orchard Books (London, England), 2005.

Norman the Demon Doorman, Orchard Books (London, England), 2005.

Vanessa, the Werewolf Hairdresser, Orchard Books (London, England), 2005.

Bert the Fairies' Fashion Expert, Orchard Books (London, England), 2005.

Iddy Bogey the Ogre Yogi, Orchard Books (London, England), 2005.

Adaptations

Dumb Creatures was adapted as a television film.

Sidelights

Working with a range of popular illustrators that includes Tony Ross, Adam Stower, Susan Varley, Paul Korky, Adrian Reynolds, and Margaret Chimberlain, British children's writer Jeanne Willis is the talent behind dozens of critically acclaimed books for children that instruct as well as amuse. A former advertising executive and author of television scripts, Willis has also written poetry and novels for preteen and adolescent readers, among them *Naked without a Hat, Shamanka, Grandad and John,* and *The Goffins: Puppets and Plays.* Like several of her picture books, her humorous "Dr. Xargle" picture-book series has been in continuous publication since first appearing in the late 1980s.

Growing up in suburban England as the daughter of teachers, Willis developed a fascination for wildlife, particularly reptiles and toads. "I belonged to the World Wildlife Guard (now the Worldwide Guard for Wildlife)," she once recalled, "and had a bedroom full of strange creatures—locusts, stick insects, newts, caterpillars, etc. The fascination with these beasts has remained with me all my life. Indeed when I got married our blessing was held in the Aquarium at the London Zoo

Jeanne Willis teams up with illustrator Tony Ross in the humorous beginning reader **Susan Laughs.** (Illustration copyright © 1999 by Tony Ross. Reproduced by permission of Andersen Press, London.)

in front of the shark tank." Willis also developed an early talent for creative writing. "I had a very vivid imagination as a child," explained the author. "I think I felt everything deeply, and in many respects that was good. My happiness, my excitements, seemed to be bigger emotions than other children felt. The bad side of the coin is obvious: deep hurt, dreadful fears. . . . Because I was not confidently articulate, I exorcised these intense feelings on paper. I still do. One day somebody pointed out that such things were commercially viable, so they found their way into stories."

Willis first won acclaim for her "Professor Xargle" series of science books for the early elementary grades. Initially released in England, each has been published under a revised title for U.S. audiences. The premise is the same throughout the series: the misinformed alien professor of the title tries to explain the odd life forms on Earth. He takes a scientific tone, but his lectures are full of comical errors. In *Dr. Xargle's Book of Earthlets,* for example, the professor strains to enlighten his class of fellow aliens about infant humans, while in *Dr. Xargle's Book of Earth Hounds* he discusses dogs on the planet and how humans spread newspapers on the floor for their young "houndlets" to read. The professor tackles the subject of cats in *Dr. Xargle's Book of Earth Tiggers,* telling his class that felines' bizarre behavior includes planting "brown stinkseeds" that never grow and leaving "squishy puddings" on the stairs, through which humans then trod. Willis's "writing is fresh and fun, the scope of her imagination limitless," enthused a *Publishers Weekly* critic reviewing the U.S. edition, *Earth Tigerlets, as Explained by Professor Xargle.*

In *Dr. Xargle's Book of Earth Mobiles* Xargle enlightens the class on the various modes of transportation on Earth, such as the very popular "stinkfumer," his term for the automobile. *Dr. Xargle's Book of Earth Weather* tackles meteorology. Humans, the professor explains, cope with wet weather by growing large rubber feet that they then have difficulty removing. During hot weather, they enjoy lying in what appear to be nests of brown sugar. "Subtle as well as slapstick humor will appeal to a wide variety of ages," noted Claudia Cooper in her assessment of *Earth Weather, as Explained by Professor Xargle* for *School Library Journal. Dr. Xargle's Book of Earth Relations,* the last title in the series, was published in the United States as *Relativity, as Explained by Professor Xargle.* Here the alien academic talks about human families and how they "belong to each other whether they like it or not."

Willis noted that her "Dr. Xargle" series is simply the result of realizing how absurd human and animal behavior is, and also a desire to believe in "the alien." "I'm sure they exist. In fact, I'm sure they're here already. I often get the feeling I'm on the wrong planet, so perhaps I'm one."

In *The Rascally Cake* Willis presents the rhyming tale of Rufus and his attempt to bake a Christmas cake. He uses so many dreadful ingredients that the batter whips

Willis takes readers on an imaginative journey in **The Boy Who Lost His Belly Button,** *featuring whimsical art by Tony Ross.* (Illustration copyright © 2000 by Tony Ross. Reproduced by permission of Andersen Press, London.)

up into a monster and chases him. Wendy Timothy, in her review for *School Librarian,* called *The Rascally Cake* "wonderfully horrid." Willis also uses humor in *The Pet Person,* a book about a dog's birthday wish for a "person" of his own. His dog parents try to dissuade him, reminding him that such creatures often develop revolting habits, such as eating at the table. In *Sloth's Shoes,* Willis describes a birthday party in the jungle for Sloth, who is so slow in getting there that he misses the party entirely. In *Tinkerbill,* little Sally learns her parents are expecting a brother or sister for her. Unhappy about this coming change, the girl makes a wish and believes it comes true when her new infant brother shows signs that he is a fairy. Andrea Rayner, writing in *School Librarian,* called *Tinkerbill* "a funny story about sibling rivalry" and one that "is not censorious about the child's jealousy."

Willis also creates an amusing storyline in *What Did I Look like When I Was a Baby?* After a little boy asks his mother the title question, she replies that he looked bald and wrinkled like his grandfather. Across the subsequent pages, young animals in the jungle posit the same question to their mothers. Only the bullfrog is traumatized by the photograph of himself as a tadpole, and his friends must sing a song to get him to come out of hiding. "Ross's cartoon-like illustrations complement the puns and double entendres in the text," noted a *Publishers Weekly* reviewer.

Featuring artwork by Ross, *The Boy Who Lost His Belly Button* was described as "another whimsical offering from Willis," by *School Library Journal* reviewer Carolyn Janssen. In this quirky tale, a child wakes up one

day to find that his navel has disappeared, and he ventures out into the jungle to look for it. The boy asks the help of various animals, including a gorilla, lion, elephant, and even a mouse, each of whom displays its own belly button. The boy's quest culminates in a scene that possesses "a cinematic-like tension," according to a *Publishers Weekly* critic. Another Willis-Ross collaboration, *Susan Laughs,* is a rhyming tale about a little girl and her everyday activities and various moods; only on the last page is the girl shown to be confined to a wheelchair. Hazel Rochman, writing in *Booklist,* noted that the story's message is conveyed "without being condescending or preachy."

A scruffy old mutt teaches a pack of frisky young puppies some new skills in *Old Dog,* a multigenerational tale that combines Ross's scratchy cartoon drawings with what London *Guardian* contributor Julia Eccleshare described as a "warm-hearted story about not underestimating your aged grandparents." Two sedentary friends indulge in their twin hobbies of sleeping and eating, with humorous results in *Flabby Cat and Slobby Dog,* and here Willis's warning to the exercise-averse is paired with water-color-and-line art by Ross that "displays its customary energy and wry wit."

Willis shrinks her story down to mouse size in *Cottonball Colin,* as a tiny rodent resists being catered to and worried over by his overprotective mother. When the cotton-covered mouseling is mistaken for a snowball on one of his rare trips outside the mouse house, he winds up in a series of adventures that transforms his world and allays his mother's concerns. "Children will relate to Colin's steps toward independence," predicted Linda Ludke in her *School Library Journal* review of *Cottonball Colin,* and a *Publishers Weekly* critic cited Ross's illustrations when dubbing the picture book "another winner from a standout British team."

Illustrated by Varley, *The Boy Who Thought He Was a Teddy Bear: A Fairy Tale* focuses on a boy who spends his growing-up years with a group of bears after being deposited with them by fairies. When the bears return him to his human mother, the lad discovers that being a human is just as much fun. Another fanciful tale, Willis's *The Bog Baby,* comes to life in artwork by Gwen Millward and follows a woman's recollection of the time she and her sister visited Bluebell Wood and discovered a blobbish blue winged creature. Although they brought the big-eyed youngling home and tried to recreate its natural habitat, it languished under their care and reminded them that wild things need to stay wild. "Imaginatively adding a touch of magic," *The Bog Baby* features a theme "budding naturalists might take to heart," observed John Peters in his review of the story for *Booklist,* and Sara Paulson-Yarovoy noted that Willis's "child-voiced . . . narrative transports readers into the squelches and squeaks of tromping through the mud and spring plants." *The Bog Baby* "asks readers to consider not only the importance of leaving wild things wild but [also] the possibility of magic," asserted a *Kirkus Reviews* writer.

Willis collaborates with artist Adrian Reynolds on several picture books, among them **I'm Sure I Saw a Dinosaur.** (Illustration copyright © 2011 by Adrian Reynolds. Reproduced by permission of Andersen Press, an imprint of Random House (UK), a division of Random House, Inc.)

That's Not Funny!, *Who's in the Bathroom?*, and *I'm Sure I Saw a Dinosaur* find Willis teaming up with Reynolds to share several silly scenarios, all in rhyme. Published in the United Kingdom as *Who's in the Loo?*, *Who's in the Bathroom?* find two children standing outside a public toilet, imagining who or what could be inside, taking such a long time about its business. Their imaginative foray into toilet humor encompasses a host of animal characters, and Reynolds' "exuberant cartoons enliven the story," according to *School Library Journal* contributor Suzanne Myers Harold.

I'm Sure I Saw a Dinosaur encourages children to think twice before believing implausible statements, while in *That's Not Funny!* the author-illustrator team "tackles laughing at other people's misfortunes," according to *School Librarian* contributor Diana Barnes. A *Kirkus Reviews* writer dubbed *I'm Sure I Saw a Dinosaur* "another slyly disquieting outing from the creators of *Who's in the Bathroom?* and a *Publishers Weekly* reviewer observed of *That's Not Funny!:* "those looking for a morality lesson won't find it—this story is all about the pratfall."

As in her work with Reynolds, animals figure in many of Willis's stories for the very young. In *Never Too Little to Love* a tiny mouse stacks one thing on top of another to reach the object of its affection, while the award-winning *Tadpole's Promise* finds a caterpillar and a polliwog vowing to love each other and promising never to change. In *Mommy Do You Love Me?* Little Chick tests the limits of Mother Hen's affection, while in *Gorilla! Gorilla!* another mother—this time a mouse—misinterprets the intent of the gorilla who follows her across the world in an attempt to return her lost baby. As *School Library Journal* contributor Kathleen Kelly MacMillan noted, in addition to being a fine story, *Gorilla! Gorilla!* "subtly conveys a great message about prejudices."

Among her many picture books, Willis has created a series geared for very young readers about to embark on the preschool adventure, her intent to help them learn the rules of the classroom. Illustrated by Mark Birchall, *Parrot Goes to Playschool* features a parrot who talks incessantly, but finally gets his beak shut temporarily when he eats his elephant classmate's caramels. In *Take Turns, Penguin!* an ostrich teacher does not seem to notice Penguin's self-centeredness, so the other animal classmates step in to solve the problem themselves. Other titles in the series include *No Biting, Panther!*, *No Biting, Puma!*, and *Be Gentle, Python!* The author also pushes the envelope in teacher-student dynamics with her rhyming *I Hate School*. Here protagonist Honor Brown proclaims the mistreatment of her teachers. A *Publishers Weekly* reviewer wrote of the book that children will "identify with and chuckle at her sense of drama."

Mick Stokes is the narrator of Willis's *The Truth or Something*, a young-adult novel set in postwar London. Mick grew up not knowing what happened to his baby sister. He is also ignorant of the truth about his father, a man who eventually sexually molests him, and his unstable mother, who serves time in jail. Eventually, Mick learns about his life and his large family, then moves on to find his place in the world. *School Library Journal* reviewer Todd Morning wrote that *The Truth or Something* "brilliantly captures a child's voice and point of view, subtly changing as the boy matures into an adolescent." In *Booklist* Anne O'Malley described Willis's story as "a powerful novel with an appealing protagonist who struggles with the cruel hand dealt to him."

Willis's award-winning novel *Naked without a Hat* is the story of Will Avery, a developmentally slow nineteen year old who leaves home and his mother to live with roommates Rocko, James, and landlady Chrissy. Willis also makes another friend in Zara, an Irish gypsy with whom he has a sexual relationship. *The Adventures of Jimmy Scar* follows Jimmy as he is taken in by Gemma Diamond, a young girl who avoids being placed in foster care, and learns self-sufficiency from a female hermit named Monti, who lives in the forest. In *When Stephanie Smiled* Willis demonstrates how the smile of a girl can brighten the mood and academic performance of a young boy.

Turning to verse, Willis's *Toffee Pockets* features poems about grandparents and grandchildren and was described by *Books for Keeps* contributor Judith Sharman as "easy to read and comforting to hear." Willis also uses rhyme to entertain young readers in *In Search of the Hidden Giant*. In this story, a narrator and his sister trek through a forest determined to find the giant they believe lives there. They find many clues: tree roots, they assume, are strands of his hair, while the crackling of tree branches overhead seem to signify his presence to them. A *Publishers Weekly* critic noted that *In Search of the Giant* is deliberately vague, but "it often exemplifies a way of seeing that naturally delights children."

Discussing her work as a storyteller, Willis once remarked that her tales "arrive in my head when they're ready, sometimes they write themselves. I [once started] . . . a novel, but suddenly the characters started to misbehave and I lost control of them. It was quite frightening, it was a little like dabbling with the occult. If they were alter-egos, then they were better destroyed. I didn't want to be a part of their world."

"I have been interested in writing for as long as I can remember," Willis more-recently commented. "I'm not sure what started it, but I have been doing it since I was five without a break. I have preserved copies of my first ever work of fiction written in 1965 in pencil and stitched together with a needle and green cotton.

"What influences my work? Pretty much everything—everywhere I go, everything I see, everyone I talk to can be turned into a story. I have too much material. It is exhausting. I pray for Writers Block (and I bet my editors do too). I usually write from nine in the morn-

ing til three in the afternoon. If I'm writing a novel, I may do nights and forget to go to bed. I usually have several books on the go at any time—a mixture of novels, picture books and novelty books.

"The most surprising thing I've learned as a writer is that the books I work at the least are the best loved."

Biographical and Critical Sources

PERIODICALS

Booklist, July, 1994, Julie Corsaro, review of *In Search of the Giant,* p. 1956; June 1, 1998, Annie Ayres, review of *Sloth's Shoes,* p. 1785; August, 2000, Hazel Rochman, review of *Susan Laughs,* p. 2151; December 1, 2000, Gillian Engberg, review of *Be Quiet, Parrot!,* and *Take Turns, Penguin!,* p. 727; December 15, 2000, Connie Fletcher, review of *What Did I Look like When I Was a Baby?,* p. 829; March 15, 2002, Kay Weisman, review of *I Want to Be a Cowgirl,* p. 1265; June 1, 2002, Anne O'Malley, review of *The Truth or Something,* p. 1710; July, 2004, Michael Cart, review of *Naked without a Hat,* p. 1835; February 1, 2005, Ilene Cooper, review of *Never Too Little to Love,* p. 966; February 1, 2007, Ilene Cooper, review of *Delilah D. at the Library,* p. 49; March 15, 2008, Randall Enos, review of *Mommy Do You Love Me?,* p. 56; September 1, 2009, John Peters, review of *The Bog Baby,* p. 95.

Books, April-May, 1996, review of *The Pet Person,* p. 26; summer, 1998, review of *The Wind in the Wallows,* p. 19.

Books for Keeps, March, 1993, Gill Roberts, review of *Dr. Xargle's Book of Earth Tiggers,* p. 11; May, 1993, Jeff Hynds, review of *In Search of the Hidden Giant,* p. 36; November, 1993, Judith Sharman, review of *Toffee Pockets,* p. 11, and Jessica Yates, review of *The Long Blue Blazer,* p. 26; May, 1994, Jill Bennett, review of *Dr. Xargle's Book of Earth Weather,* p. 12; July, 1995, Jill Bennett, review of *Dr. Xargle's Book of Earth Relations,* p. 11; July, 1999, Margaret Mallett, review of *Tom's Lady of the Lamp,* p. 3.

Books for Young Children, summer, 1991, Leonie Bennett, review of *The Tale of Mucky Mabel,* p. 5.

Guardian (London, England), January 7, 2004, Dina Rabinovitch, "Author of the Month: Jeanne Willis."

Horn Book, September, 1994, Hanna B. Zeiger, review of *In Search of the Giant,* p. 582; July-August, 2002, Susan P. Bloom, review of *The Truth or Something,* p. 474.

Junior Bookshelf, December, 1994, review of *The Rascally Cake,* p. 209; April, 1995, review of *In Search of the Hidden Giant,* p. 69; September-October, 2006, Susan Dove Lempke, review of *Gorilla! Gorilla!,* p. 573.

Kirkus Reviews, June 1, 1991, review of *Earth Tigerlets, as Explained by Professor Xargle,* p. 738; December 1, 1991, review of *Earth Mobiles, as Explained by Professor Xargle,* p. 1541; May 1, 2002, review of *The Truth or Something,* p. 670; August 15, 2002, re-

view of *The Boy Who Thought He Was a Teddy Bear: A Fairy Tale,* p. 1239; April 15, 2003, review of *Don't Let Go!,* p. 613; April, 2004, review of *Naked without a Hat,* p. 403; June 15, 2004, review of *I Hate School,* p. 583; May 15, 2005, review of *Tadpole's Promise,* p. 597; May 1, 2006, review of *Gorilla! Gorilla!,* p. 470; March 1, 2007, reviews of *Who's in the Bathroom?* and *Delilah D. at the Library,* both p. 234; January 1, 2008, review of *Cottonball Colin;* January 15, 2008, review of *Mommy Do You Love Me?;* August 15, 2009, review of *Flabby Cat and Slobby Dog;* September 1, 2009, review of *The Bog Baby;* June 15, 2010, review of *Old Dog;* August 1, 2010, review of *That's Not Funny!;* July 1, 2011, review of *I'm Sure I Saw a Dinosaur.*

Publishers Weekly, June 7, 1991, review of *Earth Tigerlets, as Explained by Professor Xargle,* p. 64; May 30, 1994, review of *In Search of the Giant,* p. 56; February 23, 1998, review of *Sloth's Shoes,* p. 76; May 22, 2000, review of *The Boy Who Lost His Belly Button,* p. 91; October 2, 2000, review of *What Did I Look like When I Was a Baby?,* p. 81; February 4, 2002, review of *I Want to Be a Cowgirl,* p. 76; May 20, 2002, review of *The Truth or Something,* p. 68; August 12, 2002, review of *The Boy Who Thought He Was a Teddy Bear,* p. 299; September 9, 2002, review of *Sleepover!: The Best Ever Party Kit,* p. 71; April 7, 2003, review of *Don't Let Go!,* p. 66; May 31, 2004, review of *Naked without a Hat,* p. 75; June 28, 2004, review of *I Hate School,* p. 49; December 6, 2004, review of *Never Too Little to Love,* p. 59; May 9, 2005, review of *Misery Moo,* p. 70; May 15, 2005, review of *Tadpole's Promise,* p. 597; January 21, 2008, review of *Cottonball Colin,* p. 169; February 25, 2008, review of *Mommy Do You Love Me?,* p. 78; August 31, 2009, review of *Flabby Cat and Slobby Dog,* p. 58; October 12, 2009, review of *The Bog Baby,* p. 47; September 13, 2010, review of *That's Not Funny!,* p. 43.

Reading Today, August, 2000, Lynne T. Burke, review of *Susan Laughs,* p. 32; April-May, 2006, David L. Richardson, review of *Tadpole's Promise,* p. 32.

School Librarian, August, 1992, Margaret Banerjee, review of *Toffee Pockets,* p. 111; April, 1994, Wendy Timothy, review of *The Rascally Cake,* p. 154; February, 1996, Teresa Scragg, review of *The Monster Storm,* p. 17; February, 1997, Trevor Dickinson, review of *The Pink Hare,* p. 22; April, 1999, Andrea Rayner, review of *Tinkerbill,* p. 201; winter, 2010, Diana Barnes, review of *That's Not Funny!,* p. 224; spring, 2010, Sybil Hannavy, review of *Big Bad Bun,* p. 32; summer, 2010, Martin Axford, review of *Caterpillar Dreams,* p. 94; spring, 2011, Janette Perkins, review of *The Nanny Goat's Kid,* p. 32.

School Library Journal, April, 1991, John Peters, review of *Earth Hounds, as Explained by Professor Xargle,* p. 106; August, 1991, Rachel S. Fox, review of *Earth Tigerlets, as Explained by Professor Xargle,* p. 157; March, 1992, Joan McGrath, review of *Earth Mobiles, as Explained by Professor Xargle,* p. 226; April, 1993, Claudia Cooper, review of *Earth Weather, as Explained by Professor Xargle,* p. 104; March, 1995, Ronald Jobe, review of *Relativity, as Explained by*

Professor Xargle, p. 195; August, 1998, Christy Norris Blanchette, review of *Sloth's Shoes,* p. 147; April, 1999, Carol Schene, review of *What Do You Want to Be, Brian?,* p. 110; May, 2000, Carolyn Janssen, review of *The Boy Who Lost His Belly Button,* p. 158; November, 2000, Linda M. Kenton, review of *Susan Laughs,* p. 137; January, 2001, Kathy M. Newby, reviews of *Be Quiet, Parrot!* and *Take Turns, Penguin!,* p. 112; September, 2001, Melinda Piehler, review of *Be Gentle, Python!,* p. 209; May, 2002, Todd Morning, review of *The Truth or Something,* p. 163; July, 2002, Ruth Semrau, review of *I Want to Be a Cowgirl,* p. 102; December, 2002, Barbara Buckley, review of *The Boy Who Thought He Was a Teddy Bear,* p. 112; June, 2004, Johanna Lewis, review of *Naked without a Hat,* p. 152; August, 2004, Marian Creamer, review of *I Hate School,* p. 104; September, 2004, Sally R. Dow, review of *When Stephanie Smiled,* p. 182; October, 2004, Beth Jones, review of *The Adventures of Jimmy Scar,* p. 182; May, 2005, Joy Fleishhacker, review of *Tadpole's Promise,* p. 104; June, 2005, Rachel G. Payne, review of *Misery Moo,* p. 131; July, 2006, Kathleen Kelly MacMillan, review of *Gorilla! Gorilla!,* p. 90; March, 2007, Grace Oliff, review of *Delilah D. at the Library,* and Suzanne Myers Harold, review of *Who's in the Bathroom?,* both p. 191; April, 2008, Anne Parker, review of *Mommy Do You Love Me?,* and Linda Ludke, review of *Cottonball Colin,* both p. 126; October, 2009, Susan E. Murray, review of *Flabby Cat and Slobby Dog,* p. 108; October, 2010, Catherine Callegari, review of *That's Not Funny!,* p. 96.

ONLINE

Jeanne Willis Home Page, http://jeannewillis.com (January 1, 2012).

Rod Hall Agency, Ltd. Web site, http://www.rodhallagency.com/ (August 22, 2006), "Jeanne Willis."

Teen Reads Web site, http:// www.teenreads.com/ (August 22, 2006), Renee Kirchner, review of *Naked without a Hat.*

Walker Books Web site, http:// www.walkerbooks.co.uk/ (August 22, 2006), "Jeanne Willis."*

Y-Z

YOUNG, Karen Romano 1959-

Personal

Born November 21, 1959, in Ithaca, NY; daughter of William S. (a computer consultant) and Carol (a registered nurse) Romano; married Mark C. Young (a publisher), April 10, 1982; children: Bethany, Samuel, Emily. *Education:* Syracuse University, B.S. (education), 1981; attended Pennsylvania Academy of Fine Arts, School of Visual Arts, and Western Connecticut State University. *Politics:* Democrat.

Addresses

Home—Bethel, CT. *Agent*—Faye Bender, Faye Bender Literary Agency, 337 W. 76th St., No. E1, New York, NY 10023. *E-mail*—wrenyoung@gmail.com.

Career

Writer and editor. Scholastic News, New York, NY, assistant editor, 1981-82, associate editor, 1982-83; Weston Woods Studios, Weston, CT, marketing associate, 1983-84; freelance writer and editor, 1983—. Instructor for Leader of the Young Writers Workshop, 1997—; Western Connecticut State University, member of adjunct faculty, 2007—; Connecticut Writing Project fellow, 2009—. Member of committee, Ocean Research Interactive Observatory Networks (ORION), 2004-06; education consultant and shipboard education coordinator aboard research vessel *Atlantis* and deep submergence vehicle *Alvin,* 2004, 2008; Maritime Aquarium, Norwalk, CT, educator, 2006-07.

Karen Romano Young (Photograph by Michael Duffy. Reproduced by permission of Karen Romano Young.)

Member

PEN, Society of Children's Book Writers and Illustrators, Authors Guild, National Marine Educators Association, National Association of Science Writers.

Awards, Honors

Best Books for Young Adults designation, American Library Association (ALA), and Best Children's Books of the Year selection, Bank Street College of Education, both 1999, both for *The Beetle and Me;* Best Books for Young Adults designation, ALA, 2000, for *Video; Smithsonian* Best Book Award, and Oppenheimer Toy Portfolio Gold Medal, both 2002, both for *Small Worlds;* work-in-progress grant for nonfiction, Society of Children's Book Writers and Illustrators, 2004; merit award, Bookbinders' Guild of New York, 2005, for *Cobwebs;* Connecticut Council for Culture and Tourism grant for

fiction, 2005; Woods Hole Oceanographic Institution Ocean Science journalism fellowship, 2007; Connecticut Book Award, 2011, for *Doodlebug*.

Writings

(With Marlene Barron) *Ready, Set, Read and Write: Sixty Playful Activities for You and Your Child to Share,* illustrated by Elaine Yabroudy, Wiley (Hoboken, NJ), 1995.

(With Marlene Barron) *Ready, Set, Count: Sixty Playful Activities for You and Your Child to Share,* illustrated by Elaine Yabroudy, Wiley (Hoboken, NJ), 1995.

(With Marlene Barron) *Ready, Set, Cooperate: Sixty Playful Activities for You and Your Child to Share,* Wiley (Hoboken, NJ), 1996.

(With Marlene Barron) *Ready, Set, Explore: Sixty Playful Activities for You and Your Child to Share,* Wiley (Hoboken, NJ), 1996.

The Ice's Edge: The Story of a Harp Seal Pup, illustrated by Brian Shaw, Soundprints (Norwalk, CT), 1996.

Guinness Record Breakers, Guinness Media, 1997.

Arctic Investigations: Exploring the Frozen Ocean, Raintree Steck-Vaughn (Austin, TX), 2000.

Small Worlds: Maps and Mapmaking, illustrated by Ingo Fast, Scholastic (New York, NY), 2002.

(Self-illustrated) *Across the Wide Ocean: The Why, How, and Where of Navigation for Humans and Animals at Sea,* Greenwillow (New York, NY), 2007.

Angels Are Everywhere: What They Are, Where They Come from, and What They Do, illustrated by Nathan Hale, Simon & Schuster (New York, NY), 2009.

Contributor to reference works, including *Inventions and Discoveries,* Facts on File, 1993; *The World and Its Peoples,* Brown Reference, 2005; and *The World Almanac Book of Records,* World Almanac Education Group, 2007. Contributor to educational materials and to periodicals, including *Oceanus, Cricket,* and *Science News.*

"SCIENCE FAIR WINNERS" SERIES

Bug Science: Twenty Projects and Experiments about Arthropods: Insects, Arachnids, Algae, Worms, and Other Small Creatures, illustrated by David Goldin, National Geographic (Washington, DC), 2009.

Crime Scene Science: Twenty Projects and Experiments about Clues, Crimes, Criminals, and Other Mysterious Things, illustrated by David Goldin, National Geographic (Washington, DC), 2009.

Experiments to Do on Your Family: Twenty Projects and Experiments about Sisters, Brothers, Parents, Pets, and the Rest of the Gang, illustrated by David Goldin, National Geographic (Washington, DC), 2010.

Junkyard Science: Twenty Projects and Experiments about Junk, Garbage, Waste, Things We Don't Need Anymore, and Ways to Recycle or Reuse It—or Lose It, illustrated by David Goldin, National Geographic (Washington, DC), 2010.

YOUNG-ADULT NOVELS

The Beetle and Me: A Love Story, Greenwillow (New York, NY), 1999.

Video, Greenwillow (New York, NY), 1999.

Outside In, Greenwillow (New York, NY), 2001.

Cobwebs, Greenwillow (New York, NY), 2004.

(Self-illustrated) *Doodlebug: A Novel in Doodles* (graphic novel), Feiwel & Friends (New York, NY), 2010.

Adaptations

The Beetle and Me was adapted for audiobook, Recorded Books, 2001.

Sidelights

Karen Romano Young demonstrates her versatility as a writer and artist in such works as *Across the Wide Ocean: The Why, How, and Where of Navigation for Humans and Animals at Sea,* a self-illustrated nonfiction title, and the graphic novel *Doodlebug: A Novel in Doodles.* Beginning her career as a writer and editor for a current-events magazine, Young moved to writing book-length nonfiction before tackling her first young-adult novel, *The Beetle and Me: A Love Story,* published in 1999. Young's tale captured the hearts of critics with its deft blend of romance and coming-of-age themes peopled by surprising and likable characters. She has followed this success with several other books, among them *Small Worlds: Maps and Mapmaking* and *Crime Scene Science: Twenty Projects and Experiments about Clues, Crimes, Criminals, and Other Mysterious Things.*

Born in upstate New York in 1959, Young grew up in southern New England. "I have been an avid reader since I was a very young child," the author once recalled to *SATA,* "and my parents and grandparents all loved to read to all of us children. There's no better preparation for a writer than so very much joyful reading."

"I always wanted to be a writer and I was always writing something," Young added. "Along the way I tried art, film, teaching, biology, nursing, library science, marketing, and more. Through a piece of luck—and a friend or two—I found myself walking into an interview at Scholastic. It was my first visit to a children's publishing house. I have never looked back."

In *The Beetle and Me* fifteen-year-old Daisy sets her heart on restoring the old Volkswagen Beetle rusting in an outbuilding on the family farm, despite the discouragement she receives from the other crack mechanics in her family. The seven chapters correspond to seven months in the life of its protagonist, as she stubbornly refuses all offers of help to fix up the car. Meanwhile, Daisy endures the disappointment of finding out that the boy she has a crush on is more interested in her boisterous cousin, as well as the realization that Billy,

an old friend and fellow car buff, is in love with her. "Young shows many types of love: mature love; intense and unrequited teen love; and steady, slow-growing someday love," observed Cindy Darling Codell in her review of *The Beetle and Me* for *School Library Journal,* adding praise for Young's ability to create "strong, likable female characters who still find men very attractive." A *Publishers Weekly* critic predicted that "readers of both sexes are sure to be swept up in the vibrant characterizations, finely nuanced emotions and detailed auto arcana" in *The Beetle and Me.*

In *Video* Young takes a darker turn, focusing on the consequences that play out after high schooler Eric Gooch secretly videotapes fellow classmate Janine Gagnon for his spring term project and discovers that the girl's solitary treks into the wetlands near her home are also witnessed by a suspicious older man. The narrative alternates between first-person accounts of Eric and Janine that detail each teen's view of events. "The author creates a compelling picture of Janine as a once popular girl, fallen from favor, and her simultaneous craving for solitude and attention," remarked a *Publishers Weekly* reviewer of *Video.*

Set in 1968, during the Vietnam War era, *Outside In* focuses on preteen Cherie Witkowski, whose job as a newspaper carrier makes her aware of existing social and political divisiveness. The upheaval reflected in newspaper headlines is reflected in Cherie's own life: the arrival of another sibling forces the family to move, a girl her age is abducted from a nearby town, and Cherie herself struggles with the emotional ups and downs of a budding romance. In *Booklist* Ann O'Malley praised Young's depiction of Cherie's parents, who "come across as sensitive, loving, and involved . . . without being saintly," while in *School Library Journal* Connie Tyrrell Burns wrote that, although Cherie's emotional "paralysis" seems dramatic, *Outside In* "adeptly paints an authentic picture of the '60s." Young "excels at creating spunky and capable young female protagonists," concluded Paula Rohrlick in *Kliatt,* "and at evoking family life in all its confusion."

Cobwebs finds sixteen-year-old Brooklynite Nancy somewhat mystified about her quirky yet loving family, each member of which seems to have some sort of spider-like quality. Her elderly grandparents, who live upstairs in the family's brownstone, are healers whose treatments utilize the cobweb strands they produce. Her mother, an agoraphobic, is a weaver, while her father, Ned—full name, Arachnid—is able to generate sticky ropes that can suspend him from high buildings. Nancy's biracial parents love each other but live apart during the warmer months, when Ned sets up temporary digs on a nearby rooftop. While Nancy moves freely between the homes of her relatives, strange restrictions are placed on her after she reaches adolescence; for example, she is not allowed to shave her legs like other girls her age. Noting that "spider puns and inferences abound," a *Kirkus Reviews* contributor wrote of *Cob-*

webs that readers will enjoy the tale's "supernatural" elements and share Nancy's fascination with a haunting homeless boy named Dion. In *School Library Journal* Johanna Lewis praised Young's text as "simple and graceful," while Jennifer Mattson predicted in *Booklist* that creative-minded teen readers will enjoy the novel's "poetic, free-verse narrative, and the imaginative, comic book-inspired premise" of Young's complex story.

The graphic-novel *Doodlebug* centers on a youngster who learns to cope with life's difficulties through her art. When her family moves from Southern California to San Francisco, Doreen "Dodo" Bussey chronicles her journey in a notebook, rechristening herself "Doodlebug" in honor of her creative efforts. A twelve year old who was expelled from her previous school, Doreen blames herself for her family's upheaval and is disappointed when she once again finds herself in trouble with her new teachers due to her constant doodling in class. Doreen, however, recognizes that these actions actually help her control her attention deficit disorder without resorting to Ritalin. Young's use of drawings, scribbles, lettering, and diagrams are "an integral part

Karen Romano Young's antic cartoons entice readers through each turn of the page in **Doodlebug: A Novel in Doodles.** *(Illustration copyright © 2010 by Karen Romano Young. Reproduced by permission of Feiwel & Friends, an imprint of St. Martin's Press.)*

of the tale," according to *Booklist* reviewer Kat Kan. Writing in *School Library Journal*, Richelle Roth Boone maintained that Doreen's narrative "voice is genuine and will especially resonate with those who have similar problems," while a *Kirkus Reviews* critic wrote that *Doodlebug* offers not only "a heartening view of a resourceful child but also a telling testament to the power of creativity."

Young has channeled her love for marine science into several nonfiction books, among them *Arctic Investigations: Exploring the Frozen Ocean*, which describes the Woods Hole Oceanographic Institution's research in the Arctic. Ocean science also comes into play in a grand overview of the world of mapping in the award-winning *Small Worlds: Map and Mapmaking*. In 2004 Young was aboard the research vessel *Atlantis* as it explored the rift zone at the East Pacific Rise, a region located nine degrees north of the equator. This trip, part of the Extreme mission led by Craig Cary of the University of Delaware, involved diving in a submarine two miles down to the ocean floor for a first-hand look at the rift zone—including tall chimneys belching hot lava and the unique creatures that make their home in this environment. These discoveries led to *Across the Wide Ocean*, Young's first self-illustrated work. Here she covers a variety of topics—from whale tracking to the mapping of currents—while following a loggerhead turtle, a container ship, a sailboat, a shark, and a nuclear submarine as they travel through the Atlantic. In *School Library Journal* Patricia Manning described *Across the Wide Ocean* as "a colorful look at a subject not often thought about, but one that many will find fascinating when they do."

Young's "Science Fair Winners" series, aimed at middle-grade readers and featuring illustrations by David Goldin, presents ideas for experiments, workshops, and projects that are relevant to students' everyday lives. In *Junkyard Science: Twenty Projects and Experiments about Junk, Garbage, Waste, Things We Don't Need Anymore, and Ways to Recycle or Reuse It—or Lose It* readers learn how to measure the cost-effectiveness of batteries, while in *Experiments to Do on Your Family: Twenty Projects and Experiments about Sisters, Brothers, Parents, Pets, and the Rest of the Gang* Young presents a method of tracking how a cold virus travels from person to person. The author's "casual writing style and Goldin's playful illustrations make the books and the projects approachable," remarked *Booklist* critic Miriam Aronin.

In addition to her fiction and nonfiction, Young has co-authored activity books for younger children that are based on Montessori teaching methods. Reviewing *Ready, Set, Count* and *Ready, Set, Cooperate*, Kevin Wayne Booe predicted in *School Library Journal* that "parents will probably have as much fun with these activities as their children will."

Regarding her role as an author, Young once told *SATA:* "I think that when you're a writer you're alive to the world in a very special way. Although the years of junior high and high school were not particularly marvelous times in my life, I remember what I thought and saw and felt then most clearly. So must of the stories I write about are those years in my characters' lives."

Biographical and Critical Sources

PERIODICALS

Booklist, April 15, 1999, Jean Franklin, review of *The Beetle and Me: A Love Story*, p. 1523; April 1, 2002, Anne O'Malley, review of *Outside In*, p. 1320; January 1, 2005, Jennifer Mattson, review of *Cobwebs*, p. 864; October 1, 2009, Daniel Kraus, review of *Crime Scene Science: Twenty Projects and Experiments about Clues, Crimes, Criminals, and Other Mysterious Things*, p. 53; September 15, 2010, Kat Kan, review of *Doodlebug: A Novel in Doodles*, p. 66; December 1, 2010, Miriam Aronin, reviews of *Experiments to Do on Your Family: Twenty Projects and Experiments about Sisters, Brothers, Parents, Pets, and the Rest of the Gang* and *Junkyard Science: Twenty Projects and Experiments about Junk, Garbage, Waste, Things We Don't Need Anymore, and Ways to Recycle or Reuse It—or Lose It*, both p. 42.

Kirkus Reviews, May 1, 2002, review of *Outside In*, p. 670; October 15, 2004, review of *Cobwebs*, p. 1015; April 15, 2007, review of *Across the Wide Ocean: The Why, How, and Where of Navigation for Humans and Animals at Sea*; June 15, 2010, review of *Doodlebug*.

Kliatt, May, 2002, Paula Rohrlick, review of *Outside In*, p. 15; November, 2004, Claire Rosser, review of *Cobwebs*, p. 13.

Publishers Weekly, May 3, 1999, review of *The Beetle and Me*, p. 77; June 28, 1999, Jennifer M. Brown "Karen Romano Young," p. 25; September 13, 1999, review of *Video*, p. 85; May 13, 2002, review of *Outside In*, p. 71.

School Library Journal, August, 1996, Kevin Wayne Booe, reviews of *Ready, Set, Count: Sixty Playful Activities for You and Your Child to Share* and *Ready, Set, Read, and Write: Sixty Playful Activities for You and Your Child to Share*, both p. 36; May, 1999, Cindy Darling Codell, review of *The Beetle and Me*, p. 133; April, 2000, Frances E. Millhouser, review of *Arctic Investigations: Exploring the Frozen Ocean*, p. 157; May, 2002, Connie Tyrrell Burns, review of *Outside In*, p. 164; June, 2003, David Pauli, review of *Small Worlds: Maps and Mapmaking*, p. 174; January, 2005, Johanna Lewis, review of *Cobwebs*, p. 139; July, 2007, Patricia Manning, review of *Across the Wide Ocean*, p. 122; January, 2010, Ann W. Moore, review of *Angels Are Everywhere: What They Are, Where They Come From, and What They Do*, p. 126; March, 2010, Christine Markley, reviews of *Bug Science: Twenty Projects and Experiments about Arthropods: Insects, Arachnids, Algae, Worms, and Other Small Creatures* and *Crime Scene Science*, both p. 182; January, 2011, Richelle Roth Boone, review of *Doodlebug*, p. 120.

ONLINE

HarperCollins Web site, http://www.harpercollins.com/ (December 15, 2011), "Karen Romano Young."

Karen Romano Young Home Page, http://www.karen romanoyoung.com (December 15, 2011).

Karen Romano Young Web log, http://thedoodlingdesk. blogspot.com (December 15, 2011).*

*   *   *

ZAPPITELLO, Beth

Personal

Born in OH; married Brian Zappitello; children: Ajax, Hopper.

Addresses

Home—Portland, OR.

Career

Writer. Works in advertising and marketing.

Writings

(With J. Patrick Lewis) *First Dog,* illustrated by Tim Bowers, Sleeping Bear Press (Chelsea, MI), 2009.
(With J. Patrick Lewis) *First Dog's White House Christmas,* illustrated by Tim Bowers, Sleeping Bear Press (Ann Arbor, MI), 2010.

Biographical and Critical Sources

PERIODICALS

Kirkus Reviews, September 1, 2010, review of *First Dog's White House Christmas.*
School Library Journal, August, 2009, Gay Lynn Van Vleck, review of *First Dog,* p. 79; October, 2010, Eva Mitnick, review of *First Dog's White House Christmas,* p. 74.

ONLINE

Sleeping Bear Web site, http://www.sleepingbearpress. com/ (December 29, 2011), "Beth Zappitello."*

Illustrations Index

(In the following index, the number of the *volume* in which an illustrator's work appears is given *before* the colon, and the *page number* on which it appears is given *after* the colon. For example, a drawing by Adams, Adrienne appears in Volume 2 on page 6, another drawing by her appears in Volume 3 on page 80, another drawing in Volume 8 on page 1, and so on and so on. . . .)

YABC

Index references to *YABC* refer to listings appearing in the two-volume *Yesterday's Authors of Books for Children,* also published by Gale. *YABC* covers prominent authors and illustrators who died prior to 1960.

A

Aas, Ulf *5:* 174
Abbe, S. van
    See van Abbe, S.
Abel, Raymond *6:* 122; *7:* 195; *12:* 3; *21:* 86; *25:* 119
Abelliera, Aldo *71:* 120
Abolafia, Yossi *60:* 2; *93:* 163; *152:* 202
Abrahams, Hilary *26:* 205; *29:* 24, 25; *53:* 61
Abrams, Kathie *36:* 170
Abrams, Lester *49:* 26
Abulafia, Yossi *154:* 67; *177:* 3
Accardo, Anthony *191:* 3, 8
Accornero, Franco *184:* 8
Accorsi, William *11:* 198
Acedera, Kei *235:* 110
Acs, Laszlo *14:* 156; *42:* 22
Acuna, Ed *198:* 79
Adams, Adrienne *2:* 6; *3:* 80; *8:* 1; *15:* 107; *16:* 180; *20:* 65; *22:* 134, 135; *33:* 75; *36:* 103, 112; *39:* 74; *86:* 54; *90:* 2, 3
Adams, Connie J. *129:* 68
Adams, John Wolcott *17:* 162
Adams, Kathryn *224:* 1
Adams, Lynn *96:* 44
Adams, Norman *55:* 82
Adams, Pam *112:* 1, 2
Adams, Sarah *98:* 126; *164:* 180
Adams, Steve *209:* 64
Adamson, George *30:* 23, 24; *69:* 64
Addams, Charles *55:* 5
Addison, Kenneth *192:* 173; *231:* 166
Addy, Sean *180:* 8; *222:* 31
Ade, Rene *76:* 198; *195:* 162
Adinolfi, JoAnn *115:* 42; *176:* 2; *217:* 79
Adkins, Alta *22:* 250
Adkins, Jan *8:* 3; *69:* 4; *144:* 2, 3, 4; *210:* 11, 17, 18, 19
Adl, Shirin *225:* 2
Adler, Kelynn *195:* 47
Adler, Peggy *22:* 6; *29:* 31
Adler, Ruth *29:* 29
Adlerman, Daniel *163:* 2
Adragna, Robert *47:* 145
Agard, Nadema *18:* 1
Agee, Jon *116:* 8, 9, 10; *157:* 4; *196:* 3, 4, 5, 6, 7, 8
Agre, Patricia *47:* 195
Aguirre, Alfredo *152:* 218
Ahl, Anna Maria *32:* 24

Ahlberg, Allan *68:* 6, 7, 9; *165:* 5; *214:* 9
Ahlberg, Janet *68:* 6, 7, 9; *214:* 9
Ahlberg, Jessica *229:* 2, 191
Aicher-Scholl, Inge *63:* 127
Aichinger, Helga *4:* 5, 45
Aitken, Amy *31:* 34
Ajhar, Brian *207:* 126; *220:* 2
Akaba, Suekichi *46:* 23; *53:* 127
Akasaka, Miyoshi *YABC 2:* 261
Akib, Jamel *181:* 13; *182:* 99; *220:* 74
Akino, Fuku *6:* 144
Alain *40:* 41
Alajalov *2:* 226
Albert, Chris *200:* 64
Alborough, Jez *86:* 1, 2, 3; *149:* 3
Albrecht, Jan *37:* 176
Albright, Donn *1:* 91
Alcala, Alfredo *91:* 128
Alcantará, Felipe Ugalde *171:* 186
Alcorn, John *3:* 159; *7:* 165; *31:* 22; *44:* 127; *46:* 23, 170
Alcorn, Stephen *110:* 4; *125:* 106; *128:* 172; *150:* 97; *160:* 188; *165:* 48; *201:* 113; *203:* 39; *207:* 3; *226:* 25
Alcott, May *100:* 3
Alda, Arlene *44:* 24; *158:* 2
Alden, Albert *11:* 103
Aldridge, Andy *27:* 131
Aldridge, George *105:* 125
Aldridge, Sheila *192:* 4
Alejandro, Cliff *176:* 75
Alex, Ben *45:* 25, 26
Alexander, Claire *228:* 2
Alexander, Ellen *91:* 3
Alexander, Lloyd *49:* 34
Alexander, Martha *3:* 206; *11:* 103; *13:* 109; *25:* 100; *36:* 131; *70:* 6, 7; *136:* 3, 4, 5; *169:* 120; *230:* 78
Alexander, Paul *85:* 57; *90:* 9
Alexeieff, Alexander *14:* 6; *26:* 199
Alfano, Wayne *80:* 69
Aliki
    See Brandenberg, Aliki
Alko, Selina *218:* 2; *235:* 187
Allamand, Pascale *12:* 9
Allan, Judith *38:* 166
Alland, Alexandra *16:* 255
Allen, Gertrude *9:* 6
Allen, Graham *31:* 145
Allen, Jonathan *131:* 3, 4; *177:* 8, 9, 10
Allen, Joy *168:* 185; *217:* 6, 7

Allen, Pamela *50:* 25, 26, 27, 28; *81:* 9, 10; *123:* 4, 5
Allen, Raul *207:* 94
Allen, Rick *236:* 174
Allen, Rowena *47:* 75
Allen, Thomas B. *81:* 101; *82:* 248; *89:* 37; *104:* 9
Allen, Tom *85:* 176
Allender, David *73:* 223
Alley, R.W. *80:* 183; *95:* 187; *156:* 100, 153; *169:* 4, 5; *179:* 17
Allison, Linda *43:* 27
Allon, Jeffrey *119:* 174
Allport, Mike *71:* 55
Almquist, Don *11:* 8; *12:* 128; *17:* 46; *22:* 110
Aloise, Frank *5:* 38; *10:* 133; *30:* 92
Alsenas, Linas *186:* 2
Alter, Ann *206:* 4, 5
Althea
    See Braithwaite, Althea
Altschuler, Franz *11:* 185; *23:* 141; *40:* 48; *45:* 29; *57:* 181
Alvin, John *117:* 5
Ambrus, Victor G. *1:* 6, 7, 194; *3:* 69; *5:* 15; *6:* 44; *7:* 36; *8:* 210; *12:* 227; *14:* 213; *15:* 213; *22:* 209; *24:* 36; *28:* 179; *30:* 178; *32:* 44, 46; *38:* 143; *41:* 25, 26, 27, 28, 29, 30, 31, 32; *42:* 87; *44:* 190; *55:* 172; *62:* 30, 144, 145, 148; *86:* 99, 100, 101; *87:* 66, 137; *89:* 162; *134:* 160
Ames, Lee J. *3:* 12; *9:* 130; *10:* 69; *17:* 214; *22:* 124; *151:* 13; *223:* 69
Amini, Mehrdokht *211:* 119
Amon, Aline *9:* 9
Amoss, Berthe *5:* 5
Amstutz, André *152:* 102; *214:* 11, 16; *223:* 99
Amundsen, Dick *7:* 77
Amundsen, Richard E. *5:* 10; *24:* 122
Ancona, George *12:* 11; *55:* 144; *145:* 7; *208:* 13
Anderson, Alasdair *18:* 122
Andersen, Bethanne *116:* 167; *162:* 189; *175:* 17; *191:* 4, 5; *218:* 20
Anderson, Bob *139:* 16
Anderson, Brad *33:* 28
Anderson, Brian *211:* 8
Anderson, C.W. *11:* 10
Anderson, Carl *7:* 4
Anderson, Catherine Corley *72:* 2

Anderson, Cecil *127:* 152
Anderson, David Lee *118:* 176
Anderson, Derek *169:* 9; *174:* 180
Anderson, Doug *40:* 111
Anderson, Erica *23:* 65
Anderson, G.E. *223:* 181
Anderson, Laurie *12:* 153, 155
Anderson, Lena *99:* 26
Anderson, Peggy Perry *179:* 2
Anderson, Sara *173:* 3
Anderson, Scoular *138:* 13; *201:* 6
Anderson, Stephanie *225:* 3
Anderson, Susan *90:* 12
Anderson, Tara *188:* 132; *211:* 115
Anderson, Wayne *23:* 119; *41:* 239; *56:* 7; *62:* 26; *147:* 6; *202:* 4, 5
Andreasen, Daniel *86:* 157; *87:* 104; *103:* 201, 202; *159:* 75; *167:* 106, 107; *168:* 184; *180:* 247; *186:* 9; *212:* 101; *220:* 110, 111; *221:* 56; *227:* 3, 4, 5, 6; *234:* 214
Andrew, Ian *111:* 37; *116:* 12; *166:* 2
Andrew, John *22:* 4
Andrews, Benny *14:* 251; *31:* 24; *57:* 6, 7; *183:* 8
Andrews, Vaughn *166:* 28
Anelay, Henry *57:* 173
Angel, Marie *47:* 22
Angelo, Valenti *14:* 8; *18:* 100; *20:* 232; *32:* 70
Anglund, Joan Walsh *2:* 7, 250, 251; *37:* 198, 199, 200
Anholt, Catherine *74:* 8; *131:* 7; *141:* 5
Anholt, Laurence *141:* 4
Anno, Mitsumasa *5:* 7; *38:* 25, 26, 27, 28, 29, 30, 31, 32; *77:* 3, 4; *157:* 10, 11
Antal, Andrew *1:* 124; *30:* 145
Antram, David *152:* 133
Apostolou, Christy Hale
  See Hale, Christy
Apple, Margot *33:* 25; *35:* 206; *46:* 81; *53:* 8; *61:* 109; *64:* 21, 22, 24, 25, 27; *71:* 176; *77:* 53; *82:* 245; *92:* 39; *94:* 180; *96:* 107; *152:* 4, 5; *162:* 192, 194; *173:* 44; *214:* 21, 22, 23, 24
Appleyard, Dev *2:* 192
Aragones, Sergio *48:* 23, 24, 25, 26, 27
Araneus *40:* 29
Arbo, Cris *103:* 4; *220:* 4, 5
Archambault, Matt *85:* 173; *138:* 19, 20; *143:* 33; *145:* 144; *179:* 103; *187:* 7; *219:* 2
Archer, Janet *16:* 69; *178:* 156
Ardizzone, Edward *1:* 11, 12; *2:* 105; *3:* 258; *4:* 78; *7:* 79; *10:* 100; *15:* 232; *20:* 69,178; *23:* 223; *24:* 125; *28:* 25, 26, 27, 28, 29, 30, 31,33, 34, 35, 36, 37; *31:* 192, 193; *34:* 215, 217; *60:* 173; *64:* 145; *87:* 176; *YABC 2:* 25
Arena, Jill *176:* 49
Arenella, Roy *14:* 9
Argemi, David *197:* 2
Argent, Kerry *103:* 56; *138:* 17; *158:* 134
Arihara, Shino *201:* 98
Arisman, Marshall *162:* 50
Armer, Austin *13:* 3
Armer, Laura Adams *13:* 3
Armer, Sidney *13:* 3
Armitage, David *47:* 23; *99:* 5; *155:* 4
Armitage, Eileen *4:* 16
Armstrong, George *10:* 6; *21:* 72
Armstrong, Shelagh *102:* 114; *224:* 4
Armstrong-Ellis, Carey *185:* 196
Arno, Enrico *1:* 217; *2:* 22, 210; *4:* 9; *5:* 43; *6:* 52; *29:* 217, 219; *33:* 152; *35:* 99; *43:* 31, 32, 33; *45:* 212, 213, 214; *72:* 72; *74:* 166; *100:* 169
Arnold, Alli *187:* 40, 41
Arnold, Andrew *219:* 155; *221:* 155
Arnold, Caroline *174:* 5
Arnold, Emily *76:* 7, 9, 10
Arnold, Katya *115:* 11; *168:* 2, 3
Arnold, Tedd *116:* 14; *133:* 152; *160:* 5; *208:* 24, 25, 26, 176

Arnosky, Jim *22:* 20; *70:* 9, 10, 11; *118:* 3, 5; *160:* 8, 10; *189:* 5, 7, 8, 9, 10; *217:* 11, 12, 13, 14
Arnsteen, Katy Keck *105:* 97; *116:* 145
Arsenault, Isabelle *207:* 7; *226:* 109
Arrowood, Clinton *12:* 193; *19:* 11; *65:* 210
Artell, Mike *89:* 8
Arting, Fred J. *41:* 63
Artzybasheff, Boris *13:* 143; *14:* 15; *40:* 152, 155
Aruego, Ariane *6:* 4
Aruego, José *4:* 140; *6:* 4; *7:* 64; *33:* 195; *35:* 208; *68:* 16, 17; *75:* 46; *93:* 91, 92; *94:* 197; *109:* 65, 67; *125:* 2, 3, 4, 5; *127:* 188; *143:* 25; *178:* 17, 19, 74; *188:* 166; *202:* 164; *231:* 176
Arzoumanian, Alik *177:* 12; *194:* 115
Asare, Meshack *86:* 9; *139:* 19
Ascensios, Natalie *105:* 139
Asch, Frank *5:* 9; *66:* 2, 4, 6, 7, 9, 10; *102:* 18, 19,21; *154:* 12
Ashby, Gail *11:* 135
Ashby, Gil *146:* 4
Ashby, Gwynneth *44:* 26
Ashley, C.W. *19:* 197
Ashmead, Hal *8:* 70
Ashton, Tim *211:* 204
Aska, Warabe *56:* 10
Assel, Steven *44:* 153; *77:* 22, 97
Astrop, John *32:* 56
Atene, Ann *12:* 18
Atherton, Lisa *38:* 198
Atkinson, Allen *60:* 5
Atkinson, J. Priestman *17:* 275
Atkinson, Janet *86:* 147; *103:* 138
Atkinson, Mike *127:* 74
Atkinson, Wayne *40:* 46
Attard, Karl *196:* 22, 23
Attebery, Charles *38:* 170
Atwell, Debby *150:* 6
Atwood, Ann *7:* 9
Aubrey, Meg Kelleher *77:* 159
Auch, Herm *173:* 7, 8
Auch, Mary Jane *173:* 7
Augarde, Steve *25:* 22; *159:* 7; *210:* 43, 44
Austerman, Miriam *23:* 107
Austin, Cary *234:* 171
Austin, Margot *11:* 16
Austin, Dawn *234:* 117
Austin, Robert *3:* 44
Austin, Virginia *81:* 205; *127:* 221; *232:* 190
Auth, Tony *51:* 5; *192:* 18
Avendano, Dolores *158:* 74
Avedon, Richard *57:* 140
Averill, Esther *1:* 17; *28:* 39, 40, 41
Avilés, Martha *218:* 6
Axeman, Lois *2:* 32; *11:* 84; *13:* 165; *22:* 8; *23:* 49; *61:* 116; *101:* 124
Axtel, David *155:* 110
Ayer, Jacqueline *13:* 7
Ayer, Margaret *15:* 12; *50:* 120
Ayers, Alan *91:* 58; *107:* 169
Ayliffe, Alex *95:* 164; *237:* 68
Ayto, Russell *111:* 5; *112:* 54; *206:* 7, 8; *213:* 56
Azarian, Mary *112:* 9, 10; *114:* 129; *117:* 171; *137:* 163; *171:* 4, 5; *181:* 161; *188:* 128; *232:* 174

B

B.T.B.
  See Blackwell, Basil T.
Baasansuren, Bolormaa *216:* 40
Babbitt, Bradford *33:* 158
Babbitt, Natalie *6:* 6; *8:* 220; *68:* 20; *70:* 242, 243; *194:* 8, 9
Baca, Maria *104:* 5
Bacchus, Andy *94:* 87

Bacha, Andy *109:* 169
Bachelet, Gilles *196:* 18
Bachem, Paul *48:* 180; *67:* 65; *144:* 206; *234:* 113
Back, Adam *63:* 125
Back, George *31:* 161
Backes, Nick *190:* 72
Backhouse, Colin *78:* 142
Bacon, Bruce *4:* 74
Bacon, Paul *7:* 155; *8:* 121; *31:* 55; *50:* 42; *56:* 175; *62:* 82, 84
Bacon, Peggy *2:* 11, 228; *46:* 44
Baek, Matthew J. *169:* 95; *202:* 8
Baer, Julie *161:* 2
Baicker-McKee, Carol *177:* 15; *180:* 215
Bailey, Peter *58:* 174; *87:* 221; *194:* 12
Bailey, Sheila *155:* 11
Baker, Alan *22:* 22; *61:* 134; *93:* 11, 12; *146:* 6, 7, 10
Baker, Charlotte *2:* 12
Baker, Garin *89:* 65
Baker, Jeannie *23:* 4; *88:* 18, 19, 20
Baker, Jim *22:* 24
Baker, Joe *82:* 188; *111:* 55; *124:* 70; *197:* 73
Baker, Keith *179:* 6, 7; *222:* 36
Baker, Leslie *112:* 214; *132:* 103, 246; *180:* 74, 246; *234:* 213
Baker-Smith, Grahame *223:* 10; *225:* 132
Baldacci, Rudy *184:* 9
Baldridge, Cyrus LeRoy *19:* 69; *44:* 50
Baldus, Jackie *216:* 81
Baldus, Zachary *152:* 231; *187:* 60
Balet, Jan *11:* 22
Balian, Lorna *9:* 16; *91:* 16
Balit, Christina *102:* 24; *159:* 9; *162:* 118, 119; *212:* 2, 3
Ballantyne, R.M. *24:* 34
Ballis, George *14:* 199
Balouch, Kristen *176:* 11
Baltzer, Hans *40:* 30
Banbery, Fred *58:* 15
Bancroft, Bronwyn *216:* 42
Banfill, A. Scott *98:* 7; *112:* 59
Bang, Molly *24:* 37, 38; *69:* 8, 9, 10; *111:* 7,9, 10, 11; *140:* 11; *158:* 37, 38, 39; *195:* 3; *215:* 11, 12, 13, 14
Banik, Yvette Santiago *21:* 136
Banks, Erin Bennett *211:* 12
Banner, Angela
  See Maddison, Angela Mary
Bannerman, Helen *19:* 13, 14
Banning, Greg *202:* 98
Bannon, Laura *6:* 10; *23:* 8
Bantock, Nick *74:* 229; *95:* 6
Banyai, Istvan *185:* 209; *193:* 14, 16; *209:* 155; *223:* 166, 167
Baptist, Michael *37:* 208
Baracca, Sal *135:* 206
Baranaski, Marcin *182:* 113
Barasch, Lynne *126:* 16; *186:* 15
Barbarin, Lucien C., Jr. *89:* 88
Barbour, Karen *96:* 5; *74:* 209; *170:* 16
Bare, Arnold Edwin *16:* 31
Bare, Colleen Stanley *32:* 33
Barger, Jan *147:* 11
Bargery, Geoffrey *14:* 258
Barkat, Jonathan *149:* 177; *164:* 254; *181:* 106; *184:* 186; *196:* 11; *198:* 148
Barker, Carol *31:* 27
Barker, Cicely Mary *49:* 50, 51
Barkley, James *4:* 13; *6:* 11; *13:* 112
Barks, Carl *37:* 27, 28, 29, 30, 31, 32, 33, 34
Barling, Joy *62:* 148
Barling, Tom *9:* 23
Barlow, Gillian *62:* 20
Barlow, Perry *35:* 28
Barlowe, Dot *30:* 223
Barlowe, Wayne *37:* 72; *84:* 43; *105:* 5
Barnard, Bryn *88:* 53; *13:* 55; *169:* 13; *193:* 194
Barneda, David *206:* 11

Barner, Bob *29:* 37; *128:* 33; *136:* 19, 20; *177:* 27
Barnes, Hiram P. *20:* 28
Barnes, Tim *137:* 28
Barnes-Murphy, Rowan *88:* 22
Barnett, Charles II *175:* 150
Barnett, Ivan *70:* 14
Barnett, Moneta *16:* 89; *19:* 142; *31:* 102; *33:* 30, 31, 32; *41:* 153; *61:* 94, 97
Barney, Maginel Wright *39:* 32, 33, 34; *YABC 2:* 306
Barnum, Jay Hyde *11:* 224; *20:* 5; *37:* 189, 190
Baron, Alan *80:* 3; *89:* 123
Barr, George *60:* 74; *69:* 64
Barragán, Paula S. *134:* 116; *186:* 158; *216:* 43, 44, 197; *232:* 133
Barrall, Tim *115:* 152
Barraud, Martin *189:* 38
Barrauds *33:* 114
Barrer-Russell, Gertrude *9:* 65; *27:* 31
Barret, Robert *85:* 134
Barrett, Angela *40:* 136, 137; *62:* 74; *75:* 10; *76:* 142; *144:* 137; *145:* 14; *223:* 14
Barrett, Jennifer *58:* 149
Barrett, John E. *43:* 119
Barrett, Moneta *74:* 10
Barrett, Peter *55:* 169; *86:* 111
Barrett, Robert *62:* 145; *77:* 146; *82:* 35
Barrett, Ron *14:* 24; *26:* 35
Barron, John N. *3:* 261; *5:* 101; *14:* 220
Barrow, Ann *136:* 27
Barrows, Walter *14:* 268
Barry, Ethelred B. *37:* 79; *YABC 1:* 229
Barry, James *14:* 25
Barry, Katharina *2:* 159; *4:* 22
Barry, Robert E. *6:* 12
Barry, Scott *32:* 35
Barshaw, Ruth McNally *203:* 9
Bartenbach, Jean *40:* 31
Barth, Ernest Kurt *2:* 172; *3:* 160; *8:* 26; *10:* 31
Bartholomew, Caty *208:* 153
Bartholomew, Marie *200:* 66
Bartlett, Alison *101:* 88; *165:* 93; *209:* 51
Barton, Byron *8:* 207; *9:* 18; *23:* 66; *80:* 181; *90:* 18, 19, 20, 21; *126:* 29, 30
Barton, Harriett *30:* 71
Barton, Jill *129:* 108; *135:* 120; *145:* 185, 189; *184:* 177; *224:* 142, 143
Barton, Patrice *226:* 14
Bartram, Robert *10:* 42
Bartram, Simon *218:* 8
Bartsch, Jochen *8:* 105; *39:* 38
Bascove, Barbara *45:* 73
Base, Graeme *101:* 15, 16, 17, 18; *162:* 8, 10, 12
Baseman, Gary *174:* 12
Bash, Barbara *132:* 9
Basic, Zdenko *235:* 176
Baskin, Leonard *30:* 42, 43, 46, 47; *49:* 125, 126, 128, 129,133; *173:* 120
Bass, Saul *49:* 192
Bassett, Jeni *40:* 99; *64:* 30
Basso, Bill *99:* 139; *189:* 134
Batchelor, Joy *29:* 41, 47, 48
Bate, Norman *5:* 16
Bates, Amy June *188:* 170; *189:* 27, 28
Bates, Leo *24:* 35
Batet, Carmen *39:* 134
Batherman, Muriel *31:* 79; *45:* 185
Battaglia, Aurelius *50:* 44
Batten, John D. *25:* 161, 162
Batten, Mary *162:* 14, 15
Battles, Asa *32:* 94, 95
Bauer, Carla *193:* 6
Bauer, Jutta *150:* 32
Bauernschmidt, Marjorie *15:* 15
Baum, Allyn *20:* 10
Baum, Willi *4:* 24, 25; *7:* 173
Bauman, Leslie *61:* 121

Baumann, Jill *34:* 170
Baumhauer, Hans *11:* 218; *15:* 163, 165, 167
Baxter, Glen *57:* 100
Baxter, Leon *59:* 102
Baxter, Robert *87:* 129
Bayer, Herbert *181:* 16
Bayley, Dorothy *37:* 195
Bayley, Nicola *40:* 104; *41:* 34, 35; *69:* 15; *129:* 33, 34, 35
Baylin, Mark *158:* 233
Baynes, Pauline *2:* 244; *3:* 149; *13:* 133, 135,137, 141; *19:* 18, 19, 20; *32:* 208, 213, 214; *36:* 105, 108; *59:* 12, 13, 14, 16, 17, 18, 20; *100:* 158, 159, 243; *133:* 3, 4
Beach, Lou *150:* 150; *207:* 117, 118
Beaky, Suzanne *232:* 11
Beame, Rona *12:* 40
Bean, Jonathan *196:* 102
Bear's Heart *73:* 215
Beard, Alex *222:* 40
Beard, Dan *22:* 31, 32
Beard, J.H. *YABC 1:* 158
Bearden, Romare *9:* 7; *22:* 35
Beardshaw, Rosalind *169:* 22; *190:* 22; *224:* 12; *225:* 6, 7, 8; *226:* 71
Beardsley, Aubrey *17:* 14; *23:* 181; *59:* 130, 131
Bearman, Jane *29:* 38
Beaton, Cecil *24:* 208
Beaton, Clare *125:* 28; *208:* 67; *220:* 10, 11, 12
Beauce, J.A. *18:* 103
Beaujard, Sophie *81:* 54
Beavers, Ethen *225:* 9
Beccia, Carlyn *189:* 29
Bechtold, Lisze *208:* 29
Beck, Andrea *226:* 16
Beck, Charles *11:* 169; *51:* 173
Beck, Ian *138:* 27; *182:* 150; *190:* 25; *225:* 130
Beck, Melinda *203:* 112
Beck, Ruth *13:* 11
Becker, Harriet *12:* 211
Beckerman, Jonathan *208:* 194
Beckett, Sheilah *25:* 5; *33:* 37, 38
Beckhoff, Harry *1:* 78; *5:* 163
Beckhorn, Susan Williams *189:* 32
Beckman, Kaj *45:* 38, 39, 40, 41
Beckman, Per *45:* 42, 43
Beddows, Eric *72:* 70
Bedford, F.D. *20:* 118, 122; *33:* 170; *41:* 220, 221,230, 233
Bee, Joyce *19:* 62
Bee, William *188:* 6
Beeby, Betty *25:* 36
Beech, Carol *9:* 149
Beech, Mark *192:* 122
Beek *25:* 51, 55, 59
Beeke, Tiphanie *177:* 127; *204:* 140; *212:* 178; *218:* 102
Beekman, Doug *125:* 146, 148
Beerbohm, Max *24:* 208
Beeson, Bob *108:* 57
Begin, Mary Jane *82:* 13; *206:* 13
Beha, Philippe *172:* 85
Behr, Joyce *15:* 15; *21:* 132; *23:* 161
Behrens, Hans *5:* 97
Beier, Ellen *135:* 170; *139:* 47; *183:* 164; *221:* 177; *222:* 151
Beingessner, Laura *220:* 14
Beinicke, Steve *69:* 18
Beisner, Monika *46:* 128, 131; *112:* 127
Belden, Charles J. *12:* 182
Belina, Renate *39:* 132
Bell, Corydon *3:* 20
Bell, Graham *54:* 48
Bell, Julia *151:* 214
Bell, Julie *159:* 172; *165:* 18
Bell, Thomas P. *76:* 182
Bellamy, Glen *127:* 15
Beltran, Alberto *43:* 37

Bemelmans, Ludwig *15:* 19, 21; *100:* 27
Ben-Ami, Doron *75:* 96; *84:* 107; *108:* 132; *110:* 63; *159:* 157; *197:* 142; *233:* 122
Bendall-Brunello, John *150:* 4; *157:* 163; *185:* 3, 4; *203:* 5; *237:* 101
Benda, Wladyslaw T. *15:* 256; *30:* 76, 77; *44:* 182
Bender, Robert *77:* 162; *79:* 13; *160:* 23
Bendick, Jeanne *2:* 24; *68:* 27, 28
Benioff, Carol *121:* 42; *175:* 23; *232:* 12
Benner, Cheryl *80:* 11
Bennett, Charles H. *64:* 6
Bennett, Erin Susanne *165:* 216
Bennett, F.I. *YABC 1:* 134
Bennett, James *146:* 240
Bennett, Jill *26:* 61; *41:* 38, 39; *45:* 54
Bennett, Rainey *15:* 26; *23:* 53
Bennett, Richard *15:* 45; *21:* 11, 12, 13; *25:* 175
Bennett, Susan *5:* 55
Benny, Mike *142:* 78; *203:* 13, 14; *207:* 85
Benoit, Elise *77:* 74
Benson, Linda *60:* 130; *62:* 91; *75:* 101; *79:* 156; *134:* 129
Benson, Patrick *68:* 162; *147:* 17, 18, 19, 20
Bentley, Carolyn *46:* 153
Bentley, James *149:* 30
Bentley, Roy *30:* 162
Benton, Jim *172:* 22
Benton, Thomas Hart *2:* 99
Bereal, JaeMe *228:* 16
Berelson, Howard *5:* 20; *16:* 58; *31:* 50
Berenstain, Jan *12:* 47; *64:* 33, 34, 36, 37, 38, 40, 42, 44; *135:* 25, 28, 31, 35
Berenstain, Stan *12:* 47; *64:* 33, 34, 36, 37, 38, 40, 42, 44; *135:* 25, 28, 31, 35
Berenzy, Alix *65:* 13; *73:* 6; *78:* 115
Berg, Joan *1:* 115; *3:* 156; *6:* 26, 58
Berg, Ron *36:* 48, 49; *48:* 37, 38; *67:* 72
Bergen, David *115:* 44; *207:* 34
Berger, Barbara *77:* 14
Berger, Carin *185:* 6; *232:* 14
Berger, Joe *221:* 9
Berger, William M. *14:* 143; *YABC 1:* 204
Bergherr, Mary *74:* 170; *151:* 123
Bergin, Mark *114:* 8, 9; *143:* 95; *160:* 26, 27
Bergstreser, Douglas *69:* 76
Bergum, Constance R. *121:* 14, 15; *208:* 31, 32, 33; *209:* 176
Bering, Claus *13:* 14
Berkeley, Jon *139:* 218
Berkowitz, Jeanette *3:* 249
Berman, Paul *66:* 14
Berman, Rachel *217:* 26
Bernal, Richard *154:* 176
Bernadette
   See Watts, Bernadette
Bernard, Gary *216:* 71
Bernardin, James *112:* 24; *167:* 94; *227:* 14, 15
Bernasconi, Pablo *183:* 10, 11
Bernatene, Poly *235:* 193
Bernath, Stefen *32:* 76
Berner, Rotraut Susanne *214:* 32
Bernhard, Durga *80:* 13
Bernstein, Michel J. *51:* 71
Bernstein, Ted *38:* 183; *50:* 131
Bernstein, Zena *23:* 46
Berridge, Celia *86:* 63
Berrill, Jacquelyn *12:* 50
Berry, Erick
   See Best, Allena
Berry, Holly *205:* 116; *210:* 49, 50
Berry, William D. *14:* 29; *19:* 48
Berry, William A. *6:* 219
Berson, Harold *2:* 17, 18; *4:* 28, 29, 220; *9:* 10; *12:* 19; *17:* 45; *18:* 193; *22:* 85; *34:* 172; *44:* 120; *46:* 42; *80:* 240
Bertholf, Bret *187:* 9; *189:* 32, 33
Berton, Patsy *99:* 16
Bertschmann, Harry *16:* 1

Besco, Don *70:* 99
Beskow, Elsa *20:* 13, 14, 15
Bess, Clayton *63:* 94
Best, Allena *2:* 26; *34:* 76
Betera, Carol *74:* 68
Bethell, Thomas N. *61:* 169
Bethers, Ray *6:* 22
Betteridge, Deirdre *214:* 34
Bettina
  See Ehrlich, Bettina
Betts, Ethel Franklin *17:* 161, 164, 165; *YABC 2:* 47
Betz, Rudolf *59:* 161
Bewick, Thomas *16:* 40, 41, 43, 44, 45, 47; *54:* 150; *YABC 1:* 107
Beyer, Paul J. III *74:* 24
Bezencon, Jacqueline *48:* 40
Biamonte, Daniel *40:* 90
Bianchi, John *91:* 19
Bianco, Pamela *15:* 31; *28:* 44, 45, 46
Bible, Charles *13:* 15
Bice, Clare *22:* 40
Biedrzycki, David *186:* 170; *219:* 7
Bierman, Don *57:* 184
Biggers, John *2:* 123
Biggs, Brian *192:* 38; *196:* 15; *207:* 170
Bikadoroff, Roxanna *201:* 74
Bileck, Marvin *3:* 102; *40:* 36, 37
Bilibin, Ivan *61:* 8, 9, 12, 13, 14, 15, 151, 152, 154, 162
Billington, Patrick *98:* 71
Billout, Guy *144:* 38, 39
Bimen, Levent *5:* 179
Binch, Caroline *81:* 18; *140:* 15, 16; *144:* 115; *211:* 82
Binder, Hannes *169:* 163
Bing, Christopher *126:* 34
Binger, Bill *121:* 46
Binks, Robert *25:* 150
Binzen, Bill *24:* 47
Birch, Reginald *15:* 150; *19:* 33, 34, 35, 36; *37:* 196,197; *44:* 182; *46:* 176; *YABC 1:* 84; *2:* 34, 39
Birch, Wendy *223:* 70
Birchall, Mark *123:* 188
Bird, Esther Brock *1:* 36; *25:* 66
Birdsong, Keith *167:* 85; *219:* 105
Birkett, Georgie *204:* 121
Birkett, Rachel *78:* 206
Birling, Paul *109:* 30
Birmingham, Christian *132:* 243; *143:* 114; *209:* 58; *220:* 20
Birmingham, Lloyd P. *12:* 51; *83:* 13
Biro, Val *1:* 26; *41:* 42; *60:* 178; *67:* 23, 24; *84:* 242, 243
Bischoff, Ilse *44:* 51
Bishop, Don *199:* 133
Bishop, Gavin *97:* 17, 18; *144:* 42, 44; *216:* 52, 55, 56, 57
Bishop, Kathleen Wong *115:* 67
Bishop, Rich *56:* 43
Bite, I. *60:* 14
Bittinger, Ned *93:* 117; *205:* 115
Bjorklund, Lorence *3:* 188, 252; *7:* 100; *9:* 113; *10:* 66; *19:* 178; *33:* 122, 123; *35:* 36, 37, 38, 39,41, 42, 43; *36:* 185; *38:* 93; *47:* 106; *66:* 194; *YABC 1:* 242
Björkman, Steve *91:* 199; *160:* 110; *198:* 18; *218:* 188; *223:* 20, 21; *236:* 56
Blabey, Aaron *214:* 35
Black Sheep *164:* 100
Blackburn, Loren H. *63:* 10
Blackall, Sophie *194:* 140; *209:* 157; *231:* 31, 115; *237:* 172
Blackford, John *137:* 105; *180:* 36
Blackwell, Basil T. *YABC 1:* 68, 69
Blackwood, Freya *199:* 9
Blackwood, Gary L. *118:* 17
Blades, Ann *16:* 52; *37:* 213; *50:* 41; *69:* 21; *99:* 215
Blair, Jay *45:* 46; *46:* 155

Blaisdell, Elinore *1:* 121; *3:* 134; *35:* 63
Blake, Anne Catharine *189:* 71
Blake, Francis *198:* 4
Blake, Quentin *3:* 170; *10:* 48; *13:* 38; *21:* 180; *26:* 60; *28:* 228; *30:* 29, 31; *40:* 108; *45:* 219; *46:* 165, 168; *48:* 196; *52:* 10, 11, 12,13, 14, 15, 16, 17; *73:* 41, 43; *78:* 84, 86; *80:* 250, 251; *84:* 210, 211, 212; *87:* 177; *96:* 24, 26, 28; *124:* 79; *125:* 32, 34; *181:* 139; *211:* 26, 27; *227:* 176; *229:* 167
Blake, Robert J. *37:* 90; *53:* 67; *54:* 23; *160:* 28, 29
Blake, William *30:* 54, 56, 57, 58, 59, 60
Blakeslee, Lys *218:* 11, 105
Blanchard, N. Taylor *82:* 140
Blass, Jacqueline *8:* 215
Blazek, Scott R. *91:* 71
Blecha, Aaron *233:* 17
Bleck, Cathie *118:* 116
Bleck, Linda *204:* 124
Blegvad, Erik *2:* 59; *3:* 98; *5:* 117; *7:* 131; *11:* 149; *14:* 34, 35; *18:* 237; *32:* 219; *60:* 106; *66:* 16, 17, 18, 19; *70:* 233; *76:* 18; *82:* 106; *87:* 45; *100:* 188; *129:* 125; *132:* 17, 18, 19, 20; *176:* 14; *200:* 100; *YABC 1:* 201
Blessen, Karen *93:* 126
Bliss, Corinne Demas *37:* 38
Bliss, Harry *196:* 27, 28, 29
Blitt, Barry *179:* 199; *187:* 13; *225:* 198
Bloch, Lucienne *10:* 12
Blondon, Herve *129:* 48; *183:* 22
Bloom, Lloyd *35:* 180; *36:* 149; *47:* 99; *62:* 117; *68:* 231; *72:* 136; *75:* 185; *83:* 99; *108:* 19; *229:* 114
Bloom, Suzanne *172:* 23, 24; *232:* 17
Blossom, Dave *34:* 29
Blumenschein, E.L. *YABC 1:* 113, 115
Blumer, Patt *29:* 214
Blundell, Kim *29:* 36
Bluthenthal, Diana Cain *93:* 32; *104:* 106; *177:* 26; *232:* 21
Blythe, Benjamin *128:* 7
Blythe, Gary *112:* 52; *181:* 166; *182:* 64; *185:* 7; *186:* 116, 117
Boake, Kathy *176:* 185
Board, Perry *171:* 99
Boardman, Gwenn *12:* 60
Boase, Susan *224:* 53
Boatwright, Phil *211:* 195
Bober, Richard *125:* 145; *132:* 40
Bobri *30:* 138; *47:* 27
Bock, Vera *1:* 187; *21:* 41
Bock, William Sauts *8:* 7; *14:* 37; *16:* 120; *21:* 141; *36:* 177; *62:* 203
Bodecker, N(iels) M(ogens) *8:* 13; *14:* 2; *17:* 55, 56, 57; *73:* 22, 23, 24
Boehm, Linda *40:* 31
Bogacki, Tomek *138:* 31, 32; *144:* 123; *202:* 13
Bogan, Paulette *197:* 152; *201:* 17
Bogdan, Florentina *107:* 43
Bohdal, Susi *22:* 44; *101:* 20
Bohlen, Nina *58:* 13
Boies, Alex *96:* 53
Bok, Chip *205:* 16
Bolam, Emily *101:* 216; *159:* 12; *205:* 59
Bolian, Polly *3:* 270; *4:* 30; *13:* 77; *29:* 197
Bolle, Frank *87:* 100; *208:* 101
Bollen, Roger *79:* 186; *83:* 16
Bolling, Vickey *114:* 44
Bollinger, Peter *101:* 7; *128:* 198; *172:* 26
Bolognese, Don *2:* 147, 231; *4:* 176; *7:* 146; *17:* 43; *23:* 192; *24:* 50; *34:* 108; *36:* 133; *71:* 24, 25; *103:* 131; *129:* 39, 40
Bolster, Rob *186:* 169
Bolton, A.T. *57:* 158
Bond, Arnold *18:* 116
Bond, Barbara Higgins *21:* 102
Bond, Bruce *52:* 97
Bond, Felicia *38:* 197; *49:* 55, 56; *89:* 170; *90:* 171; *126:* 37

Bond, Higgins *177:* 22, 23; *209:* 175; *220:* 22, 23, 24
Bone, J. *230:* 11, 181
Bonn, Pat *43:* 40
Bonner, Hannah *197:* 13, 14
Bonners, Susan *41:* 40; *85:* 36; *94:* 99, 100; *151:* 105, 106
Bonnet, Rosalinde *230:* 79
Bono, Mary *184:* 73
Bonsall, Crosby *23:* 6
Booker, Philip *225:* 16
Boon, Debbie *103:* 6; *144:* 188
Boon, Emilie *86:* 23, 24
Boone, Debbie *165:* 77
Boore, Sara *60:* 73
Bootman, Colin *155:* 13; *159:* 35; *174:* 192; *222:* 128
Booth, Franklin *YABC 2:* 76
Booth, George *191:* 13
Booth, Graham *32:* 193; *37:* 41, 42
Borda, Juliette *102:* 188
Bordier, Georgette *16:* 54
Boren, Tinka *27:* 128
Borges, Jose Francisco *119:* 62
Borja, Robert *22:* 48
Born, Adolf *49:* 63
Bornstein, Ruth *14:* 44; *88:* 45, 46; *107:* 30
Borten, Helen *3:* 54; *5:* 24
Bosin, Blackbear *69:* 104
Bossom, Naomi *35:* 48
Bostock, Mike *83:* 221; *114:* 14; *188:* 205
Boston, Peter *19:* 42
Bosustow, Stephen *34:* 202
Boszko, Ron *75:* 47
Bottner, Barbara *14:* 46
Boucher, Joelle *41:* 138
Boulat, Pierre *44:* 40
Boulet, Susan Seddon *50:* 47
Bouma, Paddy *118:* 25; *128:* 16
Bour, Daniele *66:* 145
Bourke-White, Margaret *15:* 286, 287; *57:* 102
Boutavant, Marc *200:* 136
Boutet de Monvel, M. *30:* 61, 62, 63, 65
Bowen, Betsy *105:* 222
Bowen, Richard *42:* 134
Bowen, Ruth *31:* 188
Bower, Ron *29:* 33
Bowers, David *95:* 38; *115:* 20; *127:* 169, 170; *165:* 57; *207:* 11
Bowers, Tim *185:* 35; *201:* 41; *218:* 13
Bowman, Claire *174:* 177
Bowman, Eric *151:* 23
Bowman, Leslie *85:* 203; *105:* 108; *116:* 76; *128:* 234; *182:* 24, 25
Bowman, Peter *146:* 214, 215; *150:* 115
Bowser, Carolyn Ewing *22:* 253
Boxall, Ed *178:* 28
Boyd, Aaron *158:* 242
Boyd, Patti *45:* 31
Boyle, Eleanor Vere *28:* 50, 51
Boynton, Sandra *57:* 13, 14, 15; *107:* 36, 37; *152:* 12, 13, 14
Bozzo, Frank *4:* 154
Brabbs, Derry *55:* 170
Brace, Eric *132:* 193, 194; *152:* 71; *184:* 195; *197:* 6; *201:* 54; *233:* 160
Brackers de Hugo, Pierre *115:* 21
Bradford, June *158:* 138
Bradford, Ron *7:* 157
Bradley, David P. *69:* 105
Bradley, Richard D. *26:* 182
Bradley, William *5:* 164
Brady, Irene *4:* 31; *42:* 37; *68:* 191
Bragg, Michael *32:* 78; *46:* 31
Bragg, Ruth Gembicki *77:* 18
Brainerd, John W. *65:* 19
Braithwaite, Althea *23:* 12, 13; *119:* 16
Brak, Syd *146:* 187
Bralds, Braldt *90:* 28; *91:* 151
Bram, Elizabeth *30:* 67
Bramley, Peter *4:* 3

Brandenberg, Aliki *2:* 36, 37; *24:* 222; *35:* 49, 50, 51,52, 53, 54, 56, 57; *75:* 15, 17; *92:* 205; *113:* 18, 19, 20; *157:* 28; *156:* 111
Brandenburg, Alexa *75:* 19
Brandenburg, Jim *47:* 58; *150:* 212
Brandi, Lillian *31:* 158
Brandon, Brumsic, Jr. *9:* 25
Brannen, Sarah S. *202:* 15; *216:* 199
Bransom, Paul *17:* 121; *43:* 44
Braren, Loretta Trezzo *87:* 193
Brassard, France *186:* 22
Braun, Wendy *80:* 17, 18; *213:* 14
Brautigam, Don *115:* 175, 176; *225:* 109
Brazell, Derek *75:* 105; *79:* 9
Breathed, Berkeley *86:* 27, 28, 29; *161:* 13, 14; *229:* 10, 11, 12
Breckenreid, Julia *192:* 209
Breen, Steve *186:* 23
Brennan, Steve *83:* 230; *101:* 184
Brenner, Fred *22:* 85; *36:* 34; *42:* 34
Brett, Bernard *22:* 54
Brett, Harold M. *26:* 98, 99, 100
Brett, Jan *30:* 135; *42:* 39; *71:* 31, 32; *130:* 23, 24, 25, 26, 27; *171:* 15, 16; *234:* 32, 34, 35, 36, 37
Brewer, Paul *106:* 115; *145:* 202; *230:* 13
Brewer, Sally King *33:* 44
Brewster, Patience *40:* 68; *45:* 22, 183; *51:* 20; *66:* 144; *89:* 4; *97:* 30, 31; *212:* 99
Brick, John *10:* 15
Brickman, Robin D. *131:* 88; *142:* 150; *155:* 18; *178:* 109; *184:* 32
Bridge, David R. *45:* 28
Bridgman, L.J. *37:* 77
Bridwell, Norman *4:* 37; *138:* 36, 37, 40
Brierley, Louise *91:* 22; *96:* 165; *183:* 51
Briggs, Harry *172:* 187
Briggs, Raymond *10:* 168; *23:* 20, 21; *66:* 29, 31, 32; *131:* 28, 29; *184:* 15, 16
Brigham, Grace A. *37:* 148
Bright, Robert *24:* 55
Brighton, Catherine *107:* 39; *206:* 23
Brinckloe, Julie *13:* 18; *24:* 79, 115; *29:* 35; *63:* 140; *81:* 131
Brion *47:* 116
Brisley, Joyce L. *22:* 57
Brisson, James F. *110:* 60
Brittingham, Geoffrey *88:* 37
Brix-Henker, Silke *81:* 194
Broadway, Hannah *208:* 104
Brock, Charles E. *15:* 97; *19:* 247, 249; *23:* 224, 225; *36:* 88; *42:* 41, 42, 43, 44, 45; *100:* 189; *YABC 1:* 194, 196, 203
Brock, Emma *7:* 21
Brock, Henry Matthew *15:* 81; *16:* 141; *19:* 71; *34:* 115; *40:* 164; *42:* 47, 48, 49; *49:* 66
Brocksopp, Arthur *57:* 157
Broda, Ron *136:* 180; *174:* 123
Brodkin, Gwen *34:* 135
Brodovitch, Alexi *52:* 22
Bromhall, Winifred *5:* 11; *26:* 38
Bromley, Lizzy *159:* 179; *237:* 150
Bronson, Linda *150:* 210; *174:* 133; *203:* 16, 17; *225:* 178
Brooke, L. Leslie *16:* 181, 182, 183, 186; *17:* 15, 16, 17; *18:* 194
Brooker, Christopher *15:* 251
Brooker, Kyrsten *111:* 94; *140:* 28; *162:* 111; *175:* 108; *186:* 42, 225; *199:* 12; *201:* 30; *219:* 98
Brooks, Erik *166:* 52; *182:* 30; *232:* 139; *236:* 40, 41
Brooks, Karen Stormer *186:* 110; *220:* 65
Brooks, Maya Itzna *92:* 153
Brooks, Ron *94:* 15; *197:* 188; *212:* 6, 7, 8, 9
Brooks, S.G. *178:* 127
Broomfield, Maurice *40:* 141
Brotman, Adolph E. *5:* 21
Brown, Bill *235:* 139
Brown, Buck *45:* 48

Brown, Calef *179:* 18; *210:* 206; *217:* 30, 31; *225:* 201
Brown, Christopher *62:* 124, 125, 127, 128
Brown, Craig *73:* 28; *84:* 65; *224:* 18
Brown, Dan *61:* 167; *115:* 183, 184; *116:* 28, 29; *193:* 190; *200:* 21, 23
Brown, David *7:* 47; *48:* 52
Brown, Denise *11:* 213
Brown, Don *172:* 29
Brown, Elbrite *195:* 39; *198:* 5
Brown, Ford Madox *48:* 74
Brown, Gayle *224:* 184
Brown, Hunter *191:* 111, 112; *234:* 105, 107
Brown, Judith Gwyn *1:* 45; *7:* 5; *8:* 167; *9:* 182, 190; *20:* 16, 17, 18; *23:* 142; *29:* 117; *33:* 97; *36:* 23, 26; *43:* 184; *48:* 201, 223; *49:* 69; *86:* 227; *110:* 188; *153:* 7
Brown, Kathryn *98:* 26
Brown, Lisa *187:* 175; *234:* 39
Brown, Laurie Krasny *99:* 30
Brown, Leo *225:* 18
Brown, Marc (Tolon) *10:* 17, 197; *14:* 263; *51:* 18; *53:* 11, 12, 13, 15, 16, 17; *75:* 58; *80:* 24, 25, 26; *82:* 261; *99:* 29; *145:* 22, 23, 25, 27; *162:* 198; *224:* 136
Brown, Marcia *7:* 30; *25:* 203; *47:* 31, 32, 33, 34, 35,36, 37, 38, 39, 40, 42, 43, 44; *YABC 1:* 27
Brown, Margery W. *5:* 32, 33; *10:* 3
Brown, Martin *101:* 43
Brown, Mary Barrett *97:* 74
Brown, Palmer *36:* 40
Brown, Paul *25:* 26; *26:* 107
Brown, Richard *61:* 18; *67:* 30
Brown, Rick *78:* 71; *150:* 154; *224:* 16
Brown, Robert S. *85:* 33
Brown, Rod *157:* 142; *232:* 32, 33
Brown, Ruth *55:* 165; *86:* 112, 113; *105:* 16, 17, 18; *171:* 178
Brown, Trevor *99:* 160; *139:* 247; *189:* 206
Browne, Anthony *45:* 50, 51, 52; *61:* 21, 22, 23, 24, 25; *105:* 21, 22, 23, 25
Browne, Dik *8:* 212; *67:* 32, 33, 35, 37, 39
Browne, Gordon *16:* 97; *64:* 114, 116, 117, 119, 121
Browne, Hablot K. *15:* 65, 80; *21:* 14, 15, 16, 17, 18, 19,20; *24:* 25
Browne, Jane *165:* 222
Browning, Coleen *4:* 132
Browning, Diane *233:* 30
Browning, Mary Eleanor *24:* 84
Bruce, Robert *23:* 23
Brude, Dick *48:* 215
Bruel, Nick *166:* 41; *205:* 17, 18
Brule, Al *3:* 135
Brumbeau, Jeff *157:* 29
Bruna, Dick *43:* 48, 49, 50; *76:* 27, 28
Brundage, Frances *19:* 244
Brunhoff, Jean de *24:* 57, 58
Brunhoff, Laurent de *24:* 60; *71:* 35, 36, 37
Brunkus, Denise *84:* 50; *123:* 117; *178:* 209; *193:* 99; *204:* 10, 11, 12; *209:* 202
Brunson, Bob *43:* 135
Bryan, Ashley *31:* 44; *72:* 27, 28, 29; *107:* 92; *116:* 192; *132:* 24; *178:* 33, 34, 35; *208:* 83
Bryant, Laura J. *176:* 36; *183:* 168; *214:* 141; *222:* 49, 152
Bryant, Michael *93:* 74
Brychta, Alex *21:* 21
Bryer, Diana *107:* 121
Bryson, Bernarda *3:* 88, 146; *39:* 26; *44:* 185; *131:* 40
Buba, Joy *12:* 83; *30:* 226; *44:* 56
Buchanan, George *166:* 198
Buchanan, Lilian *13:* 16
Buchanan, Rachel *171:* 71
Bucholtz-Ross, Linda *44:* 137
Buchs, Thomas *40:* 38
Buck, Margaret Waring *3:* 30
Buckhardt, Marc *172:* 59
Buckley, Mike *166:* 180

Budwine, Greg *175:* 172
Buehner, Mark *104:* 12, 15; *105:* 160; *119:* 98; *157:* 188; *159:* 39, 40, 43; *192:* 111; *219:* 13, 14, 15, 16; *221:* 17, 18, 19
Buehr, Walter *3:* 31
Buell, Carl *222:* 68
Buff, Conrad *19:* 52, 53, 54
Buff, Mary *19:* 52, 53
Bull, Charles Livingston *18:* 207; *88:* 175, 176
Bullen, Anne *3:* 166, 167
Buller, Jon *205:* 21
Bullock, Kathleen *77:* 24
Bumgarner-Kirby, Claudia *77:* 194
Burbank, Addison *37:* 43
Burchard, Peter Duncan *3:* 197; *5:* 35; *6:* 158, 218; *143:* 17
Burckhardt, Marc *94:* 48; *110:* 89; *196:* 41; *199:* 116
Burden, Andrea *227:* 26
Burger, Carl *3:* 33; *45:* 160, 162
Burgeson, Marjorie *19:* 31
Burgess, Anne *76:* 252
Burgess, Gelett *32:* 39, 42
Burgess, Mark *157:* 31
Burke, Jim *179:* 19; *185:* 63
Burke, Phillip *95:* 117
Burkert, Nancy Ekholm *18:* 186; *22:* 140; *24:* 62, 63,64, 65; *26:* 53; *29:* 60, 61; *46:* 171; *YABC 1:* 46
Burkhardt, Bruce *142:* 86
Burkhardt, Melissa A. *142:* 86
Burleson, Joe *104:* 35; *172:* 139; *227:* 124
Burn, Doris *6:* 172
Burn, Jeffrey *89:* 125; *152:* 132
Burn, Ted
 See Burn, Thomas E.
Burn, Thomas E. *151:* 41; *232:* 40
Burnard, Damon *115:* 23
Burnett, Lindy *210:* 59
Burnett, Virgil *44:* 42
Burningham, John *9:* 68; *16:* 60, 61; *59:* 28, 29, 30,31, 32, 33, 35; *111:* 18, 19, 21; *160:* 37; *225:* 21, 24
Burns, Howard M. *12:* 173
Burns, Jim *47:* 70; *86:* 32; *91:* 197; *123:* 16
Burns, M.F. *26:* 69
Burns, Raymond *9:* 29
Burns, Robert *24:* 106
Burr, Dan *65:* 28; *108:* 134; *164:* 203; *182:* 68
Burr, Dane *12:* 2
Burra, Edward *YABC 2:* 68
Burrell, Galen *56:* 76
Burri, Rene *41:* 143; *54:* 166
Burridge, Marge Opitz *14:* 42
Burris, Burmah *4:* 81
Burroughs, John Coleman *41:* 64
Burroughs, Studley O. *41:* 65
Burton, Marilee Robin *46:* 33
Burton, Virginia Lee *2:* 43; *44:* 49, 51; *100:* 46, 47; *YABC 1:* 24; *147:* 56
Buscema, Stephanie *232:* 34
Bush, Timothy *228:* 138
Busoni, Rafaello *1:* 186; *3:* 224; *6:* 126; *14:* 5; *16:* 62, 63
Butchkes, Sidney *50:* 58
Butler, Geoff *94:* 20
Butler, Ralph *116:* 212
Butterfield, Ned *1:* 153; *27:* 128; *79:* 63
Butterworth, Ian *184:* 48, 49
Butterworth, Nick *106:* 43, 44; *149:* 34
Buxton, John *123:* 12
Buzelli, Christopher *105:* 149
Buzonas, Gail *29:* 88
Buzzell, Russ W. *12:* 177
Byard, Carole *39:* 44; *57:* 18, 19, 20; *60:* 60; *61:* 93, 96; *69:* 210; *78:* 246; *79:* 227
Byars, Betsy *46:* 35
Byfield, Barbara Ninde *8:* 18
Byfield, Graham *32:* 29
Bynum, Janie *176:* 50

Byrd, Robert *13:* 218; *33:* 46; *158:* 70; *212:* 100; *226:* 39, 40; *229:* 102; *232:* 167
Byrd, Samuel *123:* 104

C

Cabat, Erni *74:* 38
Cabban, Vanessa *138:* 73; *176:* 39; *185:* 65; *227:* 70
Cabrera, Jane *103:* 24; *152:* 27; *182:* 33, 34
Caceres, Ana Palmero *198:* 106
Caddy, Alice *6:* 41
Cady, Harrison *17:* 21, 23; *19:* 57, 58
Caffrey, Aileen *72:* 223; *141:* 154
Cairns, Julia *177:* 37
Caldecott, Randolph *16:* 98, 103; *17:* 32, 33, 36, 38, 39; *26:* 90; *100:* 49, 50; *YABC 2:* 172
Calder, Alexander *18:* 168
Calderón, Gloria *179:* 5
Calderon, W. Frank *25:* 160
Caldwell, Ben *105:* 75; *149:* 60; *195:* 61
Caldwell, Clyde *98:* 100; *116:* 39; *208:* 145
Caldwell, Doreen *23:* 77; *71:* 41
Caldwell, John *46:* 225
Call, Greg *126:* 135; *165:* 49; *182:* 105, 163; *197:* 18, 19; *200:* 159; *209:* 166; *212:* 161; *229:* 122; *236:* 129
Callahan, Kevin *22:* 42
Callahan, Philip S. *25:* 77
Callan, Jamie *59:* 37
Callen, Liz *231:* 37
Calo, Marcos *236:* 151
Calvert, Rosemary *218:* 96
Calvin, James *61:* 92
Camburn-Bracalente, Carol A. *118:* 22
Cameron, Chad *190:* 144
Cameron, Julia Margaret *19:* 203
Cameron, Scott *99:* 18
Camm, Martin *140:* 208, 209, 210
Campbell, Ann *11:* 43; *123:* 182; *183:* 68
Campbell, Bill *89:* 39
Campbell, Ken *126:* 143; *205:* 162
Campbell, Robert *55:* 120
Campbell, Rod *51:* 27; *98:* 34
Campbell, Walter M. *YABC 2:* 158
Camps, Luis *28:* 120, 121; *66:* 35
Canga, C.B. *187:* 165
Caniglia, Jeremy *201:* 89
Cann, Helen *124:* 50; *141:* 78; *170:* 138; *179:* 22, 23
Cannell, Jon *196:* 43
Cannon, Janell *78:* 25; *128:* 40
Canright, David *36:* 162
Cantone, AnnaLaura *182:* 146; *196:* 80
Canty, Thomas *85:* 161; *92:* 47; *113:* 192; *134:* 60; *185:* 117
Canyon, Christopher *150:* 44; *151:* 112
Cáparo, Antonio Javier *204:* 128; *218:* 88; *220:* 114; *221:* 167; *227:* 125; *231:* 154
Caple, Laurie *228:* 9
Caporale, Wende *70:* 42
Capp, Al *61:* 28, 30, 31, 40, 41, 43, 44
Cappon, Manuela *154:* 64; *218:* 149
Caras, Peter *36:* 64
Caraway, Caren *57:* 22
Caraway, James *3:* 200, 201
Carbe, Nino *29:* 183
Cardinale, Christopher *231:* 38
Cares, Linda *67:* 176
Carigiet, Alois *24:* 67
Carle, Eric *4:* 42; *11:* 121; *12:* 29; *65:* 32,33, 34, 36; *73:* 63, 65; *163:* 55, 56
Carling, Amelia Lau *164:* 46
Carlino, Angela *168:* 43; *188:* 20
Carlson, Nancy L. *41:* 116; *56:* 25; *90:* 45; *144:* 48, 50; *213:* 24, 25, 26
Carluccio, Maria *175:* 129; *221:* 119
Carmi, Giora *79:* 35; *149:* 40; *208:* 126

Carpenter, Nancy *76:* 128; *86:* 173; *89:* 171; *131:* 186; *134:* 8; *138:* 215; *153:* 204; *159:* 93; *165:* 232; *211:* 134; *216:* 113
Carr, Archie *37:* 225
Carrick, Donald *5:* 194; *39:* 97; *49:* 70; *53:* 156; *63:* 15, 16, 17, 18, 19, 21; *80:* 131; *86:* 151; *118:* 24
Carrick, Malcolm *28:* 59, 60
Carrick, Paul *118:* 26; *194:* 28
Carrick, Valery *21:* 47
Carrier, Lark *71:* 43
Carroll, Jim *88:* 211; *140:* 177; *153:* 99; *195:* 75; *236:* 88
Carroll, Lewis
    See Dodgson, Charles L.
Carroll, Michael *72:* 5
Carroll, Pamela *84:* 68; *128:* 214; *199:* 130
Carroll, Ruth *7:* 41; *10:* 68
Carter, Abby *81:* 32; *97:* 121; *102:* 61; *163:* 139; *164:* 125; *184:* 22, 23; *191:* 85; *222:* 51; *233:* 84, 94
Carter, Barbara *47:* 167, 169
Carter, David A. *114:* 24, 25; *170:* 42, 43; *228:* 29
Carter, Don *124:* 54; *184:* 100; *192:* 43, 44, 45
Carter, Harry *22:* 179
Carter, Helene *15:* 38; *22:* 202, 203; *YABC 2:* 220, 221
Carter, Penny *173:* 91
Cartlidge, Michelle *49:* 65; *96:* 50, 51
Cartwright, Reg *63:* 61, 62; *78:* 26; *143:* 4
Cartwright, Shannon *176:* 81
Carty, Leo *4:* 196; *7:* 163; *58:* 131
Cary *4:* 133; *9:* 32; *20:* 2; *21:* 143
Cary, Page *12:* 41
Casale, Paul *71:* 63; *109:* 122; *136:* 28
Case, Chris *209:* 23
Case, Sandra E. *16:* 2
Caseley, Judith *87:* 36; *159:* 47, 48, 49
Casilla, Robert *78:* 7; *167:* 124; *211:* 41; *212:* 165
Casino, Steve *85:* 193
Cassel, Lili
    See Wronker, Lili Cassel
Cassel-Wronker, Lili
    See Wronker, Lili Cassel
Cassels, Jean *8:* 50; *150:* 119; *173:* 37; *186:* 182
Cassen, Melody *140:* 51
Cassity, Don *104:* 24
Cassler, Carl *75:* 137, 138; *82:* 162
Casson, Hugh *65:* 38, 40, 42, 43
Castellon, Federico *48:* 45, 46, 47, 48
Castle, Jane *4:* 80
Castro L., Antonio *84:* 71; *226:* 43
Casu, Danny "casroc" *201:* 10
Catalano, Dominic *94:* 79; *163:* 60, 61; *162:* 54
Catalanotto, Peter *63:* 170; *70:* 23; *71:* 182; *72:* 96; *74:* 114; *76:* 194, 195; *77:* 7; *79:* 157; *80:* 28, 67; *83:* 157; *85:* 27; *108:* 11; *113:* 30, 31, 33, 34, 36; *114:* 27, 28, 29; *117:* 53; *124:* 168; *159:* 54, 55; *195:* 19, 20, 21, 22, 24, 174; *200:* 156; *207:* 103; *209:* 184; *226:* 4
Catania, Tom *68:* 82
Cather, Carolyn *3:* 83; *15:* 203; *34:* 216
Catlin, George *214:* 172
Catrow, David *117:* 179; *152:* 31, 33; *173:* 24; *206:* 29; *231:* 107; *236:* 154
Catusanu, Mircea *222:* 53
Cauley, Lorinda Bryan *44:* 135; *46:* 49
Cayard, Bruce *38:* 67
Cazet, Denys *52:* 27; *99:* 39, 40; *163:* 65, 66; *191:* 25, 27, 28
Ceccoli, Nicoletta *181:* 39; *188:* 99; *199:* 118; *209:* 6
Cecil, Randy *127:* 132, 133; *187:* 16, 17; *191:* 168; *209:* 5; *223:* 37, 38; *224:* 83; *233:* 156
Cellini, Joseph *2:* 73; *3:* 35; *16:* 116; *47:* 103

Cepeda, Joe *90:* 62; *109:* 91; *134:* 172; *159:* 57, 58, 164; *197:* 157; *203:* 69, 95; *215:* 38, 39, 40
Chabrian, Debbi *45:* 55
Chabrian, Deborah *51:* 182; *53:* 124; *63:* 107; *75:* 84; *79:* 85; *82:* 247; *89:* 93; *101:* 197; *212:* 13
Chagnon, Mary *37:* 158
Chalmers, Mary *3:* 145; *13:* 148; *33:* 125; *66:* 214
Chamberlain, Christopher *45:* 57
Chamberlain, Margaret *46:* 51; *106:* 89; *188:* 193; *212:* 16, 17; *224:* 181
Chamberlain, Nigel *78:* 140
Chambers, C.E. *17:* 230
Chambers, Dave *12:* 151
Chambers, Jill *134:* 110
Chambers, Mary *4:* 188
Chambliss, Maxie *42:* 186; *56:* 159; *93:* 163, 164; *103:* 178; *186:* 33, 34; *196:* 39; *223:* 182; *235:* 21
Champlin, Dale *136:* 124
Chan, Harvey *96:* 236; *99:* 153; *143:* 218; *179:* 144; *211:* 219
Chan, Peter *207:* 21; *221:* 39; *235:* 110
Chandler, David P. *28:* 62
Chaney, Howard *139:* 27
Chang, Warren *101:* 209
Chapel, Jody *68:* 20
Chapman, C.H. *13:* 83, 85, 87
Chapman, Frederick T. *6:* 27; *44:* 28
Chapman, Gaye *203:* 133
Chapman, Gaynor *32:* 52, 53
Chapman, Jane *145:* 186; *150:* 56; *166:* 220; *174:* 202; *176:* 43, 44; *179:* 131; *202:* 189; *212:* 20, 21, 22; *216:* 123, 225; *221:* 181, 182
Chapman, Lynne *175:* 31; *197:* 25; *208:* 44
Chapman-Crane, Jeff *220:* 101
Chappell, Warren *3:* 172; *21:* 56; *27:* 125
Charles, Donald *30:* 154, 155
Charlip, Remy *4:* 48; *34:* 138; *68:* 53, 54; *119:* 29, 30; *210:* 63, 64
Charlot, Jean *1:* 137, 138; *8:* 23; *14:* 31; *48:* 151; *56:* 21
Charlot, Martin *64:* 72
Charlton, Michael *34:* 50; *37:* 39
Charmatz, Bill *7:* 45
Chartier, Normand *9:* 36; *52:* 49; *66:* 40; *74:* 220; *145:* 169; *168:* 91; *177:* 108
Chase, Lynwood M. *14:* 4
Chast, Roz *97:* 39, 40; *212:* 25
Chastain, Madye Lee *4:* 50
Chateron, Ann *152:* 19
Chatterton, Martin *68:* 102; *152:* 19; *225:* 42
Chau, Tungwai *140:* 35
Chauncy, Francis *24:* 158
Chayka, Doug *145:* 97; *177:* 150; *196:* 46; *212:* 58
Chee, Cheng-Khee *79:* 42; *81:* 224; *180:* 245; *234:* 212
Chen, Chih-sien *90:* 226
Chen, Tony *6:* 45; *19:* 131; *29:* 126; *34:* 160
Chen, Wendy *221:* 76
Chen, Yong *183:* 34
Cheney, T.A. *11:* 47
Cheng, Andrea *205:* 28
Cheng, Judith *36:* 45; *51:* 16
Chermayeff, Ivan *47:* 53
Cherry, David *93:* 40
Cherry, Lynne *34:* 52; *65:* 184; *87:* 111; *99:* 46, 47
Chesak, Lina *135:* 118
Chess, Victoria *12:* 6; *33:* 42, 48, 49; *40:* 194; *41:* 145; *69:* 80; *72:* 100; *92:* 33, 34; *104:* 167
Chessa, Francesca *233:* 40
Chessare, Michele *41:* 50; *56:* 48; *69:* 145
Chesterton, G.K. *27:* 43, 44, 45, 47
Chestnutt, David *47:* 217

Chesworth, Michael *75:* 24, 152; *88:* 136; *94:* 25; *98:* 155; *160:* 42; *207:* 23, 24, 25; *214:* 145
Chetham, Celia *134:* 34
Chetwin, Grace *86:* 40
Cheung, Irving *158:* 96
Chevalier, Christa *35:* 66
Chew, Ruth *7:* 46; *132:* 147
Chewning, Randy *92:* 206
Chichester Clark, Emma *72:* 121; *77:* 212; *78:* 209; *87:* 143; *117:* 37, 39, 40; *144:* 138; *156:* 24, 25; *209:* 26
Chifflart *47:* 113, 127
Child, Lauren *119:* 32; *183:* 30, 31
Chin, Alex *28:* 54
Chitwood, Susan Tanner *163:* 16
Cho, Shinta *8:* 126
Chodos-Irvine, Margaret *52:* 102, 103, 107; *152:* 44
Choi, Yangsook *171:* 134; *173:* 135; *178:* 38, 39, 40
Choksi, Nishant *222:* 54
Chollat, Emilie *170:* 203
Chollick, Jay *25:* 175
Choma, Christina *99:* 169
Chomey, Steve *188:* 53
Chorao, Kay *7:* 200, 201; *8:* 25; *11:* 234; *33:* 187; *35:* 239; *69:* 35; *70:* 235; *123:* 174; *193:* 179; *215:* 43, 44, 45, 46; *229:* 174
Chorney, Steve *221:* 63
Chow, Frances J. Soo Ping *206:* 36
Chowdhury, Subrata *62:* 130; *162:* 22, 23
Christelow, Eileen *38:* 44; *83:* 198, 199; *90:* 57, 58; *184:* 26
Christensen, Bonnie *93:* 100; *153:* 67; *213:* 29, 30
Christensen, Gardell Dano *1:* 57
Christensen, James C. *140:* 226
Christiana, David *90:* 64; *135:* 13; *171:* 7; *195:* 26, 27; *237:* 12
Christiansen, Per *40:* 24
Christie, R. Gregory *116:* 107; *127:* 20, 21; *162:* 179; *164:* 114; *165:* 137; *174:* 157; *179:* 172; *185:* 17, 18, 19; *200:* 2; *204:* 85; *215:* 207; *218:* 57; *220:* 80, 130; *225:* 45, 46, 47; *226:* 211; *231:* 113; *235:* 167
Christy, Howard Chandler *17:* 163, 164, 165, 168, 169; *19:* 186, 187; *21:* 22, 23, 24, 25
Christy, Jana *194:* 21
Chronister, Robert *23:* 138; *63:* 27; *69:* 167
Chu, Carol *237:* 108
Church, Caroline Jayne *179:* 27; *219:* 28, 29
Church, Frederick *YABC 1:* 155
Chute, Marchette *1:* 59
Chwast, Jacqueline *1:* 63; *2:* 275; *6:* 46, 47; *11:* 125; *12:* 202; *14:* 235
Chwast, Seymour *3:* 128, 129; *18:* 43; *27:* 152; *92:* 79; *96:* 56, 57, 58; *146:* 32, 33; *197:* 99
Cieslawski, Steve *101:* 142; *127:* 116; *158:* 169, 171; *190:* 174; *212:* 85; *228:* 123
Cinelli, Lisa *146:* 253
Cirlin, Edgard *2:* 168
Clairin, Georges *53:* 109
Clapp, John *105:* 66; *109:* 58; *126:* 7; *129:* 148; *130:* 165; *195:* 48; *220:* 102
Clark, Brenda *119:* 85; *153:* 55
Clark, David *77:* 164; *134:* 144, 145; *216:* 66, 67
Clark, Emma Chichester
    See Chichester Clark, Emma
Clark, Robert *227:* 170
Clark, Victoria *35:* 159
Clarke, Greg *169:* 134; *215:* 47, 115; *237:* 119
Clarke, Gus *72:* 226; *134:* 31
Clarke, Harry *23:* 172, 173
Clarke, Peter *75:* 102
Claverie, Jean *38:* 46; *88:* 29
Clavis, Philippe Goossens *182:* 167
Clay, Wil *203:* 29
Clayton, Elaine *159:* 60; *209:* 32

Clayton, Robert *9:* 181
Cleary, Brian P. *186:* 37
Cleaver, Elizabeth *8:* 204; *23:* 36
Cleland, Janet *225:* 111; *226:* 48
Cleland, T.M. *26:* 92
Clemens, Peter *61:* 125
Clement, Charles *20:* 38
Clement, Gary *186:* 79; *191:* 32
Clement, Janet *182:* 50
Clement, Nathan *200:* 30
Clement, Rod *97:* 42; *234:* 68, 69
Clement, Stephen *88:* 3
Clementson, John *84:* 213
Clemesha, David *192:* 49, 50
Cleminson, Kate *221:* 26
Clevin, Jorgen *7:* 50
Clifford, Judy *34:* 163; *45:* 198
Clokey, Art *59:* 44
Clouse, Dennis *187:* 158
Clouse, James *84:* 15
Clouse, Nancy L. *78:* 31; *114:* 90; *225:* 117
Clover, Peter *152:* 45
Cneut, Carll *156:* 166; *165:* 67; *197:* 26
Coalson, Glo *9:* 72, 85; *25:* 155; *26:* 42; *35:* 212; *53:* 31; *56:* 154; *94:* 37, 38, 193
Cober, Alan E. *17:* 158; *32:* 77; *49:* 127
Cober-Gentry, Leslie *92:* 111
Cocca-Leffler, Maryann *80:* 46; *136:* 60; *139:* 193; *194:* 31, 33, 34
Cochran, Bobbye *11:* 52
Cochran, Josh *221:* 27
CoConis, Ted *4:* 41; *46:* 41; *51:* 104
Cocozza, Chris *87:* 18; *110:* 173; *111:* 149
Cockroft, Jason *152:* 20
Coerr, Eleanor *1:* 64; *67:* 52
Coes, Peter *35:* 172
Cogancherry, Helen *52:* 143; *69:* 131; *77:* 93; *78:* 220; *109:* 204; *110:* 129; *203:* 92
Coggins, Jack *2:* 69
Cohen, Alix *7:* 53
Cohen, Lisa *225:* 49
Cohen, Miriam *155:* 23, 24
Cohen, Nancy R. *165:* 35
Cohen, Santiago *164:* 26; *215:* 52, 199
Cohen, Sheldon *105:* 33, 34; *166:* 46, 47
Cohen, Vincent O. *19:* 243
Cohen, Vivien *11:* 112
Coker, Paul *51:* 172
Colbert, Anthony *15:* 41; *20:* 193
Colby, C.B. *3:* 47
Cole, Babette *58:* 172; *96:* 63, 64; *155:* 29
Cole, Brock *68:* 223; *72:* 36, 37, 38, 192; *127:* 23; *136:* 64, 65; *197:*
Cole, Gwen *87:* 185
Cole, Henry *178:* 120; *181:* 42, 43; *189:* 60; *213:* 35, 36; *222:* 139
Cole, Herbert *28:* 104
Cole, Michael *59:* 46
Cole, Olivia H.H. *1:* 134; *3:* 223; *9:* 111; *38:* 104
Cole, Rachael *209:* 39
Colin, Paul *102:* 59; *123:* 118; *126:* 152; *192:* 129; *234:* 129
Colley, Jacqui *202:* 20
Collicott, Sharleen *98:* 39; *143:* 29, 30
Collier, Bryan *126:* 54; *151:* 166; *174:* 16, 17, 18; *204:* 18, 19; *208:* 84; *211:* 143; *228:* 128
Collier, David *13:* 127
Collier, John *27:* 179; *208:* 154
Collier, Steven *50:* 52
Collier-Morales, Roberta *168:* 61
Collins, Heather *66:* 84; *67:* 68; *81:* 40; *98:* 192, 193; *129:* 95, 96, 98
Collins, Matt *167:* 90; *231:* 9
Collins, Ross *140:* 23, 24; *200:* 36, 37; *209:* 54
Colman, Audrey *146:* 161

Colón, Raul *108:* 112; *113:* 5; *117:* 167; *134:* 112; *146:* 23; *159:* 92; *166:* 73; *180:* 107; *186:* 156; *190:* 6; *193:* 24, 205; *202:* 21, 22, 23; *217:* 68; *220:* 126, 157; *226:* 118; *227:* 165; *232:* 122
Colonna, Bernard *21:* 50; *28:* 103; *34:* 140; *43:* 180; *78:* 150
Comport, Sally Wern *117:* 169; *169:* 104; *190:* 42; *207:* 50
Conahan, Carolyn *215:* 17
Conde, J.M. *100:* 120
Condon, Grattan *54:* 85 Condon, Ken *161:* 44; *195:* 28, 29
Cone, Ferne Geller *39:* 49
Cone, J. Morton *39:* 49
Conklin, Paul *43:* 62
Connelly, Gwen *212:* 30
Connelly, James *198:* 12
Connolly, Howard *67:* 88
Connolly, Jerome P. *4:* 128; *28:* 52
Connolly, Peter *47:* 60
Conoly, Walle *110:* 224
Conover, Chris *31:* 52; *40:* 184; *41:* 51; *44:* 79; *213:* 39
Conroy, Melissa *226:* 54
Constantin, Pascale *207:* 159
Contreras, Gerry *72:* 9
Converse, James *38:* 70
Conway *62:* 62
Conway, Michael *69:* 12; *81:* 3; *92:* 108
Cook, Ande *188:* 135
Cook, G.R. *29:* 165
Cook, Joel *108:* 160
Cook, Lynette *228:* 211
Cookburn, W.V. *29:* 204
Cooke, Donald E. *2:* 77
Cooke, Tom *52:* 118
Coomaraswamy, A.K. *50:* 100
Coombs, Charles *43:* 65
Coombs, Deborah *139:* 175
Coombs, Patricia *2:* 82; *3:* 52; *22:* 119; *51:* 32, 33, 34, 35, 36, 37, 38, 39, 40, 42, 43
Cooney, Barbara *6:* 16, 17, 50; *12:* 42; *13:* 92; *15:* 145; *16:* 74, 111; *18:* 189; *23:* 38, 89, 93; *32:* 138; *38:* 105; *59:* 48, 49, 51, 52, 53; *74:* 222; *81:* 100; *91:* 25; *96:* 71, 72, 74; *100:* 149; *YABC 2:* 10
Cooper, Elisha *157:* 38, 39; *234:* 45, 46, 47
Cooper, Floyd *79:* 95; *81:* 45; *84:* 82; *85:* 74; *91:* 118; *96:* 77, 78; *103:* 149; *144:* 54; *145:* 151; *159:* 198; *176:* 133, 134; *187:* 26, 27, 28, 29; *188:* 22; *199:* 175; *219:* 66; *227:* 38, 39, 40, 42
Cooper, Heather *50:* 39
Cooper, Helen *102:* 42, 43, 44
Cooper, Mario *24:* 107
Cooper, Marjorie *7:* 112
Cope, Jane *61:* 201; *108* 52
Copeland, Mark *180:* 12
Copelman, Evelyn *8:* 61; *18:* 25
Copley, Heather *30:* 86; *45:* 57
Corace, Jen *208:* 48
Corbett, Grahame *30:* 114; *43:* 67
Corbett, Tom *234:* 99
Corbino, John *19:* 248
Corcos, Lucille *2:* 223; *10:* 27; *34:* 66
Cordell, Matthew *197:* 93; *199:* 20, 21
Córdova, Amy *220:* 194
Corey, Robert *9:* 34
Corlass, Heather *10:* 7
Cornell, James *27:* 60
Cornell, Jeff *11:* 58
Cornell, Laura *94:* 179; *95:* 25
Corr, Christopher *204:* 98
Corral, Ridrigs *212:* 87
Corrigan, Barbara *8:* 37
Corrigan, Patrick *145:* 149
Corwin, Judith Hoffman *10:* 28
Corwin, Oliver *191:* 119
Cory, Fanny Y. *20:* 113; *48:* 29
Cosentino, Ralph *169:* 32

Cosgrove, Margaret *3:* 100; *47:* 63; *82:* 133
Costabel, Eva Deutsch *45:* 66, 67
Costanza, John *58:* 7, 8, 9
Costello, Chris *86:* 78
Costello, David F. *23:* 55
Côté, Geneviéve *184:* 37, 39; *210:* 256; *211:* 151
Cote, Nancy *126:* 139; *156:* 101; *174:* 101; *182:* 53, 54, 55; *222:* 49
Cottenden, Jeff *190:* 45
Couch, Greg *94:* 124; *110:* 13; *162:* 31; *168:* 149; *199:* 22; *216:* 144; *229:* 103
Councell, Ruth Tietjen *79:* 29
Courtney, Cathy *58:* 69, 144; *59:* 15; *61:* 20, 87
Courtney, R. *35:* 110
Counihan, Claire *133:* 106
Cousineau, Normand *89:* 180; *112:* 76; *227:* 75
Cousins, Lucy *172:* 53, 54; *205:* 34, 35
Couture, Christin *41:* 209
Covarrubias, Miguel *35:* 118, 119, 123, 124, 125
Coville, Katherine *32:* 57; *36:* 167; *92:* 38
Covington, Neverne *113:* 87
Cowdrey, Richard *169:* 170; *178:* 205; *204:* 22, 23; *215:* 31
Cowell, Cressida *140:* 39
Cowell, Lucinda *77:* 54
Cowles, Rose *203:* 164, 167
Cox *43:* 93
Cox, Charles *8:* 20
Cox, David *56:* 37; *90:* 63; *119:* 38
Cox, Palmer *24:* 76, 77
Cox, Paul *226:* 57, 58
Cox, Steve *140:* 96
Coxe, Molly *69:* 44
Coxon, Michele *158:* 80
Crabb, Gordon *70:* 39
Crabtree, Judith *98:* 42
Craft, Kinuko *22:* 182; *36:* 220; *53:* 122, 123, 148,149; *74:* 12; *81:* 129; *86:* 31; *89:* 139; *127:* 27, 28, 29; *132:* 142; *139:* 38
Craig, Daniel *177:* 67; *180:* 11; *185:* 203; *211:* 212; *224:* 27; *229:* 59
Craig, David *136:* 198; *205:* 37; *236:* 188
Craig, Helen *49:* 76; *62:* 70, 71, 72; *69:* 141; *94:* 42, 43, 44; *112:* 53; *135:* 101, 102; *213:* 45, 46, 47, 55, 81, 82
Crane, Alan H. *1:* 217
Crane, H.M. *13:* 111
Crane, Jack *43:* 183
Crane, Jordan *174:* 21
Crane, Walter *18:* 46, 47, 48, 49, 53, 54, 56, 57, 59, 60, 61; *22:* 128; *24:* 210, 217; *100:* 70, 71
Cravath, Lynne Avril *98:* 45; *182:* 58, 59; *216:* 48; *219:* 61; *220:* 124; *224:* 183; *228:* 74; *229:* 89
Crawford, Allen *212:* 181
Crawford, Denise *137:* 213
Crawford, Will *43:* 77
Credle, Ellis *1:* 69
Czekaj, Jef *217:* 44; *218:* 77
Czernecki, Stefan *154:* 104; *178:* 68, 69
Cresci, Anne *232:* 148
Crespi, Francesca *87:* 90
Cressy, Michael *124:* 55; *203:* 132
Crews, Donald *32:* 59, 60; *76:* 42, 43, 44
Crews, Nina *97:* 49
Crichlow, Ernest *74:* 88; *83:* 203
Crilley, Mark *210:* 71
Croft, James *150:* 57
Crofut, Bob *80:* 87; *81:* 47
Crofut, Susan *23:* 61
Croll, Carolyn *80:* 137; *102:* 52; *235:* 166
Cross, Peter *56:* 78; *63:* 60, 65
Crossman, David A. *219:* 38
Crowe, Elizabeth *88:* 144
Crowell, Pers *3:* 125

Cruikshank, George *15:* 76, 83; *22:* 74, 75, 76, 77, 78, 79,80, 81, 82, 84, 137; *24:* 22, 23
Crump, Fred H. *11:* 62
Cruz, Ray *6:* 55; *70:* 234; *123:* 173; *172:* 192
Csatari, Joe *44:* 82; *55:* 152; *63:* 25, 28; *102:* 58
Cuetara, Mittie *158:* 85
Cuffari, Richard *4:* 75; *5:* 98; *6:* 56; *7:* 13,84, 153; *8:* 148, 155; *9:* 89; *11:* 19; *12:* 55, 96,114; *15:* 51, 202; *18:* 5; *20:* 139; *21:* 197; *22:* 14, 192; *23:* 15, 106; *25:* 97; *27:* 133; *28:* 196; *29:* 54; *30:* 85; *31:* 35; *36:* 101; *38:* 171; *42:* 97; *44:* 92, 192; *45:* 212, 213; *46:* 36, 198; *50:* 164; *54:* 80, 136, 137, 145; *56:* 17; *60:* 63; *66:* 49, 50; *70:* 41; *71:* 132; *77:* 157; *78:* 58, 149; *79:* 120; *85:* 2, 152
Cugat, Xavier *19:* 120
Cumings, Art *35:* 160
Cummings, Chris *29:* 167
Cummings, Michael *159:* 142
Cummings, Pat *42:* 61; *61:* 99; *69:* 205; *71:* 57,58; *78:* 24, 25; *93:* 75; *107:* 49, 50; *164:* 259; *203:* 45, 46
Cummings, Richard *24:* 119
Cummings, Terrance *227:* 49, 172
Cummings, Troy *236:* 83
Cunette, Lou *20:* 93; *22:* 125
Cunningham, Aline *25:* 180
Cunningham, David *11:* 13
Cunningham, Imogene *16:* 122, 127
Cunningham, Kelley *176:* 159
Cupples, Pat *107:* 12; *126:* 109; *182:* 13; *198:* 68; *217:* 21, 22
Curlee, Lynn *98:* 48; *141:* 39; *190:* 48
Currey, Anna *190:* 145; *202:* 130, 132
Curry, John Steuart *2:* 5; *19:* 84; *34:* 36; *144:* 126
Curry, Tom *127:* 131; *185:* 25, 26
Curtis, Bruce *23:* 96; *30:* 88; *36:* 22
Curtis, Neil *167:* 30
Curtis, Stacy *205:* 38
Cusack, Margaret *58:* 49, 50, 51
Cushman, Doug *65:* 57; *101:* 39, 40; *133:* 179; *157:* 45; *186:* 157; *210:* 76, 77; *232:* 132
Cutting, Ann *196:* 194
Cyrus, Kurt *132:* 39; *179:* 36, 37; *236:* 61, 62
Czechowski, Alicia *95:* 21; *171:* 37
Czernecki, Stefan *117:* 173

D

Dabcovich, Lydia *25:* 105; *40:* 114; *99:* 75, 76
Dacey, Bob *82:* 175; *152:* 65
d'Achille, Gino *127:* 175, 176
Daigneault, Sylvie *236:* 65
Daily, Don *78:* 197; *220:* 154
Dain, Martin J. *35:* 75
Dale, Penny *127:* 224; *151:* 57; *160:* 89; *197:* 75; *232:* 188
Dale, Rae *72:* 197
Daley, Joann *50:* 22
Dalton, Anne *40:* 62; *63:* 119
Dalton, Max *234:* 2, 52
Daly, Deborah M. *74:* 213
Daly, Jim *103:* 60; *150:* 48
Daly, Jude *138:* 118, 119; *213:* 41; *222:* 56, 57
Daly, Nicholas *37:* 53; *76:* 48, 49
Daly, Niki *107:* 15; *114:* 38, 39, 40; *164:* 86; *192:* 53; *198:* 26, 27
Daly, Paul *97:* 205
Dalziel, Brothers *33:* 113
D'Amato, Alex *9:* 48; *20:* 25
D'Amato, Janet *9:* 48; *20:* 25; *26:* 118
D'Amico, Steve *170:* 52
Danalis, Johnny *167:* 27
D'Andrea, Domenick *183:* 108
Daniel, Alan *23:* 59; *29:* 110; *76:* 50, 53, 55, 56; *153:* 76 *115:* 74; *134:* 70
Daniel, Lea *76:* 53, 55; *153:* 76

Daniel, Lewis C. *20:* 216
Daniels, Beau *73:* 4
Daniels, Steve *22:* 16
Daniels, Stewart *56:* 12
Dann, Bonnie *31:* 83
Dann, Penny *82:* 128
Danska, Herbert *24:* 219
Danyell, Alice *20:* 27
Darbyshire, Kristen *218:* 41
Dardik, Helen *208:* 200
Darley, F.O.C. *16:* 145; *19:* 79, 86, 88, 185; *21:* 28,36; *35:* 76, 77, 78, 79, 80, 81; *YABC 2:* 175
Darling, Lois *3:* 59; *23:* 30, 31
Darling, Louis *1:* 40, 41; *2:* 63; *3:* 59; *23:* 30,31; *43:* 54, 57, 59; *121:* 53
Darnell, K.L. *210:* 247
Darrow, David R. *84:* 101
Darrow, Whitney, Jr. *13:* 25; *38:* 220, 221
Darwin, Beatrice *43:* 54
Darwin, Len *24:* 82
Dastolfo, Frank *33:* 179
Dauber, Liz *1:* 22; *3:* 266; *30:* 49
Daugherty, James *3:* 66; *8:* 178; *13:* 27, 28, 161; *18:* 101; *19:* 72; *29:* 108; *32:* 156; *42:* 84; *YABC 1:* 256; *2:* 174
d'Aulaire, Edgar Parin *5:* 51; *66:* 53
d'Aulaire, Ingri Parin *5:* 51; *66:* 53
Davalos, Felipe *99:* 197; *159:* 66; *174:* 163; *235:* 52
Davenier, Christine *125:* 88; *127:* 32; *128:* 152; *179:* 39, 40; *216:* 84, 85, 86, 87; *218:* 62, 63; *224:* 73; *237:* 51
Davick, Linda *151:* 124; *208:* 187
David, Jacques-Louis *193:* 22
David, Jonathan *19:* 37
Davidson, Kevin *28:* 154
Davidson, Raymond *32:* 61
Davie, Helen K. *77:* 48, 49
Davies, Andy Robert *205:* 169
Davies, Lottie *214:* 69
Davis, Allen *20:* 11; *22:* 45; *27:* 222; *29:* 157; *41:* 99; *47:* 99; *50:* 84; *52:* 105
Davis, Bette J. *15:* 53; *23:* 95
Davis, Dimitris *45:* 95
Davis, Eleanor *209:* 33
Davis, Hendon *151:* 122
Davis, Jack E. *145:* 139; *175:* 84, 85; *208:* 102; *210:* 81, 82; *213:* 151
Davis, Jim *32:* 63, 64
Davis, Katie *152:* 52, 53, 54; *208:* 52
Davis, Lambert *110:* 23, 24; *176:* 58; *237:* 20
Davis, Marguerite *31:* 38; *34:* 69, 70; *100:* 34; *YABC 1:* 126, 230
Davis, Natalie *235:* 196
Davis, Nelle *69:* 191
Davis, Paul *78:* 214
Davis, Rich *206:* 38
Davis, Stuart *211:* 69
Davis, Yvonne LeBrun *94:* 144
Davisson, Virginia H. *44:* 178
DaVolls, Andy *85:* 53
Dawson, Diane *24:* 127; *42:* 126; *52:* 130; *68:* 104
Dawson, Janine *215:* 198
Dawson, Willow *208:* 54; *216:* 119
Day, Alexandra *67:* 59; *97:* 54; *166:* 65; *169:* 40; *197:* 50, 51, 52, 54
Day, Larry *169:* 88; *185:* 59; *227:* 55
Day, Rob *94:* 110; *127:* 24; *197:* 32
Dean, Bob *19:* 211
Dean, David *192:* 55
de Angeli, Marguerite *1:* 77; *27:* 62, 65, 66, 67, 69, 70, 72; *100:* 75, 76; *YABC 1:* 166
DeArmond, Dale *70:* 47
Deas, Michael *27:* 219, 221; *30:* 156; *67:* 134; *72:* 24; *75:* 155; *84:* 206; *88:* 124
Deas, Rich *191:* 87; *193:* 10; *212:* 79
deBarros, Jim *196:* 60
Debon, Nicolas *151:* 60; *177:* 46
de Bosschere, Jean *19:* 252; *21:* 4; *186:* 44, 45

De Bruyn, M(onica) G. *13:* 30, 31
Decker, C.B. *172:* 120; *215:* 94
De Cuir, John F. *1:* 28, 29
Deeter, Catherine *74:* 110; *103:* 150; *137:* 50
Degen, Bruce *40:* 227, 229; *57:* 28, 29; *56:* 156; *75:* 229; *76:* 19; *81:* 36, 37; *92:* 26; *93:* 199; *97:* 56, 58, 59; *124:* 40; *147:* 39, 40, 41; *168:* 23; *205:* 45, 46; *231:* 46, 47, 48, 49
De Grazia *14:* 59; *39:* 56, 57
DeGrazio, George *88:* 40
deGroat, Diane *9:* 39; *18:* 7; *23:* 123; *28:* 200, 201; *31:* 58, 59; *34:* 151; *41:* 152; *43:* 88; *46:* 40, 200; *49:* 163; *50:* 89; *52:* 30, 34; *54:* 43; *63:* 5; *70:* 136; *71:* 99; *73:* 117,156; *77:* 34; *85:* 48; *86:* 201; *87:* 142; *90:* 72, 73, 143; *95:* 182; *111:* 123; *118:* 160; *126:* 8; *130:* 130; *138:* 93, 94; *169:* 46, 47
de Groot, Lee *6:* 21
Deines, Brian *110:* 139; *220:* 36, 37
DeJohn, Marie *89:* 78
Dekhteryov, B. *61:* 158
de Kiefte, Kees *94:* 107
Delacre, Lulu *36:* 66; *156:* 35; *202:* 10, 53; *209:* 36
Delaney, A. *21:* 78
Delaney, Michael *180:* 16
Delaney, Molly *80:* 43
Delaney, Ned *28:* 68; *56:* 80; *102:* 11
DeLapine, Jim *79:* 21
De La Roche Saint Andre, Anne *75:* 37
de Larrea, Victoria *6:* 119, 204; *29:* 103; *72:* 203; *87:* 199
Delehanty, Joan W. *223:* 165
DeLeon, Melanie *210:* 43
Delessert, Étienne *7:* 140; *46:* 61, 62, 63, 65, 67, 68; *130:* 38, 39, 40, 41, 42; *179:* 46, 47, 48, 49; *YABC 2:* 209
Delezenne, Christine *186:* 126
Delinois, Alix *228:* 40
Del Negro, Janice *196:* 161
Delon, Melanie *216:* 30
DeLorenzo, Christopher *154:* 149
Delulio, John *15:* 54
DeLuna, Tony *88:* 95
Demarest, Chris L. *45:* 68, 69, 70; *73:* 172, 173, 176; *78:* 106; *82:* 48, 49; *89:* 212; *92:* 86; *128:* 57, 58; *175:* 46, 48
De Mejo, Oscar *40:* 67
De Muth, Roger *205:* 184; *221:* 35
Demi *11:* 135; *15:* 245; *66:* 129, 130; *89:* 216; *102:* 66, 67, 68; *210:* 86, 87, 89
Denetsosie, Hoke *13:* 126; *82:* 34
Denise, Christopher *147:* 43, 44; *176:* 101; *193:* 35, 36, 37; *201:* 37
Dennis, Morgan *18:* 68, 69; *64:* 89
Dennis, Wesley *2:* 87; *3:* 111; *11:* 132; *18:* 71, 72, 73, 74; *22:* 9; *24:* 196, 200; *46:* 178; *69:* 94, 96; *129:* 62
Denos, Julia *202:* 26
Denslow, W.W. *16:* 84, 85, 86, 87; *18:* 19, 20, 24; *29:* 211; *100:* 21
Denton, Kady MacDonald *110:* 82; *130:* 70; *181:* 54, 55, 56; *192:* 75
Denton, Phil *220:* 6
Denton, Terry *72:* 163; *174:* 26; *186:* 52; *196:* 83, 84
DePalma, Mary Newell *132:* 114; *139:* 75; *185:* 30, 31; *186:* 121; *213:* 62
dePaola, Tomie *8:* 95; *9:* 93; *11:* 69; 25; 103; *28:* 157; *29:* 80; *39:* 52, 53; *40:* 226; *46:* 187; *59:* 61, 62, 63, 64, 65, 66, 67, 68, 69, 71, 72, 74; *62:* 19; *108:* 63, 67, 68, 70; *155:* 62, 64, 66; *180:* 105; *200:* 47, 48, 49, 50; *226:* 116
Deraney, Michael J. *77:* 35; *78:* 148
deRosa, Dee *70:* 48; *71:* 210; *91:* 78
Dervaux, Isabelle *111:* 117
DeSaix, Deborah Durland *180:* 15; *188:* 24
De Saulles, Tony *119:* 39
de Sève, Peter *146:* 261; *207:* 78; *219:* 42
Deshaprabhu, Meera Dayal *86:* 192

Desimini, Lisa *86:* 68; *94:* 47; *96:* 7; *104:* 107; *125:* 194; *131:* 180; *172:* 56; *216:* 89, 90
de St. Menin, Charles *70:* 17
Detmold, Edward J. *22:* 104, 105, 106, 107; *35:* 120; *64:* 5; *YABC 2:* 203
Detrich, Susan *20:* 133
Deutermann, Diana *77:* 175
DeVelasco, Joseph E. *21:* 51
de Veyrac, Robert *YABC 2:* 19
DeVille, Edward A. *4:* 235
de Visser, John *55:* 119
Devito, Bert *12:* 164
Devlin, Harry *11:* 74; *74:* 63, 65; *136:* 77, 78
Dewan, Ted *108:* 73; *157:* 55; *165:* 129; *226:* 67, 68, 69
Dewar, Nick *133:* 122
Dewdney, Anna *184:* 43, 44; *232:* 46, 47, 48
Dewey, Ariane *7:* 64; *33:* 195; *35:* 208; *68:* 16,17; *75:* 46; *93:* 91; *94:* 197; *109:* 65, 66, 67; *125:* 2, 3, 4, 5; *127:* 188; *143:* 25; *178:* 17, 19, 74; *188:* 166; *202:* 164; *231:* 176
Dewey, Jennifer (Owings) *58:* 54; *64:* 214; *65:* 207; *88:* 169; *103:* 45
Dewey, Kenneth *39:* 62; *51:* 23; *56:* 163
de Zanger, Arie *30:* 40
Diakité, Baba Wagué *174:* 28
Diamond, Donna *21:* 200; *23:* 63; *26:* 142; *35:* 83, 84, 85, 86, 87, 88, 89; *38:* 78; *40:* 147; *44:* 152; *50:* 144; *53:* 126; *69:* 46, 47, 48, 201; *71:* 133; *123:* 19
Dias, Ron *71:* 67
Diaz, David *80:* 213; *96:* 83, 84; *108:* 228; *110:* 29; *149:* 106; *150:* 63; *179:* 160; *184:* 95, 97; *189:* 51, 52, 53; *221:* 86; *229:* 37, 38, 39, 40
di Bartolo, Jim *225:* 53
Dibley, Glin *138:* 83; *141:* 128; *211:* 162; *221:* 61
DiCesare, Joe *70:* 38; *71:* 63, 106; *79:* 214; *93:* 147; *116:* 217; *143:* 111; *166:* 57
Dick, John Henry *8:* 181
Dickens, Frank *34:* 131
Dickey, Robert L. *15:* 279
Dickson, Mora *84:* 21
Didier, Sam *166:* 114
Dietz, James *128:* 223; *193:* 136
di Fate, Vincent *37:* 70; *90:* 11; *93:* 60; *109:* 219, 220
Di Fiori, Lawrence *10:* 51; *12:* 190; *27:* 97; *40:* 219; *93:* 57; *130:* 45
Digby, Desmond *97:* 180
Dignan, James *196:* 143; *234:* 136
Di Grazia, Thomas *32:* 66; *35:* 241
Dillard, Annie *10:* 32
Dillard, Sarah *136:* 186; *217:* 53
Dillon, Corinne B. *1:* 139
Dillon, Diane *4:* 104, 167; *6:* 23; *13:* 29; *15:* 99; *26:* 148; *27:* 136, 201; *51:* 29, 48, 51, 52, 53, 54,55, 56, 57, 58, 59, 60, 61, 62; *54:* 155; *56:* 69; *58:* 127,128; *61:* 95; *62:* 27; *64:* 46; *68:* 3; *69:* 209; *74:* 89; *79:* 92; *86:* 89; *92:* 28, 177; *93:* 7, 210; *94:* 239, 240; *97:* 167; *106:* 58, 59,61, 64; *107:* 3; *139:* 246; *167:* 77; *189:* 202; *191:* 191; *194:* 45, 46, 48, 49
Dillon, Leo *4:* 104, 167; *6:* 23; *13:* 29; *15:* 99; *26:* 148; *27:* 136, 201; *51:* 29, 48, 51, 52, 53, 54,55, 56, 57, 58, 59, 60, 61, 62; *54:* 155; *56:* 69; *58:* 127,128; *61:* 95; *62:* 27; *64:* 46; *68:* 3; *69:* 209; *74:* 89; *79:* 92; *86:* 89; *92:* 28, 177; *93:* 7, 210; *94:* 239, 240; *97:* 167; *106:* 58, 59,61, 64; *107:* 3; *139:* 246; *167:* 77; *189:* 202; *191:* 191; *194:* 45, 46, 48, 49
Dillon, Sharon Saseen *59:* 179, 188
DiMaccio, Gerald *121:* 80
DiMaggio, Joe *36:* 22
DiMassi, Gina *169:* 17
Dinan, Carol *25:* 169; *59:* 75
Dines, Glen *7:* 66, 67

Dinesen, Thomas *44:* 37
Dinh, Pham Viet *167:* 184
Dinnerstein, Harvey *42:* 63, 64, 65, 66, 67, 68; *50:* 146
Dinsdale, Mary *10:* 65; *11:* 171
Dinyer, Eric *86:* 148; *109:* 163; *110:* 239; *124:* 11; *150:* 69; *170:* 4; *171:* 30
Dion, Nathalie *170:* 124; *213:* 52
DiPucchio, Kelly *230:* 3
DiRocco, Carl *181:* 23
DiSalvo-Ryan, DyAnne *59:* 77; *62:* 185; *117:* 46; *144:* 64; *150:* 153; *186:* 162
Disney, Walt *28:* 71, 72, 73, 76, 77, 78, 79, 80, 81, 87, 88, 89,90, 91, 94
DiTerlizzi, Tony *105:* 7; *147:* 22; *154:* 31, 32, 33; *214:* 74; *236:* 33
Divito, Anna *83:* 159
Dixon, Don *74:* 17; *109:* 196
Dixon, Larry *127:* 125
Dixon, Maynard *20:* 165
Dizin, Pascal *230:* 25, 26
Doares, Robert G. *20:* 39
Dob, Bob *205:* 14
Dobias, Frank *22:* 162
Dobrin, Arnold *4:* 68
Dobson, Steven Gaston *102:* 103
Docherty, Thomas *218:* 45, 46
Dockray, Tracy *139:* 77
Docktor, Irv *43:* 70
Dodd, Ed *4:* 69
Dodd, Emma *203:* 57
Dodd, Julie *74:* 73
Dodd, Lynley *35:* 92; *86:* 71; *132:* 45, 46, 47
Dodge, Bill *96:* 36; *118:* 7, 8, 9; *133:* 135
Dodgson, Charles L. *20:* 148; *33:* 146; *YABC 2:* 98
Dodson, Bert *9:* 138; *14:* 195; *42:* 55; *54:* 8; *60:* 49; *101:* 125
Dodson, Emma *235:* 43
Dodson, Liz Brenner *105:* 117; *111:* 15
Dohanos, Stevan *16:* 10
Dolce, J. Ellen *74:* 147; *75:* 41
Dolch, Marguerite P. *50:* 64
Dolesch, Susanne *34:* 49
Dollar, Diane *57:* 32
Dolobowsky, Mena *81:* 54
Dolson, Hildegarde *5:* 57
Domanska, Janina *6:* 66, 67; *YABC 1:* 166
Domi *134:* 113
Dominguez, El *53:* 94
Domjan, Joseph *25:* 93
Domm, Jeffrey C. *84:* 69; *135:* 70
Donahey, William *68:* 209
Donahue, Dorothy *76:* 170
Donahue, Vic *2:* 93; *3:* 190; *9:* 44
Donald, Elizabeth *4:* 18
Donalty, Alison *149:* 195, 196, 197
Donato *85:* 59; *149:* 204; *191:* 19
Donato, Michael A. *200:* 143
Doner, Kim *208:* 10
Doney, Todd L.W. *87:* 12; *93:* 112; *98:* 135; *101:* 57; *104:* 40; *118:* 163; *135:* 162, 163; *151:* 18; *227:* 79; *236:* 74
Donna, Natalie *9:* 52
Donohue, Dorothy *95:* 2; *132:* 30; *176:* 54, 55; *178:* 77, 78, 79
Donovan, Jane Monroe *237:* 28
Dooling, Michael *82:* 19; *105:* 55; *106:* 224; *125:* 135; *171:* 46; *172:* 12; *176:* 120; *197:* 89; *220:* 39, 40
Doran, Ben-Ami *128:* 189
Doran, Colleen *211:* 48
Dore, Gustave *18:* 169, 172, 175; *19:* 93, 94, 95, 96, 97, 98,99, 100, 101, 102, 103, 104, 105; *23:* 188; *25:* 197, 199
Doremus, Robert *6:* 62; *13:* 90; *30:* 95, 96, 97; *38:* 97
Dorfman, Ronald *11:* 128
Doriau *86:* 59; *91:* 152

Dorman, Brandon *197:* 35; *204:* 6; *210:* 104; *212:* 95; *216:* 156; *222:* 133; *234:* 92; *237:* 117
Dormer, Frank W. *200:* 55; *222:* 48; *237:* 124
Dorros, Arthur *78:* 42, 43; *91:* 28
Doruyter, Karel *165:* 105
dos Santos, Joyce Audy *57:* 187, 189
Doty, Roy *28:* 98; *31:* 32; *32:* 224; *46:* 157; *82:* 71; *142:* 7
Doucet, Bob *132:* 238; *169:* 159
Dougherty, Charles *16:* 204; *18:* 74
Doughty, Rebecca *177:* 174; *222:* 159
Doughty, Thomas *118:* 31; *140:* 60
Douglas, Aaron *31:* 103
Douglas, Allen *223:* 53; *230:* 148
Douglas, Carole Nelson *73:* 48
Douglas, Goray *13:* 151
Dow, Brian *150:* 92
Dowd, Jason *132:* 51, 52; *164:* 244
Dowd, Vic *3:* 244; *10:* 97
Dowden, Anne Ophelia *7:* 70, 71; *13:* 120
Dowdy, Mrs. Regera *29:* 100
Downard, Barry *202:* 32
Downes, Belinda *180:* 29
Downing, Julie *60:* 140; *81:* 50; *86:* 200; *99:* 129
Doyle, Janet *56:* 31
Doyle, Richard *21:* 31, 32, 33; *23:* 231; *24:* 177; *31:* 87
Draper, Angie *43:* 84
Drath, Bill *26:* 34
Drawson, Blair *17:* 53; *126:* 65
Dray, Matt *177:* 47
Drescher, Henrik *105:* 60, 62, 63; *172:* 72
Drescher, Joan *30:* 100, 101; *35:* 245; *52:* 168; *137:* 52
Dressell, Peggy *186:* 41
Drew, Janet *201:* 177
Drew, Patricia *15:* 100
Dronzek, Laura *199:* 28, 29; *207:* 69
Drummond, Allan *209:* 41
Drummond, V.H. *6:* 70
Drury, Christian Potter *105:* 97; *186:* 224
Dubanevich, Arlene *56:* 44
Dubin, Jill *205:* 56; *217:* 25
Dubois, Claude K. *196:* 2
Dubois, Gerard *182:* 9
DuBurke, Randy *187:* 89; *222:* 136; *224:* 35
Ducak, Danilo *99:* 130; *108:* 214
Duchesne, Janet *6:* 162; *79:* 8
Duda, Jana *102:* 155; *209:* 134
Dudash, C. Michael *32:* 122; *77:* 134; *82:* 149; *212:* 93, 94
Duddle, Jonny *233:* 118
Duer, Douglas *34:* 177
Duewell, Kristina *195:* 76
Duffy, Daniel Mark *76:* 37; *101:* 196; *108:* 147, 148
Duffy, Joseph *38:* 203
Duffy, Pat *28:* 153
Dugan, Karen *181:* 26; *202:* 35
Dugin, Andrej *77:* 60
Dugina, Olga *77:* 60
Duke, Chris *8:* 195; *139:* 164
Duke, Kate *87:* 186; *90:* 78, 79, 80, 81; *192:* 21, 59, 60, 61, 63
Duke, Marion *165:* 87
Dulac, Edmund *19:* 108, 109, 110, 111, 112, 113, 114, 115, 117; *23:* 187; *25:* 152; *YABC 1:* 37; *2:* 147
Dulac, Jean *13:* 64
Dumas, Philippe *52:* 36, 37, 38, 39, 40, 41, 42, 43, 45; *119:* 40, 41, 42
Dunaway, Nancy *108:* 161
Dunbar, James *76:* 63
Dunbar, Polly *181:* 60, 61; *211:* 51, 52, 53; *212:* 42; *233:* 6
Duncan, Beverly *72:* 92
Duncan, John *116:* 94
Dunn, H.T. *62:* 196
Dunn, Harvey *34:* 78, 79, 80, 81

Dunn, Iris *5:* 175
Dunn, Phoebe *5:* 175
Dunne, Jeanette *72:* 57, 173, 222
Dunnick, Regan *176:* 51; *178:* 83, 84; *219:* 36; *224:* 144; *229:* 83
Dunnington, Tom *3:* 36; *18:* 281; *25:* 61; *31:* 159; *35:* 168; *48:* 195; *79:* 144; *82:* 230
Dunn-Ramsey, Marcy *117:* 131
Dunrea, Olivier *59:* 81; *118:* 53, 54; *124:* 43; *233:* 63, 64, 66
Duntze, Dorothee *88:* 28; *160:* 76
Dupasquier, Philippe *86:* 75; *104:* 76; *151:* 63
duPont, Lindsay Harper *207:* 39
DuQuette, Keith *90:* 83; *155:* 73, 74
Durand, Delphine *200:* 56
Durham, Sarah *192:* 248
Durney, Ryan *208:* 122
Duroussy, Nathalie *146:* 150
Durrell, Julie *82:* 62; *94:* 62
Dusíková, Maja *223:* 49
Dutz *6:* 59
Duvoisin, Roger *2:* 95; *6:* 76, 77; *7:* 197; *28:* 125; *30:* 101, 102, 103, 104, 105, 107; *47:* 205; *84:* 254
Dyer, Dale *141:* 71
Dyer, Jane *75:* 219; *129:* 28; *147:* 49, 50, 51; *168:* 121; *190:* 4; *191:* 57, 59, 60; *203:* 4
Dyer, Sarah *212:* 40
Dypold, Pat *15:* 37

E

E.V.B.
   See Boyle, Eleanor Vere (Gordon)
Eachus, Jennifer *29:* 74; *82:* 201; *164:* 153
Eadie, Bob *63:* 36
Eagle, Bruce *95:* 119
Eagle, Ellen *82:* 121; *89:* 3
Eagle, Jeremy *141:* 71
Eagle, Michael *11:* 86; *20:* 9; *23:* 18; *27:* 122; *28:* 57; *34:* 201; *44:* 189; *73:* 9; *78:* 235; *85:* 43
Earl-Bridges, Michele *159:* 128
Earle, Edwin *56:* 27
Earle, Olive L. *7:* 75
Earle, Vana *27:* 99
Earley, Lori *132:* 2; *186:* 4; *195:* 8
Early, Margaret *72:* 59
East, Jacqueline *218:* 198; *224:* 38
East, Stella *131:* 223
Eastman, P.D. *33:* 57
Easton, Reginald *29:* 181
Eaton, Tom *4:* 62; *6:* 64; *22:* 99; *24:* 124
Eaves, Edward *224:* 13
Ebbeler, Jeffrey *193:* 62; *206:* 45; *236:* 55
Ebel, Alex *11:* 89
Eberbach, Andrea *192:* 115
Ebert, Len *9:* 191; *44:* 47
Echevarria, Abe *37:* 69
Echo Hawk, Bunky *187:* 192
Eckersley, Maureen *48:* 62
Eckert, Horst *72:* 62
Ede, Janina *33:* 59
Edens, Cooper *49:* 81, 82, 83, 84, 85; *112:* 58
Edens, John *109:* 115
Edgar, Sarah E. *41:* 97
Edgerton, Perky *195:* 144
Edliq, Emily S. *131:* 107
Edrien *11:* 53
Edwards, Freya *45:* 102
Edwards, George Wharton *31:* 155
Edwards, Gunvor *2:* 71; *25:* 47; *32:* 71; *54:* 106
Edwards, Jeanne *29:* 257
Edwards, Linda Strauss *21:* 134; *39:* 123; *49:* 88, 89
Edwards, Michelle *152:* 62, 63
Edwards, Wallace *170:* 55
Egan, Tim *155:* 76, 77, 78

Egge, David *102:* 71
Eggenhofer, Nicholas *2:* 81
Eggleton, Bob *74:* 40; *81:* 190, 191; *105:* 6; *121:* 183; *149:* 203; *166:* 215
Egielski, Richard *11:* 90; *16:* 208; *33:* 236; *38:* 35; *49:* 91, 92, 93, 95, 212, 213, 214, 216; *79:* 122; *106:* 67, 68, 69; *134:* 135; *144:* 244; *163:* 82, 84; *207:* 125; *225:* 200
Ehlert, Lois *35:* 97; *69:* 51; *112:* 7; *113:* 208; *128:* 63, 64, 65; *172:* 77, 79, 80; *220:* 43, 44, 45, 46, 47, 48; *237:* 33, 34, 35, 36, 37, 38
Ehrlich, Bettina *1:* 83
Eitan, Ora *160:* 165
Eichenberg, Fritz *1:* 79; *9:* 54; *19:* 248; *23:* 170; *24:* 200; *26:* 208; *50:* 67, 68, 69, 70, 71, 72, 73,74, 75, 77, 79, 80, 81; *60:* 165; *100:* 137; *YABC 1:* 104, 105; *2:* 213
Einsel, Naiad *10:* 35; *29:* 136
Einsel, Walter *10:* 37
Einzig, Susan *3:* 77; *43:* 78; *67:* 155; *129:* 154
Eisner, Will *165:* 82, 83
Eitzen, Allan *9:* 56; *12:* 212; *14:* 226; *21:* 194; *38:* 162; *76:* 218
Eldridge, H. *54:* 109
Eldridge, Harold *43:* 83
Elgaard, Greta *19:* 241
Elgin, Kathleen *9:* 188; *39:* 69
Eliopoulos, Chris *234:* 56
Ellacott, S.E. *19:* 118
Elliot, David *192:* 26; *208:* 62, 63
Elliott, Mark *93:* 69; *105:* 108; *107:* 123; *140:* 53; *165:* 189; *173:* 67; *195:* 95; *203:* 67; *210:* 99; *221:* 57, 70; *230:* 147; *236:* 186
Elliott, Sarah M. *14:* 58
Ellis, Carson *216:* 210
Ellis, Dianne *130:* 208
Ellis, Jan Davey *88:* 50; *115:* 80
Ellis, Richard *130:* 47, 48
Ellison, Chris *196:* 66; *199:* 131; *207:* 193
Ellison, Pauline *55:* 21
Ellwand, David *213:* 60
Elmer, Richard *78:* 5
Elmore, Larry *90:* 8
Elschner, Géraldine *183:* 38
Elwell, Peter *195:* 150
Elwell, Tristan *110:* 39; *121:* 182; *127:* 46; *137:* 144; *141:* 173; *151:* 236; *158:* 264; *167:* 119, 120, 121; *169:* 20; *190:* 12; *202:* 16; *226:* 6; *233:* 181
Elzbieta *88:* 80, 81
Ember, Kathi *214:* 147; *234:* 58
Emberley, Ed *8:* 53; *70:* 53, 54; *146:* 65, 69, 70; *218:* 50
Emberley, Rebecca *218:* 50
Emberley, Michael *34:* 83; *80:* 72; *119:* 47, 48; *147:* 100; *158:* 115; *189:* 62, 64; *203:* 87, 89; *232:* 51, 52, 54
Emerling, Dorothy *104:* 27
Emery, Leslie *49:* 187
Emmett, Bruce *49:* 147; *80:* 175; *101:* 206; *220:* 200
Emond, Stephen *231:* 59
Emry-Perrott, Jennifer *61:* 57
Emshwiller, Ed *174:* 45
Endle, Kate *191:* 167; *207:* 41; *233:* 155
Engel, Christiane *231:* 61
Engel, Diana *70:* 57
Engle, Mort *38:* 64
Englebert, Victor *8:* 54
English, Mark *101:* 207; *220:* 201
Enik, Ted *142:* 39
Enos, Randall *20:* 183
Enright, Maginel Wright *19:* 240, 243; *39:* 31, 35, 36
Enrique, Romeo *34:* 135
Ensor, Barbara *180:* 30
Epstein, Stephen *50:* 142, 148
Erdogan, Buket *174:* 179
Erdrich, Louise *141:* 62
Erhard, Walter *1:* 152

Erickson, Jim _196:_ 190; _233:_ 173
Erickson, Phoebe _11:_ 83; _59:_ 85
Erikson, Mel _31:_ 69
Eriksson, Eva _63:_ 88, 90, 92, 93; _203:_ 99; _207:_ 44
Ering, Timothy Basil _131:_ 100; _176:_ 63, 64; _202:_ 29; _204:_ 8
Erlbruch, Wolf _181:_ 66
Ernst, Lisa Campbell _47:_ 147; _95:_ 47; _154:_ 46, 47, 48; _164:_ 88; _212:_ 45
Esco, Jo _61:_ 103
Escourido, Joseph _4:_ 81
Escrivá, Viví _119:_ 51; _181:_ 36
Essakalli, Julie Klear _200:_ 58
Este, Kirk _33:_ 111
Estep, David _73:_ 57
Estes, Eleanor _91:_ 66
Estoril, Jean _32:_ 27
Estrada, Pau _74:_ 76
Estrada, Ric _5:_ 52, 146; _13:_ 174
Etchemendy, Teje _38:_ 68
Etheredges, the _73:_ 12
Etienne, Kirk-Albert _145:_ 184
Ets, Marie Hall _2:_ 102
Ettlinger, Doris _171:_ 98; _186:_ 106; _197:_ 126; _214:_ 125
Eulalie _YABC 2:_ 315
Eustace, David _224:_ 24
Evangelista, Theresa M. _213:_ 67
Evans, Greg _73:_ 54, 55, 56; _143:_ 40, 41
Evans, Katherine _5:_ 64
Evans, Leslie _144:_ 227; _207:_ 57; _214:_ 88; _221:_ 28
Evans, Shane W. _159:_ 142; _160:_ 190; _168:_ 39; _188:_ 88; _189:_ 66, 67, 68; _229:_ 150
Everitt, Betsy _151:_ 110
Ewart, Claire _76:_ 69; _145:_ 59, 60
Ewing, Carolyn _66:_ 143; _79:_ 52
Ewing, Juliana Horatia _16:_ 92
Eyolfson, Norman _98:_ 154

F

Fabian, Limbert _136:_ 114
Facklam, Paul _132:_ 62
Falconer, Ian _125:_ 66; _179:_ 59
Falconer, Pearl _34:_ 23
Falkenstern, Lisa _70:_ 34; _76:_ 133; _78:_ 171; _127:_ 16; _191:_ 151
Fallone, Gianluca _231:_ 23
Falls, C.B. _1:_ 19; _38:_ 71, 72, 73, 74
Falter, John _40:_ 169, 170
Falwell, Cathryn _118:_ 77; _137:_ 185; _196:_ 71, 72
Fancher, Lou _138:_ 219; _141:_ 64; _144:_ 199; _177:_ 51; _214:_ 95; _221:_ 63; _228:_ 42, 43, 44; _230:_ 44, 45, 46
Fanelli, Sara _89:_ 63; _126:_ 69
Faria, Rosana _150:_ 143
Faricy, Patrick _185:_ 182; _212:_ 61
Farooqi, Musharraf Ali _207:_ 46
Farmer, Andrew _49:_ 102
Farmer, Peter _24:_ 108; _38:_ 75
Farnsworth, Bill _93:_ 189; _116:_ 147; _124:_ 8; _135:_ 52; _146:_ 242, 243, 244; _182:_ 176; _186:_ 31, 83, 84, 85; _191:_ 197; _222:_ 2
Farquharson, Alexander _46:_ 75
Farrell, Darren _228:_ 45
Farrell, David _40:_ 135
Farrell, Russell _196:_ 38
Farris, David _74:_ 42
Fasolino, Teresa _118:_ 145
Fatigati, Evelyn _24:_ 112
Fatus, Sophie _182:_ 74; _190:_ 218; _225:_ 131
Faul-Jansen, Regina _22:_ 117
Faulkner, Jack _6:_ 169
Faulkner, Matt _161:_ 174; _167:_ 75
Faust, Anke _230:_ 166
Fava, Rita _2:_ 29

Fax, Elton C. _1:_ 101; _4:_ 2; _12:_ 77; _25:_ 107
Fay _43:_ 93
Fearing, Mark _223:_ 142; _224:_ 39, 40
Fearnley, Jan _153:_ 82, 83; _205:_ 63, 64, 65
Fearrington, Ann _146:_ 80
Federspiel, Marian _33:_ 51
Fedorov, Nickolai Ivanovich _110:_ 102
Feelings, Tom _5:_ 22; _8:_ 56; _12:_ 153; _16:_ 105; _30:_ 196; _49:_ 37; _61:_ 101; _69:_ 56, 57; _93:_ 74; _105:_ 88
Fehr, Terrence _21:_ 87
Feiffer, Jules _3:_ 91; _8:_ 58; _61:_ 66, 67, 70, 74, 76,77, 78; _111:_ 47, 48, 49, 50; _132:_ 122; _157:_ 62; _201:_ 48, 49, 50; _230:_ 66
Feigeles, Neil _41:_ 242
Feldman, Elyse _86:_ 7
Feller, Gene _33:_ 130
Fellows, Muriel H. _10:_ 42
Felstead, Cathie _116:_ 85
Felts, Shirley _33:_ 71; _48:_ 59
Fennell, Tracy _171:_ 69
Fennelli, Maureen _38:_ 181
Fenton, Carroll Lane _5:_ 66; _21:_ 39
Fenton, Mildred Adams _5:_ 66; _21:_ 39
Ferguson, Peter _177:_ 30, 31; _181:_ 154; _197:_ 4; _199:_ 40; _215:_ 104; _221:_ 66; _229:_ 15, 16; _236:_ 98; _237:_ 153
Ferguson, Walter W. _34:_ 86
Fernandes, Eugenie _77:_ 67; _205:_ 68
Fernandes, Stanislaw _70:_ 28
Fernandez, Fernando _77:_ 57
Fernandez, Laura _73:_ 153; _101:_ 117; _131:_ 222; _170:_ 119; _175:_ 182
Ferrari, Alex _188:_ 121
Ferrington, Susan _172:_ 22
Fetz, Ingrid _11:_ 67; _12:_ 52; _16:_ 205; _17:_ 59; _29:_ 105; _30:_ 108, 109; _32:_ 149; _43:_ 142; _56:_ 29; _60:_ 34; _85:_ 48; _87:_ 146
Fiammenghi, Gioia _9:_ 66; _11:_ 44; _12:_ 206; _13:_ 57, 59; _52:_ 126, 129; _66:_ 64; _85:_ 83; _91:_ 161; _166:_ 169
Fiedler, Joseph Daniel _96:_ 42; _113:_ 173; _129:_ 164; _146:_ 17; _159:_ 68; _162:_ 104
Field, Rachel _15:_ 113
Fielding, David _70:_ 124
Fieser, Stephen _152:_ 36
Fine, Howard _145:_ 159; _159:_ 64; _165:_ 134; _174:_ 129; _181:_ 68
Fine, Peter K. _43:_ 210
Finger, Helen _42:_ 81
Fink, Sam _18:_ 119
Finlay, Winifred _23:_ 72
Finney, Pat _79:_ 215
Fiore, Peter _99:_ 196; _125:_ 139; _144:_ 225; _160:_ 169; _180:_ 72; _212:_ 103
Fiorentino, Al _3:_ 240
Firehammer, Karla _174:_ 202; _221:_ 183; _228:_ 84
Firmin, Charlotte _29:_ 75; _48:_ 70
Firmin, Peter _58:_ 63, 64, 65, 67, 68, 70, 71
Firth, Barbara _81:_ 208; _127:_ 218; _179:_ 62; _232:_ 189
Fischel, Lillian _40:_ 204
Fischer, Hans _25:_ 202
Fischer, Scott M. _207:_ 37; _217:_ 29
Fischer-Nagel, Andreas _56:_ 50
Fischer-Nagel, Heiderose _56:_ 50
Fisher, Carolyn _154:_ 50
Fisher, Chris _79:_ 62; _158:_ 248; _188:_ 195
Fisher, Cynthia _117:_ 45; _137:_ 118; _195:_ 40; _235:_ 126
Fisher, Jeffrey _142:_ 80
Fisher, Leonard Everett _3:_ 6; _4:_ 72, 86; _6:_ 197; _9:_ 59; _16:_ 151, 153; _23:_ 44; _27:_ 134; _29:_ 26; _34:_ 87, 89, 90, 91, 93, 94, 95, 96; _40:_ 206; _50:_ 150; _60:_ 158; _73:_ 68, 70, 71, 72, 73; _176:_ 71, 72, 73; _208:_ 131; _YABC 2:_ 169
Fisher, Lois _20:_ 62; _21:_ 7
Fisher, Valorie _177:_ 55; _214:_ 92
Fisk, Nicholas _25:_ 112

Fitschen, Marilyn _2:_ 20, 21; _20:_ 48
Fitz-Maurice, Jeff _175:_ 2
Fitzgerald, F.A. _15:_ 116; _25:_ 86, 87
Fitzgerald, Joanne _157:_ 153, 154; _198:_ 34, 35
Fitzgerald, Royce _205:_ 5
Fitzhugh, Louise _1:_ 94; _9:_ 163; _45:_ 75, 78
Fitzhugh, Susie _11:_ 117
Fitzpatrick, Jim _109:_ 130
Fitzpatrick, Marie-Louise _125:_ 69, 70; _189:_ 72, 73
Fitzsimmons, Arthur _14:_ 128
Fix, Philippe _26:_ 102
Flack, Marjorie _21:_ 67; _100:_ 93; _YABC 2:_ 122
Flagg, James Montgomery _17:_ 227
Flavin, Teresa _132:_ 115; _186:_ 119
Flax, Zeona _2:_ 245
Fleetwood, Tony _171:_ 51
Fleishman, Seymour _14:_ 232; _24:_ 87
Fleming, Denise _71:_ 179; _81:_ 58; _126:_ 71, 72, 73; _173:_ 52, 53
Fleming, Guy _18:_ 41
Flesher, Vivienne _85:_ 55
Fletcher, Claire _80:_ 106; _157:_ 159
Flint, Russ _74:_ 80
Floate, Helen _111:_ 163
Floca, Brian _155:_ 88, 89; _190:_ 10, 66, 67
Floethe, Richard _3:_ 131; _4:_ 90
Floherty, John J., Jr. _5:_ 68
Flook, Helen _160:_ 81
Flora, James _1:_ 96; _30:_ 111, 112
Florczak, Robert _166:_ 51
Florian, Douglas _19:_ 122; _83:_ 64, 65; _125:_ 71, 72, 74, 76; _128:_ 130; _177:_ 58, 60; _226:_ 119
Flory, Jane _22:_ 111
Flower, Renee _125:_ 109
Floyd, Gareth _1:_ 74; _17:_ 245; _48:_ 63; _62:_ 35,36, 37, 39, 40, 41; _74:_ 245; _79:_ 56
Fluchere, Henri A. _40:_ 79
Flynn, Alice _183:_ 2
Flynn, Barbara _7:_ 31; _9:_ 70
Fogarty, Thomas _15:_ 89
Foley, Greg _190:_ 69
Folger, Joseph _9:_ 100
Folkard, Charles _22:_ 132; _29:_ 128, 257, 258
Foott, Jeff _42:_ 202
Forberg, Ati _12:_ 71, 205; _14:_ 1; _22:_ 113; _26:_ 22; _48:_ 64, 65
Ford, A.G. _230:_ 40; _231:_ 69
Ford, George _24:_ 120; _31:_ 70, 177; _58:_ 126; _81:_ 103; _107:_ 91; _136:_ 100; _194:_ 47; _208:_ 81; _218:_ 66; _237:_ 57, 58
Ford, Gilbert _199:_ 10
Ford, H.J. _16:_ 185, 186
Ford, Jason _174:_ 119
Ford, Pamela Baldwin _27:_ 104
Fordham, John _168:_ 160, 161
Foreman, Michael _2:_ 110, 111; _67:_ 99; _73:_ 78, 79, 80,81, 82; _93:_ 146; _135:_ 55, 56, 57; _184:_ 58, 59; _216:_ 100, 101, 102, 103; _225:_ 144
Forrester, Victoria _40:_ 83
Forsey, Chris _140:_ 210
Fortnum, Peggy _6:_ 29; _20:_ 179; _24:_ 211; _26:_ 76, 77, 78; _39:_ 78; _58:_ 19, 21, 23, 27; _YABC 1:_ 148
Fortune, Eric _191:_ 52
Foster, Brad W. _34:_ 99
Foster, Genevieve _2:_ 112
Foster, Gerald L. _7:_ 78; _198:_ 40
Foster, Jon _146:_ 18; _198:_ 7; _237:_ 140
Foster, Laura Louise _6:_ 79
Foster, Marian Curtis _23:_ 74; _40:_ 42
Foster, Sally _58:_ 73, 74
Fotheringham, Edwin _219:_ 32
Foucher, Adele _47:_ 118
Foust, Mitch _168:_ 50
Fowler, Jim _184:_ 190
Fowler, Mel _36:_ 127
Fowler, Richard _87:_ 219
Fowles, Shelley _165:_ 127; _205:_ 72
Fox, Charles Phillip _12:_ 84
Fox, Christyan _188:_ 36

Fox, Jim 6: 187
Fox, Nathan 208: 64
Fox-Davies, Sarah 76: 150; 182: 63; 199: 42, 43
Frace, Charles 15: 118
Frailey, Joy 72: 108
Frame, Paul 2: 45, 145; 9: 153; 10: 124; 21: 71; 23: 62; 24: 123; 27: 106; 31: 48; 32: 159; 34: 195; 38: 136; 42: 55; 44: 139; 60: 39, 40, 41, 42, 43, 44, 46; 73: 183
Frampton, David 85: 72; 102: 33; 139: 182; 152: 37; 189: 171
Francis, Guy 198: 164; 224: 91; 225: 65
Francois, Andre 25: 117
Francoise
   See Seignobosc, Francoise
Frank, Lola Edick 2: 199
Frank, Mary 4: 54; 34: 100
Franke, Phil 45: 91
Frankel, Alona 66: 70
Frankel, Julie 40: 84, 85, 202
Frankenberg, Robert 22: 116; 30: 50; 38: 92, 94, 95; 68: 111
Frankfeldt, Gwen 84: 223; 110: 92
Frankland, David 169: 137; 182: 164; 201: 159; 224: 7; 231: 27; 236: 37; 237: 152
Franklin, Ashton 165: 144; 225: 107
Franklin, John 24: 22
Franson, Leanne R. 111: 57, 58; 151: 7; 223: 63, 64, 158
Frascino, Edward 9: 133; 29: 229; 33: 190; 48: 80, 81, 82, 83, 84, 85, 86
Frasconi, Antonio 6: 80; 27: 208; 53: 41, 43, 45, 47,48; 68: 145; 73: 226; 131: 68
Fraser, Betty 2: 212; 6: 185; 8: 103; 31: 72,73; 43: 136; 111: 76
Fraser, Eric 38: 78; 41: 149, 151
Fraser, F.A. 22: 234
Fraser, James 171: 68
Fraser, Mary Ann 137: 63; 214: 98
Frasier, Debra 69: 60; 112: 67; 182: 81, 82, 83
Fraustino, Lisa Rowe 146: 87
Frazee, Marla 72: 98; 105: 79, 80; 151: 67, 68; 164: 165; 171: 190, 191; 187: 53, 54, 55, 56, 143; 222: 173; 225: 68, 69, 70; 226: 180
Frazetta, Frank 41: 72; 58: 77, 78, 79, 80, 81, 82, 83
Frazier, Craig 177: 63; 221: 47
Freas, John 25: 207
Fredrickson, Mark 103: 33
Freeland, Michael J. 118: 115
Freeman, Don 2: 15; 13: 249; 17: 62, 63, 65, 67, 68; 18: 243; 20: 195; 23: 213, 217; 32: 155; 55: 129
Freeman, Irving 67: 150
Freeman, Laura 144: 111; 200: 62, 63
Freeman, Pietri 140: 223
Freeman, Tom 167: 118
Freeman, Tor 164: 93
Fregosi, Claudia 24: 117
Fremaux, Charlotte Murray 138: 29; 141: 95
French, Fiona 6: 82, 83; 75: 61; 109: 170; 132: 79, 80, 81, 82
French, Martin 163: 4
French, S. Terrell 216: 106
Frendak, Rodney 126: 97, 98
Freschet, Gina 175: 73
Freynet, Gilbert 72: 221
Friar, Joanne 237: 41
Fried, Janice 202: 121
Frieden, Sarajo 213: 119
Friedman, Judith 43: 197; 131: 221
Friedman, Marvin 19: 59; 42: 86
Frinta, Dagmar 36: 42
Frith, Michael K. 15: 138; 18: 120
Fritz, Ronald 46: 73; 82: 124
Fromm, Lilo 29: 85; 40: 197
Frost, A.B. 17: 6, 7; 19: 123, 124, 125, 126, 127, 128, 129,130; 100: 119; YABC 1: 156, 157, 160; 2: 107

Frost, Helen 183: 51
Frost, Kristi 118: 113; 231: 114
Frost, Michael 151: 209; 209: 44; 212: 70
Froud, Brian 150: 82, 83
Froud, Wendy 151: 237
Fry, Guy 2: 224
Fry, Rosalie 3: 72; YABC 2: 180, 181
Fry, Rosalind 21: 153, 168
Fryer, Elmer 34: 115
Fuchs, Bernie 110: 10; 162: 46
Fuchs, Erich 6: 84
Fuchshuber, Annegert 43: 96
Fucile, Tony 221: 48
Fufuka, Mahiri 32: 146
Fuge, Charles 144: 91, 93
Fujikawa, Gyo 39: 75, 76; 76: 72, 73, 74
Fulford, Deborah 23: 159
Fuller, Margaret 25: 189
Fulweiler, John 93: 99
Funai, Mamoru 38: 105
Funfhausen, Christian 196: 30
Funk, Tom 7: 17, 99
Furchgott, Terry 29: 86
Furness, William Henry, Jr. 94: 18
Furukawa, Mel 25: 42
Fusari, Erika 164: 227

                        G

Gaadt, David 78: 212; 121: 166; 201: 171
Gaadt, George 71: 9
Gaber, Susan 99: 33; 115: 57, 58; 164: 195; 169: 61, 62, 63; 185: 50, 51; 188: 124
Gaberell, J. 19: 236
Gable, Brian 195: 68, 69
Gabler, Mirko 99: 71; 195: 32
Gabor, Tim 216: 61
Gackenbach, Dick 19: 168; 41: 81; 48: 89, 90, 91, 92,93, 94; 54: 105; 79: 75, 76, 77
Gad, Victor 87: 161
Gaetano, Nicholas 23: 209
Gaffney-Kessell, Walter 94: 219; 174: 188
Gag, Flavia 17: 49, 52
Gag, Wanda 100: 101, 102; YABC 1: 135, 137, 138, 141, 143
Gagnon, Cecile 11: 77; 58: 87
Gaillard, Jason 200: 69; 204: 74
Gal, Laszlo 14: 127; 52: 54, 55, 56; 65: 142; 68: 150; 81: 185; 96: 104, 105
Gal, Susan 228: 58
Galazinski, Tom 55: 13
Galbraith, Ben 200: 70
Galdone, Paul 1: 156, 181, 206; 2: 40, 241; 3: 42,144; 4: 141; 10: 109, 158; 11: 21; 12: 118, 210; 14: 12; 16: 36, 37; 17: 70, 71, 72, 73, 74; 18: 111, 230; 19: 183; 21: 154; 22: 150, 245; 33: 126; 39: 136, 137; 42: 57; 51: 169; 55: 110; 66: 80, 82, 139; 72: 73; 100: 84
Gale, Cathy 140: 22; 143: 52; 213: 166
Gall, Chris 176: 79, 80
Gallagher, Jack 187: 100
Gallagher, S. Saelig 105: 154; 198: 91
Gallagher, Sears 20: 112Gallagher-Cole, Mernie 206: 56
Galloway, Ewing 51: 154
Galouchka, Annouchka Gravel 95: 55; 182: 40
Galster, Robert 1: 66
Galsworthy, Gay John 35: 232
Galvez, Daniel 125: 182
Gamble, Kim 112: 64, 65; 124: 77; 183: 40, 42, 43, 56, 57; 187: 170
Gammell, Stephen 7: 48; 13: 149; 29: 82; 33: 209; 41: 88; 50: 185, 186, 187; 53: 51, 52, 53, 54, 55, 56,57, 58; 54: 24, 25; 56: 147, 148, 150; 57: 27, 66; 81: 62, 63; 87: 88; 89: 10; 106: 223; 126: 2; 128: 71, 73, 74, 77; 154: 34; 211: 210; 226: 80, 81, 82
Gamper, Ruth 84: 198

Gampert, John 58: 94
Ganly, Helen 56: 56
Gannett, Ruth Chrisman 3: 74; 18: 254; 33: 77, 78
Gannon, Ned 205: 6
Gantschev, Ivan 45: 32
Garafano, Marie 73: 33
Garbot, Dave 131: 106
Garbutt, Bernard 23: 68
Garcia 37: 71
Garcia, Geronimo 222: 73
Garcia, Manuel 74: 145
Garcia-Franco, Rebecca 173: 46
Gardiner, Lindsey 178: 128; 186: 137
Gardner, Earle 45: 167
Gardner, Joan 40: 87
Gardner, Joel 40: 87, 92
Gardner, John 40: 87
Gardner, Lucy 40: 87
Gardner, Richard
   See Cummings, Richard
Gardner, Sally 171: 177; 177: 66, 68; 229: 58
Gargiulo, Frank 84: 158
Garland, Michael 36: 29; 38: 83; 44: 168; 48: 78, 221, 222; 49: 161; 60: 139; 71: 6, 11; 72: 229; 74: 142; 89: 187; 93: 183; 104: 110; 131: 55; 139: 209; 168: 56; 208: 72, 73, 75
Garland, Peggy 60: 139
Garland, Sarah 62: 45; 135: 67, 68; 171: 118
Garn, Aimee 75: 47
Garner, Joan 128: 170
Garneray, Ambroise Louis 59: 140
Garnett, Eve 3: 75
Garnett, Gary 39: 184
Garns, Allen 80: 125; 84: 39; 165: 231; 209: 44
Garófoli, Viviana 186: 123
Garraty, Gail 4: 142; 52: 106
Garrett, Agnes 46: 110; 47: 157
Garrett, Edmund H. 20: 29
Garrett, Tom 107: 194; 215: 179
Garrick, Jacqueline 67: 42, 43; 77: 94
Garrison, Barbara 19: 133; 104: 146; 109: 87
Garro, Mark 108: 131; 128: 210
Garvey, Robert 98: 222
Garza, Carmen Lomas 80: 211; 182: 86
Garza, Xavier 184: 64
Gates, Frieda 26: 80
Gaughan, Jack 26: 79; 43: 185
Gaver, Becky 20: 61
Gavril, David 211: 196
Gawing, Toby 72: 52
Gay, Marie-Louise 68: 76, 77, 78; 102: 136; 126: 76, 78, 81, 83; 127: 55, 56; 179: 70, 72, 73, 74; 224: 81
Gay, Zhenya 19: 135, 136
Gaydos, Tim 62: 201
Gazsi, Ed 80: 48
Gazso, Gabriel 73: 85
Geary, Clifford N. 1: 122; 9: 104; 51: 74
Geary, Rick 142: 44, 46
Gee, Frank 33: 26
Geehan, Wayne 157: 181
Geer, Charles 1: 91; 3: 179; 4: 201; 6: 168; 7: 96; 9: 58; 10: 72; 12: 127; 39: 156,157, 158, 159, 160; 42: 88, 89, 90, 91; 55: 111, 116
Geerinck, Manuel 173: 128
Gehm, Charlie 36: 65; 57: 117; 62: 60, 138
Geis, Alissa Imre 189: 77; 233: 93
Geisel, Theodor Seuss 1: 104, 105, 106; 28: 108, 109, 110,111, 112, 113; 75: 67, 68, 69, 70, 71; 89: 127, 128; 100: 106, 107, 108
Geisert, Arthur 92: 67, 68; 133: 72, 73, 74; 165: 97, 98; 171: 64, 65; 237: 45, 46, 47, 48
Geldart, William 15: 121; 21: 202
Genia 4: 84
Gentry, Cyrille R. 12: 66
Genzo, John Paul 136: 74
George, Jean 2: 113
George, Lindsay Barrett 95: 57; 155: 97, 98

Geraghty, Paul *130:* 60, 61
Gerard, Jean Ignace *45:* 80
Gerard, Rolf *27:* 147, 150
Gerber, Mark *61:* 105
Gerber, Mary Jane *112:* 124; *171:* 56
Gerber, Stephanie *71:* 195
Gerdstein, Mordecai *169:* 105
Gergely, Tibor *54:* 15, 16
Geritz, Franz *17:* 135
Gerlach, Geff *42:* 58
Gerrard, Roy *47:* 78; *90:* 96, 97, 98, 99
Gerritsen, Paula *177:* 69; *217:* 166
Gershinowitz, George *36:* 27
Gerstein, Mordicai *31:* 117; *47:* 80, 81, 82, 83, 84, 85, 86; *51:* 173; *69:* 134; *107:* 122; *142:* 49, 52; *165:* 209; *176:* 119; *178:* 95, 97, 99; *215:* 173; *222:* 76
Gervase *12:* 27
Geter, Tyrone *146:* 249; *150:* 86
Getz, Arthur *32:* 148
Gévry, Claudine *188:* 47
Gewirtz, Bina *61:* 81
Giancola, Donato *95:* 146; *164:* 226; *229:* 181
Gibala-Broxholm, Scott *205:* 76; *219:* 186
Gibbons, Gail *23:* 78; *72:* 77, 78, 79; *82:* 182; *104:* 65; *160:* 99, 100; *201:* 59, 60, 62
Gibbs, Tony *40:* 95
Gibran, Kahlil *32:* 116
Gibson, Barbara Leonard *205:* 77; *212:* 151
Gider, Iskender *81:* 193
Giebfried, Rosemary *170:* 135
Giesen, Rosemary *34:* 192, 193
Giffard, Hannah *83:* 70
Gifford, Carrie *236:* 67, 68
Giguere, George *20:* 111
Gilbert, John *19:* 184; *54:* 115; *YABC 2:* 287
Gilbert, W.S. *36:* 83, 85, 96
Gilbert, Yvonne *116:* 70; *128:* 84; *149:* 119; *185:* 69; *192:* 25; *195:* 81
Gilchrist, Jan Spivey *72:* 82, 83, 84, 85, 87; *77:* 90; *105:* 89, 91; *130:* 63, 64; *155:* 105, 107; *182:* 67
Giles, Will *41:* 218
Gili, Phillida *70:* 73
Gill, Margery *4:* 57; *7:* 7; *22:* 122; *25:* 166; *26:* 146, 147
Gillen, Denver *28:* 216
Gillette, Henry J. *23:* 237
Gilliam, Stan *39:* 64, 81
Gillies, Chuck *62:* 31
Gilliland, Jillian *87:* 58
Gillman, Alec *98:* 105
Gilman, Esther *15:* 124
Gilman, Phoebe *104:* 70, 71
Gilpin, Stephen *213:* 68; *236:* 116
Ginsberg, Sari *111:* 184
Ginsburg, Max *62:* 59; *68:* 194 *Girard, Roge 161:* 30
Girouard, Patrick *155:* 100; *218:* 165
Giovanopoulos, Paul *7:* 104; *60:* 36
Giovine, Sergio *79:* 12; *93:* 118; *139:* 118; *205:* 114
Gist, E.M. *206:* 60
Githens, Elizabeth M. *5:* 47
Gladden, Scott *99:* 108; *103:* 160; *193:* 46, 47
Gladstone, Gary *12:* 89; *13:* 190
Gladstone, Lise *15:* 273
Glanzman, Louis S. *2:* 177; *3:* 182; *36:* 97, 98; *38:* 120, 122; *52:* 141, 144; *71:* 191; *91:* 54, 56
Glaser, Byron *154:* 59, 60
Glaser, Milton *3:* 5; *5:* 156; *11:* 107; *30:* 26; *36:* 112; *54:* 141; *151:* 70
Glass, Andrew *36:* 38; *44:* 133; *48:* 205; *65:* 3; *68:* 43, 45; *90:* 104, 105; *150:* 89; *223:* 73, 74
Glass, Marvin *9:* 174
Glasser, Judy *41:* 156; *56:* 140; *69:* 79; *72:* 101
Glasser, Robin Preiss *123:* 176; *152* 40; *172:* 194; *235:* 78

Glattauer, Ned *5:* 84; *13:* 224; *14:* 26
Glauber, Uta *17:* 76
Gleeson, J.M. *YABC 2:* 207
Glegg, Creina *36:* 100
Glienke, Amelie *63:* 150
Gliewe, Unada *3:* 78, 79; *21:* 73; *30:* 220
Gliori, Debi *72:* 91; *138:* 82; *162:* 37; *189:* 79, 81, 82
Glovach, Linda *7:* 105
Gobbato, Imero *3:* 180, 181; *6:* 213; *7:* 58; *9:* 150; *18:* 39; *21:* 167; *39:* 82, 83; *41:* 137, 251; *59:* 177
Goble, Paul *25:* 121; *26:* 86; *33:* 65; *69:* 68, 69; *131:* 79, 80
Goble, Warwick *46:* 78, 79; *194:* 143
Godal, Eric *36:* 93
Godbey, Cory *221:* 154
Godkin, Celia *145:* 84, 86
Godfrey, Michael *17:* 279
Godon, Ingrid *166:* 163; *186:* 99
Goede, Irene *208:* 87
Goembel, Ponder *42:* 124; *237:* 171
Goffe, Toni *61:* 83, 84, 85; *89:* 11; *90:* 124; *178:* 118
Goffstein, M.B. *8:* 71; *70:* 75, 76, 77
Golbin, Andre *15:* 125
Gold, Robert *166:* 151, 152
Goldfeder, Cheryl *11:* 191
Goldfinger, Jennifer P. *185:* 71
Goldman, Todd H. *221:* 50, 51
Goldsborough, June *5:* 154, 155; *8:* 92, *14:* 226; *19:* 139; *54:* 165
Goldsmith, Robert *110:* 77
Goldstein, Barry *198:* 147
Goldstein, Leslie *5:* 8; *6:* 60; *10:* 106
Goldstein, Nathan *1:* 175; *2:* 79; *11:* 41, 232; *16:* 55
Goldstrom, Robert *98:* 36; *145:* 51, 52; *233:* 56
Golembe, Carla *79:* 80, 81; *136:* 91; *144:* 113; *193:* 53
Golin, Carlo *74:* 112
Gomez, Elena *188:* 122; *191:* 72
Gomez, Elizabeth *127:* 70; *133:* 76
Gomi, Taro *64:* 102; *103:* 74, 76
Gon, Adriano *101:* 112
Gonsalves, Ron *178:* 213; *212:* 196
Gonzalez, Maya Christina *104:* 3; *136:* 92; *215:* 4, 5
Gonzalez, Thomas *226:* 157
Gonzalez, Yolanda *212:* 65
Good, Karen Hillard *212:* 143; *214:* 103
Goodall, John S. *4:* 92, 93; *10:* 132; *66:* 92, 93; *YABC 1:* 198
Goode, Diane *15:* 126; *50:* 183; *52:* 114, 115; *76:* 195; *84:* 94; *99:* 141; *114:* 76, 77, 78; *170:* 99, 101; *225:* 80, 81, 82, 83, 84
Goodelman, Aaron *40:* 203
Goodenow, Earle *40:* 97
Goodfellow, Peter *62:* 95; *94:* 202
Goodman, Joan Elizabeth *50:* 86
Goodman, Vivienne *82:* 251; *146:* 181, 182
Goodnow, Patti *117:* 33
Goodrich, Carter *221:* 52, 53
Goodwin, Harold *13:* 74
Goodwin, Philip R. *18:* 206
Goor, Nancy *39:* 85, 86
Goor, Ron *39:* 85, 86
Goossens, Philippe *195:* 71
Gorbachev, Valeri *89:* 96; *112:* 97; *143:* 63, 64; *184:* 66, 67, 68, 101; *222:* 84, 85, 86, 87
Gordon, David *216:* 159
Gordon, Gwen *12:* 151
Gordon, Margaret *4:* 147; *5:* 48, 49; *9:* 79
Gordon, Mike *101:* 62, 63, 64
Gordon, Russell *136:* 204; *137:* 214; *228:* 34
Gordon, Walter *138:* 9
Gore, Leonid *89:* 51; *94:* 74; *136:* 8; *158:* 117; *166:* 136; *168:* 36; *170:* 107; *181:* 94; *185:* 73; *222:* 89, 90, 91, 92; *235:* 10, 11
Gorecka-Egan, Erica *18:* 35

Gorey, Edward *1:* 60, 61; *13:* 169; *18:* 192; *20:* 201; *29:* 90, 91, 92, 93, 94, 95, 96, 97, 98, 99, 100; *30:* 129; *32:* 90; *34:* 200, *65:* 48; *68:* 24, 25; *69:* 79; *70:* 80, 82, 83, 84; *85:* 136; *127:* 62
Gorman, Mike *222:* 167
Gorsline, Douglas *1:* 98; *6:* 13; *11:* 113; *13:* 104; *15:* 14; *28:* 117, 118; *YABC 1:* 15
Gorton, Julia *108:* 94; *178:* 81, 82; *234:* 145
Gosfield, Josh *118:* 165, 166; *149:* 67
Gosner, Kenneth *5:* 135
Gosney, Joy *167:* 142
Gotlieb, Jules *6:* 127
Goto, Scott *115:* 86; *136:* 69; *203:* 77, 78
Gott, Barry *197:* 95; *212:* 102
Gottlieb, Dale *67:* 162; *107:* 16; *149:* 6
Goudey, Ray *97:* 86
Gough, Alan *91:* 57
Gough, Philip *23:* 47; *45:* 90
Gould, Chester *49:* 112, 113, 114, 116, 117, 118
Gould, Jason *151:* 232
Gourbault, Martine *177:* 159
Govern, Elaine R. *26:* 94
Gower, Teri *102:* 184
Gowing, Toby *60:* 25; *63:* 33; *78:* 70, 252; *83:* 228; *86:* 187; *93:* 145; *108:* 133; *110:* 217; *184:* 125; *225:* 142
Grabianski *20:* 144
Grabianski, Janusz *39:* 92, 93, 94, 95
Graboff, Abner *35:* 103, 104
Graef, Renée *61:* 188; *72:* 207; *204:* 45; *210:* 249
Grafe, Max *156:* 173; *178:* 237; *192:* 240; *198:* 51
Graham, A.B. *11:* 61
Graham, Bob *101:* 66, 67, 68; *151:* 74, 75; *187:* 65, 67, 68, 70
Graham, Georgia *188:* 3; *190:* 75
Graham, L. *7:* 108
Graham, Margaret Bloy *11:* 120; *18:* 305, 307
Graham, Mark *88:* 208; *159:* 153; *182:* 3
Grahame-Johnstone, Janet *13:* 61
Grahame-Johnstone, Anne *13:* 61
Grainger, Sam *42:* 95
Gralley, Jean *166:* 86
Gramatky, Hardie *1:* 107; *30:* 116, 119, 120, 122, 123
Gran, Julie *168:* 118
Granahan, Julie *84:* 84
GrandPré, Mary *84:* 131; *109:* 199; *118:* 76; *180:* 65; *184:* 70, 71, 180; *192:* 87; *215:* 24; *229:* 68, 69, 70
Grandström, Brita *176:* 139
Grandville, J.J. *45:* 81, 82, 83, 84, 85, 86, 87, 88; *47:* 125; *64:* 10
Granger, Paul *39:* 153
Granström, Brita *162:* 35; *167:* 46; *224:* 56, 57
Grant, (Alice) Leigh *10:* 52; *15:* 131; *20:* 20; *26:* 119; *48:* 202
Grant, Gordon *17:* 230, 234; *25:* 123, 124, 125, 126; *52:* 69; *YABC 1:* 164
Grant, Melvyn *159:* 186; *187:* 170: 48, 49; *213:* 168, 169; *226:* 163
Grant, Michelle *210:* 95
Grant, Renee *77:* 40
Grant, Shirley *109:* 45
Graves, Elizabeth *45:* 101
Graves, Keith *167:* 89; *191:* 74; *216:* 34; *223:* 103
Gray, Harold *33:* 87, 88
Gray, Les *82:* 76; *83:* 232
Gray, Reginald *6:* 69
Gray, Steve *226:* 206; *231:* 77, 78
Greco, Tony *184:* 6
Greder, Armin *76:* 235
Green, Ann Canevari *62:* 48
Green, Eileen *6:* 97
Green, Elizabeth Shippen *139:* 109
Green, Jonathan *86:* 135; *105:* 109; *221:* 73
Green, Ken *111:* 68

Green, Michael *32:* 216
Green, Robina *87:* 138
Green, Jonathan *157:* 105
Greene, Jeffrey *117:* 93
Greenaway, Kate *17:* 275; *24:* 180; *26:* 107; *41:* 222, 232; *100:* 115, 116; *YABC 1:* 88, 89; *2:* 131, 133, 136,138, 139, 141
Greenberg, Melanie Hope *72:* 93; *80:* 125; *101:* 174; *133:* 180; *186:* 189; *214:* 105
Greenseid, Diane *178:* 106, 107
Greenstein, Elaine *150:* 100
Greenwald, Sheila *1:* 34; *3:* 99; *8:* 72
Greger, Carol *76:* 86
Gregorian, Joyce Ballou *30:* 125
Gregory, Emilian *177:* 146; *187:* 10
Gregory, Fran *130:* 4; *140:* 93
Gregory, Frank M. *29:* 107
Greiffenhagen, Maurice *16:* 137; *27:* 57; *YABC 2:* 288
Greiner, Robert *6:* 86
Gretter, J. Clemens *31:* 134
Gretz, Susanna *7:* 114
Gretzer, John *1:* 54; *3:* 26; *4:* 162; *7:* 125; *16:* 247; *18:* 117; *28:* 66; *30:* 85, 211; *33:* 235; *56:* 16
Grey, Mini *166:* 90; *192:* 71
Grey Owl *24:* 41
Gri *25:* 90
Grieder, Walter *9:* 84
Griesbach/Martucci *59:* 3
Grifalconi, Ann *2:* 126; *3:* 248; *11:* 18; *13:* 182; *46:* 38; *50:* 145; *66:* 99, 100, 101, 104, 106; *69:* 38; *70:* 64; *87:* 128; *90:* 53; *93:* 49; *128:* 48; *133:* 79, 81; *210:* 111
Griffin, Gillett Good *26:* 96
Griffin, James *30:* 166
Griffin, John Howard *59:* 186
Griffin, Rachel *131:* 23
Griffith, Gershom *94:* 214
Griffiths, Dave *29:* 76
Griffiths, Dean *168:* 180; *169:* 182
Grimly, Gris *186:* 102; *192:* 112; *197:* 86; *219:* 34
Grimsdell, Jeremy *83:* 75
Grimwood, Brian *82:* 89
Gringhuis, Dirk *6:* 98; *9:* 196
Gripe, Harald *2:* 127; *74:* 98
Grisha *3:* 71
Grobler, Piet *201:* 100
Grohmann, Susan *84:* 97
Gropper, William *27:* 93; *37:* 193
Gros *60:* 199
Grose, Helen Mason *YABC 1:* 260; *2:* 150
Grossman, Nancy *24:* 130; *29:* 101
Grossman, Robert *11:* 124; *46:* 39
Groth, John *15:* 79; *21:* 53, 54; *83:* 230
Grover, Lorie Ann *168:* 59
Grubb, Lisa *160:* 116
Grue, Lisa *187:* 193
Gruelle, Johnny *35:* 107
Gschwind, William *11:* 72
Guarnaccia, Steven *201:* 170, 173; *233:* 73
Guay-Mitchell, Rebecca *110:* 95, 96; *135:* 240; *180:* 76; *181:* 71, 73; *216:* 77
Guback, Georgia *88:* 102
Gudeon, Karla *212:* 67
Guerguerion, Claudine *105:* 73
Guevara, Susan *97:* 87; *167:* 49; *194:* 54
Guggenheim, Hans *2:* 10; *3:* 37; *8:* 136
Guhathaakurta, Ajanta *183:* 199
Guida, Lisa Chauncy *172:* 188
Guilbeau, Honore *22:* 69
Guillette, Joseph *137:* 37
Guisewite, Cathy *57:* 52, 53, 54, 56, 57
Gukova, Julia *95:* 104; *154:* 103; *168:* 195
Gundersheimer, Karen *35:* 240; *82:* 100
Gunderson, Nick *57:* 120
Gunnella *192:* 144
Gurney, James *76:* 97; *86:* 32

Gurney, John Steven *75:* 39, 82; *110:* 175; *143:* 67, 68; *169:* 172; *217:* 50, 88; *227:* 86, 87, 88; *228:* 139, 140, 141
Gusman, Annie *38:* 62
Gustafson, Scott *34:* 111; *43:* 40
Gustavson, Adam *104:* 10; *171:* 183; *176:* 87; *197:* 94; *204:* 35; *219:* 187
Guthridge, Bettina *108:* 79; *186:* 92
Guthrie, R. Dale *64:* 143
Guthrie, Robin *20:* 122
Gutierrez, Akemi *172:* 87; *205:* 135
Gutierrez, Alan *136:* 31, 32
Gutierrez, Rudy *97:* 162; *203:* 79; *216:* 158
Gutmann, Bessie Pease *73:* 93, 94
Gwynne, Fred *41:* 94, 95
Gyberg, Bo-Erik *38:* 131

H

Haas, Irene *17:* 77; *87:* 46; *96:* 117
Hack, Konrad *51:* 127
Hader, Berta H. *16:* 126
Hader, Elmer S. *16:* 126
Haeffele, Deborah *76:* 99
Haemer, Alan *62:* 109
Hafner, Marylin *22:* 196, 216; *24:* 44; *30:* 51; *35:* 95; *51:* 25, 160, 164; *86:* 16; *105:* 196; *121:* 93, 94; *149:* 208, 209; *179:* 82, 83, 84, 115; *190:* 200; *201:* 29; *217:* 91
Hagerty, Sean *62:* 181
Hague, Michael *32:* 128; *48:* 98, 99, 100, 101, 103, 105,106, 107, 108, 109, 110; *49:* 121; *51:* 105; *64:* 14, 15; *79:* 134; *80:* 91, 92; *83:* 135; *100:* 241; *102:* 29; *129:* 101, 103, 104; *185:* 80, 81, 82; *215:* 89
Hair, Jonathan *115:* 135
Halas, John *29:* 41, 47, 48
Haldane, Roger *13:* 76; *14:* 202
Hale, Bruce *203:* 83
Hale, Christy *79:* 124; *84:* 200; *114:* 201; *128:* 2, 3; *146:* 203; *158:* 243; *167:* 99; *179:* 87
Hale, Irina *26:* 97
Hale, James Graham *88:* 207
Hale, Kathleen *17:* 79; *66:* 114, 116, 118
Hale, Nathan *210:* 115, 116; *214:* 179
Haley, Amanda *205:* 82, 83
Haley, Gail E. *43:* 102, 103, 104, 105; *78:* 65, 67; *136:* 106, 107
Hall, Amanda *96:* 110
Hall, Angus *224:* 192
Hall, August N. *217:* 74
Hall, Chuck *30:* 189
Hall, Douglas *15:* 184; *43:* 106, 107; *86:* 100; *87:* 82; *129:* 72
Hall, H. Tom *1:* 227; *30:* 210
Hall, Melanie *116:* 48, 49; *169:* 77, 78; *219:* 170; *228:* 65, 66, 67
Hall, Michael *228:* 69
Hall, Sydney P. *31:* 89
Hall, Tim *164:* 196; *202:* 41
Hall, Vicki *20:* 24
Hallinan, P.K. *39:* 98
Hallman, Tom *98:* 166
Hally, Greg *101:* 200; *151:* 224
Halperin, Wendy Anderson *96:* 151; *125:* 96, 97, 98, 99; *139:* 22; *140:* 84; *200:* 77, 78; *210:* 157; *215:* 65; *228:* 24, 76
Halpern, Joan *10:* 25
Halpern, Shari *174:* 172
Halpin, Abigail *236:* 94
Halsey, Megan *96:* 172; *114:* 185; *180:* 8; *185:* 85
Halstead, Virginia *125:* 105
Halverson, Janet *49:* 38, 42, 44
Hallensleben, Georg *134:* 5, 6; *172:* 17
Hallett, Mark *220:* 63
Hamanaka, Sheila *71:* 100
Hamann, Brad *78:* 151
Hamann, Sigune *104:* 115

Hamberger, John *6:* 8; *8:* 32; *14:* 79; *34:* 136; *88:* 78
Hamil, Tom *14:* 80; *43:* 163
Hamilton, Bill and Associates *26:* 215
Hamilton, Helen S. *2:* 238
Hamilton, J. *19:* 83, 85, 87
Hamilton, Laurie *116:* 210
Hamilton, Todd Cameron *84:* 15
Hamlin, Janet *97:* 136; *124:* 90; *137:* 157; *182:* 117
Hamlin, Louise *71:* 135
Hammill, Matt *206:* 65
Hammond, Chris *21:* 37
Hammond, Elizabeth *5:* 36, 203
Hampshire, Michael *5:* 187; *7:* 110, 111; *48:* 150; *51:* 129
Hampson, Denman *10:* 155; *15:* 130
Hampton, Blake *41:* 244
Handford, Martin *64:* 105, 106, 107, 109
Handforth, Thomas *42:* 100, 101, 102, 103, 104, 105, 107
Handville, Robert *1:* 89; *38:* 76; *45:* 108, 109
Hane, Roger *17:* 239; *44:* 54
Haney, Elizabeth Mathieu *34:* 84
Hanke, Karen *234:* 71
Hanke, Ted *71:* 10
Hankinson, Phil *181:* 164
Hanley, Catherine *8:* 161
Hann, Jacquie *19:* 144
Hanna, Cheryl *91:* 133
Hanna, Wayne A. *67:* 145
Hannon, Mark *38:* 37
Hanrahan, Kelly-Anne *203:* 142
Hansen, Gaby *159:* 11; *186:* 25; *224:* 11
Hansen, Mia *149:* 76
Hanson, Glen *229:* 84
Hanson, Joan *8:* 76; *11:* 139
Hanson, Peter E. *52:* 47; *54:* 99, 100; *73:* 21; *84:* 79; *116:* 144
Hansson, Gunilla *64:* 111, 112
Harbour, Elizabeth *221:* 68
Hardcastle, Nick *121:* 82; *175:* 185; *222:* 135
Hardy, David A. *9:* 96; *119:* 74
Hardy, Paul *YABC 2:* 245
Hargis, Wes *219:* 70 Haring, Keith *145:* 65
Harlan, Jerry *3:* 96
Harlin, Greg *89:* 194; *103:* 82; *118:* 161; *121:* 167; *182:* 76; *201:* 172; *215:* 76
Harman, Dominic *206:* 48
Harness, Cheryl *106:* 80; *131:* 87; *178:* 111; *200:* 39
Harnischfeger *18:* 121
Harper, Arthur *YABC 2:* 121
Harper, Betty *126:* 90
Harper, Jamie *174:* 71; *214:* 212
Harper, Piers *79:* 27; *105:* 102; *161:* 67
Harrington, Glenn *82:* 18; *94:* 66, 68; *185:* 118
Harrington, Jack *83:* 162
Harrington, Richard *5:* 81
Harris, Andrew N. *191:* 78
Harris, Jim *127:* 130; *183:* 4
Harris, John *83:* 25
Harris, Nick *86:* 177
Harris, Susan Yard *42:* 121
Harrison, Florence *20:* 150, 152
Harrison, Harry *4:* 103
Harrison, Jack *28:* 149
Harrison, Mark *105:* 157; *165:* 190
Harrison, Ted *56:* 73
Harsh, Fred *72:* 107
Harston, Jerry *105:* 143
Hart, Lewis *98:* 115
Hart, Thomas *181:* 165
Hart, William *13:* 72
Hartland, Jessie *171:* 80, 81; *186:* 165; *223:* 58
Hartung, Susan Kathleen *150:* 107, 108; *173:* 106; *175:* 106; *192:* 78; *211:* 19
Hartelius, Margaret *10:* 24
Hartshorn, Ruth *5:* 115; *11:* 129

Harvey, Amanda *145:* 44
Harvey, Bob *48:* 219
Harvey, Gerry *7:* 180
Harvey, Lisa *97:* 21
Harvey, Paul *88:* 74
Harvey, Roland *71:* 88; *123:* 63; *179:* 94; *218:* 94; *219:* 74
Haskamp, Steve *195:* 36; *229:* 29
Hassall, Joan *43:* 108, 109
Hassell, Hilton *YABC 1:* 187
Hassett, John *162:* 59
Hasselriis, Else *18:* 87; *YABC 1:* 96
Hastings, Glenn *89:* 183
Hastings, Ian *62:* 67
Hauman, Doris *2:* 184; *29:* 58, 59; *32:* 85, 86, 87
Hauman, George *2:* 184; *29:* 58, 59; *32:* 85, 86, 87
Hausherr, Rosmarie *15:* 29
Haverfield, Mary *225:* 87
Hawkes, Kevin *78:* 72; *104:* 198; *105:* 197; *112:* 109; *126:* 87; *144:* 88; *149:* 210; *150:* 110, 135; *156:* 94; *164:* 35; *186:* 18; *190:* 197; *198:* 152; *201:* 70, 71, 72; *220:* 99; *221:* 90, 92, 93; *234:* 195
Hawkins, Jacqui *112:* 86; *162:* 64
Hawkinson, John *4:* 109; *7:* 83; *21:* 64
Hawkinson, Lucy *21:* 64
Hawthorne, Mike *140:* 228
Haxton, Elaine *28:* 131
Haydock, Robert *4:* 95
Hayes, Geoffrey *26:* 111; *44:* 133; *91:* 85; *207:* 63
Hayes, Karel *207:* 65
Haynes, Max *72:* 107
Hays, Michael *73:* 207; *83:* 93; *139:* 197; *146:* 202, 250; *202:* 47
Haywood, Carolyn *1:* 112; *29:* 104
Heale, Jonathan *104:* 117
Healy, Daty *12:* 143
Healy, Deborah *58:* 181, 182; *101:* 111
Heap, Sue *102:* 207; *150:* 113, 114; *187:* 84, 85, 87
Hearn, Diane Dawson *79:* 99; *113:* 13; *209:* 71, 72; *211:* 106
Hearon, Dorothy *34:* 69
Heaslip, William *57:* 24, 25
Hechtkopf, H. *11:* 110
Heck, Ed *173:* 81
Hector, Julian *205:* 85
Hedderwick, Mairi *30:* 127; *32:* 47; *36:* 104; *77:* 86; *145:* 91, 93, 95
Heffernan, Phil *146:* 197; *195:* 172; *218:* 123
Hefter, Richard *28:* 170; *31:* 81, 82; *33:* 183
Hehenberger, Shelly *126:* 91
Heigh, James *22:* 98
Heighway, Richard *25:* 160; *64:* 4
Heighway-Bury, Robin *159:* 89
Heine, Helme *67:* 86; *135:* 91, 92
Heinly, John *45:* 113
Hellard, Susan *81:* 21; *204:* 82; *209:* 92
Hellebrand, Nancy *26:* 57
Heller, Linda *46:* 86
Heller, Ruth M. *66:* 125; *77:* 30, 32
Hellmuth, Jim *38:* 164
Helms, Georgeann *33:* 62
Helquist, Brett *142:* 203; *146:* 133, 134; *156:* 10; *173:* 25; *180:* 106; *187:* 90, 91; *193:* 12; *224:* 186; *226:* 117; *229:* 76, 77, 78
Helweg, Hans *41:* 118; *50:* 93; *58:* 22, 26
Hemingway, Edward *212:* 71
Hemphill, Helen *179:* 95
Henba, Bobbie *90:* 195
Henderling, Lisa *214:* 65
Henderson, Dave *73:* 76; *75:* 191, 192, 193, 194; *82:* 4
Henderson, D.F. *216:* 77
Henderson, Douglas *103:* 68
Henderson, Kathy *55:* 32; *155:* 118
Henderson, Keith *35:* 122
Henderson, Meryl *127:* 58, 60; *169:* 81; *228:*

Hendra, Sue *235:* 95
Hendricks, Donald *235:* 142
Hendrix, John *187:* 133; *208:* 106, 107, 108; *216:* 115
Hendry, Linda *80:* 104; *83:* 83; *164:* 216; *233:* 11
Hengeveld, Dennis *142:* 86
Henkes, Kevin *43:* 111; *108:* 106, 107, 108
Henneberger, Robert *1:* 42; *2:* 237; *25:* 83
Henriquez, Celeste *103:* 137
Henriquez, Elsa *82:* 260
Henriquez, Emile F. *89:* 88; *211:* 56
Henry, Everett *29:* 191
Henry, Matthew *117:* 58
Henry, Paul *93:* 121; *194:* 125
Henry, Rohan *217:* 77
Henry, Thomas *5:* 102
Hensel *27:* 119
Henshaw, Jacqui *141:* 127
Henstra, Friso *8:* 80; *36:* 70; *40:* 222; *41:* 250; *73:* 100, 101
Henterly, Jamichael *93:* 4
Heo, Yumi *89:* 85, 86; *94:* 89, 90; *146:* 40, 137, 138; *163:* 227; *201:* 192
Hepple, Norman *28:* 198
Herbert, Helen *57:* 70
Herbert, Jennifer *189:* 47
Herbert, Wally *23:* 101
Herbster, Mary Lee *9:* 33
Herder, Edwin *182:* 104
Herge
   See Remi, Georges
Hermansen, Pal *133:* 113
Hermanson, Dennis *10:* 55
Hermes, Gertrude *54:* 161
Herr, Margo *57:* 191
Herr, Susan *83:* 163
Herriman, George *140:* 74, 75, 76, 77, 78
Herriman, Lisa *87:* 190
Herring, Michael *121:* 76; *182:* 103
Herrington, Roger *3:* 161
Herscovici, C. *165:* 240
Hescox, Richard *85:* 86; *90:* 30; *139:* 35
Heslop, Mike *38:* 60; *40:* 130
Hess, Lydia J. *85:* 17
Hess, Mark *111:* 146; *113:* 207
Hess, Paul *134:* 47; *166:* 133; *193:* 13
Hess, Richard *42:* 31
Hester, Ronnie *37:* 85
Heuser, Olga J. *121:* 116
Heusser, Sibylle *168:* 195
Heustis, Louise L. *20:* 28
Hewgill, Jody *201:* 90
Hewitson, Jennifer *74:* 119; *124:* 167
Hewitt, Kathryn *80:* 126; *149:* 105; *184:* 93; *196:* 36; *229:* 99
Hewitt, Margaret *84:* 112
Heyduck-Huth, Hilde *8:* 82
Heyer, Carol *74:* 122; *130:* 72, 73; *192:* 35; *203:* 78
Heyer, Hermann *20:* 114, 115
Heyer, Marilee *102:* 108
Heyman, Ken *8:* 33; *34:* 113
Heyne, Ulrike *146:* 151
Heywood, Karen *48:* 114
Hickling, P.B. *40:* 165
Hickman, Stephen *85:* 58; *136:* 33; *171:* 128
Hierstein, Judith *56:* 40; *162:* 168; *212:* 72; *227:* 46
Higashi, Sandra *154:* 59, 60
Higginbottom, J. Winslow *8:* 170; *29:* 105, 106
Higgins, Chester *101:* 79
Higham, David *50:* 104
Hilb, Nora *176:* 8
Hild, Anja *215:* 194
Hildebrandt, Greg *8:* 191; *55:* 35, 36, 38, 39, 40, 42, 46; *172:* 110
Hildebrandt, Tim *8:* 191; *55:* 44, 45, 46
Hilder, Rowland *19:* 207

Hill, Eric *66:* 127, 128; *133:* 91
Hill, Gregory *35:* 190
Hill, Pat *49:* 120
Hillenbrand, Will *84:* 115; *92:* 76, 80; *93:* 131; *104:* 168; *128:* 137; *145:* 187; *146:* 184; *147:* 105, 106, 107; *152:* 59; *184:* 179; *195:* 34, 180; *196:* 125; *210:* 122, 123, 124; *217:* 62; *224:* 145
Hilliard, Richard *183:* 74
Hillier, Matthew *45:* 205
Hillman, Priscilla *48:* 115
Hills, Tad *113:* 4; *137:* 147; *173:* 83; *208:* 199
Himler, Ronald *6:* 114; *7:* 162; *8:* 17, 84, 125; *14:* 76; *19:* 145; *26:* 160; *31:* 43; *38:* 116; *41:* 44, 79; *43:* 52; *45:* 120; *46:* 43; *54:* 44, 83; *58:* 180; *59:* 38; *68:* 146; *69:* 231; *70:* 98; *71:* 177, 178; *77:* 219; *79:* 212; *83:* 62; *89:* 5; *91:* 160; *92:* 91, 92, 93; *94:* 93; *95:* 69, 174, 194; *99:* 99, 112; *113:* 92; *118:* 114; *137:* 73, 74, 77, 167; *163:* 99; *165:* 138; *178:* 9, 220; *183:* 77, 79, 80, 81; *184:* 80, 83; *215:* 151; *231:* 11, 112; *234:* 76, 77, 78, 80; *237:* 54, 55
Himmelman, John *47:* 109; *65:* 87; *94:* 96, 97; *159:* 85; *221:* 79, 80, 81, 82
Hinds, Bill *37:* 127, 130
Hines, Anna Grossnickle *51:* 90; *74:* 124; *95:* 78, 79,80, 81
Hines, Bob *135:* 149, 150
Hirao, Amiko *203:* 98
Hiroko *99:* 61
Hiroshige *25:* 71
Hirsh, Marilyn *7:* 126
Hiscock, Bruce *137:* 80, 81; *204:* 51, 53
Hissey, Jane *103:* 90; *130:* 81
Hitch, Jeff *99:* 206; *128:* 86
Hitz, Demi *11:* 135; *15:* 245; *66:* 129, 130; *152:* 94, 95
Hnizdovsky, Jacques *32:* 96; *76:* 187
Ho, David *227:* 32
Ho, Kwoncjan *15:* 132
Hoban, Lillian *1:* 114; *22:* 157; *26:* 72; *29:* 53; *40:* 105, 107, 195; *41:* 80; *69:* 107, 108; *71:* 98; *77:* 168; *106:* 50; *113:* 86; *136:* 118
Hoban, Tana *22:* 159; *104:* 82, 83, 85
Hobbie, Holly *225:* 90, 91
Hobbie, Jocelyn *190:* 78; *196:* 92
Hobbie, Nathaniel *196:* 92
Hobbs, Leigh *166:* 95
Hoberman, Norman *5:* 82
Hobson, Sally *77:* 185
Hockerman, Dennis *39:* 22; *56:* 23
Hodgell, P.C. *42:* 114
Hodges, C. Walter *2:* 139; *11:* 15; *12:* 25; *23:* 34; *25:* 96; *38:* 165; *44:* 197; *45:* 95; *100:* 57; *YABC 2:* 62, 63
Hodges, David *9:* 98
Hodgetts, Victoria *43:* 132
Hofbauer, Imre *2:* 162
Hoff, Syd *9:* 107; *10:* 128; *33:* 94; *72:* 115,116, 117, 118; *138:* 114, 115
Hoffman, Rosekrans *15:* 133; *50:* 219; *63:* 97
Hoffman, Sanford *38:* 208; *76:* 174; *88:* 160, 161; *151:* 156
Hoffmann, Felix *9:* 109
Hoffnung, Gerard *66:* 76, 77
Hofsinde, Robert *21:* 70
Hogan, Inez *2:* 141
Hogan, Jamie *192:* 94; *198:* 177; *237:* 107
Hogarth, Burne *41:* 58; *63:* 46, 48, 49, 50, 52, 53, 54, 55,56
Hogarth, Paul *41:* 102, 103, 104; *YABC 1:* 16
Hogarth, William *42:* 33
Hogenbyl, Jan *1:* 35
Hogner, Nils *4:* 122; *25:* 144
Hogrogian, Nonny *3:* 221; *4:* 106, 107; *5:* 166; *7:* 129; *15:* 2; *16:* 176; *20:* 154; *22:* 146; *25:* 217; *27:* 206; *74:* 127, 128, 129, 149, 152; *127:* 99; *YABC 2:* 84, 94
Hokanson, Lars *93:* 111; *172:* 137; *212:* 88
Hokusai *25:* 71

Hol, Colby *126:* 96
Holberg, Richard *2:* 51
Holbrook, Kathy *107:* 114
Holdcroft, Tina *38:* 109; *227:* 99, 100, 160
Holden, Caroline *55:* 159
Holder, Heidi *36:* 99; *64:* 9
Holder, Jim *204:* 163
Holder, Jimmy *151:* 224; *233:* 175; *234:* 82, 83
Holderness, Grizelda *215:* 107
Hole, Stian *204:* 55
Holiday, Henry *YABC 2:* 107
Holl, F. *36:* 91
Holland, Brad *45:* 59, 159
Holland, Gay W. *128:* 105; *225:* 76
Holland, Janice *18:* 118
Holland, Marion *6:* 116
Holland, Richard *216:* 109, 124
Holldobler, Turid *26:* 120
Holliday, Keaf *144:* 236
Holling, Holling C. *15:* 136, 137
Hollinger, Deanne *12:* 116
Holm, Sharon Lane *114:* 84; *115:* 52
Holmes, B. *3:* 82
Holmes, Bea *7:* 74; *24:* 156; *31:* 93
Holmes, Dave *54:* 22
Holmes, Lesley *135:* 96
Holmgren, George Ellen *45:* 112
Holmlund, Heather D. *150:* 140
Holt, Norma *44:* 106
Holt, Pater *151:* 188
Holtan, Gene *32:* 192
Holub, Joan *149:* 72; *229:* 82
Holyfield, John *149:* 231; *227:* 101; *230:* 9
Holz, Loretta *17:* 81
Hom, Nancy *79:* 195
Homar, Lorenzo *6:* 2
Homer, Winslow *128:* 8; *YABC 2:* 87
Honey, Elizabeth *112:* 95, 96; *137:* 93, 94
Honeywood, Varnette P. *110:* 68, 70
Hong, Lily Toy *76:* 104
Honigman, Marian *3:* 2
Honore, Paul *42:* 77, 79, 81, 82
Hood, Alun *69:* 145, 218; *72:* 41; *80:* 226; *87:* 4; *95:* 139
Hood, Susan *12:* 43
Hook, Christian *104:* 103
Hook, Frances *26:* 188; *27:* 127
Hook, Jeff *14:* 137; *103:* 105
Hook, Richard *26:* 188
Hooks *63:* 30
Hooper, Hadley *177:* 145
Hoover, Carol A. *21:* 77
Hoover, Russell *12:* 95; *17:* 2; *34:* 156
Hope, James *141:* 116
Hopkins, Chris *99:* 127
Hopkinson, Leigh *202:* 70
Hopman, Philip *178:* 184
Hoppe, Paul *209:* 85
Hoppin, Augustus *34:* 66
Horacek, Judy *211:* 86
Horacek, Petr *163:* 117; *214:* 113
Horder, Margaret *2:* 108; *73:* 75
Horen, Michael *45:* 121
Horne, Daniel *73:* 106; *91:* 153; *109:* 127; *110:* 232; *164:* 176
Horne, Richard *111:* 80
Horowitz, Dave *204:* 58
Horse, Harry *128:* 195; *169:* 86
Horstman, Lisa *219:* 79
Horton, Anthony *211:* 98
Horvat, Laurel *12:* 201
Horvath, David *192:* 95
Horvath, Ferdinand Kusati *24:* 176
Horvath, Maria *57:* 171
Horwitz, Richard *57:* 174
Hotchkiss, De Wolfe *20:* 49
Hough, Charlotte *9:* 112; *13:* 98; *17:* 83; *24:* 195
Houlihan, Ray *11:* 214
House, Caroline *183:* 121

Housman, Laurence *25:* 146, 147
Houston, James *13:* 107; *74:* 132, 134, 135
Hovland, Gary *88:* 172; *171:* 148
Hoyt, Eleanor *158:* 231
How, W.E. *20:* 47
Howard, Alan *16:* 80; *34:* 58; *45:* 114
Howard, Arthur *165:* 111, 112; *190:* 5; *229:* 30
Howard, J.N. *15:* 234
Howard, John *33:* 179
Howard, Kim *116:* 71
Howard, Paul *142:* 126, 129; *144:* 187
Howard, Rob *40:* 161
Howarth, Daniel *170:* 34; *222:* 97, 98; *224:* 20; *225:* 77; *234:* 189
Howe, John *79:* 101; *80:* 150; *115:* 47; *176:* 106; *207:* 32, 35
Howe, Phillip *79:* 117; *175:* 115
Howe, Stephen *1:* 232
Howell, Karen *119:* 123
Howell, Pat *15:* 139
Howell, Troy *23:* 24; *31:* 61; *36:* 158; *37:* 184; *41:* 76, 235; *48:* 112; *56:* 13; *57:* 3; *59:* 174; *63:* 5; *74:* 46; *89:* 188; *90:* 231; *95:* 97; *98:* 130; *99:* 189; *153:* 156, 157, 158; *176:* 104; *199:* 96, 98; *222:* 65
Howells, Tania *229:* 87
Howes, Charles *22:* 17
Hoyt, Ard *145:* 141; *190:* 82; *207:* 148
Hranilovich, Barbara *127:* 51
Hu, Ying-Hwa *116:* 107; *152:* 236; *173:* 171
Huang, Benrei *137:* 55
Huang, Zhong-Yang *117:* 30, 32; *213:* 18
Hubbard, Woodleigh Marx *98:* 67; *115:* 79; *160:* 138; *214:* 120
Hubbell, Patricia *222:* 31
Hubley, Faith *48:* 120, 121, 125, 130, 131, 132, 134
Hubley, John *48:* 125, 130, 131, 132, 134
Hudak, Michal *143:* 74
Hudnut, Robin *14:* 62
Huerta, Catherine *76:* 178; *77:* 44, 45; *90:* 182; *210:* 202
Huffaker, Sandy *10:* 56
Huffman, Joan *13:* 33
Huffman, Tom *13:* 180; *17:* 212; *21:* 116; *24:* 132; *33:* 154; *38:* 59; *42:* 147
Hughes, Arthur *20:* 148, 149, 150; *33:* 114, 148, 149
Hughes, Darren *95:* 44
Hughes, David *36:* 197
Hughes, Shirley *1:* 20, 21; *7:* 3; *12:* 217; *16:* 163; *29:* 154; *63:* 118; *70:* 102, 103, 104; *73:* 169; *88:* 70; *110:* 118, 119; *159:* 103
Hugo, Victor *47:* 112
Huliska-Beith, Laura *204:* 108; *220:* 137; *232:* 97, 98
Hull, Cathy *78:* 29
Hull, Richard *95:* 120; *123:* 175; *172:* 195
Hulsmann, Eva *16:* 166
Hume, Lachie *189:* 93
Hummel, Berta *43:* 137, 138, 139
Hummel, Lisl *29:* 109; *YABC 2:* 333, 334
Humphrey, Henry *16:* 167
Humphreys, Graham *25:* 168
Humphries, Tudor *76:* 66; *80:* 4; *124:* 4, 5; *226:* 112
Huneck, Stephen *183:* 88, 89
Hunt, James *2:* 143
Hunt, Jonathan *84:* 120
Hunt, Paul *119:* 104; *129:* 135; *139:* 160; *173:* 112
Hunt, Robert *110:* 206, 235; *147:* 136, 137; *170:* 3; *211:* 76; *226:* 189
Hunt, Scott *190:* 143; *233:* 172
Hunter, Anne *133:* 190; *178:* 150
Huntington, Amy *180:* 99
Hurd, Clement *2:* 148, 149; *64:* 127, 128, 129, 131, 133, 134,135, 136; *100:* 37, 38
Hurd, Peter *24:* 30, 31,; *YABC 2:* 56
Hurd, Thacher *46:* 88, 89; *94:* 114, 115, 116; *123:* 81, 82, 84; *219:* 82

Hurlimann, Ruth *32:* 99
Hurst, Carol Otis *185:* 92
Hurst, Elise *221:* 98
Hurst, Philip *196:* 79
Hurst, Tracey *192:* 238
Hussar, Michael *114:* 113; *117:* 159
Hustler, Tom *6:* 105
Hutchins, Laurence *55:* 22
Hutchins, Pat *15:* 142; *70:* 106, 107, 108; *178:* 131, 132
Hutchinson, Sascha *95:* 211
Hutchinson, William M. *6:* 3, 138; *46:* 70
Hutchison, Paula *23:* 10
Hutton, Clarke *YABC 2:* 335
Hutton, Kathryn *35:* 155; *89:* 91
Hutton, Warwick *20:* 91
Huyette, Marcia *29:* 188
Hyatt, John *54:* 7
Hyatt, Mitch *178:* 162
Hyde, Maureen *82:* 17; *121:* 145, 146
Hyman, David *117:* 64
Hyman, Miles *210:* 132
Hyman, Trina Schart *1:* 204; *2:* 194; *5:* 153; *6:* 106; *7:* 138, 145; *8:* 22; *10:* 196; *13:* 96; *14:* 114; *15:* 204; *16:* 234; *20:* 82; *22:* 133; *24:* 151; *25:* 79, 82; *26:* 82; *29:* 83; *31:* 37, 39; *34:* 104; *38:* 84, 100, 128; *41:* 49; *43:* 146; *46:* 91, 92, 93, 95, 96, 97, 98, 99, 100, 101, 102, 103, 104, 105,108, 109, 111, 197; *48:* 60, 61; *52:* 32; *60:* 168; *66:* 38; *67:* 214; *72:* 74; *75:* 92; *79:* 57; *82:* 95, 238; *89:* 46; *95:* 91, 92, 93; *100:* 33, 199; *132:* 12; *147:* 33, 35, 36; *167:* 58, 60; *177:* 189, 190; *211:* 188; *236:* 128

I

Ibarra, Rosa *147:* 91
Ibatoulline, Bagram *156:* 48; *174:* 33, 82; *202:* 30; *211:* 213; *224:* 84; *225:* 98, 99; *232:* 60; *237:* 163
Ichikawa, Satomi *29:* 152; *41:* 52; *47:* 133, 134,135, 136; *78:* 93, 94; *80:* 81; *146:* 143, 145, 146; *208:* 117, 118, 119
Ide, Jacqueline *YABC 1:* 39
Idle, Molly Schaar *223:* 95
Ignatow, Amy *233:* 91
Ilsley, Velma *3:* 1; *7:* 55; *12:* 109; *37:* 62; *38:* 184
Imai, Ayano *190:* 85, 86
in den Bosch, Nicole *150:* 204
Inga *1:* 142
Ingman, Bruce *134:* 50; *182:* 91, 92; *214:* 10
Ingpen, Robert *109:* 103, 104; *132:* 138; *137:* 177; *166:* 103; *181:* 140; *229:* 169
Ingraham, Erick *21:* 177; *84:* 256; *103:* 66
Inkpen, Mick *99:* 104, 105; *106:* 44
Innerst, Stacy *149:* 104; *232:* 101, 102
Innocenti, Roberto *21:* 123; *96:* 122; *159:* 111, 197; *199:* 176
Inoue, Yosuke *24:* 118
Iofin, Michael *97:* 157
Iosa, Ann *63:* 189
Ipcar, Dahlov *1:* 124, 125; *49:* 137, 138, 139, 140, 141, 142,143, 144, 145; *147:* 122, 124, 126
Irvin, Fred *13:* 166; *15:* 143, 144; *27:* 175
Irving, Jay *45:* 72
Irving, Laurence *27:* 50
Isaac, Joanne *21:* 76
Isaacs, Gary *170:* 188
Isadora, Rachel *43:* 159, 160; *54:* 31; *79:* 106, 107,108; *121:* 100, 102; *165:* 116, 117; *204:* 61, 63, 64
Ishmael, Woodi *24:* 111; *31:* 99
Isol *220:* 73
Ives, Ruth *15:* 257
Iwai, Melissa *149:* 233; *183:* 92; *199:* 115
Iwamura, Kazuo *213:* 87

J

Jabar, Cynthia *101:* 201; *210:* 134, 135
Jack, Colin *234:* 53
Jackness, Andrew *94:* 237
Jackson, Julian *91:* 104, 106
Jackson, Michael *43:* 42
Jackson, Shelley *79:* 71; *99:* 109; *187:* 82
Jacob, Murv *89:* 30
Jacobi, Kathy *62:* 118
Jacobs, Barbara *9:* 136
Jacobs, Lou, Jr. *9:* 136; *15:* 128
Jacobsen, Laura *176:* 98; *177:* 85, 86
Jacobson, Rick *131:* 222; *170:* 119; *222:* 52
Jacobus, Tim *79:* 140; *109:* 126; *129:* 180
Jacques, Robin *1:* 70; *2:* 1; *8:* 46; *9:* 20; *15:* 187; *19:* 253; *32:* 102, 103, 104; *43:* 184; *73:* 135; *YABC 1:* 42
Jaeggi, Yoshiko *186:* 184
Jaffee, Al *66:* 131, 132
Jago *216:* 122
Jagr, Miloslav *13:* 197
Jahn-Clough, Lisa *88:* 114; *152:* 104; *193:* 70, 71
Jahnke, Robert *84:* 24
Jainschigg, Nicholas *80:* 64; *91:* 138; *95:* 63; *99:* 25; *108:* 50; *171:* 41
Jakesevic, Nenad *85:* 102; *226:* 215
Jakobsen, Kathy *116:* 83
Jakubowski, Charles *14:* 192
Jambor, Louis *YABC 1:* 11
James, Ann *73:* 50; *82:* 113; *158:* 61; *183:* 44
James, Brian *140:* 91
James, Curtis E. *182:* 93
James, Derek *35:* 187; *44:* 91; *61:* 133; *74:* 2; *80:* 57; *86:* 88; *130:* 30; *179:* 29; *218:* 31
James, Gilbert *YABC 1:* 43
James, Gordon C. *195:* 89
James, Harold *2:* 151; *3:* 62; *8:* 79; *29:* 113; *51:* 195; *74:* 90
James, Kennon *126:* 211
James, Rhian Nest *234:* 63
James, Robin *50:* 106; *53:* 32, 34, 35
James, Simon *202:* 73, 74; *233:* 161
James, Will *19:* 150, 152, 153, 155, 163
Janosch
    See Eckert, Horst
Janovitch, Marilyn *68:* 168
Janovitz, Marilyn *87:* 187; *130:* 198; *194:* 91
Jansons, Inese *48:* 117
Jansson, Alexander *216:* 59; *234:* 29
Jansson, Tove *3:* 90; *41:* 106, 108, 109, 110, 111, 113, 114
Jaques, Faith *7:* 11, 132, 133; *21:* 83, 84; *69:* 114,116; *73:* 170
Jaques, Frances Lee *29:* 224
Jarka, Jeff *221:* 94
Jarrett, Clare *201:* 77
Jarrie, Martin *219:* 86
Jauss, Anne Marie *1:* 139; *3:* 34; *10:* 57, 119; *11:* 205; *23:* 194
Jay, Alison *158:* 97, 98; *183:* 126, 127; *196:* 95, 96, 97, 98; *200:* 72, 73, 74; *212:* 39
Jeffers, Oliver *175:* 111; *213:* 89
Jeffers, Susan *17:* 86, 87; *25:* 164, 165; *26:* 112; *50:* 132, 134, 135; *70:* 111, 112, 113; *137:* 107, 108, 109, 110, 111; *202:* 77, 78
Jefferson, Louise E. *4:* 160
Jenkin-Pearce, Susie *78:* 16
Jenkins, Debra Reid *85:* 202; *114:* 89; *173:* 134; *225:* 116
Jenkins, Jean *98:* 79, 102
Jenkins, Leonard *157:* 169; *167:* 128; *189:* 96, 97; *190:* 89
Jenkins, Patrick *72:* 126
Jenkins, Steve *124:* 177; *154:* 90, 91, 92, 93; *185:* 194; *188:* 81, 82, 83, 84, 85, 86; *218:* 67, 69, 70, 71, 72
Jenks, Aleta *73:* 117; *124:* 225
Jenkyns, Chris *51:* 97

Jensen, Bruce *95:* 39
Jensinius, Kirsten *56:* 58
Jeram, Anita *89:* 135; *102:* 122, 123; *129:* 112; *154:* 96, 97, 98; *164:* 154; *203:* 123, 124; *219:* 88, 89, 90, 91
Jernigan, E. Wesley *85:* 92
Jerome, Elaine *227:* 45
Jerome, Karen A. *72:* 194
Jeruchim, Simon *6:* 173; *15:* 250
Jeschke, Susan *20:* 89; *39:* 161; *41:* 84; *42:* 120
Jessel, Camilla *29:* 115
Jessell, Tim *159:* 3; *177:* 87; *181:* 95; *205:* 4; *213:* 74; *223:* 187; *225:* 102; *226:* 190
Jeyaveeran, Ruth *182:* 100
Jiang, Cheng An *109:* 108
Jiang, Wei *109:* 108
Jimenez, Maria *77:* 158; *93:* 127
Jobling, Curtis *138:* 74
Jocelyn, Marthe *118:* 83; *137:* 219; *163:* 119, 120; *198:* 62
Joerns, Consuelo *38:* 36; *44:* 94
John, Diana *12:* 209
John, Helen *1:* 215; *28:* 204
Johns, Elizabeth *127:* 33
Johns, Jasper *61:* 172
Johns, Jeanne *24:* 114
Johnson, Adrian *143:* 50
Johnson, Bruce *9:* 47
Johnson, Cathy *92:* 136; *218:* 112
Johnson, Crockett
    See Leisk, David
Johnson, D. William *23:* 104
Johnson, D.B. *183:* 98, 139
Johnson, David A. *175:* 18; *191:* 91; *218:* 19
Johnson, Gillian *175:* 164; *217:* 215; *215:* 99
Johnson, Harper *1:* 27; *2:* 33; *18:* 302; *19:* 61; *31:* 181; *44:* 46, 50, 95
Johnson, Ingrid *37:* 118
Johnson, James Ralph *1:* 23, 127
Johnson, James David *12:* 195
Johnson, Jane *48:* 136
Johnson, Joel Peter *98:* 18; *128:* 111; *201:* 13; *213:* 189; *234:* 172
Johnson, John E. *34:* 133
Johnson, Kevin *72:* 44
Johnson, Kevin Eugene *109:* 215
Johnson, Larry *47:* 56; *123:* 107; *159:* 203
Johnson, Layne *187:* 94; *209:* 63; *222:* 100, 101; *233:* 123
Johnson, Margaret S. *35:* 131
Johnson, Meredith Merrell *71:* 181; *83:* 158; *89:* 103; *104:* 88
Johnson, Milton *1:* 67; *2:* 71; *26:* 45; *31:* 107; *60:* 112; *68:* 96
Johnson, Pamela *16:* 174; *52:* 145; *62:* 140; *73:* 116; *85:* 64
Johnson, Paul Brett *83:* 95; *132:* 119
Johnson, Stephen T. *80:* 15; *131:* 35; *141:* 96; *145:* 40; *164:* 187; *175:* 32; *189:* 99, 100; *208:* 43
Johnson, Steve *138:* 219; *141:* 64; *144:* 199; *177:* 51; *214:* 95; *221:* 63; *228:* 42, 43, 44; *230:* 44, 45, 46
Johnson, William R. *38:* 91
Johnson-Petrov, Arden *115:* 206
Johnston, David McCall *50:* 131, 133
Johnston, Lynne *118:* 85, 87, 89; *216:* 127, 128, 131
Johnstone, Anne *8:* 120; *36:* 89
Johnstone, Janet Grahame *8:* 120; *36:* 89
Jolivet, Joëlle *231:* 71
Jonas, Ann *50:* 107, 108, 109; *135:* 113
Jones, Bob *71:* 5; *77:* 199
Jones, Carol *5:* 131; *72:* 185, 186; *153:* 111, 112
Jones, Chuck *53:* 70, 71
Jones, Curtis *211:* 144
Jones, Davy *89:* 176
Jones, Douglas B. *185:* 192; *202:* 82
Jones, Elizabeth Orton *18:* 124, 126, 128, 129

Jones, Harold *14:* 88; *52:* 50
Jones, Holly *127:* 3
Jones, Jeff *41:* 64
Jones, Laurian *25:* 24, 27
Jones, Margaret *74:* 57
Jones, Noah Z. *182:* 37; *203:* 159
Jones, Randy *131:* 104
Jones, Richard *127:* 222
Jones, Robert *25:* 67
Jones, Tim *237:* 104
Jones, Wilfred *35:* 115; *YABC 1:* 163
Jordan, Charles *89:* 58
Jordan, Jess *158:* 136; *203:* 111
Jordan, Martin George *84:* 127
Jordan, Richard *84:* 36
Jorgenson, Andrea *91:* 111
Jorisch, Stéphane *153:* 56, 193; *177:* 29; *178:* 138, 139; *187:* 23; *211:* 182
Joseph, James *53:* 88
Josse, Annabelle *234:* 88
Joudrey, Ken *64:* 145; *78:* 6
Joyce, William *72:* 131, 132, 133, 134; *73:* 227; *145:* 37
Joyner, Jerry *34:* 138
Joyner, Loraine M. *209:* 17
Joysmith, Brenda *210:* 237
Juan, Ana *175:* 38; *179:* 111, 112; *213:* 9
Juarez, Fernando *233:* 26
Jucker, Sita *5:* 93
Judge, Lita *192:* 99; *234:* 97
Judkis, Jim *37:* 38
Juhasz, Victor *31:* 67
Julian, Sean *236:* 113
Jullian, Philippe *24:* 206; *25:* 203
Jung, Tom *91:* 217
Junge, Alexandra *183:* 37
Junge, Walter *67:* 150
Jupo, Frank *7:* 148, 149
Jurisch, Stephane *154:* 105
Justice, Martin *34:* 72

K

Kabatova-Taborska, Zdenka *107:* 153
Kachik, John *165:* 230
Kaczman, James *156:* 98; *235:* 86
Kadair, Deborah Ousley *184:* 45, 89
Kahl, David *74:* 95; *97:* 35; *109:* 174; *110:* 213; *198:* 15
Kahl, M.P. *37:* 83
Kahl, Virginia *48:* 138
Kahn, Katherine Janus *90:* 135; *211:* 155; *218:* 75, 76; *220:* 89,90
Kakimoo, Kozo *11:* 148
Kalett, Jim *48:* 159, 160, 161
Kalin, Victor *39:* 186
Kalis, Jennifer *207:* 82; *219:* 62
Kalman, Maira *96:* 131, 132; *137:* 115
Kalmenoff, Matthew *22:* 191
Kalow, Gisela *32:* 105
Kamen, Gloria *1:* 41; *9:* 119; *10:* 178; *35:* 157; *78:* 236; *98:* 82
Kaminsky, Jef *102:* 153
Kandell, Alice *35:* 133
Kane, Henry B. *14:* 90; *18:* 219, 220
Kane, Robert *18:* 131
Kanfer, Larry *66:* 141
Kangas, Juli *200:* 88
Kappes, Alfred *28:* 104
Karalus, Bob *41:* 157
Karas, G. Brian *80:* 60; *99:* 179; *115:* 41; *118:* 50; *136:* 168; *145:* 166; *149:* 245; *159:* 65; *171:* 192; *178:* 142, 143; *202:* 38; *209:* 142; *222:* 106, 107, 108, 109; *225:* 62; *235:* 53
Karasz, Ilonka *128:* 163
Karlin, Eugene *10:* 63; *20:* 131
Karlin, Nurit *63:* 78; *103:* 110
Karpinski, Tony *134:* 160
Kasamatsu, Shiro *139:* 155

Kasparavicius, Kestutis *139:* 210
Kassian, Olena *64:* 94
Kastner, Jill *79:* 135; *117:* 84, 85
Kasuya, Masahiro *41:* 206, 207; *51:* 100
Kasza, Keiko *191:* 99, 100, 101, 102, 103
Katona, Robert *21:* 85; *24:* 126
Katz, Avi *199:* 55
Katz, Karen *158:* 123; *232:* 108, 109, 110
Kauffer, E. McKnight *33:* 103; *35:* 127; *63:* 67
Kaufman, Angelika *15:* 156
Kaufman, Joe *33:* 119
Kaufman, John *13:* 158
Kaufman, Stuart *62:* 64; *68:* 226; *137:* 44
Kaufmann, John *1:* 174; *4:* 159; *8:* 43, 1; *10:* 102; *18:* 133, 134; *22:* 251
Kaye, Graham *1:* 9; *67:* 7, 8
Kaye, M.M. *62:* 95
Kazalovski, Nata *40:* 205
Keane, Bil *4:* 135
Kearney, David *72:* 47; *121:* 83
Keating, Pamel T. *77:* 37
Keats, Ezra Jack *3:* 18, 105, 257; *14:* 101, 102; *33:* 129; *57:* 79, 80, 82, 83, 84, 87
Keegan, Charles *166:* 211
Keegan, Marcia *9:* 122; *32:* 93
Keeler, Patricia A. *81:* 56; *183:* 102, 103
Keely, Jack *119:* 95
Keely, John *26:* 104; *48:* 214
Keen, Eliot *25:* 213
Keep, Richard C. *170:* 122
Keeping, Charles *9:* 124, 185; *15:* 28, 134; *18:* 115; *44:* 194, 196; *47:* 25; *52:* 3; *54:* 156; *69:* 123, 124; *74:* 56; *155:* 9
Keeter, Susan *168:* 46; *183:* 192; *237:* 64
Keith, Eros *4:* 98; *5:* 138; *31:* 29; *43:* 220; *52:* 91, 92, 93, 94; *56:* 64, 66; *60:* 37; *79:* 93
Keleinikov, Andrei *65:* 101, 102
Kelen, Emery *13:* 115
Keller, A.J. *62:* 198
Keller, Arthur I. *26:* 106
Keller, Dick *36:* 123, 125
Keller, Holly *45:* 79; *76:* 118, 119, 120, 121; *108:* 137, 138, 140; *157:* 117, 118, 119; *216:* 136
Keller, Katie *79:* 222; *93:* 108
Keller, Laurie *196:* 105, 106
Keller, Ronald *45:* 208
Kelley, Gary *183:* 105; *216:* 78; *217:* 95, 96, 97
Kelley, Marty *211:* 91
Kelley, True *41:* 114, 115; *42:* 137; *75:* 35; *92:* 104, 105; *124:* 62; *130:* 100, 101; *179:* 120, 121, 122; *192:* 251
Kellogg, Steven *8:* 96; *11:* 207; *14:* 130; *20:* ; *201:* 38 58; *29:* 140, 141; *30:* 35; *41:* 141; *57:* 89, 90, 92,93, 94, 96; *59:* 182; *73:* 141; *77:* 129; *130:* 105, 106; *177:* 94, 95, 96, 97; *199:* 57; *217:* 61; *YABC 1:* 65, 73
Kelly, Billy *158:* 143
Kelly, Geoff *97:* 196; *112:* 25
Kelly, Irene *147:* 134; *210:* 144, 145
Kelly, Jennifer *230:* 137
Kelly, John *194:* 186
Kelly, Joseph *174:* 94
Kelly, Kathleen M. *71:* 109
Kelly, Laura *89:* 217
Kelly, True *163:* 87
Kelly, Walt *18:* 136, 137, 138, 139, 140, 141, 144, 145, 146, 148, 149
Kemble, E.W. *34:* 75; *44:* 178; *YABC 2:* 54, 59
Kemly, Kathleen *209:* 165
Kemp-Welsh, Lucy *24:* 197; *100:* 214
Kendall, Jane *150:* 105; *186:* 109
Kendall, Peter *152:* 85
Kendrick, Dennis *79:* 213
Kennaway, Adrienne *60:* 55, 56; *171:* 88, 89
Kennedy, Anne *212:* 34
Kennedy, Doug *189:* 104
Kennedy, Paul Edward *6:* 190; *8:* 132; *33:* 120

Kennedy, Richard *3:* 93; *12:* 179; *44:* 193; *100:* 15; *YABC 1:* 57
Kent, Jack *24:* 136; *37:* 37; *40:* 81; *84:* 89; *86:* 150; *88:* 77
Kent, Rockwell *5:* 166; *6:* 129; *20:* 225, 226, 227,229; *59:* 144
Kenyon, Tony *81:* 201; *127:* 74; *231:* 86
Kepes, Juliet *13:* 119
Kerins, Anthony *76:* 84
Kerr, Judity *24:* 137
Kerr, Phyllis Forbes *72:* 141
Kessler, Leonard *1:* 108; *7:* 139; *14:* 107, 227; *22:* 101; *44:* 96; *67:* 79; *82:* 123
Kest, Kristin *168:* 99; *173:* 23
Kesteven, Peter *35:* 189
Ketcham, Hank *28:* 140, 141, 142
Kettelkamp, Larry *2:* 164
Key, Alexander *8:* 99
Khalsa, Dayal Kaur *62:* 99
Kiakshuk *8:* 59
Kid, Tom *207:* 54
Kidd, Chip *94:* 23
Kidd, Richard *152:* 110
Kidd, Tom *64:* 199; *81:* 189; *185:* 173
Kiddell-Monroe, Joan *19:* 201; *55:* 59, 60; *87:* 174; *121:* 112
Kidder, Harvey *9:* 105; *80:* 41
Kidwell, Carl *43:* 145
Kieffer, Christa *41:* 89
Kiesler, Kate *110:* 105; *136:* 142
Kiff, Ken *40:* 45
Kilaka, John *223:* 107
Kilbride, Robert *37:* 100
Kilby, Don *141:* 144
Killen, Nicola *236:* 115
Kim, David *201:* 79; *202:* 97
Kim, Glenn *99:* 82
Kimball, Anton *78:* 114; *119:* 105
Kimball, Yeffe *23:* 116; *37:* 88
Kimber, Murray *171:* 91
Kimmel, Warren *176:* 112
Kincade, Orin *34:* 116
Kindersley, Barnabas *96:* 110
Kindred, Wendy *7:* 151
King, Colin *53:* 3
King, Robin *10:* 164, 165
King, Stephen Michael *141:* 31; *197:* 191; *218:* 81, 82
King, Tara Calahan *139:* 172
King, Tony *39:* 121
Kingman, Dong *16:* 287; *44:* 100, 102, 104
Kingsley, Charles *YABC 2:* 182
Kingston, Julie *147:* 14
Kingston, Maxine Hong *53:* 92
Kinney, Jeff *187:* 97
Kipling, John Lockwood *YABC 2:* 198
Kipling, Rudyard *YABC 2:* 196
Kipniss, Robert *29:* 59
Kirchherr, Astrid *55:* 23
Kirchhoff, Art *28:* 136
Kirk, Daniel *153:* 115, 116, 117; *173:* 101; *196:* 113, 114, 115, 116
Kirk, David *117:* 88, 89; *161:* 97, 98
Kirk, Ruth *5:* 96
Kirk, Steve *170:* 37
Kirk, Tim *32:* 209, 211; *72:* 89; *83:* 49
Kirmse, Marguerite *15:* 283; *18:* 153
Kirsch, Vincent X. *124:* 207
Kirschner, Ruth *22:* 154
Kirwan, Wednesday *198:* 73
Kish, Ely *73:* 119; *79:* 2
Kitamura, Satoshi *62:* 102; *98:* 91; *101:* 147; *138:* 2; *143:* 83, 85, 86; *201:* 83; *223:* 3, 4
Kiss, Andrew *168:* 115
Kitchel, JoAnn E. *133:* 32
Kitchen, Bert *70:* 126; *193:* 49
Kittelsen, Theodor *62:* 14
Kiuchi, Tatsuro *114:* 71
Kiwak, Barbara *172:* 135
Klahr, Susan *176:* 196
Klapholz, Mel *13:* 35

Klassen, J. *234:* 196
Klee, Jutte *209:* 136
Klein, Bill *89:* 105
Klein, Robert *55:* 77
Klein, Suzanna *63:* 104
Kleinman, Zalman *28:* 143
Kleven, Elisa *173:* 96, 97; *217:* 100, 102
Kliban, B. *35:* 137, 138
Kline, Michael *127:* 66
Klinger, Shula *230:* 55
Klise, M. Sarah *180:* 117, 118; *181:* 97; *221:* 100, 102; *235:* 117, 118
Knabel, Lonnie *73:* 103; *75:* 187, 228; *194:* 216
Kneen, Maggie *140:* 139; *221:* 104, 105
Knight, Ann *34:* 143
Knight, Christopher *13:* 125
Knight, Hilary *1:* 233; *3:* 21; *15:* 92, 158, 159; *16:* 258, 259, 260; *18:* 235; *19:* 169; *35:* 242; *46:* 167; *52:* 116; *69:* 126, 127; *132:* 129; *YABC 1:* 168, 169, 172
Knorr, Laura *200:* 91
Knorr, Peter *126:* 92, 93
Knotts, Howard *20:* 4; *25:* 170; *36:* 163
Knutson, Barbara *112:* 134; *202:* 108
Knutson, Kimberley *115:* 90
Kobayashi, Ann *39:* 58
Kochalka, James *196:* 120, 121, 122
Kocsis, J.C.
    See Paul, James
Kodman, Stanislawa *201:* 85; *224:* 72
Koehler, Hanne Lore *176:* 203
Koehn, Ilse *34:* 198; *79:* 123
Koelsch, Michael *99:* 182; *107:* 164; *109:* 239; *138:* 142; *150:* 94; *176:* 105; *187:* 63; *198:* 63; *230:* 204
Koering, Ursula *3:* 28; *4:* 14; *44:* 5; *64:* 140,141; *85:* 46
Koerner, Henry
    See Koerner, W.H.D.
Koerner, W.H.D. *14:* 216; *21:* 88, 89, 90, 91; *23:* 211
Koetsch, Mike *166:* 68
Koffler, Camilla *36:* 113
Kogan, Deborah Ray *161:* 101, 102
Koide, Yasuko *50:* 114
Kolado, Karen *102:* 228
Kolesova, Juliana *217:* 81; *222:* 185; *229:* 183; *237:* 16
Komarck, Michael *227:* 48
Komoda, Kiyo *9:* 128; *13:* 214
Kompaneyets, Marc *169:* 92
Konashevich, Vladimir *61:* 160
Konashevicha, V. *YABC 1:* 26
Konigsburg, E.L. *4:* 138; *48:* 141, 142, 144, 145; *94:* 129, 130; *126:* 129, 130, 131; *194:* 95, 98
Kono, Erin Eitter *177:* 99
Kooiker, Leonie *48:* 148
Koonook, Simon *65:* 157
Koontz, Robin Michal *136:* 155
Koopmans, Loek *101:* 121
Kopelke, Lisa *154:* 107
Kopper, Lisa *72:* 152, 153; *105:* 135, 136
Korach, Mimi *1:* 128, 129; *2:* 52; *4:* 39; *5:* 159; *9:* 129; *10:* 21; *24:* 69
Koren, Edward *5:* 100; *65:* 65, 67
Kosaka, Fumi *164:* 130
Koscielniak, Bruce *99:* 122; *153:* 120, 121, 122
Koshkin, Alexander *92:* 180
Kossin, Sandy *10:* 71; *23:* 105
Kostin, Andrej *26:* 204
Kosturko, Bob *164:* 56
Kotzky, Brian *68:* 184
Kovacevic, Zivojin *13:* 247
Kovalski, Maryann *58:* 120; *84:* 88; *97:* 124, 125, 126; *158:* 3; *186:* 80
Kozjan, Drazen *209:* 99; *231:* 130; *236:* 28
Krahn, Fernando *2:* 257; *34:* 206; *49:* 152
Krall, Dan *218:* 84, 85

Kramek, Oren *231:* 119
Kramer, Anthony *33:* 81
Kramer, David *96:* 162; *109:* 132; *150:* 220
Kramer, Frank *6:* 121
Krantz, Kathy *35:* 83
Kratter, Paul *139:* 65
Kraus, Robert *13:* 217; *65:* 113; *93:* 93, 94
Krause, Jon *176:* 62
Krauss, Trisha *174:* 10
Kredel, Fritz *6:* 35; *17:* 93, 94, 95, 96; *22:* 147; *24:* 175; *29:* 130; *35:* 77; *YABC 2:* 166, 300
Kreloff, Eliot *189:* 107, 108; *205:* 182
Krementz, Jill *17:* 98; *49:* 41
Krenina, Katya *117:* 106; *125:* 133; *176:* 117; *221:* 107
Kresin, Robert *23:* 19
Kretschmar, Sonia *226:* 97
Krieger, Salem *54:* 164
Kriegler, Lyn *73:* 29
Krinitz, Esther Nisenthal *193:* 196
Krommes, Beth *128:* 141; *149:* 136; *181:* 100, 101; *184:* 105; *188:* 125; *208:* 135; *209:* 185
Krone, Mike *101:* 71
Kronheimer, Ann *135:* 119
Krosoczka, Jarrett J. *155:* 142; *200:* 93, 94
Kruck, Gerald *88:* 181
Krudop, Walter Lyon *199:* 19
Krupinski, Loretta *67:* 104; *102:* 131; *161:* 105, 106
Krupp, Robin Rector *53:* 96, 98
Krush, Beth *1:* 51, 85; *2:* 233; *4:* 115; *9:* 61; *10:* 191; *11:* 196; *18:* 164, 165; *32:* 72; *37:* 203; *43:* 57; *60:* 102, 103, 107, 108, 109
Krush, Joe *2:* 233; *4:* 115; *9:* 61; *10:* 191; *11:* 196; *18:* 164, 165; *32:* 72, 91; *37:* 203; *43:* 57; *60:* 102, 103, 107, 108, 109
Krych, Duane *91:* 43
Krykorka, Vladyana *96:* 147; *143:* 90, 91; *168:* 14
Kubick, Dana *165:* 91; *212:* 104, 105, 212
Kubinyi, Laszlo *4:* 116; *6:* 113; *16:* 118; *17:* 100; *28:* 227; *30:* 172; *49:* 24, 28; *54:* 23; *167:* 149
Kubricht, Mary *73:* 118
Kucharik, Elena *139:* 31
Kuchera, Kathleen *84:* 5
Kuhn, Bob *17:* 91; *35:* 235
Kulikov, Boris *163:* 185; *185:* 23; *205:* 99, 100; *217:* 160; *235:* 190
Kulka, Joe *188:* 110
Kukalis, Romas *90:* 27; *139:* 37
Kuklin, Susan *63:* 82, 83, 84
Kunhardt, Dorothy *53:* 101
Kunhardt, Edith *67:* 105, 106
Kunstler, Mort *10:* 73; *32:* 143
Kurchevsky, V. *34:* 61
Kurczok, Belinda *121:* 118
Kurelek, William *8:* 107
Kuriloff, Ron *13:* 19
Kurisu, Jane *160:* 120
Kurilla, Renée *231:* 117
Kuskin, Karla *2:* 170; *68:* 115, 116; *111:* 116
Kutzer, Ernst *19:* 249
Kuzma, Steve *57:* 8; *62:* 93
Kuznetsova, Berta *74:* 45
Kvasnosky, Laura McGee *93:* 103; *142:* 83; *182:* 108
Kwas, Susan Estelle *179:* 116; *217:* 90
Kyong, Yunmee *165:* 139

L

LaBlanc, Andre *24:* 146
Laboccetta, Mario *27:* 120
LaBrose, Darcie *157:* 134
Labrosse, Darcia *58:* 88; *108:* 77; *178:* 89; *236:* 126
LaCava, Vince *95:* 118

Laceky, Adam *32:* 121
Lacis, Astra *85:* 117
Lacome, Julie *174:* 96, 97
La Croix *YABC 2:* 4
Ladd, London *206:* 50
Ladwig, Tim *98:* 212; *117:* 76; *215:* 32; *223:* 111, 112
La Farge, Margaret *47:* 141
LaFave, Kim *64:* 177; *72:* 39; *97:* 146; *99:* 172; *106:* 123; *149:* 126; *196:* 128, 129
Lafontaine, Roger *167:* 158
Lafrance, Marie *197:* 109
Lagarrigue, Jerome *136:* 102; *187:* 81
Laimgruber, Monika *11:* 153
Laínez, René Colato *226:* 50
Laio, Jimmy *213:* 57
Laite, Gordon *1:* 130, 131; *8:* 209; *31:* 113; *40:* 63; *46:* 117
Laliberté, Louise-Andrée *169:* 98
LaMarche, Jim *46:* 204; *61:* 56; *94:* 69; *114:* 22; *129:* 163; *162:* 78, 80
Lamb, Jim *10:* 117
Lambase, Barbara *101:* 185; *150:* 221; *166:* 234
Lambert, J.K. *38:* 129; *39:* 24
Lambert, Sally Anne *133:* 191
Lambert, Saul *23:* 112; *33:* 107; *54:* 136
Lambert, Stephen *109:* 33; *174:* 99
Lambo, Don *6:* 156; *35:* 115; *36:* 146
Lamont, Priscilla *236:* 182
Lamontagne, Jacques *166:* 227
Lamut, Sonja *57:* 193
Lamut, Sonya *85:* 102
Landa, Peter *11:* 95; *13:* 177; *53:* 119
Landau, Jacob *38:* 111
Landis, Joan *104:* 23; *203:* 32; *235:* 33
Landon, Lucinda *79:* 31
Landshoff, Ursula *13:* 124
Landström, Lena *146:* 165, 166
Landström, Olof *146:* 166, 168; *170:* 22; *232:* 22
Lane, Daniel *112:* 60
Lane, John R. *8:* 145
Lane, John *15:* 176, 177; *30:* 146
Lane, Nancy *166:* 74
Lang, G.D. *48:* 56
Lang, Gary *73:* 75
Lang, Glenna *221:* 113
Lang, Jerry *18:* 295
Langdon, Bryan *186:* 187; *191:* 113, 114, 115; *233:* 98, 100
Lange, Dorothea *50:* 141
Langley, Jonathan *162:* 128
Langner, Nola *8:* 110; *42:* 36
Lanino, Deborah *105:* 148
Lantz, Paul *1:* 82, 102; *27:* 88; *34:* 102; *45:* 123
Larkin, Bob *84:* 225
Laroche, Giles *126:* 140; *146:* 81; *221:* 116, 117
LaRochelle, David *171:* 97
Larrañaga, Ana Martín *229:* 106
Larrecq, John *44:* 108; *68:* 56
Larsen, Suzanne *1:* 13
Larson, Gary *57:* 121, 122, 123, 124, 125, 126, 127
Larsson, Carl *35:* 144, 145, 146, 147, 148, 149, 150, 152, 153, 154
Larsson, Karl *19:* 177
Lartitegui, Ana G. *105:* 167
LaRue, Jenna *167:* 20
La Rue, Michael D. *13:* 215
Lasker, Joe *7:* 186, 187; *14:* 55; *38:* 115; *39:* 47; *83:* 113, 114, 115
Latham, Barbara *16:* 188, 189; *43:* 71
Lathrop, Dorothy *14:* 117, 118, 119; *15:* 109; *16:* 78, 79, 81; *32:* 201, 203; *33:* 112; *YABC 2:* 301
Latimer, Miriam *234:* 205; *235:* 122
Lattimore, Eleanor Frances *7:* 156
Lauden, Claire *16:* 173

Lauden, George, Jr. *16:* 173
Laune, Paul *2:* 235; *34:* 31
Laure, Jason *49:* 53; *50:* 122
Lauter, Richard *63:* 29; *67:* 111; *77:* 198
Lavallee, Barbara *74:* 157; *92:* 154; *96:* 126; *145:* 193; *166:* 125, 126; *186:* 155; *192:* 172; *231:* 165; *232:* 131
Lave, Fitz Hugh *59:* 139
Lavis, Steve *43:* 143; *87:* 137, 164, 165; *222:* 161; *225:* 121
Layton, Neal *152:* 120, 121; *182:* 65; *187:* 103, 105, 106
Law, Jenny *201:* 31
Lawrason, June *168:* 30
Lawrence, John *25:* 131; *30:* 141; *44:* 198, 200; *214:* 7
Lawrence, Stephen *20:* 195
Lawson, Carol *6:* 38; *42:* 93, 131; *174:* 56; *189:* 89; *209:* 59
Lawson, George *17:* 280
Lawson, Robert *5:* 26; *6:* 94; *13:* 39; *16:* 11; *20:* 100, 102, 103; *54:* 3; *66:* 12; *100:* 144, 145; *YABC 2:* 222, 224, 225, 227, 228, 229, 230, 231, 232, 233, 234, 235, 237, 238, 239, 240, 241
Layfield, Kathie *60:* 194
Lazare, Jerry *44:* 109; *74:* 28
Lazarevich, Mila *17:* 118
Lazarus, Claire *103:* 30
Lazarus, Keo Felker *21:* 94
Lazzaro, Victor *11:* 126
Lea, Bob *166:* 208; *203:* 108
Lea, Tom *43:* 72, 74
Leacroft, Richard *6:* 140
Leaf, Munro *20:* 99
Leake, Donald *70:* 41
Leander, Patricia *23:* 27
Lear, Edward *18:* 183, 184, 185
Lear, Rebecca *149:* 46
Lebenson, Richard *6:* 209; *7:* 76; *23:* 145; *44:* 191; *87:* 153
Le Cain, Errol *6:* 141; *9:* 3; *22:* 142; *25:* 198; *28:* 173; *68:* 128, 129; *86:* 49
Lechon, Daniel *113:* 211
Leder, Dora *129:* 172
Ledger, Bill *181:* 58
Leduc, Bernard *102:* 36
Lee, Alan *62:* 25, 28
Lee, Bryce *99:* 60; *101:* 195; *196:* 53
Lee, Chinlun *181:* 138; *182:* 112
Lee, Declan *191:* 20
Lee, Dom *83:* 118, 120; *93:* 123; *121:* 121, 126; *146:* 174, 175, 206, 207; *174:* 204
Lee, Doris *13:* 246; *32:* 183; *44:* 111
Lee, Hector Viveros *115:* 96
Lee, Ho Baek *200:* 160
Lee, Huy Voun *217:* 106
Lee, Jeanne M. *158:* 56
Lee, Jared *93:* 200; *157:* 229; *215:* 113, 191, 192, 193; *228:* 177
Lee, Jody *81:* 121; *82:* 225; *91:* 155; *100:* 182
Lee, Jody A. *127:* 124, 126, 127
　See also Lee, Jody
Lee, Manning de V. *2:* 200; *17:* 12; *27:* 87; *37:* 102, 103, 104; *YABC 2:* 304
Lee, Margaret *213:* 179
Lee, Marie G. *138:* 157
Lee, Paul *97:* 100; *105:* 72, 209; *109:* 177; *128:* 113; *202:* 45
Lee, Robert J. *3:* 97; *67:* 124
Lee, Victor *96:* 228; *105:* 182; *140:* 196; *208:* 191
Lee, Virginia *208:* 139, 140; *218:* 28
Leech, Dorothy *98:* 76
Leech, John *15:* 59
Leedy, Loreen *84:* 142; *128:* 144, 145, 146; *175:* 125, 126, 127
Leeman, Michael *44:* 157
Leeming, Catherine *87:* 39
Lees, Harry *6:* 112
LeFever, Bill *88:* 220, 221

Legenisel *47:* 111
Legrand, Edy *18:* 89, 93
Lehman, Barbara *73:* 123; *170:* 130
Lehrman, Rosalie *2:* 180
Leichman, Seymour *5:* 107
Leick, Bonnie *205:* 104
Leighton, Clare *25:* 130; *33:* 168; *37:* 105, 106, 108,109
Leisk, David *1:* 140, 141; *11:* 54; *30:* 137, 142, 143,144
Leister, Bryan *89:* 45; *106:* 37; *114:* 67; *149:* 236; *222:* 181; *237:* 142
Leloir, Maurice *18:* 77, 80, 83, 99
Lemaître, Pascal *144:* 175; *176:* 130; *189:* 135; *225:* 124, 125
Lemieux, Michele *100:* 148; *139:* 153
Lemke, Horst *14:* 98; *38:* 117, 118, 119
Lemke, R.W. *42:* 162
Lemon, David Gwynne *9:* 1
LeMoult, Adolph *82:* 116
Lenn, Michael *136:* 89
Lennon, John *114:* 100
Lennox, Elsie *95:* 163; *143:* 160
Lenski, Lois *1:* 144; *26:* 135, 137, 139, 141; *100:* 153, 154
Lent, Blair *1:* 116, 117; *2:* 174; *3:* 206, 207; *7:* 168, 169; *34:* 62; *68:* 217; *133:* 101; *183:* 60
Leon, Jana *226:* 214
Leonard, David *212:* 149
Leonard, Richard *91:* 128
Leonard, Tom *207:* 95; *219:* 55
Leone, Leonard *49:* 190
Lerner, Carol *86:* 140, 141, 142
Lerner, Judith *116:* 138
Lerner, Sharon *11:* 157; *22:* 56
Leroux-Hugon, Helene *132:* 139
Leslie, Cecil *19:* 244
Lessac, Frané *80:* 182, 207; *96:* 182; *202:* 58; *209:* 104
Lessing, Erich *167:* 52; *173:* 60
Lester, Alison *50:* 124; *90:* 147, 148; *129:* 130; *218:* 91, 93
Lester, Mike *208:* 50
Lethcoe, Jason *191:* 116, 117
Le Tord, Bijou *49:* 156; *95:* 112
Leutz, Emanuel *165:* 27
Levai, Blaise *39:* 130
Levert, Mireille *211:* 101
Levin, Ted *12:* 148
Levine, David *43:* 147, 149, 150, 151, 152; *64:* 11
Levine, Joe *71:* 88; *219:* 74
Levine, Marge *81:* 127
Levinson, David *178:* 232
Levit, Herschel *24:* 223
Levstek, Ljuba *131:* 192; *134:* 216; *149:* 65; *168:* 180
Levy, Jessica Ann *19:* 225; *39:* 191
Levy, Lina *117:* 126
Lewin, Betsy *32:* 114; *48:* 177; *90:* 151; *91:* 125; *92:* 85; *115:* 105; *169:* 110, 111; *178:* 47; *186:* 188; *194:* 201; *222:* 120; *226:* 139
Lewin, Ted *4:* 77; *8:* 168; *20:* 110; *21:* 99,100; *27:* 110; *28:* 96, 97; *31:* 49; *45:* 55; *48:* 223; *60:* 20, 119, 120; *62:* 139; *66:* 108; *71:* 12; *72:* 21; *74:* 226; *76:* 139, 140, 141; *77:* 82; *79:* 87; *85:* 49, 177; *86:* 55; *88:* 182; *93:* 28, 29; *94:* 34, 182, 194; *99:* 156; *104:* 8; *115:* 123; *118:* 74; *119:* 114, 116; *131:* 54; *145:* 99; *165:* 151; *177:* 75; *178:* 42; *190:* 30; *192:* 86; *195:* 101, 102; *203:* 52; *222:* 119; *226:* 136, 137, 138, 139
Lewis, Allen *15:* 112
Lewis, Anthony *227:* 114
Lewis, E.B. *88:* 143; *93:* 109; *119:* 79; *124:* 113; *128:* 49; *151:* 167; *168:* 110; *173:* 121; *174:* 66; *176:* 7; *184:* 150; *185:* 191; *211:* 108, 109, 110, 111; *223:* 17
Lewis, H.B. *170:* 124
Lewis, J. Patrick *162:* 83

Lewis, Jan *81:* 22
Lewis, Kim *136:* 165; *217:* 109, 111
Lewis, Richard W. *52:* 25
Lewis, Robin Baird *98:* 193
Lew-Vriethoff, Joanne *225:* 181
Leydon, Rita Floden *21:* 101
Li, Xiojun *187:* 172
Liao, Jimmy *202:* 100
Lichtenheld, Tom *152:* 125, 126; *222:* 160; *224:* 9
Lieblich, Irene *22:* 173; *27:* 209, 214
Lieder, Rick *108:* 197; *199:* 58, 59, 60
Lies, Brian *92:* 40; *141:* 101; *150:* 138; *190:* 97, 98, 99,
Liese, Charles *4:* 222
Liew, Sonny *219:* 108
Life, Kay *79:* 49
Lifton, Robert Jay *66:* 154
Lightburn, Ron *86:* 153; *91:* 122
Lightfoot, Norman R. *45:* 47
Lignell, Lois *37:* 114
Lill, Debra *121:* 70
Lilly, Charles *8:* 73; *20:* 127; *48:* 53; *72:* 9,16; *77:* 98; *102:* 94
Lilly, Ken *37:* 224
Lim, John *43:* 153
Limona, Mercedes *51:* 183
Lin, Grace *143:* 217; *162:* 86, 87; *174:* 185
Lincoln, Patricia Henderson *27:* 27; *78:* 127
Lindahn, Ron *84:* 17
Lindahn, Val *84:* 17
Lindberg, Howard *10:* 123; *16:* 190
Lindberg, Jeffrey *64:* 77; *77:* 71; *79:* 54; *80:* 149; *174:* 109; *179:* 52
Linden, Seymour *18:* 200, 201; *43:* 140
Lindenbaum, Pija *144:* 143; *183:* 113
Linder, Richard *27:* 119
Lindman, Maj *43:* 154
Lindsay, Norman *67:* 114
Lindsay, Vachel *40:* 118
Lindstrom, Jack *145:* 118
Line, Les *27:* 143
Linell
   See Smith, Linell
Lintern, Tom *228:* 101
Lionni, Leo *8:* 115; *72:* 159, 160, 161
Lipinsky, Lino *2:* 156; *22:* 175
Lippincott, Gary A. *70:* 35; *119:* 118; *220:* 105, 106, 107
Lippman, Peter *8:* 31; *31:* 119, 120, 160
Lisi, Victoria *89:* 145
Lisker, Emily *169:* 114
Lisker, Sonia O. *16:* 274; *31:* 31; *44:* 113, 114
Lisowski, Gabriel *47:* 144; *49:* 157
Lissim, Simon *17:* 138
Little, Ed *89:* 145; *151:* 53
Little, Harold *16:* 72
Little, Mary E. *28:* 146
Littlewood, Karen *165:* 126; *211:* 112
Litty, Julie *111:* 63
Litwin, Mike *235:* 59, 136
Litzinger, Rosanne *151:* 101; *176:* 118; *196:* 133, 134, 135; *208:* 129; *209:* 147
Liu, Lesley *143:* 72
Lively, Lorna *19:* 216
Livingston, Susan *95:* 22
Liwska, Renata *164:* 113; *199:* 25, 69; *220:* 79
Ljungkvist, Laura *180:* 120
Llerena, Carlos Antonio *19:* 181
Lloyd, Errol *11:* 39; *22:* 178
Lloyd, Megan *77:* 118; *80:* 113; *97:* 75; *117:* 94, 95; *189:* 121, 122; *208:* 128; *211:* 72
Lloyd, Sam *183:* 116, 117
Lo, Beth *165:* 154
Lo, Koon-chiu *7:* 134
Loates, Glen *63:* 76
Lobel, Anita *6:* 87; *9:* 141; *18:* 248; *55:* 85,86, 87, 88, 93, 104; *60:* 67; *78:* 263; *82:* 110; *96:* 157, 159; *101:* 84; *132:* 35; *162:* 93, 94

Lobel, Arnold *1:* 188, 189; *5:* 12; *6:* 147; *7:* 167, 209; *18:* 190, 191; *25:* 39, 43; *27:* 40; *29:* 174; *52:* 127; *55:* 89, 91, 94, 95, 97, 98, 99, 100, 101, 102,103, 105, 106; *60:* 18, 31; *66:* 181, 183; *75:* 57; *82:* 246; *136:* 146
Lobel, Gillian *190:* 21
Lobo, Jen *229:* 53
Locker, Thomas *109:* 134
Lodge, Bernard *107:* 125, 126; *153:* 93
Loeb, Jeph *153:* 177
Lodge, Jo *112:* 119
Loefgren, Ulf *3:* 108
Loescher, Ann *20:* 108
Loescher, Gil *20:* 108
Loew, David *93:* 184; *171:* 120; *211:* 187
Lofting, Hugh *15:* 182, 183; *100:* 161, 162
Lofts, Pamela *60:* 188
Loh, George *38:* 88
Lomberg, Jon *58:* 160
Lonette, Reisie *11:* 211; *12:* 168; *13:* 56; *36:* 122; *43:* 155
Long, Ethan *168:* 146; *178:* 12; *182:* 120, 121; *196:* 124; *223:* 116, 117; *235:* 127
Long, Laurel *162:* 135; *190:* 11; *203:* 113, 114; *228:* 212
Long, Loren *99:* 176; *172:* 65; *182:* 78; *188:* 114, 115
Long, Melinda *152:* 128
Long, Miles *115:* 174
Long, Sally *42:* 184
Long, Sylvia *74:* 168; *132:* 63; *179:* 134
Longoni, Eduardo *73:* 86
Longtemps, Ken *17:* 123; *29:* 221; *69:* 82
Looser, Heinz *YABC 2:* 208
Lopez, Loretta *190:* 100
López, Rafael *197:* 160; *198:* 85
Lopshire, Robert *6:* 149; *21:* 117; *34:* 166; *73:* 13; *233:* 103
Lord, John Vernon *21:* 104; *23:* 25; *51:* 22
Lorenz, Albert *40:* 146; *115:* 127
Lorenzen, Geoffrey *229:* 24
Loretta, Sister Mary *33:* 73
Lorraine, Walter H. *3:* 110; *4:* 123; *16:* 192; *103:* 119
Los, Marek *146:* 22; *193:* 23
Loss, Joan *11:* 163
Louderback, Walt *YABC 1:* 164
Loughridge, Stuart *214:* 131
Louis, Catherine *212:* 186
Lousada, Sandra *40:* 138
Louth, Jack *149:* 252; *151:* 191, 192
Love, Judy *173:* 43; *196:* 40; *235:* 24
Lovelock, Brian *214:* 132, 197
Low, Joseph *14:* 124, 125; *18:* 68; *19:* 194; *31:* 166; *80:* 239
Low, William *62:* 175; *80:* 147; *112:* 194; *150:* 202; *169:* 175; *177:* 110; *192:* 27
Lowe, Vicky *177:* 130
Lowenheim, Alfred *13:* 65, 66
Lowenstein, Sallie *116:* 90, 91
Lowery, Mike *227:* 115
Lowitz, Anson *17:* 124; *18:* 215
Lowrey, Jo *8:* 133
Loxton, Daniel *229:* 109
Lubach, Vanessa *142:* 152
Lubell, Winifred *1:* 207; *3:* 15; *6:* 151
Lubin, Leonard B. *19:* 224; *36:* 79, 80; *45:* 128, 129,131, 132, 133, 134, 135, 136, 137, 139, 140, 141; *70:* 95; *YABC2:* 96
Lucas, David *208:* 148
Lucht, Irmgard *82:* 145
Ludwig, Helen *33:* 144, 145
Luebs, Robin *212:* 109
Lufkin, Raymond *38:* 138; *44:* 48
Luhrs, Henry *7:* 123; *11:* 120
Lujan, Tonita *82:* 33
Lum, Bernice *230:* 70
Lupo, Dom *4:* 204
Lustig, Loretta *30:* 186; *46:* 134, 135, 136, 137
Lutes, Jason *210:* 163

Luthardt, Kevin *172:* 125, 126; *217:* 2
Luxbacher, Irene *153:* 145; *219:* 112, 113
Luzak, Dennis *52:* 121; *99:* 142
Lydbury, Jane *82:* 98
Lydecker, Laura *21:* 113; *42:* 53
Lynch, Charles *16:* 33
Lynch, Marietta *29:* 137; *30:* 171
Lynch, P.J. *126:* 228; *129:* 110; *132:* 247; *183:* 64; *207:* 184; *213:* 100, 101, 102; *237:* 164
Lyne, Alison Davis *188:* 118, 198
Lyon, Carol *102:* 26
Lyon, Elinor *6:* 154
Lyon, Fred *14:* 16
Lyon, Lea *212:* 110
Lyon, Tammie *175:* 170
Lyons, Oren *8:* 193
Lyster, Michael *26:* 41

M

Maas, Dorothy *6:* 175
Maas, Julie *47:* 61
Macaulay, David *46:* 139, 140, 141, 142, 143, 144, 145, 147, 149, 150; *72:* 167, 168, 169; *137:* 129, 130, 131, 132
MacCarthy, Patricia *69:* 141
Macdonald, Alister *21:* 55
Macdonald, Roberta *19:* 237; *52:* 164
MacDonald, Norman *13:* 99
MacDonald, Ross *201:* 103
MacDonald, Suse *54:* 41; *109* 138; *130:* 156; *193:* 106, 107, 109, 110
Mace, Varian *49:* 159
MacEachern, Stephen *206:* 2
Macguire, Robert Reid *18:* 67
Machetanz, Fredrick *34:* 147, 148
MacInnes, Cat *236:* 51
MacInnes, Ian *35:* 59
MacIntyre, Elisabeth *17:* 127, 128
Mack, Jeff *161:* 128; *194:* 119, 120; *219:* 67; *225:* 135
Mack, Stan *17:* 129; *96:* 33
Mackay, Donald *17:* 60
MacKaye, Arvia *32:* 119
Mackenzie, Robert *204:* 78
Mackenzie, Stuart *73:* 213
MacKenzie, Garry *33:* 159
Mackie, Clare *87:* 134
Mackinlay, Miguel *27:* 22
MacKinstry, Elizabeth *15:* 110; *42:* 139, 140, 141, 142, 143,144, 145
MacLeod, Lee *91:* 167
Maclise, Daniel *YABC 2:* 257
Macnaughton, Tina *182:* 145; *218:* 106, 107
MacRae, Tom *181:* 112
Madden, Don *3:* 112, 113; *4:* 33, 108, 155; *7:* 193; *78:* 12; *YABC 2:* 211
Maddison, Angela Mary *10:* 83
Madrid, Erwin *229:* 117
Madsen, Jim *146:* 259; *152:* 237; *184:* 106; *197:* 21; *202:* 103, 104; *233:* 38
Maestro, Giulio *8:* 124; *12:* 17; *13:* 108; *25:* 182; *54:* 147; *59:* 114, 115, 116, 117, 118, 121, 123, 124, 125,126, 127; *68:* 37, 38; *106:* 129, 130, 131, 136, 137, 138
Maffia, Daniel *60:* 200
Maggio, Viqui *58:* 136, 181; *74:* 150; *75:* 90; *85:* 159; *90:* 158; *109:* 184; *193:* 113
Magnus, Erica *77:* 123
Magnuson, Diana *28:* 102; *34:* 190; *41:* 175
Magoon, Scott *181:* 104; *217:* 165; *222:* 126
Magovern, Peg *103:* 123; *218:* 164
Maguire, Sheila *41:* 100
Magurn, Susan *91:* 30
Mahony, Will *37:* 120
Mahony, Will *85:* 116
Mahood, Kenneth *24:* 141
Mahurin, Matt *164:* 225; *175:* 95; *189:* 37; *196:* 14; *209:* 163; *229:* 179

Maik, Henri *9:* 102
Maione, Heather *106:* 5; *178:* 8; *189:* 126, 127; *193:* 58
Mair, J. Sonia *237:* 84
Maisto, Carol *29:* 87
Maitland, Antony *1:* 100, 176; *8:* 41; *17:* 246; *24:* 46; *25:* 177, 178; *32:* 74; *60:* 65, 195; *67:* 156; *87:* 131; *101:* 110
Majewski, Dawn W. *169:* 95
Mak, Kam *72:* 25; *75:* 43; *87:* 186; *97:* 24; *102:* 154; *149:* 195; *186:* 28; *209:* 132
Makie, Pam *37:* 117
Maktima, Joe *116:* 191
Maland, Nick *99:* 77
Male, Alan *132:* 64
Malone, James Hiram *84:* 161
Malone, Nola Langner *82:* 239
Malone, Peter *191:* 121, 122, 123
Malsberg, Edward *51:* 175
Malvern, Corinne *2:* 13; *34:* 148, 149
Manchess, Gregory *165:* 241; *203:* 119
Mancusi, Stephen *63:* 198, 199
Mandelbaum, Ira *31:* 115
Manders, John *138:* 152, 155; *188:* 171; *190:* 92; *199:* 5; *217:* 52; *219:* 35; *219:* 115, 116, 117
Mandine, Selma *228:* 103
Manet, Edouard *23:* 170
Mangiat, Jeff *173:* 127
Mangurian, David *14:* 133
Manham, Allan *42:* 109; *77:* 180; *80:* 227
Manley, Matt *103:* 167; *117:* 98; *172:* 49; *212:* 207
Manna, Giovanni *178:* 44
Manniche, Lise *31:* 121
Manning, Jane *96:* 203; *233:* 107
Manning, Jo *63:* 154
Manning, Lawrence *191:* 153
Manning, Maurie J. *211:* 116
Manning, Mick *176:* 139; *224:* 57
Manning, Samuel F. *5:* 75
Mantel, Richard *57:* 73; *63:* 106; *82:* 255
Mantha, John *205:* 164; *217:* 117
Maraja *15:* 86; *YABC 1:* 28; *2:* 115
Marcellino, Fred *20:* 125; *34:* 222; *53:* 125; *58:* 205; *61:* 64, 121, 122; *68:* 154, 156, 157, 158, 159; *72:* 25; *86:* 184; *98:* 181; *118:* 129, 130, 131; *149:* 218; *194:* 7
Marchesi, Stephen *34:* 140; *46:* 72; *50:* 147; *66:* 239; *70:* 33; *73:* 18, 114, 163; *77:* 47, 76,147; *78:* 79; *80:* 30; *81:* 6; *89:* 66; *93:* 21,130; *94:* 94; *97:* 66; *98:* 96; *114:* 115, 116
Marchiori, Carlos *14:* 60
Marciano, John Bemelmans *118:* 133; *167:* 110, 111, 112
Marconi, Guilherme *220:* 143
Marcus, Barry David *139:* 248; *145:* 18
Maren, Julie *199:* 73
Margules, Gabriele *21:* 120
Mariana
    See Foster, Marian Curtis
Mariano, Michael *52:* 108
Marino, Dorothy *6:* 37; *14:* 135
Mario, Heide Stetson *101:* 202
Maris, Ron *71:* 123
Maritz, Nicolaas *85:* 123
Mark, Mona *65:* 105; *68:* 205; *116:* 213
Markham, R.L. *17:* 240
Marklew, Gilly *211:* 118
Marks, Alan *104:* 104; *109:* 182; *164:* 92; *185:* 134; *187:* 120, 121, 122; *218:* 114, 115; *230:* 165
Marks, Cara *54:* 9
Marks, Colin *203:* 129
Marokvia, Artur *31:* 122
Marquez, Susan *108:* 121; *219:* 95
Marrella, Maria Pia *62:* 116
Marriott, Pat *30:* 30; *34:* 39; *35:* 164, 165, 166; *44:* 170; *48:* 186, 187, 188, 189, 191, 192, 193; *91:* 92

Mars, W.T. *1:* 161; *3:* 115; *4:* 208, 225; *5:* 92, 105, 186; *8:* 214; *9:* 12; *13:* 121; *27:* 151; *31:* 180; *38:* 102; *48:* 66; *62:* 164, 165; *64:* 62; *68:* 229; *79:* 55
Marschall, Ken *85:* 29
Marsh, Christine *3:* 164
Marsh, James *73:* 137
Marsh, Reginald *17:* 5; *19:* 89; *22:* 90, 96
Marshall, Anthony D. *18:* 216
Marshall, Felicia *170:* 190
Marshall, James *6:* 160; *40:* 221; *42:* 24, 25, 29; *51:* 111, 112, 113, 114, 115, 116, 117, 118, 119, 120, 121; *64:* 13; *75:* 126, 127, 128, 129; *102:* 10, 12; *216:* 26, 28
Marshall, Janet *97:* 154
Marstall, Bob *55:* 145; *84:* 153, 170; *104:* 145; *154:* 166, 167, 168
Martchenko, Michael *50:* 129, 153, 155, 156, 157; *83:* 144,145; *154:* 137, 138, 139
Marten, Ruth *129:* 52
Martin, Brad *199:* 186
Martin, Charles E. *70:* 144
Martin, Courtney A. *214:* 28
Martin, David Stone *24:* 232; *62:* 4
Martin, Fletcher *18:* 213; *23:* 151
Martin, Rene *7:* 144; *42:* 148, 149, 150
Martin, Richard E. *51:* 157; *131:* 203
Martin, Ron *32:* 81
Martin, Stefan *8:* 68; *32:* 124, 126, *56:* 33
Martin, Whitney *166:* 137
Martinez, Ed *58:* 192; *72:* 231; *77:* 33; *80:* 214; *167:* 123
Martinez, John *6:* 113; *118:* 13; *139:* 143
Martinez, Sergio *158:* 190; *220:* 156
Martini, Angela *183:* 161; *226:* 195
Martiniere, Stephan *171:* 130
Marton, Jirina *95:* 127, 128; *144:* 145; *230:* 73, 74, 75
Martorell, Antonio *84:* 6; *97:* 161
Martucci, Griesbach *52:* 106
Marvin, Frederic *83:* 86
Marx, Robert F. *24:* 143
Marzollo, Jean *190:* 127
Masefield, Judith *19:* 208, 209
Masheris, Robert *78:* 51
Masiello, Ralph *186:* 171; *214:* 134
Mason, George F. *14:* 139
Mason, Robert *84:* 96
Masse, Josée *208:* 45; *217:* 19; *221:* 134; *234:* 184
Massey, Barbara *68:* 142
Massie, Diane Redfield *16:* 194
Massie, Kim *31:* 43
Massini, Sarah *213:* 79
Mataya, David *121:* 66
Mathers, Petra *119:* 135; *163:* 104; *176:* 143, 144; *187:* 142; *196:* 101
Mathewuse, James *51:* 143
Mathieu, Joseph *14:* 33; *39:* 206; *43:* 167; *56:* 180; *79:* 126; *94:* 147; *185:* 140; *236:* 57
Matje, Martin *169:* 177, 178; *172:* 180
Matsubara, Naoko *12:* 121
Matsuda, Shizu *13:* 167
Matsuoka, Mei *192:* 135; *214:* 84
Matte, L'Enc *22:* 183
Mattelson, Marvin *36:* 50, 51
Matheson, Jenny *180:* 132; *222:* 153
Matthews, Elizabeth *194:* 128; *223:* 35
Matthews, F. Leslie *4:* 216
Matthews, Tina *190:* 130
Mattingly, David *71:* 76, 77; *82:* 64; *91:* 216, 217; *109:* 25
Matulay, Laszlo *5:* 18; *43:* 168
Matus, Greta *12:* 142
Maughan, Bill *181:* 31; *211:* 211
Mauldin, Bill *27:* 23
Mauterer, Erin Marie *119:* 5
Mawicke, Tran *9:* 137; *15:* 191; *47:* 100
Mawson, Matt *74:* 115
Max, Peter *45:* 146, 147, 148, 149, 150
Maxie, Betty *40:* 135

Maxwell, John Alan *1:* 148
May, Katie *225:* 128
May, Steve *204:* 30
Mayan, Earl *7:* 193
Maydak, Michael S. *220:* 117
Mayer, Bill *200:* 138
Mayer, Danuta *117:* 103
Mayer, Marianna *32:* 132
Mayer, Mercer *11:* 192; *16:* 195, 196; *20:* 55, 57; *32:* 129, 130, 132, 133, 134; *41:* 144, 248, 252; *58:* 186; *73:* 140, 142, 143; *137:* 137, 138
Mayforth, Hal *166:* 77
Mayhew, James *85:* 121; *138:* 187; *149:* 140; *204:* 81
Mayhew, Richard *3:* 106
Mayo, Gretchen Will *38:* 81; *84:* 166
Mays, Victor *5:* 127; *8:* 45, 153; *14:* 245; *23:* 50; *34:* 155; *40:* 79; *45:* 158; *54:* 91; *66:* 240
Mazal, Chanan *49:* 104
Maze, Deborah *71:* 83
Mazellan, Ron *75:* 97, 98; *210:* 169
Mazetti, Alan *112:* 72
Mazille, Capucine *96:* 168
Mazza, Adriana Saviozzi *19:* 215
Mazzella, Mary Jo *82:* 165
Mazzetti, Alan *45:* 210
McAfee, Steve *135:* 146; *167:* 176; *191:* 84; *210:* 117; *218:* 34; *233:* 86
McAlinden, Paul *112:* 128
McBride, Angus *28:* 49; *103:* 40
McBride, Will *30:* 110
McCaffery, Janet *38:* 145
McCall, Bruce *209:* 119
McCallum, Graham *78:* 78
McCallum, Stephen *141:* 143; *156:* 5; *166:* 228
McCann, Gerald *3:* 50; *4:* 94; *7:* 54; *41:* 121
McCarthy, Dan *174:* 74
McCarthy, Linda *177:* 128; *218:* 104
McCarthy, Meghan *168:* 134; *199:* 74
McCauley, Adam *157:* 36; *184:* 199; *193:* 100; *209:* 122
McCay, Winsor *41:* 124, 126, 128, 129, 130, 131; *134:* 77, 79
McClary, Nelson *1:* 111
McClements, George *196:* 146
McClennan, Connie *210:* 181
McClintock, Barbara *57:* 135; *95:* 130; *146:* 190; *213:* 3, 5, 107, 108
McClintock, Theodore *14:* 141
McCloskey, Robert *1:* 184, 185; *2:* 186, 187; *17:* 209; *39:* 139, 140, 141, 142, 143, 146, 147, 148; *85:* 150, 151; *100:* 172, 173, 174
McClung, Robert *2:* 189; *68:* 166, 167
McClure, Gillian *31:* 132; *150:* 53
McClure, Nikki *218:* 120
McConnel, Jerry *31:* 75, 187
McConnell, Mary *102:* 49
McCord, Kathleen Garry *78:* 236
McCormack, John *66:* 193
McCormick, A.D. *35:* 119
McCormick, Dell J. *19:* 216
McCoy, Glenn *212:* 132
McCrady, Lady *16:* 198; *39:* 127
McCrea, James *3:* 122; *33:* 216
McCrea, Ruth *3:* 122; *27:* 102; *33:* 216
McCue, Lisa *65:* 148, 149; *77:* 54; *80:* 132; *175:* 33; *177:* 133, 135; *212:* 136, 137, 138
McCully, Emily Arnold *2:* 89; *4:* 120, 121, 146, 197; *5:* 2, 129; *7:* 191; *11:* 122; *15:* 210; *33:* 23; *35:* 244; *37:* 122; *39:* 88; *40:* 103; *50:* 30,31, 32, 33, 34, 35, 36, 37; *52:* 89, 90; *57:* 6; *62:* 3; *70:* 195; *86:* 82; *96:* 192; *97:* 93; *110:* 143,144; *117:* 47; *167:* 96; *210:* 175, 176; *225:* 179; *231:* 157
McCurdy, Michael *13:* 153; *24:* 85; *81:* 160; *82:* 157, 158; *86:* 125; *97:* 92; *117:* 178; *132:* 6; *147:* 159, 160; *237:* 92, 93, 94
McCusker, Paul *99:* 19

McDaniel, Jerry *132:* 135
McDaniel, Preston *160:* 206; *170:* 139
McDermott, Beverly Brodsky *11:* 180
McDermott, Gerald *16:* 201; *74:* 174, 175; *163:* 150, 151
McDermott, Mike *96:* 187
McDonald, Jill *13:* 155; *26:* 128
McDonald, Mercedes *169:* 118
McDonald, Ralph J. *5:* 123, 195
McDonnell, Flora *146:* 199, 200
McDonnell, Patrick *179:* 153, 154; *221:* 136, 137, 138
McDonough, Don *10:* 163
McElligott, Matt *196:* 147
McElmurry, Jill *137:* 148; *163:* 141; *202:* 186
McElrath-Eslick, Lori *129:* 145; *142:* 21; *173:* 123; *202:* 194; *204:* 88, 89
McEntee, Dorothy *37:* 124
McEwan, Keith *88:* 116; *165:* 122, 123
McEwen, Katharine *169:* 34
McFall, Christie *12:* 144
McFeely, Daniel *160:* 213
McGaw, Laurie *109:* 243; *143:* 216; *211:* 218
McGee, Barbara *6:* 165
McGee, Marni *163:* 153
McGillvray, Kim *158:* 171; *165:* 213; *186:* 183; *190:* 175
McGinley-Nally, Sharon *131:* 19
McGinnis, Robert *110:* 113; *177:* 80
McGovern, Tara *98:* 171
McGraw, Sheila *83:* 146
McGregor, Barbara *200:* 155
McGregor, Malcolm *23:* 27
McGrory, Anik *193:* 120
McGuire, Robert *204:* 57; *209:* 86
McGuirk, Leslie *152:* 159
McHale, John *138:* 190
McHenry, E.B. *193:* 122
McHugh, Tom *23:* 64
McIntosh, Jon *42:* 56
McKay, Donald *2:* 118; *32:* 157; *45:* 151, 152
McKean, Dave *150:* 71; *174:* 156; *197:* 83, 118; *229:* 45, 46
McKeating, Eileen *44:* 58
McKee, David *10:* 48; *21:* 9; *70:* 154, 155, 107: 139, 140, 141; *134:* 218; *158:* 148, 149, 150, 151; *228:* 171
McKee, Diana *109:* 185
McKelvey, Patrick *164:* 141
McKendry, Joe *170:* 136
McKeveny, Tom *164:* 60; *173:* 79
McKie, Roy *7:* 44
McKie, Todd *205:* 181
McKillip, Kathy *30:* 153
McKinney, Ena *26:* 39
McKinnon, James *136:* 75
McKowen, Scott *172:* 63; *202:* 49
McLachlan, Edward *5:* 89
McLaren, Chesley *133:* 53; *213:* 112; *219:* 31
McLaren, Kirsty *123:* 99; *124:* 226
Mclean, Andrew *113:* 117, 118, 120, 121; *172:* 130, 131
Mclean, Janet *172:* 130
McLean, Meg *94:* 196
McLean, Sammis *32:* 197
McLean, Wilson *90:* 29; *113:* 195
McLoughlin, John C. *47:* 149
McLoughlin, Wayne *102:* 230; *134:* 178; *216:* 196
McMahon, Robert *36:* 155; *69:* 169
McManus, Shawn *85:* 71
McMenemy, Sarah *156:* 139; *211:* 93; *224:* 139; *226:* 152
McMillan, Bruce *22:* 184
McMullan, James *40:* 33; *67:* 172; *87:* 142; *99:* 63, 64; *189:* 133; *196:* 51
McMullen, Nigel *146:* 177
McNeely, Tom *162:* 55
McNaught, Harry *12:* 80; *32:* 136
McNaughton, Colin *39:* 149; *40:* 108; *92:* 144, 145, 146; *134:* 104, 106; *211:* 122, 123, 124

McNicholas, Maureen *38:* 148
McNicholas, Shelagh *173:* 61; *191:* 125, 126
McPhail, David *14:* 105; *23:* 135; *37:* 217, 218, 220,221; *47:* 151, 152, 153, 154, 155, 156, 158, 159, 160, 162, 163, 164; *71:* 211; *81:* 139, 140, 142; *86:* 123; *132:* 150; *140:* 129, 131, 132; *183:* 134, 135, 137; *189:* 132; *219:* 121, 122, 123, 124, 125; *231:* 158
McPhee, Richard B. *41:* 133
McPheeters, Neal *78:* 132; *86:* 90; *99:* 162; *111:* 141; *142:* 162; *231:* 146
McQuade, Jacqueline *124:* 223
McQueen, Lucinda *28:* 149; *41:* 249; *46:* 206; *53:* 103
McQuillan, Mary *153:* 97; *200:* 140
McVay, Tracy *11:* 68
McVicker, Charles *39:* 150
McWilliam, Howard *219:* 135
Mead, Ben Carlton *43:* 75
Meade, Holly *90:* 102; *94:* 101; *149:* 8; *151:* 107
Mecray, John *33:* 62
Meddaugh, Susan *20:* 42; *29:* 143; *41:* 241; *77:* 50; *84:* 173, 174, 175, 176, 177, 178; *125:* 160, 161, 162; *176:* 148, 149, 150, 151
Meehan, Dennis B. *56:* 144
Meents, Len W. *73:* 147, 150
Meers, Tony *99:* 113
Meisel, Paul *98:* 137; *124:* 18; *162:* 180; *179:* 16; *181:* 62; *194:* 154; *221:* 5; *224:* 100, 101, 102, 133; *231:* 25
Melanson, Luc *149:* 229; *198:* 97, 98; *221:* 166
Melendez, Francisco *72:* 180
Melling, David *202:* 199
Melnychuk, Monika *153:* 65
Melo, Esperança *196:* 90
Melo, John *16:* 285; *58:* 203
Meloni, Maria Teresa *98:* 62
Meltzer, Ericka
    See O'Rourke, Ericka
Menasco, Milton *43:* 85
Menchin, Scott *188:* 129; *234:* 139
Mendelson, Steven T. *86:* 154
Mendelssohn, Felix *19:* 170
Mendola, Christopher *88:* 223
Meng, Heinz *13:* 158
Merian, Maria Sibylla *140:* 88
Mero, Lee *34:* 68
Merrell, David *205:* 3
Merrill, Frank T. *16:* 147; *19:* 71; *YABC 1:* 226, 229,273
Merriman, Rachel *98:* 108; *114:* 122; *149:* 142
Merveille, David *200:* 142
Meryman, Hope *27:* 41
Meryweather, Jack *10:* 179
Meseldzija, Petar *168:* 97
Meserve, Jessica *184:* 137; *211:* 127
Messick, Dale *64:* 150, 151, 152
Meth, Harold *24:* 203
Meyer, Alex Eben *226:* 60
Meyer, Herbert *19:* 189
Meyer, Renate *6:* 170
Meyers, Bob *11:* 136
Meyers, Nancy *172:* 124
Meynell, Louis *37:* 76
Micale, Albert *2:* 65; *22:* 185
Miccuci, Charles *82:* 163; *144:* 150
Micich, Paul *164:* 163
Middleton, Charlotte *230:* 81
Middleton, Jeffrey *177:* 173; *222:* 157
Middleton, Joshua *208:* 146; *219:* 24
Middleton-Sandford, Betty *2:* 125
Mieke, Anne *45:* 74
Mighell, Patricia *43:* 134
Miglio, Paige *101:* 203; *151:* 223; *201:* 118, 119; *204:* 162
Mikec, Larry *204:* 125

Mikolaycak, Charles 9: 144; 12: 101; 13: 212; 21: 121; 22: 168; 30: 187; 34: 103, 150; 37: 183; 43: 179; 44: 90; 46: 115, 118, 119; 49: 25; 78: 121, 122, 205, 207; 81: 4
Milelli, Pascal 129: 66; 135: 153; 187: 45; 235: 47
Miles, Elizabeth 117: 77
Miles, Jennifer 17: 278
Milgrim, David 158: 157; 187: 125, 126, 128; 223: 124, 125, 126, 127
Milhous, Katherine 15: 193; 17: 51
Millais, John E. 22: 230, 231
Millar, H.R. YABC: 194, 195, 203
Millard, C.E. 28: 186
Millard, Kerry 105: 124; 204: 93, 94
Miller, Don 15: 195; 16: 71; 20: 106; 31: 178
Miller, Edna 29: 148
Miller, Edward 115: 64; 183: 140, 141; 218: 129, 130, 131
Miller, Frank J. 25: 94
Miller, Grambs 18: 38; 23: 16
Miller, Ian 99: 128
Miller, Jane 15: 196
Miller, Marcia 13: 233
Miller, Marilyn 1: 87; 31: 69; 33: 157
Miller, Mitchell 28: 183; 34: 207
Miller, Phil 175: 150
Miller, Shane 5: 140
Miller, Virginia 81: 206
Miller, Woody 233: 153; 236: 146
Millman, Isaac 172: 18
Mills, Elaine 72: 181
Mills, Judith Christine 130: 168, 169
Mills, Lauren 92: 170
Mills, Yaroslava Surmach 35: 169, 170; 46: 114
Millsap, Darrel 51: 102
Milone, Karen 89: 169; 222: 149
Milord, Susan 147: 163, 164; 200: 144
Milot, René 226: 127
Milton, Debbie 162: 161
Mims, Ashley 170: 51
Min, Willemien 222: 62
Miner, Julia 98: 69
Minor, Wendell 39: 188; 52: 87; 56: 171; 58: 116; 62: 56; 66: 109; 74: 93; 78: 129; 94: 67; 117: 12, 13; 124: 84, 86; 136: 121; 164: 168, 169; 170: 71; 199: 79, 80, 81, 82; 217: 63; 223: 149; 226: 90, 91, 92
Minter, Daniel 176: 154; 179: 177
Mirocha, Paul 81: 133; 192: 148; 194: 36
Misako Rocks! 192: 149, 150
Mitchell, Judith 109: 117
Mitchell, Mark 91: 208
Mitchell, Tracy 190: 15
Mitgutsch, Ali 76: 161
Mitsuhashi, Yoko 45: 153
Miyake, Yoshi 38: 141
Mizumura, Kazue 10: 143; 18: 223; 36: 159
Mochi, Ugo 8: 122; 38: 150
Mock, Paul 55: 83; 123: 32
Modarressi, Mitra 90: 236; 126: 168; 173: 165, 166; 200: 147, 148
Modell, Frank 39: 152
Mogenson, Jan 74: 183
Mohn, Susan 89: 224
Mohr, Mark 133: 201
Mohr, Nicholasa 8: 139; 113: 127
Molan, Christine 60: 177; 84: 183
Moldon, Peter L. 49: 168
Molk, Laurel 92: 150; 230: 217, 219
Mollica, Gene 197: 11
Momaday, N. Scott 48: 159
Mombourquette, Paul 112: 91; 126: 142
Monk, Julie 165: 231; 191: 96
Monks, Lydia 189: 136, 137
Monroe, Chris 219: 133
Monroy, Manuel 199: 192
Montalto, Luisa 233: 79
Montgomery, Lucy 150: 126
Montgomery, Michael G. 208: 159

Montgomery-Higham, Amanda 169: 131
Monteiel, David 201: 95
Montiel, David 69: 106; 84: 145
Montijo, Rhode 193: 164
Montresor, Beni 2: 91; 3: 138; 38: 152, 153, 154,155, 156, 157, 158, 159, 160; 68: 63
Montserrat, Pep 128: 135; 181: 119; 184: 53
Moon, Carl 25: 183, 184, 185
Moon, Eliza 14: 40
Moon, Ivan 22: 39; 38: 140
Moore, Adrienne 67: 147
Moore, Agnes Kay Randall 43: 187
Moore, Cyd 117: 107, 108; 159: 137, 138; 186: 148, 149, 151; 203: 15; 214: 138, 139; 233: 111, 112, 113, 115
Moore, Gustav 127: 181, 182; 170: 162, 163
Moore, Jackie 128: 79
Moore, Janet 63: 153
Moore, Margie 176: 156; 221: 125; 224: 106, 107
Moore, Mary 29: 160
Moore, Patrick 184: 121
Moore, Sean L. 237: 98
Moore, Yvette 101: 11, 12; 154: 141
Mora, Giovanni 179: 127; 184: 11
Mora, Raul Mina 20: 41
Moraes, Odilon 102: 144
Morales, Magaly 225: 137; 233: 28
Morales, Yuyi 154: 144; 226: 120; 236: 121
Moran, Rosslyn 111: 26
Moran, Tom 60: 100
Mordan, C.B. 193: 115
Mordvinoff, Nicolas 15: 179
Moreno, René King 169: 59; 190: 133, 209; 212: 52
Morgan, Barbara 169: 116
Morgan, Jacqui 58: 57
Morgan, Mary 114: 133, 134, 135; 123: 11; 213: 115, 116, 117
Morgan, Tom 42: 157
Morgan, Pierr 173: 148
Morgenstern, Michael 158: 7, 57; 171: 103; 174: 60; 226: 12; 233: 5
Morice, Dave 93: 142
Morin, Paul 73: 132; 79: 130; 88: 140; 137: 143
Moriuchi, Mique 177: 203
Morozumi, Atsuko 110: 155; 217: 126, 127
Morrill, Leslie 18: 218; 29: 177; 33: 84; 38: 147; 42: 127; 44: 93; 48: 164, 165, 167, 168, 169, 170,171; 49: 162; 63: 136, 180; 70: 72; 71: 70, 91,92; 72: 228; 80: 163, 164, 165; 90: 121; 121: 88; 178: 117
Morrill, Rowena A. 84: 16; 98: 163
Morris 47: 91
Morris, Frank 55: 133; 60: 28; 76: 2
Morris, Harry O. 119: 138
Morris, Jackie 128: 194; 144: 119; 151: 146; 202: 126, 127; 204: 83; 211: 80; 214: 163
Morris, Jennifer E. 179: 157
Morris, Oradel Nolen 128: 180
Morris, Tony 62: 146; 70: 97
Morrison, Bill 42: 116; 66: 170; 69: 40
Morrison, Gordon 87: 150; 113: 93; 128: 181, 182; 183: 144, 145, 146
Morrison, Frank 169: 162; 205: 156; 224: 121; 226: 154
Morrison, Taylor 159: 144, 145; 187: 131
Morrow, Gray 2: 64; 5: 200; 10: 103, 114; 14: 175
Morse, Scott 200: 149, 150
Morstad, Julie 232: 137
Morton, Lee Jack 32: 140
Morton, Marian 3: 185
Mosberg, Hilary 117: 195; 118: 164; 149: 55
Moser, Barry 56: 68, 117, 118, 119, 120, 121, 122, 123, 124; 59: 141; 60: 160; 79: 91, 147, 149, 151, 152; 82: 81; 90: 118; 91: 35;

95: 210; 97: 91, 93; 102: 152; 126: 4; 128: 175; 133: 141; 138: 167, 171, 174; 153: 205; 174: 130; 185: 152, 154; 195: 163; 204: 115; 209: 201
Moser, Cara 90: 118; 138: 167
Moses, Grandma 18: 228
Moses, Will 178: 170, 171
Moskof, Martin Stephen 27: 152
Mosley, Francis 57: 144
Moss, Donald 11: 184
Moss, Geoffrey 32: 198
Moss, Marissa 71: 130; 104: 127; 163: 156; 216: 164, 165, 166
Most, Bernard 48: 173; 91: 142, 143; 134: 120
Mourning, Tuesday 205: 25; 220: 68; 221: 42; 236: 91
Mowll, Joshua 188: 133
Mowry, Carmen 50: 62
Moxley, Sheila 96: 174; 169: 26; 206: 16
Moyers, William 21: 65
Moyler, Alan 36: 142
Mozley, Charles 9: 87; 20: 176, 192, 193; 22: 228; 25: 205; 33: 150; 43: 170, 171, 172, 173, 174; YABC2: 89
Mueller, Hans Alexander 26: 64; 27: 52, 53
Mugnaini, Joseph 11: 35; 27: 52, 53; 35: 62
Mujica, Rick 72: 67; 88: 95; 111: 53; 180: 185; 197: 70
Mullen, Douglas 180: 178
Muller, Robin 86: 161
Muller, Steven 32: 167
Muller, Jorg 35: 215; 67: 138, 139
Mulock, Julie 163: 112
Mullins, Edward S. 10: 101
Mullins, Patricia 51: 68
Multer, Scott 80: 108
Munari, Bruno 15: 200
Munch, Edvard 140: 143
Munowitz, Ken 14: 148; 72: 178, 179
Muñoz, Claudio 208: 161
Munoz, William 42: 160
Munro, Roxie 58: 134; 136: 177; 137: 218; 184: 133, 134; 223: 130, 132, 133
Munsinger, Lynn 33: 161; 46: 126; 71: 92; 82: 80; 89: 218; 92: 125; 94: 157, 158, 159, 160; 98: 196; 103: 198; 142: 143; 145: 133, 134, 136; 153: 203; 176: 162; 177: 140, 141, 142; 189: 113, 114, 116, 117; 201: 42; 221: 148, 149,150
Munson, Russell 13: 9
Munster, Sebastian 166: 107
Munzar, Barbara 149: 75
Murdocca, Salvatore 73: 212; 98: 132; 111: 168; 157: 228; 164: 257
Murphy, Bill 5: 138; 130: 170
Murphy, Jill 37: 142; 70: 166; 142: 132, 134
Murphy, Kelly 130: 212; 143: 119; 176: 158; 190: 135
Murphy, Liz 210: 183; 212: 157
Murphy, Mary 196: 158
Murphy, Tom 192: 40
Murr, Karl 20: 62
Murray, Joe 175: 37
Murray, Ossie 43: 176
Mussino, Attilio 29: 131; 100: 164
Mutchler, Dwight 1: 25
Myers, Bernice 9: 147; 36: 75; 81: 146, 147, 148
Muth, Jon J. 165: 169; 167: 109; 190: 227; 193: 59; 228: 206
Myers, Christopher 183: 150; 193: 139
Myers, Duane O. 99: 145
Myers, Tim 147: 168
Myers, V.G. 142: 41
Myers, Lou 11: 2

N

Na, Il Sung *231:* 136
Nachreiner, Tom *29:* 182
Nacht, Merle *65:* 49
Nadler, Ellis *88:* 91
Nagle, Shane *180:* 223
Nagy, Ian *195:* 64
Naifeh, Ted *236:* 34
Najaka, Marlies *62:* 101
Nakai, Michael *30:* 217; *54:* 29
Nakata, Hiroe *157:* 156; *162:* 30; *205:* 124, 125
Nakatani, Chiyoko *12:* 124
Narahashi, Keiko *77:* 188; *82:* 213; *115:* 142, 143, 144
Nascimbene, Yan *133:* 128; *173:* 132, 133
Nash, Lesa *87:* 135
Nash, Linell *46:* 175
Nash, Scott *130:* 36; *188:* 196; *224:* 180
Naso, John *33:* 183
Nason, Thomas W. *14:* 68
Nasser, Muriel *48:* 74
Nast, Thomas *21:* 29; *28:* 23; *51:* 132, 133, 134, 135,136, 137, 138, 139, 141
Nasta, Vincent *78:* 185
Natale, Vincent *76:* 3; *78:* 125; *112:* 47; *166:* 81; *174:* 189; *185:* 212; *197:* 59; *218:* 35
Natchev, Alexi *96:* 177
Nathan, Charlott *125:* 151
Nathan, Cheryl *150:* 104; *186:* 112
Natti, Susanna *20:* 146; *32:* 141, 142; *35:* 178; *37:* 143; *71:* 49; *93:* 98; *125:* 166, 168; *126:* 228; *151:* 6; *178:* 8; *188:* 106; *231:* 10
Navarra, Celeste Scala *8:* 142
Naylor, Penelope *10:* 104
Nazz, James *72:* 8
Nebel, M. *45:* 154
Neebe, William *7:* 93
Needham, Dave *196:* 85
Needler, Jerry *12:* 93
Neel, Alice *31:* 23
Neely, Beth *119:* 184
Neely, Keith R. *46:* 124
Neff, Leland *78:* 74
Negri, Rocco *3:* 213; *5:* 67; *6:* 91, 108; *12:* 159
Negrin, Fabian *174:* 125; *175:* 15; *223:* 91
Neidigh, Sherry *128:* 53; *204:* 101, 102, 103; *222:* 95
Neilan, Eujin Kim *180:* 241; *200:* 151, 152
Neill, John R. *18:* 8, 10, 11, 21, 30; *100:* 22
Neilsen, Cliff *158:* 131; *177:* 112, 121; *209:* 8; *215:* 150; *230:* 62
Neilsen, Terese *116:* 74
Nelson, Craig *62:* 151; 153; *183:* 86; *236:* 103
Nelson, Gail White *68:* 140
Nelson, Jennifer *129:* 152; *199:* 132
Nelson, Kadir *151:* 185; *154:* 146, 147; *157:* 189, 222; *181:* 122, 124; *197:* 155; *213:* 122, 123, 124
Nelson, Melissa *224:* 87
Nelson, S.D. *131:* 34; *181:* 126, 127; *228:* 23
Ness, Evaline *1:* 164, 165; *2:* 39; *3:* 8; *10:* 147; *12:* 53; *26:* 150, 151, 152, 153; *49:* 30, 31, 32; *56:* 30; *60:* 113
Neubecker, Robert *170:* 143; *214:* 157; *233:* 25; *234:* 209
Neville, Vera *2:* 182
Nevins, Daniel *191:* 173
Nevwirth, Allan *79:* 168
Newberry, Clare Turlay *1:* 170
Newbold, Greg *108:* 125; *145:* 199; *151:* 23; *193:* 178; *197:* 10; *199:* 92, 93
Newfeld, Frank *14:* 121; *26:* 154
Newhouse, Maxwell *232:* 144
Newland, Gillian *220:* 132
Newman, Andy *149:* 61; *195:* 63
Newman, Ann *43:* 90

Newman, Barbara Johansen *191:* 137, 138; *231:* 13
Newquist, H.P. *235:* 156
Newsham, Ian *143:* 162
Newsom, Carol *40:* 159; *44:* 60; *47:* 189; *65:* 29; *70:* 192; *80:* 36; *85:* 137, 138; *92:* 167; *191:* 82; *233:* 83
Newsom, Tom *49:* 149; *71:* 13, 62; *75:* 156; *91:* 113
Newton, Jill *83:* 105; *200:* 154
Newton, Vanessa Brantley *236:* 180
Nez, John *218:* 136
Ng, Michael *29:* 171
Ng, Simon *167:* 7
Ngui, Marc *229:* 50
Nguyen, Vincent *189:* 49; *226:* 160; *229:* 172
Nichols, Sandy *219:* 103
Nicholson, William *15:* 33, 34; *16:* 48
Nickens, Bessie *104:* 153
Nicklaus, Carol *45:* 194; *62:* 132, 133
Nickle, John *181:* 128
Nickless, Will *16:* 139
Nicholas, Corasue *154:* 20
Nicolas *17:* 130, 132, 133; *YABC 2:* 215
Niebrugge, Jane *6:* 118
Nielsen, Cliff *95:* 207, 208; *105:* 58; *114:* 112; *124:* 12; *125:* 91, 92; *132:* 224; *135:* 187; *136:* 40; *137:* 168; *145:* 54; *149:* 28; *158:* 129; *165:* 64, 158; *168:* 169; *170:* 6; *175:* 114, 116; *187:* 75, 76; *194:* 107; *197:* 172; *201:* 14; *208:* 192; *211:* 186; *216:* 215; *217:* 67; *224:* 61, 62; *230:* 21; *233:* 58, 59; *236:* 136
Nielsen, Jon *6:* 100; *24:* 202
Nielsen, Kay *15:* 7; *16:* 211, 212, 213, 215, 217; *22:* 143; *YABC 1:* 32, 33
Niemann, Christoph *191:* 141
Nikola-Lisa, W. *180:* 180
Niland, Deborah *25:* 191; *27:* 156; *135:* 50; *172:* 143
Niland, Kilmeny *25:* 191; *75:* 143
Nino, Alex *59:* 145
Ninon *1:* 5; *38:* 101, 103, 108
Nissen, Rie *44:* 35
Nithael, Mark *158:* 237
Nivola, Claire A. *78:* 126; *140:* 147; *208:* 164
Nixon, K. *14:* 152
Nobati, Eugenia *194:* 118
Noble, Louise *61:* 170
Noble, Marty *97:* 168; *125:* 171
Noble, Trinka Hakes *39:* 162; *84:* 157
Nobles, Scott *226:* 159
Noda, Takayo *168:* 143
Noguchi, Yoshie *30:* 99
Nolan, Dennis *42:* 163; *67:* 163; *78:* 189; *82:* 225; *83:* 26; *92:* 169, 170; *103:* 166; *111:* 35; *112:* 213; *127:* 171; *166:* 161; *194:* 218
Noll, Sally *82:* 171
Nolte, Larry *121:* 63, 65
Nones, Eric Jon *61:* 111; *76:* 38; *77:* 177
Noonan, Daniel *100:* 224
Noonan, Julia *4:* 163; *7:* 207; *25:* 151; *91:* 29; *95:* 149; *231:* 163
Norcia, Ernie *108:* 155; *140:* 47
Nordenskjold, Birgitta *2:* 208
Noreika, Robert *173:* 20; *217:* 24
Norling, Beth *149:* 153, 154; *209:* 77
Norman, Elaine *77:* 72, 176; *94:* 35; *136:* 63; *178:* 42; *236:* 104
Norman, Mary *36:* 138, 147
Norman, Michael *12:* 117; *27:* 168
Normandin, Luc *227:* 180
Northway, Jennifer *85:* 96
Nostlinger, Christiana *162:* 131
Novak, Linda *166:* 205
Novak, Matt *104:* 132, 133; *165:* 173, 174; *204:* 104, 106
Novelli, Luca *61:* 137
Novgorodoff, Danica *215:* 133
Nugent, Cynthia *106:* 189; *205:* 126, 127; *209:* 180

Numberman, Neil *220:* 133
Numeroff, Laura Joffe *28:* 161; *30:* 177
Nurse, Chris *164:* 91
Nussbaumer, Paul *16:* 219; *39:* 117
Nutt, Ken *72:* 69; *97:* 170
Nyce, Helene *19:* 219
Nygren, Tord *30:* 148; *127:* 164

O

Oakley, Graham *8:* 112; *30:* 164, 165; *84:* 188,189, 190, 191, 192
Oakley, Thornton *YABC 2:* 189
Oberheide, Heide *118:* 37
Obligado, Lilian *2:* 28, 66, 67; *6:* 30; *14:* 179; *15:* 103; *25:* 84; *61:* 138, 139, 140, 141, 143
Oblinski, Rafael *190:* 139
Obrant, Susan *11:* 186
O'Brien, Anne Sibley *53:* 116, 117; *155:* 115; *213:* 127; *224:* 71; *227:* 9
O'Brien, John *41:* 253; *72:* 12; *89:* 59, 60; *98:* 16; *161:* 185; *169:* 16; *180:* 196; *228:* 38
O'Brien, Patrick *193:* 142, 143, 144
O'Brien, Teresa *87:* 89
O'Brien, Tim *93:* 25; *136:* 94; *164:* 57; *169:* 57; *173:* 55; *175:* 86; *184:* 192; *191:* 134; *193:* 137; *210:* 159; *224:* 28, 29; *229:* 140; *232:* 166
O'Clair, Dennis *127:* 25
O'Connor, George *183:* 153; *228:* 113, 114
Odell, Carole *35:* 47
Odem, Mel *99:* 164; *167:* 84, 87
O'Donohue, Thomas *40:* 89
Oechsli, Kelly *5:* 144, 145; *7:* 115; *8:* 83, 183; *13:* 117; *20:* 94; *81:* 199
Ofer, Avi *208:* 143
Offen, Hilda *42:* 207
Offermann, Andrea *233:* 108
Ogden, Bill *42:* 59; *47:* 55
Ogg, Oscar *33:* 34
Ogle, Nancy Gray *163:* 144
Ohi, Ruth *90:* 175, 177; *131:* 63; *135:* 106; *175:* 107; *179:* 55
Ohlsson, Ib *4:* 152; *7:* 57; *10:* 20; *11:* 90; *19:* 217; *41:* 246; *82:* 106; *92:* 213
Ohtomo, Yasuo *37:* 146; *39:* 212, 213
O'Keefe, Jennifer *136:* 184
O'Kelley, Mattie Lou *36:* 150
Olbinski, Rafal *149:* 27; *158:* 77; *203:* 36; *235:* 36
Oldland, Nicholas *223:* 136
O'Leary, Chris *208:* 166
Olander, Johan *231:* 138
Oleynikov, Igor *202:* 134
Oliver, Isaac *171:* 182
Oliver, Jenni *23:* 121; *35:* 112
Oliver, Narelle *152:* 192; *197:* 129, 130
Oller, Erika *128:* 186; *134:* 126; *234:* 146
Olschewski, Alfred *7:* 172
Olsen, Ib Spang *6:* 178, 179; *81:* 164
Olson, Alan *77:* 229
Olson, Julie *233:* 120
Olson-Brown, Ellen *183:* 154
Olugebefola, Ademola *15:* 205
O'Malley, Kevin *94:* 180; *106:* 8; *113:* 108; *136:* 70; *157:* 193; *191:* 146; *203:* 78; *217:* 84; *230:* 115, 117, 118
O'Neil, Dan IV *7:* 176
O'Neill, Catharine *72:* 113; *84:* 78; *134:* 153
O'Neill, Jean *22:* 146
O'Neill, Martin *187:* 39; *203:* 118
O'Neill, Michael J. *54:* 172
O'Neill, Rose *48:* 30, 31
O'Neill, Steve *21:* 118
Ono, Chiyo *7:* 97
Onoda, Yuta *237:* 136
Orbaan, Albert *2:* 31; *5:* 65, 171; *9:* 8; *14:* 241; *20:* 109
Orbach, Ruth *21:* 112

Orback, Craig *197:* 132
Orfe, Joan *20:* 81
Org, Ed *119:* 93
Ormai, Stella *72:* 129
Ormerod, Jan *55:* 124; *70:* 170, 171; *90:* 39; *132:* 172, 173, 174; *147:* 98
Ormsby, Virginia H. *11:* 187
O'Rourke, Ericka *108:* 216; *117:* 194; *111:* 142; *119:* 194; *137:* 152; *150:* 134; *167:* 64; *172:* 164; *188:* 163; *191:* 172; *201:* 15; *203:* 75; *209:* 130; *219:* 99
O'Rourke, Ericka Meltzer
　　See O'Rourke, Ericka
Orozco, Jose Clemente *9:* 177
Orr, Forrest W. *23:* 9
Orr, N. *19:* 70
Ortiz, Vilma *88:* 158
Osborn, Kathy *152:* 232; *199:* 101, 102; *206:* 67
Osborn, Robert *65:* 49
Osborne, Billie Jean *35:* 209
Osmond, Edward *10:* 111
Ostow, David *223:* 138
O'Sullivan, Tom *3:* 176; *4:* 55; *78:* 195
Otani, June *124:* 42; *156:* 53
Otis, Rebecca *185:* 92
Ottley, Matt *147:* 221; *171:* 133
Otto, Svend *22:* 130, 141; *67:* 188, 189
Oudry, J.B. *18:* 167
Oughton, Taylor *5:* 23; *104:* 136
Overeng, Johannes *44:* 36
Overlie, George *11:* 156
Owens, Carl *2:* 35; *23:* 521
Owens, Gail *10:* 170; *12:* 157; *19:* 16; *22:* 70; *25:* 81; *28:* 203, 205; *32:* 221, 222; *36:* 132; *46:* 40; *47:* 57; *54:* 66, 67, 68, 69, 70, 71, 72, 73; *71:* 100; *73:* 64; *77:* 157; *80:* 32; *82:* 3; *99:* 226; *224:* 198
Owens, Mary Beth *113:* 202, 203; *191:* 148, 149
Owens, Nubia *84:* 74
Oxenbury, Helen *3:* 150, 151; *24:* 81; *68:* 174, 175,176; *81:* 209; *84:* 213, 245; *129:* 56; *149:* 159; *184:* 181; *224:* 147
Oz, Robin *88:* 167; *185:* 181

P

Padgett, Jim *12:* 165
Page, Gail *205:* 128
Page, Homer *14:* 145
Page, Mark *162:* 70
Paget, Sidney *24:* 90, 91, 93, 95, 97
Paget, Walter *64:* 122
Paillot, Jim *173:* 89
Pajouhesh, Noushin *160:* 121
Pak *12:* 76
Pak, Yu Cha *86:* 174
Paladino, Lance *134:* 30
Palazzo, Tony *3:* 152, 153
Palecek, Josef *56:* 136; *89:* 158
Palen, Debbie *135:* 88; *195:* 148, 149
Palencar, John Jude *84:* 12, 45; *85:* 87; *92:* 187; *99:* 128; *110:* 204; *150:* 122; *171:* 86; *207:* 36
Palin, Nicki *81:* 201; *89:* 161
Palisi, Heather *231:* 109
Palladino, David *4:* 113; *40:* 176, 177, 178, 179, 181,224, 225; *50:* 138; *78:* 186
Pallarito, Don *43:* 36
Palmer, Carol *158:* 230; *195:* 187
Palmer, Gary *232:* 39
Palmer, Heidi *15:* 207; *29:* 102
Palmer, Jan *42:* 153; *82:* 161
Palmer, Judd *153:* 160, 161
Palmer, Juliette *6:* 89; *15:* 208
Palmer, Kate Salley *104:* 143; *154:* 169
Palmer, Lemuel *17:* 25, 29

Palmisciano, Diane *110:* 62; *162:* 26; *202:* 138, 139
Palmquist, Eric *38:* 133
Pamintuan, Macky *214:* 160
Panesis, Nicholas *3:* 127
Panter, Gary *182:* 191
Panton, Doug *52:* 99
Paparone, Pamela *129:* 174
Papas, William *11:* 223; *50:* 160
Papin, Joseph *26:* 113
Papish, Robin Lloyd *10:* 80
Papp, Robert *198:* 41; *205:* 130; *219:* 53
Paradis, Susan *40:* 216
Paraquin, Charles H. *18:* 166
Pardo DeLange, Alex *179:* 128; *211:* 135, 136
Paris, Peter *31:* 127
Parisi, Elizabeth B. *141:* 82; *164:* 57
Park, Nick *113:* 143
Park, Seho *39:* 110
Park, W.B. *22:* 189
Parker, Ant *82:* 87, 88; *104:* 121
Parker, Buzz *227:* 154
Parker, Jake *227:* 138
Parker, Lewis *2:* 179
Parker, Nancy Winslow *10:* 113; *22:* 164; *28:* 47, 144; *52:* 7; *69:* 153; *91:* 171, 174; *132:* 175
Parker, Robert *4:* 161; *5:* 74; *9:* 136; *29:* 39
Parker, Robert Andrew *11:* 81; *29:* 186; *39:* 165; *40:* 25; *41:* 78; *42:* 123; *43:* 144; *48:* 182; *54:* 140; *74:* 141; *91:* 24; *111:* 115; *151:* 201; *154:* 156; *200:* 163, 164; *211:* 67
Parker-Rees, Guy *149:* 145; *193:* 149, 150
Parkin, Trevor *140:* 151
Parkins, David *114:* 123; *146:* 176; *176:* 168; *192:* 107; *218:* 139, 140, 141, 148; *224:* 92
Parkinson, Kathy *71:* 143; *144:* 234
Parkinson, Keith *70:* 66
Parks, Gordon, Jr. *33:* 228
Parlato, Stephen *222:* 137
Parnall, Peter *5:* 137; *16:* 221; *24:* 70; *40:* 78; *51:* 130; *69:* 17, 155; *136:* 22, 23, 24
Parnall, Virginia *40:* 78
Paros, Jennifer *210:* 197
Parow, Lorraine *158:* 127
Parr, Todd *134:* 139, 140; *179:* 163, 164, 165
Parra, John *225:* 150; *232:* 134
Parrish, Anne *27:* 159, 160
Parrish, Dillwyn *27:* 159
Parrish, Maxfield *14:* 160, 161, 164, 165; *16:* 109; *18:* 12, 13; *YABC 1:* 149, 152, 267; *2:* 146, 149
Parry, David *26:* 156
Parry, Marian *13:* 176; *19:* 179
Parsons, Garry *197:* 135
Partch, Virgil *45:* 163, 165
Pascal, David *14:* 174
Paschkis, Julie *177:* 153, 154; *220:* 140, 141; *231:* 64
Pasquier, J.A. *16:* 91
Pastel, Elyse *201:* 123
Pasternak, Robert *119:* 53
Paterson, Diane *13:* 116; *39:* 163; *59:* 164, 165, 166,167; *72:* 51, 53; *129:* 175; *177:* 156, 157
Paterson, Helen *16:* 93
Patkau, Karen *112:* 123
Paton, Jane *15:* 271; *35:* 176
Patricelli, Leslie *207:* 129; *236:* 155, 156
Patrick, John *139:* 190
Patrick, Pamela *90:* 160; *93:* 211; *105:* 12
Patrick, Tom *190:* 103
Patterson, Geoffrey *54:* 75
Patterson, Robert *25:* 118
Patti, Joyce *187:* 145, 146
Patz, Nancy *111:* 40; *154:* 161; *214:* 80
Paul, James *4:* 130; *23:* 161
Paul, Korky *102:* 85
Paull, Grace *24:* 157; *87:* 127
Paulsen, Ruth Wright *79:* 160, 164; *189:* 146; *231:* 150

Pavlov, Elena *80:* 49
Payne, Adam S. *135:* 166
Payne, C.F. *145:* 138, 140; *179:* 168
Payne, Joan Balfour *1:* 118
Payne, Tom *170:* 27
Payson, Dale *7:* 34; *9:* 151; *20:* 140; *37:* 22
Payzant, Charles *21:* 147
Peacock, Phyllis Hornung *230:* 124
Peacock, Ralph *64:* 118
Peake, Mervyn *22:* 136, 149; *23:* 162, 163, 164; *YABC2:* 307
Pearce, Carl *228:* 107; *229:* 148
Pearson, Larry *38:* 225
Pearson, Tracey Campbell *64:* 163, 164, 167, 168, 169; *118:* 51; *156:* 169, 171, 172; *163:* 140; *219:* 140, 141, 142, 143
Peat, Fern B. *16:* 115
Peck, Anne Merriman *18:* 241; *24:* 155
Peck, Beth *66:* 242; *79:* 166; *80:* 136; *91:* 34; *95:* 9; *101:* 77; *164:* 197; *190:* 170
Peddicord, Jane Ann *199:* 106
Pedersen, Janet *193:* 152; *217:* 57; *218:* 15; *228:* 85
Pedersen, Judy *66:* 217; *121:* 36; *172:* 67
Pedersen, Vilhelm *YABC 1:* 40
Pederson, Sharleen *12:* 92
Pedlar, Elaine *161:* 45
Peek, Merle *39:* 168
Peet, Bill *2:* 203; *41:* 159, 160, 161, 162, 163; *78:* 158, 159, 160, 161
Peguero, Adrian *116:* 133
Peguero, Gerard *116:* 133
Peirce, Lincoln *232:* 150
Pels, Winslow Pinney *55:* 126
Peltier, Leslie C. *13:* 178
Peltzer, Marc *202:* 92
Penberthy, Mark *171:* 78
Pendle, Alexy *7:* 159; *13:* 34; *29:* 161; *33:* 215; *86:* 62
Pendola, Joanne *76:* 203; *81:* 125; *105:* 181; *178:* 152, 153
Pene du Bois, William *4:* 70; *10:* 122; *26:* 61; *27:* 145, 211; *35:* 243; *41:* 216; *68:* 180, 181; *73:* 45
Penfound, David *102:* 185
Pennington, Eunice *27:* 162
Peppe, Mark *28:* 142
Peppe, Rodney *4:* 164, 165; *74:* 187, 188, 189
Pepper, Hubert *64:* 143
Percy, Graham *63:* 2
Pericoli, Matteo *178:* 177
Perini, Ben *173:* 77
Perkins, David *60:* 68
Perkins, Lucy Fitch *72:* 199
Perkins, Lynne Rae *172:* 146; *212:* 153
Perl, Susan *2:* 98; *4:* 231; *5:* 44, 45, 118; *6:* 199; *8:* 137; *12:* 88; *22:* 193; *34:* 54, 55; *52:* 128; *YABC 1:* 176
Perlman, Janet *222:* 141
Perrone, Donna *78:* 166
Perry, Marie Fritz *165:* 180
Perry, Patricia *29:* 137; *30:* 171
Perry, Roger *27:* 163
Perske, Martha *46:* 83; *51:* 108, 147
Persson, Stina *175:* 166
Pesek, Ludek *15:* 237
Petach, Heidi *149:* 166; *200:* 207
Peters, David *72:* 205; *182:* 116
Petersen, Jeff *181:* 95
Petersham, Maud *17:* 108, 147, 148, 149, 150, 151, 152, 153
Petersham, Miska *17:* 108, 147, 148, 149, 150, 151, 152, 153
Peterson, Eric *109:* 125
Peterson, Nisse *99:* 27
Peterson, R.F. *7:* 101
Peterson, Russell *7:* 130
Petie, Haris *2:* 3; *10:* 41, 118; *11:* 227; *12:* 70
Petit-Roulet, Philippe *227:* 12
Petricic, Dusan *153:* 75, 76, 77; *170:* 12; *172:* 13; *176:* 170; *179:* 56

Petrides, Heidrun *19:* 223
Petrone, Valeria *159:* 160; *171:* 92; *186:* 173; *204:* 49; *216:* 208; *220:* 98; *233:* 126
Petrosino, Tamara *177:* 40; *193:* 154, 155
Petruccio, Steven James *67:* 159; *127:* 5
Pettingill, Ondre *64:* 181; *70:* 64; *222:* 167, 168
Peyo *40:* 56, 57
Peyton, K.M. *15:* 212
Pfeifer, Herman *15:* 262
Pfister, Marcus *83:* 165, 166, 167; *146:* 152; *150:* 160; *207:* 132, 134, 135, 136
Pfloog, Jan *124:* 60
Pham, LeUyen *160:* 48; *175:* 154, 156; *179:* 149; *201:* 124, 125, 126, 127; *204:* 28; *208:* 206; *217:* 92; *234:* 215; *237:* 110, 111, 112
Phelan, Matt *182:* 160; *184:* 222; *215:* 140, 141; *221:* 157; *231:* 28
Phillipps, J.C. *218:* 142
Phillips, Craig *70:* 151; *207:* 74; *221:* 159; *229:* 22
Phillips, Douglas *1:* 19
Phillips, F.D. *6:* 202
Phillips, Gary R. *223:* 23
Phillips, Louise *133:* 67
Phillips, Matt *184:* 173
Phillips, Thomas *30:* 55
Philpot, Glyn *54:* 46
Phiz
See Browne, Hablot K.
Piatti, Celestino *16:* 223
Pica, Steve *115:* 181
Picarella, Joseph *13:* 147
Picart, Gabriel *121:* 165; *201:* 169
Picasso, Pablo *228:* 131
Pichon, Liz *174:* 139
Pickard, Charles *12:* 38; *18:* 203; *36:* 152
Picken, George A. *23:* 150
Pickens, David *22:* 156
Pickering, Jimmy *195:* 152; *197:* 163
Pien, Lark *222:* 143, 144
Pienkowski, Jan *6:* 183; *30:* 32; *58:* 140, 141, 142,143, 146, 147; *73:* 3; *87:* 156, 157; *131:* 189
Pieper, Christiane *200:* 168
Pignataro, Anna *163:* 220; *223:* 143 Pile, Emma *218:* 156 Pileggi, Steve *145:* 122
Pilkey, Dav *68:* 186; *115:* 164, 166; *166:* 173, 174, 175
Pimlott, John *10:* 205
Pincus, Harriet *4:* 186; *8:* 179; *22:* 148; *27:* 164, 165; *66:* 202
Pini, Wendy *89:* 166
Pinkett, Neil *60:* 8
Pinkney, Brian *81:* 184, 185; *94:* 107; *113:* 146, 147; *117:* 121, 166; *132:* 145; *158:* 108, 191; *160:* 189; *200:* 8
Pinkney, Jerry *8:* 218; *10:* 40; *15:* 276; *20:* 66; *24:* 121; *33:* 109; *36:* 222; *38:* 200; *41:* 165, 166, 167, 168, 169, 170, 171, 173, 174; *44:* 198; *48:* 51; *53:* 20; *56:* 61, 68; *58:* 184; *60:* 59; *61:* 91; *71:* 146, 148, 149; *72:* 17; *73:* 149; *74:* 159,192; *75:* 45; *80:* 206; *81:* 44; *85:* 144; *95:* 50; *107:* 158, 159, 160; *108:* 164; *112:* 114, 115; *133:* 58; *195:* 140; *227:* 131
Pinkwater, Daniel Manus *8:* 156; *46:* 180, 181, 182, 185, 188, 189, 190; *151:* 161 *76:* 178, 179, 180; *210:* 203
Pinkwater, Manus
See Pinkwater, Daniel Manus
Pinkwater, Jill *114:* 160, 161; *158:* 179; *188:* 143, 145, 146
Pinto, Ralph *10:* 131; *45:* 93
Pinto, Sara *200:* 165
Pinon, Mark *74:* 22
Piven, Hanoch *173:* 142; *236:* 157, 158, 159
Pistolesi *73:* 211
Pitcairn, Ansel *188:* 10; *227:* 20
Pittman, Helena Clare *71:* 151

Pitz, Henry C. *4:* 168; *19:* 165; *35:* 128; *42:* 80; *YABC 2:* 95, 176
Pitzenberger, Lawrence J. *26:* 94
Pitzer, Susanna *181:* 131
Place, François *218:* 42
Plant, Andrew *214:* 166
Player, Stephen *82:* 190
Plecas, Jennifer *84:* 201; *106:* 124; *149:* 168; *205:* 180; *220:* 81; *229:* 152, 153, 154
Ploog, Mike *180:* 19
Plowden, David *52:* 135, 136
Plume, Ilse *170:* 149
Plummer, William *32:* 31
Podevin, Jean François *184:* 185
Podwal, Mark *56:* 170, 173; *101:* 154, 155, 157; *149:* 176; *160:* 194; *224:* 127, 128, 129
Pogany, Willy *15:* 46, 49; *19:* 222, 256; *25:* 214; *44:* 142, 143, 144, 145, 146, 147, 148
Pohrt, Tom *67:* 116; *104:* 80; *152:* 199; *195:* 154; *199:* 85
Poirson, V.A. *26:* 89
Polacco, Patricia *74:* 195, 196, 197, 198; *123:* 121, 122, 123; *180:* 189, 190, 191, 193, 194; *212:* 168, 170, 171
Polgreen, John *21:* 44
Polhemus, Coleman *210:* 209
Politi, Leo *1:* 178; *4:* 53; *21:* 48; *47:* 173,174, 176, 178, 179, 180, 181
Pollack, Barbara *219:* 60
Pollema-Cahill, Phyllis *123:* 126
Pollen, Samson *64:* 80
Polonsky, Arthur *34:* 168
Polseno, Jo *1:* 53; *3:* 117; *5:* 114; *17:* 154; *20:* 87; *32:* 49; *41:* 245
Pomaska, Anna *117:* 148
Pons, Bernadette *184:* 100
Ponter, James *5:* 204
Poole, Colin *111:* 27
Poortvliet, Rien *6:* 212; *65:* 165, 166, 167
Pope, Kevin *183:* 158
Popp, Wendy *72:* 122; *158:* 68
Poppel, Hans *71:* 154, 155
Porfirio, Guy *76:* 134
Portal, Colette *6:* 186; *11:* 203
Porter, George *7:* 181
Porter, Janice Lee *136:* 175; *164:* 37
Porter, John *113:* 47
Porter, Pat Grant *84:* 112; *125:* 101
Porter, Sue *146:* 246, 247; *213:* 139, 140, 141; *221:* 91
Porter, Walter *124:* 175
Porto, James *221:* 14
Posada, Mia *187:* 151
Posen, Michael *175:* 82
Post, R.K. *233:* 60
Posthuma, Sieb *150:* 163
Postier, Jim *202:* 140; *204:* 25
Postma, Lidia *79:* 17
Potter, Beatrix *100:* 194, 195; *132:* 179, 180, 181, 182; *YABC 1:* 208, 209, 210, 212, 213
Potter, Giselle *117:* 123; *143:* 44; *144:* 170, 197; *149:* 7; *150:* 165; *187:* 152, 153; *190:* 198; *196:* 152; *200:* 12; *225:* 60; *227:* 105; *235:* 150
Potter, Katherine *104:* 147; *171:* 135; *173:* 136; *217:* 130, 131
Potter, Miriam Clark *3:* 162
Poulin, Stephane *98:* 140, 141
Poullis, Nick *146:* 210
Powell, Constance Buffington *174:* 141
Powell, Gary *151:* 208
Powell, Ivan *67:* 219
Power, Margaret *105:* 122
Powers, Daniel *161:* 173
Powers, Richard M. *1:* 230; *3:* 218; *7:* 194; *26:* 186
Powledge, Fred *37:* 154
Powzyk, Joyce *74:* 214
Poydar, Nancy *96:* 149; *190:* 180, 181, 182
Pracher, Richard *91:* 166
Prachaticka, Marketa *126:* 126

Prange, Beckie *181:* 169; *236:* 173, 175
Prap, Lila *177:* 165
Prater, John *103:* 142, 143, 144; *149:* 172
Pratt, Charles *23:* 29
Pratt, Christine Joy *214:* 167
Pratt, George *116:* 208; *212:* 37
Pratt, Pierre *150:* 73; *166:* 183; *168:* 172; *201:* 27; *208:* 171, 172, 173
Prebenna, David *73:* 174
Press, Jenny *116:* 95
Preston, Mark *152:* 162
Pretro, Korinna *91:* 126
Prevost, Mikela *209:* 111
Price, Christine *2:* 247; *3:* 163, 253; *8:* 166
Price, Cynthia *118:* 156
Price, Edward *33:* 34
Price, Garrett *1:* 76; *2:* 42
Price, Hattie Longstreet *17:* 13
Price, Nick *216:* 173; *220:* 7
Price, Norman *YABC 1:* 129
Price, Willard *48:* 184
Priceman, Marjorie *81:* 171; *136:* 169; *156:* 200; *168:* 153, 154; *188:* 45; *226:* 7; *234:* 160, 161, 163, 164; *235:* 74
Priestley, Alice *168:* 33; *227:* 142
Priestley, Chris *198:* 144
Prigmore, Shane *234:* 166
Primavera, Elise *26:* 95; *58:* 151; *73:* 37; *80:* 79; *86:* 156; *105:* 161; *213:* 157; *230:* 132, 133, 134
Primrose, Jean *36:* 109
Prince, Alison *86:* 188, 189
Prince, Leonora E. *7:* 170
Pritchett, Shelley *116:* 148
Prittie, Edwin J. *YABC 1:* 120
Proimos, James *176:* 4; *217:* 132, 133, 134
Proimos, John *173:* 144
Prosmitsky, Jenya *132:* 33
Provensen, Alice *37:* 204, 215, 222; *70:* 176, 177, 178, 180; *71:* 213; *147:* 184; *191:* 190
Provensen, Martin *37:* 204, 215, 222; *70:* 176, 177, 178, 180; *71:* 213; *191:* 190
Pucci, Albert John *44:* 154
Pudlo *8:* 59
Puggaard, Ulla *196:* 25
Pullen, Zachary *211:* 161; *235:* 21
Pulver, Harry, Jr. *129:* 159
Pulver, Robin *160:* 4
Punchatz, Don *99:* 57
Purdy, Susan *8:* 162
Pursell, Weimer *55:* 18
Purston, Oliver *229:* 156
Purtscher, Alfons *97:* 6
Purvis, Leland *232:* 156
Puskas, James *5:* 141
Pyk, Jan *7:* 26; *38:* 123
Pyle, Charles S. *99:* 149; *191:* 83; *233:* 20, 21; *233:* 85
Pyle, Howard *16:* 225, 226, 227, 228, 230, 231, 232, 235; *24:* 27; *34:* 124, 125, 127, 128; *59:* 132; *100:* 198

Q

Quackenbush, Robert *4:* 190; *6:* 166; *7:* 175, 178; *9:* 86; *11:* 65, 221; *41:* 154; *43:* 157; *70:* 185, 186; *71:* 137; *85:* 47; *92:* 148; *133:* 154, 164, 169
Qualls, Sean *177:* 167, 168; *193:* 43; *228:* 108; *233:* 128, 129; *235:* 152
Quennell, Marjorie (Courtney) *29:* 163, 164
Quidor, John *19:* 82
Quirk, John *62:* 170
Quirk, Thomas *12:* 81

R

Rackham, Arthur *15:* 32, 78, 214-227; *17:* 105, 115; *18:* 233; *19:* 254; *20:* 151; *22:* 129, 131, 132, 133; *23:* 175; *24:* 161, 181; *26:* 91; *32:* 118; *64:* 18; *100:* 9, 16, 203, 204; *YABC 1:* 25, 45, 55, 147; *2:* 103, 142, 173, 210
Racz, Michael *56:* 134
Raczka, Bob *191:* 155, 156
Radcliffe, Andrew *82:* 215
Rader, Laura *101:* 219; *197:* 147; *203:* 53
Radunsky, Vladimir *177:* 170; *192:* 30
Radzinski, Kandy *212:* 174
Rafilson, Sidney *11:* 172
Raglin, Tim *125:* 24
Raible, Alton *1:* 202, 203; *28:* 193; *35:* 181; *110:* 207
Raine, Patricia *82:* 74; *88:* 154
Ramá, Sue *173:* 45; *185:* 186; *190:* 184; *237:* 123
Ramhorst, John *117:* 11
Ramirez, Gladys *177:* 19
Ramirez, Jose *207:* 27
Ramsey, James *16:* 41
Ramsey, Marcy Dunn *82:* 11; *180:* 186
Ramus, Michael *51:* 171
Rand, Paul *6:* 188
Rand, Ted *67:* 9, 10, 121, 123; *74:* 190; *84:* 170; *103:* 170; *112:* 6; *114:* 73; *139:* 168; *143:* 194; *156:* 154; *161:* 9, 10; *200:* 38; *204:* 7
Randazzo, Tony *81:* 98
Randell, William *55:* 54
Rane, Walter *93:* 144; *143:* 109; *184:* 126
Rankin, Joan *163:* 40; *212:* 176
Rankin, Laura *176:* 173, 174; *179:* 150; *236:* 163
Ransome, Arthur *22:* 201
Ransome, James E. *74:* 137; *75:* 80; *84:* 181; *94:* 108; *117:* 115; *123:* 128, 129, 130; *158:* 101, 102; *159:* 205; *178:* 188, 189, 190; *216:* 114; *227:* 146, 148, 149, 150
Rantz, Don *119:* 184
Rao, Anthony *28:* 126
Raphael, Elaine *23:* 192; *71:* 24, 25
Rappaport, Eva *6:* 190
Raschka, Chris *80:* 187, 189, 190; *97:* 211; *115:* 210; *117:* 151, 152, 153, 154; *143:* 195; *145:* 153; *166:* 190, 191; *170:* 114; *207:* 140, 143, 144, 145; *208:* 82; *220:* 85
Rash, Andy *158:* 178; *162:* 172; *210:* 204; *219:* 145; *226:* 194
Raskin, Ellen *2:* 208, 209; *4:* 142; *13:* 183; *22:* 68; *29:* 139; *36:* 134; *38:* 173, 174, 175, 176, 177, 178,179, 180, 181; *60:* 163; *86:* 81
Rathmann, Peggy *93:* 32; *94:* 168; *157:* 212, 214
Ratkus, Tony *77:* 133
Rattray, Gail *227:* 96
Ratzkin, Lawrence *40:* 143
Rau, Margaret *9:* 157
Raverat, Gwen *YABC 1:* 152
Ravid, Joyce *61:* 73
Ravielli, Anthony *1:* 198; *3:* 168; *11:* 143
Ravilious, Robin *77:* 169
Rawlins, Donna *72:* 198; *73:* 15, 129
Rawlins, Janet *76:* 79
Rawlings, Steve *143:* 139; *151:* 54; *208:* 150
Rawlinson, Debbie *75:* 132
Ray, Deborah Kogan *8:* 164; *29:* 238; *50:* 112, 113; *62:* 119; *78:* 191; *203:* 149, 150, 151
Ray, Jane *96:* 166; *97:* 104; *152:* 208; *190:* 221; *196:* 165
Ray, Ralph *2:* 239; *5:* 73
Rayann, Omar *162:* 205; *186:* 29, 30
Rayevsky, Robert *64:* 17; *70:* 173; *80:* 204; *117:* 79; *190:* 187, 188
Raymond, Larry *31:* 108; *97:* 109
Rayner, Hugh *151:* 170

Rayner, Mary *22:* 207; *47:* 140; *72:* 191; *87:* 171, 172; *192:* 104
Rayner, Shoo
　　See Rayner, Hugh
Raynes, John *71:* 19
Raynor, Dorka *28:* 168
Raynor, Paul *24:* 73
Rayyan, Omar *110:* 222; *112:* 17; *125:* 131
Razzi, James *10:* 127
Read, Alexander D. *20:* 45
Reader, Dennis *71:* 157
Reasoner, Charles *53:* 33, 36, 37
Rebenshied, Shane *203:* 76; *215:* 124; *237:* 155
Reczuch, Karen *115:* 132; *145:* 131
Redlich, Ben *163:* 221; *198:* 193
Reddy, Mike *203:* 67
Reed, Joseph *116:* 139
Reed, Lynn Rowe *115:* 173; *171:* 146; *208:* 177; *215:* 144, 145
Reed, Mike *211:* 147; *215:* 131
Reed, Tom *34:* 171
Reeder, Colin *74:* 202; *77:* 113
Rees, Mary *134:* 219
Reese, Bob *60:* 135
Reeve, Philip *171:* 50
Reeves, Eira B. *130:* 173, 174; *141:* 151
Reeves, Rick *181:* 179
Reeves, Rosie *202:* 200
Regan, Dana *117:* 116
Regan, Laura *103:* 198; *153:* 206
Reichert, Renée *169:* 127
Reid, Barbara *82:* 178; *92:* 17; *93:* 169, 170; *222:* 45
Reid, Stephen *19:* 213; *22:* 89
Reim, Melanie *104:* 151; *150:* 98
Reinert, Kirk *89:* 138; *195:* 129
Reinertson, Barbara *44:* 150; *62:* 103
Reiniger, Lotte *40:* 185
Reisberg, Mira *119:* 2
Reisch, Jesse *158:* 130
Reiser, Lynn *81:* 175; *138:* 184; *180:* 200
Reiss, John J. *23:* 193
Relf, Douglas *3:* 63
Relyea, C.M. *16:* 29; *31:* 153
Remi, Georges *13:* 184
Remington, Frederic *19:* 188; *41:* 178, 179, 180, 181, 183,184, 185, 186, 187, 188; *62:* 197
Remkiewicz, Frank *67:* 102; *77:* 171; *80:* 130; *113:* 107; *152:* 116; *152:* 211, 212; *157:* 148; *217:* 120, 138, 139, 140, 141
Rendon, Maria *116:* 141; *192:* 134; *134:* 152
Renfro, Ed *79:* 176
Renier, Aaron *202:* 141; *207:* 119
Renlie, Frank *11:* 200
Reschofsky, Jean *7:* 118
Rethi *60:* 181
Rethi, Lili *2:* 153; *36:* 156
Reusswig, William *3:* 267
Revell, Cindy *195:* 93
Rex, Adam *156:* 172; *169:* 91; *186:* 178, 179; *215:* 103; *223:* 11; *225:* 154
Rex, Michael *157:* 147; *191:* 159, 160; *221:* 124
Rey, H.A. *1:* 182; *26:* 163, 164, 166, 167, 169; *69:* 172, 173, 174, 175; *86:* 195, 196, 197; *100:* 211; *YABC 2:* 17
Rey, Luis V. *201:* 162
Reynish, Jenny *222:* 155
Reynolds, Adrian *192:* 159, 160; *237:* 178
Reynolds, Doris *5:* 71; *31:* 77
Reynolds, Peter H. *142:* 12; *179:* 175, 176; *202:* 113, 114; *226:* 30, 166, 167; *228:* 132
Rhead, Louis *31:* 91; *100:* 228
Rhodes, Andrew *38:* 204; *50:* 163; *54:* 76; *61:* 123, 124; *87:* 200
Ribbons, Ian *3:* 10; *37:* 161; *40:* 76
Ricci, Regolo *93:* 22; *164:* 148
Rice, Elizabeth *2:* 53, 214
Rice, Eve *34:* 174, 175; *91:* 172

Rice, James *22:* 210; *93:* 173
Rich, Anna *212:* 180
Rich, Martha *195:* 16
Richards, Chuck *170:* 154
Richards, George *40:* 116, 119, 121; *44:* 179
Richards, Henry *YABC 1:* 228, 231
Richardson, Ernest *2:* 144
Richardson, Frederick *18:* 27, 31
Richardson, John *110:* 88
Richman, Hilda *26:* 132
Richmond, George *24:* 179
Riddell, Chris *114:* 170, 195; *166:* 179; *199:* 164, 166, 167; *218:* 146, 148; *219:* 149, 150, 152, 153; *228:* 125
Riddle, Tohby *74:* 204; *151:* 179; *223:* 154, 156
Riding, Peter *63:* 195
Rieniets, Judy King *14:* 28
Riger, Bob *2:* 166
Riggio, Anita *73:* 191; *85:* 63; *137:* 184; *172:* 165
Rigano, Giovanni *219:* 45
Riley, Jon *74:* 70
Riley, Kenneth *22:* 230
Riley, Terry *203:* 100
Riley-Webb, Charlotte *153:* 143; *235:* 14, 161, 162
Rim, Sujean *225:* 157
Rinaldi, Angelo *165:* 60, 69; *227:* 53
Ringgold, Faith *71:* 162; *114:* 173, 174, 176; *187:* 160, 161, 163
Ringi, Kjell *12:* 171
Rios, Tere
　　See Versace, Marie
Rioux, Jo *215:* 110; *226:* 170
Ripper, Charles L. *3:* 175
Ripplinger, Henry *117:* 31
Ritchie, Scot *217:* 145
Ritchie, William *74:* 183
Ritter, John *175:* 14
Ritz, Karen *41:* 117; *72:* 239; *87:* 125; *102:* 7; *106:* 6
Rivas, Victor *209:* 193; *226:* 144
Rivers, Ruth *178:* 193
Rivkin, Jay *15:* 230
Rivoche, Paul *45:* 125
Roach, Marilynne *9:* 158
Robbin, Jodi *44:* 156, 159
Robbins, Frank *42:* 167
Robbins, Ken *147:* 191, 192; *234:* 182
Robbins, Ruth *52:* 102
Roberton, Fiona *230:* 142
Roberts, Cliff *4:* 126
Roberts, David *154:* 4, 6; *191:* 162; *196:* 184; *197:* 105; *210:* 257
Roberts, Doreen *4:* 230; *28:* 105
Roberts, Jim *22:* 166; *23:* 69; *31:* 110
Roberts, Tony *109:* 195, 214
Roberts, W. *22:* 2, 3
Robertson, M.P. *197:* 153
Robins, Arthur *137:* 172; *151:* 225; *204:* 161
Robinson, Aminah Brenda Lynn *86:* 205; *103:* 55; *159:* 175
Robinson, Charles [1870-1937] *17:* 157, 171, 172, 173, 175, 176; *24:* 207; *25:* 204; *YABC 2:* 308, 309, 310, 331
Robinson, Charles *3:* 53; *5:* 14; *6:* 193; *7:* 150; *7:* 183; *8:* 38; *9:* 81; *13:* 188; *14:* 248, 249; *23:* 149; *26:* 115; *27:* 48; *28:* 191; *32:* 28; *35:* 210; *36:* 37; *48:* 96; *52:* 33; *53:* 157; *56:* 15; *62:* 142; *77:* 41; *111:* 148
Robinson, Fiona *225:* 158
Robinson, Jerry *3:* 262
Robinson, Joan G. *7:* 184
Robinson, Lolly *90:* 227
Robinson, T.H. *17:* 179, 181, 182, 183; *29:* 254
Robinson, W. Heath *17:* 185, 187, 189, 191, 193, 195, 197, 199, 202; *23:* 167; *25:* 194; *29:* 150; *YABC 1:* 44; *2:* 183

Rocco, John *187:* 4; *188:* 151; *208:* 180, 181, 182; *213:* 94; *222:* 34
Roche, Christine *41:* 98
Roche, Denis *99:* 184; *180:* 32; *196:* 168
Roche, P.K. *57:* 151, 152
Rocker, Fermin *7:* 34; *13:* 21; *31:* 40; *40:* 190,191
Rocklen, Margot *101:* 181
Rockwell, Anne *5:* 147; *33:* 171, 173; *71:* 166, 167,168; *114:* 183, 184; *194:* 152, 155; *235:* 170
Rockwell, Gail *7:* 186
Rockwell, Harlow *33:* 171, 173, 175
Rockwell, Lizzy *114:* 182; *162:* 182; *185:* 189; *233:* 134, 135, 136; *235:* 171
Rockwell, Norman *23:* 39, 196, 197, 199, 200, 203, 204, 207; *41:* 140, 143; *123:* 47; *YABC 2:* 60
Rockwood, Richard *119:* 75
Rodanas, Kristina *156:* 183, 184; *221:* 127
Rodegast, Roland *43:* 100
Rodgers, Frank *69:* 177
Rodriguez, Albert G. *182:* 50
Rodriguez, Christina *184:* 12; *225:* 94
Rodriguez, Edel *204:* 86
Rodriguez, Joel *16:* 65
Rodriguez, Robert *145:* 145; *212:* 33
Rodriguez-Howard, Pauline *177:* 18
Roe, Monika *210:* 94
Roeckelein, Katrina *134:* 223
Roennfeldt, Robert *66:* 243
Roever, J.M. *4:* 119; *26:* 170
Roffey, Maureen *33:* 142, 176, 177
Rogasky, Barbara *46:* 90
Rogé *173:* 160; *233:* 138
Rogers, Carol *2:* 262; *6:* 164; *26:* 129
Rogers, Chris M. *150:* 59; *196:* 61
Rogers, Forest *87:* 160; *101:* 76
Rogers, Frances *10:* 130
Rogers, Gregory *104:* 76; *126:* 57; *171:* 26
Rogers, Jacqueline *78:* 249; *80:* 34; *86:* 54 *103:* 70; *115:* 72; *129:* 173; *131:* 57, 225; *143:* 211; *153:* 100; *193:* 186; *203:* 51; *213:* 144, 145, 146; *214:* 142; *234:* 173; *236:* 91
Rogers, Sherry *191:* 66
Rogers, Walter S. *31:* 135, 138; *67:* 65, 168; *100:* 81
Rogers, William A. *15:* 151, 153, 154; *33:* 35
Rogoff, Barbara *95:* 20
Rohmann, Eric *103:* 152; *198:* 151
Rojankovsky, Feodor *6:* 134, 136; *10:* 183; *21:* 128,129, 130; *25:* 110; *28:* 42; *68:* 120
Rolfsen, Alf *62:* 15
Rolston, Steve *209:* 154; *223:* 113
Romain, Trevor *134:* 157
Roman, Barbara J. *103:* 171
Romas *114:* 111; *165:* 63
Romano, Robert *64:* 68
Romero, Alejandro *187:* 185
Roos, Maryn *168:* 198; *225:* 160; *226:* 143
Root, Barry *80:* 212; *90:* 196; *146:* 78; *156:* 165; *159:* 161; *182:* 18, 172; *232:* 160, 161, 162
Root, Kimberly Bulcken *86:* 72; *98:* 21; *108:* 111; *127:* 114; *159:* 162; *176:* 134; *192:* 163
Roper, Bob *65:* 153
Roraback, Robin *111:* 156
Rorer, Abigail *43:* 222; *85:* 155
Rosales, Melodye *80:* 35
Rosamilia, Patricia *36:* 120
Rose, Carl *5:* 62
Rose, David S. *29:* 109; *70:* 120
Rose, Gerald *68:* 200, 201; *86:* 48
Rose, Naomi C. *228:* 136
Rose, Ted *93:* 178
Rosen, Elizabeth *205:* 137
Rosenbaum, Jonathan *50:* 46
Rosenberg, Amye *74:* 207, 208
Rosenberry, Vera *87:* 22, 26; *144:* 212, 213; *158:* 120; *219:* 163, 164
Rosenblum, Richard *11:* 202; *18:* 18

Rosenstiehl, Agnès *203:* 153
Rosier, Lydia *16:* 236; *20:* 104; *21:* 109; *22:* 125; *30:* 151, 158; *42:* 128; *45:* 214; *77:* 227, 228
Rosing, Jens *85:* 142
Ross
    See Thomson, Ross
Ross, Christine *83:* 172, 173
Ross, Clare Romano *3:* 123; *21:* 45; *48:* 199
Ross, Dave *32:* 152; *57:* 108
Ross, Graham *199:* 4
Ross, Herbert *37:* 78
Ross, John *3:* 123; *21:* 45
Ross, Johnny *32:* 190
Ross, Larry *47:* 168; *60:* 62
Ross, Ruth *109:* 233
Ross, Tony *17:* 204; *56:* 132; *65:* 176, 177, 179; *90:* 123; *123:* 186, 187, 190; *130:* 188, 190, 191, 192; *132:* 242; *174:* 159; *176:* 181, 182, 183; *202:* 198; *225:* 168, 170; *237:* 176, 177
Rossetti, Dante Gabriel *20:* 151, 153
Rostant, Larry *180:* 221; *194:* 108; *195:* 96; *197:* 12; *207:* 53; *210:* 189; *226:* 22; *234:* 154
Roth, Arnold *4:* 238; *21:* 133
Roth, Julie Jersild *180:* 206
Roth, Marci *135:* 223
Roth, R.G. *184:* 59
Roth, Rob *105:* 98; *146:* 41
Roth, Robert *176:* 159
Roth, Roger *61:* 128; *190:* 192
Roth, Ruby *216:* 185
Roth, Susan L. *80:* 38; *93:* 78; *134:* 165, 166; *181:* 145, 146
Rothenberg, Joani Keller *162:* 190, 191
Rothman, Michael *139:* 62; *184:* 34 *Rotman, Jeffrey L.* *145:* 30
Rotondo, Pat *32:* 158
Roughsey, Dick *35:* 186
Rouille, M. *11:* 96
Rounds, Glen *8:* 173; *9:* 171; *12:* 56; *32:* 194; *40:* 230; *51:* 161, 162, 166; *56:* 149; *70:* 198, 199; *YABC 1:* 1, 2, 3; *112:* 163
Roundtree, Katherine *114:* 88; *168:* 102
Rovetch, Lissa *201:* 164
Rowan, Evadne *52:* 51
Rowe, Eric *111:* 161
Rowe, Gavin *27:* 144; *72:* 47; *88:* 201
Rowe, John *132:* 70, 71; *180:* 126
Rowell, Kenneth *40:* 72
Rowen, Amy *52:* 143
Rowena *116:* 101
Rowland, Andrew *164:* 136
Rowland, Jada *83:* 73
Rowles, Daphne *58:* 24
Roy, Jeroo *27:* 229; *36:* 110
Royo *118:* 32; *144:* 105, 106, 108; *165:* 19; *166:* 166
Rubbino, Salvatore *220:* 147
Rubel, Nicole *18:* 255; *20:* 59; *81:* 66, 67; *95:* 169, 170; *119:* 60; *135:* 177, 179, 180; *169:* 68; *181:* 150
Rubel, Reina *33:* 217
Rud, Borghild *6:* 15
Ruddell, Gary *110:* 238; *116:* 207
Rudolph, Norman Guthrie *17:* 13
Rue, Leonard Lee III *37:* 164
Rueda, Claudia *183:* 170, 171
Ruelle, Karen Gray *126:* 193
Ruff, Donna *50:* 173; *72:* 203; *78:* 49; *80:* 120,121; *93:* 162; *164:* 121
Ruffins, Reynold *10:* 134, 135; *41:* 191, 192, 193, 194, 195, 196; *125:* 187, 188, 189; *162:* 197
Ruhlin, Roger *34:* 44
Rui, Paolo *217:* 115
Ruiz, Art *95:* 154; *110:* 91
Rumford, James *193:* 167
Runnerstroem, Bengt Arne *75:* 161
Ruse, Margaret *24:* 155

Rush, Ken *98:* 74
Rush, Peter *42:* 75
Russell, Charles M. *167:* 171
Russell, E.B. *18:* 177, 182
Russell, Jim *53:* 134
Russell, Natalie *218:* 170, 171
Russell, P. Craig *80:* 196; *146:* 102; *162:* 186
Russo, Marisabina *84:* 51; *106:* 164; *151:* 183; *188:* 153, 154, 155, 156
Russo, Susan *30:* 182; *36:* 144
Russon, Mary *87:* 145
Ruth, Greg *183:* 125
Ruth, Rod *9:* 161
Rutherford, Alexa *110:* 108
Rutherford, Jenny *78:* 5
Rutherford, Meg *25:* 174; *34:* 178, 179; *69:* 73; *72:* 31
Rutland, Jonathan *31:* 126
Ruurs, Margriet *147:* 195
Ruzzier, Sergio *159:* 176, 177; *163:* 184; *210:* 214, 216
Ryan, Amy *188:* 50
Ryan, Will *86:* 134
Rycroft, Nina *228:* 143
Ryden, Hope *8:* 176
Rylant, Cynthia *112:* 170, 172
Rymer, Alta M. *34:* 181
Ryniak, Christopher *178:* 11
Rystedt, Rex *49:* 80

S

Saaf, Chuck *49:* 179
Saaf, Donald *101:* 220; *124:* 180
Sabaka, Donna R. *21:* 172
Sabin, Robert *45:* 35; *60:* 30; *99:* 161; *223:* 29
Sabuda, Robert *170:* 166, 167, 168
Sacker, Amy *16:* 100
Sadler, Sonia Lynn *230:* 42, 163
Saelig, S.M. *129:* 73; *173:* 59
Saffioti, Lino *36:* 176; *48:* 60; *223:* 26
Saflund, Birgitta *94:* 2
Sagsoorian, Paul *12:* 183; *22:* 154; *33:* 106; *87:* 152
Sahara, Tony *168:* 106; *177:* 181; *178:* 228; *186:* 132; *207:* 89; *231:* 54; *236:* 107, 109
Sahlberg, Myron *57:* 165
Saidens, Amy *145:* 162; *191:* 131; *210:* 129
Saint Exupery, Antoine de *20:* 157
Saint James, Synthia *152:* 220; *188:* 90; *200:* 7
Sakai, Komako *213:* 148
Saldutti, Denise *39:* 186; *57:* 178
Sale, Morton *YABC 2:* 31
Sale, Tim *153:* 177
Salerno, Steven *150:* 79; *176:* 188; *202:* 39; *216:* 190; *235:* 55
Salter, George *72:* 128, 130
Saltzberg, Barney *135:* 184, 185; *194:* 160; *233:* 147, 148
Saltzman, David *86:* 209
Salwowski, Mark *71:* 54
Salzman, Yuri *86:* 12
Sambourne, Linley *YABC 2:* 181
Sampson, Katherine *9:* 197
Samson, Anne S. *2:* 216
San Souci, Daniel *40:* 200; *96:* 199, 200; *113:* 171; *157:* 149; *170:* 69; *192:* 167, 168; *220:* 152; *221:* 126
Sancha, Sheila *38:* 185
Sanchez, Enrique O. *155:* 84
Sand, George X. *45:* 182
Sandberg, Lasse *15:* 239, 241
Sanders, Beryl *39:* 173
Sanderson, Ruth *21:* 126; *24:* 53; *28:* 63; *33:* 67; *41:* 48, 198, 199, 200, 201, 202, 203; *43:* 79; *46:* 36,44; *47:* 102; *49:* 58; *62:* 121, 122; *85:* 3; *109:* 207, 208, 209, 210; *172:* 157, 158; *223:* 85; *224:* 152, 153, 154

Sandia *119:* 74
Sandin, Joan *4:* 36; *6:* 194; *7:* 177; *12:* 145,185; *20:* 43; *21:* 74; *26:* 144; *27:* 142; *28:* 224, 225; *38:* 86; *41:* 46; *42:* 35; *59:* 6; *80:* 136; *94:* 188; *140:* 116; *153:* 179, 180; *197:* 168; *232:* 6
Sandland, Reg *39:* 215
Sandoz, Edouard *26:* 45, 47
Sanford, John *66:* 96, 97
Sanger, Amy Wilson *205:* 140
Sankey, Tom *72:* 103
Sano, Kazuhiko *153:* 208; *195:* 171; *203:* 21; *221:* 71
Santat, Dan *188:* 160; *221:* 62; *223:* 163; *224:* 157, 158, 159
Santiago, Wilfred *210:* 48
Santore, Charles *54:* 139; *200:* 171, 172
Santoro, Christopher *74:* 215
Santoro, Scott *236:* 166
Santos, Jesse J. *99:* 24
Sapieha, Christine *1:* 180
Saport, Linda *123:* 137, 138; *215:* 29
Sara
    See De La Roche Saint Andre, Anne
Sarcone-Roach, Julia *215:* 158
Sardinha, Rick *175:* 151
Sarg, Tony *YABC 2:* 236
Sargent, Claudia *64:* 181
Sargent, Robert *2:* 217
Saris *1:* 33
Sarony *YABC 2:* 170
Saroff, Phyllis V. *202:* 160
Sasaki, Goro *170:* 46; *237:* 23
Sasaki, Ellen Joy *216:* 49
Sasek, Miroslav *16:* 239, 240, 241, 242
Sassman, David *9:* 79
Sattler, Jennifer Gordon *218:* 175
Satty *29:* 203, 205
Sauber, Robert *40:* 183; *76:* 256; *78:* 154; *87:* 92
Saunders, Dave *85:* 163, 164, 165
Savadier, Elivia *84:* 50; *145:* 45; *164:* 206; *228:* 146
Savage, Naomi *56:* 172
Savage, Steele *10:* 203; *20:* 77; *35:* 28
Savage, Stephen *174:* 182
Savio *76:* 4
Savitt, Sam *8:* 66, 182; *15:* 278; *20:* 96; *24:* 192; *28:* 98
Sawyer, Kem Knapp *84:* 228, 229
Say, Allen *28:* 178; *69:* 182, 183, 232; *110:* 194, 195,196; *161:* 154, 155
Sayles, Elizabeth *82:* 93; *105:* 155; *109:* 116; *180:* 64; *220:* 160, 161; *232:* 177
Scabrini, Janet *13:* 191; *44:* 128
Scalora, Suza *224:* 160
Scanlan, Peter *83:* 27; *153:* 165; *187:* 149
Scanlon, Paul *83:* 87
Scannell, Reece *105:* 105
Scarry, Huck *35:* 204, 205
Scarry, Richard *2:* 220, 221; *18:* 20; *35:* 193, 194, 195,196, 197, 198, 199, 200, 201, 202; *75:* 165, 167, 168
Schachner, Judith Byron *88:* 180; *92:* 163; *93:* 102; *142:* 82; *178:* 199, 200; *190:* 140; *228:* 83
Schade, Susan *205:* 21
Schaeffer, Mead *18:* 81, 94; *21:* 137, 138, 139; *47:* 128
Schaffer, Amanda *90:* 206
Schallau, Daniel *222:* 164
Schanzer, Rosalyn *138:* 192, 193
Scharl, Josef *20:* 132; *22:* 128
Scheel, Lita *11:* 230
Scheffler, Axel *180:* 23, 24; *230:* 169, 170
Scheib, Ida *29:* 28
Schermer, Judith *30:* 184
Schick, Eleanor *82:* 210, 211; *144:* 222
Schick, Joel *16:* 160; *17:* 167; *22:* 12; *27:* 176; *31:* 147, 148; *36:* 23; *38:* 64; *45:* 116, 117; *52:* 5, 85; *104:* 159

Schields, Gretchen *75:* 171, 203
Schindelman, Joseph *1:* 74; *4:* 101; *12:* 49; *26:* 51; *40:* 146; *56:* 158; *73:* 40
Schindler, Edith *7:* 22
Schindler, S.D. *38:* 107; *46:* 196; *74:* 162; *75:* 172, 173; *99:* 133; *112:* 177; *118:* 185, 186; *121:* 71; *136:* 159; *143:* 45; *149:* 120; *156:* 30; *169:* 135; *171:* 161, 162, 163; *172:* 9; *186:* 163; *194:* 109; *195:* 35; *198:* 170, 171, 172; *237:* 121
Schlesinger, Bret *7:* 77
Schlossberg, Elisabeth *221:* 161
Schmid, Eleanore *12:* 188; *126:* 196, 197
Schmid, Paul *231:* 169
Schmiderer, Dorothy *19:* 224
Schmidt, Bill *73:* 34; *76:* 220, 222, 224
Schmidt, Elizabeth *15:* 242
Schmidt, George Paul *132:* 122
Schmidt, Karen Lee *54:* 12; *71:* 174; *92:* 56; *94:* 190, 191; *127:* 103
Schmidt, Lynette *76:* 205
Schmitz, Tamara *207:* 147
Schneider, Christine M. *171:* 165
Schneider, Howie *181:* 159
Schneider, Katy *237:* 128
Schneider, Rex *29:* 64; *44:* 171
Schnurr, Edward *170:* 62
Schoberle, Cecile *80:* 200; *92:* 134; *218:* 113
Schoenherr, Ian *32:* 83; *173:* 41; *235:* 174
Schoenherr, John *1:* 146, 147, 173; *3:* 39, 139; *17:* 75; *29:* 72; *32:* 83; *37:* 168, 169, 170; *43:* 164, 165; *45:* 160, 162; *51:* 127; *66:* 196, 197, 198; *68:* 83; *72:* 240; *75:* 225; *88:* 176
Scholder, Fritz *69:* 103
Schomburg, Alex *13:* 23
Schongut, Emanuel *4:* 102; *15:* 186; *47:* 218, 219; *52:* 147, 148, 149, 150; *185:* 27
Schoonover, Frank *17:* 107; *19:* 81, 190, 233; *22:* 88,129; *24:* 189; *31:* 88; *41:* 69; *YABC 2:* 282, 316
Schories, Pat *164:* 210; *232:* 170, 171, 172
Schottland, Miriam *22:* 172
Schramm, Ulrik *2:* 16; *14:* 112
Schreiber, Elizabeth Anne *13:* 193
Schreiber, Ralph W. *13:* 193
Schreiter, Rick *14:* 97; *23:* 171; *41:* 247; *49:* 131
Schroades, John *214:* 129
Schroeder, Binette *56:* 128, 129
Schroeder, E. Peter *12:* 112
Schroeder, Ted *11:* 160; *15:* 189; *30:* 91; *34:* 43
Schrotter, Gustav *22:* 212; *30:* 225
Schubert, Dieter *101:* 167, 168; *217:* 151, 152, 153, 155
Schubert, Ingrid *217:* 151, 152, 153, 155
Schubert-Gabrys, Ingrid *101:* 167, 168
Schucker, James *31:* 163
Schuett, Stacey *72:* 137; *208:* 204
Schulder, Lili *146:* 29
Schulke, Debra *57:* 167
Schulke, Flip *57:* 167
Schulz, Barbara *167:* 24
Schulz, Charles M. *10:* 137, 138, 139, 140, 141, 142; *118:* 192, 193, 194, 196, 199
Schutzer, Dena *109:* 32
Schwark, Mary Beth *51:* 155; *72:* 175
Schwartz, Amy *47:* 191; *82:* 100; *83:* 178, 179, 180,181; *129:* 107; *131:* 197, 198; *189:* 166, 168; *226:* 174
Schwartz, Carol *124:* 41; *130:* 199
Schwartz, Charles *8:* 184
Schwartz, Daniel *46:* 37
Schwartz, Joanie *124:* 170
Schwartzberg, Joan *3:* 208
Schwarz, Viviane *204:* 132
Schweitzer, Iris *2:* 137; *6:* 207
Schweninger, Ann *29:* 172; *82:* 246; *159:* 202, 168; *166:* 211; *193*
Schwinger, Laurence *84:* 44; *91:* 61

Scofield, Penrod *61:* 107; *62:* 160
Scott, Anita Walker *7:* 38
Scott, Art *39:* 41
Scott, Frances Gruse *38:* 43
Scott, Jane Wooster *226:* 181
Scott, Julian *34:* 126
Scott, Roszel *33:* 238
Scott, Sally *87:* 27
Scott, Steve *166:* 230, 231; *171:* 93
Scott, Trudy *27:* 172
Scotton, Rob *214:* 183
Scrace, Carolyn *143:* 95, 96
Scrambly, Crab *198:* 196
Scribner, Joanne *14:* 236; *29:* 78; *33:* 185; *34:* 208; *78:* 75; *164:* 237; *203:* 73
Scrofani, Joseph *31:* 65; *74:* 225
Scroggs, Kirk *187:* 169
Seaman, Mary Lott *34:* 64
Searle, Ronald *24:* 98; *42:* 172, 173, 174, 176, 177, 179; *66:* 73, 74; *70:* 205, 206, 207
Searle, Townley *36:* 85
Sebree, Charles *18:* 65
Sedacca, Joseph M. *11:* 25; *22:* 36
Seder, Jason *108:* 102
Seeger, Laura Vaccaro *172:* 162
Seegmiller, Don *174:* 57
Seely, David *164:* 173
Seeley, Laura L. *97:* 105
Segal, John *178:* 202
Segar, E.C. *61:* 179, 181
Segur, Adrienne *27:* 121
Seibold, J. Otto *83:* 188, 190, 191; *149:* 212, 214, 215, 216; *196:* 177, 179; *215:* 204
Seignobosc, Francoise *21:* 145, 146
Sejima, Yoshimasa *8:* 187
Selig, Sylvie *13:* 199
Seltzer, Isadore *6:* 18; *133:* 59
Seltzer, Meyer *17:* 214
Selven, Maniam *144:* 133
Selway, Martina *169:* 157
Selznick, Brian *79:* 192; *104:* 25; *117:* 175; *126:* 156; *134:* 171; *158:* 76, 78; *169:* 70; *171:* 172, 173; *191:* 106; *192:* 130; *197:* 158; *203:* 35; *205:* 92; *210:* 219, 220, 221, 222; *234:* 130
Sempe, Jean-Jacques *47:* 92; *YABC 2:* 109
Sendak, Maurice *1:* 135, 190; *3:* 204; *7:* 142; *15:* 199; *17:* 210; *27:* 181, 182, 183, 185, 186, 187, 189,190, 191, 192, 193, 194, 195, 197, 198, 199, 203; *28:* 181, 182; *32:* 108; *33:* 148, 149; *35:* 238; *44:* 180, 181; *45:* 97, 99; *46:* 174; *73:* 225; *91:* 10, 11 *YABC1:* 167; *113:* 163, 165, 167, 168; *118:* 153; *127:* 161
Senders, Marci *180:* 79
Sengler, Johanna *18:* 256
Senn, Steve *60:* 145
Seredy, Kate *1:* 192; *14:* 20, 21; *17:* 210
Sergeant, John *6:* 74
Serra, Sebastía *212:* 215
Servello, Joe *10:* 144; *24:* 139; *40:* 91; *70:* 130, 131; *146:* 159
Seton, Ernest Thompson *18:* 260-269, 271
Seuss, Dr.
    See Geisel, Theodor
Severin, John Powers *7:* 62
Sewall, Marcia *15:* 8; *22:* 170; *37:* 171, 172, 173; *39:* 73; *45:* 209; *62:* 117; *69:* 185, 186; *71:* 212; *90:* 232; *96:* 127; *102:* 101; *107:* 129; *119:* 176, 177, 178, 180
Seward, James *70:* 35
Seward, Prudence *16:* 243
Sewell, Helen *3:* 186; *15:* 308; *33:* 102; *38:* 189, 190, 191, 192
Seymour, Stephen *54:* 21
Sfar, Joann *182:* 183
Shachat, Andrew *82:* 179
Shadbolt, Robert *203:* 68
Shahn, Ben *39:* 178; *46:* 193
Shalansky, Len *38:* 167
Shanks, Anne Zane *10:* 149

Shannon, David *57:* 137; *107:* 184; *112:* 216; *135:* 12; *152:* 223, 224, 225; *158:* 192; *212:* 159, 160, 163; *228:* 162, 163, 164, 165; *237:* 9
Sharkey, Niamh *213:* 152
Sharp, Paul *52:* 60
Sharp, William *6:* 131; *19:* 241; *20:* 112; *25:* 141
Sharratt, Nick *102:* 207, 208; *104:* 163; *153:* 198; *175:* 176; *192:* 208; *199:* 141, 142, 143, 184, 187, 188
Shaw, Barclay *74:* 14, 16; *118:* 138
Shaw, Charles *21:* 135; *38:* 187; *47:* 124; *126:* 219
Shaw, Charles G. *13:* 200
Shaw, Hannah *227:* 163, 164
Shaw-Smith, Emma *144:* 117
Shea, Bob *231:* 170, 171
Shea, Edmund *56:* 19
Shearer, Ted *43:* 193, 194, 195, 196
Sheban, Chris *182:* 185; *190:* 102, 104; *202:* 28; *204:* 112, 114; *209:* 150; *210:* 107; *220:* 103; *224:* 185
Shecter, Ben *16:* 244; *25:* 109; *33:* 188, 191; *41:* 77
Shed, Greg *74:* 94; *84:* 204; *129:* 149, *167:* 91; *179:* 192; *223:* 104
Sheeban, Chris *144:* 190; *158:* 163
Shefcik, James *48:* 221, 222; *60:* 141
Shefelman, Karl *58:* 168
Shefelman, Tom *204:* 137
Shefts, Joelle *48:* 210
Shein, Bob *139:* 189
Sheinkin, Stephen *204:* 139
Shekerjian, Haig *16:* 245
Shekerjian, Regina *16:* 245; *25:* 73
Sheldon, David *184:* 174; *185:* 204; *211:* 189
Shelley, John *186:* 223
Shemie, Bonnie *96:* 207
Shenton, Edward *45:* 187, 188, 189; *YABC 1:* 218, 219, 221
Shepard, Ernest H. *3:* 193; *4:* 74; *16:* 101; *17:* 109; *25:* 148; *33:* 152, 199, 200, 201, 202, 203, 204, 205, 206,207; *46:* 194; *98:* 114; *100:* 111, 178, 179, 217, 219, 220,221; *YABC 1:* 148, 153, 174, 176, 180, 181
Shepard, Mary *4:* 210; *22:* 205; *30:* 132, 133; *54:* 150, 152, 153, 157, 158; *59:* 108, 109, 111; *100:* 246
Shepherd, Amanda *198:* 14
Shepherd, Irana *171:* 112
Sheppard, Kate *195:* 176
Shepperson, Rob *96:* 153; *177:* 163; *178:* 204; *197:* 34; *205:* 108
Sheridan, Brian *196:* 193
Sherman, Theresa *27:* 167
Sherwan, Earl *3:* 196
Shields, Charles *10:* 150; *36:* 63
Shields, Leonard *13:* 83, 85, 87
Shiffman, Lena *139:* 167; *168:* 136
Shiga, Jason *228:* 168
Shigley, Neil K. *66:* 219
Shillabeer, Mary *35:* 74
Shilston, Arthur *49:* 61; *62:* 58
Shimin, Symeon *1:* 93; *2:* 128, 129; *3:* 202; *7:* 85; *11:* 177; *12:* 139; *13:* 202, 203; *27:* 138; *28:* 65; *35:* 129; *36:* 130; *48:* 151; *49:* 59; *56:* 63, 65, 153
Shimizu, Yuko *215:* 197
Shine, Andrea *104:* 165; *128:* 34
Shinn, Everett *16:* 148; *18:* 229; *21:* 149, 150, 151; *24:* 218
Shinn, Florence Scovel *63:* 133, 135
Shore, Robert *27:* 54; *39:* 192, 193; *YABC 2:* 200
Shortall, Leonard *4:* 144; *8:* 196; *10:* 166; *19:* 227, 228, 229, 230; *25:* 78; *28:* 66, 167; *33:* 127; *52:* 125; *73:* 12, 212
Shortt, T.M. *27:* 36
Shpitalnik, Vladimir *83:* 194
Shroades, John *230:* 24

Shropshire, Sandy *170:* 191
Shtainments, Leon *32:* 161
Shulevitz, Uri *3:* 198, 199; *17:* 85; *22:* 204; *27:* 212; *28:* 184; *50:* 190, 191, 192, 193, 194, 195, 196,197, 198, 199, 201; *106:* 181, 182, 183; *165:* 203, 205; *166:* 138
Shulman, Dee *180:* 140
Shupe, Bobbi *139:* 80, 81
Shute, A.B. *67:* 196
Shute, Linda *46:* 59; *74:* 118
Siberell, Anne *29:* 193
Sibley, Don *1:* 39; *12:* 196; *31:* 47
Sibthorp, Fletcher *94:* 111, 112
Sidjakov, Nicolas *18:* 274
Siebel, Fritz *3:* 120; *17:* 145
Siebold, J. Otto *158:* 227
Siegel, Hal *74:* 246
Sieger, Ted *189:* 172
Siegl, Helen *12:* 166; *23:* 216; *34:* 185, 186
Silin-Palmer, Pamela *184:* 102
Sill, John *140:* 194; *141:* 157; *221:* 163; *222:* 171
Sills, Joyce *5:* 199
Silva, Simon *108:* 122
Silver, Maggie *85:* 210
Silveria, Gordon *96:* 44
Silverstein, Alvin *8:* 189
Silverstein, Shel *33:* 211; *92:* 209, 210
Silverstein, Virginia *8:* 189
Silvey, Joe *135:* 203
Simard, Rémy *95:* 156; *221:* 144
Siminovich, Laura *219:* 172
Simmons, Elly *110:* 2; *127:* 69; *134:* 181
Simon, Eric M. *7:* 82
Simon, Hilda *28:* 189
Simon, Howard *2:* 175; *5:* 132; *19:* 199; *32:* 163, 164, 165
Simont, Marc *2:* 119; *4:* 213; *9:* 168; *13:* 238,240; *14:* 262; *16:* 179; *18:* 221; *26:* 210; *33:* 189, 194; *44:* 132; *58:* 122; *68:* 117; *73:* 204, 205, 206; *74:* 221; *126:* 199, 200; *133:* 195; *163:* 40; *164:* 128; *223:* 28
Simpson, Martin *233:* 168
Sims, Agnes *54:* 152
Sims, Blanche *44:* 116; *57:* 129; *75:* 179, 180; *77:* 92; *104:* 192; *152:* 117; *156:* 160; *160:* 70; *168:* 174, 175; *198:* 17; *236:* 54
Singer, Edith G. *2:* 30
Singer, Gloria *34:* 56; *36:* 43
Singer, Julia *28:* 190
Singh, Jen *178:* 146
Singh, Nikhil *234:* 54
Sinquette, Jaclyn *215:* 83
Siomades, Lorianne *134:* 45; *204:* 48; *217:* 157
Siracusa, Catherine *68:* 135; *82:* 218
Sisson, Stephanie Roth *136:* 171, 172; *237:* 131
Sís, Peter *67:* 179, 181, 183, 184, 185; *96:* 96, 98; *106:* 193, 194, 195; *149:* 224, 226; *180:* 177; *192:* 180, 182; *222:* 64
Sivard, Robert *26:* 124
Sivertson, Liz *116:* 84
Skardinski, Stanley *23:* 144; *32:* 84; *66:* 122; *84:* 108
Slack, Michael *185:* 108; *189:* 173, 174
Slackman, Charles B. *12:* 201
Slade, Christian *193:* 187; *204:* 134; *234:* 59
Slade, Paul *61:* 170
Slark, Albert *99:* 212; *205:* 161
Slater, Rod *25:* 167
Slavin, Bill *182:* 14, 15; *196:* 90; *199:* 148, 149, 150; *217:* 20; *235:* 45; *237:* 69
Sloan, Joseph *16:* 68
Sloane, Eric *21:* 3; *52:* 153, 154, 155, 156, 157, 158, 160
Sloat, Teri *164:* 231
Slobodkin, Louis *1:* 200; *3:* 232; *5:* 168; *13:* 251; *15:* 13, 88; *26:* 173, 174, 175, 176, 178, 179; *60:* 180
Slobodkina, Esphyr *1:* 201

Slonim, David *166:* 167, 168
Small, David *50:* 204, 205; *79:* 44; *95:* 189, 190, 191; *126:* 203, 204; *136:* 119; *143:* 201, 202, 203; *144:* 246; *150:* 5; *161:* 176; *183:* 181, 182, 183, 184; *200:* 211; *212:* 86; *216:* 202, 203, 204; *230:* 222; *232:* 95
Small, W. *33:* 113
Smalley, Janet *1:* 154
Smath, Jerry *198:* 179, 180
Smedley, William T. *34:* 129
Smee, David *14:* 78; *62:* 30
Smee, Nicola *167:* 156
Smith, A.G., Jr. *35:* 182
Smith, Ali *204:* 68
Smith, Alvin *1:* 31, 229; *13:* 187; *27:* 216; *28:* 226; *48:* 149; *49:* 60
Smith, Andy *188:* 20; *207:* 151
Smith, Anne *194:* 147
Smith, Anne Warren *41:* 212
Smith, Barry *75:* 183
Smith, Brian *200:* 183
Smith, Carl *36:* 41
Smith, Cat Bowman *146:* 39; *164:* 219; *201:* 55, 184
Smith, Craig *97:* 197; *172:* 175; *206:* 40; *215:* 19; *217:* 129; *220:* 145
Smith, Donald A. *178:* 7
Smith, Doris Susan *41:* 139
Smith, Douglas *189:* 159; *213:* 170
Smith, Duane *171:* 152; *208:* 97
Smith, E. Boyd *19:* 70; *22:* 89; *26:* 63; *YABC 1:* 4, 5, 240, 248, 249
Smith, Edward J. *4:* 224
Smith, Elwood H. *157:* 231; *181:* 79; *203:* 160, 161, 162; *231:* 108; *236:* 176, 177, 178
Smith, Eunice Young *5:* 170
Smith, Gary *113:* 216
Smith, George *102:* 169
Smith, Howard *19:* 196
Smith, J. Gerard *95:* 42
Smith, Jacqueline Bardner *27:* 108; *39:* 197
Smith, Jay J. *61:* 119
Smith, Jeff *93:* 191
Smith, Jessie Willcox *15:* 91; *16:* 95; *18:* 231; *19:* 57, 242; *21:* 29, 156, 157, 158, 159, 160, 161; *34:* 65; *100:* 223; *YABC 1:* 6; *2:* 180, 185, 191, 311, 325
Smith, Jos. A. *52:* 131; *72:* 120; *74:* 151; *84:* 147, 148; *85:* 146; *87:* 96; *94:* 219; *96:* 97; *104:* 33; *108:* 126, 127, 128; *111:* 140; *136:* 145; *181:* 173; *200:* 213; *201:* 94; *231:* 148; *237:* 85
Smith, Kenneth R. *47:* 182
Smith, Keri *216:* 60
Smith, Kevin Warren *89:* 112
Smith, Kristin *209:* 197
Smith, L.H. *35:* 174
Smith, Lane *76:* 211, 213; *88:* 115; *105:* 202, 203,204, 205; *131:* 207; *160:* 217, 221; *179:* 183, 184, 185, 186; *199:* 122, 123, 124, 126; *224:* 164
Smith, Lee *29:* 32
Smith, Linell Nash *2:* 195
Smith, Maggie Kaufman *13:* 205; *35:* 191; *110:* 158; *178:* 226; *190:* 204; *209:* 145; *235:* 179, 180
Smith, Mavis *101:* 219
Smith, Moishe *33:* 155
Smith, Philip *44:* 134; *46:* 203
Smith, Ralph Crosby *2:* 267; *49:* 203
Smith, Robert D. *5:* 63
Smith, Sally J. *84:* 55
Smith, Susan Carlton *12:* 208
Smith, Terry *12:* 106; *33:* 158
Smith, Virginia *3:* 157; *33:* 72
Smith, William A. *1:* 36; *10:* 154; *25:* 65
Smith-Moore, J.J. *98:* 147
Smolinski, Dick *84:* 217
Smoljan, Joe *112:* 201
Smollin, Mike *39:* 203
Smyth, Iain *105:* 207

Smyth, M. Jane *12:* 15
Smythe, Fiona *151:* 213
Smythe, Theresa *141:* 37
Snair, Andy *176:* 4
Sneed, Brad *125:* 25; *191:* 175, 176; *211:* 194; *232:* 152
Snow, Sarah *228:* 47
Snyder, Andrew A. *30:* 212
Snyder, Betsy *230:* 173
Snyder, Jerome *13:* 207; *30:* 173
Snyder, Joel *28:* 163
So, Meilo *162:* 201; *208:* 188
Soentpiet, Chris K. *97:* 208; *110:* 33; *159:* 184; *161:* 10; *163:* 130
Sofia *1:* 62; *5:* 90; *32:* 166; *86:* 43
Sofilas, Mark *93:* 157
Sogabe, Aki *207:* 153; *221:* 110
Sohn, Jiho *182:* 78
Sokol, Bill *37:* 178; *49:* 23
Sokolov, Kirill *34:* 188
Solbert, Ronni *1:* 159; *2:* 232; *5:* 121; *6:* 34; *17:* 249
Solomon, Michael *174:* 115
Solonevich, George *15:* 246; *17:* 47
Soloviov, Michael *223:* 122
Soma, Liana *81:* 118
Soman, David *90:* 122; *102:* 126; *140:* 120; 93; *188:* 43, 89; *200:* 180, 181; *235:* 72
Sommer, Robert *12:* 211
Song, Jae *203:* 27
Soo, Kean *201:* 185
Sorel, Edward *4:* 61; *36:* 82; *65:* 191, 193; *126:* 214
Sorensen, Henri *196:* 58
Sorensen, Henrik *62:* 16
Sorensen, Svend Otto *22:* 130, 141; *67:* 188, 189
Sorra, Kristin *155:* 80; *229:* 85
Sosa, Hernan *198:* 66
Sostre, Maria *187:* 36
Sotomayor, Antonio *11:* 215
Souhami, Jessica *112:* 128; *176:* 193
Sousa, Natalie C. *209:* 89
Souza, Diana *71:* 139
Sovak, Jan *115:* 190
Sowards, Ben *215:* 62
Soyer, Moses *20:* 177
Spaenkuch, August *16:* 28
Spafford, Suzy *160:* 228
Spain, Valerie *105:* 76
Spain, Sunday Sahara *133:* 204
Spalenka, Greg *149:* 69; *151:* 228; *184:* 195; *191:* 21; *196:* 12; *198:* 181, 182, 201; *208:* 92; *236:* 95
Spanfeller, James *1:* 72, 149; *2:* 183; *19:* 230, 231,232; *22:* 66; *36:* 160, 161; *40:* 75; *52:* 166; *76:* 37
Spangler, Brie *212:* 188
Sparks, Mary Walker *15:* 247
Spearing, Craig J. *228:* 172
Spears, Rick *182:* 187; *220:* 67
Speidel, Sandra *78:* 233; *94:* 178; *134:* 180; *210:* 67
Speirs, John *67:* 178
Spence, Geraldine *21:* 163; *47:* 196
Spence, Jim *38:* 89; *50:* 102
Spencer, Laurie *113:* 12
Spencer, Mark *57:* 170
Spengler, Kenneth J. *146:* 256
Sperling, Andrea *133:* 182
Spiegel, Beth *184:* 203
Spiegel, Doris *29:* 111
Spiegelman, Art *109:* 227
Spier, Jo *10:* 30
Spier, Peter *3:* 155; *4:* 200; *7:* 61; *11:* 78; *38:* 106; *54:* 120, 121, 122, 123, 124, 125, 126, 127, 128, 129, 130,131, 132, 133, 134
Spilka, Arnold *5:* 120; *6:* 204; *8:* 131
Spires, Ashley *231:* 96

Spirin, Gennady *95:* 196, 197; *113:* 172; *128:* 9; *129:* 49; *134:* 210; *153:* 9; *204:* 143, 144, 145; *220:* 153
Spiro, Ruth *208:* 197
Spivak, I. Howard *8:* 10; *13:* 172
Spohn, David *72:* 233
Spohn, Kate *87:* 195; *147:* 201, 202
Spollen, Christopher J. *12:* 214
Spooner, Malcolm *40:* 142
Spoor, Mike *220:* 92
Spowart, Robin *82:* 228; *92:* 149; *133:* 131; *176:* 163; *177:* 183, 184; *217:* 123, 124
Sprague, Kevin *150:* 60; *196:* 62
Spranger, Nina *201:* 199
Sprattler, Rob *12:* 176
Spring, Bob *5:* 60
Spring, Ira *5:* 60
Springer, Harriet *31:* 92
Spudvilas, Anne *110:* 74; *197:* 192; *199:* 154
Spurll, Barbara *78:* 199; *88:* 141, 142; *99:* 215
Spurrier, Steven *28:* 198
Spuvilas, Anne *85:* 114
Spy
  See Ward, Leslie
Squires, Stuart *127:* 74
St. Aubin, Bruno *179:* 54
St. John, J. Allen *41:* 62
Staake, Bob *209:* 168, 169; *229:* 132
Stabin, Victor *101:* 131; *164:* 158
Stadler, John *62:* 33; *204:* 149
Stadnyk, Greg *212:* 55
Staffan, Alvin E. *11:* 56; *12:* 187
Stahl, Ben *5:* 181; *12:* 91; *49:* 122; *71:* 128; *87:* 206; *112:* 107
Stair, Gobin *35:* 214
Stallwood, Karen *73:* 126
Stamaty, Mark Alan *12:* 215; *230:* 175
Stammen, JoEllen McAllister *113:* 14
Stamp, Jørgen *225:* 184
Stampnick, Ken *51:* 142
Stanbridge, Joanne *150:* 91
Stanley, Diane *3:* 45; *37:* 180; *80:* 217, 219
Stanley, Sanna *145:* 228
Star, Lindsay *219:* 39
Starcke, Helmut *86:* 217
Stark, Ken *197:* 102
Starr, Branka *73:* 25
Stasiak, Krystyna *49:* 181; *64:* 194
Staub, Leslie *103:* 54
Stauffer, Brian *220:* 123
Staunton, Ted *112:* 192
Stawicki, Matt *164:* 250
Stead, Erin E. *232:* 179
Stead, L. *55:* 51, 56
Steadman, Broeck *97:* 185, 186; *99:* 56; *121:* 48; *208:* 190
Steadman, Henry *211:* 130
Steadman, Ralph *32:* 180; *123:* 143, 145
Stearn, Nick *183:* 26
Stearn, Todd *218:* 179
Steckler, June *90:* 178
Steele, Robert Gantt *169:* 174
Steichen, Edward *30:* 79
Steig, William *18:* 275, 276; *70:* 215, 216, 217, 218; *111:* 173, 174, 175, 176, 177
Stein, David Ezra *211:* 168
Stein, Harve *1:* 109
Steinberg, Saul *47:* 193
Steinel, William *23:* 146
Steiner, Charlotte *45:* 196
Steiner, Joan *110:* 219; *199:* 160, 161
Steirnagel, Michael *80:* 56
Stemp, Eric *60:* 184
Stengel, Christopher *229:* 200; *232:* 57; *237:* 135
Stephens, Alice Barber *66:* 208, 209
Stephens, Charles H. *YABC 2:* 279
Stephens, Pam *198:* 69
Stephens, Pat *126:* 110; *128:* 101
Stephens, William M. *21:* 165
Stephenson, Kristina *224:* 169

Steptoe, Javaka *151:* 203, 204; *190:* 169; *213:* 163, 164
Steptoe, John *8:* 197; *57:* 9; *63:* 158, 159, 160, 161,163, 164, 165, 166, 167; *96:* 4; *105:* 87
Stern, Simon *15:* 249, 250; *17:* 58; *34:* 192, 193
Sterret, Jane *53:* 27
Stetsios, Debbie *165:* 108, 109
Steven, Kat *158:* 237
Stevens, David *62:* 44
Stevens, Helen *189:* 31; *207:* 83
Stevens, Janet *40:* 126; *57:* 10, 11; *80:* 112; *90:* 221, 222; *109:* 156; *130:* 34; *166:* 202; *176:* 53, 116; *193:* 199, 200, 202; *208:* 127; *212:* 182
Stevens, Mary *11:* 193; *13:* 129; *43:* 95
Stevenson, Harvey *66:* 143; *80:* 201, 221; *153:* 60; *191:* 166; *233:* 154
Stevenson, James *42:* 182, 183; *51:* 163; *66:* 184; *71:* 185, 187, 188; *78:* 262; *87:* 97; *113:* 182, 183,184, 185; *161:* 182, 183
Stevenson, Sucie *92:* 27; *104:* 194, 195; *112:* 168; *160:* 202; *194:* 172, 173; *195:* 166
Stewart, April Blair *75:* 210
Stewart, Arvis *33:* 98; *36:* 69; *60:* 118; *75:* 91; *127:* 4
Stewart, Charles *2:* 205
Stewart, Joel *151:* 205; *211:* 170, 171; *229:* 168
Stieg, William *172:* 58
Stiles, Fran *26:* 85; *78:* 56; *82:* 150
Stillman, Susan *44:* 130; *76:* 83
Stimpson, Tom *49:* 171
Stimson, James *208:* 46
Stinemetz, Morgan *40:* 151
Stinson, Paul *110:* 86
Stirnweis, Shannon *10:* 164
Stites, Joe *86:* 96
Stobbs, William *1:* 48, 49; *3:* 68; *6:* 20; *17:* 117, 217; *24:* 150; *29:* 250; *60:* 179; *87:* 204, 205,206
Stock, Catherine *37:* 55; *65:* 198; *72:* 7; *99:* 225; *114:* 197, 198, 199; *126:* 3; *145:* 161; *161:* 82; *173:* 149; *208:* 210; *214:* 192, 194; *224:* 196, 197
Stockman, Jack *113:* 24
Stoeke, Janet Morgan *90:* 225; *136:* 196; *202:* 182, 183
Stoerrle, Tom *55:* 147
Stolp, Jaap *49:* 98
Stolp, Todd *89:* 195
Stone, David L. *87:* 154
Stone, David *9:* 173
Stone, David K. *4:* 38; *6:* 124; *9:* 180; *43:* 182; *60:* 70
Stone, Helen V. *6:* 209
Stone, Helen *44:* 121, 122, 126
Stone, Kazuko G. *134:* 43
Stone, Kyle M. *202:* 185
Stone, Phoebe *86:* 212; *134:* 213; *162:* 188; *205:* 145
Stone, Steve *166:* 213; *208:* 185; *220:* 57,58; *224:* 124
Stone, Tony *150:* 34, 35
Storms, Patricia *217:* 163
Storrings, Michael *191:* 108; *216:* 217
Stoud, Virginia A. *89:* 31
Stover, Jill *82:* 234
Stower, Adam *217:* 89; *227:* 53
Strachan, Bruce *205:* 146
Stratton, Helen *33:* 151
Stratton-Porter, Gene *15:* 254, 259, 263, 264, 268, 269
Straub, Matt *192:* 176; *229:* 176
Straub, Phillip *197:* 22; *233:* 36
Streano, Vince *20:* 173
Street, Janet Travell *84:* 235
Streeter, Clive *121:* 2
Strickland, Shadra *209:* 179; *233:* 177
Stringer, Lauren *129:* 187; *154:* 172, 173; *161:* 127; *183:* 187, 188; *232:* 153

Strodl, Daniel *47:* 95
Strogart, Alexander *63:* 139
Stromoski, Rick *111:* 179; *124:* 161, 190
Strong, Joseph D., Jr. *YABC 2:* 330
Stroyer, Poul *13:* 221
Strugnell, Ann *27:* 38
Struzan, Drew *117:* 6
Stubbs, William *73:* 196
Stubis, Talivaldis *5:* 182, 183; *10:* 45; *11:* 9; *18:* 304; *20:* 127
Stubley, Trevor *14:* 43; *22:* 219; *23:* 37; *28:* 61; *87:* 26
Stuck, Marion *104:* 44
Stuecklen, Karl W. *8:* 34, 65; *23:* 103
Stull, Betty *11:* 46
Stutzman, Mark *119:* 99
Stutzmann, Laura *73:* 185
Suarez, Maribel *162:* 208; *200:* 202; *237:* 170
Suave, Gordon *209:* 66
Suba, Susanne *4:* 202, 203; *14:* 261; *23:* 134; *29:* 222; *32:* 30
Sue, Majella Lue *209:* 182; *212:* 146
Sueling, Barbara *98:* 185
Sueling, Gwenn *98:* 186
Sugarman, Tracy *3:* 76; *8:* 199; *37:* 181, 182
Sugimoto, Yugo *170:* 144; *223:* 137
Sugita, Yutaka *36:* 180, 181
Suh, John *80:* 157
Sullivan, Dorothy *89:* 113
Sullivan, Edmund J. *31:* 86
Sullivan, James F. *19:* 280; *20:* 192
Sully, Tom *104:* 199, 200; *182:* 77
Sumichrast, Jozef *14:* 253; *29:* 168, 213
Sumiko *46:* 57
Summers, Leo *1:* 177; *2:* 273; *13:* 22
Summers, Mark *118:* 144
Summers, Mike *190:* 176
Sutton, Judith *94:* 164
Svarez, Juan *56:* 113
Svendsen, Mark *181:* 176
Svolinsky, Karel *17:* 104
Swain, Carol *172:* 182
Swain, Su Zan Noguchi *21:* 170
Swan, Susan *22:* 220, 221; *37:* 66; *60:* 146; *145:* 205; *181:* 168; *236:* 172
Swann, Susan *86:* 55
Swanson, Karl *79:* 65; *89:* 186
Swarner, Kristina *203:* 62; *215:* 184
Swayne, Sam *53:* 143, 145
Swayne, Zoa *53:* 143, 145
Swearingen, Greg *152:* 56; *165:* 135; *173:* 2; *224:* 32; *225:* 188
Sweat, Lynn *25:* 206; *57:* 176; *73:* 184; *168:* 178
Sweet, Darrell K. *60:* 9; *69:* 86; *74:* 15; *75:* 215; *76:* 130, 131; *81:* 96, 122; *82:* 253; *83:* 11; *84:* 14; *85:* 37; *89:* 140; *90:* 6; *91:* 137,139; *95:* 160, 161; *126:* 25; *185:* 175; *195:* 132
Sweet, Darrell K. *1:* 163; *4:* 136; *164:* 175
Sweet, Melissa *71:* 94; *72:* 172; *111:* 82; *139:* 53, 58; *141:* 88; *142:* 231; *155:* 121; *159:* 121, 122; *172:* 185; *188:* 127; *209:* 81; *211:* 174, 175; *218:* 21; *235:* 54
Sweet, Ozzie *31:* 149, 151, 152
Sweetland, Robert *12:* 194
Swiatkowska, Gabi *132:* 43; *175:* 139; *180:* 218; *183:* 176
Swope, Martha *43:* 160; *56:* 86, 87, 89
Sylvada, Peter *154:* 174
Sylvester, Natalie G. *22:* 222
Syme, Hugh *232:* 8
Szafran, Gene *24:* 144
Szasz, Susanne *13:* 55, 226; *14:* 48
Szekeres, Cyndy *2:* 218; *5:* 185; *8:* 85; *11:* 166; *14:* 19; *16:* 57, 159; *26:* 49, 214; *34:* 205; *60:* 150, 151, 152, 153, 154; *73:* 224; *74:* 218; *131:* 213, 215
Szpura, Beata *81:* 68; *119:* 65; *168:* 201
Szuc, Jeff *220:* 188

T

Taback, Simms *40:* 207; *52:* 120; *57:* 34; *80:* 241; *104:* 202, 203; *170:* 176, 177; *205:* 183
Taber, Patricia *75:* 124
Tabor, Nancy Maria Grande *89:* 210; *161:* 188
Taddei, Richard *112:* 13, 14
Tadgell, Nicole *150:* 77; *161:* 20; *177:* 186; *209:* 16; *220:* 190, 191; *235:* 90
Tadiello, Ed *133:* 200
Tafuri, Nancy *39:* 210; *75:* 199, 200; *92:* 75; *130:* 215, 216, 217
Tailfeathers, Gerald *86:* 85
Tait, Douglas *12:* 220; *74:* 105, 106
Takabayashi, Mari *113:* 112; *130:* 22; *156:* 169
Takahashi, Hideko *136:* 160; *187:* 6; *209:* 152, 187
Takakjian, Portia *15:* 274
Takashima, Shizuye *13:* 228
Talarczyk, June *4:* 173
Talbott, Hudson *84:* 240; *163:* 100; *212:* 191, 192, 193
Tallarico, Tony *116:* 197
Tallec, Olivier *218:* 4
Tallon, Robert *2:* 228; *43:* 200, 201, 202, 203, 204, 205,206, 207, 209
Tamaki, Jillian *201:* 188
Tamas, Szecsko *29:* 135
Tamburine, Jean *12:* 222
Tanaka, Yoko *215:* 187; *234:* 106
Tancredi, Sharon *215:* 127
Tandy, H.R. *13:* 69
Tandy, Russell H. *65:* 9; *100:* 30, 131
Tang, Charles *81:* 202; *90:* 192
Tang, Susan *80:* 174; *108:* 158
Tang, You-shan *63:* 100
Tankersley, Paul *69:* 206; *133:* 219
Tannenbaum, Robert *48:* 181
Tanner, Jane *87:* 13; *97:* 37
Tanner, Tim *72:* 192; *84:* 35
Tanobe, Miyuki *23:* 221
Tarabay, Sharif *110:* 149; *113:* 123; *169:* 83
Tarkington, Booth *17:* 224, 225
Tarlow, Phyllis *61:* 198
Tate, Don *159:* 141, 191; *183:* 69; *186:* 120
Tauss, Herbert *95:* 179
Tauss, Marc *117:* 160; *126:* 155; *178:* 221; *197:* 7; *223:* 168
Tavares, Matt *159:* 192, 193; *198:* 188, 189, 190; *199:* 86
Taxali, Gary *234:* 199
Taylor, Ann *41:* 226
Taylor, Dahl *129:* 157
Taylor, Geoff *93:* 156; *197:* 173, 175; *204:* 151, 152
Taylor, Isaac *41:* 228
Taylor, Jennifer *226:* 128; *232:* 154
Taylor, Mike *143:* 99, 100
Teague, Mark *83:* 6; *139:* 241; *170:* 180, 181; *205:* 150, 151
Teale, Edwin Way *7:* 196
Teason, James *1:* 14
Teckentrup, Britta *200:* 191, 192
Teeple, Lyn *33:* 147
Tee-Van, Helen Damrosch *10:* 176; *11:* 182
Teevee, Ningeokuluk *223:* 173
Teicher, Dick *50:* 211
Teichman, Mary *77:* 220; *124:* 208; *127:* 22; *197:* 33
Telgemeier, Raina *228:* 180, 181, 182
Temertey, Ludmilla *96:* 232; *104:* 43, 45; *109:* 244
Tempest, Margaret *3:* 237, 238; *88:* 200
Temple, Frances *85:* 185, 186, 187
Temple, Herbert *45:* 201
Templeton, Owen *11:* 77
ten Cate, Marijke *183:* 193
Tenggren, Gustaf *18:* 277, 278, 279; *19:* 15; *28:* 86; *YABC2:* 145
TenNapel, Doug *234:* 200

Tennent, Julie *81:* 105
Tenneson, Joyce *153:* 166
Tenney, Gordon *24:* 204
Tenniel, John *74:* 234, 235; *100:* 89; *YABC 2:* 99; *153:* 63
Teplin, Scott *231:* 180
Tepper, Matt *116:* 80
Terkel, Ari *103:* 162
Terry, Michael *180:* 209; *233:* 166
Terry, Will *131:* 73; *205:* 155; *223:* 105
Teskey, Donald *71:* 51
Tessler, Manya *200:* 193
Thacher, Mary M. *30:* 72
Thackeray, William Makepeace *23:* 224, 228
Thamer, Katie *42:* 187
Tharlet, Eve *146:* 149
Thelwell, Norman *14:* 201
Theobalds, Prue *40:* 23
Theurer, Marilyn Churchill *39:* 195
Thiesing, Lisa *89:* 134; *95:* 202; *156:* 190; *159:* 195
Thiewes, Sam *133:* 114
Thisdale, François *223:* 55
Thistlethwaite, Miles *12:* 224
Thollander, Earl *11:* 47; *18:* 112; *22:* 224
Thomas, Allan *22:* 13
Thomas, Art *48:* 217
Thomas, Eric *28:* 49
Thomas, Harold *20:* 98
Thomas, Jacqui *125:* 95
Thomas, Jan *197:* 180; *226:* 198
Thomas, Mark *42:* 136
Thomas, Martin *14:* 255
Thomas, Middy *177:* 114; *230:* 63
Thompson, Arthur *34:* 107
Thompson, Carol *85:* 189; *95:* 75; *102:* 86; *147:* 166; *189:* 179, 180, 181; *190:* 84; *207:* 18
Thompson, Colin *95:* 204
Thompson, Ellen *51:* 88, 151; *60:* 33; *67:* 42; *77:* 148; *78:* 75, 219; *79:* 122, 170; *84:* 219; *85:* 97; *87:* 37; *88:* 192, 194; *89:* 80; *93:* 37; *98:* 59; *132:* 14; *236:* 72, 73
Thompson, George W. *22:* 18; *28:* 150; *33:* 135
Thompson, John *58:* 201; *102:* 226; *124:* 154; *128:* 228; *129:* 157; *150:* 49; *185:* 160; *191:* 192; *224:* 110; *236:* 101
Thompson, Julie *44:* 158
Thompson, Katherine *132:* 146
Thompson, K. Dyble *84:* 6
Thompson, Miles *152:* 77
Thompson, Sharon *74:* 113; *158:* 60; *165:* 87
Thomson, Arline K. *3:* 264
Thomson, Bill *186:* 160
Thomson, Hugh *26:* 88
Thomson, Ross *36:* 179
Thorkelson, Gregg *95:* 183, 184; *98:* 58; *165:* 30, 31; *225:* 31, 32
Thorn, Lori *189:* 119
Thornberg, Dan *104:* 125
Thornburgh, Rebecca McKillip *143:* 37
Thorne, Diana *25:* 212
Thornhill, Jan *77:* 213
Thorpe, Peter *58:* 109
Thorvall, Kerstin *13:* 235
Threadgall, Colin *77:* 215
Thurber, James *13:* 239, 242, 243, 245, 248, 249
Thurman, Mark *63:* 173; *168:* 116
Tibbles, Jean-Paul *115:* 200
Tibbles, Paul *45:* 23
Tibo, Gilles *67:* 207; *107:* 199, 201
Tichenor, Tom *14:* 207
Tichnor, Richard *90:* 218
Tiegreen, Alan *36:* 143; *43:* 55, 56, 58; *77:* 200; *94:* 216, 217; *121:* 54, 59
Tierney, Tom *113:* 198, 200, 201
Tildes, Phyllis Limbacher *210:* 240
Tilley, Debbie *102:* 134; *133:* 226; *137:* 101; *159:* 96; *190:* 211, 212; *213:* 51

Tillman, Nancy *211:* 129, 178
Tillotson, Katherine *224:* 175
Tilney, F.C. *22:* 231
Timbs, Gloria *36:* 90
Timmins, Harry *2:* 171
Timmons, Bonnie *194:* 189
Tinkelman, Murray *12:* 225; *35:* 44
Titherington, Jeanne *39:* 90; *58:* 138; *75:* 79; *135:* 161
Tjader, Ella *209:* 14
Tobin, Nancy *145:* 197
Toddy, Irving *172:* 144
Tokunbo, Dimitrea *181:* 183; *187:* 182, 183; *226:* 209
Tolbert, Jeff *128:* 69
Toledo, Francisco *197:* 182; *198:* 199
Toledo, Natalia *197:* 182
Tolford, Joshua *1:* 221
Tolkien, J.R.R. *2:* 243; *32:* 215
Tolman, Marije *195:* 43
Tolmie, Ken *15:* 292
Tomei, Lorna *47:* 168, 171
Tomes, Jacqueline *2:* 117; *12:* 139
Tomes, Margot *1:* 224; *2:* 120, 121; *16:* 207; *18:* 250; *20:* 7; *25:* 62; *27:* 78, 79; *29:* 81, 199; *33:* 82; *36:* 186, 187, 188, 189, 190; *46:* 129; *56:* 71; *58:* 183; *70:* 228; *75:* 73, 75; *80:* 80; *83:* 97; *90:* 205
Tommaso, Rich *200:* 198
Tommorow, Tom *223:* 176
Toner, Raymond John *10:* 179
Tong, Gary *66:* 215
Tongier, Stephen *82:* 32
Tooke, Susan *173:* 162
Toothill, Harry *6:* 54; *7:* 49; *25:* 219; *42:* 192
Toothill, Ilse *6:* 54
Topaz, Ksenia *224:* 94
Topolski, Feliks *44:* 48
Torbert, Floyd James *22:* 226
Torgersen, Don *55:* 157
Torline, Kevin *169:* 171
Tormey, Bertram M. *75:* 3, 4
Torrecilla, Pablo *176:* 207
Torres, Leyla *156:* 199, 201
Torrey, Helen *87:* 41
Torrey, Marjorie *34:* 105
Torrey, Richard *189:* 182; *205:* 24
Toschik, Larry *6:* 102
Totten, Bob *13:* 93
Townsend, Michael *231:* 183
Toy, Julie *128:* 112
Trachok, Cathy *131:* 16; *228:* 10
Tracy, Libba *82:* 24
Trago, Keith *158:* 253
Trail, Lee *55:* 157
Trang, To Ngoc *167:* 180
Trang, Winson *89:* 151
Trapani, Iza *116:* 202; *214:* 203
Travers, Bob *49:* 100; *63:* 145
Treatner, Meryl *95:* 180
Tremain, Ruthven *17:* 238
Tresilian, Stuart *25:* 53; *40:* 212
Trez, Alain *17:* 236
Trezzo, Loretta *86:* 45
Trier, Walter *14:* 96
Trimby, Elisa *47:* 199
Trinkle, Sally *53:* 27
Triplett, Gina *182:* 193; *188:* 100; *198:* 38
Tripp, F.J. *24:* 167
Tripp, Wallace *2:* 48; *7:* 28; *8:* 94; *10:* 54,76; *11:* 92; *31:* 170, 171; *34:* 203; *42:* 57; *60:* 157; *73:* 182
Trivas, Irene *53:* 4; *54:* 168; *82:* 46, 101
Trnka, Jiri *22:* 151; *43:* 212, 213, 214, 215; *YABC 1:* 30, 31
Trondheim, Lewis *182:* 183
Troughton, Joanna *37:* 186; *48:* 72
Troyer, Johannes *3:* 16; *7:* 18
Trudeau, G.B. *35:* 220, 221, 222; *48:* 119, 123, 126, 127,128, 129, 133; *168:* 189

Trueman, Matthew *165:* 208; *183:* 191; *220:* 61; *222:* 174
Truesdell, Sue *55:* 142; *108:* 219, 220; *212:* 202; *220:* 78
Tryon, Leslie *84:* 7; *139:* 214; *143:* 10; *181:* 10
Tseng, Jean *72:* 195; *94:* 102; *119:* 126; *151:* 106; *173:* 138, 139; *200:* 158
Tseng, Mou-sien *72:* 195; *94:* 102; *119:* 126; *151:* 106; *173:* 138, 139; *200:* 158
Tsinajinie, Andy *2:* 62
Tsinganos, Jim *180:* 142
Tsugami, Kyuzo *18:* 198, 199
Tucker, Ezra *156:* 31
Tuckwell, Jennifer *17:* 205
Tudor, Bethany *7:* 103
Tudor, Tasha *18:* 227; *20:* 185, 186, 187; *36:* 111; *69:* 196, 198; *100:* 44; *YABC 2:* 46, 314; *160:* 234
Tuerk, Hanne *71:* 201
Tugeau, Jeremy *199:* 170; *203:* 96
Tulloch, Maurice *24:* 79
Tunis, Edwin *1:* 218, 219; *28:* 209, 210, 211, 212
Tunnicliffe, C.F. *62:* 176; *177:* 178, 179; 181
Turkle, Brinton *1:* 211, 213; *2:* 249; *3:* 226; *11:* 3; *16:* 209; *20:* 22; *50:* 23; *67:* 50; *68:* 65; *79:* 205, 206, 207; *128:* 47; *YABC 1:* 79
Turnbull, Christopher J. *143:* 99, 100
Turner, Gwenda *59:* 195
Turner, Helen *203:* 154
Turska, Krystyna *12:* 103; *31:* 173, 174, 175; *56:* 32,34; *100:* 66
Tusa, Tricia *72:* 242; *111:* 180, 181; *157:* 165; *164:* 186; *189:* 40; *201:* 9; *207:* 163, 164; *233:* 132; *237:* 103
Tusan, Stan *6:* 58; *22:* 236, 237
Tuschman, Richard *219:* 100; *224:* 188; *225:* 175; *231:* 149
Tworkov, Jack *47:* 207
Tyers, Jenny *89:* 220
Tylden-Wright, Jenny *114:* 119
Tyrol, Adelaide Murphy *103:* 27
Tyrrell, Frances *107:* 204
Tzimoulis, Paul *12:* 104

U

Uchida, Yoshiko *1:* 220
Uderzo *47:* 88
Udovic, David *189:* 185; *195:* 201
Ueno, Noriko *59:* 155
Ugliano, Natascia *196:* 186
Ulm, Robert *17:* 238
Ulrich, George *73:* 15; *75:* 136, 139; *99:* 150
Ulriksen, Mark *101:* 58; *182:* 43; *210:* 243
Unada *84:* 67; *227:* 80
    See Gliewe, Unada
Underhill, Liz *53:* 159
Underwood, Beck *192:* 36
Underwood, Clarence *40:* 166
Unger, Jim *67:* 208
Ungerer, Tomi *5:* 188; *9:* 40; *18:* 188; *29:* 175; *33:* 221, 222, 223, 225; *71:* 48; *106:* 209, 210, 211, 212
Unwin, Nora S. *3:* 65, 234, 235; *4:* 237; *44:* 173, 174; *YABC 1:* 59; *2:* 301
Unzner, Christa *230:* 186
Upitis, Alvis *145:* 179
Urban, Helle *149:* 243
Urbanovic, Jackie *86:* 86; *189:* 186, 187
Urberuaga, Emilio *219:* 110, 175
U'ren, Andrea *213:* 177; *232:* 175
Uris, Jill *49:* 188, 197
Ursell, Martin *50:* 51
Utpatel, Frank *18:* 114
Utz, Lois *5:* 190

V

Vagin, Vladimir *66:* 10; *142:* 215
Vaillancourt, Francois *107:* 199
Vainio, Pirkko *123:* 157, 158
Valério, Geraldo *180:* 225; *194:* 116
Vallejo, Boris *62:* 130; *72:* 212; *91:* 38; *93:* 61
Van Abbe, S. *16:* 142; *18:* 282; *31:* 90; *YABC 2:* 157, 161
Van Allsburg, Chris *37:* 205, 206; *53:* 161, 162, 163, 165,166, 167, 168, 169, 170, 171; *105:* 215, 216, 217, 218; *156:* 176, 177, 178
Vance, James *65:* 28
Van Der Linde, Henry *99:* 17
van der Meer, Ron *98:* 204, 205
van der Meer, Atie *98:* 204, 205
Vandivert, William *21:* 175
Van Dongen, H.R. *81:* 97
Van Dusen, Chris W. *173:* 169; *228:* 192
Vane, Mitch *210:* 160; *218:* 152
Van Everen, Jay *13:* 160; *YABC 1:* 121
Van Fleet, John *165:* 12, 13
Van Frankenhuyzen, Gijsbert *145:* 230; *149:* 164; *184:* 151; *210:* 248
van Genechten, Guido *165:* 226
van Haeringen, Annemarie *193:* 206
Van Horn, William *43:* 218
van Hout, Mies *195:* 191; *207:* 58
van Kampen, Vlasta *194:* 217
van Lawick, Hugo *62:* 76, 79
Van Lieshout, Maria *201:* 196; *223:* 119
Van Loon, Hendrik Willem *18:* 285, 289, 291
Van Munching, Paul *83:* 85
van Ommen, Sylvia *186:* 192
Van Patter, Bruce *183:* 195
Van Rynbach, Iris *102:* 192
Van Sciver, Ruth *37:* 162
VanSeveren, Joe *63:* 182
Van Stockum, Hilda *5:* 193
Van Vleet, John *213:* 180
Van Wassenhove, Sue *202:* 193
Van Wely, Babs *16:* 50; *79:* 16
Van Wright, Cornelius *72:* 18; *102:* 208; *116:* 107; *152:* 236; *173:* 170, 171; *199:* 185
Van Zyle, Jon *103:* 125; *160:* 181, 182; *176:* 199, 200; *221:* 128; *232:* 125
Vardzigulyants, Ruben *90:* 54
Varga, Judy *29:* 196
Vargo, Kurt *79:* 224
Varley, Susan *61:* 199; *63:* 176, 177; *101:* 148; *134:* 220
Varon, Sara *195:* 208
Vasconcellos, Daniel *80:* 42
Vasiliu, Mircea *2:* 166, 253; *9:* 166; *13:* 58; *68:* 42
Vaughn, Frank *34:* 157
Vavra, Robert *8:* 206
Vawter, Will *17:* 163
Vayas, Diana *71:* 61
Vazquez, Carlos *125:* 184
Veeder, Larry *18:* 4
Velasquez, Eric *45:* 217; *61:* 45; *63:* 110, 111; *88:* 162; *90:* 34, 144; *94:* 213; *107:* 147; *132:* 192; *138:* 213; *159:* 126; *181:* 184; *184:* 96; *191:* 16; *192:* 234; *208:* 37; *214:* 81; *226:* 201, 203, 212; *237:* 59
Velasquez, Jose A. *63:* 73
Velez, Walter *71:* 75; *91:* 154; *121:* 181; *168:* 49; *207:* 52
Velthuijs, Max *110:* 228, 229
Vendrell, Carme Sole *42:* 205
Venezia, Mike *54:* 17
Venti, Anthony Bacon *124:* 103; *126:* 26
Venturo, Piero *61:* 194, 195
Ver Beck, Frank *18:* 16, 17
Verkaaik, Ben *110:* 209
Verling, John *71:* 27
Verney, John *14:* 225; *75:* 8
Vernon, Ursula *204:* 157
Verrier, Suzanne *5:* 20; *23:* 212

Verroken, Sarah *223:* 178
Versace, Marie *2:* 255
Verstraete, Randy *108:* 193
Vess, Charles *215:* 201; *233:* 182
Vestal, H.B. *9:* 134; *11:* 101; *27:* 25; *34:* 158
Vestergaard, Hope *190:* 203
Vicatan *59:* 146
Vickrey, Robert *45:* 59, 64
Victor, Joan Berg *30:* 193
Vieceli, Emma *210:* 245
Viereck, Ellen *3:* 242; *14:* 229
Vigna, Judith *15:* 293; *102:* 194, 195, 196, 197
Vila, Laura *207:* 172
Vilato, Gaspar E. *5:* 41
Villeneuve, Anne *230:* 189
Villiard, Paul *51:* 178
Vimnera, A. *23:* 154
Vincent, Eric *34:* 98
Vincent, Felix *41:* 237
Vincent, Gabrielle *121:* 175
Vip *45:* 164
Viskupic, Gary *83:* 48
Vitale, Stefano *109:* 71, 107; *114:* 219, 220; *123:* 106; *138:* 232; *180:* 228, 229; *212:* 38; *225:* 191, 192, 193
Vivas, Julie *51:* 67, 69; *96:* 225; *197:* 190; *199:* 71
Voake, Charlotte *114:* 221, 222; *180:* 232
Vo-Dinh, Mai *16:* 272; *60:* 191
Vogel, Ilse-Margret *14:* 230
Voigt, Erna *35:* 228
Vojnar, Kamil *95:* 31; *114:* 4; *115:* 62; *121:* 90; *124:* 72; *130:* 31; *141:* 81; *146:* 196; *150:* 123; *158:* 5, 6; *158:* 154; *171:* 119, 188; *179:* 15; *180:* 112; *203:* 74; *223:* 30; *229:* 43; *230:* 199; *231:* 53, 121, 122; *233:* 3, 4
Vojtech, Anna *42:* 190; *108:* 222, 223; *150:* 203; *174:* 173; *228:* 21; *234:* 181
von Buhler, Cynthia *149:* 237; *162:* 177; *177:* 205; *180:* 77; *185:* 214, 215, 216; *235:* 168; *237:* 144
von Roehl, Angela *126:* 191
von Schmidt, Eric *8:* 62; *50:* 209, 210
von Schmidt, Harold *30:* 80
Vosburgh, Leonard *1:* 161; *7:* 32; *15:* 295, 296; *23:* 110; *30:* 214; *43:* 181
Voss, Tom *127:* 104
Voter, Thomas W. *19:* 3, 9
Vroman, Tom *10:* 29
Vulliamy, Clara *72:* 65
Vyner, Tim *228:* 198

W

Waber, Bernard *47:* 209, 210, 211, 212, 213, 214; *95:* 215, 216, 217; *156:* 203, 205, 206, 207
Waber, Paulis *231:* 189
Wachenje, Benjamin *194:* 170
Wack, Jeff *95:* 140; *110:* 90
Wagner, John *8:* 200; *52:* 104
Wagner, Ken *2:* 59
Wagner, Michael *211:* 159
Wahman, Wendy *218:* 186
Waide, Jan *29:* 225; *36:* 139
Wainwright, Jerry *14:* 85
Waites, Joan *171:* 2; *226:* 184
Wakeen, Sandra *47:* 97
Wakiyama, Hanako *171:* 96; *192:* 236; *200:* 16
Waldherr, Kris *81:* 186
Waldman, Bruce *15:* 297; *43:* 178
Waldman, Neil *35:* 141; *50:* 163; *51:* 180; *54:* 78; *77:* 112; *79:* 162; *82:* 174; *84:* 5, 56, 106; *94:* 232, 233, 234; *96:* 41; *111:* 139; *113:* 9; *118:* 30; *142:* 220, 223; *203:* 173, 174
Waldrep, Richard *111:* 147; *198:* 202
Waldron, Kevin *230:* 191

Walker, Brian *144:* 128
Walker, Charles *1:* 46; *4:* 59; *5:* 177; *11:* 115; *19:* 45; *34:* 74; *62:* 168; *72:* 218
Walker, Dugald Stewart *15:* 47; *32:* 202; *33:* 112
Walker, Gil *8:* 49; *23:* 132; *34:* 42
Walker, Jeff *55:* 154; *123:* 116
Walker, Jim *10:* 94
Walker, Mort *8:* 213
Walker, Norman *41:* 37; *45:* 58
Walker, Stephen *12:* 229; *21:* 174
Walker, Steve *231:* 119
Wallace, Beverly Dobrin *19:* 259
Wallace, Chad *229:* 198
Wallace, Cly *87:* 93
Wallace, Ian *53:* 176, 177; *56:* 165, 166; *58:* 4; *98:* 4; *101:* 191; *112:* 124; *141:* 197, 198, 199, 200; *151:* 212; *219:* 180, 182
Wallace, John *105:* 228
Wallace, Nancy Elizabeth *141:* 204; *186:* 195, 197, 199; *222:* 191, 192, 193, 194
Wallenta, Adam *123:* 180
Waller, S.E. *24:* 36
Wallner, Alexandra *15:* 120; *156:* 183
Wallner, John C. *9:* 77; *10:* 188; *11:* 28; *14:* 209; *31:* 56, 118; *37:* 64; *51:* 186, 187, 188, 189, 190, 191,192, 193, 194, 195; *52:* 96; *53:* 23, 26; *71:* 99; *73:* 158; *89:* 215; *141:* 9
Wallner, John *162:* 17
Wallower, Lucille *11:* 226
Walotsky, Ron *93:* 87
Walsh, Ellen Stoll *99:* 209; *147:* 219; *194:* 194, 195, 196
Walsh, Rebecca *158:* 193; *217:* 169, 170
Walsh, Vivian *149:* 215; *158:* 227
Walters, Anita *205:* 163
Walters, Audrey *18:* 294
Walther, Tom *31:* 179
Walton, Garry *69:* 149
Walton, Tony *11:* 164; *24:* 209; *153:* 8; *177:* 73; *237:* 50, 52
Waltrip, Lela *9:* 195
Waltrip, Mildred *3:* 209; *37:* 211
Waltrip, Rufus *9:* 195
Wan *12:* 76
Wan, Shelly *212:* 131
Wang, Lin *221:* 179
Wang, Shaoli *216:* 220
Wang, Suling *191:* 183; *213:* 194
Warburton, Sarah *154:* 187
Wappers, G. *121:* 40
Ward, Chad Michael *217:* 121
Ward, Fred *52:* 19
Ward, Helen *72:* 244; *144:* 240, 242
Ward, John *42:* 191; *96:* 54; *97:* 110; *123:* 105; *124:* 71; *173:* 66; *221:* 55
Ward, Keith *2:* 107; *132:* 69
Ward, Leslie *34:* 126; *36:* 87
Ward, Lynd *1:* 99, 132, 133, 150; *2:* 108, 158, 196, 259; *18:* 86; *27:* 56; *29:* 79, 187, 253, 255; *36:* 199,200, 201, 202, 203, 204, 205, 206, 207, 209; *43:* 34; *56:* 28; *60:* 116; *100:* 65
Ward, Peter *37:* 116
Waring, Geoff *172:* 84
Warhola, James *92:* 5; *115:* 85, 87; *118:* 174, 175, 177; *176:* 84; *187:* 189, 190; *223:* 102
Warner, Bob *230:* 5
Warner, Ben *159:* 171
Warner, Peter *14:* 87
Warner, Sally *214:* 210
Warnes, Tim *175:* 159; *202:* 188; *216:* 224
Warnick, Elsa *113:* 223
Warren, Betsy *2:* 101
Warren, Jim *85:* 81
Warren, Marion Cray *14:* 215
Warshaw, Jerry *30:* 197, 198; *42:* 165
Wasden, Kevin *102:* 162
Washington, Nevin *20:* 123
Washington, Phyllis *20:* 123
Wasserman, Amy L. *92:* 110; *209:* 95

Waterman, Stan *11:* 76
Watkins-Pitchford, D.J. *6:* 215, 217
Watling, James *67:* 210; *78:* 112; *101:* 81; *117:* 189, 190; *127:* 119, 120
Watson, Aldren A. *2:* 267; *5:* 94; *13:* 71; *19:* 253; *32:* 220; *42:* 193, 194, 195, 196, 197, 198, 199, 200, 201; *YABC 2:* 202
Watson, G. *83:* 162
Watson, Gary *19:* 147; *36:* 68; *41:* 122; *47:* 139
Watson, J.D. *22:* 86
Watson, Jesse Joshua *197:* 124; *199:* 181; *202:* 136
Watson, Karen *11:* 26
Watson, Mary *117:* 193
Watson, Richard Jesse *62:* 188, 189; *211:* 201
Watson, Wendy *5:* 197; *13:* 101; *33:* 116; *46:* 163; *64:* 12; *74:* 242, 243; *91:* 21; *142:* 228; *215:* 79
Watt, Mélanie *136:* 206; *193:* 211
Wattenberg, Jane *174:* 200; *185:* 46; *187:* 108
Watterson, Bill *66:* 223, 225, 226
Watts, Bernadette *4:* 227; *103:* 182, 183; *230:* 193, 194, 195
Watts, James *59:* 197; *74:* 145; *86:* 124
Watts, John *37:* 149
Watts, Leslie Elizabeth *150:* 207; *165:* 106; *209:* 67
Watts, Sarah *234:* 115
Watts, Stan *116:* 205
Weatherby, Mark Alan *77:* 141
Web, Hannah *228:* 215
Webb, Jennifer *110:* 79
Webb, Lanny *142:* 175
Webb, Sophie *135:* 214
Webber, Helen *3:* 141
Webber, Irma E. *14:* 238
Weber, Erik *56:* 19, 20
Weber, Florence *40:* 153
Weber, Jill *127:* 227, 228; *189:* 163; *208:* 157; *209:* 190, 191; *216:* 46
Weber, Roland *61:* 204
Weber, Sam *190:* 227
Weber, William J. *14:* 239
Webster, Jean *17:* 241
Weeks, Sarah *162:* 39
Wegman, William *78:* 243
Wegner, Fritz *14:* 250; *20:* 189; *44:* 165; *86:* 62
Weidenear, Reynold H. *21:* 122
Weigel, Jeff *170:* 193
Weihs, Erika *4:* 21; *15:* 299; *72:* 201; *107:* 207, 208
Weil, Lisl *7:* 203; *10:* 58; *21:* 95; *22:* 188,217; *33:* 193
Weiman, Jon *50:* 162, 165; *52:* 103; *54:* 78, 79, 81; *78:* 80; *82:* 107; *93:* 82; *97:* 69; *105:* 179; *193:* 65
Weiner, Greg *215:* 21
Weiner, Sandra *14:* 240
Weiner, Scott *55:* 27
Weinhaus, Karen Ann *53:* 90; *71:* 50; *86:* 124
Weinman, Brad *197:* 20; *233:* 35
Weinstock, Robert *204:* 165, 166
Weisgard, Leonard *1:* 65; *2:* 191, 197, 204, 264, 265; *5:* 108; *21:* 42; *30:* 200, 201, 203, 204; *41:* 47; *44:* 125; *53:* 25; *85:* 196, 198, 200, 201; *100:* 139,207; *YABC 2:* 13
Weisman, David *173:* 47
Weiss, Ellen *44:* 202
Weiss, Emil *1:* 168; *7:* 60
Weiss, Harvey *1:* 145, 223; *27:* 224, 227; *68:* 214; *76:* 245, 246, 247
Weiss, Nicki *33:* 229
Weissman, Bari *49:* 72; *90:* 125; *139:* 142
Weitzman, David L. *172:* 199
Welch, Sheila Kelly *130:* 221
Welkes, Allen *68:* 218
Wellington, Monica *99:* 223; *157:* 259, 260, 261; *222:* 197, 198, 199, 200
Welliver, Norma *76:* 94

Wellner, Fred *127:* 53
Wells, Frances *1:* 183
Wells, H.G. *20:* 194, 200
Wells, Haru *53:* 120, 121
Wells, Robert E. *184:* 208
Wells, Rosemary *6:* 49; *18:* 297; *60:* 32; *66:* 203; *69:* 215, 216; *114:* 227; *118:* 149, 150; *156:* 188, 189, 190, 191; *207:* 180, 181, 182, 183; *237:* 159, 161, 162
Wells, Rufus III *56:* 111, 113
Wells, Susan *22:* 43
Wendelin, Rudolph *23:* 234
Wengenroth, Stow *37:* 47
Weninger, Brigitte *189:* 192, 194
Werenskiold, Erik *15:* 6; *62:* 17
Werner, Honi *24:* 110; *33:* 41; *88:* 122
Werth, Kurt *7:* 122; *14:* 157; *20:* 214; *39:* 128
Wesson,
West, Harry A. *124:* 38; *227:* 16
Westcott, Nadine Bernard *68:* 46; *84:* 49; *86:* 133; *106:* 199; *111:* 78; *113:* 111; *130:* 224; *139:* 54; *158:* 256; *194:* 199
Westerberg, Christine *29:* 226
Westerduin, Anne *105:* 229
Westerman, Johanna *162:* 206
Weston, Martha *29:* 116; *30:* 213; *33:* 85, 100; *53:* 181, 182, 183, 184; *77:* 95; *80:* 152; *119:* 196,197, 198, 199; *127:* 189; *133:* 196; *209:* 199
Wetherbee, Margaret *5:* 3
Wexler, Jerome *49:* 73; *150:* 129
Whalley, Peter *50:* 49
Whamond, Dave *222:* 203
Whatley, Bruce *186:* 93, 95; *207:* 127; *213:* 183, 184
Wheatley, Arabelle *11:* 231; *16:* 276
Wheeler, Cindy *49:* 205
Wheeler, Dora *44:* 179
Wheelright, Rowland *15:* 81; *YABC 2:* 286
Whelan, Michael *56:* 108; *70:* 27, 29, 67, 68, 148; *74:* 18; *84:* 14; *91:* 195, 196; *95:* 147; *98:* 150, 151; *106:* 157; *113:* 218, 220; *116:* 99, 100
Whelan, Patrick *135:* 145
Whistler, Rex *16:* 75; *30:* 207, 208
White, Beth *216:* 139
White, Craig *110:* 130; *119:* 193; *130:* 33; *179:* 31
White, David Omar *5:* 56; *18:* 6
White, Joan *83:* 225
White, Lee *221:* 176; *223:* 188, 189, 190
White, Martin *51:* 197; *85:* 127
Whitear *32:* 26
Whitehead, Beck *86:* 171
Whitehead, Jenny *221:* 16
Whitehead, S.B. *154:* 132
Whithorne, H.S. *7:* 49
Whitman, Candace *208:* 208
Whitney, George Gillett *3:* 24
Whitney, Jean *99:* 53
Whitson, Paul *102:* 161
Whittam, Geoffrey *30:* 191
Whyte, Mary *96:* 127; *232:* 39
Wiberg, Harald *38:* 127; *93:* 215
Wick, Walter *77:* 128
Wickstrom, Sylvie *106:* 87; *169:* 180; *214:* 110
Wickstrom, Thor *200:* 205
Widener, Terry *105:* 230; *106:* 7; *163:* 23; *200:* 17; *209:* 195; *231:* 12
Wiese, Kurt *3:* 255; *4:* 206; *14:* 17; *17:* 18, 19; *19:* 47; *24:* 152; *25:* 212; *32:* 184; *36:* 211,213, 214, 215, 216, 217, 218; *45:* 161; *100:* 92
Wiesner, David *33:* 47; *51:* 106; *57:* 67; *58:* 55; *64:* 78, 79, 81; *69:* 233; *72:* 247, 248, 249, 251,252, 253, 254; *83:* 134; *104:* 31; *117:* 197, 199, 200, 202; *139:* 223, 224; *151:* 51; *181:* 189, 190
Wiesner, William *4:* 100; *5:* 200, 201; *14:* 262
Wight, Eric *218:* 190; *232:* 195

Wiggins, George *6:* 133
Wijngaard, Juan *111:* 36; *114:* 124; *227:* 136; *230:* 202
Wikkelsoe, Otto *45:* 25, 26
Wikland, Ilon *5:* 113; *8:* 150; *38:* 124, 125, 130; *127:* 162
Wikler, Madeline *114:* 233
Wilbur, C. Keith, M.D. *27:* 228
Wilburn, Kathy *53:* 102; *68:* 234
Wilcox, Cathy *105:* 123
Wilcox, J.A.J. *34:* 122
Wilcox, Lydia *207:* 187
Wilcox, R. Turner *36:* 219
Wild, Jocelyn *46:* 220, 221, 222; *80:* 117
Wilde, George *7:* 139
Wildish, Lee *231:* 34, 193
Wildsmith, Brian *16:* 281, 282; *18:* 170, 171; *66:* 25; *69:* 224, 225, 227; *77:* 103; *83:* 218; *124:* 214,217, 219
Wildsmith, Mike *140:* 229
Wilhelm, Hans *58:* 189, 191; *73:* 157; *77:* 127; *135:* 229, 230, 233, 234; *196:* 209
Wilkin, Eloise *36:* 173; *49:* 208, 209, 210
Wilkinson, Barry *50:* 213
Wilkinson, Gerald *3:* 40
Wilkon, Jozef *31:* 183, 184; *71:* 206, 207, 209; *133:* 222
Wilks, Mike *34:* 24; *44:* 203; *224:* 193
Willems, Mo *154:* 245, 246, 247; *180:* 236, 237, 239; *228:* 204, 208
Willey, Bee *103:* 129; *139:* 159; *173:* 115
Willhoite, Michael A. *71:* 214
William, Maria *168:* 51
Williams, Berkeley, Jr. *64:* 75
Williams, Ferelith Eccles *22:* 238
Williams, Garth *1:* 197; *2:* 49, 270; *4:* 205; *15:* 198, 302, 304, 307; *16:* 34; *18:* 283, 298, 299, 300, 301; *29:* 177, 178, 179, 232, 233, 241, 242, 243, 244, 245, 248; *40:* 106; *66:* 229, 230, 231, 233, 234; *71:* 192; *73:* 218, 219, 220; *78:* 261; *100:* 251, 252, 255; *136:* 117; *YABC 2:* 15, 16, 19
Williams, J. Scott *48:* 28
Williams, Jennifer *102:* 201
Williams, Jenny *60:* 202; *81:* 21; *88:* 71
Williams, Kent *180:* 18
Williams, Kit *44:* 206, 207, 208, 209, 211, 212
Williams, Marcia *97:* 214; *159:* 208, 209
Williams, Maureen *12:* 238
Williams, Patrick *14:* 218
Williams, Richard *44:* 93; *72:* 229; *74:* 133; *78:* 155, 237; *91:* 178; *110:* 212; *136:* 201, 202, 203; *152:* 115
Williams, Sam *124:* 222; *153:* 11; *177:* 201, 202; *180:* 34; *212:* 49; *232:* 155
Williams, Sophy *135:* 236
Williams, Vera B. *53:* 186, 187, 188, 189; *102:* 201, 202, 203; *210:* 65
Williamson, Alex *177:* 180; *205:* 50
Williamson, Mel *60:* 9
Willingham, Fred *104:* 206; *154:* 157
Willis, Adam *181:* 75; *209:* 11
Willmore, J.T. *54:* 113, 114
Wilsdorf, Anne *180:* 122; *189:* 124; *191:* 195
Wilson, Anne *160:* 114; *224:* 199, 200
Wilson, Charles Banks *17:* 92; *43:* 73
Wilson, Connie *113:* 179
Wilson, Dagmar *10:* 47
Wilson, Dawn *67:* 161; *81:* 120; *113:* 158
Wilson, Edward A. *6:* 24; *16:* 149; *20:* 220, 221; *22:* 87; *26:* 67; *38:* 212, 214, 215, 216, 217
Wilson, Forrest *27:* 231
Wilson, Gahan *35:* 234; *41:* 136
Wilson, George *76:* 87
Wilson, Helen Miranda *140:* 61
Wilson, Jack *17:* 139
Wilson, Janet *77:* 154; *96:* 114; *99:* 219, 220; *153:* 64 *106:* 122; *130:* 210; *145:* 178; *173:* 64
Wilson, John *22:* 240

Wilson, Maurice *46:* 224
Wilson, Patten *35:* 61
Wilson, Peggy *15:* 4; *84:* 20
Wilson, Phil *181:* 29
Wilson, Rowland B. *30:* 170
Wilson, Sarah *50:* 215
Wilson, Tom *33:* 232
Wilson, W.N. *22:* 26
Wilson-Max, Ken *170:* 196; *180:* 181
Wilton, Nicholas *103:* 52; *183:* 111
Wilwerding, Walter J. *9:* 202
Wimmer, Mike *63:* 6; *70:* 121; *75:* 186; *76:* 21,22, 23; *91:* 114; *97:* 45, 68; *98:* 28; *107:* 130; *146:* 21; *149:* 47; *173:* 126; *193:* 21, 25; *194:* 204, 205
Winborn, Marsha *78:* 34; *99:* 70; *192:* 20
Winch, John *165:* 233
Winchester, Linda *13:* 231
Wind, Betty *28:* 158
Windham, Kathryn Tucker *14:* 260
Windham, Sophie *184:* 212
Winfield, Alison *115:* 78; *214:* 121
Winfield, Wayne *72:* 23
Wing, Gary *64:* 147
Wing, Ron *50:* 85
Wingerter, Linda S. *132:* 199; *174:* 181; *200:* 196
Winick, Judd *124:* 227, 228, 229
Winn-Lederer, Ilene *202:* 91
Winnick, Karen B. *211:* 207
Winslow, Will *21:* 124
Winstead, Rosie *180:* 243
Winsten, Melanie Willa *41:* 41
Winter, Jeanette *151:* 240, 241, 242; *184:* 215, 217, 218, 219
Winter, Milo *15:* 97; *19:* 221; *21:* 181, 203, 204, 205; *64:* 19; *YABC 2:* 144
Winter, Paula *48:* 227
Winter, Susan *163:* 177; *182:* 201; *226:* 173
Winters, Greg *70:* 117
Winters, Nina *62:* 194
Wise, Louis *13:* 68
Wiseman, Ann *31:* 187
Wiseman, B. *4:* 233
Wishnefsky, Phillip *3:* 14
Wiskur, Darrell *5:* 72; *10:* 50; *18:* 246
Wisnewski, Andrea *234:* 210
Wisniewski, David *95:* 220, 221
Wisniewski, Robert *95:* 10; *119:* 192
Withee, Maureen *225:* 42
Witschonke, Alan *153:* 149, 150
Witt, Dick *80:* 244
Wittmann, Patrick *162:* 204
Wittman, Sally *30:* 219
Wittner, Dale *99:* 43
Wittwer, Hala *158:* 267; *195:* 80
Woehr, Lois *12:* 5
Wohlberg, Meg *12:* 100; *14:* 197; *41:* 255
Wohnoutka, Mike *137:* 68; *190:* 199; *195:* 218; *205:* 132; *221:* 6; *230:* 206, 207
Wojtowycz, David *167:* 168
Woldin, Beth Weiner *34:* 211
Wolf, Elizabeth *133:* 151; *208:* 175
Wolf, J. *16:* 91
Wolf, Janet *78:* 254
Wolf, Linda *33:* 163
Wolfe, Corey *72:* 213
Wolfe, Frances *216:* 227
Wolfe, Gillian *199:* 193
Wolff, Ashley *50:* 217; *81:* 216; *156:* 216, 217; *170:* 57; *174:* 174; *184:* 72; *203:* 181, 182, 183, 184
Wolff, Glenn *178:* 230
Wolff, Jason *213:* 186
Wolfhard, Steve *235:* 199
Wolfsgruber, Linda *166:* 61
Wondriska, William *6:* 220
Wong, Janet S. *98:* 225; *152:* 43
Wong, Ken *224:* 23
Wong, Nicole *174:* 13; *214:* 216; *215:* 25
Wonsetler, John C. *5:* 168

Wood, Audrey *50:* 221, 222, 223; *81:* 219, 221; *198:* 206
Wood, Don *50:* 220, 225, 226, 228, 229; *81:* 218, 220; *139:* 239, 240
Wood, Grant *19:* 198
Wood, Heather *133:* 108
Wood, Ivor *58:* 17
Wood, Jakki *211:* 209
Wood, Muriel *36:* 119; *77:* 167; *171:* 55; *187:* 46; *235:* 49
Wood, Myron *6:* 220
Wood, Owen *18:* 187; *64:* 202, 204, 205, 206, 208, 210
Wood, Rob *193:* 48
Wood, Ruth *8:* 11
Woodbridge, Curtis *133:* 138; *204:* 113
Wooding, Sharon L. *66:* 237
Woodruff, Liza *132:* 239; *182:* 46, 204
Woodruff, Thomas *171:* 73
Woods, John, Jr. *109:* 142
Woods, Maria *227:* 69
Woodson, Jack *10:* 201
Woodson, Jacqueline *94:* 242
Woodward, Alice *26:* 89; *36:* 81
Wool, David *26:* 27
Wooley, Janet *112:* 75; *227:* 74
Woolman, Steven *106:* 47; *163:* 73
Wooten, Vernon *23:* 70; *51:* 170
Worboys, Evelyn *1:* 166, 167
Word, Reagan *103:* 204
Wormell, Christopher *154:* 251; *202:* 206
Worth, Jo *34:* 143
Worth, Wendy *4:* 133
Wosmek, Frances *29:* 251
Wrenn, Charles L. *38:* 96; *YABC 1:* 20, 21
Wright, Barbara Mullarney *98:* 161
Wright, Cliff *168:* 203
Wright, Dare *21:* 206
Wright-Frierson, Virginia *58:* 194; *110:* 246
Wright, George *YABC 1:* 268
Wright, Joseph *30:* 160
Wronker, Lili Cassel *3:* 247; *10:* 204; *21:* 10
Wu, Donald *200:* 18
Wummer, Amy *154:* 181; *168:* 150; *176:* 85; *201:* 202, 203; *218:* 154
Wyant, Alexander Helwig *110:* 19
Wyatt, David *97:* 9; *101:* 44; *114:* 194; *140:* 20; *167:* 13; *188:* 48; *227:* 60
Wyatt, Stanley *46:* 210
Wyeth, Andrew *13:* 40; *YABC 1:* 133, 134
Wyeth, Jamie *41:* 257
Wyeth, N.C. *13:* 41; *17:* 252, 253, 254, 255, 256, 257, 258, 259, 264, 265, 266, 267, 268; *18:* 181; *19:* 80, 191, 200; *21:* 57, 183; *22:* 91; *23:* 152; *24:* 28, 99; *35:* 61; *41:* 65; *100:* 206; *YABC1:* 133, 223; *2:* 53, 75, 171, 187, 317
Wyman, Cherie R. *91:* 42
Wynne, Patricia J. *210:* 260; *223:* 184

X

Xuan, YongSheng *119:* 202, 207, 208; *140:* 36; *187:* 21; *226:* 221, 227, 230, 232, 233

Y

Yaccarino, Dan *141:* 208, 209; *147:* 171; *192:* 244, 245; *207:* 168
Yakovetic, Joe *59:* 202; *75:* 85
Yalowitz, Paul *93:* 33; *211:* 92
Yamaguchi, Marianne *85:* 118
Yamasaki, James *167:* 93
Yang, Belle *170:* 198
Yang, Jay *1:* 8; *12:* 239
Yanok, Johnny *236:* 192
Yap, Weda *6:* 176
Yaroslava
    See Mills, Yaroslava Surmach
Yashima, Taro *14:* 84
Yates, John *74:* 249, 250
Yates, Kelly *208:* 214
Yayo *178:* 88; *226:* 235
Yeatts, Tabatha *215:* 210
Yee, Cora *166:* 233
Yee, Wong Herbert *115:* 216, 217; *172:* 204, 205; *194:* 59
Yelchin, Eugene *204:* 4; *232:* 198
Yeo, Brad *135:* 121; *192:* 106
Yerxa, Leo *181:* 195
Yezerski, Thomas F. *162:* 29
Ylla
    See Koffler, Camilla
Yohn, F.C. *23:* 128; *YABC 1:* 269
Yoo, Taeeun *191:* 198
Yorinks, Adrienne *144:* 248; *200:* 214
Yorke, David *80:* 178
Yoshida, Toshi *77:* 231
Yoshikawa, Sachiko *168:* 104; *177:* 28; *181:* 196, 197; *225:* 115
Youll, Paul *91:* 218
Youll, Stephen *92:* 227; *118:* 136, 137; *164:* 248; *202:* 92
Young, Amy L. *185:* 218; *190:* 46
Young, Cybéle *167:* 9
Young, Ed *7:* 205; *10:* 206; *40:* 124; *63:* 142; *74:* 250, 251, 252, 253; *75:* 227; *81:* 159; *83:* 98; *94:* 154; *115:* 160; *137:* 162; *YABC 2:* 242; *173:* 174, 175, 176; *205:* 29; *212:* 82; *221:* 72
Young, Karen Romano *237:* 184
Young, Mary O'Keefe *77:* 95; *80:* 247; *134:* 214; *140:* 213; *211:* 223, 225
Young, Ned *233:* 187
Young, Noela *8:* 221; *89:* 231; *97:* 195; *230:* 145, 146
Young, Paul *190:* 222; *225:* 38
Young, Selina *153:* 12; *201:* 204, 205
Yuen, Sammy, Jr. *223:* 46; *236:* 32
Yum, Hyewon *211:* 228
Yun, Cheng Mung *60:* 143
Yung, Jennifer *220:* 136

Z

Zacharow, Christopher *88:* 98
Zacks, Lewis *10:* 161
Zadig *50:* 58
Zaffo, George *42:* 208
Zagwyn, Deborah Turney *138:* 227
Zahares, Wade *193:* 219
Zaid, Barry *50:* 127; *51:* 201
Zaidenberg, Arthur *34:* 218, 219, 220
Zahedi, Morteza *232:* 2
Zalben, Jane Breskin *7:* 211; *79:* 230, 231, 233; *170:* 202
Zallinger, Jean *4:* 192; *8:* 8, 129; *14:* 273; *68:* 36; *80:* 254; *115:* 219, 220, 222
Zallinger, Rudolph F. *3:* 245
Zakanitch, Robert Rahway *231:* 195
Zakrajsek, Molly *177:* 146
Zappa, Ahmet *180:* 250
Zebot, George *83:* 214
Zecca, Katherine *207:* 195
Zeck, Gerry *40:* 232
Zeff, Joe *181:* 98; *221:* 101
Zeifert, Harriet *154:* 265, 267
Zeiring, Bob *42:* 130
Zeldich, Arieh *49:* 124; *62:* 120
Zeldis, Malcah *86:* 239; *94:* 198; *146:* 265, 266
Zelinsky, Paul O. *14:* 269; *43:* 56; *49:* 218-223; *53:* 111; *68:* 195; *102:* 219, 222, 221, 222; *154:* 255, 256, 257; *171:* 141; *185:* 96
Zelvin, Diana *72:* 190; *76:* 101; *93:* 207
Zemach, Kaethe *149:* 250
Zemach, Margot *3:* 270; *8:* 201; *21:* 210, 211; *27:* 204, 205, 210; *28:* 185; *49:* 22, 183, 224; *53:* 151; *56:* 146; *70:* 245, 246; *92:* 74
Zeman, Ludmila *153* 212
Zemsky, Jessica *10:* 62
Zepelinsky, Paul *35:* 93
Zerbetz, Evon *127:* 34; *158:* 109
Zezejl, Daniel *197:* 74
Zhang, Ange *101:* 190; *172:* 41
Zhang, Son Nang *163:* 113; *170:* 206
Ziegler, Jack *84:* 134
Zimdars, Berta *129:* 155
Zimet, Jay *147:* 94; *152:* 74; *196:* 75
Zimic, Tricia *72:* 95
Zimmer, Dirk *38:* 195; *49:* 71; *56:* 151; *65:* 214; *84:* 159; *89:* 26; *147:* 224
Zimmer, Tracie Vaughn *169:* 183
Zimmerman, Andrea *192:* 49, 50
Zimmermann, H. Werner *101:* 223; *112:* 197
Zimnik, Reiner *36:* 224
Zingone, Robin *180:* 134; *236:* 147, 148
Zinkeisen, Anna *13:* 106
Zinn, David *97:* 97
Zoellick, Scott *33:* 231
Zollars, Jaime *190:* 190
Zonia, Dhimitri *20:* 234, 235
Zorn, Peter A., Jr. *142:* 157
Zudeck, Darryl *58:* 129; *63:* 98; *80:* 52
Zug, Mark *88:* 131; *204:* 169
Zulewski, Tim *164:* 95; *232:* 59
Zuma *99:* 36
Zvorykin, Boris *61:* 155
Zweifel, Francis *14:* 274; *28:* 187
Zwerger, Lisbeth *54:* 176, 178; *66:* 246, 247, 248; *130:* 230, 231, 232, 233; *181:* 92; *194:* 224, 225, 226
Zwinger, Herman H. *46:* 227
Zwolak, Paul *67:* 69, 71, 73, 74

Author Index

The following index gives the number of the volume in which an author's biographical sketch, Autobiography Feature, Brief Entry, or Obituary appears.

This index includes references to all entries in the following series, which are also published by Gale.

YABC—*Yesterday's Authors of Books for Children: Facts and Pictures about Authors and Illustrators of Books for Young People from Early Times to 1960*
CLR—*Children's Literature Review: Excerpts from Reviews, Criticism, and Commentary on Books for Children*
SAAS—*Something about the Author Autobiography Series*

A

Aardema, Verna 1911-2000 107
  Obituary 119
  Earlier sketches in SATA 4, 68
  See also CLR 17
  See also SAAS 8
Aaron, Chester 1923- 216
  Autobiography Feature 216
  Earlier sketches in SATA 9, 74
  See also SAAS 12
Aaseng, Nate
  See Aaseng, Nathan
Aaseng, Nathan 1953- 236
  Autobiography Feature 236
  Brief entry 38
  Earlier sketches in SATA 51, 88, 172
  See also CLR 54
  See also SAAS 12
Abadzis, Nick 1965- 193
Abalos, Rafael 1956-
  See Abalos, Rafael
Abalos, Rafael 1956- 197
Abbas, Jailan 1952- 91
Abbey, Lynn
  See Abbey, Marilyn Lorraine
Abbey, Marilyn Lorraine 1948- 156
Abbott, Alice
  See Borland, Kathryn Kilby
  and Speicher, Helen Ross S(mith)
Abbott, Jacob 1803-1879 22
Abbott, Manager Henry
  See Stratemeyer, Edward L.
Abbott, R(obert) Tucker 1919-1995 61
  Obituary 87
Abbott, Sarah
  See Zolotow, Charlotte
Abbott, Tony 1952- 205
  Earlier sketch in SATA 159
Abdelsayed, Cindy 1962- 123
Abdul, Raoul 1929- 12
Abeele, Veronique van den 196
Abel, Raymond 1911- 12
Abell, Kathleen 1938- 9
Abelove, Joan 110
Abels, Harriette S(heffer) 1926- 50
Abercrombie, Barbara 1939- 182
  Earlier sketch in SATA 16

Abercrombie, Barbara Mattes
  See Abercrombie, Barbara
Abercrombie, Lynn
  See Sorrells, Walter
Abernethy, Robert G(ordon) 1927- 5
Abisch, Roslyn Kroop 1927- 9
Abisch, Roz
  See Abisch, Roslyn Kroop
Ablow, Gail 1962- 198
Abodaher, David J. (Naiph) 1919- 17
Abolafia, Yossi 1944-
  See Abulafia, Yossi
Abolivier, Aurelie 219
Abouzeid, Chris 175
Abrahall, Clare Hoskyns
  See Hoskyns-Abrahall, Clare (Constance Drury)
Abrahams, Hilary (Ruth) 1938- 29
Abrahams, Peter 1947- 194
Abrahams, Robert David 1905-1998 4
Abramovitz, Anita (Zeltner Brooks) 1914- 5
Abrams, Joy 1941- 16
Abrams, Lawrence F. 58
  Brief entry 47
Abramson, Andra Serlin 237
Abrashkin, Raymond 1911-1960 50
Abulafia, Yossi 1944- 177
  Brief entry 46
  Earlier sketch in SATA 60
Acampora, Paul 175
Accardo, Anthony 191
Acer, David 206
Achebe, Albert Chinualumogu
  See Achebe, Chinua
Achebe, Chinua 1930- 40
  Brief entry 38
  Earlier sketch in SATA 38
  See also CLR 156
Acheson, Alison 1964- 222
Ackerman, Diane 1948- 102
Ackerman, Eugene (Francis) 1888-1974 10
Ackerman, Karen 1951- 126
Ackerman, Peter 234
Ackerman, Susan Yoder 1945- 92
Ackison, Wendy Wassink 1956- 103
Ackley, Peggy Jo 1955- 58
Ackroyd, Peter 1949- 153
Acorn, John (Harrison) 1958- 79
Acredolo, Linda (Potter) 1947- 159

Acs, Laszlo (Bela) 1931- 42
  Brief entry 32
Acuff, Selma Boyd 1924- 45
Ada, Alma Flor 1938- 222
  Autobiography Feature 222
  Earlier sketches in SATA 43, 84, 143, 181
  See also CLR 62
Adair, Gilbert 1944- 98
Adair, Ian 1942- 53
Adair, Margaret Weeks (?)-1971 10
Adam, Cornel
  See Lengyel, Cornel Adam
Adam, Mark
  See Alexander, Marc
Adam, Paul 1958- 231
Adam, Robert 1948- 93
Adams, Adrienne 1906- 90
  Earlier sketch in SATA 8
  See also CLR 73
Adams, Andy 1859-1935
  See YABC 1
Adams, Barbara Johnston 1943- 60
Adams, Beth 236
Adams, Bruin
  See Ellis, Edward S.
Adams, Captain Bruin
  See Ellis, Edward S.
Adams, Captain J. F. C.
  See Ellis, Edward S.
Adams, Dale
  See Quinn, Elisabeth
Adams, Daniel
  See Nicole, Christopher
Adams, Debra
  See Speregen, Devra Newberger
Adams, Diane 1960- 217
Adams, Douglas 1952-2001 116
  Obituary 128
Adams, Douglas Noel
  See Adams, Douglas
Adams, Edith
  See Shine, Deborah
Adams, Florence 1932- 61
Adams, Georgie 1945- 216
Adams, Harriet S(tratemeyer) 1892(?)-1982 .. 1
  Obituary 29
Adams, Harrison
  See Rathborne, St. George (Henry)
  and Stratemeyer, Edward L.

Adams, Hazard 1926- 6
Adams, Hazard Simeon
 See Adams, Hazard
Adams, John Anthony 1944- 67
Adams, Kathryn 224
Adams, Laurie 1941- 33
Adams, Lowell
 See Joseph, James (Herz)
Adams, Nicholas
 See Pine, Nicholas
Adams, Nicholas
 See Smith, Sherwood
Adams, Nicholas
 See Doyle, Debra
 and Macdonald, James D.
Adams, Pam 1919- 112
Adams, Pamela
 See Adams, Pam
Adams, Richard 1920- 69
 Earlier sketch in SATA 7
 See also CLR 121
Adams, Richard George
 See Adams, Richard
Adams, Ruth Joyce 14
Adams, S.J.
 See Selzer, Adam
Adams, Tricia
 See Kite, Pat
Adams, William Taylor 1822-1897 28
Adam Smith, Janet (Buchanan) 1905-1999 .. 63
Adamson, Gareth 1925-1982(?) 46
 Obituary 30
Adamson, George 1906-1989
 Obituary 63
Adamson, George (Worsley) 1913-2005 30
Adamson, Graham
 See Groom, Arthur William
Adamson, Joy(-Friederike Victoria)
 1910-1980 11
 Obituary 22
Adamson, Wendy Writson 1942- 22
Addasi, Maha 1968- 205
Addison, Kenneth 1949(?)-2005 187
Addison, Kenneth L.
 See Addison, Kenneth
Addona, Angelo F. 1925- 14
Addy, Sean 1976- 222
Addy, Sharon Hart 1943- 192
 Earlier sketch in SATA 108
Addy, Ted
 See Winterbotham, R(ussell) R(obert)
Adelberg, Doris
 See Orgel, Doris
Adelson, Leone 1908- 11
Adinolfi, JoAnn 176
Adkins, Jan 1944- 210
 Autobiography Feature 210
 Earlier sketches in SATA 8, 69, 144
 See also CLR 77
 See also SAAS 19
Adl, Shirin 1975- 225
Adler, C. S. 1932- 126
 Earlier sketches in SATA 26, 63, 102
 See also CLR 78
 See also SAAS 15
Adler, Carole Schwerdtfeger
 See Adler, C. S.
Adler, David A. 1947- 231
 Earlier sketches in SATA 14, 70, 106, 151,
 178
 See also CLR 108
Adler, Emily 230
Adler, Irene
 See Penzler, Otto
 and Storr, Catherine (Cole)
Adler, Irving 1913- 29
 Autobiography Feature 164
 Earlier sketch in SATA 1
 See also CLR 27
 See also SAAS 15
Adler, Larry 1939- 36

Adler, Peggy 22
Adler, Ruth 1915-1968 1
Adlerman, Daniel (Ezra) 1963- 163
 Earlier sketch in SATA 96
Adlerman, Kim
 See Adlerman, Kimberly M(arie)
Adlerman, Kimberly M(arie) 1964- 163
 Earlier sketch in SATA 96
Adoff, Arnold 1935- 96
 Earlier sketches in SATA 5, 57
 See also CLR 7
 See also SAAS 15
Adoff, Jaime 163
Adoff, Jaime Levi
 See Adoff, Jaime
Adorjan, Carol (Madden) 1934- 71
 Earlier sketch in SATA 10
Adornetto, Alexandra 1992- 236
Adrian, Frances
 See Polland, Madeleine A(ngela Cahill)
Adrian, Mary
 See Jorgensen, Mary Venn
Adshead, Gladys L(ucy) 1896-1985 3
Aesop 620(?)B.C.-560(?)B.C. 64
 See also CLR 14
Aesop, Abraham
 See Newbery, John
Affabee, Eric
 See Stine, R.L.
Agapida, Fray Antonio
 See Irving, Washington
Agard, John 1949- 223
 Earlier sketch in SATA 138
Agard, Nadema 1948- 18
Agarwal, Deepa 1947- 141
Agee, Jon 1960- 196
 Earlier sketches in SATA 116, 157
Agell, Charlotte 1959- 214
 Earlier sketches in SATA 99, 150
Agent Orange
 See Moseley, James W(illett)
Aghill, Gordon
 See Garrett, Randall
 and Silverberg, Robert
Agle, Nan Hayden 1905- 3
 See also SAAS 10
Agnew, Edith J(osephine) 1897-1988 11
Agnew, Lincoln 222
Agonito, Joseph 177
Agonito, Rosemary 1937- 177
Aguilar, David 214
Aguilar, David A.
 See Aguilar, David
Ahearn, Janet Reed 236
Ahern, Margaret McCrohan 1921- 10
Ahl, Anna Maria 1926- 32
Ahlberg, Allan 1938- 214
 Brief entry 35
 Earlier sketches in SATA 68, 120, 165
 See also CLR 18
Ahlberg, Janet 1944-1994 120
 Brief entry 32
 Obituary 83
 Earlier sketch in SATA 68
 See also CLR 18
Ahlberg, Jessica 1980- 229
Aho, Julia Kay
 See Kay, Julia
Aichinger, Helga 1937- 4
Aiken, Clarissa (M.) Lorenz 1899-1992 12
 Obituary 109
Aiken, Conrad 1889-1973 30
 Earlier sketch in SATA 3
Aiken, Conrad Potter
 See Aiken, Conrad
Aiken, Joan (Delano) 1924-2004 73
 Autobiography Feature 109
 Obituary 152
 Earlier sketches in SATA 2, 30
 See also CLR 90
 See also SAAS 1

Aillaud, Cindy Lou 1955- 184
Ainsley, Alix
 See Steiner, Barbara A(nnette)
Ainsworth, Catherine Harris 1910- 56
Ainsworth, Norma 1911-1987 9
Ainsworth, Ruth (Gallard) 1908- 73
 Earlier sketch in SATA 7
Ainsworth, William Harrison 1805-1882 24
Aistrop, Jack 1916- 14
Aitken, Amy 1952- 54
 Brief entry 40
Aitken, Dorothy 1916- 10
Aitmatov, Chingiz 1928-2008 56
Aitmatov, Chingiz Torekulovich
 See Aitmatov, Chingiz
Ajhar, Brian 1957- 220
Akaba, Suekichi 1910- 46
Akbarpour, Ahmad 1970- 232
Akers, Floyd
 See Baum, L. Frank
Akib, Jamel 181
Akin, Sara Laux 236
Aks, Patricia 1926-1994 68
al Abdullah, Rania
 See Rania, Queen of Jordan
Alagoa, Ebiegberi Joe 1933- 108
Alain
 See Brustlein, Daniel
Alajalov, Constantin 1900-1987
 Obituary 53
Alalou, Ali 203
Alalou, Elizabeth 203
Alan, David
 See Horsfield, Alan
Alan, Robert
 See Silverstein, Robert Alan
Alarcon, Francisco X. 1954- 215
 Earlier sketch in SATA 104
Alarcon, Francisco Xavier
 See Alarcon, Francisco X.
Alarcon, Karen Beaumont
 See Beaumont, Karen
Albee, Sarah 1962- 231
Albert, Burton 1936- 22
Albert, Louise 1928- 157
Albert, Michael 1966- 202
Albert, Richard E. 1909-1999 82
Albert, Susan Wittig 1940- 107
Alberts, Frances Jacobs 1907-1989 14
Albertson, Susan
 See Wojciechowski, Susan
Albion, Lee Smith 29
Alborough, Jez 1959- 149
 Earlier sketch in SATA 86
Albrecht, Lillie (Vanderveer H.)
 1894-1985 12
Albyn, Carole Lisa 1955- 83
Alchemy, Jack
 See Gershator, David
Alcock, Gudrun 1908- 56
 Brief entry 33
Alcock, Vivien (Dolores) 1924-2003 76
 Brief entry 38
 Obituary 148
 Earlier sketch in SATA 45
 See also CLR 26
Alcorn, John 1935- 31
 Brief entry 30
Alcorn, Stephen 1958- 207
 Earlier sketch in SATA 110
Alcott, Louisa May 1832-1888 100
 See also YABC 1
 See also CLR 109
Alda, Arlene 1933- 205
 Brief entry 36
 Earlier sketches in SATA 44, 106, 158
 See also CLR 93
Alden, Isabella (Macdonald) 1841-1930 115
 See also YABC 2
Alden, Sue
 See Francis, Dorothy

Alderman, Clifford Lindsey 1902-1988 3
Alderson, Sue Ann 1940- 59
  Brief entry 48
Alding, Peter
  See Jeffries, Roderic
Aldis, Dorothy (Keeley) 1896-1966 2
Aldiss, Brian W. 1925- 34
Aldiss, Brian Wilson
  See Aldiss, Brian W.
Aldon, Adair
  See Meigs, Cornelia Lynde
Aldous, Allan (Charles) 1911- 27
Aldrich, Ann
  See Meaker, Marijane
Aldrich, Bess Streeter 1881-1954
  See CLR 70
Aldrich, Thomas (Bailey) 1836-1907 114
  Earlier sketch in SATA 17
Aldridge, (Harold Edward) James 1918- 87
Aldridge, Josephine Haskell 14
Aldridge, Sheila 1974- 192
Aleas, Richard
  See Ardai, Charles
Alegria, Malin 1974(?)- 190
Alegria, Ricardo E(nrique) 1921- 6
Aleksin, Anatolii Georgievich 1924- 36
Alenov, Lydia 1948- 61
Alex, Ben (a pseudonym) 1946- 45
Alex, Marlee (a pseudonym) 1948- 45
Alexander, Alma 1963- 217
Alexander, Anna B(arbara Cooke) 1913- 1
Alexander, Anne
  See Alexander, Anna B(arbara Cooke)
Alexander, Claire 228
Alexander, Ellen 1938- 91
Alexander, Frances (Laura) 1888-1979 4
Alexander, Heather 1967- 232
Alexander, Janet 1907-1994 97
  Earlier sketch in SATA 1
Alexander, Jill S. 1964- 223
Alexander, Jill Shurbet
  See Alexander, Jill S.
Alexander, Jocelyn Anne Arundel 1930- 22
Alexander, Linda 1935- 2
Alexander, Lloyd 1924-2007 135
  Obituary 182
  Earlier sketches in SATA 3, 49, 81, 129
  See also CLR 48
  See also SAAS 19
Alexander, Lloyd Chudley
  See Alexander, Lloyd
Alexander, Marc 1929- 117
Alexander, Martha 1920- 136
  Earlier sketches in SATA 11, 70
Alexander, Rae Pace
  See Alexander, Raymond Pace
Alexander, Raymond Pace 1898-1974 22
Alexander, R.C. 232
Alexander, Robert 200
Alexander, Robert C.
  See Alexander, R.C.
Alexander, Rod
  See Pellowski, Michael (Joseph)
Alexander, Sally Hobart 1943- 84
Alexander, Sue 1933-2008 136
  Obituary 195
  Earlier sketches in SATA 12, 89
  See also SAAS 15
Alexander, Vincent Arthur 1925-1980
  Obituary 23
Alexeieff, Alexandre A. 1901-1979 14
Alger, Horatio, Jr.
  See Stratemeyer, Edward L.
Alger, Horatio, Jr. 1832-1899 16
  See also CLR 170
Alger, Leclaire (Gowans) 1898-1969 15
Aliki
  See Brandenberg, Aliki
Alkema, Chester Jay 1932- 12
Al-Khalili, Jim 1962- 124
Alkiviades, Alkis 1953- 105

Alko, Selina 1968- 218
Alkouatli, Claire 186
Allaby, John Michael
  See Allaby, Michael
Allaby, Michael 1933- 167
Allamand, Pascale 1942- 12
Allan, Mabel Esther 1915-1998 75
  Earlier sketches in SATA 5, 32
  See also CLR 43
  See also SAAS 11
Allan, Nicholas 1956- 123
  Earlier sketch in SATA 79
Allan-Meyer, Kathleen 1918- 51
  Brief entry 46
Allard, Harry, Jr. 1928- 216
  Earlier sketches in SATA 42, 102
  See also CLR 85
Allard, Harry G.
  See Allard, Harry, Jr.
Allee, Marjorie Hill 1890-1945 17
Allen, Adam
  See Epstein, Beryl
  and Epstein, Samuel
Allen, Alex B.
  See Heide, Florence Parry
Allen, Allyn
  See Eberle, Irmengarde
Allen, Betsy
  See Harrison, Elizabeth (Allen) Cavanna
Allen, Bob 1961- 76
Allen, Constance
  See Albee, Sarah
Allen, Gertrude E(lizabeth) 1888-1984 9
Allen, Grace
  See Hogarth, Grace (Weston Allen)
Allen, Jeffrey (Yale) 1948- 42
Allen, John
  See Perry, Ritchie (John Allen)
Allen, Jonathan 1957- 177
  Earlier sketch in SATA 131
Allen, Jonathan Dean
  See Allen, Jonathan
Allen, Joy 1948- 217
Allen, Judy (Christina) 1941- 124
  Earlier sketch in SATA 80
Allen, Kenneth S. 1913-1981 56
Allen, Leroy 1912- 11
Allen, Linda 1925- 33
Allen, Marjorie 1931- 22
Allen, Maury 1932-2010 26
Allen, Merritt Parmelee 1892-1954 22
Allen, Nancy Kelly 1949- 171
  Earlier sketch in SATA 127
Allen, Nina (Stroemgren) 1935- 22
Allen, Pamela (Kay) 1934- 123
  Earlier sketches in SATA 50, 81
  See also CLR 44
Allen, Raul 205
Allen, Rodney F. 1938-1999 27
Allen, Roger MacBride 1957- 105
Allen, Ruth
  See Peterson, Esther (Allen)
Allen, Samuel W(ashington) 1917- 9
Allen, T. D.
  See Allen, Terril Diener
Allen, Terril Diener 1908- 35
Allen, Terry D.
  See Allen, Terril Diener
Allen, Thomas B. 1929- 193
  Earlier sketches in SATA 45, 140
Allen, Thomas Benton
  See Allen, Thomas B.
Allen, Tom
  See Allen, Thomas B.
Allende, Isabel 1942- 163
  See also CLR 171
Allerton, Mary
  See Govan, (Mary) Christine Noble
Alley, Robert W.
  See Alley, R.W.

Alley, R.W. 211
  Earlier sketch in SATA 169
Alley, Zoe B. 214
Alleyn, Ellen
  See Rossetti, Christina
Allington, Richard L(loyd) 1947- 39
  Brief entry 35
Allison, Amy 1956- 138
Allison, Bob 14
Allison, Diane Worfolk 78
Allison, Jennifer 173
Allison, Linda 1948- 43
Allison, Margaret
  See Klam, Cheryl
Allman, Barbara 1950- 137
Allmendinger, David F(rederick), Jr. 1938- . 35
Allred, Alexandra Powe 1965- 144
Allred, Gordon T(hatcher) 1930- 10
Allsop, Kenneth 1920-1973 17
Allsopp, Sophie 188
Alma, Ann 1946- 201
Almedingen, E. M.
  See Almedingen, Martha Edith von
Almedingen, Martha Edith von 1898-1971 3
Almon, Russell
  See Clevenger, William R.
  and Downing, David A(lmon)
Almond, David 1951- 233
  Earlier sketches in SATA 114, 158
  See also CLR 168
Almond, Linda Stevens 1881(?)-1987
  Obituary 50
Almquist, Don 1929- 11
Alonzo, Sandra 199
Alphin, Elaine Marie 1955- 232
  Autobiography Feature 139
  Earlier sketches in SATA 80, 130, 139
Alsenas, Linas 1979- 186
Alsop, Mary O'Hara 1885-1980 34
  Obituary 24
  Earlier sketch in SATA 2
Alter, Anna 1974- 206
  Earlier sketch in SATA 135
Alter, Judith 1938- 101
  Earlier sketch in SATA 52
Alter, Judith MacBain
  See Alter, Judith
Alter, Judy
  See Alter, Judith
Alter, Robert Edmond 1925-1965 9
Alter, Stephen 1956- 187
Althea
  See Braithwaite, Althea
Altman, Linda Jacobs 1943- 21
Altman, Suzanne
  See Orgel, Doris
  and Schecter, Ellen
Alton, Steve 169
Altschuler, Franz 1923- 45
Altsheler, Joseph A(lexander) 1862-1919
  See YABC 1
Alvarez, John
  See del Rey, Lester
Alvarez, Joseph A. 1930- 18
Alvarez, Julia 1950- 129
al-Windawi, Thura
  See Windawi, Thura al-
Alyer, Philip A.
  See Stratemeyer, Edward L.
Amado, Elisa 193
Amann, Janet 1951- 79
Amateau, Gigi 1964- 233
Amato, Carol A. 1942- 92
Amato, Mary 1961- 178
  Earlier sketch in SATA 140
Ambrose, Stephen E. 1936-2002 138
  Earlier sketch in SATA 40
Ambrose, Stephen Edward
  See Ambrose, Stephen E.
Ambrus, Gyozo Laszlo 1935- 1
  See also SAAS 4

Ambrus, Victor G.
See Ambrus, Gyozo Laszlo
Amend, Bill 1962- 147
Amerman, Lockhart 1911-1969 3
Ames, Evelyn 1908-1990 13
Obituary 64
Ames, Gerald 1906-1993 11
Obituary 74
Ames, Lee J. 1921-2011 151
Earlier sketch in SATA 3
Ames, Lee Judah
See Ames, Lee J.
Ames, Mildred 1919-1994 85
Earlier sketches in SATA 22, 81
Amico, Tom 1960(?)- 176
Amit, Ofra 1966- 205
Ammon, Richard 1942- 124
Amon, Aline 1928- 9
Amory, Jay
See Lovegrove, James
Amoss, Berthe 1925- 112
Earlier sketch in SATA 5
Amstutz, Andre 1925- 214
Anastasio, Dina 1941- 94
Brief entry 30
Earlier sketch in SATA 37
Anaya, Rudolfo 1937-
See CLR 129
Anaya, Rudolfo A.
See Anaya, Rudolfo
Anaya, Rudolpho Alfonso
See Anaya, Rudolfo
Anckarsvard, Karin Inez Maria 1915-1969 6
Ancona, George 1929- 208
Autobiography Feature 208
Earlier sketches in SATA 12, 85, 145, 192
See also SAAS 18
Anders, C. J.
See Bennett, Cherie
Anders, Isabel 1946- 101
Anders, Lou 176
Andersdatter, Karla M. 1938- 34
Andersen, Bethanne 1954- 191
Andersen, Hans Christian 1805-1875 100
See also YABC 1
See also CLR 113
Andersen, Ted
See Boyd, Waldo T.
Andersen, Yvonne 1932- 27
Anderson, Bernice G(oudy) 1894-1997 33
Anderson, Bob 1944- 139
Earlier sketch in SATA 136
Anderson, Brad 1924- 33
Brief entry 31
Anderson, Bradley Jay
See Anderson, Brad
Anderson, Brian 1974- 211
Anderson, C. C.
See Anderson, Catherine Corley
Anderson, C(larence) W(illiam) 1891-1971 . 11
Anderson, Carolyn Dunn
See Dunn, Carolyn
Anderson, Catherine C.
See Anderson, Catherine Corley
Anderson, Catherine Corley 1909-2001 72
See Lee, Cora
Anderson, Clifford
See Gardner, Richard (M.)
Anderson, Daryl Shon 1963- 93
Anderson, Dave
See Anderson, David
Anderson, David 1929- 60
Anderson, Derek 1969- 169
Anderson, Eloise Adell 1927- 9
Anderson, George
See Groom, Arthur William
Anderson, Grace Fox 1932- 43
Anderson, J(ohn) R(ichard) L(ane)
1911-1981 15
Obituary 27
Anderson, Jessica Lee 1980- 224

Anderson, Jodi Lynn 182
Anderson, John David 197
Anderson, John L. 1905- 2
Anderson, Joy 1928- 1
Anderson, Kevin J. 1962- 117
Earlier sketch in SATA 74
Anderson, Kevin James
See Anderson, Kevin J.
Anderson, Kirsty 1978- 108
Anderson, K.J.
See Moesta, Rebecca
Anderson, Laurie Halse 1961- 186
Earlier sketches in SATA 95, 132
See also CLR 138
Anderson, LaVere Francis Shoenfelt
1907-1998 27
Anderson, Leone Castell 1923- 53
Brief entry 49
Anderson, Lisa G. 1963- 108
Anderson, Lonzo
See Anderson, John L.
Anderson, Lucia (Lewis) 1922- 10
Anderson, Madelyn Klein 1926-2005 28
Anderson, Margaret J. 1931- 234
Autobiography Feature 234
Earlier sketch in SATA 27
See also SAAS 8
Anderson, Marilyn D. 1943- 144
Anderson, Mary 1939- 82
Earlier sketch in SATA 7
See also SAAS 23
Anderson, Matthew Tobin
See Anderson, M.T.
Anderson, Mona 1910-2004 40
Anderson, Mrs. Melvin
See Anderson, Catherine Corley
Anderson, M.T. 1968- 182
Earlier sketches in SATA 97, 146
Anderson, Norman Dean 1928- 22
Anderson, Peggy Perry 1953- 179
Earlier sketch in SATA 84
Anderson, Poul 1926-2001 90
Autobiography Feature 106
Brief entry 39
See also CLR 58
Anderson, Poul William
See Anderson, Poul
Anderson, Rachel 1943- 86
Earlier sketch in SATA 34
See also SAAS 18
Anderson, Rebecca J.
See Anderson, R.J.
Anderson, Rebecca M.
See Moesta, Rebecca
Anderson, Rebecca Moesta
See Moesta, Rebecca
Anderson, Richard
See Anderson, J(ohn) R(ichard) L(ane)
Anderson, R.J. 1970(?)- 216
Anderson, Sara 173
Anderson, Scoular 201
Anderson, (Tom) Scoular 138
Anderson, Stephanie 1976- 225
Anderson, Susan 1952- 90
Anderson, Thomas Scoular
See Anderson, Scoular
Anderson, W. B.
See Schultz, James Willard
Anderson, Wayne 1946- 202
Earlier sketches in SATA 56, 147
Andersson, Kenneth 1970- 200
Andre, Evelyn M. 1924- 27
Andre, Evelyn Marie
See Andre, Evelyn M.
Andreasen, Dan 227
Earlier sketch in SATA 186
Andreassen, Karl
See Boyd, Waldo T.
Andreassi, K. Robert
See DeCandido, Keith R.A.

Andree, Louise
See Coury, Louise Andree
Andres, Kristina 1971- 233
Andrew, Ian 1962- 166
Earlier sketch in SATA 116
Andrew, Ian Peter
See Andrew, Ian
Andrew, Prudence (Hastings) 1924- 87
Andrews, Benny 1930-2006 31
Obituary 178
Andrews, Eleanor Lattimore
See Lattimore, Eleanor Frances
Andrews, Elton V.
See Pohl, Frederik
Andrews, F(rank) Emerson 1902-1978 22
Andrews, J(ames) S(ydney) 1934- 4
Andrews, Jan 1942- 167
Brief entry 49
Earlier sketches in SATA 58, 98
Andrews, Julie 1935- 153
Earlier sketch in SATA 7
See also CLR 85
Andrews, Laura
See Coury, Louise Andree
Andrews, Roy Chapman 1884-1960 19
Andrews, Tamra 1959- 129
Andrews, V(irginia) C(leo) 1924(?)-1986
Obituary 50
Andrews, Wendy
See Sharmat, Marjorie Weinman
Andrews, William G. 1930- 74
Andrews, William George
See Andrews, William G.
Andrezel, Pierre
See Blixen, Karen
Andriani, Renee
See Williams-Andriani, Renee
Andriola, Alfred J. 1912-1983
Obituary 34
Andrist, Ralph K. 1914-2004 45
Andronik, Catherine M. 189
Andryszewski, Tricia 1956- 148
Earlier sketch in SATA 88
Anelli, Melissa 1979- 215
Angaramo, Roberta 1974- 229
Angel, Ann 1952- 192
Angel, Carl 178
Angel, Marie 1923- 47
Angeles, Peter A. 1931- 40
Angeletti, Roberta 1964- 124
Angeli, Marguerite (Lofft) de
See de Angeli, Marguerite (Lofft)
Angell, Judie 1937- 78
Earlier sketch in SATA 22
See also CLR 33
Angell, Madeline 1919- 18
Angelo, Valenti 1897- 14
Angelou, Maya 1928- 136
Earlier sketch in SATA 49
See also CLR 53
Angier, Bradford -1997 12
Angle, Kimberly Greene 203
Angle, Paul M(cClelland) 1900-1975
Obituary 20
Anglund, Joan Walsh 1926- 2
See also CLR 94
Ango, Fan D.
See Longyear, Barry B(rookes)
Angrist, Stanley W(olff) 1933- 4
Anhalt, Ariela 1990(?)- 227
Anholt, Catherine 1958- 131
Earlier sketch in SATA 74
Anholt, Laurence 1959- 141
Earlier sketch in SATA 74
Aninno, J.G.
See Annino, Jan Godown
Anita
See Daniel, Anita
Anmar, Frank
See Nolan, William F.

Annett, Cora
　See Scott, Cora Annett (Pipitone)
Annie-Jo
　See Blanchard, Patricia
　and Suhr, Joanne
Annino, Jan Godown 1952- 228
Annixter, Jane
　See Sturtzel, Jane Levington
Annixter, Paul
　See Sturtzel, Howard A(llison)
Anno, Mitsumasa 1926- 157
　Earlier sketches in SATA 5, 38, 77
　See also CLR 122
Anrooy, Francine Van
　See Van Anrooy, Francine
Ansary, Mir Tamim 1948- 140
Anstey, Caroline 1958- 81
Antell, Will D. 1935- 31
Anthony, Barbara
　See Barber, Antonia
Anthony, C. L.
　See Smith, Dorothy Gladys
Anthony, Edward 1895-1971 21
Anthony, Joelle 232
Anthony, John
　See Beckett, Ronald Brymer
　and Ciardi, John (Anthony)
　and Sabini, John Anthony
Anthony, Joseph Patrick 1964- 103
Anthony, Patricia 1947- 109
Anthony, Piers 1934- 129
　Autobiography Feature 129
　Earlier sketch in SATA 84
　See also CLR 118
　See also SAAS 22
Anthony, Susan C(arol) 1953- 87
Anticaglia, Elizabeth 1939- 12
Antieau, Kim 214
Antilles, Kem
　See Moesta, Rebecca
Antle, Nancy 1955- 102
Antolini, Margaret Fishback 1904-1985
　Obituary 45
Anton, Michael J(ames) 1940- 12
Antonacci, Robert J(oseph) 1916- 45
　Brief entry 37
Anvil, Christopher 1925-2009 102
Anzaldua, Gloria (Evanjelina) 1942-2004
　Obituary 154
Aoki, Hisako 1942- 45
Aoyagi, Nora 229
Apfel, Necia H(alpern) 1930- 51
　Brief entry 41
Aphrodite, J.
　See Livingston, Carole
Apikuni
　See Schultz, James Willard
Apostolina, M. 184
Apostolina, Michael
　See Apostolina, M.
Apostolou, Christine Hale 1955- 179
　Earlier sketches in SATA 82, 128
Appel, Allen (R.) 1945- 115
Appel, Benjamin 1907-1977 39
　Obituary 21
Appel, Martin 1948- 45
Appel, Martin Eliot
　See Appel, Martin
Appel, Marty
　See Appel, Martin
Appelbaum, Diana Muir Karter 1953- 132
Appelbaum, Susannah 234
Appelt, Kathi 1954- 190
　Earlier sketches in SATA 83, 129
Apperley, Dawn 1969- 135
Appiah, Peggy 1921-2006 84
　Earlier sketch in SATA 15
　See also SAAS 19
Apple, Margot 214
　Brief entry 42
　Earlier sketches in SATA 64, 152

Applebaum, Stan 1922- 45
Applegate, K.A.
　See Applegate, Katherine
Applegate, Katherine 1956- 196
　Earlier sketches in SATA 109, 162
　See also CLR 90
Applegate, Katherine Alice
　See Applegate, Katherine
Appleton, Victor
　See Barrett, Neal, Jr.
　and Doyle, Debra
　and Stratemeyer, Edward L.
　and Vardeman, Robert E.
Appollo 1969- 214
Appollodorus, Olivier
　See Appollo
Apsler, Alfred 1907-1982 10
Aragones, Sergio 1937- 48
　Brief entry 39
Arato, Rona 233
Araujo, Frank P. 1937- 86
Arbo, Cris 1950- 220
　Earlier sketch in SATA 103
Arbuckle, Dorothy Fry 1910-1982
　Obituary 33
Arbuthnot, May Hill 1884-1969 2
Archambault, John 163
　Earlier sketches in SATA 67, 112
Archambault, Matthew 1968- 219
Archbold, Rick 1950- 97
Archer, Colleen Rutherford 1949- 164
Archer, Frank
　See O'Connor, Richard
Archer, Jules 1915- 85
　Earlier sketch in SATA 4
　See also SAAS 5
Archer, Lily 1981- 193
Archer, Marion Fuller 1917- 11
Archer, Nathan
　See Watt-Evans, Lawrence
Archer, Peggy 1947- 199
Archibald, Joe
　See Archibald, Joseph S(topford)
Archibald, Joseph S(topford) 1898-1986 3
　Obituary 47
Ard, William
　See Jakes, John
Ardagh, Philip 1961- 154
Ardai, Charles 1969- 85
Arden, Barbi
　See Stoutenburg, Adrien (Pearl)
Arden, William
　See Lynds, Dennis
Ardizzone, Edward (Jeffrey Irving)
　1900-1979 28
　Obituary 21
　Earlier sketch in SATA 1
　See also CLR 3
Ardley, Neil 1937- 121
　Earlier sketch in SATA 43
Ardley, Neil Richard
　See Ardley, Neil
Arehart-Treichel, Joan 1942- 22
Arena, Felice 1968- 151
Arenella, Roy 1939- 14
Arevamirp, Esile
　See Primavera, Elise
Argent, Kerry 1960- 138
Arguelles, Francisco Xavier
　See Stork, Francisco X.
Argueta, Jorge 179
Arihara, Shino 1973- 201
Arkin, Alan 1934- 59
　Brief entry 32
Arkin, Alan Wolf
　See Arkin, Alan
Arksey, Neil 158
Arlen, Leslie
　See Nicole, Christopher
Arley, Robert
　See Jackson, Mike

Armer, Alberta (Roller) 1904-1986 9
Armer, Laura Adams 1874-1963 13
Armistead, John 1941- 130
Armitage, David 1943- 155
　Brief entry 38
　Earlier sketch in SATA 99
Armitage, Frank
　See Carpenter, John
Armitage, Ronda (Jacqueline) 1943- 155
　Brief entry 38
　Earlier sketches in SATA 47, 99
Armour, Richard (Willard) 1906-1989 14
　Obituary 61
Armstrong, Alan 1939- 172
Armstrong, Alan W.
　See Armstrong, Alan
Armstrong, George D. 1927- 10
Armstrong, Gerry (Breen) 1929- 10
Armstrong, Jeannette (C.) 1948- 102
Armstrong, Jennifer 1961- 165
　Autobiography Feature 120
　Earlier sketches in SATA 77, 111
　See also CLR 66
　See also SAAS 24
Armstrong, Louise 43
　Brief entry 33
Armstrong, Martin Donisthorpe
　1882-1974 115
Armstrong, Matthew 1975- 188
Armstrong, Matthew S.
　See Armstrong, Matthew
Armstrong, Ralph Richard
　See Armstrong, Richard
Armstrong, Richard 1903-1986 11
Armstrong, Shelagh 1961- 224
Armstrong, William H(oward) 1914-1999 4
　Obituary 111
　See also CLR 117
　See also SAAS 7
Armstrong-Ellis, Carey (Fraser) 1956- 145
Armstrong-Hodgson, Shelagh
　See Armstrong, Shelagh
Arndt, Ursula (Martha H.) 56
　Brief entry 39
Arneson, D(on) J(on) 1935- 37
Arnett, Caroline
　See Cole, Lois Dwight
Arnett, Jack
　See Goulart, Ron
Arnette, Robert
　See Silverberg, Robert
Arno, Enrico 1913-1981 43
　Obituary 28
Arnold, Ann 1953(?)- 207
Arnold, Caroline 1944- 228
　Brief entry 34
　Earlier sketches in SATA 36, 85, 131, 174
　See also CLR 61
　See also SAAS 23
Arnold, Elizabeth 1944- 164
Arnold, Elliott 1912-1980 5
　Obituary 22
Arnold, Emily 1939- 210
　Autobiography Feature 134
　Earlier sketches in SATA 5, 50, 76, 110, 134
　See also CLR 46
　See also SAAS 7
Arnold, Gillian Clare
　See Cross, Gillian
Arnold, Katya 1947- 168
　Earlier sketches in SATA 82, 115
Arnold, Louise 175
Arnold, Louise Claire
　See Arnold, Louise
Arnold, Marsha Diane 1948- 147
　Earlier sketch in SATA 93
Arnold, Nick 1961- 113
Arnold, Oren 1900-1980 4
Arnold, Susan (Riser) 1951- 58
Arnold, Tedd 1949- 208
　Earlier sketches in SATA 69, 116, 160

Arnoldy, Julie
  See Bischoff, Julia Bristol
Arnosky, James Edward 1946- 189
  Earlier sketches in SATA 70, 118
  See also CLR 93
Arnosky, Jim
  See Arnosky, James Edward
Arnott, Kathleen 1914- 20
Arnov, Boris, Jr. 1926- 12
Arnow, Harriette (Louisa) Simpson
  1908-1986 42
  Obituary 47
Arnsteen, Katy Keck 1934- 68
Arnstein, Helene S(olomon) 1915- 12
Arntson, Herbert E(dward) 1911-1982 12
Aroner, Miriam 82
Aronin, Ben 1904-1980
  Obituary 25
Aronson, Marc 1950- 189
  Autobiography Feature 189
  Earlier sketches in SATA 126, 175
Aronson, Marc Henry
  See Aronson, Marc
Aronson, Sarah 196
Aronson, Virginia 1954- 122
Arora, Shirley (Lease) 1930- 2
Arrasmith, Patrick 176
Arrick, Fran
  See Angell, Judie
Arrigan, Mary 1943- 142
Arrington, Aileen 183
Arrington, Stephen L. 1948- 97
Arrington, Stephen Lee
  See Arrington, Stephen L.
Arrley, Richmond
  See Delany, Samuel R., Jr.
Arrou-Vignod, Jean-Philippe 1958- 218
Arrowood, (McKendrick Lee) Clinton
  1939- 19
Arrowsmith, Pat 1930- 59
Arsenault, Isabelle 1978- 207
Artell, Mike 1948- 183
  Earlier sketches in SATA 89, 134
Arthur, A.C.
  See Arthur, Artist
Arthur, Artist 235
Arthur, Artist C.
  See Arthur, Artist
Arthur, Robert (Andrew) 1909-1969
  See Arthur, Robert, (Jr.)
Arthur, Robert, (Jr.) 1909-1969 118
Arthur, Ruth M(abel) 1905-1979 26
  Earlier sketch in SATA 7
Artis, Vicki Kimmel 1945- 12
Artzybasheff, Boris (Miklailovich)
  1899-1965 14
Aruego, Ariane
  See Dewey, Ariane
Aruego, Jose 1932- 178
  Earlier sketches in SATA 6, 68, 125
  See also CLR 5
Aruego, Jose Espiritu
  See Aruego, Jose
Arundel, Honor (Morfydd) 1919-1973 4
  Obituary 24
  See also CLR 35
Arundel, Jocelyn
  See Alexander, Jocelyn Anne Arundel
Arvey, Michael 1948- 79
Arzoumanian, Alik 177
Asare, Meshack (Yaw) 1945- 139
  Earlier sketch in SATA 86
Asaro, Catherine 1955- 165
  Earlier sketch in SATA 101
Asaro, Catherine Ann 1955-
  See Asaro, Catherine
Asay, Donna Day 1945- 127
Asbjornsen, Peter Christen 1812-1885 15
  See also CLR 104
Asch, Frank 1946- 154
  Earlier sketches in SATA 5, 66, 102

Ash, Jutta 1942- 38
Ashabranner, Brent 1921- 166
  Earlier sketches in SATA 1, 67, 130
  See also CLR 28
  See also SAAS 14
Ashabranner, Brent Kenneth
  See Ashabranner, Brent
Ashbless, William
  See Blaylock, James P.
  and Powers, Tim
Ashby, Gil 1958- 146
Ashby, Gwynneth 1922- 44
Ashby, Ruth 170
Ashby, Yvonne 1955- 121
Ashe, Arthur (Robert, Jr.) 1943-1993 65
  Obituary 87
Ashe, Geoffrey (Thomas) 1923- 17
  Autobiography Feature 125
Ashe, Mary Ann
  See Lewis, Mary
Asher, Bridget
  See Baggott, Julianna
Asher, Sandra Fenichel
  See Asher, Sandy
Asher, Sandy 1942- 71
  Autobiography Feature 158
  Brief entry 34
  Earlier sketch in SATA 36
  See also SAAS 13
Asheron, Sara
  See Moore, Lilian
Ashey, Bella
  See Breinburg, Petronella
Ashford, Daisy
  See Ashford, Margaret Mary
Ashford, Jeffrey
  See Jeffries, Roderic
Ashford, Margaret Mary 1881-1972 10
Ashland, Monk 1972- 207
Ashley, Bernard (John) 1935- 155
  Brief entry 39
  Earlier sketches in SATA 47, 79
  See also CLR 4
Ashley, Elizabeth
  See Salmon, Annie Elizabeth
Ashley, Ray
  See Abrashkin, Raymond
Ashman, Linda 1960- 203
  Earlier sketch in SATA 150
Ashton, Lorayne
  See Gottfried, Theodore Mark
Ashton, Warren T.
  See Adams, William Taylor
Asimov, Isaac 1920-1992 74
  Earlier sketches in SATA 1, 26
  See also CLR 79
Asinof, Eliot 1919-2008 6
Asinof, Eliot Tager
  See Asinof, Eliot
Aska, Warabe
  See Masuda, Takeshi
Askani, Tanja 1962- 227
Asprin, Robert 1946-2008 92
Asprin, Robert L.
  See Asprin, Robert
Asprin, Robert Lynn
  See Asprin, Robert
Asquith, Cynthia Mary Evelyn (Charteris)
  1887-1960 107
Asquith, Ros 153
Astley, Juliet
  See Lofts, Norah (Robinson)
Aston, Dianna Hutts 1964- 176
Aston, James
  See White, T(erence) H(anbury)
Ata, Te 1895-1995 119
Atene, Ann
  See Atene, (Rita) Anna
Atene, (Rita) Anna 1922- 12
Atheling, William, Jr.
  See Blish, James

Atkins, Catherine 160
Atkins, Jeannine 1953- 172
  Earlier sketch in SATA 113
Atkinson, Allen G. 1953(?)-1987 60
  Brief entry 46
  Obituary 55
Atkinson, Elizabeth 215
Atkinson, Elizabeth Jane
  See Atkinson, Elizabeth
Atkinson, M. E.
  See Frankau, Mary Evelyn Atkinson
Atkinson, Margaret Fleming 14
Atteberry, Kevan J. 186
Attema, Martha 1949- 156
  Earlier sketch in SATA 94
Atticus
  See Davies, Hunter
  and Fleming, Ian
  and Pawle, Gerald Strachan
  and Wilson, (Thomas) Woodrow
Atwater, Florence 1896-1979 66
  Earlier sketch in SATA 16
  See also CLR 19
Atwater, Florence Hasseltine Carroll
  See Atwater, Florence
Atwater, Montgomery Meigs 1904-1976 15
Atwater, Richard 1892-1948 66
  Brief entry 27
  Earlier sketch in SATA 54
  See also CLR 19
Atwater, Richard Tupper
  See Atwater, Richard
Atwater-Rhodes, Amelia 1984- 170
  Earlier sketch in SATA 124
Atwell, Debby 1953- 150
  Earlier sketch in SATA 87
Atwood, Ann (Margaret) 1913-1992 7
Atwood, Margaret 1939- 170
  Earlier sketch in SATA 50
Atwood, Margaret Eleanor
  See Atwood, Margaret
Aubrey, Meg Kelleher 1963- 83
Aubry, Claude B. 1914-1984 29
  Obituary 40
Auch, Herm 173
Auch, Mary Jane 173
  Earlier sketch in SATA 138
Auch, M.J.
  See Auch, Mary Jane
Auclair, Joan 1960- 68
Auel, Jean
  See Auel, Jean M.
Auel, Jean M. 1936- 91
Auel, Jean Marie
  See Auel, Jean M.
Auer, Martin 1951- 77
Augarde, Steve 1950- 210
  Earlier sketches in SATA 25, 159
Augarde, Steven Andre
  See Augarde, Steve
Augelli, John P(at) 1921- 46
Augustine, Mildred
  See Benson, Mildred
Ault, Phil
  See Ault, Phillip H(alliday)
Ault, Phillip H(alliday) 1914- 23
Ault, Rosalie Sain 1942- 38
Ault, Roz
  See Ault, Rosalie Sain
Aung, (Maung) Htin 1909- 21
Auntie Deb
  See Coury, Louise Andree
Auntie Louise
  See Coury, Louise Andree
Aunt Weedy
  See Alcott, Louisa May
Auseon, Andrew 1976- 217
  Earlier sketch in SATA 166
Austen, Carrie
  See Bennett, Cherie
Austen, Catherine 1965- 223

Austin, Carrie
  See Seuling, Barbara
Austin, Elizabeth S. 1907-1977 5
Austin, Harry
  See McInerny, Ralph
Austin, Margot 1909(?)-1990 11
  Obituary 66
Austin, Michael 178
Austin, Oliver L(uther), Jr. 1903-1988 7
  Obituary 59
Austin, Patricia 1950- 137
Austin, R. G.
  See Gelman, Rita Golden
  and Lamb, Nancy
Austin, Virginia 1951- 152
  Earlier sketch in SATA 80
Auteur, Hillary
  See Gottfried, Theodore Mark
Auth, Tony
  See Auth, William Anthony, Jr.
Auth, William Anthony, Jr. 1942- 192
Autry, Gloria Diener
  See Allen, Terril Diener
Auvil, Peggy A 1954- 122
Auvil, Peggy Appleby
  See Auvil, Peggy A
Avasthi, Swati 1971- 231
Aveni, Anthony F. 1938- 181
Aveni, Anthony Francis
  See Aveni, Anthony F.
Averbeck, Jim 1963- 201
Averill, Esther (Holden) 1902-1992 28
  Obituary 72
  Earlier sketch in SATA 1
Avery, A. A.
  See Montgomery, Rutherford George
Avery, Al
  See Montgomery, Rutherford George
Avery, Gillian 1926- 137
  Autobiography Feature 137
  Earlier sketches in SATA 7, 75
  See also SAAS 6
Avery, Gillian Elise
  See Avery, Gillian
Avery, Kay 1908- 5
Avery, Lorraine
  See Older, Effin
  and Older, Jules
Avery, Lynn
  See Cole, Lois Dwight
Avi 1937- 226
  Earlier sketches in SATA 14, 71, 108, 156,
  190
  See also CLR 68
Aviles, Martha 218
Avishai, Susan 1949- 82
Avraham, Kate Aver 227
Avril, Francois 1961- 191
Avril, Lynne
  See Cravath, Lynne W.
Awdry, Christopher Vere 1940- 67
Awdry, Wilbert Vere 1911-1997 94
  See also CLR 23
Axelrod, Amy 131
Axelsen, Stephen 1953- 165
Axton, David
  See Koontz, Dean
Ayars, James S(terling) 1898-1986 4
Aye, A. K.
  See Edwards, Hazel (Eileen)
Ayer, Eleanor H. 1947-1998 121
  Earlier sketch in SATA 78
Ayer, Jacqueline 1930- 13
Ayer, Margaret (?)-1981 15
Aylesworth, Jim 1943- 213
  Earlier sketches in SATA 38, 89, 139
  See also CLR 89
Aylesworth, Thomas G(ibbons) 1927-1995 .. 88
  Earlier sketch in SATA 4
  See also CLR 6
  See also SAAS 17

Ayliffe, Alex 190
Aylward, Marcus
  See Alexander, Marc
Aymar, Brandt 1911- 22
Ayme, Marcel (Andre) 1902-1967 91
  See also CLR 25
Ayres, Becky
  See Hickox, Rebecca (Ayres)
Ayres, Katherine 1947- 187
Ayres, Pam 1947- 90
Ayres, Patricia Miller 1923-1985
  Obituary 46
Aytmatov, Chingiz
  See Aitmatov, Chingiz
Ayto, Russell 1960- 206
  Earlier sketches in SATA 111, 166
Azaid
  See Zaidenberg, Arthur
Azar, Penny 1952- 121
Azarian, Mary 1940- 171
  Earlier sketch in SATA 112
Azore, Barbara 1934- 188

B

Baasansuren, Bolormaa 1982- 216
Baastad, Babbis Friis
  See Friis-Baastad, Babbis Ellinor
Bab
  See Gilbert, W(illiam) S(chwenck)
Babbis, Eleanor
  See Friis-Baastad, Babbis Ellinor
Babbitt, Lucy Cullyford 1960- 85
Babbitt, Natalie 1932- 194
  Earlier sketches in SATA 6, 68, 106
  See also CLR 141
  See also SAAS 5
Babbitt, Natalie Zane Moore
  See Babbitt, Natalie
Babcock, Chris 1963- 83
Babcock, Dennis 1948- 22
Babcock, Dennis Arthur
  See Babcock, Dennis
Baber, Carolyn Stonnell 1936- 96
Baboni, Elena 198
Baca, Ana 1967- 191
Baca, Maria 1951- 104
Baccalario, Pierdomenico 1974- 222
Bach, Alice (Hendricks) 1942- 93
  Brief entry 27
  Earlier sketch in SATA 30
Bach, Bellamy
  See Windling, Terri
Bach, Mary 1960- 125
Bach, Richard 1936- 13
Bach, Richard David
  See Bach, Richard
Bache, Ellyn 1942- 124
Bachel, Beverly K. 1957- 142
Bachelet, Gilles 1952- 196
Bachem, Paul 231
Bachman, Fred 1949- 12
Bachman, Richard
  See King, Stephen
Bachorz, Pam 1973- 226
Bachrach, Deborah 1943- 80
Bacigalupi, Paolo 1973- 230
Backus, James Gilmore 1913-1989
  Obituary 63
Backus, Jim
  See Backus, James Gilmore
Bacmeister, Rhoda W(arner) 1893-1991 11
Bacon, Betty
  See Bacon, Elizabeth
Bacon, Elizabeth 1914-2001 3
  Obituary 131
Bacon, Joan Chase
  See Bowden, Joan Chase

Bacon, Josephine Dodge (Daskam)
  1876-1961 48
Bacon, Margaret Frances
  See Bacon, Peggy
Bacon, Margaret Hope 1921- 6
Bacon, Martha Sherman 1917-1981 18
  Obituary 27
  See also CLR 3
Bacon, Melvin 1950- 93
Bacon, Melvin L.
  See Bacon, Melvin
Bacon, Peggy 1895-1987 50
Bacon, R(onald) L(eonard) 1924- 84
  Earlier sketch in SATA 26
Baddiel, Ivor 1963- 210
Baden, Robert 1936- 70
Baden-Powell, Robert (Stephenson Smyth)
  1857-1941 16
Badoe, Adwoa 237
Badt, Karin L(uisa) 1963- 91
Bae, Hyun-Joo 186
Baehr, Kingsley M. 1937- 89
Baehr, Patricia 1952- 65
Baehr, Patricia Goehner
  See Baehr, Patricia
Baek, Matthew J. 1971- 202
Baer, Jill
  See Gilbert, (Agnes) Joan (Sewell)
Baer, Judy 1951- 71
Baer, Julie 1960- 161
Baer-Block, Roxanna 172
Baerg, Harry J(ohn) 1909-1996 12
Baeten, Lieve 1954- 83
Bagert, Brod 1947- 191
  Earlier sketch in SATA 80
Baggette, Susan K. 1942- 126
Baggott, Julianna 1969- 197
Bagnold, Enid 1889-1981 25
  Earlier sketch in SATA 1
Baguley, Elizabeth 1959- 199
Bahlke, Valerie Worth -1994
  See Worth, Valerie
Bahous, Sally 1939- 86
Bahr, Mary (Madelyn) 1946- 95
Bahr, Robert 1940- 38
Bahti, Tom 1926-1972 57
  Brief entry 31
Bai, Durga 211
Baicker-McKee, Carol 1958- 177
Bailey, Alice Cooper 1890-1978 12
Bailey, Anne 1958- 71
Bailey, Bernadine (Freeman) 1901-1995 14
Bailey, Carolyn Sherwin 1875-1961 14
Bailey, Debbie 1954- 123
Bailey, Donna (Veronica Anne) 1938- 68
Bailey, Jane H(orton) 1916- 12
Bailey, John (Robert) 1940- 52
Bailey, Len 193
Bailey, Linda 1948- 217
  Earlier sketches in SATA 107, 182
Bailey, Maralyn Collins (Harrison) 1941- 12
Bailey, Matilda
  See Radford, Ruby L(orraine)
Bailey, Maurice Charles 1932- 12
Bailey, Pearl (Mae) 1918-1990 81
Bailey, Peter 1946- 194
Bailey, Ralph Edgar 1893-1982 11
Bailey, Sheila (Lucas) 1960- 155
Baillie, Allan 1943- 151
  Earlier sketch in SATA 87
  See also CLR 49
  See also SAAS 21
Baillie, Allan Stuart
  See Baillie, Allan
Baines, John (David) 1943- 71
Bains, Larry
  See Sabin, Louis
Baird, Alison 1963- 138
Baird, Bil 1904-1987 30
  Obituary 52

Baird, Thomas (P.) 1923-1990 45
  Brief entry 39
  Obituary 64
Baird, William Britton
  See Baird, Bil
Baity, Elizabeth Chesley 1907-1989 1
Baiul, Oksana 1977- 108
Bajoria, Paul 1964- 187
Bakeless, John (Edwin) 1894-1978 9
Bakeless, Katherine Little 1895-1992 9
Baker, Alan 1951- 146
  Earlier sketches in SATA 22, 93
Baker, Augusta 1911-1998 3
Baker, Barbara 1947- 192
Baker, Betty Lou 1928-1987 73
  Obituary 54
  Earlier sketch in SATA 5
Baker, Carin Greenberg 1959- 79
Baker, Charlotte 1910- 2
Baker, Christina
  See Kline, Christina Baker
Baker, Christopher W. 1952- 144
Baker, Deirdre 1955- 195
Baker, E.D. 237
  Earlier sketch in SATA 190
Baker, (Mary) Elizabeth (Gillette) 1923- 7
Baker, Gayle Cunningham 1950- 39
Baker, James W. 1924- 65
  Earlier sketch in SATA 22
Baker, James W. 1926- 122
Baker, Janice E(dla) 1941- 22
Baker, Jeanette 178
Baker, Jeannie 1950- 156
  Earlier sketches in SATA 23, 88
  See also CLR 28
Baker, Jeffrey J(ohn) W(heeler) 1931- 5
Baker, Jim
  See Baker, James W.
Baker, Keith 1953- 222
  Earlier sketch in SATA 179
Baker, Ken 1962- 133
Baker, Laura Nelson 1911- 3
Baker, Margaret 1890-1965 4
Baker, Margaret J(oyce) 1918- 12
  See also SAAS 8
Baker, Mary Gladys Steel 1892-1974 12
Baker, (Robert) Michael (Graham) 1938- 4
Baker, Nina (Brown) 1888-1957 15
Baker, Pamela J. 1947- 66
Baker, Rachel 1904-1978 2
  Obituary 26
Baker, Roberta 206
Baker, Rosalie F. 1945- 166
Baker, Samm Sinclair 1909-1997 12
  Obituary 96
Baker, Sharon Reiss 1962- 207
Baker, Susan (Catherine) 1942-1991 29
Baker-Smith, Grahame 223
Balaam
  See Lamb, G(eoffrey) F(rederick)
Balan, Bruce 1959- 113
Balcavage, Dynise 1965- 137
Balch, Glenn 1902-1989 3
  Obituary 83
  See also SAAS 11
Baldacci, David 1960- 184
Baldacci, David G.
  See Baldacci, David
  and Baldacci, David
Balderose, Nancy Ward 1952- 93
Balderson, Margaret 1935- 151
Baldini, Michelle 205
Baldry, Cherith 1947- 167
  Earlier sketch in SATA 72
Balducci, Carolyn 1946- 5
Balducci, Carolyn Feleppa
  See Balducci, Carolyn
Baldwin, Alex
  See Griffin, W. E. B.
Baldwin, Anne Norris 1938- 5
Baldwin, Clara 11

Baldwin, Gordo
  See Baldwin, Gordon C(ortis)
Baldwin, Gordon C(ortis) 1908-1983 12
Baldwin, James 1841-1925 24
Baldwin, James 1924-1987 9
  Obituary 54
Baldwin, Louis 1919- 110
Baldwin, Margaret
  See Weis, Margaret
Baldwin, Stan(ley C.) 1929- 62
  Brief entry 28
Bales, Carol Ann 1940- 57
  Brief entry 29
Balet, Jan (Bernard) 1913- 11
Balgassi, Haemi 1971- 131
Balian, Lorna 1929- 91
  Earlier sketch in SATA 9
Balit, Christina 1961- 212
  Earlier sketches in SATA 102, 159
Ball, Duncan 1941- 73
Ball, Zachary
  See Janas, Frankie-Lee
  and Masters, Kelly R(ay)
Ballantine, Lesley Frost
  See Frost, Lesley
Ballantyne, R(obert) M(ichael) 1825-1894 ... 24
  See also CLR 137
Ballard, James G.
  See Ballard, J.G.
Ballard, James Graham
  See Ballard, J.G.
Ballard, Jane
  See Gorman, Carol
Ballard, J.G. 1930-2009 93
  Obituary 203
Ballard, Jim G.
  See Ballard, J.G.
Ballard, John 1945- 110
Ballard, Lowell C(lyne) 1904-1986 12
  Obituary 49
Ballard, (Charles) Martin 1929- 1
Ballard, Mignon F. 1934- 64
  Brief entry 49
Ballard, Mignon Franklin
  See Ballard, Mignon F.
Ballard, Robert D(uane) 1942- 85
  See also CLR 60
Ballard, Robin 1965- 126
Balliett, Blue 1955- 156
Ballinger, Bryan 1968- 161
Ballouhey, Pierre 1944- 90
Balog, Cyn 221
Balogh, Penelope 1916-1975 1
  Obituary 34
Balouch, Kristen 176
Balow, Tom 1931- 12
Baltazzi, Evan S(erge) 1921- 90
Balterman, Marcia Ridlon 1942- 22
Baltimore, J.
  See Catherall, Arthur
Baltzer, Hans (Adolf) 1900- 40
Balzano, Jeanne (Koppel) 1912- 7
Bambara, Toni Cade 1939-1995 112
Bamfylde, Walter
  See Bevan, Tom
Bamman, Henry A. 1918- 12
Banat, D. R.
  See Bradbury, Ray
Bancks, Tristan 1974- 231
Bancroft, Bronwyn 1958- 216
Bancroft, Griffing 1907-1999 6
Bancroft, Laura
  See Baum, L. Frank
Bandel, Betty 1912- 47
Baner, Skulda Vanadis 1897-1964 10
Banerjee, Anjali 174
Banfill, A. Scott 1956- 98
Bang, Betsy 1912- 48
  Brief entry 37
Bang, Garrett
  See Bang, Molly

Bang, Molly 1943- 215
  Earlier sketches in SATA 24, 69, 111, 158
  See also CLR 8
Bang, Molly Garrett
  See Bang, Molly
Bang-Campbell, Monika 1975(?)- 195
  Earlier sketch in SATA 140
Banjo, The
  See Paterson, A(ndrew) B(arton)
Banke, Cecile de
  See de Banke, Cecile
Banks, Erin Bennett 1978- 211
Banks, Kate 1960- 200
  Earlier sketches in SATA 134, 172
Banks, Laura Stockton Voorhees 1908(?)-1980
  Obituary 23
Banks, Lynne Reid
  See Reid Banks, Lynne
Banks, Merry 197
Banks, Michael A. 1951- 101
Banks, Paul 1952- 174
Banks, Sara
  See Harrell, Sara Gordon
Banks, Sara Jeanne Gordon Harrell
  See Harrell, Sara Gordon
Bannatyne-Cugnet, Elizabeth Jo-Anne
  See Bannatyne-Cugnet, Jo
Bannatyne-Cugnet, Jo 1951- 101
Banner, Angela
  See Maddison, Angela Mary
Bannerman, Helen (Brodie Cowan Watson)
  1862(?)-1946 19
  See also CLR 144
Banning, Evelyn I. 1903-1993 36
Bannon, Laura (?)-1963 6
Bannor, Brett 1959- 143
Bansch, Helga 1957- 224
Banta, Susan 181
Bantock, Nick 1950(?)- 95
Banyai, Istvan 193
Barakat, Ibtisam 1963- 186
Barasch, Lynne 1939- 186
  Earlier sketches in SATA 74, 126
Baratz-Logsted, Lauren 235
Barbalet, Margaret 1949- 77
Barbary, James
  See Baumann, Amy Beeching
  and Beeching, Jack
Barbash, Shepard 1957- 84
Barbauld, Anna Laetitia 1743-1825
  See CLR 160
Barbe, Walter Burke 1926- 45
Barber, Alison 222
Barber, Antonia 1932- 163
  Earlier sketch in SATA 29
Barber, Atiim Kiambu
  See Barber, Tiki
Barber, Lynda
  See Graham-Barber, Lynda
Barber, Lynda Graham
  See Graham-Barber, Lynda
Barber, Richard (William) 1941- 35
Barber, Ronde 1975- 182
Barber, Tiki 1975- 182
Barbera, Joe 1911-2006 51
  Obituary 179
Barbera, Joseph
  See Barbera, Joe
Barbera, Joseph Roland
  See Barbera, Joe
Barberis, Juan C(arlos) 1920- 61
Barbour, Karen 1956- 170
  Earlier sketches in SATA 63, 121
Barbour, Ralph Henry 1870-1944 16
Barclay, Bill
  See Moorcock, Michael
Barclay, Isabel
  See Dobell, I(sabel) M(arian) B(arclay)
Barclay, William Ewert
  See Moorcock, Michael

Barclay, William Ewert
  See Moorcock, Michael
Bardhan-Quallen, Sudipta 1977- *214*
  Earlier sketch in SATA *168*
Bardoe, Cheryl *181*
Bare, Arnold Edwin 1920- *16*
Bare, Colleen Stanley *32*
Bar-el, Dan *199*
Barenholtz, Bernard 1914-1989
  Obituary *64*
Bargar, Gary W. 1947-1985 .... *63*
Barger, Jan 1948- *147*
Barish, Matthew 1907-2000 .... *12*
Barkan, Joanne *127*
  Earlier sketch in SATA *77*
Barker, Albert W. 1900- *8*
Barker, Carol (Minturn) 1938- *31*
Barker, Cicely Mary 1895-1973 .... *49*
  Brief entry *39*
  See also CLR *88*
Barker, Claire 1969- *237*
Barker, Melvern 1907-1989 .... *11*
Barker, S. Omar 1894-1985 .... *10*
Barker, Squire Omar
  See Barker, S. Omar
Barker, Will 1913-1983 .... *8*
Barkin, Carol 1944- *52*
  Earlier sketch in SATA *42*
Barklem, Jill 1951- *96*
  See also CLR *31*
Barkley, Brad *178*
Barkley, James Edward 1941- *6*
Barks, Carl 1901-2000 .... *37*
Barley, Janet Crane 1934- *95*
Barlow, Steve 1952- *211*
Barnaby, Ralph S(tanton) 1893-1986 .... *9*
Barnard, A. M.
  See Alcott, Louisa May
Barnard, Bryn 1956- *169*
  Earlier sketch in SATA *115*
Barne, Kitty
  See Barne, Marion Catherine
Barne, Marion Catherine 1883-1957 .... *97*
Barneda, David *206*
Barner, Bob 1947- *136*
  Earlier sketch in SATA *29*
Barnes, Dawn 1957- *175*
Barnes, Derrick *191*
Barnes, Derrick D.
  See Barnes, Derrick
Barnes, (Frank) Eric Wollencott 1907-1962 . *22*
Barnes, Joyce Annette 1958- *85*
Barnes, Laura T. 1958- *119*
Barnes, Loutricia
  See Barnes-Svarney, Patricia L(ou)
Barnes, Malcolm 1909(?)-1984
  Obituary *41*
Barnes, Michael 1934- *55*
Barnes-Murphy, Frances 1951- *88*
Barnes-Murphy, Rowan 1952- *88*
Barnes-Svarney, Patricia L(ou) 1953- *67*
Barnet, Nancy 1954- *84*
Barnett, Ivan 1947- *70*
Barnett, Lincoln (Kinnear) 1909-1979 .... *36*
Barnett, Mac *223*
Barnett, Moneta 1922-1976 .... *33*
Barnett, Naomi 1927- *40*
Barney, Maginel Wright 1881(?)-1966 .... *39*
  Brief entry *32*
Barnhart, Clarence L(ewis) 1900-1993 .... *48*
  Obituary *78*
Barnholdt, Lauren 1980(?)- *232*
Barnhouse, Rebecca 1961- *225*
Barnouw, Adriaan Jacob 1877-1968
  Obituary *27*
Barnouw, Victor 1915-1989 .... *43*
  Brief entry *28*
Barnstone, Willis 1927- *20*
Barnum, Jay Hyde 1888(?)-1962 .... *20*
Barnum, P. T., Jr.
  See Stratemeyer, Edward L.

Barnum, Richard *67*
  Earlier sketch in SATA *1*
Barnum, Theodore
  See Stratemeyer, Edward L.
Barnwell, Ysaye M. 1946- *200*
Baron, Kathi 1956- *226*
Baron, Kathy 1954- *90*
Baron, Virginia Olsen 1931- *46*
  Brief entry *28*
Barr, Donald 1921-2004 .... *20*
  Obituary *152*
Barr, George 1907-1992 .... *2*
Barr, Jene 1922-1985 .... *16*
  Obituary *42*
Barr, Nevada 1952- *126*
  Earlier sketch in SATA *115*
Barragan, Paula 1963- *216*
Barratt, Mark 1954- *224*
Barrer, Gertrude
  See Barrer-Russell, Gertrude
Barrer-Russell, Gertrude 1921- *27*
Barrett, Angela 1955- *223*
Barrett, Angela (Jane) 1955- *145*
  Earlier sketch in SATA *75*
Barrett, Ethel *87*
  Brief entry *44*
Barrett, Joyce Durham 1943- *138*
Barrett, Judi
  See Barrett, Judith
Barrett, Judith 1941- *204*
  Earlier sketch in SATA *26*
  See also CLR *98*
Barrett, Robert T. 1949- *234*
  Earlier sketch in SATA *92*
Barrett, Ron 1937- *14*
Barrett, Susan (Mary) 1938- *113*
Barrett, Tracy 1955- *207*
  Earlier sketches in SATA *84, 115, 156*
Barrett, William E(dmund) 1900-1986
  Obituary *49*
Barretta, Gene *214*
  Earlier sketch in SATA *176*
Barretton, Grandall
  See Garrett, Randall
Barrie, Baronet
  See Barrie, J. M.
Barrie, J. M. 1860-1937 .... *100*
  See also YABC *1*
  See also CLR *124*
Barrie, James Matthew
  See Barrie, J. M.
Barringer, William 1940-1996 .... *153*
Barrington, Michael
  See Moorcock, Michael
Barris, George 1925- *47*
Barrol, Grady
  See Bograd, Larry
Barron, Rex 1951- *84*
Barron, T.A. 1952- *192*
  Earlier sketches in SATA *83, 126*
  See also CLR *86*
Barron, Thomas Archibald
  See Barron, T.A.
Barron, Tom
  See Barron, T.A.
Barrow, Lloyd H. 1942- *73*
Barrows, Annie 1962- *180*
Barry, Dan 1958- *177*
Barry, Dana (Marie Malloy) 1949- *139*
Barry, James P(otvin) 1918- *14*
Barry, Katharina Watjen 1936- *4*
Barry, Robert 1931- *6*
Barry, Robert Everett
  See Barry, Robert
Barry, Scott 1952- *32*
Barry, Sheila Anne -2003 .... *91*
Barshaw, Ruth McNally *203*
Bartell, Susan S. *175*
Bartenbach, Jean 1918- *40*
Barth, Edna 1914-1980 .... *7*
  Obituary *24*

Barth, Kelly L. 1964- *152*
Barthelme, Donald 1931-1989 .... *7*
  Obituary *62*
Barth-Grozinger, Inge 1950- *185*
Bartholomew, Barbara 1941- *86*
  Brief entry *42*
Bartholomew, Jean
  See Beatty, Patricia (Robbins)
Bartlett, Alison *153*
Bartlett, Philip A. *1*
Bartlett, Robert Merrill 1899-1995 .... *12*
Bartoletti, Susan Campbell 1958- *237*
  Earlier sketches in SATA *88, 129, 135, 173*
Barton, Byron 1930- *126*
  Earlier sketches in SATA *9, 90*
Barton, Chris *224*
Barton, Jill(ian) 1940- *75*
Barton, May Hollis *67*
  Earlier sketch in SATA *1*
Barton, Pat
  See Arrowsmith, Pat
Barton, Patrice 1955- *226*
Bartos-Hoeppner, Barbara 1923- *5*
Bartram, Simon *218*
  Earlier sketch in SATA *156*
Bartsch, Jochen 1906- *39*
Baruch, Dorothy W(alter) 1899-1962 .... *21*
Barunga, Albert 1912(?)-1977 .... *120*
Baryshnikov, Mikhail 1948- *192*
Bas, Rutger
  See Rutgers van der Loeff-Basenau, An(na)
  Maria Margaretha
Base, Graeme 1958- *162*
  Earlier sketches in SATA *67, 101*
  See also CLR *22*
Base, Graeme Rowland
  See Base, Graeme
Baseman, Gary 1960- *174*
Bash, Barbara 1948- *132*
Basher
  See Basher, Simon
Basher, Simon *235*
Bashevis, Isaac
  See Singer, Isaac Bashevis
Bashevis, Yitskhok
  See Singer, Isaac Bashevis
Bashista, Adrienne Ehlert *203*
Basile, Gloria Vitanza 1929- *180*
Baskin, Leonard 1922-2000 .... *120*
  Brief entry *27*
  Earlier sketch in SATA *30*
Baskin, Nora Raleigh 1961- *189*
  Earlier sketch in SATA *129*
Bason, Lillian 1913- *20*
Bass, Hester 1956- *223*
Bass, L.G.
  See Geringer, Laura
Bassett, Jeni 1959- *64*
  Brief entry *43*
Bassett, John Keith
  See Keating, Lawrence A.
Bassett, Lisa 1958- *61*
Bassil, Andrea
  See Nilsen, Anna
Bastyra, Judy *108*
Basye, Dale E. *205*
Bataille, Marion 1963- *209*
Bat-Ami, Miriam 1950- *150*
  Autobiography Feature *150*
  Earlier sketches in SATA *82, 122*
Bate, Lucy 1939-1993 .... *18*
Bate, Norman (Arthur) 1916- *5*
Bateman, Colin 1962- *172*
Bateman, Donna M. *190*
Bateman, Teresa 1957- *216*
  Earlier sketches in SATA *112, 168*
Bates, Amy June *189*
Bates, Barbara S(nedeker) 1919- *12*
Bates, Betty
  See Bates, Elizabeth
Bates, Dianne 1948- *147*

Bates, Elizabeth 1921- 19
Bates, Ivan 175
Bates, Katharine Lee 1859-1929 113
Bates, Martine
  See Leavitt, Martine
Bateson, Catherine 1960- 197
  Earlier sketch in SATA 157
Batey, Tom 1946- 52
  Brief entry 41
Bath, Kevin P.
  See Bath, K.P.
Bath, K.P. 1959- 171
Batherman, Muriel
  See Sheldon, Muriel
Batson, Larry 1930- 35
Batt, Tanya Robyn 1970- 131
Battaglia, Aurelius 1910- 50
  Brief entry 33
Batten, H(arry) Mortimer 1888-1958 25
Batten, Mary 1937- 162
  Earlier sketches in SATA 5, 102
Batterberry, Ariane Ruskin 1935- 13
Batterberry, Michael Carver 1932-2010 32
Battle-Lavert, Gwendolyn 1951- 155
  Earlier sketches in SATA 85, 131
Battles, (Roxy) Edith 1921- 7
Baudouy, Michel-Aime 1909- 7
Bauer, A.C.E. 201
Bauer, Caroline Feller 1935- 98
  Brief entry 46
  Earlier sketch in SATA 52
  See also SAAS 24
Bauer, Fred 1934- 36
Bauer, Helen 1900-1988 2
Bauer, Joan 1951- 160
  Earlier sketch in SATA 117
Bauer, Jutta 1955- 150
Bauer, Marion Dane 1938- 192
  Autobiography Feature 144
  Earlier sketches in SATA 20, 69, 113, 144
  See also SAAS 9
Bauer, Michael Gerard 1955(?)- 167
Bauer, Steven 1948- 125
Bauerschmidt, Marjorie 1926- 15
Baughman, Dorothy 1940- 61
Baum, Allyn Z(elton) 1924-1997 98
  Earlier sketch in SATA 20
Baum, L. Frank
  See Thompson, Ruth Plumly
Baum, L. Frank 1856-1919 100
  Earlier sketch in SATA 18
  See also CLR 107
Baum, Louis 1948- 182
  Brief entry 52
  Earlier sketch in SATA 64
Baum, Louis F.
  See Baum, L. Frank
Baum, Lyman Frank
  See Baum, L. Frank
Baum, Maxie 188
Baum, Willi 1931- 4
Bauman, Beth Ann 1964- 220
Baumann, Amy Beeching 1922- 10
Baumann, Amy Brown Beeching
  See Baumann, Amy Beeching
Baumann, Hans 1914- 2
  See also CLR 35
Baumann, Kurt 1935- 21
Baumgartner, Barbara 1939- 86
Baurys, Flo 1938- 122
Baurys, Florence
  See Baurys, Flo
Bausum, Ann 173
Bawden, Nina 1925- 132
  Earlier sketches in SATA 4, 72
  See also CLR 51
  See also SAAS 16
Bawden, Nina Mary Mabey
  See Bawden, Nina
Baxter, Andy
  See Dakin, Glenn

Baxter, Roberta 1952- 219
Baxter, Valerie
  See Meynell, Laurence Walter
Bay, Jeanette Graham 1928- 88
Bayer, Harold
  See Gregg, Andrew K.
Bayer, Jane E. (?)-1985
  Obituary 44
Bayley, Nicola 1949- 129
  Earlier sketches in SATA 41, 69
Baylor, Byrd 1924- 136
  Earlier sketches in SATA 16, 69
  See also CLR 3
Baynes, Pauline 1922-2008 133
  Obituary 196
  Earlier sketches in SATA 19, 59
Baynes, Pauline Diana
  See Baynes, Pauline
Bayoc, Cbabi 186
Bayrock, Fiona 215
BB
  See Watkins-Pitchford, Denys James
Beach, Charles
  See Reid, (Thomas) Mayne
Beach, Charles Amory 1
Beach, Edward L. 1918-2002 12
  Obituary 140
Beach, Edward Latimer
  See Beach, Edward L.
Beach, Lisa 1957- 111
Beach, Lynn
  See Lance, Kathryn
Beach, Stewart T(aft) 1899-1979 23
Beachcroft, Nina 1931- 18
Beagle, Peter S. 1939- 130
  Earlier sketch in SATA 60
Beagle, Peter Soyer
  See Beagle, Peter S.
Beaglehole, Helen 1946- 117
Beake, Lesley 1949- 209
Beaky, Suzanne 1971- 230
Beale, Fleur 107
Bealer, Alex W(inkler III) 1921-1980 8
  Obituary 22
Beales, Valerie 1915- 74
Beals, Carleton 1893-1979 12
Beals, Frank Lee 1881-1972
  Obituary 26
Beam, Matt 1970- 187
Beame, Rona 1934- 12
Beamer, Charles 1942- 43
Beamer, George Charles, Jr.
  See Beamer, Charles
Bean, Jonathan 1979- 194
Bean, Normal
  See Burroughs, Edgar Rice
Beaney, Jan
  See Udall, Jan Beaney
Beaney, Jane
  See Udall, Jan Beaney
Bear, Carolyn
  See Rayban, Chloe
Bear, Greg 1951- 105
  Earlier sketch in SATA 65
Bear, Gregory Dale
  See Bear, Greg
Bearanger, Marie
  See Messier, Claire
Beard, Alex 1970- 222
Beard, Charles A(ustin) 1874-1948 18
Beard, Dan(iel Carter) 1850-1941 22
Beard, Darleen Bailey 1961- 96
Bearden, Romare (Howard) 1914(?)-1988 ... 22
  Obituary 56
Beardmore, Cedric
  See Beardmore, George
Beardmore, George 1908-1979 20
Beardshaw, Rosalind 1969- 225
  Earlier sketch in SATA 190
Beardsley, Martyn R. 1957- 150
Bearman, Jane (Ruth) 1917- 29

Bearn, Emily 220
Beaton, Clare 1947- 220
  Earlier sketch in SATA 125
Beatty, Elizabeth
  See Holloway, Teresa (Bragunier)
Beatty, Hetty Burlingame 1907-1971 5
Beatty, Jerome, Jr. 1918- 5
Beatty, John (Louis) 1922-1975 6
  Obituary 25
Beatty, Patricia (Robbins) 1922-1991 73
  Obituary 68
  Earlier sketches in SATA 1, 30
  See also SAAS 4
Beaty, Andrea 186
Beaty, Mary (T.) 1947- 146
Beaudoin, Sean 210
Beauford, Jhenne Tyler
  See Beauford, Tyler
Beauford, Tyler 1990- 225
Beaufort, Simon
  See Gregory, Susanna
  and Riffenburgh, Beau
Beaumont, Karen 1954- 204
Beavers, Ethen 1971- 225
Beccia, Carlyn 189
Bechard, Margaret 1953- 164
  Earlier sketch in SATA 85
Bechtel, Louise Seaman 1894-1985 4
  Obituary 43
Bechtold, Lisze 208
Beck, Andrea 1956- 226
Beck, Barbara L. 1927- 12
Beck, Ian 1947- 190
  Earlier sketch in SATA 138
  See Beck, Ian Archibald
Beck, Peggy 1949- 171
Beck, Scott 197
Becker, Beril 1901-1999 11
Becker, Bonny 184
Becker, Deborah Zimmett 1955- 138
Becker, Helaine 1961- 142
Becker, John (Leonard) 1901- 12
Becker, John E(mil) 1942- 148
Becker, Joyce 1936- 39
Becker, May Lamberton 1873-1958 33
Becker, Neesa 1951- 123
Becker, Shari 174
Beckerman, Chad W. 198
Beckett, Sheilah 1913- 33
Beckhorn, Susan Williams 1953- 189
Beckles Willson, Robina 1930- 27
Beckman, Delores 1914-1994 51
Beckman, Gunnel 1910- 6
  See also CLR 25
  See also SAAS 9
Beckman, Kaj
  See Beckman, Karin
Beckman, Karin 1913- 45
Beckman, Per (Frithiof) 1913- 45
Bedard, Michael 1949- 154
  Earlier sketch in SATA 93
  See also CLR 35
Beddor, Frank 194
Beddows, Eric
  See Nutt, Ken
Bedford, A. N.
  See Watson, Jane Werner
Bedford, Annie North
  See Watson, Jane Werner
Bedford, David 224
  Earlier sketch in SATA 159
Bedford, David J.
  See Bedford, David
Bedoukian, Kerop 1907-1981 53
Bee, Jay
  See Brainerd, John W(hiting)
Bee, William 188
Beebe, B. F.
  See Johnson, B. F.
Beebe, (Charles) William 1877-1962 19
Beeby, Betty 1923- 25

Beech, Mark 1971- *191*
Beech, Webb
  See Griffin, W. E. B.
Beecham, Jahnna *161*
Beechcroft, William
  See Hallstead, William F(inn III)
Beeching, Jack 1922- *14*
Beeke, Tiphanie *219*
  Earlier sketch in SATA *163*
Beeler, Janet
  See Shaw, Janet
Beeler, Nelson F(rederick) 1910-1978 .... *13*
Beere, Peter 1951- *97*
Beers, Dorothy Sands 1917- *9*
Beers, Lorna 1897-1989 .... *14*
Beers, V(ictor) Gilbert 1928- *130*
  Earlier sketch in SATA *9*
Beeton, Max
  See Redding, Robert Hull
Begay, Shonto 1954- *137*
Begaye, Lisa Shook
  See Beach, Lisa
Begin, Mary Jane 1963- *82*
Begin-Callanan, Mary Jane
  See Begin, Mary Jane
Begley, Kathleen A. 1948- *21*
Begley, Kathleen Anne
  See Begley, Kathleen A.
Beguine, Anna
  See Saintcrow, Lilith
Beha, Eileen *221*
Beha, Philippe *211*
Behan, Leslie
  See Gottfried, Theodore Mark
Behler, Deborah A. 1947- *145*
Behler, John L. 1943-2006 .... *145*
  Obituary *173*
Behler, John Luther
  See Behler, John L.
Behn, Harry 1898-1973 .... *2*
  Obituary *34*
Behnke, Frances L. *8*
Behr, Joyce 1929- *15*
Behrens, Andy *228*
Behrens, June York 1925- *19*
Behrman, Carol H(elen) 1925- *144*
  Earlier sketch in SATA *14*
Beifuss, John, (Jr.) 1959- *92*
Beil, Karen Magnuson 1950- *221*
  Earlier sketch in SATA *124*
Beil, Michael D. *226*
Beiler, Edna 1923- *61*
Beingessner, Laura 1965- *220*
Beinicke, Steve 1956- *69*
Beirne, Barbara 1933- *71*
Beiser, Arthur 1931- *22*
Beiser, Germaine 1931- *11*
Belair, Richard L. 1934- *45*
Belaney, Archibald Stansfeld 1888-1938 ...... *24*
  See also CLR *32*
Belasen, Amy 1983- *213*
Belbin, David 1958- *164*
  Earlier sketch in SATA *106*
Belden, Wilanne Schneider 1925- *56*
Belford, Kevin *236*
Belfrage, Sally 1936-1994 .... *65*
  Obituary *79*
Belknap, B. H.
  See Ellis, Edward S.
Belknap, Boynton
  See Ellis, Edward S.
Belknap, Boynton M.D.
  See Ellis, Edward S.
Bell, Anthea 1936- *148*
  Earlier sketch in SATA *88*
Bell, Cathleen Davitt 1971- *203*
Bell, Cece *202*
Bell, Clare (Louise) 1952- *99*
Bell, Corydon Whitten 1894-1980 .... *3*
Bell, David Owen 1949- *99*

Bell, Emerson
  See Stratemeyer, Edward L.
Bell, Emily Mary
  See Cason, Mabel Earp
Bell, Frank
  See Benson, Mildred
Bell, Gertrude (Wood) 1911-1987 .... *12*
Bell, Gina
  See Balzano, Jeanne (Koppel)
Bell, Hilari 1958- *226*
  Earlier sketches in SATA *151, 197*
Bell, Jadrien
  See Golden, Christie
Bell, Janet
  See Clymer, Eleanor
Bell, Janet Cheatham 1937- *127*
Bell, Krista 1950- *215*
  Earlier sketch in SATA *126*
Bell, Krista Anne Blakeney
  See Bell, Krista
Bell, Margaret E(lizabeth) 1898-1990 .... *2*
Bell, Mary Reeves 1946- *88*
Bell, Norman (Edward) 1899- *11*
Bell, Raymond Martin 1907-1999 .... *13*
Bell, Siobhan *177*
Bell, Thelma Harrington 1896-1985 .... *3*
Bell, William 1945- *90*
  See also CLR *91*
Bellairs, John (Anthony) 1938-1991 .... *160*
  Obituary *66*
  Earlier sketches in SATA *2, 68*
  See also CLR *37*
Beller, Susan Provost 1949- *128*
  Earlier sketch in SATA *84*
  See also CLR *106*
Bellingham, Brenda 1931- *99*
  Brief entry *51*
Bello, Rosario de
  See De Bello, Rosario
Belloc, Hilaire 1870-1953 .... *112*
  See also YABC *1*
  See also CLR *102*
Belloc, Joseph Hilaire Pierre Sebastien Rene
  Swanton
  See Belloc, Hilaire
Belloc, Joseph Peter Rene Hilaire
  See Belloc, Hilaire
Belloc, Joseph Pierre Hilaire
  See Belloc, Hilaire
Belloli, Andrea P. A. 1947- *86*
Bell-Rehwoldt, Sheri 1962- *199*
Bellville, Cheryl Walsh 1944- *54*
  Brief entry *49*
Bell-Zano, Gina
  See Balzano, Jeanne (Koppel)
Belpre, Pura 1899-1982 .... *16*
  Obituary *30*
Belting, Natalia Maree 1915-1997 .... *6*
Belton, John Raynor 1931- *22*
Belton, Sandra 1939- *186*
  Earlier sketches in SATA *85, 134*
Belton, Sandra Yvonne
  See Belton, Sandra
Beltran, Alberto 1923- *43*
Beltran-Hernandez, Irene 1945- *74*
Belvedere, Lee
  See Grayland, Valerie (Merle Spanner)
Bemelmans, Ludwig 1898-1962 .... *100*
  Earlier sketch in SATA *15*
  See also CLR *93*
Bemis, John Claude *234*
Benander, Carl D. 1941- *74*
Benary, Margot
  See Benary-Isbert, Margot
Benary-Isbert, Margot 1889-1979 .... *2*
  Obituary *21*
  See also CLR *12*
Benasutti, Marion 1908-1992 .... *6*
Benatar, Raquel 1955- *167*

Benchley, Nathaniel (Goddard) 1915-1981 .. *25*
  Obituary *28*
  Earlier sketch in SATA *3*
Benchley, Peter 1940-2006 .... *164*
  Earlier sketches in SATA *3, 89*
Benchley, Peter Bradford
  See Benchley, Peter
Bendall-Brunello, John *185*
Bender, Edna 1941- *92*
Bender, Esther 1942- *88*
Bender, Lucy Ellen 1942- *22*
Bender, Robert 1962- *160*
  Earlier sketch in SATA *79*
Bendick, Jeanne 1919- *135*
  Earlier sketches in SATA *2, 68*
  See also CLR *5*
  See also SAAS *4*
Bendick, Robert L(ouis) 1917- *11*
Bendinger, Jessica 1966- *233*
Benedetto, William R. 1928- *180*
Benedetto, William Ralph
  See Benedetto, William R.
Benedict, Andrew
  See Arthur, Robert, (Jr.)
Benedict, Dorothy Potter 1889-1979 .... *11*
  Obituary *23*
Benedict, Lois Trimble 1902-1967 .... *12*
Benedict, Rex 1920-1995 .... *8*
Benedict, Stewart H(urd) 1924- *26*
Beneduce, Ann Keay *128*
Benet, Laura 1884-1979 .... *3*
  Obituary *23*
Benet, Stephen Vincent 1898-1943
  See YABC *1*
Benet, Sula 1906-1982 .... *21*
  Obituary *33*
Ben-Ezer, Ehud 1936- *122*
Benezra, Barbara (Beardsley) 1921- *10*
Benham, Leslie 1922- *48*
Benham, Lois (Dakin) 1924- *48*
Benham, Mary Lile 1914-1991 .... *55*
Benioff, Carol *232*
Benjamin, E. M. J.
  See Bache, Ellyn
Benjamin, Floella 1949- *206*
Benjamin, Nora
  See Kubie, Nora Gottheil Benjamin
Benjamin, Saragail Katzman 1953- *86*
Benner, Cheryl 1962- *80*
Benner, Judith Ann 1942- *94*
Bennett, Alice
  See Ziner, Florence
Bennett, Artie *227*
Bennett, Cherie 1960- *158*
  Earlier sketch in SATA *97*
Bennett, Dorothea
  See Young, Dorothea Bennett
Bennett, Erin Susanne
  See Banks, Erin Bennett
Bennett, Holly 1957- *181*
Bennett, James (W.) 1942- *153*
  Autobiography Feature *153*
  Earlier sketches in SATA *93, 148*
Bennett, Jay 1912- *87*
  Brief entry *27*
  Earlier sketch in SATA *41*
  See also SAAS *4*
Bennett, Jill (Crawford) 1934- *41*
Bennett, John 1865-1956
  See YABC *1*
Bennett, Kelly 1958- *231*
Bennett, Kelly Goldman
  See Bennett, Kelly
Bennett, Penelope (Agnes) 1938- *94*
Bennett, Rachel
  See Hill, Margaret (Ohler)
Bennett, Rainey 1907-1998 .... *15*
  Obituary *111*
Bennett, Richard 1899- *21*
Bennett, Russell H(oradley) 1896- *25*
Bennett, Veronica 1953- *178*

Bennett, William (John) 1943- 102
Benning, Elizabeth
  See Rice, Bebe Faas
Benny, Mike 1964- 203
Benson, Amber 1977- 235
Benson, Elizabeth P(olk) 1924- 65
Benson, Kathleen 1947- 183
  Earlier sketches in SATA 62, 111
Benson, Linda M(aria) 1959- 84
Benson, Mildred 1905-2002 100
  Obituary 135
  Earlier sketches in SATA 1, 65, 67
Benson, Mildred Augustine Wirt
  See Benson, Mildred
Benson, Mildred Wirt
  See Benson, Mildred
Benson, Millie
  See Benson, Mildred
Benson, Patrick 1956- 147
Benson, Sally 1900-1972 35
  Obituary 27
  Earlier sketch in SATA 1
Bentley, Judith (McBride) 1945- 89
  Earlier sketch in SATA 40
Bentley, Karen
  See Taschek, Karen
Bentley, Nancy (L.) 1946- 78
Bentley, Nicolas Clerihew 1907-1978
  Obituary 24
Bentley, Phyllis Eleanor 1894-1977 6
  Obituary 25
Bentley, Roy 1947- 46
Bentley, William (George) 1916- 84
Bently, Peter 1960- 221
Benton, Jim 1963- 172
ben Uzair, Salem
  See Horne, Richard Henry Hengist
Ben-Zvi, Rebeccca Tova
  See O'Connell, Rebecca
Bercaw, Edna Coe 1961- 124
Berck, Judith 1960- 75
Bereal, JaeMe 1959(?)- 228
Berelson, Howard 1940- 5
Berends, Polly Berrien 1939- 50
  Brief entry 38
Berenstain, Jan 1923- 135
  Earlier sketches in SATA 12, 64, 129
  See also CLR 150
  See also SAAS 20
Berenstain, Janice
  See Berenstain, Jan
Berenstain, Michael 1951- 220
  Earlier sketch in SATA 45
Berenstain, Mike
  See Berenstain, Michael
Berenstain, Stan 1923-2005 135
  Obituary 169
  Earlier sketches in SATA 12, 64, 129
  See also CLR 150
  See also SAAS 20
Berenstain, Stanley
  See Berenstain, Stan
Berenzy, Alix 1957- 168
  Earlier sketch in SATA 65
Beresford, Elisabeth 1928-2010 141
  Earlier sketches in SATA 25, 86
  See also SAAS 20
Berg, Adriane G(ilda) 1948- 152
Berg, Dave
  See Berg, David
Berg, David 1920-2002 27
  Obituary 137
Berg, Elizabeth 1948- 104
Berg, Jean Horton 1913-1995 6
Berg, Joan
  See Victor, Joan Berg
Berg, Ron 1952- 48
Bergaust, Erik 1925-1978 20
Bergel, Colin J. 1963- 137
Bergen, Joyce 1949- 95
Berger, Barbara (Helen) 1945- 77

Berger, Carin 232
  Earlier sketch in SATA 185
Berger, Gilda 1935- 88
  Brief entry 42
Berger, Joe 1970- 221
Berger, Josef 1903-1971 36
Berger, Lou 1950- 213
Berger, Melvin H. 1927- 158
  Autobiography Feature 124
  Earlier sketches in SATA 5, 88
  See also CLR 32
  See also SAAS 2
Berger, Phil 1942-2001 62
Berger, Samantha 1969- 140
Berger, Samantha Allison
  See Berger, Samantha
Berger, Terry 1933- 8
Bergey, Alyce 1934- 45
Bergey, Alyce Mae
  See Bergey, Alyce
Bergin, Mark 1961- 160
  Earlier sketch in SATA 114
Berglin, Ruth Marie 1970- 181
Bergman, Donna 1934- 73
Bergman, Mara 1956- 196
Bergman, Tamar 1939- 95
Bergren, Lisa T.
  See Bergren, Lisa Tawn
Bergren, Lisa Tawn 200
Bergsma, Jody Lynn 163
Bergstein, Rita M. 211
Bergum, Constance R. 1952- 208
  Earlier sketch in SATA 121
Berk, Ari 208
Berk, Josh 1976- 227
Berkebile, Fred D(onovan) 1900-1978
  Obituary 26
Berkeley, Jon 1962- 204
Berkes, Marianne 217
  Earlier sketch in SATA 173
Berkey, Barry Robert 1935- 24
Berkowitz, Freda Pastor 1908-1994 12
Berkus, Clara Widess 1909- 78
Berlan, Kathryn Hook 1946- 78
Berlfein, Judy Reiss 1958- 79
Berlin, Eric 1968- 195
Berliner, Don 1930- 33
Berliner, Franz 1930- 13
Berlitz, Charles (L. Frambach) 1914-2003 ... 32
  Obituary 151
Berman, Len 1947- 229
Berman, Linda 1948- 38
Berman, Paul (Lawrence) 1949- 66
Berman, Rachel 1946- 217
Berna, Paul 1910-1994 15
  Obituary 78
  See also CLR 19
Bernadette
  See Watts, Bernadette
Bernard, Bruce 1928-2000 78
  Obituary 124
Bernard, George I. 1949- 39
Bernard, Jacqueline (de Sieyes) 1921-1983 ... 8
  Obituary 45
Bernard, Patricia 1942- 181
  Earlier sketch in SATA 106
Bernard, Trish
  See Bernard, Patricia
Bernardin, James 1966- 227
  Earlier sketch in SATA 112
Bernardo, Anilu 184
Bernards, Neal 1963- 71
Bernasconi, Pablo 1973- 183
Bernays, Anne 1930- 32
Berner, Rotraut Susanne 1948- 214
Bernhard, Durga T. 1961- 80
Bernhard, Emery 1950- 80
Bernheimer, Kate 201
Bernier-Grand, Carmen T. 1947- 202
Bernstein, Daryl (Evan) 1976- 81
Bernstein, Joanne E(ckstein) 1943- 15

Bernstein, Jonathan 217
Bernstein, Margery 1933- 114
Bernstein, Nina 1949- 180
Bernstein, Theodore M(enline) 1904-1979 ... 12
  Obituary 27
Berrien, Edith Heal
  See Heal, Edith
Berrill, Jacquelyn (Batsel) 1905- 12
Berrington, John
  See Brownjohn, Alan
Berry, B. J.
  See Berry, Barbara J.
Berry, Barbara J. 1937- 7
Berry, Erick
  See Best, (Evangel) Allena Champlin
Berry, Holly 1957- 210
Berry, James 1924- 110
  Earlier sketch in SATA 67
  See also CLR 143
Berry, Jane Cobb 1915(?)-1979
  Obituary 22
Berry, Joy 1944- 58
  Brief entry 46
Berry, Joy Wilt
  See Berry, Joy
Berry, Julie 1974- 218
Berry, Lynne 190
Berry, William D(avid) 1926- 14
Bersani, Shennen 1961- 164
Berson, Harold 1926- 4
Bertagna, Julie 1962- 151
Bertholf, Bret 189
Bertin, Charles-Francois
  See Berlitz, Charles (L. Frambach)
Bertolet, Paul
  See McLaughlin, Frank
Berton, Pierre (Francis de Marigny)
  1920-2004 99
  Obituary 158
Bertrand, Cecile 1953- 76
Bertrand, Diane Gonzales 1956- 177
  Earlier sketch in SATA 106
Bertrand, Lynne 1963- 164
  Earlier sketch in SATA 81
Beskow, Elsa (Maartman) 1874-1953 20
  See also CLR 17
Bess, Clayton
  See Locke, Robert
Besson, Luc 1959- 199
Best, (Evangel) Allena Champlin 1892-1974 . 2
  Obituary 25
Best, Cari 1951- 200
  Earlier sketches in SATA 107, 149
Best, (Oswald) Herbert 1894-1980 2
Bestall, A(lfred) E(dmeades) 1892-1986 97
  Obituary 48
Betancourt, Jeanne 1941- 148
  Brief entry 43
  Earlier sketches in SATA 55, 96
Beth, Mary
  See Miller, Mary Beth
Bethancourt, T. Ernesto
  See Paisley, Tom
Bethel, Dell 1929- 52
Bethell, Jean (Frankenberry) 1922- 8
Bethers, Ray 1902-1973 6
Bethke, Bruce Raymond 1955- 114
Bethlen, T.D.
  See Silverberg, Robert
Bethune, J. G.
  See Ellis, Edward S.
Bethune, J. H.
  See Ellis, Edward S.
Betteridge, Anne
  See Potter, Margaret
Betteridge, Deirdre 214
Bettina
  See Ehrlich, Bettina Bauer
Bettmann, Otto Ludwig 1903-1998 46
Bettoli, Delana 187

Betts, James
  See Haynes, Betsy
Betz, Eva Kelly 1897-1968 .... *10*
Bevan, Tom 1868-1930(?)
  See YABC 2
Bevis, Mary 1939- *202*
Bewick, Thomas 1753-1828 .... *16*
Beyer, Audrey White 1916- *9*
Beyer, Paul J. III 1950- *74*
Beynon, John
  See Harris, John (Wyndham Parkes Lucas)
  Beynon
Bezencon, Jacqueline (Buxcel) 1924- *48*
Bhatia, Jamunadevi 1919- *48*
Bhatia, June
  See Bhatia, Jamunadevi
Bial, Morrison David 1917- *62*
Bial, Raymond 1948- *225*
  Earlier sketches in SATA *76, 116, 165*
Biala
  See Brustlein, Janice Tworkov
Biale, Rachel 1952- *99*
Bialk, Elisa
  See Krautter, Elisa (Bialk)
Bianchi, John 1947- *91*
Bianchi, Robert S(teven) 1943- *92*
Bianco, Margery
  See Bianco, Margery Williams
Bianco, Margery Williams 1881-1944 .... *15*
  See also CLR *146*
Bianco, Pamela 1906- *28*
Bibby, Violet 1908-1996 .... *24*
Bible, Charles 1937- *13*
Bibo, Bobette
  See Gugliotta, Bobette
Bice, Clare 1909-1976 .... *22*
Bickerstaff, Isaac
  See Swift, Jonathan
Bidner, Jenni 1963- *193*
Biedrzycki, David 1955- *219*
Biegel, Paul 1925- *79*
  Earlier sketch in SATA *16*
  See also CLR *27*
  See also SAAS *18*
Biemiller, Carl L(udwig), Jr.) 1912-1979 ..... *40*
  Obituary *21*
Bienenfeld, Florence L(ucille) 1929- *39*
Bierhorst, John (William) 1936- *149*
  Autobiography Feature *149*
  Earlier sketches in SATA *6, 91*
  See also SAAS *10*
Biggar, Joan R. 1936- *120*
Biggar, Joan Rawlins
  See Biggar, Joan R.
Biggle, Lloyd, Jr. 1923-2002 .... *65*
Biggs, Brian 1968- *192*
Bilal, Abdel W(ahab) 1970- *92*
Bilbrough, Norman 1941- *111*
Bildner, Phil *230*
  Earlier sketch in SATA *173*
Bileck, Marvin 1920- *40*
Bilibin, Ivan (Iakolevich) 1876-1942 .... *61*
Bill, Alfred Hoyt 1879-1964 .... *44*
Bill, Tannis *228*
Billam, Rosemary 1952- *61*
Billings, Charlene W(interer) 1941- *41*
Billingsley, Franny 1954- *235*
  Earlier sketch in SATA *132*
Billington, Elizabeth T(hain) *50*
  Brief entry *43*
Billout, Guy (Rene) 1941- *144*
  Earlier sketch in SATA *10*
  See also CLR *33*
Bilson, Geoffrey 1938-1987 .... *99*
Binch, Caroline (Lesley) 1947- *140*
  Earlier sketch in SATA *81*
Bing, Christopher (H.) *126*
Bingham, Caroline 1962- *158*
Bingham, Jane M. 1941- *163*
Bingham, Jane Marie
  See Bingham, Jane M.

Bingham, Janet 1959- *200*
Bingham, Kelly 1967- *207*
Bingham, Sam 1944- *96*
Bingham, Samuel A.
  See Bingham, Sam
Bingley, Margaret (Jane Kirby) 1947- *72*
Binkley, Anne
  See Rand, Ann (Binkley)
Binzen, Bill
  See Binzen, William
Binzen, William *24*
Birch, David (W.) 1913-1996 .... *89*
Birch, Reginald B(athurst) 1856-1943 .... *19*
Birchman, David 1949- *72*
Birchmore, Daniel A. 1951- *92*
Bird, Carmel 1940- *124*
Bird, E(lzy) J(ay) 1911- *58*
Birdsall, Jeanne 1951- *231*
Birdsall, Jeanne 1952(?)- *170*
Birdseye, Tom 1951- *148*
  Earlier sketches in SATA *66, 98*
Birenbaum, Barbara 1941- *65*
Birmingham, Christian 1970- *220*
Birmingham, Lloyd P(aul) 1924- *83*
  Earlier sketch in SATA *12*
Birmingham, Ruth
  See Sorrells, Walter
Birney, Betty G. 1947- *169*
  Earlier sketch in SATA *98*
Biro, B.
  See Biro, B. S.
Biro, B. S. 1921- *1*
  See also CLR *28*
  See also SAAS *13*
Biro, Val
  See Biro, B. S.
Birtha, Becky 1948- *229*
Bischoff, Julia Bristol 1899-1970 .... *12*
Bishop, Bonnie 1943- *37*
Bishop, Claire Huchet 1899(?)-1993 .... *14*
  Obituary *74*
  See also CLR *80*
Bishop, Courtney
  See Ruemmler, John D(avid)
Bishop, Curtis (Kent) 1912-1967 .... *6*
Bishop, Elizabeth 1911-1979
  Obituary *24*
Bishop, Gavin 1946- *216*
  Earlier sketches in SATA *97, 144*
Bishop, Kathleen Wong 1954- *120*
Bishop, Kathy
  See Bishop, Kathleen Wong
Bishop, Nic 1955- *161*
  Earlier sketch in SATA *107*
Bishop, Rudine Sims *224*
Bisset, Donald 1910-1995 .... *86*
  Earlier sketch in SATA *7*
Bisson, Terry 1942- *99*
Bisson, Terry Ballantine
  See Bisson, Terry
Bitter, Gary G(len) 1940- *22*
Bixby, William (Courtney) 1920-1986 .... *6*
  Obituary *47*
Bjoerk, Christina 1938- *99*
  Earlier sketch in SATA *67*
  See also CLR *22*
Bjork, Christina
  See Bjoerk, Christina
Bjorklund, Lorence F. 1913-1978 .... *35*
  Brief entry *32*
Bjorkman, Lauren *222*
Bjorkman, Steve *223*
  Earlier sketch in SATA *163*
Blabey, Aaron 1975(?)- *214*
Black, Algernon David 1900-1993 .... *12*
  Obituary *76*
Black, Holly 1971- *236*
  Earlier sketches in SATA *147, 210*
Black, Irma Simonton 1906-1972 .... *2*
  Obituary *25*
Black, Joe 1959- *224*

Black, Rabbi Joe
  See Black, Joe
Black, Kat *217*
Black, Katherine
  See Black, Kat
Black, Mansell
  See Trevor, Elleston
Black, MaryAnn
  See Easley, MaryAnn
Black, Susan Adams 1953- *40*
Blackall, Bernie 1956- *126*
Blackall, Sophie *231*
  Earlier sketch in SATA *182*
Blackburn, Claire
  See Altman, Linda Jacobs
Blackburn, John(ny) Brewton 1952- *15*
Blackburn, Joyce Knight 1920- *29*
Blacker, Terence 1948- *194*
Blacker, Tina
  See Louise, Tina
Blackett, Veronica Heath 1927- *12*
Blackie, Jean Cutler 1943- *79*
Blacklin, Malcolm
  See Chambers, Aidan
Blacklock, Dyan 1951- *112*
Blackman, Malorie 1962- *196*
  Earlier sketches in SATA *83, 128*
Blackton, Peter
  See Wilson, Lionel
Blackwood, Alan 1932- *70*
Blackwood, Freya *199*
Blackwood, Gary
  See Blackwood, Gary L.
Blackwood, Gary L. 1945- *226*
  Earlier sketches in SATA *72, 118, 169*
Blade, Alexander
  See Garrett, Randall
  and Hamilton, Edmond
  and Silverberg, Robert
Bladek, John 1963(?)- *237*
Blades, Ann (Sager) 1947- *69*
  Earlier sketch in SATA *16*
  See also CLR *15*
Bladow, Suzanne Wilson 1937- *14*
Blaine, Chris
  See Gardner, Craig Shaw
Blaine, John
  See Goodwin, Harold L(eland)
Blaine, Marge
  See Blaine, Margery Kay
Blaine, Margery Kay 1937- *11*
Blair, Alison
  See Lerangis, Peter
Blair, Anne Denton 1914-1993 .... *46*
Blair, David Nelson 1954- *80*
Blair, Eric
  See Orwell, George
Blair, Jay 1953- *45*
Blair, Lucile
  See Yeakley, Marjory Hall
Blair, Margaret Whitman 1951- *227*
  Earlier sketch in SATA *124*
Blair, Mary 1911-1978 .... *195*
Blair, Pauline Hunter
  See Clarke, Pauline
Blair, Ruth Van Ness 1912-1999 .... *12*
Blair, Shannon
  See Kaye, Marilyn
Blair, Walter 1900-1992 .... *12*
  Obituary *72*
Blaisdell, Bob
  See Blaisdell, Robert
Blaisdell, Robert 1959- *105*
Blake, Bronwyn 1940- *149*
Blake, Francis *198*
Blake, Jon 1954- *171*
  Earlier sketch in SATA *78*
Blake, Olive
  See Supraner, Robyn

Blake, Quentin 1932- *211*
   Earlier sketches in SATA *9, 52, 96, 125*
   See also CLR *31*
Blake, Robert 1949- *42*
Blake, Robert J. *160*
Blake, Stephanie *233*
   See Pearl, Jacques Bain
Blake, Walker E.
   See Griffin, W. E. B.
Blake, William 1757-1827 .... *30*
   See also CLR *52*
Blakely, Gloria 1950- *139*
Blakely, Roger K. 1922- *82*
Blakeney, Jay D.
   See Chester, Deborah
Blakeslee, Lys 1985- *218*
Blakey, Nancy 1955- *94*
Blanc, Esther S. 1913-1997 .... *66*
Blanc, Mel 1908-1989
   Obituary *64*
Blanchard, Patricia *125*
Blanchet, M(uriel) Wylie 1891-1961 .... *106*
Blanco, Richard L(idio) 1926- *63*
Bland, E.
   See Nesbit, E.
Bland, Edith Nesbit
   See Nesbit, E.
Bland, Fabian
   See Nesbit, E.
Blane, Gertrude
   See Blumenthal, Gertrude
Blank, Clarissa Mabel 1915-1965 .... *62*
Blankenship, LeeAnn 1944- *181*
Blassingame, Wyatt Rainey 1909-1985 .... *34*
   Obituary *41*
   Earlier sketch in SATA *1*
Blatchford, Claire H. 1944- *94*
Blau, Aljoscha 1972- *233*
Blauer, Ettagale 1940- *49*
Blecha, Aaron *233*
Bleck, Linda *207*
Bledsoe, Glen L. 1951- *108*
Bledsoe, Glen Leonard
   See Bledsoe, Glen L.
Bledsoe, Karen E. 1962- *167*
   Earlier sketch in SATA *108*
Bledsoe, Karen Elizabeth
   See Bledsoe, Karen E.
Bledsoe, Lucy Jane 1957- *162*
   Earlier sketch in SATA *97*
Bleeker, Sonia
   See Zim, Sonia Bleeker
Blegen, Daniel M. 1950- *92*
Blegvad, Erik 1923- *132*
   Earlier sketches in SATA *14, 66*
Blegvad, Lenore 1926- *176*
   Earlier sketches in SATA *14, 66*
Bleiman, Andrew *237*
Blessing, Charlotte *223*
Bley, Anette 1967- *188*
Blish, James 1921-1975 .... *66*
Blish, James Benjamin
   See Blish, James
Blishen, Edward (William) 1920-1996 .... *66*
   Obituary *93*
   Earlier sketch in SATA *8*
Bliss, Corinne Demas
   See Demas, Corinne
Bliss, Frederick
   See Card, Orson Scott
Bliss, Gillian
   See Paton Walsh, Jill
Bliss, Harry 1964- *196*
   Earlier sketch in SATA *156*
Bliss, Reginald
   See Wells, H. G.
Bliss, Ronald G(ene) 1942- *12*
Blitt, Barry *187*
Bliven, Bruce, Jr. 1916-2002 .... *2*
Blixen, Karen 1885-1962 .... *44*
Blizzard, Gladys S. (?)-1992 .... *79*

Blobaum, Cindy 1966- *123*
Bloch, Lucienne 1909-1999 .... *10*
Bloch, Marie Halun 1910-1998 .... *6*
   See also SAAS *9*
Bloch, Robert (Albert) 1917-1994 .... *12*
   Obituary *82*
Bloch, Serge 1956- *213*
Blochman, Lawrence G(oldtree)
   1900-1975 .... *22*
Block, Francesca Lia 1962- *213*
   Earlier sketches in SATA *80, 116, 158*
   See also CLR *116*
   See also SAAS *21*
Block, Irvin 1917- *12*
Blomgren, Jennifer (Alice) 1954- *136*
Blonder, Terry Joyce
   See Golson, Terry
Blood, Charles Lewis 1929- *28*
Bloom, Barbara Lee 1943- *146*
Bloom, Freddy 1914-2000 .... *37*
   Obituary *121*
Bloom, Lloyd 1947- *108*
   Brief entry *43*
Bloom, Suzanne 1950- *232*
   Earlier sketch in SATA *172*
Bloomfield, Michaela 1966- *70*
Bloor, Edward 1950- *201*
   Earlier sketches in SATA *98, 155*
Bloor, Edward William
   See Bloor, Edward
Blos, Joan W. 1928- *153*
   Autobiography Feature *153*
   Brief entry *27*
   Earlier sketches in SATA *33, 69, 109*
   See also CLR *18*
   See also SAAS *11*
Blos, Joan Winsor
   See Blos, Joan W.
Bloss, Josie 1981- *232*
Blough, Glenn O(rlando) 1907-1995 .... *1*
Blue, Rose 1931- *166*
   Autobiography Feature *117*
   Earlier sketches in SATA *5, 91, 93*
   See also SAAS *24*
Blue, Zachary
   See Stine, R.L.
Bluemle, Elizabeth *209*
Bluggage, Oranthy
   See Alcott, Louisa May
Blumberg, Leda 1956- *59*
Blumberg, Rhoda 1917- *123*
   Earlier sketches in SATA *35, 70*
   See also CLR *21*
Blume, Judy 1938- *195*
   Earlier sketches in SATA *2, 31, 79, 142*
   See also CLR *69*
Blume, Judy Sussman
   See Blume, Judy
Blume, Lesley M.M. 1975- *180*
Blumenthal, Deborah *204*
   Earlier sketch in SATA *161*
Blumenthal, Gertrude 1907-1971
   Obituary *27*
Blumenthal, Shirley 1943- *46*
Blutig, Eduard
   See Gorey, Edward (St. John)
Bly, Janet 1945- *43*
Bly, Janet Chester
   See Bly, Janet
Bly, Stephen A(rthur) 1944- *116*
   Earlier sketch in SATA *43*
Blyler, Allison Lee 1966- *74*
Blythe, Gary 1959- *185*
Blyton, Carey 1932-2002 .... *9*
   Obituary *138*
Blyton, Enid 1897-1968 .... *25*
   See also CLR *31*
Blyton, Enid Mary
   See Blyton, Enid
Bo, Ben
   See Richardson, V.A.

Boardman, Fon Wyman, Jr. 1911-2000 .... *6*
Boardman, Gwenn R.
   See Petersen, Gwenn Boardman
Boase, Susan *226*
Boase, Wendy 1944-1999 .... *28*
   Obituary *110*
Boatner, Mark Mayo III 1921- *29*
Bobbe, Dorothie de Bear 1905-1975 .... *1*
   Obituary *25*
Bober, Natalie S. 1930- *134*
   Earlier sketch in SATA *87*
   See also SAAS *23*
Bobette, Bibo
   See Gugliotta, Bobette
Bobri, Vladimir V. 1898-1986 .... *47*
   Brief entry *32*
Bobritsky, Vladimir
   See Bobri, Vladimir V.
Bochak, Grayce 1956- *76*
Bock, Hal
   See Bock, Harold I.
Bock, Harold I. 1939- *10*
Bock, William Sauts Netamux'we 1939- *14*
Bodanis, David *179*
Bode, Janet 1943-1999 .... *96*
   Obituary *118*
   Earlier sketch in SATA *60*
Bode, N.E.
   See Baggott, Julianna
Bodecker, N(iels) M(ogens) 1922-1988 .... *73*
   Obituary *54*
   Earlier sketch in SATA *8*
Bodeen, S. A. 1965- *158*
   Earlier sketch in SATA *114*
Boden, Hilda
   See Bodenham, Hilda Morris
Bodenham, Hilda Morris 1901- *13*
Bodett, Thomas Edward 1955- *70*
Bodett, Tom
   See Bodett, Thomas Edward
Bodie, Idella F(allaw) 1925- *89*
   Earlier sketch in SATA *12*
Bodker, Cecil
   See Bodker, Cecil
Bodker, Cecil 1927- *133*
   Earlier sketch in SATA *14*
   See also CLR *23*
Bodsworth, (Charles) Fred(erick) 1918- *27*
Boeckman, Charles 1920- *12*
Boegehold, Betty (Doyle) 1913-1985
   Obituary *42*
Boelts, Maribeth 1964- *200*
   Earlier sketches in SATA *78, 163*
Boerst, William J. 1939- *170*
   Earlier sketch in SATA *121*
Boesch, Mark J(oseph) 1917- *12*
Boesen, Victor 1908- *16*
Bogacki, Tomek 1950- *214*
   Earlier sketch in SATA *138*
Bogaerts, Gert 1965- *80*
Bogan, Paulette 1960- *201*
   Earlier sketch in SATA *129*
Bogart, Jo Ellen 1945- *222*
   Earlier sketch in SATA *92*
   See also CLR *59*
Boggs, Ralph Steele 1901-1994 .... *7*
Bograd, Larry 1953- *89*
   Earlier sketch in SATA *33*
   See also SAAS *21*
Bogue, Gary 1938- *195*
Bogue, Gary L.
   See Bogue, Gary
Bohdal, Susi 1951- *101*
   Earlier sketch in SATA *22*
Bohlen, Nina 1931- *58*
Bohlmeijer, Arno 1956- *94*
Bohner, Charles (Henry) 1927- *62*
Bohnhoff, Maya Kaathryn 1954- *88*
Boie, Kirsten 1950- *221*
Boiger, Alexandra *178*
Boissard, Janine 1932- *59*

Bojunga, Lygia
    See Nunes, Lygia Bojunga
Bojunga-Nunes, Lygia
    See Nunes, Lygia Bojunga
Bok, Arthur
    See Bok, Chip
Bok, Chip 1952- 205
Bolam, Emily 1969- 206
Boland, Janice 98
Bolden, Tonya 1959- 227
    Earlier sketches in SATA *79, 138, 188*
Bolden, Tonya Wilyce
    See Bolden, Tonya
Boles, Paul Darcy 1916-1984 9
    Obituary 38
Bolger, Kevin 233
Bolian, Polly 1925- 4
Bollen, Roger 1941(?)- 83
    Brief entry 29
Bolliger, Max 1929- 7
Bollinger, Max 1929- 167
Bollinger, Peter 172
Bolognese, Don(ald Alan) 1934- 129
    Earlier sketches in SATA *24, 71*
Bolognese, Elaine 1933- 23
Bolotin, Norman (Phillip) 1951- 93
Bolton, Carole 1926- 6
Bolton, Elizabeth
    See St. John, Nicole
Bolton, Evelyn
    See Bunting, Eve
Bonar, Veronica
    See Bailey, Donna (Veronica Anne)
Bond, B. J.
    See Heneghan, James
Bond, Bruce 1939- 61
Bond, Felicia 1954- 219
    Earlier sketches in SATA *49, 126*
Bond, Gladys Baker 1912- 14
Bond, Higgins 1951- 220
    Earlier sketches in SATA *83, 177*
Bond, J. Harvey
    See Winterbotham, R(ussell) R(obert)
Bond, (Thomas) Michael 1926- 157
    Earlier sketches in SATA *6, 58*
    See also CLR *95*
    See also SAAS *3*
Bond, Nancy 1945- 159
    Autobiography Feature 159
    Earlier sketches in SATA *22, 82*
    See also CLR *11*
    See also SAAS *13*
Bond, Nancy Barbara
    See Bond, Nancy
Bond, Rebecca 1972- 214
    Earlier sketch in SATA *130*
Bond, Ruskin 1934- 87
    Earlier sketch in SATA *14*
    See also CLR *171*
Bondie, J. D.
    See Cunningham, Chet
Bondoux, Anne-Laure 1971- 175
Bone, Ian 1956- 158
    Earlier sketch in SATA *117*
Bone, J. 230
Bone, Jason
    See Bone, J.
Bonehill, Captain Ralph
    See Stratemeyer, Edward L.
Bonestell, Chesley 1888-1986
    Obituary 48
Bonham, Barbara Thomas 1926- 7
Bonham, Frank 1914-1989 49
    Obituary 62
    Earlier sketch in SATA *1*
    See also SAAS *3*
Boniface, William 1963- 182
    Earlier sketch in SATA *102*
Bonino, Louise
    See Williams, Louise Bonino
Bonk, John J. 189

Bonn, Pat
    See Bonn, Patricia Carolyn
Bonn, Patricia Carolyn 1948- 43
Bonner, Hannah 197
Bonner, Mary Graham 1890-1974 19
Bonner, Mike 1951- 121
Bonners, Susan 1947- 85
    Brief entry 48
Bonnet, Rosalinde 1978- 226
Bonnett-Rampersaud, Louise 173
Bonning, Tony 1948- 169
Bonsall, Crosby Barbara (Newell)
    1921-1995 23
    Obituary 84
Bonsall, Joseph S. 1948- 119
Bonsignore, Joan 1959- 140
Bontemps, Arna 1902-1973 44
    Obituary 24
    Earlier sketch in SATA *2*
    See also CLR *6*
Bontemps, Arnaud Wendell
    See Bontemps, Arna
Bonzon, Paul-Jacques 1908-1978 22
Boock, Paula 1964- 134
Booher, Dianna Daniels 1948- 33
Book, Rick 1949- 119
Book, Rita
    See Holub, Joan
Bookman, Charlotte
    See Zolotow, Charlotte
Boon, Debbie 1960- 103
Boon, Emilie (Laetitia) 1958- 86
Boone, Charles Eugene
    See Boone, Pat
Boone, Pat 1934- 7
Booraem, Ellen 211
Boorman, Linda 1940- 46
Boorman, Linda Kay
    See Boorman, Linda
Boorstin, Daniel J(oseph) 1914-2004 52
Boos, Ben 1971- 206
Booth, Coe 187
Booth, Ernest Sheldon 1915-1984 43
Booth, George 1926- 191
Booth, Graham (Charles) 1935- 37
Bootman, Colin 159
Borden, Louise 1949- 190
    Autobiography Feature 141
    Earlier sketches in SATA *68, 104, 141*
Bordier, Georgette 1924- 16
Borgman, James
    See Borgman, Jim
Borgman, James Mark
    See Borgman, Jim
Borgman, Jim 1954- 122
Borgo, Lacy Finn 1972- 194
Boring, Mel 1939- 168
    Earlier sketch in SATA *35*
Borja, Corinne 1929- 22
Borja, Robert 1923- 22
Borland, Hal
    See Borland, Harold Glen
Borland, Harold Glen 1900-1978 5
    Obituary 24
Borland, Kathryn Kilby 1916- 16
Borlenghi, Patricia 1951- 79
Born, Adolf 1930- 49
Bornstein, Ruth Lercher
    See Bornstein-Lercher, Ruth
Bornstein-Lercher, Ruth 1927- 88
    Autobiography Feature 107
    Earlier sketch in SATA *14*
Borris, Albert 221
Borski, Lucia Merecka 18
Borten, Helen Jacobson 1930- 5
Bortolotti, Dan 1969- 157
Borton, Elizabeth
    See Trevino, Elizabeth B(orton) de
Borton, Lady 1942- 98
Borton de Trevino, Elizabeth
    See Trevino, Elizabeth B(orton) de

Bortstein, Larry 1942-2010 16
Bortz, Alfred B(enjamin) 1944- 139
    Earlier sketch in SATA *74*
Bortz, Fred
    See Bortz, Alfred B(enjamin)
Bosch, Pseudonymous 199
Bosco, Jack
    See Holliday, Joseph
Bose, Mitali
    See Perkins, Mitali
Boshell, Gordon 1908-1991 15
Boshinski, Blanche 1922- 10
Bosman, Paul 1929- 107
Bosse, Malcolm (Joseph, Jr.) 1926-2002 136
    Earlier sketch in SATA *35*
Bosserman, Charles Phillip
    See Bosserman, Phillip
Bosserman, Phillip 1931- 84
Bossley, Michele Martin 1969- 219
Bossom, Naomi 1933- 35
Bostock, Mike 1962- 114
Boston, L(ucy) M(aria Wood) 1892-1990 19
    Obituary 64
    See also CLR *3*
Bostrom, Kathleen (Susan) Long 1954- 139
Bostrom, Kathy
    See Bostrom, Kathleen (Susan) Long
Boswell, Addie 208
Boswell, Addie Kay
    See Boswell, Addie
Bosworth, J. Allan 1925- 19
Bothwell, Jean (?)-1977 2
Botkin, B(enjamin) A(lbert) 1901-1975 40
Botsford, Ward 1927-2004 66
Botting, Douglas (Scott) 1934- 43
Bottner, Barbara 1943- 232
    Autobiography Feature 121
    Earlier sketches in SATA *14, 93, 170*
    See also SAAS *26*
Bottone, Frank G., Jr. 1969- 141
Bouchard, David 1952- 213
    Earlier sketch in SATA *117*
Boucher, (Clarence) Carter 1954- 129
Boudelang, Bob
    See Pell, Ed(ward)
Boughton, Richard 1954- 75
Boulet, Susan Seddon 1941- 50
Boulle, Pierre 1912-1994 22
    Obituary 78
Boulle, Pierre Francois Marie-Louis
    See Boulle, Pierre
Boulton, Jane 1921- 91
Bouma, Paddy 1947- 128
Bour, Daniele 1939- 62
Bourbonniere, Sylvie 1966- 182
Bourdon, David 1934-1998 46
Bourgeois, Paulette 1951- 153
Bourne, Lesley
    See Marshall, Evelyn
Bourne, Miriam Anne 1931-1989 16
    Obituary 63
Boutavant, Marc 1970- 200
Boutet de Monvel, (Louis) M(aurice)
    1850(?)-1913 30
    See also CLR *32*
Bouwman, Heather M.
    See Bouwman, H.M.
Bouwman, H.M. 209
Bova, Ben 1932- 133
    Earlier sketches in SATA *6, 68*
    See also CLR *96*
Bova, Benjamin William
    See Bova, Ben
Bovaird, Anne E(lizabeth) 1960- 90
Bow, Erin 1972- 237
Bow, Patricia 1946- 168
Bowden, Joan Chase 1925- 51
    Brief entry 38
Bowe, Julie 1962- 194
Bowen, Alexandria Russell 97

Bowen, Andy Russell
  See Bowen, Alexandria Russell
Bowen, Anne 1952- 202
  Earlier sketch in SATA 170
Bowen, Betty Morgan
  See West, Betty
Bowen, Catherine (Shober) Drinker
  1897-1973 7
Bowen, David
  See Bowen, Joshua David
Bowen, Fred 1953- 233
  Earlier sketch in SATA 136
Bowen, Joshua David 1930- 22
Bowen, Rhys
  See Quin-Harkin, Janet
Bowen, Robert Sydney 1900-1977 52
  Obituary 21
Bowermaster, Jon 1954- 135
  Earlier sketch in SATA 77
Bowers, Richard J.
  See Bowers, Rick
Bowers, Rick 1952- 227
Bowers, Terrell L. 1945- 101
Bowers, Terry
  See Bowers, Terrell L.
Bowers, Tim 218
  Earlier sketch in SATA 185
Bowie, C. W.
  See Old, Wendie C(orbin)
  and Wirths, Claudine (Turner) G(ibson)
Bowie, Jim
  See Norwood, Victor G(eorge) C(harles)
  and Stratemeyer, Edward L.
Bowkett, Stephen 1953- 67
Bowler, Jan Brett
  See Brett, Jan
Bowler, Tim 1953- 209
  Earlier sketch in SATA 149
Bowman, Catherine
  See Smith, Cat Bowman
Bowman, Crystal 1951- 105
Bowman, James Cloyd 1880-1961 23
Bowman, John S(tewart) 1931- 16
Bowman, Kathleen (Gill) 1942- 52
  Brief entry 40
Bowman, Leslie
  See Bowman, Leslie W.
Bowman, Leslie W. 182
Bowsher, Melodie 195
Boxall, Ed 178
Boyce, Frank Cottrell 182
Boyce, George A(rthur) 1898- 19
Boyd, Candy Dawson 1946- 72
  See also CLR 50
Boyd, Pauline
  See Schock, Pauline
Boyd, Selma
  See Acuff, Selma Boyd
Boyd, Waldo T. 1918- 18
Boyden, Linda 1948- 143
Boyer, Allen B. 1963- 153
Boyer, Robert E(rnst) 1929- 22
Boyes, Vivien 1952- 106
Boyes, Vivien Elizabeth
  See Boyes, Vivien
Boyle, Ann (Peters) 1916- 10
Boyle, Bob 232
Boyle, Eleanor Vere (Gordon) 1825-1916 28
Boyle, Robert II
  See Boyle, Bob
Boyle, Robert H. 1928- 65
Boylston, Helen Dore 1895-1984 23
  Obituary 39
Boyne, John 1971- 181
Boynton, Sandra (Keith) 1953- 152
  Brief entry 38
  Earlier sketches in SATA 57, 107
  See also CLR 105
Boz
  See Dickens, Charles
Bozarth, Jan 227

Braasch, Gary 201
Bracegirdle, Paul
  See Bracegirdle, P.J.
Bracegirdle, P.J. 236
Bracken, Alexandra 1987- 233
Bracken, Charles
  See Pellowski, Michael (Joseph)
Brackers de Hugo, Pierre 1960- 115
Brackett, Dolli Tingle 1911-1993 137
Brackett, Virginia 1950- 166
  Earlier sketch in SATA 121
Brackett, Virginia Roberts Meredith
  See Brackett, Virginia
Bradbury, Bianca (Ryley) 1908-1982 56
  Earlier sketch in SATA 3
Bradbury, Edward P.
  See Moorcock, Michael
Bradbury, Ray 1920- 123
  Earlier sketches in SATA 11, 64
Bradbury, Ray Douglas
  See Bradbury, Ray
Bradby, Marie 161
Bradfield, Carl 1942- 91
Bradford, Ann (Liddell) 1917- 56
  Brief entry 38
Bradford, Barbara Taylor 1933- 66
Bradford, Chris 1974- 215
Bradford, Emma
  See Perrin, Pat
Bradford, Karleen 1936- 96
  Earlier sketch in SATA 48
Bradford, Lois J(ean) 1936- 36
Bradford, Richard (Roark) 1932-2002 59
  Obituary 135
Bradford, Sally
  See Bradford, Barbara Taylor
Bradley, Duane
  See Sanborn, Duane
Bradley, Kimberly Brubaker 1967- 179
Bradley, Marion Zimmer 1930-1999 139
  Obituary 116
  Earlier sketch in SATA 90
  See also CLR 158
Bradley, Timothy J. 193
Bradley, Virginia 1912- 23
Bradley, Will
  See Strickland, Brad
Bradman, Tony 1954- 152
  Earlier sketch in SATA 81
Bradshaw, Gillian (Joan) 1949- 118
Bradshaw, Gillian 1956- 127
Bradshaw, Gillian Marucha
  See Bradshaw, Gillian
Bradstreet, T. J.
  See Thesman, Jean
Brady, Esther Wood 1905-1987 31
  Obituary 53
Brady, Irene 1943- 4
Brady, Kimberley S. 1953- 101
Brady, Kimberley Smith
  See Brady, Kimberley S.
Brady, Lillian 1902- 28
Braeuner, Shellie 1966(?)- 233
Bragdon, Elspeth MacDuffie 1897-1980 6
Bragdon, Lillian Jacot 24
Brager, Bruce L. 1949- 146
Bragg, Georgia 225
Bragg, Mabel Caroline 1870-1945 24
Bragg, Michael 1948- 46
Bragg, Ruth Gembicki 1943- 77
Brahm, Sumishta 1954- 58
Brailsford, Frances
  See Wosmek, Frances
Brainerd, John W(hiting) 1918- 65
Braithwaite, Althea 1940- 23
  Autobiography Feature 119
  See also SAAS 24
Brallier, Jess M. 1953- 226
Bram, Elizabeth 1948- 30
Bramsen, Carin 227
Bramsen, Kirsten 228

Brancato, Robin F. 1936- 97
  See also CLR 32
  See also SAAS 9
Brancato, Robin Fidler
  See Brancato, Robin F.
Branch, Muriel Miller 1943- 152
  Earlier sketch in SATA 94
Brand, Christianna
  See Lewis, Mary
Brand, Rebecca
  See Charnas, Suzy McKee
Brande, Robin 194
Brandel, Marc 1919- 71
Brandenberg, Alexa (Demetria) 1966- 97
Brandenberg, Aliki 1929- 157
  Earlier sketches in SATA 2, 35, 75, 113
  See also CLR 71
Brandenberg, Franz 1932- 75
  Earlier sketches in SATA 8, 35
Brandenburg, Jim 1945- 87
Brandhorst, Carl T(heodore) 1898-1988 23
Brandis, Marianne 1938- 149
  Earlier sketches in SATA 59, 96
Brandon, Brumsic, Jr. 1927- 9
Brandon, Curt
  See Bishop, Curtis (Kent)
Brandreth, Gyles 1948- 28
Brandreth, Gyles Daubeney
  See Brandreth, Gyles
Brandt, Catharine 1905-1997 40
Brandt, Keith
  See Sabin, Louis
Brandt, Sue R(eading) 1916- 59
Branfield, John (Charles) 1931- 11
Branford, Henrietta 1946-1999 106
Branley, Franklyn M(ansfield) 1915-2002 .. 136
  Earlier sketches in SATA 4, 68
  See also CLR 13
  See also SAAS 16
Brannen, Sarah S. 202
Branscum, Robbie (Tilley) 1937-1997 72
  Obituary 96
  Earlier sketch in SATA 23
  See also SAAS 17
Bransom, (John) Paul 1885-1979 43
Brashares, Ann 1967- 188
  Earlier sketch in SATA 145
  See also CLR 113
Brassard, France 1963- 186
Braswell, E.J.
  See Lynn, Tracy
Braswell, Elizabeth J.
  See Lynn, Tracy
Braswell, Liz
  See Lynn, Tracy
Bratton, Helen 1899-1986 4
Bratun, Katy 1950- 160
  Earlier sketch in SATA 83
Braude, Michael 1936- 23
Braun, Lilian Jackson 1916(?)-2011 109
Brautigan, Richard 1935-1984 56
Brautigan, Richard Gary
  See Brautigan, Richard
Bray, Libba 1964- 203
  Earlier sketch in SATA 159
Bray, Martha E.
  See Bray, Libba
Braymer, Marjorie Elizabeth 1911-1988 6
Brazil, Angela 1869(?)-1947
  See CLR 157
Breathed, Berke 1957- 161
  Earlier sketch in SATA 86
  See Breathed, Berkeley
Breathed, Berkeley 229
  See Breathed, Berke
Breathed, Guy Berkeley
  See Breathed, Berke
Brecht, Edith 1895-1975 6
  Obituary 25
Breck, Vivian
  See Breckenfeld, Vivian Gurney

Breckenfeld, Vivian Gurney 1895-1992 .... *1*
Breda, Tjalmar
    See DeJong, David C(ornel)
Bredeson, Carmen 1944- *163*
    Earlier sketch in SATA *98*
Breen, M.E. *216*
Breen, Molly
    See Breen, M.E.
Breen, Steve 1970- *186*
Breinburg, Petronella 1927- *11*
    See also CLR *31*
Breisky, William J(ohn) 1928- *22*
Brenaman, Miriam *172*
Brenna, Beverley 1962- *226*
Brennan, Caitlin
    See Tarr, Judith
Brennan, Gale (Patrick) 1927- *64*
    Brief entry *53*
Brennan, Herbie 1940- *214*
    Autobiography Feature *214*
    Earlier sketches in SATA *140, 183*
Brennan, J. H.
    See Brennan, Herbie
Brennan, James Herbert
    See Brennan, Herbie
Brennan, Jan
    See Brennan, Herbie
Brennan, Joseph Lomas 1903-2000 .... *6*
Brennan, Linda Crotta 1952- *130*
Brennan, Sarah Rees 1983- *221*
Brennan, Tim
    See Conroy, John Wesley
Brennan-Nelson, Denise *203*
Brenner, Anita 1905-1974 .... *56*
Brenner, Barbara (Johnes) 1925- *124*
    Earlier sketches in SATA *4, 42, 76*
    See also SAAS *14*
Brenner, Fred 1920- *36*
    Brief entry *34*
Brent, Hope 1935(?)-1984
    Obituary *39*
Brent, Stuart 1912-2010 .... *14*
Breskin, Jane
    See Zalben, Jane Breskin
Breslin, Theresa *128*
    Autobiography Feature *128*
    Earlier sketch in SATA *70*
Breslow, Maurice 1935- *72*
Breslow, Maurice A
    See Breslow, Maurice
Breslow, Susan 1951- *69*
Brett, Bernard 1925- *22*
Brett, Grace N(eff) 1900-1975 .... *23*
Brett, Jan 1949- *234*
    Earlier sketches in SATA *42, 71, 130, 171*
    See also CLR *27*
Brett, Jan Churchill
    See Brett, Jan
Brett Bowler, Jan
    See Brett, Jan
Brewer, Heather 1973- *196*
Brewer, James D. 1951- *108*
Brewer, Paul 1950- *230*
Brewer, Sally King 1947- *33*
Brewster, Benjamin
    See Folsom, Franklin (Brewster)
Brewster, Hugh 1950- *191*
    Earlier sketch in SATA *95*
Brewster, Patience 1952- *97*
Brewton, John E(dmund) 1898-1982 .... *5*
Brezenoff, Steve 1974- *236*
Brezenoff, Steven
    See Brezenoff, Steve
Breznak, Irene *218*
Brian, Dennis 1971- *229*
Brian, Janeen (Paulette) 1948- *141*
Briant, Ed *218*
    Earlier sketch in SATA *180*
Brick, John 1922-1973 .... *10*
Brickman, Robin D. 1954- *155*

Bride, Nadja
    See Nobisso, Josephine
Bridgers, Sue Ellen 1942- *90*
    Autobiography Feature *109*
    Earlier sketch in SATA *22*
    See also CLR *18*
    See also SAAS *1*
Bridges, Laurie
    See Bruck, Lorraine
Bridges, Ruby (Nell) 1954- *131*
Bridges, William (Andrew) 1901-1984 .... *5*
Bridwell, Norman (Ray) 1928- *138*
    Earlier sketches in SATA *4, 68*
    See also CLR *96*
Brier, Howard M(axwell) 1903-1969 .... *8*
Brierley, (Louise) 1958- *59*
Briggs, Katharine Mary 1898-1980 .... *101*
    Obituary *25*
Briggs, Peter 1921-1975 .... *39*
    Obituary *31*
Briggs, Raymond 1934- *184*
    Earlier sketches in SATA *23, 66, 131*
    See also CLR *168*
Briggs, Raymond Redvers
    See Briggs, Raymond
Bright, Paul 1949- *231*
    Earlier sketch in SATA *182*
Bright, Robert Sr.) 1902-1988 .... *63*
    Obituary *60*
    Earlier sketch in SATA *24*
Bright, Robert Douglas
    See Bright, Robert Sr.)
Bright, Sarah
    See Shine, Deborah
Brightfield, Richard 1927- *65*
    Brief entry *53*
Brightfield, Rick
    See Brightfield, Richard
Brighton, Catherine 1943- *206*
    Earlier sketches in SATA *65, 107*
Brill, Marlene Targ 1945- *124*
    Earlier sketch in SATA *77*
Brimberg, Stanlee 1947- *9*
Brimner, Larry Dane 1949- *232*
    Autobiography Feature *112*
    Earlier sketches in SATA *79, 170*
Brin, David 1950- *65*
Brin, Ruth Firestone 1921- *22*
Brinckloe, Julie 1950- *13*
Brinckloe, Julie Lorraine
    See Brinckloe, Julie
Brindel, June (Rachuy) 1919- *7*
Brindle, Max
    See Fleischman, Sid
Brindze, Ruth 1903-1984 .... *23*
Brink, Carol Ryrie 1895-1981 .... *100*
    Obituary *27*
    Earlier sketches in SATA *1, 31*
    See also CLR *149*
Brinsmead, H. F.
    See Brinsmead, H(esba) F(ay)
Brinsmead, H. F(ay)
    See Brinsmead, H(esba) F(ay)
Brinsmead, H(esba) F(ay) 1922- *78*
    Earlier sketch in SATA *18*
    See also CLR *47*
    See also SAAS *5*
Briquebec, John
    See Rowland-Entwistle, (Arthur) Theodore
    (Henry)
Brisbane, Henry R.
    See Ellis, Edward S.
Brisco, P. A.
    See Matthews, Patricia
Brisco, Patty
    See Matthews, Patricia
    and Matthews, Clayton (Hartley)
Briscoe, Jill (Pauline) 1935- *56*
    Brief entry *47*
Brisley, Joyce Lankester 1896-1978 .... *22*
    Obituary *84*

Brissenden, Connie
    See Brissenden, Constance
Brissenden, Constance 1947- *150*
Brisson, Pat 1951- *177*
    Autobiography Feature *133*
    Earlier sketches in SATA *67, 128, 133*
Bristow, David *237*
Bristow, David L.
    See Bristow, David
Britt, Albert 1874-1969
    Obituary *28*
Britt, Dell 1934- *1*
Brittain, Bill
    See Brittain, William
Brittain, C. Dale 1948- *82*
Brittain, William 1930- *76*
    Earlier sketch in SATA *36*
    See also SAAS *7*
Brittingham, Geoffrey (Hugh) 1959- *76*
Brittney, L. *209*
Britton, Kate
    See Stegeman, Janet Allais
Britton, Louisa
    See McGuire, Leslie (Sarah)
Britton, Rick 1952- *82*
Bro, Margueritte (Harmon) 1894-1977 .... *19*
    Obituary *27*
Broach, Elise 1963- *173*
Broadhead, Helen Cross 1913- *25*
Broadway, Hannah *208*
Brochmann, Elizabeth 1938- *41*
Brock, Betty (Carter) 1923-2003 .... *4*
    Obituary *150*
Brock, C(harles) E(dmund) 1870-1938 .... *42*
    Brief entry *32*
Brock, Delia
    See Ephron, Delia
Brock, Emma L(illian) 1886-1974 .... *8*
Brock, H(enry) M(atthew) 1875-1960 .... *42*
Brockett, Eleanor Hall 1913-1967 .... *10*
Brockman, C(hristian) Frank 1902-1985 ...... *26*
Brockmeier, Kevin 1972- *176*
Broda, Ron 1954- *209*
Broderick, Dorothy M. 1929- *5*
Brodeur, Ruth Wallace
    See Wallace-Brodeur, Ruth
Brodie, Sally
    See Cavin, Ruth
Brodien-Jones, Chris
    See Brodien-Jones, Christine
Brodien-Jones, Christine 1950- *233*
Brodsky, Beverly
    See McDermott, Beverly Brodsky
Brody, Wendy
    See Staub, Wendy Corsi
Broekel, Rainer Lothar
    See Broekel, Ray
Broekel, Ray 1923- *38*
Broekstra, Lorette 1964- *189*
    Earlier sketch in SATA *124*
Brogden, Sherryl
    See Jordan, Sherryl
Broger, Achim
    See Broger, Achim
Broger, Achim 1944- *31*
Broida, Marian *154*
Brokamp, Marilyn 1920- *10*
Broman, Fred
    See Moseley, James W(illett)
Bromely, Anne C. 1950- *234*
Bromhall, Winifred *26*
Brommer, Gerald F(rederick) 1927- *28*
Brondfield, Jerome 1913-1998 .... *22*
Brondfield, Jerry
    See Brondfield, Jerome
Bronner, Stephen Eric 1949- *101*
Bronowski, Jacob 1908-1974 .... *55*
Bronson, Alice
    See Watkins, Dawn L.
Bronson, Linda *203*

Bronson, Lynn
  See Lampman, Evelyn Sibley
Bronson, Wilfrid Swancourt 1894-1985
  Obituary *43*
Brook, Judith (Penelope) 1926- *59*
  Brief entry *51*
Brook, Judy
  See Brook, Judith (Penelope)
Brooke, L(eonard) Leslie 1862-1940 .... *17*
  See also CLR 20
Brooke, William J. 1946- *139*
Brooke-Haven, P.
  See Wodehouse, P. G.
Brooker, Kyrsten *199*
Brookins, Dana 1931- *28*
Brooks, Anita
  See Abramovitz, Anita (Zeltner Brooks)
Brooks, Bill 1939- *59*
Brooks, Bruce 1950- *112*
  Brief entry *53*
  Earlier sketch in SATA 72
  See also CLR 25
Brooks, Caryl 1924- *84*
Brooks, Charlotte K(endrick) 1918-1998 ..... *24*
  Obituary *112*
Brooks, Erik 1972- *236*
  Earlier sketches in SATA 152, 182
Brooks, George
  See Baum, L. Frank
Brooks, Gwendolyn 1917-2000 .... *6*
  Obituary *123*
  See also CLR 27
Brooks, Gwendolyn Elizabeth
  See Brooks, Gwendolyn
Brooks, Jerome 1931- *23*
Brooks, Kevin 1959- *197*
  Earlier sketch in SATA 150
Brooks, Kevin M.
  See Brooks, Kevin
Brooks, Laurie *209*
Brooks, Lester 1924- *7*
Brooks, Martha 1944- *134*
  Autobiography Feature *134*
  Earlier sketches in SATA 68, 121
Brooks, Maurice (Graham) 1900- *45*
Brooks, Polly Schoyer 1912- *12*
Brooks, Ron 1948- *212*
  Brief entry *33*
  Earlier sketch in SATA 94
Brooks, Ronald George
  See Brooks, Ron
Brooks, Terry 1944- *60*
Brooks, Walter R(ollin) 1886-1958 .... *17*
Brooks-Hill, Helen (Mason) 1908-1994 .... *59*
Broome, Errol 1937- *158*
  Earlier sketch in SATA 105
Brophy, Nannette 1963- *73*
Brosnan, James Patrick 1929- *14*
Brosnan, Jim
  See Brosnan, James Patrick
Brostoff, Anita 1931- *132*
Brothers Grimm
  See Grimm, Jacob Ludwig Karl
  and Grimm, Wilhelm Karl
Brothers Hildebrandt, The
  See Hildebrandt, Greg
  and Hildebrandt, Tim
Broun, Emily
  See Sterne, Emma Gelders
Brouwer, S. W.
  See Brouwer, Sigmund (W.)
Brouwer, Sigmund (W.) 1959- *109*
Brow, Thea 1934- *60*
Brower, Millicent *8*
Brower, Pauline 1929- *22*
Browin, Frances Williams 1898-1986 .... *5*
Brown, Alan
  See Brown, Alan James
Brown, Alan James 1947- *232*
Brown, Alexis
  See Baumann, Amy Beeching

Brown, Anne Ensign 1937- *61*
Brown, Beverly Swerdlow *97*
Brown, Bill
  See Brown, William L(ouis)
Brown, Billye Walker
  See Cutchen, Billye Walker
Brown, Bob
  See Brown, Robert Joseph
Brown, Buck 1936- *45*
Brown, Calef *217*
  Earlier sketch in SATA 179
Brown, Cassie 1919-1986 .... *55*
Brown, Charlotte Lewis *181*
Brown, Conrad 1922- *31*
Brown, Craig 1947- *224*
Brown, Craig 1947- *224*
  Earlier sketch in SATA 73
Brown, Craig McFarland
  See Brown, Craig
Brown, David
  See Brown, David A(lan)
  and Myller, Rolf
Brown, Dee 1908-2002 .... *110*
  Obituary *141*
  Earlier sketch in SATA 5
Brown, Dee Alexander
  See Brown, Dee
Brown, Don 1949- *200*
  Earlier sketch in SATA 172
Brown, Drew T. III 1955- *83*
Brown, Drollene P. 1939- *53*
Brown, Elbrite *198*
Brown, Eleanor Frances 1908-1987 .... *3*
Brown, Elizabeth Ferguson 1937- *153*
Brown, Elizabeth M(yers) 1915- *43*
Brown, Fern G. 1918- *34*
Brown, (Robert) Fletch 1923- *42*
Brown, Fornan 1901-1996 .... *71*
  Obituary *88*
Brown, George Earl 1883-1964 .... *11*
Brown, George Mackay 1921-1996 .... *35*
Brown, Irene Bennett 1932- *3*
Brown, Irving
  See Adams, William Taylor
Brown, Ivor (John Carnegie) 1891-1974 .... *5*
  Obituary *26*
Brown, Jane Clark 1930- *81*
Brown, Janet Mitsui *87*
Brown, Jennifer 1972- *227*
Brown, Jo 1964- *170*
Brown, Joanne 1933- *147*
Brown, Joe David 1915-1976 .... *44*
Brown, Joseph E(dward) 1929- *59*
  Brief entry *51*
Brown, Judith Gwyn 1933- *20*
Brown, Kathryn 1955- *168*
  Earlier sketch in SATA 98
Brown, Kathy
  See Brown, Kathryn
Brown, Ken (James) *129*
Brown, Kevin 1960- *101*
Brown, Laurene Krasny 1945- *99*
  Earlier sketch in SATA 54
Brown, Laurie Krasny
  See Brown, Laurene Krasny
Brown, Leo *225*
Brown, Lisa *234*
Brown, Lloyd Arnold 1907-1966 .... *36*
Brown, Mahlon A.
  See Ellis, Edward S.
Brown, Marc (Tolon) 1946- *145*
  Earlier sketches in SATA 10, 53, 80
  See also CLR 29
Brown, Marcia (Joan) 1918- *47*
  Earlier sketch in SATA 7
  See also CLR 12
Brown, Margaret Wise 1910-1952 .... *100*
  See also YABC 2
  See also CLR 107
Brown, Margery (Wheeler) *78*
  Earlier sketch in SATA 5

Brown, Marion Marsh 1908-2001 .... *6*
Brown, Monica 1969- *233*
Brown, Myra Berry 1918- *6*
Brown, Palmer 1919- *36*
Brown, Pamela (Beatrice) 1924-1989 .... *5*
  Obituary *61*
Brown, Paul 1942- *221*
Brown, Peter 1979- *178*
Brown, Rachel W.N. 1947- *203*
Brown, Reeve Lindbergh
  See Lindbergh, Reeve
Brown, Richard
  See Brown, Rick
Brown, Richard E.
  See Brown, Rick
Brown, Rick 1946- *226*
  Earlier sketch in SATA 61
Brown, Robert Joseph 1907-1989 .... *14*
Brown, Rod 1961- *232*
Brown, Roderick (Langmere) Haig-
  See Haig-Brown, Roderick (Langmere)
Brown, Rosalie
  See Moore, Rosalie (Gertrude)
Brown, Roswell
  See Webb, Jean Francis (III)
Brown, Roy (Frederick) 1921-1982 .... *51*
  Obituary *39*
Brown, Ruth 1941- *170*
  Earlier sketch in SATA 105
Brown, Scott 1971- *134*
Brown, Sue Ellen 1954- *81*
Brown, Tameka Fryer *235*
Brown, Tricia 1954- *114*
Brown, Vinson 1912-1991 .... *19*
Brown, Walter R(eed) 1929- *19*
Brown, Will
  See Ainsworth, William Harrison
Brown, William L(ouis) 1910-1964 .... *5*
Browne, Anthony 1946- *163*
  Brief entry *44*
  Earlier sketches in SATA 45, 61, 105
  See also CLR 156
Browne, Anthony Edward Tudor
  See Browne, Anthony
Browne, Dik
  See Browne, Richard Arthur Allen
Browne, Hablot Knight 1815-1882 .... *21*
Browne, Matthew
  See Rands, William Brighty
Browne, Nicki M.
  See Browne, N.M.
Browne, Nicky Matthews
  See Browne, N.M.
Browne, N.M. 1960- *167*
Browne, Richard Arthur Allen 1917-1989 ... *67*
  Brief entry *38*
Browne, Vee F. 1956- *214*
  Earlier sketch in SATA 90
Browning, Diane *233*
Browning, Robert 1812-1889
  See YABC 1
  See also CLR 97
Browning, Tom 1949- *226*
Brownjohn, Alan 1931- *6*
Brownlee, Walter 1930- *62*
Brownlie, Betty 1946- *159*
Brownlow, Kevin 1938- *65*
Brownlow, Mike *183*
Brownridge, William R(oy) 1932- *94*
Broyles, Anne 1953- *201*
Bruce, Dorita Fairlie 1885-1970
  Obituary *27*
Bruce, Harry 1934- *77*
Bruce, Mary 1927- *1*
Bruchac, Joseph III
  See Bruchac, Joseph
Bruchac, Joseph 1942- *228*
  Autobiography Feature *176*
  Earlier sketches in SATA 42, 89, 131, 176
  See also CLR 46

Bruchac, Margaret M.
See Bruchac, Marge
Bruchac, Marge 181
Bruck, Lorraine 1921- 55
Brief entry 46
Bruel, Nick 205
Earlier sketch in SATA 166
Bruel, Robert O. 1929-2002 189
Bruemmer, Fred 1929- 47
Brugman, Alyssa (F.) 1974- 152
Brumbeau, Jeff 1955- 157
Bruna, Dick 1927- 76
Brief entry 30
Earlier sketch in SATA 43
See also CLR 7
Brunelle, Lynn 233
Brunhoff, Jean de 1899-1937 24
See also CLR 116
Brunhoff, Laurent de 1925- 150
Earlier sketches in SATA 24, 71
See also CLR 116
Brunkus, Denise 204
Bruno, Elsa Knight 1935-2009 221
Brunskill, Elizabeth Ann Flatt
See Flatt, Lizann
Brush, Karen A(lexandra) 1960- 85
Brussel-Smith, Bernard 1914- 58
Brust, Steven 1955- 121
Earlier sketch in SATA 86
Brust, Steven Karl Zoltan
See Brust, Steven
Brustlein, Daniel 1904- 40
Brustlein, Janice Tworkov -2000 40
Obituary 126
Brutschy, Jennifer 1960- 84
Bryan, Ashley 1923- 178
Earlier sketches in SATA 31, 72, 132
See also CLR 66
Bryan, Ashley F.
See Bryan, Ashley
Bryan, Dorothy M. 1896(?)-1984
Obituary 39
Bryan, Jennifer 190
Bryan, Kathleen
See Tarr, Judith
Bryan, Sean 192
Bryant, Bernice (Morgan) 1908-1976 11
Bryant, Jen 1960- 218
Earlier sketches in SATA 94, 175
Bryant, Jennifer
See Bryant, Jen
Bryant, Jennifer Fisher
See Bryant, Jen
Bryant, Laura J. 176
Brychta, Alex 1956- 21
Brynie, Faith H. 1946- 113
Brynie, Faith Hickman
See Brynie, Faith H.
Bryson, Bernarda 1903-2004 9
Buba, Joy Flinsch 1904- 44
Buchan, Bryan 1945- 36
Buchan, John 1875-1940
See YABC 2
Buchan, Stuart 1942-1987
Obituary 54
Buchanan, Debby 1952- 82
Buchanan, Deborah Leevonne
See Buchanan, Debby
Buchanan, Jane 1956- 160
Buchanan, Lang
See Buchanan, Michael
Buchanan, Lang
See Lang, Diane
Buchanan, Michael 1955- 235
Buchanan, Michael David
See Buchanan, Michael
Buchanan, Paul 1959- 116
Buchanan, Sue 1939- 139
Buchheimer, Naomi Barnett
See Barnett, Naomi
Buchignani, Walter 1965- 84

Buchmann, Stephen L. 194
Buchwald, Art 1925-2007 10
Buchwald, Arthur
See Buchwald, Art
Buchwald, Emilie 1935- 7
Buck, Gisela 1941- 101
Buck, Lewis 1925- 18
Buck, Margaret Waring 1905-1997 3
Buck, Nola
See Godwin, Laura
Buck, Pearl S. 1892-1973 25
Earlier sketch in SATA 1
Buck, Pearl Sydenstricker
See Buck, Pearl S.
Buck, Siegfried 1941- 101
Buckalew, Clare B.
See Dunkle, Clare B.
Buckeridge, Anthony (Malcolm)
1912-2004 85
Earlier sketch in SATA 6
Buckholtz, Eileen (Garber) 1949- 54
Brief entry 47
Buckingham, Royce 1966- 210
Buckingham, Royce Scott
See Buckingham, Royce
Buckler, Ernest 1908-1984 47
Buckless, Andrea K. 1968- 117
Buckley, Helen E(lizabeth) 1918- 90
Earlier sketch in SATA 2
Buckley, James, Jr. 1963- 166
Earlier sketch in SATA 114
Buckley, Michael 229
Earlier sketch in SATA 177
Buckley, Susan 184
Buckley, Susan Washburn
See Buckley, Susan
Buckley-Archer, Linda 185
Buckmaster, Henrietta
See Stephens, Henrietta Henkle
Bucks, Brad
See Holub, Joan
Budd, E. S.
See Sirimarco, Elizabeth
Budd, Lillian (Peterson) 1897-1989 7
Budhos, Marina 236
Earlier sketch in SATA 173
Budhos, Marina Tamar
See Budhos, Marina
Buehler, Stephanie Jona 1956- 83
Buehner, Caralyn 1963- 219
Earlier sketches in SATA 104, 159
Buehner, Mark 1959- 221
Earlier sketches in SATA 104, 159
Buehr, Walter Franklin 1897-1971 3
Buell, Ellen Lewis
See Cash, Ellen Lewis Buell
Buell, Janet 1952- 185
Earlier sketch in SATA 106
Buergel, Paul-Hermann H. 1949- 83
Buettner, Dan 1960- 95
Buff, Conrad 1886-1975 19
Buff, Mary (E. Marsh) 1890-1970 19
Buffett, Jimmy 1946- 110
Earlier sketch in SATA 76
Buffie, Margaret 1945- 161
Earlier sketches in SATA 71, 107
See also CLR 39
Bugbee, Emma 1888(?)-1981
Obituary 29
Bugni, Alice 1951- 122
Bujold, Lois McMaster 1949- 136
Bulfinch, Thomas 1796-1867 35
Bulion, Leslie 1958- 209
Earlier sketch in SATA 161
Bull, Angela (Mary) 1936- 45
Bull, Emma 1954- 190
Autobiography Feature 103
Earlier sketch in SATA 99
Bull, Norman John 1916- 41
Bull, Peter (Cecil) 1912-1984
Obituary 39

Bull, Schuyler M. 1974- 138
Bulla, Clyde R. 1914-2007 139
Obituary 182
Earlier sketches in SATA 2, 41, 91
See also SAAS 6
Bullard, Lisa 1961- 142
Bullen, Alexandra 227
Buller, Jon 205
Bullock, Kathleen (Mary) 1946- 77
Bullock, Robert (D.) 1947- 92
Bulpin, (Barbara) Vicki 92
Bulwer-Lytton, Edward 1803-1873 23
Bulwer-Lytton, Edward George Earle Lytton
See Bulwer-Lytton, Edward
Bumstead, Kathleen Mary 1918-1987 53
Bundles, A'Lelia Perry 1952- 76
Bunge, Daniela 1973- 207
Bunin, Catherine 1967- 30
Bunin, Sherry 1925- 30
Bunkers, Suzanne L. 1950- 136
Bunting, A.E.
See Bunting, Eve
Bunting, Anne Evelyn
See Bunting, Eve
Bunting, Eve 1928- 235
Earlier sketches in SATA 18, 64, 110, 158,
196
See also CLR 82
Bunting, Glenn (Davison) 1957- 22
Bunyan, John 1628-1688
See CLR 124
Bupp, Walter
See Garrett, Randall
Burack, Sylvia K. 1916-2003 35
Obituary 143
Burbank, Addison (Buswell) 1895-1961 37
Burch, Joann J(ohansen) 75
Burch, Robert J(oseph) 1925- 74
Earlier sketch in SATA 1
See also CLR 63
Burchard, Peter Duncan 1921- 143
Earlier sketches in SATA 5, 74
See also SAAS 13
Burchard, S. H.
See Burchard, Sue
Burchard, Sue 1937- 22
Burchardt, Nellie 1921- 7
Burckhardt, Marc 1962- 196
Burden, Andrea 1969-2009 227
Burdett, Lois 117
Burdick, Eugene (Leonard) 1918-1965 22
Burford, Eleanor
See Hibbert, Eleanor Alice Burford
Burg, Ann E. 1954- 217
Burg, Shana 1968- 204
Burgan, Michael 1960- 167
Earlier sketch in SATA 118
Burger, Carl 1888-1967 9
Burgess, Ann Marie
See Gerson, Noel Bertram
Burgess, Barbara Hood 1926- 69
Burgess, Em
See Burgess, Mary Wyche
Burgess, (Frank) Gelett 1866-1951 32
Brief entry 30
Burgess, Mark 157
Burgess, Mary Wyche 1916- 18
Burgess, Melvin 1954- 198
Earlier sketches in SATA 96, 146
Burgess, Michael
See Gerson, Noel Bertram
Burgess, Robert F(orrest) 1927- 4
Burgess, Starling
See Tudor, Tasha
Burgess, Thornton Waldo 1874-1965 17
Burgess, Trevor
See Trevor, Elleston
Burgwyn, Mebane Holoman 1914-1992 7
Burke, David 1927- 46
Burke, Diana G.
See Gallagher, Diana G.

Burke, Diana Gallagher
  See Gallagher, Diana G.
Burke, Dianne O'Quinn 1940- 89
Burke, Janine 1952- 139
Burke, Jim 1973- 179
Burke, John
  See O'Connor, Richard
Burke, Katie 1953- 168
Burke, Patrick 1958- 114
Burke, Ralph
  See Garrett, Randall
  and Silverberg, Robert
Burkert, Nancy Ekholm 1933- 24
  See also SAAS 14
Burkett, D. Brent 194
Burke-Weiner, Kimberly 1962- 95
Burks, Brian 1955- 95
Burland, Brian (Berkeley) 1931- 34
Burland, C. A.
  See Burland, Cottie (Arthur)
Burland, Cottie (Arthur) 1905-1983 5
Burleigh, Robert 1936- 193
  Earlier sketches in SATA 55, 98, 146
Burlingame, (William) Roger 1889-1967 2
Burman, Alice Caddy 1896(?)-1977
  Obituary 24
Burman, Ben Lucien 1896-1984 6
  Obituary 40
Burn, Doris 1923- 1
Burn, Ted
  See Burn, Thomas E.
Burn, Thomas E. 1940- 150
Burnard, Damon 1963- 115
Burnett, Constance Buel 1893-1975 36
Burnett, Frances Eliza Hodgson
  See Burnett, Frances Hodgson
Burnett, Frances Hodgson 1849-1924 100
  See also YABC 2
  See also CLR 122
Burnett, Lindy 210
Burnett Bossi, Lisa 193
Burney, Anton
  See Hopkins, (Hector) Kenneth
Burnford, Sheila (Philip Cochrane Every)
  1918-1984 3
  Obituary 38
  See also CLR 2
Burnham, Gretchen
  See Sprague, Gretchen
Burnham, Nicole 1970- 161
Burnham, Niki
  See Burnham, Nicole
Burnham, Sophy 1936- 65
Burningham, John 1936- 225
  Earlier sketches in SATA 16, 59, 111, 160
  See also CLR 9
Burningham, Robin Yoko
  See Racoma, Robin Yoko
Burningham, Sarah O'Leary 216
Burns, Diane L. 1950- 81
  See also SAAS 24
Burns, Eloise Wilkin
  See Wilkin, Eloise
Burns, Florence M. 1905-1988 61
Burns, Khephra 1950- 92
Burns, Loree Griffin 193
Burns, Marilyn 1941- 96
  Brief entry 33
Burns, Olive Ann 1924-1990 65
Burns, Patrick 1968- 227
Burns, Paul C. 5
Burns, Ray
  See Burns, Raymond (Howard)
Burns, Raymond (Howard) 1924- 9
Burns, Theresa 1961- 84
Burns, T.R.
  See Rayburn, Tricia
Burns, William A. 1909-1999 5
Burr, Dan 1951- 65
Burr, Dan 1960- 219
Burr, Lonnie 1943- 47

Burrell, Roy E(ric) C(harles) 1923- 72
Burroughs, Edgar Rice 1875-1950 41
  See also CLR 157
Burroughs, Jean Mitchell 1908- 28
Burroughs, Polly 1925- 2
Burroway, Janet 1936- 23
Burroway, Janet Gay
  See Burroway, Janet
Burstein, Chaya M(alamud) 1923- 64
Burstein, Fred 1950- 83
Burstein, John 1949- 54
  Brief entry 40
Burstein, Stanley M.
  See Burstein, Stanley Mayer
Burstein, Stanley Mayer 1941- 175
Bursztynski, Sue 1953- 114
Burt, Jesse Clifton 1921-1976 46
  Obituary 20
Burt, Olive Woolley 1894-1981 4
Burtinshaw, Julie 185
Burton, Gennett 1945- 95
Burton, Hester (Wood-Hill) 1913-2000 74
  Earlier sketch in SATA 7
  See also CLR 1
  See also SAAS 8
Burton, Leslie
  See McGuire, Leslie (Sarah)
Burton, Marilee Robin 1950- 82
  Earlier sketch in SATA 46
Burton, Maurice 1898-1992 23
Burton, Rebecca 1970- 183
Burton, Robert (Wellesley) 1941- 22
Burton, Virginia Lee 1909-1968 100
  Earlier sketch in SATA 2
  See also CLR 11
Burton, William H(enry) 1890-1964 11
Busby, Ailie 192
Busby, Cylin 1970- 118
Busby, Edith (A. Lake) (?)-1964
  Obituary 29
Busby, John 1942- 209
Buscaglia, (Felice) Leo(nardo) 1924-1998 ... 65
Buscaglia, Leo F.
  See Buscaglia, (Felice) Leo(nardo)
Buscema, Stephanie 232
Busch, Phyllis S. 1909- 30
Bush, Anne Kelleher
  See Kelleher, Anne
Bush, Catherine 1961- 128
Bush, Jenna 1981- 208
Bush, Laura 1946- 208
Bushmiller, Ernest Paul 1905-1982 31
Bushmiller, Ernie
  See Bushmiller, Ernest Paul
Bushnell, Jack 1952- 86
Busoni, Rafaello 1900-1962 16
Buss, Helen M.
  See Clarke, Margaret
Busse, Sarah Martin 194
Busselle, Rebecca 1941- 80
Bustard, Anne 1951- 173
Butcher, Kristin 1951- 140
Butenko, Bohdan 1931- 90
Butler, Beverly Kathleen 1932- 7
Butler, Bill
  See Butler, William Vivian
  and Butler, Ernest Alton
  and Butler, William Huxford
Butler, Charles 1963- 175
  Earlier sketch in SATA 121
Butler, Charles Cadman
  See Butler, Charles
Butler, Dori Hillestad 1965- 207
  Earlier sketch in SATA 164
Butler, Dorothy 1925- 73
Butler, Geoff 1945- 94
Butler, John 1952- 225
Butler, M. Christina 1934- 224
  Earlier sketches in SATA 72, 170
Butler, Octavia 1947-2006 84
  See also CLR 65

Butler, Octavia E.
  See Butler, Octavia
Butler, Octavia Estelle
  See Butler, Octavia
Butler, Vivian
  See Butler, William Vivian
Butler, William
  See Butler, William Vivian
Butler, William Vivian 1927-1987 79
Butterfield, Moira 1960- 219
Butters, Dorothy Gilman
  See Gilman, Dorothy
Butterworth, Emma Macalik 1928- 43
Butterworth, Nick 1946- 149
  Earlier sketch in SATA 106
Butterworth, Oliver 1915-1990 1
  Obituary 66
Butterworth, W. E.
  See Griffin, W. E. B.
Butterworth, William E.
  See Griffin, W. E. B.
Butterworth, William Edmund III
  See Griffin, W. E. B.
Button, Lana 1968- 229
Butts, Ed 1951- 177
Butts, Edward P.
  See Butts, Ed
Butts, Ellen R. 1942- 93
Butts, Ellen Rubinstein
  See Butts, Ellen R.
Butzer, C. M. 1974- 212
Buxton, Ralph
  See Silverstein, Alvin
  and Silverstein, Virginia B.
Buzzeo, Toni 1951- 215
  Earlier sketch in SATA 135
Byalick, Marcia 1947- 141
  Earlier sketch in SATA 97
Byard, Carole (Marie) 1941- 57
Byars, Betsy 1928- 223
  Autobiography Feature 108
  Earlier sketches in SATA 4, 46, 80, 163
  See also CLR 72
  See also SAAS 1
Byars, Betsy Cromer
  See Byars, Betsy
Byfield, Barbara Ninde 1930-1988 8
Byman, Jeremy 1944- 129
Bynum, Janie 133
Byrd, Elizabeth 1912-1989 34
Byrd, Nicole
  See Zach, Cheryl (Byrd)
Byrd, Robert 1942- 226
  Earlier sketches in SATA 33, 112, 158
Byrd, Robert John
  See Byrd, Robert
Byrd, Tim 1964- 216
Byrne, Gayle 218
Byrne, Mary Gregg 1951- 162

C

C. 3. 3.
  See Wilde, Oscar
C. E. M.
  See Mastrangelo, Charles E(lmer)
Cabaniss, J(ames) Allen 1911-1997 5
Cabat, Erni 1914- 74
Cabban, Vanessa 1971- 176
Cable, Mary 1920- 9
Cabot, Meg 1967- 217
  Earlier sketches in SATA 127, 175
  See also CLR 85
Cabot, Meggin
  See Cabot, Meg
Cabot, Meggin Patricia
  See Cabot, Meg
Cabot, Patricia
  See Cabot, Meg

Cabral, O. M.
    See Cabral, Olga
Cabral, Olga 1909- 46
Cabrera, Cozbi A. 1963- 177
Cabrera, Jane 1968- 182
    Earlier sketches in SATA *103, 152*
Cabrera, Marcela 1966- 90
Caddy, Alice
    See Burman, Alice Caddy
Cade, Toni
    See Bambara, Toni Cade
Cadena, Beth 222
Cadmus and Harmonia
    See Buchan, John
Cadnum, Michael 1949- 225
    Earlier sketches in SATA *87, 121, 165*
    See also CLR *78*
Caduto, Michael J. 1955- 103
Cadwallader, Sharon 1936- 7
Cady, (Walter) Harrison 1877(?)-1970 19
Caffey, Donna (J.) 1954- 110
Cagle, Malcolm W(infield) 1918- 32
Cahn, Rhoda 1922- 37
Cahn, William 1912-1976 37
Cain, Arthur H(omer) 1913-1981 3
Cain, Christopher
    See Fleming, Thomas
Cain, Sheridan 1952- 186
Caine, Geoffrey
    See Walker, Robert W.
Caines, Jeannette (Franklin) 1938- 78
    Brief entry 43
    See also CLR *24*
Cairns, Trevor 1922- 14
Calabro, Marian 1954- 79
Caldecott, Moyra 1927- 22
Caldecott, Randolph (J.) 1846-1886 100
    Earlier sketch in SATA *17*
    See also CLR *110*
Calder, Charlotte 1952- 125
Calder, David 1932-1997 105
Calder, Lyn
    See Calmenson, Stephanie
Calder, Marie D(onais) 1948- 96
Calderone-Stewart, Lisa
    See Calderone-Stewart, Lisa-Marie
Calderone-Stewart, Lisa-Marie 1958- 123
Caldwell, Ben 1973- 230
Caldwell, Doreen (Mary) 1942- 71
Caldwell, John C(ope) 1913-1984 7
Caletti, Deb 1963- 221
    Earlier sketch in SATA *171*
Calhoun, B. B. 1961- 98
Calhoun, Chad
    See Barrett, Neal, Jr.
    and Cunningham, Chet
    and Goulart, Ron
Calhoun, Dia 1959- 183
    Earlier sketch in SATA *129*
Calhoun, Mary
    See Wilkins, Mary Huiskamp
Calhoun, T.B.
    See Bisson, Terry
Cali, Davide 1972- 190
Calif, Ruth 1922- 67
Calkhoven, Laurie 1959- 229
Calkins, Franklin
    See Stratemeyer, Edward L.
Call, Greg 197
Call, Hughie Florence 1890-1969 1
Callahan, Dorothy M. 1934- 39
    Brief entry 35
Callahan, Dorothy Monahan
    See Callahan, Dorothy M.
Callahan, Philip Serna 1923- 25
Callahan, Sean 1965- 222
Callan, Jamie 1954- 59
Callan, Jim 1951- 181
Callaway, Bernice (Anne) 1923- 48
Callaway, Kathy 1943- 36

Callen, Larry
    See Callen, Lawrence Willard, Jr.
Callen, Lawrence Willard, Jr. 1927- 19
Callen, Liz 1951- 231
Callery, Sean 233
Calley, Karin 1965- 92
Calmenson, Stephanie 1952- 211
    Brief entry 37
    Earlier sketches in SATA *51, 84, 139*
Calonita, Jen 216
Calvert, Elinor H.
    See Lasell, Elinor H.
Calvert, John
    See Leaf, (Wilbur) Munro
Calvert, Pam 1966- 205
Calvert, Patricia 1931- 132
    Earlier sketches in SATA *45, 69*
    See also SAAS *17*
Camburn, Carol A.
    See Camburn-Bracalente, Carol A.
Camburn-Bracalente, Carol A. 1962- 118
Cameron, Ann 1943- 129
    Earlier sketches in SATA *27, 89*
    See also SAAS *20*
Cameron, Edna M. 1905-1999 3
Cameron, Eleanor (Frances) 1912-1996 25
    Obituary 93
    Earlier sketch in SATA *1*
    See also CLR *72*
    See also SAAS *10*
Cameron, Elizabeth
    See Nowell, Elizabeth Cameron
Cameron, Elizabeth Jane 1910-1976 32
    Obituary 30
Cameron, Ian
    See Payne, Donald Gordon
Cameron, M(alcolm) G(ordon) Graham
    See Graham-Cameron, M(alcolm) G(ordon)
Cameron, M. Graham
    See Graham-Cameron, M(alcolm) G(ordon)
Cameron, Mike Graham
    See Graham-Cameron, M(alcolm) G(ordon)
Cameron, Natalie Russell
    See Russell, Natalie
Cameron, Polly 1928- 2
Cameron, Scott 1962- 84
Camp, Charles L. 1893-1975
    Obituary 31
Camp, Lindsay 1957- 133
Camp, Madeleine L'Engle
    See L'Engle, Madeleine
Camp, Walter (Chauncey) 1859-1925
    See YABC *1*
Campbell, (Elizabeth) Andrea 1963- 50
Campbell, Ann R. 1925- 11
Campbell, Bill 1960- 89
Campbell, Bruce
    See Epstein, Samuel
Campbell, Camilla 1905-1992 26
Campbell, Carole R. 1939- 125
Campbell, Hope 1925- 20
Campbell, Hugh 1930- 90
Campbell, Jane
    See Edwards, Jane Campbell
Campbell, Julie
    See Tatham, Julie Campbell
Campbell, Patricia J(ean) 1930- 45
Campbell, Patty
    See Campbell, Patricia J(ean)
Campbell, Peter A. 1948- 99
Campbell, R. W.
    See Campbell, Rosemae Wells
Campbell, Robin
    See Strachan, Ian
Campbell, Rod 1945- 98
    Brief entry 44
    Earlier sketch in SATA *51*
Campbell, Rosemae Wells 1909- 1
Campbell, Sarah C. 1966- 207
Camper, Cathy 1956- 170
Campion, Nardi Reeder 1917-2007 22

Campling, Elizabeth 1948- 53
Campos, Maria de Fatima 229
Campoy, F. Isabel 1946- 181
    Earlier sketch in SATA *143*
Camps, Luis 1928- 66
Canales, Viola 1957- 141
Candell, Victor 1903-1977
    Obituary 24
Canfield, Dorothea F.
    See Fisher, Dorothy (Frances) Canfield
Canfield, Dorothea Frances
    See Fisher, Dorothy (Frances) Canfield
Canfield, Dorothy
    See Fisher, Dorothy (Frances) Canfield
Canfield, Jack 1944- 164
Canfield, Jane White 1897-1984 32
    Obituary 38
Canfield, Muriel 1935- 94
Canga, C.B. 1976- 216
Canga, Chris
    See Canga, C.B.
Caniff, Milton 1907-1988
    Obituary 58
Caniff, Milton Arthur Paul
    See Caniff, Milton
Cann, Helen 1969- 179
    Earlier sketch in SATA *124*
Cann, Kate 1954- 152
    Earlier sketch in SATA *103*
Cannan, Joanna
    See Pullein-Thompson, Joanna Maxwell
Cannell, Jon 196
Cannell, Jonathan C.
    See Cannell, Jon
Cannon, A.E. 202
    Earlier sketches in SATA *93, 163*
Cannon, Ann Edwards
    See Cannon, A.E.
Cannon, Bettie (Waddell) 1922- 59
Cannon, Curt
    See Hunter, Evan
Cannon, Eileen E(mily) 1948- 119
Cannon, Frank
    See Mayhar, Ardath
Cannon, Janell 1957- 128
    Earlier sketch in SATA *78*
    See also CLR *120*
Cannon, Marian G. 1923- 85
Cannon, Taffy
    See Cannon, Eileen E(mily)
Cantone, AnnaLaura 182
Cantrell, Julie 1973- 217
Canusi, Jose
    See Barker, S. Omar
Canyon, Christopher 1966- 150
    Earlier sketch in SATA *104*
Caparo, Antonio
    See Caparo, Antonio Javier
Caparo, Antonio Javier 205
Capek, Michael 1947- 142
    Earlier sketch in SATA *96*
Capes, Bernard (Edward Joseph)
    1854-1918 116
Caple, Kathy 193
Caple, Laurie 1958- 201
Caplin, Alfred Gerald 1909-1979 61
    Obituary 21
Caponigro, John Paul 1965- 84
Capote, Truman 1924-1984 91
Capozzola, Michael 234
Capp, Al
    See Caplin, Alfred Gerald
Cappel, Constance 1936- 22
Cappetta, Cynthia 1949- 125
Cappo, Nan Willard 1955- 143
Capps, Benjamin (Franklin) 1922- 9
Cappy Dick
    See Cleveland, George
Captain Kangaroo
    See Keeshan, Robert J.

Captain Wheeler
 See Ellis, Edward S.
Captain Young of Yale
 See Stratemeyer, Edward L.
Capucilli, Alyssa Satin 1957- 203
 Earlier sketches in SATA 115, 163
Capucine
 See Mazille, Capucine
Carafoli, Marci
 See Balterman, Marcia Ridlon
Caraher, Kim(berley Elizabeth) 1961- 105
Caraker, Mary 1929- 74
Caras, Roger A(ndrew) 1928-2001 12
 Obituary 127
Caravantes, Peggy 1935- 140
Caraway, Caren 1939- 57
Carbone, Elisa 1954- 173
 Earlier sketches in SATA 81, 137
Carbone, Elisa Lynn
 See Carbone, Elisa
Carbonnier, Jeanne 1894-1974 3
 Obituary 34
Card, Orson Scott 1951- 127
 Earlier sketch in SATA 83
 See also CLR 116
Cardinale, Christopher 231
Cardon, Laurent 1962- 230
Care, Felicity
 See Coury, Louise Andree
Carew, Jan 1925- 51
 Brief entry 40
Carew, Jan Rynveld
 See Carew, Jan
Carey, Benedict 1960- 219
Carey, Bonnie
 See Marshall, Bonnie C.
Carey, Charles W., Jr. 1951- 170
Carey, Ernestine Gilbreth 1908-2006 2
 Obituary 177
Carey, Janet Lee 1954(?)- 225
 Earlier sketch in SATA 185
Carey, Lisa 110
Carey, M. V.
 See Carey, Mary V(irginia)
Carey, Mary V(irginia) 1925-1994 44
 Brief entry 39
Carey, Peter 1943- 94
Carey, Peter Philip
 See Carey, Peter
Carey, Valerie Scho 1949- 60
Carheden, Goorel Kristina
 See Naaslund, Goorel Kristina
Carigiet, Alois 1902-1985 24
 Obituary 47
 See also CLR 38
Carini, Edward 1923- 9
Carkeet, David 1946- 75
Carle, Eric 1929- 163
 Earlier sketches in SATA 4, 65, 120
 See also CLR 72
 See also SAAS 6
Carleton, Captain L. C.
 See Ellis, Edward S.
Carleton, Captain Latham C.
 See Ellis, Edward S.
Carleton, Latham C.
 See Ellis, Edward S.
Carley, V(an Ness) Royal 1906-1976
 Obituary 20
Carling, Amelia Lau 1949- 164
 Earlier sketch in SATA 119
Carlisle, Carolyn
 See Hawes, Louise
Carlisle, Clark
 See Holding, James (Clark Carlisle, Jr.)
Carlisle, Olga Andreyev 1930- 35
Carlock, Miriam
 See Eyerly, Jeannette
Carls, Claudia 1978- 198
Carlsen, G(eorge) Robert 1917- 30
Carlsen, Ruth C(hristoffer) 1918- 2

Carlson, Bernice Wells 1910- 8
Carlson, Christopher C. 202
Carlson, Dale (Bick) 1935- 1
Carlson, Daniel (Bick) 1960- 27
Carlson, Kirsten 1968- 192
Carlson, Kirsten M.
 See Carlson, Kirsten
Carlson, Laurie 1952- 173
 Earlier sketch in SATA 101
Carlson, Laurie Winn
 See Carlson, Laurie
Carlson, Melody 1956- 171
 Earlier sketch in SATA 113
Carlson, Nancy 1953- 213
 Brief entry 45
 Earlier sketches in SATA 56, 90, 144
Carlson, Nancy L.
 See Carlson, Nancy
Carlson, Natalie Savage 1906-1997 68
 Earlier sketch in SATA 2
 See also SAAS 4
Carlson, Susan Johnston 1953- 88
Carlson, Vada F. 1897- 16
Carlstrom, Nancy White 1948- 215
 Brief entry 48
 Earlier sketches in SATA 53, 92, 156
Carlton, Keith
 See Robertson, Keith (Carlton)
Carlton, Susan 1960- 195
Carluccio, Maria 236
Carlyon, Richard 55
Carman, Bill
 See Carman, William
Carman, Patrick 1966- 233
 Earlier sketches in SATA 161, 197
Carman, William 223
Carmer, Carl (Lamson) 1893-1976 37
 Obituary 30
Carmer, Elizabeth Black 1904- 24
Carmi, Giora 1944- 149
 Earlier sketch in SATA 79
Carmichael, Carrie
 See Carmichael, Harriet
Carmichael, Clay 218
Carmichael, Harriet 40
Carmody, Isobelle 1958- 191
 Earlier sketch in SATA 161
Carmody, Isobelle Jane
 See Carmody, Isobelle
Carney, Elizabeth 1981- 199
Carney, Jeff 1962- 196
Carney, Mary Lou 1949- 170
Carol, Bill J.
 See Knott, William C(ecil, Jr.)
Caron, Romi
 See Caron-Kyselkova', Romana
Caron-Kyselkova', Romana 1967- 94
Caroselli, Remus F(rancis) 1916- 36
Carpelan, Bo 1926- 8
Carpelan, Bo Gustaf Bertelsson
 See Carpelan, Bo
Carpenter, (John) Allan 1917- 81
 Earlier sketch in SATA 3
Carpenter, Angelica Shirley 1945- 153
 Earlier sketch in SATA 71
Carpenter, Frances 1890-1972 3
 Obituary 27
Carpenter, John 1948- 58
Carpenter, John Howard
 See Carpenter, John
Carpenter, Johnny
 See Carpenter, John
Carpenter, Nancy 215
Carpenter, Nancy Sippel
 See Carpenter, Nancy
Carpenter, Patricia (Healy Evans) 1920- 11
Carr, Glyn
 See Styles, (Frank) Showell
Carr, Harriett H(elen) 1899-1977 3
Carr, Jan 1953- 132
 Earlier sketch in SATA 89

Carr, M. J.
 See Carr, Jan
Carr, Mary Jane 1899-1988 2
 Obituary 55
Carr, Philippa
 See Hibbert, Eleanor Alice Burford
Carr, Roger Vaughan 1937- 95
Carrel, Annette Felder 1929- 90
Carrick, Carol (Hatfield) 1935- 118
 Earlier sketches in SATA 7, 63
 See also SAAS 18
Carrick, Donald (F.) 1929-1989 63
 Earlier sketch in SATA 7
Carrick, Malcolm 1945- 28
Carrick, Paul 1972- 194
Carrier, Lark 1947- 71
 Brief entry 50
Carrier, Roch 1937- 166
 Earlier sketch in SATA 105
Carrighar, Sally 1898-1985 24
Carrillo, Patricia S.
 See Carrillo, P.S.
Carrillo, P.S. 209
Carrington, G. A.
 See Cunningham, Chet
Carrington, Marsha Gray 1954- 168
 Earlier sketch in SATA 111
Carris, Joan 1938- 182
 Brief entry 42
 Earlier sketch in SATA 44
Carris, Joan Davenport
 See Carris, Joan
Carroll, Curt
 See Bishop, Curtis (Kent)
Carroll, Elizabeth
 See Barkin, Carol
 and James, Elizabeth
Carroll, James Christopher 1960- 235
Carroll, Jaye
 See Carroll, Michael
Carroll, Jenny
 See Cabot, Meg
Carroll, (Archer) Latrobe 1894-1996 7
Carroll, Laura
 See Parr, Lucy
Carroll, Lewis 1832-1898 100
 See also YABC 2
 See also CLR 108
Carroll, Michael 1966- 203
Carroll, Raymond 1924- 86
 Brief entry 47
Carruth, Hayden 1921-2008 47
 Obituary 197
Carryl, Charles E. 1841-1920 114
Carryl, Charles Edward
 See Carryl, Charles E.
Carse, Robert 1902-1971 5
Carson, J(ohn) Franklin 1920-1981 1
 Obituary 107
Carson, Mary Kay 1964- 200
 Earlier sketch in SATA 150
Carson, Rachel 1907-1964 23
Carson, Rachel Louise
 See Carson, Rachel
Carson, Rosalind
 See Chittenden, Margaret
Carson, S. M.
 See Gorsline, (Sally) Marie
Carson, William C. 1928- 154
Carter, Abby 222
 Earlier sketch in SATA 184
Carter, Alden R 1947- 137
 Earlier sketch in SATA 67
 See also CLR 22
 See also SAAS 18
Carter, Alden Richardson
 See Carter, Alden R
Carter, Andy 1948- 134
Carter, Angela 1940-1992 66
 Obituary 70

Carter, Angela Olive
  See Carter, Angela
Carter, Anne Laurel 1953- 209
  Earlier sketch in SATA *135*
Carter, Asa Earl
  See Carter, Forrest
Carter, Avis Murton
  See Allen, Kenneth S.
Carter, Bruce
  See Hough, Richard (Alexander)
Carter, Carol S(hadis) 1948- *124*
Carter, David A. 1957- *228*
  Earlier sketches in SATA *114, 170*
Carter, Don 1958- *192*
  Earlier sketch in SATA *124*
Carter, Dorothy Sharp 1921- 8
Carter, Forrest 1927(?)-1979 .... *32*
Carter, Helene 1887-1960 .... *15*
Carter, (William) Hodding, Jr. 1907-1972 ...... *2*
  Obituary *27*
Carter, James Earl, Jr.
  See Carter, Jimmy
Carter, Jimmy 1924- *79*
Carter, Katharine J(ones) 1905-1984 .... *2*
Carter, Lin(wood Vrooman) 1930-1988 .... *91*
Carter, Mike 1936- *138*
Carter, Nick
  See Avallone, Michael (Angelo, Jr.)
  and Ballard, (Willis) Todhunter
  and Crider, Bill
  and Cassiday, Bruce (Bingham)
  and Chastain, Thomas
  and Dey, Frederic (Merrill) Van Rensselaer
  and Garside, Jack
  and Hayes, Ralph E(ugene)
  and Henderson, M(arilyn) R(uth)
  and Lynds, Dennis
  and Lynds, Gayle (Hallenbeck)
  and Randisi, Robert J.
  and Rasof, Henry
  and Stratemeyer, Edward L.
  and Smith, Martin Cruz
  and Swain, Dwight V(reeland)
  and Vardeman, Robert E.
  and Wallmann, Jeffrey M(iner)
  and White, Lionel
Carter, Peter 1929- *57*
Carter, Phyllis Ann
  See Eberle, Irmengarde
Carter, Samuel (Thomson) III 1904-1988 .... *37*
  Obituary *60*
Carter, Scott William *231*
Carter, Timothy 1972- *224*
Carter, William E. 1926-1983 .... *1*
  Obituary *35*
Cartlidge, Michelle 1950- *96*
  Brief entry *37*
  Earlier sketch in SATA *49*
Cartner, William Carruthers 1910- *11*
Cartwright, Ann 1940- *78*
Cartwright, Reg(inald Ainsley) 1938- *64*
Cartwright, Sally 1923- *9*
Carusone, Al 1949- *89*
Carvell, Marlene *172*
Carver, John
  See Gardner, Richard (M.)
Carwell, L'Ann
  See McKissack, Patricia C.
Cary
  See Cary, Louis F(avreau)
Cary, Barbara Knapp 1912(?)-1975
  Obituary *31*
Cary, Kate 1967(?)- *174*
Cary, Louis F(avreau) 1915- *9*
Caryl, Jean
  See Kaplan, Jean Caryl Korn
Casanova, Mary 1957- *186*
  Earlier sketches in SATA *94, 136*
Cascone, A.G.
  See Cascone, Annette
  and Cascone, Gina

Cascone, Annette 1960- *103*
Cascone, Gina 1955- *103*
Case, Chris 1976- *209*
Case, Marshal T(aylor) 1941- 9
Case, Michael
  See Howard, Robert West
Caseley, Judith 1951- *159*
  Brief entry *53*
  Earlier sketch in SATA *87*
Casewit, Curtis W(erner) 1922-2002 .... *4*
Casey, Barbara (Louise) 1944- *147*
  Earlier sketch in SATA *79*
Casey, Brigid 1950- 9
Casey, Tina 1959- *141*
Cash, Ellen Lewis Buell 1905-1989
  Obituary *64*
Cash, John Carter 1970- *218*
Cash, Megan Montague *160*
Cashore, Kristin 1976(?)- *206*
Casilla, Robert 1959- *211*
  Earlier sketches in SATA *75, 146*
Cason, Mabel Earp 1892-1965 .... *10*
Cass, Joan E(velyn) *1*
Cass-Beggs, Barbara 1904- *62*
Cassedy, Patrice (Rinaldo) 1953- *149*
Cassedy, Sylvia 1930-1989 .... *77*
  Obituary *61*
  Earlier sketch in SATA *27*
  See also CLR *26*
Cassel, Lili
  See Wronker, Lili Cassel
Cassels, Jean *173*
Cassidy, Anne 1952- *166*
Cassidy, Anne Josephine
  See Cassidy, Anne
Cassidy, Cathy 1962- *183*
Cassidy, Kay *232*
Cassino, Mark *228*
Casson, Hugh Maxwell 1910-1999 .... *65*
  Obituary *115*
Cassutt, Michael 1954- *78*
Cassutt, Michael Joseph
  See Cassutt, Michael
Castaldi, Elicia *194*
Castaldo, Nancy Fusco 1962- *151*
  Earlier sketch in SATA *93*
Castaneda, Omar S. 1954- *71*
Castell, Megan
  See Williams, Jeanne
Castellanos, Jane Mollie Robinson
  1913-2001 9
Castellon, Federico 1914-1971 .... *48*
Castellucci, Cecil 1969- *176*
Castillo, Edmund L. 1924-2005 .... *1*
  Obituary *167*
Castillo, Lauren *195*
Castle, Lee
  See Ogan, George F.
  and Ogan, Margaret E. (Nettles)
Castle, Paul
  See Howard, Vernon (Linwood)
Castle, Robert
  See Hamilton, Edmond
Castro L., Antonio 1941- *226*
Castrovilla, Selene 1966- *186*
Caswell, Brian 1954- *171*
  Earlier sketch in SATA *97*
Caswell, Deanna *223*
Caswell, Helen (Rayburn) 1923- *12*
Catalano, Dominic 1956- *163*
  Earlier sketch in SATA *76*
Catalano, Grace (A.) 1961- *99*
Catalanotto, Peter 1959- *195*
  Autobiography Feature *113*
  Earlier sketches in SATA *70, 114, 159*
  See also CLR *68*
  See also SAAS *25*
Catanese, P.W. 1961- *227*
  Earlier sketch in SATA *179*
Cate, Annette LeBlanc *196*

Cate, Dick
  See Cate, Richard Edward Nelson
Cate, Richard Edward Nelson 1932- *28*
Cather, Willa 1873-1947 .... *30*
  See also CLR *98*
Catherall, Arthur 1906-1980 .... *74*
  Earlier sketches in SATA *3, 4*
Cathon, Laura E(lizabeth) 1908-1991 .... *27*
Catlett, Elizabeth 1919(?)- *82*
Catlin, Wynelle 1930- *13*
Catlow, Nikalas
  See Catlow, Niki
Catlow, Niki 1975- *193*
Cato, Heather *105*
Cato, Sheila *114*
Catran, Ken 1944- *190*
Catrow, David
  See Catrow, David J. III
Catrow, David J. III *206*
  Earlier sketch in SATA *152*
Catt, Louis
  See French, Vivian
Cattell, James 1954- *123*
Catton, (Charles) Bruce 1899-1978 .... *2*
  Obituary *24*
Catusanu, Mircea *222*
Catz, Max
  See Glaser, Milton
Caudell, Marian 1930- *52*
Caudill, Rebecca 1899-1985 .... *1*
  Obituary *44*
Cauley, Lorinda Bryan 1951- *46*
  Brief entry *43*
Caulfield, Peggy F. 1926-1987
  Obituary *53*
Cauman, Samuel 1910-1971 .... *48*
Causley, Charles (Stanley) 1917-2003 .... *66*
  Obituary *149*
  Earlier sketch in SATA *3*
  See also CLR *30*
Cavallaro, Ann (Abelson) 1918- *62*
Cavallo, Diana 1931- *7*
Cavanagh, Helen (Carol) 1939- *98*
  Brief entry *37*
  Earlier sketch in SATA *48*
Cavanah, Frances 1899-1982 .... *31*
  Earlier sketch in SATA *1*
Cavanna, Betty
  See Harrison, Elizabeth (Allen) Cavanna
Cavanna, Elizabeth
  See Harrison, Elizabeth (Allen) Cavanna
Cave, Kathryn 1948- *123*
  Earlier sketch in SATA *76*
Cave, Patrick 1965- *234*
Cavendish, Grace
  See Finney, Patricia
Cavendish, Peter
  See Horler, Sydney
Caveney, Philip 1951- *219*
Caveney, Philip Richard
  See Caveney, Philip
Cavin, Ruth 1918-2011 .... *38*
Cavin, Ruth Brodie
  See Cavin, Ruth
Cavoukian, Raffi 1948- *68*
Cawley, Winifred 1915- *13*
Cazeau, Charles J(ay) 1931- *65*
Cazet, Denys 1938- *191*
  Brief entry *41*
  Earlier sketches in SATA *52, 99, 163*
Cazzola, Gus 1934- *73*
Cebulash, Mel 1937- *91*
  Earlier sketch in SATA *10*
Ceccoli, Nicoletta *181*
Cecil, Randy 1968- *223*
  Earlier sketch in SATA *187*
Cecka, Melanie *199*
Ceder, Georgiana Dorcas -1985 .... *10*
Celenza, Anna Harwell *133*
Celestino, Martha Laing
  See Laing, Martha

Cepeda, Joe 215
Earlier sketch in SATA 159
Cerf, Bennett (Alfred) 1898-1971 7
Cerf, Christopher (Bennett) 1941- 2
Cermak, Martin
See Duchacek, Ivo D(uka)
Cerullo, Mary M. 1949- 145
Earlier sketch in SATA 86
Cervantes, Jennifer 234
Cervon, Jacqueline
See Moussard, Jacqueline
Cetin, Frank Stanley 1921- 2
Chabon, Michael 1963- 145
Chabrian, Deborah
See Chabrian, Deborah L.
Chabrian, Deborah L. 212
Chaconas, D.J.
See Chaconas, Dori
Chaconas, Dori 1938- 208
Earlier sketches in SATA 145, 175
Chaconas, Doris J.
See Chaconas, Dori
Chadda, Sarwat 224
Chadwick, Lester 67
Earlier sketch in SATA 1
Chaffee, Allen 3
Chaffin, Lillie D(orton) 1925- 4
Chaikin, Miriam 1924- 152
Earlier sketches in SATA 24, 102
Chall, Marsha Wilson 150
Challand, Helen J(ean) 1921- 64
Challans, Mary
See Renault, Mary
Chalmers, Mary (Eileen) 1927- 6
See also SAAS 14
Chamberlain, Barbara A.
See Azore, Barbara
Chamberlain, Margaret 1954- 212
Earlier sketch in SATA 46
Chamberlin, Kate 1945- 105
Chamberlin, Mary 1960- 177
Chamberlin, Rich 177
Chamberlin, Richard
See Chamberlin, Rich
Chambers, Aidan 1934- 171
Earlier sketches in SATA 1, 69, 108
See also CLR 151
See also SAAS 12
Chambers, Bradford 1922-1984
Obituary 39
Chambers, Catherine E.
See St. John, Nicole
Chambers, John W. 1933- 57
Brief entry 46
Chambers, Kate
See St. John, Nicole
Chambers, Margaret Ada Eastwood 1911- 2
Chambers, Peggy
See Chambers, Margaret Ada Eastwood
Chambers, Robert W(illiam) 1865-1933 107
Chambliss, Maxie 186
Champlin, Susan 1961- 225
Chan, Gillian 1954- 147
Earlier sketch in SATA 102
Chan, Peter 1980(?)- 207
Chance, James T.
See Carpenter, John
Chance, John T.
See Carpenter, John
Chance, Stephen
See Turner, Philip (William)
Chandler, Caroline A(ugusta) 1906-1979 22
Obituary 24
Chandler, David P. 1933- 28
Chandler, David Porter
See Chandler, David P.
Chandler, Edna Walker 1908-1982 11
Obituary 31
Chandler, Jennifer
See Westwood, Jennifer
Chandler, Karen 1959- 122

Chandler, Kristen 230
Chandler, Linda S(mith) 1929- 39
Chandler, Pauline 175
Chandler, Robert 1953- 40
Chandler, Ruth Forbes 1894-1978 2
Obituary 26
Chandonnet, Ann F. 1943- 92
Chaney, Jill 1932- 87
Chang, Chih-Wei 1966- 111
Chang, Cindy 1968- 90
Chang, Grace 1961- 226
Chang, Margaret 1941- 71
Chang, Margaret Scrogin
See Chang, Margaret
Chang, Raymond 1939- 142
Earlier sketches in SATA 71, 142 PEN
Chanin, Michael 1952- 84
Channel, A. R.
See Catherall, Arthur
Chapian, Marie 1938- 29
Chapin, Alene Olsen Dalton 1915(?)-1986
Obituary 47
Chapin, Tom 1945- 83
Chapman, Allen 67
Earlier sketch in SATA 1
Chapman, Cheryl O(rth) 1948- 80
Chapman, (Constance) Elizabeth (Mann)
1919- 10
Chapman, Gaye 1970- 200
Chapman, Gaye Coralie
See Chapman, Gaye
Chapman, Gaynor 1935- 32
Chapman, Gillian 1955- 120
Chapman, Jane 1970- 212
Earlier sketches in SATA 122, 176
Chapman, Jean 104
Earlier sketch in SATA 34
See also CLR 65
Chapman, John Stanton Higham 1891-1972
Obituary 27
Chapman, Lee
See Bradley, Marion Zimmer
Chapman, Linda 1969- 223
Chapman, Lynne 1960- 197
Chapman, Lynne F(erguson) 1963- 150
Earlier sketch in SATA 94
Chapman, Maristan
See Chapman, John Stanton Higham
Chapman, Vera (Ivy May) 1898-1996 33
Chapman, Walker
See Silverberg, Robert
Chappell, Audrey 1954- 72
Chappell, Crissa-Jean 198
Chappell, Warren 1904-1991 68
Obituary 67
Earlier sketch in SATA 6
See also SAAS 10
Chapra, Mimi 182
Charbonneau, Eileen 1951- 118
Earlier sketch in SATA 84
Charbonnet, Gabrielle 1961- 227
Earlier sketch in SATA 81
Chardiet, Bernice 1927(?)- 27
Chardiet, Bernice Kroll
See Chardiet, Bernice
Charest, Emily MacLachlan 198
Charles, Donald
See Meighan, Donald Charles
Charles, Louis
See Stratemeyer, Edward L.
Charles, Nicholas
See Kuskin, Karla
Charles, Nicholas J.
See Kuskin, Karla
Charles, Norma 153
Charles, Veronika Martenova 182
Charlip, Remy 1929- 119
Earlier sketches in SATA 4, 68
See also CLR 8
Charlot, Jean 1898-1979 8
Obituary 31

Charlot, Martin 1944- 64
Charlot, Martin Day
See Charlot, Martin
Charlton, Michael (Alan) 1923- 34
Charlton-Trujillo, e.E. 189
Charmatz, Bill 1925-2005 7
Charnas, Suzy McKee 1939- 110
Earlier sketch in SATA 61
Charosh, Mannis 1906- 5
Chartier, Normand L. 1945- 66
Chase, Alice
See McHargue, Georgess
Chase, Alyssa 1965- 92
Chase, Andra 1942- 91
Chase, Emily
See Aks, Patricia
and Garwood, Julie
and Sachs, Judith
and White, Carol
Chase, Mary (Coyle) 1907-1981 17
Obituary 29
Chase, Mary Ellen 1887-1973 10
Chase, Paula 214
Chase, Richard 1904-1988 64
Obituary 56
Chase, Samantha
See Glick, Ruth
Chast, Roz 1954- 212
Earlier sketch in SATA 97
Chastain, Madye Lee 1908-1989 4
Chataway, Carol 1955- 140
Chatterjee, Debjani 1952- 83
Chatterton, Martin 1961- 225
Chauncy, Nan(cen Beryl Masterman)
1900-1970 6
See also CLR 6
Chaundler, Christine 1887-1972 1
Obituary 25
Chayka, Doug 196
Chbosky, Stephen 1972- 164
Cheaney, Janie B.
See Cheaney, J.B.
Cheaney, J.B. 1950- 188
Chee, Cheng-Khee 1934- 79
Cheese, Chloe 1952- 118
Chekhonte, Antosha
See Chekhov, Anton
Chekhov, Anton 1860-1904 90
Chekhov, Anton Pavlovich
See Chekhov, Anton
Chelushkin, Kirill 1968- 186
Chen, Anthony 1929- 6
Chen, Chih-Yuan 1975- 216
Earlier sketch in SATA 155
Chen, Ju-Hong 1941- 78
Chen, Pauline 1966- 202
Chen, Sara
See Odgers, Sally Farrell
Chen, Tony
See Chen, Anthony
Chen, Yong 1963- 183
Chen, Yuan-tsung 1932- 65
Chen, Zhiyuan
See Chen, Chih-Yuan
Chenault, Nell
See Smith, Linell Nash
Chen Chih-Yuan
See Chen, Chih-Yuan
Chenery, Janet (Dai) 1923- 25
Cheney, Cora 1916-1999 3
Obituary 110
Cheney, Glenn (Alan) 1951- 99
Cheney, Lynne V. 1941- 152
Cheney, Lynne Vincent
See Cheney, Lynne V.
Cheney, Ted
See Cheney, Theodore Albert
Cheney, Theodore A. Rees
See Cheney, Theodore Albert
Cheney, Theodore Albert 1928- 11

Cheng, Andrea 1957- 205
Earlier sketches in SATA *128, 172*
Cheng, Christopher 1959- 173
Earlier sketch in SATA *106*
Cheng, Judith 1955- 36
Cheng, Shan
See Jiang, Cheng An
Cheripko, Jan 1951- 155
Earlier sketch in SATA *83*
Chermayeff, Ivan 1932- 47
Chernenko, Dan
See Turtledove, Harry
Chernett, Dan 224
Chernoff, Dorothy A.
See Ernst, (Lyman) John
Chernoff, Goldie Taub 1909- 10
Cherry, Carolyn Janice
See Cherryh, C.J.
Cherry, Lynne 1952- 99
Earlier sketch in SATA *34*
Cherryh, C.J. 1942- 172
Earlier sketch in SATA *93*
Cherryholmes, Anne
See Price, Olive
Cheshire, Simon 236
Earlier sketch in SATA *172*
Chesler, Bernice 1932-2002 59
Chess, Victoria (Dickerson) 1939- 92
Earlier sketch in SATA *33*
Chessa, Francesca 233
Earlier sketch in SATA *191*
Chester, Deborah 1957- 85
Chester, Kate
See Guccione, Leslie Davis
Chesterton, G. K. 1874-1936 27
Chesterton, Gilbert Keith
See Chesterton, G. K.
Chesworth, Michael 207
Earlier sketch in SATA *160*
Chetin, Helen 1922- 6
Chetwin, Grace 86
Brief entry 50
Chevalier, Christa 1937- 35
Chevalier, Tracy 1962- 128
Chew, Ruth 1920-2010 7
Chichester Clark, Emma 1955- 209
Earlier sketches in SATA *117, 156, 69*
Chidsey, Donald Barr 1902-1981 3
Obituary 27
Chiefari, Janet D. 1942- 58
Chien, Catia 193
Chien-min, Lin
See Rumford, James
Child, L. Maria
See Child, Lydia Maria
Child, Lauren 1965- 183
Earlier sketches in SATA *119, 160*
Child, Lincoln 1957- 113
Child, Lincoln B.
See Child, Lincoln
Child, Lydia Maria 1802-1880 67
Child, Mrs.
See Child, Lydia Maria
Child, Philip 1898-1978 47
Children's Shepherd, The
See Westphal, Arnold Carl
Childress, Alice 1920-1994 81
Earlier sketches in SATA *7, 48*
See also CLR *14*
Childs, H(alla) Fay (Cochrane) 1890-1971 1
Obituary 25
Childs, Tera Lynn 1976- 235
Chilton, Charles (Frederick William)
1917- 102
Chima, Cinda Williams 226
Earlier sketch in SATA *192*
Chimaera
See Farjeon, Eleanor
Chin, Jason 1978- 218
Chin, Richard (M.) 1946- 52
Chinery, Michael 1938- 26

Chin-Lee, Cynthia 1958- 102
Chin-Lee D., Cynthia
See Chin-Lee, Cynthia
Chippendale, Lisa A. 158
Chipperfield, Joseph Eugene 1912-1980(?) .. 87
Earlier sketch in SATA *2*
Chisholm, P. F.
See Finney, Patricia
Chislett, Gail (Elaine) 1948- 58
Chittenden, Elizabeth F. 1903-1999 9
Chittenden, Margaret 1935- 28
Chittum, Ida 1918- 7
Chitwood, Suzanne Tanner 1958- 160
Chmielarz, Sharon Lee 1940- 72
Choate, Judith (Newkirk) 1940- 30
Chocolate, Debbi 1954- 223
Earlier sketch in SATA *96*
Chocolate, Deborah H. Newton
See Chocolate, Debbi
Chodos-Irvine, Margaret 211
Earlier sketch in SATA *152*
Choi, Sook Nyul 1937- 73
Autobiography Feature 126
See also CLR *53*
Choi, Yangsook 178
Choksi, Nishant 1975- 222
Choldenko, Gennifer 1957- 182
Earlier sketch in SATA *135*
Chorao, Kay 1936- 215
Chorao, (Ann Mc)Kay (Sproat) 1936- 162
Earlier sketches in SATA *8, 69*
Choron, Sandra (Zena Samelson) 1950- 146
Choung, Eun-hee 199
Chown, Marcus 1959- 137
Choyce, Lesley 1951- 165
Earlier sketch in SATA *94*
Choyce, Lesley Willis
See Choyce, Lesley
Chrisman, Arthur Bowie 1889-1953 124
See also YABC *1*
Christelow, Eileen 1943- 184
Autobiography Feature 120
Brief entry 35
Earlier sketches in SATA *38, 90*
Christensen, Bonnie 1951- 213
Earlier sketches in SATA *110, 157*
Christensen, Gardell Dano 1907-1991 ... 1
Christensen, Laurie
See Steding, Laurie
Christesen, Barbara 1940- 40
Christgau, Alice Erickson 1902-1977 13
Christian, Mary Blount 1933- 9
Christiana, David 195
Christie, Agatha 1890-1976 36
Christie, Agatha Mary Clarissa
See Christie, Agatha
Christie, Ann Philippa
See Pearce, Philippa
Christie, Gregory
See Christie, R. Gregory
Christie, Peter 1962- 236
Christie, Philippa
See Pearce, Philippa
Christie, R. Gregory 1971- 225
Earlier sketches in SATA *127, 185*
Christopher, John
See Youd, Samuel
Christopher, Louise
See Hale, Arlene
Christopher, Matt(hew Frederick)
1917-1997 80
Obituary 99
Earlier sketches in SATA *2, 47*
See also CLR *119*
See also SAAS *9*
Christopher, Milbourne 1914(?)-1984 46
Christy, Howard Chandler 1873-1952 ... 21
Chrustowski, Rick 176
Chrystie, Frances N(icholson) 1904-1986 ... 60
Chu, Daniel 1933- 11
Chui, Vince 1975- 236

Chukovsky, Kornei (Ivanovich) 1882-1969 . 34
Earlier sketch in SATA *5*
Church, Caroline Jayne 219
Earlier sketch in SATA *179*
Church, Richard 1893-1972 3
Churchill, E(lmer) Richard 1937- 11
Churchill, Elizabeth
See Hough, Richard (Alexander)
Chute, B(eatrice) J(oy) 1913-1987 2
Obituary 53
Chute, Marchette (Gaylord) 1909-1994 ... 1
Chwast, Jacqueline 1932- 6
Chwast, Seymour 1931- 146
Earlier sketches in SATA *18, 96*
Ciardi, John (Anthony) 1916-1986 65
Obituary 46
Earlier sketch in SATA *1*
See also CLR *19*
See also SAAS *26*
Ciccone, Madonna Louise Veronica
See Madonna
Ciddor, Anna 1957- 213
Ciment, James D. 1958- 140
Cirrone, Dorian 182
Cisneros, Sandra 1954-
See CLR *123*
Citra, Becky 1954- 137
Citrin, Michael 1965(?)- 183
Claflin, Willy 1944- 208
Clair, Andree 19
Clampett, Bob 1914(?)-1985 44
Obituary 38
Clampett, Robert
See Clampett, Bob
Clapp, John 1968- 109
Clapp, Patricia 1912- 74
Earlier sketch in SATA *4*
See also SAAS *4*
Clare, Ellen
See Sinclair, Olga
Clare, Helen
See Clarke, Pauline
Claremont, Chris 1950- 87
Claremont, Christopher Simon
See Claremont, Chris
Clark, Ann Nolan 1896-1995 82
Obituary 87
Earlier sketch in SATA *4*
See also CLR *16*
See also SAAS *16*
Clark, Champ 1923-2002 47
Clark, Christopher (Anthony) Stuart
See Stuart-Clark, Christopher (Anthony)
Clark, Clara Gillow 1951- 154
Earlier sketch in SATA *84*
Clark, David
See Hardcastle, Michael
Clark, David Allen
See Ernst, (Lyman) John
Clark, Emma Chichester
See Chichester Clark, Emma
Clark, Frank J(ames) 1922- 18
Clark, Garel
See Garelick, May
Clark, Halsey
See Deming, Richard
Clark, Joan
See Benson, Mildred
Clark, Joan 1934- 182
Earlier sketches in SATA *59, 96*
Clark, Karen Henry 237
Clark, Leonard 1905-1981 30
Obituary 29
Clark, M. R.
See Clark, Mavis Thorpe
Clark, Margaret (D.) 1943- 126
Clark, Margaret Goff 1913- 82
Earlier sketch in SATA *8*
Clark, Mary Higgins 1929- 46

Clark, Mavis Thorpe 1909-1999 .... *74*
  Earlier sketch in SATA *8*
  See also CLR *30*
  See also SAAS *5*
Clark, Merle
  See Gessner, Lynne
Clark, Patricia Denise
  See Robins, Patricia
Clark, Patricia Finrow 1929- *11*
Clark, Ronald Harry 1904-1999 .... *193*
Clark, Ronald William 1916-1987 .... *2*
  Obituary *52*
Clark, Sherryl 1956- *149*
Clark, Van D(eusen) 1909-1974 .... *2*
Clark, Virginia
  See Gray, Patricia (Clark)
Clark, Walter Van Tilburg 1909-1971 .... *8*
Clarke, Arthur
  See Clarke, Arthur C.
Clarke, Arthur C. 1917-2008 .... *115*
  Obituary *191*
  Earlier sketches in SATA *13, 70*
  See also CLR *119*
Clarke, Arthur Charles
  See Clarke, Arthur C.
Clarke, Clorinda 1917- *7*
Clarke, Elizabeth L. 1934- *103*
Clarke, Greg 1959- *215*
Clarke, Gus 1948- *134*
Clarke, J.
  See Clarke, Judith
Clarke, James Hall
  See Rowland-Entwistle, (Arthur) Theodore
  (Henry)
Clarke, Joan B. 1921- *42*
  Brief entry *27*
Clarke, John
  See Laklan, Carli
  and Sontup, Dan(iel)
Clarke, Judith 1943- *164*
  Earlier sketches in SATA *75, 110*
  See also CLR *61*
Clarke, Julia 1950- *138*
Clarke, Kenneth 1957- *107*
Clarke, Lea
  See Rowland-Entwistle, (Arthur) Theodore
  (Henry)
Clarke, Margaret 1941-
  See CLR *99*
Clarke, Mary Stetson 1911-1994 .... *5*
Clarke, Michael
  See Newlon, (Frank) Clarke
Clarke, Pauline 1921- *131*
  Earlier sketch in SATA *3*
  See also CLR *28*
Clarkson, E(dith) Margaret 1915- *37*
Clarkson, Ewan 1929- *9*
Clarkson, Karen *233*
Claudia, Susan
  See Goulart, Ron
  and Johnston, William
Claverie, Jean 1946- *38*
Clay, Patrice 1947- *47*
Clay, Wil *203*
Clayman, Deborah Paula
  See Da Costa, Deborah
Claypool, Jane
  See Miner, Jane Claypool
Clayton, Elaine 1961- *209*
  Earlier sketches in SATA *94, 159*
Clayton, Lawrence (Otto, Jr.) 1945- *75*
Clayton, Sally Pomme *218*
Clayton, Sandra 1951- *110*
Cle, Troy *202*
Clea, Super
  See Hantman, Clea
Cleary, Beverly 1916- *121*
  Earlier sketches in SATA *2, 43, 79*
  See also CLR *72*
  See also SAAS *20*

Cleary, Beverly Atlee Bunn
  See Cleary, Beverly
Cleary, Brian P. 1959- *186*
  Earlier sketches in SATA *93, 132*
Cleaver, Bill
  See Cleaver, William J.
Cleaver, Carole 1934- *6*
Cleaver, Elizabeth (Ann Mrazik)
  1939-1985 .... *23*
  Obituary *43*
  See also CLR *13*
Cleaver, Hylton Reginald 1891-1961 .... *49*
Cleaver, Vera 1919-1993 .... *76*
  Earlier sketch in SATA *22*
  See also CLR *6*
Cleaver, Vera Allen
  See Cleaver, Vera
Cleaver, William J. 1920-1981 .... *22*
  Obituary *27*
  See also CLR *6*
Cleishbotham, Jebediah
  See Scott, Sir Walter
Cleland, Janet *226*
Cleland, Mabel
  See Widdemer, Mabel Cleland
Clem, Margaret H(ollingsworth) 1923- *90*
Clemens, James
  See Rollins, James
Clemens, Samuel
  See Twain, Mark
Clemens, Samuel Langhorne
  See Twain, Mark
Clemens, Virginia Phelps 1941- *35*
Clement, Gary *191*
Clement, Janet *182*
Clement, Nathan 1966- *200*
Clement, Priscilla Ferguson 1942- *171*
Clement, Rod *97*
Clement-Moore, Rosemary *229*
  Earlier sketch in SATA *188*
Clements, Andrew 1949- *235*
  Earlier sketches in SATA *104, 158, 203*
Clements, Bruce 1931- *178*
  Earlier sketches in SATA *27, 94*
Clemesha, David *192*
Cleminson, Katie *221*
Clemons, Elizabeth
  See Nowell, Elizabeth Cameron
Clerk, N. W.
  See Lewis, C. S.
Cleveland, Bob
  See Cleveland, George
Cleveland, George 1903(?)-1985
  Obituary *43*
Cleveland-Peck, Patricia *80*
Cleven, Cathrine
  See Cleven, Kathryn Seward
Cleven, Kathryn Seward *2*
Clevenger, William R. 1954- *84*
Clevenger, William Russell
  See Clevenger, William R.
Clevin, Joergen 1920- *7*
Clevin, Jorgen
  See Clevin, Joergen
Clewes, Dorothy (Mary) 1907-2003 .... *86*
  Obituary *138*
  Earlier sketch in SATA *1*
Clifford, David
  See Rosenberg, Eth Clifford
Clifford, Eth
  See Rosenberg, Eth Clifford
Clifford, Harold B(urton) 1893-1988 .... *10*
Clifford, Margaret Cort 1929- *1*
Clifford, Martin
  See Hamilton, Charles (Harold St. John)
Clifford, Mary Louise Beneway 1926- *23*
Clifford, Peggy
  See Clifford, Margaret Cort
Clifford, Rachel Mark
  See Lewis, Brenda Ralph

Clifton, Lucille 1936-2010 .... *128*
  Earlier sketches in SATA *20, 69*
  See also CLR *5*
Clifton, Thelma Lucille
  See Clifton, Lucille
Climo, Shirley 1928- *166*
  Autobiography Feature *110*
  Brief entry *35*
  Earlier sketches in SATA *39, 77*
  See also CLR *69*
Cline-Ransome, Lesa *201*
Clinton, Catherine 1952- *203*
Clinton, Cathryn 1957- *136*
Clinton, Dirk
  See Silverberg, Robert
Clinton, Jon
  See Prince, J(ack) H(arvey)
Clippinger, Carol *193*
Clish, (Lee) Marian 1946- *43*
Clive, Clifford
  See Hamilton, Charles (Harold St. John)
Clokey, Art 1921- *59*
Cloudsley-Thompson, J(ohn) L(eonard)
  1921- *19*
Clouse, Nancy L. 1938- *78*
Clover, Peter 1952- *215*
  Earlier sketch in SATA *152*
Clutha, Janet
  See Frame, Janet
Clutha, Janet Paterson Frame
  See Frame, Janet
Clymer, Eleanor 1906-2001 .... *85*
  Obituary *126*
  Earlier sketch in SATA *9*
  See also SAAS *17*
Clyne, Patricia (Edwards) *31*
Cneut, Carll 1969- *197*
Coalson, Glo 1946- *94*
  Earlier sketch in SATA *26*
Coates, Anna 1958- *73*
Coates, Belle 1896-1986 .... *2*
Coates, Ruth Allison 1915- *11*
Coats, Alice M(argaret) 1905-1976 .... *11*
Coatsworth, Elizabeth (Jane) 1893-1986 .... *100*
  Obituary *49*
  Earlier sketches in SATA *2, 56*
  See also CLR *2*
Cobalt, Martin
  See Mayne, William
Cobb, Jane
  See Berry, Jane Cobb
Cobb, Mary 1931- *88*
Cobb, Vicki 1938- *136*
  Autobiography Feature *136*
  Earlier sketches in SATA *8, 69, 131*
  See also CLR *2*
  See also SAAS *6*
Cobbett, Richard
  See Pluckrose, Henry
Cober, Alan E(dwin) 1935-1998 .... *7*
  Obituary *101*
Cobham, Sir Alan
  See Hamilton, Charles (Harold St. John)
Coburn, Jake 1978- *155*
Cocagnac, Augustin Maurice(-Jean) 1924- *7*
Cocca-Leffler, Maryann 1958- *194*
  Earlier sketches in SATA *80, 136*
Cochran, Bill *187*
Cochran, Bobbye A. 1949- *11*
Cochran, Josh *221*
Cochran, Thomas 1955- *198*
Cochrane, Hamilton E.
  See Cochrane, Mick
Cochrane, Mick 1956- *215*
Cockcroft, Jason *217*
Cockett, Mary *3*
Cocks, Peter *204*
Cocovini, Abby *202*
Coddell, Esme Raji
  See Codell, Esme Raji
Codell, Esme Raji 1968- *160*

Cody, C. S.
  See Waller, Leslie
Cody, Jess
  See Cunningham, Chet
Cody, Matthew 229
Coe, Anne (E.) 1949- 95
Coe, Douglas
  See Epstein, Beryl
  and Epstein, Samuel
Coe, Lloyd 1899(?)-1976
  Obituary 30
Coen, Rena Neumann 1925- 20
Coerr, Eleanor (Beatrice) 1922- 67
  Earlier sketch in SATA *1*
Cofer, Judith Ortiz 1952- 164
  Earlier sketch in SATA *110*
Coffelt, Nancy 1961- 189
Coffey, Brian
  See Koontz, Dean
Coffin, Geoffrey
  See Mason, F(rancis) van Wyck
Coffin, M. T.
  See Stanley, George Edward
Coffin, M.T.
  See Stanley, George Edward
Coffman, Ramon Peyton 1896-1989 4
Cogan, Karen 1954- 125
Coggins, Jack (Banham) 1911-2006 2
Cohagan, Carolyn 1972- 228
Cohen, Barbara 1932-1992 77
  Obituary 74
  Earlier sketch in SATA *10*
  See also SAAS *7*
Cohen, Daniel (E.) 1936- 70
  Earlier sketch in SATA *8*
  See also CLR *43*
  See also SAAS *4*
Cohen, Deborah Bodin 1968- 180
Cohen, Jan Barger
  See Barger, Jan
Cohen, Jene Barr
  See Barr, Jene
Cohen, Joan Lebold 1932- 4
Cohen, Judith Love 1933- 78
Cohen, Lisa 1963- 225
Cohen, Miriam 1926-1955 155
  Earlier sketches in SATA *29, 106*
  See also SAAS *11*
Cohen, Nora 75
Cohen, Paul 1945- 58
Cohen, Paul S.
  See Cohen, Paul
Cohen, Peter Zachary 1931- 150
  Earlier sketch in SATA *4*
Cohen, Robert Carl 1930- 8
Cohen, Santiago 1954- 215
Cohen, Sholom 1951- 94
Cohn, Angelo 1914-1997 19
Cohn, Diana 194
Cohn, Rachel 1968- 228
  Earlier sketch in SATA *161*
Coit, Margaret Louise 1922-2003 2
  Obituary 142
Colasanti, Susane 1973- 214
Colato Lainez, Rene 1970- 226
  Earlier sketch in SATA *176*
Colbert, Anthony 1934-2007 15
Colbert, Nancy A. 1936- 139
Colby, C(arroll) B(urleigh) 1904-1977 35
  Earlier sketch in SATA *3*
Colby, Jean Poindexter 1909-1993 23
Cole, Annette
  See Steiner, Barbara A(nnette)
Cole, Babette 1949- 155
  Earlier sketches in SATA *61, 96*
Cole, Betsy 1940- 83
Cole, Brock 1938- 200
  Earlier sketches in SATA *72, 136*
  See also CLR *18*
Cole, Davis
  See Elting, Mary

Cole, Hannah 1954- 74
Cole, Henry 1955- 213
  Earlier sketch in SATA *181*
Cole, Jack -1974
  See Stewart, John
Cole, Jackson
  See Curry, Thomas Albert
  and Germano, Peter B.
  and Heckelmann, Charles N(ewman)
  and Newton, D(wight) B(ennett)
  and Schisgall, Oscar
Cole, Jennifer
  See Zach, Cheryl (Byrd)
Cole, Joanna 1944- 231
  Brief entry 37
  Earlier sketches in SATA *49, 81, 120, 168*
  See also CLR *40*
Cole, Lois Dwight 1903-1979 10
  Obituary 26
Cole, Michael 1947- 59
Cole, Samantha
  See Cole, Stephen
Cole, Sheila 1939- 171
  Earlier sketches in SATA *24, 95*
Cole, Sheila R.
  See Cole, Sheila
Cole, Sheila Rotenberg
  See Cole, Sheila
Cole, Stephen 1971- 230
  Earlier sketch in SATA *161*
Cole, Steve
  See Cole, Stephen
Cole, William (Rossa) 1919-2000 71
  Earlier sketch in SATA *9*
  See also SAAS *9*
Coleman, Andrew
  See Pine, Nicholas
Coleman, Clare
  See Bell, Clare (Louise)
  and Easton, M(alcolm) Coleman
Coleman, Janet Wyman 184
Coleman, Loren 1947- 164
Coleman, Loren Elwood, Jr.
  See Coleman, Loren
Coleman, Mary Ann 1928- 83
Coleman, Michael
  See Jones, Allan Frewin
Coleman, Michael 1946- 199
  Autobiography Feature 133
  Earlier sketches in SATA *108, 133*
Coleman, Rowan 187
Coleman, William L(eRoy) 1938- 49
  Brief entry 34
Coleman, Wim 1926- 212
Coles, Robert 1929- 23
Coles, Robert Martin
  See Coles, Robert
Colfer, Eoin 1965- 197
  Earlier sketch in SATA *148*
  See also CLR *112*
Colin, Ann
  See Ure, Jean
Collard, Sneed B. III 1959- 184
  Earlier sketches in SATA *84, 139*
Colledge, Anne 1939- 142
Colley, Jacqui 1965- 202
Collicott, Sharleen 1937- 143
  Earlier sketch in SATA *98*
Collicutt, Paul 229
Collier, Bryan 204
  Earlier sketches in SATA *126, 174*
Collier, Christopher 1930- 70
  Earlier sketch in SATA *16*
  See also CLR *126*
Collier, Ethel 1903-1999 22
Collier, James Lincoln 1928- 166
  Earlier sketches in SATA *8, 70*
  See also CLR *126*
  See also SAAS *21*
Collier, Jane
  See Collier, Zena

Collier, Kristi 182
Collier, Steven 1942- 61
Collier, Zena 1926- 23
Collings, Gillian 1939- 102
Collington, Peter 1948- 99
  Earlier sketch in SATA *59*
Collins, Ace 1953- 82
Collins, Andrew J.
  See Collins, Ace
Collins, B. R. 1981- 214
Collins, David R(aymond) 1940-2001 121
  Earlier sketch in SATA *7*
Collins, Heather 1946- 81
Collins, Hunt
  See Hunter, Evan
Collins, Michael
  See Lynds, Dennis
Collins, Michael 1930- 58
Collins, Pat Lowery 1932- 217
  Earlier sketches in SATA *31, 151*
Collins, Paul 1954- 126
Collins, Ross 1972- 200
Collins, Ruth Philpott 1890-1975
  Obituary 30
Collins, Suzanne 1963(?)- 224
  Earlier sketch in SATA *180*
Collins, Yvonne 194
Collinson, A. S.
  See Collinson, Alan S.
Collinson, Alan S. 1934- 80
Collinson, Roger (Alfred) 1936- 133
Collison, Linda 1953- 185
Collodi, Carlo 1826-1890 100
  Earlier sketch in SATA *29*
  See also CLR *120*
Colloms, Brenda 1919- 40
Colman, Hila 1909-2008 53
  Earlier sketch in SATA *1*
  See also SAAS *14*
Colman, Morris 1899(?)-1981
  Obituary 25
Colman, Penny (Morgan) 1944- 160
  Autobiography Feature 160
  Earlier sketches in SATA *77, 114*
Colman, Warren (David) 1944- 67
Coloma, Cindy
  See Martinusen-Coloma, Cindy
Colombo, John Robert 1936- 50
Colon, Raul 156
Colon, Raul 1952- 202
Colonius, Lillian 1911-1992 3
Colorado, Antonio J.
  See Colorado (Capella), Antonio J(ulio)
Colorado (Capella), Antonio J(ulio)
  1903-1994 23
  Obituary 79
Colquhoun, Glenn 1964- 165
Colston, Fifi E. 1960- 150
Colt, Martin
  See Epstein, Beryl
  and Epstein, Samuel
Colum, Padraic 1881-1972 15
  See also CLR *36*
Columbus, Chris 1959- 97
Columbus, Christopher
  See Columbus, Chris
Columella
  See Moore, Clement Clarke
Colver, Anne 1908- 7
Colvin, James
  See Moorcock, Michael
Colwell, Eileen (Hilda) 1904-2002 2
Colwyn, Stewart
  See Pepper, Frank S.
Coman, Carolyn 1951- 197
  Earlier sketch in SATA *127*
Combres, Elisabeth 1967- 226
Combs, Lisa M.
  See McCourt, Lisa
Combs, Robert
  See Murray, John

Comfort, Jane Levington
See Sturtzel, Jane Levington
Comfort, Mildred Houghton 1886-1976 .... *3*
Comins, Ethel M(ae) *11*
Comins, Jeremy 1933- *28*
Commager, Henry Steele 1902-1998 .... *23*
Obituary *102*
Comora, Madeleine *190*
Compere, Mickie
See Davidson, Margaret
Compestine, Ying Chang 1963- *187*
Earlier sketch in SATA *140*
Comport, Sally Wern *190*
Compton, Patricia A. 1936- *75*
Comte, The Great
See Hawkesworth, Eric
Comus
See Ballantyne, R(obert) M(ichael)
Comyns, Nance
See Comyns-Toohey, Nantz
Comyns-Toohey, Nantz 1956- *86*
Conahan, Carolyn
See Conahan, Carolyn Digby
Conahan, Carolyn Digby 1961- *216*
Conan Doyle, Arthur
See Doyle, Sir Arthur Conan
Condie, Ally *204*
Condie, Allyson B.
See Condie, Ally
Condit, Martha Olson 1913- *28*
Condon, Bill 1949- *142*
Condon, Judith *83*
Condon, Ken *195*
Condy, Roy 1942- *96*
Cone, Ferne Geller 1921- *39*
Cone, Molly (Lamken) 1918- *151*
Autobiography Feature *151*
Earlier sketches in SATA *1, 28, 115*
See also SAAS *11*
Cone, Patrick 1954- *89*
Coney, Michael G. 1932-2005 .... *61*
Obituary *170*
Coney, Michael Greatrex
See Coney, Michael G.
Coney, Mike
See Coney, Michael G.
Conford, Ellen 1942- *162*
Earlier sketches in SATA *6, 68, 110*
See also CLR *71*
Conger, Lesley
See Suttles, Shirley (Smith)
Conklin, Gladys Plemon 1903- *2*
Conklin, Paul S. 1929(?)-2003 .... *43*
Brief entry *33*
Obituary *147*
Conkling, Hilda 1910-1986 .... *23*
Conlan, Kathleen Elizabeth 1950- *145*
Conlan, Kathy
See Conlan, Kathleen Elizabeth
Conley, Robyn 1963- *125*
Conley-Weaver, Robyn
See Conley, Robyn
Conlon-McKenna, Marita 1956- *71*
Conly, Jane Leslie 1948- *164*
Earlier sketches in SATA *80, 112*
Conly, Robert Leslie
See O'Brien, Robert C.
Connell, Kirk
See Chapman, John Stanton Higham
Connell, Tom *206*
Connelly, Gwen 1952- *212*
Connelly, Marc(us Cook) 1890-1980
Obituary *25*
Connolly, Jerome P(atrick) 1931- *8*
Connolly, Pat 1943- *74*
Connolly, Peter 1935- *105*
Earlier sketch in SATA *47*
Conover, Chris 1950- *213*
Earlier sketch in SATA *31*
Conquest, Owen
See Hamilton, Charles (Harold St. John)

Conrad, Joseph 1857-1924 .... *27*
Conrad, Pam 1947-1996 .... *133*
Brief entry *49*
Obituary *90*
Earlier sketches in SATA *52, 80*
See also CLR *18*
See also SAAS *19*
Conroy, Jack
See Conroy, John Wesley
Conroy, John Wesley 1899-1990 .... *19*
Obituary *65*
Conroy, Melissa 1969- *226*
Conroy, Robert
See Goldston, Robert (Conroy)
Constable, Kate 1966- *172*
Constant, Alberta Wilson 1908-1981 .... *22*
Obituary *28*
Constantin, Pascale *185*
Conway, Celeste *210*
Conway, David 1970- *213*
Conway, Diana C. 1943- *91*
Conway, Diana Cohen
See Conway, Diana C.
Conway, Gordon
See Hamilton, Charles (Harold St. John)
Cook, Ande *192*
Cook, Bernadine 1924- *11*
Cook, Fred J(ames) 1911-2003 .... *2*
Obituary *145*
Cook, Glen 1944- *171*
Earlier sketch in SATA *108*
Cook, Glen Charles
See Cook, Glen
Cook, Hugh 1956- *85*
Cook, Hugh, Walter Gilbert
See Cook, Hugh
Cook, Jean Thor 1930- *94*
Cook, Joel 1934- *79*
Cook, Joseph Jay 1924- *8*
Cook, Lisa Broadie *157*
Cook, Lyn
See Waddell, Evelyn Margaret
Cook, Roy
See Silverberg, Robert
Cook, Sally *207*
Cook, Trish *175*
Cooke, Ann
See Cole, Joanna
Cooke, Arthur
See Lowndes, Robert A(ugustine) W(ard)
Cooke, Barbara
See Alexander, Anna B(arbara Cooke)
Cooke, David Coxe 1917- *2*
Cooke, Donald Ewin 1916-1985 .... *2*
Obituary *45*
Cooke, Frank E. 1920- *87*
Cooke, Jean (Isobel Esther) 1929- *74*
Cooke, John Estes
See Baum, L. Frank
Cooke, Trish 1962- *129*
Cookson, Catherine (McMullen) 1906-1998 .. *9*
Obituary *116*
Cooley, Beth *210*
Cooley, Elizabeth
See Cooley, Beth
Cooley, Regina Francoise 1940- *177*
Coolidge, Olivia E(nsor) 1908- *26*
Earlier sketch in SATA *1*
Cooling, Wendy *169*
Earlier sketch in SATA *111*
Coombs, Charles I(ra) 1914-1994 .... *43*
Earlier sketch in SATA *3*
See also SAAS *15*
Coombs, Chick
See Coombs, Charles I(ra)
Coombs, Jonathan *204*
Coombs, Kate *190*
Coombs, Patricia 1926- *51*
Earlier sketch in SATA *3*
See also SAAS *22*

Cooney, Barbara 1917-2000 .... *96*
Obituary *123*
Earlier sketches in SATA *6, 59*
See also CLR *23*
Cooney, Caroline B. 1947- *218*
Brief entry *41*
Earlier sketches in SATA *48, 80, 113, 130, 179*
Cooney, Doug *181*
Cooney, Nancy Evans 1932- *42*
Coontz, Otto 1946- *33*
Cooper, Ann (Catharine) 1939- *104*
Cooper, Dutch
See Kuyper, Sjoerd
Cooper, Elisha 1971- *234*
Earlier sketches in SATA *99, 157*
Cooper, Elizabeth Keyser -1992 .... *47*
Cooper, Floyd *227*
Earlier sketches in SATA *96, 144, 187*
See also CLR *60*
Cooper, Gordon 1932- *23*
Cooper, Helen 1963- *169*
Earlier sketch in SATA *102*
Cooper, Henry S. F., Jr. 1933- *65*
Cooper, Henry Spotswood Fenimore, Jr.
See Cooper, Henry S. F., Jr.
Cooper, Ilene 1948- *145*
Earlier sketches in SATA *66, 97*
Cooper, James Fenimore 1789-1851 .... *19*
See also CLR *105*
Cooper, John R. *1*
Cooper, Kay 1941- *11*
Cooper, Lee Pelham 1926- *5*
Cooper, Lester (Irving) 1919-1985 .... *32*
Obituary *43*
Cooper, Lettice (Ulpha) 1897-1994 .... *35*
Obituary *82*
Cooper, Louise 1952-2009 .... *152*
Cooper, Mark A. 1963- *235*
Cooper, M.E.
See Davis, Maggie S.
Cooper, M.E.
See Lerangis, Peter
Cooper, Melrose
See Kroll, Virginia L.
Cooper, Michael L. 1950- *181*
Earlier sketches in SATA *79, 117*
Cooper, Michelle 1969- *226*
Cooper, Patrick 1949- *134*
Cooper, Susan 1935- *151*
Earlier sketches in SATA *4, 64, 104*
See also CLR *161*
See also SAAS *6*
Cooper, Susan Mary
See Cooper, Susan
Cope, Jane U(rsula) 1949- *108*
Copeland, Helen 1920- *4*
Copeland, Mark 1956- *180*
Copeland, Paul W. *23*
Coplans, Peta 1951- *84*
Copley (Diana) Heather Pickering 1918- *45*
Coppard, A(lfred) E(dgar) 1878-1957
See YABC *1*
Copper, Melinda 1952- *172*
Copper, Melinda McConnaughey
See Copper, Melinda
Corace, Jen *208*
Coralie
See Anderson, Catherine Corley
Corbett, Grahame *43*
Brief entry *36*
Corbett, Scott 1913- *42*
Earlier sketch in SATA *2*
See also CLR *1*
See also SAAS *2*
Corbett, Sue *174*
Corbett, W(illiam) J(esse) 1938- *102*
Brief entry *44*
Earlier sketch in SATA *50*
See also CLR *19*

Corbin, Sabra Lee
  See Malvern, Gladys
Corbin, William
  See McGraw, William Corbin
Corbman, Marjorie 1987- 179
Corby, Dan
  See Catherall, Arthur
Corcoran, Barbara (Asenath) 1911-2003 77
  Autobiography Feature 125
  Earlier sketch in SATA 3
  See also CLR 50
  See also SAAS 20
Corcos, Lucille 1908-1973 10
Cordell, Alexander
  See Graber, Alexander
Cordell, Matthew 1975- 199
Corder, Zizou
  See Young, Louisa
Cordova, Amy 232
Corella, Joseph
  See Odgers, Sally Farrell
Coren, Alan 1938-2007 32
  Obituary 187
Corey, Dorothy 23
Corey, Shana 1974- 219
  Earlier sketch in SATA 133
Corfe, Thomas Howell 1928- 27
Corfe, Tom
  See Corfe, Thomas Howell
Corfield, Robin Bell 1952- 74
Corke, Estelle 1969- 220
Corlett, William 1938-2005 46
  Brief entry 39
Cormack, M(argaret) Grant 1913- 11
Cormack, Maribelle B. 1902-1984 39
Cormier, Robert 1925-2000 83
  Obituary 122
  Earlier sketches in SATA 10, 45
  See also CLR 167
Cormier, Robert Edmund
  See Cormier, Robert
Cornelius, Carol 1942- 40
Cornelius, Kay 1933- 157
Cornell, J.
  See Cornell, Jeffrey
Cornell, James (Clayton, Jr.) 1938- 27
Cornell, Jean Gay 1920- 23
Cornell, Jeffrey 1945- 11
Cornell, Laura 189
Cornish, D.M. 1972- 185
Cornish, Sam(uel James) 1935- 23
Cornwall, Nellie
  See Sloggett, Nellie
Cornwell, Autumn 195
Corr, Christopher 1955- 189
Correa, E. Shan
  See Correa, Shan
Correa, Shan 233
Correy, Lee
  See Stine, G(eorge) Harry
Corrick, James A. 1945- 76
Corrigan, (Helen) Adeline 1909- 23
Corrigan, Barbara 1922- 8
Corrigan, Eireann 1977- 163
Corrin, Sara 1918- 86
  Brief entry 48
Corrin, Stephen 86
  Brief entry 48
Corriveau, Art 231
Corsi, Wendy
  See Staub, Wendy Corsi
Cort, M. C.
  See Clifford, Margaret Cort
Cort, Margaret
  See Clifford, Margaret Cort
Corwin, Judith H(offman) 1946- 10
Corwin, Oliver
  See Corwin, Oliver J.
Corwin, Oliver J. 206
Cory, Rowena
  See Lindquist, Rowena Cory

Cosby, Bill 1937- 110
  Earlier sketch in SATA 66
Cosby, William Henry, Jr.
  See Cosby, Bill
  and Cosby, Bill
Cosentino, Ralph 169
Cosgrave, John O'Hara II 1908-1968
  Obituary 21
Cosgrove, Margaret (Leota) 1926- 47
Cosgrove, Stephen E(dward) 1945- 53
  Brief entry 40
Coskey, Evelyn 1932- 7
Cosner, Shaaron 1940- 43
Cossi, Olga 1921- 216
  Earlier sketches in SATA 67, 102
Costa Bates, Janet 1959- 237
Costabel, Eva Deutsch 1924- 45
Costabel-Deutsch, Eva
  See Costabel, Eva Deutsch
Costales, Amy 1974- 227
Coste, Marion 1938- 183
Costello, David 174
Costello, David F(rancis) 1904-1990 23
Cte, Genevieve 1964- 184
Cote, Nancy 1952- 182
Cott, Jonathan 1942- 23
Cottam, Clarence 1899-1974 25
Cotten, Cynthia 188
Cottin, Menena 1950- 213
Cottle, Joan 1960- 135
Cottler, Joseph 1899-1996 22
Cottonwood, Joe 1947- 92
Cottrell, Leonard 1913-1974 24
Cottringer, Anne 1952- 150
  Earlier sketch in SATA 97
Couch, Greg 199
Coulman, Valerie 1969- 161
Couloumbis, Akila 1932-2009 225
Couloumbis, Audrey 173
Counsel, June 1926- 70
Countryman, The
  See Whitlock, Ralph
Courlander, Harold 1908-1996 6
  Obituary 88
Coursen, Valerie 1965(?)- 102
Courtis, Stuart Appleton 1874-1969
  Obituary 29
Courtland, Tyler
  See Stevens, Serita
Courtney, Dayle
  See Goldsmith, Howard
Coury, Louise Andree 1895(?)-1983
  Obituary 34
Cousins, Linda 1946- 90
Cousins, Lucy 1964- 205
  Earlier sketch in SATA 172
Cousins, Margaret 1905-1996 2
  Obituary 92
Cousteau, Jacques 1910-1997 98
  Earlier sketch in SATA 38
Cousteau, Jacques-Yves
  See Cousteau, Jacques
Couture, Christin 1951- 73
Couvillon, Jacques 195
Coventry, Susan 233
Coverly, Dave 1964- 223
Covert, Ralph 1968- 197
Coville, Bruce 1950- 216
  Autobiography Feature 155
  Earlier sketches in SATA 32, 77, 118, 155
Covington, Dennis 109
Covington, Linda
  See Windsor, Linda
Cowan, Catherine 121
Cowan, Rebecca M.
  See Moesta, Rebecca
Cowan, Rebecca Moesta
  See Moesta, Rebecca
Coward, Fiona 1963- 178
Cowdrey, Richard 1959- 204
Cowell, Cressida 1966- 140

Cowen, Eve
  See Werner, Herma
Cowen, Ida 1898-1993 64
Cowie, Leonard W(allace) 1919- 4
Cowles, Kathleen
  See Krull, Kathleen
Cowley, Cassia Joy
  See Cowley, Joy
Cowley, Joy 1936- 164
  Autobiography Feature 118
  Earlier sketches in SATA 4, 90
  See also CLR 55
  See also SAAS 26
Cowley, Marjorie 1925- 111
Cox, (Christopher) Barry 1931- 62
Cox, Clinton 1934- 108
  Earlier sketch in SATA 74
Cox, David 1933- 56
Cox, David Dundas
  See Cox, David
Cox, Donald William 1921- 23
Cox, Jack
  See Cox, John Roberts
Cox, John Roberts 1915-1981 9
Cox, Judy 1954- 236
  Earlier sketches in SATA 117, 160, 198
Cox, Marion Monroe 1898-1983
  Obituary 34
Cox, Palmer 1840-1924 24
  See also CLR 24
Cox, Paul 1957- 226
Cox, Vic 1942- 88
Cox, Vicki 1945- 158
Cox, Victoria 1945- 44
Cox, Wallace 1924-1973 25
Cox, Wally
  See Cox, Wallace
Cox, William R(obert) 1901-1988 46
  Brief entry 31
  Obituary 57
Coxe, Molly 1959- 101
  Earlier sketch in SATA 69
Coxon, Michele 1950- 158
  Earlier sketch in SATA 76
Coy, Harold 1902-1986 3
Coy, John 1958- 233
  Earlier sketches in SATA 120, 171
Craats, Rennay 1973- 131
Crabtree, Judith 1928- 98
  Earlier sketch in SATA 63
Crabtree, Julie 1970- 214
Cracker, Edward E.B.
  See Odgers, Sally Farrell
Craft, Elizabeth 1971(?)- 204
Craft, K. Y.
  See Craft, Kinuko Y.
Craft, Kinuko Y. 1940- 127
  Earlier sketch in SATA 65
Craft, Kinuko Yamabe
  See Craft, Kinuko Y.
Craft, Ruth 1935- 87
  Brief entry 31
Craig, A. A.
  See Anderson, Poul
Craig, Alisa
  See MacLeod, Charlotte (Matilda)
Craig, David
  See James, Bill
Craig, Helen 1934- 213
  Earlier sketches in SATA 46, 49, 94
Craig, Joe 1979- 198
Craig, Joe Alexander
  See Craig, Joe
Craig, John Eland
  See Chipperfield, Joseph Eugene
Craig, John Ernest 1921- 23
Craig, Kit
  See Reed, Kit
Craig, M. F.
  See Craig, Mary (Francis) Shura
Craig, M. Jean 17

Craig, M. S.
    See Craig, Mary (Francis) Shura
Craig, Margaret (Maze) 1911-1964 9
Craig, Mary
    See Craig, Mary (Francis) Shura
Craig, Mary Shura
    See Craig, Mary (Francis) Shura
Craig, Mary (Francis) Shura 1923-1991 86
    Obituary 65
    Earlier sketch in SATA 6
    See also SAAS 7
Craig, Ruth 1922- 95
Craik, Mrs.
    See Craik, Dinah Maria (Mulock)
Craik, Dinah Maria (Mulock) 1826-1887 34
Crandall, Court 1965- 175
Crandell, Rachel 1943- 152
Crane, Barbara (Joyce) 1934- 31
Crane, Carol 1933- 232
Crane, Caroline 1930- 11
Crane, Jordan 1973- 174
Crane, M. A.
    See Wartski, Maureen (Ann Crane)
Crane, Royston Campbell 1901-1977
    Obituary 22
Crane, Stephen 1871-1900
    See YABC 2
    See also CLR 132
Crane, Stephen Townley
    See Crane, Stephen
Crane, Walter 1845-1915 100
    Earlier sketch in SATA 18
    See also CLR 56
Crane, William D(wight) 1892-1976 1
Cranfield, Ingrid 1945- 74
Cranshaw, Stanley
    See Fisher, Dorothy (Frances) Canfield
Crary, Elizabeth (Ann) 1942- 99
    Brief entry 43
Crary, Margaret (Coleman) 1906-1986 9
Craste, Marc 201
Cravath, Lynne Avril
    See Cravath, Lynne W.
Cravath, Lynne W. 1951- 182
    Earlier sketches in SATA 98, 148
Craven, Thomas 1889-1969 22
Crawford, Brent 1975- 220
Crawford, Charles P. 1945- 28
Crawford, Deborah 1922- 6
Crawford, John E(dmund) 1904-1971 3
Crawford, K(aren) Michael 1959- 155
Crawford, Laura 1977(?)- 227
Crawford, Mel 1925- 44
    Brief entry 33
Crawford, Phyllis 1899- 3
Crawley, Dave 177
Cray, Roberta
    See Emerson, Ru
Crayder, Dorothy 7
Crayder, Teresa
    See Colman, Hila
Crayon, Geoffrey
    See Irving, Washington
Craz, Albert G. 1926- 24
Creagh, Kelly 234
Crebbin, June 1938- 169
    Earlier sketch in SATA 80
Crecy, Jeanne
    See Williams, Jeanne
Credle, Ellis 1902-1998 1
Creech, Sharon 1945- 226
    Earlier sketches in SATA 94, 139, 172
    See also CLR 164
Creeden, Sharon 1938- 91
Creel, Ann Howard 1953- 187
Creighton, (Mary) Helen 1899-1989
    Obituary 64
Creighton, Jill 1949- 96
Crelin, Bob 1959(?)- 221
Crenson, Victoria 1952- 159
    Earlier sketch in SATA 88

Cresp, Gael 1954- 119
Crespo, George 1962- 82
Cresswell, Helen 1934-2005 79
    Obituary 168
    Earlier sketches in SATA 1, 48
    See also CLR 18
    See also SAAS 20
Cressy, Michael 1955- 124
Cressy, Mike
    See Cressy, Michael
Cretan, Gladys (Yessayan) 1921- 2
Cretzmeyer, Stacy (Megan) 1959- 124
Crew, Gary 1947- 163
    Earlier sketches in SATA 75, 110
    See also CLR 42
Crew, Helen (Cecilia) Coale 1866-1941
    See YABC 2
Crew, Linda (Jean) 1951- 137
    Earlier sketch in SATA 71
Crewe, Megan 1980- 225
Crews, Donald 1938- 76
    Brief entry 30
    Earlier sketch in SATA 32
    See also CLR 7
Crews, Nina 1963- 158
    Earlier sketch in SATA 97
Crichton, John Michael
    See Crichton, Michael
Crichton, Michael 1942-2008 88
    Obituary 199
    Earlier sketch in SATA 9
Crider, Allen Billy
    See Crider, Bill
Crider, Bill 1941- 99
Crilley, Mark 1966- 210
    Autobiography Feature 148
    Earlier sketches in SATA 120, 148
Crilley, Paul 1975- 227
Crimi, Carolyn 1959- 219
    Earlier sketch in SATA 176
Cripps, Enid Margaret
    See Appiah, Peggy
Crisler, Curtis L. 188
Crisman, Ruth 1914- 73
Crisp, Marta Marie
    See Crisp, Marty
Crisp, Marty 1947- 128
Crispin, A(nn) C(arol) 1950- 86
Crist, James J. 1961- 168
Cristall, Barbara 79
Crist-Evans, Craig 1954- 153
Crocker, Carter 193
Crocker, Nancy 1956- 185
Crofford, Emily (Ardell) 1927- 61
Crofut, William E. III 1934- 23
Croggon, Alison 1962- 194
Croll, Carolyn 1945- 102
    Brief entry 52
    Earlier sketch in SATA 56
Croman, Dorothy Young
    See Rosenberg, Dorothy
Cromie, Alice Hamilton 1914-2000 24
Cromie, William J(oseph) 1930- 4
Crompton, Anne Eliot 1930- 73
    Earlier sketch in SATA 23
Crompton, Richmal
    See Lamburn, Richmal Crompton
Cronbach, Abraham 1882-1965 11
Crone, Ruth 1919-2003 4
Cronin, A(rchibald) J(oseph) 1896-1981 47
    Obituary 25
Cronin, Doreen (A.) 125
Cronin, Doreen 1966(?)- 178
    See also CLR 136
Cronin, Doreen A.
    See Cronin, Doreen
Cronn-Mills, Kirstin 1968- 224
Crook, Beverly Courtney 38
    Brief entry 35
Crook, Connie Brummel 1930- 168
    Earlier sketch in SATA 98

Crook, Constance
    See Crook, Connie Brummel
Crosby, Alexander L. 1906-1980 2
    Obituary 23
Crosby, Harry C.
    See Anvil, Christopher
Crosby, Margaret
    See Rathmann, Peggy
Crosher, G. R. 14
Cross, Gilbert B. 1939- 60
    Brief entry 51
Cross, Gillian 1945- 178
    Autobiography Feature 178
    Earlier sketches in SATA 38, 71, 110, 165
    See also CLR 28
Cross, Gillian Clare
    See Cross, Gillian
Cross, Helen Reeder
    See Broadhead, Helen Cross
Cross, Peter 1951- 95
Cross, Sarah 216
Cross, Shauna 1976(?)- 196
Cross, Tom 1954- 146
Cross, Verda 1914- 75
Cross, Wilbur Lucius III 1918- 2
Crossingham, John 1974- 226
Crossland, Caroline 1964- 83
Crossley-Holland, Kevin 1941- 165
    Earlier sketches in SATA 5, 74, 120
    See also CLR 84
    See also SAAS 20
Crossley-Holland, Kevin John William
    See Crossley-Holland, Kevin
Crossman, David A. 1951- 219
Crouch, Karen Hillard
    See Good, Karen Hillard
Crouch, Marcus 1913-1996 4
Crout, George C(lement) 1917- 11
Crow, Donna Fletcher 1941- 40
Crow, Francis Luther
    See Luther, Frank
Crow, Kristyn 208
Crowe, Andrew 111
Crowe, Carole 1943- 204
Crowe, Chris 206
Crowe, Ellie 203
Crowe, John
    See Lynds, Dennis
Crowe, (Bettina) Peter Lum 1911- 6
Crowell, Grace Noll 1877-1969 34
Crowell, Pers 1910-1990 2
Crowell, Robert Leland 1909-2001 63
Crowfield, Christopher
    See Stowe, Harriet Beecher
Crowley, Arthur 1945- 38
Crowley, Arthur McBlair
    See Crowley, Arthur
Crowley, Cath 1971- 233
Crowley, James 1969- 237
Crowley, John 1942- 140
    Earlier sketch in SATA 65
Crowley, Suzanne 1963- 196
Crowley, Suzanne Carlisle
    See Crowley, Suzanne
Crownfield, Gertrude 1867-1945
    See YABC 1
Crowther, James Gerald 1899-1983 14
Crowther, Kitty 1970- 220
Crowther, Robert 1948- 163
Croza, Laurel 233
Cruikshank, George 1792-1878 22
    See also CLR 63
Cruise, Robin 1951- 179
Crum, Shutta 192
    Earlier sketch in SATA 134
Crummel, Susan Stevens 1949- 176
    Earlier sketch in SATA 130
Crump, Fred H., Jr. 1931- 76
    Earlier sketch in SATA 11
Crump, J(ames) Irving 1887-1979 57
    Obituary 21

Crump, William D(rake) 1949- 138
Crunden, Reginald
  See Cleaver, Hylton Reginald
Crunk, T.
  See Crunk, Tony
Crunk, Tony 1956- 130
Crutcher, Chris 1946- 196
  Earlier sketches in SATA *52, 99, 153*
  See also CLR *159*
Crutcher, Christopher C.
  See Crutcher, Chris
Cruz, Ray(mond) 1933- 6
Cruz Martinez, Alejandro (?)-1987 74
Crystal, Billy 1947- 154
Crystal, William
  See Crystal, Billy
Ctvrtek, Vaclav 1911-1976
  Obituary 27
Cuate, Melodie A. 219
Cuetara, Mittie 1957- 158
  Earlier sketch in SATA *106*
Cuffari, Richard 1925-1978 66
  Obituary 25
  Earlier sketch in SATA *6*
Cuffe-Perez, Mary 1946- 199
Culbertson, Kim 1974- 235
Cullen, Countee 1903-1946 18
Cullen, Lynn 1955- 190
Culliford, Pierre 1928-1992 40
  Obituary 74
Cullinan, Bernice E(llinger) 1926- 135
Culp, Louanna McNary 1901-1965 2
Culper, Felix
  See McCaughrean, Geraldine
Cumbaa, Stephen 1947- 72
Cumming, Peter 1951- 168
Cumming, Primrose Amy 1915- 24
Cumming, Robert 1945- 65
Cummings, Betty Sue 1918- 15
  See also SAAS *9*
Cummings, Gillian 1961- 233
Cummings, John Michael 1963(?)- 216
Cummings, Mary 1951- 185
Cummings, Parke 1902-1987 2
  Obituary 53
Cummings, Pat 1950- 203
  Earlier sketches in SATA *42, 71, 107*
  See also CLR *48*
  See also SAAS *13*
Cummings, Phil 1957- 232
  Earlier sketches in SATA *74, 123*
Cummings, Priscilla 1951- 237
  Earlier sketches in SATA *129, 170*
Cummings, Richard
  See Gardner, Richard (M.)
Cummings, Terrance 227
Cummings, Troy 232
Cummins, Julie 200
Cummins, Maria Susanna 1827-1866
  See YABC *1*
Cumpliano, Ina 207
Cuneo, Mary Louise -2001 85
Cunliffe, John Arthur 1933- 86
  Earlier sketch in SATA *11*
Cunliffe, Marcus (Falkner) 1922-1990 37
  Obituary 66
Cunnane, Kelly 175
Cunningham, Bob
  See May, Julian
Cunningham, Captain Frank
  See Glick, Carl (Cannon)
Cunningham, Cathy
  See Cunningham, Chet
Cunningham, Chet 1928- 23
Cunningham, Dale S(peers) 1932- 11
Cunningham, Dru 91
Cunningham, E. V.
  See Fast, Howard
Cunningham, Julia (Woolfolk) 1916- 132
  Earlier sketches in SATA *1, 26*
  See also SAAS *2*

Cunningham, Lawrence J. 1943- 125
Cunningham, Virginia
  See Holmgren, Virginia C(unningham)
Cunxin, Li 1961- 220
Cupala, Holly 235
Curiae, Amicus
  See Fuller, Edmund (Maybank)
Curie, Eve 1904-2007 1
  Obituary 188
Curlee, Lynn 1947- 190
  Earlier sketches in SATA *98, 141*
Curley, Daniel 1918-1988 23
  Obituary 61
Curley, Marianne 1959- 175
  Earlier sketch in SATA *131*
Currey, Anna 194
Currie, Robin 1948- 120
Currie, Stephen 1960- 132
  Earlier sketch in SATA *82*
Curry, Ann (Gabrielle) 1934- 72
Curry, Jane L(ouise) 1932- 138
  Autobiography Feature 138
  Earlier sketches in SATA *1, 52, 90*
  See also CLR *31*
  See also SAAS *6*
Curry, Peggy Simson 1911-1987 8
  Obituary 50
Curry, Tom 185
Curtis, Bruce (Richard) 1944- 30
Curtis, Chara M(ahar) 1950- 78
Curtis, Christopher Paul 1953- 187
  Earlier sketches in SATA *93, 140*
  See also CLR *172*
Curtis, Gavin 1965- 107
Curtis, Jamie Lee 1958- 144
  Earlier sketch in SATA *95*
  See also CLR *88*
Curtis, Jennifer Keats 185
Curtis, Marci 160
Curtis, Munzee
  See Caseley, Judith
Curtis, Neil 1950-2006 202
Curtis, Patricia 1921- 101
  Earlier sketch in SATA *23*
Curtis, Peter
  See Lofts, Norah (Robinson)
Curtis, Philip (Delacourt) 1920- 62
Curtis, Richard 1937- 29
Curtis, Richard Alan
  See Curtis, Richard
Curtis, Richard Hale
  See Deming, Richard
  and Levinson, Leonard
  and Rothweiler, Paul Roger
Curtis, Stacy 205
Curtis, Wade
  See Pournelle, Jerry
Curtiss, A(rlene) B. 1934- 90
Cusack, Margaret 1945- 58
Cushman, Doug 1953- 210
  Earlier sketches in SATA *65, 101, 157*
Cushman, Jerome 2
Cushman, Karen 1941- 147
  Earlier sketch in SATA *89*
  See also CLR *55*
Cusick, John M. 236
Cusick, Richie Tankersley 1952- 231
  Earlier sketches in SATA *67, 140*
Cusimano, Maryann K.
  See Love, Maryann Cusimano
Cutbill, Andy 1972- 201
Cutchen, Billye Walker 1930- 15
Cutchins, Judy 1947- 59
Cutler, Daniel S. 1951- 78
Cutler, Daniel Solomon
  See Cutler, Daniel S.
Cutler, Ebbitt 1923- 9
Cutler, Ivor 1923-2006 24
  Obituary 174
Cutler, Jane 1936- 162
  Earlier sketches in SATA *75, 118*

Cutler, May Ebbitt
  See Cutler, Ebbitt
Cutler, Samuel
  See Folsom, Franklin (Brewster)
Cutlip, Kimbra L(eigh-Ann) 1964- 128
Cutrate, Joe
  See Spiegelman, Art
Cutt, W(illiam) Towrie 1898-1981 16
  Obituary 85
Cuyler, Margery 1948- 229
  Earlier sketches in SATA *39, 99, 156, 195*
Cuyler, Margery Stuyvesant
  See Cuyler, Margery
Cuyler, Stephen
  See Bates, Barbara S(nedeker)
Cypess, Leah 233
Cyrus, Kurt 1954- 236
  Earlier sketches in SATA *132, 179*
Czajkowski, James
  See Rollins, James
Czekaj, Jef 1969- 217
Czernecki, Stefan 1946- 178

D

Daagnese, Joseph 228
Dabba Smith, Frank 174
Dabcovich, Lydia 99
  Brief entry 47
  Earlier sketch in SATA *58*
Dace, Dolores B(oelens) 1929- 89
Da Costa, Deborah 193
Daddo, Andrew 1967- 198
Dadey, Debbie 1959- 217
  Earlier sketches in SATA *73, 136*
Dahl, Borghild (Margarethe) 1890-1984 7
  Obituary 37
Dahl, Roald 1916-1990 73
  Obituary 65
  Earlier sketches in SATA *1, 26*
  See also CLR *111*
Dahlberg, Maurine F. 1951- 171
Dahlstedt, Marden (Stewart) 1921-1983 8
  Obituary 110
Dahme, Joanne 206
Daigneault, Sylvie 236
Dain, Martin J. 1924-2000 35
Dakin, Glenn 1960- 224
Dakos, Kalli 1950- 115
  Earlier sketch in SATA *80*
Dale, Anna 1971- 170
Dale, Gary
  See Reece, Colleen L.
Dale, George E.
  See Asimov, Isaac
Dale, Jack
  See Holliday, Joseph
Dale, Kim 1957- 123
Dale, Margaret J(essy) Miller 1911- 39
Dale, Mitzi
  See Hemstock, Gillian
Dale, Norman
  See Denny, Norman (George)
Dale, Penny 1954- 151
  Earlier sketch in SATA *70*
Daley, Michael J. 170
Dalgliesh, Alice 1893-1979 17
  Obituary 21
  See also CLR *62*
Dalkey, Kara 1953- 132
Dalkey, Kara Mia
  See Dalkey, Kara
Dallas, Ruth 1919- 86
Dalmas, John
  See Jones, John R(obert)
Dalton, Alene
  See Chapin, Alene Olsen Dalton
Dalton, Annie 1948- 140
  Earlier sketch in SATA *40*

Dalton, Kit
  See Cunningham, Chet
Dalton, Max 234
Dalton, Pamela
  See Johnson, Pamela
Dalton, Sean
  See Chester, Deborah
Dalton, Sheila 1949- 108
D'Aluisio, Faith 1957- 205
Daly, James 217
Daly, Jim
  See Stratemeyer, Edward L.
Daly, Jude 1951- 222
  Earlier sketch in SATA 177
Daly, Kathleen N(orah) 124
  Brief entry 37
Daly, Maureen 1921-2006 129
  Obituary 176
  Earlier sketch in SATA 2
  See also CLR 96
  See also SAAS 1
Daly, Nicholas
  See Daly, Niki
Daly, Niki 1946- 198
  Earlier sketches in SATA 37, 76, 114, 164
  See also CLR 41
  See also SAAS 21
D'Amato, Alex 1919- 20
D'Amato, Janet (Potter) 1925- 9
Damerow, Gail 1944- 83
Damerow, Gail Jane
  See Damerow, Gail
D'Amico, Carmela 170
D'Amico, Steve 170
Damrell, Liz 1956- 77
Damrosch, Helen
  See Tee-Van, Helen Damrosch
Dana, Barbara 1940- 218
  Earlier sketch in SATA 22
Dana, Richard Henry, Jr. 1815-1882 26
Danachair, Caoimhin O
  See Danaher, Kevin
Danaher, Kevin 1913-2002 22
Danakas, John 1963- 94
Danalis, John 236
Dandi
  See Mackall, Dandi Daley
D'Andrea, Kate
  See Steiner, Barbara A(nnette)
Daneshvari, Gitty 236
Dangerfield, Balfour
  See McCloskey, (John) Robert
Daniel, Alan 1939- 76
  Brief entry 53
Daniel, Anita 1893(?)-1978 23
  Obituary 24
Daniel, Anne
  See Steiner, Barbara A(nnette)
Daniel, Becky 1947- 56
Daniel, Claire 1949- 164
Daniel, Colin
  See Windsor, Patricia
Daniel, Hawthorne 1890- 8
Daniel, (Donna) Lee 1944- 76
Daniel, Rebecca
  See Daniel, Becky
Daniels, Guy 1919-1989 11
  Obituary 62
Daniels, Kit
  See Diver, Lucienne
Daniels, Lucy
  See Oldfield, Jenny
Daniels, Max
  See Gellis, Roberta
Daniels, Olga
  See Sinclair, Olga
Daniels, Patricia 1955- 93
Daniels, Zoe
  See Laux, Constance
Dank, Gloria Rand 1955- 56
  Brief entry 46

Dank, Leonard D(ewey) 1929- 44
Dank, Milton 1920- 31
Dann, Max 1955- 62
Danneberg, Julie 1958- 173
Dantz, William R.
  See Philbrick, Rodman
Danzig, Dianne 213
Danziger, Paula 1944-2004 149
  Brief entry 30
  Obituary 155
  Earlier sketches in SATA 36, 63, 102
  See also CLR 20
Darby, Gene Kegley
  See Darby, Jean (Kegley)
Darby, J. N.
  See Govan, (Mary) Christine Noble
Darby, Jean (Kegley) 1921- 68
Darby, Patricia (Paulsen) 14
Darby, Ray(mond) 1912-1982 7
Darbyshire, Kristen 218
d'Arcy, Willard
  See Cox, William R(obert)
Dare, Geena
  See McNicoll, Sylvia (Marilyn)
D'arge, Mackie 218
Darian, Shea 1959- 97
Daringer, Helen Fern 1892-1986 1
Darke, Marjorie 1929- 87
  Earlier sketch in SATA 16
Darley, F(elix) O(ctavius) C(arr)
  1822-1888 35
Darling, David J. 1953- 60
  Brief entry 44
Darling, Kathy
  See Darling, Mary Kathleen
Darling, Lois (MacIntyre) 1917-1989 3
  Obituary 64
Darling, Louis, (Jr.) 1916-1970 3
  Obituary 23
Darling, Mary Kathleen 1943- 124
  Earlier sketches in SATA 9, 79
Darling, Sandra Louise Woodward
  See Day, Alexandra
Darnell, K(athryn) L(ynne) 1955- 150
Darroll, Sally
  See Odgers, Sally Farrell
Darrow, Sharon 181
Darrow, Whitney, (Jr.) 1909-1999 13
  Obituary 115
Darwin, Len
  See Darwin, Leonard
Darwin, Leonard 1916- 24
Dasent, Sir George Webbe 1817-1896 62
  Brief entry 29
Dash, Joan 1925- 142
Daskam, Josephine Dodge
  See Bacon, Josephine Dodge (Daskam)
D'ath, Justin 1953- 174
  Earlier sketch in SATA 106
Dauer, Rosamond 1934- 23
Daugherty, Charles Michael 1914- 16
Daugherty, James (Henry) 1889-1974 13
  See also CLR 78
Daugherty, Richard D(eo) 1922- 35
Daugherty, Sonia Medwedeff (?)-1971
  Obituary 27
d'Aulaire, Edgar Parin 1898-1986 66
  Obituary 47
  Earlier sketch in SATA 5
  See also CLR 21
d'Aulaire, Ingri 1904-1980 66
  Obituary 24
  Earlier sketch in SATA 5
  See also CLR 21
d'Aulaire, Ingri Mortenson Parin
  See d'Aulaire, Ingri
Dave, Dave
  See Berg, David
Daveluy, Paule Cloutier 1919- 11
Davenier, Christine 1961- 216
  Earlier sketches in SATA 127, 179

Davenport, John 1960- 156
Daves, Michael 1938- 40
David, A. R.
  See David, A(nn) Rosalie
David, A(nn) Rosalie 1946- 103
David, Jonathan
  See Ames, Lee J.
David, Keren 1963- 236
David, Lawrence 1963- 165
  Earlier sketch in SATA 111
David, Peter 1956- 72
David, Peter Allen
  See David, Peter
David, Rosalie
  See David, A(nn) Rosalie
Davidson, Alice Joyce 1932- 54
  Brief entry 45
Davidson, Basil 1914-2010 13
Davidson, (Marie) Diane 1924- 91
Davidson, Hugh
  See Hamilton, Edmond
Davidson, Jessica 1915-1986 5
Davidson, Judith 1953- 40
Davidson, Lionel 1922-2009 87
Davidson, Margaret 1936- 5
Davidson, Marion
  See Garis, Howard R.
Davidson, Mary R. 1885-1973 9
Davidson, Mary S. 1940- 61
Davidson, Mickie
  See Davidson, Margaret
Davidson, Nicole
  See Jensen, Kathryn
Davidson, R.
  See Davidson, Raymond
Davidson, Raymond 1926- 32
Davidson, Rosalie 1921- 23
Davie, Helen K(ay) 1952- 148
  Earlier sketch in SATA 77
Davies, Andrew (Wynford) 1936- 27
Davies, Andy Robert 200
Davies, Bettilu D(onna) 1942- 33
Davies, Hunter 1936- 55
  Brief entry 45
Davies, Jacqueline 1962- 186
  Earlier sketch in SATA 155
Davies, Joan 1934- 50
  Brief entry 47
Davies, Nicola 1958- 182
  Earlier sketches in SATA 99, 150
Davies, Peter J(oseph) 1937- 52
Davies, Sumiko 1942- 46
Davis, (A.) Aubrey 1949- 153
Davis, Barbara Steincrohn
  See Davis, Maggie S.
Davis, Bette J. 1923- 15
Davis, Burke 1913- 4
Davis, Christopher 1928- 6
Davis, D(elbert) Dwight 1908-1965 33
Davis, Daniel S(heldon) 1936- 12
Davis, David R. 1948- 106
Davis, Donald 1944- 169
  Earlier sketch in SATA 93
Davis, Donald D.
  See Davis, Donald
Davis, Eleanor 1983(?)- 209
Davis, Emma
  See Davis, Maggie S.
Davis, Gibbs 1953- 102
  Brief entry 41
  Earlier sketch in SATA 46
Davis, Grania 1943- 88
  Brief entry 50
Davis, H(arold) L(enoir) 1896-1960 114
Davis, Heather 1970- 221
Davis, Hubert J(ackson) 1904-1997 31
Davis, Jack E. 210
Davis, Jacky 204
Davis, James Robert 1945- 32
Davis, Jenny 1953- 74

Davis, Jim
　See Davis, James Robert
Davis, Julia 1900(?)-1993 6
　Obituary 75
Davis, Karen (Elizabeth) 1944- 109
Davis, Katie 1959(?)- 208
　Earlier sketch in SATA 152
Davis, Lambert 176
Davis, Leslie
　See Guccione, Leslie Davis
Davis, Louise Littleton 1921- 25
Davis, Maggie S. 1943- 57
Davis, Marguerite 1889- 34
Davis, Mary L(ee) 1935- 9
Davis, Mary Octavia 1901-1976 6
Davis, Nancy 1958(?)- 229
Davis, Nelle 1958- 73
Davis, Ossie 1917-2005 81
　See also CLR 56
Davis, Paxton 1925-1994 16
Davis, Rich 1958- 206
Davis, Robert 1881-1949
　See YABC 1
Davis, Robin W(orks) 1962- 87
Davis, Russell Gerard 1922- 3
Davis, Tanita S. 212
Davis, Tim(othy N.) 1957- 94
Davis, Tony 1961- 222
Davis, Verne Theodore 1889-1973 6
Davis, Yvonne 1927- 115
Davol, Marguerite W. 1928- 146
　Earlier sketch in SATA 82
DaVolls, Andy (P.) 1967- 85
DaVolls, Linda 1966- 85
Davys, Sarah
　See Manning, Rosemary
Dawes, Claiborne 1935- 111
Dawson, Arthur L. 207
Dawson, Elmer A. 67
　Earlier sketch in SATA 1
Dawson, Imogen (Zoe) 1948- 126
　Earlier sketch in SATA 90
Dawson, Janine 1957- 196
Dawson, Mary 1919- 11
Dawson, Scott 233
Dawson, Willow 1975- 208
Day, A(rthur) Grove 1904-1994 59
Day, Alexandra 1941- 197
　Autobiography Feature 197
　Earlier sketches in SATA 67, 97, 169
　See also CLR 22
　See also SAAS 19
Day, Beth (Feagles) 1924- 33
Day, Donna
　See Asay, Donna Day
Day, Edward C. 1932- 72
Day, Jon 1936(?)- 79
Day, Karen 187
Day, Larry 1956- 227
　Earlier sketch in SATA 181
Day, Nancy 1953- 140
Day, Nancy Raines 1951- 148
　Earlier sketch in SATA 93
Day, Shirley 1962- 94
Day, Susie 1975- 231
Day, Thomas 1748-1789
　See YABC 1
Day, Trevor 1955- 124
Dazey, Agnes J(ohnston) 2
Dazey, Frank M. 2
Deacon, Alexis 1978- 139
Deacon, Eileen
　See Geipel, Eileen
Deacon, Richard
　See McCormick, (George) Donald (King)
Deadman, Ronald 1919-1988(?)
　Obituary 56
Deak, Erzsi 1959- 152
Dean, Anabel 1915- 12
Dean, Carolee 1962- 148
Dean, Claire 215

Dean, David 1976- 192
Dean, Karen Strickler 1923- 49
Dean, Ruth (Brigham) 1947- 145
Dean, Zoey
　See Bennett, Cherie
de Angeli, Marguerite (Lofft) 1889-1987 ... 100
　Obituary 51
　Earlier sketches in SATA 1, 27
　See also CLR 1
Deans, Karen 195
Deans, Sis Boulos 1955- 136
　Earlier sketch in SATA 78
DeArmand, Frances Ullmann 1904(?)-1984 . 10
　Obituary 38
DeArmond, Dale 1914- 70
DeArmond, Dale Burlison
　See DeArmond, Dale
Deary, Terry 1946- 171
　Brief entry 41
　Earlier sketches in SATA 51, 101
Deaver, Julie Reece 1953- 68
de Banke, Cecile 1889-1965 11
De Bello, Rosario 1923- 89
Debon, Nicolas 186
　Earlier sketch in SATA 151
de Bono, Edward 1933- 66
de Brissac, Malcolm
　See Dickinson, Peter
de Brunhoff, Jean
　See Brunhoff, Jean de
De Brunhoff, Laurent
　See Brunhoff, Laurent de
De Bruyn, Monica G. 1952- 13
De Bruyn, Monica Jean Grembowicz
　See De Bruyn, Monica G.
DeBry, Roger K. 1942- 91
de Camp, Catherine Crook 1907-2000 83
　Earlier sketch in SATA 12
de Camp, L. Sprague 1907-2000 83
　Earlier sketch in SATA 9
de Camp, Lyon Sprague
　See de Camp, L. Sprague
DeCandido, Keith R.A. 112
Dechausay, Sonia E. 94
Decker, C.B. 172
Decker, Cynthia B.
　See Decker, C.B.
Decker, Duane 1910-1964 5
Decker, Timothy 1974- 197
DeClements, Barthe 1920- 131
　Earlier sketches in SATA 35, 71
　See also CLR 23
DeClements, Barthe Faith
　See DeClements, Barthe
de Clercq Zubli, Rita la Fontaine 1929- 199
de Conte, Sieur Louis
　See Twain, Mark
Dedman, Stephen 108
Dee, Barbara 1958- 220
Dee, Catherine 1964- 138
Dee, Ruby
　See Wallace, Ruby Ann
Deeble, Jason 1979- 221
Deedy, Carmen Agra 1960- 196
Deedy, John 1923- 24
Deegan, Paul Joseph 1937- 48
　Brief entry 38
Deem, James M. 1950- 191
　Autobiography Feature 191
　Earlier sketches in SATA 75, 134
Deem, James Morgan
　See Deem, James M.
Deeter, Catherine 1947- 137
DeFelice, Cynthia 1951- 165
　Earlier sketches in SATA 79, 121
DeFelice, Cynthia C.
　See DeFelice, Cynthia
Defoe, Daniel 1660(?)-1731 22
　See also CLR 164
de Fombelle, Timothee
　See Fombelle, Timothee de

DeFord, Deborah H. 123
deFrance, Anthony
　See DiFranco, Anthony (Mario)
Degen, Bruce 1945- 205
　Brief entry 47
　Earlier sketches in SATA 57, 97, 147
DeGering, Etta (Belle) Fowler 1898-1996 7
Degman, Lori 234
De Goldi, Kate 1959- 123
De Goldi, Kathleen Domenica
　See De Goldi, Kate
de Goursac, Olivier 1959- 184
De Grazia, Ettore 1909-1982 39
De Grazia, Ted
　See De Grazia, Ettore
deGroat, Diane 1947- 169
　Earlier sketches in SATA 31, 90
deGros, J. H.
　See Villiard, Paul
de Grummond, Lena Young 62
　Earlier sketch in SATA 6
de Hamel, Joan Littledale 1924- 86
De Haven, Tom 1949- 72
de Hugo, Pierre
　See Brackers de Hugo, Pierre
Deines, Brian 1955- 220
Deiss, Joseph Jay 1912-1999 12
de Jenkins, Lyll Becerra 1925-1997 102
DeJong, David C(ornel) 1905-1967 10
de Jong, Dola
　See de Jong, Dorothea Rosalie
de Jong, Dorothea Rosalie 1911-2003 7
　Obituary 149
DeJong, Meindert 1906-1991 2
　Obituary 68
　See also CLR 73
DeJonge, Joanne E. 1943- 56
Deka, Connie
　See Laux, Constance
de Kay, Ormonde (Jr.) 1923-1998 7
　Obituary 106
DeKeyser, Stacy 1959- 214
de Kiriline, Louise
　See Lawrence, Louise de Kiriline
Dekker, Carl
　See Laffin, John (Alfred Charles)
　and Lynds, Dennis
deKruif, Paul (Henry) 1890-1971 50
　Earlier sketch in SATA 5
Delacre, Lulu 1957- 209
　Earlier sketches in SATA 36, 156
DeLaCroix, Alice 1940- 195
　Earlier sketch in SATA 75
de la Cruz, Melissa 1971- 179
De la Garza, Phyllis 1942- 169
De Lage, Ida 1918- 11
de la Mare, Walter (John) 1873-1956 16
　See also CLR 148
Delaney, Harry 1932- 3
Delaney, Joseph 1945- 172
Delaney, M.C.
　See Delaney, Michael
Delaney, Michael 1955- 180
　Earlier sketch in SATA 96
Delaney, Michael Clark
　See Delaney, Michael
Delaney, Ned 1951- 28
Delaney, Thomas Nicholas III
　See Delaney, Ned
DeLange, Alex Pardo
　See Pardo DeLange, Alex
Delano, Hugh 1933- 20
Delano, Marfe Ferguson 215
Delany, Samuel R., Jr. 1942- 92
Delany, Samuel Ray
　See Delany, Samuel R., Jr.
de la Pena, Matt 205
De La Ramee, Marie Louise 1839-1908 20
de la Roche, Mazo 1879-1961 64
De La Roche Saint Andre, Anne 1950- 75
de Las Casas, Dianne 1970- 221

Delaune, (Jewel) Lynn (de Grummond) 7
DeLaurentis, Louise Budde 1920- 12
del Barco, Lucy Salamanca 1900(?)-1989
    Obituary 64
Delderfield, Eric R(aymond) 1909-1995 14
Delderfield, Ronald Frederick 1912-1972 20
DeLeeuw, Adele (Louise) 1899-1988 30
    Obituary 56
    Earlier sketch in SATA 1
De Leon, Nephtali 1945- 97
Delessert, Etienne 1941- 179
    Brief entry 27
    Earlier sketches in SATA 46, 130
    See also CLR 81
Delgado, James P. 1958- 122
Delinois, Alix 228
de Lint, Charles 1951- 207
    Earlier sketches in SATA 115, 157
de Lint, Charles Henri Diederick Hofsmit
    See de Lint, Charles
Delmar, Roy
    See Wexler, Jerome (LeRoy)
Del Negro, Janice M. 197
Deloria, Vine, Jr. 1933-2005 21
    Obituary 171
Deloria, Vine Victor, Jr.
    See Deloria, Vine, Jr.
del Rey, Lester 1915-1993 22
    Obituary 76
Delrio, Martin
    See Doyle, Debra
    and Macdonald, James D.
Delton, Judy 1931-2001 77
    Obituary 130
    Earlier sketch in SATA 14
    See also SAAS 9
Delulio, John 1938- 15
Delvig, Lou
    See Vigan, Delphine de
Delving, Michael
    See Williams, Jay
de Marcken, Gail 186
Demarest, Chris L. 1951- 175
    Brief entry 44
    Earlier sketches in SATA 45, 82, 128
Demarest, Christopher Lynn
    See Demarest, Chris L.
Demarest, Doug
    See Barker, Will
De Mari, Silvana 1953- 193
Demas, Corinne 1947- 203
    Earlier sketches in SATA 37, 131
Demas, Vida 1927- 9
Dematons, Charlotte 1957- 203
DeMatteis, J.M. 1953- 180
DeMatteis, John Marc
    See DeMatteis, J.M.
De Mejo, Oscar 1911-1992 40
Demers, Dominique 1956- 177
de Messieres, Nicole 1930- 39
DeMeulemeester, Linda 1956- 230
Demi 1942- 210
    Earlier sketches in SATA 11, 66, 102, 152
    See also CLR 58
Demijohn, Thom
    See Disch, Thomas M.
    and Sladek, John
Deming, Richard 1915-1983 24
Deming, Sarah 191
de Monfreid, Dorothee 1973- 189
Demuth, Patricia Brennan 1948- 84
    Brief entry 51
De Muth, Roger 1948- 221
Dendinger, Roger E. 1952- 158
Denenberg, Barry 1940- 175
Dengler, Marianna (Herron) 1935- 103
Dengler, Sandy 1939- 54
    Brief entry 40
Denim, Sue
    See Pilkey, Dav
Denise, Anika 210

Denise, Christopher 1968- 193
    Earlier sketch in SATA 147
Denman, K.L. 1957- 186
Denmark, Harrison
    See Zelazny, Roger
Dennard, Deborah 1953- 136
    Earlier sketch in SATA 78
Denney, Diana 1910-2000 25
    Obituary 120
Dennis, Morgan 1891(?)-1960 18
Dennis, Wesley 1903-1966 18
Denniston, Elinore 1900-1978
    Obituary 24
Denny, Norman (George) 1901-1982 43
Denos, Julia 202
Denslow, Sharon Phillips 1947- 142
    Earlier sketch in SATA 68
Denslow, W(illiam) W(allace) 1856-1915 16
    See also CLR 15
Dent, Grace 1973- 187
Denton, Kady MacDonald 181
    Earlier sketches in SATA 66, 110
    See also CLR 71
Denton, Terry 1950- 186
Denver, Walt
    See Redding, Robert Hull
    and Sherman, Jory (Tecumseh)
Denzel, Justin F(rancis) 1917-1999 46
    Brief entry 38
Denzer, Ann Wiseman
    See Wiseman, Ann (Sayre)
DePalma, Mary Newell 1961- 185
    Earlier sketch in SATA 139
De Palma, Toni 199
dePaola, Thomas Anthony 1934- 200
    Earlier sketches in SATA 11, 59, 108, 155
    See also CLR 81
    See also SAAS 15
dePaola, Tomie
    See dePaola, Thomas Anthony
deParrie, Paul 1949- 74
DePauw, Linda Grant 1940- 24
De Pretto, Lorenzo 1966- 225
de Quidt, Jeremy 237
DeRan, David 1946- 76
Derby, Ken 1956- 181
Derby, Kenneth R.
    See Derby, Ken
Derby, Pat 1942- 172
Derby, Sally 1934- 189
    Earlier sketches in SATA 89, 132
de Regniers, Beatrice Schenk (Freedman)
    1914-2000 68
    Obituary 123
    Earlier sketch in SATA 2
    See also SAAS 6
Dereske, Jo 1947- 72
Deriso, Christine Hurley 1961- 210
Derleth, August (William) 1909-1971 5
Derman, Martha (Winn) 74
Derman, Sarah Audrey 1915- 11
DeRoberts, Lyndon
    See Silverstein, Robert Alan
Derom, Dirk 1980- 224
de Roo, Anne Louise 1931-1997 84
    Earlier sketch in SATA 25
    See also CLR 63
deRosa, Dee 70
Derrick, Lionel
    See Cunningham, Chet
Derrickson, Jim 1959- 141
Derry Down Derry
    See Lear, Edward
Derting, Kimberly 1968- 231
Dervaux, Isabelle 1961- 106
Derwent, Lavinia 14
Desai, Anita 1937- 126
    Earlier sketch in SATA 63
DeSaix, Deborah Durland 188
De Saulles, Tony 1958- 119
Desbarats, Peter 1933- 39

de Selincourt, Aubrey 1894-1962 14
de Seve, Peter 1958- 219
de Seve, Randall 198
Deshpande, Chris 1950- 69
Desimini, Lisa 1964- 216
    Earlier sketches in SATA 86, 148
Desjarlais, John 1953- 71
Desjarlais, John J.
    See Desjarlais, John
Desmoinaux, Christel 1967- 149
    Earlier sketch in SATA 103
Desmond, Adrian 1947- 51
Desmond, Adrian J.
    See Desmond, Adrian
Desmond, Adrian John
    See Desmond, Adrian
Desmond, Alice Curtis 1897-1990 8
Desnoettes, Caroline 183
DeSpain, Pleasant 1943- 87
Desputeaux, Helene 1959- 95
Dessen, Sarah 1970- 172
    Earlier sketch in SATA 120
Detine, Padre
    See Olsen, Ib Spang
de Trevino, Elizabeth B.
    See Trevino, Elizabeth B(orton) de
de Trevino, Elizabeth Borton
    See Trevino, Elizabeth B(orton) de
Detwiler, Susan Dill 1956- 58
Deuker, Carl 1950- 196
    Earlier sketches in SATA 82, 150
Deutsch, Babette 1895-1982 1
    Obituary 33
Deutsch, Eva Costabel
    See Costabel, Eva Deutsch
Deutsch, Helen 1906-1992 76
Deutsch, Kurt
    See Singer, Kurt D.
De Valera, Sinead 1879(?)-1975
    Obituary 30
Devaney, John 1926-1994 12
de Varennes, Monique 1947- 168
de Varona, Frank J. 1943- 83
Devereux, Frederick L(eonard), Jr.
    1914-1993 9
Devi, Nila
    See Woody, Regina Jones
DeVillers, Julia 1967- 227
deVinck, Christopher 1951- 85
DeVita, James 195
DeVito, Cara 1956- 80
Devlin, Dorothy Wende
    See Devlin, Wende
Devlin, Harry 1918-2001 136
    Earlier sketches in SATA 11, 74
Devlin, Wende 1918-2002 74
    Earlier sketch in SATA 11
Devon, Paddie 1953- 92
Devons, Sonia 1974- 72
Devorah-Leah 111
de Vos, Gail 1949- 122
de Vries, Anke 1936- 222
DeVries, Douglas 1933- 122
De Waard, E(lliott) John 1935- 7
Dewan, Ted 1961- 226
    Earlier sketches in SATA 108, 157
Dewdney, Anna 232
    Earlier sketch in SATA 184
Dewdney, Selwyn (Hanington) 1909-1979 ... 64
DeWeese, Gene
    See DeWeese, Thomas Eugene
DeWeese, Jean
    See DeWeese, Thomas Eugene
DeWeese, Thomas Eugene 1934- 46
    Brief entry 45
Dewey, Ariane 1937- 178
    Earlier sketches in SATA 7, 109
Dewey, Jennifer (Owings) 1941- 103
    Brief entry 48
    Earlier sketch in SATA 58
Dewey, Kenneth Francis 1940- 39

Dewin, Howie
　See Howie, Betsy
De Wire, Elinor 1953- *180*
deWit, Dorothy (May Knowles) 1916-1980 . *39*
　Obituary *28*
Dexter, Alison 1966- *125*
Dexter, John
　See Bradley, Marion Zimmer
Deyneka, Anita 1943- *24*
Deyrup, Astrith Johnson 1923- *24*
Dezern, Chad *201*
de Zubizarreta, Alma
　See Ada, Alma Flor
Dhami, Narinder 1958- *152*
Dhondy, Farrukh 1944- *152*
　Earlier sketch in SATA *65*
　See also CLR *41*
Diakite, Baba Wague 1961- *174*
Diakite, Penda 1993(?)- *174*
Diamand, Emily 1971- *227*
Diamond, Arthur 1957- *76*
Diamond, Donna 1950- *69*
　Brief entry *30*
　Earlier sketch in SATA *35*
Diamond, Petra
　See Sachs, Judith
Diamond, Rebecca
　See Sachs, Judith
Dias, Earl Joseph 1916- *41*
Dias, Ron 1937- *71*
Diaz, David 1959(?)- *229*
　Earlier sketches in SATA *96, 150, 189*
　See also CLR *65*
di Bartolo, Jim *225*
Dibley, Glin *188*
DiCamillo, Kate 1964- *202*
　Earlier sketches in SATA *121, 163*
　See also CLR *117*
Di Certo, J(oseph) J(ohn) 1933- *60*
DiCianni, Ron 1952- *107*
Dick, Trella Lamson 1889-1974 .... *9*
Dickens, Charles 1812-1870 .... *15*
　See also CLR *162*
Dickens, Charles John Huffam
　See Dickens, Charles
Dickens, Frank
　See Huline-Dickens, Frank William
Dickens, Monica (Enid) 1915-1992 .... *4*
　Obituary *74*
Dickerson, Roy Ernest 1886-1965
　Obituary *26*
Dickinson, Emily 1830-1886 .... *29*
Dickinson, Emily Elizabeth
　See Dickinson, Emily
Dickinson, Mary 1949- *48*
　Brief entry *41*
Dickinson, Mary-Anne
　See Rodda, Emily
Dickinson, Peter 1927- *229*
　Earlier sketches in SATA *5, 62, 95, 150*
　See also CLR *125*
Dickinson, Peter Malcolm de Brissac
　See Dickinson, Peter
Dickinson, Susan 1931- *8*
Dickinson, Terence 1943- *102*
Dickinson, W(illiam) Croft 1897-1963 .... *13*
Dickson, Gordon R. 1923-2001 .... *77*
Dickson, Gordon Rupert
　See Dickson, Gordon R.
Dickson, Helen
　See Reynolds, Helen Mary Greenwood Campbell
Dickson, Naida 1916- *8*
Diehn, Gwen 1943- *80*
Dierssen, Andreas 1962- *190*
Diesen, Deborah 1967- *200*
Dieterich, Michele M. 1962- *78*
Dietz, David H(enry) 1897-1984 .... *10*
　Obituary *41*
Dietz, Lew 1907-1997 .... *11*
　Obituary *95*

Diffily, Deborah *159*
Di Fiori, Larry
　See Di Fiori, Lawrence
Di Fiori, Lawrence 1934- *130*
DiFranco, Anthony (Mario) 1945- *42*
Digby, Anne 1935- *72*
Digges, Jeremiah
　See Berger, Josef
Digman, Kristina 1959- *176*
D'Ignazio, Fred 1949- *39*
　Brief entry *35*
D'Ignazio, Frederick
　See D'Ignazio, Fred
Di Grazia, Thomas (?)-1983 .... *32*
Dijkstra, Lida 1961- *195*
Dikty, Julian May
　See May, Julian
Dillard, Annie 1945- *140*
　Earlier sketch in SATA *10*
Dillard, Kristine 1964- *113*
Dillard, Polly Hargis 1916- *24*
Dillard, Sarah 1961- *217*
Diller, Harriett 1953- *78*
Dillon, Anna
　See Scott, Michael
Dillon, Barbara 1927- *44*
　Brief entry *39*
Dillon, Diane 1933- *194*
　Earlier sketches in SATA *15, 51, 106*
　See also CLR *44*
Dillon, Diane Claire
　See Dillon, Diane
Dillon, Eilis 1920-1994 .... *74*
　Autobiography Feature *105*
　Obituary *83*
　Earlier sketch in SATA *2*
　See also CLR *26*
Dillon, Jana (a pseudonym) 1952- *117*
Dillon, Leo 1933- *194*
　Earlier sketches in SATA *15, 51, 106*
　See also CLR *44*
Dillon, Sharon Saseen
　See Saseen, Sharon (Dillon)
Dils, Tracey E. 1958- *83*
Dilson, Jesse 1914-1988 .... *24*
Dinan, Carolyn *59*
　Brief entry *47*
Dines, Carol 1956- *175*
Dines, (Harry) Glen 1925-1996 .... *7*
Dinesen, Isak
　See Blixen, Karen
Dinessi, Alex
　See Schembri, Jim
Dinneen, Betty 1929- *61*
Dinnerstein, Harvey 1928- *42*
Dinsdale, Tim(othy Kay) 1924-1987 .... *11*
Dion, Nathalie 1964- *213*
Dionne, Erin 1975- *217*
Diop, Birago (Ismael) 1906-1989
　Obituary *64*
Diouf, Sylviane A. *168*
Diouf, Sylviane Anna
　See Diouf, Sylviane A.
DiPucchio, Kelly *204*
　Earlier sketch in SATA *159*
Dirk
　See Gringhuis, Richard H.
Dirks, Wilhelmina 1916- *59*
Dirks, Willy
　See Dirks, Wilhelmina
Dirtmeister
　See Tomecek, Steve
DiSalvo, DyAnne 1960- *144*
　Earlier sketch in SATA *59*
DiSalvo-Ryan, DyAnne
　See DiSalvo, DyAnne
Disch, Thomas M. 1940-2008 .... *92*
　Obituary *195*
　See also CLR *18*
　See also SAAS *15*

Disch, Thomas Michael
　See Disch, Thomas M.
Disch, Tom
　See Disch, Thomas M.
Disher, Garry 1949- *125*
　Earlier sketch in SATA *81*
Disney, Walt(er Elias) 1901-1966 .... *28*
　Brief entry *27*
Ditchfield, Christin 1973- *226*
　Earlier sketch in SATA *189*
DiTerlizzi, Tony 1969- *214*
　Earlier sketch in SATA *154*
DiTerlooney, Tiny
　See DiTerlizzi, Tony
Divakaruni, Chitra Banerjee 1956- *222*
　Earlier sketch in SATA *160*
Di Valentin, Maria (Amelia) Messuri
　1911-1985 .... *7*
Diver, Lucienne 1971- *218*
Divine, Arthur Durham 1904-1987
　Obituary *52*
Divine, David
　See Divine, Arthur Durham
Divine, L. *229*
Dixon, Ann 1954- *212*
　Earlier sketches in SATA *77, 127*
Dixon, Ann Renee
　See Dixon, Ann
Dixon, Dougal 1947- *190*
　Earlier sketches in SATA *45, 127*
Dixon, Franklin W.
　See Barrett, Neal, Jr.
　and Goulart, Ron
　and Lantz, Francess L(in)
　and Lerangis, Peter
　and McFarlane, Leslie
　and Stanley, George Edward
　and Stratemeyer, Edward L.
Dixon, Jeanne 1936- *31*
Dixon, Paige
　See Corcoran, Barbara (Asenath)
Dixon, Peter L(ee) 1931- *6*
Dixon, Rachel 1952- *74*
Dizin, Pascal *230*
Djoleto, (Solomon Alexander) Amu 1929- ... *80*
d'Lacey, Chris 1949- *227*
　Earlier sketch in SATA *165*
Doak, Annie
　See Dillard, Annie
Doane, Pelagie 1906-1966 .... *7*
Dob, Bob *207*
Dobell, I(sabel) M(arian) B(arclay)
　1909-1998 .... *11*
Dobie, J(ames) Frank 1888-1964 .... *43*
Dobkin, Alexander 1908-1975
　Obituary *30*
Dobler, Lavinia G. 1910- *6*
Dobrin, Arnold 1928- *4*
Dobson, Jill 1969- *140*
Dobson, Julia 1941- *48*
Dobson, Mary 1954- *117*
DoCampo, Valeria 1976- *217*
Docherty, James
　See Docherty, Jimmy
Docherty, Jimmy 1976- *204*
Docherty, Thomas 1955- *218*
Dockery, Wallene T. 1941- *27*
Dockray, Tracy 1962- *139*
Dockrey, Karen 1955- *103*
Doctor, Bernard
　See Doctor, Bernard Aquina
Doctor, Bernard Aquina 1950- *81*
Doctor X
　See Nourse, Alan E(dward)
Dodd, Ed(ward Benton) 1902-1991 .... *4*
　Obituary *68*
Dodd, Emma 1969- *203*
Dodd, Lynley (Stuart) 1941- *132*
　Earlier sketches in SATA *35, 86*
　See also CLR *62*
Dodd, Marty 1921- *142*

Dodd, Quentin 1972- 137
Dodds, Bill 1952- 78
Dodds, Dayle Ann 1952- 201
  Earlier sketches in SATA 75, 150
Doder, Josh 1968- 187
Dodge, Bertha S(anford) 1902-1995 8
Dodge, Fremont
  See Grimes, Lee
Dodge, Gil
  See Hano, Arnold
Dodge, Mary (Elizabeth) Mapes
  1831(?)-1905 100
  Earlier sketch in SATA 21
  See also CLR 62
Dodgson, Charles Lutwidge
  See Carroll, Lewis
Dodson, Emma 235
Dodson, Kenneth MacKenzie 1907-1999 11
Dodson, Susan 1941- 50
  Brief entry 40
Doerrfeld, Cori 1964- 214
Dogar, Sharon 1962- 211
Dogyear, Drew
  See Gorey, Edward (St. John)
Doherty, Berlie 1943- 111
  Earlier sketch in SATA 72
  See also CLR 21
  See also SAAS 16
Doherty, Charles Hugh 1913- 6
Doherty, Craig A. 1951- 169
  Earlier sketch in SATA 83
Doherty, Katherine M(ann) 1951- 83
Doherty, Kieran 1945- 164
Dokas, Dara 1968- 216
Dokey, Cameron 1956- 97
Dolamore, Jaclyn 1982- 227
Dolan, Edward F(rancis), Jr. 1924- 94
  Brief entry 31
  Earlier sketch in SATA 45
Dolan, Ellen M(eara) 1929-1998 88
Dolan, Sean J. 1958- 74
Dolce, J. Ellen 1948- 75
Dolch, Edward William 1889-1961 50
Dolch, Marguerite Pierce 1891-1978 50
Dollar, Diane (Hills) 1933- 57
Dolson, Hildegarde
  See Lockridge, Hildegarde (Dolson)
Domanska, Janina 1913(?)-1995 68
  Obituary 84
  Earlier sketch in SATA 6
  See also CLR 40
  See also SAAS 18
Dominguez, Angel 1953- 76
Dominguez, Angela N. 1982- 219
Domino, John
  See Averill, Esther (Holden)
Domjan, Joseph (Spiri) 1907-1992 25
Domm, Jeffrey C. 1958- 84
Donahue, Dorothy 178
Donald, Rhonda Lucas 1962- 147
Donalds, Gordon
  See Shirreffs, Gordon D(onald)
Donaldson, Bryna
  See Stevens, Bryna
Donaldson, Gordon 1913-1993 64
  Obituary 76
Donaldson, Joan 1953- 227
  Earlier sketch in SATA 78
Donaldson, Julia 1948- 226
  Earlier sketches in SATA 82, 132, 180
Donaldson, Stephen R. 1947- 121
Donaldson, Stephen Reeder
  See Donaldson, Stephen R.
Doner, Kim 1955- 208
  Earlier sketch in SATA 91
Doney, Todd L. W. 1959- 104
Dong-Sung, Kim 1970- 195
Dong-Sung Kim
  See Dong-Sung, Kim
Donkin, Andrew 219
Donkin, Nance (Clare) 1915- 95

Donna, Natalie 1934-1979 9
Donnelly, Elfie 1950-
  See CLR 104
Donnelly, Jennifer 1963- 154
Donnelly, Matt 1972- 148
Donnio, Sylviane 188
Donofrio, Beverly 1950- 209
Donoghue, Emma 1969- 101
Donohue, Moira Rose 1954- 201
Donoughue, Carol 1935- 139
Donovan, Frank (Robert) 1906-1975
  Obituary 30
Donovan, Gail 1962- 217
Donovan, Jane Monroe 237
Donovan, John 1928-1992 72
  Brief entry 29
  See also CLR 3
Donovan, Mary Lee 1961- 86
Donovan, William
  See Berkebile, Fred D(onovan)
Donze, Mary Terese 1911- 89
Doob, Leonard W(illiam) 1909-2000 8
Doodler, Todd H.
  See Goldman, Todd Harris
Dooley, Norah 1953- 74
Dooley, Sarah 236
Dooling, Michael 1958- 220
  Earlier sketch in SATA 105
Dor, Ana
  See Ceder, Georgiana Dorcas
Doran, Colleen 1963- 211
Dore, (Louis Christophe Paul) Gustave
  1832-1883 19
Doremus, Robert 1913-2010 30
Doren, Marion (Walker) 1928- 57
Dorenkamp, Michelle 1957- 89
Dorflinger, Carolyn 1953- 91
Dorfman, Joaquin 1979- 180
Dorfman, Joaquin Emiliano
  See Dorfman, Joaquin
Dorian, Edith M(cEwen) 1900-1983 5
Dorian, Harry
  See Hamilton, Charles (Harold St. John)
Dorian, Marguerite 7
Dorin, Patrick C(arberry) 1939- 59
  Brief entry 52
Dorman, Brandon 194
Dorman, Michael 1932- 7
Dorman, N. B. 1927- 39
Dormer, Frank W. 200
Dorris, Michael 1945-1997 75
  Obituary 94
  See also CLR 58
Dorris, Michael A.
  See Dorris, Michael
Dorris, Michael Anthony
  See Dorris, Michael
Dorritt, Susan
  See Schlein, Miriam
Dorros, Alex 1991- 194
Dorros, Arthur 1950- 168
  Earlier sketches in SATA 78, 122
  See also CLR 42
  See also SAAS 20
Dorros, Arthur M.
  See Dorros, Arthur
Dorson, Richard M(ercer) 1916-1981 30
Doss, Helen (Grigsby) 1918- 20
Doss, Margot Patterson 6
dos Santos, Joyce Audy 1949- 57
  Brief entry 42
Dothers, Anne
  See Chess, Victoria (Dickerson)
Dotlich, Rebecca Kai 1951- 182
Dottig
  See Grider, Dorothy
Dotts, Maryann J. 1933- 35
Doty, Jean Slaughter 1929- 28
Doty, Roy 1922- 28
Doubtfire, Dianne (Abrams) 1918- 29

Doucet, Sharon Arms 1951- 144
  Autobiography Feature 144
  Earlier sketch in SATA 125
Dougherty, Charles 1922- 18
Dougherty, Terri (L.) 1964- 146
Doughty, Rebecca 1955- 174
Douglas, Allen 223
Douglas, Blaise 1960- 101
Douglas, Carole Nelson 1944- 73
Douglas, Garry
  See Kilworth, Garry
Douglas, James McM.
  See Griffin, W. E. B.
Douglas, Kathryn
  See Ewing, Kathryn
Douglas, Leonard
  See Bradbury, Ray
Douglas, Lola
  See Zeises, Lara M.
Douglas, Marjory Stoneman 1890-1998 10
Douglas, Michael
  See Bright, Robert Sr.)
Douglas, Michael
  See Crichton, Michael
Douglas, Shirley Stewart
  See Tepper, Sheri S.
Douglass, Barbara 1930- 40
Douglass, Frederick 1817(?)-1895 29
Douglass, Keith
  See Cunningham, Chet
Douty, Esther M(orris) 1909-1978 8
  Obituary 23
Dow, Emily R. 1904-1987 10
Dow, Vicki
  See McVey, Vicki
Dowd, John David 1945- 78
Dowd, Siobhan 1960-2007 204
Dowdell, Dorothy (Florence) Karns 1910- 12
Dowden, Anne Ophelia Todd 1907-2007 7
  Obituary 180
  See also SAAS 10
Dowdey, Landon Gerald 1923- 11
Dowdy, Mrs. Regera
  See Gorey, Edward (St. John)
Dowell, Frances O'Roark 1964- 205
  Earlier sketch in SATA 157
Dower, Laura 1967- 185
Dowling, Terry 1947- 101
Downard, Barry 1956- 202
Downer, Ann 1960- 155
Downer, Marion 1892(?)-1971 25
Downes, Belinda 1962- 180
Downey, Fairfax D(avis) 1893-1990 3
  Obituary 66
Downey, Lisa 214
Downey, Lynn 1961- 185
Downham, Jenny 1964- 192
Downie, John 1931- 87
Downie, Mary Alice 1934- 171
  Earlier sketches in SATA 13, 87
Downie, Mary Alice Dawe
  See Downie, Mary Alice
Downing, David A(lmon) 1958- 84
Downing, Erin 1976- 237
Downing, Johnette 184
Downing, Julie 1956- 148
  Earlier sketch in SATA 81
Downing, Paula E. 1951- 80
Downing, Warwick
  See Downing, Wick
Downing, Wick 1931- 138
Dowswell, Paul 1957- 184
Doyle, A. Conan
  See Doyle, Sir Arthur Conan
Doyle, Sir Arthur Conan 1859-1930 24
  See also CLR 106
Doyle, Brian 1935- 156
  Earlier sketches in SATA 67, 104
  See also CLR 22
  See also SAAS 16

Doyle, Charlotte 1937- *178*
  Earlier sketch in SATA *94*
Doyle, Charlotte Lackner
  See Doyle, Charlotte
Doyle, Conan
  See Doyle, Sir Arthur Conan
Doyle, Debra 1952- *165*
  Earlier sketch in SATA *105*
Doyle, Donovan
  See Boegehold, Betty (Doyle)
Doyle, Eugenie 1952- *225*
Doyle, John
  See Graves, Robert
Doyle, Malachy 1954- *165*
  Earlier sketch in SATA *120*
  See also CLR *83*
Doyle, Richard 1824-1883 .... *21*
Doyle, Sir A. Conan
  See Doyle, Sir Arthur Conan
Dr. A
  See Asimov, Isaac
  and Silverstein, Alvin
  and Silverstein, Virginia B.
Dr. Alphabet
  See Morice, Dave
Dr. Fred
  See Bortz, Alfred B(enjamin)
Dr. Laura
  See Schlessinger, Laura (Catherine)
Dr. Seuss 1904-1991 .... *100*
  Obituary *67*
  Earlier sketches in SATA *1, 28, 75*
  See also CLR *100*
Dr. Zed
  See Penrose, Gordon
Drabble, Margaret 1939- *48*
Drackett, Phil(ip Arthur) 1922- *53*
Draco, F.
  See Davis, Julia
Dracup, Angela 1943- *74*
Dragisic, Patricia *116*
Dragonwagon, Crescent 1952- *186*
  Autobiography Feature *186*
  Earlier sketches in SATA *11, 41, 75, 133*
  See also SAAS *14*
Drake, David 1945- *85*
Drake, David Allen
  See Drake, David
Drake, Frank
  See Hamilton, Charles (Harold St. John)
Drake, Jane 1954- *235*
  Earlier sketch in SATA *82*
Drake, Salamanda
  See Barlow, Steve
Drakeford, Dale B 1952- *113*
Drakeford, Dale Benjamin
  See Drakeford, Dale B
Draper, Hastings
  See Jeffries, Roderic
Draper, Sharon
  See Draper, Sharon M.
Draper, Sharon M. 1948- *195*
  Autobiography Feature *146*
  Earlier sketches in SATA *98, 146*
  See also CLR *57*
Draper, Sharon Mills
  See Draper, Sharon M.
Drapier, M. B.
  See Swift, Jonathan
Drawson, Blair 1943- *126*
  Earlier sketch in SATA *17*
Dray, Matt 1967- *177*
Dray, Matthew Frederick
  See Dray, Matt
Dresang, Eliza (Carolyn Timberlake) 1941- . *19*
Drescher, Henrik 1955- *172*
  Earlier sketches in SATA *67, 105*
  See also CLR *20*
Drescher, Joan E(lizabeth) 1939- *137*
  Earlier sketch in SATA *30*
Dressen-McQueen, Stacey *191*

Dreves, Veronica R. 1927-1986
  Obituary *50*
Drew, Patricia 1938- *15*
Drew, Patricia Mary
  See Drew, Patricia
Drewery, Mary 1918- *6*
Drewery, Melanie 1970- *165*
Drewry, Henry N(athaniel) 1924- *138*
Dreyer, Ellen *177*
Drial, J. E.
  See Laird, Jean E(louise)
Drimmer, Frederick 1916-2000 .... *60*
  Obituary *124*
Driskill, J. Lawrence 1920- *90*
Driskill, Larry
  See Driskill, J. Lawrence
Driving Hawk, Virginia
  See Sneve, Virginia Driving Hawk
Dron, Laura
  See Matthews, L. S.
Dronzek, Laura *199*
Drucker, Malka 1945- *214*
  Brief entry *29*
  Earlier sketches in SATA *39, 111*
Drucker, Olga Levy 1927- *79*
Druitt, Tobias
  See Purkiss, Diane
Drummond, Allan 1957- *209*
Drummond, Karona 1965- *220*
Drummond, V(iolet) H(ilda) 1911-2000 .... *6*
Drummond, Walter
  See Silverberg, Robert
Drury, Clare Marie
  See Hoskyns-Abrahall, Clare (Constance Drury)
Drury, Roger W(olcott) 1914-1996 .... *15*
Druse, Eleanor
  See King, Stephen
Dryden, Pamela
  See St. John, Nicole
D.T., Hughes
  See Hughes, Dean
Duane, Diane 1952- *233*
  Brief entry *46*
  Earlier sketches in SATA *58, 95, 145*
Dubanevich, Arlene 1950- *56*
Dubelaar, Thea 1947- *60*
Dubin, Jill *205*
du Blane, Daphne
  See Groom, Arthur William
Duble, Kathleen Benner 1958- *164*
Dubois, Claude K. 1960- *196*
DuBois, Rochelle Holt 1946- *41*
Du Bois, Shirley Graham 1907(?)-1977 .... *24*
  See Graham, Shirley
Du Bois, W. E. B. 1868-1963 .... *42*
Du Bois, William Edward Burghardt
  See Du Bois, W. E. B.
du Bois, William Pene
  See Pene du Bois, William (Sherman)
Duboise, Novella 1911-1999 .... *88*
Dubosarsky, Ursula 1961- *193*
  Earlier sketches in SATA *107, 147*
DuBose, LaRocque (Russ) 1926- *2*
Dubrovin, Vivian 1931- *139*
  Earlier sketch in SATA *65*
DuBurke, Randy *224*
  Earlier sketch in SATA *172*
Ducey, Jean Sparks 1915- *93*
Duchacek, Ivo D(uka) 1913-1988
  Obituary *55*
Du Chaillu, Paul (Belloni) 1835(?)-1903 ..... *26*
Ducharme, Dede Fox
  See Ducharme, Lilian Fox
Ducharme, Lilian Fox 1950- *122*
Ducornet, Erica 1943- *7*
Ducornet, Rikki
  See Ducornet, Erica
Duddle, Jonny 1971(?)- *219*
Duden, Jane 1947- *136*

Duder, Tessa 1940- *117*
  Earlier sketch in SATA *80*
  See also CLR *43*
  See also SAAS *23*
Dudley, Helen
  See Hope Simpson, Jacynth
Dudley, Martha Ward 1909(?)-1985
  Obituary *45*
Dudley, Nancy
  See Cole, Lois Dwight
Dudley, Robert
  See Baldwin, James
Dudley, Ruth H(ubbell) 1905-2001 .... *11*
Dudley-Smith, T.
  See Trevor, Elleston
Due, Linnea A. 1948- *64*
Dueck, Adele 1955- *97*
Dueland, Joy V(ivian) *27*
Duerr, Gisela 1968- *89*
Duey, Kathleen 1950- *199*
  Earlier sketch in SATA *132*
Dufault, Joseph Ernest Nephtali
  See James, Will(iam Roderick)
Duff, Annis (James) 1904(?)-1986
  Obituary *49*
Duff, Maggie
  See Duff, Margaret K(app)
Duff, Margaret K(app) 1916-2003 .... *37*
  Obituary *144*
Duffey, Betsy 1953- *236*
  Earlier sketches in SATA *80, 131*
Duffie, Charles 1960- *144*
Duffield, Katy S. 1961- *147*
Duffy, Carol Ann 1955- *165*
  Earlier sketch in SATA *95*
Duffy Stone, Heather *217*
Dugan, Jack
  See Griffin, W. E. B.
Dugan, John Kevin
  See Griffin, W. E. B.
Dugan, Karen *202*
Dugan, Karen M.
  See Dugan, Karen
Dugan, Michael (Gray) 1947- *15*
Duggan, Alfred Leo 1903-1964 .... *25*
Duggan, Maurice 1922-1974 .... *40*
  Obituary *30*
Duggan, Maurice Noel
  See Duggan, Maurice
Dugger, Elizabeth L.
  See Kanell, Beth
Duggleby, John 1952- *94*
Dugin, Andrej 1955- *77*
Dugina, Olga 1964- *77*
du Jardin, Rosamond Neal 1902-1963 .... *2*
Duka, Ivo
  See Duchacek, Ivo D(uka)
Duke, Kate 1956- *192*
  Earlier sketches in SATA *90, 148*
  See also CLR *51*
Duke, Will
  See Gault, William Campbell
Dulac, Edmund 1882-1953 .... *19*
Dumas, Alexandre (pere) 1802-1870 .... *18*
  See also CLR *134*
Dumas, Jacqueline 1946- *55*
Dumas, Philippe 1940- *119*
  Earlier sketch in SATA *52*
du Maurier, Daphne 1907-1989 .... *27*
  Obituary *60*
Dumbleton, Mike 1948- *206*
  Earlier sketches in SATA *73, 124*
Dunbar, Fiona 1961- *167*
Dunbar, Joyce 1944- *213*
  Earlier sketches in SATA *76, 112, 162*
Dunbar, Paul Laurence 1872-1906 .... *34*
Dunbar, Polly 1980(?)- *211*
  Earlier sketch in SATA *181*
Dunbar, Robert E(verett) 1926- *32*
Duncan, Alexandra
  See Moore, Ishbel (Lindsay)

Duncan, Alice Faye 1967- *168*
  Earlier sketch in SATA *95*
Duncan, Gregory
  See McClintock, Marshall
Duncan, Jane
  See Cameron, Elizabeth Jane
Duncan, Julia K.
  See Benson, Mildred
Duncan, Lois 1934- *219*
  Autobiography Feature *141*
  Earlier sketches in SATA *1, 36, 75, 133, 141*
  See also CLR *129*
  See also SAAS *2*
Duncan, Norman 1871-1916
  See YABC *1*
Duncan, Terence
  See Nolan, William F.
Duncombe, Frances (Riker) 1900-1994 .... *25*
  Obituary *82*
Dungy, Anthony
  See Dungy, Tony
Dungy, Tony 1955- *206*
Dunham, Montrew 1919- *162*
Dunham, Montrew Goetz
  See Dunham, Montrew
Dunkle, Clare B. 1964- *223*
  Earlier sketch in SATA *155*
Dunlap, Julie 1958- *84*
Dunleavy, Deborah 1951- *133*
Dunlop, Agnes M. R. (?)-1982 .... *87*
Dunlop, Eileen (Rhona) 1938- *76*
  Earlier sketch in SATA *24*
  See also SAAS *12*
Dunmore, Helen 1952- *201*
Dunn, Anne M. 1940- *107*
Dunn, Carolyn 1965- *208*
Dunn, Harvey T(homas) 1884-1952 .... *34*
Dunn, Herb
  See Gutman, Dan
Dunn, John M. (III) 1949- *93*
Dunn, Judy
  See Spangenberg, Judith Dunn
Dunn, Mary Lois 1930- *6*
Dunnahoo, Terry Janson 1927- *7*
Dunne, Jeanette 1952- *72*
Dunne, Kathleen 1933- *126*
Dunne, Marie
  See Clark, Ann Nolan
Dunne, Mary Collins 1914- *11*
Dunne, Mary Jo
  See Dunne, Mary Collins
Dunnett, Kaitlyn
  See Emerson, Kathy Lynn
Dunnett, Margaret (Rosalind) 1909-1977 ..... *42*
Dunnick, Regan *178*
Dunning, John Harris 1974- *234*
Dunphy, Madeleine 1962- *219*
Dunrea, Olivier 1953- *233*
  Brief entry *46*
  Earlier sketches in SATA *59, 118, 160*
Dunrea, Olivier Jean-Paul Dominique
  See Dunrea, Olivier
Dunstan Muller, Rachel *221*
Dunton, Dorothy 1912- *92*
Dupasquier, Philippe 1955- *151*
  Earlier sketch in SATA *86*
duPont, Lindsay *207*
duPont, Lindsay Harper
  See duPont, Lindsay
DuPrau, Jeanne 1944- *215*
  Earlier sketch in SATA *144*
Dupuy, T(revor) N(evitt) 1916-1995 .... *4*
  Obituary *86*
DuQuette, Keith 1960- *155*
  Earlier sketch in SATA *90*
Duran, Gloria 1924- *171*
Duran, Gloria Bradley
  See Duran, Gloria
Duranceau, Suzanne 1952- *162*
Durand, Delphine 1971- *200*
Durand, Hallie 1964(?)- *216*

Durango, Julia 1967- *215*
  Earlier sketch in SATA *173*
Durant, Alan 1958- *214*
  Earlier sketches in SATA *121, 165*
Durant, John 1902- *27*
Durbin, William 1951- *174*
  Earlier sketch in SATA *143*
Durell, Ann 1930- *66*
Durkee, Sarah *173*
Durney, Ryan *205*
Durrant, Lynda 1954- *212*
  Earlier sketches in SATA *96, 148*
Durrant, Sabine *210*
Durrell, Gerald (Malcolm) 1925-1995 .... *8*
  Obituary *84*
Durrell, Julie 1955- *94*
Durrett, Deanne 1940- *144*
  Earlier sketch in SATA *92*
Durst, Sarah Beth 1974- *203*
Dusikova, Maja 1946- *223*
Du Soe, Robert C. 1892-1958
  See YABC *2*
Dussling, Jennifer 1970- *143*
  Earlier sketch in SATA *96*
DuTemple, Lesley A. 1952- *113*
Dutton, Sandra *191*
Dutz
  See Davis, Mary Octavia
Duval, Katherine
  See James, Elizabeth
Duval, Kathy 1946- *181*
Duvall, Aimee
  See Thurlo, Aimee
  and Thurlo, David
Duvall, Evelyn Millis 1906- *9*
Duvall, Jill D. 1932- *102*
Duvall, Jill Donovan
  See Duvall, Jill D.
Duvoisin, Roger (Antoine) 1904-1980 .... *30*
  Obituary *23*
  Earlier sketch in SATA *2*
  See also CLR *23*
Dwiggins, Don(ald J.) 1913-1988 .... *4*
  Obituary *60*
Dwight, Allan
  See Cole, Lois Dwight
Dwyer, Deanna
  See Koontz, Dean
Dwyer, K.R.
  See Koontz, Dean
Dyck, Peter J. 1914- *75*
Dyer, Alan 1953- *218*
Dyer, Hadley 1973- *229*
Dyer, James (Frederick) 1934- *37*
Dyer, Jane *191*
  Earlier sketch in SATA *147*
Dyer, Sarah 1978- *212*
Dyer, Sarah L.
  See Dyer, Sarah
Dyess, John (Foster) 1939- *76*
Dygard, Thomas J. 1931-1996 .... *97*
  Obituary *92*
  Earlier sketch in SATA *24*
  See also SAAS *15*
Dyke, John 1935- *35*

E

E. V. L.
  See Lucas, E(dward) V(errall)
Eagar, Frances (Elisabeth Stuart)
  1940-1978 .... *11*
  Obituary *55*
Eager, Edward (McMaken) 1911-1964 .... *17*
  See also CLR *43*
Eager, George 1921- *56*
Eager, George B.
  See Eager, George
Eagland, Jane *237*

Eagle, Ellen 1953- *61*
Eagle, Kin
  See Adlerman, Daniel (Ezra)
  and Adlerman, Kimberly M(arie)
Eagle, Mike 1942- *11*
Eamer, Claire 1947- *222*
Earle, Olive L(ydia) 1888-1982 .... *7*
Earle, William
  See Johns, W(illiam) E(arle)
Earls, Nick 1963- *156*
  Earlier sketch in SATA *95*
Early, Jack
  See Scoppettone, Sandra
Early, Jon
  See Johns, W(illiam) E(arle)
Early, Margaret 1951- *72*
Earnest, Peter 1934- *222*
Earnshaw, Brian 1929- *17*
Earnshaw, Micky 1939- *88*
Earnshaw, Spencer Wright
  See Earnshaw, Micky
Easley, MaryAnn *94*
Eason, Alethea 1957- *197*
East, Jacqueline *224*
Eastman, Charles A(lexander) 1858-1939
  See YABC *1*
Eastman, P(hilip) D(ey) 1909-1986 .... *33*
  Obituary *46*
Easton, Kelly 1960- *192*
  Earlier sketch in SATA *141*
Eastwick, Ivy (Ethel) O(live) *3*
Eaton, Anne T(haxter) 1881-1971 .... *32*
Eaton, Anthony 1971- *167*
Eaton, George L.
  See Verral, Charles Spain
Eaton, Janet
  See Givens, Janet E(aton)
Eaton, Jeanette 1886-1968 .... *24*
Eaton, Maxwell III 1981- *199*
Eaton, Tom 1940- *22*
Ebbeler, Jeff
  See Ebbeler, Jeffrey
Ebbeler, Jeffrey 1974- *206*
Ebbitt, Carolyn Q. 1974(?)- *225*
Ebel, Alex 1927- *11*
Eber, Dorothy (Margaret) Harley 1930- *27*
Eberhart, Sheri S.
  See Tepper, Sheri S.
Eberle, Irmengarde 1898-1979 .... *2*
  Obituary *23*
Eble, Diane 1956- *74*
Eboch, Chris *113*
Eccles Williams, Ferelith 1920- *22*
Echeverria-Bis, Olivia *217*
Echeverria Gyorkos, Charmaine *216*
Echlin, Kim 1955- *166*
Eckblad, Edith Berven 1923- *23*
Ecke, Wolfgang 1927-1983
  Obituary *37*
Eckert, Allan W. 1931- *91*
  Brief entry *27*
  Earlier sketch in SATA *29*
  See also SAAS *21*
Eckert, Horst 1931- *72*
  Earlier sketch in SATA *8*
  See also CLR *26*
Ecklar, Julia (Marie) 1964- *112*
Eddings, David 1931-2009 .... *91*
Eddings, David Carroll
  See Eddings, David
Ede, Janina 1937- *33*
Edell, Celeste *12*
Edelman, Lily (Judith) 1915-1981 .... *22*
Edelson, Edward 1932- *51*
Edens, Cooper 1945- *166*
  Earlier sketches in SATA *49, 112*
Edens, (Bishop) David 1926- *39*
Edey, Maitland A(rmstrong) 1910-1992 .... *25*
  Obituary *71*
Edgerton, Perky *196*

Edgeworth, Maria 1768-1849 21
  See also CLR *153*
Edgson, Alison *211*
Edgy, Wardore
  See Gorey, Edward (St. John)
Edison, Theodore
  See Stratemeyer, Edward L.
Edler, Tim(othy) 1948- 56
Edmiston, Jim 1948- 80
Edmonds, I(vy) G(ordon) 1917- 8
Edmonds, Walter D(umaux) 1903-1998 27
  Obituary 99
  Earlier sketch in SATA *1*
  See also SAAS *4*
Edmund, Sean
  See Pringle, Laurence
Edsall, Marian (Stickney) 1920- 8
Edwards, Al
  See Nourse, Alan E(dward)
Edwards, Anne 1927- 35
Edwards, Audrey 1947- 52
  Brief entry 31
Edwards, Becky (Jane) 1966- *125*
Edwards, Bertram
  See Edwards, Herbert Charles
Edwards, Bronwen Elizabeth
  See Rose, Wendy
Edwards, Cecile Pepin 1916- 25
Edwards, David 1962- *198*
Edwards, Dorothy 1914-1982 88
  Obituary 31
  Earlier sketch in SATA *4*
Edwards, F. E.
  See Nolan, William F.
Edwards, Frank B. 1952- 93
Edwards, Gunvor 32
Edwards, Harvey 1929- 5
Edwards, Hazel (Eileen) 1945- *135*
Edwards, Herbert Charles 1912- 12
Edwards, Jane Campbell 1932- 10
Edwards, Julia
  See Stratemeyer, Edward L.
Edwards, Julie
  See Andrews, Julie
Edwards, Julie Andrews
  See Andrews, Julie
Edwards, June
  See Bhatia, Jamunadevi
Edwards, Linda Strauss 1948- 49
  Brief entry 42
Edwards, Margaret (Alexander) 1902-1988
  Obituary 56
Edwards, Michelle 1955- *152*
  Earlier sketch in SATA *70*
Edwards, Monica le Doux Newton
  1912-1998 12
Edwards, Olwen
  See Gater, Dilys
Edwards, Page (Lawrence, Jr.) 1941-1999 ... 59
Edwards, Pamela Duncan *189*
Edwards, R. T.
  See Goulart, Ron
Edwards, Sally (Cary) 1929- 7
Edwards, Samuel
  See Gerson, Noel Bertram
Edwards, Wallace 1957(?)- *170*
Edwardson, Debby Dahl *223*
Eeckhout, Emmanuelle 1976- *208*
Egan, E. W. 1922- 35
Egan, Edward Welstead
  See Egan, E. W.
Egan, Kerry *175*
Egan, Lorraine Hopping 1960- *134*
  Earlier sketch in SATA *91*
Egan, Tim 1957- *191*
  Earlier sketches in SATA *89, 155*
Egermeier, Elsie E(milie) 1890-1986 65
Eggenberger, David 1918- 6
Eggleston, Edward 1837-1902 27
Egielski, Richard 1952- *220*
  Earlier sketches in SATA *11, 49, 106, 163*

Egypt, Ophelia Settle 1903-1984 .... *16*
  Obituary *38*
Ehlert, Lois 1934- *237*
  Earlier sketches in SATA *35, 69, 128, 172*
  See also CLR *28*
Ehlert, Lois Jane
  See Ehlert, Lois
Ehling, Katalin Olah 1941- 93
Ehrenberg, Pamela 1972- *219*
Ehrenfreund, Norbert 1921- 86
Ehrenhaft, Daniel 1970- *185*
Ehrenhaft, Daniel Parker
  See Ehrenhaft, Daniel
Ehrhardt, Karen 1963- *184*
Ehrlich, Amy 1942- *217*
  Earlier sketches in SATA *25, 65, 96, 132*
Ehrlich, Bettina Bauer 1903-1985 .... *1*
Ehrlich, Fred *205*
Ehrlich, Fred M.D.
  See Ehrlich, Fred
Ehrlich, H. M.
  See Ziefert, Harriet
Eichenberg, Fritz 1901-1990 .... *50*
  Earlier sketch in SATA *9*
Eichler, Margrit 1942- *35*
Eichner, James A. 1927- *4*
Eidson, Thomas 1944- *112*
Eifert, Virginia (Louise) S(nider) 1911-1966 . *2*
Eige, (Elizabeth) Lillian 1915- *65*
Eiken, J. Melia 1967- *125*
Einhorn, Edward 1970- *204*
Einsel, Naiad *10*
Einsel, Walter 1926- *10*
Einzig, Susan 1922- *43*
Eiseman, Alberta 1925- *15*
Eisenberg, Azriel (Louis) 1903-1985 .... *12*
Eisenberg, Lisa 1949- *155*
  Brief entry *50*
  Earlier sketch in SATA *57*
Eisenberg, Phyllis Rose 1924- *41*
Eisner, Vivienne
  See Margolis, Vivienne
Eisner, Will 1917-2005 .... *165*
  Earlier sketch in SATA *31*
Eisner, William Erwin
  See Eisner, Will
Eitzen, Allan 1928- *9*
Eitzen, Ruth (Carper) 1924- *9*
Ekwensi, C. O. D.
  See Ekwensi, Cyprian
Ekwensi, Cyprian 1921-2007 .... *66*
Ekwensi, Cyprian Odiatu Duaka
  See Ekwensi, Cyprian
Elam, Richard M(ace, Jr.) 1920- *9*
Elborn, Andrew
  See Clements, Andrew
  and Clements, Andrew
Elboz, Stephen 1956- *152*
Eldin, Peter 1939- *154*
Eldon, Kathy 1946- *107*
Eldridge, Marion *199*
Eley, Robin *219*
Elfman, Blossom 1925- *8*
Elgin, Kathleen 1923- *39*
Elia
  See Lamb, Charles
Elio
  See Eliopoulos, Chris
Eliopoulos, Chris *234*
Eliot, A. D.
  See Jewett, Sarah Orne
Eliot, Alice
  See Jewett, Sarah Orne
Eliot, Anne
  See Cole, Lois Dwight
Eliot, Dan
  See Silverberg, Robert
Elish, Dan 1960- *204*
  Earlier sketches in SATA *68, 129*
Elisha, Ron 1951- *104*

Elisofon, Eliot 1911-1973
  Obituary *21*
Elkeles, Simone 1970- *187*
Elkin, Benjamin 1911-1995 .... *3*
Elkins, Dov Peretz 1937- *5*
Ellacott, S(amuel) E(rnest) 1911- *19*
Elleman, Barbara 1934- *147*
Ellen, Jaye
  See Nixon, Joan Lowery
Eller, Scott
  See Holinger, William (Jacques)
  and Shepard, Jim
Ellery, Amanda *216*
Ellestad, Myrvin
  See Ellestad, Myrvin H.
Ellestad, Myrvin H. 1921- *120*
Elliot, Bruce
  See Field, Edward
Elliot, David 1952- *208*
  Earlier sketch in SATA *122*
Elliott, Bruce
  See Field, Edward
Elliott, David 1947- *201*
  Earlier sketch in SATA *163*
Elliott, Don
  See Silverberg, Robert
Elliott, Elizabeth Shippen Green
  See Green, Elizabeth Shippen
Elliott, Janice 1931-1995 .... *119*
Elliott, Joey
  See Houk, Randy
Elliott, Laura Malone 1957- *197*
Elliott, L.M.
  See Elliott, Laura Malone
Elliott, Louise *111*
Elliott, Mark 1949- *210*
Elliott, Odette 1939- *75*
Elliott, Patricia 1946- *176*
Elliott, Sarah M(cCarn) 1930- *14*
Elliott, (Robert) Scott 1970- *153*
Elliott, William
  See Bradbury, Ray
Elliott, Zetta *206*
Ellis, (Mary) Amabel (Nassau Strachey)
  Williams
  See Williams-Ellis, (Mary) Amabel (Nassau
  Strachey)
Ellis, Ann Dee *210*
Ellis, Anyon
  See Rowland-Entwistle, (Arthur) Theodore
  (Henry)
Ellis, Carson 1975- *190*
Ellis, Carson Friedman
  See Ellis, Carson
Ellis, Deborah 1960- *235*
  Earlier sketches in SATA *129, 187*
Ellis, E. S.
  See Ellis, Edward S.
Ellis, Edward S. 1840-1916
  See YABC *1*
Ellis, Edward Sylvester
  See Ellis, Edward S.
Ellis, Ella Thorp 1928- *127*
  Earlier sketch in SATA *7*
  See also SAAS *9*
Ellis, Harry Bearse 1921-2004 .... *9*
Ellis, Helen *232*
Ellis, Herbert
  See Wilson, Lionel
Ellis, Julie 1961- *227*
Ellis, Mel(vin Richard) 1912-1984 .... *7*
  Obituary *39*
Ellis, Richard 1938- *130*
Ellis, Sarah 1952- *179*
  Earlier sketches in SATA *68, 131*
  See also CLR *42*
Ellison, Chris *196*
Ellison, Elizabeth Stow 1970- *209*
Ellison, Emily *114*
Ellison, Lucile Watkins 1907(?)-1979 ...... *50*
  Obituary *22*

Ellison, Virginia H(owell) 1910- 4
Ellsberg, Edward 1891-1983 7
Ellsworth, Loretta 1954- 199
Ellsworth, Mary Ellen (Tressel) 1940- 146
Ellwand, David 1965(?)- 213
Elmer, Robert 1958- 154
    Earlier sketch in SATA 99
Elmore, (Carolyn) Patricia 1933- 38
    Brief entry 35
El-Moslimany, Ann P(axton) 1937- 90
Elsammak, Ariane 236
Elschner, Geraldine 1954- 183
Elspeth
    See Bragdon, Elspeth MacDuffie
Elster, Jean Alicia 1953- 150
Elting, Mary 1906- 88
    Earlier sketch in SATA 2
    See also SAAS 20
Elvgren, Jennifer Riesmeyer 179
Elwart, Joan Potter 1927- 2
Elwell, Peter 220
Elwood, Ann 1931- 55
    Brief entry 52
Elwood, Roger 1943-2007 58
Ely, Lesley 212
Elya, Susan Middleton 1955- 235
    Earlier sketches in SATA 106, 159, 202
Elzbieta 88
Ember, Kathi 234
    Earlier sketch in SATA 190
Emberley, Barbara A. 1932- 146
    Earlier sketches in SATA 8, 70
    See also CLR 5
Emberley, Barbara Anne
    See Emberley, Barbara A.
Emberley, Ed 1931- 146
    Earlier sketches in SATA 8, 70
    See also CLR 81
Emberley, Edward Randolph
    See Emberley, Ed
Emberley, Michael 1960- 232
    Earlier sketches in SATA 34, 80, 119, 189
Emberley, Rebecca 1958- 218
Embry, Margaret Jacob 1919-1975 5
Emecheta, Buchi 1944- 66
    See also CLR 158
Emecheta, Florence Onye Buchi
    See Emecheta, Buchi
Emerson, Alice B.
    See Benson, Mildred
Emerson, Kate
    See Emerson, Kathy Lynn
Emerson, Kathy Lynn 1947- 63
Emerson, Kevin 209
Emerson, Ru 1944- 107
    Earlier sketch in SATA 70
Emerson, Sally 1952- 111
Emerson, William K(eith) 1925- 25
Emert, Phyllis R. 1947- 93
Emert, Phyllis Raybin
    See Emert, Phyllis R.
Emery, Anne (McGuigan) 1907- 33
    Earlier sketch in SATA 1
Emmens, Carol Ann 1944- 39
Emmett, Jonathan 1965- 188
    Earlier sketch in SATA 138
Emmons, Della (Florence) Gould 1890-1983
    Obituary 39
Emond, Stephen 1979(?)- 231
Emory, Jerry 1957- 96
Emrich, Duncan (Black Macdonald)
    1908-1970(?) 11
Emshwiller, Carol 1921- 174
    Autobiography Feature 174
Emshwiller, Carol Fries
    See Emshwiller, Carol
Emslie, M. L.
    See Simpson, Myrtle L(illias)

Ende, Michael (Andreas Helmuth)
    1929-1995 130
    Brief entry 42
    Obituary 86
    Earlier sketch in SATA 61
    See also CLR 138
Enderle, Dotti 1954- 203
    Earlier sketch in SATA 145
Enderle, Judith (Ann) Ross 1941- 89
    Autobiography Feature 114
    Earlier sketch in SATA 38
    See also SAAS 26
Endle, Kate 207
Enell, Trinka (Gochenour) 1951- 79
Enfield, Carrie
    See Smith, Susan Vernon
Engdahl, Sylvia Louise 1933- 4
    Autobiography Feature 122
    See also CLR 2
    See also SAAS 5
Engel, Christiane 231
Engel, Diana 1947- 70
Engelbreit, Mary 1952- 169
Engelhart, Margaret S. 1924- 59
Engelmann, Kim (V.) 1959- 87
England, George Allan 1877-1936 102
Englart, Mindi Rose 1965- 146
Engle, Eloise
    See Paananen, Eloise (Katherine)
Engle, Margarita 1951- 231
    Earlier sketch in SATA 193
Englebert, Victor 1933- 8
English, James W(ilson) 1915- 37
English, Karen 202
Engstrom, Elizabeth 1951- 110
Enright, D(ennis) J(oseph) 1920-2002 25
    Obituary 140
Enright, Dominique 194
Enright, Elizabeth (Wright) 1909-1968 9
    See also CLR 4
Ensor, Barbara 180
Ensor, Robert (T.) 1922- 93
Enthoven, Sam 1974- 187
Entwistle, (Arthur) Theodore (Henry) Rowland
    See Rowland-Entwistle, (Arthur) Theodore
    (Henry)
Enys, Sarah L.
    See Sloggett, Nellie
Epanya, Christian A(rthur Kingue) 1956- 91
Ephraim, Shelly S(chonebaum) 1952- 97
Ephron, Delia 1944- 197
    Brief entry 50
    Earlier sketch in SATA 65
Epler, Doris M. 1928- 73
Epp, Margaret A(gnes) 1913- 20
Eppenstein, Louise (Kohn) 1892-1987
    Obituary 54
Epple, Anne Orth 1927- 20
Epstein, Adam Jay 1975- 235
Epstein, Anne Merrick 1931- 20
Epstein, Beryl 1910- 31
    Earlier sketch in SATA 1
    See also CLR 26
    See also SAAS 17
Epstein, Beryl M. Williams
    See Epstein, Beryl
Epstein, Perle S(herry) 1938- 27
Epstein, Rachel S. 1941- 102
Epstein, Robin 1972- 230
Epstein, Samuel 1909-2000 31
    Earlier sketch in SATA 1
    See also CLR 26
    See also SAAS 17
Erdman, Loula Grace 1905(?)-1976 1
Erdoes, Richard 1912- 33
    Brief entry 28
Erdogan, Buket 187
Erdrich, Karen Louise
    See Erdrich, Louise
Erdrich, Louise 1954- 141
    Earlier sketch in SATA 94

Erickson, Betty J. 1923- 97
Erickson, Betty Jean
    See Erickson, Betty J.
Erickson, John R. 1943- 136
    Earlier sketch in SATA 70
Erickson, Jon 1948- 141
Erickson, Phoebe 59
Erickson, Russell E(verett) 1932- 27
Erickson, Sabra Rollins 1912-1995 35
Erickson, Walter
    See Fast, Howard
Ericson, Walter
    See Fast, Howard
Ericsson, Jennifer A. 170
Erikson, Mel 1937- 31
Eriksson, Eva 1949- 207
Ering, Timothy Basil 176
Erlanger, Baba
    See Trahey, Jane
Erlbach, Arlene 1948- 160
    Earlier sketches in SATA 78, 115
Erlbruch, Wolf 1948- 181
Erlich, Lillian (Feldman) 1910-1983 10
Erlings, Fridrik 1962- 196
Erlingsson, Friorik
    See Erlings, Fridrik
Ermatinger, James W. 1959- 170
Ernest, William
    See Berkebile, Fred D(onovan)
Ernst, (Lyman) John 1940- 39
Ernst, Kathleen
    See Ernst, Kathleen
Ernst, Kathleen 1959- 162
Ernst, Kathryn (Fitzgerald) 1942- 25
Ernst, Lisa Campbell 1957- 212
    Brief entry 44
    Earlier sketches in SATA 55, 95, 154
Erskine, Kathryn 193
Ervin, Janet Halliday 1923- 4
Erwin, Will
    See Eisner, Will
Esbaum, Jill 213
    Earlier sketch in SATA 174
Esbensen, Barbara J(uster) 1925-1996 97
    Brief entry 53
    Earlier sketch in SATA 62
Eschbacher, Roger 160
Eschmeyer, R. E. 1898-1989 29
Escriva, Vivi 182
Eseki, Bruno
    See Mphahlele, Es'kia
Esekie, Bruno
    See Mphahlele, Es'kia
Eshmeyer, Reinhart Ernst
    See Eschmeyer, R. E.
Eskridge, Ann E. 1949- 84
Espeland, Pamela (Lee) 1951- 128
    Brief entry 38
    Earlier sketch in SATA 52
Espinosa, Laura 203
Espinosa, Leo 203
Espriella, Don Manuel Alvarez
    See Southey, Robert
Espy, Willard R(ichardson) 1910-1999 38
    Obituary 113
Essakalli, Julie Klear 200
Essrig, Harry 1912- 66
Estep, Irene Compton 5
Esterl, Arnica 1933- 77
Estes, Eleanor (Ruth) 1906-1988 91
    Obituary 56
    Earlier sketch in SATA 7
    See also CLR 70
Estoril, Jean
    See Allan, Mabel Esther
Estrada, Pau 1961- 200
    Earlier sketch in SATA 74
Etchemendy, Nancy 1952- 166
    Earlier sketch in SATA 38
Etchemendy, Nancy Elise Howell
    See Etchemendy, Nancy

Etchison, Birdie L(ee) 1937- 38
Etchison, Craig 1945- 133
Etherington, Frank 1945- 58
Etnier, Jennifer L. 227
Eton, Robert
See Meynell, Laurence Walter
Ets, Marie Hall 1893-1984 2
See also CLR 33
Ettlinger, Doris 1950- 173
Eugnia, Maria 222
Eulberg, Elizabeth 1975- 227
Eunson, (John) Dale 1904-2002 5
Obituary 132
Evan, Frances Y. 1951- 167
Evanoff, Vlad 1916- 59
Evans, Cambria 1981- 178
Evans, Douglas 1953- 144
Earlier sketch in SATA 93
Evans, Eva (Knox) 1905-1998 27
Evans, Freddi Williams 1957- 211
Earlier sketch in SATA 134
Evans, Greg 1947- 143
Earlier sketch in SATA 73
Evans, Hubert Reginald 1892-1986 118
Obituary 48
Evans, Katherine (Floyd) 1901-1964 5
Evans, Larry
See Evans, Laurence Chubb
Evans, Laurence Chubb 1939- 88
Evans, Lawrence Watt
See Watt-Evans, Lawrence
Evans, Leslie 1953- 214
Evans, Lezlie 180
Evans, Mari 1923- 10
Evans, Mark 19
Evans, Nancy 1950- 65
Evans, Nate 201
Evans, Patricia Healy
See Carpenter, Patricia (Healy Evans)
Evans, (Alice) Pearl 1927- 83
Evans, Shane W. 189
Evans, Shirlee 1931- 58
Evans, Tabor
See Cameron, Lou
and Knott, William C(ecil, Jr.)
and Wallmann, Jeffrey M(iner)
and Whittington, Harry (Benjamin)
Evarts, Esther
See Benson, Sally
Evarts, Hal G., (Jr.) 1915-1989 6
Everett, Gail
See Hale, Arlene
Evernden, Margery 1916- 5
Eversole, Robyn 1971- 74
Eversole, Robyn H.
See Eversole, Robyn
Eversole, Robyn Harbert
See Eversole, Robyn
Evslin, Bernard 1922-1993 83
Brief entry 28
Obituary 77
Earlier sketch in SATA 45
Ewart, Claire 1958- 145
Earlier sketch in SATA 76
Ewart, Franzeska G. 1950- 205
Ewen, David 1907-1985 4
Obituary 47
Ewing, Juliana (Horatia Gatty) 1841-1885 ... 16
See also CLR 78
Ewing, Kathryn 1921- 20
Eyerly, Jeannette 1908-2008 86
Obituary 196
Earlier sketch in SATA 4
See also SAAS 10
Eyerly, Jeannette Hyde
See Eyerly, Jeannette
Eyre, Dorothy
See McGuire, Leslie (Sarah)
Eyre, Frank 1910-1988
Obituary 62
Eyre, Katherine Wigmore 1901-1970 *Volume 26*

Ezzell, Marilyn 1937- 42
Brief entry 38

F

Fabe, Maxene 1943- 15
Faber, Doris (Greenberg) 1924- 78
Earlier sketch in SATA 3
Faber, Harold 1919-2010 5
Fabre, Jean Henri (Casimir) 1823-1915 22
Fabry, Glenn 1961- 205
Facklam, Margaret
See Thomas, Peggy
Facklam, Margery (Metz) 1927- 132
Earlier sketches in SATA 20, 85
Fadden, David Kanietakeron 196
Fadiman, Clifton (Paul) 1904-1999 11
Obituary 115
Fagan, Cary 1957- 186
Fagan, Deva 220
Fahs, Sophia Blanche Lyon 1876-1978 102
Failing, Barbara Larmon 182
Fain, Sarah 1971- 204
Fair, David 1952- 96
Fair, Sylvia 1933- 13
Fairfax-Lucy, Brian (Fulke Cameron-Ramsay)
1898-1974 6
Obituary 26
Fairfield, Flora
See Alcott, Louisa May
Fairlie, Gerard 1899-1983
Obituary 34
Fairman, Joan A(lexandra) 1935- 10
Faithfull, Gail 1936- 8
Falcone, L.M. 1951- 231
Earlier sketch in SATA 155
Falcone, Lucy M.
See Falcone, L.M.
Falconer, Ian 1959- 179
Earlier sketch in SATA 125
See also CLR 146
Falconer, James
See Kirkup, James
Falconer, Lee N.
See May, Julian
Falkner, Brian 1962- 206
Falkner, Leonard 1900-1977 12
Fall, Andrew
See Arthur, Robert, (Jr.)
Fall, Thomas
See Snow, Donald Clifford
Faller, Regis 1968- 187
Falls, C(harles) B(uckles) 1874-1960 38
Brief entry 27
Falls, Kat 232
Falls, Kathleen Moynihan
See Falls, Kat
Falstein, Louis 1909-1995 37
Falvey, David 1982- 222
Falwell, Cathryn 1952- 196
Fancher, Lou 1960- 228
Earlier sketch in SATA 177
Fanelli, Sara 1969- 126
Earlier sketch in SATA 89
Fanning, Leonard M(ulliken) 1888-1967 5
Fantaskey, Beth 1965- 217
Faralla, Dana 1909- 9
Faralla, Dorothy W.
See Faralla, Dana
Farb, Peter 1929-1980 12
Obituary 22
Farber, Norma 1909-1984 75
Obituary 38
Earlier sketch in SATA 25
Fardell, John 1967- 195
Fardell, John William
See Fardell, John
Faria, Rosana 213

Farish, Terry 1947- 146
Earlier sketch in SATA 82
Farjeon, (Eve) Annabel 1919-2004 11
Obituary 153
Farjeon, Eleanor 1881-1965 2
See also CLR 34
Farley, Carol (J.) 1936- 137
Earlier sketch in SATA 4
Farley, Terri 165
Farley, Walter (Lorimer) 1915-1989 132
Earlier sketches in SATA 2, 43
Farlow, James O(rville, Jr.) 1951- 75
Farmer, Jacqueline 210
Farmer, Nancy 1941- 161
Earlier sketches in SATA 79, 117
Farmer, Patti 1948- 79
Farmer, Penelope (Jane) 1939- 105
Brief entry 39
Earlier sketch in SATA 40
See also CLR 8
See also SAAS 22
Farmer, Peter 1950- 38
Farmer, Philip Jose
See Farmer, Philip Jose
Farmer, Philip Jose 1918-2009 93
Obituary 201
Farmer, Philipe Jos
See Farmer, Philip Jose
Farnham, Burt
See Clifford, Harold B(urton)
Farnsworth, Bill 1958- 186
Earlier sketches in SATA 84, 135
Farooqi, Musharraf Ali 1968- 207
Farquhar, Margaret C(utting) 1905-1988 13
Farquharson, Alexander 1944- 46
Farquharson, Martha
See Finley, Martha
Farr, Diana 82
Earlier sketch in SATA 3
Farr, Finis (King) 1904-1982 10
Farr, Richard 1960- 209
Farrar, Jill
See Morris, Jill
Farrar, Susan Clement 1917- 33
Farrell, Ben
See Cebulash, Mel
Farrell, Darren 228
Farrell, John 1951- 204
Farrell, Patrick
See Odgers, Sally Farrell
Farrell, Sally
See Odgers, Sally Farrell
Farrer, Vashti 167
Farrington, Benjamin 1891-1974
Obituary 20
Farrington, S(elwyn) Kip, Jr. 1904-1983 20
Farris, Christine King 1927- 206
Farshtey, Greg(ory T.) 1965- 148
Farthing, Alison 1936- 45
Brief entry 36
Farthing-Knight, Catherine 1933- 92
Fassler, Joan (Grace) 1931- 11
Fast, Howard 1914-2003 7
Autobiography Feature 107
Fast, Howard Melvin
See Fast, Howard
Fasulo, Michael 1963- 83
Fatchen, Max 1920- 84
Earlier sketch in SATA 20
See also SAAS 20
Fate, Marilyn
See Collins, Paul
Father Goose
See Ghigna, Charles
Fatigati, Evelyn 1948- 24
Fatigati, Frances Evelyn
See Fatigati, Evelyn
Fatio, Louise 1904-1993 6
Fatus, Sophie 1957- 182
Faulhaber, Martha 1926- 7
Faulkner, Anne Irvin 1906- 23

Faulkner, Frank
    See Ellis, Edward S.
Faulkner, Nancy
    See Faulkner, Anne Irvin
Faulknor, Cliff(ord Vernon) 1913- 86
Faust, Anke 1971- 230
Favole, Robert J(ames) 1950- 125
Fawcett, Katie Pickard 229
Fax, Elton Clay 1909-1993 25
Faxon, Lavinia
    See Russ, Lavinia (Faxon)
Feagles, Anita M.
    See Feagles, Anita MacRae
Feagles, Anita MacRae 1927- 9
Feagles, Elizabeth
    See Day, Beth (Feagles)
Feague, Mildred H. 1915- 14
Fearing, Mark 1968- 224
Fearnley, Jan 1965- 205
    Earlier sketch in SATA *153*
Fearrington, Ann (Peyton) 1945- 146
Fecher, Constance
    See Heaven, Constance (Christina)
Feder, Chris Welles 1938- 81
Feder, Harriet K. 1928- 73
Feder, Paula (Kurzband) 1935- 26
Federici, Debbie 1965- 175
Federici, Debbie Tanner
    See Federici, Debbie
Feelings, Muriel 1938- 16
    See also CLR *5*
    See also SAAS *8*
Feelings, Muriel Lavita Grey
    See Feelings, Muriel
Feelings, Thomas 1933-2003 69
    Obituary 148
    Earlier sketch in SATA *8*
    See also CLR *58*
    See also SAAS *19*
Feelings, Tom
    See Feelings, Thomas
Fehler, Gene 1940- 201
    Earlier sketch in SATA *74*
Fehrenbach, T(heodore) R(eed, Jr.) 1925- 33
Feiffer, Jules 1929- 201
    Earlier sketches in SATA *8, 61, 111, 157*
Feiffer, Jules Ralph
    See Feiffer, Jules
Feiffer, Kate 1964- 206
    Earlier sketch in SATA *170*
Feig, Barbara Krane 1937- 34
Feig, Paul 221
Feikema, Feike
    See Manfred, Frederick (Feikema)
Feil, Hila 1942- 12
Feilen, John
    See May, Julian
Feinberg, Barbara Jane 1938- 123
    Earlier sketch in SATA *58*
Feinberg, Barbara Silberdick
    See Feinberg, Barbara Jane
Feinstein, John 1956- 195
    Earlier sketch in SATA *163*
Feldman, Anne (Rodgers) 1939- 19
Feldman, Elane 79
Feldman, Eve B. 221
Feldman, Jody 200
Felin, M. Sindy 194
Felix
    See Vincent, Felix
Fell, Derek 1939- 167
Fell, Derek John
    See Fell, Derek
Fellowes, Julian 1950- 198
Fellows, Muriel H. 10
Fellows, Stan 1957- 177
Fellows, Stanley
    See Fellows, Stan
Felsen, Henry Gregor 1916-1995 1
    See also SAAS *2*
Felstead, Cathie 1954- 192

Feltenstein, Arlene 1934- 119
Feltenstine, Arlene H.
    See Feltenstein, Arlene
Felton, Harold William 1902-1991 1
Felton, Ronald Oliver 1909- 3
Felts, Shirley 1934- 33
Felts, Susannah 1973- 214
Fenderson, Lewis H., Jr. 1907-1983 47
    Obituary 37
Fenner, Carol (Elizabeth) 1929-2002 89
    Obituary 132
    Earlier sketch in SATA *7*
    See also SAAS *24*
Fenner, Phyllis R(eid) 1899-1982 1
    Obituary 29
Fensham, Elizabeth 169
Fenten, Barbara D(oris) 1935- 26
Fenten, D(onald) X. 1932- 4
Fenton, Carroll Lane 1900-1969 5
Fenton, Edward 1917-1995 7
    Obituary 89
Fenton, Joe 213
Fenton, Mildred Adams 1899-1995 21
Fenwick, Patti
    See Grider, Dorothy
Feravolo, Rocco Vincent 1922- 10
Ferber, Brenda A. 1967- 184
Ferber, Edna 1887-1968 7
Fergus, Charles 114
Ferguson, Alane 1957- 182
    Earlier sketch in SATA *85*
Ferguson, Bob
    See Ferguson, Robert Bruce
Ferguson, Cecil 1931- 45
Ferguson, Pamela
    See Ferguson, Pamela Ellen
Ferguson, Pamela Ellen 1943- 234
Ferguson, Peter 1968- 199
Ferguson, Robert Bruce 1927-2001 13
Ferguson, Sarah 1959- 180
    Earlier sketches in SATA *66, 110*
Ferguson, Sarah Margaret
    See Ferguson, Sarah
Ferguson, Walter (W.) 1930- 34
Fergusson, Erna 1888-1964 5
Fermi, Laura 1907-1977 6
    Obituary 28
Fern, Eugene A. 1919-1987 10
    Obituary 54
Fern, Tracey E. 202
Fernandes, Eugenie 1943- 205
    Earlier sketches in SATA *77, 139*
Fernandez, Laura 1960- 171
Ferraiolo, Jack D. 208
Ferrari, Maria 123
Ferrari, Michael 223
Ferrari, Michael J.
    See Ferrari, Michael
Ferreiro, Carmen 1958- 158
Ferrell, Nancy Warren 1932- 70
Ferrer, Isabel
    See Riu, Isabel Ferrer
Ferri, Giuliano 1965- 197
Ferrier, Lucy
    See Penzler, Otto
Ferris, Helen Josephine 1890-1969 21
Ferris, James Cody
    See McFarlane, Leslie
Ferris, Jean 1939- 202
    Brief entry 50
    Earlier sketches in SATA *56, 105, 149*
Ferris, Jeri Chase 1937- 84
Ferry, Charles 1927- 92
    Earlier sketch in SATA *43*
    See also CLR *34*
    See also SAAS *20*
Fetz, Ingrid 1915- 30
Feydy, Anne Lindbergh
    See Sapieyevski, Anne Lindbergh
Fiammenghi, Gioia 1929- 66
    Earlier sketch in SATA *9*

Fiarotta, Noel
    See Ficarotta, Noel
Fiarotta, Phyllis
    See Ficarotta, Phyllis
Ficarotta, Noel 1944- 15
Ficarotta, Phyllis 1942- 15
Fichter, George S. 1922-1993 7
Ficocelli, Elizabeth 189
Fidler, Kathleen (Annie) 1899-1980 87
    Obituary 45
    Earlier sketch in SATA *3*
Fiedler, Jean(nette Feldman) 4
Fiedler, Joseph Daniel 159
Fiedler, Lisa 185
Field, Dorothy 1944- 97
Field, Edward 1924- 109
    Earlier sketch in SATA *8*
Field, Elinor Whitney 1889-1980
    Obituary 28
Field, Eugene 1850-1895 16
Field, Gans T.
    See Wellman, Manly Wade
Field, James 1959- 113
Field, Peter
    See Drago, Harry Sinclair
    and Dresser, Davis
    and Mann, E(dward) B(everly)
Field, Rachel (Lyman) 1894-1942 15
    See also CLR *21*
Fielding, Kate
    See Oldfield, Jenny
Fields, Bryan W. 1958(?)- 188
Fields, Lisa 1984(?)- 216
Fields, Terri 1948- 191
Fields, T.S.
    See Fields, Terri
Fienberg, Anna 1956- 183
    Earlier sketch in SATA *112*
Fiery, Ann
    See Barrows, Annie
Fife, Dale (Odile Hollerbach) 1901- 18
Fighter Pilot, A
    See Johnston, H(ugh) A(nthony) S(tephen)
Figler, Jeanie 1949- 123
Figley, Marty Rhodes 1948- 158
    Earlier sketch in SATA *88*
Figueredo, D(anilo) H. 1951- 155
Figueroa, Pablo 1938- 9
Fijan, Carol 1918- 12
Filderman, Diane E(lizabeth) 1959- 87
Files, Meg 1946- 107
Fillmore, Parker H(oysted) 1878-1944
    See YABC *1*
Filstrup, Chris
    See Filstrup, E(dward) Christian
Filstrup, E(dward) Christian 1942- 43
Filstrup, Janie
    See Merrill, Jane
Finbarr, Desmond
    See Zobel Nolan, Allia
Finchler, Judy 1943- 230
    Earlier sketch in SATA *93*
Finder, Martin
    See Salzmann, Siegmund
Findlay, Jamieson 1958- 169
Findon, Joanne 1957- 161
Fine, Anne 1947- 197
    Earlier sketches in SATA *29, 72, 111, 160*
    See also CLR *25*
    See also SAAS *15*
Fine, Edith Hope 169
Fine, Howard 1961- 181
Fine, Jane
    See Ziefert, Harriet
Finger, Charles J(oseph) 1869(?)-1941 42
Fink, William B(ertrand) 1916- 22
Finke, Blythe Foote 1922- 26
Finkel, George (Irvine) 1909-1975 8
Finkelstein, Norman H. 1941- 220
    Earlier sketches in SATA *73, 137*

Finkelstein, Norman Henry
    See Finkelstein, Norman H.
Finlay, Alice Sullivan 1946- 82
Finlay, Winifred Lindsay Crawford
    (McKissack) 1910-1989 23
Finlayson, Ann 1925- 8
Finley, Martha 1828-1909 43
    See also CLR 148
Finley, Mary Peace 1942- 83
Finn, Mary 208
Finney, Jack 1911-1995 109
Finney, Patricia 1958- 163
Finney, Shan 1944- 65
Finney, Walter Braden
    See Finney, Jack
Firer, Ben Zion
    See Firer, Benzion
Firer, Benzion 1914- 64
Fireside, Bryna J. 1932- 73
Firmin, Charlotte 1954- 29
Firmin, Peter 1928- 58
    Earlier sketch in SATA 15
Firth, Barbara 179
Fischbach, Julius 1894-1988 10
Fischer, John
    See Fluke, Joanne
Fischer, R.J.
    See Fluke, Joanne
Fischer, Scott M. 1971- 195
Fischer-Nagel, Andreas 1951- 56
Fischer-Nagel, Heiderose 1956- 56
Fischler, Shirley (Walton) 66
Fischler, Stan(ley I.) 66
    Brief entry 36
Fischtrom, Harvey 1933-1974 3
Fishback, Margaret
    See Antolini, Margaret Fishback
Fishbone, Greg R. 195
Fisher, Aileen (Lucia) 1906-2002 73
    Obituary 143
    Earlier sketches in SATA 1, 25
    See also CLR 49
Fisher, Barbara 1940- 44
    Brief entry 34
Fisher, Carolyn 1968- 154
Fisher, Catherine 1957- 155
Fisher, Chris 1958- 80
Fisher, Clavin C(argill) 1912- 24
Fisher, Cynthia 195
Fisher, Dorothy (Frances) Canfield 1879-1958
    See YABC 1
    See also CLR 71
Fisher, Gary L. 1949- 86
Fisher, John 1909-1996 15
Fisher, John Oswald Hamilton
    See Fisher, John
Fisher, Laura Harrison 1934- 5
Fisher, Leonard Everett 1924- 176
    Autobiography Feature 122
    Earlier sketches in SATA 4, 34, 73, 120
    See also CLR 18
    See also SAAS 1
Fisher, Lois I. 1948- 38
    Brief entry 35
Fisher, Margery (Turner) 1913-1992 20
    Obituary 74
Fisher, Marshall Jon 1963- 113
Fisher, Nikki
    See Strachan, Ian
Fisher, Robert (Tempest) 1943- 47
Fisher, Suzanne
    See Staples, Suzanne Fisher
Fisher, Valorie 214
    Earlier sketch in SATA 177
Fishman, Cathy Goldberg 1951- 106
Fisk, Nicholas
    See Higginbottom, David
Fisk, Pauline 1948- 160
    Earlier sketch in SATA 66
Fiske, Tarleton
    See Bloch, Robert (Albert)

Fisscher, Catharina G. M. 1958- 142
Fisscher, Tiny
    See Fisscher, Catharina G. M.
Fitch, Clarke
    See Sinclair, Upton
Fitch, John IV
    See Cormier, Robert
Fitch, Sheree 1956- 178
    Earlier sketch in SATA 108
Fitschen, Dale 1937- 20
Fitzalan, Roger
    See Trevor, Elleston
Fitzgerald, Captain Hugh
    See Baum, L. Frank
FitzGerald, Cathleen 1932-1987
    Obituary 50
Fitzgerald, Dawn 175
Fitzgerald, Edward Earl 1919-2001 20
Fitzgerald, F(rancis) A(nthony) 1940- 15
Fitzgerald, Joanne 1956- 198
Fitzgerald, John D(ennis) 1907(?)-1988 20
    Obituary 56
    See also CLR 1
Fitzgerald, Merni Ingrassia 1955- 53
Fitzgibbon, Terry 1948- 121
Fitzhardinge, Joan Margaret 1912- 73
    Earlier sketch in SATA 2
    See also CLR 5
    See also SAAS 3
Fitzhugh, Louise (Perkins) 1928-1974 45
    Obituary 24
    Earlier sketch in SATA 1
    See also CLR 72
Fitzhugh, Percy Keese 1876-1950 65
Fitzmaurice, Kathryn 217
Fitzpatrick, Becca 1979- 224
Fitzpatrick, Marie-Louise 1962- 189
    Earlier sketch in SATA 125
FitzRalph, Matthew
    See McInerny, Ralph
Fitz-Randolph, Jane (Currens) 1915- 51
Fitzsimons, Cecilia 1952- 97
Fitzsimons, Cecilia A.L.
    See Fitzsimons, Cecilia
Fixmer, Elizabeth 237
Flack, Marjorie 1897-1958 100
    See also YABC 2
    See also CLR 28
Flack, Naomi John White -1999 40
    Brief entry 35
Flake, Sharon G. 166
Flanagan, John 1944- 180
Flanagan, John Anthony
    See Flanagan, John
Flannery, Kate
    See De Goldi, Kate
Flatt, Lizann 1966- 88
Fleagle, Gail S(hatto) 1940- 117
Fleetwood, Jenni 1947- 80
Fleischer, Jane
    See Oppenheim, Joanne
Fleischhauer-Hardt, Helga 1936- 30
Fleischman, Albert Sidney
    See Fleischman, Sid
Fleischman, John 1948- 145
Fleischman, Paul 1952- 156
    Brief entry 32
    Earlier sketches in SATA 39, 72, 110
    See also CLR 66
    See also SAAS 20
Fleischman, Sid 1920-2010 185
    Earlier sketches in SATA 8, 59, 96, 148
    See also CLR 15
Fleischner, Jennifer 1956- 188
    Earlier sketch in SATA 93
Fleisher, Paul 1948- 132
    Earlier sketch in SATA 81
Fleisher, Robbin 1951-1977 52
    Brief entry 49
Fleishman, Seymour 1918- 66
    Brief entry 32

Fleming, A. A.
    See Arthur, Robert, (Jr.)
Fleming, Alice Mulcahey 1928- 9
Fleming, Candace 1962- 225
    Earlier sketches in SATA 94, 143, 190
Fleming, Denise 1950- 173
    Earlier sketches in SATA 81, 126
Fleming, Elizabeth P. 1888-1985
    Obituary 48
Fleming, Ian 1908-1964 9
Fleming, Ian Lancaster
    See Fleming, Ian
Fleming, Ronald Lee 1941- 56
Fleming, Sally
    See Walker, Sally M.
Fleming, Stuart
    See Knight, Damon (Francis)
Fleming, Susan 1932- 32
Fleming, Thomas 1927- 8
Fleming, Thomas James
    See Fleming, Thomas
Fleming, Virginia (Edwards) 1923- 84
Flesch, Y.
    See Flesch, Yolande
Flesch, Yolande 1950- 55
Flesch, Yolande Catarina
    See Flesch, Yolande
Fletcher, Charlie 220
Fletcher, Charlie May Hogue 1897-1977 3
Fletcher, Colin 1922-2007 28
Fletcher, Dirk
    See Cunningham, Chet
Fletcher, George U.
    See Pratt, (Murray) Fletcher
Fletcher, Helen Jill 1910- 13
Fletcher, Ralph 1953- 195
    Earlier sketches in SATA 105, 149
    See also CLR 104
Fletcher, Ralph J.
    See Fletcher, Ralph
Fletcher, Richard E. 1917(?)-1983
    Obituary 34
Fletcher, Rick
    See Fletcher, Richard E.
Fletcher, Susan 1951- 181
    Earlier sketches in SATA 70, 110
Fletcher, Susan Clemens
    See Fletcher, Susan
Fleur, Paul
    See Pohl, Frederik
Flexner, James Thomas 1908-2003 9
Flinn, Alex 1966- 198
    Earlier sketch in SATA 159
Flint, Helen 1952- 102
Flint, Russ 1944- 74
Flitner, David, Jr. 1949- 7
Flitner, David Perkins
    See Flitner, David, Jr.
Floca, Brian 190
    Earlier sketch in SATA 155
Floethe, Louise Lee 1913-1988 4
Floethe, Richard 1901-1998 4
Floherty, John Joseph 1882-1964 25
Flood, Bo
    See Flood, Nancy Bo
Flood, Nancy Bo 1945- 233
    Earlier sketch in SATA 130
Flood, Pansie Hart 1964- 140
Flood, William 1942- 129
Flooglebuckle, Al
    See Spiegelman, Art
Flora, James (Royer) 1914-1998 30
    Obituary 103
    Earlier sketch in SATA 1
    See also SAAS 6
Flores-Galbis, Enrique 1952- 186
Florian, Douglas 1950- 177
    Earlier sketches in SATA 19, 83, 125
Flory, Jane Trescott 1917- 22
Flournoy, Valerie 1952- 95

Flournoy, Valerie Rose
See Flournoy, Valerie
Flowerdew, Phyllis -1994 33
Flowers, Pam 1946- 136
Flowers, Sarah 1952- 98
Floyd, Gareth 1940- 62
Brief entry 31
Fluchere, Henri 1914-1991 40
Fluke, Joanne 1943- 88
Flutsztejn-Gruda, Ilona 1930- 170
Flynn, Barbara 1928- 9
Flynn, Jackson
See Bensen, Donald R.
and Shirreffs, Gordon D(onald)
Flynn, Nicholas
See Odgers, Sally Farrell
Flynn, Pat 1968- 214
Flynn, Patrick
See Flynn, Pat
Flynn, Rachel 1953- 171
Earlier sketch in SATA 109
Flynn, Warren (G.) 1950- 154
Fodor, R. V. 1944- 25
Fodor, Ronald Victor
See Fodor, R. V.
Fogelin, Adrian 1951- 175
Earlier sketch in SATA 129
Foley, (Anna) Bernice Williams 1902-1987 . 28
Foley, Greg E. 1969- 236
Earlier sketch in SATA 190
Foley, June 1944- 44
Foley, (Mary) Louise Munro 1933- 106
Brief entry 40
Earlier sketch in SATA 54
Foley, Rae
See Denniston, Elinore
Folke, Will
See Bloch, Robert (Albert)
Follett, Helen Thomas 1884(?)-1970
Obituary 27
Folsom, Franklin (Brewster) 1907-1995 5
Obituary 88
Folsom, Michael (Brewster) 1938-1990 40
Obituary 88
Fombelle, Timothee de 1973- 218
Fontenot, Mary Alice 1910-2003 91
Obituary 209
Earlier sketch in SATA 34
Fontes, Justine 172
Fontes, Ron 1952- 183
Foon, Dennis 1951- 119
Fooner, Michael 22
Foote, Timothy (Gilson) 1926- 52
Forberg, Ati
See Forberg, Beate Gropius
Forberg, Beate Gropius 1925- 22
Forbes, Anna 1954- 101
Forbes, Bryan 1926- 37
Forbes, Cabot L.
See Hoyt, Edwin P(almer), Jr.
Forbes, Esther 1891-1967 100
Earlier sketch in SATA 2
See also CLR 147
Forbes, Graham B. 1
Forbes, Kathryn
See McLean, Kathryn (Anderson)
Forbes, Robert
See Arthur, Robert, (Jr.)
Ford, A.G. 231
Ford, Albert Lee
See Stratemeyer, Edward L.
Ford, Barbara 56
Brief entry 34
Ford, Bernette 212
Ford, Bernette G.
See Ford, Bernette
Ford, B.G.
See Ford, Bernette
Ford, Brian J(ohn) 1939- 49
Ford, Carolyn 1938- 98

Ford, Carolyn Mott
See Ford, Carolyn
Ford, Christine 1953- 176
Ford, David
See Baldacci, David
and Baldacci, David
Ford, David B.
See Baldacci, David
Ford, David Baldacci
See Baldacci, David
Ford, Elbur
See Hibbert, Eleanor Alice Burford
Ford, Ellen 1949- 89
Ford, George (Jr.) 31
Ford, Hilary
See Youd, Samuel
Ford, Hildegarde
See Morrison, Velma Ford
Ford, Jerome W. 1949- 78
Ford, Jerry
See Ford, Jerome W.
Ford, John C. 1971- 221
Ford, Juwanda G(ertrude) 1967- 102
Ford, Marcia
See Radford, Ruby L(orraine)
Ford, Nancy K(effer) 1906-1961
Obituary 29
Ford, Peter 1936- 59
Ford, S. M.
See Uhlig, Susan
Forde, Catherine 1961- 170
Foreman, Mark 199
Foreman, Michael 1938- 216
Earlier sketches in SATA 2, 73, 129, 135, 184
See also CLR 32
See also SAAS 21
Foreman, Wilmoth 1939- 153
Forest, Antonia 1915-2003 29
Obituary 149
Forest, Dial
See Gault, William Campbell
Forest, Heather 1948- 185
Earlier sketch in SATA 120
Forester, C. S. 1899-1966 13
Forester, Cecil Scott
See Forester, C. S.
Forester, Victoria 214
Forler, Nan 223
Forman, Brenda 1936- 4
Forman, James
See Forman, James D.
Forman, James D. 1932-2009 70
Earlier sketch in SATA 8
Forman, James Douglas
See Forman, James D.
Forman, Mark L.
See Forman, M.L.
Forman, M.L. 1964- 215
Forman, Ruth 1970- 186
Formento, Alison 228
Forrest, Elizabeth
See Salsitz, Rhondi Vilott
Forrest, Mary
See Pausacker, Jenny
Forrest, Sybil
See Markun, Patricia Maloney
Forrestal, Elaine 1941- 165
Earlier sketch in SATA 117
Forrester, Frank H. 1919(?)-1986
Obituary 52
Forrester, Helen
See Bhatia, Jamunadevi
Forrester, Jade
See Pausacker, Jenny
Forrester, Marian
See Schachtel, Roger
Forrester, Sandra 1949- 166
Earlier sketch in SATA 90
Forrester, Victoria 1940- 40
Brief entry 35
Forsee, (Frances) Aylesa -1986 1

Forsey, Chris 1950- 59
Forshay-Lunsford, Cin 1965- 60
Forster, E. M. 1879-1970 57
Forster, Edward Morgan
See Forster, E. M.
Forsyth, Kate 1966- 154
Fort, Paul
See Stockton, Francis Richard
Forte, Maurizio 1961- 110
Fortey, Richard 1946- 109
Fortey, Richard A.
See Fortey, Richard
Fortey, Richard Alan
See Fortey, Richard
Forth, Melissa D(eal) 96
Fortnum, Peggy
See Nuttall-Smith, Margaret Emily Noel
Fortune, Eric 182
Forward, Robert L(ull) 1932-2002 82
Fosberry, Jennifer 235
Foster, Alan Dean 1946- 70
Foster, Brad W. 1955- 34
Foster, Doris Van Liew 1899-1993 10
Foster, E(lizabeth) C(onnell) 1902- 9
Foster, Elizabeth 1902- 12
Foster, Elizabeth 1905-1963 10
Foster, F. Blanche 1919- 11
Foster, G(eorge) Allen 1907-1969 26
Foster, Genevieve (Stump) 1893-1979 2
Obituary 23
See also CLR 7
Foster, Gerald L. 198
Foster, Hal
See Foster, Harold
Foster, Harold 1892-1982 31
Foster, Jeanne
See Williams, Jeanne
Foster, John
See Foster, John L(ouis)
and Furcolo, Foster
Foster, John (Thomas) 1925- 8
Foster, John L(ouis) 1941- 102
Foster, Juliana 196
Foster, Laura Louise (James) 1918- 6
Foster, Leila Merrell 1929- 73
Foster, Lynne 1937- 74
Foster, Margaret Lesser 1899(?)-1979
Obituary 21
Foster, Marian Curtis 1909-1978 23
Foster, Mark 1961- 197
Foster, Sally 58
Fotheringham, Edwin 201
Foulds, E. V.
See Foulds, Elfrida Vipont
Foulds, Elfrida Vipont 1902-1992 52
Fountas, Angela Jane 180
Fourie, Corlia 1944- 91
Fourth Brother, The
See Aung, (Maung) Htin
Fowke, Edith (Margaret) 1913-1996 14
Fowles, John 1926-2005 22
Obituary 171
Fowles, John Robert
See Fowles, John
Fowles, Shelley 1956- 205
Fox, Aileen 1907-2005 58
Obituary 170
Fox, Aileen Mary
See Fox, Aileen
Fox, Annie 1950- 175
Fox, Charles Philip 1913-2003 12
Obituary 150
Fox, Christyan 188
Fox, Diane 188
Fox, Eleanor
See St. John, Wylly Folk
Fox, Fontaine Talbot, Jr. 1884-1964
Obituary 23
Fox, Fred 1903(?)-1981
Obituary 27

Fox, Freeman
  See Hamilton, Charles (Harold St. John)
Fox, Geoffrey 1941- 73
Fox, Grace
  See Anderson, Grace Fox
Fox, Helen 1962- 181
Fox, Karen C. 1969- 229
Fox, Larry 30
Fox, Lee 1958- 227
Fox, Lorraine 1922-1976 27
  Earlier sketch in SATA 11
Fox, Louisa
  See Kroll, Virginia L.
Fox, Mary Virginia 1919- 152
  Brief entry 39
  Earlier sketches in SATA 44, 88
Fox, Mem 1946- 211
  Earlier sketches in SATA 51, 103, 155
  See also CLR 80
Fox, Merrion Frances
  See Fox, Mem
Fox, Michael W(ilson) 1937- 15
Fox, Norma Diane
  See Mazer, Norma Fox
Fox, Paula 1923- 167
  Earlier sketches in SATA 17, 60, 120
  See also CLR 96
Fox, Robert J. 1927- 33
Fox, Robert Joseph
  See Fox, Robert J.
Fox-Davies, Sarah 1956- 199
Foyt, Victoria .... 187.
Fradin, Dennis
  See Fradin, Dennis Brindell
Fradin, Dennis Brindell 1945- 185
  Earlier sketches in SATA 29, 90, 135
Fradin, Judith Bloom 1945- 185
  Earlier sketches in SATA 90, 152
Frailey, Paige (Menefee) 1965- 82
Frame, Janet 1924-2004 119
Frame, Janet Paterson
  See Frame, Janet
Frame, Paul 1913-1994 60
  Brief entry 33
  Obituary 83
Frances, Miss
  See Horwich, Frances R(appaport)
Franchere, Ruth 18
Francis, Charles
  See Holme, Bryan
Francis, Dee
  See Haas, Dorothy F.
Francis, Dorothy 1926- 127
  Earlier sketch in SATA 10
Francis, Dorothy B.
  See Francis, Dorothy
Francis, Dorothy Brenner
  See Francis, Dorothy
Francis, Guy 225
Francis, Jaye
  See Pausacker, Jenny
Francis, Pamela (Mary) 1926- 11
Franck, Eddie
  See Cooke, Frank E.
Franco, Betsy 223
  Earlier sketches in SATA 150, 188
Franco, Eloise (Bauder) 1910- 62
Franco, Johan (Henri Gustave) 1908-1988 ... 62
Franco, Marjorie 38
Franco, Tom 224
Francois, Andre 1915-2005 25
Francoise
  See Seignobosc, Francoise
Frank, Anne 1929-1945 87
  Brief entry 42
  See also CLR 101
Frank, Annelies Marie
  See Frank, Anne
Frank, Daniel B. 1956- 55
Frank, Emily R.
  See Frank, E.R.

Frank, E.R. 1967- 157
Frank, Helene
  See Vautier, Ghislaine
Frank, Hillary 1976- 148
Frank, John 199
Frank, Josette 1893-1989 10
  Obituary 63
Frank, Lucy 1947- 166
  Earlier sketch in SATA 94
Frank, Mary 1933- 34
Frank, R., Jr.
  See Ross, Frank (Xavier), Jr.
Frankau, Mary Evelyn Atkinson 1899-1974 .. 4
Frankel, Alona 1937- 66
Frankel, Bernice 9
Frankel, Edward 1910- 44
Frankel, Ellen 1951- 78
Frankel, Julie 1947- 40
  Brief entry 34
Frankenberg, Robert 1911- 22
Frankland, David 207
Franklin, Cheryl J. 1955- 70
Franklin, Harold 1926- 13
Franklin, Kristine L. 1958- 124
  Earlier sketch in SATA 80
Franklin, Lance
  See Lantz, Francess L(in)
Franklin, Madeleine
  See L'Engle, Madeleine
Franklin, Madeleine L'Engle
  See L'Engle, Madeleine
Franklin, Madeleine L'Engle Camp
  See L'Engle, Madeleine
Franklin, Max
  See Deming, Richard
Franklin, Steve
  See Stevens, Franklin
Franson, Leanne 1963- 223
  Earlier sketch in SATA 111
Franson, Scott E. 1966- 192
Franzen, Nils-Olof 1916- 10
Frascino, Edward 48
  Brief entry 33
  See also SAAS 9
Frasconi, Antonio 1919- 131
  Earlier sketches in SATA 6, 53
  See also SAAS 11
Fraser, Betty
  See Fraser, Elizabeth Marr
Fraser, Elizabeth Marr 1928- 31
Fraser, Eric (George) 1902-1983 38
Fraser, Mary Ann 1959- 214
  Earlier sketches in SATA 76, 137
  See also SAAS 23
Fraser, Wynnette (McFaddin) 1925- 90
Frasier, Debra 1953- 182
  Earlier sketches in SATA 69, 112
Fraustino, Lisa Rowe 1961- 146
  Autobiography Feature 146
  Earlier sketch in SATA 84
Frazee, Marla 1958- 225
  Earlier sketches in SATA 105, 151, 187
Frazer, Megan 1977- 221
Frazetta, Frank 1928-2010 58
Frazier, Angie 234
Frazier, Craig 1955- 221
  Earlier sketch in SATA 177
Frazier, Neta (Osborn) Lohnes 1890-1990 7
Frazier, Sundee T. 1968- 198
Frazier, Sundee Tucker
  See Frazier, Sundee T.
Frederic, Mike
  See Cox, William R(obert)
Frederick, Heather Vogel 207
Fredericks, Anthony D. 1947- 113
Freed, Alvyn M. 1913-1993 22
Freedman, Benedict 1919- 27
Freedman, Claire 227
  Earlier sketch in SATA 185
Freedman, Deborah 1960- 191
Freedman, Jeff 1953- 90

Freedman, Nancy 1920-2010 27
Freedman, Russell 1929- 235
  Earlier sketches in SATA 16, 71, 123, 175
  See also CLR 71
Freedman, Russell Bruce
  See Freedman, Russell
Freeman, Barbara C. 1906-1999 28
Freeman, Barbara Constance
  See Freeman, Barbara C.
Freeman, Bill
  See Freeman, William Bradford
Freeman, Don 1908-1978 17
  See also CLR 90
Freeman, Ira Maximilian 1905-1987 21
Freeman, Kimberley
  See Wilkins, Kim
Freeman, Laura 200
Freeman, Lucy (Greenbaum) 1916-2004 24
Freeman, Mae 1907-1985 25
Freeman, Mae Blacker
  See Freeman, Mae
Freeman, Marcia S. 1937- 102
Freeman, Marcia Sheehan
  See Freeman, Marcia S.
Freeman, Martha 1956- 201
  Earlier sketches in SATA 101, 152
Freeman, Nancy 1932- 61
Freeman, Peter J.
  See Calvert, Patricia
Freeman, Roy 235
Freeman, Sarah (Caroline) 1940- 66
Freeman, Tor 1977- 164
Freeman, VicToria
  See Freeman, Tor
Freeman, William Bradford 1938- 58
  Brief entry 48
Fregosi, Claudia (Anne Marie) 1946- 24
Freitas, Donna 1972- 205
French, Allen 1870-1946
  See YABC 1
French, Dorothy Kayser 1926- 5
French, Fiona 1944- 132
  Earlier sketches in SATA 6, 75
  See also CLR 37
  See also SAAS 21
French, Jackie 186
  Autobiography Feature 139
  Earlier sketches in SATA 108, 139
  See French, Jackie Anne
  and French, Jacqueline Anne
French, Kathryn
  See Mosesson, Gloria R(ubin)
French, Martin 176
French, Michael 1944- 49
  Brief entry 38
French, Paul
  See Asimov, Isaac
French, S. Terrell 216
French, Simon 1957- 147
  Earlier sketch in SATA 86
French, Vivian 209
  Earlier sketch in SATA 165
French, Wendy 1972- 234
Frenette, Liza 126
Freschet, Gina 1960- 175
  Earlier sketch in SATA 139
Frewer, Glyn (M.) 1931- 11
Frey, Darcy 98
Freymann, Saxton 1958(?)- 178
Freymann-Weyr, Garret 1965- 145
Freymann-Weyr, Rhoda Garret Michaela
  See Freymann-Weyr, Garret
Friar, Joanne 237
Friar, Joanne H.
  See Friar, Joanne
Frick, C. H.
  See Irwin, Constance (H.) Frick
Frick, Constance
  See Irwin, Constance (H.) Frick
Fricke, Aaron 1962- 89
Fridell, Ron 1943- 124

Fried, Janice *197*
Frieden, Sarajo *232*
Friedlander, Joanne K(ohn) 1930- *9*
Friedman, Aimee 1979- *189*
Friedman, D. Dina 1957- *180*
Friedman, Debra 1955- *150*
Friedman, Estelle (Ehrenwald) 1920- *7*
Friedman, Frieda 1905- *43*
Friedman, Hal *230*
    See Friedman, Harold
Friedman, Ina R(osen) 1926- *136*
    Brief entry *41*
    Earlier sketch in SATA *49*
Friedman, Jerrold David
    See Gerrold, David
Friedman, Judi 1935- *59*
Friedman, Laurie 1964- *219*
    Earlier sketches in SATA *138, 179*
Friedman, Marvin 1930- *42*
    Brief entry *33*
Friedman, Robin 1968- *219*
    Earlier sketch in SATA *162*
Friedmann, Stan 1953- *80*
Friedrich, Otto (Alva) 1929-1995 .... *33*
Friedrich, Priscilla 1927- *39*
Friend, Catherine 1957(?)- *194*
Friend, David Michael 1975- *195*
Friend, Natasha 1972- *184*
Friendlich, Dick
    See Friendlich, Richard J.
Friendlich, Richard J. 1909- *11*
Friermood, Elisabeth Hamilton 1903-1992 .... *5*
Friesen, Bernice (Sarah Anne) 1966- *105*
Friesen, Gayle 1960- *200*
    Earlier sketch in SATA *109*
Friesen, Jonathan 1967(?)- *206*
Friesner, Esther 1951- *207*
    Earlier sketches in SATA *71, 168*
Friesner, Esther M.
    See Friesner, Esther
Friis-Baastad, Babbis Ellinor 1921-1970 .... *7*
Frimmer, Steven 1928- *31*
Frischmuth, Barbara 1941- *114*
Friskey, Margaret (Richards) 1901-1995 .... *5*
Fritts, Mary Bahr
    See Bahr, Mary (Madelyn)
Fritz, Jean (Guttery) 1915- *163*
    Autobiography Feature *122*
    Earlier sketches in SATA *1, 29, 72, 119*
    See also CLR *96*
    See also SAAS *2*
Froehlich, Margaret W(alden) 1930- *56*
Frois, Jeanne 1953- *73*
Froissart, Jean 1338(?)-1410(?) *28*
Froman, Elizabeth Hull 1920-1975 .... *10*
Froman, Robert (Winslow) 1917- *8*
Fromental, Jean-Luc 1950- *231*
Fromm, Lilo 1928- *29*
Frommer, Harvey 1937- *41*
Frost, A(rthur) B(urdett) 1851-1928 .... *19*
Frost, Elizabeth
    See Frost-Knappman, Elizabeth
Frost, Erica
    See Supraner, Robyn
Frost, Helen 1949- *194*
    Autobiography Feature *194*
    Earlier sketches in SATA *157, 183*
Frost, Helen Marie
    See Frost, Helen
Frost, Lesley 1899-1983 .... *14*
    Obituary *34*
Frost, Robert 1874-1963 .... *14*
    See also CLR *67*
Frost, Robert Lee
    See Frost, Robert
Frost, Shelley 1960- *138*
Frost-Knappman, Elizabeth 1943- *179*
Froud, Brian 1947- *150*
Fry, Annette R(iley) *89*
Fry, Christopher 1907-2005 .... *66*
Fry, Edward Bernard 1925- *35*

Fry, Rosalie Kingsmill 1911-1992 .... *3*
    See also SAAS *11*
Fry, Virginia Lynn 1952- *95*
Frye, Sally
    See Moore, Elaine
Fuchs, Bernie 1932- *162*
    Earlier sketch in SATA *95*
Fuchs, Erich 1916- *6*
Fuchshuber, Annegert 1940- *43*
Fucile, Tony *221*
Fuerst, Jeffrey B. 1956- *143*
Fuertes, Gloria 1918-1998 .... *115*
Fuge, Charles 1966- *144*
    Earlier sketch in SATA *74*
Fujikawa, Gyo 1908-1998 .... *76*
    Brief entry *30*
    Obituary *110*
    Earlier sketch in SATA *39*
    See also CLR *25*
    See also SAAS *16*
Fujita, Tamao 1905-1999 .... *7*
Fujiwara, Kim 1957- *81*
Fujiwara, Michiko 1946- *15*
Fuka, Vladimir 1926-1977
    Obituary *27*
Fulcher, Jennifer
    See Westwood, Jennifer
Fuller, Catherine Leuthold 1916- *9*
Fuller, Edmund (Maybank) 1914- *21*
Fuller, Iola
    See McCoy, Iola Fuller
Fuller, John G(rant, Jr.) 1913-1990 .... *65*
Fuller, Kathleen
    See Gottfried, Theodore Mark
Fuller, Lois Hamilton 1915- *11*
Fuller, Margaret 1810-1850 .... *25*
Fuller, Maud
    See Petersham, Maud
Fuller, Roy (Broadbent) 1912-1991 .... *87*
Fuller, Sarah Margaret
    See Fuller, Margaret
Fults, John Lee 1932- *33*
Funk, Thompson 1911- *7*
Funk, Tom
    See Funk, Thompson
Funke, Cornelia 1958- *209*
    Earlier sketches in SATA *154, 174*
    See also CLR *145*
Funke, Cornelia Caroline
    See Funke, Cornelia
Funke, Lewis 1912-1992 .... *11*
Fuqua, Jonathon Scott 1966- *141*
Furbee, Mary R.
    See Furbee, Mary Rodd
Furbee, Mary Rodd 1954- *138*
Furchgott, Terry 1948- *29*
Furlong, Monica (Mavis) 1930-2003 .... *86*
    Obituary *142*
Furlonger, Patricia
    See Wrightson, Patricia
Furman, Gertrude Lerner Kerman 1909- *21*
Furniss, Tim 1948- *49*
Furrow, Robert 1985- *172*
Furukawa, Toshi 1924- *24*
Fusco, Kimberly Newton *236*
Fusillo, Archimede 1962- *137*
Fussell, Sandy 1960- *234*
Futcher, Jane P. 1947- *76*
Futehali, Zahida
    See Whitaker, Zai
Fyleman, Rose (Amy) 1877-1957 .... *21*
Fyson, Jenny Grace
    See Fyson, J.G.
Fyson, J.G. 1904-1998 .... *42*

G

Gaan, Margaret 1914- *65*
Gaber, Susan 1956- *169*
    Earlier sketch in SATA *115*
Gaberman, Judie Angell
    See Angell, Judie
Gabhart, Ann
    See Gabhart, Ann H.
Gabhart, Ann H. 1947- *75*
Gable, Brian 1949- *195*
Gabler, Mirko 1951- *77*
Gabriel, Adriana
    See Rojany, Lisa
Gabrys, Ingrid Schubert
    See Schubert-Gabrys, Ingrid
Gackenbach, Dick 1927- *79*
    Brief entry *30*
    Earlier sketch in SATA *48*
Gadd, Jeremy 1949- *116*
Gaddis, Vincent H. 1913-1997 .... *35*
Gadler, Steve J. 1905-1985 .... *36*
Gaeddert, Lou Ann (Bigge) 1931- *103*
    Earlier sketch in SATA *20*
Gaeddert, Louann
    See Gaeddert, Lou Ann (Bigge)
Gaer, Joseph 1897-1969 .... *118*
Gaer, Yossef
    See Gaer, Joseph
Gaetz, Dayle Campbell 1947- *138*
Gaffney, Timothy R. 1951- *170*
    Earlier sketch in SATA *69*
Gaffron, Norma 1931- *97*
Gaffron, Norma Bondeson
    See Gaffron, Norma
Gag, Flavia 1907-1979
    Obituary *24*
Gag, Wanda (Hazel) 1893-1946 .... *100*
    See also YABC *1*
    See also CLR *150*
Gage, Brian *162*
Gage, Wilson
    See Steele, Mary Q(uintard Govan)
Gagliano, Eugene M. 1946- *150*
Gagliardo, Ruth Garver 1895(?)-1980
    Obituary *22*
Gagnon, Cecile 1936- *58*
Gaillard, Jason 1965- *200*
Gaiman, Neil 1960- *228*
    Earlier sketches in SATA *85, 146, 197*
    See also CLR *109*
Gaiman, Neil Richard
    See Gaiman, Neil
Gainer, Cindy 1962- *74*
Gaines, Ernest J. 1933- *86*
    See also CLR *62*
Gaines, Ernest James
    See Gaines, Ernest J.
Gaither, Gloria 1942- *127*
Gal, Laszlo 1933- *96*
    Brief entry *32*
    Earlier sketch in SATA *52*
    See also CLR *61*
Gal, Susan *228*
Galbraith, Ben 1980- *200*
Galbraith, Kathryn O. 1945- *219*
    Earlier sketch in SATA *85*
Galbraith, Kathryn Osebold
    See Galbraith, Kathryn O.
Galdone, Paul 1907(?)-1986 .... *66*
    Obituary *49*
    Earlier sketch in SATA *17*
    See also CLR *16*
Galindo, Claudia 1979- *203*
Galinsky, Ellen 1942- *23*
Gall, Chris 1961- *176*
Gallagher, Diana G. 1946- *153*
Gallagher, Lurlene Nora
    See McDaniel, Lurlene
Gallagher-Cole, Mernie 1958- *206*

Gallant, Roy A(rthur) 1924- *110*
  Earlier sketches in SATA *4, 68*
  See also CLR *30*
Gallardo, Evelyn 1948- *78*
Gallaz, Christophe 1948- *162*
  See also CLR *126*
Gallego Garcia, Laura 1977- *173*
Gallico, Paul 1897-1976 .... *13*
Gallico, Paul William
  See Gallico, Paul
Gallo, Donald R. 1938- *112*
  Autobiography Feature *104*
Gallo, Donald Robert
  See Gallo, Donald R.
Galloway, Owateka (S.) 1981- *121*
Galloway, Priscilla 1930- *227*
  Earlier sketches in SATA *66, 112*
Gallup, Joan 1957- *128*
Galouchko, Annouchka Gravel 1960- *95*
Galt, Thomas Franklin, Jr. 1908-1989 .... *5*
Galt, Tom
  See Galt, Thomas Franklin, Jr.
Galvin, Matthew R. 1950- *93*
Galvin, Matthew Reppert
  See Galvin, Matthew R.
Gamble, Kim 1952- *183*
  Earlier sketches in SATA *81, 124*
Gambrell, Jamey *82*
Gamerman, Martha 1941- *15*
Gammell, Stephen 1943- *226*
  Earlier sketches in SATA *53, 81, 128*
  See also CLR *83*
Ganly, Helen (Mary) 1940- *56*
Gannett, Ruth Chrisman (Arens)
  1896-1979 .... *33*
Gannett, Ruth Stiles 1923- *3*
Gannij, Joan *208*
Gannij, Joan Levine
  See Gannij, Joan
Gannon, Ned 1974- *205*
Gannon, Robert Haines 1931- *8*
Gano, Lila 1949- *76*
Gans, Roma 1894-1996 .... *45*
  Obituary *93*
Gant, Matthew
  See Hano, Arnold
Gantner, Susan (Verble) 1939- *63*
Gantos, Jack 1951- *169*
  Earlier sketches in SATA *20, 81, 119*
  See also CLR *85*
Gantos, John Bryan, Jr.
  See Gantos, Jack
Ganz, Yaffa 1938- *61*
  Brief entry *52*
Garafano, Marie 1942- *84*
Garant, Andre J. 1968- *123*
Garbe, Ruth Moore
  See Moore, Ruth (Ellen)
Garber, Esther
  See Lee, Tanith
Garcia, Cristina 1958- *208*
Garcia, Emma 1969- *198*
Garcia, Geronimo 1960- *222*
Garcia, Kami 1972- *229*
Garcia, Yolanda P. 1952- *113*
Garcia, Yolanda Pacheco
  See Garcia, Yolanda P.
Gard, Janice
  See Latham, Jean Lee
Gard, Joyce
  See Reeves, Joyce
Gard, Robert Edward 1910-1992 .... *18*
  Obituary *74*
Gard, (Sanford) Wayne 1899-1986
  Obituary *49*
Gardam, Jane 1928- *130*
  Brief entry *28*
  Earlier sketches in SATA *39, 76*
  See also CLR *12*
  See also SAAS *9*

Gardam, Jane Mary
  See Gardam, Jane
Gardella, Tricia 1944- *96*
Garden, Nancy 1938- *147*
  Autobiography Feature *147*
  Earlier sketches in SATA *12, 77, 114*
  See also CLR *51*
  See also SAAS *8*
Gardiner, John Reynolds 1944-2006 .... *64*
  Obituary *174*
Gardiner, Lindsey 1971- *144*
Gardner, Craig Shaw 1949- *99*
Gardner, Dic
  See Gardner, Richard (M.)
Gardner, Graham *159*
Gardner, Hugh 1910-1986
  Obituary *49*
Gardner, Jane Mylum 1946- *83*
Gardner, Jeanne LeMonnier 1925- *5*
Gardner, John, Jr. 1933-1982 .... *40*
  Obituary *31*
Gardner, John Champlin, Jr.
  See Gardner, John, Jr.
Gardner, John E(dward) 1917- *192*
Gardner, Lyn *192*
Gardner, Martin 1914-2010 .... *142*
  Earlier sketch in SATA *16*
Gardner, Miriam
  See Bradley, Marion Zimmer
Gardner, Richard (M.) 1931- *24*
Gardner, Richard A(lan) 1931-2003 .... *13*
  Obituary *144*
Gardner, Sally *229*
  Earlier sketch in SATA *177*
Gardner, Sandra 1940- *70*
Gardner, Scot 1968- *143*
Gardner, Sheldon 1934- *33*
Gardner, Ted
  See Gardner, Theodore Roosevelt II
Gardner, Theodore Roosevelt
  See Gardner, Theodore Roosevelt II
Gardner, Theodore Roosevelt II 1934- *84*
Garelick, May 1910-1989 .... *19*
Garfield, James B. 1881-1984 .... *6*
  Obituary *38*
Garfield, Leon 1921-1996 .... *76*
  Obituary *90*
  Earlier sketches in SATA *1, 32*
  See also CLR *166*
Garfinkle, Debra L.
  See Garfinkle, D.L.
Garfinkle, D.L. *187*
Garis, Howard R. 1873-1962 .... *13*
Garis, Howard Roger
  See Garis, Howard R.
Garland, Mark 1953- *79*
Garland, Mark A.
  See Garland, Mark
Garland, Michael 1952- *208*
  Earlier sketch in SATA *168*
Garland, Sarah 1944- *135*
  Earlier sketch in SATA *62*
Garland, Sherry 1948- *145*
  Autobiography Feature *145*
  Earlier sketches in SATA *73, 114*
Garner, Alan 1934- *69*
  Autobiography Feature *108*
  Earlier sketch in SATA *18*
  See also CLR *130*
Garner, David 1958- *78*
Garner, Eleanor Ramrath 1930- *122*
Garner, James Finn 1960(?)- *92*
Garnet, A. H.
  See Slote, Alfred
Garnett, Eve C. R. 1900-1991 .... *3*
  Obituary *70*
Garofoli, Viviana 1970- *186*
Garou, Louis P.
  See Bowkett, Stephen
Garraty, John A. 1920-2007 .... *23*
  Obituary *189*

Garraty, John Arthur
  See Garraty, John A.
Garren, Devorah-Leah
  See Devorah-Leah
Garret, Maxwell R. 1917- *39*
Garretson, Dee *236*
Garretson, Victoria Diane
  See Cox, Victoria
Garrett, Helen 1895- *21*
Garrett, Randall 1927-1987 .... *180*
Garrett, Richard 1920- *82*
Garrigue, Sheila 1931- *21*
Garrison, Barbara 1931- *163*
  Earlier sketch in SATA *19*
Garrison, Frederick
  See Sinclair, Upton
Garrison, Mary 1952- *146*
Garrison, Peter
  See Gardner, Craig Shaw
Garrison, Webb B(lack) 1919-2000 .... *25*
Garrity, Jennifer Johnson 1961- *124*
Garrity, Linda K. 1947- *128*
Garsee, Jeannine *199*
Garst, Doris Shannon 1894-1981 .... *1*
Garst, Shannon
  See Garst, Doris Shannon
Garth, Will
  See Hamilton, Edmond
  and Kuttner, Henry
Garthwaite, Marion H(ook) 1893-1981 .... *7*
Garton, Malinda D(ean) (?)-1976
  Obituary *26*
Garvie, Maureen 1944- *175*
Garvie, Maureen McCallum
  See Garvie, Maureen
Garza, Carmen Lomas 1948- *182*
Garza, Xavier *184*
Gascoigne, Bamber 1935- *62*
Gaskins, Pearl Fuyo 1957- *134*
Gasperini, Jim 1952- *54*
  Brief entry *49*
Gater, Dilys 1944- *41*
Gates, Doris 1901-1987 .... *34*
  Obituary *54*
  Earlier sketch in SATA *1*
  See also SAAS *1*
Gates, Frieda 1933- *26*
Gates, Susan 1950- *153*
Gates, Viola R. 1931- *101*
Gathorne-Hardy, Jonathan G. 1933- *124*
  Earlier sketch in SATA *26*
Gatti, Anne 1952- *103*
Gatty, Juliana Horatia
  See Ewing, Juliana (Horatia Gatty)
Gauch, Patricia Lee 1934- *228*
  Earlier sketches in SATA *26, 80*
  See also CLR *56*
  See also SAAS *21*
Gauch, Sarah *223*
Gaudasinska, Elzbieta 1943- *190*
Gaul, Randy 1959- *63*
Gault, Clare 1925- *36*
Gault, Frank 1926-1982 .... *36*
  Brief entry *30*
Gault, William Campbell 1910-1995 .... *8*
Gauthier, Gail 1953- *203*
  Earlier sketches in SATA *118, 160*
Gaver, Becky
  See Gaver, Rebecca
Gaver, Rebecca 1952- *20*
Gavin, Jamila 1941- *223*
  Earlier sketches in SATA *96, 125*
Gay, Amelia
  See Hogarth, Grace (Weston Allen)
Gay, Francis
  See Gee, H(erbert) L(eslie)
Gay, Kathlyn 1930- *144*
  Earlier sketch in SATA *9*

Gay, Marie-Louise 1952- *179*
  Earlier sketches in SATA *68, 126*
  See also CLR 27
  See also SAAS *21*
Gay, Michel 1947- *162*
Gay, Zhenya 1906-1978 .... *19*
Gaze, Gillian
  See Barklem, Jill
Gear, Kathleen M. O'Neal
  See Gear, Kathleen O'Neal
Gear, Kathleen O'Neal 1954- *224*
  Earlier sketches in SATA *71, 166*
Gear, W. Michael 1955- *224*
  Earlier sketches in SATA *71, 166*
Geary, Rick 1946- *142*
Geason, Susan 1946- *122*
Gedalof, Robin
  See McGrath, Robin
Gedge, Pauline (Alice) 1945- *101*
Gee, H(erbert) L(eslie) 1901-1977
  Obituary *26*
Gee, Maurice 1931- *227*
  Earlier sketches in SATA *46, 101*
  See also CLR 56
Gee, Maurice Gough
  See Gee, Maurice
Geehan, Wayne (E.) 1947- *107*
Geer, Charles 1922- *42*
  Brief entry *32*
Geeslin, Campbell 1925- *163*
  Earlier sketch in SATA *107*
Gehman, Mary W. 1923- *86*
Gehr, Mary 1910(?)-1997 .... *32*
  Obituary *99*
Geipel, Eileen 1932- *30*
Geis, Alissa Imre 1976- *189*
Geis, Darlene Stern 1918(?)-1999 .... *7*
  Obituary *111*
Geisel, Helen 1898-1967 .... *26*
Geisel, Theodor Seuss
  See Dr. Seuss
Geisert, Arthur 1941- *237*
  Brief entry *52*
  Earlier sketches in SATA *56, 92, 133, 171*
  See also CLR 87
  See also SAAS 23
Geisert, Arthur Frederick
  See Geisert, Arthur
Geisert, Bonnie 1942- *165*
  Earlier sketch in SATA *92*
Geist, Ken *191*
Gelber, Lisa *210*
Geldart, William 1936- *15*
Gelinas, Paul J. 1904-1996 .... *10*
Gellis, Roberta 1927- *128*
Gellis, Roberta Leah Jacobs
  See Gellis, Roberta
Gellman, Marc *112*
Gelman, Amy 1961- *72*
Gelman, Jan 1963- *58*
Gelman, Rita Golden 1937- *131*
  Brief entry *51*
  Earlier sketch in SATA *84*
Gelman, Steve 1934- *3*
Gemignani, Tony 1973- *220*
Gemming, Elizabeth 1932- *11*
Gendel, Evelyn W. 1916(?)-1977
  Obituary *27*
Gennaro, Joseph F., Jr. 1924- *53*
Gennaro, Joseph Francis, Jr.
  See Gennaro, Joseph F., Jr.
Gentieu, Penny *204*
Gentile, Petrina 1969- *91*
Gentle, Mary 1956- *48*
Gentleman, David (William) 1930- *7*
Gentry, Marita *215*
Geoghegan, Adrienne 1962- *143*
George, Barbara
  See Katz, Bobbi
George, Emily
  See Katz, Bobbi

George, Gail
  See Katz, Bobbi
George, Jean
  See George, Jean Craighead
George, Jean C.
  See George, Jean Craighead
George, Jean Craighead 1919- *226*
  Earlier sketches in SATA *2, 68, 124, 170*
  See also CLR *136*
George, Jessica Day 1976- *210*
George, John L(othar) 1916- *2*
George, Kristine O'Connell 1954- *156*
  Earlier sketch in SATA *110*
George, Lindsay Barrett 1952- *206*
  Earlier sketches in SATA *95, 155*
George, S. C. 1898- *11*
George, Sally
  See Orr, Wendy
George, Sidney Charles
  See George, S. C.
George, Twig C. 1950- *114*
George, W(illiam) Lloyd 1900(?)-1975
  Obituary *30*
Georgiou, Constantine 1927- *7*
Georgiou, Theo
  See Odgers, Sally Farrell
Geraghty, Paul 1959- *130*
Gerard, Jean Ignace Isidore 1803-1847 .... *45*
Geras, Adele 1944- *180*
  Autobiography Feature *180*
  Earlier sketches in SATA *23, 87, 129, 173*
  See also SAAS *21*
Geras, Adele Daphne Weston
  See Geras, Adele
Gerber, Carole 1947- *207*
Gerber, Linda *213*
Gerber, Merrill Joan 1938- *170*
  Autobiography Feature *170*
  Earlier sketches in SATA *64, 127*
Gerber, Perren 1933- *104*
Gerberg, Mort 1931- *64*
Gergely, Tibor 1900-1978 .... *54*
  Obituary *20*
Geringer, Laura 1948- *232*
  Earlier sketches in SATA *29, 94, 164*
Gerler, William R(obert) 1917-1996 .... *47*
Gerrard, Jean 1933- *51*
Gerrard, Roy 1935-1997 .... *90*
  Brief entry *45*
  Obituary *99*
  Earlier sketch in SATA *47*
  See also CLR 23
Gerritsen, Paula 1956- *177*
Gerrold, David 1944- *144*
  Earlier sketch in SATA *66*
Gersh, A.
  See Gersh, Amanda
Gersh, Amanda *235*
Gershator, David 1937- *180*
Gershator, Phillis 1942- *235*
  Earlier sketches in SATA *90, 158, 188*
Gershon, Dann 1955- *187*
Gershon, Gina 1962- *187*
Gerson, Corinne 1927- *37*
Gerson, Mary-Joan *136*
  Earlier sketch in SATA *79*
Gerson, Noel Bertram 1914-1988 .... *22*
  Obituary *60*
Gerstein, Mordicai 1935- *222*
  Brief entry *36*
  Earlier sketches in SATA *47, 81, 142, 178*
  See also CLR *102*
Gertridge, Allison 1967- *132*
Gervais, Bernadette 1959- *80*
Gervay, Susanne *183*
Gesner, Clark 1938-2002 .... *40*
  Obituary *143*
Gessner, Lynne 1919- *16*
Geter, Tyrone *150*
Getz, David 1957- *91*
Getzinger, Donna 1968- *128*

Geus, Mireille 1964- *207*
Gevirtz, Eliezer 1950- *49*
Gevry, Claudine *188*
Gewe, Raddory
  See Gorey, Edward (St. John)
Ghan, Linda (R.) 1947- *77*
Ghent, Natale 1962- *148*
Gherman, Beverly 1934- *123*
  Earlier sketch in SATA *68*
Ghigna, Charles 1946- *153*
  Earlier sketch in SATA *108*
Giacobbe, Beppe 1953- *174*
Giambastiani, Kurt R. A. 1958- *141*
Giannini, Enzo 1946- *68*
Gibala-Broxholm, Scott 1959(?)- *205*
Gibbons, Alan 1953- *198*
  Earlier sketch in SATA *124*
Gibbons, Faye 1938- *103*
  Earlier sketch in SATA *65*
Gibbons, Gail 1944- *201*
  Earlier sketches in SATA *23, 72, 104, 160*
  See also CLR 8
  See also SAAS 12
Gibbons, Gail Gretchen
  See Gibbons, Gail
Gibbons, Kaye 1960- *117*
Gibbs, Adrea 1960- *126*
Gibbs, Alonzo (Lawrence) 1915-1992 .... *5*
Gibbs, (Cecilia) May 1877-1969
  Obituary *27*
Gibbs, Stuart 1969- *230*
Gibbs, Tony
  See Gibbs, Wolcott, Jr.
Gibbs, Wolcott, Jr. 1935- *40*
Giblin, James Cross 1933- *197*
  Earlier sketches in SATA *33, 75, 122*
  See also CLR 29
  See also SAAS 12
Gibson, Andrew (William) 1949- *72*
Gibson, Barbara L. *205*
Gibson, Barbara Leonard
  See Gibson, Barbara L.
Gibson, Betty 1911- *75*
Gibson, Jo
  See Fluke, Joanne
Gibson, Josephine
  See Hine, Sesyle Joslin
  and Hine, Al(fred Blakelee)
Gibson, Marley 1966- *225*
Gibson, Sarah P. 1962- *211*
Gibson, William 1914-2008 .... *66*
  Obituary *199*
Gibson, William Ford
  See Gibson, William
Gidal, Nachum
  See Gidal, Tim Nachum
Gidal, Sonia (Epstein) 1922- *2*
Gidal, Tim Nachum 1909-1996 .... *2*
Gidalewitsch, Nachum
  See Gidal, Tim Nachum
Gideon, Melanie 1963- *175*
Giegling, John A(llan) 1935- *17*
Gifaldi, David 1950- *209*
  Earlier sketch in SATA *76*
Giff, Patricia Reilly 1935- *203*
  Earlier sketches in SATA *33, 70, 121, 160*
Giffard, Hannah 1962- *83*
Gifford, Carrie *224*
Gifford, Clive 1966- *198*
Gifford, Griselda 1931- *171*
  Earlier sketch in SATA *42*
Gifford, Kerri 1961- *91*
Gifford, Peggy 1952- *191*
Gilani, Fawzia
  See Gilani-Williams, Fawzia
Gilani-Williams, Fawzia 1967- *231*
Gilbert, Ann
  See Taylor, Ann
Gilbert, Anne Yvonne 1951- *185*
Gilbert, Barbara Snow 1954- *97*

Gilbert, Catherine
  See Murdock, Catherine Gilbert
Gilbert, Frances
  See Collings, Gillian
Gilbert, Harriett 1948- 30
Gilbert, (Agnes) Joan (Sewell) 1931- 10
Gilbert, John (Raphael) 1926- 36
Gilbert, Nan
  See Gilbertson, Mildred Geiger
Gilbert, Roby Goodale 1966- 90
Gilbert, Ruth Gallard Ainsworth
  See Ainsworth, Ruth (Gallard)
Gilbert, Sara (Dulaney) 1943- 82
  Earlier sketch in SATA *11*
Gilbert, Sheri L. 157
Gilbert, Suzie 1956- 97
Gilbert, W(illiam) S(chwenck) 1836-1911 ... 36
Gilbert, Yvonne
  See Gilbert, Anne Yvonne
Gilbertson, Mildred Geiger 1908-1988 2
Gilbreath, Alice 1921- 12
Gilbreth, Frank B., Jr. 1911-2001 2
Gilbreth, Frank Bunker
  See Gilbreth, Frank B., Jr.
Gilchrist, Jan Spivey 1949- 130
  Earlier sketch in SATA *72*
Gilden, Mel 1947- 97
Giles, Gail 196
  Earlier sketch in SATA *152*
Giles, Stephen M. 236
Gilfond, Henry 2
Gilge, Jeanette 1924- 22
Gili, Phillida 1944- 70
Gill, Derek (Lewis Theodore) 1919-1997 9
Gill, Margery Jean 1925- 22
Gill, Shelley 176
Gill, Stephen 1932- 63
Gillespie, Carol Ann 1951- 158
Gillett, Mary (Bledsoe) 7
Gillette, Henry Sampson 1915- 14
Gillette, J. Lynett 1946- 103
Gillette, Jan Lynett
  See Gillette, J. Lynett
Gilley, Jeremy 1969- 174
Gillham, Bill
  See Gillham, W(illiam) E(dwin) C(harles)
Gillham, W(illiam) E(dwin) C(harles)
  1936- 42
Gilliam, Stan 1946- 39
  Brief entry 35
Gilliland, Alexis A. 1931- 72
Gilliland, Alexis Arnaldus
  See Gilliland, Alexis A.
Gilliland, (Cleburne) Hap 1918- 92
Gilliland, Judith Heide 180
Gillmor, Don 1954- 127
Gilman, Dorothy 1923- 5
Gilman, Esther 1925- 15
Gilman, Laura Anne 178
Gilman, Phoebe 1940-2002 104
  Obituary 141
  Earlier sketch in SATA *58*
Gilmore, Iris 1900-1982 22
Gilmore, Kate 1931- 87
Gilmore, Mary (Jean Cameron) 1865-1962 . 49
Gilmore, Rachna 1953- 209
Gilmore, Susan 1954- 59
Gilpin, Stephen 213
  Earlier sketch in SATA *177*
Gilroy, Beryl (Agatha) 1924- 80
Gilson, Barbara
  See Gilson, Charles James Louis
Gilson, Charles James Louis 1878-1943
  See YABC 2
Gilson, Jamie 1933- 176
  Brief entry 34
  Earlier sketches in SATA *37, 91*
Gimpel, Carolyn
  See Hart, Carolyn
Ginsberg, Blaze 1987- 222

Ginsburg, Mirra 1909-2000 92
  Earlier sketch in SATA *6*
  See also CLR *45*
Giovanni, Nikki 1943- 208
  Earlier sketches in SATA *24, 107*
  See also CLR *73*
Giovanni, Yolanda Cornelia
  See Giovanni, Nikki
Giovanni, Yolande Cornelia
  See Giovanni, Nikki
Giovanni, Yolande Cornelia, Jr.
  See Giovanni, Nikki
Giovanopoulos, Paul (Arthur) 1939- 7
Gipson, Billie
  See Letts, Billie
Gipson, Fred(erick Benjamin) 1908-1973 2
  Obituary 24
Girard, Linda (Walvoord) 1942- 41
Giraudon, David 1975- 215
Girion, Barbara 1937- 78
  Earlier sketch in SATA *26*
  See also SAAS *14*
Girl, Nerdy
  See Castellucci, Cecil
Girouard, Patrick 1957- 155
Girzone, Joseph F. 1930- 76
Girzone, Joseph Francis
  See Girzone, Joseph F.
Gise, Joanne
  See Mattern, Joanne
Gist, E.M. 206
Gittings, Jo (Grenville) Manton 1919- 3
Gittings, Robert (William Victor) 1911-1992 . 6
  Obituary 70
Givens, Janet E(aton) 1932- 60
Givner, Joan 1936- 171
Givner, Joan Mary
  See Givner, Joan
Gladstone, Eve
  See Werner, Herma
Gladstone, Gary 1935- 12
Gladstone, M(yron) J. 1923- 37
Glanville, Brian (Lester) 1931- 42
Glanzman, Louis S. 1922- 36
Glaser, Byron 1954- 154
Glaser, Dianne E(lizabeth) 1937- 50
  Brief entry 31
Glaser, Isabel Joshlin 1929- 94
Glaser, Linda 225
Glaser, Milton 1929- 151
  Earlier sketch in SATA *11*
Glaser, Shirley 151
Glaspell, Susan 1882(?)-1948
  See YABC 2
Glass, Andrew 1949- 223
  Brief entry 46
  Earlier sketches in SATA *90, 150*
Glass, Linzi 175
Glass, Linzi Alex
  See Glass, Linzi
Glasscock, Amnesia
  See Steinbeck, John
Glasser, Robin Preiss 1956- 235
Glassman, Bruce 1961- 76
Glatt, Lisa 1963- 217
Glauber, Uta (Heil) 1936- 17
Glazer, Thomas (Zachariah) 1914-2003 9
Glazer, Tom
  See Glazer, Thomas (Zachariah)
Gleasner, Diana (Cottle) 1936- 29
Gleason, Judith 1929- 24
Gleason, Katherine (A.) 1960- 104
Gleeson, Libby 1950- 142
  Autobiography Feature 142
  Earlier sketches in SATA *82, 118*
Gleiter, Jan 1947- 111
Gleitzman, Morris 1953- 234
  Earlier sketches in SATA *88, 156*
  See also CLR *88*
Glen, Maggie 1944- 88
Glendinning, Richard 1917-1988 24

Glendinning, Sally
  See Glendinning, Sara W(ilson)
Glendinning, Sara W(ilson) 1913-1993 24
Glenn, John W. 195
Glenn, Mel 1943- 93
  Brief entry 45
  Earlier sketch in SATA *51*
  See also CLR *51*
Glenn, Patricia Brown 1953- 86
Glenn, Sharlee 159
Glenn, Sharlee Mullins
  See Glenn, Sharlee
Glennon, Karen M. 1946- 85
Gles, Margaret Breitmaier 1940- 22
Glick, Carl (Cannon) 1890-1971 14
Glick, Ruth 1942- 125
Glick, Ruth Burtnick
  See Glick, Ruth
Glick, Virginia Kirkus 1893-1980
  Obituary 23
Gliewe, Unada (Grace) 1927- 3
Glimmerveen, Ulco 1958- 85
Glines, Carroll V(ane), Jr. 1920- 19
Gliori, Debi 1959- 189
  Earlier sketches in SATA *72, 138*
Globe, Leah Ain 1900- 41
Glori Ann
  See Blakely, Gloria
Glovach, Linda 1947- 105
  Earlier sketch in SATA *7*
Glover, Denis (James Matthews) 1912-1980 . 7
Glubok, Shirley (Astor) 146
  Autobiography Feature 146
  Earlier sketches in SATA *6, 68*
  See also CLR *1*
  See also SAAS *7*
Gluck, Felix 1923-1981
  Obituary 25
Glyman, Caroline A. 1967- 103
Glynne-Jones, William 1907-1977 11
Gobbato, Imero 1923- 39
Gobbletree, Richard
  See Quackenbush, Robert M(ead)
Goble, Dorothy 26
Goble, Paul 1933- 131
  Earlier sketches in SATA *25, 69*
  See also CLR *21*
Goble, Warwick (?)-1943 46
Godden, (Margaret) Rumer 1907-1998 36
  Obituary 109
  Earlier sketch in SATA *3*
  See also CLR *20*
  See also SAAS *12*
Gode, Alexander
  See Gode von Aesch, Alexander (Gottfried
  Friedrich)
Gode von Aesch, Alexander (Gottfried
  Friedrich) 1906-1970 14
Godfrey, Jane
  See Bowden, Joan Chase
Godfrey, Martyn
  See Godfrey, Martyn N.
  and Godfrey, Martyn N.
Godfrey, Martyn N. 1949-2000 95
  See also CLR *57*
Godfrey, William
  See Youd, Samuel
Godkin, Celia 1948- 145
  Earlier sketch in SATA *66*
Godkin, Celia Marilyn
  See Godkin, Celia
Godon, Ingrid 1958- 186
Godown, Jan
  See Annino, Jan Godown
Godwin, Laura 1956- 179
Godwin, Sam
  See Pirotta, Saviour
Godwin, Sarah Massini
  See Massini, Sarah
Goede, Irene 1966- 208
Goedecke, Christopher (John) 1951- 81

Goekler, Susan
  See Wooley, Susan Frelick
Goembel, Ponder 204
Goertzen, Glenda 172
Goettel, Elinor 1930- 12
Goetz, Delia 1898-1996 22
  Obituary 91
Goffe, Toni 1936- 61
Goffstein, Brooke
  See Goffstein, Marilyn Brooke
Goffstein, M. B.
  See Goffstein, Marilyn Brooke
Goffstein, Marilyn Brooke 1940- 70
  Earlier sketch in SATA 8
  See also CLR 3
Goforth, Ellen
  See Francis, Dorothy
Gogol, Sara 1948-2004 80
Goh, Chan Hon 1969- 145
Going, Kelly L.
  See Going, K.L.
Going, Kelly Louise
  See Going, K.L.
Going, K.L. 199
  Earlier sketch in SATA 156
Golann, Cecil Paige 1921-1995 11
Golbin, Andree 1923- 15
Gold, Alison Leslie 1945- 104
Gold, August 1955- 215
Gold, Bernice 150
Gold, Phyllis
  See Goldberg, Phyllis
Gold, Robert S(tanley) 1924- 63
Gold, Sharlya 9
Gold, Susan
  See Gold, Susan Dudley
Gold, Susan Dudley 1949- 147
Goldbach, Veronica 1980- 220
Goldberg, Grace 1956- 78
Goldberg, Herbert S. 1926- 25
Goldberg, Jacob 1943- 94
Goldberg, Jake
  See Goldberg, Jacob
Goldberg, Myla 1972(?)- 210
Goldberg, Phyllis 1941- 21
Goldberg, Stan J. 1939- 26
Goldberg, Susan 1948- 71
Goldberg, Whoopi 1955- 119
Goldberger, Judith M. 1948- 80
Goldblatt, Stacey 1969(?)- 191
Golden, Christie 1963- 167
  Earlier sketch in SATA 116
Goldentyer, Debra 1960- 84
Goldfeder, Cheryl
  See Pahz, Cheryl Suzanne
Goldfeder, James
  See Pahz, James Alon
Goldfeder, Jim
  See Pahz, James Alon
Goldfinger, Jennifer P. 1963- 185
Goldfrank, Helen Colodny 1912- 6
Goldin, Augusta 1906-1999 13
Goldin, Barbara Diamond 1946- 129
  Autobiography Feature 129
  Earlier sketch in SATA 92
  See also SAAS 26
Goldin, David 1963- 101
Golding, Julia 1969- 188
Golding, Theresa Martin 1960- 150
Golding, William 1911-1993
  See CLR 130
Golding, William Gerald
  See Golding, William
Goldman, Alex J. 1917- 65
Goldman, E. M. 1943- 103
Goldman, Eleanor Maureen
  See Goldman, E. M.
Goldman, Elizabeth 1949- 90
Goldman, Judy 1955- 212
Goldman, Steven 1964- 207
Goldman, Todd Harris 221

Goldring, Ann 1937- 149
Golds, Cassandra 1962- 226
Goldsborough, June 1923- 19
Goldschmidt, Judy 202
Goldsmith, Connie 1945- 147
Goldsmith, Howard 1943- 108
  Earlier sketch in SATA 24
Goldsmith, John Herman Thorburn 1903-1987
  Obituary 52
Goldsmith, Oliver 1730(?)-1774 26
Goldsmith, Ruth M. 1919- 62
Goldstein, Nathan 1927- 47
Goldstein, Philip 1910-1997 23
Goldston, Robert (Conroy) 1927- 6
Goldstone, Bruce 183
Goldstone, Lawrence A.
  See Treat, Lawrence
Goldszmit, Henryk 1878-1942 65
  See also CLR 152
Golembe, Carla 1951- 79
Golenbock, Peter 1946- 99
Goll, Reinhold W(eimar) 1897-1993 26
Gollub, Matthew 1960- 134
  Earlier sketch in SATA 83
Golson, Terry 213
Golson, Terry Blonder
  See Golson, Terry
Gomes, Filomena 1965- 183
Gomez, Elena 191
Gomez, Elizabeth 133
Gomez-Freer, Elizabeth
  See Gomez, Elizabeth
Gomi, Taro 1945- 103
  Earlier sketch in SATA 64
  See also CLR 57
Gondosch, Linda 1944- 58
Gonsalves, Rob 1959- 209
Gonyea, Mark 236
  Earlier sketch in SATA 194
Gonzales, Chuck 230
Gonzalez, Catherine Troxell 1917-2000 87
Gonzalez, Christina
  See Gonzalez, Maya Christina
Gonzalez, Christina Diaz 1969- 231
Gonzalez, Gloria 1940- 23
Gonzalez, Julie 1958- 174
Gonzalez, Julie Sehers
  See Gonzalez, Julie
Gonzalez, Lucia M. 1957- 202
Gonzalez, Maya
  See Gonzalez, Maya Christina
Gonzalez, Maya Christina 1964- 175
  Earlier sketch in SATA 115
Gonzalez, Rigoberto 1970- 147
Gonzalez, Thomas 1959- 237
Goobie, Beth 1959- 128
Good, Alice 1950- 73
Good, Clare
  See Romano, Clare
Good, Karen Hillard 214
Goodall, Daphne Machin
  See Machin Goodall, Daphne (Edith)
Goodall, Jane 1934- 111
Goodall, John S(trickland) 1908-1996 66
  Obituary 91
  Earlier sketch in SATA 4
  See also CLR 25
Goodbody, Slim
  See Burstein, John
Goode, Diane 1949- 225
  Earlier sketches in SATA 15, 84, 114, 170
Goode, Diane Capuozzo
  See Goode, Diane
Goode, Stephen Ray 1943- 55
  Brief entry 40
Goodenow, Earle 1913- 40
Goodhart, Pippa 1958- 196
  Earlier sketch in SATA 153
Goodhue, Thomas W. 1949- 143
Goodin, Sallie (Brown) 1953- 74
Goodman, Alison 1966- 111

Goodman, Deborah Lerme 1956- 50
  Brief entry 49
Goodman, Elaine 1930- 9
Goodman, Emily 217
Goodman, Joan Elizabeth 1950- 162
  Earlier sketches in SATA 50, 94
Goodman, Susan E. 1952- 181
Goodman, Walter 1927-2002 9
Goodman Koz, Paula 211
Goodrich, Carter 1959(?)- 221
Goodrich, Samuel Griswold 1793-1860 23
Goodsell, Jane Neuberger 1921(?)-1988
  Obituary 56
Goodweather, Hartley
  See King, Thomas
GoodWeather, Hartley
  See King, Thomas
Goodwin, Hal
  See Goodwin, Harold L(eland)
Goodwin, Harold L(eland) 1914-1990 51
  Obituary 65
  Earlier sketch in SATA 13
Goodwin, William 1943- 117
Goor, Nancy (Ruth Miller) 1944- 39
  Brief entry 34
Goor, Ron(ald Stephen) 1940- 39
  Brief entry 34
Goossen, Agnes
  See Epp, Margaret A(gnes)
Goossens, Philippe 1963- 195
Gootman, Marilyn E. 1944- 179
Gopnik, Adam 1956- 171
Gorbachev, Valeri 1944- 222
  Autobiography Feature 143
  Earlier sketches in SATA 98, 143, 184
Gordion, Mark
  See Turtledove, Harry
Gordon, Ad
  See Hano, Arnold
Gordon, Amy 1949- 197
  Earlier sketches in SATA 115, 156
Gordon, Bernard Ludwig 1931-2010 27
Gordon, Colonel H. R.
  See Ellis, Edward S.
Gordon, David
  See Garrett, Randall
Gordon, Donald
  See Payne, Donald Gordon
Gordon, Dorothy 1893-1970 20
Gordon, Esther S(aranga) 1935- 10
Gordon, Frederick 1
Gordon, Gaelyn 1939-1997
  See CLR 75
Gordon, Garrett
  See Garrett, Randall
Gordon, Gary
  See Edmonds, I(vy) G(ordon)
Gordon, Hal
  See Goodwin, Harold L(eland)
Gordon, Jeffie Ross
  See Enderle, Judith (Ann) Ross
  and Gordon, Stephanie Jacob
Gordon, John
  See Gesner, Clark
Gordon, John (William) 1925- 84
Gordon, Lew
  See Baldwin, Gordon C(ortis)
Gordon, Margaret (Anna) 1939- 9
Gordon, Mike 1948- 101
Gordon, Mildred 1912-1979
  Obituary 24
Gordon, Selma
  See Lanes, Selma G.
Gordon, Sheila 1927- 88
  See also CLR 27
Gordon, Shirley 1921- 48
  Brief entry 41
Gordon, Sol 1923- 11

Gordon, Stephanie Jacob 1940- 89
    Autobiography Feature 114
    Earlier sketch in SATA 64
    See also SAAS 26
Gordon, Stewart
    See Shirreffs, Gordon D(onald)
Gordons, The
    See Gordon, Mildred
    and Gordon, Gordon
Gore, Leonid 222
    Earlier sketch in SATA 185
Gorelick, Molly C(hernow) 1920-2003 9
    Obituary 153
Gorey, Edward (St. John) 1925-2000 70
    Brief entry 27
    Obituary 118
    Earlier sketch in SATA 29
    See also CLR 36
Gorham, Charles Orson 1868-1936 36
Gorham, Michael
    See Folsom, Franklin (Brewster)
Gorman, Carol 187
    Earlier sketch in SATA 150
Gorman, Jacqueline Laks 1955- 148
Gorman, Mike 206
Gormley, Beatrice 1942- 202
    Brief entry 35
    Earlier sketches in SATA 39, 127
Gorog, Judith (Katharine Allen) 1938- 75
    Earlier sketch in SATA 39
Gorrell, Gena K. 1946- 170
Gorsline, Douglas (Warner) 1913-1985 11
    Obituary 43
Gorsline, (Sally) Marie 1928- 28
Gorsline, S. M.
    See Gorsline, (Sally) Marie
Gorton, Julia 218
Gorton, Kaitlyn
    See Emerson, Kathy Lynn
Gorton, Kathy Lynn
    See Emerson, Kathy Lynn
Goryan, Sirak
    See Saroyan, William
Goschke, Julia 1973- 208
Goscinny, Rene 1926-1977 47
    Brief entry 39
    See also CLR 37
Goss, Clay(ton E.) 1946- 82
Goss, Gary 1947- 124
Goss, Mini 1963- 186
Goto, Scott 203
Gott, Barry 197
Gottesman, S. D.
    See Kornbluth, C(yril) M.
    and Lowndes, Robert A(ugustine) W(ard)
    and Pohl, Frederik
Gottfried, Ted
    See Gottfried, Theodore Mark
Gottfried, Theodore Mark 1928- 150
    Earlier sketch in SATA 85
Gottlieb, Gerald 1923- 7
Gottlieb, William P. 1917-2006 24
Gottlieb, William Paul
    See Gottlieb, William P.
Goudey, Alice E(dwards) 1898-1993 20
Goudge, Eileen 1950- 88
Goudge, Elizabeth (de Beauchamp)
    1900-1984 2
    Obituary 38
    See also CLR 94
Gough, Catherine
    See Mulgan, Catherine
Gough, Philip 1908-1986 45
Gough, Sue 1940- 106
Goulart, Ron 1933- 67
    Earlier sketch in SATA 1
Goulart, Ronald Joseph
    See Goulart, Ron
Gould, Alberta 1945- 96
Gould, Chester 1900-1985 49
    Obituary 43

Gould, Jean R(osalind) 1909-1993 11
    Obituary 77
Gould, Lilian 6
Gould, Marilyn 1928- 76
    Earlier sketch in SATA 15
Gould, Robert 154
Gould, Steven 1955- 95
Gould, Steven Charles
    See Gould, Steven
Gourley, Catherine 1950- 190
    Earlier sketch in SATA 95
Gourse, Leslie 1939-2004 89
Govan, (Mary) Christine Noble 1898-1985 ... 9
Gove, Doris 1944- 72
Govenar, Alan 1952- 189
Govenar, Alan Bruce
    See Govenar, Alan
Govern, Elaine 1939- 26
Gowen, L. Kris 1968- 156
Graaf, Peter
    See Youd, Samuel
Grab, Daphne 1971- 233
Graber, Alexander 1914-1997 98
    Earlier sketch in SATA 7
Graber, George Alexander
    See Graber, Alexander
Graber, Janet 1942- 170
Graber, Richard (Fredrick) 1927- 26
Grabianski, Janusz 1928-1976 39
    Obituary 30
Graboff, Abner 1919-1986 35
Grace, Fran(ces Jane) 45
Grace, N.B.
    See Harper, Suzanne
Grace, Theresa
    See Mattern, Joanne
Gracza, Margaret Young 1928- 56
Graduate of Oxford, A
    See Ruskin, John
Grady, Denise 1952- 189
Graeber, Charlotte Towner 106
    Brief entry 44
    Earlier sketch in SATA 56
Graef, Renee 1956- 204
Graeme, Roderic
    See Jeffries, Roderic
Graf, Michael
    See Graf, Mike
Graf, Mike 1960- 164
Grafe, Max 198
Graff, Lisa 1981- 235
    Earlier sketch in SATA 188
Graff, Polly Anne Colver
    See Colver, Anne
Graff, (S.) Stewart 1908-2009 9
Graham, Ada 1931- 11
Graham, Alastair 1945- 74
Graham, Arthur Kennon
    See Harrison, David L.
Graham, Bob 1942- 187
    Earlier sketches in SATA 63, 101, 151
    See also CLR 31
Graham, Brenda Knight 1942- 32
Graham, Charlotte
    See Bowden, Joan Chase
Graham, Christine 1952- 224
Graham, Eleanor 1896-1984 18
    Obituary 38
Graham, Ennis
    See Molesworth, Mary Louisa
Graham, Frank, Jr. 1925- 11
Graham, Georgia 1959- 190
Graham, Ian 1953- 229
    Earlier sketch in SATA 112
Graham, John 1926-2007 11
Graham, Kennon
    See Harrison, David L.
Graham, Larry
    See Graham, Lawrence
Graham, Lawrence 1962- 63

Graham, Lawrence Otis
    See Graham, Lawrence
Graham, Linda
    See Graham-Barber, Lynda
Graham, Lorenz (Bell) 1902-1989 74
    Obituary 63
    Earlier sketch in SATA 2
    See also CLR 10
    See also SAAS 5
Graham, Margaret Bloy 1920- 11
Graham, Robin Lee 1949- 7
Graham, Rosemary 236
Graham, Shirley 1896(?)-1977
    See Du Bois, Shirley Graham
Graham-Barber, Lynda 1944- 159
    Earlier sketch in SATA 42
Graham-Cameron, M.
    See Graham-Cameron, M(alcolm) G(ordon)
Graham-Cameron, M(alcolm) G(ordon)
    1931- 53
    Brief entry 45
Graham-Cameron, Mike
    See Graham-Cameron, M(alcolm) G(ordon)
Grahame, Kenneth 1859-1932 100
    See also YABC 1
    See also CLR 135
Gralley, Jean 166
Gramatky, Hardie 1907-1979 30
    Obituary 23
    Earlier sketch in SATA 1
    See also CLR 22
Grambling, Lois G. 1927- 206
    Earlier sketches in SATA 71, 148
Grambo, Rebecca L(ynn) 1963- 109
Grammer, June Amos 1927- 58
Grand, Samuel 1912-1988 42
Grandits, John 1949- 192
GrandPre, Mary 1954- 229
    Earlier sketch in SATA 184
Grandville, J. J.
    See Gerard, Jean Ignace Isidore
Grandville, Jean Ignace Isidore Gerard
    See Gerard, Jean Ignace Isidore
Granfield, Linda 1950- 160
    Earlier sketch in SATA 96
Grange, Peter
    See Nicole, Christopher
Granger, Margaret Jane 1925(?)-1977
    Obituary 27
Granger, Michele 1949- 88
Granger, Peggy
    See Granger, Margaret Jane
Granowsky, Alvin 1936- 101
Granstaff, Bill 1925- 10
Granstrom, Brita 1969- 224
    Earlier sketches in SATA 111, 167
Grant, Bruce 1893-1977 5
    Obituary 25
Grant, Cynthia D. 1950- 147
    Earlier sketches in SATA 33, 77
Grant, Eva 1907-1996 7
Grant, Evva H. 1913-1977
    Obituary 27
Grant, Gordon 1875-1962 25
Grant, Gwen(doline Ellen) 1940- 47
Grant, Judyann Ackerman 211
Grant, Katie
    See Grant, K.M.
Grant, Katie M.
    See Grant, K.M.
Grant, K.M. 230
    Earlier sketch in SATA 175
Grant, (Alice) Leigh 1947- 10
Grant, Matthew G.
    See May, Julian
Grant, Maxwell
    See Gibson, Walter B(rown)
    and Lynds, Dennis
Grant, Melvyn 183
Grant, Myrna (Lois) 1934- 21

Grant, Neil 1938- *154*
  Earlier sketch in SATA *14*
Grant, Nicholas
  See Nicole, Christopher
Grant, Richard 1948- *80*
Grant, Skeeter
  See Spiegelman, Art
Grater, Michael 1923- *57*
Gratz, Alan 1972- *212*
Graullera, Fabiola
  See Graullera Ramirez, Fabiola
Graullera Ramirez, Fabiola *225*
Gravel, Fern
  See Hall, James Norman
Gravelle, Karen 1942- *166*
  Earlier sketch in SATA *78*
Graves, Charles Parlin 1911-1972 .... *4*
Graves, Keith *191*
  Earlier sketch in SATA *156*
Graves, Robert 1895-1985 .... *45*
Graves, Robert von Ranke
  See Graves, Robert
Graves, Valerie
  See Bradley, Marion Zimmer
Gravett, Emily 1972(?)- *232*
  Earlier sketch in SATA *189*
Gray, Betsy
  See Poole, Gray Johnson
Gray, Caroline
  See Nicole, Christopher
Gray, Claudia *213*
Gray, Dianne E. *183*
Gray, Elizabeth Janet
  See Vining, Elizabeth Gray
Gray, Genevieve S(tuck) 1920-1995 .... *4*
Gray, Harold (Lincoln) 1894-1968 .... *33*
  Brief entry *32*
Gray, Jenny
  See Gray, Genevieve S(tuck)
Gray, John Lee
  See Jakes, John
Gray, Judith A. 1949- *93*
Gray, Judith Anne
  See Gray, Judith A.
Gray, Keith 1972- *151*
Gray, Kes 1960- *153*
Gray, Les 1929- *82*
Gray, Libba Moore 1937- *83*
Gray, Luli 1945- *149*
  Earlier sketch in SATA *90*
Gray, Marian
  See Pierce, Edith Gray
Gray, Nicholas Stuart 1922-1981 .... *4*
  Obituary *27*
Gray, Nigel 1941- *104*
  Earlier sketch in SATA *33*
Gray, (Lucy) Noel (Clervaux) 1898-1983 .... *47*
Gray, Patricia (Clark) *7*
Gray, Patsey
  See Gray, Patricia (Clark)
Gray, Rita *184*
Gray, Steve 1950- *231*
Graydon, Shari 1958- *158*
Grayland, V. Merle
  See Grayland, Valerie (Merle Spanner)
Grayland, Valerie (Merle Spanner) *7*
Grayson, Devin (Kalile) 1970- *119*
Grayson, Kristine
  See Rusch, Kristine Kathryn
Grayson, Paul 1946- *79*
Graystone, Lynn
  See Brennan, Joseph Lomas
Great Comte, The
  See Hawkesworth, Eric
Greaves, Margaret 1914-1995 .... *87*
  Earlier sketch in SATA *7*
Greaves, Nick 1955- *77*
Greban, Quentin 1977- *223*
Gree, Alain 1936- *28*
Green, Adam
  See Weisgard, Leonard (Joseph)

Green, Anne Canevari 1943- *62*
Green, Brian
  See Card, Orson Scott
Green, Cliff(ord) 1934- *126*
Green, Connie Jordan 1938- *80*
Green, D.
  See Casewit, Curtis W(erner)
Green, Elizabeth Shippen 1871-1954 .... *139*
Green, Hannah
  See Greenberg, Joanne (Goldenberg)
Green, Jane 1937- *9*
Green, Jessica *211*
Green, John 1977(?)- *235*
  Earlier sketch in SATA *170*
Green, Mary Moore 1906- *11*
Green, Morton 1937- *8*
Green, Norma B(erger) 1925- *11*
Green, Phyllis 1932- *20*
Green, Roger (Gilbert) Lancelyn 1918-1987 . *2*
  Obituary *53*
Green, (James Le)Roy 1948- *89*
Green, Sheila Ellen 1934- *148*
  Earlier sketches in SATA *8, 87*
Green, Timothy 1953- *91*
Greenaway, Kate 1846-1901 .... *100*
  See also YABC *2*
  See also CLR *111*
Greenbank, Anthony Hunt 1933- *39*
Greenberg, David 1954- *171*
Greenberg, David T.
  See Greenberg, David
Greenberg, Harvey R. 1935- *5*
Greenberg, Jan 1942- *211*
  Earlier sketches in SATA *61, 125*
Greenberg, Joanne (Goldenberg) 1932- *25*
Greenberg, Melanie Hope 1954- *214*
  Earlier sketch in SATA *72*
Greenberg, Polly 1932- *52*
  Brief entry *43*
Greenblat, Rodney Alan 1960- *106*
Greenburg, Dan 1936- *175*
  Earlier sketch in SATA *102*
Greene, Bette 1934- *161*
  Earlier sketches in SATA *8, 102*
  See also CLR *140*
  See also SAAS *16*
Greene, Carla 1916- *67*
  Earlier sketch in SATA *1*
Greene, Carol *102*
  Brief entry *44*
  Earlier sketch in SATA *66*
Greene, Constance C(larke) 1924- *72*
  Earlier sketch in SATA *11*
  See also CLR *62*
  See also SAAS *11*
Greene, Edgar
  See Papademetriou, Lisa
Greene, Ellin 1927- *23*
Greene, Graham 1904-1991 .... *20*
Greene, Graham Henry
  See Greene, Graham
Greene, Jacqueline Dembar 1946- *212*
  Earlier sketches in SATA *76, 131*
Greene, Laura Offenhartz 1935- *38*
Greene, Meg
  See Malvasi, Meg Greene
Greene, Michele 1962- *178*
Greene, Michele Dominguez
  See Greene, Michele
Greene, Rhonda Gowler 1955- *235*
  Earlier sketches in SATA *101, 160*
Greene, Stephanie 1950- *221*
  Earlier sketches in SATA *127, 173*
Greene, Wade 1933- *11*
Greene, Yvonne
  See Flesch, Yolande
Greenfeld, Howard (Scheinman) 1928- *140*
  Earlier sketch in SATA *19*
Greenfeld, Josh(ua Joseph) 1928- *62*

Greenfield, Eloise 1929- *155*
  Earlier sketches in SATA *19, 61, 105*
  See also CLR *38*
  See also SAAS *16*
Greenhaus, Thelma Nurenberg 1903-1984
  Obituary *45*
Greenhut, Josh
  See Mercer, Sienna
Greening, Hamilton
  See Hamilton, Charles (Harold St. John)
Greenlaw, M. Jean 1941- *107*
Greenleaf, Barbara Kaye 1942- *6*
Greenleaf, Peter 1910-1997 .... *33*
Greenlee, Sharon 1935- *77*
Greeno, Gayle 1949- *81*
Greenseid, Diane 1948- *178*
  Earlier sketch in SATA *93*
Greenspun, Adele Aron 1938- *142*
  Earlier sketch in SATA *76*
Greenstein, Elaine 1959- *150*
  Earlier sketch in SATA *82*
Greenwald, Sheila
  See Green, Sheila Ellen
Greenwood, Barbara 1940- *129*
  Earlier sketch in SATA *90*
Greenwood, Mark 1958- *202*
Greenwood, Pamela D. 1944- *115*
Greer, Richard
  See Garrett, Randall
  and Silverberg, Robert
Gregg, Andrew K. 1929- *81*
Gregg, Charles T(hornton) 1927- *65*
Gregg, Walter H(arold) 1919- *20*
Gregor, Arthur 1923- *36*
Gregor, Lee
  See Pohl, Frederik
Gregori, Leon 1919- *15*
Gregorian, Joyce Ballou 1946-1991 .... *30*
  Obituary *83*
Gregorich, Barbara 1943- *184*
  Earlier sketch in SATA *66*
Gregorowski, Christopher 1940- *30*
Gregory, Diana (Jean) 1933- *49*
  Brief entry *42*
Gregory, Harry
  See Gottfried, Theodore Mark
Gregory, Jean
  See Ure, Jean
Gregory, Kristiana 1951- *212*
  Earlier sketches in SATA *74, 136*
Gregory, Nan 1944- *192*
  Earlier sketch in SATA *148*
Gregory, Philippa 1954- *122*
Gregory, Stephen
  See Penzler, Otto
Gregory, Valiska 1940- *82*
Greif, Jean-Jacques 1944- *195*
Greisman, Joan Ruth 1937- *31*
Grendon, Stephen
  See Derleth, August (William)
Grenville, Pelham
  See Wodehouse, P. G.
Gretz, Susanna 1937- *7*
Gretzer, John *18*
Grewdead, Roy
  See Gorey, Edward (St. John)
Grey, Carol
  See Lowndes, Robert A(ugustine) W(ard)
Grey, Christopher *191*
Grey, Christopher Peter
  See Grey, Christopher
Grey, Jerry 1926- *11*
Grey, Mini *205*
  Earlier sketch in SATA *166*
Greybeard the Pirate
  See Macintosh, Brownie
Grey Owl
  See Belaney, Archibald Stansfeld
Gri
  See Denney, Diana
Gribbin, John 1946- *159*

Gribbin, John R.
  See Gribbin, John
Grice, Frederick 1910-1983 6
Grider, Dorothy 1915- 31
Gridley, Marion E(leanor) 1906-1974 35
  Obituary 26
Grieco-Tiso, Pina 1954- 108
Grieder, Walter 1924- 9
Griego, Tony A. 1955- 77
Griese, Arnold A(lfred) 1921- 9
Griessman, Annette 1962- 170
  Earlier sketch in SATA *116*
Grieve, James 1934- 146
Grifalconi, Ann 1929- 210
  Earlier sketches in SATA *2, 66, 133*
  See also CLR *35*
  See also SAAS *16*
Griffin, Adele 1970- 236
  Earlier sketches in SATA *105, 153, 195*
Griffin, Elizabeth May 1985- 89
Griffin, Gillett Good 1928- 26
Griffin, Judith Berry 34
Griffin, Kitty 1951- 137
Griffin, Peni R. 1961- 193
  Earlier sketches in SATA *67, 99*
Griffin, Steven A. 1953- 89
Griffin, Steven Arthur
  See Griffin, Steven A.
Griffin, W. E. B. 1929- 5
Griffith, Connie 1946- 89
Griffith, Gershom 1960- 85
Griffith, Helen V. 1934- 87
  Autobiography Feature 107
  Earlier sketch in SATA *39*
Griffith, Helen Virginia
  See Griffith, Helen V.
Griffith, Jeannette
  See Eyerly, Jeannette
Griffith, Saul 1974- 200
Griffiths, Andy 1961- 196
  Earlier sketch in SATA *152*
Griffiths, G(ordon) D(ouglas) 1910-1973
  Obituary 20
Griffiths, Helen 1939- 86
  Earlier sketch in SATA *5*
  See also CLR *75*
  See also SAAS *5*
Grigsby, Susan 235
Grigson, Jane (McIntire) 1928-1990 63
Grimes, Lee 1920- 68
Grimes, Nikki 1950- 218
  Earlier sketches in SATA *93, 136, 174*
  See also CLR *42*
Grimly, Gris 186
Grimm, Jacob Ludwig Karl 1785-1863 22
  See also CLR *112*
Grimm, Wilhelm Karl 1786-1859 22
  See also CLR *112*
Grimm, William C(arey) 1907-1992 14
Grimm and Grim
  See Grimm, Jacob Ludwig Karl
  and Grimm, Wilhelm Karl
Grimm Brothers
  See Grimm, Jacob Ludwig Karl
  and Grimm, Wilhelm Karl
Grimsdell, Jeremy 1942- 83
Grimshaw, Nigel (Gilroy) 1925- 23
Grimsley, Gordon
  See Groom, Arthur William
Grindley, Jane Sally
  See Grindley, Sally
Grindley, Sally 1953- 148
Gringhuis, Dirk
  See Gringhuis, Richard H.
Gringhuis, Richard H. 1918-1974 6
  Obituary 25
Grinnell, David
  See Wollheim, Donald A(llen)
Grinnell, George Bird 1849-1938 16
Grinspoon, David
  See Grinspoon, David H.

Grinspoon, David H. 1959- 156
Grinspoon, David Harry
  See Grinspoon, David H.
Gripe, Maria 1923- 74
  Earlier sketch in SATA *2*
  See also CLR *5*
Gripe, Maria Kristina
  See Gripe, Maria
Gritton, Steve 223
Grobler, Piet 1959- 201
Groch, Judith (Goldstein) 1929- 25
Grode, Redway
  See Gorey, Edward (St. John)
Groener, Carl
  See Lowndes, Robert A(ugustine) W(ard)
Groening, Matt 1954- 116
  Earlier sketch in SATA *81*
Grohmann, Susan 1948- 84
Grohskopf, Bernice 7
Grol, Lini R(icharda) 1913- 9
Grollman, Earl A. 1925- 22
Groom, Arthur William 1898-1964 10
Grooms, Duffy 1964- 169
Gross, Alan 1947- 54
  Brief entry 43
Gross, Ernie 1913- 67
Gross, Philip 1952- 164
  Earlier sketch in SATA *84*
Gross, Philip John
  See Gross, Philip
Gross, Ruth Belov 1929- 33
Gross, Sarah Chokla 1906-1976 9
  Obituary 26
Grosser, Morton 1931- 74
Grosser, Vicky 1958- 83
Grossman, Bill 1948- 126
  Earlier sketch in SATA *72*
Grossman, Nancy 1940- 29
Grossman, Patricia 1951- 73
Grossman, Robert 1940- 11
Grossmann-Hensel, Katharina 1973- 219
Grote, JoAnn A. 1951- 113
Groten, Dallas 1951- 64
Groth, John (August) 1908-1988 21
  Obituary 56
Groth-Fleming, Candace
  See Fleming, Candace
Grove, Vicki 1948- 151
  Autobiography Feature 151
  Earlier sketch in SATA *122*
Grover, Lorie Ann 1964- 168
Grover, Wayne 1934- 69
Groves, Georgina
  See Symons, (Dorothy) Geraldine
Groves, Maketa 1950- 107
Groves, Seli 77
Grubb, Lisa 160
Gruber, Michael 1940- 173
Gruber, Terry (deRoy) 1953- 66
Gruelle, John 1880-1938 35
  Brief entry 32
  See also CLR *34*
Gruelle, Johnny
  See Gruelle, John
Gruenberg, Sidonie Matsner 1881-1974 2
  Obituary 27
Gruhzit-Hoyt, Olga (Margaret) 1922- 127
  Earlier sketch in SATA *16*
Grummer, Arnold E(dward) 1923- 49
Gruner, Jessica 233
Grunewalt, Pine
  See Kunhardt, Edith
Grunwell, Jeanne Marie 1971- 147
Grupper, Jonathan 137
Gryski, Camilla 1948- 72
Guarino, Dagmar
  See Guarino, Deborah
Guarino, Deborah 1954- 68
Guarnaccia, Steven 233
Guay, Georgette (Marie Jeanne) 1952- 54
Guay, Rebecca 209

Guay-Mitchell, Rebecca
  See Guay, Rebecca
Guback, Georgia 88
Guccione, Leslie Davis 1946- 111
  Earlier sketch in SATA *72*
Guck, Dorothy 1913-2002 27
Gudeon, Karla 212
Guerny, Gene
  See Gurney, Gene
Guest, Elissa Haden 1953- 218
  Earlier sketch in SATA *125*
Guest, Jacqueline 1952- 135
Guevara, Susan 167
  Earlier sketch in SATA *97*
Gugler, Laurel Dee 95
Gugliotta, Bobette 1918-1994 7
Guianan, Eve 1965- 102
Guiberson, Brenda Z. 1946- 211
  Earlier sketch in SATA *71, 124*
Guibert, Emmanuel 1964- 181
Guile, Melanie 1949- 152
  Earlier sketch in SATA *104*
Guillaume, Jeanette G. Flierl 1899-1990 8
Guillot, Rene 1900-1969 7
  See also CLR *22*
Guisewite, Cathy 1950- 57
Guisewite, Cathy Lee
  See Guisewite, Cathy
Gulbis, Stephen 1959- 142
Gulley, Judie 1942- 58
Gump, P. Q.
  See Card, Orson Scott
Gundrey, Elizabeth 1924- 23
Gunn, James E. 1923- 35
Gunn, James Edwin
  See Gunn, James E.
Gunn, Robin Jones 1955- 84
Gunnella 1956- 197
Gunning, Monica Olwen 1930- 161
Gunston, Bill
  See Gunston, William Tudor
Gunston, William Tudor 1927- 9
Gunterman, Bertha Lisette 1886(?)-1975
  Obituary 27
Gunther, John 1901-1970
Guravich, Dan 1918- 74
Gurko, Leo 1914- 9
Gurko, Miriam 1910(?)-1988 9
  Obituary 58
Gurney, Gene 1924- 65
Gurney, James 1958- 120
  Earlier sketch in SATA *76*
Gurney, John Steven 1962- 227
  Earlier sketches in SATA *75, 143*
Gustafson, Sarah R.
  See Riedman, Sarah R(egal)
Gustafson, Scott 1956- 34
Gustavson, Adam 1974- 214
  Earlier sketch in SATA *176*
Guthrie, A(lfred) B(ertram), Jr. 1901-1991 .. 62
  Obituary 67
Guthrie, Anne 1890-1979 28
Guthrie, Donna W. 1946- 105
  Earlier sketch in SATA *63*
Gutierrez, Akemi 172
Gutierrez, Rudy 203
Gutman, Bill 128
  Brief entry 43
  Earlier sketch in SATA *67*
Gutman, Dan 1955- 221
  Earlier sketches in SATA *77, 139, 188*
Gutman, Nahum 1899(?)-1981
  Obituary 25
Gutmann, Bessie Pease 1876-1960 73
Guy, Geoffrey 1942- 153
Guy, Ginger Foglesong 1954- 171
Guy, Rosa 1925- 122
  Earlier sketches in SATA *14, 62*
  See also CLR *137*
Guy, Rosa Cuthbert
  See Guy, Rosa

Guy, Susan 1948- *149*
Guymer, (Wilhelmina) Mary 1909- *50*
Guzman, Lila 1952- *168*
Guzman, Rick 1957- *168*
Gwaltney, Doris 1932- *181*
Gwynne, Fred(erick Hubbard) 1926-1993 .... *41*
    Brief entry *27*
    Obituary *75*
Gwynne, Oscar A.
    See Ellis, Edward S.
Gwynne, Oswald A.
    See Ellis, Edward S.
Gyorkos, Charmaine Echeverria
    See Echeverria Gyorkos, Charmaine

                    H

Haab, Sherri 1964- *169*
    Earlier sketch in SATA *91*
Haar, Jaap ter
    See ter Haar, Jaap
Haarsma, P.J. *183*
Haas, Carolyn Buhai 1926- *43*
Haas, Dan 1957- *105*
Haas, Dorothy F. *46*
    Brief entry *43*
    See also SAAS *17*
Haas, Irene 1929- *96*
    Earlier sketch in SATA *17*
Haas, James E. 1943- *40*
Haas, James Edward
    See Haas, James E.
Haas, Jessie 1959- *215*
Haas, (Katherine) Jessie 1959- *135*
    Autobiography Feature *135*
    Earlier sketch in SATA *98*
Haas, Merle S. 1896(?)-1985
    Obituary *41*
Habenstreit, Barbara 1937- *5*
Haber, Karen 1955- *78*
Haber, Louis 1910-1988 .... *12*
Haber, Melissa Glenn 1969- *235*
Hacker, Randi 1951- *185*
Hacker, Randi Dawn
    See Hacker, Randi
Hackett, John Winthrop 1910-1997 .... *65*
Hacks, Peter 1928-2003
    Obituary *151*
Haddix, Margaret Peterson 1964- *224*
    Earlier sketches in SATA *94, 125, 187*
Haddon, Mark 1962- *223*
    Earlier sketch in SATA *155*
Hader, Berta (Hoerner) 1891(?)-1976 .... *16*
Hader, Elmer (Stanley) 1889-1973 .... *16*
Hadithi, Mwenye
    See Hobson, Bruce
Hadley, Franklin
    See Winterbotham, R(ussell) R(obert)
Hadley, Lee 1934-1995 .... *89*
    Brief entry *38*
    Obituary *86*
    Earlier sketch in SATA *47*
    See also CLR *40*
    See also SAAS *14*
Haeffele, Deborah 1954- *76*
Haenel, Wolfram 1956- *89*
    See also CLR *64*
Hafner, Marylin 1925- *179*
    Earlier sketches in SATA *7, 121*
Haft, Erin
    See Ehrenhaft, Daniel
Hager, Alan 1940- *176*
Hager, Alice Rogers 1894-1969
    Obituary *26*
Hager, Betty 1923- *89*
Hager, Jenna Bush
    See Bush, Jenna
Hager, Sarah *171*
Hager, Thomas 1953- *119*

Hager, Tom
    See Hager, Thomas
Hagerup, Klaus 1946- *186*
Haggard, H(enry) Rider 1856-1925 .... *16*
Haggerty, James J(oseph) 1920- *5*
Hagon, Priscilla
    See Allan, Mabel Esther
Hague, Kathleen 1949- *49*
    Brief entry *45*
Hague, Michael 1948- *185*
    Brief entry *32*
    Earlier sketches in SATA *48, 80, 129*
Hague, Michael R.
    See Hague, Michael
Hague, Susan Kathleen
    See Hague, Kathleen
Hahn, Emily 1905-1997 .... *3*
    Obituary *96*
Hahn, Hannelore *8*
Hahn, James (Sage) 1947- *9*
Hahn, Lynn 1949- *9*
Hahn, Mary Downing 1937- *208*
    Autobiography Feature *157*
    Brief entry *44*
    Earlier sketches in SATA *50, 81, 138, 157*
    See also SAAS *12*
Hahn, Michael T. 1953- *92*
Hahn, Mona Lynn
    See Hahn, Lynn
Haig, Matt 1975- *221*
Haig-Brown, Roderick (Langmere)
    1908-1976 .... *12*
    See also CLR *31*
Haight, Anne Lyon 1895-1977
    Obituary *30*
Haight, Rip
    See Carpenter, John
Haight, Sandy 1949- *79*
Haij, Vera
    See Jansson, Tove (Marika)
Hailstone, Ruth *219*
Haines, Gail Kay 1943- *11*
Haines, Margaret Ann Beck
    See Beck, Peggy
Haining, Peter 1940-2007 .... *14*
    Obituary *188*
Haining, Peter Alexander
    See Haining, Peter
Hains, Harriet
    See Watson, Carol
Hajdusiewicz, Babs Bell *163*
Hakim, Joy 1931- *173*
    Earlier sketch in SATA *83*
Halacy, D. S., Jr. 1919-2002 .... *36*
    See also SAAS *8*
Halacy, Dan
    See Halacy, D. S., Jr.
Halam, Ann
    See Jones, Gwyneth A.
Haldane, Roger John 1945- *13*
Hale, Arlene 1924-1982 .... *49*
Hale, Bruce 1957- *203*
    Earlier sketch in SATA *123*
Hale, Christy
    See Apostolou, Christine Hale
Hale, Dean 1972- *227*
Hale, Edward Everett 1822-1909 .... *16*
Hale, Glenn
    See Walker, Robert W.
Hale, Helen
    See Mulcahy, Lucille Burnett
Hale, Irina 1932- *26*
Hale, Kathleen 1898-2000 .... *66*
    Obituary *121*
    Earlier sketch in SATA *17*
Hale, Linda (Howe) 1929- *6*
Hale, Lucretia P.
    See Hale, Lucretia Peabody
Hale, Lucretia Peabody 1820-1900 .... *26*
    See also CLR *105*
Hale, Marian *194*

Hale, Nancy 1908-1988 .... *31*
    Obituary *57*
Hale, Nathan 1976- *210*
Hale, Shannon *200*
    Earlier sketch in SATA *158*
Hale, Stephanie 1973- *232*
Haley, Amanda *205*
Haley, Gail E(inhart) 1939- *161*
    Autobiography Feature *161*
    Brief entry *28*
    Earlier sketches in SATA *43, 78, 136*
    See also CLR *21*
    See also SAAS *13*
Haley, Neale *52*
Halfmann, Janet 1944- *208*
Hall, Adam
    See Trevor, Elleston
Hall, Adele 1910- *7*
Hall, Anna Gertrude 1882-1967 .... *8*
Hall, August *207*
Hall, Barbara 1961- *68*
Hall, Becky 1950- *186*
Hall, Beverly B. 1918- *95*
Hall, Borden
    See Yates, Raymond F(rancis)
Hall, Brian P(atrick) 1935- *31*
Hall, Cameron
    See del Rey, Lester
Hall, Caryl
    See Hansen, Caryl (Hall)
Hall, Donald 1928- *97*
    Earlier sketch in SATA *23*
Hall, Donald Andrew, Jr.
    See Hall, Donald
Hall, Douglas 1931- *43*
Hall, Elizabeth 1929- *77*
Hall, Elvajean 1910-1984 .... *6*
Hall, Francie 1940- *166*
Hall, James Norman 1887-1951 .... *21*
Hall, Jesse
    See Boesen, Victor
Hall, Katy
    See McMullan, Kate
Hall, Kirsten Marie 1974- *67*
Hall, Lynn 1937- *79*
    Earlier sketches in SATA *2, 47*
    See also SAAS *4*
Hall, Malcolm 1945- *7*
Hall, Marcellus *203*
Hall, Marjory
    See Yeakley, Marjory Hall
Hall, Melanie 1949- *228*
    Earlier sketches in SATA *78, 116, 169*
Hall, Michael 1954- *228*
Hall, Patricia 1940- *136*
Hall, Rosalys Haskell 1914- *7*
Hall, Teri *229*
Hall, Willis 1929-2005 .... *66*
Hallard, Peter
    See Catherall, Arthur
Hallas, Richard
    See Knight, Eric
Hall-Clarke, James
    See Rowland-Entwistle, (Arthur) Theodore
    (Henry)
Hallensleben, Georg 1958- *173*
Haller, Dorcas Woodbury 1946- *46*
Hallett, Mark 1947- *220*
    Earlier sketch in SATA *83*
Halliburton, Richard 1900-1939(?) *81*
Halliburton, Warren J. 1924- *19*
Halliday, Brett
    See Dresser, Davis
    and Johnson, (Walter) Ryerson
    and Terrall, Robert
Halliday, William R(oss) 1926- *52*
Hallin, Emily Watson 1916-1995 .... *6*
Hallinan, P. K. 1944- *39*
    Brief entry *37*
Hallinan, Patrick Kenneth
    See Hallinan, P. K.

Hallman, Ruth 1929- *43*
    Brief entry *28*
Hallowell, Tommy
    See Hill, Thomas
Hall-Quest, (Edna) Olga W(ilbourne)
    1899-1986 .... *11*
    Obituary *47*
Halls, Kelly Milner 1957- *220*
    Earlier sketch in SATA *131*
Hallstead, William F(inn III) 1924- *11*
Hallward, Michael 1889-1982 .... *12*
Halperin, Michael *156*
Halperin, Wendy Anderson 1952- *200*
    Earlier sketches in SATA *80, 125*
Halpern, Julie 1975- *198*
Halpin, Abigail *236*
Halpin, Brendan 1968- *193*
Halpin, Marlene 1927- *88*
Halse, Laurie Beth
    See Anderson, Laurie Halse
Halsell, Grace (Eleanor) 1923-2000 .... *13*
Halsey, Megan *185*
Halsted, Anna Roosevelt 1906-1975
    Obituary *30*
Halter, Jon C(harles) 1941- *22*
Halverson, Deborah *202*
Halvorson, Adeline *218*
Halvorson, Marilyn 1948- *123*
Hamalian, Leo 1920- *41*
Hamberger, John 1934- *14*
Hamblin, Dora Jane 1920- *36*
Hambly, Barbara 1951- *108*
Hambly, Barbara Joan
    See Hambly, Barbara
Hamer, Martyn
    See Eldin, Peter
Hamerstrom, Frances 1907-1998 .... *24*
Hamil, Thomas Arthur 1928- *14*
Hamill, Ethel
    See Webb, Jean Francis (III)
Hamilton, (John) Alan 1943- *66*
Hamilton, Alice
    See Cromie, Alice Hamilton
Hamilton, Anita 1919- *92*
Hamilton, Barbara
    See Hambly, Barbara
Hamilton, Buzz
    See Hemming, Roy G.
Hamilton, Carol (Jean Barber) 1935- *94*
Hamilton, Charles (Harold St. John)
    1876-1961 .... *13*
Hamilton, Charles 1913-1996 .... *65*
    Obituary *93*
Hamilton, Clive
    See Lewis, C. S.
Hamilton, Dorothy (Drumm) 1906-1983 ...... *12*
    Obituary *35*
Hamilton, Edith 1867-1963 .... *20*
Hamilton, Edmond 1904-1977 .... *118*
Hamilton, (Muriel) Elizabeth (Mollie)
    1906- *23*
Hamilton, Emma Walton 1962- *237*
    Earlier sketch in SATA *177*
Hamilton, Franklin
    See Silverberg, Robert
Hamilton, Gail
    See Corcoran, Barbara (Asenath)
    and Dodge, Mary Abigail
Hamilton, Kersten 1958- *204*
    Earlier sketch in SATA *134*
Hamilton, K.R.
    See Hamilton, Kersten
Hamilton, Martha 1953- *183*
    Earlier sketch in SATA *123*
Hamilton, Mary (E.) 1927- *55*
Hamilton, Meredith *233*
Hamilton, Mollie
    See Kaye, M.M.
Hamilton, Morse 1943-1998 .... *101*
    Earlier sketch in SATA *35*
Hamilton, Peter F. 1960- *109*

Hamilton, Priscilla
    See Gellis, Roberta
Hamilton, Ralph
    See Stratemeyer, Edward L.
Hamilton, Virginia 1936-2002 .... *123*
    Obituary *132*
    Earlier sketches in SATA *4, 56, 79*
    See also CLR *127*
Hamilton, Virginia Esther
    See Hamilton, Virginia
Hamilton-Paterson, James 1941- *82*
Hamlet, Ova
    See Lupoff, Richard A.
Hamley, D. C.
    See Hamley, Dennis
Hamley, Dennis 1935- *69*
    Earlier sketch in SATA *39*
    See also CLR *47*
    See also SAAS *22*
Hamley, Dennis C.
    See Hamley, Dennis
Hamlin, Peter J. 1970- *84*
Hamm, Diane Johnston 1949- *78*
Hammer, Charles 1934- *58*
Hammer, Richard 1928- *6*
Hammerman, Gay M(orenus) 1926- *9*
Hammill, Matt 1982- *206*
Hammond, Andrew 1970- *181*
Hammond, Ralph
    See Hammond Innes, Ralph
Hammond, Winifred G(raham) 1899-1992 ... *29*
    Obituary *107*
Hammond Innes, Ralph 1913-1998 .... *116*
Hammontree, Marie (Gertrude) 1913- *13*
Hample, Zack 1977- *161*
Hampshire, Joyce Gregorian
    See Gregorian, Joyce Ballou
Hampshire, Susan 1942- *98*
Hampson, (Richard) Denman 1929- *15*
Hampson, Frank 1918(?)-1985
    Obituary *46*
Hampton, Wilborn 1940- *196*
    Earlier sketch in SATA *156*
Hamre, Leif 1914- *5*
Hamsa, Bobbie 1944- *52*
    Brief entry *38*
Han, Jenny 1981- *175*
Han, Lu
    See Stickler, Soma Han
Han, Soma
    See Stickler, Soma Han
Han, Suzanne Crowder 1953- *89*
Hancock, Mary A. 1923- *31*
Hancock, Sibyl 1940- *9*
Hand, Elizabeth 1957- *167*
    Earlier sketch in SATA *118*
Handford, Martin (John) 1956- *64*
    See also CLR *22*
Handforth, Thomas (Schofield) 1897-1948 .. *42*
Handleman, Philip 1951- *222*
Handler, Daniel
    See Snicket, Lemony
Handville, Robert (Tompkins) 1924- *45*
Hane, Roger 1940-1974
    Obituary *20*
Hanel, Wolfram
    See Haenel, Wolfram
Haney, Lynn 1941- *23*
Hanff, Helene 1916-1997 .... *97*
    Earlier sketch in SATA *11*
Hanft, Josh 1956- *197*
Hanft, Joshua E.
    See Hanft, Josh
Hanke, Karen *234*
Hanley, Boniface Francis 1924- *65*
Hanlon, Emily 1945- *15*
Hann, Jacquie 1951- *19*
Hann, Judith 1942- *77*
Hanna, Bill
    See Hanna, William (Denby)
Hanna, Cheryl 1951- *84*

Hanna, Dan *200*
Hanna, Jack (Bushnell) 1947- *74*
Hanna, Nell(ie L.) 1908- *55*
Hanna, Paul R(obert) 1902-1988 .... *9*
Hanna, William (Denby) 1910-2001 .... *51*
    Obituary *126*
Hannam, Charles 1925- *50*
Hannan, Peter 1954- *187*
Hannigan, Katherine *170*
Hannon, Ezra
    See Hunter, Evan
Hann-Syme, Marguerite *127*
Hano, Arnold 1922- *12*
Hano, Renee Roth
    See Roth-Hano, Renee
Hanover, Terri
    See Huff, Tanya
Hansen, Amy S. *229*
Hansen, Ann Larkin 1958- *96*
Hansen, Brooks 1965- *104*
Hansen, Caryl (Hall) 1929- *39*
Hansen, Ian V. 1929- *113*
Hansen, Jennifer 1972- *156*
Hansen, Joyce 1942- *172*
    Autobiography Feature *172*
    Brief entry *39*
    Earlier sketches in SATA *46, 101*
    See also CLR *21*
    See also SAAS *15*
Hansen, Joyce Viola
    See Hansen, Joyce
Hansen, Mark Victor *112*
Hansen, Ron 1947- *56*
Hansen, Ronald Thomas
    See Hansen, Ron
Hansen, Thore 1942- *224*
Hanser, Richard (Frederick) 1909-1981 .... *13*
Hanson, Joan 1938- *8*
Hanson, Joseph E. 1894(?)-1971
    Obituary *27*
Hanson, Mary Elizabeth *188*
Hanson, Warren 1949- *155*
Hansson, Gunilla 1939- *64*
Hantman, Clea *200*
Hapka, C.A.
    See Hapka, Catherine
Hapka, Catherine *223*
Hapka, Cathy
    See Hapka, Catherine
Harald, Eric
    See Boesen, Victor
Harazin, S. A. *210*
Harbour, Elizabeth 1968- *221*
Harcourt, Ellen Knowles 1890(?)-1984
    Obituary *36*
Hard, Charlotte (Ann) 1969- *98*
Hardcastle, Michael 1933- *216*
    Brief entry *38*
    Earlier sketch in SATA *47*
Harding, Lee 1937- *32*
    Brief entry *31*
Hardinge, Frances 1973- *210*
Hardt, Helga Fleischhauer
    See Fleischhauer-Hardt, Helga
Hardwick, Richard Holmes, Jr. 1923- *12*
Hardy, Alice Dale *67*
    Earlier sketch in SATA *1*
Hardy, David A(ndrews) 1936- *9*
Hardy, Janice *222*
Hardy, Jon 1958- *53*
Hardy, LeAnne 1951- *154*
Hardy, Stuart
    See Schisgall, Oscar
Hare, Norma Q(uarles) 1924- *46*
    Brief entry *41*
Harel, Nira 1936- *154*
Harford, Henry
    See Hudson, W(illiam) H(enry)
Hargis, Wes *219*
Hargrave, Leonie
    See Disch, Thomas M.

Hargreaves, (Charles) Roger 1935-1988
  Obituary *56*
Hargrove, James 1947- *57*
  Brief entry *50*
Hargrove, Jim
  See Hargrove, James
Harik, Elsa
  See Marston, Elsa
Harik, Elsa M.
  See Marston, Elsa
Harik, Elsa Marston
  See Marston, Elsa
Hariton, Anca I. 1955- *79*
Hark, Mildred
  See McQueen, Mildred Hark
Harkaway, Hal
  See Stratemeyer, Edward L.
Harkins, Philip 1912-1997 .... *6*
  Obituary *129*
Harlan, Elizabeth 1945- *41*
  Brief entry *35*
Harlan, Glen
  See Cebulash, Mel
Harlan, Judith 1949- *135*
  Earlier sketch in SATA 74
  See also CLR 81
Harland, Richard 1947- *152*
Harlee, J. V.
  See Leese, Jennifer L.B.
Harler, Ann
  See Van Steenwyk, Elizabeth (Ann)
Harley, Avis *183*
Harley, Bill 1954- *208*
  Earlier sketch in SATA 87
Harlow, Joan Hiatt 1932- *226*
  Earlier sketch in SATA 157
Harman, Fred 1902(?)-1982
  Obituary *30*
Harman, Hugh 1903-1982
  Obituary *33*
Harmelink, Barbara (Mary) *9*
Harmer, Mabel 1894-1992 .... *45*
Harmon, Dan
  See Harmon, Daniel E(lton)
Harmon, Daniel E(lton) 1949- *157*
Harmon, Kate
  See Gibson, Marley
Harmon, Margaret 1906- *20*
Harmon, Michael 1969- *189*
Harmon, Michael B.
  See Harmon, Michael
Harmon, William (Ruth) 1938- *65*
Harnan, Terry 1920- *12*
Harness, Cheryl 1951- *178*
  Earlier sketch in SATA 131
Harnett, Cynthia (Mary) 1893-1981 .... *5*
  Obituary *32*
Harper, Anita 1943- *41*
Harper, Betty 1946- *126*
Harper, Charise
  See Harper, Charise Mericle
Harper, Charise Mericle *226*
  Earlier sketch in SATA 179
Harper, Elaine
  See Hallin, Emily Watson
Harper, Ellen
  See Noble, Marty
Harper, Jamie *174*
Harper, Jessica 1949- *148*
Harper, Jo 1932- *169*
  Earlier sketch in SATA 97
Harper, Lee *201*
Harper, Mary Wood
  See Dixon, Jeanne
Harper, Piers 1966- *161*
  Earlier sketch in SATA 105
Harper, Suzanne *194*
Harper, Wilhelmina 1884-1973 .... *4*
  Obituary *26*
Harrah, Madge 1931- *154*
Harrah, Michael 1940- *41*

Harrah, Monique
  See Harrah, Madge
Harrar, George E. 1949- *124*
Harrell, Beatrice Orcutt 1943- *93*
Harrell, Janice 1945- *70*
Harrell, Sara Gordon 1940- *26*
Harrell, Sara Jeanne Gordon
  See Harrell, Sara Gordon
Harries, Joan 1922- *39*
Harrill, Ronald 1950- *90*
Harrington, Denis J(ames) 1932- *88*
Harrington, Evelyn Davis 1911- *5*
Harrington, Janice N. 1956- *187*
Harrington, Lyn
  See Harrington, Evelyn Davis
Harris, Alan 1944- *71*
Harris, Aurand 1915-1996 .... *37*
  Obituary *91*
Harris, Bob
  See Harris, Robert J.
Harris, Carol Flynn 1933- *135*
Harris, Catherine
  See Ainsworth, Catherine Harris
Harris, Christie
  See Harris, Christie (Lucy) Irwin
Harris, Christie (Lucy) Irwin 1907-2002 ...... *74*
  Autobiography Feature *116*
  Earlier sketch in SATA 6
  See also CLR 47
  See also SAAS 10
Harris, Christine 1955- *105*
Harris, Colver
  See Colver, Anne
Harris, David 1942- *118*
Harris, David William
  See Harris, David
Harris, Dorothy Joan 1931- *153*
  Earlier sketch in SATA 13
Harris, Geraldine 1951- *54*
Harris, Geraldine Rachel
  See Harris, Geraldine
Harris, Jacqueline L. 1929- *62*
Harris, Janet 1932-1979 .... *4*
  Obituary *23*
Harris, Jesse
  See Standiford, Natalie
Harris, Joan 1946- *146*
Harris, Joe 1928- *201*
Harris, Joel Chandler 1848-1908 .... *100*
  See also YABC 1
  See also CLR 128
Harris, John (Wyndham Parkes Lucas) Beynon
  1903-1969 .... *118*
Harris, Johnson
  See Harris, John (Wyndham Parkes Lucas)
  Beynon
Harris, Jonathan 1921-1997 .... *52*
Harris, Larry Vincent 1939- *59*
Harris, Lavinia
  See St. John, Nicole
Harris, Leon A., Jr. 1926-2000 .... *4*
Harris, Lois V. *199*
Harris, Lorle K(empe) 1912-2001 .... *22*
Harris, Maria Guadalupe
  See Harris, M.G.
Harris, Marilyn
  See Springer, Marilyn Harris
Harris, Mark Jonathan 1941- *84*
  Earlier sketch in SATA 32
Harris, Mary K(athleen) 1905-1966 .... *119*
Harris, M.G. *231*
Harris, Robert J. 1955- *195*
Harris, Robie H. 1940- *203*
  Brief entry *53*
  Earlier sketches in SATA 90, 147
Harris, Robin
  See Shine, Deborah
Harris, Rosemary (Jeanne) *82*
  Earlier sketch in SATA 4
  See also CLR 30
  See also SAAS 7

Harris, Ruth Elwin 1935- *164*
Harris, Sherwood 1932-2009 .... *25*
Harris, Stephen 1959- *230*
Harris, Steven Michael 1957- *55*
Harris, Trudy 1949- *191*
  Earlier sketch in SATA 128
Harris-Filderman, Diane
  See Filderman, Diane E(lizabeth)
Harrison, C(hester) William 1913-1994 .... *35*
Harrison, Carol
  See Harrison, Carol Thompson
Harrison, Carol Thompson *113*
Harrison, David L. 1937- *186*
  Earlier sketches in SATA 26, 92, 150
Harrison, Deloris 1938- *9*
Harrison, Edward Hardy 1926- *56*
Harrison, Elizabeth (Allen) Cavanna
  1909-2001 .... *30*
  Earlier sketch in SATA 1
  See also SAAS 4
Harrison, Harry 1925- *4*
Harrison, Harry Max
  See Harrison, Harry
Harrison, Mette Ivie 1970- *236*
  Earlier sketches in SATA 149, 202
Harrison, Michael 1939- *106*
Harrison, Michelle 1979- *233*
Harrison, Molly (Hodgett) 1909-2002 .... *41*
Harrison, Sarah 1946- *63*
Harrison, Ted
  See Harrison, Edward Hardy
Harsh, Fred (T.) 1925- *72*
Harshaw, Ruth H(etzel) 1890-1968 .... *27*
Harshman, Marc 1950- *109*
  Earlier sketch in SATA 71
Hart, Alexandra 1939- *14*
Hart, Alison
  See Leonhardt, Alice
Hart, Bruce 1938-2006 .... *57*
  Brief entry *39*
Hart, Carole 1943- *57*
  Brief entry *39*
Hart, Carolyn 1936- *74*
Hart, Carolyn G.
  See Hart, Carolyn
Hart, Carolyn Gimpel
  See Hart, Carolyn
Hart, Jan Siegel 1940- *79*
Hart, Joyce 1954- *148*
Hart, Karen *185*
Hart, Lenore *171*
Hart, Philip S. 1944- *180*
Hart, Virginia 1949- *83*
Harte, Bret 1836(?)-1902 .... *26*
Harte, Francis Brett
  See Harte, Bret
Harter, Debbie 1963- *107*
Hartfield, Claire 1957- *147*
Hartinger, Brent 1964- *217*
  Earlier sketches in SATA 145, 174
Hartland, Jessie *171*
Hartley, Ellen (Raphael) 1915-1980 .... *23*
Hartley, Fred Allan III 1953- *41*
Hartley, William B(rown) 1913-1980 .... *23*
Hartling, Peter
  See Hartling, Peter
Hartling, Peter 1933- *66*
  See also CLR 29
Hartman, Bob 1955- *224*
Hartman, Carrie *226*
Hartman, Cassie *202*
Hartman, Dan 1955- *202*
Hartman, Evert 1937- *38*
  Brief entry *35*
Hartman, Jane E. 1928- *47*
Hartman, Jane Evangeline
  See Hartman, Jane E.
Hartman, Louis F(rancis) 1901-1970 .... *22*
Hartman, Rachel *174*
Hartman, Victoria 1942- *91*

Hartnett, Sonya 1968- *176*
  Earlier sketches in SATA *93, 130*
Hartry, Nancy *219*
Hartshorn, Ruth M. 1928- *11*
Hartung, Susan Kathleen *192*
  Earlier sketch in SATA *150*
Hartwig, Manfred 1950- *81*
Harvey, Alyxandra 1974- *227*
  Earlier sketch in SATA *189*
Harvey, Brett 1936- *61*
Harvey, Edith 1908(?)-1972
  Obituary *27*
Harvey, Gill *189*
Harvey, Karen D. 1935- *88*
Harvey, Roland 1945- *219*
  Earlier sketches in SATA *71, 123, 179*
Harvey-Fitzhenry, Alyxandra
  See Harvey, Alyxandra
Harwick, B. L.
  See Keller, Beverly L(ou)
Harwin, Brian
  See Henderson, LeGrand
Harwood, Pearl Augusta (Bragdon)
  1903-1998 .... *9*
Haseley, Dennis 1950- *221*
  Brief entry *44*
  Earlier sketches in SATA *57, 105, 157*
Hashmi, Kerri 1955- *108*
Haskell, Arnold L(ionel) 1903-1981(?) *6*
Haskins, James
  See Haskins, James S.
Haskins, James S. 1941-2005 .... *132*
  Autobiography Feature *132*
  Earlier sketches in SATA *9, 69, 105*
  See also CLR *39*
  See also SAAS *4*
Haskins, Jim
  See Haskins, James S.
Hasler, Eveline 1933- *181*
Hasler, Joan 1931- *28*
Hasler, Nikol 1979- *235*
Hasnat, Naheed
  See Senzai, N.H.
Hass, Robert 1941- *94*
Hassall, Joan 1906-1988 .... *43*
  Obituary *56*
Hassett, Ann 1958- *162*
Hassett, John *162*
Hassler, Jon 1933-2008 .... *19*
  Obituary *191*
Hassler, Jon Francis
  See Hassler, Jon
Hastings, Beverly
  See Barkin, Carol
  and James, Elizabeth
Hastings, Graham
  See Jeffries, Roderic
Hastings, Ian 1912- *62*
Hastings, Victor
  See Disch, Thomas M.
Haszard, Patricia Moyes 1923-2000 .... *63*
Hatch, Lynda S. 1950- *90*
Hathaway, Barbara *164*
Hathorn, Elizabeth
  See Hathorn, Libby
Hathorn, Elizabeth Helen
  See Hathorn, Libby
Hathorn, Libby 1943- *232*
  Autobiography Feature *232*
  Earlier sketches in SATA *74, 120, 156*
Hatkoff, Craig 1954- *192*
Hatlo, Jimmy 1898-1963
  Obituary *23*
Hatton, Caroline 1957- *205*
Hauff, Wilhelm 1802-1827
  See CLR *155*
Haugaard, Erik Christian 1923- *68*
  Earlier sketch in SATA *4*
  See also CLR *173*
  See also SAAS *12*
Haugaard, Kay *117*

Hauge, Lesley *234*
Haugen, Hayley Mitchell 1968- *172*
Haugen, Tormod 1945- *66*
Hauman, Doris 1898-1984 .... *32*
Hauman, George 1890-1961 .... *32*
Hauptly, Denis J. 1945- *57*
Hauptly, Denis James
  See Hauptly, Denis J.
Hauser, Jill Frankel 1950- *127*
Hauser, Margaret L(ouise) 1909- *10*
Hausherr, Rosmarie 1943- *86*
Hausman, Gerald 1945- *180*
  Earlier sketches in SATA *13, 90, 132*
  See also CLR *89*
Hausman, Gerry
  See Hausman, Gerald
Hauth, Katherine B. 1940- *99*
Hautman, Pete 1952- *173*
  Earlier sketches in SATA *82, 128*
Hautman, Peter Murray
  See Hautman, Pete
Hautzig, Deborah 1956- *106*
  Earlier sketch in SATA *31*
Hautzig, Esther Rudomin 1930-2009 .... *148*
  Earlier sketches in SATA *4, 68*
  See also CLR *22*
  See also SAAS *15*
Havel, Geoff 1955- *152*
Havel, Jennifer
  See Havill, Juanita
Havelin, Kate 1961- *143*
Haven, Paul 1971(?)- *213*
Haverfield, Mary *225*
Havighurst, Walter (Edwin) 1901-1994 .... *1*
  Obituary *79*
Haviland, Virginia 1911-1988 .... *6*
  Obituary *54*
Havill, Juanita 1949- *224*
  Earlier sketches in SATA *74, 155*
Hawes, Judy 1913- *4*
Hawes, Louise 1943- *180*
  Earlier sketch in SATA *60*
Hawk, Fran *222*
Hawke, Rosanne 1953- *165*
  Earlier sketch in SATA *124*
Hawke, Rosanne Joy
  See Hawke, Rosanne
Hawkes, Kevin 1959- *201*
  Earlier sketches in SATA *78, 150*
Hawkes, Nigel 1943- *119*
Hawkesworth, Eric 1921- *13*
Hawking, Lucy 1969- *197*
Hawkins, Aaron R. *236*
Hawkins, Arthur 1903-1985 .... *19*
Hawkins, Colin 1945- *162*
  Earlier sketch in SATA *112*
Hawkins, Jacqui *162*
  Earlier sketch in SATA *112*
Hawkins, Jimmy 1941- *188*
Hawkins, Laura 1951- *74*
Hawkins, (Helena Ann) Quail 1905-2002 ...... *6*
  Obituary *141*
Hawkins, Rachel 1979- *228*
Hawkinson, John (Samuel) 1912-1994 .... *4*
Hawkinson, Lucy (Ozone) 1924-1971 .... *21*
Hawks, Robert 1961- *85*
Hawley, Mabel C. *67*
  Earlier sketch in SATA *1*
Haworth, Danette *207*
Haworth-Attard, Barbara 1953- *215*
Hawthorne, Captain R. M.
  See Ellis, Edward S.
Hawthorne, Nathaniel 1804-1864
  See YABC *2*
  See also CLR *163*
Hay, Jeff T. *154*
Hay, John 1915-2011 .... *13*
Hay, Samantha *213*
Hay, Timothy
  See Brown, Margaret Wise
Hayashi, Leslie Ann 1954- *115*

Hayashi, Nancy 1939- *186*
  Earlier sketch in SATA *80*
Haycak, Cara 1961- *180*
Haycock, Kate 1962- *77*
Haycraft, Howard 1905-1991 .... *6*
  Obituary *70*
Haycraft, Molly Costain 1911- *6*
Hayden, Gwendolen Lampshire 1904- *35*
Hayden, Robert
  See Hayden, Robert Earl
Hayden, Robert C(arter), Jr. 1937- *47*
  Brief entry *28*
Hayden, Robert E.
  See Hayden, Robert Earl
Hayden, Robert Earl 1913-1980 .... *19*
  Obituary *26*
Hayden, Torey L. 1951- *163*
  Earlier sketch in SATA *65*
Hayden, Torey Lynn
  See Hayden, Torey L.
Hayes, Carlton J(oseph) H(untley)
  1882-1964 .... *11*
Hayes, Daniel 1952- *109*
  Earlier sketch in SATA *73*
Hayes, Geoffrey 1947- *207*
  Earlier sketches in SATA *26, 91*
Hayes, Joe 1945- *131*
  Earlier sketch in SATA *88*
Hayes, John F. 1904-1980 .... *11*
Hayes, Karel 1949- *207*
Hayes, Rosemary *227*
  Earlier sketch in SATA *158*
Hayes, Sarah 1945- *208*
Hayes, Sheila 1937- *51*
  Brief entry *50*
Hayes, Will *7*
Hayes, William D(imitt) 1913-1976 .... *8*
Haynes, Betsy 1937- *94*
  Brief entry *37*
  Earlier sketch in SATA *48*
  See also CLR *90*
Haynes, David 1955- *97*
Haynes, Linda
  See Swinford, Betty (June Wells)
Haynes, Mary 1938- *65*
Haynes, Max 1956- *72*
Hays, Anna Jane *214*
Hays, H(offmann) R(eynolds) 1904-1980 .... *26*
Hays, Thomas A.
  See Hays, Tony
Hays, Thomas Anthony
  See Hays, Tony
Hays, Tony 1957- *84*
Hays, Wilma Pitchford 1909- *28*
  Earlier sketch in SATA *1*
  See also CLR *59*
  See also SAAS *3*
Hayter, Rhonda *233*
Hayward, Linda 1943- *185*
  Brief entry *39*
  Earlier sketch in SATA *101*
Haywood, Carolyn 1898-1990 .... *75*
  Obituary *64*
  Earlier sketches in SATA *1, 29*
  See also CLR *22*
Hazelaar, Cor *217*
Hazell, Rebecca (Eileen) 1947- *141*
Hazen, Barbara Shook 1930- *178*
  Earlier sketches in SATA *27, 90*
Hazen, Lynn E. *202*
Head, Gay
  See Hauser, Margaret L(ouise)
Head, Tom 1978- *167*
Headley, Elizabeth
  See Harrison, Elizabeth (Allen) Cavanna
Headley, Justina Chen 1968- *176*
Headstrom, (Birger) Richard 1902-1985 .... *8*
Heady, Eleanor B(utler) 1917-1979 .... *8*
Heagy, William D. 1964- *76*
Heal, Edith 1903-1995 .... *7*
Heal, Gillian 1934- *89*

Heale, Jay (Jeremy Peter Wingfield) 1937- .. 84
Healey, Brooks
  See Albert, Burton
Healey, Karen 1981- 230
Healey, Larry 1927- 44
  Brief entry 42
Heap, Sue 1954- 187
  Earlier sketch in SATA *150*
Heaps, Willard A(llison) 1908-1987 26
Hearn, Diane Dawson 1952- 209
  Earlier sketch in SATA *79*
Hearn, Emily
  See Valleau, Emily
Hearn, Julie 1958- 212
  Earlier sketch in SATA *152*
Hearn, Lian
  See Rubinstein, Gillian
Hearn, Sneed
  See Gregg, Andrew K.
Hearne, Betsy 1942- 146
  Earlier sketches in SATA *38, 95*
Heath, Charles D(ickinson) 1941- 46
Heath, Veronica
  See Blackett, Veronica Heath
Heaven, Constance (Christina) 1911- 7
Hebert-Collins, Sheila 1948- 111
Hecht, George J(oseph) 1895-1980
  Obituary 22
Hecht, Henri Joseph 1922- 9
Hechtkopf, Henryk 1910- 17
Heck, Bessie (Mildred) Holland 1911-1995 . 26
Heck, Ed 1963- 173
Heckert, Connie K(aye Delp) 1948- 82
Hector, Julian 205
Hedderwick, Mairi 1939- 145
  Earlier sketches in SATA *30, 77*
Hedges, Sid(ney) G(eorge) 1897-1974 28
Hedrick, Irene Hope 1920- 175
Heelan, Jamee Riggio 1965- 146
Heerboth, Sharon
  See Leon, Sharon
Heffernan, John 1949- 168
  Earlier sketch in SATA *121*
Heffron, Dorris 1944- 68
Hefter, Richard 1942- 31
Hegamin, Tonya C. 1975- 209
Hegarty, Reginald Beaton 1906-1973 10
Hehenberger, Shelly 1968- 126
Heidbreder, Robert 1947- 196
  Earlier sketch in SATA *130*
Heidbreder, Robert K.
  See Heidbreder, Robert
Heide, Florence Parry 1919-2011 192
  Earlier sketches in SATA *32, 69, 118*
  See also CLR *60*
  See also SAAS *6*
Heiderstadt, Dorothy 1907-2001 6
Heidi Louise
  See Erdrich, Louise
Heidler, David S. 1955- 132
Heidler, David Stephen
  See Heidler, David S.
Heidler, Jeanne T. 1956- 132
Heilbroner, Joan Knapp 1922- 63
Heilbrun, Lois Hussey 1922(?)-1987
  Obituary 54
Heiligman, Deborah 1958- 193
  Earlier sketches in SATA *90, 144*
Heilman, Joan Rattner 50
Heimann, Rolf 1940- 164
  Earlier sketch in SATA *120*
Heimberg, Justin 232
Hein, Lucille Eleanor 1915-1994 20
Heine, Helme 1941- 135
  Earlier sketch in SATA *67*
  See also CLR *18*
Heinlein, Robert A. 1907-1988 69
  Obituary 56
  Earlier sketch in SATA *9*
  See also CLR *75*

Heinlein, Robert Anson
  See Heinlein, Robert A.
Heins, Ethel L(eah) 1918-1997 101
Heins, Paul 1909- 13
Heintze, Carl 1922- 26
Heinz, Bill
  See Heinz, W. C.
Heinz, Brian J. 1946- 181
  Earlier sketch in SATA *95*
Heinz, Brian James
  See Heinz, Brian J.
Heinz, W. C. 1915-2008 26
Heinz, Wilfred Charles
  See Heinz, W. C.
Heinzen, Mildred
  See Masters, Mildred
Heisel, Sharon E(laine) 1941- 125
  Earlier sketch in SATA *84*
Heitzmann, William Ray 1948- 73
Heitzmann, Wm. Ray
  See Heitzmann, William Ray
Helakoski, Leslie 178
Helberg, Shirley Adelaide Holden 1919- ... 138
Heldring, Thatcher 229
Helfer, Andrew 187
Helfer, Ralph 1937- 177
Helfman, Elizabeth S(eaver) 1911-2001 3
Helfman, Harry Carmozin 1910-1995 3
Helgerson, Joseph 1950- 181
Hellard, Susan 232
  Earlier sketch in SATA *182*
Hellberg, Hans-Eric 1927- 38
Heller, Linda 1944- 46
  Brief entry 40
Heller, Mike
  See Hano, Arnold
Heller, Ruth M. 1924- 112
  Earlier sketch in SATA *66*
Hellman, Hal
  See Hellman, Harold
Hellman, Harold 1927- 4
Helman, Andrea (Jean) 1946- 160
  Earlier sketch in SATA *107*
Helmer, Diana Star 1962- 86
Helmer, Marilyn 160
  Earlier sketch in SATA *112*
Helps, Racey 1913-1971 2
  Obituary 25
Helquist, Brett 229
  Earlier sketches in SATA *146, 187*
Helweg, Hans H. 1917- 50
  Brief entry 33
Helyar, Jane Penelope Josephine 1933- 5
  Autobiography Feature 138
  See also SAAS *2*
Hemingway, Edith M. 1950- 223
Hemingway, Edith Morris
  See Hemingway, Edith M.
Hemingway, Edward 1969(?)- 212
Hemingway, Ernest 1899-1961
  See CLR *168*
Hemingway, Ernest Miller
  See Hemingway, Ernest
Hemmant, Lynette 1938- 69
Hemming, Roy G. 1928-1995 11
  Obituary 86
Hemphill, Helen 1955- 179
Hemphill, Kris (Harrison) 1963- 118
Hemphill, Martha Locke 1904-1973 37
Hemphill, Michael 220
Hemphill, Stephanie 190
Hemstock, Gillian 1956- 173
Henba, Bobbie 1926- 87
Henbest, Nigel 1951- 55
  Brief entry 52
Henderley, Brooks 1
Henderson, Aileen Kilgore 1921- 178
Henderson, Aileen Mary
  See Fox, Aileen
Henderson, Gordon 1950- 53

Henderson, Kathy 1949- 155
  Brief entry 53
  Earlier sketches in SATA *55, 95*
Henderson, Lauren 1966- 201
Henderson, LeGrand 1901-1965 9
Henderson, Nancy Wallace 1916- 22
Henderson, Zenna (Chlarson) 1917-1983 5
Hendra, Sue 235
Hendrickson, Walter Brookfield, Jr. 1936- 9
Hendrix, John 1976- 208
Hendry, Diana 1941- 213
  Earlier sketches in SATA *68, 106*
Hendry, Frances Mary 1941- 171
  Earlier sketch in SATA *110*
Hendry, Linda (Gail) 1961- 83
Heneghan, James 1930- 160
  Earlier sketches in SATA *53, 97*
Henkes, Kevin 1960- 207
  Earlier sketches in SATA *43, 76, 108, 154*
  See also CLR *108*
Henn, Astrid 214
Hennessy, Barbara G.
  See Hennessy, B.G.
Hennessy, Barbara Gulbrandsen
  See Hennessy, B.G.
Hennessy, B.G. 1951- 175
Hennessy, Carolyn 1962- 221
Henney, Carolee Wells 1928- 102
Henriod, Lorraine 1925- 26
Henriquez, Emile F. 1937- 170
  Earlier sketch in SATA *89*
Henry, April 1959- 235
  Earlier sketch in SATA *174*
Henry, Ernest 1948- 107
Henry, Joanne Landers 1927- 6
Henry, Maeve 1960- 75
Henry, Marguerite 1902-1997 100
  Obituary 99
  See also CLR *4*
  See also SAAS *7*
Henry, Marie H. 1935- 65
Henry, Marilyn 1939- 117
Henry, Marion
  See del Rey, Lester
Henry, O. 1862-1910
  See YABC *2*
Henry, Oliver
  See Henry, O.
Henry, Rohan 217
Henry, T. E.
  See Rowland-Entwistle, (Arthur) Theodore
  (Henry)
Henschel, Elizabeth Georgie 56
Henson, Heather 206
Henson, James Maury
  See Henson, Jim
Henson, Jim 1936-1990 43
  Obituary 65
Henstra, Friso 1928- 73
  Earlier sketch in SATA *8*
  See also SAAS *14*
Hentoff, Nat(han Irving) 1925- 133
  Brief entry 27
  Earlier sketches in SATA *42, 69*
  See also CLR *52*
Henty, G(eorge) A(lfred) 1832-1902 64
  See also CLR *76*
Heo, Yumi 1964- 206
  Earlier sketches in SATA *94, 146*
Hepler, Heather 177
Herald, Kathleen
  See Peyton, Kathleen Wendy
Herb, Angela M. 1970- 92
Herbert, Cecil
  See Hamilton, Charles (Harold St. John)
Herbert, Don 1917-2007 2
  Obituary 184
Herbert, Donald Jeffrey
  See Herbert, Don

Herbert, Frank 1920-1986 37
  Obituary 47
  Earlier sketch in SATA 9
Herbert, Frank Patrick
  See Herbert, Frank
Herbert, Helen (Jean) 1947- 57
Herbert, Janis 1956- 139
Herbert, Wally 1934-2007 23
Herbert, Walter William
  See Herbert, Wally
Herbst, Judith 1947- 74
Herda, D.J. 1948- 80
Herge
  See Remi, Georges
Heritage, Martin
  See Horler, Sydney
Herkimer, L(awrence) R(ussell) 1925(?)- 42
Herlihy, Dirlie Anne 1935- 73
Herlong, Madaline
  See Herlong, M.H.
Herlong, M.H. 211
Herman, Charlotte 1937- 203
  Earlier sketches in SATA 20, 99
Hermanson, Dennis (Everett) 1947- 10
Hermes, Jules 1962- 92
Hermes, Patricia 1936- 233
  Earlier sketches in SATA 31, 78, 141, 191
Hermes, Patricia Mary
  See Hermes, Patricia
Hernandez, Natalie Nelson 1929- 123
Herndon, Ernest 91
Herold, Ann Bixby 1937- 72
Herrera, Diego
  See Yayo
Herrera, Juan Felipe 1948- 127
Herrick, Steven 1958- 209
  Earlier sketches in SATA 103, 156
Herriman, George (Joseph) 1880-1944 140
Herriot, James 1916-1995 135
  Brief entry 44
  Earlier sketch in SATA 86
  See also CLR 80
Herrmanns, Ralph 1933- 11
Herrold, Tracey
  See Dils, Tracey E.
Herron, Carolivia 1947- 203
Herron, Edward A(lbert) 1912- 4
Herschler, Mildred Barger 130
Hersey, John 1914-1993 25
  Obituary 76
Hersey, John Richard
  See Hersey, John
Hershberger, Priscilla (Gorman) 1951- 81
Hershenhorn, Esther 1945- 151
Hershey, Kathleen M. 1934- 80
Hershey, Mary 173
Hershey, Mary L.
  See Hershey, Mary
Hersom, Kathleen 1911- 73
Hertz, Grete Janus 1915- 23
Herxheimer, Sophie 1963- 220
Herzig, Alison Cragin 1935- 87
Herzog, Brad 1968- 131
Heshka, Ryan 236
Heslewood, Juliet 1951- 82
Hess, Lilo 1916- 4
Hess, Paul 1961- 134
Hesse, Hermann 1877-1962 50
Hesse, Karen 1952- 215
  Autobiography Feature 113
  Earlier sketches in SATA 74, 103, 158
  See also CLR 141
  See also SAAS 25
Hest, Amy 1950- 193
  Earlier sketches in SATA 55, 82, 129
Heuer, Karsten 1968(?)- 202
Heuer, Kenneth John 1927- 44
Heuman, William 1912-1971 21
Heuston, Kimberley 1960- 167
Heuston, Kimberley Burton
  See Heuston, Kimberley

Heuvel, Eric 1960- 224
Hewes, Agnes Danforth 1874-1963 35
Hewett, Anita 1918-1989 13
Hewett, Joan 1930- 140
  Earlier sketch in SATA 81
Hewett, Richard 1929- 81
Hewitson, Jennifer 1961- 97
Hewitt, Margaret 1961- 84
Hewitt, Sally 1949- 231
  Earlier sketch in SATA 127
Hext, Harrington
  See Phillpotts, Eden
Hey, Nigel 1936- 20
Hey, Nigel Stewart
  See Hey, Nigel
Heyduck-Huth, Hilde 1929- 8
Heyer, Carol 1950- 130
  Earlier sketch in SATA 74
Heyer, Marilee 1942- 102
  Earlier sketch in SATA 64
Heyerdahl, Thor 1914-2002 52
  Earlier sketch in SATA 2
Heyes, (Nancy) Eileen 1956- 150
  Earlier sketch in SATA 80
Heyliger, William 1884-1955
  See YABC 1
Heyman, Ken(neth Louis) 1930- 114
  Earlier sketch in SATA 34
Heyward, (Edwin) DuBose 1885-1940 21
Heywood, Karen 1946- 48
Hezlep, William (Earl) 1936- 88
Hiaasen, Carl 1953- 208
Hiatt, Shelby 226
Hibbert, Arthur Raymond
  See Hibbert, Christopher
Hibbert, Christopher 1924-2008 4
  Obituary 201
Hibbert, Eleanor Alice Burford 1906-1993 2
  Obituary 74
Hickman, Estella (Lee) 1942- 111
Hickman, Janet 1940- 127
  Earlier sketch in SATA 12
Hickman, Martha Whitmore 1925- 26
Hickman, Pamela 1958- 186
  Earlier sketch in SATA 128
Hickock, Will
  See Harrison, C(hester) William
Hickok, Lorena A. 1893-1968 20
Hickox, Rebecca (Ayres) 116
Hicks, Barbara Jean 1953- 165
Hicks, Betty 191
Hicks, Clifford B. 1920- 50
Hicks, Eleanor B.
  See Coerr, Eleanor (Beatrice)
Hicks, Faith Erin 235
Hicks, Harvey
  See Stratemeyer, Edward L.
Hicks, Peter 1952- 111
Hicyilmaz, Gaye 1947- 157
  Earlier sketch in SATA 77
Hieatt, Constance B(artlett) 1928- 4
Hiebert, Ray Eldon 1932- 13
Hierstein, Judith 212
Hierstein, Judy
  See Hierstein, Judith
Higdon, Hal 1931- 4
Higginbottom, David 1923- 87
  Earlier sketch in SATA 25
Higginbottom, J(effrey) Winslow 1945- 29
Higgins, Dalton 223
Higgins, F.E. 219
Higgins, Fiona
  See Higgins, F.E.
Higgins, Joanna 1945- 125
Higgins, Simon (Richard) 1958- 105
Higginson, Vy 79
High, Linda Oatman 1958- 188
  Autobiography Feature 188
  Earlier sketches in SATA 94, 145
High, Philip E. 1914- 119

High, Philip Empson
  See High, Philip E.
Higham, David 1949- 50
Higham, David Michael
  See Higham, David
Higham, Jon Atlas
  See Higham, Jonathan Huw
Higham, Jonathan Huw 1960- 59
Highet, Helen
  See MacInnes, Helen (Clark)
Hightman, Jason 1971(?)- 189
Hightman, J.P.
  See Hightman, Jason
Hightower, Florence Cole 1916-1981 4
  Obituary 27
Highwater, Jamake (Mamake)
  1942(?)-2001 69
  Brief entry 30
  Earlier sketch in SATA 32
  See also CLR 17
Hilb, Nora 1953- 178
Hildebrandt, Greg, Jr. 1970- 228
Hildebrandt, Greg 1939- 172
  Brief entry 33
  Earlier sketch in SATA 55
Hildebrandt, Tim 1939-2006 55
  Brief entry 33
Hildebrandt, Timothy
  See Hildebrandt, Tim
Hildebrandts, The
  See Hildebrandt, Greg
  and Hildebrandt, Tim
Hilder, Rowland 1905-1993 36
  Obituary 77
Hildick, E. W.
  See Hildick, Wallace
Hildick, Wallace 1925-2001 68
  Earlier sketch in SATA 2
  See also SAAS 6
Hilgartner, Beth 1957- 58
Hill, Alexis
  See Craig, Mary (Francis) Shura
  and Glick, Ruth
Hill, Anthony R. 1942- 164
  Earlier sketch in SATA 91
Hill, Anthony Robert
  See Hill, Anthony R.
Hill, David 1942- 152
  Earlier sketch in SATA 103
Hill, Donna (Marie) 1921- 124
  Earlier sketch in SATA 24
Hill, Douglas 1935-2007 78
  Earlier sketch in SATA 39
Hill, Douglas Arthur
  See Hill, Douglas
Hill, Elizabeth Starr 1925- 143
  Earlier sketch in SATA 24
Hill, Eric 1927- 133
  Brief entry 53
  Earlier sketch in SATA 66
  See also CLR 13
Hill, Gordon
  See Eldin, Peter
Hill, Grace Brooks 67
  Earlier sketch in SATA 1
Hill, Grace Livingston 1865-1947
  See YABC 2
Hill, Helen M(orey) 1915- 27
Hill, Isabel 225
Hill, Isabel T.
  See Hill, Isabel
Hill, John
  See Koontz, Dean
Hill, Johnson
  See Kunhardt, Edith
Hill, Judy I. R.
  See Roberts, Judy I.
Hill, Kathleen Louise 1917- 4
Hill, Kay
  See Hill, Kathleen Louise

Hill, Kirkpatrick 1938- *188*
  Earlier sketches in SATA *72, 126*
Hill, Laban
  See Hill, Laban Carrick
Hill, Laban Carrick *170*
Hill, Lee Sullivan 1958- *96*
Hill, Lorna 1902-1991 .... *12*
Hill, Margaret (Ohler) 1915- *36*
Hill, Meg
  See Hill, Margaret (Ohler)
Hill, Meredith
  See Craig, Mary (Francis) Shura
Hill, Monica
  See Watson, Jane Werner
Hill, Pamela Smith 1954- *112*
Hill, Ralph Nading 1917-1987 .... *65*
Hill, Robert W(hite) 1919-1982 .... *12*
  Obituary *31*
Hill, Ruth A.
  See Viguers, Ruth Hill
Hill, Ruth Livingston
  See Munce, Ruth Hill
Hill, Stuart 1958- *186*
Hill, Susan 1942- *183*
Hill, Susan Elizabeth
  See Hill, Susan
Hill, Susanna Leonard 1965- *193*
Hill, Thomas 1960- *82*
Hillcourt, William 1900-1992 .... *27*
Hillenbrand, Will 1960- *210*
  Earlier sketches in SATA *84, 147*
Hiller, Ilo (Ann) 1938- *59*
Hillerman, Anthony Grove
  See Hillerman, Tony
Hillerman, Tony 1925-2008 .... *6*
  Obituary *198*
Hillert, Margaret 1920- *91*
  Earlier sketch in SATA *8*
Hilliard, Richard *183*
Hillman, Ben 1957- *202*
Hillman, Elizabeth 1942- *75*
Hillman, John 1952- *120*
Hillman, Martin
  See Hill, Douglas
Hillman, Priscilla 1940- *48*
  Brief entry *39*
Hillman, Shane *200*
Hills, C.A.R. 1955- *39*
Hills, Charles Albert Reis
  See Hills, C.A.R.
Hills, Tad *237*
  Earlier sketch in SATA *173*
Hilton, Irene Pothus -1979 .... *7*
Hilton, James 1900-1954 .... *34*
Hilton, Margaret Lynette 1946- *105*
  Earlier sketch in SATA *68*
  See also CLR *25*
  See also SAAS *21*
Hilton, Nette
  See Hilton, Margaret Lynette
Hilton, Ralph 1907-1982 .... *8*
Hilton, Suzanne 1922- *4*
Hilton-Bruce, Anne
  See Hilton, Margaret Lynette
Him, George 1937-1982
  Obituary *30*
Himelblau, Linda -2005 .... *179*
Himelstein, Shmuel 1940- *83*
Himler, Ann 1946- *8*
Himler, Ronald 1937- *234*
  Earlier sketches in SATA *6, 92, 137, 183*
Himler, Ronald Norbert
  See Himler, Ronald
Himmelman, John 1959- *221*
  Earlier sketches in SATA *47, 94, 159*
Himmelman, John C.
  See Himmelman, John
Hinckley, Helen
  See Jones, Helen Hinckley
Hind, Dolores (Ellen) 1931- *53*
  Brief entry *49*

Hindin, Nathan
  See Bloch, Robert (Albert)
Hindley, Judy 1940- *179*
  Earlier sketch in SATA *120*
Hinds, P. Mignon *98*
Hinds, Patricia Mignon
  See Hinds, P. Mignon
Hine, Sesyle Joslin 1929- *2*
Hines, Anna Grossnickle 1946- *209*
  Brief entry *45*
  Earlier sketches in SATA *51, 95, 141*
  See also SAAS *16*
Hines, Gary (Roger) 1944- *136*
  Earlier sketch in SATA *74*
Hinman, Bonnie 1950- *216*
Hinojosa, Maria (de Lourdes) 1961- *88*
Hinton, Nigel 1941- *166*
Hinton, S. E. 1950- *160*
  Earlier sketches in SATA *19, 58, 115*
  See also CLR *23*
Hinton, Sam 1917-2009 .... *43*
Hinton, Susan Eloise
  See Hinton, S. E.
Hintz, Martin 1945- *128*
  Brief entry *39*
  Earlier sketch in SATA *47*
Hintz, Stephen V. 1975- *129*
Hippopotamus, Eugene H.
  See Kraus, (Herman) Robert
Hirano, Cathy 1957- *68*
Hirao, Amiko *203*
Hirsch, Karen 1941- *61*
Hirsch, Odo *157*
  Earlier sketch in SATA *111*
Hirsch, Phil 1926- *35*
Hirsch, S. Carl 1913-1990 .... *2*
  See also SAAS *7*
Hirschfelder, Arlene B. 1943- *227*
  Earlier sketches in SATA *80, 138*
Hirschi, Ron 1948- *192*
  Earlier sketches in SATA *56, 95*
Hirschmann, Linda (Ann) 1941- *40*
Hirsh, Marilyn 1944-1988 .... *7*
  Obituary *58*
Hirshberg, Al(bert Simon) 1909-1973 .... *38*
Hiscock, Bruce 1940- *204*
  Earlier sketch in SATA *57, 137*
Hiser, Constance 1950- *71*
Hiser, Iona Seibert -1998 .... *4*
Hislop, Julia Rose Catherine 1962- *74*
Hissey, Jane 1952- *130*
  Autobiography Feature *130*
  Earlier sketches in SATA *58, 103*
Hissey, Jane Elizabeth
  See Hissey, Jane
Hitchcock, Alfred (Joseph) 1899-1980 .... *27*
  Obituary *24*
Hite, Sid 1954- *175*
  Earlier sketches in SATA *75, 136*
Hitte, Kathryn 1919- *16*
Hitz, Demi
  See Demi
Hitzeroth, Deborah L. 1961- *78*
Hnizdovsky, Jacques 1915- *32*
Ho, Jannie *226*
Ho, Louise *185*
Ho, Minfong 1951- *151*
  Earlier sketches in SATA *15, 94*
  See also CLR *28*
Hoagland, Edward (Morley) 1932- *51*
Hoare, Robert J(ohn) 1921-1975 .... *38*
Hoban, Julia *217*
Hoban, Lillian 1925-1998 .... *69*
  Obituary *104*
  Earlier sketch in SATA *22*
  See also CLR *67*
Hoban, Russell 1925- *136*
  Earlier sketches in SATA *1, 40, 78*
  See also CLR *139*
Hoban, Russell Conwell
  See Hoban, Russell

Hoban, Tana 1917(?)-2006 .... *104*
  Obituary *173*
  Earlier sketches in SATA *22, 70*
  See also CLR *76*
  See also SAAS *12*
Hobart, Lois (Elaine) *7*
Hobbie, Holly 1942- *225*
  Earlier sketch in SATA *178*
  See also CLR *88*
Hobbie, Jocelyn *190*
Hobbie, Nathaniel *196*
Hobbs, Leigh 1953- *166*
Hobbs, Valerie 1941- *193*
  Autobiography Feature *145*
  Earlier sketches in SATA *93, 145*
  See also CLR *148*
Hobbs, Will 1947- *177*
  Autobiography Feature *127*
  Earlier sketches in SATA *72, 110*
  See also CLR *59*
Hobbs, William Carl
  See Hobbs, Will
Hoberman, Mary Ann 1930- *228*
  Earlier sketches in SATA *5, 72, 111, 158*
  See also CLR *22*
  See also SAAS *18*
Hobson, Bruce 1950- *62*
Hobson, Burton (Harold) 1933- *28*
Hobson, Laura Z(ametkin) 1900-1986 .... *52*
Hobson, Sally 1967- *172*
  Earlier sketch in SATA *84*
Hoce, Charley E. *174*
Hochman, David *202*
Hochschild, Arlie Russell 1940- *11*
Hockaby, Stephen
  See Mitchell, Gladys (Maude Winifred)
Hockenberry, Hope
  See Newell, Hope Hockenberry
Hodge, Deborah 1954- *163*
  Earlier sketch in SATA *122*
Hodge, P. W.
  See Hodge, Paul W(illiam)
Hodge, Paul W(illiam) 1934- *12*
Hodgell, P(atricia) C(hristine) 1951- *42*
Hodges, C. Walter 1909-2004 .... *2*
  Obituary *158*
Hodges, Carl G. 1902-1964 .... *10*
Hodges, Cyril Walter
  See Hodges, C. Walter
Hodges, Elizabeth Jamison *1*
Hodges, Margaret 1911-2005 .... *167*
  Obituary *172*
  Earlier sketches in SATA *1, 33, 75, 117*
  See also SAAS *9*
Hodges, Margaret Moore
  See Hodges, Margaret
Hodgetts, Blake Christopher 1967- *43*
Hodgkins, Fran 1964- *199*
Hodgkinson, Leigh 1975- *202*
Hodgman, Ann 1956- *198*
Hodgson, Harriet (W.) 1935- *84*
Hoehne, Marcia 1951- *89*
Hoellwarth, Cathryn Clinton
  See Clinton, Cathryn
Hoestlandt, Jo 1948- *221*
  Earlier sketch in SATA *94*
Hoestlandt, Jocelyne
  See Hoestlandt, Jo
Hoexter, Corinne K. 1927- *6*
Hoeye, Michael 1947- *136*
Hof, Marjolijn 1956- *226*
Hoff, Carol 1900-1979 .... *11*
Hoff, Mary (King) 1956- *157*
  Earlier sketch in SATA *74*
Hoff, Syd(ney) 1912-2004 .... *138*
  Obituary *154*
  Earlier sketches in SATA *9, 72*
  See also CLR *83*
  See also SAAS *4*
Hoffman, Edwin D. *49*

Hoffman, Elizabeth P(arkinson) 1921-2003
    Obituary *153*
Hoffman, Mary 1945- *211*
    Earlier sketches in SATA *59, 97, 144*
    See also SAAS *24*
Hoffman, Mat 1972- *150*
Hoffman, Nina Kiriki 1955- *160*
Hoffman, Phyllis M. 1944- *4*
Hoffman, Phyllis Miriam
    See Hoffman, Phyllis M.
Hoffman, Rosekrans 1926- *15*
Hoffmann, E(rnst) T(heodor) A(madeus)
    1776-1822 .... *27*
    See also CLR *133*
Hoffmann, Felix 1911-1975 .... *9*
Hoffmann, Heinrich 1809-1894
    See CLR *122*
Hoffmann, Margaret Jones 1910- *48*
Hoffmann, Peggy
    See Hoffmann, Margaret Jones
Hofher, Catherine Baxley 1954- *130*
Hofher, Cathy
    See Hofher, Catherine Baxley
Hofmeyr, Dianne (Louise) *138*
Hofsepian, Sylvia A. 1932- *74*
Hofsinde, Robert 1902-1973 .... *21*
Hogan, Bernice Harris 1929- *12*
Hogan, Inez 1895-1973 .... *2*
Hogan, James P. 1941-2010 .... *81*
Hogan, James Patrick
    See Hogan, James P.
Hogan, Jamie *192*
Hogan, Linda 1947- *132*
Hogan, Mary 1957- *210*
Hogarth, Burne 1911-1996 .... *89*
    Earlier sketch in SATA *63*
Hogarth, Grace (Weston Allen) 1905-1995 .. *91*
Hogarth, Jr.
    See Kent, Rockwell
Hogarth, (Arthur) Paul 1917-2001 .... *41*
Hogg, Garry 1902-1976 .... *2*
Hogg, Gary 1957- *172*
    Earlier sketch in SATA *105*
Hogner, Dorothy Childs *4*
Hogner, Nils 1893-1970 .... *25*
Hogrogian, Nonny 1932- *74*
    Autobiography Feature *127*
    Earlier sketch in SATA *7*
    See also CLR *95*
    See also SAAS *1*
Hoh, Diane 1937- *102*
    Brief entry *48*
    Earlier sketch in SATA *52*
Hoke, Helen
    See Watts, Helen L. Hoke
Hoke, Helen L.
    See Watts, Helen L. Hoke
Hoke, John 1925-2011 .... *7*
Hoke, John Lindsay
    See Hoke, John
Hokenson, Terry 1948- *193*
Hol, Coby 1943- *126*
Holabird, Katharine 1948- *213*
    Earlier sketches in SATA *62, 135*
Holaday, Bobbie 1922- *153*
Holbeach, Henry
    See Rands, William Brighty
Holberg, Ruth L(angland) 1889-1984 .... *1*
Holbrook, Kathy 1963- *107*
Holbrook, Peter
    See Glick, Carl (Cannon)
Holbrook, Sabra
    See Erickson, Sabra Rollins
Holbrook, Sara *131*
Holbrook, Stewart Hall 1893-1964 .... *2*
Holcomb, Jerry (Leona) Kimble 1927- *113*
Holcomb, Nan
    See McPhee, Norma H.
Holdcroft, Tina *227*
Holden, Elizabeth Rhoda
    See Lawrence, Louise

Holder, Jimmy 1962- *234*
Holding, James (Clark Carlisle, Jr.)
    1907-1997 .... *3*
Hole, Stian 1969- *204*
Holeman, Linda 1949- *136*
    Autobiography Feature *136*
    Earlier sketch in SATA *102*
Holgate, Doug *225*
Holinger, William (Jacques) 1944- *90*
Holisher, Desider 1901-1972 .... *6*
Holl, Adelaide Hinkle 1910- *8*
Holl, Kristi
    See Holl, Kristi D.
Holl, Kristi D. 1951- *51*
Holl, Kristi Diane
    See Holl, Kristi D.
Holland, Gay W. 1941- *128*
Holland, Isabelle (Christian) 1920-2002 .... *70*
    Autobiography Feature *103*
    Obituary *132*
    Earlier sketch in SATA *8*
    See also CLR *57*
Holland, Janice 1913-1962 .... *18*
Holland, John L(ewis) 1919- *20*
Holland, Joyce
    See Morice, Dave
Holland, Julia 1954- *106*
Holland, Lynda (H.) 1959- *77*
Holland, Lys
    See Gater, Dilys
Holland, Marion 1908-1989 .... *6*
    Obituary *61*
Holland, Richard 1976- *216*
Holland, Trish *221*
Hollander, John 1929- *13*
Hollander, Nicole 1940(?)- *101*
Hollander, Paul
    See Silverberg, Robert
Hollander, Phyllis 1928- *39*
Hollander, Zander 1923- *63*
Holldobler, Turid 1939- *26*
Holliday, Joe
    See Holliday, Joseph
Holliday, Joseph 1910- *11*
Hollihan, Kerrie Logan *235*
Holling, Holling C(lancy) 1900-1973 .... *15*
    Obituary *26*
    See also CLR *50*
Hollingsworth, Alvin C(arl) 1930- *39*
Hollingsworth, Mary 1947- *166*
    Earlier sketch in SATA *91*
Holloway, Teresa (Bragunier) 1906- *26*
Hollyer, Beatrice 1957- *226*
Hollyer, Belinda *204*
Holm, (Else) Anne (Lise) 1922-1998 .... *1*
    See also CLR *75*
    See also SAAS *7*
Holm, Jennifer L. 1968(?)- *236*
    Earlier sketches in SATA *120, 163, 183*
Holm, Matthew 1974- *174*
Holm, Sharon Lane 1955- *114*
    Earlier sketch in SATA *78*
Holman, Felice 1919- *82*
    Earlier sketch in SATA *7*
    See also SAAS *17*
Holm and Hamel
    See Holm, Jennifer L.
Holmberg, Bo R. 1945- *203*
Holme, Bryan 1913-1990 .... *26*
    Obituary *66*
Holmes, Barbara Ware 1945- *127*
    Earlier sketch in SATA *65*
Holmes, Elizabeth 1957- *191*
Holmes, Elizabeth Ann
    See Holmes, Elizabeth
Holmes, John
    See Souster, (Holmes) Raymond
Holmes, Liz
    See Holmes, Elizabeth
Holmes, Marjorie (Rose) 1910-2002 .... *43*
Holmes, Martha 1961- *72*

Holmes, Mary Tavener 1954- *199*
Holmes, Mary Z(astrow) 1943- *80*
Holmes, Oliver Wendell 1809-1894 .... *34*
Holmes, Peggy 1898- *60*
Holmes, Raymond
    See Souster, (Holmes) Raymond
Holmes, Rick
    See Hardwick, Richard Holmes, Jr.
Holmes, Sara Lewis *186*
Holmgren, Helen Jean 1930- *45*
Holmgren, Sister George Ellen
    See Holmgren, Helen Jean
Holmgren, Virginia C(unningham) 1909- *26*
Holmquist, Eve 1921- *11*
Holt, K.A.
    See Roy, Kari Anne
Holt, Kimberly Willis 1960- *223*
    Earlier sketches in SATA *122, 179*
Holt, Margaret 1937- *4*
Holt, Margaret Van Vechten (Saunders)
    1899-1963 .... *32*
Holt, Michael (Paul) 1929- *13*
Holt, Rackham
    See Holt, Margaret Van Vechten (Saunders)
Holt, Rochelle L.
    See DuBois, Rochelle Holt
Holt, Stephen
    See Thompson, Harlan
Holt, Victoria
    See Hibbert, Eleanor Alice Burford
Holtei, Christa 1953- *214*
Holton, Leonard
    See Wibberley, Leonard
Holtz, Thomas R., Jr. 1965- *203*
Holtze, Sally Holmes 1952- *64*
Holtzman, Jerome 1926-2008 .... *57*
    Obituary *194*
Holub, Joan 1956- *229*
    Earlier sketches in SATA *99, 149*
Holub, Josef 1926- *175*
Holubitsky, Katherine 1955- *165*
    Earlier sketch in SATA *121*
Holyer, Erna Maria 1925- *22*
Holyer, Ernie
    See Holyer, Erna Maria
Holyfield, John 1969- *227*
Holz, Loretta 1943- *17*
Holz, Loretta Marie
    See Holz, Loretta
Homel, David 1952- *97*
Homze, Alma C. 1932- *17*
Honey, Elizabeth 1947- *137*
    Autobiography Feature *137*
    Earlier sketch in SATA *112*
Honeycutt, Natalie 1945- *97*
Hong, Lily Toy 1958- *76*
Hong, Maxine Ting Ting
    See Kingston, Maxine Hong
Honig, Donald 1931- *18*
Honig, Donald Martin
    See Honig, Donald
Honness, Elizabeth H. 1904- *2*
Hoobler, Dorothy 1941- *161*
    Earlier sketches in SATA *28, 109*
Hoobler, Thomas *161*
    Earlier sketches in SATA *28, 109*
Hood, Joseph F. 1925- *4*
Hood, Robert E. 1926- *21*
Hood, Sarah
    See Killough, (Karen) Lee
Hook, Brendan 1963- *105*
Hook, Frances 1912-1983 .... *27*
Hook, Geoffrey R(aynor) 1928- *103*
Hook, Jeff
    See Hook, Geoffrey R(aynor)
Hook, Martha 1936- *27*
Hooker, Richard
    See Heinz, W. C.
Hooker, Ruth 1920-1998 .... *21*
hooks, bell 1952(?)- *170*
    Earlier sketch in SATA *115*

Hooks, William H(arris) 1921- 94
  Earlier sketch in SATA 16
Hoon, Patricia Easterly 1954- 90
Hooper, Byrd
  See St. Clair, Byrd Hooper
Hooper, Mary 1948- 205
  Earlier sketch in SATA 160
Hooper, Maureen Brett 1927- 76
Hooper, Meredith 1939- 159
  Earlier sketches in SATA 28, 101
Hooper, Meredith Jean
  See Hooper, Meredith
Hooper, Patricia 1941- 95
Hoopes, Lyn Littlefield 1953- 49
  Brief entry 44
Hoopes, Ned E(dward) 1932- 21
Hoopes, Roy 1922-2009 11
Hoose, Phillip 1947- 215
  Earlier sketch in SATA 137
Hoover, H(elen) M(ary) 1935- 132
  Brief entry 33
  Earlier sketches in SATA 44, 83
  See also SAAS 8
Hoover, Helen (Drusilla Blackburn)
  1910-1984 12
  Obituary 39
Hopcus, Anastasia 234
Hope, Christopher 1944- 62
Hope, Christopher David Tully
  See Hope, Christopher
Hope, Laura Lee
  See Goulart, Ron
  and Stanley, George Edward
Hope Simpson, Jacynth 1930- 12
Hopf, Alice (Martha) L(ightner) 1904-1988 ... 5
  Obituary 55
Hopgood, Tim 1961- 224
Hopkins, A. T.
  See Turngren, Annette
Hopkins, C. M.
  See Hopkins, Cathy
Hopkins, Cathy 1953- 165
Hopkins, Cathy M.
  See Hopkins, Cathy
Hopkins, Clark 1895-1976
  Obituary 34
Hopkins, Ellen 1955- 128
Hopkins, Ellen L.
  See Hopkins, Ellen
Hopkins, Jackie
  See Hopkins, Jackie Mims
Hopkins, Jackie Mims 1952- 178
  Earlier sketch in SATA 92
Hopkins, Joseph G(erard) E(dward) 1909- ... 11
Hopkins, (Hector) Kenneth 1914-1988
  Obituary 58
Hopkins, Lee Bennett 1938- 215
  Earlier sketches in SATA 3, 68, 125, 168
  See also CLR 44
  See also SAAS 4
Hopkins, Lyman
  See Folsom, Franklin (Brewster)
Hopkins, Marjorie 1911-1999 9
Hopkins, Mary R(ice) 1956- 97
Hopkinson, Amanda 1948- 84
Hopkinson, Deborah 1952- 216
  Autobiography Feature 180
  Earlier sketches in SATA 76, 108, 159, 180
  See also CLR 118
Hopman, Philip 1961- 177
Hoppe, Joanne 1932- 42
Hoppe, Matthias 1952- 76
Hoppe, Paul 209
Hopper, Nancy J. 1937- 38
  Brief entry 35
Hoppey, Tim 1958- 225
Hopping, Lorraine Jean
  See Egan, Lorraine Hopping
Horacek, Judy 1961- 211
Horacek, Petr 214
  Earlier sketch in SATA 163

Horenstein, Henry 1947- 108
Horgan, Paul (George Vincent O'Shaughnessy)
  1903-1995 13
  Obituary 84
Horlak, E.E.
  See Tepper, Sheri S.
Horler, Sydney 1888-1954 102
Horley, Alex 1970- 229
Horn, Sandra Ann 1944- 154
Hornblow, Arthur, Jr. 1893-1976 15
Hornblow, Leonora 1920-2005 18
  Obituary 171
Hornblow, Leonora Schinasi
  See Hornblow, Leonora
Horne, Constance 1927- 149
Horne, Richard 1960-2007 169
  Obituary 180
  Earlier sketch in SATA 111
Horne, Richard Henry Hengist
  1802(?)-1884 29
Horner, Althea (Jane) 1926- 36
Horner, Dave 1934- 12
Horner, Emily 1982- 233
Horner, Jack 1946- 106
Horner, John R.
  See Horner, Jack
Horner, John Robert
  See Horner, Jack
Hornik, Laurie Miller 159
Horniman, Joanne 1951- 167
  Earlier sketch in SATA 98
Hornos, Axel 1907-1994 20
Hornstein, Reuben Aaron 1912- 64
Horowitz, Anthony 1955- 236
  Earlier sketches in SATA 137, 195
Horowitz, Dave 1970- 204
  Earlier sketch in SATA 172
Horowitz, Eli 230
Horowitz, Ruth 1957- 136
Horrocks, Anita 1958- 169
Horse, Harry
  See Horne, Richard
Horsfield, Alan 1939- 153
Horstman, Lisa 1964- 219
Hort, Lenny 179
Horton, James O. 1943- 173
Horton, James Oliver
  See Horton, James O.
Horton, Joan 217
Horton, Madelyn (Stacey) 1962- 77
Horvath, Betty 1927- 4
Horvath, David 1972(?)- 192
Horvath, Polly 1957- 194
  Earlier sketches in SATA 85, 140
  See also CLR 90
Horwich, Frances R(appaport) 1908-2001 11
  Obituary 130
Horwitz, Elinor Lander 45
  Brief entry 33
Horwood, William 1944- 85
Hosford, Dorothy (Grant) 1900-1952 22
Hosford, Jessie 1892-1990 5
Hoshi, Shin'ichi 1926- 101
Hoshino, Felicia 1968- 189
Hoskyns-Abrahall, Clare (Constance
  Drury) 13
Hosler, Danamarie 1978- 184
Hossack, Sylvia 1939- 83
Hossack, Sylvie Adams
  See Hossack, Sylvia
Hosseini, Khaled 1965- 156
Hossell, Karen Price
  See Price, Karen
Hosta, Dar 192
Hostetler, Marian 1932- 91
Hostetter, Joyce Moyer 1952- 228
Houck, Carter 1924- 22
Hough, Charlotte 1924-2008 9
  Obituary 202
Hough, Helen Charlotte
  See Hough, Charlotte

Hough, Judy Taylor 1932- 63
  Brief entry 51
  Earlier sketch in SATA 56
Hough, Richard (Alexander) 1922-1999 17
Houghton, Eric 1930- 7
Houk, Randy 1944- 97
Houlehen, Robert J. 1918- 18
Houlton, Peggy Mann 1925(?)-1990 6
Household, Geoffrey 1900-1988 14
  Obituary 59
Housman, Laurence 1865-1959 25
Houston, Dick 1943- 231
  Earlier sketch in SATA 74
Houston, Gloria 138
  Autobiography Feature 138
  Earlier sketch in SATA 81
Houston, James A(rchibald) 1921-2005 74
  Obituary 163
  Earlier sketch in SATA 13
  See also CLR 3
  See also SAAS 17
Houston, James D. 1933-2009 78
  Obituary 203
Houston, James Dudley
  See Houston, James D.
Houston, James Dudley
  See Houston, James D.
Houston, Jeanne Toyo Wakatsuki
  See Houston, Jeanne Wakatsuki
Houston, Jeanne Wakatsuki 1934- 168
  Autobiography Feature 168
  Earlier sketch in SATA 78
Houston, Juanita C. 1921- 129
Houtman, Jacqueline 1960- 231
Houtman, Jacqueline Jaeger
  See Houtman, Jacqueline
Houton, Kathleen
  See Kilgore, Kathleen
Houts, Amy F. 164
Houts, Michelle 219
Hovey, Kate 158
Howard, Alan 1922- 45
Howard, Alyssa
  See Buckholtz, Eileen (Garber)
  and Glick, Ruth
  and Titchener, Louise
Howard, Arthur 1948- 212
  Earlier sketch in SATA 165
Howard, Arthur Charles
  See Howard, Arthur
Howard, Elizabeth Fitzgerald 1927- 119
  Earlier sketch in SATA 74
Howard, Ellen 1943- 184
  Earlier sketches in SATA 67, 99
Howard, Jane R(uble) 1924- 87
Howard, Norman Barry 1949- 90
Howard, P. M.
  See Howard, Pauline Rodriguez
Howard, Paul 1967- 190
  Earlier sketch in SATA 118
Howard, Pauline Rodriguez 1951- 124
Howard, Prosper
  See Hamilton, Charles (Harold St. John)
Howard, Robert West 1908-1988 5
Howard, Todd 1964- 135
Howard, Tristan
  See Currie, Stephen
Howard, Vernon (Linwood) 1918-1992 40
  Obituary 73
Howard, Warren F.
  See Pohl, Frederik
Howarth, Daniel 222
  Earlier sketch in SATA 188
Howarth, David (Armine) 1912-1991 6
  Obituary 68
Howarth, Lesley 1952- 94
Howe, Deborah 1946-1978 29
Howe, James 1946- 224
  Earlier sketches in SATA 29, 71, 111, 161
  See also CLR 9
Howe, John F. 1957- 79

Howe, Norma 1930-2011 .... *126*
Howe, Peter 1942- *214*
Howell, Pat 1947- *15*
Howell, S.
   See Styles, (Frank) Showell
Howell, Simmone 1971- *214*
Howell, Virginia
   See Ellison, Virginia H(owell)
Howells, Amanda
   See Gersh, Amanda
Howells, Tania *229*
Howes, Barbara 1914-1996 .... *5*
Howie, Betsy 1962- *215*
Howie, Diana 1945- *122*
Howie, Diana Melson
   See Howie, Diana
Howker, Janni 1957- *72*
   Brief entry *46*
   See also CLR *14*
   See also SAAS *13*
Howland, Ethan 1963- *131*
Howland, Naomi *232*
Hoxter, Holly Nicole 1983- *231*
Hoy, Linda 1946- *65*
Hoy, Nina
   See Roth, Arthur J(oseph)
Hoyle, Geoffrey 1942- *18*
Hoyt, Ard *190*
Hoyt, Edwin P(almer), Jr. 1923- *28*
Hoyt, Erich 1950- *140*
   Earlier sketch in SATA *65*
Hoyt, Olga
   See Gruhzit-Hoyt, Olga (Margaret)
Hrdlitschka, Shelley 1956- *167*
   Earlier sketch in SATA *111*
Hrdlitschka, Shelley Joanne
   See Hrdlitschka, Shelley
Hromic, Alma A.
   See Alexander, Alma
Htin Aung, U.
   See Aung, (Maung) Htin
Hu, Ying-Hwa *173*
Huang, Benrei 1959- *86*
Huang, Nathan 1982(?)- *228*
Hubalek, Linda K. 1954- *111*
Hubbard, Crystal *209*
Hubbard, Jennifer R. *227*
Hubbard, Margaret Ann
   See Priley, Margaret (Ann) Hubbard
Hubbard, Michelle Calabro 1953- *122*
Hubbard, Patricia 1945- *124*
Hubbard, Woodleigh Marx *160*
   Earlier sketch in SATA *98*
Hubbell, Patricia 1928- *186*
   Earlier sketches in SATA *8, 132*
Hubery, Julia *195*
Hubley, Faith Elliot 1924-2001 .... *48*
   Obituary *133*
Hubley, John 1914-1977 .... *48*
   Obituary *24*
Huck, Charlotte S. 1922- *136*
   Earlier sketch in SATA *82*
Hucke, Johannes 1966- *218*
Hudak, Michal 1956- *143*
Hudson, Cheryl Willis 1948- *237*
   Earlier sketches in SATA *81, 160*
Hudson, Jan 1954-1990 .... *77*
   See also CLR *40*
Hudson, Jeffery
   See Crichton, Michael
Hudson, Jeffrey
   See Crichton, Michael
Hudson, (Margaret) Kirsty 1947- *32*
Hudson, Margaret
   See Shuter, Jane (Margaret)
Hudson, W(illiam) H(enry) 1841-1922 .... *35*
Hudson, Wade 1946- *162*
   Earlier sketch in SATA *74*
Huelsmann, Eva 1928- *16*
Huerlimann, Bettina 1909-1983 .... *39*
   Obituary *34*

Huerlimann, Ruth 1939- *32*
   Brief entry *31*
Huff, Barbara A. 1929- *67*
Huff, Tanya 1957- *171*
   Earlier sketch in SATA *85*
Huff, Tanya Sue
   See Huff, Tanya
Huff, T.S.
   See Huff, Tanya
Huff, Vivian 1948- *59*
Huffaker, Sandy 1943- *10*
Huffman, Tom *24*
Huggins, Nathan Irvin 1927-1989 .... *63*
Huggins, Peter 1951- *178*
Hughes, Carol 1955- *217*
   Earlier sketch in SATA *108*
Hughes, Dean 1943- *235*
   Earlier sketches in SATA *33, 77, 139*
   See also CLR *76*
Hughes, D.T.
   See Hughes, Dean
Hughes, Eden
   See Griffin, W. E. B.
Hughes, Edward James
   See Hughes, Ted
Hughes, James Langston
   See Hughes, Langston
Hughes, Langston 1902-1967 .... *33*
   Earlier sketch in SATA *4*
   See also CLR *17*
Hughes, Libby *71*
Hughes, Matilda
   See MacLeod, Charlotte (Matilda)
Hughes, Monica 1925-2003 .... *162*
   Earlier sketches in SATA *15, 70, 119*
   See also CLR *60*
   See also SAAS *11*
Hughes, Monica Ince
   See Hughes, Monica
Hughes, Pat *197*
Hughes, Richard (Arthur Warren)
   1900-1976 .... *8*
   Obituary *25*
Hughes, Sara
   See Saunders, Susan
Hughes, Shirley 1927- *159*
   Earlier sketches in SATA *16, 70, 110*
   See also CLR *15*
Hughes, Susan 1960- *216*
Hughes, Ted 1930-1998 .... *49*
   Brief entry *27*
   Obituary *107*
   See also CLR *131*
Hughes, Thomas 1822-1896 .... *31*
   See also CLR *160*
Hughes, Virginia
   See Campbell, Hope
Hughes, Walter (Llewellyn) 1910-1993 .... *26*
Hughey, Roberta 1942- *61*
Hugo, Pierre Brackers de
   See Brackers de Hugo, Pierre
Hugo, Victor 1802-1885 .... *47*
Hugo, Victor Marie
   See Hugo, Victor
Huline-Dickens, Frank William 1931- *34*
Huling, Jan *172*
Huliska-Beith, Laura *232*
   Earlier sketch in SATA *175*
Hull, Eleanor (Means) 1913- *21*
Hull, Eric Traviss
   See Harnan, Terry
Hull, H. Braxton
   See Jacobs, Helen Hull
Hull, Jesse Redding
   See Hull, Jessie Redding
Hull, Jessie Redding 1932- *51*
Hull, Katharine 1921-1977 .... *23*
Hull, Lise (E.) 1954- *148*
Hull, Maureen 1949- *142*
Hulme, Joy N. 1922- *161*
   Earlier sketches in SATA *74, 112*

Hults, Dorothy Niebrugge 1898-2000 .... *6*
Humble, Richard 1945- *60*
Hume, Lachie *189*
Hume, Lotta Carswell *7*
Hume, Ruth Fox 1922-1980 .... *26*
   Obituary *22*
Hume, Stephen Eaton 1947- *136*
Hummel, Berta 1909-1946 .... *43*
Hummel, Sister Maria Innocentia
   See Hummel, Berta
Hummon, Marcus 1960- *213*
Humphrey, Carol Sue 1956- *167*
Humphrey, Henry (III) 1930- *16*
Humphrey, Kate
   See Forsyth, Kate
Humphrey, Sandra McLeod 1936- *95*
Humphreys, Martha 1943- *71*
Humphreys, Susan L.
   See Lowell, Susan
Humphries, Tudor 1953- *226*
Hundal, Nancy 1957- *128*
Huneck, Stephen 1949- *183*
   Earlier sketch in SATA *129*
Hungerford, Hesba Fay
   See Brinsmead, H(esba) F(ay)
Hungerford, Pixie
   See Brinsmead, H(esba) F(ay)
Hunkin, Tim 1950- *53*
Hunkin, Timothy Mark Trelawney
   See Hunkin, Tim
Hunt, Angela Elwell 1957- *159*
   Earlier sketch in SATA *75*
Hunt, Bernice 1920- *4*
Hunt, Charlotte Dumaresq
   See Demi
Hunt, Francesca
   See Holland, Isabelle (Christian)
Hunt, Irene 1907-2001 .... *91*
   Earlier sketch in SATA *2*
   See also CLR *1*
Hunt, Janie Louise 1963- *102*
Hunt, Jonathan 1966- *84*
Hunt, Joyce 1927- *31*
Hunt, Linda 1940- *39*
Hunt, Lisa B(ehnke) 1967- *84*
Hunt, Mabel Leigh 1892-1971 .... *1*
   Obituary *26*
Hunt, Morton M(agill) 1920- *22*
Hunt, Nigel
   See Greenbank, Anthony Hunt
Hunt, Peter (Leonard) 1945- *76*
Hunter, Anne B. 1966- *118*
Hunter, Bernice Thurman 1922-2002 .... *85*
   Brief entry *45*
Hunter, Bobbi Dooley 1945- *89*
Hunter, Captain Marcy
   See Ellis, Edward S.
Hunter, Chris
   See Fluke, Joanne
Hunter, Clingham M.D.
   See Adams, William Taylor
Hunter, Edith Fisher 1919- *31*
Hunter, Erin
   See Cary, Kate
Hunter, Evan 1926-2005 .... *25*
   Obituary *167*
Hunter, George E.
   See Ellis, Edward S.
Hunter, Hilda 1921- *7*
Hunter, Jana
   See Hunter, Jana Novotny
Hunter, Jana Novotny *190*
Hunter, Jim 1939- *65*
Hunter, Kristin
   See Lattany, Kristin Hunter
Hunter, Leigh
   See Etchison, Birdie L(ee)
Hunter, Lieutenant Ned
   See Ellis, Edward S.
Hunter, Linzie 1979- *227*
Hunter, Mel 1927-2004 .... *39*

Hunter, Mollie 1922- *139*
  Autobiography Feature *139*
  Earlier sketches in SATA *2, 54, 106*
  See also CLR *25*
  See also SAAS *7*
Hunter, Ned
  See Ellis, Edward S.
Hunter, Norman (George Lorimer)
  1899-1995 .... *84*
  Earlier sketch in SATA *26*
Hunter, Ryan Ann
  See Greenwood, Pamela D.
  and Macalaster, Elizabeth G.
Hunter, Sara Hoagland 1954- *98*
Hunter Blair, Pauline
  See Clarke, Pauline
Huntington, Amy 1956- *180*
  Earlier sketch in SATA *138*
Huntington, Geoffrey *145*
Huntington, Harriet E(lizabeth) 1909- *1*
Huntley, Amy *225*
Huntsberry, William E(mery) 1916- *5*
Hurd, Clement (G.) 1908-1988 .... *64*
  Obituary *54*
  Earlier sketch in SATA *2*
  See also CLR *49*
Hurd, Edith Thacher 1910-1997 .... *64*
  Obituary *95*
  Earlier sketch in SATA *2*
  See also CLR *49*
  See also SAAS *13*
Hurd, John Thacher
  See Hurd, Thacher
Hurd, Thacher 1949- *219*
  Autobiography Feature *123*
  Brief entry *45*
  Earlier sketches in SATA *46, 94*
Hurley, Jo
  See Dower, Laura
Hurley, Tonya *207*
Hurlimann, Bettina
  See Huerlimann, Bettina
Hurlimann, Ruth
  See Huerlimann, Ruth
Hurmence, Belinda 1921- *77*
  See also CLR *25*
  See also SAAS *20*
Hurst, Carol Otis 1933-2007 .... *185*
  Earlier sketch in SATA *130*
Hurt-Newton, Tania 1968- *84*
Hurwin, Davida Wills 1950- *180*
Hurwitz, Johanna 1937- *175*
  Earlier sketches in SATA *20, 71, 113*
  See also SAAS *18*
Hurwood, Bernhardt J. 1926-1987 .... *12*
  Obituary *50*
Husain, Shahrukh 1950- *108*
Huser, Glen 1943- *151*
Hutchens, Paul 1902-1977 .... *31*
Hutchins, Carleen M.
  See Hutchins, Carleen Maley
Hutchins, Carleen Maley 1911-2009 .... *9*
  Obituary *206*
Hutchins, Hazel J. 1952- *175*
  Brief entry *51*
  Earlier sketches in SATA *81, 135*
  See also SAAS *24*
Hutchins, Pat 1942- *178*
  Earlier sketches in SATA *15, 70, 111*
  See also CLR *20*
  See also SAAS *16*
Hutchins, Ross Elliott 1906- *4*
Hutchison, Linda 1942- *152*
Huthmacher, J. Joseph 1929- *5*
Hutto, Nelson (Allen) 1904-1985 .... *20*
Hutton, Kathryn 1915- *89*
Hutton, Sam
  See Jones, Allan Frewin
Hutton, Warwick 1939-1994 .... *20*
  Obituary *83*
  See also SAAS *17*

Huxley, Aldous 1894-1963 .... *63*
  See also CLR *151*
Huxley, Aldous Leonard
  See Huxley, Aldous
Huxley, Elspeth (Josceline Grant)
  1907-1997 .... *62*
  Obituary *95*
Hyde, Catherine *232*
Hyde, Catherine R.
  See Hyde, Catherine Ryan
Hyde, Catherine Ryan 1955- *224*
  Earlier sketch in SATA *141*
Hyde, Dayton O(gden) *9*
Hyde, Hawk
  See Hyde, Dayton O(gden)
Hyde, Jeannette
  See Eyerly, Jeannette
Hyde, Margaret O. 1917- *139*
  Earlier sketches in SATA *1, 42, 76*
  See also CLR *23*
  See also SAAS *8*
Hyde, Margaret Oldroyd
  See Hyde, Margaret O.
Hyde, Shelley
  See Reed, Kit
Hyde, Wayne Frederick 1922- *7*
Hylander, Clarence J(ohn) 1897-1964 .... *7*
Hyman, Miles 1962- *210*
Hyman, Paula Chase
  See Chase, Paula
Hyman, Robin 1931- *12*
Hyman, Robin Phiilip
  See Hyman, Robin
Hyman, Trina Schart 1939-2004 .... *95*
  Obituary *158*
  Earlier sketches in SATA *7, 46*
  See also CLR *50*
Hymes, Lucia M(anley) 1907-1998 .... *7*
Hyndman, Jane Andrews Lee 1912-1978 ..... *46*
  Obituary *23*
  Earlier sketch in SATA *1*
Hyndman, Robert Utley 1906-1973 .... *18*
Hynes, Pat *98*

I

Iannone, Jeanne
  See Balzano, Jeanne (Koppel)
Ibatoulline, Bagram 1965(?)- *225*
  Earlier sketch in SATA *174*
Ibbitson, John Perrie 1955- *102*
Ibbotson, Eva 1925-2010 .... *221*
  Earlier sketches in SATA *13, 103, 156*
Ibbotson, M. C(hristine) 1930- *5*
Icenoggle, Jodi 1967- *168*
Icenoggle, Jodi O.
  See Icenoggle, Jodi
Ichikawa, Satomi 1949- *208*
  Brief entry *36*
  Earlier sketches in SATA *47, 78, 146*
  See also CLR *62*
Idle, Molly Schaar *223*
Iggulden, Hal 1972- *196*
Ignatow, Amy 1977- *233*
Ignoffo, Matthew 1945- *92*
Igus, Toyomi 1953- *112*
  Earlier sketch in SATA *76*
Ihimaera, Witi (Tame) 1944- *148*
Ikeda, Daisaku 1928- *77*
Ilowite, Sheldon A. 1931- *27*
Ilsey, Dent
  See Chapman, John Stanton Higham
Ilsley, Dent
  See Chapman, John Stanton Higham
Ilsley, Velma (Elizabeth) 1918- *12*
Imai, Ayano 1980- *190*
Imai, Miko 1963- *90*
Imershein, Betsy 1953- *62*
Immel, Mary Blair 1930- *28*

Immell, Myra H. 1941- *92*
Impey, Rose 1947- *223*
  Earlier sketches in SATA *69, 152*
Ingalls, Ann *227*
Ingelow, Jean 1820-1897 .... *33*
Ingermanson, Randall 1958- *134*
Ingermanson, Randy
  See Ingermanson, Randall
Ingersoll, Norman 1928- *79*
Ingham, Colonel Frederic
  See Hale, Edward Everett
Ingman, Bruce 1963- *182*
  Earlier sketch in SATA *134*
Ingman, Nicholas 1948- *52*
Ingold, Jeanette *128*
Ingpen, Robert 1936- *166*
  Earlier sketch in SATA *109*
Ingpen, Robert Roger
  See Ingpen, Robert
Ingraham, Erick 1950- *145*
Ingraham, Leonard W(illiam) 1913-2003 .... *4*
Ingram, Scott 1948- *167*
  Earlier sketch in SATA *92*
Ingram, W. Scott
  See Ingram, Scott
Ingrams, Doreen 1906-1997 .... *97*
  Earlier sketch in SATA *20*
Ingrid, Charles
  See Salsitz, Rhondi Vilott
Ingves, Gunilla 1939- *101*
Ingves, Gunilla Anna Maria Folkesdotter
  See Ingves, Gunilla
Inkpen, Mick 1952- *154*
  Earlier sketch in SATA *99*
Innerst, Stacy *232*
Innes, (Ralph) Hammond
  See Hammond Innes, Ralph
Innes, Ralph Hammond
  See Hammond Innes, Ralph
Innes, Stephanie *220*
Innocenti, Roberto 1940- *159*
  Earlier sketch in SATA *96*
  See also CLR *126*
Innocenti and Gallaz
  See Gallaz, Christophe
  and Innocenti, Roberto
Inns, Chris *212*
Inyart, Gene
  See Namovicz, Gene Inyart
Ionesco, Eugene 1909-1994 .... *7*
  Obituary *79*
Ipcar, Dahlov (Zorach) 1917- *147*
  Autobiography Feature *147*
  Earlier sketches in SATA *1, 49*
  See also SAAS *8*
Ireland, Karin *151*
  Earlier sketch in SATA *101*
Ironside, Jetske 1940- *60*
Irvin, Fred 1914- *15*
Irvine, Georgeanne 1955- *72*
Irvine, Joan 1951- *80*
Irving, Alexander
  See Hume, Ruth Fox
Irving, Robert
  See Adler, Irving
Irving, Washington 1783-1859
  See YABC *2*
  See also CLR *97*
Irwin, Ann(abelle Bowen) 1915-1998 .... *89*
  Brief entry *38*
  Obituary *106*
  Earlier sketch in SATA *44*
  See also CLR *40*
  See also SAAS *14*
Irwin, Constance (H.) Frick 1913-1995 .... *6*
Irwin, Hadley
  See Hadley, Lee
  and Irwin, Ann(abelle Bowen)
Irwin, Keith Gordon 1885-1964 .... *11*
Isaac, Joanne 1934- *21*

Isaacs, Anne 1949- *185*
  Earlier sketch in SATA *90*
Isaacs, Jacob
  See Kranzler, George G(ershon)
Isaacson, Philip M(arshal) 1924- *87*
Isadora, Rachel 1953(?)- *204*
  Brief entry *32*
  Earlier sketches in SATA *54, 79, 121, 165*
  See also CLR *7*
Isbell, Rebecca T(emple) 1942- *125*
Isham, Charlotte H(ickock) 1912- *21*
Ishida, Jui *176*
Ish-Kishor, Judith 1892-1972 .... *11*
Ish-Kishor, Sulamith 1896-1977 .... *17*
Ishmael, Woodi 1914-1995 .... *31*
  Obituary *109*
Isle, Sue 1963- *105*
Isol 1972- *220*
Israel, Elaine 1945- *12*
Israel, Marion Louise 1882-1973
  Obituary *26*
Iterson, S(iny) R(ose) Van
  See Van Iterson, S(iny) R(ose)
Ivanko, John D. 1966- *111*
Ivanko, John Duane
  See Ivanko, John D.
Iversen, Jeremy 1980(?)- *174*
Iversen, Jeremy Watt
  See Iversen, Jeremy
Iverson, Carol (L.) 1941- *145*
Iverson, Diane 1950- *122*
Iverson, Eric G.
  See Turtledove, Harry
Ivery, Martha M. 1948- *124*
Ives, David 1951- *173*
Ives, Morgan
  See Bradley, Marion Zimmer
Ives, Penny 1956- *215*
Iwai, Melissa *183*
Iwamatsu, Jun Atsushi 1908-1994 .... *81*
  Earlier sketch in SATA *14*
  See also CLR *4*
Iwamura, Kazuo 1939- *213*
Iwasaki (Matsumoto), Chihiro 1918-1974
  See CLR *18*
Iyengar, Malathi Michelle 1954- *220*

J

Jabar, Cynthia *210*
Jablonski, Carla *184*
Jac, Lee
  See Morton, Lee Jack, Jr.
Jack, Colin *234*
Jacka, Martin 1943- *72*
Jackson, Alison 1953- *228*
  Earlier sketches in SATA *73, 108, 160*
Jackson, Anne 1896(?)-1984
  Obituary *37*
Jackson, Barry
  See Jackson, Barry E.
Jackson, Barry E. *200*
Jackson, C(aary) Paul 1902-1991 .... *6*
Jackson, Caary
  See Jackson, C(aary) Paul
Jackson, Charlotte E. (Cobden) 1903(?)-1989
  Obituary *62*
Jackson, Dave
  See Jackson, J. David
Jackson, Donna M. 1959- *206*
Jackson, Ellen 1943- *214*
  Earlier sketches in SATA *75, 115, 167*
Jackson, Ellen B.
  See Jackson, Ellen
Jackson, Garnet Nelson 1944- *87*
Jackson, Geoffrey (Holt Seymour) 1915-1987
  Obituary *53*
Jackson, Gina
  See Fluke, Joanne

Jackson, Guida M. 1930- *71*
Jackson, J. David 1944- *91*
Jackson, Jacqueline 1928- *65*
Jackson, Jacqueline Dougan
  See Jackson, Jacqueline
Jackson, Jesse 1908-1983 .... *29*
  Obituary *48*
  Earlier sketch in SATA *2*
  See also CLR *28*
Jackson, Marjorie 1928- *127*
Jackson, Melanie 1956- *141*
Jackson, Mike 1946- *91*
Jackson, Neta J. 1944- *91*
Jackson, O. B.
  See Jackson, C(aary) Paul
Jackson, Rob 1961- *176*
Jackson, Robert B(lake) 1926- *8*
Jackson, Robert Bradley
  See Jackson, Rob
Jackson, Sally
  See Kellogg, Jean (Defrees)
Jackson, Shirley 1919-1965 .... *2*
Jackson, Woody 1948- *92*
Jackson Issa, Kai *205*
Jacob, Helen Pierce 1927- *21*
Jacobin
  See Bisson, Terry
Jacobs, Deborah Lynn *187*
Jacobs, Flora Gill 1918-2006 .... *5*
  Obituary *178*
Jacobs, Francine 1935- *150*
  Brief entry *42*
  Earlier sketch in SATA *43*
Jacobs, Frank 1929- *30*
Jacobs, Helen Hull 1908-1997 .... *12*
Jacobs, Joseph 1854-1916 .... *25*
Jacobs, Judy 1952- *69*
Jacobs, Laurie A. 1956- *89*
Jacobs, Leah
  See Gellis, Roberta
Jacobs, Lee
  See Stone, Tanya Lee
Jacobs, Leland Blair 1907-1992 .... *20*
  Obituary *71*
Jacobs, Linda
  See Altman, Linda Jacobs
Jacobs, Lou(is), Jr. 1921- *2*
Jacobs, Paul DuBois *235*
Jacobs, Shannon K. 1947- *77*
Jacobs, Susan
  See Quinn, Susan
Jacobs, William Jay 1933- *89*
  Earlier sketch in SATA *28*
Jacobsen, Laura *177*
Jacobson, Andrew *235*
Jacobson, Daniel 1923- *12*
Jacobson, Jennifer
  See Jacobson, Jennifer Richard
Jacobson, Jennifer Richard 1958- *233*
  Earlier sketch in SATA *170*
Jacobson, Morris K(arl) 1906- *21*
Jacobson, Rick *170*
Jacobus, Tim 1959- *234*
Jacopetti, Alexandra
  See Hart, Alexandra
Jacques, Brian 1939-2011 .... *176*
  Earlier sketches in SATA *62, 95, 138*
  See also CLR *21*
Jacques, Robin 1920-1995 .... *32*
  Brief entry *30*
  Obituary *86*
  See also SAAS *5*
Jaekel, Susan M. 1948- *89*
Jaffe, Michele *179*
Jaffe, Michele Sharon
  See Jaffe, Michele
Jaffee, Al(lan) 1921- *66*
  Earlier sketch in SATA *37*
Jagendorf, Moritz (Adolf) 1888-1981 .... *2*
  Obituary *24*
Jago 1979- *216*

Jahn, Joseph Michael
  See Jahn, Michael
Jahn, Michael 1943- *28*
Jahn, Mike
  See Jahn, Michael
Jahn-Clough, Lisa 1967- *193*
  Earlier sketches in SATA *88, 152*
Jahsmann, Allan Hart 1916- *28*
Jakes, John 1932- *62*
Jakes, John William
  See Jakes, John
Jalali, Reza *234*
James, Andrew
  See Kirkup, James
James, Ann 1952- *168*
  Earlier sketches in SATA *82, 117*
James, Betsy *183*
James, Bill 1929- *205*
James, B.J.
  See James, Brian
James, Brian 1976- *212*
  Earlier sketch in SATA *140*
James, Bronte
  See Nash, Renea Denise
James, Captain Lew
  See Stratemeyer, Edward L.
James, Charlie 1961- *185*
James, Curtis E. *182*
James, Dynely
  See Mayne, William
James, Edwin
  See Gunn, James E.
James, Elizabeth 1942- *97*
  Earlier sketches in SATA *39, 45, 52*
James, Emily
  See Standiford, Natalie
James, Gordon C. 1973- *195*
James, Harry Clebourne 1896-1978 .... *11*
James, J. Alison 1962- *146*
  Earlier sketch in SATA *83*
James, Josephine
  See Sterne, Emma Gelders
James, Mary
  See Meaker, Marijane
James, Matt *201*
James, Philip
  See del Rey, Lester
  and Moorcock, Michael
James, Rhian Nest *235*
James, Robin 1953- *50*
James, Robin Irene
  See James, Robin
James, Simon 1961- *202*
James, T. F.
  See Fleming, Thomas
James, Tegan
  See Odgers, Sally Farrell
James, Will(iam Roderick) 1892-1942 .... *19*
Jameson, W. C. 1942- *93*
Jamieson, Ian R.
  See Goulart, Ron
Jamieson, Victoria *218*
Jamiolkowski, Raymond M. 1953- *81*
Jane, Mary Childs 1909-1991 .... *6*
Jane, Pamela *158*
Janeczko, Paul B(ryan) 1945- *155*
  Earlier sketches in SATA *53, 98*
  See also CLR *47*
  See also SAAS *18*
Janes, Edward C. 1908-1984 .... *25*
Janes, Edward Clarence
  See Janes, Edward C.
Janes, J(oseph) Robert 1935- *148*
  Brief entry *50*
  Earlier sketch in SATA *101*
Janeway, Elizabeth (Hall) 1913-2005 .... *19*
Janger, Kathleen N. 1940- *66*
Jango-Cohen, Judith 1955- *208*
Janice
  See Brustlein, Janice Tworkov
Janisch, Heinz 1960- *181*

Janni, Rebecca 229
Janosch
   See Eckert, Horst
Janover, Caroline (Davis) 1943- 141
   Earlier sketch in SATA 89
Janovitz, Marilyn 194
Jansen, Jared
   See Cebulash, Mel
Janson, Dora Jane (Heineberg) 1916- 31
Janson, H(orst) W(oldemar) 1913-1982 9
Jansson, Tove (Marika) 1914-2001 41
   Earlier sketch in SATA 3
   See also CLR 125
Janus, Grete
   See Hertz, Grete Janus
Jaques, Faith 1923-1997 97
   Earlier sketches in SATA 21, 69
Jaquith, Priscilla 1908- 51
Jaramillo, Mari-Luci 1928- 139
Jarka, Jeff 221
Jarman, Julia 1946- 198
   Earlier sketch in SATA 133
Jarman, Rosemary Hawley 1935- 7
Jarrell, Mary Von Schrader 1914- 35
Jarrell, Randall 1914-1965 7
   See also CLR 111
Jarrett, Clare 1952- 201
Jarrett, Roxanne
   See Werner, Herma
Jarrie, Martin 1953- 219
Jarrow, Gail 1952- 185
   Earlier sketch in SATA 84
Jarvis, E.K.
   See Ellison, Harlan
   and Silverberg, Robert
Jarvis, Robin 1963- 181
Jarzab, Anna 1984- 227
Jaskol, Julie 1958- 127
Jasner, W. K.
   See Watson, Jane Werner
Jassem, Kate
   See Oppenheim, Joanne
Jauss, Anne Marie 1902(?)-1991 10
   Obituary 69
Javaherbin, Mina 230
Javernick, Ellen 1938- 217
   Earlier sketch in SATA 89
Javins, Marie 1966- 212
Jay, Alison 196
Jay, Stacey 1978(?)- 231
Jayne, Lieutenant R. H.
   See Ellis, Edward S.
Jaynes, Clare
   See Mayer, Jane Rothschild
Jeake, Samuel, Jr.
   See Aiken, Conrad
Jean-Bart, Leslie 1954- 121
Jeapes, Ben 1965- 174
Jecan, Gavriel 1962- 200
Jefferds, Vincent H(arris) 1916- 59
   Brief entry 49
Jefferies, (John) Richard 1848-1887 16
Jeffers, Dawn 189
Jeffers, Oliver 1977- 213
   Earlier sketch in SATA 175
Jeffers, Susan 1942- 202
   Earlier sketches in SATA 17, 70, 129, 137
   See also CLR 30
Jefferson, Sarah
   See Farjeon, (Eve) Annabel
Jeffries, Roderic 1926- 4
Jeffries, Roderic Graeme
   See Jeffries, Roderic
Jenkin-Pearce, Susie 1943- 80
Jenkins, A. M. 1961- 174
Jenkins, Amanda McRaney
   See Jenkins, A. M.
Jenkins, Debra Reid
   See Reid Jenkins, Debra
Jenkins, Emily 1967- 174
   Earlier sketch in SATA 144

Jenkins, Jean 98
Jenkins, Jerry B. 1949- 149
Jenkins, Jerry Bruce
   See Jenkins, Jerry B.
Jenkins, Leonard 189
Jenkins, Marie M(agdalen) 1909- 7
Jenkins, Martin 1959- 216
Jenkins, M.D.
   See Jenkins, Martin
Jenkins, Patrick 1955- 72
Jenkins, Steve 1952- 218
   Earlier sketches in SATA 154, 188
Jenkins, William A(twell) 1922-1998 9
Jenkyns, Chris 1924- 51
Jennewein, James 215
Jennewein, Jim
   See Jennewein, James
Jennings, Christopher S. 1971(?)- 201
Jennings, Coleman A(lonzo) 1933- 64
Jennings, C.S.
   See Jennings, Christopher S.
Jennings, Dana Andrew 1957- 93
Jennings, Elizabeth (Joan) 1926-2001 66
Jennings, Gary 1928-1999 9
   Obituary 117
Jennings, Gary Gayne
   See Jennings, Gary
Jennings, Linda 1937- 211
Jennings, Linda M.
   See Jennings, Linda
Jennings, Patrick 1962- 205
   Earlier sketches in SATA 96, 160
Jennings, Paul 1943- 165
   Earlier sketch in SATA 88
   See also CLR 40
Jennings, Richard W. 1945- 185
   Earlier sketch in SATA 136
Jennings, Robert
   See Hamilton, Charles (Harold St. John)
Jennings, S. M.
   See Meyer, Jerome Sydney
Jennings, Sharon 1954- 231
   Earlier sketch in SATA 95
Jennings, Sharon Elizabeth
   See Jennings, Sharon
Jennison, C. S.
   See Starbird, Kaye
Jennison, Keith Warren 1911-1995 14
Jensen, Kathryn 1949- 81
Jensen, Kristine Mary 1961- 78
Jensen, Niels 1927- 25
Jensen, Vickie (Dee) 1946- 81
Jensen, Virginia Allen 1927- 8
Jenson-Elliott, Cynthia L(ouise) 1962- 143
Jeram, Anita 1965- 219
   Earlier sketches in SATA 71, 102, 154
Jerman, Jerry 1949- 89
Jernigan, E. Wesley 1940- 85
Jernigan, Gisela (Evelyn) 1948- 85
Jerome, Elaine 228
Jeschke, Susan 1942- 42
   Brief entry 27
Jessel, Camilla (Ruth) 1937- 143
   Earlier sketch in SATA 29
Jessell, Tim 225
   Earlier sketch in SATA 177
Jessey, Cornelia
   See Sussman, Cornelia Silver
Jewel
   See Kilcher, Jewel
Jewell, Nancy 1940- 109
   Brief entry 41
Jewett, Eleanore Myers 1890-1967 5
Jewett, Sarah Orne 1849-1909 15
Jewett, Theodora Sarah Orne
   See Jewett, Sarah Orne
Jezard, Alison 1919- 57
   Brief entry 34
Jiang, Cheng An 1943- 109
Jiang, Ji-li 1954- 101

Jiang, Zheng An
   See Jiang, Cheng An
Jiler, John 1946- 42
   Brief entry 35
Jimenez, Francisco 1943- 219
   Earlier sketch in SATA 108
Jinks, Catherine 1963- 207
   Earlier sketches in SATA 94, 155
Jobb, Jamie 1945- 29
Jobling, Curtis 131
Jocelyn, Ann Henning 1948- 92
Jocelyn, Marthe 1956- 198
   Earlier sketches in SATA 118, 163
Joerns, Consuelo 44
   Brief entry 33
Joey D
   See Macaulay, Teresa
Johansen, Krista V.
   See Johansen, K.V.
Johansen, K.V 1968- 186
Johansen, K.V. 1968- 186
   Earlier sketch in SATA 129
Johansson, Philip 163
John, Antony 1972- 206
John, Joyce 59
Johns, Avery
   See Cousins, Margaret
Johns, Elizabeth 1943- 88
Johns, Janetta
   See Quin-Harkin, Janet
Johns, Linda 1945- 173
Johns, W(illiam) E(arle) 1893-1968 55
Johns, Captain W. E.
   See Johns, W(illiam) E(arle)
Johnson, A.
   See Johnson, Annabell
Johnson, A. E.
   See Johnson, Annabell
   and Johnson, Edgar (Raymond)
Johnson, Angela 1961- 188
   Earlier sketches in SATA 69, 102, 150
   See also CLR 33
Johnson, Annabel
   See Johnson, Annabell
Johnson, Annabell 1921- 72
   Earlier sketch in SATA 2
Johnson, Art 1946- 123
Johnson, B. F. 1920- 1
Johnson, Benjamin F., of Boone
   See Riley, James Whitcomb
Johnson, Bettye 1858-1919
   See Rogers, Bettye
Johnson, Caryn
   See Goldberg, Whoopi
Johnson, Caryn E.
   See Goldberg, Whoopi
Johnson, Caryn Elaine
   See Goldberg, Whoopi
Johnson, Charles R. 1925- 11
Johnson, Charlotte Buel
   See von Wodtke, Charlotte Buel Johnson
Johnson, Christine 1978- 232
Johnson, Chuck
   See Johnson, Charles R.
Johnson, Crockett
   See Leisk, David (Johnson)
Johnson, D(ana) William 1945- 23
Johnson, Daniel Shahid 1954- 73
Johnson, David
   See Johnson, David A.
Johnson, David A. 1951- 191
Johnson, D.B. 1944- 183
   Earlier sketch in SATA 146
Johnson, Dianne 1960- 130
   See Johnson, Dinah
Johnson, Dinah 231
   See Johnson, Dianne
Johnson, Dolores 1949- 69
Johnson, Donald B.
   See Johnson, D.B.

Johnson, Dorothy M(arie) 1905-1984 6
  Obituary 40
Johnson, E(ugene) Harper 44
Johnson, Edgar (Raymond) 1912-1990 72
  Earlier sketch in SATA 2
Johnson, Eleanor Murdock 1892-1987
  Obituary 54
Johnson, Elizabeth 1911-1984 7
  Obituary 39
Johnson, Eric W(arner) 1918-1994 ....
  Obituary 82
  Earlier sketch in SATA 8
Johnson, Evelyne 1922- 20
Johnson, Fred 19(?)-1982 63
Johnson, Gaylord 1884-1972 7
Johnson, Gerald White 1890-1980 19
  Obituary 28
Johnson, Gillian 1963- 215
Johnson, Harper
  See Johnson, E(ugene) Harper
Johnson, Harriett 1908-1987
  Obituary 53
Johnson, James Ralph 1922- 1
Johnson, James Weldon 1871-1938 31
  See also CLR 32
Johnson, Jane 1951- 48
Johnson, Jen Cullerton 1972- 230
Johnson, Joan J. 1942- 59
Johnson, John E(mil) 1929- 34
Johnson, Johnny 1901-1995
  See Johnson, (Walter) Ryerson
Johnson, Kathleen Jeffrie 1950- 186
Johnson, Kathryn
  See Jensen, Kathryn
Johnson, La Verne B(ravo) 1925- 13
Johnson, Layne 222
  Earlier sketch in SATA 187
Johnson, Lee Kaiser 1962- 78
Johnson, Lissa H(alls) 1955- 65
Johnson, Lois Smith 1894-1993 6
Johnson, Lois Walfrid 1936- 130
  Earlier sketches in SATA 22, 91
Johnson, Margaret S(weet) 1893-1964 35
Johnson, Marguerite Annie
  See Angelou, Maya
Johnson, Mary Frances K. 1929(?)-1979
  Obituary 27
Johnson, Maud Battle 1918(?)-1985
  Obituary 46
Johnson, Maureen 1973- 232
  Earlier sketch in SATA 200
Johnson, Meredith Merrell 1952- 104
Johnson, Milton 1932- 31
Johnson, Mo 1966- 234
Johnson, Neil 1954- 135
  Earlier sketch in SATA 73
Johnson, Pamela 1949- 71
Johnson, Patricia Polin 1956- 84
Johnson, Paul Brett 1947- 132
  Earlier sketch in SATA 83
Johnson, Rebecca L. 1956- 147
  Earlier sketch in SATA 67
Johnson, Rick L. 1954- 79
Johnson, (Walter) Ryerson 1901-1995 10
  Obituary 106
Johnson, Scott 1952- 119
  Earlier sketch in SATA 76
Johnson, Sherrie 1948- 87
Johnson, Shirley K(ing) 1927- 10
Johnson, Siddie Joe 1905-1977
  Obituary 20
Johnson, Spencer 1938- 145
  Brief entry 38
Johnson, Stacie
  See Myers, Walter Dean
Johnson, Stephen T. 1964- 189
  Earlier sketches in SATA 84, 141
Johnson, Steve 1960- 230
  Earlier sketch in SATA 177
Johnson, Sue Kaiser 1963- 78

Johnson, Sylvia A. 166
  Brief entry 52
  Earlier sketch in SATA 104
Johnson, Varian 1977- 229
Johnson, William R. 38
Johnson, William Weber 1909-1992 7
Johnson-Feelings, Dianne
  See Johnson, Dianne
Johnson, Agnes Christine
  See Dazey, Agnes J(ohnston)
Johnston, Annie Fellows 1863-1931 37
Johnston, Dorothy Grunbock 1915-1979 54
Johnston, Ginny 1946- 60
Johnston, H(ugh) A(nthony) S(tephen)
  1913-1967 14
Johnston, Janet 1944- 71
Johnston, Jeffry W. 188
Johnston, Johanna 1914(?)-1982 12
  Obituary 33
Johnston, Julie 1941- 110
  Autobiography Feature 128
  Earlier sketch in SATA 78
  See also CLR 41
  See also SAAS 24
Johnston, Lynn 1947- 216
  Earlier sketch in SATA 118
Johnston, Lynn Beverley
  See Johnston, Lynn
Johnston, Mark 194
Johnston, Norma
  See St. John, Nicole
Johnston, Portia
  See Takakjian, Portia
Johnston, Susan Taylor 1942- 180
  Earlier sketches in SATA 8, 83, 128
  See Johnston, Tony
Johnston, Tim(othy Patrick) 1962- 146
Johnston, Tony 226
  See Johnston, Susan Taylor
Joinson, Carla 160
Jolin, Paula 186
Jolivet, Joelle 1965- 221
Jonas, Ann 1932- 135
  Brief entry 42
  Earlier sketch in SATA 50
  See also CLR 74
Jonell, Lynne 1956- 196
  Earlier sketch in SATA 109
Jones, Adrienne 1915-2000 82
  Earlier sketch in SATA 7
  See also SAAS 10
Jones, Allan Frewin 1954- 204
Jones, Annabel
  See Lewis, Mary
Jones, Betty Millsaps 1940- 54
Jones, Carol 1942- 153
  Earlier sketch in SATA 79
Jones, Carrie 1971- 229
  Earlier sketch in SATA 191
Jones, Charles M.
  See Jones, Chuck
Jones, Charlotte Foltz 1945- 122
  Earlier sketch in SATA 77
Jones, Chuck 1912-2002 53
  Obituary 133
Jones, Constance 112
Jones, Constance A.
  See Jones, Constance
Jones, David 1956- 202
Jones, Diana Wynne 1934-2011 234
  Earlier sketches in SATA 9, 70, 108, 160
  See also CLR 120
  See also SAAS 7
Jones, Douglas B. 202
Jones, Douglas C(lyde) 1924-1998 52
Jones, Elizabeth McDavid 155
Jones, Elizabeth Orton 1910-2005 18
  Obituary 164
Jones, Evan 1915-1996 3
Jones, Frewin
  See Jones, Allan Frewin

Jones, Geraldine
  See McCaughrean, Geraldine
Jones, Gillingham
  See Hamilton, Charles (Harold St. John)
Jones, Gwyneth A. 1952- 159
Jones, Gwyneth Ann
  See Jones, Gwyneth A.
Jones, Harold 1904-1992 14
  Obituary 72
Jones, Helen Hinckley 1903-1991 26
Jones, Helen L(ouise) 1903-1973
  Obituary 22
Jones, Hettie 1934- 42
  Brief entry 27
Jones, Hortense P. 1918- 9
Jones, J. Sydney 1948- 101
Jones, Jasmine
  See Papademetriou, Lisa
Jones, Jennifer (Berry) 1947- 90
Jones, Jessie Mae Orton 1887(?)-1983
  Obituary 37
Jones, John R(obert) 1926- 76
Jones, Jon Sydney
  See Jones, J. Sydney
Jones, Judith
  See James, Bill
Jones, Kimberly K. 1957- 187
Jones, Marcia Thornton 1958- 217
  Earlier sketches in SATA 73, 115
Jones, Martha T(annery) 1931- 130
Jones, Mary Alice 1898(?)-1980 6
Jones, McClure 34
Jones, Noah Z. 182
Jones, Patrick 1961- 210
  Earlier sketch in SATA 136
Jones, Penelope 1938- 31
Jones, Rebecca C(astaldi) 1947- 99
  Earlier sketch in SATA 33
Jones, Robin D(orothy) 1959- 80
Jones, Sanford W.
  See Thorn, John
Jones, Sylvie 185
Jones, Sylvie Michelle
  See Jones, Sylvie
Jones, Terence Graham Parry 1942- 127
  Brief entry 51
  Earlier sketch in SATA 67
Jones, Terry
  See Jones, Terence Graham Parry
Jones, Tim 237
Jones, Tim Wynne
  See Wynne-Jones, Tim
Jones, Traci L. 186
Jones, V. M. 1958- 147
Jones, Veda Boyd 1948- 119
Jones, Victoria Mary
  See Jones, V. M.
Jones, Volcano
  See Mitchell, Adrian
Jones, Weyman (B.) 1928- 4
  See also SAAS 11
Jones, William Glynne
  See Glynne-Jones, William
Jonk, Clarence 1906-1987 10
Jonsberg, Barry 1951- 168
Joos, Francoise 1956- 78
Joos, Frederic 1953- 78
Joosse, Barbara 1949- 220
  Earlier sketches in SATA 52, 96, 164
Joosse, Barbara M.
  See Joosse, Barbara
Joosse, Barbara Monnot
  See Joosse, Barbara
Jordan, Alexis Hill
  See Glick, Ruth
  and Titchener, Louise
Jordan, Anne Devereaux 1943- 80
Jordan, Chris
  See Philbrick, Rodman
Jordan, Deloris 191
Jordan, Devin 221

Jordan, Don
    See Howard, Vernon (Linwood)
Jordan, Hope Dahle 1905-1995 .... *15*
Jordan, Jael (Michal) 1949- *30*
Jordan, June 1936-2002 .... *136*
    Earlier sketch in SATA *4*
    See also CLR *10*
Jordan, June Meyer
    See Jordan, June
Jordan, Lee
    See Scholefield, Alan
Jordan, Martin George 1944- *84*
Jordan, Robert 1948-2007 .... *95*
Jordan, Robert K.
    See Jordan, Robert
Jordan, Rosa 1939- *191*
Jordan, Roslyn M. *189*
Jordan, Sherryl 1949- *122*
    Earlier sketch in SATA *71*
    See also SAAS *23*
Jordan, Shirley 1930- *154*
Jordan, Tanis 1946- *84*
Jorgensen, Ivar
    See Ellison, Harlan
    and Garrett, Randall
Jorgensen, Mary Venn -1995 .... *36*
Jorgensen, Norman 1954- *157*
Jorgenson, Ivar
    See Silverberg, Robert
Jorisch, Stephane *178*
Joseph, Anne
    See Coates, Anna
Joseph, Danielle 1973- *235*
Joseph, James (Herz) 1924- *53*
Joseph, Joan 1939- *34*
Joseph, Joseph M(aron) 1903-1979 .... *22*
Joseph, Patrick
    See O'Malley, Kevin
Josephs, Rebecca
    See Talbot, Toby
Josephson, Judith Pinkerton 1943- *198*
Josh
    See Twain, Mark
Joshua, Peter
    See Stone, Peter
Joslin, Mary 1953- *176*
Joslin, Sesyle
    See Hine, Sesyle Joslin
Joubert, Beverly 1957- *204*
Joubert, Dereck *204*
Journet, Mireille
    See Marokvia, Mireille
Joyce, Bill
    See Joyce, William
Joyce, J(ames) Avery 1902-1987 .... *11*
    Obituary *50*
Joyce, Peter 1937- *127*
Joyce, William 1957- *118*
    Brief entry *46*
    Earlier sketch in SATA *72*
    See also CLR *26*
Joyner, Jerry 1938- *34*
Juan, Ana 1961- *179*
Juarez, Fernando *230*
Juarez, Fernando Lopez
    See Juarez, Fernando
Jubb, Sophie *210*
Jubert, Herve *185*
Juby, Susan 1969- *202*
    Earlier sketch in SATA *156*
Jucker, Sita 1921- *5*
Judah, Aaron 1923- *118*
Judd, Cyril
    See Kornbluth, C(yril) M.
    and Merril, Judith
    and Pohl, Frederik
Judd, Denis (O'Nan) 1938- *33*
Judd, Frances K.
    See Benson, Mildred
Jude, Conny *81*

Judge, Lita *234*
    Earlier sketch in SATA *192*
Judson, Clara Ingram 1879-1960 .... *38*
    Brief entry *27*
Judy, Stephen
    See Tchudi, Stephen N.
Judy, Stephen N.
    See Tchudi, Stephen N.
Juhasz, Victor 1954- *177*
Jukes, Mavis 1947- *219*
    Brief entry *43*
    Earlier sketches in SATA *72, 111*
    See also SAAS *12*
Jules, Jacqueline 1956- *218*
    Earlier sketches in SATA *148, 183*
Julesberg, Elizabeth Rider Montgomery
    1902-1985 .... *34*
    Obituary *41*
    Earlier sketch in SATA *3*
Julian, Jane
    See Wiseman, David
Julian, Russell 1975- *237*
Julian, Sean *236*
Jumpp, Hugo
    See MacPeek, Walter G.
Junco, Martha Aviles
    See Aviles, Martha
Jungman, Ann *165*
Jupo, Frank J. 1904-1981 .... *7*
Jurmain, Suzanne 1945- *169*
    Earlier sketch in SATA *72*
Jurmain, Suzanne Tripp
    See Jurmain, Suzanne
Juster, Norton 1929- *220*
    Earlier sketches in SATA *3, 132*
    See also CLR *112*
Justus, May 1898-1989 .... *1*
    Obituary *106*
Jutte, Jan 1953- *231*
Juvenilia
    See Taylor, Ann

K

Kaaberbol, Lene
    See Kaaberbol, Lene
Kaaberbol, Lene 1960- *159*
Kabdebo, Tamas
    See Kabdebo, Thomas
Kabdebo, Thomas 1934- *10*
Kabibble, Osh
    See Jobb, Jamie
Kacer, Kathy 1954- *184*
    Earlier sketch in SATA *142*
Kaczman, James *156*
Kadair, Deborah Ousley *184*
Kade, Stacey *234*
Kadefors, Sara 1965- *218*
Kadesch, Robert R(udstone) 1922- *31*
Kadohata, Cynthia 1956(?)- *228*
    Earlier sketches in SATA *155, 180*
    See also CLR *121*
Kadohata, Cynthia L.
    See Kadohata, Cynthia
Kaempfert, Wade
    See del Rey, Lester
Kaestner, Erich 1899-1974 .... *14*
    See also CLR *153*
Kagawa, Julie *228*
Kahl, Jonathan (D.) 1959- *77*
Kahl, M(arvin) P(hilip) 1934- *37*
Kahl, Virginia (Caroline) 1919-2004 .... *48*
    Brief entry *38*
    Obituary *158*
Kahn, Joan 1914-1994 .... *48*
    Obituary *82*
Kahn, Katherine Janus 1942- *220*
    Earlier sketches in SATA *90, 167*

Kahn, Peggy
    See Katz, Bobbi
Kahn, Roger 1927- *37*
Kahukiwa, Robyn 1940- *134*
Kains, Josephine
    See Goulart, Ron
Kaizuki, Kiyonori 1950- *72*
Kajikawa, Kimiko *212*
Kakimoto, Kozo 1915- *11*
Kalashnikoff, Nicholas 1888-1961 .... *16*
Kalb, Jonah 1926- *23*
Kalbacken, Joan 1925- *96*
Kalechofsky, Roberta 1931- *92*
Kaler, James Otis 1848-1912 .... *15*
Kalis, Jennifer *207*
Kalish, Claire M. 1947- *92*
Kallen, Stuart A. 1955- *126*
    Earlier sketch in SATA *86*
Kallen, Stuart Arnold
    See Kallen, Stuart A.
Kallevig, Christine Petrell 1955- *164*
Kalman, Bobbie 1947- *63*
Kalman, Maira 1949- *137*
    Earlier sketch in SATA *96*
    See also CLR *32*
Kalnay, Francis 1899-1992 .... *7*
Kaloustian, Rosanne 1955- *93*
Kalow, Gisela 1946- *32*
Kalstein, Dave *175*
Kamara, Mariatu *214*
Kamen, Gloria 1923- *98*
    Earlier sketch in SATA *9*
Kamerman, Sylvia E.
    See Burack, Sylvia K.
Kamm, Josephine (Hart) 1905-1989 .... *24*
Kammerman, Sylvia K.
    See Burack, Sylvia K.
Kandel, Michael 1941- *93*
Kandell, Alice S. 1938- *35*
Kane, Bob 1916-1998 .... *120*
Kane, Henry Bugbee 1902-1971 .... *14*
Kane, Kim 1973(?)- *221*
Kane, L. A.
    See Mannetti, Lisa
Kane, Robert W. 1910- *18*
Kane, Wilson
    See Bloch, Robert (Albert)
Kanefield, Teri 1960- *135*
Kanell, Beth *215*
Kaner, Etta 1947- *198*
    Earlier sketch in SATA *126*
Kanetzke, Howard W(illiam) 1932- *38*
Kangas, Juli 1958- *200*
Kann, Elizabeth *180*
Kann, Victoria *180*
Kanninen, Barbara *196*
Kanninen, Barbara J.
    See Kanninen, Barbara
Kanoza, Muriel Canfield
    See Canfield, Muriel
Kantner, Seth 1965- *179*
Kanzawa, Toshiko
    See Furukawa, Toshi
Kanzler, John 1963- *188*
Kaplan, Andrew 1960- *78*
Kaplan, Anne Bernays
    See Bernays, Anne
Kaplan, Bess 1927- *22*
Kaplan, Boche 1926- *24*
Kaplan, Elizabeth 1956- *83*
Kaplan, Elizabeth A.
    See Kaplan, Elizabeth
Kaplan, Irma 1900- *10*
Kaplan, Jean Caryl Korn 1926- *10*
Kaplow, Robert 1954- *70*
Karageorge, Michael
    See Anderson, Poul
Karas, G. Brian 1957- *222*
    Earlier sketch in SATA *178*
Karas, George Brian
    See Karas, G. Brian

Karasz, Ilonka 1896-1981
  Obituary 29
Karen, Ruth 1922-1987 9
  Obituary 54
Kark, Nina Mary
  See Bawden, Nina
Karl, Herb 1938- 73
Karl, Jean E(dna) 1927-2000 122
  Earlier sketch in SATA 34
  See also SAAS 10
Karlin, Bernie 1927- 68
Karlin, Eugene 1918- 10
Karlin, Nurit 103
  Earlier sketch in SATA 63
Karlins, Mark 1947- 219
Karnes, Frances A. 1937- 110
Karp, Naomi J. 1926- 16
Karpinski, J. Rick
  See Karpinski, John Eric
Karpinski, John Eric 1952- 81
Karpinski, Rick
  See Karpinski, John Eric
Karr, Kathleen 1946- 212
  Earlier sketches in SATA 82, 127
Karr, Phyllis Ann 1944- 119
Karwoski, Gail 1949- 127
Karwoski, Gail Langer
  See Karwoski, Gail
Kashiwagi, Isami 1925- 10
Kaslik, Ibi
  See Kaslik, Ibolya Emma
Kaslik, Ibolya Emma 1973- 185
Kassem, Lou 1931- 62
  Brief entry 51
Kastel, Warren
  See Silverberg, Robert
Kastner, Erich
  See Kaestner, Erich
Kastner, Jill (Marie) 1964- 117
  Earlier sketch in SATA 70
Kasuya, Masahiro 1937- 51
Kasza, Keiko 1951- 191
  Earlier sketch in SATA 124
Kataphusin
  See Ruskin, John
Katchen, Carole 1944- 9
Katcher, Brian 1975- 203
Kate, Lauren 1981- 237
Kathryn
  See Searle, Kathryn Adrienne
Kato, Aya 1982- 202
Katona, Robert 1949- 21
Katsarakis, Joan Harries
  See Harries, Joan
Katz, Alan 231
  Earlier sketch in SATA 185
Katz, Avi 1949- 199
Katz, Avner 1939- 103
Katz, Bobbi 1933- 217
  Earlier sketches in SATA 12, 179
Katz, Fred(eric Phillip) 1938- 6
Katz, Jane B(resler) 1934- 33
Katz, Karen 1947- 232
  Earlier sketches in SATA 158, 195
Katz, Marjorie P.
  See Weiser, Marjorie P(hillis) K(atz)
Katz, Susan 1945- 156
Katz, Welwyn Wilton 1948- 96
  Autobiography Feature 118
  Earlier sketch in SATA 62
  See also CLR 45
Katz, William 1940- 98
Katz, William Loren 1927- 13
Kaufman, Bel 57
Kaufman, Jeff 1955- 84
Kaufman, Joe 1911-2001 33
Kaufman, Joseph
  See Kaufman, Joe
Kaufman, Mervyn D. 1932- 4
Kaufmann, Angelika 1935- 15
Kaufmann, John 1931- 18

Kaula, Edna Mason 1906-1987 13
Kaur Khalsa, Dayal
  See Khalsa, Dayal Kaur
Kavaler, Lucy 1930- 23
Kavanagh, Jack 1920- 85
Kavanagh, P(atrick) J(oseph Gregory)
  1931- 122
Kavanaugh, Ian
  See Webb, Jean Francis (III)
Kay, Alan N. 1965- 144
Kay, Elizabeth 1949- 165
Kay, Guy Gavriel 1954- 167
  Earlier sketch in SATA 121
Kay, Helen
  See Goldfrank, Helen Colodny
Kay, Jackie 1961- 165
  Earlier sketch in SATA 97
Kay, Jacqueline Margaret
  See Kay, Jackie
Kay, Julia 205
Kay, Mara 13
Kay, Verla 1946- 210
  Earlier sketch in SATA 120
Kaye, Danny 1913-1987
  Obituary 50
Kaye, Geraldine (Hughesdon) 1925- 85
  Earlier sketch in SATA 10
Kaye, Judy
  See Baer, Judy
Kaye, Marilyn 1949- 230
  Earlier sketches in SATA 56, 110
Kaye, Mary Margaret
  See Kaye, M.M.
Kaye, M.M. 1908-2004 62
  Obituary 152
Kaye, Mollie
  See Kaye, M.M.
Kaye, Peggy 1948- 143
Keach, James P. 1950- 125
Keams, Geri 1951- 117
Keane, Bil 1922- 4
Keane, Dave 1965- 216
Keaney, Brian 1954- 188
  Earlier sketch in SATA 106
Kearney, Meg 1964- 178
Kearny, Jillian
  See Goulart, Ron
Keat, Nawuth 1964- 222
Keating, Bern
  See Keating, Leo Bernard
Keating, Frank 1944- 143
Keating, Lawrence A. 1903-1966 23
Keating, Leo Bernard 1915- 10
Keats, Emma 1899(?)-1979(?) 68
Keats, Ezra Jack 1916-1983 57
  Obituary 34
  Earlier sketch in SATA 14
  See also CLR 35
Keefer, Catherine
  See Ogan, George F.
  and Ogan, Margaret E. (Nettles)
Keefer, Janice Kulyk
  See Kulyk Keefer, Janice
Keegan, Marcia 1943- 104
  Earlier sketch in SATA 9
Keehn, Sally M. 1947- 165
  Earlier sketch in SATA 87
Keel, Frank
  See Keeler, Ronald F(ranklin)
Keeler, Patricia 183
Keeler, Patricia A.
  See Keeler, Patricia
Keeler, Ronald F(ranklin) 1913-1983 47
Keely, Jack 1951- 119
Keen, Martin L. 1913-1992 4
Keenan, Sheila 1953- 95
Keene, Ann T. 1940- 86
Keene, Ann Todd
  See Keene, Ann T.

Keene, Carolyn
  See Benson, Mildred
  and Goulart, Ron
  and Lerangis, Peter
  and McFarlane, Leslie
  and Stanley, George Edward
  and Stratemeyer, Edward L.
Keens-Douglas, Richardo 1953- 154
  Earlier sketch in SATA 95
Keep, Linda Lowery
  See Lowery, Linda
Keep, Richard 1949- 170
Keep, Richard Cleminson
  See Keep, Richard
Keeping, Charles (William James)
  1924-1988 69
  Obituary 56
  Earlier sketch in SATA 9
  See also CLR 34
Keeshan, Robert J. 1927-2004 32
  Obituary 151
Keeter, Susan 237
Kehlenbeck, Angela 1959- 186
Kehoe, Tim 1970- 224
Kehret, Peg 1936- 212
  Autobiography Feature 149
  Earlier sketches in SATA 73, 108, 149
Keillor, Garrison 1942- 58
Keillor, Gary Edward
  See Keillor, Garrison
Keir, Christine
  See Pullein-Thompson, Christine
Keiser, Paige 220
Keister, Douglas 1948- 88
Keith, Doug 1952- 81
Keith, Eros 1942- 52
Keith, Hal 1934- 36
Keith, Harold (Verne) 1903-1998 74
  Earlier sketch in SATA 2
Keith, Robert
  See Applebaum, Stan
Keleinikov, Andrei 1924- 65
Kelemen, Julie 1959- 78
Kelen, Emery 1896-1978 13
  Obituary 26
Kelleam, Joseph E(veridge) 1913-1975 31
Kelleher, Anne 1959- 97
Kelleher, Annette 1950- 122
Kelleher, Daria Valerian 1955- 79
Kelleher, Victor (Michael Kitchener)
  1939- 129
  Brief entry 52
  Earlier sketch in SATA 75
  See also CLR 36
Keller, Beverly L(ou) 91
  Earlier sketch in SATA 13
Keller, Charles 1942- 82
  Earlier sketch in SATA 8
Keller, Debra 1958- 94
Keller, Dick 1923- 36
Keller, Emily 96
Keller, Gail Faithfull
  See Faithfull, Gail
Keller, Holly 1942- 216
  Brief entry 42
  Earlier sketches in SATA 76, 108, 157
  See also CLR 45
Keller, Irene (Barron) 1927-2002 36
  Obituary 139
Keller, Laurie 1961(?)- 196
Kelley, Ann 1941- 217
Kelley, Ellen A. 185
Kelley, Ellen Chavez
  See Kelley, Ellen A.
Kelley, Gary 1945- 217
  Earlier sketch in SATA 183
Kelley, J.A.
  See Kelley, Jane
Kelley, Jane 1954- 231
Kelley, Leo P(atrick) 1928- 32
  Brief entry 31

Kelley, Marty 1971- 211
Kelley, Patrick (G.) 1963- 129
Kelley, Patte 1947- 93
Kelley, True 1946- 179
Kelley, True (Adelaide) 1946- 130
  Brief entry 39
  Earlier sketches in SATA *41, 92*
Kelley, True Adelaide
  See Kelley, True
Kellin, Sally Moffet 1932- 9
Kelling, Furn L. 1914-2000 37
Kellogg, Gene
  See Kellogg, Jean (Defrees)
Kellogg, Jean (Defrees) 1916-1978 10
Kellogg, Steven 1941- 177
  Earlier sketches in SATA *8, 57, 130*
  See also CLR *6*
Kellogg, Steven Castle
  See Kellogg, Steven
Kellow, Kathleen
  See Hibbert, Eleanor Alice Burford
Kelly, C. M. O.
  See Gibbs, (Cecilia) May
Kelly, Clint 1950- 140
Kelly, Eric P(hilbrook) 1884-1960
  See YABC *1*
Kelly, Fiona
  See Coleman, Michael
  and Hendry, Frances Mary
  and Jones, Allan Frewin
  and Oldfield, Jenny
  and Welford, Sue
Kelly, Irene 1957- 210
  Earlier sketch in SATA *147*
Kelly, Jacqueline 216
Kelly, Jeff
  See Kelly, Jeffrey
Kelly, Jeffrey 1946- 65
Kelly, Jenn 1973- 236
Kelly, Jenn L.
  See Kelly, Jenn
Kelly, Joanne (W.) 1934- 87
Kelly, Kate 1958- 91
Kelly, Kathleen M. 1964- 71
Kelly, Katy 1955- 215
  Earlier sketch in SATA *169*
Kelly, Lauren
  See Oates, Joyce Carol
Kelly, Laurene 1954- 123
Kelly, Martha Rose 1914-1983 37
Kelly, Marty
  See Kelly, Martha Rose
Kelly, Mij 166
Kelly, Ralph
  See Geis, Darlene Stern
Kelly, Regina Z(immerman) 1898-1986 5
Kelly, Rosalie (Ruth) 43
Kelly, Tara 230
Kelly, Tom 1961- 191
Kelly, Walt(er Crawford) 1913-1973 18
Kelsey, Alice Geer 1896-1982 1
Kelsey, Elin 1961- 159
Kelsey, Marybeth 216
Kemly, Kathleen 1958- 197
Kemnitz, Thomas Milton, Jr. 1984- 152
Kemnitz, Tom, Jr.
  See Kemnitz, Thomas Milton, Jr.
Kemp, Gene 1926- 75
  Earlier sketch in SATA *25*
  See also CLR *29*
Kempner, Mary Jean 1913-1969 10
Kempter, Christa 1945- 187
Kempton, Jean Welch 1914- 10
Kenah, Katharine 1949- 182
Kenda, Margaret 1942- 71
Kendall, Carol (Seeger) 1917- 74
  Earlier sketch in SATA *11*
  See also SAAS *7*
Kendall, Gideon 1966- 215
Kendall, Katherine
  See Applegate, Katherine

Kendall, Lace
  See Stoutenburg, Adrien (Pearl)
Kendall, Martha E. 87
Kendall, Russ 1957- 83
Kenealy, James P. 1927- 52
  Brief entry 29
Kenealy, Jim
  See Kenealy, James P.
Kennaway, Adrienne 1945- 171
  Earlier sketch in SATA *60*
Kennedy, Anne 1955- 198
Kennedy, Anne Vittur
  See Kennedy, Anne
Kennedy, Brendan 1970- 57
Kennedy, Dana Forrest 1917- 74
Kennedy, Dorothy M(intzlaff) 1931- 53
Kennedy, Doug 1963- 189
  Earlier sketch in SATA *122*
Kennedy, Frances 1937- 192
Kennedy, James 214
Kennedy, John F. 1917-1963 11
Kennedy, John Fitzgerald
  See Kennedy, John F.
Kennedy, Joseph Charles
  See Kennedy, X. J.
Kennedy, Kim 189
Kennedy, Marlane 1962- 210
Kennedy, Pamela (J.) 1946- 87
Kennedy, Paul E(dward) 1929- 113
  Earlier sketch in SATA *33*
Kennedy, Richard (Pitt) 1910-1989
  Obituary 60
Kennedy, (Jerome) Richard 1932- 22
Kennedy, Robert 1938- 63
Kennedy, T.A. 1953- 42
  Brief entry 35
Kennedy, Teresa
  See Kennedy, T.A.
Kennedy, Teresa A.
  See Kennedy, T.A.
Kennedy, William 1928- 57
Kennedy, William Joseph
  See Kennedy, William
Kennedy, X. J. 1929- 130
  Autobiography Feature 130
  Earlier sketches in SATA *14, 86*
  See also CLR *27*
  See also SAAS *22*
Kennell, Ruth Epperson 1893-1977 6
  Obituary 25
Kennemore, Tim 1957- 220
  Earlier sketch in SATA *133*
Kennen, Ally 190
Kennett, David 1959- 206
  Earlier sketch in SATA *121*
Kennison, Ruth 202
Kenny, Ellsworth Newcomb 1909-1971
  Obituary 26
Kenny, Herbert Andrew 1912-2002 13
Kenny, Jude
  See Daly, Jude
Kenny, Kathryn
  See Bowden, Joan Chase
  and Krull, Kathleen
  and Sanderlin, Owenita (Harrah)
  and Stack, Nicolete Meredith
Kenny, Kevin
  See Krull, Kathleen
Kensinger, George
  See Fichter, George S.
Kensington, Kathryn Wesley
  See Rusch, Kristine Kathryn
Kent, Alexander
  See Reeman, Douglas Edward
Kent, David
  See Lambert, David
Kent, Deborah Ann 1948- 155
  Brief entry 41
  Earlier sketches in SATA *47, 104*
Kent, Jack
  See Kent, John Wellington

Kent, John Wellington 1920-1985 24
  Obituary 45
Kent, Lisa 1942- 90
Kent, Mallory
  See Lowndes, Robert A(ugustine) W(ard)
Kent, Margaret 1894- 2
Kent, Rockwell 1882-1971 6
Kent, Rose 188
Kent, Sherman 1903-1986 20
  Obituary 47
Kenward, Jean 1920- 42
Kenworthy, Leonard S. 1912-1991 6
Kenyon, Karen (Smith) 1938- 145
Kenyon, Kate
  See Adorjan, Carol (Madden)
  and Ransom, Candice
Kenyon, Ley 1913-1990 6
Keown, Elizabeth 78
Kepes, Juliet A(ppleby) 1919-1999 13
Kephart, Beth 1960- 196
Keplinger, Kody 1991- 237
Kerby, Johanna 235
Kerby, Mona 1951- 202
  Earlier sketch in SATA *75*
Kerigan, Florence 1896-1984 12
Kerley, Barbara 1960- 191
  Earlier sketch in SATA *138*
Kerman, Gertrude
  See Furman, Gertrude Lerner Kerman
Kerns, Thelma 1929- 116
Kerr, Anne Louise
  See Mackey, Weezie Kerr
Kerr, Bob 1951- 120
Kerr, Jessica 1901-1991 13
Kerr, (Anne-)Judith 1923-1970 24
Kerr, M. E.
  See Meaker, Marijane
Kerr, P.B.
  See Kerr, Philip
Kerr, Philip 1956- 168
Kerr, Phyllis Forbes 1942- 72
Kerr, Tom 1950- 77
Kerrin, Jessica Scott 174
Kerry, Frances
  See Kerigan, Florence
Kerry, Lois
  See Duncan, Lois
Kershen, (L.) Michael 1982- 82
Kerven, Rosalind 1954- 83
Ker Wilson, Barbara 1929- 121
  Earlier sketches in SATA *20, 70*
  See also SAAS *18*
Kerz, Anna 1947- 220
Keselman, Gabriela 1953- 128
Kesey, Ken 1935-2001 66
  Obituary 131
  See also CLR *170*
Kesey, Ken Elton
  See Kesey, Ken
Kesler, Jay 1935- 65
Kessel, Joyce Karen 1937- 41
Kessler, Cristina 190
Kessler, Ethel 1922- 44
  Brief entry 37
Kessler, Leonard P. 1921- 14
Kessler, Liz 1966- 206
Kest, Kristin 1967- 168
  Earlier sketch in SATA *118*
Kesteven, G. R.
  See Crosher, G. R.
Ketcham, Hank
  See Ketcham, Henry King
Ketcham, Henry King 1920-2001 28
  Brief entry 27
  Obituary 128
Ketcham, Sallie 1963- 124
Ketchum, Liza 1946- 132
  Earlier sketch in SATA *78*
Ketner, Mary Grace 1946- 75
Kettelkamp, Larry (Dale) 1933- 2
  See also SAAS *3*

Ketteman, Helen 1945- 223
  Earlier sketches in SATA *73, 115, 167*
Kettle, Peter
  See Glover, Denis (James Matthews)
Kevles, Bettyann Holtzmann 1938- 23
Key, Alexander (Hill) 1904-1979 8
  Obituary 23
Key, Samuel M.
  See de Lint, Charles
Key, Watt 1970- 189
Keyes, Daniel 1927- 37
Keyes, Diane 207
Keyes, Fenton 1915-1999 34
Keyes, Greg 1963- 116
Keyes, J. Gregory
  See Keyes, Greg
Keyser, Marcia 1933- 42
Keyser, Sarah
  See McGuire, Leslie (Sarah)
Khalid, Mohamed Nor
  See Lat
Khalsa, Dayal Kaur 1943-1989 62
  See also CLR *30*
Khan, Hena 214
Khan, Rukhsana 1962- 231
  Earlier sketches in SATA *118, 165*
Khanshendel, Chiron
  See Rose, Wendy
Kheirabadi, Masoud 1951- 158
Khemir, Sabiha 87
Kherdian, David 1931- 74
  Autobiography Feature 125
  Earlier sketch in SATA *16*
  See also CLR *24*
Khing, T.T. 1933- 192
Kibbe, Pat (Hosley) 60
Kidd, Diana 1933-2000 150
Kidd, Richard 1952-2008 152
  Obituary 194
Kidd, Ronald 1948- 173
  Earlier sketches in SATA *42, 92*
Kiddell, John 1922- 3
Kiddell-Monroe, Joan 1908-1972 55
Kidwell, Carl 1910- 43
Kiefer, Irene 1926- 21
Kiefer, Kathleen Balmes 1957- 142
Kiepper, Shirley Morgan 1933- 10
Kierstead, Vera M.
  See Kierstead-Farber, Vera M.
Kierstead-Farber, Vera M. 1913- 121
Kierstead-Farber, Vera May
  See Kierstead-Farber, Vera M.
Kiesel, Stanley 1925- 35
Kiesler, Kate (A.) 1971- 152
  Earlier sketch in SATA *90*
Kihn, Greg 1952- 110
Kikukawa, Cecily H(arder) 1919- 44
  Brief entry 35
Kilaka, John 1966- 223
Kilcher, Jewel 1974- 109
Kile, Joan 1940- 78
Kilgore, Kathleen 1946- 42
Kilian, Crawford 1941- 35
Killdeer, John
  See Mayhar, Ardath
Killen, Nicola 236
Killien, Christi 1956- 73
Killilea, Marie (Lyons) 1913-1991 2
Killingback, Julia 1944- 63
Killough, (Karen) Lee 1942- 64
Kilpatrick, Don 206
Kilreon, Beth
  See Walker, Barbara (Jeanne) K(erlin)
Kilworth, Garry 1941- 216
  Earlier sketch in SATA *94*
Kilworth, Garry D.
  See Kilworth, Garry
Kilworth, Garry Douglas
  See Kilworth, Garry
Kim, David 1977- 201
Kim, Dong-hwa 1950- 225

Kim, Helen 1899-1970 98
Kim, Joung Un 1970- 205
Kim, Susan 1958- 232
Kimball, Gayle 1943- 90
Kimball, Violet T(ew) 1932- 126
Kimball, Yeffe 1914-1978 37
Kimber, Murray 1964- 171
Kimble, Warren 176
Kimbrough, Emily 1899-1989 2
  Obituary 59
Kimeldorf, Martin 1948- 121
Kimeldorf, Martin R.
  See Kimeldorf, Martin
Kimenye, Barbara 1940(?)- 121
Kimmel, Elizabeth Cody 209
  Earlier sketch in SATA *170*
Kimmel, Eric A. 1946- 208
  Earlier sketches in SATA *13, 80, 125, 176*
Kimmel, Margaret Mary 1938- 43
  Brief entry 33
Kimmelman, Burt 1947- 180
Kimmelman, Leslie 1958- 211
  Earlier sketches in SATA *85, 156*
Kincaid, Jamaica 1949-
  See CLR *63*
Kincher, Jonni 1949- 79
Kincy, Karen 1986- 234
Kindl, Patrice 1951- 128
  Earlier sketch in SATA *82*
  See also CLR *132*
Kindred, Wendy (Good) 1937- 7
Kinerk, Robert 199
Kines, Pat Decker 1937- 12
King, Adam
  See Hoare, Robert J(ohn)
King, Alison
  See Martini, Teri
King, (Maria) Anna 1964- 72
King, A.S. 1970- 217
King, Billie Jean 1943- 12
King, Christine
  See Farris, Christine King
King, Christopher (L.) 1945- 84
King, (David) Clive 1924- 144
  Earlier sketch in SATA *28*
King, Colin 1943- 76
King, Cynthia 1925- 7
King, Daniel (John) 1963- 130
King, Daren 1972- 197
King, Elizabeth 1953- 83
King, Frank O. 1883-1969
  Obituary 22
King, Frank R. 1904-1999 127
King, Jane
  See Currie, Stephen
King, Jeanette (Margaret) 1959- 105
King, Larry L. 1929- 66
King, Laurie R. 1952- 88
King, Marian 1900(?)-1986 23
  Obituary 47
King, Martin Luther, Jr. 1929-1968 14
King, Mary Ellen 1958- 93
King, M.G. 1968- 236
King, Paul
  See Drackett, Phil(ip Arthur)
King, Paula
  See Downing, Paula E.
King, Stephen 1947- 161
  Earlier sketches in SATA *9, 55*
  See also CLR *124*
King, Stephen Edwin
  See King, Stephen
King, Stephen Michael 218
  Earlier sketch in SATA *157*
King, Steve
  See King, Stephen
King, Thomas 1943- 96
King, Thomas Hunt
  See King, Thomas
King, Tony 1947- 39

King, Willie Christine
  See Farris, Christine King
Kingfisher, Rupert 209
Kingman, Dong (Moy Shu) 1911-2000 44
Kingman, Lee
  See Natti, Lee
Kingsbury, Evan
  See Walker, Robert W.
Kingsland, Leslie William 1912- 13
Kingsley, Charles 1819-1875
  See YABC *2*
  See also CLR *167*
Kingsley, Emily Perl 1940- 33
Kingsley, Kaza 193
King-Smith, Dick 1922-2011 192
  Brief entry 38
  Earlier sketches in SATA *47, 80, 135*
  See also CLR *40*
Kingston, Maxine Hong 1940- 53
Kingston, Maxine Ting Ting Hong
  See Kingston, Maxine Hong
Kinkade, Sheila 1962- 229
Kinnaird, Ross 1954- 236
Kinney, C. Cle(land) 1915- 6
Kinney, Harrison 1921- 13
Kinney, Jean Stout 1912- 12
Kinney, Jeff 1971- 187
Kinsey, Elizabeth
  See Clymer, Eleanor
Kinsey, Helen 1948- 82
Kinsey-Warnock, Natalie 1956- 167
  Earlier sketches in SATA *71, 116*
Kinzel, Dorothy 1950- 57
Kinzel, Dottie
  See Kinzel, Dorothy
Kipling, Joseph Rudyard
  See Kipling, Rudyard
Kipling, Rudyard 1865-1936 100
  See also YABC *2*
  See also CLR *65*
Kippax, Frank
  See Needle, Jan
Kirby, David 1944- 78
Kirby, David K.
  See Kirby, David
Kirby, David Kirk
  See Kirby, David
Kirby, Margaret
  See Bingley, Margaret (Jane Kirby)
Kirby, Pamela F. 1952- 220
Kirby, Susan E. 1949- 62
Kirk, Connie Ann 1957- 167
Kirk, Daniel 1952- 196
  Earlier sketches in SATA *107, 153*
Kirk, David 1955- 161
  Earlier sketch in SATA *117*
Kirk, Heather 1949- 166
Kirk, Ruth (Kratz) 1925- 5
Kirkham, Dinah
  See Card, Orson Scott
Kirkland, Will
  See Hale, Arlene
Kirkpatrick, Katherine (Anne) 1964- 113
Kirkup, James 1918-2009 12
Kirkus, Virginia
  See Glick, Virginia Kirkus
Kirkwood, Kathryn
  See Fluke, Joanne
Kirsch, Vincent X. 211
Kirshenbaum, Binnie 79
Kirshner, David S. 1958- 123
Kirtland, G. B.
  See Hine, Sesyle Joslin
  and Hine, Al(fred Blakelee)
Kirwan, Wednesday 198
Kish, Eleanor M(ary) 1924- 73
Kish, Ely
  See Kish, Eleanor M(ary)
Kishida, Eriko 1929- 12
Kisinger, Grace Gelvin (Maze) 1913-1965 .. 10
Kissel, Richard 209

Kissin, Eva H. 1923- *10*
Kissinger, Rosemary K.
  See Updyke, Rosemary K.
Kistler, John M. 1967- *160*
Kitamura, Satoshi 1956- *201*
  Earlier sketches in SATA *62, 98, 143*
  See also CLR *60*
Kitanidis, Phoebe 1977- *230*
Kitchen, Bert
  See Kitchen, Herbert Thomas
Kitchen, Herbert Thomas 1940- *70*
Kite, L. Patricia
  See Kite, Pat
Kite, Pat 1940- *78*
Kitt, Tamara
  See de Regniers, Beatrice Schenk (Freedman)
Kittinger, Jo S(usenbach) 1955- *148*
  Earlier sketch in SATA *96*
Kituomba
  See Odaga, Asenath (Bole)
Kitzinger, Sheila 1929- *57*
Kiwak, Barbara 1966- *103*
Kjelgaard, James Arthur 1910-1959 .... *17*
  See also CLR *81*
Kjelgaard, Jim
  See Kjelgaard, James Arthur
Kjelle, Marylou Morano 1954- *146*
Klages, Ellen 1954- *196*
Klagsbrun, Francine (Lifton) *36*
Klaits, Barrie 1944- *52*
Klam, Cheryl *191*
Klaperman, Gilbert 1921- *33*
Klaperman, Libby Mindlin 1921-1982 ..... *33*
  Obituary *31*
Klass, David 1960- *207*
  Earlier sketches in SATA *88, 142*
Klass, Morton 1927-2001 .... *11*
Klass, Sheila Solomon 1927- *219*
  Autobiography Feature *126*
  Earlier sketches in SATA *45, 99*
  See also SAAS *26*
Klause, Annette Curtis 1953- *175*
  Earlier sketch in SATA *79*
  See also CLR *104*
Klaveness, Jan O'Donnell 1939- *86*
Kleberger, Ilse 1921- *5*
Kleeberg, Irene (Flitner) Cumming 1932- *65*
Klein, Aaron E. 1930-1998 .... *45*
  Brief entry *28*
Klein, Bill 1945- *89*
Klein, David 1919-2001 .... *59*
Klein, Frederick C. 1938- *154*
Klein, Gerda Weissmann 1924- *44*
Klein, H(erbert) Arthur *8*
Klein, James 1932- *115*
Klein, Leonore (Glotzer) 1916- *6*
Klein, Lisa 1958- *211*
Klein, Lisa M.
  See Klein, Lisa
Klein, Mina C(ooper) 1906-1979 .... *8*
Klein, Norma 1938-1989 .... *57*
  Earlier sketch in SATA *7*
  See also CLR *162*
  See also SAAS *1*
Klein, Rachel S. 1953- *105*
Klein, Robin 1936- *164*
  Brief entry *45*
  Earlier sketches in SATA *55, 80*
  See also CLR *21*
Klemin, Diana *65*
Klemm, Barry 1945- *104*
Klemm, Edward G., Jr. 1910-2001 .... *30*
Klemm, Roberta K(ohnhorst) 1884-1975 ..... *30*
Klemstein, Stacey
  See Kade, Stacey
Kleven, Elisa 1958- *217*
  Earlier sketches in SATA *76, 173*
  See also CLR *85*
Klevin, Jill Ross 1935- *39*
  Brief entry *38*

Kliban, B(ernard) 1935-1990 .... *35*
  Obituary *66*
Klier, Kimberly Wagner *208*
Klimo, Kate *214*
Klimowicz, Barbara 1927- *10*
Kline, Christina Baker 1964- *101*
Kline, James
  See Klein, James
Kline, Jim
  See Kline, Jim
Kline, Lisa Williams 1954- *143*
Kline, Suzy 1943- *193*
  Autobiography Feature *193*
  Brief entry *48*
  Earlier sketches in SATA *67, 99, 152*
Kling, Heidi R. *233*
Klinger, Shula *230*
Kliros, Thea 1935- *106*
Klise, Kate *221*
  Earlier sketch in SATA *181*
Klise, M. Sarah 1961- *235*
  Earlier sketches in SATA *128, 180*
Kloepfer, John *235*
Klots, Alexander Barrett 1903-1989
  Obituary *62*
Klug, Ron(ald) 1939- *31*
Knaak, Richard A. 1961- *166*
  Earlier sketch in SATA *86*
Knaak, Richard Allen
  See Knaak, Richard A.
Knapman, Timothy *200*
Knapp, Edward
  See Kunhardt, Edith
Knapp, Ron 1952- *34*
Knebel, Fletcher 1911-1993 .... *36*
  Obituary *75*
Kneeland, Linda Clarke 1947- *94*
Kneen, Maggie 1957- *221*
Knickerbocker, Diedrich
  See Irving, Washington
Knifesmith
  See Cutler, Ivor
Knigge, Robert (R.) 1921(?)-1987 .... *50*
Knight, Anne (Katherine) 1946- *34*
Knight, Brenda *112*
Knight, Christopher G. 1943- *96*
Knight, Damon (Francis) 1922-2002 .... *9*
  Obituary *139*
Knight, David C(arpenter) 1925-1984 ..... *14*
  See also CLR *38*
Knight, Eric 1897-1943 .... *18*
Knight, Eric Mowbray
  See Knight, Eric
Knight, Francis Edgar 1905- *14*
Knight, Frank
  See Knight, Francis Edgar
Knight, Hilary 1926- *132*
  Earlier sketches in SATA *15, 69*
Knight, Joan
  See Knight, Joan (MacPhail)
Knight, Joan (MacPhail) *159*
  Earlier sketch in SATA *82*
Knight, Kathryn Lasky
  See Lasky, Kathryn
Knight, Mallory T.
  See Hurwood, Bernhardt J.
Knight, Ruth Adams 1898-1974
  Obituary *20*
Knight, Steven 1959- *234*
Knight, Theodore O. 1946- *77*
Knobloch, Dorothea 1951- *88*
Knoepfle, John (Ignatius) 1923- *66*
Knorr, Laura 1971- *200*
Knott, Bill
  See Knott, William C(ecil, Jr.)
Knott, William C(ecil, Jr.) 1927- *3*
Knotts, Howard (Clayton, Jr.) 1922- *25*
Knowles, Anne 1933- *37*
Knowles, Jo 1970- *197*
Knowles, Johanna Beth
  See Knowles, Jo

Knowles, John 1926-2001 .... *89*
  Obituary *134*
  Earlier sketch in SATA *8*
  See also CLR *98*
Knox, Calvin M.
  See Silverberg, Robert
Knox, (Mary) Eleanor Jessie 1909-2000 ...... *59*
  Earlier sketch in SATA *30*
Knox, Elizabeth 1959- *176*
Knox, Elizabeth Fiona
  See Knox, Elizabeth
Knox, James
  See Brittain, William
Knox, Jolyne 1937- *76*
Knudsen, James 1950- *42*
Knudsen, Michelle 1974- *220*
  Earlier sketch in SATA *171*
Knudson, Mike 1965- *209*
Knudson, R. R.
  See Knudson, Rozanne
Knudson, Richard L(ewis) 1930- *34*
Knudson, Rozanne 1932-2008 .... *79*
  Earlier sketch in SATA *7*
  See also SAAS *18*
Knutson, Barbara 1959-2005 .... *166*
Knutson, Kimberley *115*
Knye, Cassandra
  See Disch, Thomas M.
Kobayashi, Masako Matsuno 1935- *6*
Kober, Shahar 1979- *213*
Koch, Dorothy Clarke 1924- *6*
Koch, Kenneth 1925-2002 .... *65*
Koch, Kenneth Jay
  See Koch, Kenneth
Koch, Phyllis (Mae) McCallum 1911- *10*
Kochalka, James 1967- *196*
Kocsis, J. C.
  See Paul, James
Koda-Callan, Elizabeth 1944- *140*
  Earlier sketch in SATA *67*
Kodera, Craig 1956- *222*
Kodman, Stanislawa *201*
Koehler, Phoebe 1955- *85*
Koehler-Pentacoff, Elizabeth 1957- *160*
  Earlier sketch in SATA *96*
Koehn, Ilse
  See Van Zwienen, Ilse Charlotte Koehn
Koeller, Carol *192*
Koenig, Viviane 1950- *80*
Koering, Ursula 1921-1976 .... *64*
Koerner, W(illiam) H(enry) D(avid)
  1878-1938 .... *21*
Koertge, Ron 1940- *209*
  Earlier sketches in SATA *53, 92, 131*
Koestler-Grack, Rachel A. 1973- *156*
Koff, Richard Myram 1926- *62*
Koffinke, Carol 1949- *82*
Kogan, Deborah
  See Kogan Ray, Deborah
Kogan Ray, Deborah 1940- *203*
  Earlier sketches in SATA *8, 50, 161*
Kogawa, Joy 1935- *99*
Kogawa, Joy Nozomi
  See Kogawa, Joy
Kogler, Jennie
  See Kogler, Jennifer Anne
Kogler, Jennifer Anne 1982(?)- *174*
Kohara, Kazuno *207*
Kohl, Herbert 1937- *47*
Kohl, Herbert R.
  See Kohl, Herbert
Kohl, MaryAnn F(aubion) 1947- *144*
  Earlier sketch in SATA *74*
Kohler, Dean Ellis 1947- *226*
Kohler, Julilly H(ouse) 1908-1976
  Obituary *20*
Kohn, Bernice
  See Hunt, Bernice
Kohn, Rita (T.) 1933- *89*
Kohner, Frederick 1905-1986 .... *10*
  Obituary *48*

Koide, Tan 1938-1986 .... *50*
Koike, Kay 1940- *72*
Koja, Kathe 1960- *199*
    Earlier sketch in SATA *155*
Koja, Stephan *198*
Kolar, Bob 1960(?)- *206*
Kolb, Larry J. 1953- *175*
Kolba, St. Tamara *22*
Kolibalova, Marketa
    See Kolibalova, Marketa
Kolibalova, Marketa 1953- *126*
Koller, Jackie French 1948- *157*
    Earlier sketches in SATA *72, 109*
    See also CLR *68*
Kolodny, Nancy J. 1946- *76*
Kolosov, Jacqueline 1967- *199*
Komaiko, Leah 1954- *164*
    Earlier sketch in SATA *97*
Komisar, Lucy 1942- *9*
Komoda, Beverly 1939- *25*
Komoda, Kiyo 1937- *9*
Kompaneyets, Marc 1974- *169*
Komroff, Manuel 1890-1974 .... *2*
    Obituary *20*
Konigsberg, Bill 1970- *207*
Konigsburg, E.L. 1930- *194*
    Earlier sketches in SATA *4, 48, 94, 126*
    See also CLR *81*
Konigsburg, Elaine Lobl
    See Konigsburg, E.L.
Koning, Hans 1921-2007 .... *5*
    Obituary *182*
Koningsberger, Hans
    See Koning, Hans
Konkle, Janet Everest 1917- *12*
Kono, Erin Eitter 1973- *177*
Konrad, Marla Stewart *218*
Konzak, Burt 1946- *151*
Koob, Theodora (J. Foth) 1918- *23*
Kooiker, Leonie
    See Kooyker-Romijn, Johanna Maria
Koons, James
    See Pernu, Dennis
Koontz, Dean 1945- *165*
    Earlier sketch in SATA *92*
    See Koontz, Dean R.
Koontz, Dean R. *225*
    See Koontz, Dean
Koontz, Dean Ray
    See Koontz, Dean
Koontz, Robin Michal 1954- *136*
    Earlier sketch in SATA *70*
Kooyker, Leonie
    See Kooyker-Romijn, Johanna Maria
Kooyker-Romijn, Johanna Maria 1927- *48*
Kooyker-Romyn, Johanna Maria
    See Kooyker-Romijn, Johanna Maria
Kopelke, Lisa 1963- *154*
Kopper, Lisa 1950- *105*
    Brief entry *51*
Kopper, Lisa Esther
    See Kopper, Lisa
Koppes, Steven N. 1957- *169*
Koppes, Steven Nelson
    See Koppes, Steven N.
Korach, Mimi 1922- *9*
Koralek, Jenny 1934- *215*
    Earlier sketches in SATA *71, 140*
Korczak, Janusz
    See Goldszmit, Henryk
Koren, Edward (Benjamin) 1935- *148*
    Earlier sketch in SATA *5*
Koren, Edward 1935- *206*
Korinets, Iurii Iosifovich
    See Korinetz, Yuri (Iosifovich)
Korinetz, Yuri (Iosifovich) 1923- *9*
    See also CLR *4*
Korman, Bernice 1937- *78*

Korman, Gordon 1963- *226*
    Brief entry *41*
    Earlier sketches in SATA *49, 81, 119, 167*
    See also CLR *25*
Korman, Gordon Richard
    See Korman, Gordon
Korman, Justine 1958- *70*
Kornblatt, Marc 1954- *147*
    Earlier sketch in SATA *84*
Kornprobst, Jacques 1937- *177*
Korte, Gene J. 1950- *74*
Korthues, Barbara 1971- *203*
Korty, Carol 1937- *15*
Koscielniak, Bruce 1947- *153*
    Earlier sketches in SATA *67, 99*
Koshin, Alexander (A.) 1952- *86*
Kositsky, Lynne 1947- *158*
Koskenmaki, Rosalie
    See Maggio, Rosalie
Koss, Amy Goldman 1954- *158*
    Earlier sketch in SATA *115*
Kossin, Sandy (Sanford) 1926- *10*
Kossman, Nina 1959- *84*
Kostecki-Shaw, Jenny Sue *203*
Kostick, Conor 1964- *186*
Kotzwinkle, William 1938- *146*
    Earlier sketches in SATA *24, 70*
    See also CLR *6*
Kouhi, Elizabeth 1917- *54*
    Brief entry *49*
Kouts, Anne 1945- *8*
Koutsky, Jan Dale 1955- *146*
Kovacs, Deborah 1954- *132*
    Earlier sketch in SATA *79*
Kovalski, Maryann 1951- *175*
    Earlier sketches in SATA *58, 97*
    See also CLR *34*
    See also SAAS *21*
Kowalski, Kathiann M. 1955- *151*
    Earlier sketch in SATA *96*
Koz, Paula G.
    See Goodman Koz, Paula
Kozjan, Drazen *209*
Kraft, Betsy Harvey 1937- *157*
Kraft, Erik P. *193*
Krahn, Fernando 1935- *49*
    Brief entry *31*
    See also CLR *3*
Krakauer, Hoong Yee Lee 1955- *86*
Krakauer, Jon 1954- *108*
Krall, Dan 1970- *218*
Kramer, Andrew *237*
Kramer, George
    See Heuman, William
Kramer, Nora 1896(?)-1984 .... *26*
    Obituary *39*
Kramer, Remi (Thomas) 1935- *90*
Krantz, Hazel (Newman) *12*
Kranzler, George G(ershon) 1916- *28*
Kranzler, Gershon
    See Kranzler, George G(ershon)
Krasilovsky, Phyllis 1926- *38*
    Earlier sketch in SATA *1*
    See also CLR *83*
    See also SAAS *5*
Krasne, Betty
    See Levine, Betty K(rasne)
Krasner, Steven 1953- *154*
Krasnesky, Thad 1969(?)- *224*
Krasno, Rena 1923- *104*
Kratman, Tom *175*
Kraus, Joanna Halpert 1937- *87*
Kraus, (Herman) Robert 1925-2001 .... *93*
    Obituary *130*
    Earlier sketches in SATA *4, 65*
    See also SAAS *11*
Krauss, Ruth 1911-1993 .... *30*
    Obituary *75*
    Earlier sketch in SATA *1*
    See also CLR *42*

Krauss, Ruth Ida
    See Krauss, Ruth
Krautter, Elisa (Bialk) 1912(?)-1990 .... *1*
    Obituary *65*
Krautwurst, Terry 1946- *79*
Kray, Robert Clement 1930- *82*
Krech, Bob 1956- *185*
Krech, Robert
    See Krech, Bob
Kredel, Fritz 1900-1973 .... *17*
Kreikemeier, Gregory Scott 1965- *85*
Kreloff, Elliot *189*
Krementz, Jill 1940- *134*
    Earlier sketches in SATA *17, 71*
    See also CLR *5*
    See also SAAS *8*
Kremer, Marcie
    See Sorenson, Margo
Krenina, Katya 1968- *221*
    Earlier sketch in SATA *101*
Krensky, Stephen 1953- *188*
    Brief entry *41*
    Earlier sketches in SATA *47, 93, 136*
Krensky, Stephen Alan
    See Krensky, Stephen
Kresh, Paul 1919-1997 .... *61*
    Obituary *94*
Kress, Nancy 1948- *147*
    Autobiography Feature *147*
    Earlier sketch in SATA *85*
Kricher, John C. 1944- *113*
Krieger, Melanie 1944- *96*
Krinitz, Esther Nisenthal 1927-2001 .... *194*
Kripke, Dorothy Karp *30*
Krisher, Trudy 1946- *160*
    Earlier sketch in SATA *86*
Krisher, Trudy B.
    See Krisher, Trudy
Krishnaswami, Uma 1956- *182*
    Earlier sketch in SATA *144*
Kristiansen, Teddy 1964- *210*
Kristiansen, Teddy H.
    See Kristiansen, Teddy
Kristof, Jane 1932- *8*
Kroeber, Theodora (Kracaw) 1897-1979 ...... *1*
Kroeger, Mary Kay 1950- *92*
Krohn, Katherine E(lizabeth) 1961- *125*
    Earlier sketch in SATA *84*
Kroll, Francis Lynde 1904-1973 .... *10*
Kroll, Steven 1941-2011 .... *212*
    Autobiography Feature *135*
    Earlier sketches in SATA *19, 66, 125, 135*
    See also SAAS *7*
Kroll, Virginia L. 1948- *225*
    Earlier sketches in SATA *76, 114, 168*
Kroll, Virginia Louisa
    See Kroll, Virginia L.
Kromhout, Rindert 1958- *189*
Krommes, Beth 1956- *208*
    Earlier sketches in SATA *128, 181*
Kronenwetter, Michael 1943- *62*
Kroniuk, Lisa
    See Berton, Pierre (Francis de Marigny)
Kropp, Paul 1948- *38*
    Brief entry *34*
    See also CLR *96*
Kropp, Paul Stephan
    See Kropp, Paul
Krosoczka, Jarrett J. 1977- *200*
    Earlier sketch in SATA *155*
Krovatin, Christopher 1985- *171*
Krudop, Walter
    See Krudop, Walter Lyon
Krudop, Walter Lyon 1966- *210*
Kruess, James
    See Kruss, James
Kruglik, Gerald *187*

Krull, Kathleen 1952- 229
   Autobiography Feature 106
   Brief entry 39
   Earlier sketches in SATA *52, 80, 149, 184*
   See also CLR *44*
Krumgold, Joseph (Quincy) 1908-1980 48
   Obituary 23
   Earlier sketch in SATA *1*
Krupinski, Loretta 1940- 161
   Earlier sketches in SATA *67, 102*
Krupnick, Karen 1947- 89
Krupp, E. C. 1944- 123
   Earlier sketch in SATA *53*
Krupp, Edwin Charles
   See Krupp, E. C.
Krupp, Robin Rector 1946- 53
Krush, Beth 1918- 18
Krush, Joe 1918-
   See Krush, Joseph P.
Krush, Joseph P. 1918- 18
Kruss, James 1926-1997 8
   See also CLR *9*
Kruusval, Catarina 1951- 201
Krykorka, Vladyana 1945- 96
Krystoforski, Andrej 1943- 196
Kubick, Dana 212
Kubie, Eleanor Gottheil
   See Kubie, Nora Gottheil Benjamin
Kubie, Nora Benjamin
   See Kubie, Nora Gottheil Benjamin
Kubie, Nora Gottheil Benjamin 1899-1988 . 39
   Obituary 59
Kubinyi, Laszlo 1937- 94
   Earlier sketch in SATA *17*
Kudlinski, Kathleen V. 1950- 213
   Earlier sketch in SATA *150*
Kuehnert, Stephanie 1979- 205
Kuenstler, Morton 1927- 10
Kuh, Charlotte 1892(?)-1985
   Obituary 43
Kuharski, Janice 1947- 128
Kuhn, Dwight 199
Kuijer, Guus 1942- 179
Kujoth, Jean Spealman 1935-1975
   Obituary 30
Kuklin, Susan 1941- 163
   Earlier sketches in SATA *63, 95*
   See also CLR *51*
Kulak, Jeff 1984(?)- 223
Kulikov, Boris 1966- 205
   Earlier sketch in SATA *170*
Kulka, Joe 188
Kulling, Monica 1952- 237
   Earlier sketch in SATA *89*
Kullman, Harry 1919-1982 35
Kulyk Keefer, Janice 1952- 132
Kumin, Maxine 1925- 12
Kumin, Maxine Winokur
   See Kumin, Maxine
Kunhardt, Dorothy (Meserve) 1901-1979 53
   Obituary 22
Kunhardt, Edith 1937- 67
Kunjufu, Jawanza 1953- 73
Kunstler, Morton
   See Kuenstler, Morton
Kuntz, J(ohn) L. 1947- 91
Kuntz, Jerry 1956- 133
Kupferberg, Herbert 1918-2001 19
Kuratomi, Chizuko 1939- 12
   See also CLR *32*
Kurczok, Belinda 1978- 121
Kurelek, William 1927-1977 8
   Obituary 27
   See also CLR *2*
Kurian, George 1928- 65
Kurilla, Renee 1981- 231
Kurjian, Judi(th M.) 1944- 127
Kurland, Gerald 1942- 13
Kurland, Michael 1938- 118
   Earlier sketch in SATA *48*

Kurland, Michael Joseph
   See Kurland, Michael
Kuroi, Ken 1947- 120
Kurokawa, Mitsuhiro 1954- 88
Kurten, Bjorn (Olof) 1924-1988 64
Kurtz, Jane 1952- 139
   Earlier sketch in SATA *91*
   See also CLR *123*
Kurtz, Katherine 1944- 182
   Earlier sketches in SATA *76, 126*
Kurtz, Katherine Irene
   See Kurtz, Katherine
Kurusa 1942- 226
Kurz, Rudolf 1952- 95
Kushner, Donn (J.) 1927- 52
   See also CLR *55*
Kushner, Ellen 1955- 202
   Earlier sketch in SATA *98*
Kushner, Ellen Ruth
   See Kushner, Ellen
Kushner, Jill Menkes 1951- 62
Kushner, Lawrence 1943- 169
   Earlier sketch in SATA *83*
Kushner, Tony 1956- 160
Kuskin, Karla 1932-2009 164
   Obituary 206
   Earlier sketches in SATA *2, 68, 111*
   See also CLR *4*
   See also SAAS *3*
Kuskin, Karla Seidman
   See Kuskin, Karla
Kusugak, Michael 1948- 143
Kusugak, Michael Arvaarluk
   See Kusugak, Michael
Kutner, Merrily 1948- 196
Kuttner, Paul 1922- 18
Kuyper, Sjoerd 1952- 177
Kuzma, Kay 1941- 39
Kvale, Velma R(uth) 1898-1979 8
Kvasnosky, Laura McGee 1951- 182
   Earlier sketches in SATA *93, 142*
Kwasney, Michelle D. 1960- 162
Kyi, Tanya Lloyd 1973- 236
Kyle, Benjamin
   See Gottfried, Theodore Mark
Kyle, Elisabeth
   See Dunlop, Agnes M. R.
Kyte, Kathy S. 1946- 50
   Brief entry 44

L

L., Barry
   See Longyear, Barry B(rookes)
L., Tommy
   See Lorkowski, Thomas V(incent)
Labatt, Mary 1944- 215
Labouisse, Eve Curie
   See Curie, Eve
Labouisse, Eve Denise
   See Curie, Eve
Lacamara, Laura 236
Lace, William W. 1942- 126
Lacey, Joshua
   See Doder, Josh
Lachenmeyer, Nathaniel 1969- 221
Lachner, Dorothea
   See Knobloch, Dorothea
Lachtman, Ofelia Dumas 1919- 179
Lackey, Mercedes 237
   See Lackey, Mercedes R.
Lackey, Mercedes R. 1950- 127
   Earlier sketch in SATA *81*
   See Lackey, Mercedes
Lackey, Mercedes Ritchie
   See Lackey, Mercedes R.
Lacoe, Addie 78
Lacombe, Benjamin 1982- 198

Lacome, Julie 1961- 174
   Earlier sketch in SATA *80*
LaCour, Nina 1982- 222
Lacy, Leslie Alexander 1937- 6
Lacy, Rick 231
Ladd, Cheryl (Jean) 1951- 113
Ladd, London 1972(?)- 206
Ladd, Louise 1943- 97
Ladd, Veronica
   See Miner, Jane Claypool
Laden, Nina 1962- 148
   Earlier sketch in SATA *85*
Lader, Lawrence 1919-2006 6
   Obituary 178
LaDoux, Rita C. 1951- 74
Ladwig, Tim 1952- 223
Ladwig, Timothy
   See Ladwig, Tim
Lady, A
   See Taylor, Ann
Lady Mears
   See Tempest, Margaret Mary
Lady of Quality, A
   See Bagnold, Enid
La Farge, Oliver 1901-1963 19
La Farge, Oliver Hazard Perry
   See La Farge, Oliver
La Farge, Phyllis 14
LaFave, Kim 196
LaFaye, A. 1970- 220
   Earlier sketches in SATA *105, 156*
LaFaye, Alexandria R.T.
   See LaFaye, A.
LaFevers, R.L. 234
   Earlier sketch in SATA *191*
LaFevers, Robin
   See LaFevers, R.L.
LaFevers, Robin L.
   See LaFevers, R.L.
Lafferty, Mur 1973- 227
Laffin, John (Alfred Charles) 1922- 31
LaFleur, Suzanne 1983- 221
LaFontaine, Bruce 1948- 176
   Earlier sketch in SATA *114*
La Fontaine, Jean de 1621-1695 18
Lafrance, Marie 1955- 197
Lager, Claude
   See Lapp, Christiane (Germain)
Lager, Marilyn 1939- 52
Lagercrantz, Rose (Elsa) 1947- 39
Lagerloef, Selma
   See Lagerlof, Selma
Lagerlof, Selma 1858-1940 15
   See also CLR *7*
Lagos, Alexander 232
Lagos, Joseph 231
Laguna, Sofie 1968- 158
LaHaye, Tim 1926- 149
LaHaye, Timothy F.
   See LaHaye, Tim
Laidlaw, Rob 205
Laiken, Deirdre S. 1948- 48
   Brief entry 40
Laiken, Deirdre Susan
   See Laiken, Deirdre S.
Laimgruber, Monika 1946- 11
Lain, Anna
   See Lamb, Nancy
Laing, Alexander (Kinnan) 1903-1976 117
Laing, Martha 1951- 39
Lairamore, Dawn 233
Laird, Christa 1944- 108
   Autobiography Feature 120
   See also SAAS *26*
Laird, Elizabeth 1943- 228
   Earlier sketches in SATA *77, 114, 159*
   See also CLR *65*
Laird, Elizabeth Mary Risk
   See Laird, Elizabeth
Laird, Jean E(louise) 1930- 38
Laite, Gordon 1925- 31

Lake, Harriet
    See Taylor, Paula (Wright)
Lake, Nick 227
Lakeman, Victoria
    See Forester, Victoria
Lakin, Patricia 1944- 190
Laklan, Carli 1907-1988 5
Laliberte, Louise-Andree 1958- 169
Lalicki, Barbara 61
Lalicki, Tom 1949- 186
Lally, Soinbhe 1945- 119
LaMarche, Jim 162
Lamb, Albert 187
Lamb, Beatrice Pitney 1904-1997 21
Lamb, Charles 1775-1834 17
Lamb, Elizabeth Searle 1917- 31
Lamb, G(eoffrey) F(rederick) 10
Lamb, Harold (Albert) 1892-1962 53
Lamb, Lynton (Harold) 1907-1977 10
Lamb, Mary Ann 1764-1847 17
Lamb, Nancy 1939- 80
Lamb, Robert (Boyden) 1941- 13
Lamba, Marie 195
Lambert, David 1932- 84
    Brief entry 49
Lambert, David Compton
    See Lambert, David
Lambert, Janet 1895(?)-1973 25
Lambert, Martha L. 113
Lambert, Saul 1928- 23
Lambert, Stephen 174
Lamburn, Richmal Crompton 1890-1969 5
Lamensdorf, Len 1930- 120
Lamensdorf, Leonard
    See Lamensdorf, Len
Laminack, Lester L. 1956- 163
    Earlier sketch in SATA 120
Lammle, Leslie 1965- 213
Lamont, Priscilla 200
Lamorisse, Albert (Emmanuel) 1922-1970 ... 23
Lampert, Emily 1951- 52
    Brief entry 49
Lamplugh, Lois 1921- 17
Lampman, Evelyn Sibley 1907-1980 87
    Obituary 23
    Earlier sketch in SATA 4
Lamprey, Louise 1869-1951
    See YABC 2
Lampton, Chris
    See Lampton, Christopher F.
Lampton, Christopher
    See Lampton, Christopher F.
Lampton, Christopher F. 67
    Brief entry 47
Lamstein, Sarah 1943- 174
    Earlier sketch in SATA 126
Lamstein, Sarah Marwil
    See Lamstein, Sarah
Lanagan, Margo 1960- 201
    Earlier sketch in SATA 163
Lancaster, Bruce 1896-1963 9
Lancaster, Matthew 1973(?)-1983
    Obituary 45
Lance, Kathryn 1943- 76
Land, Barbara (Neblett) 1923- 16
Land, Jane
    See Borland, Kathryn Kilby
    and Speicher, Helen Ross S(mith)
Land, Myrick (Ebben) 1922-1998 15
Land, Ross
    See Borland, Kathryn Kilby
    and Speicher, Helen Ross S(mith)
Landa, Norbert 1952- 218
Landau, Elaine 1948- 141
    Earlier sketches in SATA 10, 94
Landau, Jacob 1917- 38
Landeck, Beatrice 1904-1978 15
Landin, Les 1923- 2
Landis, J. D. 1942- 60
    Brief entry 52

Landis, James D.
    See Landis, J. D.
Landis, James David
    See Landis, J. D.
Landis, Jill Marie 1948- 101
Landman, Tanya 207
Landmann, Bimba 1968- 176
Landon, Dena 1978(?)- 168
Landon, Lucinda 1950- 56
    Brief entry 51
Landon, Margaret (Dorothea Mortenson)
    1903-1993 50
Landowne, Youme 1970- 211
Landry, Leo 202
Landshoff, Ursula 1908-1989 13
Landstrom, Lena 1943- 206
    Earlier sketch in SATA 146
Landstrom, Olof 1943- 146
Landy, Derek 1974- 210
Lane, Alison Hoffman 215
Lane, Carolyn 1926-1993 10
Lane, Connie
    See Laux, Constance
Lane, Dakota 1959- 166
    Earlier sketch in SATA 105
Lane, Jerry
    See Martin, Patricia Miles
Lane, John (Richard) 1932- 15
Lane, Leena 199
Lane, Margaret 1907-1994 65
    Brief entry 38
    Obituary 79
Lane, Rose Wilder 1887-1968 29
    Brief entry 28
Lanes, Selma G. 1929- 3
Lanes, Selma Gordon
    See Lanes, Selma G.
Lanfredi, Judy 1964- 83
Lang, Andrew 1844-1912 16
    See also CLR 101
Lang, Aubrey 169
Lang, Diane 234
Lang, Glenna 1951- 221
Lang, Lang 1982- 208
Lang, Paul 1948- 83
Lang, Susan S. 1950- 68
Lang, T.T.
    See Taylor, Theodore
Langart, Darrell T.
    See Garrett, Randall
Langdo, Bryan 1973- 233
    Earlier sketches in SATA 138, 191
Lange, John
    See Crichton, Michael
Lange, Karen E. 190
Lange, Suzanne 1945- 5
Langley, Andrew 1949- 166
    Earlier sketch in SATA 104
Langley, Charles P(itman) III 1949- 103
Langley, Jonathan 1952- 122
Langley, Noel 1911-1980
    Obituary 25
Langley, Wanda 173
Langner, Nola
    See Malone, Nola Langner
Langone, John (Michael) 1929- 46
    Brief entry 38
Langreuter, Jutta 1944- 122
Langrish, Katherine 177
Langsen, Richard C. 1953- 95
Langstaff, John 1920-2005 68
    Obituary 172
    Earlier sketch in SATA 6
    See also CLR 3
Langstaff, John Meredith
    See Langstaff, John
Langstaff, Launcelot
    See Irving, Washington
Langston, Laura 1958- 186

Langton, Jane 1922- 200
    Autobiography Feature 140
    Earlier sketches in SATA 3, 68, 129, 140
    See also CLR 33
    See also SAAS 5
Lanier, Sidney 1842-1881 18
Lanier, Sterling E. 1927-2007 109
Lanier, Sterling Edmund
    See Lanier, Sterling E.
Lanino, Deborah 1964- 123
Lankford, Mary D. 1932- 112
    Earlier sketch in SATA 77
Lannin, Joanne 1951- 121
Lannin, Joanne A.
    See Lannin, Joanne
Lansdale, Joe R. 1951- 116
Lansdale, Joe Richard
    See Lansdale, Joe R.
Lansing, Alfred 1921-1975 35
Lansing, Karen E. 1954- 71
Lansky, Vicki 1942- 177
Lanthier, Jennifer 1964- 204
Lantier-Sampon, Patricia 1952- 92
Lantz, Fran
    See Lantz, Frances L(in)
Lantz, Frances L(in) 1952-2004 153
    Autobiography Feature 153
    Obituary 159
    Earlier sketches in SATA 63, 109
Lantz, Paul 1908- 45
Lantz, Walter 1900-1994 37
    Obituary 79
Lanza, Barbara 1945- 101
Lapp, Christiane (Germain) 1948- 74
Lappin, Peter 1911-1999 32
Larbalestier, Justine 231
    Earlier sketch in SATA 178
Lardy, Philippe 1963- 168
LaReau, Jenna 181
LaReau, Kara 181
Larios, Julie 1949- 178
Larios, Julie Hofstrand
    See Larios, Julie
Larkin, Amy
    See Burns, Olive Ann
Larkin, Maia
    See Wojciechowska, Maia (Teresa)
Larkspur, Penelope
    See Wyatt, Valerie
Laroche, Giles 1956- 221
    Earlier sketches in SATA 71, 126
LaRochelle, David 1960- 171
    Earlier sketch in SATA 115
Larom, Henry V. 1903(?)-1975
    Obituary 30
LaRose, Linda 125
Larrabee, Lisa 1947- 84
Larranaga, Ana Martin 1969- 229
Larrecq, John M(aurice) 1926-1980 44
    Obituary 25
Larrick (Crosby), Nancy 1910-2004 4
Larsen, Anita 1942- 78
Larsen, Egon 1904- 14
Larsen, Rebecca 1944- 54
Larson, Eve
    See St. John, Wylly Folk
Larson, Gary 1950- 57
Larson, Hope 1982- 205
Larson, Ingrid D(ana) 1965- 92
Larson, Jean Russell 1930- 121
Larson, Kirby 1954- 181
    Earlier sketch in SATA 96
Larson, Norita D. 1944- 29
Larson, Norita Dittberner
    See Larson, Norita D.
Larson, William H. 1938- 10
Larsson, Carl (Olof) 1853-1919 35
LaSalle, Charles A.
    See Ellis, Edward S.
LaSalle, Charles E.
    See Ellis, Edward S.

Lasell, Elinor H. 1929- *19*
Lasell, Fen H.
    See Lasell, Elinor H.
Lasenby, Jack 1931- *172*
    Earlier sketches in SATA *65, 103*
Laser, Michael 1954- *117*
Lash, Joseph P. 1909-1987 .... *43*
Lasher, Faith B. 1921- *12*
Lasker, David 1950- *38*
Lasker, Joe
    See Lasker, Joseph Leon
Lasker, Joseph Leon 1919- *83*
    Earlier sketch in SATA *9*
    See also SAAS *17*
Laski, Marghanita 1915-1988 .... *55*
Laskin, Pamela L. 1954- *75*
Lasky, Kathryn 1944- *236*
    Earlier sketches in SATA *13, 69, 112, 157,
    210*
    See also CLR *140*
Lasky Knight, Kathryn
    See Lasky, Kathryn
Lass, Bonnie *131*
Lassalle, C. E.
    See Ellis, Edward S.
Lassiter, Mary
    See Hoffman, Mary
Lassiter, Rhiannon 1977- *157*
Lat 1951- *196*
Latham, Barbara 1896- *16*
Latham, Frank B(rown) 1910-2000 .... *6*
Latham, Irene 1971- *228*
Latham, Jean Lee 1902-1995 .... *68*
    Earlier sketch in SATA *2*
    See also CLR *50*
Latham, Mavis
    See Clark, Mavis Thorpe
Latham, Philip
    See Richardson, Robert S(hirley)
Lathrop, Dorothy P(ulis) 1891-1980 .... *14*
    Obituary *24*
Lathrop, Francis
    See Leiber, Fritz (Reuter, Jr.)
Latimer, Jim 1943- *80*
Latimer, Miriam *235*
Latta, Rich
    See Latta, Richard
Latta, Richard 1946- *113*
Latta, Sara L. 1960- *174*
Lattany, Kristin
    See Lattany, Kristin Hunter
Lattany, Kristin (Eggleston) Hunter 1931- . *154*
    Autobiography Feature *154*
    Earlier sketch in SATA *132*
Lattany, Kristin Hunter 1931-2008 .... *132*
    Earlier sketch in SATA *12*
    See also CLR *3*
    See also SAAS *10*
Lattimore, Eleanor Frances 1904-1986 .... *7*
    Obituary *48*
Lattin, Ann
    See Cole, Lois Dwight
Latyk, Olivier 1976- *234*
Lauber, Patricia (Grace) 1924- *138*
    Earlier sketches in SATA *1, 33, 75*
    See also CLR *16*
Laugesen, Malene *207*
Laugesen, Malene Reynolds
    See Laugesen, Malene
Laugesen, Mary E(akin) 1906-1995 .... *5*
Laughbaum, Steve 1945- *12*
Laughlin, Florence Young 1910-2001 .... *3*
Laughlin, Rosemary 1941- *123*
Launder, Sally *206*
Laure, Ettagale
    See Blauer, Ettagale
Laure, Jason 1940- *50*
    Brief entry *44*
Laurence, Ester Hauser 1935- *7*
Laurence, Jean Margaret Wemyss
    See Laurence, Margaret

Laurence, Margaret 1926-1987
    Obituary *50*
Laurie, Rona 1916- *55*
Laurie, Victoria *218*
Laurin, Anne
    See McLaurin, Anne
Lauritzen, Jonreed 1902-1979 .... *13*
Lauscher, Hermann
    See Hesse, Hermann
Lauture, Denize 1946- *86*
Laux, Connie
    See Laux, Constance
Laux, Constance 1952- *97*
Laux, Dorothy 1920- *49*
Lavallee, Barbara 1941- *166*
    Earlier sketch in SATA *74*
Lavender, David (Sievert) 1910-2003 .... *97*
    Obituary *145*
    Earlier sketch in SATA *64*
Lavender, William D. 1921- *143*
Laverne, Christine *175*
Lavert, Gwendolyn Battle 1951-
    See Battle-Lavert, Gwendolyn
Laverty, Donald
    See Blish, James
    and Knight, Damon (Francis)
Lavigne, Louis-Dominique 1949- *107*
Lavine, David 1928- *31*
Lavine, Sigmund Arnold 1908-1986 .... *82*
    Earlier sketch in SATA *3*
    See also CLR *35*
Lavis, Steve *225*
Lavond, Paul Dennis
    See Kornbluth, C(yril) M.
    and Lowndes, Robert A(ugustine) W(ard)
    and Pohl, Frederik
Law, Stephen *225*
Law, Stephen
    See Law, Stephen
Lawford, Paula Jane 1960- *57*
    Brief entry *53*
Lawhead, Stephen R. 1950- *109*
Lawhead, Steve
    See Lawhead, Stephen R.
Lawler, Janet *222*
Lawlor, Laurie 1953- *235*
    Earlier sketches in SATA *80, 137*
Lawlor, William
    See Lawlor, William T.
Lawlor, William T. 1951- *183*
Lawrence, Ann (Margaret) 1942-1987 .... *41*
    Obituary *54*
Lawrence, Caroline 1954- *203*
Lawrence, Iain 1955- *183*
    Earlier sketch in SATA *135*
Lawrence, J. T.
    See Rowland-Entwistle, (Arthur) Theodore
    (Henry)
Lawrence, Jerome 1915-2004 .... *65*
Lawrence, John 1933- *30*
Lawrence, Josephine 1890(?)-1978
    Obituary *24*
Lawrence, Louise 1943- *119*
    Earlier sketches in SATA *38, 78*
Lawrence, Louise de Kiriline 1894-1992 ..... *13*
Lawrence, Lynn
    See Garland, Sherry
Lawrence, Margery H. 1889-1969 .... *120*
Lawrence, Michael 1943- *132*
Lawrence, Mildred Elwood 1907-1997 .... *3*
Lawrence, R(onald) D(ouglas) 1921- *55*
Lawrinson, Julia 1969- *141*
Lawson, Amy
    See Gordon, Amy
Lawson, Carol (Antell) 1946- *42*
Lawson, Don(ald Elmer) 1917-1990 .... *9*
Lawson, Joan 1906- *55*
Lawson, Julie 1947- *126*
    Earlier sketch in SATA *79*
    See also CLR *89*
Lawson, Marion Tubbs 1896-1994 .... *22*

Lawson, Robert 1892-1957 .... *100*
    See also YABC *2*
    See also CLR *73*
Lawton, Clive A. 1951- *145*
Laxdal, Vivienne 1962- *112*
Laybourn, Emma *193*
Layburn, Joe *228*
Laycock, George (Edwin) 1921- *5*
Layne, Laura
    See Knott, William C(ecil, Jr.)
Layne, Steven L. *171*
Layson, Annelex Hofstra 1938(?)- *211*
Layton, Neal 1971- *187*
    Earlier sketch in SATA *152*
Layton, Neal Andrew
    See Layton, Neal
Lazare, Gerald John 1927- *44*
Lazare, Jerry
    See Lazare, Gerald John
Lazarevich, Mila 1942- *17*
Lazarus, Keo Felker 1913-1993 .... *21*
    Obituary *129*
Lea, Alec 1907- *19*
Lea, Bob 1952- *203*
Lea, Joan
    See Neufeld, John (Arthur)
Leach, Maria 1892-1977 .... *39*
    Brief entry *28*
Leacock, Elspeth 1946- *131*
Leacroft, Helen (Mabel Beal) 1919- *6*
Leacroft, Richard (Vallance Becher) 1914- *6*
Leaf, Margaret P. 1909(?)-1988
    Obituary *55*
Leaf, (Wilbur) Munro 1905-1976 .... *20*
    See also CLR *25*
Leaf, VaDonna Jean 1929- *26*
Leah, Devorah
    See Devorah-Leah
Leakey, Richard E(rskine Frere) 1944- *42*
Leal, Ann Haywood *216*
Leander, Ed
    See Richelson, Geraldine
Lear, Edward 1812-1888 .... *100*
    Earlier sketch in SATA *18*
    See also CLR *169*
Lears, Laurie 1955- *127*
Leasor, James 1923-2007 .... *54*
Leasor, Thomas James
    See Leasor, James
Leavitt, Jerome E(dward) 1916- *23*
Leavitt, Martine 1953- *170*
LeBar, Mary E(velyn) 1910-1982 .... *35*
LeBlanc, Annette M. 1965- *68*
LeBlanc, L(ee) 1913- *54*
LeBox, Annette 1943- *145*
Lebrun, Claude 1929- *66*
Le Cain, Errol (John) 1941-1989 .... *68*
    Obituary *60*
    Earlier sketch in SATA *6*
Lechermeier, Philippe 1968- *235*
Lechner, Jack *201*
Lechner, John 1966- *200*
Leck, James 1973- *229*
Lecourt, Nancy (Hoyt) 1951- *73*
Ledbetter, Suzann 1953- *119*
Leder, Jane Mersky 1945- *61*
    Brief entry *51*
Lederer, Muriel 1929- *48*
Lederer, William J. 1912-2009 .... *62*
Lederer, William Julius
    See Lederer, William J.
Lee, Amanda
    See Baggett, Nancy
    and Buckholtz, Eileen (Garber)
    and Glick, Ruth
Lee, Benjamin 1921- *27*
Lee, Betsy 1949- *37*
Lee, Carol
    See Fletcher, Helen Jill
Lee, Carol Ann 1969- *185*
Lee, Chinlun *182*

Lee, Cora 223
　See Anderson, Catherine Corley
Lee, Dennis (Beynon) 1939- 102
　Earlier sketch in SATA *14*
　See also CLR *3*
Lee, Dom 1959- 146
　Autobiography Feature 121
　Earlier sketch in SATA *83*
　See also SAAS *26*
Lee, Doris Emrick 1905-1983 44
　Obituary 35
Lee, Edward
　See Lee, J. Edward
Lee, Elizabeth Rogers 1940- 90
Lee, Harper 1926- 11
　See also CLR *169*
Lee, Hector Viveros 1962- 115
Lee, Howard N.
　See Goulart, Ron
Lee, Huy Voun 1969- 217
　Earlier sketch in SATA *129*
Lee, Insu 213
Lee, J. Edward 1953- 130
Lee, Jared 1943- 215
Lee, Jared D.
　See Lee, Jared
Lee, Jeanne M. 1943- 138
Lee, John R(obert) 1923-1976 27
Lee, Jordan
　See Scholefield, Alan
Lee, Joseph Edward
　See Lee, J. Edward
Lee, Julian
　See Latham, Jean Lee
Lee, Linda
　See Eyerly, Jeannette
Lee, Liz
　See Lee, Elizabeth Rogers
Lee, Lucy
　See Talbot, Charlene Joy
Lee, Lyn 1953- 128
Lee, Manning de Villeneuve 1894-1980 37
　Obituary 22
Lee, Marian
　See Clish, (Lee) Marian
Lee, Marie G. 1964- 178
　Earlier sketches in SATA *81, 130*
Lee, Marie Myung-Ok
　See Lee, Marie G.
Lee, Mary Price 1934- 82
　Earlier sketch in SATA *8*
Lee, Mildred
　See Scudder, Mildred Lee
Lee, Nelle Harper
　See Lee, Harper
Lee, Richard S. 1927- 82
Lee, Robert C. 1931- 20
Lee, Robert Edwin 1918-1994 65
　Obituary 82
Lee, Robert J. 1921- 10
Lee, Roy
　See Hopkins, Clark
Lee, Sally 1943- 67
Lee, Suzy 193
Lee, Tammie
　See Townsend, Thomas L.
Lee, Tanith 1947- 185
　Earlier sketches in SATA *8, 88, 134*
Lee, Virginia 1976- 208
Lee, Y.S. 1974- 232
Leech, Ben
　See Bowkett, Stephen
Leeds, Contance 188
Leedy, Loreen 1959- 175
　Brief entry 50
　Earlier sketches in SATA *54, 84, 128*
Leedy, Loreen Janelle
　See Leedy, Loreen
Lee-Hostetler, Jeri 1940- 63
Leekley, Thomas B(riggs) 1910-2001 *Volume 23*

Leeming, Jo Ann
　See Leeming, Joseph
Leeming, Joseph 1897-1968 26
Leemis, Ralph B. 1954- 72
Leese, Jennifer L.B. 1970- 163
Leeson, Muriel 1920- 54
Leeson, R. A.
　See Leeson, Robert (Arthur)
Leeson, Robert (Arthur) 1928- 76
　Earlier sketch in SATA *42*
Lee Tae-Jun 1904-1956(?) 194
Lee-Tai, Amy 1964- 189
Leffland, Ella 1931- 65
Leffler, Silke 197
Lefler, Irene (Whitney) 1917- 12
LeFrak, Karen 182
Le Gallienne, Eva 1899-1991 9
　Obituary 68
Legg, Gerald 1947- 143
Legg, Sarah Martha Ross Bruggeman (?)-1982
　Obituary 40
LeGrand
　See Henderson, LeGrand
Le Guin, Ursula K. 1929- 194
　Earlier sketches in SATA *4, 52, 99, 149*
　See also CLR *173*
Le Guin, Ursula Kroeber
　See Le Guin, Ursula K.
Legum, Colin 1919-2003 10
Lehman, Barbara 1963- 170
　Earlier sketch in SATA *115*
Lehman, Bob 91
Lehman, Elaine 91
Lehmann, Debra Lynn
　See Vanasse, Deb
Lehman-Wilzig, Tami 1950- 224
Lehn, Cornelia 1920- 46
Lehne, Judith Logan 1947- 93
Lehr, Delores 1920- 10
Lehr, Norma 1930- 71
Leiber, Fritz (Reuter, Jr.) 1910-1992 45
　Obituary 73
Leibold, Jay 1957- 57
　Brief entry 52
Leichman, Seymour 1933- 5
Leick, Bonnie 205
Leigh, Nila K. 1981- 81
Leigh, Tom 1947- 46
Leigh-Pemberton, John 1911-1997 35
Leighton, Clare (Veronica Hope)
　1899-1989 37
Leighton, Margaret (Carver) 1896-1987 1
　Obituary 52
Leijten, Aileen 216
Leiner, Al(an) 1938- 83
Leiner, Katherine 1949- 93
Leipold, L. Edmond 1902-1983 16
Leisk, David (Johnson) 1906-1975 30
　Obituary 26
　Earlier sketch in SATA *1*
　See also CLR *98*
Leist, Christina 226
Leister, Mary 1917- 29
Leitch, Patricia 1933- 98
　Earlier sketch in SATA *11*
Leitner, Isabella 1924- 86
Lekich, John 202
Leland, Bob 1956- 92
Leland, Robert E.
　See Leland, Bob
Leloup, Genevieve 230
Lematre, Pascal 1967- 225
　Earlier sketch in SATA *176*
Lember, Barbara Hirsch 1941- 92
LeMieux, A.C. 1954- 125
　Earlier sketch in SATA *90*
LeMieux, Anne
　See LeMieux, A.C.
LeMieux, Anne Connelly
　See LeMieux, A.C.
Lemieux, Michele 1955- 139

Lemke, Horst 1922- 38
Lemna, Don 1936- 216
Lenain, Thierry 1959- 201
Lenanton, Carola Mary Anima Oman
　See Oman, Carola (Mary Anima)
Lenard, Alexander 1910-1972
　Obituary 21
Lendroth, Susan 207
L'Engle, Madeleine 1918-2007 128
　Obituary 186
　Earlier sketches in SATA *1, 27, 75*
　See also CLR *172*
　See also SAAS *15*
L'Engle, Madeleine Camp Franklin
　See L'Engle, Madeleine
Lengyel, Cornel Adam 1915- 27
Lengyel, Emil 1895-1985 3
　Obituary 42
Lennon, John 1940-1980 114
Lennon, John Ono
　See Lennon, John
Leno, Jay 1950- 154
LeNoir, Janice 1941- 89
Lens, Sidney 1912-1986 13
　Obituary 48
Lenski, Lois 1893-1974 100
　Earlier sketches in SATA *1, 26*
　See also CLR *26*
Lent, Blair 1930-2009 133
　Obituary 200
　Earlier sketch in SATA *2*
Lent, Henry Bolles 1901-1973 17
Lent, John 1948- 108
Leodhas, Sorche Nic
　See Alger, Leclaire (Gowans)
Leokum, Arkady 1916(?)- 45
Leon, Carol Boyd 212
Leon, Sharon 1959- 79
Leonard, Alison 1944- 70
Leonard, Anna
　See Gilman, Laura Anne
Leonard, Constance (Brink) 1923- 42
　Brief entry 40
Leonard, Dutch
　See Leonard, Elmore
Leonard, Elmore 1925- 163
Leonard, Elmore John, Jr.
　See Leonard, Elmore
Leonard, Jonathan N(orton) 1903-1975 36
Leonard, Laura 1923- 75
Leonard, Tom 1955- 207
Leonetti, Mike 1958- 202
Leong, Gor Yun
　See Ellison, Virginia H(owell)
Leonhard, Herb 217
Leonhardt, Alice 1950- 234
　Earlier sketch in SATA *152*
Lerangis, Peter 1955- 171
　Earlier sketch in SATA *72*
Lerman, Josh 215
Lerner, Aaron 1920-2007 35
　Obituary 179
Lerner, Aaron Bunsen
　See Lerner, Aaron
Lerner, Carol 1927- 86
　Earlier sketch in SATA *33*
　See also CLR *34*
　See also SAAS *12*
Lerner, Gerda 1920- 65
Lerner, Harriet 1944- 101
Lerner, Marguerite Rush 1924-1987 11
　Obituary 51
Lerner, Sharon (Ruth) 1938-1982 11
　Obituary 29
Leroe, Ellen 1949- 99
　Brief entry 51
　Earlier sketch in SATA *61*
Leroe, Ellen W.
　See Leroe, Ellen
Leroe, Ellen Whitney
　See Leroe, Ellen

Leroux, Gaston 1868-1927 65
Leroux-Hugon, Helene 1955- 132
LeRoy, Gen 52
  Brief entry 36
Lerrigo, Marion Olive 1898-1968
  Obituary 29
LeShan, Eda J(oan) 1922-2002 21
  See also CLR 6
Leshem, Yossi 1947- 222
LeSieg, Theo.
  See Dr. Seuss
Lesinski, Jeanne M. 1960- 120
Leslie, Robert Franklin 1911-1990 7
Leslie, Roger 1961- 168
Leslie, Roger James
  See Leslie, Roger
Leslie, Sarah
  See McGuire, Leslie (Sarah)
LeSourd, Catherine
  See Marshall, (Sarah) Catherine (Wood)
Lessac, Frane
  See Lessac, Frane
Lessac, Frane 1954- 209
  Earlier sketches in SATA 61, 148
Lessem, Dino Don
  See Lessem, Don
Lessem, Don 1951- 182
  Earlier sketches in SATA 97, 155
Lesser, Margaret 1899(?)-1979
  Obituary 22
Lesser, Rika 1953- 53
Lester, Alison 1952- 218
  Earlier sketches in SATA 50, 90, 129
Lester, Helen 1936- 189
  Earlier sketches in SATA 46, 92, 145
Lester, Julius 1939- 157
  Earlier sketches in SATA 12, 74, 112
  See also CLR 143
Lester, Julius Bernard
  See Lester, Julius
Lester, Mike 1955- 206
  Earlier sketch in SATA 131
Le Sueur, Meridel 1900-1996 6
Leszczynski, Diana 211
Lethcoe, Jason 191
Le Tord, Bijou 1945- 95
  Earlier sketch in SATA 49
Letts, Billie 1938- 121
Letts, Elizabeth
  See Alalou, Elizabeth
Leuck, Laura 1962- 192
  Earlier sketches in SATA 85, 146
Leung, Hilary 1975- 225
Leutscher, Alfred (George) 1913- 23
Levai, Blaise 1919- 39
le Vann, Kate 237
Levchuk, Lisa 215
Leveen, Tom 230
Levenkron, Steven 1941- 86
Leverich, Kathleen 1948- 103
LeVert, John 1946- 55
Levert, Mireille 1956- 211
LeVert, William John
  See LeVert, John
Levete, Sarah 1961- 153
Levin, Betty 1927- 201
  Earlier sketches in SATA 19, 84, 137
  See also SAAS 11
Levin, Ira 1929-2007 66
  Obituary 187
Levin, Ira Marvin
  See Levin, Ira
Levin, Marcia Obrasky 1918- 13
Levin, Meyer 1905-1981 21
  Obituary 27
Levin, Miriam (Ramsfelder) 1962- 97
Levine, Abby 1943- 54
  Brief entry 52
Levine, Anna 212
Levine, Betty K(rasne) 1933- 66

Levine, David 1926-2009 43
  Brief entry 35
Levine, Edna S(imon) 35
Levine, Ellen 1939- 190
Levine, Evan 1962- 77
  Earlier sketch in SATA 74
Levine, Gail Carson 1947- 195
  Earlier sketches in SATA 98, 161
  See also CLR 85
Levine, I(srael) E. 1923-2003 12
  Obituary 146
Levine, Joan Goldman 11
Levine, Joseph 1910- 33
Levine, Kristin 1974- 213
Levine, Marge 1934- 81
Levine, Rhoda 14
Levine, Sarah 1970- 57
Levine, Shar 1953- 131
Levine-Freidus, Gail
  See Provost, Gail Levine
Levinson, Nancy Smiler 1938- 211
  Earlier sketches in SATA 33, 80, 140
Levinson, Riki 99
  Brief entry 49
  Earlier sketch in SATA 52
Levithan, David 1972- 235
  Earlier sketch in SATA 166
Levitin, Sonia 1934- 192
  Autobiography Feature 131
  Earlier sketches in SATA 4, 68, 119, 131
  See also CLR 53
  See also SAAS 2
Levitt, Sidney (Mark) 1947- 68
Levon, O. U.
  See Kesey, Ken
Levoy, Myron 1930- 49
  Brief entry 37
Levy, Barrie 112
Levy, Constance 1931- 140
  Earlier sketch in SATA 73
  See also SAAS 22
Levy, Debbie 1957- 232
Levy, Deborah Marian
  See Levy, Debbie
Levy, Elizabeth 1942- 169
  Earlier sketches in SATA 31, 69, 107
  See also SAAS 18
Levy, Janice 172
Levy, Marilyn 1937- 67
Levy, Nathan 1945- 63
Levy, Robert 1945- 82
Lewees, John
  See Stockton, Francis Richard
Lewin, Betsy 1937- 222
  Autobiography Feature 115
  Earlier sketches in SATA 32, 90, 169
Lewin, Hugh 1939- 72
  Brief entry 40
  See also CLR 9
Lewin, Ted 1935- 226
  Autobiography Feature 115
  Earlier sketches in SATA 21, 76, 119, 165,
  195
Lewis, Alice C. 1936- 46
Lewis, Alice Hudson 1895(?)-1971
  Obituary 29
Lewis, Amanda 1955- 80
Lewis, Anthony 1927- 27
Lewis, Anthony 1966- 227
  Earlier sketch in SATA 120
Lewis, Barbara A. 1943- 73
Lewis, Beverly 1949- 80
Lewis, Brenda Ralph 1932- 72
Lewis, Brian 1963- 128
Lewis, C. S. 1898-1963 100
  Earlier sketch in SATA 13
  See also CLR 173
Lewis, Claudia (Louise) 1907-2001 5
Lewis, Clive Staples
  See Lewis, C. S.
Lewis, Cynthia Copeland 1960- 111

Lewis, E. M. 123
  Earlier sketch in SATA 20
Lewis, Earl Bradley
  See Lewis, E.B.
Lewis, E.B. 1956- 211
  Earlier sketches in SATA 93, 124, 168
Lewis, Elizabeth Foreman 1892-1958 121
  See also YABC 2
Lewis, Francine
  See Wells, Helen
Lewis, Harry Sinclair
  See Lewis, Sinclair
Lewis, Hilda (Winifred) 1896-1974
  Obituary 20
Lewis, J. Patrick 1942- 205
  Earlier sketches in SATA 69, 104, 162
Lewis, Jack P(earl) 1919- 65
Lewis, Jean 1924- 61
Lewis, Jon Samuel
  See Lewis, J.S.
Lewis, Joseph Anthony
  See Lewis, Anthony
Lewis, J.S. 1972- 203
Lewis, Julinda
  See Lewis-Ferguson, Julinda
Lewis, Kevin 173
Lewis, Kim 1951- 217
  Earlier sketches in SATA 84, 136
Lewis, Linda (Joy) 1946- 67
Lewis, Lucia Z.
  See Anderson, Lucia (Lewis)
Lewis, Marjorie 1929- 40
  Brief entry 35
Lewis, Mary 1907(?)-1988 64
  Obituary 56
Lewis, Mervyn
  See Frewer, Glyn (M.)
Lewis, Michael
  See Untermeyer, Louis
Lewis, Naomi 1911-2009 144
  Earlier sketch in SATA 76
Lewis, Paeony 1960- 173
Lewis, Paul
  See Gerson, Noel Bertram
Lewis, Richard 1935- 3
Lewis, Richard 1956- 209
Lewis, Rob 1962- 72
Lewis, Roger
  See Zarchy, Harry
Lewis, Rose 209
Lewis, Rose A.
  See Lewis, Rose
Lewis, Shannon
  See Llywelyn, Morgan
Lewis, Shari 1934-1998 35
  Brief entry 30
  Obituary 104
Lewis, Sylvan R.
  See Aronson, Virginia
Lewis, Thomas P(arker) 1936- 27
Lewis, Wendy A. 1966- 150
Lewis-Ferguson, Julinda 1955- 85
Lewison, Wendy Cheyette 177
Lewiton, Mina 1904-1970 2
Lew-Vriethoff, Joanne 186
Lexau, Joan M. 130
  Earlier sketches in SATA 1, 36
Ley, Willy 1906-1969 2
Leydon, Rita (Floden) 1949- 21
Leyland, Eric (Arthur) 1911- 37
L'Hommedieu, Dorothy Keasley 1885-1961
  Obituary 29
Li, Xiao Jun 1952- 86
Liao, Jimmy 1958- 202
Liatsos, Sandra Olson 1942- 103
Libby, Alisa M. 189
Libby, Barbara M. 153
Libby, Bill
  See Libby, William M.
Libby, William M. 1927-1984 5
  Obituary 39

Liberty, Gene 1924- *3*
Lichtenheld, Tom *208*
  Earlier sketch in SATA *152*
Lichtman, Wendy 1946- *193*
Liddell, Kenneth 1912-1975 .... *63*
Liddiment, Carol *224*
Lidz, Jane *120*
Lieb, Josh 1972- *224*
Lieberman, E(dwin) James 1934- *62*
Liebers, Arthur 1913-1984 .... *12*
Lieblich, Irene 1923- *22*
Liers, Emil E(rnest) 1890-1975 .... *37*
Lies, Brian 1963- *190*
  Earlier sketch in SATA *131*
Lieshout, Elle van
  See van Lieshout, Elle
Liestman, Vicki 1961- *72*
Lietz, Gerald S. 1918- *11*
Liew, Sonny 1974- *219*
Life, Kay (Guinn) 1930- *83*
Lifton, Betty Jean 1926-2010 .... *118*
  Earlier sketch in SATA *6*
Lifton, Robert Jay 1926- *66*
Light, Steve *237*
Lightburn, Ron 1954- *91*
Lightburn, Sandra 1955- *91*
Lightner, A. M.
  See Hopf, Alice (Martha) L(ightner)
Lightner, Alice
  See Hopf, Alice (Martha) L(ightner)
Lignell, Lois 1911- *37*
Liles, Maurine Walpole 1935- *81*
Lillegard, Dee *184*
Lilley, Stephen R. 1950- *97*
Lilley, Stephen Ray
  See Lilley, Stephen R.
Lillington, Kenneth (James) 1916-1998 ...... *39*
Lilly, Nate *182*
Lilly, Ray
  See Curtis, Richard
Lim, John 1932- *43*
Liman, Ellen (Fogelson) 1936- *22*
Limb, Sue 1946- *203*
  Earlier sketch in SATA *158*
Limburg, Peter R(ichard) 1929- *13*
Lin, Grace 1974- *198*
  Earlier sketches in SATA *111, 162*
Lincoln, C(harles) Eric 1924-2000 .... *5*
Lincoln, Christopher 1952- *208*
Lincoln, Hazel *187*
Lincoln, James
  See Bates, Katharine Lee
Lindbergh, Anne
  See Sapieyevski, Anne Lindbergh
Lindbergh, Anne Morrow 1906-2001 .... *33*
  Obituary *125*
Lindbergh, Anne Spencer Morrow
  See Lindbergh, Anne Morrow
Lindbergh, Charles A(ugustus, Jr.)
  1902-1974 .... *33*
Lindbergh, Reeve 1945- *163*
  Earlier sketch in SATA *116*
Lindblom, Steven (Winther) 1946- *94*
  Brief entry *39*
  Earlier sketch in SATA *42*
Linde, Gunnel 1924- *5*
Lindenbaum, Pija 1955- *183*
  Earlier sketches in SATA *77, 144*
Lindgren, Astrid (Anna Emilia Ericsson)
  1907-2002 .... *38*
  Obituary *128*
  Earlier sketch in SATA *2*
  See also CLR *119*
Lindgren, Barbro 1937- *207*
  Brief entry *46*
  Earlier sketches in SATA *63, 120*
  See also CLR *86*
Lindman, Maj (Jan) 1886-1972 .... *43*
Lindo, Elvira 1962- *219*
Lindop, Edmund 1925- *5*
Lindquist, Jennie Dorothea 1899-1977 *Volume 13*

Lindquist, Rowena Cory 1958- *98*
Lindquist, Willis 1908-1988 .... *20*
Lindsay, Nicholas Vachel
  See Lindsay, Vachel
Lindsay, Norman Alfred William
  1879-1969 .... *67*
  See also CLR *8*
Lindsay, Vachel 1879-1931 .... *40*
Lindsey, Kathleen D(orothy) 1949- *153*
Line, David
  See Davidson, Lionel
Line, Les 1935-2010 .... *27*
Lines, Kathleen Mary 1902-1988
  Obituary *61*
Linfield, Esther *40*
Lingard, Joan (Amelia) 1932- *130*
  Autobiography Feature *130*
  Earlier sketches in SATA *8, 74, 114*
  See also CLR *89*
  See also SAAS *5*
Link, Martin 1934- *28*
Linn, Margot
  See Ziefert, Harriet
Linnea, Sharon 1956- *82*
Lintern, Tom *228*
Lion, Melissa 1976- *176*
Lionni, Leo(nard) 1910-1999 .... *72*
  Obituary *118*
  Earlier sketch in SATA *8*
  See also CLR *71*
Lipinsky de Orlov, Lino S. 1908- *22*
Lipkind, William 1904-1974 .... *15*
Lipman, David 1931-2008 .... *21*
Lipman, Matthew 1923-2010 .... *14*
Lipp, Frederick *204*
Lippincott, Bertram 1898(?)-1985
  Obituary *42*
Lippincott, Gary A. 1953- *220*
  Earlier sketches in SATA *73, 119*
Lippincott, Joseph W(harton) 1887-1976 ..... *17*
Lippincott, Sarah Lee 1920- *22*
Lippman, Peter J. 1936- *31*
Lipsyte, Robert 1938- *198*
  Earlier sketches in SATA *5, 68, 113, 161*
  See also CLR *76*
Lipsyte, Robert Michael
  See Lipsyte, Robert
Lisandrelli, Elaine Slivinski 1951- *94*
Lisker, Sonia O. 1933- *44*
Lisle, Holly 1960- *208*
  Earlier sketch in SATA *98*
Lisle, Janet Taylor 1947- *150*
  Brief entry *47*
  Earlier sketches in SATA *59, 96*
  See also SAAS *14*
Lisle, Rebecca *162*
Lisle, Seward D.
  See Ellis, Edward S.
Lisowski, Gabriel 1946- *47*
  Brief entry *31*
Liss, Howard 1922-1995 .... *4*
  Obituary *84*
Lissiat, Amy
  See Thompson, Colin
Lisson, Deborah 1941- *110*
  Earlier sketch in SATA *71*
List, Ilka Katherine 1935- *6*
Liston, Robert A. 1927- *5*
Litchfield, Ada B(assett) 1916-1999 .... *5*
Litchfield, Jo 1973- *116*
Lithgow, John 1945- *145*
Lithgow, John Arthur
  See Lithgow, John
Litowinsky, Olga 1936- *26*
Litowinsky, Olga Jean
  See Litowinsky, Olga
Littke, Lael J. 1929- *140*
  Earlier sketches in SATA *51, 83*
Little, A. Edward
  See Klein, Aaron E.
Little, Douglas 1942- *96*

Little, (Flora) Jean 1932- *149*
  Earlier sketches in SATA *2, 68, 106*
  See also CLR *4*
  See also SAAS *17*
Little, Lessie Jones 1906-1986 .... *60*
  Obituary *50*
Little, Mary E. 1912-1999 .... *28*
Littlechild, George 1958- *85*
Littledale, Freya 1929-1992 .... *74*
  Earlier sketch in SATA *2*
Littlefield, Bill 1948- *83*
Littlefield, Holly 1963- *97*
Littlesugar, Amy 1953- *176*
  Earlier sketch in SATA *122*
Littleton, Mark R. 1950- *142*
  Earlier sketch in SATA *89*
Littlewood, Karin *211*
Littman, Sarah Darer *221*
  Earlier sketch in SATA *175*
Litty, Julie 1971- *181*
Litwin, Mike *235*
Litzinger, Rosanne 1948- *196*
Liu, Cynthea *221*
Lively, Penelope 1933- *164*
  Earlier sketches in SATA *7, 60, 101*
  See also CLR *159*
Lively, Penelope Margaret
  See Lively, Penelope
Liverakos, L. A.
  See Gilman, Laura Anne
Liversidge, (Henry) Douglas 1913- *8*
Livesey, Claire (Warner) 1927- *127*
Livingston, Carole 1941- *42*
Livingston, (M.) Irene 1932- *150*
Livingston, Myra Cohn 1926-1996 .... *68*
  Obituary *92*
  Earlier sketch in SATA *5*
  See also CLR *7*
  See also SAAS *1*
Livingston, Richard R(oland) 1922- *8*
Livo, Norma J. 1929- *76*
Liwska, Renata *199*
Ljungkvist, Laura *180*
Llerena Aguirre, Carlos 1952- *19*
Llerena Aguirre, Carlos Antonio
  See Llerena Aguirre, Carlos
Llewellyn, Claire 1954- *196*
  Earlier sketches in SATA *77, 143*
Llewellyn, Grace 1964- *110*
Llewellyn, Richard
  See Llewellyn Lloyd, Richard Dafydd Vivian
Llewellyn, Sam 1948- *185*
  Earlier sketch in SATA *95*
Llewellyn, Tom 1964- *234*
Llewellyn Lloyd, Richard Dafydd Vivian
  1906-1983 .... *11*
  Obituary *37*
Llewelyn, T. Harcourt
  See Hamilton, Charles (Harold St. John)
Lloyd, Alan
  See Lloyd, A.R.
Lloyd, Alan Richard
  See Lloyd, A.R.
Lloyd, Alison 1966- *231*
Lloyd, A.R. 1927- *168*
  Earlier sketch in SATA *97*
Lloyd, David
  See Lloyd, David T.
Lloyd, David T. 1954- *167*
Lloyd, E. James
  See James, Elizabeth
Lloyd, Errol 1943- *22*
Lloyd, Hugh
  See Fitzhugh, Percy Keese
Lloyd, James
  See James, Elizabeth
Lloyd, Megan 1958- *189*
  Earlier sketches in SATA *77, 117*
Lloyd, Norman 1909-1980
  Obituary *23*

Lloyd, (Mary) Norris 1908-1993 .... *10*
    Obituary *75*
Lloyd, Saci 1967- *220*
Lloyd, Sam *183*
Lloyd, Tanya
    See Kyi, Tanya Lloyd
Lloyd-Jones, Sally 1960- *179*
Lloyd Webber, Andrew 1948- *56*
Llywelyn, Morgan 1937- *109*
Lo, Ginnie *165*
Lo, Malinda 1974- *222*
Lo, Virginia M.
    See Lo, Ginnie
Lobato, Jose Bento Monteiro 1882-1948 ... *114*
Lobel, Anita (Kempler) 1934- *162*
    Earlier sketches in SATA *6, 55, 96*
Lobel, Arnold (Stark) 1933-1987 .... *55*
    Obituary *54*
    Earlier sketch in SATA *6*
    See also CLR *5*
Lobel, Gillian *181*
Lobsenz, Amelia *12*
Lobsenz, Norman M(itchell) 1919- *6*
Lochak, Michele 1936- *39*
Lochlons, Colin
    See Jackson, C(aary) Paul
Locke, Clinton W. *1*
Locke, Elsie (Violet) 1912-2001 .... *87*
Locke, Gary 1963- *197*
Locke, Lucie 1904-1989 .... *10*
Locke, Robert 1944- *63*
    See also CLR *39*
Locker, Thomas 1937- *109*
    Earlier sketch in SATA *59*
    See also CLR *14*
Lockhart, E.
    See Jenkins, Emily
Lockridge, Hildegarde (Dolson)
    1908-1981 .... *121*
    Earlier sketch in SATA *5*
Lockwood, Mary
    See Spelman, Mary
Lodge, Bernard 1933- *215*
    Earlier sketches in SATA *33, 107*
Lodge, Jo 1966- *173*
    Earlier sketch in SATA *112*
Loeb, Jeffrey 1946- *57*
Loeb, Robert H., Jr. 1917- *21*
Loefgren, Ulf 1931- *3*
Loehfelm, Bill 1969- *153*
Loehr, Mallory *184*
Loehr, Patrick 1968(?)- *194*
Loeper, John J(oseph) 1929- *118*
    Earlier sketch in SATA *10*
Loescher, Ann Dull 1942- *20*
Loescher, Gil 1945- *20*
Loescher, Gilburt Damian
    See Loescher, Gil
Loewer, Jean Jenkins
    See Jenkins, Jean
Loewer, (Henry) Peter 1934- *98*
LoFaro, Jerry 1959- *77*
Lofo
    See Heimann, Rolf
Lofthouse, Liz *199*
Lofting, Hugh (John) 1886-1947 .... *100*
    Earlier sketch in SATA *15*
    See also CLR *143*
Lofts, Norah (Robinson) 1904-1983 .... *8*
    Obituary *36*
Logan, Alysia
    See Divine, L.
Logan, Jake
    See Knott, William C(ecil, Jr.)
    and Krepps, Robert W(ilson)
    and Pearl, Jacques Bain
    and Riefe, Alan
    and Rifkin, Shepard
    and Smith, Martin Cruz
Logan, Laura *237*

Logan, Mark
    See Nicole, Christopher
Logan, Rochelle 1954- *169*
Logsted, Greg *221*
Logston, Anne 1962- *112*
Logue, Christopher 1926- *23*
Logue, Mary 1952- *161*
    Earlier sketch in SATA *112*
Logue, Mary Louise
    See Logue, Mary
Loh, Morag 1935- *73*
Lohans, Alison 1949- *101*
Loizeaux, William *185*
Loken, Newton Clayton 1919- *26*
Lomas, Steve
    See Brennan, Joseph Lomas
Lomask, Milton (Nachman) 1909-1991 .... *20*
Lombard, Jenny *178*
Lombino, Salvatore
    See Hunter, Evan
LoMonaco, Palmyra 1932- *102*
London, Jack 1876-1916 .... *18*
    See also CLR *108*
London, Jane
    See Geis, Darlene Stern
London, John Griffith
    See London, Jack
London, Jonathan 1947- *221*
    Earlier sketches in SATA *74, 113, 157*
Lonergan, (Pauline) Joy (MacLean) 1909- ... *10*
Lonette, Reisie (Dominee) 1924- *43*
Long, Cathryn J. 1946- *89*
Long, Earlene (Roberta) 1938- *50*
Long, Emmett
    See Leonard, Elmore
Long, Ethan 1968(?)- *223*
    Earlier sketch in SATA *182*
Long, Helen Beecher *1*
Long, Judith Elaine 1953- *20*
Long, Judy
    See Long, Judith Elaine
Long, Kim 1949- *69*
Long, Laura Mooney 1892-1967
    Obituary *29*
Long, Laurel *203*
Long, Loren 1966(?)- *188*
    Earlier sketch in SATA *151*
Long, Melinda 1960- *152*
Long, Sylvia 1948- *179*
    Earlier sketch in SATA *120*
Longbeard, Frederick
    See Longyear, Barry B(rookes)
Longfellow, Henry Wadsworth 1807-1882 ... *19*
    See also CLR *99*
Longfellow, Layne 1937- *102*
Longfellow, Layne A.
    See Longfellow, Layne
Longman, Harold S. 1919- *5*
Longsworth, Polly 1933- *28*
Longtemps, Kenneth 1933- *17*
Longway, A. Hugh
    See Lang, Andrew
Longyear, Barry B(rookes) 1942- *117*
Look, Lenore *180*
Loomans, Diane 1955- *90*
Loomis, Christine *160*
    Earlier sketch in SATA *113*
Loomis, Jennifer A. 1942- *101*
Loomis, Robert D. *5*
Lopez, Angelo (Cayas) 1967- *83*
Lopez, Antonio Castro
    See Castro L., Antonio
Lopez, Barry 1945- *67*
Lopez, Barry Holstun
    See Lopez, Barry
Lopez, Jack 1950- *178*
Lopez, Loretta 1963- *190*
Lopez, Lorraine 1956- *181*
Lopez, Lorraine M.
    See Lopez, Lorraine
Lopez, Mario 1973- *226*

Lopez, Rafael 1961(?)- *198*
Lopshire, Robert 1927-2002 .... *233*
    Earlier sketch in SATA *6*
Loraine, Connie
    See Reece, Colleen L.
Lorbiecki, Marybeth 1959- *172*
    Earlier sketch in SATA *121*
Lord, Athena V. 1932- *39*
Lord, Beman 1924-1991 .... *5*
    Obituary *69*
Lord, Bette Bao 1938- *58*
    See also CLR *151*
Lord, Cynthia *182*
Lord, Doreen Mildred Douglas
    See Lord, Douglas
Lord, Douglas 1904-1992 .... *12*
Lord, Janet *204*
Lord, John Vernon 1939- *21*
Lord, Michele *201*
Lord, Nancy J.
    See Titus, Eve
Lord, Patricia C. 1927-1988
    Obituary *58*
Lord, Walter 1917-2002 .... *3*
Lorde, Diana
    See Reno, Dawn E(laine)
Lorenz, Albert 1941- *115*
Lorenzini, Carlo
    See Collodi, Carlo
Lorey, Dean 1967- *193*
Lorimer, Janet 1941- *60*
Loring, Emilie (Baker) 1864(?)-1951 .... *51*
Lorkowski, Thomas V(incent) 1950- *92*
Lorkowski, Tom
    See Lorkowski, Thomas V(incent)
Lorraine, Walter (Henry) 1929- *16*
Lorrimer, Claire
    See Robins, Patricia
Loss, Joan 1933- *11*
Lothrop, Harriet Mulford Stone 1844-1924 . *20*
Lottridge, Celia Barker 1936- *157*
    Earlier sketch in SATA *112*
LoTurco, Laura 1963- *84*
Lotz, Wolfgang 1912-1981 .... *65*
Loughridge, Stuart 1978- *214*
Louie, Ai-Ling 1949- *40*
    Brief entry *34*
Louis, Catherine 1963- *186*
Louis, Pat
    See Francis, Dorothy
Louisburgh, Sheila Burnford
    See Burnford, Sheila (Philip Cochrane Every)
Louise, Anita
    See Riggio, Anita
Louise, Tina 1934- *191*
Lourie, Helen
    See Storr, Catherine (Cole)
Lourie, Peter 1952- *183*
    Earlier sketches in SATA *82, 142*
Lourie, Peter King
    See Lourie, Peter
Love, Ann 1947- *168*
    Earlier sketch in SATA *79*
Love, D. Anne 1949- *180*
    Earlier sketches in SATA *96, 145*
Love, Douglas 1967- *92*
Love, Judith Dufour
    See Love, Judy
Love, Judy *188*
Love, Katherine (Isabel) 1907- *3*
Love, Kathleen Ann
    See Love, Ann
Love, Maryann Cusimano *223*
Love, Sandra (Weller) 1940- *26*
Lovegrove, James 1965- *216*
Lovegrove, J.M.H.
    See Lovegrove, James
Lovejoy, Jack 1937- *116*
Lovelace, Delos Wheeler 1894-1967 .... *7*
Lovelace, Maud Hart 1892-1980 .... *2*
    Obituary *23*

Lovell, Ingraham
    See Bacon, Josephine Dodge (Daskam)
Lovelock, Brian 1956- 214
Loverseed, Amanda (Jane) 1965- 75
Lovett, Margaret (Rose) 1915- 22
Low, Alice 1926- 156
    Earlier sketches in SATA *11, 76*
Low, Elizabeth Hammond 1898-1991 5
Low, Joseph 1911-2007 14
Low, Penelope Margaret
    See Lively, Penelope
Low, William 177
Lowe, Helen 1961- 206
Lowe, Jay, Jr.
    See Loeper, John J(oseph)
Lowell, Pamela 187
Lowell, Susan 1950- 206
    Earlier sketches in SATA *81, 127*
Lowenstein, Dyno 1914-1996 6
Lowenstein, Sallie 1949- 116
Lowery, Linda 1949- 151
    Earlier sketch in SATA *74*
Lowery, Mike 227
Lowery, Kate 18
Lowitz, Anson C. 1901(?)-1978 18
Lowitz, Sadyebeth Heath 1901-1969 17
Lowndes, Robert A(ugustine) W(ard)
    1916-1998 117
Lowrey, Janette Sebring 1892-1986 43
Lowry, Lois 1937- 230
    Autobiography Feature 127
    Earlier sketches in SATA *23, 70, 111, 177*
    See also CLR *72*
    See also SAAS *3*
Lowry, Lois Hammersberg
    See Lowry, Lois
Lowry, Peter 1953- 7
Lowther, George F. 1913-1975
    Obituary 30
Loxton, Daniel 1975- 229
Loyie, Larry 1933- 150
Lozansky, Edward D. 1941- 62
Lozier, Herbert 1915- 26
Lubar, David 1954- 190
    Earlier sketch in SATA *133*
Lubell, Cecil 1912-2000 6
Lubell, Winifred 1914- 6
Lubell, Winifred A. Milius
    See Lubell, Winifred
Lubin, Leonard
    See Lubin, Leonard B.
Lubin, Leonard B. 1943-1994 45
    Brief entry 37
Lubka, S. Ruth 1948- 154
Lubner, Susan 185
Luby, Thia 1954- 124
Lucado, Max (Lee) 1955- 104
Lucas, Cedric 1962- 101
Lucas, David 1966- 208
Lucas, E(dward) V(errall) 1868-1938 20
Lucas, Eileen 1956- 113
    Earlier sketch in SATA *76*
Lucas, George 1944- 56
Lucas, Jerry 1940- 33
Lucas, Margeaux 186
Lucas, Victoria
    See Plath, Sylvia
Lucashenko, Melissa 1967- 104
Luccarelli, Vincent 1923- 90
Luce, Celia (Geneva Larsen) 1914- 38
Luce, Willard (Ray) 1914-1990 38
Lucht, Irmgard 1937- 82
Lucke, Deb 202
Luckett, Dave 1951- 220
    Earlier sketches in SATA *106, 167*
Luckhardt, Mildred Corell 1898-1990 5
Ludden, Allen (Ellsworth) 1918(?)-1981
    Obituary 27
Ludel, Jacqueline 1945- 64
Ludlow, Geoffrey
    See Meynell, Laurence Walter

Ludlum, Mabel Cleland
    See Widdemer, Mabel Cleland
Ludwig, Helen 33
Ludwig, Lyndell 1923- 63
Ludwig, Trudy 1959- 209
    Earlier sketch in SATA *166*
Luebs, Robin 1949- 212
Lueders, Edward (George) 1923- 14
Luenn, Nancy 1954- 79
    Earlier sketch in SATA *51*
Lufkin, Raymond H. 1897- 38
Lugard, Flora Louisa Shaw 1852-1929 21
Luger, Harriett Mandelay 1914- 23
Luhrmann, Winifred B(ruce) 1934- 11
Luis, Earlene W. 1929- 11
Lujan, Jorge 201
Lukas, Catherine
    See Albee, Sarah
Luke, Pauline 178
Luke, Pauline R.
    See Luke, Pauline
Lum, Bernice 230
Lum, Kate 229
Lum, Peter
    See Crowe, (Bettina) Peter Lum
Lumry, Amanda (R.) 159
Lund, Deb 157
Lund, Doris Herold 1919- 12
Lunde, Darrin 202
Lundebrek, Amy 1975- 213
Lung, Chang
    See Jordan, Robert
Lunge-Larsen, Lise 1955- 184
    Earlier sketch in SATA *138*
Lunn, Carolyn (Kowalczyk) 1960- 67
Lunn, Janet (Louise Swoboda) 1928- 110
    Earlier sketches in SATA *4, 68*
    See also CLR *18*
    See also SAAS *12*
Lunsford, Cin Forshay
    See Forshay-Lunsford, Cin
Lupica, Michael
    See Lupica, Mike
Lupica, Michael Thomas
    See Lupica, Mike
Lupica, Mike 1952- 236
    Earlier sketch in SATA *177*
Lupoff, Dick
    See Lupoff, Richard A.
Lupoff, Richard A. 1935- 60
Lupoff, Richard Allen
    See Lupoff, Richard A.
Lurie, Alison 1926- 112
    Earlier sketch in SATA *46*
Lurie, Morris 1938- 72
Lussert, Anneliese 1929- 101
Lusted, Marcia Amidon 1962- 143
Lustig, Arnost 1926-2011 56
Lustig, Loretta 1944- 46
Lutes, Jason 1967- 210
Luthardt, Kevin 1973- 172
Luther, Frank 1905-1980
    Obituary 25
Luther, Rebekah (Lyn) S(tiles) 1960- 90
Luttmann, Gail
    See Damerow, Gail
Luttrell, Guy L. 1938- 22
Luttrell, Ida (Alleene) 1934- 91
    Brief entry 35
    Earlier sketch in SATA *40*
Luttrell, William (J. III) 1954- 149
Lutz, John 1939- 180
Lutz, John Thomas
    See Lutz, John
Lutz, Norma Jean 1943- 122
Lutzeier, Elizabeth 1952- 72
Lutzker, Edythe 1904-1991 5
Luxbacher, Irene 1970- 219
    Earlier sketch in SATA *153*
Luzadder, Patrick 1954- 89
Luzzati, Emanuele 1921-2007 7

Luzzatto, Paola Caboara 1938- 38
Ly, Many 1977- 208
Lybbert, Tyler 1970- 88
Lydon, Michael 1942- 11
Lyfick, Warren
    See Reeves, Lawrence F.
Lyle, Katie Letcher 1938- 8
Lynch, Chris 1962- 209
    Earlier sketches in SATA *95, 131, 171*
    See also CLR *58*
Lynch, Janet Nichols 1952- 221
Lynch, Jay 1945- 204
Lynch, Lorenzo 1932- 7
Lynch, Marietta 1947- 29
Lynch, Patricia (Nora) 1898-1972 9
    See also CLR *167*
Lynch, Patrick James
    See Lynch, P.J.
Lynch, P.J. 1962- 213
    Earlier sketches in SATA *79, 122*
Lynds, Dennis 1924-2005 47
    Brief entry 37
Lyne, Alison Davis 188
Lyngseth, Joan
    See Davies, Joan
Lynn, Elizabeth A(nne) 1946- 99
Lynn, Mary
    See Brokamp, Marilyn
Lynn, Patricia
    See Watts, Mabel Pizzey
Lynn, Sarah 237
Lynn, Tracy 175
Lyon, Elinor 1921-2008 6
    Obituary 192
Lyon, Elinor Bruce
    See Lyon, Elinor
Lyon, George Ella 1949- 207
    Autobiography Feature 148
    Earlier sketches in SATA *68, 119, 148*
Lyon, Lea 1945- 212
Lyon, Lyman R.
    See de Camp, L. Sprague
Lyons, Dorothy M(arawee) 1907-1997 3
Lyons, Grant 1941- 30
Lyons, Jayne 226
Lyons, Marcus
    See Blish, James
Lyons, Mary E. 1947- 195
    Autobiography Feature 195
    Earlier sketches in SATA *93, 142*
Lyons, Mary Evelyn
    See Lyons, Mary E.
Lystad, Mary (Hanemann) 1928- 11
Lytle, Elizabeth Stewart 1949- 79
Lytle, Robert A. 1944- 119
Lyttle, Richard B(ard) 1927- 23
Lytton, Deborah 1966- 218
Lytton, Edward G.E.L. Bulwer-Lytton Baron
    See Bulwer-Lytton, Edward
Lytton of Knebworth, Baron
    See Bulwer-Lytton, Edward

M

Ma, Wenhai 1954- 84
Maar, Leonard (Frank, Jr.) 1927- 30
Maartens, Maretha 1945- 73
Maas, Selve -1997 14
Maass, Robert 195
Mabie, Grace
    See Mattern, Joanne
Mac
    See MacManus, Seumas
    and Maccari, Ruggero
Macalaster, Elizabeth G. 1951- 115
MacAlister, Katie 159
MacAlister, V. A.
    See McKernan, Victoria

MacAllan, Andrew
 See Leasor, James
MacAodhagain, Eamon
 See Egan, E. W.
MacArthur-Onslow, Annette Rosemary
 1933- 26
Macaulay, David (Alexander) 1946- 137
 Brief entry 27
 Earlier sketches in SATA 46, 72
 See also CLR 14
Macaulay, Teresa 1947- 95
Macauley, Theresa E.
 See Macaulay, Teresa
Macavinta, Courtney 176
MacBeth, George (Mann) 1932-1992 4
 Obituary 70
MacBride, Roger Lea 1929-1995 85
MacCarter, Don 1944- 91
MacClintock, Dorcas 1932- 8
MacCready, Robin Merrow 1959(?)- 190
MacCullough, Carolyn 174
MacDonald, Alan 1958- 192
MacDonald, Amy 1951- 156
 Autobiography Feature 156
 Earlier sketches in SATA 76, 136
MacDonald, Anne Elizabeth Campbell Bard
 -1958
 See MacDonald, Betty
MacDonald, Anne Louise 1955- 217
MacDonald, Anson
 See Heinlein, Robert A.
MacDonald, Betty 1908-1958
 See YABC 1
Macdonald, Blackie
 See Emrich, Duncan (Black Macdonald)
Macdonald, Caroline 1948- 86
 Obituary 111
 See also CLR 60
Macdonald, Dwight 1906-1982 29
 Obituary 33
MacDonald, George 1824-1905 100
 Earlier sketch in SATA 33
 See also CLR 67
MacDonald, Golden
 See Brown, Margaret Wise
Macdonald, Guy 195
Macdonald, James D. 1954- 67
 Earlier sketches in SATA 81, 114, 165, 1
Macdonald, Marcia
 See Hill, Grace Livingston
MacDonald, Margaret Read 1940- 194
 Earlier sketches in SATA 94, 164
Macdonald, Marianne 1934- 113
Macdonald, Mary
 See Gifford, Griselda
Macdonald, Maryann 1947- 189
 Earlier sketch in SATA 72
MacDonald, Ross 1957- 201
Macdonald, Shelagh 1937- 25
MacDonald, Suse 1940- 193
 Brief entry 52
 Earlier sketches in SATA 54, 109
Macdonald, Wendy 217
Macdonald, Wendy M.
 See Macdonald, Wendy
Macdonald, Zillah K(atherine) 1885-1979 ... 11
MacDonnell, Megan
 See Stevens, Serita
MacDougal, John
 See Blish, James
Mace, Elisabeth 1933- 27
Mace, Varian 1938- 49
MacEachern, Stephen 206
MacEwen, Gwendolyn (Margaret)
 1941-1987 50
 Obituary 55
Macfarlan, Allan A. 1892-1982 35
MacFarlane, Iris 1922- 11
MacGill-Callahan, Sheila 1926-2000 78
MacGregor, Carol Lynn 153

MacGregor, Ellen 1906-1954 39
 Brief entry 27
MacGregor-Hastie, Roy (Alasdhair Niall)
 1929- 3
MacGrory, Yvonne 1948- 142
Machado, Ana Maria 1941- 150
MacHale, D.J. 1956- 234
 Earlier sketch in SATA 175
MacHale, Donald James
 See MacHale, D.J.
Machetanz, Frederick 1908- 34
Machin, Sue
 See Williams, Sue
Machin Goodall, Daphne (Edith) 37
Macht, Norm
 See Macht, Norman L.
Macht, Norman L. 1929- 122
Macht, Norman Lee
 See Macht, Norman L.
Macht, Norman Lee
 See Macht, Norman L.
MacInnes, Cat 236
MacInnes, Helen (Clark) 1907-1985 22
 Obituary 44
Macintosh, Brownie 1950- 98
MacIntyre, Elisabeth 1916- 17
MacIntyre, Rod
 See MacIntyre, R.P.
MacIntyre, R.P. 1947- 203
MacIntyre, R.P. 1947- 203
MacIntyre, Wendy 1947- 196
Mack, Jeff 194
Mack, L.V.
 See Kimmelman, Burt
Mack, Stan(ley) 17
Mack, Todd 168
Mack, Tracy 1968- 183
 Earlier sketch in SATA 128
Mack, W.C.
 See French, Wendy
Mack, Winnie
 See French, Wendy
Mackall, Dandi D.
 See Mackall, Dandi Daley
Mackall, Dandi Daley 1949- 218
 Earlier sketches in SATA 118, 177, 182
Mackay, Claire 1930- 97
 Autobiography Feature 124
 Earlier sketch in SATA 40
 See also CLR 43
Mackay, Constance D'Arcy (?)-1966 125
Mackay, Donald 1914-2005 81
 Obituary 173
Mackay, Donald Alexander
 See Mackay, Donald
MacKaye, Percy (Wallace) 1875-1956 32
Mackel, Kathryn 1950- 162
Mackel, Kathy
 See Mackel, Kathryn
MacKellar, William 1914- 4
Macken, JoAnn Early 1953- 201
Macken, Walter 1915-1967 36
Mackenzie, Anna 1963- 212
MacKenzie, Jill (Kelly) 1947- 75
Mackenzie, Robert 1974- 204
Mackey, Ernan
 See McInerny, Ralph
Mackey, Weezie Kerr 188
Mackie, Maron
 See McNeely, Jeannette
Mackin, Edward
 See McInerny, Ralph
MacKinnon, Bernie 1957- 69
MacKinnon Groomer, Vera 1915- 57
MacKinstry, Elizabeth 1879-1956 42
Mackler, Carolyn 1973- 231
 Earlier sketch in SATA 156
MacLachlan, Emily
 See Charest, Emily MacLachlan

MacLachlan, Patricia 1938- 229
 Brief entry 42
 Earlier sketches in SATA 62, 107, 168
 See also CLR 14
MacLane, Jack
 See Crider, Bill
MacLean, Alistair 1922(?)-1987 23
 Obituary 50
MacLean, Alistair Stuart
 See MacLean, Alistair
Maclean, Art
 See Shirreffs, Gordon D(onald)
MacLean, Christine Kole 1962- 177
MacLean, Glynne 1964- 150
MacLean, Jill 1941- 211
MacLeod, Beatrice 1910- 162
 Earlier sketch in SATA 10
MacLeod, Beatrice Beach
 See MacLeod, Beatrice
MacLeod, Charlotte (Matilda) 1922-2005 28
 Obituary 160
MacLeod, Doug 1959- 201
 Earlier sketch in SATA 60
MacLeod, Elizabeth 184
 Earlier sketch in SATA 158
MacLeod, Ellen Jane (Anderson) 1916- 14
MacManus, James
 See MacManus, Seumas
MacManus, Seumas 1869-1960 25
MacMaster, Eve (Ruth) B(owers) 1942- 46
MacMillan, Annabelle
 See Quick, Annabelle
MacMillan, Dianne M(arie) 1943- 125
 Earlier sketch in SATA 84
Macnaughton, Tina 218
 Earlier sketch in SATA 182
Macneill, Janet
 See McNeely, Jeannette
MacPeek, Walter G. 1902-1973 4
 Obituary 25
MacPhail, Catherine 1946- 197
 Earlier sketch in SATA 130
MacPherson, Margaret 1908-2001 9
 See also SAAS 4
MacPherson, Thomas George 1915-1976
 Obituary 30
MacPherson, Winnie 1930- 107
MacRae, Tom 1980- 181
Macrae, Travis
 See Feagles, Anita MacRae
MacRaois, Cormac 1944- 72
Macumber, Mari
 See Sandoz, Mari(e Susette)
Macy, Sue 1954- 227
 Earlier sketches in SATA 88, 134
Madaras, Lynda 1947- 151
Madden, Colleen 228
Madden, Colleen M.
 See Madden, Colleen
Madden, Don 1927- 3
Madden, Kerry 1961- 168
Madden-Lunsford, Kerry
 See Madden, Kerry
Maddern, Eric 1950- 166
Maddigan, Beth 1967- 174
Maddison, Angela Mary 1923- 10
 See also CLR 24
Maddock, Reginald (Bertram) 1912-1994 15
Maddox, Jake
 See Trumbauer, Lisa
Madenski, Melissa (Ann) 1949- 77
Madian, Jon 1941- 9
Madigan, Lisa Kay
 See Madigan, L.K.
Madigan, L.K. (?)-2011 224
Madison, Alan 182
Madison, Arnold 1937- 6
Madison, Bennett 220
Madison, Winifred 5
Madonna 1958- 149
Madsen, Gunnar 171

Madsen, Jim 1964- *202*
Madsen, Ross Martin 1946- *82*
Madsen, Susan A. 1954- *90*
Madsen, Susan Arrington
    See Madsen, Susan A.
Maehlqvist, Stefan 1943- *30*
Maestro, Betsy (Crippen) 1944- *106*
    Brief entry *30*
    Earlier sketch in SATA *59*
    See also CLR *45*
Maestro, Giulio 1942- *106*
    Earlier sketches in SATA *8, 59*
    See also CLR *45*
Maeterlinck, Maurice 1862-1949 .... *66*
Magee, Doug 1947- *78*
Magee, Wes 1939- *64*
Maggio, Rosalie 1943- *69*
Magid, Ken(neth Marshall) *65*
Magnus, Erica 1946- *77*
Magoon, Kekla 1980- *213*
Magoon, Scott *222*
    Earlier sketch in SATA *182*
Magorian, James 1942- *92*
    Earlier sketch in SATA *32*
Magorian, Michelle 1947- *128*
    Earlier sketch in SATA *67*
Magorian, Michelle Jane
    See Magorian, Michelle
Magovern, Peg *103*
Magsamen, Sandra 1959- *213*
Maguire, Anne
    See Nearing, Penny
Maguire, Eden *232*
Maguire, Gregory 1954- *200*
    Autobiography Feature *200*
    Earlier sketches in SATA *28, 84, 129*
    See also SAAS *22*
Maguire, Gregory Peter
    See Maguire, Gregory
Maguire, Jack 1920-2000 .... *74*
Maguire, Jesse
    See Smith, Sherwood
Maguire, Jessie
    See Smith, Sherwood
Maher, Ramona 1934- *13*
Mahlqvist, Stefan
    See Maehlqvist, Stefan
Mahon, Julia C(unha) 1916- *11*
Mahony, Elizabeth Winthrop
    See Winthrop, Elizabeth
Mahood, Kenneth 1930- *24*
Mahy, Margaret 1936- *171*
    Earlier sketches in SATA *14, 69, 119*
    See also CLR *155*
Mahy, Margaret May
    See Mahy, Margaret
Maiden, Cecil (Edward) 1902-1981 .... *52*
Maidoff, Ilka
    See List, Ilka Katherine
Maifair, Linda Lee 1947- *83*
Maik, Henri
    See Hecht, Henri Joseph
Maillu, David G(ian) 1939- *111*
Maine, Trevor
    See Catherall, Arthur
Mains, Randolph P. 1946- *80*
Maione, Heather *189*
Maiorano, Robert 1946- *43*
Mair, J. Samia *237*
Mair, Julie Samia
    See Mair, J. Samia
Maisner, Heather 1947- *89*
Maison, Della
    See Katz, Bobbi
Maitland, Antony Jasper 1935- *25*
Maitland, Barbara *102*
Mai-Wyss, Tatjana 1972- *187*
Maizel, Rebecca 1980- *236*
Maizels, Jennie *210*

Major, Kevin (Gerald) 1949- *134*
    Earlier sketches in SATA *32, 82*
    See also CLR *11*
Majure, Janet 1954- *96*
Makhijani, Pooja *188*
Makie, Pam 1943- *37*
Makowski, Silk
    See Sullivan, Silky
Makowski, Silvia Ann
    See Sullivan, Silky
Malam, John 1957- *152*
    Earlier sketch in SATA *89*
Maland, Nick *195*
Malaspina, Ann 1957- *222*
Malawer, Ted
    See Michael, Ted
Malcolm, Dan
    See Silverberg, Robert
Malcolm, Jahnna N.
    See Beecham, Jahnna
Malcolmson, Anne
    See von Storch, Anne B.
Malcolmson, David 1899-1978 .... *6*
Maletta, Dr. Arlene
    See Feltenstein, Arlene
Maley, Carleen
    See Hutchins, Carleen Maley
Mali, Jane Lawrence 1937-1995 .... *51*
    Brief entry *44*
    Obituary *86*
Malkin, Nina 1959(?)- *179*
Mallett, Jerry J. 1939- *76*
Malley, Gemma *198*
Malley, G.R.
    See Malley, Gemma
Mallory, Kenneth 1945- *185*
    Earlier sketch in SATA *128*
Mallowan, Agatha Christie
    See Christie, Agatha
Malmberg, Carl 1904-1979 .... *9*
Malmgren, Dallin 1949- *65*
Malo, John W. 1911-2000 .... *4*
Malone, James Hiram 1930- *84*
Malone, Marianne *229*
Malone, Nola Langner 1930-2003 .... *8*
    Obituary *151*
Malone, Patricia 1932- *155*
Malone, Peter 1953- *191*
Maloney, Pat
    See Markun, Patricia Maloney
Malory, Sir Thomas 1410(?)-1471(?) *59*
    Brief entry *33*
Maltbie, P.I. *237*
Maltbie, Priscilla
    See Maltbie, P.I.
Maltese, Michael 1909(?)-1981
    Obituary *24*
Malvasi, Meg Greene *143*
Malvern, Corinne 1905-1956 .... *34*
Malvern, Gladys (?)-1962 .... *23*
Mama G.
    See Davis, Grania
Mammano, Julie 1962- *202*
    Earlier sketch in SATA *107*
Mamonova, Tatyana 1943- *93*
Manchel, Frank 1935- *10*
Manchess, Gregory 1955- *203*
Manchester, William (Raymond)
    1922-2004 .... *65*
Mandabach, Brian 1962(?)- *197*
Mandel, Brett H. 1969- *108*
Mandel, Peter 1957- *87*
Mandel, Sally (Elizabeth) 1944- *64*
Mandell, Muriel (Hortense Levin) 1921- *63*
Manders, John 1957- *219*
    Earlier sketch in SATA *175*
Mandine, Selma 1973- *228*
Manes, Stephen 1949- *99*
    Brief entry *40*
    Earlier sketch in SATA *42*
Manfred, Frederick (Feikema) 1912-1994 ...... *30*

Mangin, Marie France 1940- *59*
Mangione, Gerlando 1909-1998 .... *6*
    Obituary *104*
Mangione, Jerre
    See Mangione, Gerlando
Mango, Karin N. 1936- *52*
Mangurian, David 1938- *14*
Mania, Cathy 1950- *102*
Mania, Robert 1952- *102*
Mania, Robert C., Jr.
    See Mania, Robert
Maniatty, Taramesha 1978- *92*
Maniscalco, Joseph 1926- *10*
Manivong, Laura 1967- *229*
Manley, Deborah 1932- *28*
Manley, Seon 1921- *15*
    See also CLR *3*
    See also SAAS *2*
Mann, Elizabeth 1948- *153*
Mann, Josephine
    See Pullein-Thompson, Josephine (Mary
    Wedderburn)
Mann, Kenny 1946- *91*
Mann, Pamela 1946- *91*
Mann, Patrick
    See Waller, Leslie
Mann, Peggy
    See Houlton, Peggy Mann
Mannetti, Lisa 1953- *57*
    Brief entry *51*
Mannheim, Grete (Salomon) 1909-1986 .... *10*
Manniche, Lise 1943- *31*
Manning, Jane *233*
    Earlier sketch in SATA *185*
Manning, Jane K.
    See Manning, Jane
Manning, Maurie
    See Manning, Maurie J.
Manning, Maurie J. *211*
Manning, Maurie Jo
    See Manning, Maurie J.
Manning, Mick 1959- *176*
Manning, Rosemary 1911-1988 .... *10*
Manning, Sarra *162*
Manning-Sanders, Ruth (Vernon)
    1895(?)-1988 .... *73*
    Obituary *57*
    Earlier sketch in SATA *15*
Mannion, Diane
    See Paterson, Diane
Mannis, Celeste Davidson *173*
Mannon, Warwick
    See Hopkins, (Hector) Kenneth
Manos, Helen *199*
Mansir, A. Richard 1932- *170*
Manson, Ainslie Kertland 1938- *115*
Manson, Beverlie 1945- *57*
    Brief entry *44*
Mantchev, Lisa *221*
Mantha, John 1960- *217*
Manthorpe, Helen 1958- *122*
Mantinband, Gerda (B.) 1917- *74*
Manton, Jo
    See Gittings, Jo (Grenville) Manton
Manuel, Lynn 1948- *179*
    Earlier sketch in SATA *99*
Manushkin, Fran 1942- *205*
    Earlier sketches in SATA *7, 54, 93, 166*
Manushkin, Frances
    See Manushkin, Fran
Man Without a Spleen, A
    See Chekhov, Anton
Many, Paul 1947- *210*
Many, Paul A.
    See Many, Paul
Manzano, Sonia 1950- *167*
Mapes, Mary A.
    See Ellison, Virginia H(owell)
Maple, Marilyn 1931- *80*
Mappin, Strephyn 1956- *109*

Mara, Barney
    See Roth, Arthur J(oseph)
Mara, Jeanette
    See Cebulash, Mel
Mara, Rachna
    See Gilmore, Rachna
Marais, Josef 1905-1978
    Obituary 24
Marasmus, Seymour
    See Rivoli, Mario
Marbach, Ethel
    See Pochocki, Ethel (Frances)
Marcal, Annette B.
    See Callaway, Bernice (Anne)
Marcelino
    See Agnew, Edith J(osephine)
Marcellino, Fred 1939-2001 118
    Obituary 127
    Earlier sketch in SATA 68
March, Carl
    See Fleischman, Sid
Marchant, Bessie 1862-1941
    See YABC 2
Marchant, Catherine
    See Cookson, Catherine (McMullen)
Marcher, Marion Walden 1890-1987 10
Marchesi, Stephen 1951- 114
Marchesi, Steve
    See Marchesi, Stephen
    and Older, Effin
    and Older, Jules
Marchetta, Melina 1965- 170
Marciano, John Bemelmans 1970- 167
    Earlier sketch in SATA 118
    See also CLR 93
Marco, Lou
    See Gottfried, Theodore Mark
Marcus, Leonard S. 1950- 187
    Earlier sketch in SATA 133
Marcus, Paul 1953- 82
Marcus, Rebecca B(rian) 1907- 9
Marcuse, Aida E. 1934- 89
Marek, Margot L. 1934(?)-1987
    Obituary 54
Maren, Julie 1970- 199
Margaret, Karla
    See Andersdatter, Karla M.
Margolin, Harriet
    See Ziefert, Harriet
Margolis, Jeffrey A. 1948- 108
Margolis, Leslie 187
Margolis, Richard J(ules) 1929-1991 86
    Obituary 67
    Earlier sketch in SATA 4
Margolis, Vivienne 1922- 46
Mariana
    See Foster, Marian Curtis
Marie, Geraldine 1949- 61
Mariner, Scott
    See Pohl, Frederik
Marino, Dorothy Bronson 1912- 14
Marino, Gianna 231
Marino, Jan 1936- 114
Marino, Nan 216
Marino, Nick
    See Deming, Richard
Marino, Peter 1960- 179
Marinsky, Jane 227
Mario, Anna
    See Odgers, Sally Farrell
Marion, Henry
    See del Rey, Lester
Maris, Ron 71
    Brief entry 45
Mariz, Rae 1981- 237
Mark, Jan 1943-2006 164
    Obituary 173
    Earlier sketches in SATA 22, 69, 114
    See also CLR 11
Mark, Janet Marjorie
    See Mark, Jan

Mark, Joan T. 1937- 122
Mark, Pauline (Dahlin) 1913-1997 14
Mark, Polly
    See Mark, Pauline (Dahlin)
Mark, Ted
    See Gottfried, Theodore Mark
Markel, Michelle 169
Marker, Sherry 1941- 76
Markert, Jennifer 1965- 83
Markert, Jenny
    See Markert, Jennifer
Markey, Kevin 1965- 215
Markham, Lynne 1947- 102
Markham, Marion M. 1929- 60
Markham, Wendy
    See Staub, Wendy Corsi
Markins, W. S.
    See Jenkins, Marie M(agdalen)
Markle, Sandra 1946- 218
    Brief entry 41
    Earlier sketches in SATA 57, 92, 148, 185
Markle, Sandra L.
    See Markle, Sandra
Marklew, Gilly 211
Marko, Katherine D(olores) 28
Markoosie
    See Patsauq, Markoosie
Marks, Alan 1957- 187
    Earlier sketches in SATA 77, 151
Marks, Burton 1930- 47
    Brief entry 43
Marks, Graham 158
Marks, Hannah K.
    See Trivelpiece, Laurel
Marks, J.
    See Highwater, Jamake (Mamake)
Marks, J(ames) M(acdonald) 1921- 13
Marks, Laurie J. 1957- 68
Marks, Margaret L. 1911(?)-1980
    Obituary 23
Marks, Mickey Klar -1986 12
Marks, Peter
    See Smith, Robert Kimmel
Marks, Rita 1938- 47
Marks, Stan(ley) 1938- 14
Marks-Highwater, J.
    See Highwater, Jamake (Mamake)
Markun, Patricia Maloney 1924- 15
Markusen, Bruce (Stanley Rodriguez)
    1965- 141
Marley, Louise 1952- 173
    Earlier sketch in SATA 120
Marlin, Hilda
    See Van Stockum, Hilda
Marlow, Layne 204
Marlow, Max
    See Nicole, Christopher
Marlow, Susan K. 1953- 178
Marlowe, Amy Bell 67
    Earlier sketch in SATA 1
Marlowe, Jack
    See Deary, Terry
Marlowe, Tess
    See Glick, Ruth
Marney, Dean 1952- 90
Marokvia, Artur 1909- 31
Marokvia, Mireille 1908-2008 5
    Obituary 197
Marokvia, Mireille Journet
    See Marokvia, Mireille
Marol, Jean-Claude 1946- 125
Marr, John S(tuart) 1940- 48
Marr, Melissa 1972- 189
Marric, J. J.
    See Butler, William Vivian
    and Creasey, John
Marrin, Albert 1936- 193
    Brief entry 43
    Earlier sketches in SATA 53, 90, 126
    See also CLR 53

Marriott, Alice Lee 1910-1992 31
    Obituary 71
Marriott, Janice 1946- 134
Marriott, Pat(ricia) 1920- 35
Marriott, Zoe 1982- 216
Marriott, Zoe Davina
    See Marriott, Zoe
Marroquin, Patricio
    See Markun, Patricia Maloney
Mars, W. T.
    See Mars, Witold Tadeusz J.
Mars, Witold Tadeusz J. 1912-1985 3
Marsden, Carolyn 1950- 212
    Autobiography Feature 212
    Earlier sketches in SATA 140, 175
Marsden, John 1950- 146
    Earlier sketches in SATA 66, 97
    See also CLR 34
    See also SAAS 22
Marsh, Carole 1946- 127
Marsh, Dave 1950- 66
Marsh, J. E.
    See Marshall, Evelyn
Marsh, James 1946- 73
Marsh, Jean
    See Marshall, Evelyn
Marsh, Joan F. 1923- 83
Marsh, Katherine 1974- 220
Marsh, Paul
    See Hopkins, (Hector) Kenneth
Marsh, Valerie 1954- 89
Marshall, Anthony D(ryden) 1924- 18
Marshall, Bonnie C. 1941- 141
    Earlier sketch in SATA 18
Marshall, Bridget M(ary) 1974- 103
Marshall, (Sarah) Catherine (Wood)
    1914-1983 2
    Obituary 34
Marshall, Douglas
    See McClintock, Marshall
Marshall, Edmund
    See Hopkins, (Hector) Kenneth
Marshall, Edward
    See Marshall, James
Marshall, Evelyn 1897-1991 11
Marshall, Felicity 1950- 116
Marshall, Garry 1934- 60
Marshall, H. H.
    See Jahn, Michael
Marshall, James 1942-1992 75
    Earlier sketches in SATA 6, 51
    See also CLR 21
Marshall, James Edward
    See Marshall, James
Marshall, James Vance
    See Payne, Donald Gordon
Marshall, Janet (Perry) 1938- 97
Marshall, Jeff
    See Laycock, George (Edwin)
Marshall, Kim
    See Marshall, Michael (Kimbrough)
Marshall, Michael (Kimbrough) 1948- 37
Marshall, Percy
    See Young, Percy M(arshall)
Marshall, S(amuel) L(yman) A(twood)
    1900-1977 21
Marsoli, Lisa Ann 1958- 101
    Brief entry 53
Marsten, Richard
    See Hunter, Evan
Marston, Elsa 1933- 156
Marston, Hope Irvin 1935- 127
    Earlier sketch in SATA 31
Marszalek, John F. 1939- 167
Marszalek, John Francis, Jr.
    See Marszalek, John F.
Marszalek, John Francis 1939-
    See Marszalek, John F.
Martchenko, Michael 1942- 154
    Earlier sketches in SATA 50, 95

Martel, Aimee
　See Thurlo, Aimee
　and Thurlo, David
Martel, Suzanne 1924- 99
Martignoni, Margaret E. 1908(?)-1974
　Obituary 27
Martin, Ann M. 1955- 234
　Brief entry 41
　Earlier sketches in SATA *44, 70, 126, 192*
　See also CLR *32*
Martin, Bill, Jr. 1916-2004 145
　Brief entry 40
　Earlier sketches in SATA *40, 67*
　See also CLR *97*
Martin, Charles E(lmer)
　See Mastrangelo, Charles E(lmer)
Martin, Christopher
　See Hoyt, Edwin P(almer), Jr.
Martin, C.K. Kelly 207
Martin, Claire 1933- 76
Martin, Courtney Autumn 1984- 205
Martin, David Stone 1913-1992 39
Martin, Donald
　See Honig, Donald
Martin, Dorothy 1921- 47
Martin, Dorothy McKay
　See Martin, Dorothy
Martin, Eugene 1
Martin, Eva M. 1939- 65
Martin, Frances M(cEntee) 1906-1998 36
Martin, Francesca 1947- 101
Martin, Fred 1948- 119
Martin, Fredric
　See Christopher, Matt(hew Frederick)
Martin, George Raymond Richard
　See Martin, George R.R.
Martin, George R.R. 1948- 118
Martin, J(ohn) P(ercival) 1880(?)-1966 15
Martin, Jacqueline Briggs 1945- 188
　Earlier sketches in SATA *98, 149*
Martin, Jane Read 1957- 84
Martin, Jeremy
　See Levin, Marcia Obrasky
Martin, Les
　See Schulman, L(ester) M(artin)
Martin, Linda 1961- 82
Martin, Lynne 1923- 21
Martin, Marcia
　See Levin, Marcia Obrasky
Martin, Marvin 1926- 126
Martin, Melanie
　See Pellowski, Michael (Joseph)
Martin, Nancy
　See Salmon, Annie Elizabeth
Martin, Patricia 200
Martin, Patricia A.
　See Martin, Patricia
Martin, Patricia Miles 1899-1986 43
　Obituary 48
　Earlier sketch in SATA *1*
Martin, Peter
　See Chaundler, Christine
Martin, Rafe 1946- 175
Martin, Rene 1891-1977 42
　Obituary 20
Martin, Rupert (Claude) 1905- 31
Martin, S. R.
　See Mappin, Strephyn
Martin, Stefan 1936- 32
Martin, Vicky
　See Storey, Victoria Carolyn
Martin, Webber
　See Silverberg, Robert
Martin, Wendy
　See Martini, Teri
Martin, William Ivan, Jr.
　See Martin, Bill, Jr.
Martineau, Diane 1940- 178
Martineau, Harriet 1802-1876
　See YABC *2*
Martinet, Jeanne 1958- 80

Martinez, Agnes 167
Martinez, Arturo O. 1933- 192
Martinez, Claudia Guadalupe 1978- 214
Martinez, Ed(ward) 1954- 98
Martinez, Elizabeth Conrod 1954- 85
Martinez, Rueben 1940- 232
Martinez, Victor 1954-2011 95
Martini, Angela 1972(?)- 223
Martini, Teri 1930- 3
Martini, Therese
　See Martini, Teri
Martino, Alfred C. 1964- 174
Martinson, Janis
　See Herbert, Janis
Martinusen, Cindy
　See Martinusen-Coloma, Cindy
Martinusen, Cindy McCormick
　See Martinusen-Coloma, Cindy
Martinusen-Coloma, Cindy 1970- 218
Marton, Jirina 1946- 230
　Earlier sketches in SATA *95, 144*
Marton, Pierre
　See Stone, Peter
Martson, Del
　See Lupoff, Richard A.
Martyr, Paula (Jane)
　See Lawford, Paula Jane
Maruki, Toshi 1912-2000 112
　See also CLR *19*
Marvin, Isabel R(idout) 1924- 84
Marx, Patricia Windschill
　See Marx, Trish
Marx, Robert F(rank) 1936- 24
Marx, Trish 1948- 202
　Earlier sketches in SATA *112, 160*
Marzani, Carl (Aldo) 1912-1994 12
Marzollo, Jean 1942- 190
　Autobiography Feature 190
　Earlier sketches in SATA *29, 77, 130*
　See also SAAS *15*
Masefield, John (Edward) 1878-1967 19
　See also CLR *164*
Masiello, Ralph 1961- 214
Masoff, Joy 1951- 118
Mason, Adrienne 1962- 163
Mason, Cherie 170
Mason, Edwin A. 1905-1979
　Obituary 32
Mason, Ernst
　See Pohl, Frederik
Mason, F(rancis) van Wyck 1901-1978 3
　Obituary 26
Mason, Frank W.
　See Mason, F(rancis) van Wyck
Mason, George Frederick 1904-2000 14
Mason, Miriam E(vangeline) 1900-1973 2
　Obituary 26
Mason, Prue 195
Mason, Simon 1962- 178
Mason, Tally
　See Derleth, August (William)
Mason, Van Wyck
　See Mason, F(rancis) van Wyck
Mass, Wendy 1967- 234
　Earlier sketches in SATA *158, 196*
Mass, William
　See Gibson, William
Masse, Josee 221
Masselman, George 1897-1971 19
Massey, Misty 212
Massie, Dianne Redfield 1938- 125
　Earlier sketch in SATA *16*
Massie, Elizabeth 108
Massini, Sarah 213
Masson, Sophie 1959- 179
　Earlier sketch in SATA *133*
Masters, Anthony (Richard) 1940-2003 112
　Obituary 145
Masters, Kelly R(ay) 1897-1987 3
Masters, Mildred 1932- 42

Masters, William
　See Cousins, Margaret
Masters, Zeke
　See Bensen, Donald R.
　and Goulart, Ron
Mastrangelo, Charles E(lmer) 1910-1995 70
　Earlier sketch in SATA *69*
Masuda, Takeshi 1944- 56
Matas, Carol 1949- 194
　Autobiography Feature 112
　Earlier sketch in SATA *93*
　See also CLR *52*
Matchette, Katharine E. 1941- 38
Math, Irwin 1940- 42
Mathabane, Mark 1960- 123
Mather, Kirtley F(letcher) 1888-1978 65
Mathers, Petra 1945- 176
　Earlier sketch in SATA *119*
　See also CLR *76*
Matheson, Richard (Christian) 1953- 119
Matheson, Shirlee Smith 1942- 155
Mathews, Eleanor
　See Mathews, Ellie
Mathews, Ellie 1946(?)- 193
Mathews, Janet 1914-1992 41
Mathews, Judith
　See Goldberger, Judith M.
Mathews, Louise
　See Tooke, Louise Mathews
Mathiesen, Egon 1907-1976
　Obituary 28
Mathieu, Joe 1949- 185
　Brief entry 36
　Earlier sketches in SATA *43, 94*
Mathieu, Joseph P.
　See Mathieu, Joe
Mathis, Sharon Bell 1937- 58
　Earlier sketch in SATA *7*
　See also CLR *147*
　See also SAAS *3*
Matlin, Marlee 1965- 181
Matlin, Marlee Beth
　See Matlin, Marlee
Matloff, Gregory 1945- 73
Matott, Justin 1961- 109
Matranga, Frances Carfi 1922- 78
Matray, James I. 1948- 161
Matray, James Irving
　See Matray, James I.
Matson, Emerson N(els) 1926- 12
Matson, Morgan 230
Matsui, Tadashi 1926- 8
Matsuno, Masako
　See Kobayashi, Masako Matsuno
Matsuoka, Mei 1981- 192
Matte, (Encarnacion) L'Enc 1936- 22
Mattern, Joanne 1963- 122
Mattheson, Jenny 180
Matthew, James
　See Barrie, J. M.
Matthews, Aline
　See De Wire, Elinor
Matthews, Andrew 1948- 138
Matthews, Caitlin 1952- 122
Matthews, Cecily 1945- 221
Matthews, Downs 1925- 71
Matthews, Elizabeth 1978- 194
Matthews, Ellen
　See Bache, Ellyn
Matthews, Ellen 1950- 28
Matthews, Harold Downs
　See Matthews, Downs
Matthews, Jacklyn Meek
　See Meek, Jacklyn O'Hanlon
Matthews, John (Kentigern) 1948- 116
Matthews, L. S. 183
Matthews, Laura S.
　See Matthews, L. S.
Matthews, Liz
　See Pellowski, Michael (Joseph)

Matthews, Morgan
See Pellowski, Michael (Joseph)
Matthews, Nicola
See Browne, N.M.
Matthews, Patricia 1927-2006 28
Matthews, Patricia Anne
See Matthews, Patricia
Matthews, Tina 1961- 190
Matthews, Tom L.
See Lalicki, Tom
Matthews, William Henry III 1919- 45
Brief entry 28
Matthiessen, Peter 1927- 27
Mattingley, Christobel (Rosemary) 1931- 85
Earlier sketch in SATA 37
See also CLR 24
See also SAAS 18
Matulay, Laszlo 1912- 43
Matus, Greta 1938- 12
Matzigkeit, Philip 220
Maugham, W. S.
See Maugham, W. Somerset
Maugham, W. Somerset 1874-1965 54
Maugham, William S.
See Maugham, W. Somerset
Maugham, William Somerset
See Maugham, W. Somerset
Maurer, Diane Philippoff
See Maurer-Mathison, Diane V(ogel)
Maurer, Diane Vogel
See Maurer-Mathison, Diane V(ogel)
Maurer-Mathison, Diane V(ogel) 1944- 89
Mauser, Pat Rhoads
See McCord, Patricia
Mauser, Patricia Rhoads
See McCord, Patricia
Maves, Mary Carolyn 1916- 10
Maves, Paul B(enjamin) 1913-1994 10
Mavor, Salley 1955- 125
Mawicke, Tran 1911- 15
Max 1906-1989
See Diop, Birago (Ismael)
Max, Jill
See Bennett, Kelly
Max, Peter 1939- 45
Maxon, Anne
See Best, (Evangel) Allena Champlin
Maxwell, Arthur S. 1896-1970 11
Maxwell, B.E. 1957- 211
Maxwell, Bruce E.
See Maxwell, B.E.
Maxwell, Edith 1923- 7
Maxwell, Gavin 1914-1969 65
Maxwell, Katie
See MacAlister, Katie
Maxwell, William (Keepers, Jr.) 1908-2000
Obituary 128
Maxwell-Hyslop, Miranda 1968- 154
May, Charles Paul 1920- 4
May, Elaine Tyler 1947- 120
May, J. C.
See May, Julian
May, Julian 1931- 11
May, Katie 225
May, Robert Lewis 1905-1976
Obituary 27
May, Robert Stephen 1929-1996 46
May, Robin
See May, Robert Stephen
Mayall, Beth 171
Mayberry, Florence V(irginia) Wilson 10
Maybury, Richard J. 1946- 72
Maybury, Rick
See Maybury, Richard J.
Maydak, Michael S. 1952- 220
Mayer, Agatha
See Maher, Ramona
Mayer, Albert Ignatius, Jr. 1906-1994
Obituary 29
Mayer, Ann M(argaret) 1938- 14
Mayer, Bill 200

Mayer, Danuta 1958- 117
Mayer, Hannelore Valencak 1929- 42
Mayer, Jane Rothschild 1903-2001 38
Mayer, Marianna 1945- 132
Earlier sketches in SATA 32, 83
Mayer, Mercer 1943- 137
Earlier sketches in SATA 16, 32, 73, 129
See also CLR 11
Mayerson, Charlotte Leon 36
Mayerson, Evelyn Wilde 1935- 55
Mayfield, Katherine 1958- 118
Mayfield, Sue 1963- 146
Earlier sketch in SATA 72
Mayhar, Ardath 1930- 38
Mayhew, James 1964- 204
Earlier sketches in SATA 85, 149
Maynard, Olga 1920- 40
Mayne, William 1928-2010 122
Earlier sketches in SATA 6, 68
See also CLR 123
See also SAAS 11
Mayne, William James Carter
See Mayne, William
Maynes, J. O. Rocky, Jr.
See Maynes, J. Oscar, Jr.
Maynes, J. Oscar, Jr. 1929- 38
Mayo, Gretchen Will 1936- 163
Earlier sketch in SATA 84
Mayo, Margaret 1935- 165
Earlier sketches in SATA 38, 96
Mayo, Margaret Mary
See Mayo, Margaret
Mayr, Diane 1949- 197
Mays, Lucinda L(a Bella) 1924- 49
Mays, (Lewis) Victor (Jr.) 1927- 5
Mazellan, Ron 210
Mazer, Anne 1953- 235
Earlier sketches in SATA 67, 105, 192
Mazer, Harry 1925- 167
Earlier sketches in SATA 31, 67, 105
See also CLR 16
See also SAAS 11
Mazer, Norma Fox 1931-2009 198
Earlier sketches in SATA 24, 67, 105, 168
See also CLR 23
See also SAAS 1
Mazille, Capucine 1953- 96
Mazo, Michael 223
Mazza, Adriana 1928- 19
Mazzio, Joann 1926- 74
Mbugua, Kioi Wa 1962- 83
McAfee, Carol 1955- 81
McAlister, Caroline 1960- 235
McAllister, Amanda
See Dowdell, Dorothy (Florence) Karns
and Hager, Jean
and Meaker, Eloise
McAllister, Angela 225
Earlier sketch in SATA 182
McAllister, Margaret I. 1956- 169
Earlier sketch in SATA 117
McAllister, M.I.
See McAllister, Margaret I.
McArdle, Paula 1971- 198
McArthur, Nancy 96
McAvoy, Jim 1972- 142
McBain, Ed
See Hunter, Evan
McBain, Georgina 189
McBratney, Sam 1943- 203
Earlier sketches in SATA 89, 164
See also CLR 44
McBride, Lish 237
McBrier, Michael
See Older, Effin
and Older, Jules
McCafferty, Jim 1954- 84
McCaffery, Janet 1936- 38

McCaffrey, Anne 1926- 152
Autobiography Feature 152
Earlier sketches in SATA 8, 70, 116
See also CLR 130
See also SAAS 11
McCaffrey, Anne Inez
See McCaffrey, Anne
McCaffrey, Kate 1970- 228
McCaffrey, Mary
See Szudek, Agnes S(usan) P(hilomena)
McCahan, Erin 234
McCain, Becky Ray 1954- 138
McCain, Murray (David, Jr.) 1926-1981 7
Obituary 29
McCall, Bruce 1935(?)- 209
McCall, Edith (Sansom) 1911- 6
McCall, Virginia Nielsen 1909-2000 13
McCall, Wendell
See Pearson, Ridley
McCall Smith, Alexander
See Smith, Alexander McCall
McCallum, Phyllis
See Koch, Phyllis (Mae) McCallum
McCallum, Stephen 1960- 91
McCampbell, Darlene Z. 1942- 83
McCann, Edson
See del Rey, Lester
and Pohl, Frederik
McCann, Gerald 1916- 41
McCann, Helen 1948- 75
McCannon, Dindga 41
McCants, William D. 1961- 82
McCarter, Neely Dixon 1929- 47
McCarthy, Agnes 1933- 4
McCarthy, Colin (John) 1951- 77
McCarthy, Mary 1951- 203
McCarthy, Meghan 199
Earlier sketch in SATA 168
McCarthy, Ralph F. 1950- 139
McCarthy-Tucker, Sherri N. 1958- 83
McCarty, Peter 1966- 182
McCarty, Rega Kramer 1904-1986 10
McCaslin, Nellie 1914-2005 12
McCaughrean, Geraldine 1951- 173
Earlier sketches in SATA 87, 139
See also CLR 38
McCaughren, Tom 1936- 75
McCauley, Adam 1965- 209
Earlier sketch in SATA 128
McCay, (Zenas) Winsor 1869-1934 134
Earlier sketch in SATA 41
McClafferty, Carla Killough 1958- 137
McClary, Jane Stevenson 1919-1990
Obituary 64
McCleery, Patsy R. 1925- 133
Earlier sketch in SATA 88
McClelland, Susan 214
McClements, George 196
McClintock, Barbara 1955- 213
Earlier sketches in SATA 57, 95, 146
McClintock, Marshall 1906-1967 3
McClintock, May Garelick
See Garelick, May
McClintock, Mike
See McClintock, Marshall
McClintock, Norah 226
Earlier sketch in SATA 178
McClintock, Theodore 1902-1971 14
McClinton, Leon 1933- 11
McCloskey, Kevin 1951- 79
McCloskey, (John) Robert 1914-2003 100
Obituary 146
Earlier sketches in SATA 2, 39
See also CLR 7
McCloy, James F(loyd) 1941- 59
McClung, Robert M(arshall) 1916- 135
Earlier sketches in SATA 2, 68
See also CLR 11
See also SAAS 15
McClure, Gillian Mary 1948- 31
McClure, Nikki 218

McColley, Kevin 1961- *80*
  See also SAAS *23*
McConduit, Denise Walter 1950- *89*
McConnell, James Douglas Rutherford
  1915-1988 .... *40*
  Obituary *56*
McCord, Anne 1942- *41*
McCord, David (Thompson Watson)
  1897-1997 .... *18*
  Obituary *96*
  See also CLR *9*
McCord, Jean 1924- *34*
McCord, Pat Mauser
  See McCord, Patricia
McCord, Patricia 1943- *159*
  Earlier sketch in SATA *37*
McCord, Patricia Sue Rhoads Mauser
  See McCord, Patricia
McCormack, Caren McNelly *217*
McCormick, Brooks
  See Adams, William Taylor
McCormick, Dell J. 1892-1949 .... *19*
McCormick, (George) Donald (King)
  1911-1998 .... *14*
McCormick, Edith (Joan) 1934- *30*
McCormick, Kimberly A. 1960- *153*
McCormick, Patricia 1956- *181*
  Earlier sketch in SATA *128*
McCourt, Edward (Alexander) 1907-1972
  Obituary *28*
McCourt, Lisa 1964- *214*
  Earlier sketches in SATA *117, 159*
McCourt, Malachy 1931- *126*
McCoy, Glenn 1965- *212*
McCoy, Iola Fuller *3*
McCoy, J(oseph) J(erome) 1917- *8*
McCoy, Karen Kawamoto 1953- *82*
McCoy, Lois (Rich) 1941- *38*
McCrady, Lady 1951- *16*
McCrea, James (Craig, Jr.) 1920- *3*
McCrea, Ruth (Pirman) 1921- *3*
McCreigh, James
  See Pohl, Frederik
McCrumb, Sharyn 1948- *109*
McCue, Lisa 1959- *212*
  Earlier sketches in SATA *65, 177*
McCue, Lisa Emiline
  See McCue, Lisa
McCullen, Andrew
  See Arthur, Robert, (Jr.)
McCullers, Carson 1917-1967 .... *27*
McCullers, Lula Carson Smith
  See McCullers, Carson
McCulloch, Derek (Ivor Breashur) 1897-1967
  Obituary *29*
McCulloch, John Tyler
  See Burroughs, Edgar Rice
McCulloch, Sarah
  See Ure, Jean
McCullough, David 1933- *62*
McCullough, David Gaub
  See McCullough, David
McCullough, Frances Monson 1938- *8*
McCullough, Sharon Pierce 1943- *131*
McCully, Emily Arnold
  See Arnold, Emily
McCune, Dan
  See Haas, Dorothy F.
McCunn, Ruthanne Lum 1946- *63*
McCurdy, Michael 1942- *237*
  Earlier sketches in SATA *13, 82, 147*
McCurdy, Michael Charles
  See McCurdy, Michael
McCusker, Paul 1958- *220*
McCutcheon, Elsie (Mary Jackson) 1937- ... *60*
McCutcheon, John 1952- *97*
McDaniel, Becky Bring 1953- *61*
McDaniel, Lurlene 1944- *218*
  Earlier sketches in SATA *71, 146*
McDaniels, Pellom III 1968- *121*
McDaniels, Preston 1952- *192*

McDearmon, Kay *20*
McDermott, Beverly Brodsky 1941- *11*
McDermott, Eleni *156*
McDermott, Gerald (Edward) 1941- *163*
  Earlier sketches in SATA *16, 74*
  See also CLR *9*
McDermott, Michael 1962- *76*
McDevitt, Jack 1935- *155*
  Earlier sketch in SATA *94*
McDevitt, John Charles
  See McDevitt, Jack
McDole, Carol
  See Farley, Carol (J.)
McDonald, Candice Hartsough 1982- *225*
McDonald, Collin 1943- *79*
McDonald, Gerald D(oan) 1905-1970 .... *3*
McDonald, Jamie
  See Heide, Florence Parry
McDonald, Janet 1953-2007 .... *204*
  Earlier sketch in SATA *148*
McDonald, Jill (Masefield) 1927-1982 .... *13*
  Obituary *29*
McDonald, Joyce 1946- *164*
  Earlier sketch in SATA *101*
McDonald, Lucile Saunders 1898-1992 .... *10*
McDonald, Mary Ann 1956- *84*
McDonald, Megan 1958- *202*
  Autobiography Feature *151*
  Earlier sketches in SATA *67, 99, 148, 151*
  See also CLR *94*
McDonald, Meme 1954- *112*
McDonald, Mercedes 1956- *169*
  Earlier sketch in SATA *97*
McDonald, Rae A. 1952- *201*
McDonell, Chris 1960- *138*
McDonell, Christine 1949- *225*
  Earlier sketches in SATA *34, 115*
McDonnell, Flora (Mary) 1963- *146*
  Earlier sketch in SATA *90*
McDonnell, Kathleen 1947- *186*
McDonnell, Lois Eddy 1914-2001 .... *10*
McDonnell, Patrick 1956- *221*
  Earlier sketch in SATA *179*
McDonough, Yona Zeldis 1957- *73*
McDowell, Marilyn Taylor *217*
McElligott, Matt 1968- *196*
  Earlier sketch in SATA *135*
McElligott, Matthew
  See McElligott, Matt
McElmeel, Sharron L. 1942- *128*
McElmurry, Jill *198*
  Earlier sketch in SATA *159*
McElrath, William N. 1932- *65*
McElrath-Eslick, Lori 1960- *204*
  Earlier sketch in SATA *96*
McEntee, Dorothy (Layng) 1902- *37*
McEvoy, Anne *214*
McEwen, Katherine *183*
McEwen, Robert (Lindley) 1926-1980
  Obituary *23*
McFadden, Kevin Christopher
  See Pike, Christopher
McFall, Christie 1918- *12*
McFall, Gardner 1952- *183*
McFarlan, Donald M(aitland) 1915- *59*
McFarland, Henry "Hammer"
  See McFarland, Henry O.
McFarland, Henry O. 1934- *143*
McFarland, Kenton D(ean) 1920- *11*
McFarland, Martha
  See Smith-Ankrom, M. E.
McFarlane, Leslie 1902-1977 .... *100*
  Earlier sketches in SATA *31, 1, 65, 67*
  See also CLR *118*
McFarlane, Leslie Charles
  See McFarlane, Leslie
McFarlane, Peter 1940- *95*
McFarlane, Peter William
  See McFarlane, Peter
McFarlane, Sheryl P. 1954- *86*
McFarlane, Todd 1961- *117*

McGaw, Jessie Brewer 1913-1997 .... *10*
McGee, Barbara 1943- *6*
McGee, Marni *163*
McGhee, Alison 1960- *231*
  Earlier sketch in SATA *196*
McGhee, Alison R.
  See McGhee, Alison
McGhee, Holly M.
  See Durand, Hallie
McGiffin, (Lewis) Lee (Shaffer) 1908-1978 ... *1*
McGill, Alice *159*
McGill, Marci
  See Balterman, Marcia Ridlon
McGill, Marci Ridlon
  See Balterman, Marcia Ridlon
McGill, Ormond 1913- *92*
McGinley, Jerry 1948- *116*
McGinley, Phyllis 1905-1978 .... *44*
  Obituary *24*
  Earlier sketch in SATA *2*
McGinnis, Lila S(prague) 1924- *44*
McGinty, Alice B. 1963- *202*
  Earlier sketch in SATA *134*
McGivern, Justin 1985- *129*
McGivern, Maureen Daly
  See Daly, Maureen
McGivern, Maureen Patricia Daly
  See Daly, Maureen
McGough, Elizabeth (Hemmes) 1934- *33*
McGovern, Ann 1930- *132*
  Earlier sketches in SATA *8, 69, 70*
  See also CLR *50*
  See also SAAS *17*
McGowen, Thomas E. 1927- *109*
  Earlier sketch in SATA *2*
McGowen, Tom
  See McGowen, Thomas E.
McGrady, Mike 1933- *6*
McGrath, Barbara Barbieri 1953- *230*
  Earlier sketches in SATA *108, 169*
McGrath, Robin 1949- *121*
McGrath, Thomas (Matthew) 1916-1990 ..... *41*
  Obituary *66*
McGraw, Eloise Jarvis 1915-2000 .... *67*
  Obituary *123*
  Earlier sketch in SATA *1*
  See also SAAS *6*
McGraw, William Corbin 1916-1999 .... *3*
McGreal, Elizabeth
  See Yates, Elizabeth
McGregor, Barbara 1959- *82*
McGregor, Craig 1933- *8*
McGregor, Iona 1929- *25*
McGrory, Anik *193*
McGuffey, Alexander Hamilton 1816-1896 . *60*
McGuigan, Mary Ann 1949- *228*
  Earlier sketch in SATA *106*
McGuire, Edna 1899- *13*
McGuire, Leslie (Sarah) 1945- *94*
  Brief entry *45*
  Earlier sketch in SATA *52*
McGuire, Robert *187*
McGuirk, Leslie (A.) 1960- *152*
McGurk, Slater
  See Roth, Arthur J(oseph)
McHargue, Georgess 1941-2011 .... *77*
  Earlier sketch in SATA *4*
  See also CLR *2*
  See also SAAS *5*
McHenry, E.B. 1963(?)- *193*
McHugh, (Berit) Elisabet 1941- *55*
  Brief entry *44*
McIlvaine, Jane
  See McClary, Jane Stevenson
McIlwraith, Maureen Mollie Hunter
  See Hunter, Mollie
McInerney, Judith W(hitelock) 1945- *49*
  Brief entry *46*
McInerny, Ralph 1929-2010 .... *93*
McInerny, Ralph Matthew
  See McInerny, Ralph

McKaughan, Larry (Scott) 1941- 75
McKay, Donald 1895- 45
McKay, Hilary 1959- 208
    Earlier sketches in SATA 92, 145
    See also SAAS 23
McKay, Hilary Jane
    See McKay, Hilary
McKay, Lawrence, Jr. 1948- 114
McKay, Robert W. 1921- 15
McKay, Sharon E. 1954- 165
McKay, Simon
    See Nicole, Christopher
McKean, Dave 1963- 197
McKean, David Jeff
    See McKean, Dave
McKeating, Eileen 1957- 81
McKee, David (John) 1935- 158
    Earlier sketches in SATA 70, 107
    See also CLR 38
McKee, Tim 1970- 111
McKeever, Marcia
    See Laird, Jean E(louise)
McKellar, Danica 1975- 213
McKelvey, Carole A. 1942- 78
McKelvy, Charles 1950- 124
McKendrick, Melveena (Christine) 1941- 55
McKendry, Joe 1972- 170
McKenna, Colleen O'Shaughnessy 1948- .. 136
    Earlier sketch in SATA 76
McKenzie, Dorothy Clayton 1910-1981
    Obituary 28
McKenzie, Ellen Kindt 1928- 80
McKernan, Victoria 1957- 171
McKie, Robin 112
McKillip, Patricia A. 1948- 174
    Earlier sketches in SATA 30, 80, 126
McKillip, Patricia Anne
    See McKillip, Patricia A.
McKim, Audrey Margaret 1909-1999 47
McKimmie, Chris 194
McKinley, Jennifer Carolyn Robin
    See McKinley, Robin
McKinley, Robin 1952- 229
    Brief entry 32
    Earlier sketches in SATA 50, 89, 130, 195
    See also CLR 127
McKinney, Barbara Shaw 1951- 116
McKinney, Nadine 1938- 91
McKinty, Adrian 186
McKissack, Fredrick L. 1939- 162
    Brief entry 53
    Earlier sketches in SATA 73, 117
    See also CLR 55
McKissack, Fredrick Lemuel
    See McKissack, Fredrick L.
McKissack, Patricia C. 1944- 195
    Earlier sketches in SATA 51, 73, 117, 162
    See also CLR 129
McKissack, Patricia L'Ann Carwell
    See McKissack, Patricia C.
McKissack and McKissack
    See McKissack, Fredrick L.
    and McKissack, Patricia C.
McKown, Robin (?)-1976 6
McKy, Katie 1956- 184
McLaren, Chesley 213
McLaren, Clemence 1938- 158
    Earlier sketch in SATA 105
McLaughlin, Frank 1934- 73
McLaughlin, Julie 1984- 226
McLaughlin, Lauren 209
McLaurin, Anne 1953- 27
McLean, Andrew 1946- 172
    Earlier sketch in SATA 113
McLean, Dirk 1956- 236
McLean, J. Sloan
    See Gillette, Virginia M(ary)
    and Wunsch, Josephine (McLean)
McLean, Jacqueline
    See Kolosov, Jacqueline
McLean, Janet 1946- 113

McLean, Kathryn (Anderson) 1909-1966 9
McLean, Virginia Overton 1946- 90
McLean-Carr, Carol 1948- 122
McLeish, Kenneth 1940-1997 35
McLenighan, Valjean 1947- 46
    Brief entry 40
McLennan, Connie 171
McLennan, Will
    See Wisler, G(ary) Clifton
McLeod, Bob 1951- 173
McLeod, Chum 1955- 95
McLeod, Emilie Warren 1926-1982 23
    Obituary 31
McLeod, Kirsty
    See Hudson, (Margaret) Kirsty
McLeod, Margaret Vail
    See Holloway, Teresa (Bragunier)
McLerran, Alice 1933- 137
    Earlier sketch in SATA 68
McLimans, David 1949- 182
McLoughlin, John C. 1949- 47
McMahon, Bob 1956- 208
McManus, Patrick F. 1933- 46
McManus, Patrick Francis
    See McManus, Patrick F.
McMeekin, Clark
    See McMeekin, Isabel McLennan
McMeekin, Isabel McLennan 1895-1973 3
McMenemy, Sarah 1965- 226
    Earlier sketch in SATA 156
McMillan, Bruce 1947- 192
    Earlier sketches in SATA 22, 70, 129
    See also CLR 47
McMillan, Naomi
    See Grimes, Nikki
McMorey, James L.
    See Moyer, Terry J.
McMorrow, Annalisa 1969- 104
McMullan, Jim 1934- 150
    Earlier sketch in SATA 87
McMullan, K. H.
    See McMullan, Kate
McMullan, Kate 1947- 189
    Brief entry 48
    Earlier sketches in SATA 52, 87, 132
McMullan, Kate Hall
    See McMullan, Kate
McMullan, Margaret 1960- 203
McMurtrey, Martin A(loysias) 1921- 21
McNabb, Linda 1963- 147
McNair, Kate 3
McNair, Sylvia 1924-2002 74
McNamara, Margaret C(raig) 1915-1981
    Obituary 24
McNaught, Harry 32
McNaughton, Colin 1951- 211
    Earlier sketches in SATA 39, 92, 134
    See also CLR 54
McNaughton, Janet 1953- 162
    Earlier sketch in SATA 110
McNeal, Laura 194
McNeal, Tom 194
McNeely, Jeannette 1918- 25
McNeer, May (Yonge) 1902-1994 81
    Earlier sketch in SATA 1
McNeese, Tim 1953- 139
McNeill, Janet
    See Alexander, Janet
McNicholas, Shelagh 191
McNickle, D'Arcy 1904-1977
    Obituary 22
McNickle, William D'Arcy
    See McNickle, D'Arcy
McNicoll, Sylvia (Marilyn) 1954- 113
    See also CLR 99
McNulty, Faith 1918-2005 168
    Earlier sketches in SATA 12, 84, 139
McPhail, David 1940- 219
    Brief entry 32
    Earlier sketches in SATA 47, 81, 140, 183

McPhail, David M.
    See McPhail, David
McPhail, David Michael
    See McPhail, David
McPhee, Norma H. 1928- 95
McPhee, Peter 1957- 214
McPhee, Richard B(yron) 1934- 41
McPherson, James M. 1936- 141
    Earlier sketch in SATA 16
McPherson, James Munro
    See McPherson, James M.
McQueen, Lucinda 1950- 58
    Brief entry 48
McQueen, Mildred Hark 1908-1978 12
McQuillan, Mary 200
McRae, Russell (William) 1934- 63
McShean, Gordon 1936- 41
Mc Swigan, Marie 1907-1962 24
McTavish, Sandy
    See Eyerly, Jeannette
McVeity, Jen 148
McVey, Vicki 1946- 80
McVicker, Charles (Taggart) 1930- 39
McVicker, Chuck
    See McVicker, Charles (Taggart)
McVoy, Terra Elan 220
McWhirter, A(lan) Ross 1925-1975 37
    Obituary 31
McWhirter, Norris (Dewar) 1925-2004 37
McWilliam, Howard 1977- 219
McWilliams, Karen 1943- 65
Mdurvwa, Hajara E. 1962- 92
Meacham, Margaret 1952- 203
    Earlier sketch in SATA 95
Meachum, Virginia 1918- 133
    Earlier sketch in SATA 87
Mead, Alice 1952- 146
    Earlier sketch in SATA 94
Mead, Margaret 1901-1978
    Obituary 20
Mead, Russell (M., Jr.) 1935- 10
Mead, Stella (?)-1981
    Obituary 27
Meade, Elizabeth Thomasina 1854(?)-1914(?)
    See CLR 163
Meade, Ellen
    See Roddick, Ellen
Meade, Holly 207
Meade, L. T.
    See Meade, Elizabeth Thomasina
Meade, Marion 1934- 127
    Earlier sketch in SATA 23
Meader, Stephen W(arren) 1892-1977 1
Meadmore, Susan
    See Sallis, Susan (Diana)
Meadow, Charles T(roub) 1929- 23
Meadowcroft, Enid LaMonte
    See Wright, Enid Meadowcroft (LaMonte)
Meadows, Daisy
    See Chapman, Linda
Meadows, Graham (W.) 1934- 161
Meadows, Michelle 202
Meaker, M. J.
    See Meaker, Marijane
Meaker, Marijane 1927- 160
    Autobiography Feature 111
    Earlier sketches in SATA 20, 61, 99
    See also CLR 29
    See also SAAS 1
Meaker, Marijane Agnes
    See Meaker, Marijane
Means, Florence Crannell 1891-1980 1
    Obituary 25
    See also CLR 56
Mearian, Judy Frank 1936- 49
Mebus, Scott 1974- 216
Mecca, Judy Truesdell 1955- 127
Mechling, Lauren 1978(?)- 194
Mechling, Lauren 1978(?)- 194
Mechner, Jordan 1964- 205
Medary, Marjorie 1890-1980 14

Meddaugh, Susan 1944- *176*
  Earlier sketches in SATA *29, 84, 125*
Medearis, Angela Shelf 1956- *123*
  Earlier sketch in SATA *72*
Medearis, Mary 1915- *5*
Medina, Jane 1953- *167*
  Earlier sketch in SATA *122*
Medina, Meg 1963- *212*
Medina, Nico 1982- *193*
Medlicott, Mary 1946- *88*
Mee, Charles L., Jr. 1938- *72*
  Earlier sketch in SATA *8*
Meehan, Kierin *218*
Meehl, Brian *204*
Meek, Jacklyn O'Hanlon 1933- *51*
  Brief entry *34*
Meek, S(terner St.) P(aul) 1894-1972
  Obituary *28*
Meeker, Clare Hodgson 1952- *96*
Meeker, Oden 1919(?)-1976 .... *14*
Meeker, Richard
  See Brown, Fornan
Meeks, Esther MacBain *1*
Meggs, Libby Phillips 1943- *130*
Mehdevi, Alexander (Sinclair) 1947- *7*
Mehdevi, Anne (Marie) Sinclair 1947- *8*
Mehling, Carl 1969(?)- *237*
Meidell, Sherry 1951- *73*
Meier, Minta 1906- *55*
Meighan, Donald Charles 1929- *30*
Meigs, Cornelia Lynde 1884-1973 .... *6*
  See also CLR *55*
Meilach, Dona Z(weigoron) 1926- *34*
Meilman, Philip W(arren) 1951- *79*
Meinstereifel, Ronald L. 1960- *134*
Meisel, Paul *224*
  Earlier sketch in SATA *184*
Meister, Cari *204*
Melanson, Luc *198*
Melcher, Daniel 1912-1985
  Obituary *43*
Melcher, Frederic Gershom 1879-1963
  Obituary *22*
Melcher, Marguerite Fellows 1879-1969 .... *10*
Meldrum, Christina 1969(?)- *206*
Melendez, Francisco 1964- *72*
Melhuish, Eva *199*
Melin, Grace Hathaway 1892-1973 .... *10*
Mellersh, H(arold) E(dward) L(eslie)
  1897- *10*
Melling, David *186*
Melmed, Laura Krauss *212*
Melmoth, Sebastian
  See Wilde, Oscar
Melnikoff, Pamela (Rita) *97*
Meltzer, Amy 1968- *202*
Meltzer, Milton 1915-2009 .... *201*
  Autobiography Feature *124*
  Earlier sketches in SATA *1, 50, 80, 128*
  See also CLR *13*
  See also SAAS *1*
Melville, Anne
  See Potter, Margaret
Melville, Herman 1819-1891 .... *59*
Melwood, Mary
  See Lewis, E. M.
Melzack, Ronald 1929- *5*
Memling, Carl 1918-1969 .... *6*
Menchin, Scott *234*
  Earlier sketch in SATA *188*
Mendel, Jo
  See Bond, Gladys Baker
  and Gilbertson, Mildred Geiger
Mendelson, Steven T. 1958-1995 .... *86*
Mendelson-Stevens, Serita Deborah
  See Stevens, Serita
Mendes, Valerie 1939- *157*
Mendez, Raymond A. 1947- *66*
Mendez, Simon 1975- *215*
Mendonca, Susan
  See Smith, Susan Vernon

Mendoza, George 1934- *41*
  Brief entry *39*
  See also SAAS *7*
Menendez, Shirley (C.) 1937- *146*
Meng, Cece *194*
Meng, Heinz (Karl) 1924- *13*
Mennen, Ingrid 1954- *85*
Menotti, Gian Carlo 1911-2007 .... *29*
  Obituary *180*
Menuhin, Sir Yehudi 1916-1999 .... *40*
  Obituary *113*
Menville, Douglas 1935- *64*
Menzel, Barbara Jean 1946- *63*
Menzel, Peter 1948- *207*
Mercati, Cynthia *164*
Mercati, Cynthia J.
  See Mercati, Cynthia
Mercer, Charles (Edward) 1917-1988 .... *16*
  Obituary *61*
Mercer, Jessie *21*
Mercer, Sienna *192*
Meredith, Arnold
  See Hopkins, (Hector) Kenneth
Meredith, David William
  See Miers, Earl Schenck
Meringoff, Laurene Krasny
  See Brown, Laurene Krasny
Meriwether, Louise 1923- *52*
  Brief entry *31*
Merlin, Arthur
  See Blish, James
Merlin, Christina
  See Heaven, Constance (Christina)
Merola, Caroline 1962- *236*
Merrell, Billy 1982- *222*
Merriam, Eve 1916-1992 .... *73*
  Earlier sketches in SATA *3, 40*
  See also CLR *14*
Merrill, Jane 1946- *42*
Merrill, Jane Merrill
  See Merrill, Jane
Merrill, Jean (Fairbanks) 1923- *82*
  Earlier sketch in SATA *1*
  See also CLR *52*
Merrill, Phil
  See Merrill, Jane
Merriman, Alex
  See Silverberg, Robert
Merriman, Rachel 1971- *149*
  Earlier sketch in SATA *98*
Merrit, Elizabeth
  See Goudge, Eileen
Merski, Patricia K.
  See Merski, P.K.
Merski, P.K. *172*
Mertz, Barbara
  See Peters, Elizabeth
Mertz, Barbara Gross
  See Peters, Elizabeth
Merveille, David *200*
Merz, Jennifer J. *196*
Meschel, Susan V. 1936- *83*
Meschenmoser, Sebastian 1980- *229*
Meserve, Jessica *211*
Messenger, Charles (Rynd Milles) 1942- *59*
Messer, Stephen 1972- *231*
Messick, Dale 1906-2005 .... *64*
  Brief entry *48*
Messier, Claire 1956- *103*
Messieres, Nicole de
  See de Messieres, Nicole
Messinger, Carla *198*
Messmer, Otto 1892(?)-1983 .... *37*
Messner, Kate *224*
Mesta, Gabriel
  See Moesta, Rebecca
Metaxas, Eric 1963- *211*
Metcalf, Doris H(unter) *91*
Metcalf, Suzanne
  See Baum, L. Frank
Metos, Thomas H(arry) 1932- *37*

Metter, Bert(ram Milton) 1927- *56*
Metzenthen, David 1958- *167*
  Earlier sketch in SATA *106*
Meunier, Brian 1954- *195*
Meyer, Barbara 1939- *77*
Meyer, Carolyn 1935- *142*
  Autobiography Feature *142*
  Earlier sketches in SATA *9, 70, 118*
  See also SAAS *9*
Meyer, Carolyn Mae
  See Meyer, Carolyn
Meyer, Edith Patterson 1895-1993 .... *5*
Meyer, F(ranklyn) E(dward) 1932- *9*
Meyer, Jean Shepherd *11*
Meyer, Jerome Sydney 1895-1975 .... *3*
  Obituary *25*
Meyer, June
  See Jordan, June
Meyer, Kerstin 1966- *190*
Meyer, L.A. 1942- *221*
  Earlier sketches in SATA *12, 144*
Meyer, Louis A.
  See Meyer, L.A.
Meyer, Renate 1930- *6*
Meyer, Stephenie 1973- *193*
  See also CLR *142*
Meyer, Susan E. 1940- *64*
Meyerhoff, Jenny 1972- *208*
Meyers, Susan 1942- *164*
  Earlier sketches in SATA *19, 108*
Meynell, Laurence Walter 1899-1989
  Obituary *61*
Meynier, Yvonne (Pollet) 1908- *14*
Mezey, Robert 1935- *33*
Micale, Albert 1913- *22*
Michael, James
  See Scagnetti, Jack
Michael, Jan 1947- *216*
Michael, Livi 1960- *172*
Michael, Manfred
  See Winterfeld, Henry
Michael, Olivia
  See Michael, Livi
Michael, Ted 1984- *234*
Michaelis, Antonia 1979- *215*
Michaels, Barbara
  See Peters, Elizabeth
Michaels, Jamie *195*
Michaels, Joanne Louise
  See Teitelbaum, Michael
Michaels, Kristin
  See Williams, Jeanne
Michaels, Molly
  See Untermeyer, Louis
Michaels, Neal
  See Teitelbaum, Michael
Michaels, Rune *194*
Michaels, Ski
  See Pellowski, Michael (Joseph)
Michaels, Steve 1955- *71*
Michaels, William M. 1917- *77*
Michalak, Jamie 1973- *217*
Michel, Anna 1943- *49*
  Brief entry *40*
Michel, Francois 1948- *82*
Michelin, Linda *183*
Michelson, Richard *198*
  Earlier sketch in SATA *173*
Micich, Paul *74*
Mickelson, Scott 1963- *213*
Micklish, Rita 1931- *12*
Micklos, John, Jr. 1956- *173*
  Earlier sketch in SATA *129*
Micklos J., John, Jr. 1956-
  See Micklos, John, Jr.
Micucci, Charles (Patrick, Jr.) 1959- *144*
  Earlier sketch in SATA *82*
Middleton, Charlotte *230*
Middleton, Haydn 1955- *152*
  Earlier sketch in SATA *85*

Miers, Earl Schenck 1910-1972 .... *1*
  Obituary *26*
Migdale, Lawrence 1951- *89*
Miglio, Paige 1966- *201*
Mikaelsen, Ben 1952- *173*
  Earlier sketches in SATA *73, 107*
Mikaelsen, Benjamin John
  See Mikaelsen, Ben
Miklowitz, Gloria D. 1927- *129*
  Earlier sketches in SATA *4, 68*
  See also SAAS *17*
Mikolaycak, Charles 1937-1993 .... *78*
  Obituary *75*
  Earlier sketch in SATA *9*
  See also SAAS *4*
Mild, Warren (Paul) 1922- *41*
Milelli, Pascal 1965- *135*
Miles, Betty 1928- *78*
  Earlier sketch in SATA *8*
  See also SAAS *9*
Miles, Miska
  See Martin, Patricia Miles
Miles, (Mary) Patricia 1930- *29*
Miles, Patricia A.
  See Martin, Patricia Miles
Miles, Victoria 1966- *188*
Milford, Kate 1976- *233*
Milgrim, David *223*
  Earlier sketches in SATA *158, 187*
Milgrom, Harry 1912-1978 .... *25*
Milhous, Katherine 1894-1977 .... *15*
Milich, Zoran *174*
Milios, Rita 1949- *79*
Militant
  See Sandburg, Carl
Millais, Raoul 1901- *77*
Millar, Barbara F. 1924- *12*
Millar, Margaret (Ellis Sturm) 1915-1994 .... *61*
  Obituary *79*
Millard, Glenda *203*
Millard, Kerry *204*
Millbank, Captain H. R.
  See Ellis, Edward S.
Millen, C(ynthia) M. 1955- *114*
Miller, Albert G(riffith) 1905-1982 .... *12*
  Obituary *31*
Miller, Alice Ann 1958- *150*
Miller, Alice P(atricia McCarthy) *22*
Miller, Allan 1978- *216*
Miller, Christopher 1976- *215*
Miller, Debbie 1951- *160*
  Earlier sketch in SATA *103*
  See Miller, Debbie S.
Miller, Debbie S. *232*
  See Miller, Debbie
Miller, Deborah Uchill 1944- *61*
Miller, Don 1923- *15*
Miller, Doris R.
  See Mosesson, Gloria R(ubin)
Miller, Eddie
  See Miller, Edward
Miller, Edna Anita 1920- *29*
Miller, Edward 1905-1974 .... *8*
Miller, Edward 1964- *218*
  Earlier sketch in SATA *183*
Miller, Elizabeth 1933- *41*
Miller, Ellanita 1957- *87*
Miller, Eugene 1925- *33*
Miller, Frances A. 1937- *52*
  Brief entry *46*
Miller, Heather Lynn 1971- *214*
Miller, Helen M(arkley) -1984 .... *5*
Miller, Helen Topping 1884-1960
  Obituary *29*
Miller, Jane (Judith) 1925-1989 .... *15*
Miller, Jewel 1956- *73*
Miller, John
  See Samachson, Joseph
Miller, Judi *117*
Miller, Karen 1949- *210*

Miller, Karen Hokanson
  See Miller, Karen
Miller, Kate 1948- *193*
Miller, Kirsten 1973- *185*
Miller, Louise (Rolfe) 1940- *76*
Miller, M. L. *85*
Miller, Madge 1918- *63*
Miller, Margaret J.
  See Dale, Margaret J(essy) Miller
Miller, Marilyn (Jean) 1925- *33*
Miller, Marvin *65*
Miller, Mary
  See Northcott, (William) Cecil
Miller, Mary Beth 1942- *9*
Miller, Mary Beth 1964- *185*
Miller, Maryann 1943- *73*
Miller, Natalie 1917-1976 .... *35*
Miller, Pat 1951- *214*
Miller, Robert H. 1944- *91*
Miller, Ron 1947- *185*
Miller, Ruth White
  See White, Ruth
Miller, Sandra
  See Miller, Sandy
Miller, Sandra Peden
  See Miller, Sandy
Miller, Sandy 1948- *41*
  Brief entry *35*
Miller, Sarah 1969- *175*
Miller, Virginia
  See Austin, Virginia
Miller, William R. 1959- *116*
Miller, Woody *236*
Miller Brothers
  See Miller, Allan
Milligan, Bryce 1953- *170*
Milligan, Spike
  See Milligan, Terence Alan
Milligan, Terence Alan 1918-2002 .... *29*
  Obituary *134*
  See also CLR *92*
Millington, Ada
  See Deyneka, Anita
Millman, Isaac 1933- *140*
Mills, Adam
  See Stanley, George Edward
Mills, Claudia 1954- *191*
  Brief entry *41*
  Earlier sketches in SATA *44, 89, 145*
Mills, Elaine (Rosemary) 1941- *72*
Mills, G. Riley *196*
Mills, Joyce C. 1944- *102*
Mills, Judith Christine 1956- *130*
Mills, Yaroslava Surmach 1925-2008 .... *35*
Millspaugh, Ben P. 1936- *77*
Millstead, Thomas E. *30*
Millward, Gwen *202*
Milne, A. A. 1882-1956 .... *100*
  See also YABC *1*
  See also CLR *108*
Milne, Alan Alexander
  See Milne, A. A.
Milne, Lorus J. *5*
  See also CLR *22*
  See also SAAS *18*
Milne, Margery *5*
  See also CLR *22*
  See also SAAS *18*
Milne, Terry
  See Milne, Theresa Ann
Milne, Theresa Ann 1964- *84*
Milnes, Irma McDonough 1924- *101*
Milonas, Rolf
  See Myller, Rolf
Milone, Karen
  See Dugan, Karen
Milone-Dugan, Karen
  See Dugan, Karen
Milord, Susan 1954- *200*
  Earlier sketches in SATA *74, 147*

Milotte, Alfred G(eorge) 1904-1989 .... *11*
  Obituary *62*
Milstein, Linda 1954- *80*
Milton, Ann *134*
Milton, Hilary (Herbert) 1920- *23*
Milton, John R(onald) 1924- *24*
Milton, Joyce 1946- *101*
  Brief entry *41*
  Earlier sketch in SATA *52*
Milusich, Janice *216*
Milverton, Charles A.
  See Penzler, Otto
Milway, Alex 1978- *215*
Milway, Katie Smith 1960- *203*
Minahan, John A. 1956- *92*
Minar, Barbra (Goodyear) 1940- *79*
Minard, Rosemary 1939- *63*
Minarik, Else Holmelund 1920- *127*
  Earlier sketch in SATA *15*
  See also CLR *33*
Miner, Jane Claypool 1933- *103*
  Brief entry *37*
  Earlier sketch in SATA *38*
Miner, Lewis S. 1909-1971 .... *11*
Mines, Jeanette 1948- *61*
Mines, Jeanette Marie
  See Mines, Jeanette
Minier, Nelson
  See Stoutenburg, Adrien (Pearl)
Minnitt, Ronda Jacqueline
  See Armitage, David
Minor, Wendell 1944- *199*
  Earlier sketches in SATA *78, 109, 164*
Minter, Daniel 1961- *176*
Mintonye, Grace *4*
Miranda, Anne 1954- *109*
  Earlier sketch in SATA *71*
Miranda, Inaki 1983(?)- *207*
Mirocha, Paul *192*
Mirsky, Jeannette 1903-1987 .... *8*
  Obituary *51*
Mirsky, Reba Paeff 1902-1966 .... *1*
Misako Rocks! *192*
Misenta, Marisol
  See Innes, Stephanie
Mishica, Clare 1960- *91*
Miskovits, Christine 1939- *10*
Miss Frances
  See Horwich, Frances R(appaport)
Miss Read
  See Saint, Dora Jessie
Mister Rogers
  See Rogers, Fred McFeely
Mitchard, Jacquelyn 1956- *219*
  Earlier sketches in SATA *98, 168*
Mitchell, Adrian 1932-2008 .... *166*
  Obituary *200*
  Earlier sketch in SATA *104*
Mitchell, Allison
  See Griffin, W. E. B.
Mitchell, Betty Jo
  See Mitchell, B.J.
Mitchell, B.J. 1931- *120*
Mitchell, Clyde
  See Ellison, Harlan
  and Silverberg, Robert
Mitchell, Cynthia 1922- *29*
Mitchell, (Sibyl) Elyne (Keith) 1913- *10*
Mitchell, Gladys (Maude Winifred)
  1901-1983 .... *46*
  Obituary *35*
Mitchell, Jay
  See Roberson, Jennifer
Mitchell, Joyce Slayton 1933- *142*
  Brief entry *43*
  Earlier sketch in SATA *46*
Mitchell, K. L.
  See Lamb, Elizabeth Searle
Mitchell, Kathy 1948- *59*
Mitchell, Lori 1961- *128*
Mitchell, Margaree King 1953- *84*

Mitchell, Marianne 1947- *145*
Mitchell, Rhonda *89*
Mitchell, Saundra 1974(?)- *217*
Mitchell, Stephen 1943- *199*
Mitchell, Susan
  See Mitchell, Susan K.
Mitchell, Susan K. 1972- *210*
Mitchell, Todd 1974- *191*
Mitchell, Yvonne 1925-1979
  Obituary *24*
Mitchelson, Mitch
  See Mitchelson, Peter Richard
Mitchelson, Peter Richard 1950- *104*
Mitchison, Naomi (Margaret Haldane)
  1897-1999 .... *24*
  Obituary *112*
Mitchnik, Helen 1901-1982 .... *41*
  Brief entry *35*
Mitchum, Hank
  See Knott, William C(ecil, Jr.)
  and Murray, Stuart A. P.
  and Newton, D(wight) B(ennett)
  and Sherman, Jory (Tecumseh)
Mitgutsch, Ali 1935- *76*
Mitsuhashi, Yoko *45*
  Brief entry *33*
Mitton, Jacqueline 1948- *162*
  Earlier sketches in SATA *66, 115*
Mitton, Simon 1946- *66*
Mitton, Tony 1951- *235*
  Earlier sketches in SATA *104, 149, 203*
Miura, Taro 1968- *181*
Mizner, Elizabeth Howard 1907- *27*
Mizumura, Kazue *18*
Mlynowski, Sarah 1977(?)- *236*
  Earlier sketch in SATA *180*
Mobin-Uddin, Asma *216*
  Earlier sketch in SATA *172*
Mobley, Joe A. 1945- *91*
Moche, Dinah (Rachel) L(evine) 1936- *44*
  Brief entry *40*
Mochi, Ugo (A.) 1889-1977 .... *38*
Mochizuki, Ken 1954- *146*
  Earlier sketch in SATA *81*
  See also SAAS *22*
Modarressi, Mitra 1967- *200*
  Earlier sketch in SATA *126*
Modell, Frank B. 1917- *39*
  Brief entry *36*
Modesitt, Jeanne 1953- *217*
  Earlier sketches in SATA *92, 143*
Modesitt, L.E., Jr. 1943- *164*
  Earlier sketch in SATA *91*
Modesitt, Leland Exton, Jr.
  See Modesitt, L.E., Jr.
Modrell, Dolores 1933- *72*
Moe, Barbara 1937- *20*
Moe, Jorgen (Ingebretsen) 1813-1882
  See CLR *104*
Moed-Kass, Pnina *169*
Moerbeek, Kees 1955- *98*
Moeri, Louise 1924- *93*
  Earlier sketch in SATA *24*
  See also SAAS *10*
Moesta, Rebecca 1956- *182*
Moffett, Jami 1952- *84*
Moffett, Mark W. 1957(?)- *203*
Moffett, Martha (Leatherwood) 1934- *8*
Mogensen, Suzanne A(ncher) 1946- *129*
Mohammed, Khadra *197*
Mohanty, Raja *223*
Mohn, Peter B(urnet) 1934- *28*
Mohn, Viola Kohl 1914- *8*
Mohr, Nicholasa 1938- *97*
  Autobiography Feature *113*
  Earlier sketch in SATA *8*
  See also CLR *22*
  See also SAAS *8*
Mok, Esther 1953- *93*
Molan, Christine 1943- *84*
Molarsky, Osmond 1909- *16*

Moldon, Peter L(eonard) 1937- *49*
Mole, John 1941- *103*
  Earlier sketch in SATA *36*
  See also CLR *61*
Molesworth, Mary Louisa 1839-1921 .... *98*
  See also CLR *166*
Molin, Charles
  See Mayne, William
Molina, Silvia 1946- *97*
Molk, Laurel 1957- *162*
  Earlier sketch in SATA *92*
Mollel, Tololwa M. 1952- *88*
Molloy, Anne Baker 1907-1999 .... *32*
Molloy, Michael (John) 1940- *162*
Molloy, Paul (George) 1924- *5*
Molnar, Haya Leah 1951(?)- *230*
Moloney, James 1954- *202*
  Autobiography Feature *144*
  Earlier sketches in SATA *94, 144*
Molski, Carol *215*
Momaday, N. Scott 1934- *48*
  Brief entry *30*
Momaday, Navarre Scott
  See Momaday, N. Scott
Monaco, Octavia 1963- *169*
Monagle, Bernie 1957- *121*
Moncure, Jane Belk 1926- *23*
Monjo, F(erdinand) N(icholas III)
  1924-1978 .... *16*
  See also CLR *2*
Monk, Isabell 1952- *136*
Monks, Lydia *189*
Monroe, Chris 1962- *219*
Monroe, Christine
  See Monroe, Chris
Monroe, Lyle
  See Heinlein, Robert A.
Monroe, Marion
  See Cox, Marion Monroe
Monroy, Manuel 1970- *196*
Monsell, Helen Albee 1895-1971 .... *24*
Monson-Burton, Marianne 1975- *139*
Montalbano, Andrea *231*
Montana, Bob 1920-1975
  Obituary *21*
Montanari, Eva 1977- *209*
Montecalvo, Janet *177*
Montenegro, Laura Nyman 1953- *95*
Montero, Gloria 1933- *109*
Montes, Marisa 1951- *144*
Montgomerie, Norah (Mary) 1913- *26*
Montgomery, Constance
  See Cappel, Constance
Montgomery, Elizabeth
  See Julesberg, Elizabeth Rider Montgomery
Montgomery, Elizabeth Rider
  See Julesberg, Elizabeth Rider Montgomery
Montgomery, Hugh (Edward) 1962- *146*
Montgomery, L. M. 1874-1942 .... *100*
  See also YABC *1*
  See also CLR *145*
Montgomery, Lucy Maud
  See Montgomery, L. M.
Montgomery, Michael G. 1952- *208*
Montgomery, Raymond A. (Jr.) 1936- *39*
Montgomery, Rutherford George 1894-1985 . *3*
Montgomery, Sy 1958- *184*
  Autobiography Feature *132*
  Earlier sketches in SATA *114, 132*
Montgomery, Vivian *36*
Monthei, Betty *179*
Montijo, Rhode *179*
Montileaux, Donald F. 1948- *183*
Montpetit, Charles 1958- *101*
Montresor, Beni 1926-2001 .... *38*
  Earlier sketch in SATA *3*
  See also SAAS *4*
Montserrat, Pep *181*

Monty Python
  See Chapman, Graham
  and Cleese, John (Marwood)
  and Gilliam, Terry
  and Idle, Eric
  and Jones, Terence Graham Parry
  and Palin, Michael
Moodie, Craig 1956- *172*
Moodie, Fiona 1952- *133*
Moody, Minerva
  See Alcott, Louisa May
Moody, Ralph Owen 1898-1982 .... *1*
Moon, Carl 1879(?)-1948 .... *25*
Moon, Grace (Purdie) 1877(?)-1947 .... *25*
Moon, Lily
  See Warnes, Tim
Moon, Nicola 1952- *147*
  Earlier sketch in SATA *96*
Moon, Pat 1946- *113*
Moon, Sheila 1910-1991 .... *5*
  Obituary *114*
Moon, Sheila Elizabeth
  See Moon, Sheila
Mooney, Bel 1946- *95*
Mooney, Bill 1936- *122*
Mooney, Elizabeth C(omstock) 1918-1986
  Obituary *48*
Mooney, William
  See Mooney, Bill
Moor, Emily
  See Deming, Richard
Moorcock, Michael 1939- *166*
  Earlier sketch in SATA *93*
Moorcock, Michael John
  See Moorcock, Michael
Moorcock, Michael John
  See Moorcock, Michael
Moore, Anne Carroll 1871-1961 .... *13*
Moore, Cheri
  See Ladd, Cheryl (Jean)
Moore, Clement Clarke 1779-1863 .... *18*
Moore, Cyd 1957- *233*
  Earlier sketches in SATA *83, 133, 186*
Moore, Don W. 1905(?)-1986
  Obituary *48*
Moore, Elaine 1944- *86*
Moore, Eva 1942- *103*
  Earlier sketch in SATA *20*
Moore, Ishbel (Lindsay) 1954- *140*
Moore, Jack (William) 1941- *46*
  Brief entry *32*
Moore, Janet Gaylord 1905-1992 .... *18*
Moore, Jim 1946- *42*
Moore, John Travers 1908- *12*
Moore, Lilian 1909-2004 .... *137*
  Obituary *155*
  Earlier sketch in SATA *52*
  See also CLR *15*
Moore, Liz
  See Moore, M. Elizabeth
Moore, M. Elizabeth 1959- *156*
Moore, Margaret R(umberger) 1903- *12*
Moore, Margie *224*
  Earlier sketch in SATA *176*
Moore, Marianne 1887-1972 .... *20*
Moore, Marianne Craig
  See Moore, Marianne
Moore, Patrick (Alfred Caldwell) 1923- *49*
  Brief entry *39*
  See also SAAS *8*
Moore, Patrick 1959- *184*
Moore, Perry 1971-2011 .... *193*
Moore, Peter 1963- *175*
Moore, Peter G.
  See Moore, Peter
Moore, Raina 1970- *212*
Moore, Ray (S.) 1905(?)-1984
  Obituary *37*
Moore, Regina
  See Dunne, Mary Collins
Moore, Rosalie (Gertrude) 1910-2001 .... *9*

Moore, Ruth (Ellen) 1908-1989 23
Moore, Ruth Nulton 1923- 38
Moore, S(arah) E. 23
Moore, Sarah Margaret
  See Hodges, Margaret
Moore, Sean L. 1976- 237
Moore, Stephanie Perry 1969(?)- 214
Moore, Tara 1950- 61
Moore, Yvette 1958- 154
  Earlier sketches in SATA *69, 70*
Moores, Dick
  See Moores, Richard (Arnold)
Moores, Richard (Arnold) 1909-1986
  Obituary 48
Mooser, Stephen 1941- 75
  Earlier sketch in SATA *28*
Mora, Francisco X(avier) 1952- 90
Mora, Pat 1942- 232
  Earlier sketches in SATA *92, 134, 186*
  See also CLR *58*
Mora, Patricia
  See Mora, Pat
Morais, Flavio 207
Morales, Magaly 225
Morales, Yuyi 180
  Earlier sketch in SATA *154*
Moran, Tom 1943- 60
Moranville, Sharelle Byars 196
  Earlier sketch in SATA *152*
Moray Williams, Ursula 1911-2006 3
  Obituary 177
  See also SAAS *9*
Mordecai, Martin 220
Morden, Simon 1966(?)- 211
Mordhorst, Heidi 1964- 222
Mordvinoff, Nicolas 1911-1973 17
More, Caroline
  See Cone, Molly (Lamken)
  and Strachan, Margaret Pitcairn
Moreau, Jean-Pierre
  See Jarrie, Martin
Moreno, Rene King 190
Moreton, Andrew Esq.
  See Defoe, Daniel
Morey, Charles
  See Fletcher, Helen Jill
Morey, Walt(er Nelson) 1907-1992 51
  Obituary 70
  Earlier sketch in SATA *3*
  See also SAAS *9*
Morgan, Alfred P(owell) 1889-1972 33
Morgan, Alison (Mary) 1930- 85
  Earlier sketch in SATA *30*
Morgan, Anne 1954- 121
Morgan, Christopher 1956- 199
Morgan, Clay 1950- 198
Morgan, Douglas
  See Macdonald, James D.
Morgan, Ellen
  See Bumstead, Kathleen Mary
Morgan, Geoffrey 1916- 46
Morgan, Helen (Gertrude Louise)
  1921-1990 29
Morgan, Jane
  See Cooper, James Fenimore
  and Franklin, Jane (Morgan)
  and Moren, Sally M(oore)
Morgan, Lenore H. 1908-1976 8
Morgan, Mary 1957- 213
  Earlier sketches in SATA *81, 114*
Morgan, McKayla
  See Basile, Gloria Vitanza
Morgan, Michaela
  See Basile, Gloria Vitanza
Morgan, Nicola 1961- 161
Morgan, Nina 1953- 110
Morgan, Pierr 1952- 122
  Earlier sketch in SATA *77*
Morgan, Robin (Evonne) 1941- 80
Morgan, Roxanne
  See Gentle, Mary

Morgan, Sarah (Nicola) 1959- 68
Morgan, Shirley
  See Kiepper, Shirley Morgan
Morgan, Stacy T(owle) 1959- 104
Morgan, Stevie
  See Davies, Nicola
Morgan, Tom 1942- 42
Morgan, Wendy
  See Staub, Wendy Corsi
Morgan-Vanroyen, Mary
  See Morgan, Mary
Morgenstern, Susie Hoch 1945- 133
Mori, Hana 1909-1990(?) 88
Mori, Kyoko 1957- 122
  Autobiography Feature 126
  See also CLR *64*
  See also SAAS *26*
Moriarty, Jaclyn 1968- 162
Moriarty, William J. 1930- 127
Morice, Dave 1946- 93
Morin, Isobel V. 1928- 110
Morine, Hoder
  See Conroy, John Wesley
Morley, Ben 228
Morley, Taia 199
Morley, Wilfred Owen
  See Lowndes, Robert A(ugustine) W(ard)
Morningstar, Mildred (Whaley) 1912-1997 .. 61
  Obituary 114
Morozumi, Atsuko 217
  Earlier sketch in SATA *110*
Morpurgo, Michael 1943- 225
  Earlier sketches in SATA *93, 143, 184*
  See also CLR *51*
Morrah, Dave
  See Morrah, David Wardlaw, Jr.
Morrah, David Wardlaw, Jr. 1914-1991 10
Morreale-de la Garza, Phyllis
  See De la Garza, Phyllis
Morressy, John 1930-2006 23
Morrill, Leslie H(olt) 1934-2003 48
  Brief entry 33
  Obituary 148
  See also SAAS *22*
Morris, Carla 210
Morris, Carla D.
  See Morris, Carla
Morris, Chris(topher Crosby) 1946- 66
Morris, Deborah 1956- 91
Morris, Desmond 1928- 14
Morris, Desmond John
  See Morris, Desmond
Morris, Don 1954- 83
Morris, Gerald 1963- 207
  Earlier sketches in SATA *107, 150*
Morris, Gerald Paul
  See Morris, Gerald
Morris, Gilbert (Leslie) 1929- 104
Morris, Jackie 202
  Earlier sketch in SATA *151*
Morris, Janet (Ellen) 1946- 66
Morris, Jay
  See Tatham, Julie Campbell
Morris, (Margaret) Jean 1924- 98
Morris, Jeffrey
  See Morris, Jeffrey Brandon
Morris, Jeffrey B.
  See Morris, Jeffrey Brandon
Morris, Jeffrey Brandon 1941- 92
Morris, Jennifer E. 1969- 179
Morris, Jill 1936- 165
  Earlier sketch in SATA *119*
Morris, Juddi 85
Morris, Judy K. 1936- 61
Morris, Oradel Nolen 128
Morris, Richard 1969- 224
Morris, Robert A(da) 1933- 7
Morris, William 1913-1994 29
Morrison, Angela 218
Morrison, Bill 1935- 66
  Brief entry 37

Morrison, Chloe Anthony Wofford
  See Morrison, Toni
Morrison, Dorothy Nafus 29
Morrison, Frank 1971- 226
  Earlier sketch in SATA *185*
Morrison, Gordon 1944- 183
  Earlier sketches in SATA *87, 128*
Morrison, Joan 1922- 65
Morrison, Lillian 1917- 108
  Earlier sketch in SATA *3*
Morrison, Lucile Phillips 1896- 17
Morrison, Martha A. 1948- 77
Morrison, Meighan 1966- 90
Morrison, P.R. 196
Morrison, Richard
  See Lowndes, Robert A(ugustine) W(ard)
Morrison, Robert
  See Lowndes, Robert A(ugustine) W(ard)
Morrison, Roberta
  See Webb, Jean Francis (III)
Morrison, Slade 1964-2010 228
Morrison, Susan Dudley
  See Gold, Susan Dudley
Morrison, Taylor 1971- 187
  Earlier sketches in SATA *95, 159*
Morrison, Toni 1931- 235
  Earlier sketches in SATA *57, 144*
  See also CLR *99*
Morrison, Velma Ford 1909- 21
Morrison, Wilbur Howard 1915- 64
Morrison, William
  See Samachson, Joseph
Morriss, James E(dward) 1932- 8
Morrissey, Dean 183
Morrow, Barbara Olenyik 1952- 167
Morrow, Betty
  See Bacon, Elizabeth
Morrow, Sue Anne 1966- 218
Morse, C. Scott
  See Morse, Scott
Morse, Carol
  See Yeakley, Marjory Hall
Morse, C.S.
  See Morse, Scott
Morse, Dorothy B(ayley) 1906-1979
  Obituary 24
Morse, Flo 1921- 30
Morse, Scott 1973- 200
Morse, Tony 1953- 129
Morstad, Julie 232
Mort, Vivian
  See Cromie, Alice Hamilton
Mortensen, Denise Dowling 179
Mortensen, Lori 1955- 221
Mortimer, Anne 1958- 206
  Earlier sketch in SATA *116*
Mortimer, Mary H.
  See Coury, Louise Andree
Morton, Alexandra (Hubbard) 1957- 144
Morton, Anthony
  See Arthur, Robert, (Jr.)
Morton, Christine
  See Morton-Shaw, Christine
Morton, Jane 1931- 50
Morton, Joseph C. 1932- 156
Morton, Lee Jack, Jr. 1928- 32
Morton, Miriam 1918(?)-1985 9
  Obituary 46
Morton-Shaw, Christine 1957- 211
Mosatche, Harriet 1949- 122
Mosatche, Harriet S.
  See Mosatche, Harriet
Moscow, Alvin 1925- 3
Mosel, Arlene (Tichy) 1921-1996 7
Moseley, James W(illett) 1931- 139
Moseng, Elisabeth 1967- 90
Moser, Barry 1940- 185
  Earlier sketches in SATA *56, 79, 138*
  See also CLR *49*
  See also SAAS *15*
Moser, Don(ald Bruce) 1932- 31

Moser, Laura *194*
Moser, Lisa *192*
Moses, Sheila P. 1961- *168*
Moses, Will 1956- *178*
  Earlier sketch in SATA *120*
Mosesson, Gloria R(ubin) *24*
Mosher, Richard 1949- *120*
Moskin, Marietta D(unston) 1928- *23*
Moskof, Martin Stephen 1930- *27*
Mosley, Francis 1957- *57*
Moss, Don(ald) 1920- *11*
Moss, Elaine (Dora) 1924- *57*
  Brief entry *31*
Moss, Jeff(rey) 1942-1998 .... *73*
  Obituary *106*
Moss, Marissa 1959- *216*
  Earlier sketches in SATA *71, 104, 163*
  See also CLR *134*
Moss, Miriam 1955- *202*
  Earlier sketches in SATA *76, 140*
Moss, Peggy 1966- *235*
Moss, Thylias 1954- *108*
Moss, Thylias Rebecca Brasier
  See Moss, Thylias
Most, Bernard 1937- *134*
  Brief entry *40*
  Earlier sketches in SATA *48, 91*
Mosz, Gosia 1972- *194*
Mott, Evelyn Clarke 1962- *133*
  Earlier sketch in SATA *75*
Motz, Lloyd 1909-2004 .... *20*
Mould, Chris *205*
Mould, Edwin
  See Whitlock, Ralph
Moulton, Mark Kimball *212*
Mouly, Francoise *155*
Mountain, Robert
  See Montgomery, Raymond A. (Jr.)
Mountfield, David
  See Grant, Neil
Mourlevat, Jean-Claude 1952- *187*
Mourning, Tuesday *206*
Moussard, Jacqueline 1924- *24*
Mowat, Claire 1933- *123*
Mowat, Claire Angel Wheeler
  See Mowat, Claire
Mowat, Farley 1921- *55*
  Earlier sketch in SATA *3*
  See also CLR *20*
Mowat, Farley McGill
  See Mowat, Farley
Mowll, Joshua 1970(?)- *188*
Mowry, Jess 1960- *131*
  Autobiography Feature *131*
  Earlier sketch in SATA *109*
  See also CLR *65*
Moxley, Sheila 1966- *96*
Moyer, Terry J. 1937- *94*
Moyes, Patricia
  See Haszard, Patricia Moyes
Moyler, Alan (Frank Powell) 1926- *36*
Mozelle, Shirley *179*
Mozley, Charles 1915- *43*
  Brief entry *32*
Mphahlele, Es'kia 1919-2008 .... *119*
  Obituary *198*
Mphahlele, Ezekiel
  See Mphahlele, Es'kia
Mphahlele, Zeke
  See Mphahlele, Es'kia
Mr. McGillicuddy
  See Abisch, Roslyn Kroop
Mr. Sniff
  See Abisch, Roslyn Kroop
Mr. Tivil
  See Lorkowski, Thomas V(incent)
Mr. Wizard
  See Herbert, Don
Mraz, David 1947- *219*
Mrs. Fairstar
  See Horne, Richard Henry Hengist

Muchamore, Robert 1972- *175*
Muchmore, Jo Ann 1937- *103*
Mude, O.
  See Gorey, Edward (St. John)
Mudgeon, Apeman
  See Mitchell, Adrian
Mueller, Jorg 1942- *67*
  See also CLR *43*
Mueller, Miranda R. *201*
Mueller, Virginia 1924- *28*
Muggs
  See Watkins, Lois
Muir, Diana
  See Appelbaum, Diana Muir Karter
Muir, Frank (Herbert) 1920-1998 .... *30*
Muir, Helen 1937- *65*
Muirhead, Margaret *220*
Mukerji, Dhan Gopal 1890-1936 .... *40*
  See also CLR *10*
Mulcahy, Lucille Burnett *12*
Muldrow, Diane *229*
Mulford, Philippa G. 1948- *112*
  Earlier sketch in SATA *43*
Mulford, Philippa Greene
  See Mulford, Philippa G.
Mulgan, Catherine 1931- *24*
Mulila, Vigad G.
  See Maillu, David G(ian)
Mull, Brandon 1974- *190*
Mullen, Michael 1937- *122*
Muller, Billex
  See Ellis, Edward S.
Muller, Birte 1973- *214*
Muller, Jorg
  See Mueller, Jorg
Muller, (Lester) Robin 1953- *86*
Mullin, Caryl Cude 1969- *130*
Mullins, Edward S(wift) 1922- *10*
Mullins, Hilary 1962- *84*
Mulock, Dinah Maria
  See Craik, Dinah Maria (Mulock)
Mulvihill, William Patrick 1923- *8*
Mumford, Ruth
  See Dallas, Ruth
Mumy, Bill 1954- *112*
Mun
  See Leaf, (Wilbur) Munro
Munari, Bruno 1907-1998 .... *15*
  See also CLR *9*
Munce, Ruth Hill 1898- *12*
Mundy, Simon 1954- *64*
Mundy, Simon Andrew James Hainault
  See Mundy, Simon
Munger, Nancy *170*
Munowitz, Ken 1935-1977 .... *14*
Munoz, Claudio *208*
Munoz, William 1949- *92*
  Earlier sketch in SATA *42*
Munro, Alice 1931- *29*
Munro, Alice Anne
  See Munro, Alice
Munro, Eleanor 1928- *37*
Munro, Roxie 1945- *223*
  Earlier sketches in SATA *58, 136, 184*
Munsch, Bob
  See Munsch, Robert (Norman)
Munsch, Robert (Norman) 1945- *120*
  Brief entry *48*
  Earlier sketches in SATA *50, 83*
  See also CLR *19*
Munsinger, Lynn 1951- *221*
  Earlier sketches in SATA *33, 94, 177*
Munson, Derek 1970- *139*
Munson, R. W.
  See Karl, Jean E(dna)
Munson-Benson, Tunie 1946- *15*
Munsterberg, Peggy 1921- *102*
Muntean, Michaela *182*
Munthe, Nelly 1947- *53*
Munves, James (Albert) 1922- *30*
Munzer, Martha E. 1899-1999 .... *4*

Murawski, Darlyne A. *193*
Murch, Mel
  See Manes, Stephen
Murdoch, David H(amilton) 1937- *96*
Murdoch, Patricia 1957- *192*
Murdock, Catherine Gilbert *185*
Murhall, J(acqueline) J(ane) 1964- *143*
Murphy, Barbara Beasley 1933- *130*
  Earlier sketch in SATA *5*
Murphy, Claire Rudolf 1951- *137*
  Earlier sketch in SATA *76*
Murphy, E(mmett) Jefferson 1926- *4*
Murphy, Elizabeth Ann Maureen
  See Murphy, Liz
Murphy, Jill 1949- *214*
  Earlier sketches in SATA *37, 70, 142*
  See also CLR *39*
Murphy, Jill Frances
  See Murphy, Jill
Murphy, Jim 1947- *224*
  Brief entry *32*
  Earlier sketches in SATA *37, 77, 124, 185*
  See also CLR *53*
Murphy, Joseph E., Jr. 1930- *65*
Murphy, Kelly 1977- *190*
  Earlier sketch in SATA *143*
Murphy, Liz 1964- *210*
Murphy, Louise 1943- *155*
Murphy, Mary 1961- *196*
Murphy, Pat
  See Murphy, E(mmett) Jefferson
Murphy, Patricia J. 1963- *132*
Murphy, Rita *180*
Murphy, Robert (William) 1902-1971 .... *10*
Murphy, Shirley Rousseau 1928- *126*
  Earlier sketches in SATA *36, 71*
  See also SAAS *18*
Murphy, Stuart J. 1942- *237*
  Earlier sketches in SATA *115, 157*
Murphy, Thomas Basil, Jr. 1935- *191*
Murphy, Tim
  See Murphy, Jim
Murphy, Tom
  See Murphy, Thomas Basil, Jr.
Murray, John 1923- *39*
Murray, Kirsty 1960- *165*
  Earlier sketch in SATA *108*
Murray, Marguerite 1917- *63*
Murray, Marian *5*
Murray, Martine 1965- *125*
Murray, (Judith) Michele (Freedman)
  1933-1974 .... *7*
Murray, Ossie 1938- *43*
Murray, Peter
  See Hautman, Pete
Murrow, Liza Ketchum
  See Ketchum, Liza
Musgrave, Florence 1902-1999 .... *3*
Musgrove, Margaret W(ynkoop) 1943- *124*
  Earlier sketch in SATA *26*
Musgrove, Marianne *207*
Mussey, Virginia Howell
  See Ellison, Virginia H(owell)
Mussey, Virginia T.H.
  See Ellison, Virginia H(owell)
Mussi, Sarah *206*
Mutel, Cornelia F. 1947- *74*
Muth, Jon J. *206*
  Earlier sketch in SATA *165*
Mutz
  See Kuenstler, Morton
Mwangi, Meja 1948- *174*
My Brother's Brother
  See Chekhov, Anton
Myers, Anna *220*
  Earlier sketch in SATA *160*
Myers, Arthur 1917- *91*
  Earlier sketch in SATA *35*
Myers, Bernice *81*
  Earlier sketch in SATA *9*

Myers, Caroline Elizabeth Clark
   1887-1980 28
Myers, Christopher 1975- 183
   See also CLR 97
Myers, Edward 1950- 227
   Earlier sketches in SATA 96, 172
Myers, Elisabeth P(erkins) 1918- 36
Myers, (Mary) Hortense (Powner)
   1913-1987 10
Myers, Jack 1913-2006 83
   Obituary 178
Myers, Jack Edgar
   See Myers, Jack
Myers, Laurie 232
Myers, Lou 1915-2005 81
   Obituary 171
Myers, Louis
   See Myers, Lou
Myers, R.E. 1924- 119
Myers, Robert Eugene
   See Myers, R.E.
Myers, Tim 1953- 176
   Earlier sketch in SATA 147
Myers, Timothy Joseph
   See Myers, Tim
Myers, Walter Dean 1937- 229
   Brief entry 27
   Earlier sketches in SATA 41, 71, 109, 157,
   193
   See also CLR 110
   See also SAAS 2
Myers, Walter M.
   See Myers, Walter Dean
Myklusch, Matt 236
Myller, Rolf 1926-2006 27
   Obituary 175
Myra, Harold L(awrence) 1939- 46
   Brief entry 42
Myracle, Lauren 1969- 204
   Earlier sketch in SATA 162
Myrus, Donald (Richard) 1927- 23
Mysterious Traveler, The
   See Arthur, Robert, (Jr.)

N

Na, An 149
Na, Il Sung 231
Naaslund, Goorel Kristina 1940- 170
Nadel, Laurie 1948- 74
Naden, Corinne J. 1930- 166
   Earlier sketch in SATA 79
Nadimi, Suzan 188
Nadol, Jen 228
Nagda, Ann Whitehead 199
Nagel, Andreas Fischer
   See Fischer-Nagel, Andreas
Nagel, Heiderose Fischer
   See Fischer-Nagel, Heiderose
Nagle, Shane 176
Nahoko, Uehashi
   See Uehashi, Nahoko
Naidoo, Beverley 1943- 180
   Earlier sketches in SATA 63, 135
   See also CLR 29
Nails, Jennifer 213
Naiyomah, Wilson Kimeli 1977- 226
Nakae, Noriko 1940- 59
Nakata, Hiroe 205
Nakatani, Chiyoko 1930-1981 55
   Brief entry 40
   See also CLR 30
Nally, Susan W. 1947- 90
Namioka, Lensey 1929- 157
   Autobiography Feature 116
   Earlier sketches in SATA 27, 89
   See also CLR 48
   See also SAAS 24
Namovicz, Gene Inyart 1927- 6

Nance, Andrew 210
Nanji, Shenaaz 1954- 204
   Earlier sketch in SATA 131
Nanogak Agnes 1925- 61
Napier, Mark
   See Laffin, John (Alfred Charles)
Napoli, Donna Jo 1948- 230
   Autobiography Feature 230
   Earlier sketches in SATA 92, 137, 190
   See also CLR 51
   See also SAAS 23
Napp, Daniel 1974- 204
Narahashi, Keiko 1959- 115
   Earlier sketch in SATA 79
Narayan, R. K. 1906-2001 62
Narayan, Rasipuram Krishnaswami
   See Narayan, R. K.
Nascimbene, Yan 1949- 173
   Earlier sketch in SATA 133
Nash, Bruce M(itchell) 1947- 34
Nash, Frediric Ogden
   See Nash, Ogden
Nash, Linell
   See Smith, Linell Nash
Nash, Mary (Hughes) 1925- 41
Nash, Ogden 1902-1971 46
   Earlier sketch in SATA 2
Nash, Renea Denise 1963- 81
Nast, Elsa Ruth
   See Watson, Jane Werner
Nast, Thomas 1840-1902 51
   Brief entry 33
Nastick, Sharon 1954- 41
Natale, Vince 196
Natalini, Sandro 1970- 222
Natarajan, Srividya 187
Nathan, Adele (Gutman) 1900(?)-1986
   Obituary 48
Nathan, Amy 155
   Earlier sketch in SATA 104
Nathan, Dorothy (Goldeen) (?)-1966 15
Nathan, Robert (Gruntal) 1894-1985 6
   Obituary 43
Nathanson, Laura Walther 1941- 57
Nation, Kaleb 1988- 222
Natti, Lee 1919- 67
   Earlier sketch in SATA 1
   See also SAAS 3
Natti, Susanna 1948- 125
   Earlier sketch in SATA 32
Nau, Thomas 186
Naughtie, Eleanor
   See Updale, Eleanor
Naughton, Bill
   See Naughton, William John (Francis)
Naughton, James Franklin 1957- 85
Naughton, Jim
   See Naughton, James Franklin
Naughton, William John (Francis)
   1910-1992 86
Navarra, John Gabriel 1927- 8
Nayeri, Daniel 232
Nayeri, Dina 226
Naylor, Penelope 1941- 10
Naylor, Phyllis 1933-
   See Naylor, Phyllis Reynolds
Naylor, Phyllis Reynolds 1933- 209
   Autobiography Feature 152
   See also CLR 135
   See also SAAS 10
Nazarian, Nikki
   See Nichols, Cecilia Fawn
Nazaroff, Alexander I(vanovich) 1898-1981 .. 4
Nazoa, Aquiles 1920-1976 198
Neal, Harry Edward 1906-1993 5
   Obituary 76
Neal, Michael
   See Teitelbaum, Michael
Nearing, Penny 1916- 47
   Brief entry 42

Nebel, Gustave E. 45
   Brief entry 33
Nebel, Mimouca
   See Nebel, Gustave E.
Nee, Kay Bonner 10
Needham, Kate 1962- 95
Needle, Jan 1943- 98
   Earlier sketch in SATA 30
   See also CLR 43
   See also SAAS 23
Needleman, Jacob 1934- 6
Neel, David 1960- 82
Neel, Preston 1959- 93
Neff, Henry H. 1973- 221
Negri, Rocco 1932- 12
Negrin, Fabian 1963- 189
Neidigh, Sherry 1956- 204
Neier, Aryeh 1937- 59
Neigoff, Anne 13
Neigoff, Mike 1920- 13
Neilan, Eujin Kim 1969- 200
Neilson, Frances Fullerton (Jones)
   1910-2001 14
Neimark, Anne E. 1935- 145
   Earlier sketch in SATA 4
Neimark, Paul G. 1934- 80
   Brief entry 37
Neitzel, Shirley 1941- 134
   Earlier sketch in SATA 77
Nell
   See Hanna, Nell(ie L.)
Nelscott, Kris
   See Rusch, Kristine Kathryn
Nelson, Blake 1960- 177
Nelson, Catherine Chadwick 1926- 87
Nelson, Cordner 1918-2009 54
   Brief entry 29
Nelson, Cordner Bruce
   See Nelson, Cordner
Nelson, D.A. 1970- 215
Nelson, Dawn Ann
   See Nelson, D.A.
Nelson, Drew 1952- 77
Nelson, Esther L. 1928- 13
Nelson, Jandy 229
Nelson, Jim A.
   See Stotter, Mike
Nelson, Julie L. 1970- 117
Nelson, Kadir 213
   Earlier sketches in SATA 154, 181
Nelson, Kris
   See Rusch, Kristine Kathryn
Nelson, Lawrence E(rnest) 1928-1977
   Obituary 28
Nelson, Marilyn 1946- 60
   Autobiography Feature 180
Nelson, Mary Carroll 1929- 23
Nelson, O. Terry 1941- 62
Nelson, Peter 1953- 73
Nelson, Peter N.
   See Nelson, Peter
Nelson, R. A. 197
Nelson, Richard K(ing) 1941- 65
Nelson, Robin Laura 1971- 141
Nelson, Roy Paul 1923- 59
Nelson, S.D. 181
Nelson, Sharlene (P.) 1933- 96
Nelson, Suzanne 1976- 184
Nelson, Ted (W.) 1931- 96
Nelson, Theresa 1948- 143
   Autobiography Feature 143
   Earlier sketch in SATA 79
Nelson, Vaunda Micheaux 1953- 220
Nemeth, Sally 187
Neri, G. 197
Neri, Greg
   See Neri, G.
Neri, Gregory
   See Neri, G.
Nerlove, Miriam 1959- 53
   Brief entry 49

Nesbit, E. 1858-1924 .... *100*
  See also YABC *1*
  See also CLR *70*
Nesbit, Edith
  See Nesbit, E.
Nesbit, Troy
  See Folsom, Franklin (Brewster)
Nespojohn, Katherine V(eronica) 1912-1975 . *7*
Ness, Evaline (Michelow) 1911-1986 .... *26*
  Obituary *49*
  Earlier sketch in SATA *1*
  See also CLR *6*
  See also SAAS *1*
Ness, Patrick 1971- *207*
Nestor, Larry 1940- *149*
Nestor, William P(rodromos) 1947- *49*
Nethery, Mary *93*
Neubecker, Robert *214*
  Earlier sketch in SATA *170*
Neuberger, Julia (Babette Sarah) 1950- *142*
  Earlier sketch in SATA *78*
Neufeld, John (Arthur) 1938- *131*
  Autobiography Feature *131*
  Earlier sketches in SATA *6, 81*
  See also CLR *52*
  See also SAAS *3*
Neuhaus, David 1958- *83*
Neumeyer, Peter F(lorian) 1929- *13*
Neurath, Marie (Reidemeister) 1898-1986 ..... *1*
Neuschwander, Cindy 1953- *157*
  Earlier sketch in SATA *107*
Neusner, Jacob 1932- *38*
Neville, Charles
  See Bodsworth, (Charles) Fred(erick)
Neville, Emily Cheney 1919- *1*
  See also SAAS *2*
Neville, Mary
  See Woodrich, Mary Neville
Nevins, Albert (Francis) J(erome)
  1915-1997 .... *20*
Nevius, Carol 1955- *186*
Newberger, Devra
  See Speregen, Devra Newberger
Newberry, Clare Turlay 1903-1970 .... *1*
  Obituary *26*
Newbery, John 1713-1767 .... *20*
  See also CLR *147*
Newbery, Linda 1952- *184*
  Earlier sketch in SATA *142*
Newbigging, Martha *198*
Newbold, Greg *199*
Newcomb, Ellsworth
  See Kenny, Ellsworth Newcomb
Newcombe, Eugene A. 1923-1990 .... *45*
  Brief entry *33*
Newcombe, Jack
  See Newcombe, Eugene A.
Newcome, Robert 1955- *91*
Newcome, Zita 1959- *88*
Newell, Crosby
  See Bonsall, Crosby Barbara (Newell)
Newell, Edythe W(eatherford) 1910-1989 .... *11*
Newell, Hope Hockenberry 1896-1965 .... *24*
Newfeld, Frank 1928- *26*
Newgarden, Mark 1959- *194*
Newhouse, Maxwell 1947- *232*
Newland, Gillian *220*
Newlon, (Frank) Clarke 1905(?)-1982 .... *6*
  Obituary *33*
Newman, Barbara Johansen *191*
Newman, C.J.
  See Newman, Coleman J.
Newman, Coleman J. 1935- *82*
Newman, Daisy 1904-1994 .... *27*
  Obituary *78*
Newman, Gerald 1939- *46*
  Brief entry *42*
Newman, Jeff 1976- *228*
Newman, Jerry
  See Newman, Coleman J.

Newman, Leslea 1955- *234*
  Earlier sketches in SATA *71, 128, 134*
Newman, Margaret
  See Potter, Margaret
Newman, Marjorie *146*
Newman, Matthew (Harrison) 1955- *56*
Newman, Nanette 1934- *162*
Newman, Robert (Howard) 1909-1988 .... *87*
  Obituary *60*
  Earlier sketch in SATA *4*
Newman, Shirlee P(etkin) *144*
  Earlier sketches in SATA *10, 90*
Newquist, Harvey
  See Newquist, H.P.
Newquist, H.P. 1958- *235*
Newsom, Carol 1948- *92*
  Earlier sketch in SATA *40*
Newsom, Tom 1944- *80*
Newsome, Richard 1964- *233*
Newth, Mette 1942- *140*
Newton, David E. 1933- *67*
Newton, David Edward
  See Newton, David E.
Newton, James R(obert) 1935- *23*
Newton, Jill 1964- *200*
Newton, Robert 1965- *191*
Newton, Suzanne 1936- *77*
  Earlier sketch in SATA *5*
Newton, Vanessa
  See Newton, Vanessa Brantley
Newton, Vanessa Brantley 1962(?)- *206*
Ney, John 1923- *43*
  Brief entry *33*
Nez, John *218*
  Earlier sketch in SATA *155*
Nez, John Abbott
  See Nez, John
Ng, Franklin *82*
Ngui, Marc 1972- *229*
Nguyen, Vincent *226*
  Earlier sketch in SATA *187*
Nichol, B(arrie) P(hillip) 1944-1988 .... *66*
Nicholas, Louise D.
  See Watkins, Dawn L.
Nicholls, Judith (Ann) 1941- *61*
Nicholls, Sally 1983- *209*
Nichols, Cecilia Fawn 1906-1987 .... *12*
Nichols, Grace 1950- *164*
  Earlier sketch in SATA *98*
Nichols, Janet (Louise) 1952- *67*
Nichols, Judy 1947- *124*
Nichols, Leigh
  See Koontz, Dean
Nichols, Michael 1952- *215*
Nichols, Nick
  See Nichols, Michael
Nichols, Paul
  See Hawks, Robert
Nichols, Peter
  See Youd, Samuel
Nichols, (Joanna) Ruth 1948- *15*
  See also CLR *149*
Nichols, Travis *206*
Nicholson, C. R.
  See Nicole, Christopher
Nicholson, Christina
  See Nicole, Christopher
Nicholson, Joyce Thorpe 1919-2011 .... *35*
Nicholson, Lois P. 1949- *88*
Nicholson, Robin
  See Nicole, Christopher
Nicholson, William *180*
Nicholson, William 1872-1949
  See CLR *76*
Nickel, Barbara 1966- *188*
Nickell, Joe 1944- *167*
  Earlier sketch in SATA *73*
Nickelsburg, Janet 1893-1983 .... *11*
Nickerson, Betty 1922- *14*
Nickerson, Elizabeth
  See Nickerson, Betty

Nickl, Barbara (Elisabeth) 1939- *56*
Nicklaus, Carol *62*
  Brief entry *33*
Nickle, John *181*
Nickless, Will 1902-1979(?) *66*
Nic Leodhas, Sorche
  See Alger, Leclaire (Gowans)
Nicol, Ann
  See Turnbull, Ann
Nicolas
  See Mordvinoff, Nicolas
Nicolay, Helen 1866-1954
  See YABC *1*
Nicole, Christopher 1930- *5*
Nicole, Christopher Robin
  See Nicole, Christopher
Nicoll, Helen 1937- *87*
Nicolson, Cynthia Pratt 1949- *141*
Ni Dhuibhne, Eilis 1954- *91*
Niehaus, Paddy Bouma
  See Bouma, Paddy
Nields, Nerissa 1967- *166*
Nielsen, Kay (Rasmus) 1886-1957 .... *16*
  See also CLR *16*
Nielsen, Laura F. 1960- *93*
Nielsen, Laura Farnsworth
  See Nielsen, Laura F.
Nielsen, Nancy J. 1951- *77*
Nielsen, Susin 1964- *195*
Nielsen, Virginia
  See McCall, Virginia Nielsen
Nielsen-Fernlund, Susin
  See Nielsen, Susin
Nielson, Sheila A. *234*
Niemann, Christoph 1970- *191*
Nieuwsma, Milton J(ohn) 1941- *142*
Nightingale, Sandy 1953- *76*
Nikolajeva, Maria 1952- *127*
Nikola-Lisa, W. 1951- *180*
  Earlier sketch in SATA *71*
Niland, Deborah 1951- *172*
  Earlier sketch in SATA *27*
Niland, Kilmeny *75*
Nilsen, Anna 1948- *174*
  Earlier sketch in SATA *96*
Nilsson, Eleanor 1939- *117*
  Earlier sketch in SATA *81*
  See also SAAS *23*
Nilsson, Per 1954- *159*
Nimmo, Jenny 1944- *144*
  Earlier sketch in SATA *87*
  See also CLR *44*
Nishimura, Kae *196*
Niven, Larry 1938- *171*
  Earlier sketch in SATA *95*
Niven, Laurence Van Cott
  See Niven, Larry
Niven, Laurence VanCott
  See Niven, Larry
Nivola, Claire A. 1947- *208*
  Earlier sketches in SATA *84, 140*
Nix, Garth 1963- *210*
  Earlier sketches in SATA *97, 143*
  See also CLR *68*
Nixon, Hershell Howard 1923- *42*
Nixon, Joan Lowery 1927-2003 .... *115*
  Obituary *146*
  Earlier sketches in SATA *8, 44, 78*
  See also CLR *24*
  See also SAAS *9*
Nixon, K.
  See Nixon, Kathleen Irene (Blundell)
Nixon, Kathleen Irene (Blundell)
  1894-1988(?) *14*
  Obituary *59*
Nobati, Eugenia 1968- *201*
Nobisso, Josephine 1953- *121*
  Earlier sketch in SATA *78*
Noble, Iris (Davis) 1922-1986 .... *5*
  Obituary *49*

Noble, Marty 1947- 125
  Earlier sketch in SATA 97
Noble, Trinka Hakes 1944- 197
  Brief entry 37
  Earlier sketch in SATA 123
Nobleman, Marc Tyler 1972- 203
Noda, Takayo 1961- 168
Nodelman, Perry 1942- 101
Nodset, Joan L.
  See Lexau, Joan M.
Noel Hume, Ivor 1927- 65
Noestlinger, Christine
  See Nostlinger, Christine
Noguere, Suzanne 1947- 34
Nolan, Dennis 1945- 166
  Brief entry 34
  Earlier sketches in SATA 42, 92
Nolan, Han 1956- 157
  Earlier sketch in SATA 109
Nolan, Janet 1956- 191
  Earlier sketch in SATA 145
Nolan, Jeannette Covert 1897-1974 2
  Obituary 27
Nolan, Lucy 215
Nolan, Paul T(homas) 1919- 48
Nolan, William F. 1928- 88
  Brief entry 28
Nolan, William Francis
  See Nolan, William F.
Nolen, Jerdine 1953- 157
  Earlier sketch in SATA 105
Noll, Amanda 219
Noll, Sally 1946- 82
Nolte, Jack
  See Carter, Scott William
Noonan, Brandon 1979- 184
Noonan, Diana 1960- 146
Noonan, Julia 1946- 148
  Earlier sketches in SATA 4, 95
Norac, Carl 1960- 166
Norcliffe, James 1946- 234
Norcross, John
  See Conroy, John Wesley
Nordan, Robert W(arren) 1934-2004 133
Nordhoff, Charles Bernard 1887-1947 23
Nordlicht, Lillian 29
Nordstrom, Ursula 1910-1988 3
  Obituary 57
Nordtvedt, Matilda 1926- 67
Norling, Beth 1969- 149
Norman, Charles 1904-1996 38
  Obituary 92
Norman, Geoffrey 223
Norman, Howard
  See Norman, Howard A.
Norman, Howard A. 1949- 81
Norman, James
  See Schmidt, James Norman
Norman, Jay
  See Arthur, Robert, (Jr.)
Norman, Lilith 1927- 120
  Earlier sketch in SATA 86
Norman, Mary 1931- 36
Norman, Steve
  See Pashko, Stanley
Norment, Lisa 1966- 91
Norris, Gunilla Brodde 1939- 20
North, Andrew
  See Norton, Andre
North, Anthony
  See Koontz, Dean
North, Captain George
  See Stevenson, Robert Louis
North, Captain George
  See Stevenson, Robert Louis
North, Howard
  See Trevor, Elleston
North, Joan 1920- 16
North, Milou
  See Erdrich, Louise

North, Robert
  See Withers, Carl A.
North, Sara
  See Bonham, Barbara Thomas
  and Hager, Jean
North, Sherry 201
North, Sterling 1906-1974 45
  Obituary 26
  Earlier sketch in SATA 1
Northcott, (William) Cecil 1902-1987
  Obituary 55
Northeast, Brenda V(ictoria) 1948- 106
Northmore, Elizabeth Florence 1906-1974 . 122
Norton, Alice Mary
  See Norton, Andre
Norton, Andre 1912-2005 91
  Earlier sketches in SATA 1, 43
  See also CLR 50
Norton, Browning
  See Norton, Frank R. B(rowning)
Norton, Frank R. B(rowning) 1909-1989 10
Norton, Mary 1903-1992 60
  Obituary 72
  Earlier sketch in SATA 18
  See also CLR 140
Nosredna, Trebor
  See Anderson, Bob
Nostlinger, Christine 1936- 162
  Brief entry 37
  Earlier sketch in SATA 64
  See also CLR 12
Noteboom, Erin
  See Bow, Erin
Nourse, Alan E(dward) 1928-1992 48
  See also CLR 33
Novak, Matt 1962- 204
  Brief entry 52
  Earlier sketches in SATA 60, 104, 165
Novelli, Luca 1947- 61
Novgorodoff, Danica 1982(?)- 215
Nowell, Elizabeth Cameron 12
Noyes, Deborah 1965- 194
  Earlier sketch in SATA 145
Nugent, Cynthia 1954- 205
Nugent, Nicholas 1949- 73
Numberman, Neil 1981(?)- 220
Numeroff, Laura 1953- 206
  Earlier sketches in SATA 28, 90, 142
  See also CLR 85
Numeroff Joffe, Laura
  See Numeroff, Laura
Nunes, Lygia Bojunga 1932- 154
  Earlier sketch in SATA 75
Nunn, Laura (Donna) Silverstein 1968- 124
Nurenberg, Thelma
  See Greenhaus, Thelma Nurenberg
Nurnberg, Maxwell 1897-1984 27
  Obituary 41
Nussbaumer, Paul (Edmund) 1934- 16
Nutt, Ken 1951- 163
  Earlier sketch in SATA 97
Nuttall-Smith, Margaret Emily Noel 1919- .. 26
Nuygen, Mathieu 1967- 80
Nuzum, K. A. 195
Nuzum, Kathy A.
  See Nuzum, K. A.
Nwapa, Flora (Nwanzuruaha) 1931-1993
  See CLR 162
Nyberg, (Everett Wayne) Morgan 1944- 87
Nyce, (Nellie) Helene von Strecker
  1885-1969 19
Nyce, Vera 1862-1925 19
Nye, Naomi Shihab 1952- 198
  Earlier sketches in SATA 86, 147
  See also CLR 59
Nye, Robert 1939- 6
Nyeu, Tao 206
Nyikos, Stacy A. 1969- 164
Nystrom, Carolyn 1940- 130
  Earlier sketch in SATA 67

O

O. Henry
  See Henry, O.
Oakes, Elizabeth H. 1964- 132
Oakes, Vanya 1909-1983 6
  Obituary 37
Oakley, Don(ald G.) 1927- 8
Oakley, Graham 1929- 84
  Earlier sketch in SATA 30
  See also CLR 7
Oakley, Helen (McKelvey) 1906- 10
Oaks, J. Adams 220
Oana, Katherine 1929- 53
  Brief entry 37
Oates, Eddie H. 1943- 88
Oates, Joyce Carol 1938- 159
Oates, Stephen B(aery) 1936- 59
Obed, Ellen Bryan 1944- 74
Oberdieck, Bernhard 1949- 230
Oberle, Joseph 1958- 69
Oberman, Sheldon 1949-2004 85
  Autobiography Feature 114
  Obituary 153
  See also CLR 54
  See also SAAS 26
Obligado, Lilian (Isabel) 1931- 61
  Brief entry 45
Obrant, Susan 1946- 11
O'Brian, E.G.
  See Clarke, Arthur C.
O'Brien, Anne Sibley 1952- 213
  Brief entry 48
  Earlier sketches in SATA 53, 80
O'Brien, Caragh M. 232
O'Brien, E.G.
  See Clarke, Arthur C.
O'Brien, Esse Forrester 1895(?)-1975
  Obituary 30
O'Brien, Johnny 222
O'Brien, Patrick 1960- 193
O'Brien, Robert C. 1918-1973 23
  See also CLR 2
O'Brien, Thomas C. 1938-2010 29
O'Brien, Thomas Clement
  See O'Brien, Thomas C.
O'Callaghan, Julie 1954- 113
O'Callahan, Jay 1938- 88
O'Carroll, Ryan
  See Markun, Patricia Maloney
Ochiltree, Dianne 1953- 117
Ockham, Joan Price
  See Price, Joan
O'Connell, Margaret F(orster) 1935-1977 30
  Obituary 30
O'Connell, Peg
  See Ahern, Margaret McCrohan
O'Connell, Rebecca 1968- 212
  Earlier sketch in SATA 130
O'Connor, Barbara 1950- 193
  Earlier sketch in SATA 154
O'Connor, Francine M(arie) 1930- 90
O'Connor, Genevieve A. 1914- 75
O'Connor, George 228
  Earlier sketch in SATA 183
O'Connor, Ian 1965- 188
O'Connor, Jane 1947- 186
  Brief entry 47
  Earlier sketches in SATA 59, 103, 150
O'Connor, Karen 1938- 89
  Earlier sketch in SATA 34
O'Connor, Patrick
  See Wibberley, Leonard
O'Connor, Richard 1915-1975
  Obituary 21
O'Conor, Jane 1958- 78
Odaga, Asenath (Bole) 1937- 130
  Earlier sketch in SATA 67
  See also SAAS 19
O Danachair, Caoimhin
  See Danaher, Kevin

Odanaka, Barbara *159*
O'Daniel, Janet 1921- *24*
O'Day, Cathy
  See Crane, Barbara (Joyce)
O'Dell, Scott 1898-1989 .... *134*
  Earlier sketches in SATA *12, 60*
  See also CLR *126*
Odenwald, Robert P(aul) 1899-1965 .... *11*
Odgers, Sally
  See Odgers, Sally Farrell
Odgers, Sally Farrell 1957- *139*
  Earlier sketch in SATA *72*
Odone, Jamison 1980- *209*
O'Donnell, Dick
  See Lupoff, Richard A.
  and Thompson, Don(ald Arthur)
O'Donnell, Liam 1970- *209*
Odriozola, Elena *186*
Oechsli, Kelly 1918-1999 .... *5*
Oertel, Andreas 1966- *230*
Oesterle, Virginia Rorby
  See Rorby, Ginny
Ofek, Uriel 1926- *36*
  See also CLR *28*
Ofer, Avi 1975- *207*
Offenbacher, Ami 1958- *91*
Offermann, Andrea *231*
Offill, Jenny 1968- *211*
Offit, Sidney 1928- *10*
Ofosu-Appiah, L(awrence) H(enry) 1920- ... *13*
Ogan, George F. 1912-1983 .... *13*
Ogan, M. G.
  See Ogan, George F.
  and Ogan, Margaret E. (Nettles)
Ogan, Margaret E. (Nettles) 1923-1979 .... *13*
Ogburn, Charlton (Jr.) 1911-1998 .... *3*
  Obituary *109*
Ogburn, Jacqueline K. *162*
Ogilvie, Elisabeth May 1917-2006 .... *40*
  Brief entry *29*
  Obituary *176*
Ogilvy, Gavin
  See Barrie, J. M.
Ogilvy, Ian 1943- *177*
Ogilvy, Ian Raymond
  See Ogilvy, Ian
Ogle, Lucille Edith 1904-1988
  Obituary *59*
Ogletree, Charles J. 1952- *175*
O'Green, Jennifer
  See Roberson, Jennifer
O'Green, Jennifer Roberson
  See Roberson, Jennifer
O'Hagan, Caroline 1946- *38*
O'Hanlon, Jacklyn
  See Meek, Jacklyn O'Hanlon
O'Hara, Elizabeth
  See Ni Dhuibhne, Eilis
O'Hara, Kenneth
  See Morris, (Margaret) Jean
O'Hara, Mary
  See Alsop, Mary O'Hara
O'Hara (Alsop), Mary
  See Alsop, Mary O'Hara
O'Hare, Jeff(rey A.) 1958- *105*
O'hearn, Kate *225*
Ohi, Ruth 1964- *95*
Ohiyesa
  See Eastman, Charles A(lexander)
Ohlsson, Ib 1935- *7*
Ohmi, Ayano 1959- *115*
Ohtomo, Yasuo 1946- *37*
o huigin, sean 1942- *138*
  See also CLR *75*
Oiseau
  See Moseley, James W(illett)
Oke, Janette 1935- *97*
O'Keefe, Susan Heyboer *176*
  Earlier sketch in SATA *133*
O'Keeffe, Frank 1938- *99*

O'Kelley, Mattie Lou 1908-1997 .... *97*
  Earlier sketch in SATA *36*
Okimoto, Jean Davies 1942- *103*
  Earlier sketch in SATA *34*
Okomfo, Amasewa
  See Cousins, Linda
olafsdottir, Gudrun Elin
  See Gunnella
Olaleye, Isaac O. 1941- *96*
  See also SAAS *23*
Olander, Johan 1967- *231*
Olcott, Frances Jenkins 1872(?)-1963 .... *19*
Old, Wendie C(orbin) 1943- *154*
Old Boy
  See Hughes, Thomas
Oldenburg, E(gbert) William 1936-1974 ...... *35*
Older, Effin 1942- *114*
Older, Jules 1940- *156*
  Earlier sketch in SATA *114*
Oldfield, Jenny 1949- *140*
Oldfield, Margaret J(ean) 1932- *56*
Oldfield, Pamela 1931- *86*
Oldham, June *70*
Oldham, Mary 1944- *65*
Oldland, Nicholas 1972- *223*
Olds, Elizabeth 1896-1991 .... *3*
  Obituary *66*
Olds, Helen Diehl 1895-1981 .... *9*
  Obituary *25*
Oldstyle, Jonathan
  See Irving, Washington
O'Leary, Brian (Todd) 1940- *6*
O'Leary, Chris *208*
O'Leary, Patsy B. 1937- *97*
O'Leary, Patsy Baker
  See O'Leary, Patsy B.
Oleynikov, Igor 1953- *202*
Oliphant, B.J.
  See Tepper, Sheri S.
Oliver, Burton
  See Burt, Olive Woolley
Oliver, Chad
  See Oliver, Symmes C.
Oliver, John Edward 1933- *21*
Oliver, Lauren 1982- *228*
Oliver, Lin *202*
Oliver, Marilyn Tower 1935- *89*
Oliver, Mark 1960- *214*
Oliver, Narelle 1960- *197*
  Earlier sketch in SATA *152*
Oliver, Shirley (Louise Dawkins) 1958- *74*
Oliver, Symmes C. 1928-1993 .... *101*
Oliviero, Jamie 1950- *84*
Olmsted, Lorena Ann 1890-1989 .... *13*
Olney, Ross R. 1929- *13*
Olschewski, Alfred (Erich) 1920- *7*
Olsen, Barbara *148*
Olsen, Carol 1945- *89*
Olsen, Ib Spang 1921- *81*
  Earlier sketch in SATA *6*
Olsen, Violet (Mae) 1922-1991 .... *58*
Olson, Arielle North 1932- *67*
Olson, David J. 1974- *198*
Olson, Gene 1922- *32*
Olson, Gretchen *187*
Olson, Helen Kronberg *48*
Olson, Julie 1976- *233*
Olson, Kay Melchisedech 1948- *175*
Olson, Marianne
  See Mitchell, Marianne
Olson-Brown, Ellen 1967- *183*
Olten, Manuela 1970- *197*
Olugebefola, Ademole 1941- *15*
Oluonye, Mary N(kechi) 1955- *111*
Om
  See Gorey, Edward (St. John)
O'Malley, Donough *208*
O'Malley, Kevin 1961- *230*
  Earlier sketches in SATA *157, 191*
Oman, Carola (Mary Anima) 1897-1978 ..... *35*
O'Mara, Carmel 1965- *166*

O'Mara-Horwitz, Carmel
  See O'Mara, Carmel
O'Meara, Walter (Andrew) 1897-1989 .... *65*
Ommanney, F(rancis) D(ownes) 1903-1980 . *23*
Omololu, Cynthia Jaynes *222*
O Mude
  See Gorey, Edward (St. John)
Oneal, Elizabeth 1934- *82*
  Earlier sketch in SATA *30*
  See also CLR *169*
O'Neal, Katherine Pebley 1957- *204*
O'Neal, Reagan
  See Jordan, Robert
O'Neal, Regan
  See Jordan, Robert
Oneal, Zibby
  See Oneal, Elizabeth
O'neill, Alexis 1949- *220*
O'Neill, Amanda 1951- *111*
O'Neill, Catharine *203*
O'Neill, Gerard K(itchen) 1927-1992 .... *65*
O'Neill, Judith (Beatrice) 1930- *34*
O'Neill, Mary L(e Duc) 1908(?)-1990 .... *2*
  Obituary *64*
O'Neill, Reagan
  See Jordan, Robert
Onslow, Annette Rosemary MacArthur
  See MacArthur-Onslow, Annette Rosemary
Onslow, John 1906-1985
  Obituary *47*
Onyefulu, Ifeoma 1959- *157*
  Earlier sketches in SATA *81, 115*
Opie, Iona (Margaret Balfour) 1923- *118*
  Earlier sketches in SATA *3, 63*
  See also SAAS *6*
Opie, Peter (Mason) 1918-1982 .... *118*
  Obituary *28*
  Earlier sketches in SATA *3, 63*
Oppel, Kenneth 1967- *199*
  Earlier sketches in SATA *99, 153*
Oppel, Kenneth Kerry
  See Oppel, Kenneth
Oppenheim, Joanne 1934- *174*
  Earlier sketches in SATA *5, 82, 136*
Oppenheim, Shulamith Levey 1928- *177*
Oppenheimer, Joan L(etson) 1925- *28*
Oppong, Joseph Ransford 1953- *160*
Optic, Oliver
  See Adams, William Taylor
  and Stratemeyer, Edward L.
Oram, Hiawyn 1946- *101*
  Earlier sketch in SATA *56*
Orbach, Ruth Gary 1941- *21*
Orback, Craig *197*
Orczy, Emma
  See Orczy, Baroness Emmuska
Orczy, Emma Magdalena Rosalia Maria Josefa
  See Orczy, Baroness Emmuska
Orczy, Emmuska
  See Orczy, Baroness Emmuska
Orczy, Baroness Emmuska 1865-1947 .... *40*
Orde, A.J.
  See Tepper, Sheri S.
O'Reilly, Jackson
  See Jordan, Robert
Orenstein, Denise Gosliner 1950- *157*
Orgad, Dorit 1936- *199*
Orgel, Doris 1929- *148*
  Earlier sketches in SATA *7, 85*
  See also CLR *48*
  See also SAAS *19*
Orgill, Roxane *198*
Oriolo, Joe
  See Oriolo, Joseph D.
Oriolo, Joseph D. 1913-1985
  Obituary *46*
Orlandelli, Alessandro
  See Horley, Alex
Orlean, Susan 1955- *209*
Orleans, Ilo 1897-1962 .... *10*

Orlev, Uri 1931- *135*
  Earlier sketch in SATA *58*
  See also CLR *30*
  See also SAAS *19*
Orloff, Karen Kaufman *236*
Ormai, Stella *57*
  Brief entry *48*
Ormerod, Jan 1946- *210*
  Brief entry *44*
  Earlier sketches in SATA *55, 70, 132*
  See also CLR *20*
Ormerod, Janette Louise
  See Ormerod, Jan
Ormes, Jackie
  See Ormes, Zelda J.
Ormes, Zelda J. 1914-1986
  Obituary *47*
Ormondroyd, Edward 1925- *14*
Ormsby, Virginia H(aire) 1906-1990 .... *11*
Orona-Ramirez, Kristy 1964- *189*
Orozco, Jose-Luis 1948- *179*
Orr, Katherine S(helley) 1950- *72*
Orr, Wendy 1953- *206*
  Earlier sketches in SATA *90, 141*
Orris
  See Ingelow, Jean
Orth, Richard
  See Gardner, Richard (M.)
Ortiz Cofer, Judith
  See Cofer, Judith Ortiz
Orwell, George 1903-1950 .... *29*
  See also CLR *171*
Orwin, Joanna 1944- *141*
Os, Eric van
  See van Os, Erik
Osborn, Elinor 1939- *145*
Osborn, Jacob 1981(?)- *215*
Osborn, Kathy 1955(?)- *199*
Osborn, Lois D(orothy) 1915- *61*
Osborne, Charles 1927- *59*
Osborne, Chester G(orham) 1915-1987 .... *11*
Osborne, David
  See Silverberg, Robert
Osborne, George
  See Silverberg, Robert
Osborne, Leone Neal 1914-1996 .... *2*
Osborne, Linda Barrett 1949- *215*
Osborne, Mary Pope 1949- *144*
  Earlier sketches in SATA *41, 55, 98*
  See also CLR *88*
Osceola
  See Blixen, Karen
Osgood, William E(dward) 1926- *37*
O'Shaughnessy, Darren
  See Shan, Darren
O'Shaughnessy, Ellen Cassels 1937- *78*
O'shaughnessy, Tam 1951- *221*
O'Shea, Catherine Patricia Shiels
  See O'Shea, Pat
O'Shea, Pat 1931-2007 .... *87*
  See also CLR *18*
Osmond, Edward 1900- *10*
Ossoli, Sarah Margaret
  See Fuller, Margaret
Ostendorf, (Arthur) Lloyd, (Jr.) 1921-2000 .. *65*
  Obituary *125*
Osterweil, Adam 1972- *217*
Ostow, Micol 1976- *223*
  Earlier sketch in SATA *170*
Otfinoski, Steven 1949- *116*
  Earlier sketch in SATA *56*
Otis, James
  See Kaler, James Otis
O'Toole, Thomas 1941- *71*
O'Trigger, Sir Lucius
  See Horne, Richard Henry Hengist
Otten, Charlotte
  See Otten, Charlotte F.
Otten, Charlotte F. 1926- *98*
Otten, Charlotte Fennema
  See Otten, Charlotte F.

Ottley, Matt 1962- *171*
  Earlier sketch in SATA *102*
Ottley, Reginald Leslie 1909-1985 .... *26*
  See also CLR *16*
Otto, Margaret Glover 1909-1976
  Obituary *30*
Otto, Svend
  See Soerensen, Svend Otto
Ouellet, Debbie 1954- *219*
Oughton, Jerrie (Preston) 1937- *131*
  Earlier sketch in SATA *76*
Oughton, (William) Taylor 1925- *104*
Ouida
  See De La Ramee, Marie Louise
Ousley, Odille 1896-1976 .... *10*
Outcalt, Todd 1960- *123*
Overmyer, James E. 1946- *88*
Overton, Jenny (Margaret Mary) 1942- *52*
  Brief entry *36*
Owen, Ann
  See Qualey, Marsha
Owen, Annie 1949- *75*
Owen, Caroline Dale
  See Snedeker, Caroline Dale (Parke)
Owen, Clifford
  See Hamilton, Charles (Harold St. John)
Owen, Dilys
  See Gater, Dilys
Owen, (Benjamin) Evan 1918-1984 .... *38*
Owen, (John) Gareth 1936-2002 .... *162*
  Earlier sketch in SATA *83*
  See also CLR *31*
  See also SAAS *14*
Owen, James A. *185*
Owens, Bryant 1968- *116*
Owens, Dana Elaine
  See Queen Latifah
Owens, Gail 1939- *54*
Owens, Mary Beth *191*
Owens, Thomas S(heldon) 1960- *86*
Owens, Tom
  See Owens, Thomas S(heldon)
Oxenbury, Helen 1938- *149*
  Earlier sketches in SATA *3, 68*
  See also CLR *70*
Oxendine, Bess Holland 1933- *90*
Oz, Frank (Richard) 1944- *60*
Ozer, Jerome S. 1927- *59*

P

Paananen, Eloise (Katherine) 1923-1993 .... *9*
Pace, Lorenzo 1943- *131*
Pace, Mildred Mastin 1907- *46*
  Brief entry *29*
Pachter, Hedwig (?)-1988 .... *63*
Pack, Janet 1952- *77*
Pack, Robert 1929- *118*
Packard, Edward 1931- *148*
  Earlier sketches in SATA *47, 90*
Packer, Kenneth L. 1946- *116*
Packer, Vin
  See Meaker, Marijane
Pad, Peter
  See Stratemeyer, Edward L.
Page, Eileen
  See Heal, Edith
Page, Eleanor
  See Coerr, Eleanor (Beatrice)
Page, Gail 1950- *205*
Page, Jake 1936- *81*
Page, James Keena, Jr.
  See Page, Jake
Page, Lou Williams 1912-1997 .... *38*
Page, Mary
  See Heal, Edith
Page, Robin 1943- *154*
Pagliarulo, Antonio 1977(?)- *212*
Pagnucci, Susan 1944- *90*

Pahlen, Kurt 1907-2003
  Obituary *147*
Pahz, Cheryl
  See Pahz, Cheryl Suzanne
Pahz, Cheryl Suzanne 1949- *11*
Pahz, James Alon 1943- *11*
Paice, Margaret 1920- *10*
Paige, Harry W(orthington) 1922- *41*
  Brief entry *35*
Paige, Richard
  See Koontz, Dean
Paige, Robin
  See Albert, Susan Wittig
Paillot, Jim *230*
Paine, Penelope Colville 1946- *87*
Paine, Roberta M. 1925- *13*
Paisley, Tom 1932- *11*
  See also CLR *3*
Palatini, Margie *207*
  Earlier sketches in SATA *134, 174*
Palazzo, Anthony D.
  See Palazzo, Tony
Palazzo, Tony 1905-1970 .... *3*
Palder, Edward L. 1922- *5*
Palecek, Josef 1932- *56*
Palecek, Libuse 1937- *89*
Palen, Debbie *195*
Palin, Michael 1943- *67*
Palin, Michael Edward
  See Palin, Michael
Palladini, David (Mario) 1946- *40*
  Brief entry *32*
Pallas, Norvin 1918-1983 .... *23*
Pallister, John C(lare) 1891-1980
  Obituary *26*
Pallotta, Gerard Larry
  See Pallotta, Jerry
Pallotta, Jerry 1953- *186*
Pallotta-Chiarolli, Maria 1960- *117*
Palmer, Bernard (Alvin) 1914-1998 .... *26*
Palmer, C. Everard 1930- *14*
Palmer, (Ruth) Candida 1926- *11*
Palmer, Cyril Everard
  See Palmer, C. Everard
Palmer, Don
  See Benson, Mildred
Palmer, Gary 1968- *231*
Palmer, Hap 1942- *68*
Palmer, Heidi 1948- *15*
Palmer, Helen Marion
  See Geisel, Helen
Palmer, Jessica 1953- *120*
Palmer, Judd 1972- *153*
Palmer, Juliette 1930- *15*
Palmer, Kate Salley 1946- *97*
Palmer, Maria
  See Strachan, Ian
Palmer, Maria
  See Brennan, Herbie
Palmer, Robin 1909-2000 .... *43*
Palmer, Robin 1969- *232*
Palmero Caceres, Ana *198*
Palmisciano, Diane *202*
Paltrowitz, Donna 1950- *61*
  Brief entry *50*
Paltrowitz, Donna Milman
  See Paltrowitz, Donna
Paltrowitz, Stuart 1946- *61*
  Brief entry *50*
Pamela, Todd 1950- *124*
Pamintuan, Macky *214*
  Earlier sketch in SATA *178*
Panagopoulos, Janie Lynn *149*
Panati, Charles 1943- *65*
Panchyk, Richard 1970- *138*
Panetta, George 1915-1969 .... *15*
Panetta, Joseph N. 1953- *96*
Pang, YaWen Ariel *206*
Panik, Sharon 1952- *82*
Panowski, Eileen Thompson 1920- *49*

Pansy
See Alden, Isabella (Macdonald)
Pantell, Dora (Fuchs) 39
Panter, Carol 1936- 9
Paolini, Christopher 1983- 157
See also CLR 102
Papademetriou, Lisa 175
Paparone, Pam 185
Paparone, Pamela
See Paparone, Pam
Papas, Bill
See Papas, William
Papas, William 1927-2000 50
Papashvily, George 1898-1978 17
Papashvily, Helen (Waite) 1906-1996 17
Pape, D. L.
See Pape, Donna (Lugg)
Pape, Donna (Lugg) 1930- 82
Earlier sketch in SATA 2
Paperny, Myra (Green) 1932- 51
Brief entry 33
Papineau, Lucie 1962- 224
Papp, Robert 1967- 205
Paradis, Adrian A(lexis) 1912- 67
Earlier sketch in SATA 1
See also SAAS 8
Paradis, Marjorie Bartholomew
1886(?)-1970 17
Paradiz, Valerie 1963- 176
Paratore, Coleen
See Paratore, Coleen Murtagh
Paratore, Coleen Murtagh 1958- 200
Pardo DeLange, Alex 211
Parenteau, Shirley 1935- 199
Brief entry 40
Earlier sketch in SATA 47
Parish, Margaret 1927-1988 73
Obituary 59
Earlier sketch in SATA 17
See also CLR 22
Parish, Margaret Holt
See Holt, Margaret
Parish, Peggy
See Parish, Margaret
Park, Barbara 1947- 123
Brief entry 35
Earlier sketches in SATA 40, 78
See also CLR 34
Park, Bill
See Park, W(illiam) B(ryan)
Park, Frances 1955- 171
Park, Ginger 173
Park, Janie Jaehyun 150
Park, Jordan
See Kornbluth, C(yril) M.
and Pohl, Frederik
Park, Linda Sue 1960- 200
Earlier sketches in SATA 127, 173
See also CLR 84
Park, Nick 1958- 113
Park, Rosina Ruth Lucia
See Park, Ruth
Park, Ruth 1917(?)-2010 93
Earlier sketch in SATA 25
See also CLR 51
Park, W(illiam) B(ryan) 1936- 22
Parke, Marilyn 1928- 82
Parker, Barbara Keevil 1938- 157
Parker, Daniel
See Ehrenhaft, Daniel
Parker, Elinor Milnor 1906- 3
Parker, Jake 1977- 227
Parker, Julie F. 1961- 92
Parker, Kim 1963- 174
Parker, Kristy 1957- 59
Parker, Lois M(ay) 1912-1996 30
Parker, Margot M. 1937- 52
Parker, Marjorie Blain 1960- 205
Earlier sketch in SATA 145
Parker, Mary Jessie 1948- 71

Parker, Nancy Winslow 1930- 132
Earlier sketches in SATA 10, 69
See also SAAS 20
Parker, Richard 1915-1990 14
Parker, Robert
See Boyd, Waldo T.
and Parker, Robert Andrew
Parker, Robert Andrew 1927- 200
Parker, Steve 1954- 213
Parker, Tom S. 215
Parker, Toni Trent 1947-2005 142
Obituary 169
Parker-Rees, Guy 193
Parker-Rock, Michelle 214
Parkes, Lucas
See Harris, John (Wyndham Parkes Lucas)
Beynon
Parkhill, John
See Cox, William R(obert)
Parkins, David 1955- 218
Earlier sketch in SATA 176
Parkinson, Curtis 219
Parkinson, Ethelyn M(inerva) 1906-1999 11
Parkinson, Kathryn N. 1954- 71
Parkinson, Kathy
See Parkinson, Kathryn N.
Parkinson, Siobhan
See Parkinson, Siobhan
Parkinson, Siobhan 1954- 178
Parks, Deborah A. 1948- 133
Earlier sketch in SATA 91
Parks, Edd Winfield 1906-1968 10
Parks, Gordon 1912-2006 108
Obituary 175
Earlier sketch in SATA 8
Parks, Gordon Roger Alexander
See Parks, Gordon
Parks, Peggy J. 1951- 143
Parks, PJ
See Parks, Peggy J.
Parks, Rosa 1913-2005 83
Obituary 169
Parks, Rosa Louise Lee
See Parks, Rosa
Parks, Van Dyke 1943- 62
Parlato, Stephen 1954- 222
Parley, Peter
See Goodrich, Samuel Griswold
Parlin, John
See Graves, Charles Parlin
Parme, Fabrice 1966- 191
Parnall, Peter 1936- 69
Earlier sketch in SATA 16
See also SAAS 11
Paros, Jennifer 210
Parotti, Phillip (Elliott) 1941- 109
Parr, Ann 1943- 144
Parr, Danny
See Parr, Ann
Parr, Letitia (Evelyn) 1906-1985(?) 37
Parr, Lucy 1924- 10
Parr, Todd 179
Earlier sketch in SATA 134
Parra, John 1972- 225
Parrish, Anne 1888-1957 27
Parrish, Mary
See Cousins, Margaret
Parrish, Maxfield
See Parrish, (Frederick) Maxfield
Parrish, (Frederick) Maxfield 1870-1966 14
Parry, Marian 1924- 13
Parry, Rosanne 212
Parson Lot
See Kingsley, Charles
Parsons, Alexandra 1947- 92
Parsons, Ellen
See Dragonwagon, Crescent
Parsons, Garry 197
Parsons, Martin 1951- 116
Parsons, Martin Leslie
See Parsons, Martin

Parsons, Tom
See MacPherson, Thomas George
Parsons-Yazzi, Evangeline 172
Partch, Virgil Franklin II 1916-1984 39
Obituary 39
Parton, Dolly 1946- 94
Parton, Dolly Rebecca
See Parton, Dolly
Partridge, Benjamin W., Jr. 1915-2005 28
Obituary 163
Partridge, Benjamin Waring, Jr.
See Partridge, Benjamin W., Jr.
Partridge, Cora Cheney
See Cheney, Cora
Partridge, Elizabeth 216
Earlier sketch in SATA 134
Partridge, Jenny (Lilian) 1947- 52
Brief entry 37
Pasachoff, Naomi 1947- 147
Pascal, David 1918- 14
Pascal, Francine 1938- 143
Brief entry 37
Earlier sketches in SATA 51, 80
See also CLR 25
Paschal, Nancy
See Trotter, Grace V(iolet)
Paschkis, Julie 1957- 220
Earlier sketch in SATA 177
Pascudniak, Pascal
See Lupoff, Richard A.
Pashko, Stanley 1913-1982 29
Pasqualotto, Chiara 1976- 228
Passailaigue, Thomas E.
See Paisley, Tom
Pastel, Elyse 201
Pateman, Robert 1954- 84
Patent, Dorothy Hinshaw 1940- 162
Autobiography Feature 162
Earlier sketches in SATA 22, 69, 120
See also CLR 19
See also SAAS 13
Paterson, A(ndrew) B(arton) 1864-1941 97
Paterson, Banjo
See Paterson, A(ndrew) B(arton)
Paterson, Diane 1946- 177
Brief entry 33
Earlier sketch in SATA 59
Paterson, John (Barstow) 1932- 114
Paterson, Katherine 1932- 204
Earlier sketches in SATA 13, 53, 92, 133
See also CLR 127
Paterson, Katherine Womeldorf
See Paterson, Katherine
Patience, John 1949- 90
Patneaude, David 1944- 233
Earlier sketches in SATA 85, 159
Paton, Alan 1903-1988 11
Obituary 56
Paton, Alan Stewart
See Paton, Alan
Paton, Jane (Elizabeth) 1934- 35
Paton, Priscilla 1952- 98
Paton Walsh, Gillian
See Paton Walsh, Jill
Paton Walsh, Jill 1937- 190
Autobiography Feature 190
Earlier sketches in SATA 4, 72, 109
See also CLR 128
See also SAAS 3
Patricelli, Leslie 236
Earlier sketch in SATA 207
Patrick, Susan
See Robins, Patricia
Patron, Susan 1948- 182
Earlier sketch in SATA 76
Patsauq, Markoosie 1942-
See CLR 23
Patschke, Steve 1955- 125
Patt, Beverly 231
Patten, Brian 1946- 152
Earlier sketch in SATA 29

Patterson, Charles 1935- 59
Patterson, Geoffrey 1943- 54
    Brief entry 44
Patterson, James 1947- 234
    Earlier sketches in SATA 164, 197
Patterson, James B.
    See Patterson, James
Patterson, Lillie G. -1999 88
    Earlier sketch in SATA 14
Patterson, Nancy Ruth 1944- 148
    Earlier sketch in SATA 72
Patterson, Valerie O. 223
Pattison, Darcy (S.) 1954- 126
    Earlier sketch in SATA 72
Pattou, Edith 164
Patz (Blaustein), Nancy 154
Paul, Aileen 1917- 12
Paul, Alison 196
Paul, Ann Whitford 1941- 209
    Earlier sketches in SATA 76, 110, 168
Paul, Chris 1985- 224
Paul, David (Tyler) 1934-1988
    Obituary 56
Paul, Dominique 1973- 184
Paul, Elizabeth
    See Crow, Donna Fletcher
Paul, Hamish Vigne Christie 1951- 151
    See also CLR 87
Paul, James 1936- 23
Paul, Korky
    See Paul, Hamish Vigne Christie
Paul, Robert
    See Roberts, John G(aither)
Paul, Tessa 1944- 103
Pauley, Kimberly 1973- 208
Pauli, Hertha (Ernestine) 1909-1973 3
    Obituary 26
Paull, Grace A. 1898- 24
Paulsen, Gary 1939- 231
    Earlier sketches in SATA 22, 50, 54, 79, 111,
    158, 189
    See also CLR 82
Paulson, Jack
    See Jackson, C(aary) Paul
Pauquet, Gina Ruck
    See Ruck-Pauquet, Gina
Pausacker, Jenny 1948- 72
    See also SAAS 23
Pausewang, Gudrun 1928- 165
    Earlier sketch in SATA 104
Pavel, Frances 1907- 10
Paver, Michelle 215
    Earlier sketch in SATA 170
Paxton
    See Barr, Nevada
Paxton, Thomas R. 1937- 70
Paxton, Tom
    See Paxton, Thomas R.
Paye, Won-Ldy 185
Payne, Alan
    See Jakes, John
Payne, Bernal C., Jr. 1941- 60
Payne, C. Douglas
    See Payne, C.D.
Payne, C.D. 1949- 133
Payne, C.F. 1956- 179
Payne, Chris Fox
    See Payne, C.F.
Payne, Donald Gordon 1924- 37
Payne, Emmy
    See West, Emily Govan
Payne, Nina 135
Payne, Rachel Ann
    See Jakes, John
Payson, Dale 1943- 9
Payzant, Charles 18
Paz, A.
    See Pahz, James Alon
Paz, Natalia Toledo
    See Toledo, Natalia

Paz, Zan
    See Pahz, Cheryl Suzanne
Peace, Mary
    See Finley, Mary Peace
Peacock, Louise 210
Peacock, Phyllis Hornung 1977- 230
Peacock, Shane 1957- 192
Peake, Mervyn 1911-1968 23
Peale, Norman Vincent 1898-1993 20
    Obituary 78
Pearce, Ann Philippa
    See Pearce, Philippa
Pearce, Carl 229
Pearce, Emily Smith 1975- 199
Pearce, Jackson 1984- 235
Pearce, Jacqueline 1962- 146
Pearce, Margaret 104
Pearce, Philippa 1920-2006 129
    Obituary 179
    Earlier sketches in SATA 1, 67
    See also CLR 9
Peare, Catherine Owens 1911- 9
Pearle, Ida 207
Pearsall, Shelley 1966- 190
Pearson, Gayle 1947- 119
    Earlier sketch in SATA 53
Pearson, Jean Mary
    See Gardam, Jane
Pearson, Kit 1947- 77
    Autobiography Feature 117
    See also CLR 26
Pearson, Mary E. 1955- 211
    Earlier sketch in SATA 134
Pearson, Michael Parker
    See Pearson, Mike Parker
Pearson, Mike Parker 1957- 228
Pearson, Ridley 1953- 182
Pearson, Susan 1946- 166
    Brief entry 27
    Earlier sketches in SATA 39, 91
Pearson, Tracey Campbell 1956- 219
    Earlier sketches in SATA 64, 155
Pease, (Clarence) Howard 1894-1974 2
    Obituary 25
Peavy, Linda 1943- 54
Peck, Anne Merriman 1884-1976 18
Peck, Beth 1957- 190
    Earlier sketch in SATA 79
Peck, Jan 159
Peck, Jeanie J. 1967- 147
Peck, Marshall III 1951- 92
Peck, Richard 1934- 228
    Autobiography Feature 110
    Earlier sketches in SATA 18, 55, 97, 110, 158,
    190
    See also CLR 142
    See also SAAS 2
Peck, Richard Wayne
    See Peck, Richard
Peck, Robert Newton 1928- 156
    Autobiography Feature 108
    Earlier sketches in SATA 21, 62, 111
    See also CLR 163
    See also SAAS 1
Peck, Sylvia 1953- 133
Peck-Whiting, Jeanie J.
    See Peck, Jeanie J.
Peddicord, Jane Ann 199
Pedersen, Janet 193
Pederson, Sharleen
    See Collicott, Sharleen
Pedler, Caroline 197
Peebles, Anne
    See Galloway, Priscilla
Peek, Merle 1938- 39
Peel, John 1954- 79
Peel, Norman Lemon
    See Hirsch, Phil
Peeples, Edwin A(ugustus, Jr.) 1915-1994 6
Peers, Judi 1956- 119

Peers, Judith May West
    See Peers, Judi
Peet, Bill
    See Peet, William Bartlett
Peet, Creighton B. 1899-1977 30
Peet, Mal 227
    Earlier sketch in SATA 171
Peet, Malcolm
    See Peet, Mal
Peet, William Bartlett 1915-2002 78
    Obituary 137
    Earlier sketches in SATA 2, 41
    See also CLR 12
Peete, Holly Robinson 1964- 229
Peguero, Leone 116
Peirce, Lincoln 232
Pelaez, Jill 1924- 12
Pelham, David 1938- 70
Pelikan, Judy 1941- 219
Pell, Ed(ward) 1950- 157
Pelletier, Andrew T. 195
Pelletier, Andrew Thomas
    See Pelletier, Andrew T.
Pellowski, Anne 1933- 20
Pellowski, Michael (Joseph) 1949- 151
    Brief entry 48
    Earlier sketch in SATA 88
Pellowski, Michael Morgan
    See Pellowski, Michael (Joseph)
Pelta, Kathy 1928- 18
Peltier, Leslie C(opus) 1900-1980 13
Pemberton, Bonnie 191
Pemberton, John Leigh
    See Leigh-Pemberton, John
Pembury, Bill
    See Groom, Arthur William
Pemsteen, Hans
    See Manes, Stephen
Pendennis, Arthur Esquir
    See Thackeray, William Makepeace
Pender, Lydia Podger 1907- 61
Pendery, Rosemary (Schmitz) 7
Pendle, Alexy 1943- 29
Pendle, George 1906-1977
    Obituary 28
Pendleton, Don
    See Cunningham, Chet
    and Garside, Jack
    and Jagninski, Tom
    and Krauzer, Steven M(ark)
    and Obstfeld, Raymond
Pendleton, Thomas 1965- 206
Pendziwol, Jean E. 1965- 177
Pene du Bois, William (Sherman)
    1916-1993 68
    Obituary 74
    Earlier sketch in SATA 4
    See also CLR 1
Penn, Audrey 1947- 212
Penn, Audrey 1950- 22
Penn, Ruth Bonn
    See Rosenberg, Eth Clifford
Pennac, Daniel 1944- 155
Pennage, E. M.
    See Finkel, George (Irvine)
Penner, Fred 1946- 169
    Earlier sketch in SATA 67
Penner, Frederick Ralph Cornelius
    See Penner, Fred
Penner, Lucille Recht 1942- 226
Penney, Grace Jackson 1904-2000 35
Penney, Ian 1960- 76
Penney, Sue 1957- 152
    Earlier sketch in SATA 102
Pennington, Eunice 1923- 27
Pennington, Lillian Boyer 1904-2003 45
Pennypacker, Sara 1951- 187
Penrose, Gordon 1925- 66
Penson, Mary E. 1917- 78
Penzler, Otto 1942- 38
Pepe, Phil 1935- 20

Pepe, Philip
  See Pepe, Phil
Peppe, Rodney (Darrell) 1934- 74
  Earlier sketch in SATA 4
  See also SAAS 10
Pepper, Frank S. 1910-1988
  Obituary 61
Percy, Charles Henry
  See Smith, Dorothy Gladys
Percy, Rachel 1930- 63
Perdomo, Willie 228
Perdrizet, Marie-Pierre 1952- 79
Perenyi, Constance 1954- 93
Perenyi, Constance Marie
  See Perenyi, Constance
Perera, Hilda 1926- 105
Perera, Thomas Biddle 1938- 13
Peretti, Frank E. 1951- 141
  Earlier sketch in SATA 80
Perez, L. King 1940- 199
Perez, Lana
  See Perez, Marlene
Perez, Lucia Angela 1973- 182
Perez, Marlene 170
Pericoli, Matteo 1968- 178
Perkins, Al(bert Rogers) 1904-1975 30
Perkins, Dan
  See Tomorrow, Tom
Perkins, Lucy Fitch 1865-1937 72
Perkins, Lynne Rae 1956- 212
  Earlier sketch in SATA 131, 172
Perkins, (Richard) Marlin 1905-1986 21
  Obituary 48
Perkins, Mitali 1963- 237
  Earlier sketches in SATA 88, 188
Perks, Anne-Marie 1955- 122
Perl, Erica S. 222
  Earlier sketch in SATA 188
Perl, Lila 72
  Earlier sketch in SATA 6
Perl, Susan 1922-1983 22
  Obituary 34
Perlman, Janet 1954- 222
Perlman, Rhea 1948- 183
Perlmutter, O(scar) William 1920-1975 8
Pernu, Dennis 1970- 87
Perrault, Charles 1628-1703 25
  See also CLR 134
Perret, Delphine 1980- 190
Perret, Gene (Richard) 1937- 76
Perriman, Cole
  See Perrin, Pat
Perriman, Cole
  See Coleman, Wim
  and Perrin, Pat
Perrin, Pat 212
Perrine, Mary 1913-1976 2
Perrins, Lesley 1953- 56
Perrow, Angeli 1954- 121
Perry, Andrea 1956- 190
  Earlier sketch in SATA 148
Perry, Barbara Fisher
  See Fisher, Barbara
Perry, Elizabeth 1959- 174
Perry, Elizabeth Goodwin
  See Perry, Elizabeth
Perry, John 1967- 223
Perry, M. LaVora 232
Perry, Marie Fritz 165
Perry, Patricia 1949- 30
Perry, Phyllis J(ean) 1933- 152
  Earlier sketches in SATA 60, 101
Perry, Ritchie (John Allen) 1942- 105
Perry, Roger 1933- 27
Perry, Steve(n Carl) 1947- 76
Pershall, Mary K. 1951- 172
  Earlier sketch in SATA 70
Pershing, Marie
  See Schultz, Pearle Henriksen
Perske, Robert 1927- 57

Persun, Morgan Reed
  See Watkins, Dawn L.
Perversi, Margaret 213
Petach, Heidi 149
Peter
  See Stratemeyer, Edward L.
Peters, Alexander
  See Hollander, Zander
Peters, Andrew Fusek 1965- 169
  Earlier sketch in SATA 107
Peters, Bernadette 1948- 212
Peters, Caroline
  See Betz, Eva Kelly
Peters, David
  See David, Peter
Peters, Elizabeth 1927- 49
Peters, Emma
  See Price, Karen
Peters, Gabriel
  See Matott, Justin
Peters, Julie Anne 1952- 197
  Earlier sketches in SATA 82, 128
Peters, Linda
  See Catherall, Arthur
Peters, Lisa Westberg 1951- 232
  Earlier sketches in SATA 74, 115, 161
Peters, Patricia 1953- 84
Peters, Russell M. 1929- 78
Peters, S. H.
  See Henry, O.
  and Proffitt, Nicholas
Peters, Stephanie True 1965- 224
Petersen, David 1946- 109
  Earlier sketch in SATA 62
Petersen, Gwenn Boardman 1924- 12
Petersen, P(eter) J(ames) 1941- 118
  Brief entry 43
  Earlier sketches in SATA 48, 83
Petersen, Palle 1943- 85
Petersham, Maud 1890-1971 17
  See also CLR 24
Petersham, Maud Sylvia Fuller
  See Petersham, Maud
Petersham, Miska 1888-1960 17
  See also CLR 24
Peterson, Cris 1952- 174
  Earlier sketches in SATA 84, 145
Peterson, Dawn 1934- 86
Peterson, Esther (Allen) 1934- 35
Peterson, Hans 1922- 8
Peterson, Harold L(eslie) 1922-1978 8
Peterson, Helen Stone 1910- 8
Peterson, Jean Sunde 1941- 108
Peterson, Jeanne Whitehouse 1939- 159
  Earlier sketch in SATA 29
Peterson, John 1924-2002 233
Peterson, Kathleen B. 1951- 119
Peterson, Lorraine 1940- 56
  Brief entry 44
Peterson, Mary 215
Peterson, Shelley 1952- 146
Peterson, Will
  See Cocks, Peter
Petie, Haris
  See Petty, Roberta
Petricic, Dusan 1946- 176
Petrides, Heidrun 1944- 19
Petrie, Catherine 1947- 52
  Brief entry 41
Petrone, Valeria 233
  Earlier sketch in SATA 186
Petrosino, Tamara 193
Petroski, Catherine (Ann Groom) 1939- 48
Petrovich, Michael B(oro) 1922- 40
Petrovskaya, Kyra
  See Wayne, Kyra Petrovskaya
Petruccio, Steven James 1961- 67
Petrucha, Stefan 1959- 213
Petry, Ann 1908-1997 5
  Obituary 94
  See also CLR 12

Petry, Ann Lane
  See Petry, Ann
Pettit, Jayne 1932- 108
Petty, J.T. 1977- 189
Petty, Kate 1951-2007 204
Petty, Roberta 1915- 10
Pevsner, Stella 131
  Earlier sketches in SATA 8, 77
  See also SAAS 14
Peyo
  See Culliford, Pierre
Peyton, K. M.
  See Peyton, Kathleen Wendy
Peyton, Kathleen Wendy 1929- 157
  Earlier sketches in SATA 15, 62
  See also CLR 3
  See also SAAS 17
Pfanner, (Anne) Louise 1955- 68
Pfeffer, Susan Beth 1948- 180
  Earlier sketches in SATA 4, 83
  See also CLR 11
  See also SAAS 17
Pfeffer, Wendy 1929- 204
  Earlier sketches in SATA 78, 142
Pfeiffer, Janet (B.) 1949- 96
Pfister, Marcus 207
  Earlier sketches in SATA 83, 150
  See also CLR 42
Pfitsch, Patricia Curtis 1948- 148
Pfitzenmaier, Audrey 1959- 220
Pflieger, Pat 1955- 84
Pham, LeUyen 1973- 237
  Earlier sketches in SATA 175, 201
Phelan, Mary Kay 1914- 3
Phelan, Matt 1970- 215
  Earlier sketch in SATA 172
Phelan, Terry Wolfe 1941- 56
Phelps, Ethel Johnston 1914-1984 35
Philbrick, Rodman 1951- 163
Philbrick, W. Rodman
  See Philbrick, Rodman
Philbrick, W.R.
  See Philbrick, Rodman
Philbrook, Clem(ent E.) 1917- 24
Phillipps, J.C. 218
Phillipps, Julie Christine
  See Phillipps, J.C.
Phillips, Aileen Paul
  See Paul, Aileen
Phillips, Betty Lou
  See Phillips, Elizabeth Louise
Phillips, Bob 1940- 95
Phillips, Douglas A. 1949- 161
Phillips, Elizabeth Louise 58
  Brief entry 48
Phillips, Gary R. 225
Phillips, Irv(ing W.) 1905-2000 11
  Obituary 125
Phillips, Jack
  See Sandburg, Carl
Phillips, Leon
  See Gerson, Noel Bertram
Phillips, Loretta (Hosey) 1893-1987 10
Phillips, Louis 1942- 102
  Earlier sketch in SATA 8
Phillips, Mark
  See Garrett, Randall
  and Janifer, Laurence M(ark)
Phillips, Mary Geisler 1881-1964 10
Phillips, Michael
  See Nolan, William F.
Phillips, (Woodward) Prentice 1894-1981 10
Phillpotts, Eden 1862-1960 24
Phin
  See Thayer, Ernest Lawrence
Phipson, Joan
  See Fitzhardinge, Joan Margaret
Phiz
  See Browne, Hablot Knight
Phleger, Fred B. 1909-1993 34

Phleger, Marjorie Temple 1908(?)-1986 .... *1*
  Obituary *47*
Piaget, Jean 1896-1980
  Obituary *23*
Piatti, Celestino 1922- *16*
Picard, Barbara Leonie 1917- *89*
  Earlier sketch in SATA *2*
  See also SAAS *10*
Pichon, Liz *174*
Pickard, Charles 1932- *36*
Pickering, James Sayre 1897-1969 .... *36*
  Obituary *28*
Pickering, Jimmy *195*
Pickering, Robert B. 1950- *93*
Pielichaty, Helena 1955- *142*
Pien, Lark *222*
Pienkowski, Jan (Michal) 1936- *131*
  Earlier sketches in SATA *6, 58*
  See also CLR *6*
Pierce, Edith Gray 1893-1977 .... *45*
Pierce, Katherine
  See St. John, Wylly Folk
Pierce, Meredith Ann 1958- *127*
  Brief entry *48*
  Earlier sketch in SATA *67*
  See also CLR *20*
Pierce, Ruth (Ireland) 1936- *5*
Pierce, Sharon
  See McCullough, Sharon Pierce
Pierce, Tamora 1954- *187*
  Brief entry *49*
  Earlier sketches in SATA *51, 96, 153*
Pierce, Terry *178*
Pierik, Robert 1921- *13*
Piernas-Davenport, Gail *199*
Piers, Robert
  See Anthony, Piers
Pig, Edward
  See Gorey, Edward (St. John)
Pignataro, Anna 1965- *223*
Pike, Aprilynne *218*
Pike, Bob
  See Pike, Robert W.
Pike, Christopher 1954(?)- *156*
  Earlier sketch in SATA *68*
  See also CLR *29*
Pike, Deborah 1951- *89*
Pike, E(dgar) Royston 1896-1980 .... *22*
  Obituary *56*
Pike, R. William 1956- *92*
Pike, Robert
  See Pike, Robert W.
Pike, Robert W. 1931- *102*
Pike, Robert Wilson
  See Pike, Robert W.
Pilarski, Laura 1926- *13*
Pilgrim, Anne
  See Allan, Mabel Esther
Pilkey, Dav 1966- *166*
  Earlier sketches in SATA *68, 115*
  See also CLR *160*
Pilkey, David Murray, Jr.
  See Pilkey, Dav
Pilkington, Francis Meredyth 1907-1993 ...... *4*
Pilkington, Roger (Windle) 1915-2003 .... *10*
  Obituary *144*
Pilutti, Deb *208*
Pin, Isabel 1975- *183*
Pinchot, David 1914(?)-1983
  Obituary *34*
Pincus, Harriet 1938- *27*
Pinczes, Elinor J(ane) 1940- *81*
Pine, Nicholas 1951- *91*
Pine, Tillie S(chloss) 1896-1999 .... *13*
Pini, Richard (Alan) 1950- *89*
Pini, Wendy 1951- *89*
Pinkerton, Kathrene Sutherland (Gedney)
  1887-1967
  Obituary *26*
Pinkett, Jada
  See Smith, Jada Pinkett

Pinkney, Andrea Davis 1963- *160*
  Earlier sketch in SATA *113*
Pinkney, Brian 1961- *206*
  Earlier sketches in SATA *74, 148*
  See also CLR *54*
Pinkney, Gloria Jean 1941- *212*
  Earlier sketch in SATA *85*
Pinkney, J. Brian
  See Pinkney, Brian
Pinkney, Jerry 1939- *198*
  Autobiography Feature *198*
  Brief entry *32*
  Earlier sketches in SATA *41, 71, 107, 151*
  See also CLR *43*
  See also SAAS *12*
Pinkney, John *97*
Pinkney, Sandra L. *193*
  Earlier sketch in SATA *128*
Pinkwater, D. Manus
  See Pinkwater, Daniel
Pinkwater, Daniel 1941- *210*
  Earlier sketches in SATA *8, 46, 76, 114, 158*
  See also CLR *4*
  See also SAAS *3*
Pinkwater, Daniel M.
  See Pinkwater, Daniel
Pinkwater, Daniel Manus
  See Pinkwater, Daniel
Pinkwater, Jill *188*
Pinkwater, Manus
  See Pinkwater, Daniel
Pinner, Joma
  See Werner, Herma
Pinto, Sara *200*
Pioneer
  See Yates, Raymond F(rancis)
Piowaty, Kim Kennelly 1957- *49*
Piper, Roger
  See Fisher, John
Pirner, Connie White 1955- *72*
Piro, Richard 1934- *7*
Pirot, Alison Lohans
  See Lohans, Alison
Pirotta, Saviour *184*
Pirsig, Robert M(aynard) 1928- *39*
Pita
  See Rendon, Maria
Pitcher, C.
  See Pitcher, Caroline
Pitcher, Caroline 1948- *214*
  Earlier sketch in SATA *128*
Pitcher, Caroline Nell
  See Pitcher, Caroline
Pitman, (Isaac) James 1901-1985
  Obituary *46*
Pitre, Felix 1949- *84*
Pitrone, Jean Maddern 1920- *4*
Pittman, Helena Clare 1945- *71*
Pitz, Henry C(larence) 1895-1976 .... *4*
  Obituary *24*
Pitzer, Susanna 1958- *181*
Piven, Hanoch 1963- *236*
  Earlier sketch in SATA *173*
Pixley, Marcella *194*
Pizer, Vernon 1918- *21*
Place, Francois 1957- *234*
Place, Marian T(empleton) 1910- *3*
Place, Robin (Mary) 1926- *71*
Plaidy, Jean
  See Hibbert, Eleanor Alice Burford
Plain, Belva 1919-2010 .... *62*
Plaine, Alfred R. 1898(?)-1981
  Obituary *29*
Plant, Andrew *214*
Plath, Sylvia 1932-1963 .... *96*
Platt, Chris 1959- *185*
Platt, Kin 1911- *86*
  Earlier sketch in SATA *21*
  See also SAAS *17*
Platt, Randall 1948- *95*

Platt, Randall Beth
  See Platt, Randall
Platt, Richard 1953- *218*
  Earlier sketches in SATA *120, 166*
Playfellow, Robin
  See Ellis, Edward S.
Playsted, James
  See Wood, James Playsted
Plecas, Jennifer 1966- *229*
  Earlier sketches in SATA *84, 149*
Plimpton, George 1927-2003 .... *10*
  Obituary *150*
Plimpton, George Ames
  See Plimpton, George
Plomer, William Charles Franklin
  1903-1973 .... *24*
Plotz, Helen Ratnoff 1913-2000 .... *38*
Plourde, Lynn 1955- *218*
  Earlier sketches in SATA *122, 168*
Plowden, David 1932- *52*
Plowden, Martha Ward 1948- *98*
Plowhead, Ruth Gipson 1877-1967 .... *43*
Plowman, Stephanie 1922- *6*
Pluckrose, Henry 1931-2011 .... *141*
  Earlier sketch in SATA *13*
Pluckrose, Henry Arthur
  See Pluckrose, Henry
Plum, J.
  See Wodehouse, P. G.
Plum, Jennifer
  See Kurland, Michael
Plumb, Charles P. 1900(?)-1982
  Obituary *29*
Plume, Ilse *170*
  Brief entry *43*
Plumme, Don E.
  See Katz, Bobbi
Plummer, Margaret 1911- *2*
Plum-Ucci, Carol 1957- *184*
Poblocki, Dan 1981- *224*
Pochocki, Ethel (Frances) 1925- *76*
Podendorf, Illa (E.) 1903(?)-1983 .... *18*
  Obituary *35*
Podwal, Mark 1945- *224*
  Earlier sketches in SATA *101, 160*
Podwal, Mark H.
  See Podwal, Mark
Poe, Edgar Allan 1809-1849 .... *23*
Poe, Ty (Christopher) 1975- *94*
Pogany, William Andrew 1882-1955 .... *44*
  Brief entry *30*
Pogany, Willy
  See Pogany, William Andrew
Pogue, Carolyn 1948- *223*
Pogue, David 1963- *231*
Pohl, Frederik 1919- *24*
Pohlmann, Lillian (Grenfell) 1902-1997 .... *11*
Pohrt, Tom 1953- *195*
  Earlier sketches in SATA *67, 152*
Pointon, Robert
  See Rooke, Daphne
Points, Larry G. 1945- *177*
  Earlier sketch in SATA *133*
Points, Larry Gene
  See Points, Larry G.
Pokeberry, P.J.
  See Mitchell, B.J.
POLA
  See Watson, Pauline
Polacco, Patricia 1944- *212*
  Earlier sketches in SATA *74, 123, 180*
  See also CLR *40*
Polacco, Patricia Ann
  See Polacco, Patricia
Polak, Monique 1960- *230*
  Earlier sketch in SATA *178*
Polatnick, Florence T. 1923- *5*
Polcovar, Jane 1948- *211*
Polder, Markus
  See Kruss, James
Polenghi, Evan 1961- *225*

Polese, Carolyn 1947- 58
Polese, James 1914- 87
Polette, Nancy (Jane) 1930- 42
Polhamus, Jean Burt 1928- 21
Polhemus, Coleman 210
Policoff, Stephen Phillip 1948- 77
Polikoff, Barbara G. 1929- 162
   Earlier sketch in SATA 77
Polikoff, Barbara Garland
   See Polikoff, Barbara G.
Polisar, Barry Louis 1954- 134
   Earlier sketch in SATA 77
Politi, Leo 1908-1996 47
   Obituary 88
   Earlier sketch in SATA 1
   See also CLR 29
Polking, Kirk 1925- 5
Pollack, Jill S. 1963- 88
Pollack, Merrill S. 1924-1988
   Obituary 55
Polland, Barbara K(ay) 1939- 44
Polland, Madeleine A(ngela Cahill) 1918- ... 68
   Earlier sketch in SATA 6
   See also SAAS 8
Pollema-Cahill, Phyllis 1958- 123
Pollock, Bruce 1945- 46
Pollock, Mary
   See Blyton, Enid
Pollock, Penny 1935- 137
   Brief entry 42
   Earlier sketch in SATA 44
Pollowitz, Melinda Kilborn 1944- 26
Polner, Murray 1928- 64
Polonsky, Arthur 1925- 34
Polseno, Jo 17
Pomaska, Anna 1946- 117
Pomerantz, Charlotte 1930- 177
   Earlier sketches in SATA 20, 80
Pomeroy, Pete
   See Roth, Arthur J(oseph)
Pon, Cindy 1973- 216
Pon, Cynthia 229
Pond, Alonzo W(illiam) 1894-1986 5
Pontiflet, Ted 1932- 32
Poole, Gray Johnson 1906- 1
Poole, Josephine
   See Helyar, Jane Penelope Josephine
Poole, (Jane Penelope) Josephine
   See Helyar, Jane Penelope Josephine
Poole, Lynn 1910-1969 1
Poole, Peggy 1925- 39
Pooler, Paige 235
Poon, Janice 228
Poortvliet, Rien 1932- 65
   Brief entry 37
Pope, Elizabeth Marie 1917-1992 38
   Brief entry 36
Pope, Kevin 1958- 183
Popescu, Christine
   See Pullein-Thompson, Christine
Poploff, Michelle 1956- 67
Popp, K. Wendy 91
Poppel, Hans 1942- 71
Porfirio, Guy 1958- 197
Portal, Colette 1936- 6
Porte, Barbara Ann 1943- 152
   Brief entry 45
   Earlier sketches in SATA 57, 93
Porter, A(nthony) P(eyton) 1945- 68
Porter, Connie (Rose) 1959(?)- 129
   Earlier sketch in SATA 81
Porter, Donald Clayton
   See Gerson, Noel Bertram
Porter, Eleanor H(odgman) 1868-1920
   See CLR 110
Porter, Gene Stratton
   See Stratton-Porter, Gene
Porter, Janice Lee 1953- 108
   Earlier sketch in SATA 68
Porter, Katherine Anne 1890-1980 39
   Obituary 23

Porter, Kathryn
   See Swinford, Betty (June Wells)
Porter, Pamela 1956- 193
Porter, Sheena 1935- 24
   See also SAAS 10
Porter, Sue
   See Limb, Sue
Porter, Sue 1951- 213
   Earlier sketch in SATA 76
Porter, Tracey 191
Porter, William Sydney
   See Henry, O.
Portis, Antoinette 189
Porto, Tony 1960- 153
Portteus, Eleanora Marie Manthei (?)-1983
   Obituary 36
Posada, Mia 187
Posell, Elsa Z(eigerman) -1995 3
Posesorski, Sherie 216
Posten, Margaret L(ois) 1915- 10
Postgate, Daniel 1964- 216
Posthuma, Sieb 1960- 150
Postier, Jim 1965- 202
Potok, Chaim 1929-2002 106
   Obituary 134
   Earlier sketch in SATA 33
   See also CLR 92
Potok, Herbert Harold
   See Potok, Chaim
Potok, Herman Harold
   See Potok, Chaim
Potter, Alicia 216
Potter, Beatrix 1866-1943 132
   Earlier sketch in SATA 100
   See also YABC 1
   See also CLR 165
Potter, Ellen 1973- 218
Potter, Giselle 187
   Earlier sketch in SATA 150
Potter, Helen Beatrix
   See Potter, Beatrix
Potter, Katherine 217
Potter, Margaret 1926-1998 21
   Obituary 104
Potter, Marian 1915- 9
Potter, Miriam Clark 1886-1965 3
Potter, Ryan 230
Poulin, Stephane 1961- 98
   See also CLR 28
Poulton, Kimberly 1957(?)- 136
Pournelle, Jerry 1933- 161
   Earlier sketches in SATA 26, 91
Pournelle, Jerry Eugene
   See Pournelle, Jerry
Povelite, Kay 1955- 102
Pow, Tom 1950- 163
Powe-Allred, Alexandra
   See Allred, Alexandra Powe
Powell, A. M.
   See Morgan, Alfred P(owell)
Powell, Consie 174
Powell, E. Sandy 1947- 72
Powell, E.S.
   See Powell, E. Sandy
Powell, Pamela 1960- 78
Powell, Patricia Hruby 1951- 136
Powell, Randy 1956- 118
Powell, Richard Stillman
   See Barbour, Ralph Henry
Powell, Robert (Stephenson Smyth) Baden
   See Baden-Powell, Robert (Stephenson Smyth)
Powell, Stephanie 1953- 93
Power, Margaret (M.) 1945- 125
   Earlier sketch in SATA 75
Powers, Anne
   See Schwartz, Anne Powers
Powers, Bill 1931- 52
   Brief entry 31
Powers, Daniel 1959- 164
Powers, J. L. 195

Powers, Jessica
   See Powers, J. L.
Powers, Jessica Lynn
   See Powers, J. L.
Powers, Margaret
   See Heal, Edith
Powers, Tim 1952- 107
Powers, Timothy Thomas
   See Powers, Tim
Powledge, Fred 1935- 37
Poydar, Nancy 190
Poynter, Margaret 1927- 27
Prachaticka, Marketa
   See Kolibalova, Marketa
Prachatika, Marketa
   See Kolibalova, Marketa
Prager, Arthur 44
Prager, Ellen J. 1962- 136
Prange, Beckie 172
Prap, Lila 1955- 177
Praprotnik-Zupancic, Lilijana
   See Prap, Lila
Pratchett, Terence David John
   See Pratchett, Terry
Pratchett, Terry 1948- 185
   Earlier sketches in SATA 82, 139
   See also CLR 64
Prater, John 1947- 149
   Earlier sketches in SATA 72, 103
Prato, Rodica 184
Pratt, Christine Joy 214
Pratt, (Murray) Fletcher 1897-1956 102
Pratt, Kristin Joy 1976- 87
Pratt, Pierre 1962- 208
   Earlier sketches in SATA 95, 166
Preiss, Byron 1953-2005 166
   Brief entry 42
   Earlier sketch in SATA 47
Preiss, Byron Cary
   See Preiss, Byron
Preller, James 1961- 209
   Earlier sketch in SATA 88
Prelutsky, Jack 1940- 171
   Earlier sketches in SATA 22, 66, 118
   See also CLR 115
Prentice, Amy
   See Kaler, James Otis
Prescott, Casey
   See Morris, Chris(topher Crosby)
Presnall, Judith (Ann) Janda 1943- 96
Pressler, Mirjam 1940- 155
Preston, Douglas 1956- 113
Preston, Edna Mitchell 40
Preston, Lillian Elvira 1918- 47
Preus, Margi 209
Preussler, Otfried 1923- 24
Prevert, Jacques 1900-1977
   Obituary 30
Prevert, Jacques Henri Marie
   See Prevert, Jacques
Prevost, Guillaume 1964- 192
Prevost, Mikela 203
Price, Beverley Joan 1931- 98
Price, Charlie 237
   Earlier sketch in SATA 187
Price, Christine (Hilda) 1928-1980 3
   Obituary 23
Price, Garrett 1896-1979
   Obituary 22
Price, Jennifer
   See Hoover, Helen (Drusilla Blackburn)
Price, Joan 1931- 124
Price, Jonathan (Reeve) 1941- 46
Price, Karen 1957- 125
Price, Kathy Z. 1957- 172
Price, Lucie Locke
   See Locke, Lucie
Price, Olive 1903-1991 8
Price, Susan 1955- 128
   Earlier sketches in SATA 25, 85

Price, Willard 1887-1983 .... *48*
  Brief entry *38*
Price-Groff, Claire *127*
Priceman, Marjorie 1958- *234*
  Earlier sketches in SATA *81, 120, 168*
Prichard, Katharine Susannah 1883-1969 ..... *66*
Priddy, Roger *227*
Prideaux, Tom 1908-1993 .... *37*
  Obituary *76*
Priestley, Alice 1962- *227*
  Earlier sketch in SATA *95*
Priestley, Chris 1958- *198*
Priestley, Lee (Shore) 1904-1999 .... *27*
Priestly, Doug 1954- *122*
Priestly, Douglas Michael
  See Priestly, Doug
Prieto, Mariana Beeching 1912-1999 .... *8*
Prigmore, Shane 1977- *234*
Priley, Margaret (Ann) Hubbard 1909-1992
  Obituary *130*
Primavera, Elise 1954- *230*
  Brief entry *48*
  Earlier sketches in SATA *58, 109, 185*
Prime, Derek (James) 1931- *34*
Prince, Alison (Mary) 1931- *86*
  Earlier sketch in SATA *28*
Prince, April Jones 1975- *180*
Prince, J(ack) H(arvey) 1908- *17*
Prince, Joshua *188*
Prince, Maggie *102*
Prineas, Sarah *204*
Pringle, Eric *138*
Pringle, Laurence 1935- *201*
  Autobiography Feature *201*
  Earlier sketches in SATA *4, 68, 104, 154*
  See also CLR *57*
  See also SAAS *6*
Pringle, Laurence Patrick
  See Pringle, Laurence
Prinz, Yvonne 1960- *175*
Prior, Natalie Jane 1963- *106*
Pritchett, Elaine H(illyer) 1920- *36*
Pritchett, Laura 1971- *178*
Pritchett, Laura Rose
  See Pritchett, Laura
Pritts, Kim Derek 1953- *83*
Prochazkova, Iva 1953- *68*
Proctor, Everitt
  See Montgomery, Rutherford George
Proeysen, Alf 1914-1970 .... *67*
  See also CLR *24*
Professor Scribbler
  See Hollingsworth, Mary
Proimos, James 1955- *217*
  Earlier sketch in SATA *173*
Promitzer, Rebecca *229*
Prose, Francine 1947- *198*
  Earlier sketches in SATA *101, 149*
Prosek, James 1975- *216*
Protopopescu, Orel *186*
Protopopescu, Orel Odinov
  See Protopopescu, Orel
Provensen, Alice 1918- *147*
  Earlier sketches in SATA *9, 70*
  See also CLR *11*
Provensen, Martin 1916-1987 .... *70*
  Obituary *51*
  Earlier sketch in SATA *9*
  See also CLR *11*
Provensen, Martin Elias
  See Provensen, Martin
Provenzo, Eugene (F., Jr.) 1949- *142*
  Earlier sketch in SATA *78*
Provist, d'Alain 1906-1989
  See Diop, Birago (Ismael)
Provost, Gail Levine 1944- *65*
Provost, Gary (Richard) 1944-1995 .... *66*
Proysen, Alf
  See Proeysen, Alf
Pruett, Candace (J.) 1968- *157*
Pryor, Bonnie H. 1942- *69*

Pryor, Boori (Monty) 1950- *112*
Pryor, Helen Brenton 1897-1972 .... *4*
Pryor, Michael 1957- *153*
Pucci, Albert John 1920- *44*
Pudney, John (Sleigh) 1909-1977 .... *24*
Pugh, Ellen (Tiffany) 1920- *7*
Pullein-Thompson, Christine 1925-2005 ...... *82*
  Obituary *172*
  Earlier sketch in SATA *3*
Pullein-Thompson, Diana
  See Farr, Diana
Pullein-Thompson, Joanna Maxwell
  1898-1961 .... *82*
Pullein-Thompson, Josephine (Mary
  Wedderburn) *82*
  Earlier sketch in SATA *3*
Pullen, Zachary *189*
Pullman, Philip 1946- *198*
  Earlier sketches in SATA *65, 103, 150*
  See also CLR *84*
  See also SAAS *17*
Pullman, Philip Nicholas
  See Pullman, Philip
Pulver, Harry, Jr. 1960- *129*
Pulver, Robin 1945- *208*
  Earlier sketches in SATA *76, 133*
Puner, Helen W(alker) 1915-1989 .... *37*
  Obituary *63*
Purdy, Carol 1943- *120*
  Earlier sketch in SATA *66*
Purdy, Susan G(old) 1939- *8*
Purkiss, Diane 1961- *194*
Purmell, Ann 1953- *206*
  Earlier sketch in SATA *147*
Purnell, Idella 1901-1982 .... *120*
Purscell, Phyllis 1934- *7*
Purtill, Richard L. 1931- *53*
Purvis, Leland *232*
Pushker, Gloria 1927- *162*
  Earlier sketch in SATA *75*
Pushker, Gloria Teles
  See Pushker, Gloria
Pushkin, Aleksandr Sergeevich
  See Pushkin, Alexander
Pushkin, Alexander 1799-1837 .... *61*
Putnam, Alice 1916- *61*
Putnam, Arthur Lee
  See Alger, Horatio, Jr.
Putnam, Peter B(rock) 1920-1998 .... *30*
  Obituary *106*
Puttapipat, Niroot *199*
Puttock, Simon *178*
Puvilland, Alex *205*
Puvilland, Alexandre
  See Puvilland, Alex
Puybaret, Eric 1976- *299*
  Earlier sketch in SATA *195*
Pyle, Charles S. 1954(?)- *229*
Pyle, Chuck
  See Pyle, Charles S.
Pyle, Howard 1853-1911 .... *100*
  Earlier sketch in SATA *16*
  See also CLR *117*
Pyle, Katharine 1863-1938 .... *66*
Pyne, Mable Mandeville 1903-1969 .... *9*
Pyrnelle, Louise-Clarke 1850-1907 .... *114*

Q

Quackenbush, Robert M(ead) 1929- *133*
  Autobiography Feature *133*
  Earlier sketches in SATA *7, 70*
  See also CLR *122*
  See also SAAS *7*
Qualey, Marsha 1953- *124*
  Earlier sketch in SATA *79*
Qualls, Sean *233*
  Earlier sketch in SATA *177*
Quammen, David 1948- *7*

Quark, Jason
  See Eldin, Peter
Quarles, Benjamin 1904-1996 .... *12*
Quarles, Benjamin Arthur
  See Quarles, Benjamin
Quatermass, Martin
  See Carpenter, John
Quattlebaum, Mary 1958- *185*
  Earlier sketches in SATA *88, 134*
Quay, Emma *173*
  Earlier sketch in SATA *119*
Queen, Ellery
  See Deming, Richard
  and Dannay, Frederic
  and Davidson, Avram (James)
  and Fairman, Paul W.
  and Flora, Fletcher
  and Holding, James (Clark Carlisle, Jr.)
  and Hoch, Edward D.
  and Kane, Henry
  and Lee, Manfred B.
  and Marlowe, Stephen
  and Powell, (Oval) Talmage
  and Sheldon, Walter J(ames)
  and Sturgeon, Theodore (Hamilton)
  and Tracy, Don(ald Fiske)
  and Vance, Jack
Queen Latifah 1970- *185*
Quennell, Marjorie Courtney 1884-1972 ...... *29*
Quentin
  See Sheldon, David
Quentin, Brad
  See Bisson, Terry
Quest, (Edna) Olga W(ilbourne) Hall
  See Hall-Quest, (Edna) Olga W(ilbourne)
Quick, Annabelle 1922-1986 .... *2*
Quigg, Jane (Hulda) (?)-1986
  Obituary *49*
Quigley, Sarah 1976- *220*
Quill, Monica
  See McInerny, Ralph
Quimby, Laura *237*
Quin-Harkin, Janet 1941- *165*
  Earlier sketches in SATA *18, 90, 119*
Quin-Harkin, Janet Elizabeth
  See Quin-Harkin, Janet
Quinlan, Susan E. 1954- *88*
Quinlan, Susan Elizabeth
  See Quinlan, Susan E.
Quinn, Elisabeth 1881-1962 .... *22*
Quinn, Pat 1947- *130*
Quinn, Patrick 1950- *73*
Quinn, Rob 1972- *138*
Quinn, Spencer
  See Abrahams, Peter
Quinn, Susan 1940- *30*
Quinn, Susan Taft
  See Quinn, Susan
Quinn, Theodora K.
  See Kroeber, Theodora (Kracaw)
Quinn, Vernon
  See Quinn, Elisabeth
Quirk, Anne (E.) 1956- *99*
Quixley, Jim 1931- *56*
Quyth, Gabriel
  See Jennings, Gary

R

Ra, Carol F. 1939- *76*
Raab, Evelyn 1951- *129*
Rabb, Margo 1972- *188*
Rabb, M.E.
  See Rabb, Margo
Rabe, Berniece (Louise) 1928- *148*
  Autobiography Feature *148*
  Earlier sketches in SATA *7, 77*
  See also SAAS *10*
Rabe, Olive H(anson) (?)-1968 .... *13*

Rabin, Staton 1958- *162*
　Earlier sketch in SATA *84*
Rabinowich, Ellen 1946- 29
Rabinowitz, Sandy 1954- 52
　Brief entry *39*
Rachlin, Carol K(ing) 1919- *64*
Rachlin, Harvey 1951- 47
Rachlin, Harvey Brant
　See Rachlin, Harvey
Rachlin, Nahid *64*
Rachlis, Eugene (Jacob) 1920-1986
　Obituary *50*
Rackham, Arthur 1867-1939 .... *100*
　Earlier sketch in SATA *15*
　See also CLR *57*
Racoma, Robin Yoko 1953- *207*
Raczka, Bob 1963- *228*
　Earlier sketches in SATA *163, 191*
Radencich, Marguerite C. 1952-1998 .... *79*
Rader, Laura *197*
Radford, Ruby L(orraine) 1891-1971 .... *6*
Radin, Ruth Yaffe 1938- *107*
　Brief entry *52*
　Earlier sketch in SATA *56*
Radlauer, David 1952- *28*
Radlauer, Edward 1921- *15*
Radlauer, Ruth Shaw 1926- *98*
　Earlier sketch in SATA *15*
Radley, Gail 1951- *112*
　Earlier sketch in SATA *25*
Radunsky, Vladimir *177*
Radzinski, Kandy 1948- *212*
Rae, Gwynedd 1892-1977 .... *37*
Raebeck, Lois 1921- *5*
Rael, Elsa Okon 1927-
　See CLR *84*
Raffi
　See Cavoukian, Raffi
Raftery, Gerald (Bransfield) 1905-1986 .... *11*
Ragan-Reid, Gale 1956- *90*
Rahaman, Vashanti 1953- *98*
Rahn, Joan Elma 1929- *27*
Rai, Bali 1971- *152*
Raible, Alton (Robert) 1918- *35*
Raiff, Stan 1930- *11*
Railsback, Lisa *230*
Raines, Shirley C(arol) 1945- *128*
Rainey, W. B.
　See Blassingame, Wyatt Rainey
Rake, Jody 1961- *157*
Rallison, Janette 1966- *183*
Ralston, Jan
　See Dunlop, Agnes M. R.
Rama, Sue *190*
Ramal, Walter
　See de la Mare, Walter (John)
Ramanujan, A(ttipat) K(rishnaswami)
　1929-1993 .... *86*
Rame, David
　See Divine, Arthur Durham
Ramirez, Jose 1967- *198*
Ramirez, Orlando L. 1972- *194*
Ramos, Jorge 1958- *205*
Ramstad, Ralph L. 1919- *115*
Ramthun, Bonnie *214*
Rana, Indi
　See Rana, Indira Higham
Rana, Indira Higham 1944- *82*
Rana, J.
　See Bhatia, Jamunadevi
Ranadive, Gail 1944- *10*
Rand, Ann (Binkley) *30*
Rand, Gloria 1925- *156*
　Earlier sketch in SATA *101*
Rand, Paul 1914-1996 .... *6*
Randall, Carrie
　See Ransom, Candice
Randall, David 1972- *167*
Randall, Florence Engel 1917-1997 *Volume 5*

Randall, Janet
　See Young, Janet Randall
　and Young, Robert W(illiam)
Randall, Robert
　See Garrett, Randall
　and Silverberg, Robert
Randall, Ruth (Elaine) Painter 1892-1971 ..... *3*
Randell, Beverley
　See Price, Beverley Joan
Randle, Kristen D. 1952- 92
　Autobiography Feature *119*
　See also SAAS *24*
Randle, Kristen Downey
　See Randle, Kristen D.
Randolph, Boynton M.D.
　See Ellis, Edward S.
Randolph, Ellen
　See Rawn, Melanie
Randolph, Geoffrey
　See Ellis, Edward S.
Randolph, J. H.
　See Ellis, Edward S.
Randolph, Lieutenant J. H.
　See Ellis, Edward S.
Rands, William Brighty 1823-1882 .... *17*
Raney, Ken 1953- *74*
Rania, Queen of Jordan 1970- *233*
Rankin, Joan 1940- *212*
　Earlier sketches in SATA *88, 148*
Rankin, Laura 1953(?)- *236*
　Earlier sketch in SATA *176*
Ranney, Agnes V. 1916-1985 .... *6*
Ransom, Candice 1952- *222*
　Brief entry *49*
　Earlier sketches in SATA *52, 89, 135, 183*
Ransom, Jeanie Franz 1957- *187*
Ransome, Arthur (Michell) 1884-1967 .... *22*
　See also CLR *8*
Ransome, James E. 1961- *227*
　Earlier sketches in SATA *76, 123, 178*
　See also CLR *86*
Rant, Tol E.
　See Longyear, Barry B(rookes)
Rao, Rohitash *218*
Raphael, Elaine
　See Bolognese, Elaine
Raposo, Joseph Guilherme 1938-1989
　Obituary *61*
Rapp, Adam 1968- *148*
Rappaport, Doreen *211*
　Earlier sketch in SATA *151*
Rappaport, Eva 1924- *6*
Rappoport, Ken 1935- *167*
　Earlier sketch in SATA *89*
Rarick, Carrie 1911-2002 .... *41*
Raschka, Chris 1959- *207*
　Earlier sketches in SATA *80, 117, 166*
Raschka, Christopher
　See Raschka, Chris
Rascol, Sabina I. *159*
Rash, Andy *219*
　Earlier sketch in SATA *162*
Raskin, Edith Lefkowitz 1908-1987 .... *9*
Raskin, Ellen 1928-1984 .... *139*
　Earlier sketches in SATA *2, 38*
　See also CLR *12*
Raskin, Joseph 1897-1982 .... *12*
　Obituary *29*
Rathjen, Carl Henry 1909-1984 .... *11*
Rathmann, Peggy 1953- *157*
　Earlier sketch in SATA *94*
　See also CLR *77*
Ratliff, Thomas M. 1948- *118*
Ratner, Sue Lynn
　See Alexander, Sue
Rattigan, Jama Kim 1951- *99*
Ratto, Linda Lee 1952- *79*
Rattray, Simon
　See Trevor, Elleston
Ratz de Tagyos, Paul 1958- *198*
　Earlier sketch in SATA *76*

Rau, Dana Meachen 1971- *218*
　Earlier sketches in SATA *94, 167*
Rau, Margaret 1913- *168*
　Earlier sketch in SATA *9*
　See also CLR *8*
Rauch, Mabel Thompson 1888-1972
　Obituary *26*
Raucher, Herman 1928- *8*
Raude, Karina *199*
Rauh, Sherry
　See North, Sherry
Raum, Elizabeth 1949- *155*
Raut, Radhashyam *222*
Rave, Friederike 1970- *231*
Raven, Margot Theis *184*
RavenWolf, Silver 1956- *155*
Ravielli, Anthony 1916-1997 .... *3*
　Obituary *95*
Ravilious, Robin 1944- *77*
Ravishankar, Anushka 1961- *200*
Rawding, F(rederick) W(illiam) 1930- *55*
Rawlings, Marjorie Kinnan 1896-1953 .... *100*
　See also YABC *1*
　See also CLR *63*
Rawlins, Donna 1956- *206*
Rawlinson, Julia *212*
　Earlier sketch in SATA *175*
Rawls, (Woodrow) Wilson 1913-1984 .... *22*
　See also CLR *81*
Rawlyk, George Alexander 1935- *64*
Rawn, Melanie 1954- *98*
Rawn, Melanie Robin
　See Rawn, Melanie
Rawson, Katherine 1955- *190*
Ray, Carl 1943-1978 .... *63*
Ray, Deborah
　See Kogan Ray, Deborah
Ray, Delia 1963- *179*
　Earlier sketch in SATA *70*
Ray, Irene
　See Sutton, Margaret Beebe
Ray, Jane 1960- *196*
　Earlier sketches in SATA *72, 152*
Ray, JoAnne 1935- *9*
Ray, Mary (Eva Pedder) 1932- *127*
　Earlier sketch in SATA *2*
Ray, Mary Lyn 1946- *154*
　Earlier sketch in SATA *90*
Rayban, Chloe 1944- *167*
Rayburn, Tricia *234*
Rayevsky, Robert 1955- *190*
　Earlier sketch in SATA *81*
Raymond, James Crossley 1917-1981
　Obituary *29*
Raymond, Robert
　See Alter, Robert Edmond
Rayner, Catherine *204*
Rayner, Hugh *151*
Rayner, Mary 1933- *87*
　Earlier sketch in SATA *22*
　See also CLR *41*
Rayner, Shoo
　See Rayner, Hugh
Rayner, William 1929- *55*
　Brief entry *36*
Raynor, Dorka *28*
Raynor, Gemma 1985- *216*
Rayson, Steven 1932- *30*
Rayyan, Omar 1968- *216*
Razzell, Arthur (George) 1925- *11*
Razzell, Mary (Catherine) 1930- *102*
Razzi, James 1931- *10*
Read, Elfreida 1920- *2*
Read, Nicholas 1956- *146*
Read, Piers Paul 1941- *21*
Reade, Deborah 1949- *69*
Reader, Dennis 1929- *71*
Reading, Richard P(atrick) 1962- *161*
Readman, Jo 1958- *89*
Ready, Kirk L(ewis) 1943- *39*
Reaney, James 1926-2008 .... *43*

Reaney, James Crerar
See Reaney, James
Reardon, Joyce
See Pearson, Ridley
Reaver, Chap 1935-1993 69
Obituary 77
Reaver, Herbert R.
See Reaver, Chap
Reaves, J. Michael
See Reaves, (James) Michael
Reaves, (James) Michael 1950- 99
Reber, Deborah 189
Recorvits, Helen 191
Redding, Robert Hull 1919- 2
Redekopp, Elsa 61
Redlich, Ben 1977- 181
Redsand, Anna 1948- 184
Redway, Ralph
See Hamilton, Charles (Harold St. John)
Redway, Ridley
See Hamilton, Charles (Harold St. John)
Reece, Colleen L. 1935- 116
Reece, Gabrielle 1970- 108
Reed, Amy 1979- 223
Reed, Betty Jane 1921- 4
Reed, Dallas
See Pendleton, Thomas
Reed, E.
See Evans, Mari
Reed, Gwendolyn E(lizabeth) 1932- 21
Reed, Kit 1932- 184
Autobiography Feature 184
Earlier sketches in SATA 34, 116
Reed, Lynn Rowe 215
Earlier sketch in SATA 171
Reed, Mike 1951- 211
Reed, Neil 1961- 99
Reed, Talbot Baines 1852-1893
See CLR 76
Reed, Thomas (James) 1947- 34
Reed, William Maxwell 1871-1962 15
Reeder, Carolyn 1937- 97
Earlier sketch in SATA 66
See also CLR 69
Reeder, Colin (Dawson) 1938- 74
Reeder, Colonel Red
See Reeder, Russell P(otter), Jr.
Reeder, Russell P(otter), Jr. 1902-1998 4
Obituary 101
Reeder, Stephanie Owen 1951- 102
Reed-Jones, Carol 1955- 112
Reef, Catherine 1951- 223
Earlier sketches in SATA 73, 128, 189
Reekie, Jocelyn (Margaret) 1947- 145
Reeman, Douglas Edward 1924- 63
Brief entry 28
Rees, Celia 1949- 124
Rees, David (Bartlett) 1936-1993 69
Obituary 76
Earlier sketch in SATA 36
See also SAAS 5
Rees, Douglas 1947- 237
Earlier sketch in SATA 169
Rees, Ennis (Samuel, Jr.) 1925-2009 3
Rees, (George) Leslie (Clarence)
1905-2000 105
Obituary 135
Reese, Bob
See Reese, Robert A.
Reese, Carolyn Johnson 1938- 64
Reese, Della 1931(?)- 114
Reese, Lyn
See Reese, Carolyn Johnson
Reese, Robert A. 1938- 60
Brief entry 53
Reese, (John) Terence 1913-1996 59
Reeve, Joel
See Cox, William R(obert)
Reeve, Kirk 1934- 117
Reeve, Philip 1966- 201
Earlier sketch in SATA 170

Reeve, Rosie 188
Earlier sketch in SATA 186
Reeves, Dia 1977- 227
Reeves, Faye Couch 1953- 76
Reeves, James
See Reeves, John Morris
Reeves, Jeni 1947- 111
Reeves, John Morris 1909-1978 87
Earlier sketch in SATA 15
Reeves, Joyce 1911- 17
Reeves, Lawrence F. 1926- 29
Reeves, Ruth Ellen
See Ranney, Agnes V.
Regan, Dian Curtis 1950- 224
Autobiography Feature 149
Earlier sketches in SATA 75, 133, 149
Regehr, Lydia 1903-1991 37
Reger, James P. 1952- 106
Reger, Rob 1969- 227
Reggiani, Renee 1925- 18
Rehm, Karl M. 1935- 72
Reibstein, Mark 211
Reich, Ali
See Katz, Bobbi
Reich, Susanna 1954- 214
Earlier sketch in SATA 113
Reiche, Dietlof 1941- 159
Reichert, Edwin C(lark) 1909-1988
Obituary 57
Reichert, Mickey Zucker
See Reichert, Miriam Zucker
Reichert, Miriam Zucker 1962- 85
Reichert, Renee 172
Reichhold, Jane(t E.) 1937- 147
Reid, Alastair 1926- 46
Reid, Barbara 1922- 21
Reid, Barbara (Jane) 1957- 93
See also CLR 64
Reid, Desmond
See Moorcock, Michael
and McNeilly, Wilfred (Glassford)
Reid, Eugenie Chazal 1924- 12
Reid, John Calvin 21
Reid, (Thomas) Mayne 1818-1883 24
Reid, Meta Mayne 1905-1991 58
Brief entry 36
Reid, Robin (Nicole) 1969- 145
Reid Banks, Lynne 1929- 165
Earlier sketches in SATA 22, 75, 111
See also CLR 86
Reider, Katja 1960- 126
Reid Jenkins, Debra 1955- 87
Reidy, Jean 228
Reiff, Stephanie Ann 1948- 47
Brief entry 28
Reig, June 1933- 30
Reigot, Betty Polisar 1924- 55
Brief entry 41
Reilly, Joan 195
Reim, Melanie (K.) 1956- 104
Reinach, Jacquelyn (Krasne) 1930-2000 28
Reiner, Carl 1922- 151
Reiner, William B(uck) 1910-1976 46
Obituary 30
Reinfeld, Fred 1910-1964 3
Reinhardt, Dana 1971- 175
Reinhart, Matthew 1971- 197
Earlier sketch in SATA 161
Reiniger, Lotte 1899-1981 40
Obituary 33
Reinsma, Carol 1949- 91
Reinstedt, Randall A. 1935- 101
Reinstedt, Randy
See Reinstedt, Randall A.
Reisberg, Mira 1955- 82
Reisberg, Veg
See Reisberg, Mira
Reiser, Lynn 1944- 180
Earlier sketches in SATA 81, 138
Reiser, Lynn Whisnant
See Reiser, Lynn

Reisgies, Teresa (Maria) 1966- 74
Reiss, Johanna 1929(?)- 18
See also CLR 19
Reiss, Johanna de Leeuw
See Reiss, Johanna
Reiss, John J. 23
Reiss, Kathryn 1957- 144
Earlier sketch in SATA 76
Reit, Seymour Victory 1918-2001 21
Obituary 133
Reit, Sy
See Reit, Seymour Victory
Relf, Patricia 1954- 134
Earlier sketch in SATA 71
Remark, Erich Paul
See Remarque, Erich Maria
Remarque, Erich Maria 1898-1970
See CLR 159
Remi, Georges 1907-1983 13
Obituary 32
See also CLR 114
Remington, Frederic S(ackrider)
1861-1909 41
Remkiewicz, Frank 1939- 217
Earlier sketches in SATA 77, 152
Rempt, Fiona 1973- 198
Remy, Georges
See Remi, Georges
Renaud, Anne 1957- 211
Renaud, Bernadette 1945- 66
Renault, Mary 1905-1983 23
Obituary 36
Rendell, Joan 28
Rendina, Laura (Jones) Cooper 1902- 10
Rendon, Marcie R. 1952- 97
Rendon, Maria 1965- 116
Renee, Janina 1956- 140
Renfro, Ed 1924- 79
Renick, Marion (Lewis) 1905-1983 1
Renier, Aaron 1977- 202
Renken, Aleda 1907- 27
Renlie, Frank H. 1936- 11
Rennert, Laura Joy 224
Rennert, Richard Scott 1956- 67
Rennison, Louise 1951- 149
Reno, Dawn E(laine) 1953- 130
Rensie, Willis
See Eisner, Will
Renton, Cam
See Armstrong, Richard
Renvoize, Jean 5
Resau, Laura 1973- 230
Earlier sketch in SATA 190
Resciniti, Angelo G. 1952- 75
Resnick, Michael David
See Resnick, Mike
Resnick, Mike 1942- 159
Earlier sketches in SATA 38, 106
Resnick, Seymour 1920- 23
Retla, Robert
See Alter, Robert Edmond
Rettig, Liz 199
Rettstatt, Chris
See Ashland, Monk
Reuter, Bjarne (B.) 1950- 142
Earlier sketch in SATA 68
Reuter, Carol (Joan) 1931- 2
Revena
See Wright, Betty Ren
Revsbech, Vicki
See Liestman, Vicki
Rex, Adam 225
Earlier sketch in SATA 186
Rex, Michael 191
Rey, H. A. 1898-1977 100
Earlier sketches in SATA 1, 26, 69
See also CLR 93
Rey, Hans Augusto
See Rey, H. A.
Rey, Luis V. 1955- 201

Rey, Margret 1906-1996 86
  Obituary 93
  Earlier sketch in SATA 26
  See also CLR 93
Rey, Margret Elisabeth
  See Rey, Margret
Reyher, Becky
  See Reyher, Rebecca Hourwich
Reyher, Rebecca Hourwich 1897-1987 18
  Obituary 50
Reynish, Jenny 222
Reynold, Ann
  See Bernardo, Anilu
Reynolds, Aaron 1970- 197
Reynolds, Adrian 1963- 192
Reynolds, C. Buck 1957- 107
Reynolds, Dickson
  See Reynolds, Helen Mary Greenwood Camp-
  bell
Reynolds, Helen Mary Greenwood Campbell
  1884-1969
  Obituary 26
Reynolds, Jan 1956- 180
Reynolds, John
  See Whitlock, Ralph
Reynolds, Madge
  See Whitlock, Ralph
Reynolds, Malvina 1900-1978 44
  Obituary 24
Reynolds, Marilyn 1935- 121
  See also SAAS 23
Reynolds, Marilyn M.
  See Reynolds, Marilyn
Reynolds, Marilynn 1940- 141
  Earlier sketch in SATA 80
Reynolds, Pamela 1923- 34
Reynolds, Peter H. 1961- 226
  Earlier sketch in SATA 128
Reynolds, Peter J. 1961- 179
Reynolds, Susan 179
Rhine, Richard
  See Silverstein, Alvin
  and Silverstein, Virginia B.
Rhoades, Diane 1952- 90
Rhodes, Bennie (Loran) 1927- 35
Rhodes, Donna McKee 1962- 87
Rhodes, Frank Harold Trevor 1926- 37
Rhuday-Perkovich, Olugbemisola 227
Rhue, Morton
  See Strasser, Todd
Rhyne, Nancy 1926- 66
Rhynes, Martha E. 1939- 141
Ribbons, Ian 1924- 37
  Brief entry 30
  See also SAAS 3
Ricciuti, Edward R(aphael) 1938- 10
Rice, Alice (Caldwell) Hegan 1870-1942 63
Rice, Bebe Faas 1932- 89
Rice, Charles D(uane) 1910-1971
  Obituary 27
Rice, Dale R. 1948- 42
Rice, Dale Richard
  See Rice, Dale R.
Rice, Dick
  See Rice, R. Hugh
Rice, Earle (Wilmont), Jr. 1928- 151
  Earlier sketch in SATA 92
Rice, Edward 1918-2001 47
  Brief entry 42
Rice, Elizabeth 1913-1976 2
Rice, Eve 1951- 91
  Earlier sketch in SATA 34
Rice, Eve Hart
  See Rice, Eve
Rice, Inez 1907- 13
Rice, James 1934- 93
  Earlier sketch in SATA 22
Rice, John F. 1958- 82
Rice, R. Hugh 1929- 115
Rice, Richard H.
  See Rice, R. Hugh

Rich, Anna 1956- 212
Rich, Barbara
  See Graves, Robert
Rich, Elaine Sommers 1926- 6
Rich, Josephine Bouchard 1912- 10
Rich, Louise Dickinson 1903-1991 54
  Obituary 67
Rich, Naomi 217
Richard, Adrienne 1921- 5
  See also SAAS 9
Richard, James Robert
  See Bowen, Robert Sydney
Richards, Chuck 1957- 170
Richards, Frank
  See Hamilton, Charles (Harold St. John)
Richards, Hilda
  See Hamilton, Charles (Harold St. John)
Richards, Jackie 1925- 102
Richards, Jame 230
Richards, Jean 1940- 135
Richards, Justin 169
Richards, Kay
  See Baker, Susan (Catherine)
Richards, Laura E(lizabeth Howe) 1850-1943
  See YABC 1
  See also CLR 54
Richards, Leigh
  See King, Laurie R.
Richards, Marlee
  See Brill, Marlene Targ
Richards, Norman 1932- 48
Richards, R(onald) C(harles) W(illiam)
  1923- 59
  Brief entry 43
Richards, Walter Alden (Jr.) 1907-1988
  Obituary 56
Richardson, Andrew (William) 1986- 120
Richardson, Carol 1932- 58
Richardson, Frank Howard 1882-1970
  Obituary 27
Richardson, Grace Lee
  See Dickson, Naida
Richardson, Jean (Mary) 59
Richardson, Judith Benet 1941- 77
Richardson, Nigel 1957- 187
Richardson, Robert S(hirley) 1902-1981 8
Richardson, Sandy 1949- 116
Richardson, V.A. 189
Richardson, Willis 1889-1977 60
Richelson, Geraldine 1922- 29
Richemont, Enid 1940- 82
Richler, Mordecai 1931-2001 98
  Brief entry 27
  Earlier sketch in SATA 44
  See also CLR 17
Richman, Sophia 1941- 142
Rich-McCoy, Lois
  See McCoy, Lois (Rich)
Richmond, Robin 1951- 75
Richoux, Pat(ricia) 1927- 7
Richter, Alice 1941- 30
Richter, Conrad (Michael) 1890-1968 3
Richter, Hans Peter 1925-1993 6
  See also CLR 21
  See also SAAS 11
Richter, Jutta 1955- 184
Rickard, Graham 1949- 71
Rico, Don(ato) 1917-1985
  Obituary 43
Riddell, Chris 1962- 219
  Earlier sketches in SATA 114, 166
Riddell, Christopher Barry
  See Riddell, Chris
Riddell, Edwina 1955- 82
Ridden, Brian 1934- 123
  See Ridden, Brian John
Riddle, Tohby 1965- 223
  Earlier sketches in SATA 74, 151
Riddleburger, Sam 202
Riddles, Libby 1956- 140
Ride, Sally 1951- 219

Ride, Sally Kristen
  See Ride, Sally
Rideout, Sandy 194
Rider, D. F.
  See Perrin, Pat
Rider, David F.
  See Perrin, Pat
Ridge, Antonia (Florence) (?)-1981 7
  Obituary 27
Ridge, Martin 1923-2003 43
Ridley, Philip 171
  Earlier sketch in SATA 88
Ridlon, Marci
  See Balterman, Marcia Ridlon
Riedman, Sarah R(egal) 1902-1995 1
Riehecky, Janet 1953- 164
Ries, Lori 237
  Earlier sketch in SATA 185
Riesenberg, Felix, Jr. 1913-1962 23
Rieu, E(mile) V(ictor) 1887-1972 46
  Obituary 26
Riffenburgh, Beau 1955- 175
Rigg, Sharon
  See Creech, Sharon
Riggenbach, Holly
  See Black, Holly
Riggio, Anita 1952- 148
  Earlier sketch in SATA 73
Riggs, Shannon 190
Riggs, Sidney Noyes 1892-1975
  Obituary 28
Riggs, Stephanie 1964- 138
Riglietti, Serena 1969- 189
Rigney, James Oliver, Jr.
  See Jordan, Robert
Rikhoff, Jean 1928- 9
Rikki
  See Ducornet, Erica
Riley, James A. 1939- 97
Riley, James Whitcomb 1849-1916 17
Riley, Jocelyn 1949- 60
  Brief entry 50
Riley, Jocelyn Carol
  See Riley, Jocelyn
Riley, Linda Capus 1950- 85
Riley, Martin 1948- 81
Riley-Webb, Charlotte 1948- 235
Rim, Sujean 225
Rimbauer, Steven
  See Pearson, Ridley
Rimes, (Margaret) LeAnn 1982- 154
Rinaldi, Ann 1934- 202
  Brief entry 50
  Earlier sketches in SATA 51, 78, 117, 161
  See also CLR 46
Rinard, Judith E(llen) 1947- 140
  Earlier sketch in SATA 44
Rinck, Maranke 1976- 214
Rinder, Lenore 1949- 92
Ring, Elizabeth 1920- 79
Ringdahl, Mark
  See Longyear, Barry B(rookes)
Ringgold, Faith 1930- 187
  Earlier sketches in SATA 71, 114
  See also CLR 30
Ringi, Kjell (Arne Soerensen) 1939- 12
Rinkoff, Barbara Jean (Rich) 1923-1975 4
  Obituary 27
Rinn, Miriam 1946- 127
Riordan, James 1936- 95
Riordan, Rick 208
  Earlier sketch in SATA 174
Rios, Tere
  See Versace, Marie Teresa Rios
Rioux, Jo 226
Rioux, Jo-Anne
  See Rioux, Jo
Ripken, Cal, Jr. 1960- 215
  Earlier sketch in SATA 114
Ripken, Calvin Edward, Jr.
  See Ripken, Cal, Jr.

Ripley, Catherine 1957- 82
Ripley, Elizabeth Blake 1906-1969 5
Ripper, Charles L(ewis) 1929- 3
Ripper, Chuck
  See Ripper, Charles L(ewis)
Rippin, Sally 220
Riq
  See Atwater, Richard
Rish, David 1955- 110
Riskind, Mary 1944- 60
Rissinger, Matt 1956- 93
Rissman, Art
  See Sussman, Susan
Rissman, Susan
  See Sussman, Susan
Ritchie, Barbara Gibbons 14
Ritchie, Scot 1954- 217
Ritter, Felix
  See Kruss, James
Ritter, John H. 1951- 215
  Earlier sketches in SATA *129, 137*
Ritter, Lawrence S(tanley) 1922-2004 58
  Obituary 152
Ritthaler, Shelly 1955- 91
Ritts, Paul 1920(?)-1980
  Obituary 25
Ritz, Karen 1957- 202
  Earlier sketch in SATA *80*
Riu, Isabel Ferrer 1969- 222
Rivera, Geraldo (Miguel) 1943- 54
  Brief entry 28
Rivera, Guadalupe
  See Rivera Marin, Guadalupe
Rivera Marin, Guadalupe 1924- 224
Rivers, Elfrida
  See Bradley, Marion Zimmer
Rivers, Karen 1970- 131
Riverside, John
  See Heinlein, Robert A.
Rivkin, Ann 1920- 41
Rivoli, Mario 1943- 10
Roach, Marilynne K. 1946- 9
Roach, Marilynne Kathleen
  See Roach, Marilynne K.
Roach, Portia
  See Takakjian, Portia
Robb, Don 1937- 194
Robb, Laura 1937- 95
Robberecht, Thierry 1960- 182
Robbins, Frank 1917-1994(?) 42
  Brief entry 32
Robbins, Jacqui 221
Robbins, Ken 1945- 219
  Brief entry 53
  Earlier sketches in SATA *94, 147*
Robbins, Raleigh
  See Hamilton, Charles (Harold St. John)
Robbins, Ruth 1917(?)- 14
Robbins, Tony
  See Pashko, Stanley
Robbins, Wayne
  See Cox, William R(obert)
Robel, S. L.
  See Fraustino, Lisa Rowe
Roberson, Jennifer 1953- 72
Roberson, John R(oyster) 1930- 53
Robert, Adrian
  See St. John, Nicole
Roberton, Fiona 230
Roberts, Bethany 202
  Earlier sketch in SATA *133*
Roberts, Bruce (Stuart) 1930- 47
  Brief entry 39
Roberts, Charles G(eorge) D(ouglas)
  1860-1943 88
  Brief entry 29
  See also CLR *33*
Roberts, David
  See Cox, John Roberts
Roberts, David 1970- 191
Roberts, Diane 1937- 184

Roberts, Elizabeth 1944- 80
Roberts, Elizabeth Madox 1886-1941 33
  Brief entry 27
  See also CLR *100*
Roberts, Jim
  See Bates, Barbara S(nedeker)
Roberts, Jody 218
Roberts, John G(aither) 1913-1993 27
Roberts, Judy I. 1957- 93
Roberts, Katherine 1962- 152
Roberts, Ken 223
  See Lake, Kenneth R(obert)
Roberts, Laura Peyton 232
Roberts, M. L.
  See Mattern, Joanne
Roberts, Marion 1966- 212
Roberts, Nancy Correll 1924- 52
  Brief entry 28
Roberts, Priscilla 1955- 184
Roberts, Terence
  See Sanderson, Ivan T(erence)
Roberts, Willo Davis 1928-2004 150
  Autobiography Feature 150
  Obituary 160
  Earlier sketches in SATA *21, 70, 133*
  See also CLR *95*
  See also SAAS *8*
Robertson, Barbara (Anne) 1931- 12
Robertson, Don 1929-1999 8
  Obituary 113
Robertson, Dorothy Lewis 1912- 12
Robertson, Ellis
  See Ellison, Harlan
  and Silverberg, Robert
Robertson, James I., Jr. 1930- 182
Robertson, James Irvin
  See Robertson, James I., Jr.
Robertson, Janet (E.) 1935- 68
Robertson, Jennifer Sinclair 1942-1998 12
Robertson, Jenny
  See Robertson, Jennifer Sinclair
Robertson, Keith (Carlton) 1914-1991 85
  Obituary 69
  Earlier sketch in SATA *1*
  See also SAAS *15*
Robertson, Mark
  See Robertson, M.P.
Robertson, M.P. 1965- 197
Robertson, Stephen
  See Walker, Robert W.
Robertus, Polly M. 1948- 212
  Earlier sketch in SATA *73*
Robeson, Kenneth
  See Dent, Lester
  and Goulart, Ron
Robeson, Kenneth
  See Johnson, (Walter) Ryerson
Robinet, Harriette Gillem 1931- 104
  Earlier sketch in SATA *27*
  See also CLR *64*
Robins, Deri 1958- 166
  Earlier sketch in SATA *117*
Robins, Patricia 1921- 117
Robins, Rollo, Jr.
  See Ellis, Edward S.
Robins, Seelin
  See Ellis, Edward S.
Robinson, Adjai 1932- 8
Robinson, Aminah Brenda Lynn 1940- 159
  Earlier sketch in SATA *77*
Robinson, Barbara (Webb) 1927- 84
  Earlier sketch in SATA *8*
Robinson, C(harles) A(lexander), Jr.
  1900-1965 36
Robinson, Charles 1870-1937 17
Robinson, Charles 1931- 6
Robinson, Dorothy W. 1929- 54
Robinson, Elizabeth Keeler 1959- 204
Robinson, Eve
  See Tanselle, Eve
Robinson, Fiona 1965- 225

Robinson, Glen 1953- 92
Robinson, Glendal P.
  See Robinson, Glen
Robinson, Jan M. 1933- 6
Robinson, Jean O. 1934- 7
Robinson, Joan (Mary) G(ale Thomas)
  1910-1988 7
Robinson, Kim Stanley 1952- 109
Robinson, Lee 1948- 110
Robinson, Lloyd
  See Silverberg, Robert
Robinson, Lynda S(uzanne) 1951- 107
Robinson, Marileta 1942- 32
Robinson, Maudie Millian Oller 1914- 11
Robinson, Maurice R(ichard) 1895-1982
  Obituary 29
Robinson, Nancy K(onheim) 1942-1994 91
  Brief entry 31
  Obituary 79
  Earlier sketch in SATA *32*
Robinson, Ray 1920- 23
Robinson, Raymond Kenneth
  See Robinson, Ray
Robinson, Shari
  See McGuire, Leslie (Sarah)
Robinson, Sharon 1950- 197
  Earlier sketch in SATA *162*
Robinson, Spider 1948- 118
Robinson, Sue
  See Robinson, Susan Maria
Robinson, Susan Maria 1955- 105
Robinson, Susan Patricia
  See Gates, Susan
Robinson, Suzanne
  See Robinson, Lynda S(uzanne)
Robinson, T(homas) H(eath) 1869-1950 17
Robinson, Tim 1963- 205
Robinson, (Wanda) Veronica 1926- 30
Robinson, W(illiam) Heath 1872-1944 17
Robison, Bonnie 1924- 12
Robison, Nancy L(ouise) 1934- 32
Robles, Harold E. 1948- 87
Robottom, John 1934- 7
Robson, Eric 1939- 82
Roca, Francois 1971- 200
Rocco, John 1967- 188
Roche, A. K.
  See Abisch, Roslyn Kroop
  and Kaplan, Boche
Roche, Denis 1967- 196
  Earlier sketch in SATA *99*
Roche, Denis Mary
  See Roche, Denis
Roche, Luane 1937- 170
Roche, P(atricia) K. 1935- 57
  Brief entry 34
Roche, Terry
  See Poole, Peggy
Rochman, Hazel 1938- 105
Rock, Lois
  See Joslin, Mary
Rock, Maxine 1940- 108
Rocker, Fermin 1907- 40
Rockliff, Mara 224
Rocklin, Joanne 1946- 134
  Earlier sketch in SATA *86*
Rockwell, Anne 1934- 235
  Earlier sketches in SATA *33, 71, 114, 162,
  194*
  See also SAAS *19*
Rockwell, Anne F.
  See Rockwell, Anne
Rockwell, Anne Foote
  See Rockwell, Anne
Rockwell, Bart
  See Pellowski, Michael (Joseph)
Rockwell, Harlow 1910-1988 33
  Obituary 56
Rockwell, Lizzy 1961- 233
  Earlier sketch in SATA *185*
Rockwell, Norman (Percevel) 1894-1978 23

Rockwell, Thomas 1933- *231*
Earlier sketches in SATA *7, 70*
See also CLR *6*
Rockwood, Joyce 1947- *39*
Rockwood, Roy
See McFarlane, Leslie
and Stratemeyer, Edward L.
Rodanas, Kristina 1952- *155*
Rodari, Gianni 1920-1980
See CLR *24*
Rodd, Kathleen Tennant
See Rodd, Kylie Tennant
Rodd, Kylie Tennant 1912-1988 .... *57*
Obituary *55*
Earlier sketch in SATA *6*
Rodda, Emily 1948- *230*
Earlier sketches in SATA *97, 146*
See also CLR *32*
Roddenberry, Eugene Wesley 1921-1991 ..... *45*
Obituary *69*
Roddenberry, Gene
See Roddenberry, Eugene Wesley
Roddick, Ellen 1936- *5*
Roddie, Shen *153*
Roddy, Lee 1921- *57*
Rodenas, Paula *73*
Rodgers, Frank 1944- *69*
Rodgers, Mary 1931- *130*
Earlier sketch in SATA *8*
See also CLR *20*
Rodman, Emerson
See Ellis, Edward S.
Rodman, Eric
See Silverberg, Robert
Rodman, Maia
See Wojciechowska, Maia (Teresa)
Rodman, Mary Ann *185*
Rodman, (Cary) Selden 1909-2002 .... *9*
Rodowsky, Colby 1932- *164*
Earlier sketches in SATA *21, 77, 120*
See also SAAS *22*
Rodowsky, Colby F.
See Rodowsky, Colby
Rodriguez, Alejo 1941- *83*
Rodriguez, Alex 1975- *189*
Rodriguez, Beatrice 1969- *230*
Rodriguez, Christina 1981- *177*
Rodriguez, Edel 1971- *196*
Rodriguez, Luis J. 1954- *125*
Rodriguez, Rachel *180*
Rodriguez, Rachel Victoria
See Rodriguez, Rachel
Roeder, Virginia Marsh 1926- *98*
Roehrig, Catharine H. 1949- *67*
Roennfeldt, Robert 1953- *78*
Roessel-Waugh, C. C.
See Waugh, Carol-Lynn Rossel
and Waugh, Charles G(ordon)
Roets, Lois F. 1937- *91*
Roever, J(oan) M(arilyn) 1935- *26*
Rofes, Eric 1954-2006 .... *52*
Rofes, Eric Edward 1954-2006
See Rofes, Eric
Roffey, Maureen 1936- *33*
Rogak, Lisa 1962- *80*
Rogak, Lisa Angowski
See Rogak, Lisa
Rogan, S. Jones *199*
Rogan, Sally Jones
See Rogan, S. Jones
Rogasky, Barbara 1933- *144*
Earlier sketch in SATA *86*
Roge 1972- *233*
Rogers, (Thomas) Alan (Stinchcombe)
1937- *81*
Earlier sketch in SATA *2*
Rogers, Bettye 1858-1919 .... *103*
Rogers, Cindy 1950- *89*
Rogers, Emma 1951- *74*
Rogers, Frances 1888-1974 .... *10*

Rogers, Fred McFeely 1928-2003 .... *33*
Obituary *138*
Rogers, Gregory 1957- *211*
Rogers, Hal
See Sirimarco, Elizabeth
Rogers, Jacqueline 1958- *213*
Rogers, Jean 1919- *55*
Brief entry *47*
Rogers, Matilda 1894-1976 .... *5*
Obituary *34*
Rogers, Pamela 1927- *9*
Rogers, Paul 1950- *98*
Earlier sketch in SATA *54*
Rogers, Robert
See Hamilton, Charles (Harold St. John)
Rogers, Sherry *193*
Rogers, W(illiam) G(arland) 1896-1978 .... *23*
Rohan, M. S.
See Rohan, Michael Scott
Rohan, Michael Scott 1951- *98*
Rohan, Mike Scott
See Rohan, Michael Scott
Rohmann, Eric 1957- *171*
See also CLR *100*
Rohmer, Harriet 1938- *56*
Rohrer, Doug 1962- *89*
Rojan
See Rojankovsky, Feodor (Stepanovich)
Rojankovsky, Feodor (Stepanovich)
1891-1970 .... *21*
Rojany, Lisa *94*
Rokeby-Thomas, Anna E(lma) 1911- *15*
Roland, Albert 1925-2002 .... *11*
Roland, Mary
See Lewis, Mary
Roleff, Tamara L. 1959- *143*
Rolerson, Darrell A(llen) 1946- *8*
Roll, Winifred 1909-1998 .... *6*
Rollins, Charlemae Hill 1897-1979 .... *3*
Obituary *26*
Rollins, James 1961- *216*
Rollock, Barbara T(herese) 1924- *64*
Rolston, Steve 1978- *209*
Romack, Janice Reed
See LeNoir, Janice
Romain, Trevor *134*
Romanenko, Vitaliy 1962- *101*
Romano, Christy
See Romano, Christy Carlson
Romano, Christy Carlson 1984- *210*
Romano, Clare 1922- *111*
Earlier sketch in SATA *48*
Romano, Louis G. 1921- *35*
Romano, Melora A. 1966- *118*
Romano, Ray 1957- *170*
Romano, Raymond
See Romano, Ray
Romijn, Johanna Maria Kooyker
See Kooyker-Romijn, Johanna Maria
Romyn, Johanna Maria Kooyker
See Kooyker-Romijn, Johanna Maria
Rong, Yu 1970- *174*
Rongen, Bjoern 1906- *10*
Rongen, Bjorn
See Rongen, Bjoern
Ronson, Mark
See Alexander, Marc
Rood, Ronald (N.) 1920- *12*
Rook, Sebastian
See Jeapes, Ben
Rooke, Daphne 1914-2009 .... *12*
Rooke, Daphne Marie
See Rooke, Daphne
Rooney, Ronnie 1970- *212*
Roop, Connie 1951- *167*
Brief entry *49*
Earlier sketches in SATA *54, 116*
Roop, Constance Betzer
See Roop, Connie

Roop, Peter 1951- *167*
Brief entry *49*
Earlier sketches in SATA *54, 116*
Roop, Peter G.
See Roop, Peter
Roop, Peter Geiger
See Roop, Peter
Roos, Maryn *225*
Roos, Stephen 1945- *128*
Brief entry *41*
Earlier sketches in SATA *47, 77*
Roosa, Karen 1961- *218*
Roose-Evans, James 1927- *65*
Roosevelt, Eleanor 1884-1962 .... *50*
Root, Barry *232*
Earlier sketch in SATA *182*
Root, Betty *84*
Root, Kimberly Bulcken *192*
Root, Phyllis 1949- *224*
Brief entry *48*
Earlier sketches in SATA *55, 94, 145, 184*
Root, Shelton L., Jr. 1923-1986
Obituary *51*
Roper, Laura (Newbold) Wood 1911-2003 .. *34*
Obituary *150*
Roper, Robert 1946- *142*
Earlier sketch in SATA *78*
Roraback, Robin (Ellan) 1964- *111*
Rorby, Ginny 1944- *94*
Rorer, Abigail 1949- *85*
Rosaler, Maxine *208*
Rosamel, Godeleine de 1968- *151*
Roscoe, D(onald) T(homas) 1934- *42*
Rose, Anne *8*
Rose, Deborah Lee 1955- *185*
Earlier sketches in SATA *71, 124*
Rose, Elizabeth (Jane Pretty) 1933- *68*
Brief entry *28*
Rose, Florella
See Carlson, Vada F.
Rose, Gerald (Hembdon Seymour) 1935- *68*
Brief entry *30*
Rose, Malcolm 1953- *168*
Earlier sketch in SATA *107*
Rose, Nancy A.
See Sweetland, Nancy A(nn)
Rose, Naomi C. *228*
Rose, Ted 1940- *93*
Rose, Wendy 1948- *12*
Rosen, Elizabeth 1961- *205*
Rosen, Lillian (Diamond) 1928- *63*
Rosen, Marvin 1933- *161*
Rosen, Michael 1946- *229*
Brief entry *40*
Earlier sketches in SATA *48, 84, 137, 181*
See also CLR *45*
Rosen, Michael J. 1954- *199*
Earlier sketch in SATA *86*
Rosen, Michael Wayne
See Rosen, Michael
Rosen, Sidney 1916- *1*
Rosen, Winifred 1943- *8*
Rosenbaum, Maurice 1907-1987 .... *6*
Rosenberg, Amye 1950- *74*
Rosenberg, Dorothy 1906- *40*
Rosenberg, Eth Clifford 1915- *92*
See also SAAS *22*
Rosenberg, Jane 1949- *58*
Rosenberg, Liz 1958- *129*
Earlier sketch in SATA *75*
Rosenberg, Maxine B(erta) 1939- *93*
Brief entry *47*
Earlier sketch in SATA *55*
Rosenberg, Nancy 1931- *4*
Rosenberg, Sharon 1942- *8*
Rosenberry, Vera 1948- *219*
Earlier sketches in SATA *83, 144*
Rosenblatt, Arthur
See Rosenblatt, Arthur S.
Rosenblatt, Arthur S. 1938- *68*
Brief entry *45*

Rosenblatt, Lily 1956- 90
Rosenbloom, Joseph 1928- 21
Rosenblum, Richard 1928- 11
Rosenburg, John M. 1918- 6
Rosenfeld, Dina 1962- 99
Rosenstiehl, Agnes 1941- 203
Rosenthal, Amy Krouse 1965- 222
    Earlier sketch in SATA 177
Rosenthal, Betsy R. 1957- 178
Rosenthal, Harold 1914-1999 35
Rosenthal, M(acha) L(ouis) 1917-1996 59
Rosenthal, Marc 1949- 193
Rosenthal, Mark A(lan) 1946- 64
Rosing, Norbert 1953- 196
Rosman, Steven M 1956- 81
Rosman, Steven Michael
    See Rosman, Steven M
Rosoff, Meg 1956- 209
    Earlier sketch in SATA 160
Ross, Alan
    See Warwick, Alan R(oss)
Ross, Christine 1950- 172
    Earlier sketch in SATA 83
Ross, Clare
    See Romano, Clare
Ross, Dana Fuller
    See Cockrell, Amanda
    and Gerson, Noel Bertram
Ross, Dave
    See Ross, David
Ross, David 1896-1975 49
    Obituary 20
Ross, David 1949- 133
    Earlier sketch in SATA 32
Ross, Deborah J.
    See Wheeler, Deborah
Ross, Diana
    See Denney, Diana
Ross, Edward S(hearman) 1915- 85
Ross, Eileen 1950- 115
Ross, Frank (Xavier), Jr. 1914- 28
Ross, Jane 1961- 79
Ross, John 1921- 45
Ross, Judy 1942- 54
Ross, Katharine Reynolds
    See Ross, Kathy
Ross, Kathy 1948- 169
    Earlier sketch in SATA 89
Ross, Kent 1956- 91
Ross, Lillian Hammer 1925- 72
Ross, Michael Elsohn 1952- 170
    Earlier sketches in SATA 80, 127
Ross, Pat(ricia Kienzle) 1943- 53
    Brief entry 48
Ross, Ramon R(oyal) 1930- 62
Ross, Stewart 1947- 134
    Earlier sketch in SATA 92
    See also SAAS 23
Ross, Sylvia 1937- 231
Ross, Tom 1958- 84
Ross, Tony 1938- 225
    Earlier sketches in SATA 17, 65, 130, 176
Ross, Wilda 1915- 51
    Brief entry 39
Rossel, Seymour 1945- 28
Rossell, Judith 1953- 187
Rossel-Waugh, C. C.
    See Waugh, Carol-Lynn Rossel
Rossetti, Christina 1830-1894 20
    See also CLR 115
Rossetti, Christina Georgina
    See Rossetti, Christina
Rossi, Joyce 1943- 116
Rossotti, Hazel Swaine 1930- 95
Rostkowski, Margaret I. 1945- 59
Rostoker-Gruber, Karen 229
Roth, Arnold 1929- 21
Roth, Arthur J(oseph) 1925-1993 43
    Brief entry 28
    Obituary 75
    See also SAAS 11

Roth, Carol 222
Roth, David 1940- 36
Roth, Julie Jersild 180
Roth, Matthue 1978(?)- 174
Roth, R.G.
    See Roth, Robert
Roth, Rob
    See Roth, Robert
Roth, Robert 1965- 230
Roth, Roger 190
Roth, Ruby 1983(?)- 216
Roth, Stephanie
    See Sisson, Stephanie Roth
Roth, Susan L. 181
    Earlier sketch in SATA 134
Rothberg, Abraham 1922-2011 59
Roth-Hano, Renee 1931- 85
Rothkopf, Carol Z. 1929- 4
Rothman, Joel 1938- 7
Rotner, Shelley 1951- 169
    Earlier sketch in SATA 76
Rottman, S.L. 1970- 157
    Earlier sketch in SATA 106
Rottman, Susan Lynn
    See Rottman, S.L.
Roueche, Berton 1911-1994 28
Roughsey, Dick 1921(?)-1985 35
    See also CLR 41
Roughsey, Goobalathaldin
    See Roughsey, Dick
Rounds, Glen (Harold) 1906-2002 112
    Obituary 141
    Earlier sketches in SATA 8, 70
Rourke, Constance Mayfield 1885-1941
    See YABC 1
Rouss, Sylvia 211
Rovetch, Gerda 1925(?)- 202
Rovetch, L. Bob
    See Rovetch, Lissa
Rovetch, Lissa 201
Rowan, Deirdre
    See Williams, Jeanne
Rowe, Jennifer
    See Rodda, Emily
Rowe, John A. 1949- 198
    Earlier sketch in SATA 146
Rowe, Viola Carson 1903-1969
    Obituary 26
Rowh, Mark 1952- 90
Rowland, Florence Wightman 1900-1997 8
    Obituary 108
Rowland-Entwistle, (Arthur) Theodore (Henry)
    1925- 94
    Earlier sketch in SATA 31
Rowling, J.K. 1965- 174
    Earlier sketch in SATA 109
    See also CLR 112
Rowling, Joanne Kathleen
    See Rowling, J.K.
Rowsome, Frank (Howard), Jr. 1914-1983 .. 36
Roy, Gabrielle 1909-1983 104
Roy, Jacqueline 1954- 74
Roy, James 1968- 218
Roy, Jennifer
    See Roy, Jennifer Rozines
Roy, Jennifer Rozines 1967- 178
Roy, Jessie Hailstalk 1895-1986
    Obituary 51
Roy, Kari Anne 1977(?)- 221
Roy, Liam
    See Scarry, Patricia (Murphy)
Roy, Ron 1940- 228
    Brief entry 35
    Earlier sketches in SATA 40, 110
Roybal, Laura 1956- 85
Roybal, Laura Husby
    See Roybal, Laura
Royds, Caroline 1953- 55
Royston, Angela 1945- 230
    Earlier sketches in SATA 120, 169
Rozakis, Laurie E. 1952- 84

Rozen, Anna 1960- 206
Rubbino, Salvatore 1970- 220
Rubel, David 1961- 223
Rubel, Nicole 1953- 181
    Earlier sketches in SATA 18, 95, 135
Rubin, Eva Johanna 1925- 38
Rubin, Susan Goldman 1939- 182
    Earlier sketches in SATA 84, 132
Rubin, Vicky 1964- 193
Rubinetti, Donald 1947- 92
Rubinger, Ami 1953- 225
Rubinstein, Gillian 1942- 158
    Autobiography Feature 116
    Earlier sketches in SATA 68, 105
    See also CLR 35
    See also SAAS 25
Rubinstein, Gillian Margaret
    See Rubinstein, Gillian
Rubinstein, Patricia -2003
    See Forest, Antonia
Rubinstein, Patricia Giulia Caulfield Kate
    See Forest, Antonia
Rubinstein, Robert E(dward) 1943- 49
Rublowsky, John M(artin) 1928- 62
Rubright, Lynn 1936- 171
Ruby, Laura 227
    Earlier sketches in SATA 155, 181
Ruby, Lois 1942- 184
    Autobiography Feature 105
    Brief entry 34
    Earlier sketches in SATA 35, 95
Ruby, Lois F.
    See Ruby, Lois
Ruchlis, Hy(man) 1913-1992 3
    Obituary 72
Ruckdeschel, Liz 214
Rucker, Mike 1940- 91
Ruckman, Ivy 1931- 93
    Earlier sketch in SATA 37
Ruck-Pauquet, Gina 1931- 40
    Brief entry 37
Ruddell, Deborah 1949- 210
Ruditis, Paul 190
Rudley, Stephen 1946- 30
Rudolph, Marguerita 1908- 21
Rudomin, Esther
    See Hautzig, Esther Rudomin
Rue, Ginger 236
Rue, Leonard Lee III 1926- 142
    Earlier sketch in SATA 37
Rue, Nancy 1951- 233
Rue, Nancy N.
    See Rue, Nancy
Rue, Nancy Naylor
    See Rue, Nancy
Rueda, Claudia 183
Ruedi, Norma Paul
    See Ainsworth, Norma
Ruelle, Karen Gray 1957- 209
    Earlier sketches in SATA 84, 126
Ruemmler, John D(avid) 1948- 78
Ruepp, Krista 1947- 143
Ruffell, Ann 1941- 30
Ruffins, Reynold 1930- 125
    Earlier sketch in SATA 41
Rugg, Jim 206
Ruggles, Lucy
    See Williams, Kathryn
Rugoff, Milton 1913- 30
Ruhen, Olaf 1911-1989 17
Rui, Paolo 1962- 217
Rukeyser, Muriel 1913-1980
    Obituary 22
Rumbaut, Hendle 1949- 84
Rumford, James 1948- 193
    Earlier sketch in SATA 116
Rumsey, Marian (Barritt) 1928- 16
Rumstuckle, Cornelius
    See Brennan, Herbie
Runholt, Susan 216
Runnerstroem, Bengt Arne 1944- 75

Runyan, John
  See Palmer, Bernard (Alvin)
Runyon, Brent *217*
Runyon, Catherine 1947- *62*
Ruoff, A. LaVonne Brown 1930- *76*
Rupp, Rebecca *185*
Rusch, Elizabeth 1966- *198*
Rusch, Kris
  See Rusch, Kristine Kathryn
Rusch, Kristine Kathryn 1960- *113*
Rush, Alison 1951- *41*
Rush, Peter 1937- *32*
Rushdie, Ahmed Salman
  See Rushdie, Salman
Rushdie, Salman 1947-
  See CLR *125*
Rushford, Patricia H(elen) 1943- *134*
Rushmore, Helen 1898-1994 .... *3*
Rushmore, Robert (William) 1926-1986 .... *8*
  Obituary *49*
Ruskin, Ariane
  See Batterberry, Ariane Ruskin
Ruskin, John 1819-1900 .... *24*
Russ, Lavinia (Faxon) 1904-1992 .... *74*
Russell, Charlotte
  See Rathjen, Carl Henry
Russell, Ching Yeung 1946- *107*
Russell, Don(ald Bert) 1899-1986
  Obituary *47*
Russell, Franklin (Alexander) 1926- *11*
Russell, Gertrude Barrer
  See Barrer-Russell, Gertrude
Russell, Helen Ross 1915- *8*
Russell, James 1933- *53*
Russell, Jim
  See Russell, James
Russell, Joan Plummer 1930- *139*
Russell, Natalie 1972- *218*
Russell, P(hilip) Craig 1951- *162*
  Earlier sketch in SATA *80*
Russell, Patrick
  See Sammis, John
Russell, Paul (Gary) 1942- *57*
Russell, Sarah
  See Laski, Marghanita
Russell, Sharman Apt 1954- *123*
Russell, Solveig Paulson 1904-1985 .... *3*
Russo, Marisabina 1950- *188*
  Earlier sketches in SATA *106, 151*
Russo, Monica J. 1950- *83*
Russo, Susan 1947- *30*
Russon, Penni 1974- *179*
Rutgers van der Loeff, An
  See Rutgers van der Loeff-Basenau, An(na)
  Maria Margaretha
Rutgers van der Loeff-Basenau, An(na) Maria
  Margaretha 1910- *22*
Ruth, Rod 1912-1987 .... *9*
Rutherford, Douglas
  See McConnell, James Douglas Rutherford
Rutherford, Meg 1932- *34*
Ruthin, Margaret
  See Catherall, Arthur
Rutkoski, Marie 1977- *219*
Rutland, J. *232*
Rutland, Jarrett
  See Rutland, J.
Rutledge, Jill Zimmerman 1951- *155*
Rutz, Viola Larkin 1932- *12*
Ruurs, Margriet 1952- *215*
  Earlier sketches in SATA *97, 147*
Ruzicka, Rudolph 1883-1978
  Obituary *24*
Ruzzier, Sergio 1966- *210*
  Earlier sketch in SATA *159*
Ryan, Betsy
  See Ryan, Elizabeth (Anne)
Ryan, Candace *234*
Ryan, Cheli Duran *20*
Ryan, Darlene 1958- *176*
Ryan, Elizabeth (Anne) 1943- *30*

Ryan, Jeanette
  See Mines, Jeanette
Ryan, John 1921-2009 .... *22*
Ryan, John Gerald Christopher
  See Ryan, John
Ryan, Margaret 1950- *166*
  Earlier sketch in SATA *78*
Ryan, Mary E. 1953- *61*
Ryan, Mary Elizabeth
  See Ryan, Mary E.
Ryan, Pam Munoz 1951- *197*
  Earlier sketch in SATA *134*
Ryan, Patrick 1957- *138*
Ryan, Peter (Charles) 1939- *15*
Ryan, Rob 1962- *237*
Ryan-Lush, Geraldine 1949- *89*
Rybakov, Anatoli (Naumovich) 1911-1998 .. *79*
  Obituary *108*
Rybakov, Anatolii (Naumovich)
  See Rybakov, Anatoli (Naumovich)
Rybolt, Thomas R. 1954- *62*
Rybolt, Thomas Roy
  See Rybolt, Thomas R.
Rybolt, Tom
  See Rybolt, Thomas R.
Rycroft, Nina *228*
Rydberg, Ernest E(mil) 1901-1993 .... *21*
Rydberg, Lou(isa Hampton) 1908- *27*
Rydell, Katy 1942- *91*
Rydell, Wendell
  See Rydell, Wendy
Rydell, Wendy *4*
Ryden, Hope *91*
  Earlier sketch in SATA *8*
Ryder, Joanne 1946- *226*
  Brief entry *34*
  Earlier sketches in SATA *65, 122, 163*
  See also CLR *37*
Ryder, Pamela
  See Lamb, Nancy
Rye, Anthony
  See Youd, Samuel
Rylant, Cynthia 1954- *195*
  Brief entry *44*
  Earlier sketches in SATA *50, 76, 112, 160*
  See also CLR *86*
  See also SAAS *13*
Rymer, Alta May 1925- *34*
Rymond, Lynda Gene *199*

S

S. L. C.
  See Twain, Mark
S., Svend Otto
  See Soerensen, Svend Otto
Saaf, Donald W(illiam) 1961- *124*
Saal, Jocelyn
  See Sachs, Judith
Sabbeth, Carol (Landstrom) 1957- *125*
Saberhagen, Fred 1930-2007 .... *89*
  Obituary *184*
  Earlier sketch in SATA *37*
Saberhagen, Fred T.
  See Saberhagen, Fred
Saberhagen, Fred Thomas
  See Saberhagen, Fred
Saberhagen, Frederick Thomas
  See Saberhagen, Fred
Sabin, Edwin L(egrand) 1870-1952
  See YABC *2*
Sabin, Francene *27*
Sabin, Lou
  See Sabin, Louis
Sabin, Louis 1930- *27*
Sabre, Dirk
  See Laffin, John (Alfred Charles)
Sabuda, Robert (James) 1965- *120*
  Earlier sketch in SATA *81*

Sabuda, Robert 1965- *170*
Sabuda, Robert James
  See Sabuda, Robert
Sachar, Louis 1954- *154*
  Brief entry *50*
  Earlier sketches in SATA *63, 104*
  See also CLR *161*
Sachs, Elizabeth-Ann 1946- *48*
Sachs, Judith 1947- *52*
  Brief entry *51*
Sachs, Marilyn 1927- *164*
  Autobiography Feature *110*
  Earlier sketches in SATA *3, 68*
  See also CLR *2*
  See also SAAS *2*
Sachs, Marilyn Stickle
  See Sachs, Marilyn
Sackett, S(amuel) J(ohn) 1928- *12*
Sackson, Sid 1920- *16*
Sacre, Antonio 1968- *152*
Saddler, Allen
  See Richards, R(onald) C(harles) W(illiam)
Saddler, K. Allen
  See Richards, R(onald) C(harles) W(illiam)
Sadie, Stanley 1930-2005 .... *14*
Sadie, Stanley John
  See Sadie, Stanley
Sadiq, Nazneen
  See Sheikh, Nazneen
Sadler, Catherine Edwards 1952- *60*
  Brief entry *45*
Sadler, Marilyn (June) 1950- *79*
Sadler, Mark
  See Lynds, Dennis
Sadler, Sonia Lynn *230*
Saffer, Barbara *144*
Sagan, Carl 1934-1996 .... *58*
  Obituary *94*
Sagan, Carl Edward
  See Sagan, Carl
Sage, Angie 1952- *197*
Sage, Juniper
  See Brown, Margaret Wise
  and Hurd, Edith Thacher
Sagsoorian, Paul 1923- *12*
Said, S.F. 1967- *174*
Saidman, Anne 1952- *75*
Saint, Dora Jessie 1913- *10*
St. Anthony, Jane *175*
St. Antoine, Sara L. 1966- *84*
St. Clair, Byrd Hooper 1905-1976
  Obituary *28*
St. Crow, Lili
  See Saintcrow, Lilith
Saintcrow, Lilith 1976- *221*
Saint-Exupery, Antoine de 1900-1944 .... *20*
  See also CLR *142*
Saint-Exupery, Antoine Jean Baptiste Marie
  Roger de
  See Saint-Exupery, Antoine de
St. George, Judith 1931- *161*
  Earlier sketches in SATA *13, 99*
  See also CLR *57*
  See also SAAS *12*
St. George, Judith Alexander
  See St. George, Judith
St. James, Blakely
  See Gottfried, Theodore Mark
  and Platt, Charles
St. James, Blakely
  See Griffin, W. E. B.
St. James, Sierra
  See Rallison, Janette
Saint James, Synthia 1949- *152*
  Earlier sketch in SATA *84*
St. John, Lauren 1966- *214*
St. John, Nicole *143*
  Autobiography Feature *143*
  Earlier sketches in SATA *29, 89*
  See also CLR *46*
  See also SAAS *7*

St. John, Patricia Mary 1919-1993
  Obituary 79
St. John, Philip
  See del Rey, Lester
St. John, Wylly Folk 1908-1985 10
  Obituary 45
St. Max, E. S.
  See Ellis, Edward S.
St. Meyer, Ned
  See Stratemeyer, Edward L.
St. Mox, E. A.
  See Ellis, Edward S.
St. Myer, Ned
  See Stratemeyer, Edward L.
St. Tamara
  See Kolba, St. Tamara
Saito, Michiko
  See Fujiwara, Michiko
Sakai, Komako 1966- 213
Sakaki, Ichiro 1969- 192
Sakamoto, Miki 198
Sakers, Don 1958- 72
Sakharnov, S.
  See Sakharnov, Svyatoslav
Sakharnov, Svyatoslav 1923- 65
Sakharnov, Svyatoslav Vladimirovich
  See Sakharnov, Svyatoslav
Saksena, Kate 148
Sakurai, Gail 1952- 153
  Earlier sketch in SATA 87
Salamanca, Lucy
  See del Barco, Lucy Salamanca
Salas, Laura Purdie 1966- 216
Salassi, Otto R(ussell) 1939-1993 38
  Obituary 77
Salat, Cristina 82
Saldana, Rene, Jr. 186
Saldutti, Denise 1953- 39
Sale, Tim 1956- 153
Salem, Kay 1952- 92
Salerni, Dianne K. 231
Salerno, Steven 176
Salinger, J.D. 1919-2010 67
  See also CLR 18
Salinger, Jerome David
  See Salinger, J.D.
Salisbury, Graham 1944- 234
  Earlier sketches in SATA 76, 108, 161, 195
Salisbury, Joyce E(llen) 1944- 138
Salkey, (Felix) Andrew (Alexander)
  1928-1995 118
  Earlier sketch in SATA 35
Salley, Coleen 166
Sallis, Susan (Diana) 1929- 55
Salmieri, Daniel 1983- 208
Salmon, Annie Elizabeth 1899- 13
Salmon, Dena K. 1959(?)- 219
Salonen, Roxane Beauclair 1968- 184
Salsi, Lynn 1947- 130
Salsitz, R. A. V.
  See Salsitz, Rhondi Vilott
Salsitz, Rhondi Vilott 115
Salten, Felix
  See Salzmann, Siegmund
Salter, Cedric
  See Knight, Francis Edgar
Salter, Sydney 220
Saltman, Judith 1947- 64
Saltzberg, Barney 1955- 233
  Earlier sketches in SATA 135, 194
Saltzman, David (Charles Laertes)
  1967-1990 86
Salvadori, Mario (George) 1907-1997 97
  Earlier sketch in SATA 40
Salwood, F.K.
  See Kilworth, Garry
Salzer, L. E.
  See Wilson, Lionel
Salzman, Marian 1959- 77
Salzmann, Siegmund 1869-1945 25
Samachson, Dorothy (Mirkin) 1914-1997 3

Samachson, Joseph 1906-1980 3
  Obituary 52
Sammis, John 1942- 4
Sampson, Emma (Keats) Speed 1868-1947 . 68
Sampson, Fay 1935- 151
  Brief entry 40
  Earlier sketch in SATA 42
Sampson, Fay Elizabeth
  See Sampson, Fay
Sampson, Jeff 1982- 232
Sampson, Michael 1952- 143
  Earlier sketch in SATA 95
Samson, Anne S(tringer) 1933- 2
Samson, Joan 1937-1976 13
Samson, Suzanne M. 1959- 91
Samuels, Barbara 199
Samuels, Charles 1902-1982 12
Samuels, Cynthia K(alish) 1946- 79
Samuels, Gertrude 1910(?)-2003 17
  Obituary 147
Sanborn, Duane 1914-1996 38
Sancha, Sheila 1924- 38
Sanchez, Alex 1957- 151
Sanchez, Anita 1956- 209
Sanchez, Sonia 1934- 136
  Earlier sketch in SATA 22
  See also CLR 18
Sanchez-Silva, Jose Maria 1911- 132
  Earlier sketch in SATA 16
  See also CLR 12
Sand, George X. 45
Sandak, Cass R(obert) 1950-2001 51
  Brief entry 37
Sandberg, (Karin) Inger 1930- 15
Sandberg, Karl C. 1931- 35
Sandberg, Lasse (E. M.) 1924- 15
Sandburg, Carl 1878-1967 8
  See also CLR 67
Sandburg, Carl August
  See Sandburg, Carl
Sandburg, Charles
  See Sandburg, Carl
Sandburg, Charles A.
  See Sandburg, Carl
Sandburg, Helga 1918- 3
  See also SAAS 10
Sandell, Lisa Ann 1977- 175
Sandemose, Iben 1950- 211
Sander, Heather L. 1947- 157
Sanderlin, George 1915- 4
Sanderlin, Owenita (Harrah) 1916- 11
Sanders, Betty Jane
  See Monthei, Betty
Sanders, Nancy I. 1960- 141
  Earlier sketch in SATA 90
Sanders, Scott Russell 1945- 109
  Earlier sketch in SATA 56
Sanders, Winston P.
  See Anderson, Poul
Sanderson, Irma 1912- 66
Sanderson, Ivan T(erence) 1911-1973 6
Sanderson, Margaret Love
  See Keats, Emma
  and Sampson, Emma (Keats) Speed
Sanderson, Ruth 1951- 224
  Earlier sketches in SATA 41, 109, 172
Sanderson, Ruth L.
  See Sanderson, Ruth
Sanders-Wells, Linda 220
Sand-Eveland, Cyndi 211
Sandin, Joan 1942- 197
  Earlier sketches in SATA 12, 94, 153
Sandison, Janet
  See Cameron, Elizabeth Jane
Sandler, Martin W. 216
  Earlier sketch in SATA 160
Sandom, J. Gregory
  See Welsh, T.K.
Sandom, J.G.
  See Welsh, T.K.
Sandoz, Mari(e Susette) 1900-1966 5

Sanford, Agnes (White) 1897-1976 61
Sanford, Doris 1937- 69
Sanford, Rose
  See Simmonds, Posy
Sanger, Amy Wilson 1967- 205
Sanger, Marjory Bartlett 1920- 8
San Jose, Christine 1929- 167
Sankey, Alice (Ann-Susan) 1910- 27
Sansone, Adele 1953- 230
San Souci, Daniel 192
  Earlier sketch in SATA 96
San Souci, Robert D. 1946- 220
  Earlier sketches in SATA 40, 81, 117, 158
  See also CLR 43
Santamaria, Benjamin 1955- 184
Santat, Dan 224
  Earlier sketch in SATA 188
Santesson, Hans Stefan 1914(?)-1975
  Obituary 30
Santiago, Esmeralda 1948- 129
Santopolo, Jill 214
Santore, Charles 1935- 200
Santoro, C.
  See Santoro, Christopher
Santoro, Christopher 218
Santoro, Scott 1956- 236
Santos, Helen
  See Griffiths, Helen
Santrey, Louis
  See Sabin, Louis
Santucci, Barbara 1948- 130
Sapergia, Barbara 1943- 181
Sapet, Kerrily 1972- 214
Sapieyevski, Anne Lindbergh 1940-1993 81
  Brief entry 32
  Earlier sketches in SATA 35, 78
Saport, Linda 1954- 123
Sapp, Allen 1929- 151
Sarac, Roger
  See Caras, Roger A(ndrew)
Sarah, Duchess of York
  See Ferguson, Sarah
Sarasin, Jennifer
  See Sachs, Judith
Sarcone-Roach, Julia 215
Sardinha, Rick 192
Sarg, Anthony Frederick
  See Sarg, Tony
Sarg, Tony 1882-1942
  See YABC 1
Sargent, Pamela 1948- 78
  Earlier sketch in SATA 29
Sargent, Robert 1933- 2
Sargent, Sarah 1937- 44
  Brief entry 41
Sargent, Shirley 1927-2004 11
Sarnoff, Jane 1937- 10
Saroff, Phyllis V. 202
Saroyan, William 1908-1981 23
  Obituary 24
Sartell, Debra 229
Sarton, Eleanor May
  See Sarton, May
Sarton, May 1912-1995 36
  Obituary 86
Sasaki, Chris 182
Sasaki, Ellen Joy 206
Saseen, Sharon (Dillon) 1949- 59
Sasek, Miroslav 1916-1980 16
  Obituary 23
  See also CLR 4
Sasso, Sandy Eisenberg 1947- 162
  Earlier sketches in SATA 86, 116
Sathre, Vivian 1952- 133
  Earlier sketch in SATA 79
Satterfield, Charles
  See del Rey, Lester
  and Pohl, Frederik
Sattgast, L. J.
  See Sattgast, Linda J.
Sattgast, Linda J. 1953- 91

Sattler, Helen Roney 1921-1992 .... *74*
  Earlier sketch in SATA *4*
  See also CLR *24*
Sattler, Jennifer
  See Sattler, Jennifer Gordon
Sattler, Jennifer Gordon *218*
Sauer, Julia Lina 1891-1983 .... *32*
  Obituary *36*
Sauer, Tammi 1972- *223*
Sauerwein, Leigh 1944- *155*
Saul, Carol P. 1947- *117*
  Earlier sketch in SATA *78*
Saul, John 1942- *98*
Saul, John W.
  See Saul, John
Saul, John Woodruff III
  See Saul, John
Saul, (Ellen) Wendy 1946- *42*
Saulnier, Karen Luczak 1940- *80*
Saunders, Caleb
  See Heinlein, Robert A.
Saunders, Dave 1939- *85*
Saunders, Julie 1939- *85*
Saunders, (William) Keith 1910-1994 .... *12*
Saunders, Rubie (Agnes) 1929- *21*
Saunders, Steven
  See Jones, Allan Frewin
Saunders, Susan 1945- *96*
  Brief entry *41*
  Earlier sketch in SATA *46*
Saunders-Smith, Gail 1952- *169*
Sauvain, Philip Arthur 1933- *111*
Savadier, Elivia 1950- *228*
  Earlier sketches in SATA *79, 164*
Savage, Alan
  See Nicole, Christopher
Savage, Blake
  See Goodwin, Harold L(eland)
Savage, Candace 1949- *142*
Savage, Deborah 1955- *76*
Savage, Jeff 1961- *97*
Savage, Katharine James 1905-1989
  Obituary *61*
Savage, Stephen 1965- *194*
Savage, Thomas 1915-2003
  Obituary *147*
Savageau, Cheryl 1950- *96*
Savery, Constance (Winifred) 1897-1999 .... *1*
Saville, Andrew
  See Taylor, Andrew
Saville, (Leonard) Malcolm 1901-1982 .... *23*
  Obituary *31*
Saviozzi, Adriana
  See Mazza, Adriana
Savitt, Sam 1917-2000 .... *8*
  Obituary *126*
Savitz, Harriet May 1933-2008 .... *72*
  Earlier sketch in SATA *5*
  See also SAAS *26*
Sawicki, Mary 1950- *90*
Sawyer, (Frederick) Don(ald) 1947- *72*
Sawyer, Kem Knapp 1953- *84*
Sawyer, Kim Vogel *233*
Sawyer, Robert J. 1960- *149*
  Earlier sketch in SATA *81*
Sawyer, Robert James
  See Sawyer, Robert J.
Sawyer, Ruth 1880-1970 .... *17*
  See also CLR *36*
Saxby, H.M.
  See Saxby, (Henry) Maurice
Saxby, (Henry) Maurice 1924- *71*
Saxon, Andrew
  See Arthur, Robert, (Jr.)
Saxon, Antonia
  See Sachs, Judith
Say, Allen 1937- *161*
  Earlier sketches in SATA *28, 69, 110*
  See also CLR *135*
Sayers, Frances Clarke 1897-1989 .... *3*
  Obituary *62*

Sayles, Elizabeth 1956- *220*
  Earlier sketches in SATA *108, 163*
Saylor-Marchant, Linda 1963- *82*
Sayre, April Pulley 1966- *233*
  Earlier sketches in SATA *88, 131, 191*
Sazer, Nina 1949- *13*
Scabrini, Janet 1953- *13*
Scagell, Robin 1946- *107*
Scagnetti, Jack 1924- *7*
Scaletta, Kurtis 1968- *215*
Scalora, Suza *224*
Scamander, Newt
  See Rowling, J.K.
Scamell, Ragnhild 1940- *180*
  Earlier sketch in SATA *77*
Scandiffio, Laura *227*
Scanlon, Elizabeth Garton
  See Scanlon, Liz Garton
Scanlon, Liz Garton *226*
Scanlon, Marion Stephany *11*
Scannel, John Vernon
  See Scannell, Vernon
Scannell, Vernon 1922-2007 .... *59*
  Obituary *188*
Scarborough, Elizabeth
  See Scarborough, Elizabeth Ann
Scarborough, Elizabeth Ann 1947- *171*
  Earlier sketch in SATA *98*
Scarf, Maggi
  See Scarf, Maggie
Scarf, Maggie 1932- *5*
Scariano, Margaret M. 1924- *86*
Scarlett, Susan
  See Streatfeild, Noel
Scarrow, Alex 1966- *236*
Scarry, Huck
  See Scarry, Richard McClure, Jr.
Scarry, Patricia (Murphy) 1924- *2*
Scarry, Patsy
  See Scarry, Patricia (Murphy)
Scarry, Richard (McClure) 1919-1994 .... *75*
  Obituary *90*
  Earlier sketches in SATA *2, 35*
  See also CLR *41*
Scarry, Richard McClure, Jr. 1953- *35*
Schachner, Judith Byron 1951- *178*
  Earlier sketch in SATA *88*
Schachner, Judy
  See Schachner, Judith Byron
Schachtel, Roger 1949- *38*
Schachtel, Roger Bernard
  See Schachtel, Roger
Schade, Susan *189*
Schaedler, Sally *116*
Schaefer, Carole Lexa *173*
Schaefer, Jack (Warner) 1907-1991 .... *66*
  Obituary *65*
  Earlier sketch in SATA *3*
Schaefer, Lola M. 1950- *183*
  Earlier sketches in SATA *91, 144*
Schaeffer, Mead 1898- *21*
Schaeffer, Susan Fromberg 1940-2011 .... *22*
Schaer, Brigitte 1958- *112*
Schallau, Daniel 1966- *222*
Schaller, George
  See Schaller, George B.
Schaller, George B. 1933- *30*
Schaller, George Beals
  See Schaller, George B.
Schanzer, Rosalyn (Good) 1942- *138*
  Earlier sketch in SATA *77*
Schatell, Brian *66*
  Brief entry *47*
Schechter, Betty (Goodstein) 1921- *5*
Schechter, Simone
  See Elkeles, Simone
Schecter, Ellen 1944- *85*
Scheeder, Louis 1946- *141*
Scheer, Julian (Weisel) 1926-2001 .... *8*
Scheerger, Sarah Lynn
  See Lynn, Sarah

Scheffer, Victor B(lanchard) 1906- *6*
Scheffler, Axel 1957- *230*
  Earlier sketch in SATA *180*
Scheffler, Ursel 1938- *81*
Scheffrin-Falk, Gladys 1928- *76*
Scheidl, Gerda Marie 1913- *85*
Scheier, Michael 1943- *40*
  Brief entry *36*
Schell, Mildred 1922- *41*
Schell, Orville (Hickok) 1940- *10*
Scheller, Melanie 1953- *77*
Schellie, Don 1932- *29*
Schembri, Jim 1962- *124*
Schembri, Pamela 1969- *195*
Schemm, Mildred Walker 1905-1998 .... *21*
  Obituary *103*
Schenker, Dona 1947- *133*
  Earlier sketch in SATA *68*
Scher, Paula 1948- *47*
Scherer, Jeffrey *194*
Scherf, Margaret 1908-1979 .... *10*
Schermer, Judith (Denise) 1941- *30*
Schertle, Alice 1941- *231*
  Earlier sketches in SATA *36, 90, 145, 192*
Schick, Alice 1946- *27*
Schick, Eleanor 1942- *144*
  Earlier sketches in SATA *9, 82*
Schick, Joel 1945- *31*
  Brief entry *30*
Schields, Gretchen 1948- *75*
Schiff, Ken(neth Roy) 1942- *7*
Schiller, Andrew 1919- *21*
Schiller, Barbara (Heyman) 1928- *21*
Schiller, Pamela (Byrne) *127*
Schindel, John 1955- *213*
  Earlier sketches in SATA *77, 115*
Schindelman, Joseph 1923- *67*
  Brief entry *32*
Schindler, S.D. 1952- *198*
  Brief entry *50*
  Earlier sketches in SATA *75, 118, 171*
Schindler, Steven D.
  See Schindler, S.D.
Schinto, Jeanne 1951- *93*
Schisgall, Oscar 1901-1984 .... *12*
  Obituary *38*
Schlaepfer, Gloria G. 1931- *154*
Schlee, Ann 1934- *44*
  Brief entry *36*
Schleichert, Elizabeth 1945- *77*
Schlein, Miriam 1926-2004 .... *130*
  Obituary *159*
  Earlier sketches in SATA *2, 87*
  See also CLR *41*
Schlesinger, Arthur M., Jr. 1917-2007 .... *61*
  Obituary *181*
  See Schlesinger, Arthur Meier
Schlesinger, Arthur Meier 1888-1965
Schlesinger, Laura (Catherine) 1947- *160*
  Earlier sketch in SATA *110*
Schlitz, Laura Amy *232*
  Earlier sketch in SATA *184*
Schloat, G. Warren, Jr. 1914-2000 .... *4*
Schlossberg, Elisabeth *221*
Schmais, Libby *227*
Schmatz, Pat *197*
Schmid, Eleonore 1939- *126*
  Earlier sketches in SATA *12, 84*
Schmid, Paul *231*
Schmid, Susan Maupin *208*
Schmiderer, Dorothy 1940- *19*
Schmidt, Annie M. G. 1911-1995 .... *67*
  Obituary *91*
  See also CLR *22*
Schmidt, C.A. *196*
Schmidt, Diane 1953- *70*
Schmidt, Elizabeth 1915- *15*
Schmidt, Gary D. 1957- *193*
  Earlier sketches in SATA *93, 135*
Schmidt, James Norman 1912-1983 .... *21*

Schmidt, Karen Lee 1953- *185*
  Earlier sketch in SATA *94*
Schmidt, Lynette 1952- *76*
Schmitz, Tamara *207*
Schneider, Antonie 1954- *167*
  Earlier sketch in SATA *89*
Schneider, Christine M. 1972(?)- *171*
  Earlier sketch in SATA *120*
Schneider, Dick
  See Schneider, Richard H.
Schneider, Elisa
  See Kleven, Elisa
Schneider, Herman 1905-2003 .... *7*
  Obituary *148*
Schneider, Howie -2007 .... *181*
Schneider, Josh 1980- *196*
Schneider, Katy *237*
Schneider, Laurie
  See Adams, Laurie
Schneider, Nina 1913-2007 .... *2*
  Obituary *186*
Schneider, Nina Zimet
  See Schneider, Nina
Schneider, Rex 1937- *44*
Schneider, Richard H. 1922- *171*
Schneider, Richard Henry
  See Schneider, Richard H.
Schneider, Robyn 1986- *187*
Schnirel, James R. 1931- *14*
Schnitter, Jane T. 1958- *88*
Schnitzlein, Danny *134*
Schnur, Steven 1952- *144*
  Earlier sketch in SATA *95*
Schnurre, Wolfdietrich 1920-1989
  Obituary *63*
Schoberle, Cecile 1949- *80*
Schock, Pauline 1928- *45*
Schoell, William 1951- *160*
Schoen, Barbara (Taylor) 1924-1993 .... *13*
Schoenherr, Ian *235*
  Earlier sketch in SATA *177*
Schoenherr, John 1935-2010 .... *66*
  Earlier sketch in SATA *37*
  See also SAAS *13*
Schoenherr, John Carl
  See Schoenherr, John
Schofield, Sandy
  See Rusch, Kristine Kathryn
Scholastica, Sister Mary
  See Jenkins, Marie M(agdalen)
Scholefield, A. T.
  See Scholefield, Alan
Scholefield, Alan 1931- *66*
Scholefield, Edmund O.
  See Griffin, W. E. B.
Scholey, Arthur 1932- *28*
Scholz, Jackson Volney 1897-1986
  Obituary *49*
Schon, Nick 1955- *223*
Schone, Virginia *22*
Schongut, Emanuel 1936- *184*
  Brief entry *36*
  Earlier sketch in SATA *52*
Schoonover, Frank (Earle) 1877-1972 .... *24*
Schoor, Gene 1921- *3*
Schories, Pat 1952- *232*
  Earlier sketches in SATA *116, 164*
Schorr, Melissa 1972- *194*
Schorr, Melissa Robin
  See Schorr, Melissa
Schott, Jane A. 1946- *172*
Schotter, Roni *190*
  Earlier sketches in SATA *105, 149*
Schrader, Dave 1967(?)- *225*
Schraff, Anne E(laine) 1939- *92*
  Earlier sketch in SATA *27*
Schram, Penninah 1934- *219*
  Earlier sketch in SATA *119*
Schrank, Joseph 1900-1984
  Obituary *38*
Schrecengost, Maity 1938- *118*

Schrecengost, S. Maitland
  See Schrecengost, Maity
Schreck, Karen
  See Schreck, Karen Halvorsen
Schreck, Karen Halvorsen 1962- *185*
Schrecker, Judie 1954- *90*
Schreiber, Elizabeth Anne (Ferguson)
  1947- *13*
Schreiber, Ralph W(alter) 1942- *13*
Schreiner, Samuel A(gnew), Jr. 1921- *70*
Schroades, John *214*
Schroder, Monika 1965- *229*
Schroeder, Alan 1961- *98*
  Earlier sketch in SATA *66*
Schroeder, Binette
  See Nickl, Barbara (Elisabeth)
Schroeder, Russell (K.) 1943- *146*
Schroeder, Ted 1931(?)-1973
  Obituary *20*
Schubert, Dieter 1947- *217*
  Earlier sketches in SATA *62, 101*
Schubert, Ingrid 1953- *217*
Schubert, Leda 1945(?)- *232*
  Earlier sketch in SATA *181*
Schubert, Leda Deirdre
  See Schubert, Leda
Schubert-Gabrys, Ingrid 1953- *101*
  Earlier sketch in SATA *62*
Schuelein-Steel, Danielle
  See Steel, Danielle
Schuelein-Steel, Danielle Fernande
  See Steel, Danielle
Schuerger, Michele R. *110*
Schuett, Stacey 1960- *168*
  Earlier sketch in SATA *75*
Schulke, Flip Phelps Graeme 1930- *57*
Schulman, Arlene 1961- *105*
Schulman, Janet 1933- *208*
  Earlier sketches in SATA *22, 137*
Schulman, L(ester) M(artin) 1934- *13*
Schulte, Elaine L(ouise) 1934- *36*
Schultz, Betty K(epka) 1932- *125*
Schultz, Gwendolyn *21*
Schultz, James Willard 1859-1947
  See YABC *1*
Schultz, Pearle Henriksen 1918- *21*
Schulz, Charles M. 1922-2000 .... *10*
  Obituary *118*
Schulz, Charles Monroe
  See Schulz, Charles M.
Schumacher, Julie 1958- *191*
Schumaker, Ward 1943- *96*
Schuman, Michael A. 1953- *134*
  Earlier sketch in SATA *85*
Schur, Maxine
  See Schur, Maxine Rose
Schur, Maxine Rose 1948- *135*
  Autobiography Feature *135*
  Brief entry *49*
  Earlier sketches in SATA *53, 98*
Schurfranz, Vivian 1925- *13*
Schutzer, A. I. 1922- *13*
Schuyler, Pamela R. 1948- *30*
Schwabach, Karen *185*
Schwager, Tina 1964- *110*
Schwandt, Stephen (William) 1947- *61*
Schwark, Mary Beth 1954- *51*
Schwartz, Alvin 1927-1992 .... *56*
  Obituary *71*
  Earlier sketch in SATA *4*
  See also CLR *89*
Schwartz, Amy 1954- *189*
  Brief entry *41*
  Earlier sketches in SATA *47, 83, 131*
  See also CLR *25*
  See also SAAS *18*
Schwartz, Anne Powers 1913-1987 .... *10*
Schwartz, Carol 1954- *77*
Schwartz, Charles W(alsh) 1914- *8*
Schwartz, David M. 1951- *110*
  Earlier sketch in SATA *59*

Schwartz, David Martin
  See Schwartz, David M.
Schwartz, Elizabeth Reeder 1912- *8*
Schwartz, Ellen 1949- *117*
Schwartz, Jerome L.
  See Lawrence, Jerome
Schwartz, Joanne 1960- *220*
Schwartz, Joel L. 1940- *54*
  Brief entry *51*
Schwartz, John 1957- *232*
Schwartz, Joyce R. 1950- *93*
Schwartz, Julius 1907-2004 .... *45*
Schwartz, Perry 1942- *75*
Schwartz, Sheila (Ruth) 1929- *27*
Schwartz, Stephen (Lawrence) 1948- *19*
Schwartz, Virginia Frances 1950- *184*
  Earlier sketch in SATA *131*
Schwarz, Silvia Tessa Viviane
  See Schwarz, Viviane
Schwarz, Viviane 1977- *204*
Schwarz, (Silvia Tessa) Viviane 1977- *141*
Schweitzer, Byrd Baylor
  See Baylor, Byrd
Schweitzer, Iris *59*
  Brief entry *36*
Schweninger, Ann 1951- *168*
  Earlier sketches in SATA *29, 98*
Schwerin, Doris H(alpern) 1922- *64*
Schy, Yael *197*
Scieszka, Jon 1954- *199*
  Earlier sketches in SATA *68, 105, 160*
  See also CLR *107*
Scillian, Devin *199*
  Earlier sketch in SATA *128*
Scioscia, Mary (Hershey) 1926- *63*
Sciurba, Katie 1957- *196*
Scofield, Penrod 1933- *62*
  Obituary *78*
Scoggin, Margaret C(lara) 1905-1968 .... *47*
  Brief entry *28*
Scoltock, Jack 1942- *141*
  Earlier sketch in SATA *72*
Scoppettone, Sandra 1936- *92*
  Earlier sketch in SATA *9*
Scot, Michael
  See Rohan, Michael Scott
Scot-Bernard, P.
  See Bernard, Patricia
Scotland, Jay
  See Jakes, John
Scott, Alastair
  See Allen, Kenneth S.
Scott, Ann Herbert 1926- *140*
  Autobiography Feature *140*
  Brief entry *29*
  Earlier sketches in SATA *56, 94*
Scott, Bill
  See Scott, William N(eville)
Scott, Bill 1920(?)-1985
  Obituary *46*
Scott, Cora Annett (Pipitone) 1931- *11*
Scott, Dan
  See Barker, S. Omar
Scott, Elaine 1940- *198*
  Earlier sketches in SATA *36, 90, 164*
Scott, Elizabeth 1972- *194*
Scott, Inara *236*
Scott, Jack Denton 1915-1995 .... *83*
  Earlier sketch in SATA *31*
  See also CLR *20*
  See also SAAS *14*
Scott, Jane (Harrington) 1931- *55*
Scott, Jane Wooster 1939- *226*
Scott, Jennifer Power 1968- *230*
Scott, Jessica
  See De Wire, Elinor
Scott, John 1912-1976 .... *14*
Scott, John Anthony 1916- *23*
Scott, John M(artin) 1913- *12*
Scott, Mary
  See Mattern, Joanne

Scott, Melissa 1960- *109*
Scott, Michael 1959- *211*
Scott, Michael Peter
    See Scott, Michael
Scott, Mike
    See Scott, Michael
Scott, Richard
    See Rennert, Richard Scott
Scott, Roney
    See Gault, William Campbell
Scott, Sally 1909-1978 .... *43*
Scott, Sally 1948- *44*
Scott, Sally Elisabeth
    See Scott, Sally
Scott, W. N.
    See Scott, William N(eville)
Scott, Sir Walter 1771-1832
    See YABC *2*
    See also CLR *154*
Scott, Warwick
    See Trevor, Elleston
Scott, William N(eville) 1923- *87*
Scotti, Anna
    See Coates, Anna
Scotton, Rob 1960- *214*
    Earlier sketch in SATA *177*
Scribner, Charles, Jr. 1921-1995 .... *13*
    Obituary *87*
Scribner, Joanne L. 1949- *33*
Scribner, Kimball 1917- *63*
Scrimger, Richard 1957- *164*
    Earlier sketch in SATA *119*
Scrimsher, Lila Gravatt 1897-1974
    Obituary *28*
Scroder, Walter K. 1928- *82*
Scroggs, Kirk *187*
Scruggs, Sandy 1961- *89*
Scudder, Brooke 1959- *154*
Scudder, Mildred Lee 1908- *6*
    See also SAAS *12*
Scull, Marie-Louise 1943-1993 .... *77*
Scuro, Vincent 1951- *21*
Seabrooke, Brenda 1941- *148*
    Earlier sketches in SATA *30, 88*
Seagraves, D.B.
    See Seagraves, Donny Bailey
Seagraves, Donny
    See Seagraves, Donny Bailey
Seagraves, Donny Bailey 1951- *224*
Seaman, Augusta Huiell 1879-1950 .... *31*
Seamands, Ruth 1916- *9*
Searcy, Margaret Zehmer 1926- *54*
    Brief entry *39*
Searight, Mary W(illiams) 1918- *17*
Searle, Kathryn Adrienne 1942- *10*
Searle, Ronald 1920- *70*
    Earlier sketch in SATA *42*
Searle, Ronald William Fordham
    See Searle, Ronald
Sears, Stephen W. 1932- *4*
Seaskull, Cecil
    See Castellucci, Cecil
Sebastian, Lee
    See Silverberg, Robert
Sebestyen, Igen
    See Sebestyen, Ouida
Sebestyen, Ouida 1924- *140*
    Earlier sketch in SATA *39*
    See also CLR *17*
    See also SAAS *10*
Sebrey, Mary Ann 1951- *62*
Sechrist, Elizabeth Hough 1903-1991 .... *2*
Sederman, Marty *211*
Sedges, John
    See Buck, Pearl S.
Sedgwick, Marcus 1968- *197*
    Earlier sketch in SATA *160*
Sedita, Francesco 1974- *235*
Seed, Cecile Eugenie 1930- *86*
    Earlier sketch in SATA *8*
    See also CLR *76*

Seed, Jenny
    See Seed, Cecile Eugenie
Seed, Sheila Turner 1937(?)-1979
    Obituary *23*
Seeger, Elizabeth 1889-1973
    Obituary *20*
Seeger, Laura Vaccaro *200*
    Earlier sketch in SATA *172*
Seeger, Pete 1919- *139*
    Earlier sketch in SATA *13*
Seeger, Peter R.
    See Seeger, Pete
Seeley, Laura L. 1958- *71*
Seever, R.
    See Reeves, Lawrence F.
Sefozo, Mary 1925- *82*
Sefton, Catherine
    See Waddell, Martin
Segal, John *178*
Segal, Joyce 1940- *35*
Segal, Lore 1928- *228*
    Autobiography Feature *228*
    Earlier sketches in SATA *4, 66, 163*
    See also SAAS *11*
Segal, Lore Groszmann
    See Segal, Lore
Segar, E(lzie) C(risler) 1894-1938 .... *61*
Segovia, Andres 1893(?)-1987
    Obituary *52*
Seguin, Marilyn W(eymouth) 1951- *91*
Seguin-Fontes, Marthe 1924- *109*
Seibold, J. Otto 1960- *196*
    Earlier sketches in SATA *83, 149*
    See also SAAS *22*
Seidel, Ross *95*
Seidelman, James Edward 1926- *6*
Seiden, Art(hur) *107*
    Brief entry *42*
Seidensticker, John 1944- *200*
Seidler, Ann (G.) 1925- *131*
Seidler, Tor 1952- *149*
    Brief entry *46*
    Earlier sketches in SATA *52, 98*
Seidman, Karla
    See Kuskin, Karla
Seidman, Laurence Ivan 1925- *15*
Seigel, Kalman 1917-1998 .... *12*
    Obituary *103*
Seignobosc, Françoise 1897-1961 .... *21*
Seinfeld, Jerry 1954- *146*
Seitz, Jacqueline 1931- *50*
Seixas, Judith S. 1922- *17*
Sejima, Yoshimasa 1913- *8*
Selberg, Ingrid (Maria) 1950- *68*
Selden, George
    See Thompson, George Selden
Selden, Neil R(oy) 1931- *61*
Self, Margaret Cabell 1902-1996 .... *24*
Selfors, Suzanne 1963- *193*
Selick, Henry 1952- *183*
Selig, Sylvie 1942- *13*
Selkirk, Jane
    See Chapman, John Stanton Higham
Sellers, Naomi
    See Flack, Naomi John White
Sellier, Marie 1953- *212*
Selman, LaRue W. 1927- *55*
Selsam, Millicent E(llis) 1912-1996 .... *29*
    Obituary *92*
    Earlier sketch in SATA *1*
    See also CLR *1*
Seltzer, Meyer 1932- *17*
Seltzer, Richard 1946- *41*
Seltzer, Richard Warren, Jr.
    See Seltzer, Richard
Selvadurai, Shyam 1965(?)- *171*
Selway, Martina 1940- *169*
    Earlier sketch in SATA *74*
Selzer, Adam 1980- *229*
    Earlier sketch in SATA *192*

Selznick, Brian 1966- *210*
    Earlier sketches in SATA *79, 117, 171*
Semel, Nava 1954- *107*
Semloh
    See Holmes, Peggy
Sendak, Jack 1924(?)-1995 .... *28*
Sendak, Maurice 1928- *165*
    Earlier sketches in SATA *1, 27, 113*
    See also CLR *131*
Sendak, Maurice Bernard
    See Sendak, Maurice
Sender, Ruth M(insky) 1926- *62*
Sengler, Johanna 1924- *18*
Senir, Mirik
    See Snir, Mirik
Senisi, Ellen B. 1951- *116*
Senisi, Ellen Babinec
    See Senisi, Ellen B.
Senn, J(oyce) A(nn) 1941- *115*
Senn, Steve 1950- *60*
    Brief entry *48*
Sensel, Joni 1962- *204*
Senzai, N.H. *233*
Serafini, Frank *201*
Serage, Nancy 1924- *10*
Seredy, Kate 1899-1975 .... *1*
    Obituary *24*
    See also CLR *10*
Serfozo, Mary 1925- *194*
Serlin, Andra
    See Abramson, Andra Serlin
Seroff, Victor I(ilyitch) 1902-1979 .... *12*
    Obituary *26*
Serra, Sebastia 1966- *202*
Serraillier, Ian (Lucien) 1912-1994 .... *73*
    Obituary *83*
    Earlier sketch in SATA *1*
    See also CLR *2*
    See also SAAS *3*
Serros, Michele *175*
Serros, Michele M.
    See Serros, Michele
Servello, Joe 1932- *10*
Service, Pamela F. 1945- *222*
    Earlier sketch in SATA *64*
Service, Robert
    See Service, Robert W.
Service, Robert W. 1874(?)-1958 .... *20*
Serwadda, W(illiam) Moses 1931- *27*
Serwer-Bernstein, Blanche L(uria)
    1910-1997 .... *10*
Sescoe, Vincent E. 1938- *123*
Seskin, Steve 1953- *211*
Seth, Mary
    See Lexau, Joan M.
Seton, Anya 1904(?)-1990 .... *3*
    Obituary *66*
Seton, Ernest (Evan) Thompson 1860-1946 . *18*
    See also CLR *59*
Seton-Thompson, Ernest
    See Seton, Ernest (Evan) Thompson
Seuling, Barbara 1937- *220*
    Autobiography Feature *220*
    Earlier sketches in SATA *10, 98, 145, 193*
    See also SAAS *24*
Seuss, Dr.
    See Dr. Seuss
Severn, Bill
    See Severn, William Irving
Severn, David
    See Unwin, David S.
Severn, William Irving 1914- *1*
Sewall, Marcia 1935- *119*
    Earlier sketches in SATA *37, 69*
Seward, Prudence 1926- *16*
Sewell, Anna 1820-1878 .... *100*
    Earlier sketch in SATA *24*
    See also CLR *17*
Sewell, Helen (Moore) 1896-1957 .... *38*
Sexton, Anne 1928-1974 .... *10*

Sexton, Anne Harvey
See Sexton, Anne
Sexton, Brenda 1957- 237
Seymour, Alta Halverson 10
Seymour, Jane 1951- 139
Seymour, Tres 1966- 164
Earlier sketch in SATA 82
Sfar, Joann 1971- 182
Shachtman, Tom 1942- 49
Shackleton, C.C.
See Aldiss, Brian W.
Shader, Rachel
See Sofer, Barbara
Shadow, Jak
See Sutherland, Jon
Shadyland, Sal
See Cooper, Louise
Shafer, Audrey 183
Shafer, Robert E(ugene) 1925- 9
Shaffer, Terea 1968- 79
Shahan, Sherry 1949- 216
Earlier sketches in SATA 92, 134
Shahn, Ben(jamin) 1898-1969
Obituary 21
Shahn, Bernarda Bryson
See Bryson, Bernarda
Shaik, Fatima 114
Shalant, Phyllis 1949- 150
Shan, Darren 1972- 199
Earlier sketches in SATA 129, 168
Shan, D.B.
See Shan, Darren
Shanahan, Lisa 199
Shanberg, Karen
See Shragg, Karen (I.)
Shane, Harold Gray 1914-1993 36
Obituary 76
Shange, Ntozake 1948- 157
Shanks, Ann Zane (Kushner) 10
Shannon, David 1959- 228
Earlier sketches in SATA 107, 152
See also CLR 87
Shannon, George 1952- 202
Earlier sketches in SATA 35, 94, 143
Shannon, George William Bones
See Shannon, George
Shannon, Jacqueline 63
Shannon, Margaret
See Silverwood, Margaret Shannon
Shannon, Monica 1905(?)-1965 28
Shannon, Terry
See Mercer, Jessie
Shannon, Terry Miller 1951- 148
Shapiro, Irwin 1911-1981 32
Shapiro, Jody Fickes 1940- 193
Shapiro, Karen Jo 1964- 186
Shapiro, Michelle 1961- 196
Shapiro, Milton J. 1926- 32
Shapiro, Tricia
See Andryszewski, Tricia
Shapiro, Zachary 1970- 213
Shapp, Charles M(orris) 1906-1989
Obituary 61
Shapp, Martha Glauber 1910- 3
Sharenow, Robert 193
Sharfman, Amalie 14
Sharkey, Niamh 213
Sharma, Partap 1939- 15
Sharma, Rashmi
See Singh, Rashmi Sharma
Sharman, Alison
See Leonard, Alison
Sharmat, Marjorie Weinman 1928- 133
Earlier sketches in SATA 4, 33, 74
Sharmat, Mitchell 1927- 127
Earlier sketch in SATA 33
Sharp, Anne Wallace 1947- 144
Sharp, Luke
See Alkiviades, Alkis

Sharp, Margery 1905-1991 29
Obituary 67
Earlier sketch in SATA 1
See also CLR 27
Sharp, Zerna A. 1889-1981
Obituary 27
Sharpe, Jon
See Duncan, Alice
and Knott, William C(ecil, Jr.)
and Messman, Jon
Sharpe, Mitchell R(aymond) 1924- 12
Sharpe, Susan 1946- 71
Sharratt, Nick 1962- 199
Earlier sketches in SATA 104, 153
Shasha, Mark 1961- 80
Shattuck, Roger 1923-2005 64
Obituary 174
Shattuck, Roger Whitney
See Shattuck, Roger
Shaw, Arnold 1909-1989 4
Obituary 63
Shaw, Carolyn V. 1934- 91
Shaw, Charles (Green) 1892-1974 13
Shaw, Evelyn S. 1927- 28
Shaw, Flora Louisa
See Lugard, Flora Louisa Shaw
Shaw, Hannah 1982(?)- 227
Shaw, Janet 1937- 146
Earlier sketch in SATA 61
See also CLR 96
Shaw, Janet Beeler
See Shaw, Janet
Shaw, Liane 1959- 222
Shaw, Lisa
See Rogak, Lisa
Shaw, Margret 1940- 68
Shaw, Mary 1965- 180
Shaw, Nancy 1946- 162
Earlier sketch in SATA 71
Shaw, Ray 7
Shaw, Richard 1923- 12
Shawn, Frank S.
See Goulart, Ron
Shay, Art
See Shay, Arthur
Shay, Arthur 1922- 4
Shay, Lacey
See Shebar, Sharon Sigmond
Shea, Bob 231
Earlier sketch in SATA 188
Shea, George 1940- 54
Brief entry 42
Shea, Pegi Deitz 1960- 172
Earlier sketches in SATA 77, 137
Shearer, Alex 1949- 204
Shearer, John 1947- 43
Brief entry 27
See also CLR 34
Shearer, Ted 1919- 43
Shearing, Leonie 1972- 184
Sheban, Chris 182
Shebar, Sharon Sigmond 1945- 36
Shecter, Ben 1935- 16
Shecter, Vicky Alvear 1961- 234
Shedd, Warner 1934- 147
Earlier sketch in SATA 87
Sheedy, Alexandra Elizabeth 1962- 39
Earlier sketch in SATA 19
Sheehan, Ethna 1908-2000 9
Sheehan, Patty 1945- 77
Sheehan, Sean 1951- 154
Earlier sketch in SATA 86
Sheen, Barbara 1949- 143
Shefelman, Janice 1930- 205
Earlier sketches in SATA 58, 129
Shefelman, Janice Jordan
See Shefelman, Janice
Shefelman, Tom 1927- 204
Earlier sketch in SATA 58
Sheffer, H. R.
See Abels, Harriette S(heffer)

Sheffield, Charles 1935-2002 109
Sheffield, Janet N. 1926- 26
Sheikh, Nazneen 1944- 101
Sheinkin, Steve 1968- 204
Sheinmel, Alyssa B. 233
Sheinmel, Courtney 1977- 211
Shekerjian, Regina Tor 16
Shelby, Anne 1948- 85
Autobiography Feature 121
See also SAAS 26
Sheldon, Ann
See Antle, Nancy
Sheldon, Ann 67
Earlier sketch in SATA 1
Sheldon, Aure 1917-1976 12
Sheldon, David 185
Sheldon, Deyan 181
Sheldon, John
See Bloch, Robert (Albert)
Sheldon, Muriel 1926- 45
Brief entry 39
Shell, Barry 1951- 176
Shelley, Frances
See Wees, Frances Shelley
Shelley, John 1959- 202
Shelley, Mary
See Shelley, Mary Wollstonecraft
Shelley, Mary Wollstonecraft 1797-1851 29
See also CLR 133
Shelton, Paula Young 1961- 227
Shelton, William Roy 1919-1995 5
Obituary 129
Shemie, Bonnie (Jean Brenner) 1949- 96
Shemin, Margaretha (Hoeneveld) 1928- 4
Shen, Michele 1953- 173
Shenker, Michele
See Shen, Michele
Shenton, Edward 1895-1977 45
Shepard, Aaron 1950- 187
Earlier sketches in SATA 75, 113
Shepard, Ernest Howard 1879-1976 100
Obituary 24
Earlier sketches in SATA 3, 33
See also CLR 27
Shepard, James R.
See Shepard, Jim
Shepard, Jim 1956- 164
Earlier sketch in SATA 90
Shepard, Mary
See Knox, (Mary) Eleanor Jessie
Shephard, Esther 1891-1975 5
Obituary 26
Shepherd, Amanda 201
Shepherd, Donna Walsh
See Walsh Shepherd, Donna
Shepherd, Elizabeth 4
Shepherd, Irana 173
Shepherd, Roni
See Shepherd, Irana
Sheppard, Kate 195
Shepperson, Rob 178
Sherburne, Zoa (Lillian Morin) 1912-1995 3
See also SAAS 18
Sherk-Savage, Candace
See Savage, Candace
Sherlock, Patti 71
Sherman, D(enis) R(onald) 1934- 48
Brief entry 29
Sherman, Diane (Finn) 1928- 12
Sherman, Elizabeth
See Friskey, Margaret (Richards)
Sherman, Harold (Morrow) 1898-1987 37
Obituary 137
Sherman, Josepha 163
Earlier sketch in SATA 75
Sherman, Michael
See Lowndes, Robert A(ugustine) W(ard)
Sherman, Nancy
See Rosenberg, Nancy
Sherman, Pat 174

Sherman, Peter Michael
   See Lowndes, Robert A(ugustine) W(ard)
Sherrard, Valerie 1957- *141*
Sherrard, Valerie Anne
   See Sherrard, Valerie
Sherrod, Jane
   See Singer, Jane Sherrod
Sherry, Clifford J. 1943- 84
Sherry, (Dulcie) Sylvia 1932- *122*
   Earlier sketch in SATA 8
Sherwan, Earl 1917- 3
Sherwood, Jonathan
   See London, Jonathan
Sheth, Kashmira *186*
Shetterly, Will 1955- 78
   Autobiography Feature *106*
Shetterly, William Howard
   See Shetterly, Will
Shiefman, Vicky 1942- 22
Shields, Brenda Desmond (Armstrong)
   1914- 37
Shields, Carol Diggory *174*
Shields, Charles 1944- 10
Shields, Gillian *203*
Shiels, Barbara
   See Adams, Barbara Johnston
Shiffman, Lena 1957- *101*
Shiga, Jason 1976- *228*
Shiina, Makoto 1944- 83
Shimin, Symeon 1902-1984 .... *13*
Shimko, Bonnie 1941- *191*
Shine, Andrea 1955- *104*
Shine, Deborah 1932- 71
Shinn, Everett 1876-1953 .... *21*
Shinn, Sharon 1957- *229*
   Earlier sketches in SATA *110, 164*
Shipp, Josh 1982- *236*
Shippen, Katherine B(inney) 1892-1980 .... *1*
   Obituary 23
   See also CLR 36
Shippey, T. A. 1943- *143*
Shippey, Thomas Alan
   See Shippey, T. A.
Shipton, Eric Earle 1907-1977 .... *10*
Shipton, Jonathan 1948- *215*
Shipton, Paul 1963- *196*
Shiraz, Yasmin *173*
Shirer, William L. 1904-1993 45
   Obituary 78
   See Shirer, William Lawrence
Shirley, Debra *203*
Shirley, Gayle C 1955- 96
Shirley, Gayle Corbett
   See Shirley, Gayle C
Shirley, Jean 1919- 70
Shirreffs, Gordon D(onald) 1914-1996 .... *11*
Shirts, Morris A(lpine) 1922- 63
Shlichta, Joe 1968- 84
Shmurak, Carole B. 1944- *118*
Sholokhov, Mikhail 1905-1984
   Obituary 36
Sholokhov, Mikhail Aleksandrovich
   See Sholokhov, Mikhail
Shore, Diane Z. *215*
   Earlier sketch in SATA *179*
Shore, Diane ZuHone
   See Shore, Diane Z.
Shore, June Lewis 30
Shore, Nancy 1960- *124*
Shore, Robert 1924- 39
Short, Michael 1937- 65
Short, Roger
   See Arkin, Alan
Shortall, Leonard W. *19*
Shortt, Tim(othy Donald) 1961- 96
Shotwell, Louisa Rossiter 1902-1993 3
Shoulders, Michael 1954- *216*
Shoup, Barbara 1947- *156*
   Earlier sketch in SATA *86*
   See also SAAS 24
Shoveller, Herb *184*

Showalter, Jean B(reckinridge) *12*
Showell, Ellen Harvey 1934- 33
Showers, Paul C. 1910-1999 92
   Obituary *114*
   Earlier sketch in SATA *21*
   See also CLR 6
   See also SAAS 7
Shpakow, Tanya 1959(?)- 94
Shpitalnik, Vladimir 1964- 83
Shragg, Karen (I.) 1954- *142*
Shreeve, Elizabeth 1956- *156*
Shreve, Susan
   See Shreve, Susan Richards
Shreve, Susan Richards 1939- *152*
   Brief entry *41*
   Earlier sketches in SATA *46, 95*
Shriver, Jean Adair 1932- 75
Shriver, Maria 1955- *134*
Shriver, Maria Owings
   See Shriver, Maria
Shrode, Mary
   See Hollingsworth, Mary
Shtainmets, Leon 32
Shub, Elizabeth 1915(?)-2004 5
Shuken, Julia 1948- 84
Shulevitz, Uri 1935- *165*
   Earlier sketches in SATA *3, 50, 106*
   See also CLR 61
Shulman, Alix Kates 1932- 7
Shulman, Dee 1957- *146*
Shulman, Irving 1913-1995 .... *13*
Shulman, Lisa *202*
Shulman, Mark 1962- *184*
Shulman, Max 1919-1988
   Obituary 59
Shulman, Milton 1913-2004
   Obituary *154*
Shulman, Neil B(arnett) 1945- 89
Shulman, Polly *235*
Shumsky, Zena
   See Collier, Zena
Shura, Mary Francis
   See Craig, Mary (Francis) Shura
Shusterman, Neal 1962- *201*
   Autobiography Feature *140*
   Earlier sketches in SATA *85, 121, 140*
Shuter, Jane (Margaret) 1955- *151*
   Earlier sketch in SATA *90*
Shuttlesworth, Dorothy Edwards 3
Shwartz, Susan (Martha) 1949- 94
Shyer, Christopher 1961- 98
Shyer, Marlene Fanta *13*
Siberell, Anne 29
Sibley, Don 1922- *12*
Siburt, Ruth 1951- *121*
Siculan, Daniel 1922- *12*
Siddals, Mary McKenna *232*
Siddon, Barbara
   See Bradford, Barbara Taylor
Sidgwick, Ethel 1877-1970 .... *116*
Sidjakov, Nicolas 1924- *18*
Sidman, Joyce 1956- *236*
   Earlier sketches in SATA *145, 181*
Sidney, Frank
   See Warwick, Alan R(oss)
Sidney, Margaret
   See Lothrop, Harriet Mulford Stone
Siebert, Diane 1948- *189*
Siegal, Aranka 1930- 88
   Brief entry *37*
Siegel, Beatrice 36
Siegel, Helen
   See Siegl, Helen
Siegel, Randolph
   See Siegel, Randy
Siegel, Randy *234*
Siegel, Robert 1939- 39
Siegel, Robert Harold
   See Siegel, Robert
Siegel, Siena Cherson 1967(?)- *185*
Siegelson, Kim L. 1962- *114*

Sieger, Ted 1958- *189*
Siegl, Helen 1924- 34
Siepmann, Mary Aline
   See Wesley, Mary (Aline)
Sierra, Judy 1945- *195*
   Earlier sketches in SATA *104, 162*
Sieswerda, Paul L. 1942- *147*
Sievert, Terri
   See Dougherty, Terri (L.)
Sigsawa, Keiichi 1972- *211*
Silas
   See McCay, (Zenas) Winsor
Silcock, Sara Lesley 1947- *12*
Silin-Palmer, Pamela *184*
Sill, Cathryn 1953- *221*
   Earlier sketches in SATA *74, 141*
Sill, John 1947- *222*
   Earlier sketches in SATA *74, 140*
Sillitoe, Alan 1928-2010 .... *61*
Sills, Leslie (Elka) 1948- *129*
Silly, E. S.
   See Kraus, (Herman) Robert
Silsbe, Brenda 1953- *73*
Silva, Joseph
   See Goulart, Ron
Silvano, Wendi 1962- *223*
Silver, Jago
   See Jago
Silver, Maggie *216*
Silver, Ruth
   See Chew, Ruth
Silverberg, Robert 1935- *91*
   Autobiography Feature *104*
   Earlier sketch in SATA *13*
   See also CLR 59
Silverman, Erica 1955- *222*
   Earlier sketches in SATA *78, 112, 165*
Silverman, Janis L. 1946- *127*
Silverman, Mel(vin Frank) 1931-1966 9
Silverman, Robin L. 1954- 96
Silverman, Robin Landew
   See Silverman, Robin L.
Silverstein, Alvin 1933- *124*
   Earlier sketches in SATA *8, 69*
   See also CLR 25
Silverstein, Herma 1945- *106*
Silverstein, Robert Alan 1959- *124*
   Earlier sketch in SATA *77*
Silverstein, Shel 1932-1999 92
   Brief entry *27*
   Obituary *116*
   Earlier sketch in SATA *33*
   See also CLR 96
Silverstein, Sheldon Allan
   See Silverstein, Shel
Silverstein, Virginia B. 1937- *124*
   Earlier sketches in SATA *8, 69*
   See also CLR 25
Silverstein, Virginia Barbara Opshelor
   See Silverstein, Virginia B.
Silverthorne, Elizabeth 1930- *35*
Silverwood, Margaret Shannon 1966- *137*
   Earlier sketch in SATA *83*
Silvey, Diane F. 1946- *135*
Sim, David 1953- *162*
Sim, Dorrith M. 1931- 96
Simak, Clifford D(onald) 1904-1988
   Obituary 56
Simard, Remy 1959- *168*
Siminovich, Lorena 1976(?)- *219*
Simmie, Lois (Ann) 1932- *106*
Simmonds, Posy 1945- *130*
   See also CLR 23
Simmonds, Rosemary Elizabeth
   See Simmonds, Posy
Simmons, Andra 1939- *141*
Simmons, Elly 1955- *134*
Simmons, Michael 1970- *185*
Simms, Laura 1947- *117*
Simner, Janni Lee *113*

Simon, Charlie May
   See Fletcher, Charlie May Hogue
Simon, Francesca 1955- *111*
Simon, Gabriel 1972- *118*
Simon, Hilda Rita 1921- *28*
   See also CLR 39
Simon, Howard 1903-1979 .... *32*
   Obituary *21*
Simon, Joe
   See Simon, Joseph H.
Simon, Joseph H. 1913- *7*
Simon, Martin P(aul William) 1903-1969 .... *12*
Simon, Mina Lewiton
   See Lewiton, Mina
Simon, Norma (Feldstein) 1927- *129*
   Earlier sketches in SATA *3, 68*
Simon, Seymour 1931- *202*
   Earlier sketches in SATA *4, 73, 138*
   See also CLR 63
Simon, Shirley (Schwartz) 1921- *11*
Simon, Solomon 1895-1970 .... *40*
Simonetta, Linda 1948- *14*
Simonetta, Sam 1936- *14*
Simons, Barbara B(rooks) 1934- *41*
Simont, Marc 1915- *126*
   Earlier sketches in SATA *9, 73*
Simpson, Colin 1908-1983 .... *14*
Simpson, Harriette
   See Arnow, Harriette (Louisa) Simpson
Simpson, Jacynth Hope
   See Hope Simpson, Jacynth
Simpson, Lesley 1963- *150*
Simpson, Margaret 1943- *128*
Simpson, Myrtle L(illias) 1931- *14*
Sims, Blanche *168*
   Earlier sketch in SATA *75*
Sims, Blanche L.
   See Sims, Blanche
Sims, Rudine
   See Bishop, Rudine Sims
Simundsson, Elva 1950- *63*
Sinclair, Clover
   See Gater, Dilys
Sinclair, Emil
   See Hesse, Hermann
Sinclair, Jeff 1958- *77*
Sinclair, Olga 1923- *121*
Sinclair, Rose
   See Smith, Susan Vernon
Sinclair, Upton 1878-1968 .... *9*
Sinclair, Upton Beall
   See Sinclair, Upton
Singer, A.L.
   See Lerangis, Peter
Singer, Arthur 1917-1990 .... *64*
Singer, Isaac
   See Singer, Isaac Bashevis
Singer, Isaac Bashevis 1904-1991 .... *27*
   Obituary *68*
   Earlier sketch in SATA *3*
   See also CLR 1
Singer, Jane Sherrod 1917-1985 .... *4*
   Obituary *42*
Singer, Julia 1917- *28*
Singer, Kurt D. 1911-2005 .... *38*
   Obituary *172*
Singer, Marilyn 1948- *234*
   Autobiography Feature *158*
   Brief entry *38*
   Earlier sketches in SATA *48, 80, 125, 158, 201*
   See also CLR 48
   See also SAAS 13
Singer, Muff 1942-2005 .... *104*
   Obituary *160*
Singer, Nicky 1956- *194*
Singer, Susan (Mahler) 1941- *9*
Singh, Rashmi Sharma 1952- *90*
Singleton, Linda Joy 1957- *166*
   Earlier sketch in SATA *88*

Singleton, L.J.
   See Singleton, Linda Joy
Singleton, Sarah 1966- *214*
Sinykin, Sheri
   See Sinykin, Sheri Cooper
Sinykin, Sheri Cooper 1950- *142*
   Autobiography Feature *142*
   Earlier sketches in SATA *72, 133*
Sinykin, Sheril Terri Cooper
   See Sinykin, Sheri Cooper
Siomades, Lorianne *217*
Sipiera, Paul P., (Jr.) 1948- *144*
   Earlier sketch in SATA *89*
Siracusa, Catherine (Jane) 1947- *82*
Sirett, Dawn (Karen) 1966- *88*
Sirimarco, Elizabeth 1966- *158*
Sirof, Harriet 1930- *94*
   Earlier sketch in SATA *37*
Sirois, Allen L. 1950- *76*
Sirvaitis (Chernyaev), Karen (Ann) 1961- ... *79*
Sis, Peter 1949- *192*
   Earlier sketch in SATA *149*
   See also CLR 110
Sisson, Rosemary Anne 1923- *11*
Sisson, Stephanie Roth *237*
   Earlier sketch in SATA *202*
Sister Mary Terese
   See Donze, Mary Terese
Sita, Lisa 1962- *87*
Sitarski, Anita *200*
Sitomer, Alan Lawrence *174*
Sitomer, Harry 1903-1985 .... *31*
Sitomer, Mindel 1903-1987 .... *31*
Sittenfeld, Curtis 1975(?)- *164*
Sive, Helen R(obinson) 1951- *30*
Sivulich, Sandra (Jeanne) Stroner 1941- *9*
Siy, Alexandra *193*
Skarmeta, Antonio 1940- *57*
Skeers, Linda 1958- *207*
Skelly, James R(ichard) 1927- *17*
Skelton, Matthew 1971- *185*
Skinner, Constance Lindsay 1877-1939
   See YABC 1
Skinner, Cornelia Otis 1901-1979 .... *2*
Skipper, G. C. 1939- *46*
   Brief entry *38*
Sklansky, Amy E(dgar) 1971- *145*
Sklansky, Amy E. 1971- *204*
Skofield, James *95*
   Brief entry *44*
Skold, Betty Westrom 1923- *41*
Skorpen, Liesel Moak 1935- *3*
Skott, Maria
   See Nikolajeva, Maria
Skovron, Jon 1976- *229*
Skrypuch, Marsha Forchuk 1954- *134*
Skultety, Nancy Laney 1960- *175*
Skurzynski, Gloria 1930- *145*
   Autobiography Feature *145*
   Earlier sketches in SATA *8, 74, 122*
   See also SAAS 9
Skurzynski, Gloria Joan
   See Skurzynski, Gloria
Skutch, Robert 1925- *89*
Skye, Maggie
   See Werner, Herma
Skye, Obert *200*
   Earlier sketch in SATA *170*
Slack, Michael 1969- *189*
Slackman, Charles B. 1934- *12*
Slade, Arthur G. 1967- *221*
   Earlier sketches in SATA *106, 149*
Slade, Arthur Gregory
   See Slade, Arthur G.
Slade, Christian 1974- *193*
Slade, Richard 1910-1971 .... *9*
Slade, Suzanne 1964- *226*
Slangerup, Erik Jon 1969- *130*
Slate, Joseph 1928- *174*
   Earlier sketches in SATA *38, 122*

Slate, Joseph Frank
   See Slate, Joseph
Slater, Dashka 1963- *179*
Slater, David Michael 1970- *212*
Slater, Ray
   See Lansdale, Joe R.
Slaughter, Hope 1940- *84*
Slaughter, Jean
   See Doty, Jean Slaughter
Slaughter, Tom 1955- *152*
Slavicek, Louise Chipley 1956- *144*
Slavin, Bill 1959- *199*
   Earlier sketches in SATA *76, 148*
Slaymaker, Melissa Eskridge 1958- *158*
Slayton, Fran Cannon *221*
Sleator, William 1945-2011 .... *208*
   Earlier sketches in SATA *3, 68, 118, 161*
   See also CLR 128
Sleator, William Warner III
   See Sleator, William
Slegers, Liesbet 1975- *154*
Sleigh, Barbara 1906-1982 .... *86*
   Obituary *30*
   Earlier sketch in SATA *3*
Slepian, Jan 1921- *85*
   Brief entry *45*
   Earlier sketch in SATA *51*
   See also SAAS 8
Slepian, Janice B.
   See Slepian, Jan
Slicer, Margaret O. 1920- *4*
Slier, Debby
   See Shine, Deborah
Sloan, Brian 1966- *172*
Sloan, Carolyn 1937- *116*
   Earlier sketch in SATA *58*
Sloan, Glenna 1930- *120*
Sloan, Glenna Davis
   See Sloan, Glenna
Sloane, Eric 1910(?)-1985 .... *52*
   Obituary *42*
Sloane, Todd 1955- *88*
Sloat, Teri 1948- *164*
   Earlier sketches in SATA *70, 106*
Slobodkin, Florence Gersh 1905-1994 .... *5*
   Obituary *107*
Slobodkin, Louis 1903-1975 .... *26*
   Earlier sketch in SATA *1*
Slobodkina, Esphyr 1908-2002 .... *1*
   Obituary *135*
   See also SAAS 8
Sloggett, Nellie 1851-1923 .... *44*
Slonim, David 1966- *207*
Sloss, Lesley Lord 1965- *72*
Slote, Alfred 1926- *72*
   Earlier sketch in SATA *8*
   See also CLR 4
   See also SAAS 21
Slote, Elizabeth 1956- *80*
Small, Charlie
   See Ward, Nick
Small, David 1945- *216*
   Brief entry *46*
   Earlier sketches in SATA *50, 95, 126, 183*
   See also CLR 53
Small, Ernest
   See Lent, Blair
Small, Mary 1932- *165*
Small, Terry 1942- *75*
Smallcomb, Pam 1954- *159*
Smallman, Steve *227*
   Earlier sketch in SATA *197*
Smalls, Irene
   See Smalls-Hector, Irene
Smalls-Hector, Irene 1950- *146*
   Earlier sketch in SATA *73*
   See also CLR 103
Smallwood, Norah (Evelyn) 1910(?)-1984
   Obituary *41*
Smaridge, Norah (Antoinette) 1903-1994 ...... *6*
Smath, Jerry 1933- *198*

Smee, Nicola 1948- *167*
  Earlier sketch in SATA 76
Smiley, Virginia Kester 1923- *2*
Smit, Noelle 1972- *199*
Smith, Alexander McCall 1948- *179*
  Earlier sketch in SATA 73
Smith, Andrew 1959- *209*
Smith, Andrew Anselmo
  See Smith, Andrew
Smith, Andy J. 1975- *207*
Smith, Anne Warren 1938- *41*
  Brief entry *34*
Smith, Barry (Edward Jervis) 1943- *75*
Smith, Beatrice S(chillinger) *12*
Smith, Betsy Covington 1937- *55*
  Earlier sketch in SATA 43
Smith, Betty (Wehner) 1904-1972 .... *6*
Smith, Bradford 1909-1964 .... *5*
Smith, Brenda 1946- *82*
Smith, C. Pritchard
  See Hoyt, Edwin P(almer), Jr.
Smith, Caesar
  See Trevor, Elleston
Smith, Cat Bowman 1939- *201*
Smith, Charles R., Jr. 1969- *203*
  Earlier sketch in SATA 159
Smith, Craig 1955- *172*
  Earlier sketches in SATA 81, 117
Smith, Cynthia Leitich 1967- *215*
  Earlier sketch in SATA 152
Smith, D. James 1955- *176*
Smith, Danna *216*
Smith, Danna Kessimakis
  See Smith, Danna
Smith, Datus C(lifford), Jr. 1907-1999 .... *13*
  Obituary *116*
Smith, Debra 1955- *89*
Smith, Derek 1943- *141*
Smith, Dick King
  See King-Smith, Dick
Smith, D.J.
  See Smith, D. James
Smith, Dodie
  See Smith, Dorothy Gladys
Smith, Doris Buchanan 1934-2002 .... *75*
  Obituary *140*
  Earlier sketch in SATA 28
  See also SAAS 10
Smith, Dorothy Gladys 1896-1990 .... *82*
  Obituary *65*
Smith, Dorothy Stafford 1905- *6*
Smith, Duane 1974- *202*
Smith, E(lmer) Boyd 1860-1943
  See YABC 1
Smith, E(dric) Brooks 1917- *40*
Smith, Elwood H. 1941- *236*
  Earlier sketch in SATA 203
Smith, Emily Wing 1980- *215*
Smith, Emma 1923- *52*
  Brief entry *36*
Smith, (Katherine) Eunice (Young)
  1902-1993 .... *5*
Smith, Frances C(hristine) 1904-1986 .... *3*
Smith, Gary R. 1932- *14*
Smith, Geof 1969- *102*
Smith, George Harmon 1920- *5*
Smith, Gordon 1951- *184*
Smith, Greg Leitich *152*
Smith, H(arry) Allen 1907-1976
  Obituary *20*
Smith, Helene 1937- *142*
Smith, Hope Anita *202*
Smith, Howard E(verett), Jr. 1927- *12*
Smith, Hugh L(etcher) 1921-1968 .... *5*
Smith, Icy 1966- *228*
Smith, Imogene Henderson 1922- *12*
Smith, Jacqueline B. 1937- *39*
Smith, Jada Pinkett 1971- *161*
Smith, James Noel 1950- *193*
Smith, Janet (Buchanan) Adam
  See Adam Smith, Janet (Buchanan)

Smith, Janice Lee 1949- *155*
  Earlier sketch in SATA 54
Smith, Jean
  See Smith, Frances C(hristine)
Smith, Jean Pajot 1945- *10*
Smith, Jeff 1958- *161*
  Earlier sketch in SATA 93
Smith, Jeff Allen
  See Smith, Jeff
Smith, Jeffrey Alan
  See Smith, Jeff
Smith, Jenny 1963- *90*
Smith, Jessie
  See Kunhardt, Edith
Smith, Jessie Willcox 1863-1935 .... *21*
  See also CLR 59
Smith, Jim W.W. *231*
Smith, Joan (Mary) 1933- *54*
  Brief entry *46*
Smith, Johnston
  See Crane, Stephen
Smith, Jos A. 1936- *181*
  Earlier sketches in SATA 73, 120
Smith, Joseph Arthur
  See Smith, Jos A.
Smith, Judie R. 1936- *80*
Smith, Kirsten 1970- *210*
Smith, Lafayette
  See Higdon, Hal
Smith, Lane 1959- *224*
  Earlier sketches in SATA 76, 131, 179
  See also CLR 47
Smith, Lee
  See Albion, Lee Smith
Smith, Lendon H(oward) 1921- *64*
Smith, Lillian H(elena) 1887-1983
  Obituary *32*
Smith, Linda 1949- *177*
Smith, Linell Nash 1932- *2*
Smith, Lucia B. 1943- *30*
Smith, Maggie 1965- *235*
  Earlier sketch in SATA 190
Smith, Margaret Emily Noel Nuttall
  See Nuttall-Smith, Margaret Emily Noel
Smith, Marion Hagens 1913- *12*
Smith, Marion Jaques 1899-1987 .... *13*
Smith, Mary Ellen *10*
Smith, Marya 1945- *78*
Smith, Mike
  See Smith, Mary Ellen
Smith, Nancy Covert 1935- *12*
Smith, Norman F. 1920- *70*
  Earlier sketch in SATA 5
Smith, Patricia Clark 1943- *96*
Smith, Pauline C.
  See Arthur, Robert, (Jr.)
Smith, Pauline C(oggeshall) 1908-1994 .... *27*
Smith, Philip Warren 1936- *46*
Smith, R. Alexander McCall
  See Smith, Alexander McCall
Smith, Rebecca 1946- *123*
Smith, Robert Kimmel 1930- *77*
  Earlier sketch in SATA 12
Smith, Robert Paul 1915-1977 .... *52*
  Obituary *30*
Smith, Roland 1951- *193*
  Earlier sketches in SATA 115, 161
Smith, Rosamond
  See Oates, Joyce Carol
Smith, Ruth Leslie 1902- *2*
Smith, Samantha 1972-1985
  Obituary *45*
Smith, Sandra Lee 1945- *75*
Smith, Sarah Stafford
  See Smith, Dorothy Stafford
Smith, Sharon 1947- *82*
Smith, Sherri L. 1971- *156*
Smith, Sherwood 1951- *206*
  Autobiography Feature *206*
  Earlier sketches in SATA 82, 140

Smith, Shirley Raines
  See Raines, Shirley C(arol)
Smith, Susan Carlton 1923- *12*
Smith, Susan Mathias 1950- *43*
  Brief entry *35*
Smith, Susan Vernon 1950- *48*
  Brief entry *45*
Smith, Tim(othy R.) 1945- *151*
Smith, Ursula 1934- *54*
Smith, Vian (Crocker) 1920-1969 .... *11*
Smith, Wanda VanHoy 1926- *65*
Smith, Ward
  See Goldsmith, Howard
Smith, Wendy
  See French, Wendy
Smith, William A. 1918- *10*
Smith, William Jay 1918- *154*
  Autobiography Feature *154*
  Earlier sketches in SATA 2, 68
  See also SAAS 22
Smith, Winsome 1935- *45*
Smith, Z.Z.
  See Westheimer, David
Smith-Ankrom, M. E. 1942- *130*
Smith-Griswold, Wendy 1955- *88*
Smith Hernandez, Duncan Tonatiuh
  See Tonatiuh, Duncan
Smith-Rex, Susan J. 1950- *94*
Smithsen, Richard
  See Pellowski, Michael (Joseph)
Smithson, Ryan 1985- *216*
Smits, Teo
  See Smits, Theodore R(ichard)
Smits, Theodore R(ichard) 1905-1996 .... *45*
  Brief entry *28*
Smolinski, Dick 1932- *86*
Smothers, Ethel Footman 1944- *149*
  Earlier sketch in SATA 76
Smucker, Anna Egan 1948- *209*
Smucker, Barbara 1915-2003 .... *130*
  Earlier sketches in SATA 29, 76
  See also CLR 10
  See also SAAS 11
Smucker, Barbara Claassen
  See Smucker, Barbara
Smyth, Iain 1959- *105*
Snedeker, Caroline Dale (Parke) 1871-1956
  See YABC 2
Sneed, Brad *191*
Sneider, Marian 1932-2005 .... *197*
Snell, Gordon 1933(?)- *228*
Snell, Nigel (Edward Creagh) 1936- *57*
  Brief entry *40*
Snellgrove, L(aurence) E(rnest) 1928- *53*
Snelling, Dennis (Wayne) 1958- *84*
Sneve, Virginia Driving Hawk 1933- *95*
  Earlier sketch in SATA 8
  See also CLR 2
Snicket, Lemony 1970- *215*
  Earlier sketches in SATA 126, 187
  See also CLR 79
Sniegoski, Thomas E. *195*
Sniegoski, Tom
  See Sniegoski, Thomas E.
Snir, Eleyor *225*
Snir, Mirik 1948- *226*
Snodgrass, Mary Ellen 1944- *75*
Snodgrass, Quentin Curtius
  See Twain, Mark
Snodgrass, Thomas Jefferson
  See Twain, Mark
Snook, Barbara (Lillian) 1913-1976 .... *34*
Snow, Alan 1959- *190*
Snow, Carol 1965- *208*
Snow, Donald Clifford 1917-1979 .... *16*
Snow, Dorothea J(ohnston) 1909- *9*
Snow, Richard F. 1947- *52*
  Brief entry *37*
Snow, Richard Folger
  See Snow, Richard F.
Snow, Sarah *229*

Author Index

Snyder, Anne 1922-2001 4
   Obituary *125*
Snyder, Bernadette McCarver 1930- *97*
Snyder, Betsy *230*
Snyder, Carol 1941- *35*
Snyder, Gerald S(eymour) 1933- *48*
   Brief entry *34*
Snyder, Jerome 1916-1976
   Obituary *20*
Snyder, Laurel 1974- *209*
Snyder, Midori 1954- *106*
Snyder, Paul A. 1946- *125*
Snyder, Zilpha Keatley 1927- *226*
   Autobiography Feature *163*
   Earlier sketches in SATA *1, 28, 75, 110, 163*
   See also CLR *121*
   See also SAAS *2*
Snyderman, Reuven K. 1922- 5
So, Meilo *162*
Sobel, June 1950- *149*
Soble, Jennie
   See Cavin, Ruth
Sobol, Donald J. 1924- *132*
   Earlier sketches in SATA *1, 31, 73*
   See also CLR *4*
Sobol, Harriet Langsam 1936- *47*
   Brief entry *34*
Sobol, Richard *211*
Sobol, Rose 1931- *76*
Sobott-Mogwe, Gaele 1956- *97*
Soderberg, Erin Kate
   See Downing, Erin
Soderlind, Arthur E(dwin) 1920- *14*
Soentpiet, Chris K. 1970- *159*
   Earlier sketch in SATA *97*
Soerensen, Svend Otto 1916- *67*
Sofer, Barbara 1949- *109*
Sofer, Rachel
   See Sofer, Barbara
Softly, Barbara Frewin 1924- *12*
Sogabe, Aki *207*
Soglow, Otto 1900-1975
   Obituary *30*
Sohl, Frederic J(ohn) 1916- *10*
Sohr, Daniel 1973- *190*
Sokol, Bill
   See Sokol, William
Sokol, William 1923- *37*
Sokolov, Kirill 1930- *34*
Solbert, Romaine G. 1925- 2
Solbert, Ronni
   See Solbert, Romaine G.
Solheim, James *233*
   Earlier sketch in SATA *133*
Solomon, Heather M. *188*
Solomon, Joan 1930- *51*
   Brief entry *40*
Solomons, Ikey Esquir
   See Thackeray, William Makepeace
Solonevich, George 1915-2003 .... *15*
Solot, Mary Lynn 1939- *12*
Solov'ev, Mikhail
   See Soloviov, Michael
Soloviov, Michael 1972- *222*
Soman, David 1965- *200*
Somerlott, Robert 1928-2001 .... *62*
Somers, Kevin *205*
Somervill, Barbara A(nn) 1948- *140*
Sommer, Angela
   See Sommer-Bodenburg, Angela
Sommer, Carl 1930- *175*
   Earlier sketch in SATA *126*
Sommer, Elyse 1929- 7
Sommer, Robert 1929- *12*
Sommer-Bodenburg, Angela 1948- *113*
   Earlier sketch in SATA *63*
Sommerdorf, Norma 1926- *131*
Sommerdorf, Norma Jean
   See Sommerdorf, Norma
Sommerfelt, Aimee 1892-1975 5
Son, John *160*

Sones, Sonya *131*
Sonneborn, Ruth (Cantor) 1899-1974 4
   Obituary *27*
Sonnenblick, Jordan 1969- *223*
   Earlier sketch in SATA *185*
   See also CLR *144*
Sonnenmark, Laura A. 1958- *73*
Soo, Kean *201*
Sopko, Eugen 1949- *58*
Sorel, Edward 1929- *126*
   Brief entry *37*
   Earlier sketch in SATA *65*
Sorensen, Henri 1950- *115*
   Earlier sketch in SATA *77*
Sorensen, Svend Otto
   See Soerensen, Svend Otto
Sorensen, Virginia 1912-1991 2
   Obituary *72*
   See also SAAS *15*
Sorenson, Jane 1926- *63*
Sorenson, Margo 1946- *96*
Sorley Walker, Kathrine *41*
Sorra, Kristin *185*
Sorrells, Walter *177*
Sorrentino, Joseph N. 1937- 6
Sortor, June Elizabeth 1939- *12*
Sortor, Toni
   See Sortor, June Elizabeth
Sosa, Hernan 1977- *203*
Soskin, V. H.
   See Ellison, Virginia H(owell)
Soto, Gary 1952- *174*
   Earlier sketches in SATA *80, 120*
   See also CLR *38*
Sotomayor, Antonio 1902-1985 .... *11*
Souci, Robert D. San
   See San Souci, Robert D.
Souders, Taryn 1977- *237*
Soudley, Henry
   See Wood, James Playsted
Souhami, Jessica *176*
Soule, Gardner (Bosworth) 1913-2000 .... *14*
Soule, Jean Conder 1919- *10*
Soup, Cuthbert
   See Swallow, Gerry
Souster, (Holmes) Raymond 1921- *63*
South, Sheri Cobb 1959- *82*
Southall, Ivan 1921-2008 .... *134*
   Autobiography Feature *134*
   Earlier sketches in SATA *3, 68*
   See also CLR *165*
   See also SAAS *3*
Southall, Ivan Francis
   See Southall, Ivan
Southey, Robert 1774-1843 .... *54*
Southgate, Vera *54*
Souza, Janet
   See Tashjian, Janet
Sovak, Jan 1953- *115*
Sowden, Celeste
   See Walters, Celeste
Sowter, Nita *69*
Spafford, Suzy 1945- *160*
Spagnoli, Cathy 1950- *134*
   Earlier sketch in SATA *79*
Spain, Sahara Sunday 1991- *133*
Spain, Susan Rosson *185*
Spalding, Andrea 1944- *150*
   Earlier sketch in SATA *101*
Spalenka, Greg 1958- *198*
Spanfeller, James J. 1930- *19*
   See also SAAS *8*
Spanfeller, Jim
   See Spanfeller, James J.
Spangenberg, Judith Dunn 1942- 5
Spangler, Brie *212*
Spanyol, Jessica 1965- *206*
   Earlier sketch in SATA *137*
Spar, Jerome 1918- *10*
Sparks, Barbara 1942- *78*

Sparks, Beatrice (Mathews) 1918- *44*
   Brief entry *28*
   See also CLR *139*
Sparks, Mary W. 1920- *15*
Spaulding, Douglas
   See Bradbury, Ray
Spaulding, Leonard
   See Bradbury, Ray
Spaulding, Norma *107*
Speare, Elizabeth George 1908-1994 .... *62*
   Obituary *83*
   Earlier sketch in SATA *5*
   See also CLR *8*
Spearing, Craig J. *228*
Spearing, Judith (Mary Harlow) 1922- 9
Spears, Rick *182*
Speck, Katie *196*
Speck, Nancy 1959- *104*
Specking, Inez 1890-1960(?) *11*
Speed, Nell
   See Keats, Emma
   and Sampson, Emma (Keats) Speed
Speed, Nell (Ewing) 1878-1913 .... *68*
Speer, Bonnie Stahlman 1929- *113*
Speer-Lyon, Tammie L. 1965- *89*
Speicher, Helen Ross S(mith) 1915- *8*
Speir, Nancy 1958- *210*
   Earlier sketch in SATA *81*
Spelling, Tori 1973- *236*
Spelling, Victoria Davey
   See Spelling, Tori
Spellman, John W(illard) 1934- *14*
Spellman, Roger G.
   See Cox, William R(obert)
Spelman, Cornelia Maude 1946- *144*
   Earlier sketch in SATA *96*
Spelman, Mary 1934- *28*
Spelvin, George
   See Lerangis, Peter
   and Phillips, David Atlee
Spence, Cynthia
   See Eble, Diane
Spence, Eleanor (Rachel) 1928- *21*
   See also CLR *26*
Spence, Geraldine 1931- *47*
Spencer, Ann 1918- *10*
Spencer, Britt *206*
Spencer, Cornelia
   See Yaukey, Grace S(ydenstricker)
Spencer, Donald D(ean) 1931- *41*
Spencer, Elizabeth 1921- *14*
Spencer, Leonard G.
   See Garrett, Randall
   and Silverberg, Robert
Spencer, William 1922- 9
Spencer, Zane A(nn) 1935- *35*
Spengler, Margaret *223*
Sper, Emily 1957- *142*
Speregen, Devra Newberger 1964- *84*
Sperling, Dan(iel Lee) 1949- *65*
Sperry, Armstrong W. 1897-1976 1
   Obituary *27*
Sperry, Raymond
   See Garis, Howard R.
Sperry, Raymond, Jr. 1
Spetter, Jung-Hee 1969- *134*
Spicer, Dorothy Gladys -1975 .... *32*
Spiegel, Beth *184*
Spiegelman, Art 1948- *158*
   Earlier sketch in SATA *109*
Spiegelman, Judith M. 5
Spielberg, Steven 1947- *32*
Spier, Peter (Edward) 1927- *54*
   Earlier sketch in SATA *4*
   See also CLR *5*
Spilhaus, Athelstan (Frederick) 1911-1998 .. *13*
   Obituary *102*
Spilka, Arnold 1917- 6
Spillane, Frank Morrison
   See Spillane, Mickey

Spillane, Mickey 1918-2006 .... *66*
  Obituary *176*
Spillebeen, Geert 1956- *225*
Spinelli, Eileen 1942- *225*
  Earlier sketches in SATA *38, 101, 150, 186*
Spinelli, Jerry 1941- *195*
  Earlier sketches in SATA *39, 71, 110, 158*
  See also CLR *82*
Spink, Reginald (William) 1905-1994 .... *11*
Spinka, Penina Keen 1945- *72*
Spinner, Stephanie 1943- *234*
  Earlier sketches in SATA *38, 91, 132*
Spinossimus
  See White, William, Jr.
Spiotta-DiMare, Loren *173*
Spires, Ashley 1978- *183*
Spires, Elizabeth 1952- *215*
  Earlier sketches in SATA *71, 111*
Spiridellis, Gregg 1971(?)- *199*
Spirin, Gennadii
  See Spirin, Gennady
Spirin, Gennadij
  See Spirin, Gennady
Spirin, Gennady 1948- *204*
  Earlier sketches in SATA *95, 134*
  See also CLR *88*
Spiro, Ruth *208*
Spivak, Dawnine *101*
Spizman, Robyn Freedman *194*
Spohn, David 1948- *72*
Spohn, Kate 1962- *147*
  Earlier sketch in SATA *87*
Spollen, Christopher 1952- *12*
Spooner, Michael (Tim) 1954- *92*
Spoor, Mike *218*
Spowart, Robin 1947- *177*
  Earlier sketch in SATA *82*
Spradlin, Michael P. *235*
  Earlier sketch in SATA *204*
Sprague, Gretchen 1926-2003 .... *27*
Spranger, Nina 1969- *203*
Spratt, R.A. *235*
Spratt, Rachel
  See Spratt, R.A.
Sprengel, Artie
  See Lerangis, Peter
Sprigge, Elizabeth (Miriam Squire)
  1900-1974 .... *10*
Spring, (Robert) Howard 1889-1965 .... *28*
Springer, Kristina *226*
Springer, Margaret 1941- *78*
Springer, Marilyn Harris 1931- *47*
Springer, Nancy 1948- *222*
  Earlier sketches in SATA *65, 110, 172*
Springstubb, Tricia 1950- *78*
  Brief entry *40*
  Earlier sketch in SATA *46*
Spudvilas, Anne 1951- *199*
  Earlier sketch in SATA *94*
Spurll, Barbara 1952- *78*
Spurr, Elizabeth *172*
Spykman, E(lizabeth) C(hoate) 1896-1965 .. *10*
  See also CLR *35*
Spyri, Johanna (Heusser) 1827-1901 .... *100*
  Earlier sketch in SATA *19*
  See also CLR *115*
Squires, Janet *215*
Squires, Phil
  See Barker, S. Omar
Srba, Lynne *98*
Sreenivasan, Jyotsna 1964- *101*
S-Ringi, Kjell
  See Ringi, Kjell (Arne Soerensen)
Staake, Bob 1957- *209*
Stacey, Cherylyn 1945- *96*
Stacy, Donald
  See Pohl, Frederik
Stadler, John *204*
Stadtler, Bea 1921- *17*
Stafford, Jean 1915-1979
  Obituary *22*

Stafford, Liliana 1950- *141*
Stafford, Paul 1966- *116*
Stahl, Ben(jamin) 1910-1987 .... *5*
  Obituary *54*
Stahl, Hilda 1938-1993 .... *48*
  Obituary *77*
Stahler, David, Jr. *218*
  Earlier sketch in SATA *162*
Staib, Walter *233*
Staines, Bill 1949- *213*
Stainton, Sue *187*
Stair, Gobin (John) 1912- *35*
Stalder, Valerie *27*
Stamaty, Mark Alan 1947- *230*
  Earlier sketch in SATA *12*
Stambler, Irwin 1924- *5*
Stamp, Jorgen 1969- *225*
Stampler, Ann Redisch *209*
Standiford, Natalie 1961- *169*
  Earlier sketch in SATA *81*
Stanek, Lou Willett 1931- *63*
Stang, Judit 1921-1977 .... *29*
Stang, Judy
  See Stang, Judit
Stangl, (Mary) Jean 1928- *67*
Stanhope, Eric
  See Hamilton, Charles (Harold St. John)
Stankevich, Boris 1928- *2*
Stanley, Diane 1943- *213*
  Brief entry *32*
  Earlier sketches in SATA *37, 80, 115, 164*
  See also CLR *46*
  See also SAAS *15*
Stanley, Elizabeth 1947- *206*
Stanley, George Edward 1942-2011 .... *228*
  Earlier sketches in SATA *53, 111, 157, 1, 67*
Stanley, Jerry 1941- *127*
  Earlier sketch in SATA *79*
Stanley, Mandy *165*
Stanley, Robert
  See Hamilton, Charles (Harold St. John)
Stanley, Sanna 1962- *145*
Stanli, Sue
  See Meilach, Dona Z(weigoron)
Stanstead, John
  See Groom, Arthur William
Stanton, Karen 1960- *190*
Stanton, Schuyler
  See Baum, L. Frank
Staples, Suzanne Fisher 1945- *207*
  Earlier sketches in SATA *70, 105, 151*
  See also CLR *137*
Stapleton, Marjorie (Winifred) 1932- ... *28*
Stapp, Arthur D(onald) 1906-1972 .... *4*
Starbird, Kaye 1916- *6*
  See also CLR *60*
Stark, Evan 1942- *78*
Stark, James
  See Goldston, Robert (Conroy)
Stark, Ken 1943- *199*
Stark, Ulf 1944- *124*
Starke, Ruth (Elaine) 1946- *129*
Starkey, Marion L(ena) 1901-1991 .... *13*
Starmer, Aaron 1976- *226*
Starr, Ward
  See Manes, Stephen
Starret, William
  See McClintock, Marshall
Starr Taylor, Bridget 1959- *99*
Stasiak, Krystyna *49*
Staub, Frank 1949- *116*
Staub, Frank Jacob
  See Staub, Frank
Staub, Wendy Corsi 1964- *114*
Stauffacher, Sue 1961- *236*
  Earlier sketches in SATA *155, 199*
Stauffer, Don
  See Berkebile, Fred D(onovan)
Staunton, Schuyler
  See Baum, L. Frank

Staunton, Ted 1956- *167*
  Earlier sketch in SATA *112*
Stead, Erin E. 1982- *232*
Stead, Judy *210*
Stead, Philip C.
  See Stringer, Helen
Stead, Philip Christian *225*
Stead, Rebecca 1968(?)- *228*
  Earlier sketch in SATA *188*
Steadman, Ralph 1936- *123*
  Earlier sketch in SATA *32*
Steadman, Ralph Idris
  See Steadman, Ralph
Stearman, Kaye 1951- *118*
Stearn, Ted 1961- *218*
Stearns, Monroe (Mather) 1913-1987 .... *5*
  Obituary *55*
Steckler, Arthur 1921-1985 .... *65*
Steding, Laurie 1953- *119*
Steel, Danielle 1947- *66*
Steel, Danielle Fernande
  See Steel, Danielle
Steele, Addison II
  See Lupoff, Richard A.
Steele, Alexander 1958- *116*
Steele, Henry Maxwell
  See Steele, Max
Steele, Mary 1930- *94*
Steele, Mary Q(uintard Govan) 1922-1992 .. *51*
  Obituary *72*
  Earlier sketch in SATA *3*
Steele, Max 1922-2005 .... *168*
  Earlier sketch in SATA *10*
Steele, Philip 1948- *140*
  Earlier sketch in SATA *81*
Steele, William O(wen) 1917-1979 .... *51*
  Obituary *27*
  Earlier sketch in SATA *1*
Steelhammer, Ilona 1952- *98*
Steelsmith, Shari 1962- *72*
Stefanik, Alfred T. 1939- *55*
Steffanson, Con
  See Cassiday, Bruce (Bingham)
  and Goulart, Ron
Steffens, Bradley 1955- *166*
  Earlier sketch in SATA *77*
Steffensmeier, Alexander 1977- *195*
Stegeman, Janet Allais 1923- *49*
  Brief entry *49*
Steggall, Susan 1967- *182*
Steig, William 1907-2003 .... *111*
  Obituary *149*
  Earlier sketches in SATA *18, 70*
  See also CLR *103*
Steig, William H.
  See Steig, William
Stein, David Ezra *211*
  Earlier sketch in SATA *180*
Stein, Janet 1955- *218*
Stein, M(eyer) L(ewis) 1920- *6*
Stein, Mathilde 1969- *195*
Stein, Mini *2*
Stein, R(ichard) Conrad 1937- *154*
  Earlier sketches in SATA *31, 82*
Stein, Wendy 1951- *77*
Steinbeck, John 1902-1968 .... *9*
  See also CLR *172*
Steinbeck, John Ernst
  See Steinbeck, John
Steinberg, Alfred 1917-1995 .... *9*
Steinberg, David 1962- *200*
Steinberg, D.J.
  See Steinberg, David
Steinberg, Fannie 1899-1990 .... *43*
Steinberg, Fred J. 1933- *4*
Steinberg, Phillip Orso 1921- *34*
Steinberg, Rafael (Mark) 1927- *45*
Steinberg, Saul 1914-1999 .... *67*
Steincrohn, Maggie
  See Davis, Maggie S.

Steiner, Barbara A(nnette) 1934- 83
  Earlier sketch in SATA *13*
  See also SAAS *13*
Steiner, Charlotte 1900-1981 45
Steiner, George 1929- 62
Steiner, Joan 199
  Earlier sketch in SATA *110*
Steiner, Jorg
  See Steiner, Jorg
Steiner, Jorg 1930- 35
Steiner, K. Leslie
  See Delany, Samuel R., Jr.
Steiner, Stan(ley) 1925-1987 14
  Obituary 50
Steinmetz, Karen 235
Steins, Richard 1942- 79
Stem, Jacqueline 1931- 110
Stemple, Heidi E.Y. 1966- 214
Stemple, Jason 179
Steneman, Shep 1945- 132
Stengel, Joyce A. 1938- 158
Stephanie, Gordon
  See Gordon, Stephanie Jacob
Stephens, Alice Barber 1858-1932 66
Stephens, Casey
  See Wagner, Sharon B.
Stephens, Helen 1972- 234
Stephens, Henrietta Henkle 1909-1993 6
Stephens, J.B.
  See Lynn, Tracy
Stephens, Mary Jo 1935- 8
Stephens, Rebecca 1961- 141
Stephens, Reed
  See Donaldson, Stephen R.
Stephens, Suzanne
  See Kirby, Susan E.
Stephens, William M(cLain) 1925- 21
Stephensen, A. M.
  See Manes, Stephen
Stephenson, Kristina 224
Stephenson, Lynda 1941- 179
Stephenson, Lynda A.
  See Stephenson, Lynda
Stepp, Ann 1935- 29
Stepto, Michele 1946- 61
Steptoe, Javaka 1971- 213
  Earlier sketch in SATA *151*
Steptoe, John (Lewis) 1950-1989 63
  Earlier sketch in SATA *8*
  See also CLR *12*
Sterling, Brett
  See Bradbury, Ray
  and Hamilton, Edmond
  and Samachson, Joseph
Sterling, Dorothy 1913-2008 83
  Autobiography Feature 127
  Obituary 200
  Earlier sketch in SATA *1*
  See also CLR *1*
  See also SAAS *2*
Sterling, Helen
  See Watts, Helen L. Hoke
Sterling, Philip 1907-1989 8
  Obituary 63
Sterling, Shirley (Anne) 1948- 101
Stern, Ellen Norman 1927- 26
Stern, Judith M. 1951- 75
Stern, Madeleine
  See Stern, Madeleine B.
Stern, Madeleine B. 1912-2007 14
Stern, Madeleine Bettina
  See Stern, Madeleine B.
Stern, Maggie 1953- 156
Stern, Philip Van Doren 1900-1984 13
  Obituary 39
Stern, Simon 1943- 15
Sterne, Emma Gelders 1894- 6
Steurt, Marjorie Rankin 1888-1978 10
Stevens, April 1963- 208
Stevens, Bryna 1924- 65
Stevens, Carla M(cBride) 1928- 13

Stevens, Chambers 1968- 128
Stevens, Diane 1939- 94
Stevens, Franklin 1933- 6
Stevens, Greg
  See Cook, Glen
Stevens, Gwendolyn 1944- 33
Stevens, Helen 209
Stevens, Jan Romero 1953- 95
Stevens, Janet 1953- 193
  Earlier sketches in SATA *90, 148*
Stevens, Kathleen 1936- 49
Stevens, Leonard A. 1920- 67
Stevens, Lucile Vernon 1899-1994 59
Stevens, Margaret Dean
  See Aldrich, Bess Streeter
Stevens, Patricia Bunning 1931- 27
Stevens, Peter
  See Geis, Darlene Stern
Stevens, Serita 1949- 70
Stevens, Serita Deborah
  See Stevens, Serita
Stevens, Serita Mendelson
  See Stevens, Serita
Stevens, Shira
  See Stevens, Serita
Stevenson, Anna (M.) 1905- 12
Stevenson, Augusta 1869(?)-1976 2
  Obituary 26
Stevenson, Burton Egbert 1872-1962 25
Stevenson, Drew 1947- 60
Stevenson, Emma 207
Stevenson, Harvey 1960- 148
  Earlier sketch in SATA *80*
Stevenson, James 1929- 195
  Brief entry 34
  Earlier sketches in SATA *42, 71, 113, 161*
  See also CLR *17*
Stevenson, Janet 1913- 8
Stevenson, Robert Louis 1850-1894 100
  See also YABC *2*
  See also CLR *107*
Stevenson, Robert Louis Balfour
  See Stevenson, Robert Louis
Stevenson, Sucie
  See Stevenson, Sucie
Stevenson, Sucie 1956- 194
  Earlier sketch in SATA *104*
Stewart, A(gnes) C(harlotte) 15
Stewart, Amber 181
Stewart, Chantal 1945- 173
  Earlier sketch in SATA *121*
Stewart, Charles
  See Zurhorst, Charles (Stewart, Jr.)
Stewart, Eleanor
  See Porter, Eleanor H(odgman)
Stewart, Elisabeth J(ane) 1927- 93
Stewart, Elizabeth Laing 1907- 6
Stewart, Gail B. 1949- 141
Stewart, George Rippey 1895-1980 3
  Obituary 23
Stewart, Jennifer J. 1960- 128
Stewart, Jennifer Jenkins
  See Stewart, Jennifer J.
Stewart, Joel 211
  Earlier sketch in SATA *151*
Stewart, John 1920- 14
Stewart, Mary (Florence Elinor) 1916- 12
Stewart, Mary Rainbow
  See Stewart, Mary (Florence Elinor)
Stewart, Melissa 1968- 209
  Earlier sketches in SATA *111, 167*
Stewart, Paul 1955- 199
  Earlier sketches in SATA *114, 163*
Stewart, Robert Neil 1891-1972 7
Stewart, Sarah 143
Stewart, Scott
  See Zaffo, George J.
Stewart, Trenton Lee 1970- 216
Stewart, W(alter) P. 1924- 53
Stewart, Whitney 1959- 167
  Earlier sketch in SATA *92*

Stewig, John Warren 1937- 162
  Earlier sketches in SATA *26, 110*
Stickler, Soma Han 1942- 128
Stidworthy, John 1943- 63
Stiefvater, Maggie 1981- 237
Stiegemeyer, Julie 180
Stier, Catherine 198
Stiles, Martha Bennett 108
  Earlier sketch in SATA *6*
Still, James 1906-2001 29
  Obituary 127
Stille, Darlene R. 1942- 170
  Earlier sketch in SATA *126*
Stille, Darlene Ruth
  See Stille, Darlene R.
Stillerman, Marci 104
Stillerman, Robbie 1947- 12
Stilley, Frank 1918- 29
Stilton, Geronimo 158
Stimpson, Gerald
  See Mitchell, Adrian
Stimson, James 1964- 213
Stine, Catherine 165
Stine, G(eorge) Harry 1928-1997 136
  Earlier sketch in SATA *10*
Stine, Jovial Bob
  See Stine, R.L.
Stine, R.L. 1943- 194
  Earlier sketches in SATA *31, 76, 129*
  See also CLR *111*
Stine, Robert Lawrence
  See Stine, R.L.
Stinetorf, Louise (Allender) 1900-1992 10
Stinson, Kathy 1952- 98
Stirling, Arthur
  See Sinclair, Upton
Stirling, Ian 1941- 77
Stirling, Nora B(romley) 1900-1997 3
Stirnweis, Shannon 1931- 10
Stobbs, William 1914-2000 17
  Obituary 120
Stock, Carolmarie 1951- 75
Stock, Catherine 1952- 214
  Earlier sketches in SATA *65, 114, 158*
Stockdale, Susan 1954- 206
  Earlier sketch in SATA *98*
Stockham, Peter (Alan) 1928- 57
Stockton, Francis Richard 1834-1902 44
  Brief entry 32
Stockton, Frank R.
  See Stockton, Francis Richard
Stockwell-Moniz, Marc J. 1954- 164
Stoddard, Edward G. 1923- 10
Stoddard, Hope 1900-1987 6
Stoddard, Sandol 1927- 98
  Earlier sketch in SATA *14*
Stoehr, Shelley 1969- 107
Stoeke, Janet Morgan 1957- 202
  Earlier sketches in SATA *90, 136*
Stohl, Margaret 227
Stohner, Anu 1952- 179
Stoiko, Michael 1919- 14
Stojic, Manya 1967- 156
Stoker, Abraham
  See Stoker, Bram
Stoker, Bram 1847-1912 29
Stokes, Cedric
  See Beardmore, George
Stokes, Jack (Tilden) 1923- 13
Stokes, Olivia Pearl 1916- 32
Stolarz, Laurie Faria 1972- 203
Stolz, Mary 1920-2006 133
  Obituary 180
  Earlier sketches in SATA *10, 71*
  See also SAAS *3*
Stolz, Mary Slattery
  See Stolz, Mary
Stone, Alan
  See Svenson, Andrew E(dward)
Stone, David K(arl) 1922- 9
Stone, David Lee 1978- 166

Stone, Eugenia 1879-1971 7
Stone, Gene
  See Stone, Eugenia
Stone, Helen V(irginia) 6
Stone, Idella Purnell
  See Purnell, Idella
Stone, Ikey
  See Purnell, Idella
Stone, Irving 1903-1989 3
  Obituary 64
Stone, Jeff 178
Stone, Jon 1931-1997 39
  Obituary 95
Stone, Josephine Rector
  See Dixon, Jeanne
Stone, Kyle M. 1972- 202
Stone, Lesley
  See Trevor, Elleston
Stone, Mary Hanlon 231
Stone, Peter 1930-2003 65
  Obituary 143
Stone, Phoebe 205
  Earlier sketch in SATA *134*
Stone, Raymond 1
Stone, Rosetta
  See Dr. Seuss
Stone, Tanya Lee 1965- 217
  Earlier sketch in SATA *182*
Stonehouse, Bernard 1926- 140
  Earlier sketches in SATA *13, 80*
Stones, (Cyril) Anthony 1934- 72
Stong, Phil(ip Duffield) 1899-1957 32
Stoops, Erik D(aniel) 1966- 142
  Earlier sketch in SATA *78*
Stoppelmoore, Cheryl Jean
  See Ladd, Cheryl (Jean)
Stops, Sue 1936- 86
Storace, Patricia 193
Storad, Conrad J. 1957- 119
Storey, Margaret 1926- 9
Storey, Victoria Carolyn 1945- 16
Stork, Francisco
  See Stork, Francisco X.
Stork, Francisco X. 1953- 210
Storme, Peter
  See Stern, Philip Van Doren
Storms, Patricia 1963- 217
Storr, Catherine (Cole) 1913-2001 87
  Obituary 122
  Earlier sketch in SATA *9*
Story, Josephine
  See Loring, Emilie (Baker)
Stotko, Mary-Ann 1960- 154
Stott, Ann 219
Stott, Dorothy (M.) 1958- 99
  Earlier sketch in SATA *67*
Stott, Dot
  See Stott, Dorothy (M.)
Stotter, Mike 1957- 108
Stotts, Stuart 227
Stout, Shawn K. 226
Stout, William 1949- 132
Stoutenburg, Adrien (Pearl) 1916-1982 3
Stoutland, Allison 1963- 130
Stover, Allan C(arl) 1938- 14
Stover, Jill (Griffin) 1958- 82
Stover, Marjorie Filley 1914- 9
Stowe, Harriet Beecher 1811-1896
  See YABC *1*
  See also CLR *131*
Stowe, Harriet Elizabeth Beecher
  See Stowe, Harriet Beecher
Stowe, Leland 1899-1994 60
  Obituary 78
Stowe, Rosetta
  See Ogan, George F.
  and Ogan, Margaret E. (Nettles)
Stower, Adam 229
  Earlier sketch in SATA *195*
Strachan, Bruce 1959- 205
Strachan, Ian 1938- 85

Strachan, Linda 167
Strachan, Margaret Pitcairn 1908-1998 14
Strahinich, H. C.
  See Strahinich, Helen C.
Strahinich, Helen C. 1949- 78
Strait, Treva Adams 1909-2002 35
Strand, Mark 1934- 41
Strange, Philippa
  See Coury, Louise Andree
Stranger, Joyce
  See Wilson, Joyce M.
Strangis, Joel 1948- 124
Strannigan, Shawn 1956- 93
Strannigan, Shawn Alyne
  See Strannigan, Shawn
Strasnick, Lauren 222
Strasser, Todd 1950- 215
  Earlier sketches in SATA *41, 45, 71, 107, 153*
  See also CLR *11*
Stratemeyer, Edward L. 1862-1930 100
  Earlier sketches in SATA *1, 67*
  See also CLR *166*
  See Adams, Harrison
Stratford, Philip 1927- 47
Stratton, Allan 1951- 178
Stratton, J. M.
  See Whitlock, Ralph
Stratton, Thomas
  See Coulson, Robert S(tratton)
  and DeWeese, Thomas Eugene
Stratton-Porter, Gene 1863-1924 15
  See also CLR *87*
Strauss, Gwen 1963- 77
Strauss, Joyce 1936- 53
Strauss, Linda Leopold 1942- 127
Strauss, Susan (Elizabeth) 1954- 75
Strayer, E. Ward
  See Stratemeyer, Edward L.
Streano, Vince(nt Catello) 1945- 20
Streatfeild, Mary Noel
  See Streatfeild, Noel
Streatfeild, Noel 1897(?)-1986 20
  Obituary 48
  See also CLR *83*
Street, Janet Travell 1959- 84
Street, Julia Montgomery 1898-1993 11
Streissguth, Thomas 1958- 116
Strelkoff, Tatiana 1957- 89
Stren, Patti 1949- 88
  Brief entry 41
  See also CLR *5*
Strete, Craig Kee 1950- 96
  Earlier sketch in SATA *44*
Stretton, Barbara (Humphrey) 1936- 43
  Brief entry 35
Strickland, Brad 1947- 200
  Earlier sketches in SATA *83, 137, 142*
Strickland, Craig (A.) 1956- 102
Strickland, Dorothy S(alley) 1933- 89
Strickland, Michael R. 1965- 144
  Earlier sketch in SATA *83*
Strickland, Shadra 209
Strickland, Tessa 173
Strickland, William Bradley
  See Strickland, Brad
Striegel, Jana 1955- 140
Striegel-Wilson, Jana
  See Striegel, Jana
Striker, Lee
  See Clark, Margaret (D.)
Striker, Susan 1942- 63
Stringam, Jean 1945- 233
Stringer, Helen 225
Stringer, Lauren 1957- 183
  Earlier sketch in SATA *129*
Stroeyer, Poul 1923- 13
Stromoski, Rick 1958- 111
Strong, Charles
  See Epstein, Beryl
  and Epstein, Samuel

Strong, David
  See McGuire, Leslie (Sarah)
Strong, Jeremy 1949- 175
  Earlier sketches in SATA *36, 105*
Strong, J.J.
  See Strong, Jeremy
Strong, Pat
  See Hough, Richard (Alexander)
Strong, Stacie 1965- 74
Stroud, Bettye 1939- 165
  Earlier sketch in SATA *96*
Stroud, Jonathan 1970- 213
  Earlier sketches in SATA *102, 159*
  See also CLR *134*
Stroyer, Poul
  See Stroeyer, Poul
Strug, Kerri 1977- 108
Stryer, Andrea Stenn 1938- 192
Stryker, Daniel
  See Morris, Chris(topher Crosby)
  and Stump, Jane Barr
Stuart, David
  See Hoyt, Edwin P(almer), Jr.
Stuart, Derek
  See Foster, John L(ouis)
Stuart, Forbes 1924- 13
Stuart, Ian
  See MacLean, Alistair
Stuart, Jesse (Hilton) 1906-1984 2
  Obituary 36
Stuart, Ruth McEnery 1849(?)-1917 116
Stuart, Sheila
  See Baker, Mary Gladys Steel
Stuart-Clark, Christopher (Anthony) 1940- .. 32
Stuber, Barbara 1951- 234
Stubis, Talivaldis 1926- 5
Stubley, Trevor (Hugh) 1932- 22
Stuchner, Joan Betty 209
Stucky, Naomi R. 1922- 72
Stucley, Elizabeth
  See Northmore, Elizabeth Florence
Stultifer, Morton
  See Curtis, Richard
Sture-Vasa, Mary
  See Alsop, Mary O'Hara
Sturges, Philemon 174
Sturman, Jennifer 237
Sturtevant, Katherine 1950- 180
  Earlier sketch in SATA *130*
Sturton, Hugh
  See Johnston, H(ugh) A(nthony) S(tephen)
Sturtzel, Howard A(llison) 1894-1985 1
Sturtzel, Jane Levington 1903-1996 1
Stutley, D(oris) J(ean) 1959- 142
Stutson, Caroline 1940- 234
  Earlier sketch in SATA *104*
Stuve-Bodeen, Stephanie
  See Bodeen, S. A.
Stux, Erica 1929- 140
Styles, (Frank) Showell 1908- 10
Stynes, Barbara White 133
Suarez, Maribel 1952- 201
Suba, Susanne 4
Suber, Melissa 213
Subond, Valerie
  See Grayland, Valerie (Merle Spanner)
Sudbery, Rodie 1943- 42
Sudyka, Diana 208
Sue, Majella Lue 209
Suen, Anastasia 1956(?)- 157
Sufrin, Mark 1925- 76
Sugarman, Joan G. 1917- 64
Sugarman, Tracy 1921- 37
Sugita, Yutaka 1930- 36
Suhl, Yuri (Menachem) 1908-1986 8
  Obituary 50
  See also CLR *2*
  See also SAAS *1*
Suhr, Joanne 129
Suid, Murray 1942- 27
Sullivan, Edward T. 206

Sullivan, George (Edward) 1927- *147*
  Earlier sketches in SATA *4, 89*
Sullivan, Jacqueline Levering *203*
Sullivan, Jody
  See Rake, Jody
Sullivan, Kathryn A. 1954- *141*
Sullivan, Mary Ann 1954- *63*
Sullivan, Mary W(ilson) 1907- *13*
Sullivan, Pat
  See Messmer, Otto
Sullivan, Paul 1939- *106*
Sullivan, Sarah G. 1953- *179*
Sullivan, Silky 1940- *101*
Sullivan, Sue
  See Sullivan, Susan E.
Sullivan, Susan E. 1962- *123*
Sullivan, Thomas Joseph, Jr. 1947- *16*
Sullivan, Tom
  See Sullivan, Thomas Joseph, Jr.
Sully, Tom 1959- *104*
Suma, Nova Ren *223*
Sumichrast, Jozef 1948- *29*
Sumiko
  See Davies, Sumiko
Summerforest, Ivy B.
  See Kirkup, James
Summers, Barbara 1944- *182*
Summers, Cassia Joy
  See Cowley, Joy
Summers, James L(evingston) 1910-1973 .... *57*
  Brief entry *28*
Summertree, Katonah
  See Windsor, Patricia
Summy, Barrie *208*
Sumner, William 1971- *229*
Sun, Chyng Feng 1959- *90*
Sunderlin, Sylvia (S.) 1911-1997 .... *28*
  Obituary *99*
Sung, Betty Lee *26*
Supeene, Shelagh Lynne 1952- *153*
Supplee, Suzanne *204*
Supraner, Robyn 1930- *101*
  Earlier sketch in SATA *20*
Supree, Burt(on) 1941-1992 .... *73*
Surface, Mary Hall 1958- *126*
Surge, Frank 1931- *13*
Susac, Andrew 1929- *5*
Susi, Geraldine Lee 1942- *98*
Sussman, Cornelia Silver 1914-1999 .... *59*
Sussman, Irving 1908-1996 .... *59*
Sussman, Michael 1953- *217*
Sussman, Michael B.
  See Sussman, Michael
Sussman, Susan 1942- *48*
Sutcliff, Rosemary 1920-1992 .... *78*
  Obituary *73*
  Earlier sketches in SATA *6, 44*
  See also CLR *138*
Sutcliffe, Jane 1957- *138*
Sutherland, Colleen 1944- *79*
Sutherland, Efua (Theodora Morgue)
  1924-1996 .... *25*
Sutherland, Jon 1958- *167*
Sutherland, Jonathan D.
  See Sutherland, Jon
Sutherland, Jonathan David
  See Sutherland, Jon
Sutherland, Margaret 1941- *15*
Sutherland, Zena Bailey 1915-2002 .... *37*
  Obituary *137*
Suttles, Shirley (Smith) 1922- *21*
Sutton, Ann (Livesay) 1923- *31*
Sutton, Eve(lyn Mary) 1906-1992 .... *26*
Sutton, Felix 1910(?)-1973 .... *31*
Sutton, Jane 1950- *52*
  Brief entry *43*
Sutton, Larry M(atthew) 1931- *29*
Sutton, Margaret Beebe 1903-2001 .... *1*
  Obituary *131*
Sutton, Myron Daniel 1925- *31*
Sutton, Roger 1956- *93*

Sutton, Sally 1973- *214*
Suzanne, Jamie
  See Hawes, Louise
  and Lantz, Francess L(in)
  and Singleton, Linda Joy
  and Zach, Cheryl (Byrd)
Suzuki, David 1936- *138*
Suzuki, David Takayoshi
  See Suzuki, David
Svendsen, Mark 1962- *181*
  Earlier sketch in SATA *120*
Svendsen, Mark Nestor
  See Svendsen, Mark
Svenson, Andrew E(dward) 1910-1975 .... *2*
  Obituary *26*
Swaab, Neil 1978- *191*
Swaim, Jessica 1950- *202*
Swain, Carol 1962- *172*
Swain, Gwenyth 1961- *134*
  Earlier sketch in SATA *84*
Swain, Ruth
  See Swain, Ruth Freeman
Swain, Ruth Freeman 1951- *161*
  Earlier sketch in SATA *119*
Swain, Su Zan (Noguchi) 1916- *21*
Swain, Wilson 1976- *225*
Swallow, Gerry *227*
Swallow, Pamela Curtis *178*
Swamp, Jake 1941- *98*
Swan, Susan 1944- *108*
  Earlier sketch in SATA *22*
Swann, Brian (Stanley Frank) 1940- *116*
Swann, E.L.
  See Lasky, Kathryn
Swann, Ruth Rice 1920- *84*
Swanson, Diane 1944- *203*
Swanson, Helen M(cKendry) 1919- *94*
Swanson, June 1931- *76*
Swanson, Susan Marie *209*
Swanson, Wayne 1942- *167*
Swarner, Kristina 1965- *215*
Swarthout, Glendon (Fred) 1918-1992 .... *26*
Swarthout, Kathryn 1919- *7*
Swayne, Sam(uel F.) 1907- *53*
Swayne, Zoa (Lourana) 1905- *53*
Swearingen, Greg 1976- *225*
Sweat, Lynn 1934- *168*
  Earlier sketch in SATA *57*
Swede, George 1940- *67*
Sweeney, James B(artholomew) 1910-1999 . *21*
Sweeney, Joyce 1955- *167*
  Earlier sketches in SATA *65, 68, 108*
Sweeney, Joyce Kay
  See Sweeney, Joyce
Sweeney, Karen O'Connor
  See O'Connor, Karen
Sweeney, Matthew (Gerard) 1952- *156*
Sweet, Melissa 1956- *211*
  Earlier sketch in SATA *172*
Sweet, Sarah C.
  See Jewett, Sarah Orne
Sweetland, Nancy A(nn) 1934- *48*
Swender, Jennifer *235*
Swenson, Allan A(rmstrong) 1933- *21*
Swenson, May 1919-1989 .... *15*
Swentzell, Rina 1939- *79*
Swiatkowska, Gabi 1971(?)- *180*
Swift, Bryan
  See Knott, William C(ecil, Jr.)
Swift, David
  See Kaufmann, John
Swift, Hildegarde Hoyt 1890(?)-1977
  Obituary *20*
Swift, Jonathan 1667-1745 .... *19*
  See also CLR *161*
Swift, Merlin
  See Leeming, Joseph
Swiger, Elinor Porter 1927- *8*
Swinburne, Laurence (Joseph) 1924- *9*
Swinburne, Stephen R. 1952- *231*
  Earlier sketches in SATA *150, 188*

Swinburne, Steve
  See Swinburne, Stephen R.
Swindells, Robert (Edward) 1939- *150*
  Brief entry *34*
  Earlier sketches in SATA *50, 80*
  See also SAAS *14*
Swinford, Betty (June Wells) 1927- *58*
Swinford, Bob
  See Swinford, Betty (June Wells)
Swithen, John
  See King, Stephen
Switzer, Ellen 1923- *48*
Swope, Sam *156*
Swope, Samuel
  See Swope, Sam
Sybesma, Jetske
  See Ironside, Jetske
Sydney, Frank
  See Warwick, Alan R(oss)
Sydor, Colleen 1960- *207*
Sykes, Julie 1963- *202*
Sylvada, Peter 1964- *202*
Sylver, Adrienne *230*
Sylvester, Natalie G(abry) 1922- *22*
Syme, (Neville) Ronald 1913-1992 .... *87*
  Earlier sketch in SATA *2*
Symes, R. F. *77*
Symes, Ruth Louise 1962- *179*
Symons, (Dorothy) Geraldine 1909- *33*
Symons, Stuart
  See Stanley, George Edward
Symynkywicz, Jeffrey B. 1954- *87*
Symynkywicz, Jeffrey Bruce
  See Symynkywicz, Jeffrey B.
Synge, (Phyllis) Ursula 1930- *9*
Sypher, Lucy Johnston 1907- *7*
Szasz, Suzanne (Shorr) 1915-1997 .... *13*
  Obituary *99*
Szekeres, Cyndy 1933- *157*
  Autobiography Feature *157*
  Earlier sketches in SATA *5, 60, 131*
  See also SAAS *13*
Szekessy, Tanja *98*
Szpura, Beata 1961- *93*
Szuc, Jeff 1975- *220*
Szudek, Agnes S(usan) P(hilomena) *57*
  Brief entry *49*
Szulc, Tad 1926-2001 .... *26*
Szydlow, Jarl
  See Szydlowski, Mary Vigliante
Szydlowski, Mary Vigliante 1946- *94*
Szymanski, Lois 1957- *91*

T

Taback, Simms 1932- *170*
  Brief entry *36*
  Earlier sketches in SATA *40, 104*
  See also CLR *100*
Taber, Gladys (Bagg) 1899-1980
  Obituary *22*
Tabor, Nancy Maria Grande 1949- *161*
  Earlier sketch in SATA *89*
Tabrah, Ruth Milander 1921- *14*
Tacang, Brian *213*
Tackach, James 1953- *123*
Tackach, James M.
  See Tackach, James
Tadgell, Nicole 1969- *220*
  Earlier sketch in SATA *177*
Tafolla, Carmen 1951- *220*
Tafolla, Mary Carmen
  See Tafolla, Carmen
Tafuri, Nancy 1946- *192*
  Autobiography Feature *192*
  Earlier sketches in SATA *39, 75, 130*
  See also CLR *74*
  See also SAAS *14*
Tagg, Christine Elizabeth 1962- *138*

Tagliaferro, Linda *173*
Taha, Karen T(erry) 1942- *156*
  Earlier sketch in SATA *71*
Tai, Sharon O. 1963- *153*
Tait, Douglas 1944- *12*
Takabayashi, Mari 1960- *156*
  Earlier sketch in SATA *115*
Takahashi, Hideko *209*
Takahashi, Rumiko 1957- *163*
Takakjian, Portia 1930- *15*
Takashima, Misako
  See Misako Rocks!
Takashima, Shizuye 1928- *13*
Takayama, Sandi 1962- *106*
Takeda, Pete(r M.) 1964- *148*
Tal, Eve 1947- *176*
Talbert, Marc (Alan) 1953- *154*
  Autobiography Feature *154*
  Earlier sketches in SATA *68, 99*
Talbot, Charlene Joy 1928- *10*
Talbot, Toby 1928- *14*
Talbott, Hudson 1949- *212*
  Earlier sketches in SATA *84, 131*
Talifero, Gerald 1950- *75*
Talker, T.
  See Rands, William Brighty
Tallarico, Tony 1933- *116*
Tallcott, Emogene *10*
Tallec, Olivier 1970- *197*
Tallis, Robyn
  See Smith, Sherwood
Tallon, Robert 1939- *43*
  Brief entry *28*
Talmadge, Marian *14*
Tamaki, Jillian 1980- *201*
Tamar, Erika 1934- *150*
  Earlier sketches in SATA *62, 101*
Tamarin, Alfred H. 1913-1980 .... *13*
Tamburine, Jean 1930- *12*
Tames, Richard (Lawrence) 1946- *102*
  Earlier sketch in SATA *67*
Tamminga, Frederick W(illiam) 1934- *66*
Tammuz, Benjamin 1919-1989
  Obituary *63*
Tan, Amy 1952- *75*
Tan, Amy Ruth
  See Tan, Amy
Tan, Shaun 1974- *198*
Tanaka, Beatrice 1932- *76*
Tanaka, Shelley *214*
  Earlier sketch in SATA *136*
Tanaka, Yoko 1947- *215*
Tang, Charles 1948- *81*
Tang, Greg *172*
Tang, You-Shan 1946- *53*
Tania B.
  See Blixen, Karen
Tankard, Jeremy 1973- *191*
Tannen, Mary 1943- *37*
Tannenbaum, Beulah Goldstein 1916- *3*
Tannenbaum, D(onald) Leb 1948- *42*
Tanner, Jane 1946- *74*
Tanner, Lian 1951- *237*
Tanner, Louise S(tickney) 1922-2000 .... *9*
Tanobe, Miyuki 1937- *23*
Tanselle, Eve 1933- *125*
Tapio, Pat Decker
  See Kines, Pat Decker
Tapp, Kathy Kennedy 1949- *88*
  Brief entry *50*
Tarbescu, Edith 1939- *107*
Tarkington, (Newton) Booth 1869-1946 .... *17*
Tarpley, Natasha A(nastasia) 1971- *147*
Tarr, Judith 1955- *237*
  Earlier sketches in SATA *64, 149*
Tarry, Ellen 1906-2008 .... *16*
  See also CLR *26*
  See also SAAS *16*
Tarshis, Jerome 1936- *9*
Tarshis, Lauren *187*
Tarsky, Sue 1946- *41*

Taschek, Karen 1956- *185*
Tashjian, Jake 1994- *234*
Tashjian, Janet 1956- *151*
  Earlier sketch in SATA *102*
Tashjian, Virginia A. 1921-2008 .... *3*
Tasker, James 1908- *9*
Tate, Don(ald E.) *159*
Tate, Eleanora E. 1948- *191*
  Earlier sketches in SATA *38, 94*
  See also CLR *37*
Tate, Eleanora Elaine
  See Tate, Eleanora E.
Tate, Ellalice
  See Hibbert, Eleanor Alice Burford
Tate, Joan 1922- *86*
  Earlier sketch in SATA *9*
  See also SAAS *20*
Tate, Mary Anne
  See Hale, Arlene
Tate, Nikki *134*
Tate, Richard
  See Masters, Anthony (Richard)
Tate, Suzanne 1930- *91*
Tatham, Betty *142*
Tatham, Campbell
  See Elting, Mary
Tatham, Julie
  See Tatham, Julie Campbell
Tatham, Julie Campbell 1908-1999 .... *80*
Tavares, Matt *198*
  Earlier sketch in SATA *159*
Tavares, Victor 1971- *176*
Taves, Isabella 1915- *27*
Taxali, Gary 1968- *234*
Tayleur, Karen 1961- *213*
Taylor, Alastair 1959- *130*
Taylor, Andrew 1951- *70*
Taylor, Andrew John Robert
  See Taylor, Andrew
Taylor, Ann 1782-1866 .... *41*
  Brief entry *35*
Taylor, Audilee Boyd 1931- *59*
Taylor, Barbara J. 1927- *10*
Taylor, Ben
  See Strachan, Ian
Taylor, Brooke *205*
Taylor, Carl 1937-2010 .... *14*
Taylor, Carrie-Jo
  See Taylor, C.J.
Taylor, Cheryl Munro 1957- *96*
Taylor, C.J. 1952- *224*
Taylor, Cora (Lorraine) 1936- *103*
  Earlier sketch in SATA *64*
  See also CLR *63*
Taylor, Dave 1948- *78*
Taylor, David
  See Taylor, Dave
Taylor, David 1900-1965 .... *10*
Taylor, Debbie A. 1955- *169*
Taylor, Eleanor 1969- *206*
Taylor, Elizabeth 1912-1975 .... *13*
Taylor, Florance Walton *9*
Taylor, Florence M(arian Tompkins)
  1892-1983 .... *9*
Taylor, Gage 1942-2000 .... *87*
Taylor, Geoff 1946- *204*
Taylor, G.P. 1958(?)- *216*
  Earlier sketch in SATA *156*
Taylor, Graham Peter
  See Taylor, G.P.
Taylor, Greg 1951- *221*
Taylor, Herb(ert Norman, Jr.) 1942-1987 ..... *22*
  Obituary *54*
Taylor, J. David
  See Taylor, Dave
Taylor, Jane 1783-1824 .... *41*
  Brief entry *35*
Taylor, Jerry D(uncan) 1938- *47*
Taylor, John Robert
  See Taylor, Andrew

Taylor, Judy
  See Hough, Judy Taylor
Taylor, Kenneth N. 1917-2005 .... *26*
Taylor, Kenneth Nathaniel
  See Taylor, Kenneth N.
Taylor, Kim *180*
Taylor, L(ester) B(arbour), Jr. 1932- *27*
Taylor, Lois Dwight Cole
  See Cole, Lois Dwight
Taylor, Louise Todd 1939- *47*
Taylor, Margaret 1950- *106*
Taylor, Mark 1927- *32*
  Brief entry *28*
Taylor, Mildred D. 1943- *135*
  See also CLR *144*
  See also SAAS *5*
Taylor, Mildred Delois
  See Taylor, Mildred D.
Taylor, Paula (Wright) 1942- *48*
  Brief entry *33*
Taylor, Peter Lane *210*
Taylor, Robert Lewis 1912-1998 .... *10*
Taylor, Sean 1965- *192*
Taylor, Susan Champlin
  See Champlin, Susan
Taylor, Sydney (Brenner) 1904(?)-1978 .... *28*
  Obituary *26*
  Earlier sketch in SATA *1*
Taylor, Theodore 1921-2006 .... *128*
  Obituary *177*
  Earlier sketches in SATA *5, 54, 83*
  See also CLR *30*
  See also SAAS *4*
Taylor, William 1938- *164*
  Earlier sketches in SATA *78, 113*
  See also CLR *63*
Taylor-Butler, Christine 1959- *218*
Tazewell, Charles 1900-1972 .... *74*
Tchana, Katrin
  See Tchana, Katrin Hyman
Tchana, Katrin H.
  See Tchana, Katrin Hyman
Tchana, Katrin Hyman 1963- *177*
  Earlier sketch in SATA *125*
Tchekhov, Anton
  See Chekhov, Anton
Tchen, Richard *120*
Tchudi, Stephen N. 1942- *55*
Teague, Bob
  See Teague, Robert
Teague, David *235*
Teague, Mark 1963- *205*
  Earlier sketches in SATA *68, 99, 170*
Teague, Mark Christopher
  See Teague, Mark
Teague, Robert 1929- *32*
  Brief entry *31*
Teal, Val 1902-1997 .... *10*
  Obituary *114*
Teal, Valentine M.
  See Teal, Val
Teale, Edwin Way 1899-1980 .... *7*
  Obituary *25*
Teasdale, Sara 1884-1933 .... *32*
Tebbel, John (William) 1912-2004 .... *26*
Teckentrup, Britta 1969- *200*
Tedesco, P.R.
  See Naylor, Phyllis Reynolds
Teensma, Lynne Bertrand
  See Bertrand, Lynne
Tee-Van, Helen Damrosch 1893-1976 .... *10*
  Obituary *27*
Teevee, Ningeokuluk 1963- *223*
Tegner, Bruce 1928- *62*
Teitelbaum, Michael 1953- *116*
  Earlier sketch in SATA *59*
Tejima
  See Tejima, Keizaburo
Tejima, Keizaburo 1931- *139*
  See also CLR *20*
Telander, Todd (G.) 1967- *88*

Teleki, Geza 1943- 45
Telemaque, Eleanor Wong 1934- 43
Telescope, Tom
    See Newbery, John
Telgemeier, Raina 1977- 228
Tellegen, Toon 1941- 229
Teller, Janne 1964- 230
Tellis, Annabel 1967- 191
Temkin, Sara Anne Schlossberg 1913-1996 . 26
Temko, Florence 13
Tempest, Margaret Mary 1892-1982
    Obituary 33
Templar, Maurice
    See Groom, Arthur William
Temple, Arthur
    See Northcott, (William) Cecil
Temple, Charles 1947- 79
Temple, Frances (Nolting) 1945-1995 85
Temple, Herbert 1919- 45
Temple, Paul
    See McConnell, James Douglas Rutherford
Temple, William F(rederick) 1914-1989 107
Tenggren, Gustaf 1896-1970 18
    Obituary 26
Tennant, Kylie
    See Rodd, Kylie Tennant
Tennant, Veronica 1947- 36
TenNapel, Doug 1966- 234
Tenneshaw, S.M.
    See Beaumont, Charles
    and Garrett, Randall
    and Silverberg, Robert
Tenniel, John 1820-1914 74
    Brief entry 27
    See also CLR 146
Teplin, Scott 231
Tepper, Sheri S. 1929- 113
Tepper, Yona 1941- 228
Terada, Alice M. 1928- 90
Terban, Marvin 1940- 54
    Brief entry 45
Teresi, Judith M.
    See Goldberger, Judith M.
ter Haar, Jaap 1922- 6
    See also CLR 15
Terhune, Albert Payson 1872-1942 15
Terkel, Susan N(eiburg) 1948- 103
    Earlier sketch in SATA 59
Terlouw, Jan (Cornelis) 1931- 30
Terrazzini, Daniela Jaglenka 218
Terrell, John Upton 1900-1988
    Obituary 60
Terrill, Beth 198
Terrill, Elizabeth
    See Terrill, Beth
Terris, Susan 1937- 77
    Earlier sketch in SATA 3
Terry, Luther L(eonidas) 1911-1985 11
    Obituary 42
Terry, Margaret
    See Dunnahoo, Terry Janson
Terry, Michael 1947- 233
Terry, Walter 1913-1982 14
Terry, Will 1966- 205
Terzian, James P. 1915- 14
Tessendorf, K(enneth) C(harles) 1925-2003 . 75
    Obituary 142
Tessler, Manya 200
Tessler, Stephanie Gordon
    See Gordon, Stephanie Jacob
Testa, Dom 208
Tester, Sylvia Root 1939- 64
    Brief entry 37
Tether, (Cynthia) Graham 1950- 46
    Brief entry 36
Tetzner, Lisa 1894-1963 169
Thach, James Otis 1969- 195
Thacher, Mary McGrath 1933- 9
Thackeray, William Makepeace 1811-1863 .. 23
Thake, Richard 1938- 237

Thaler, Michael C.
    See Thaler, Mike
Thaler, Mike 1936- 215
    Brief entry 47
    Earlier sketches in SATA 56, 93
Thaler, Shmuel 1958- 126
    Earlier sketch in SATA 72
Thamer, Katie 1955- 42
Thane, Elswyth 1900-1984(?) 32
Tharp, Louise (Marshall) Hall 1898-1992 3
    Obituary 129
Tharp, Tim 1957- 189
Thayer, Ernest Lawrence 1863-1940 60
Thayer, Jane
    See Woolley, Catherine
Thayer, Marjorie 1908-1992 74
    Brief entry 37
Thayer, Peter
    See Wyler, Rose
Thelwell, Norman 1923-2004 14
Themerson, Stefan 1910-1988 65
Thermes, Jennifer 1966- 155
Theroux, Paul 1941- 109
    Earlier sketch in SATA 44
Theroux, Paul Edward
    See Theroux, Paul
Thesman, Jean 124
    Earlier sketch in SATA 74
The Tjong-Khing
    See Khing, T.T.
Thieda, Shirley Ann 1943- 13
Thiele, Colin 1920-2006 125
    Earlier sketches in SATA 14, 72
    See also CLR 27
    See also SAAS 2
Thiele, Colin Milton
    See Thiele, Colin
Thiesing, Lisa 1958- 159
    Earlier sketch in SATA 95
Thimmesh, Catherine 189
Thiry, Joan (Marie) 1926- 45
Thisdale, Francois 1964- 222
Thistlethwaite, Miles 1945- 12
Thollander, Earl 1922- 22
Thomas, Abigail 1941- 112
Thomas, Andrea
    See Hill, Margaret (Ohler)
Thomas, Art(hur Lawrence) 1952- 48
    Brief entry 38
Thomas, Carroll
    See Ratliff, Thomas M.
    and Shmurak, Carole B.
Thomas, Cassia 236
Thomas, Dylan 1914-1953 60
Thomas, Dylan Marlais
    See Thomas, Dylan
Thomas, Egbert S.
    See Ellis, Edward S.
Thomas, Estelle Webb 1899-1982 26
Thomas, Frances 1943- 171
    Earlier sketch in SATA 92
Thomas, Garen 213
Thomas, H. C.
    See Keating, Lawrence A.
Thomas, Ianthe 1951- 139
    Brief entry 42
    See also CLR 8
Thomas, J. F.
    See Fleming, Thomas
Thomas, Jan 1958- 226
    Earlier sketch in SATA 197
Thomas, Jane Resh 1936- 171
    Earlier sketches in SATA 38, 90
Thomas, Jerry D. 1959- 91
Thomas, Joan Gale
    See Robinson, Joan (Mary) G(ale Thomas)
Thomas, Joyce Carol 1938- 210
    Autobiography Feature 137
    Earlier sketches in SATA 40, 78, 123, 137
    See also CLR 19
    See also SAAS 7

Thomas, Lee
    See Floren, Lee
    and Pendleton, Thomas
Thomas, Lowell Jackson, Jr. 1923- 15
Thomas, Margaret
    See Thomas, Peggy
Thomas, Meredith 1963- 119
Thomas, Michael
    See Wilks, Michael Thomas
Thomas, Middy 1931- 191
Thomas, Patricia 1934- 199
    Earlier sketch in SATA 51
Thomas, Peggy 174
Thomas, Rob 1965- 97
Thomas, Scott 1959- 147
Thomas, Velma Maia 1955- 171
Thomas, Vernon (Arthur) 1934- 56
Thomas, Victoria
    See DeWeese, Thomas Eugene
    and Kugi, Constance Todd
Thomasma, Kenneth R. 1930- 90
Thomason, Mark 215
Thomassie, Tynia 1959- 92
Thompson, Alicia 1984- 224
Thompson, Brenda 1935- 34
Thompson, Carol 1951- 189
    Earlier sketch in SATA 85
Thompson, China
    See Lewis, Mary
Thompson, Colin 1942- 198
    Earlier sketches in SATA 95, 163
Thompson, David H(ugh) 1941- 17
Thompson, Eileen
    See Panowski, Eileen Thompson
Thompson, George Selden 1929-1989 73
    Obituary 63
    Earlier sketch in SATA 4
    See also CLR 8
Thompson, Harlan 1894-1987 10
    Obituary 53
Thompson, Hilary 1943- 56
    Brief entry 49
Thompson, Joanna Maxwell Pullein
    See Pullein-Thompson, Joanna Maxwell
Thompson, Julian F(rancis) 1927- 155
    Brief entry 40
    Earlier sketches in SATA 55, 99
    See also CLR 24
    See also SAAS 13
Thompson, K(athryn Carolyn) Dyble
    1952- 82
Thompson, Kate 1956- 204
Thompson, Kay 1912(?)-1998 16
    See also CLR 22
Thompson, Lauren 1962- 200
    Earlier sketches in SATA 132, 174
Thompson, Lauren Stevens
    See Thompson, Lauren
Thompson, Megan Lloyd
    See Lloyd, Megan
Thompson, Richard 1951- 184
Thompson, Ruth Plumly 1891-1976 66
Thompson, Sharon 1952- 119
Thompson, Sharon Elaine
    See Thompson, Sharon
Thompson, Stith 1885-1976 57
    Obituary 20
Thompson, Vivian L(aubach) 1911- 3
Thomson, Bill 1963- 187
Thomson, Celia
    See Lynn, Tracy
Thomson, David (Robert Alexander)
    1914-1988 40
    Obituary 55
Thomson, Melissa 1979- 205
Thomson, Pat 1939- 122
    Earlier sketch in SATA 77
Thomson, Peggy 1922- 31
Thomson, Sarah L. 212
    Earlier sketch in SATA 178
Thon, Melanie Rae 1957- 132

Thong, Roseanne *174*
Thor, Annika 1950- *222*
Thorburn, John
    See Goldsmith, John Herman Thorburn
Thorn, John 1947- *59*
Thorndyke, Helen Louise
    See Benson, Mildred
Thorne, Ian
    See May, Julian
Thorne, Jean Wright
    See May, Julian
Thornhill, Jan 1955- *148*
    Earlier sketch in SATA 77
Thornton, Hall
    See Silverberg, Robert
Thornton, W. B.
    See Burgess, Thornton Waldo
Thornton, Yvonne S. 1947- *96*
Thornton, Yvonne Shirley
    See Thornton, Yvonne S.
Thorpe, E(ustace) G(eorge) 1916- *21*
Thorpe, J. K.
    See Nathanson, Laura Walther
Thorvall, Kerstin 1925- *13*
Thorvall-Falk, Kerstin
    See Thorvall, Kerstin
Thrasher, Crystal (Faye) 1921- *27*
Threadgall, Colin 1941- *77*
Three Little Pigs
    See Lantz, Francess L(in)
Thum, Gladys 1920- *26*
Thum, Marcella *28*
    Earlier sketch in SATA 3
Thundercloud, Katherine
    See Witt, Shirley Hill
Thurber, James 1894-1961 .... *13*
Thurber, James Grover
    See Thurber, James
Thurlo, Aimee *161*
Thurlo, David *161*
Thurman, Judith 1946- *33*
Thurman, Mark (Gordon Ian) 1948- *63*
Thwaite, Ann (Barbara Harrop) 1932- *14*
Tibbetts, Peggy *127*
Tibbles, Jean-Paul 1958- *115*
Tibo, Gilles 1951- *107*
    Earlier sketch in SATA 67
Tiburzi, Bonnie 1948- *65*
Ticheburn, Cheviot
    See Ainsworth, William Harrison
Tichenor, Tom 1923-1992 .... *14*
Tichnor, Richard 1959- *90*
Tichy, William 1924- *31*
Tickle, Jack
    See Chapman, Jane
Tidholm, Anna-Clara 1946- *223*
Tiegreen, Alan F. 1935- *94*
    Brief entry *36*
Tierney, Fiona *229*
Tierney, Frank M. 1930- *54*
Tierney, Tom 1928- *113*
Tiffault, Benette W. 1955- *77*
Tildes, Phyllis Limbacher 1945- *210*
Tiller, Ruth L. 1949- *83*
Tilley, Debbie *190*
Tillman, Nancy *211*
Tillotson, Katherine *224*
Tilly, Nancy 1935- *62*
Tilton, Madonna Elaine 1929- *41*
Tilton, Rafael
    See Tilton, Madonna Elaine
Timberlake, Amy *156*
Timberlake, Carolyn
    See Dresang, Eliza (Carolyn Timberlake)
Timmers, Leo 1970- *190*
Timmins, Jeffrey Stewart 1979- *227*
Timmins, William F(rederick) *10*
Tinbergen, Niko(laas) 1907-1988
    Obituary *60*
Tincknell, Cathy *194*
Tiner, John Hudson 1944- *32*

Tingle, Dolli (?)-
    See Brackett, Dolli Tingle
Tingle, Rebecca *174*
Tingle, Tim *208*
Tingum, Janice 1958- *91*
Tinkelman, Murray 1933- *12*
Tinkham, Kelly A. *188*
Tinkle, (Julien) Lon 1906-1980 .... *36*
Tinling, Marion (Rose) 1904- *140*
Tipene, Tim 1972- *141*
Tippett, James S(terling) 1885-1958 .... *66*
Tirone Smith, Mary-Ann 1944- *143*
Titcomb, Gordon *237*
Titlebaum, Ellen *195*
Titler, Dale M(ilton) 1926- *35*
    Brief entry *28*
Titmarsh, Michael Angelo
    See Thackeray, William Makepeace
Titus, Eve 1922- *2*
Tjia, Sherwin 1975- *204*
Tjong Khing, The 1933- *76*
Tobias, Katherine
    See Gottfried, Theodore Mark
Tobias, Tobi 1938- *82*
    Earlier sketch in SATA 5
    See also CLR 4
Tobin, James *226*
Tocci, C. Lee 1958- *220*
Tocci, Cynthia Lee
    See Tocci, C. Lee
Tocher, Timothy *228*
Todd, Anne Ophelia
    See Dowden, Anne Ophelia Todd
Todd, Barbara 1961- *173*
Todd, Barbara K(eith) 1917- *10*
Todd, Chuck *195*
Todd, H(erbert) E(atton) 1908-1988 .... *84*
    Earlier sketch in SATA 11
Todd, Loreto 1942- *30*
Todd, Pamela *212*
Todd, Peter
    See Hamilton, Charles (Harold St. John)
Toews, Miriam 1964- *165*
Tofel, Richard J. 1957- *140*
Toffler-Corrie, Laura *237*
Toft, Di 1958- *233*
Toft, Kim Michelle 1960- *170*
Tokunbo, Dimitrea *187*
Tolan, Stephanie S. 1942- *142*
    Earlier sketches in SATA 38, 78
Toland, John (Willard) 1912-2004 .... *38*
Tolbert, Steve 1944- *143*
Toledo, Francisco 1940- *198*
Toledo, Natalia 1967- *197*
Tolkien, J. R. R. 1892-1973 .... *100*
    Obituary *24*
    Earlier sketches in SATA 2, 32
    See also CLR 152
Tolkien, John Ronald Reuel
    See Tolkien, J. R. R.
Toll, Emily
    See Cannon, Eileen E(mily)
Toll, Nelly S. 1935- *78*
Tolland, W. R.
    See Heitzmann, William Ray
Tolles, Martha 1921- *76*
    Earlier sketch in SATA 8
Tolliver, Ruby C(hangos) 1922- *110*
    Brief entry *41*
    Earlier sketch in SATA 55
Tolmie, Kenneth Donald 1941- *15*
Tolstoi, Lev
    See Tolstoy, Leo
Tolstoy, Leo 1828-1910 .... *26*
Tolstoy, Count Leo
    See Tolstoy, Leo
Tolstoy, Leo Nikolaevich
    See Tolstoy, Leo
Tomalin, Ruth *29*
Tomaselli, Rosa
    See Pausacker, Jenny

Tomecek, Steve *172*
Tomes, Margot (Ladd) 1917-1991 .... *70*
    Brief entry *27*
    Obituary *69*
    Earlier sketch in SATA 36
Tomey, Ingrid 1943- *77*
Tomfool
    See Farjeon, Eleanor
Tomic, Tomislav 1977- *202*
Tomkins, Jasper
    See Batey, Tom
Tomline, F. Latour
    See Gilbert, W(illiam) S(chwenck)
Tomlinson, Heather *192*
Tomlinson, Jill 1931-1976 .... *3*
    Obituary *24*
Tomlinson, Reginald R(obert) 1885-1979(?)
    Obituary *27*
Tomlinson, Theresa 1946- *165*
    Earlier sketch in SATA 103
    See also CLR 60
Tommaso, Rich 1970(?)- *200*
Tomorrow, Tom 1961- *223*
Tompert, Ann 1918- *139*
    Earlier sketches in SATA 14, 89
Tompkins, Troy
    See Cle, Troy
Tonatiuh, Duncan *231*
Toner, Raymond John 1908-1986 .... *10*
Tong, Gary S. 1942- *66*
Tong, Paul *188*
Took, Belladonna
    See Chapman, Vera (Ivy May)
Tooke, Louise Mathews 1950- *38*
Tooke, Susan *173*
Toonder, Martin
    See Groom, Arthur William
Toothaker, Roy Eugene 1928- *18*
Tooze, Ruth (Anderson) 1892-1972 .... *4*
Topaz, Ksenia *212*
Topek, Susan Remick 1955- *78*
Topping, Audrey R(onning) 1928- *14*
Tor, Regina
    See Shekerjian, Regina Tor
Torbert, Floyd James 1922- *22*
Torgersen, Don Arthur 1934- *55*
    Brief entry *41*
Torley, Luke
    See Blish, James
Torrecilla, Pablo 1967- *206*
Torres, Andres Segovia
    See Segovia, Andres
Torres, Daniel 1958- *102*
Torres, J. 1969- *230*
Torres, John A. 1965- *163*
    Earlier sketch in SATA 94
Torres, John Albert
    See Torres, John A.
Torres, Joseph
    See Torres, J.
Torres, Laura 1967- *146*
    Earlier sketch in SATA 87
Torres, Leyla 1960- *155*
Torrey, Rich
    See Torrey, Richard
Torrey, Richard *189*
Torrie, Malcolm
    See Mitchell, Gladys (Maude Winifred)
Toten, Teresa 1955- *99*
Totham, Mary
    See Breinburg, Petronella
Touponce, William F. 1948- *114*
Tournier, Michel 1924- *23*
Tournier, Michel Edouard
    See Tournier, Michel
Towle, Ben 1970- *228*
Towle, Wendy 1963- *79*
Towne, Mary
    See Spelman, Mary
Townley, Rod
    See Townley, Roderick

Townley, Roderick 1942- *177*
Townsend, Brad W. 1962- *91*
Townsend, John Rowe 1922- *132*
    Autobiography Feature *132*
    Earlier sketches in SATA *4, 68*
    See also CLR *2*
    See also SAAS *2*
Townsend, Michael 1981- *231*
    Earlier sketch in SATA *194*
Townsend, Sue 1946- *93*
    Brief entry *48*
    Earlier sketch in SATA *55*
Townsend, Susan Lilian
    See Townsend, Sue
Townsend, Thomas L. 1944- *59*
Townsend, Tom
    See Townsend, Thomas L.
Townsend, Wendy 1962- *201*
Townson, Hazel *134*
Toye, William Eldred 1926- *8*
Traherne, Michael
    See Watkins-Pitchford, Denys James
Trahey, Jane 1923-2000 .... *36*
    Obituary *120*
Trapani, Iza 1954- *214*
    Earlier sketches in SATA *80, 116*
Trapp, Maria Augusta von
    See von Trapp, Maria Augusta
Travers, P(amela) L(yndon) 1899-1996 ...... *100*
    Obituary *90*
    Earlier sketches in SATA *4, 54*
    See also CLR *93*
    See also SAAS *2*
Travis, Lucille *133*
    Earlier sketch in SATA *88*
Treadgold, Mary 1910-2005 .... *49*
Trease, (Robert) Geoffrey 1909-1998 .... *60*
    Obituary *101*
    Earlier sketch in SATA *2*
    See also CLR *42*
    See also SAAS *6*
Treat, Lawrence 1903-1998 .... *59*
Tredez, Alain 1926- *17*
Tredez, Denise 1930- *50*
Treece, Henry 1912-1966 .... *2*
    See also CLR *2*
Tregarthen, Enys
    See Sloggett, Nellie
Tregaskis, Richard 1916-1973 .... *3*
    Obituary *26*
Treherne, Katie Thamer 1955- *76*
Trell, Max 1900-1996 .... *14*
    Obituary *108*
Tremain, Ruthven 1922- *17*
Trembath, Don 1963- *168*
    Earlier sketch in SATA *96*
Tremens, Del
    See MacDonald, Amy
Trent, Robbie 1894-1988 .... *26*
Trent, Timothy
    See Malmberg, Carl
Treseder, Terry Walton 1956- *68*
Tresilian, (Cecil) Stuart 1891-(?) *40*
Tresselt, Alvin 1916-2000 .... *7*
    See also CLR *30*
Trevino, Elizabeth B(orton) de 1904- *29*
    Earlier sketch in SATA *1*
    See also SAAS *5*
Trevor, Elleston 1920-1995 .... *28*
Trevor, Frances
    See Teasdale, Sara
Trevor, Glen
    See Hilton, James
Trevor, (Lucy) Meriol 1919-2000 .... *113*
    Obituary *122*
    Earlier sketch in SATA *10*
Trewellard, J.M. *195*
Trewellard, Juliet
    See Trewellard, J.M.
Trez, Alain
    See Tredez, Alain

Trez, Denise
    See Tredez, Denise
Trezise, Percy 1923-
    See CLR *41*
Trezise, Percy James
    See Trezise, Percy
Triggs, Tony D. 1946- *70*
Trimble, Marshall I(ra) 1939- *93*
Trimby, Elisa 1948- *47*
    Brief entry *40*
Tring, A. Stephen
    See Meynell, Laurence Walter
Triplett, Gina *229*
Tripp, Eleanor B(aldwin) 1936- *4*
Tripp, Janet 1942- *108*
Tripp, Jenny *188*
Tripp, John
    See Moore, John Travers
Tripp, Nathaniel 1944- *101*
Tripp, Paul 1916-2002 .... *8*
    Obituary *139*
Tripp, Valerie 1951- *168*
    Earlier sketch in SATA *78*
Tripp, Wallace (Whitney) 1940- *31*
Trivelpiece, Laurel 1926- *56*
    Brief entry *46*
Trivett, Daphne Harwood 1940- *22*
Trivizas, Eugene 1946- *84*
Trnka, Jiri 1912-1969 .... *43*
    Brief entry *32*
Trollope, Anthony 1815-1882 .... *22*
Trost, Lucille W(ood) 1938- *149*
    Earlier sketch in SATA *12*
Trott, Betty 1933- *91*
Trotter, Deborah W. *184*
Trotter, Grace V(iolet) 1900-1991 .... *10*
Trottier, Maxine 1950- *175*
    Earlier sketch in SATA *131*
Troughton, Joanna (Margaret) 1947- *37*
Trout, Kilgore
    See Farmer, Philip Jose
Trout, Richard E. *123*
Trudeau, Garretson Beekman
    See Trudeau, G.B.
Trudeau, Garry
    See Trudeau, G.B.
Trudeau, Garry B.
    See Trudeau, G.B.
Trudeau, G.B. 1948- *168*
    Earlier sketch in SATA *35*
Trueit, Trudi
    See Trueit, Trudi Strain
Trueit, Trudi Strain 1963- *179*
Trueman, Matthew *183*
Trueman, Terry 1947- *178*
    Earlier sketch in SATA *132*
Truesdell, Judy
    See Mecca, Judy Truesdell
Truesdell, Sue
    See Truesdell, Susan G.
Truesdell, Susan G. *212*
    Brief entry *45*
    Earlier sketch in SATA *108*
Trumbauer, Lisa 1963- *228*
    Earlier sketch in SATA *149*
Trumbauer, Lisa Trutkoff
    See Trumbauer, Lisa
Truss, Jan 1925- *35*
Truss, Lynne 1955(?)- *194*
Tryon, Leslie *194*
    Earlier sketch in SATA *139*
Tubb, Jonathan N. 1951- *78*
Tubb, Kristin O'Donnell 1971- *209*
Tubby, I. M.
    See Kraus, (Herman) Robert
Tucker, Allan James
    See James, Bill
Tucker, Caroline
    See Nolan, Jeannette Covert
Tucker, James
    See James, Bill

Tudor, Edward
    See Browne, Anthony
Tudor, Tasha 1915-2008 .... *160*
    Obituary *205*
    Earlier sketches in SATA *20, 69*
    See also CLR *13*
Tuerk, Hanne 1951- *71*
Tugeau, Jeremy *199*
Tulloch, Richard 1949- *180*
    Earlier sketch in SATA *76*
Tulloch, Richard George
    See Tulloch, Richard
Tulloch, Shirley *169*
Tully, John (Kimberley) 1923- *14*
Tumanov, Vladimir A. 1961- *138*
Tung, Angela 1972- *109*
Tunis, Edwin (Burdett) 1897-1973 .... *28*
    Obituary *24*
    Earlier sketch in SATA *1*
    See also CLR *2*
Tunis, John R(oberts) 1889-1975 .... *37*
    Brief entry *30*
Tunnell, Michael
    See Tunnell, Michael O.
Tunnell, Michael O. 1950- *157*
    Earlier sketch in SATA *103*
Tunnell, Michael O'Grady
    See Tunnell, Michael O.
Tunnicliffe, C(harles) F(rederick)
    1901-1979 .... *62*
Turck, Mary C. 1950- *144*
Turk, Hanne
    See Tuerk, Hanne
Turk, Ruth 1917- *82*
Turkle, Brinton 1915- *79*
    Earlier sketch in SATA *2*
Turlington, Bayly 1919-1977 .... *5*
    Obituary *52*
Turnbull, Agnes Sligh 1888-1982 .... *14*
Turnbull, Ann 1943- *160*
    Earlier sketch in SATA *18*
Turnbull, Ann Christine
    See Turnbull, Ann
Turnbull, Susan *222*
Turner, Alice K. 1940- *10*
Turner, Ann 1945- *188*
    Autobiography Feature *188*
    Earlier sketches in SATA *14, 77, 113, 178*
Turner, Ann Warren
    See Turner, Ann
Turner, Bonnie 1932- *75*
Turner, Elizabeth 1774-1846
    See YABC *2*
Turner, Glennette Tilley 1933- *183*
    Earlier sketch in SATA *71*
Turner, Josie
    See Crawford, Phyllis
Turner, Megan Whalen 1965- *174*
    Earlier sketch in SATA *94*
Turner, Pamela S. 1957- *211*
Turner, Philip (William) 1925- *83*
    Earlier sketch in SATA *11*
    See also CLR *89*
    See also SAAS *6*
Turner, Robyn 1947- *77*
Turner, Sheila R.
    See Seed, Sheila Turner
Turngren, Annette 1902(?)-1980
    Obituary *23*
Turngren, Ellen (?)-1964 .... *3*
Turska, Krystyna (Zofia) 1933- *31*
    Brief entry *27*
Turteltaub, H. N.
    See Turtledove, Harry
Turtledove, Harry 1949- *166*
    Earlier sketch in SATA *116*
Turtledove, Harry Norman
    See Turtledove, Harry
Tusa, Tricia 1960- *207*
    Earlier sketches in SATA *72, 111*
Tusiani, Joseph 1924- *45*

Tuttle, Cameron *237*
Tuxbury, Larry 1969- *235*
Twain, Mark 1835-1910 .... *100*
    See also YABC 2
    See also CLR *156*
Tweit, Susan J 1956- *94*
Tweit, Susan Joan
    See Tweit, Susan J
Tweton, D. Jerome 1933- *48*
Twinem, Neecy 1958- *92*
Twohill, Maggie
    See Angell, Judie
Tworkov, Jack 1900-1982 .... *47*
    Obituary *31*
Tyche
    See Papademetriou, Lisa
Tyers, Jenny 1969- *89*
Tyers, Kathy 1952- *82*
Tyler, Anne 1941- *173*
    Earlier sketches in SATA *7, 90*
Tyler, Linda
    See Tyler, Linda W(agner)
Tyler, Linda W(agner) 1952- *65*
Tyler, Vicki 1952- *64*
Tyne, Joel
    See Schembri, Jim
Tyrrell, Frances 1959- *107*

U

Ubell, Earl 1926-2007 .... *4*
    Obituary *182*
Uchida, Yoshiko 1921-1992 .... *53*
    Obituary *72*
    Earlier sketch in SATA *1*
    See also CLR *56*
    See also SAAS *1*
Udall, Jan Beaney 1938- *10*
Uden, (Bernard Gilbert) Grant 1910- *26*
Uderzo, Albert 1927-
    See CLR *37*
Udovic, David 1950- *189*
Udovic, Jane Morris 1947- *224*
Udry, Janice May 1928- *152*
    Earlier sketch in SATA *4*
Uegaki, Chieri 1969- *211*
    Earlier sketch in SATA *153*
Uehashi, Nahoko 1962- *215*
Ueno, Noriko
    See Nakae, Noriko
Ugliano, Natascia *196*
Uhlberg, Myron *174*
Uhlig, Richard 1970- *195*
Uhlig, Susan 1955- *129*
Ulam, S(tanislaw) M(arcin) 1909-1984 .... *51*
Ullman, Barb Bentler *210*
Ullman, James Ramsey 1907-1971 .... *7*
Ulm, Robert 1934-1977 .... *17*
Ulmer, Louise 1943- *53*
Ulmer, Wendy K. 1950- *201*
Ulrich, Maureen 1958- *206*
Ulriksen, Mark 1957- *210*
Ulyatt, Kenneth 1920- *14*
Umansky, Kaye 1946- *224*
    Earlier sketches in SATA *158, 188*
Unada
    See Gliewe, Unada (Grace)
Uncle Carter
    See Boucher, (Clarence) Carter
Uncle Eric
    See Maybury, Richard J.
Uncle Gus
    See Rey, H. A.
Uncle Mac
    See McCulloch, Derek (Ivor Breashur)
Uncle Ray
    See Coffman, Ramon Peyton
Uncle Shelby
    See Silverstein, Shel

Underhill, Alice Mertie (Waterman)
    1900-1971 .... *10*
Underhill, Liz 1948- *53*
    Brief entry *49*
Underwood, Deborah 1962- *206*
Unger, Harlow G. 1931- *75*
Unger, Harlow Giles
    See Unger, Harlow G.
Unger, Jim 1937- *67*
Ungerer, (Jean) Thomas 1931- *106*
    Earlier sketches in SATA *5, 33*
    See also CLR *77*
Ungerer, Tomi 1931-
    See Ungerer, (Jean) Thomas
Unkelbach, Kurt 1913-1992 .... *4*
Unnerstad, Edith (Totterman) 1900-1982 .... *3*
    See also CLR *36*
Unobagha, Uzo *139*
Unrau, Ruth 1922- *9*
Unstead, R(obert) J(ohn) 1915-1988 .... *12*
    Obituary *56*
Unsworth, Walt(er) 1928- *4*
Untermeyer, Bryna Ivens 1909-1985 .... *61*
Untermeyer, Louis 1885-1977 .... *37*
    Obituary *26*
    Earlier sketch in SATA *2*
Unwin, David S. 1918-2010 .... *14*
Unwin, David Storr
    See Unwin, David S.
Unwin, Nora S(picer) 1907-1982 .... *3*
    Obituary *49*
Unzner, Christa 1958- *230*
    Earlier sketches in SATA *80, 141*
Unzner-Fischer, Christa
    See Unzner, Christa
Updale, Eleanor 1953- *175*
Updyke, Rosemary K. 1924- *103*
Upitis, Alvis *109*
Urbain, Cat 1956- *211*
Urbain, Catherine
    See Urbain, Cat
Urban, Helle (Denise) 1957- *149*
Urban, Linda *199*
Urbanovic, Jackie *189*
Urberuaga, Emilio 1954- *219*
Urbigkit, Cat 1965- *196*
Urdahl, Catherine *215*
Ure, Jean 1943- *192*
    Autobiography Feature *192*
    Earlier sketches in SATA *48, 78, 129*
    See also CLR *34*
    See also SAAS *14*
U'Ren, Andrea 1968- *213*
    Earlier sketch in SATA *142*
Uris, Leon 1924-2003 .... *49*
    Obituary *146*
Uris, Leon Marcus
    See Uris, Leon
Ursu, Anne *177*
Ury, Allen B. 1954- *98*
Uschan, Michael V. 1948- *129*
Usher, Margo Scegge
    See McHargue, Georgess
Usher, Mark David
    See Usher, M.D.
Usher, M.D. 1966- *221*
Uslan, Michael E. 1951- *169*
Uston, Ken(neth Senzo) 1935-1987 .... *65*
Uttley, Alice Jane 1884-1976 .... *88*
    Obituary *26*
    Earlier sketch in SATA *3*
Uttley, Alison
    See Uttley, Alice Jane
Utz, Lois (Marie) 1932-1986 .... *5*
    Obituary *50*

V

Vaeth, J. Gordon 1921- *17*
Vaeth, Joseph Gordon
    See Vaeth, J. Gordon
Vagin, Vladimir (Vasilevich) 1937- *142*
Vail, Rachel 1966- *201*
    Earlier sketches in SATA *94, 163*
Vainio, Pirkko 1957- *123*
    Earlier sketch in SATA *76*
Valen, Nanine 1950- *21*
Valencak, Hannelore
    See Mayer, Hannelore Valencak
Valens, Amy 1946- *70*
Valens, E(vans) G(ladstone), Jr. 1920-1992 ... *1*
Valentine, Johnny *72*
Valentine, Madeline *236*
Valerio, Geraldo 1970- *180*
Valgardson, W. D. 1939- *151*
    Earlier sketch in SATA *101*
Valgardson, William Dempsey
    See Valgardson, W. D.
Valleau, Emily 1925- *51*
Vamos, Samantha R. *215*
Van Abbe, Salaman 1883-1955 .... *18*
Van Allsburg, Chris 1949- *156*
    Earlier sketches in SATA *37, 53, 105*
    See also CLR *113*
Van Anrooy, Francine 1924- *2*
Van Anrooy, Frans
    See Van Anrooy, Francine
Vanasse, Deb 1957- *170*
Van Buren, David *203*
Van Camp, Katie 1981- *222*
Vance, Cynthia *207*
Vance, Eleanor Graham 1908-1985 .... *11*
Vance, Gerald
    See Garrett, Randall
    and Silverberg, Robert
Vance, Marguerite 1889-1965 .... *29*
Vance-Abrams, Cynthia
    See Vance, Cynthia
VanCleave, Janice 1942- *116*
    Autobiography Feature *123*
    Earlier sketch in SATA *75*
Vandenburg, Mary Lou 1943- *17*
Vander Boom, Mae M. *14*
Vander-Els, Betty 1936- *63*
van der Heide, Iris 1970- *183*
van der Linde, Laurel 1952- *78*
van der Linden, Martijn 1979- *214*
van der Meer, Ron 1945- *98*
Vanderpool, Clare 1964- *232*
van de Ruit, John 1975- *199*
Van der Veer, Judy 1912-1982 .... *4*
    Obituary *33*
Vanderwal, Andrew H. 1956- *219*
Vanderwerff, Corrine 1939- *117*
Vander Zee, Ruth *199*
    Earlier sketch in SATA *159*
Vande Velde, Vivian 1951- *211*
    Earlier sketches in SATA *62, 95, 141*
    See also CLR *145*
Vandivert, Rita (Andre) 1905-1986 .... *21*
Van Draanen, Wendelin *207*
    Earlier sketch in SATA *122*
Van Dusen, Chris *228*
    Earlier sketch in SATA *173*
Van Duyn, Janet 1910- *18*
Van Dyne, Edith
    See Baum, L. Frank
    and Sampson, Emma (Keats) Speed
    and van Zantwijk, Rudolf (Alexander
    Marinus)
Vane, Mitch
    See Vane, Mitchelle
Vane, Mitchelle *176*
van Eekhout, Greg *232*
van Etten, David
    See Levithan, David
van Frankenhuyzen, Gijsbert 1951- *132*

Van Genechten, Guido 1957- *165*
van Haeringen, Annemarie *193*
Van Hook, Beverly 1941- *99*
Van Hook, Beverly H.
   See Van Hook, Beverly
Van Hook, Beverly Hennen
   See Van Hook, Beverly
Van Horn, William 1939- *43*
van Hout, Mies 1962- *178*
Van Iterson, S(iny) R(ose) *26*
Van Kampen, Vlasta 1943- *163*
   Earlier sketch in SATA *54*
Van Laan, Nancy 1939- *214*
   Earlier sketch in SATA *105*
van Lawick-Goodall, Jane
   See Goodall, Jane
Van Leeuwen, Jean 1937- *211*
   Autobiography Feature *141*
   Earlier sketches in SATA *6, 82, 132, 141*
   See also SAAS *8*
van Lhin, Erik
   See del Rey, Lester
van Lieshout, Elle 1963- *217*
van Lieshout, Maria *201*
Van Loon, Hendrik Willem 1882-1944 .... *18*
van Ommen, Sylvia 1978- *186*
VanOosting, James 1951- *170*
Van Orden, M(erton) D(ick) 1921- *4*
van Os, Erik 1963- *217*
Van Patter, Bruce *183*
Van Reek, Wouter *204*
Van Rensselaer, Alexander (Taylor Mason)
   1892-1962 .... *14*
Van Riper, Guernsey, Jr. 1909-1995 .... *3*
van Rossum, Heleen 1962- *174*
Van Rynbach, Iris 1952- *102*
Vansant, Rhonda Joy Edwards 1950- *92*
Van Steenwyk, Elizabeth (Ann) 1928- *89*
   Earlier sketch in SATA *34*
Van Stockum, Hilda 1908-2006 .... *5*
   Obituary *179*
van Straaten, Harmen 1961- *218*
   Earlier sketch in SATA *195*
Van Tuyl, Barbara 1940- *11*
van Vogt, A(lfred) E(lton) 1912-2000 .... *14*
   Obituary *124*
Van Wassenhove, Sue 1951- *202*
Van Woerkom, Dorothy (O'Brien)
   1924-1996 .... *21*
Van Wormer, Joe
   See Van Wormer, Joseph Edward
Van Wormer, Joseph Edward 1913-1998 ...... *35*
Van Wright, Cornelius *173*
Van Zwienen, Ilse Charlotte Koehn
   1929-1991 .... *34*
   Brief entry *28*
   Obituary *67*
Van Zyle, Jon 1942- *176*
   Earlier sketch in SATA *84*
Varela, Barry *180*
Varga, Judy
   See Stang, Judit
Varley, Dimitry V. 1906-1984 .... *10*
Varley, Susan 1961- *134*
   Earlier sketch in SATA *63*
Varon, Sara *195*
Vasileva, Tatiana
   See Wassiljewa, Tatjana
Vasiliev, Valery 1949- *80*
Vasilieva, Tatiana
   See Wassiljewa, Tatjana
Vasiliu, Mircea 1920- *2*
Vass, George 1927- *57*
   Brief entry *31*
Vaughan, Carter A.
   See Gerson, Noel Bertram
Vaughan, Harold Cecil 1923- *14*
Vaughan, Marcia (K.) 1951- *159*
   Earlier sketches in SATA *60, 95*
Vaughan, Richard 1947- *87*
Vaughan, Sam 1928- *14*

Vaughn, Ruth 1935- *14*
Vaught, Susan 1965- *195*
Vaupel, Robin *198*
Vautier, Ghislaine 1932- *53*
Vavra, Robert James 1935- *8*
Vecsey, George Spencer 1939- *9*
Vedral, Joyce L(auretta) 1943- *65*
Vega, Denise *216*
   Earlier sketch in SATA *174*
Vega, Denise B.
   See Vega, Denise
Vega, Diego
   See Adkins, Jan
Veglahn, Nancy (Crary) 1937- *5*
Vejjajiva, Jane 1963- *189*
Velasquez, Crystal *228*
Velasquez, Eric *226*
   Earlier sketch in SATA *192*
Velasquez, Gloria 1949- *229*
   Earlier sketch in SATA *113*
Velthuijs, Max 1923-2005 .... *110*
   Obituary *160*
   Earlier sketch in SATA *53*
Venable, Alan (Hudson) 1944- *8*
Venable, Colleen A.F. 1980- *233*
Venezia, Mike 1945- *150*
Venner, Grace Chang
   See Chang, Grace
Ventura, Anthony
   See Pellowski, Michael (Joseph)
Ventura, Piero (Luigi) 1937- *61*
   Brief entry *43*
   See also CLR *16*
Venuti, Kristin Clark *237*
Vequin, Capini
   See Quinn, Elisabeth
Verba, Joan Marie 1953- *78*
Verboven, Agnes 1951- *103*
verDorn, Bethea (Stewart) 1952- *76*
Vere, Ed *197*
Verissimo, Erico (Lopes) 1905-1975 .... *113*
Verne, Jules 1828-1905 .... *21*
   See also CLR *88*
Verne, Jules Gabriel
   See Verne, Jules
Verner, Gerald 1897(?)-1980
   Obituary *25*
Verney, John 1913-1993 .... *14*
   Obituary *75*
Verniero, Joan C. 1949- *181*
Vernon, (Elda) Louise A(nderson) 1914- *14*
Vernon, Rosemary
   See Smith, Susan Vernon
Vernon, Ursula *204*
Vernor, D.
   See Casewit, Curtis W(erner)
Verr, Harry Coe
   See Kunhardt, Edith
Verral, Charles Spain 1904-1990 .... *11*
   Obituary *65*
Verrillo, Erica 1953- *199*
Verrillo, Erica F.
   See Verrillo, Erica
Verroken, Sarah 1982- *223*
Verrone, Robert J. 1935(?)-1984
   Obituary *39*
Versace, Marie Teresa Rios 1917- *2*
Vertreace, Martha M(odena) 1945- *78*
Vesey, A(manda) 1939- *62*
Vesey, Mark (David) 1958- *123*
Vesey, Paul
   See Allen, Samuel W(ashington)
Vess, Charles 1951- *215*
Vestergaard, Hope *178*
Vestly, Anne-Cath(arina) 1920-2008 .... *14*
   See also CLR *99*
Vevers, (Henry) Gwynne 1916-1988 .... *45*
   Obituary *57*
Viator, Vacuus
   See Hughes, Thomas
Viau, Nancy *208*

Vicar, Henry
   See Felsen, Henry Gregor
Vick, Helen Hughes 1950- *88*
Vicker, Angus
   See Felsen, Henry Gregor
Vickers, Sheena 1960- *94*
Vickery, Kate
   See Kennedy, T.A.
Victor, Edward 1914- *3*
Victor, Joan Berg 1942- *30*
Vidrine, Beverly Barras 1938- *188*
   Earlier sketch in SATA *103*
Vieceli, Emma 1979- *210*
Viereck, Ellen K. 1928- *14*
Viereck, Phillip 1925- *3*
Viergutz, Dina Nayeri
   See Nayeri, Dina
Viertel, Janet 1915- *10*
Vigan, Delphine de 1966- *236*
Vigliante, Mary
   See Szydlowski, Mary Vigliante
Vigna, Judith 1936- *102*
   Earlier sketch in SATA *15*
Viguers, Ruth Hill 1903-1971 .... *6*
Vila, Laura *207*
Vilela, Fernando 1973- *216*
Villareal, Ray *187*
Villasenor, Edmund
   See Villasenor, Victor E.
Villasenor, Edmundo
   See Villasenor, Victor E.
Villasenor, Victor
   See Villasenor, Victor E.
Villasenor, Victor E. 1940- *171*
Villasenor, Victor Edmundo
   See Villasenor, Victor E.
Villeneuve, Anne *230*
Villiard, Paul 1910-1974 .... *51*
   Obituary *20*
Villiers, Alan (John) 1903-1982 .... *10*
Vilott, Rhondi
   See Salsitz, Rhondi Vilott
Vincent, Amy
   See Gray, Claudia
Vincent, Eric Douglas 1953- *40*
Vincent, Erin 1969- *188*
Vincent, Felix 1946- *41*
Vincent, Gabrielle 1928-2000 .... *121*
   Earlier sketch in SATA *61*
   See also CLR *13*
Vincent, Mary Keith
   See St. John, Wylly Folk
Vincent, Rachel 1978- *222*
Vincent, William R.
   See Heitzmann, William Ray
Vinegar, Tom
   See Gregg, Andrew K.
Vinest, Shaw
   See Longyear, Barry B(rookes)
Vinge, Joan (Carol) D(ennison) 1948- *113*
   Earlier sketch in SATA *36*
Vining, Elizabeth Gray 1902-1999 .... *6*
   Obituary *117*
Vinson, Kathryn 1911-1995 .... *21*
Vinton, Iris 1906(?)-1988 .... *24*
   Obituary *55*
Viola, Herman J(oseph) 1938- *126*
Viorst, Judith 1931- *172*
   Earlier sketches in SATA *7, 70, 123*
   See also CLR *90*
Vip
   See Partch, Virgil Franklin II
Vipont, Charles
   See Foulds, Elfrida Vipont
Vipont, Elfrida
   See Foulds, Elfrida Vipont
Viramontes, Helena Maria 1954-
   See CLR *285*
Viscott, David S(teven) 1938-1996 .... *65*
Visser, W(illem) F(rederik) H(endrik)
   1900-1968 .... *10*

Vitale, Stefano 1958- 225
Earlier sketches in SATA *114, 180*
Vivas, Julie 1947- 96
Vivelo, Jackie 1943- 63
Vivelo, Jacqueline J.
See Vivelo, Jackie
Vivelo, Jacqueline Jean
See Vivelo, Jackie
Vivian, Siobhan 1979(?)- 215
Vizzini, Ned 1981- 179
Earlier sketch in SATA *125*
Vlahos, Olivia 1924- 31
Vlasic, Bob
See Hirsch, Phil
Voake, Charlotte 180
Earlier sketch in SATA *114*
Voake, Steve 1961- 178
Vo-Dinh, Mai 1933- 16
Vogel, Carole Garbuny 1951- 231
Earlier sketches in SATA *70, 105*
Vogel, Ilse-Margret 1914-2001 14
See also CLR *170*
Vogel, John H., Jr. 1950- 18
Vogt, Esther Loewen 1915-1999 14
Vogt, Gregory L. 94
Vogt, Marie Bollinger 1921- 45
Vohwinkel, Astrid 1969- 207
Voight, Virginia Frances 1909-1989 8
Voigt, Cynthia 1942- 160
Brief entry 33
Earlier sketches in SATA *48, 79, 116*
See also CLR *141*
Voigt, Erna 1925- 35
Voigt-Rother, Erna
See Voigt, Erna
Vojtech, Anna 1946- 108
Earlier sketch in SATA *42*
Vollstadt, Elizabeth Weiss 1942- 121
Volponi, Paul 228
Earlier sketch in SATA *175*
Volting, Dr. R.E.
See Lerangis, Peter
Von Ahnen, Katherine 1922- 93
von Buhler, Cynthia 185
Vondra, J. Gert
See Vondra, Josef
Vondra, Josef 1941- 121
Vondra, Josef Gert
See Vondra, Josef
Von Gunden, Kenneth 1946- 113
Von Hagen, Victor Wolfgang 1908-1985 29
von Klopp, Vahrah
See Malvern, Gladys
von Schmidt, Eric 1931-2007 50
Brief entry 36
Obituary 181
von Storch, Anne B. 1910- 1
von Trapp, Maria Augusta 1905-1987 16
von Wodtke, Charlotte Buel Johnson
1918-1982 46
von Ziegesar, Cecily 1970- 161
Vos, Ida 1931-2006 121
Earlier sketch in SATA *69*
See also CLR *85*
Vosburgh, Leonard (W.) 1912- 15
Votaw, Carol 1961- 201
Voyle, Mary
See Manning, Rosemary
Vrettos, Adrienne Maria 187
Vriens, Jacques 1946- 151
Vugteveen, Verna Aardema
See Aardema, Verna
Vulture, Elizabeth T.
See Gilbert, Suzie
Vuong, Lynette Dyer 1938- 110
Earlier sketch in SATA *60*
Vyner, Tim 1963- 228

W

Waas, Uli
See Waas-Pommer, Ulrike
Waas-Pommer, Ulrike 1949- 85
Waber, Bernard 1924- 155
Brief entry 40
Earlier sketches in SATA *47, 95*
See also CLR *55*
Waber, Paulis 231
Wachtel, Shirley Russak 1951- 88
Wachter, Oralee (Roberts) 1935- 61
Brief entry 51
Waddell, Evelyn Margaret 1918- 10
Waddell, Martin 1941- 232
Autobiography Feature 129
Earlier sketches in SATA *43, 81, 127, 129*
See also CLR *31*
See also SAAS *15*
Waddy, Lawrence 1912-2010 91
Waddy, Lawrence Heber
See Waddy, Lawrence
Wade, Mary Dodson 1930- 151
Earlier sketch in SATA *79*
Wade, Suzanne
See Kirby, Susan E.
Wade, Theodore E., Jr. 1936- 37
Wademan, Peter John 1946- 122
Wademan, Spike
See Wademan, Peter John
Wadsworth, Ginger 1945- 223
Earlier sketches in SATA *103, 157*
Wagenheim, Kal 1935- 21
Wagner, Hilary 237
Wagner, Michele R. 1975- 157
Wagner, Sharon B. 1936- 4
Wagoner, David (Russell) 1926- 14
Wahl, Jan (Boyer) 1933- 132
Earlier sketches in SATA *2, 34, 73*
See also SAAS *3*
Wahl, Mats 1945- 186
Wahman, Wendy 218
Waide, Jan 1952- 29
Wainscott, John Milton 1910-1981 53
Wainwright, Debra 218
Wainwright, Richard M. 1935- 91
Wainwright, Ruth
See Symes, Ruth Louise
Wait, Lea 1946- 137
Waite, Judy 174
Waite, Judy Bernard
See Bernard, Patricia
Waite, Michael
See Waite, Michael P.
Waite, Michael P. 1960- 101
Waite, P(eter) B(usby) 1922- 64
Waites, Joan C. 187
Waitley, Douglas 1927- 30
Wakefield, Jean L.
See Laird, Jean E(louise)
Wakin, Daniel (Joseph) 1961- 84
Wakin, Edward 1927- 37
Wakiyama, Hanako 1966- 192
Walck, Henry Z. 1908(?)-1984
Obituary 40
Walden, Amelia Elizabeth 3
Walden, Mark 188
Waldherr, Kris 1963- 76
Waldman, Bruce 1949- 15
Waldman, Neil 1947- 203
Earlier sketches in SATA *51, 94, 142*
Waldrep, Richard 198
Waldron, Ann Wood 1924-2010 16
Waldron, Kathleen Cook 176
Waldron, Kevin 1979- 230
Wales, Dirk 1931- 205
Walgren, Judy 1963- 118
Walker, Addison
See Walker, Mort
Walker, Addison Mort
See Walker, Mort

Walker, Alice 1944- 31
Walker, Alice Malsenior
See Walker, Alice
Walker, Anna 223
Walker, Barbara (Jeanne) K(erlin) 1921- 80
Earlier sketch in SATA *4*
Walker, Barbara M(uhs) 1928- 57
Walker, (James) Braz(elton) 1934-1983 45
Walker, David 1965- 197
Walker, David G(ordon) 1926- 60
Walker, David Harry 1911-1992 8
Obituary 71
Walker, Diana 1925- 9
Walker, Diane Marie Catherine
See Walker, Kate
Walker, Dick
See Pellowski, Michael (Joseph)
Walker, Frank 1931-2000 36
Walker, Holly Beth
See Bond, Gladys Baker
Walker, Kate 1950- 165
Earlier sketch in SATA *82*
Walker, Kathrine Sorley
See Sorley Walker, Kathrine
Walker, Kristin 228
Walker, Lou Ann 1952- 66
Brief entry 53
Walker, Louise Jean 1891-1976
Obituary 35
Walker, Mary Alexander 1927- 61
Walker, Mildred
See Schemm, Mildred Walker
Walker, Mort 1923- 8
Walker, Pamela 1948- 142
Earlier sketch in SATA *24*
Walker, Paul Robert 1953- 154
Walker, Robert W. 1948- 66
Walker, Robert Wayne
See Walker, Robert W.
Walker, Sally M. 1954- 221
Earlier sketch in SATA *135*
Walker, Stephen J. 1951- 12
Walker, Steve 232
Walker-Blondell, Becky 1951- 89
Wallace, Barbara Brooks 1922- 136
Earlier sketches in SATA *4, 78*
See also CLR *150*
See also SAAS *17*
Wallace, Beverly Dobrin 1921- 19
Wallace, Bill 1947- 169
Brief entry 47
Earlier sketches in SATA *53, 101*
Wallace, Carol 1948- 218
Wallace, Chad 229
Wallace, Daisy
See Cuyler, Margery
Wallace, Ian 1950- 219
Earlier sketches in SATA *53, 56, 141*
See also CLR *37*
Wallace, John 1966- 155
Earlier sketch in SATA *105*
Wallace, John A(dam) 1915-2004 3
Obituary 155
Wallace, Karen 1951- 188
Earlier sketches in SATA *83, 139*
Wallace, Nancy Elizabeth 1948- 222
Earlier sketches in SATA *141, 186*
Wallace, Nigel
See Hamilton, Charles (Harold St. John)
Wallace, Paula S. 153
Wallace, Rich 1957- 233
Earlier sketches in SATA *117, 158, 196*
Wallace, Robert 1932-1999 47
Brief entry 37
Wallace, Ruby Ann 1923(?)- 77
Wallace, Sandra Neil 236
Wallace, William Keith
See Wallace, Bill
Wallace-Brodeur, Ruth 1941- 169
Brief entry 41
Earlier sketches in SATA *51, 88*

Wallenfels, Stephen 232
Wallenta, Adam 1974- 123
Waller, Leslie 1923-2007 20
Walley, Byron
    See Card, Orson Scott
Walliams, David 1971- 227
Wallis, Diz 1949- 77
Wallis, G. McDonald
    See Campbell, Hope
Wallner, Alexandra 1946- 156
    Brief entry 41
    Earlier sketches in SATA *51, 98*
Wallner, John C. 1945- 133
    Earlier sketches in SATA *10, 51*
Wallower, Lucille 11
Walrod, Amy 1973(?)- 182
Walsh, Ann 1942- 176
    Earlier sketch in SATA *62*
Walsh, Ellen Stoll 1942- 194
    Earlier sketches in SATA *49, 99, 147*
Walsh, George Johnston 1889-1981 53
Walsh, Gillian Paton
    See Paton Walsh, Jill
Walsh, Jill Paton
    See Paton Walsh, Jill
Walsh, Joanna 1970- 182
Walsh, Lawrence 1942- 170
Walsh, Marissa 1972- 195
Walsh, Mary Caswell 1949- 118
Walsh, Mitzy
    See Walsh, Marissa
Walsh, Pat 1954- 237
Walsh, Rebecca 217
Walsh, Suella 170
Walsh, V. L.
    See Walsh, Vivian
Walsh, Vivian 1960- 120
Walsh Shepherd, Donna 1948- 78
Walter, Frances V. 1923- 71
Walter, Mildred Pitts 1922- 133
    Brief entry 45
    Earlier sketch in SATA *69*
    See also CLR *61*
    See also SAAS *12*
Walter, Villiam Christian
    See Andersen, Hans Christian
Walter, Virginia
    See Walter, Virginia A.
Walter, Virginia A. 134
Walters, Audrey 1929- 18
Walters, Celeste 1938- 126
Walters, Eric 1957- 205
    Earlier sketches in SATA *99, 155*
Walters, Eric Robert
    See Walters, Eric
Walters, Gregory 1964- 213
Walters, Helen B. (?)-1987
    Obituary 50
Walters, Hugh
    See Hughes, Walter (Llewellyn)
Walther, Thomas A. 1950- 31
Walther, Tom
    See Walther, Thomas A.
Waltner, Elma 1912-1987 40
Waltner, Willard H. 1909- 40
Walton, Darwin McBeth 1926- 119
Walton, Fiona L. M. 1959- 89
Walton, Richard J. 1928- 4
Walton, Rick 1957- 204
    Earlier sketch in SATA *101, 151*
Waltrip, Lela (Kingston) 1904-1995 9
Waltrip, Mildred 1911- 37
Waltrip, Rufus (Charles) 1898-1988 9
Walworth, Nancy Zinsser 1917- 14
Wang, Gabrielle 212
Wang, Lin 1973- 221
Wang, Shaoli 216
Wangerin, Walter, Jr. 1944- 98
    Brief entry 37
    Earlier sketch in SATA *45*

Waniek, Marilyn
    See Nelson, Marilyn
Waniek, Marilyn Nelson 1946-
    See Nelson, Marilyn
Wannamaker, Bruce
    See Moncure, Jane Belk
Warbler, J. M.
    See Cocagnac, Augustin Maurice(-Jean)
Warburg, Sandol Stoddard
    See Stoddard, Sandol
Warburton, Tom 1968(?)- 218
Ward, David 1967- 213
Ward, E. D.
    See Gorey, Edward (St. John)
    and Lucas, E(dward) V(errall)
Ward, Ed
    See Stratemeyer, Edward L.
Ward, Helen 1962- 206
    Earlier sketches in SATA *72, 144*
Ward, Jay 1920-1989
    Obituary 63
Ward, Jennifer 1963- 226
    Earlier sketch in SATA *146*
Ward, John (Stanton) 1917- 42
Ward, Jonas
    See Ard, William
    and Cox, William R(obert)
    and Garfield, Brian (Francis Wynne)
Ward, Lindsay M. 236
Ward, Lynd (Kendall) 1905-1985 36
    Obituary 42
    Earlier sketch in SATA *2*
Ward, Martha (Eads) 5
Ward, Melanie
    See Curtis, Richard
    and Lynch, Marilyn
Ward, Nicholas John
    See Ward, Nick
Ward, Nick 1955- 190
Ward, Rachel 1964- 229
Ward, Tom
    See Stratemeyer, Edward L.
Wardell, Dean
    See Prince, J(ack) H(arvey)
Wardlaw, Lee 1955- 115
    Earlier sketch in SATA *79*
Ware, Cheryl 1963- 101
Ware, Chris 1967- 140
Ware, Leon (Vernon) 1909-1976 4
Wargin, Kathy-jo 1964- 210
    Earlier sketch in SATA *145*
Warhola, James 1955- 187
Warman, Jessica 1981- 225
Warner, Frank A. 67
    Earlier sketch in SATA *1*
Warner, Gertrude Chandler 1890-1979 9
    Obituary 73
Warner, J(ohn) F. 1929- 75
Warner, Lucille Schulberg 30
Warner, Marsha 232
Warner, Matt
    See Fichter, George S.
Warner, Oliver (Martin Wilson) 1903-1976 . 29
Warner, Sally 1946- 214
    Earlier sketch in SATA *131*
Warner, Sunny (B.) 1931- 108
Warnes, Tim 1971- 216
    Earlier sketches in SATA *116, 166*
Warnes, Timothy
    See Warnes, Tim
Warnick, Elsa 1942- 113
Warren, Andrea 1946- 98
Warren, Betsy
    See Warren, Elizabeth Avery
Warren, Billy
    See Warren, William Stephen
Warren, Cathy 1951- 62
    Brief entry 46
Warren, Elizabeth
    See Supraner, Robyn

Warren, Elizabeth Avery 1916- 46
    Brief entry 38
Warren, Jackie M. 1953- 135
Warren, Joshua P(aul) 1976- 107
Warren, Joyce W(illiams) 1935- 18
Warren, Mary Phraner 1929- 10
Warren, Robert Penn 1905-1989 46
    Obituary 63
Warren, Scott S. 1957- 79
Warren, William Stephen 1882-1968 9
Warrick, Patricia Scott 1925- 35
Warriner, John 1907(?)-1987
    Obituary 53
Warsh
    See Warshaw, Jerry
Warshaw, Jerry 1929- 30
Warshaw, Mary 1931- 89
Warshofsky, Fred 1931- 24
Warshofsky, Isaac
    See Singer, Isaac Bashevis
Wartski, Maureen (Ann Crane) 1940- 50
    Brief entry 37
Warwick, Alan R(oss) 1900-1973 42
Wa-sha-quon-asin
    See Belaney, Archibald Stansfeld
Wa-Sha-Quon-Asin
    See Belaney, Archibald Stansfeld
Washburn, Bradford 1910-2007 38
    Obituary 181
Washburn, Henry Bradford, Jr.
    See Washburn, Bradford
Washburn, Jan(ice) 1926- 63
Washburn, Lucia 193
Washburne, Carolyn Kott 1944- 86
Washburne, Heluiz Chandler 1892-1970 10
    Obituary 26
Washington, Booker T. 1856-1915 28
Washington, Donna L. 1967- 159
    Earlier sketch in SATA *98*
Wasserman, Robin 1978- 207
Wasserstein, Wendy 1950-2006 94
    Obituary 174
Wassiljewa, Tatjana 1928- 106
Watanabe, Etsuko 1968- 219
Watanabe, Shigeo 1928- 131
    Brief entry 32
    Earlier sketch in SATA *39*
    See also CLR *8*
Waters, John F(rederick) 1930- 4
Waters, Summer
    See Sykes, Julie
Waters, Tony 1958- 75
Waterton, Betty 1923- 99
    Brief entry 34
    Earlier sketch in SATA *37*
Waterton, Betty Marie
    See Waterton, Betty
Watkins, Dawn L. 126
Watkins, Gloria Jean
    See hooks, bell
Watkins, Lis
    See Watkins, Liselotte
Watkins, Liselotte 1971- 215
Watkins, Lois 1930- 88
Watkins, Peter 1934- 66
Watkins, Yoko Kawashima 1933- 93
Watkins-Pitchford, Denys James
    1905-1990 87
    Obituary 66
    Earlier sketch in SATA *6*
    See also SAAS *4*
Watling, James 1933- 117
    Earlier sketch in SATA *67*
Watson, Aldren A(uld) 1917- 42
    Brief entry 36
Watson, Amy Zakrzewski 1965- 76
Watson, B. S.
    See Teitelbaum, Michael
Watson, Carol 1949- 78
Watson, C.G. 193

Watson, Clyde 1947- 68
　Earlier sketch in SATA 5
　See also CLR 3
Watson, Geoff 1978- 237
Watson, Helen Orr 1892-1978
　Obituary 24
Watson, James 1936- 106
　Earlier sketch in SATA 10
Watson, Jane Werner 1915- 54
　Earlier sketch in SATA 3
Watson, Jesse Joshua 199
Watson, John H.
　See Farmer, Philip Jose
Watson, Mary 1953- 117
Watson, N. Cameron 1955- 81
Watson, Nancy Dingman 32
Watson, Pauline 1925- 14
Watson, Renee 1978- 233
Watson, Richard F.
　See Silverberg, Robert
Watson, Richard Jesse 1951- 211
　Earlier sketch in SATA 62
Watson, Sally (Lou) 1924- 3
Watson, Sasha 211
Watson, Stephanie 1979- 237
Watson, Wendy (McLeod) 1942- 142
　Earlier sketches in SATA 5, 74
Watson Taylor, Elizabeth 1915- 41
Watt, Melanie 1975- 193
　Earlier sketch in SATA 136
Watt, Thomas 1935- 4
Wattenberg, Jane 174
Watterson, Bill 1958- 66
Watt-Evans, Lawrence 1954- 121
Watts, Bernadette 1942- 230
　Earlier sketches in SATA 4, 103
Watts, Ephraim
　See Horne, Richard Henry Hengist
Watts, Franklin (Mowry) 1904-1978 46
　Obituary 21
Watts, Helen L. Hoke 1903-1990
　Obituary 65
Watts, Irene N(aemi) 1931- 111
　Earlier sketch in SATA 56
Watts, Isaac 1674-1748 52
Watts, James K(ennedy) M(offitt) 1955- 59
Watts, Jeri Hanel 1957- 170
Watts, Julia 1969- 103
Watts, Leander 1956- 146
Watts, Leslie Elizabeth 1961- 168
Watts, Mabel Pizzey 1906-1994 11
Watts, Nigel 1957-1999 121
Watts, Sarah 1986- 234
Waugh, C. C. Roessel
　See Waugh, Carol-Lynn Rossel
　and Waugh, Charles G(ordon)
Waugh, Carol-Lynn Rossel 1947- 41
Waugh, Dorothy -1996 11
Waugh, Sylvia 1935- 169
Waugh, Virginia
　See Sorensen, Virginia
Wax, Wendy A. 1963- 219
　Earlier sketches in SATA 73, 163
Wayland, April Halprin 1954- 143
　Earlier sketch in SATA 78
　See also SAAS 26
Wayland, Patrick
　See O'Connor, Richard
Wayne, (Anne) Jenifer 1917-1982 32
Wayne, Kyra Petrovskaya 1918- 8
Wayne, Richard
　See Decker, Duane
Wayshak, Deborah Noyes
　See Noyes, Deborah
Waystaff, Simon
　See Swift, Jonathan
Weales, Gerald (Clifford) 1925- 11
Weary, Ogdred
　See Gorey, Edward (St. John)
Weatherford, Carole Boston 1956- 226
　Earlier sketches in SATA 138, 181

Weatherill, Cat 203
Weatherly, Lee 1967- 192
Weatherly, Myra 1926- 130
Weatherly, Myra S.
　See Weatherly, Myra
Weaver, Brian M.
　See Numberman, Neil
Weaver, Harriett E. 1908-1993 65
Weaver, Janice 236
Weaver, John L. 1949- 42
Weaver, Robyn
　See Conley, Robyn
Weaver, Robyn M.
　See Conley, Robyn
Weaver, Tess 197
Weaver, Ward
　See Mason, F(rancis) van Wyck
Weaver, Will 1950- 217
　Earlier sketches in SATA 88, 109, 161
Weaver, William Weller
　See Weaver, Will
Weaver-Gelzer, Charlotte 1950- 79
Webb, Christopher
　See Wibberley, Leonard
Webb, Jacqueline
　See Pearce, Margaret
Webb, Jacquelyn
　See Pearce, Margaret
　and Pearce, Margaret
Webb, Jean Francis (III) 1910-1991 35
Webb, Kaye 1914- 60
Webb, Lois Sinaiko 1922- 82
Webb, Margot 1934- 67
Webb, Sarah 235
Webb, Sharon 1936-2010 41
Webb, Sophie 1958- 135
Webber, Andrew Lloyd
　See Lloyd Webber, Andrew
Webber, Desiree Morrison 1956- 170
Webber, Irma E(leanor Schmidt)
　1904-1995 14
Weber, Alfons 1921- 8
Weber, Bruce 1942- 120
　Earlier sketch in SATA 73
Weber, Debora 1955- 58
Weber, Dennis J. 1951- 234
Weber, EdNah New Rider 1919(?)- 168
Weber, Elka 1968- 219
Weber, Jill 1950- 209
　Earlier sketch in SATA 127
Weber, Judith E(ichler) 1938- 64
Weber, Ken(neth J.) 1940- 90
Weber, Lenora Mattingly 1895-1971 2
　Obituary 26
Weber, Lisa K. 217
Weber, Lori 1959- 220
Weber, Michael 1945- 87
Weber, Penny 235
Weber, Sandra 1961- 158
Weber, William J(ohn) 1927- 14
Webster, Alice Jane Chandler 1876-1916 17
Webster, David 1930- 11
Webster, Frank V. 67
　Earlier sketch in SATA 1
Webster, Gary
　See Garrison, Webb B(lack)
Webster, James 1925-1981 17
　Obituary 27
Webster, Jean
　See Webster, Alice Jane Chandler
Wechsler, Doug 189
Wechsler, Herman J. 1904-1976
　Obituary 20
Wechter, Nell (Carolyn) Wise 1913-1989 .. 127
　Earlier sketch in SATA 60
Weck, Thomas L. 1942- 62
Wedd, Kate
　See Gregory, Philippa
Weddle, Ethel Harshbarger 1897-1996 11
Wedekind, Annie 204

Weeks, Sarah 194
　Earlier sketch in SATA 158
Weems, David B(urnola) 1922- 80
Wees, Frances Shelley 1902-1982 58
Weevers, Peter 1944- 59
Wegen, Ronald 1946-1985 99
Wegman, William (George) 1943- 135
　Earlier sketches in SATA 78, 129
Wegner, Fritz 1924- 20
Wehrman, Vicki 223
Weidhorn, Manfred 1931- 60
Weidt, Maryann N. 1944- 85
Weigel, Jeff 1958- 170
Weigelt, Udo 1960- 201
　Earlier sketch in SATA 168
Weihs, Erika 1917-2010 107
　Earlier sketch in SATA 15
Weik, Mary Hays 1898(?)-1979 3
　Obituary 23
Weil, Ann Yezner 1908-1969 9
Weil, Lisl 1910- 7
Weilerstein, Sadie Rose 1894-1993 3
　Obituary 75
Weill, Cynthia 1959- 167
Wein, Elizabeth E. 1964- 151
　Earlier sketch in SATA 82
Wein, Elizabeth Eve
　See Wein, Elizabeth E.
Wein, Hallie
　See Zobel Nolan, Allia
Weinberg, Larry
　See Weinberg, Lawrence (E.)
Weinberg, Lawrence (E.) 92
　Brief entry 48
Weinberger, Tanya 1939- 84
Weiner, Sandra 1922- 14
Weingarten, Lynn 217
Weingarten, Violet (Brown) 1915-1976 3
　Obituary 27
Weingartner, Charles 1922- 5
Weinheimer, Beckie 1958- 186
Weinstein, Bruce 1960- 220
Weinstein, Bruce M.
　See Weinstein, Bruce
Weinstein, Ellen Slusky 1959- 200
Weinstein, Muriel Harris 215
Weinstein, Nina 1951- 73
Weinstock, Robert 1967- 204
Weir, Bob 1947- 76
Weir, Diana (R.) Loiewski 1958- 111
Weir, Joan S(herman) 1928- 99
Weir, LaVada 2
Weir, Rosemary (Green) 1905-1994 21
Weir, Wendy 1949- 76
Weis, Margaret 1948- 164
　Earlier sketches in SATA 38, 92
Weisberger, Bernard A(llen) 1922- 21
Weisburd, Stefi 1957- 202
Weise, Patty 236
Weiser, Marjorie P(hillis) K(atz) 1934- 33
Weisgard, Leonard (Joseph) 1916-2000 85
　Obituary 122
　Earlier sketches in SATA 2, 30
　See also SAAS 19
Weiss, Adelle 1920- 18
Weiss, Ann E(dwards) 1943- 69
　Earlier sketch in SATA 30
　See also SAAS 13
Weiss, Edna
　See Barth, Edna
Weiss, Ellen 1953- 44
Weiss, Harvey 1922- 76
　Earlier sketches in SATA 1, 27
　See also CLR 4
　See also SAAS 19
Weiss, Jaqueline Shachter 1926- 65
Weiss, Malcolm E. 1928- 3
Weiss, Margaret Edith
　See Weis, Margaret
Weiss, Miriam
　See Schlein, Miriam

Weiss, Mitch 1951- *183*
  Earlier sketch in SATA *123*
Weiss, Nicki 1954- *86*
  Earlier sketch in SATA *33*
Weiss, Renee Karol 1923- *5*
Weissberger, Ela 1930- *181*
Weissberger, Ela Stein
  See Weissberger, Ela
Weissenborn, Hellmuth 1898-1982
  Obituary *31*
Weissman, Elissa Brent *217*
Weitzman, David L. 1936- *172*
  Earlier sketch in SATA *122*
Wekesser, Carol A. 1963- *76*
Welber, Robert *26*
Welch, Amanda (Jane) 1945- *75*
Welch, D'Alte Aldridge 1907-1970
  Obituary *27*
Welch, Holly *206*
Welch, Jean-Louise
  See Kempton, Jean Welch
Welch, Pauline
  See Bodenham, Hilda Morris
Welch, Ronald
  See Felton, Ronald Oliver
Welch, Sheila Kelly 1945- *130*
Welch, Willy 1952- *93*
Weldin, Frauke 1969- *188*
Welford, Sue 1942- *75*
Weller, George 1907-2002 .... *31*
  Obituary *140*
Weller, George Anthony
  See Weller, George
Welling, Peter J. 1947- *135*
Wellington, Monica 1957- *222*
  Earlier sketches in SATA *67, 99, 157*
Wellman, Alice 1900-1984 .... *51*
  Brief entry *36*
Wellman, Manly Wade 1903-1986 .... *6*
  Obituary *47*
Wellman, Paul I. 1898-1966 .... *3*
Wellman, Paul Iselin
  See Wellman, Paul I.
Wellman, Sam 1939- *122*
Wellman, Samuel
  See Wellman, Sam
Wells, H. G. 1866-1946 .... *20*
  See also CLR *133*
Wells, Helen
  See Campbell, Hope
Wells, Helen 1910-1986 .... *49*
  Earlier sketch in SATA *2*
Wells, Herbert George
  See Wells, H. G.
Wells, J. Wellington
  See de Camp, L. Sprague
Wells, June
  See Swinford, Betty (June Wells)
Wells, Robert
  See Welsch, Roger L(ee)
Wells, Robert E. *184*
Wells, Rosemary 1943- *237*
  Earlier sketches in SATA *18, 69, 114, 156,*
  207
  See also CLR *69*
  See also SAAS *1*
Wells, Susan (Mary) 1951- *78*
Wels, Byron G(erald) 1924-1993 .... *9*
Welsbacher, Anne 1955- *89*
Welsch, Roger L(ee) 1936- *82*
Welsh, C.E.L. *234*
Welsh, Chris
  See Welsh, C.E.L.
Welsh, David
  See Hills, C.A.R.
Welsh, Mary Flynn 1910(?)-1984
  Obituary *38*
Welsh, T.K. 1956- *184*
Weltevrede, Pieter 1957- *228*
Weltner, Linda R(iverly) 1938- *38*

Welton, Jude 1955- *143*
  Earlier sketch in SATA *79*
Welty, S. F.
  See Welty, Susan F.
Welty, Susan F. 1905- *9*
Wemmlinger, Raymond *190*
Wendelin, Rudolph 1910-2000 .... *23*
Weninger, Brigitte 1960- *189*
Wensell, Ulises 1945- *229*
Wentworth, Robert
  See Hamilton, Edmond
Werlin, Nancy 1961- *161*
  Earlier sketches in SATA *87, 119*
Werner, Elsa Jane
  See Watson, Jane Werner
Werner, Herma 1926- *47*
  Brief entry *41*
Werner, Jane
  See Watson, Jane Werner
Werner, K.
  See Casewit, Curtis W(erner)
Wersba, Barbara 1932- *58*
  Autobiography Feature *103*
  Earlier sketch in SATA *1*
  See also CLR *78*
  See also SAAS *2*
Werstein, Irving 1914(?)-1971 .... *14*
Werth, Kurt 1896-1983 .... *20*
Wesley, Alison
  See Barnes, Michael
Wesley, Kathryn
  See Rusch, Kristine Kathryn
Wesley, Mary (Aline) 1912-2002 .... *66*
Wesley, Valerie Wilson 1947- *168*
  Earlier sketch in SATA *106*
Wesselhoeft, Conrad 1953- *237*
West, Andrew
  See Arthur, Robert, (Jr.)
West, Anna 1938- *40*
West, Barbara
  See Price, Olive
West, Betty 1921- *11*
West, Bruce 1951- *63*
West, C. P.
  See Wodehouse, P. G.
West, Dorothy
  See Benson, Mildred
West, Emily Govan 1919- *38*
West, Emmy
  See West, Emily Govan
West, Jacqueline 1979- *235*
West, James
  See Withers, Carl A.
West, Jerry
  See Svenson, Andrew E(dward)
West, (Mary) Jessamyn 1902-1984
  Obituary *37*
West, John
  See Arthur, Robert, (Jr.)
West, Owen
  See Koontz, Dean
West, Ward
  See Borland, Harold Glen
Westall, Robert (Atkinson) 1929-1993 .... *69*
  Obituary *75*
  Earlier sketch in SATA *23*
  See also CLR *13*
  See also SAAS *2*
Westaway, Jane 1948- *121*
Westcott, Nadine Bernard 1949- *130*
Westera, Marleen 1962- *187*
Westerberg, Christine 1950- *29*
Westerduin, Anne 1945- *105*
Westerfeld, Scott 1963- *230*
  Earlier sketch in SATA *161*
Westervelt, Virginia Veeder 1914-2005 .... *10*
Westheimer, David 1917-2005 .... *14*
  Obituary *170*
Westheimer, David Kaplan
  See Westheimer, David

Westmacott, Mary
  See Christie, Agatha
Westman, Barbara *70*
Westman, Paul (Wendell) 1956- *39*
Westmoreland, William C. 1914-2005 .... *63*
Westmoreland, William Childs
  See Westmoreland, William C.
Weston, Allen
  See Hogarth, Grace (Weston Allen)
  and Norton, Andre
Weston, Carol 1956- *135*
Weston, Carrie *190*
Weston, John (Harrison) 1932- *21*
Weston, Martha 1947- *119*
  Earlier sketch in SATA *53*
Weston, Robert Paul *209*
Westphal, Arnold Carl 1897- *57*
Westrup, Hugh *102*
Westwood, Jennifer 1940-2008 .... *10*
  Obituary *192*
Wexler, Jerome (LeRoy) 1923- *14*
Weyland, Jack 1940- *81*
Weyn, Suzanne 1955- *220*
  Earlier sketches in SATA *63, 101, 164*
Weyr, Garret
  See Freymann-Weyr, Garret
Wezyk, Joanna 1966- *82*
Whaley, Joyce Irene 1923- *61*
Whalin, W. Terry 1953- *93*
Whamond, Dave *222*
Wharf, Michael
  See Weller, George
Wharmby, Margot *63*
Wharton, Edith 1862-1937
  See CLR *136*
Wharton, Edith Newbold Jones
  See Wharton, Edith
Wharton, Thomas 1963- *223*
Whatley, Bruce 1954- *213*
  Earlier sketch in SATA *177*
Wheatley, Arabelle 1921- *16*
Wheatley, Nadia 1949- *147*
Wheeler, Cindy 1955- *49*
  Brief entry *40*
Wheeler, Deborah 1947- *83*
Wheeler, Janet D. *1*
Wheeler, Jill C. 1964- *136*
  Earlier sketch in SATA *86*
Wheeler, Jody 1952- *148*
  Earlier sketch in SATA *84*
Wheeler, Lisa 1963- *237*
  Earlier sketches in SATA *162, 200*
Wheeler, Opal 1898- *23*
Whelan, Elizabeth M(urphy) 1943- *14*
Whelan, Gloria 1923- *224*
  Earlier sketches in SATA *85, 128, 178*
  See also CLR *90*
Whelan, Gloria Ann
  See Whelan, Gloria
Whinnem, Reade Scott *224*
Whipple, A(ddison) B(eecher) C(olvin)
  1918- *64*
Whipple, Cal
  See Whipple, A(ddison) B(eecher) C(olvin)
Whisp, Kennilworthy
  See Rowling, J.K.
Whistler, Reginald John 1905-1944 .... *30*
Whistler, Rex
  See Whistler, Reginald John
Whitaker, Zai *183*
Whitcher, Susan (Godsil) 1952- *96*
Whitcomb, Jon 1906-1988 .... *10*
  Obituary *56*
Whitcomb, Laura 1958- *214*
  Earlier sketch in SATA *171*
White, Amy Brecount *228*
White, Anne Terry 1896-1980 .... *2*
White, Bessie (Felstiner) 1892(?)-1986
  Obituary *50*
White, Carolyn 1948- *130*

White, Dale
  See Place, Marian T(empleton)
White, Dori 1919- 10
White, E. B. 1899-1985 100
  Obituary 44
  Earlier sketches in SATA 2, 29
  See also CLR 107
White, Eliza Orne 1856-1947
  See YABC 2
White, Elwyn Brooks
  See White, E. B.
White, Florence M(eiman) 1910- 14
White, Kathryn 1956- 234
White, Kathryn Ivy
  See White, Kathryn
White, K.I.
  See White, Kathryn
White, Laurence B(arton), Jr. 1935- 10
White, Lee 223
  Earlier sketch in SATA 176
White, Martin 1943- 51
White, Nancy 1942- 126
White, Ramy Allison 67
  Earlier sketch in SATA 1
White, Robb 1909-1990 83
  Earlier sketch in SATA 1
  See also CLR 3
  See also SAAS 1
White, Ruth 1942- 186
  Autobiography Feature 186
  Earlier sketches in SATA 39, 117, 165
White, Ruth C.
  See White, Ruth
White, T(erence) H(anbury) 1906-1964 12
  See also CLR 139
White, Tekla N. 1934- 115
White, Timothy (Thomas Anthony)
  1952-2002 60
White, Tom 1923- 148
White, Tracy 235
White, Tracy A.
  See White, Tracy
White, William, Jr. 1934- 16
Whitehead, Don(ald) F. 1908-1981 4
Whitehead, Jenny 1964- 191
Whitehead, Kathy 1957- 176
Whitehouse, Arch
  See Whitehouse, Arthur George Joseph
Whitehouse, Arthur George Joseph
  1895-1979 14
  Obituary 23
Whitehouse, Elizabeth S(cott) 1893-1968 35
Whitehouse, Jeanne
  See Peterson, Jeanne Whitehouse
Whitelaw, Nancy 1933- 166
  Earlier sketch in SATA 76
Whitesel, Cheryl Aylward 162
Whiting, Sue 1960- 205
Whiting, Susan Allana
  See Whiting, Sue
Whitinger, R. D.
  See Place, Marian T(empleton)
Whitley, David 1984- 225
Whitley, Mary Ann
  See Sebrey, Mary Ann
Whitley, Peggy 1938- 140
Whitlock, Pamela 1921(?)-1982
  Obituary 31
Whitlock, Ralph 1914-1995 35
Whitman, Alice
  See Marker, Sherry
Whitman, Candace 1958- 208
Whitman, Sylvia (Choate) 1961- 135
  Earlier sketch in SATA 85
Whitman, Walt 1819-1892 20
Whitman, Walter
  See Whitman, Walt
Whitmore, Arvella 1922- 125
Whitmore, Benette 1955- 203
Whitney, Alex(andra) 1922- 14

Whitney, David C(harles) 1921- 48
  Brief entry 29
Whitney, Kim Ablon 162
Whitney, Phyllis A. 1903-2008 30
  Obituary 189
  Earlier sketch in SATA 1
  See also CLR 59
Whitney, Phyllis Ayame
  See Whitney, Phyllis A.
Whitney, Sharon 1937- 63
Whitney, Thomas P. 1917-2007 25
  Obituary 189
Whitney, Thomas Porter
  See Whitney, Thomas P.
Whittington, Mary K(athrine) 1941- 75
Whitworth, John 1945- 123
Whybrow, Ian 202
  Earlier sketch in SATA 132
Whyte, Mal(colm Kenneth, Jr.) 1933- 62
Whyte, Mary 1953- 148
  Earlier sketch in SATA 94
Whyte, Ron 1942(?)-1989
  Obituary 63
Whytock, Cherry 177
Wiater, Stanley 1953- 84
Wibbelsman, Charles J(oseph) 1945- 59
Wibberley, Leonard 1915-1983 45
  Obituary 36
  Earlier sketch in SATA 2
  See also CLR 3
Wibberley, Leonard Patrick O'Connor
  See Wibberley, Leonard
Wiberg, Harald (Albin) 1908- 93
  Brief entry 40
Wick, Walter 1953- 148
Wickberg, Susan
  See Rottman, S.L.
Wickens, Elaine 86
Wicker, Ireene 1905(?)-1987
  Obituary 55
Wickstrom, Sylvie 1960- 169
Wickstrom, Thor 1960- 200
Widdemer, Mabel Cleland 1902-1964 5
Widener, Terry 1950- 209
  Earlier sketch in SATA 105
Widerberg, Siv 1931- 10
Wiebe, Rudy 1934- 156
Wiebe, Rudy Henry
  See Wiebe, Rudy
Wieler, Diana (Jean) 1961- 109
Wiener, Lori 1956- 84
Wier, Ester (Alberti) 1910-2000 3
Wiese, Kurt 1887-1974 36
  Obituary 24
  Earlier sketch in SATA 3
  See also CLR 86
Wiesel, Elie 1928- 56
Wiesel, Eliezer
  See Wiesel, Elie
Wiesner, David 1956- 181
  Earlier sketches in SATA 72, 117, 139
  See also CLR 84
Wiesner, Portia
  See Takakjian, Portia
Wiesner, William 1899-1984 5
Wiewandt, Thomas 1945- 231
Wiggers, Raymond 1952- 82
Wiggin, Eric E. 1939- 167
  Earlier sketch in SATA 88
Wiggin, Eric Ellsworth 1939-
  See Wiggin, Eric E.
Wiggin (Riggs), Kate Douglas (Smith)
  1856-1923
  See YABC 1
  See also CLR 52
Wiggins, VeraLee (Chesnut) 1928-1995 89
Wight, Eric 1974- 232
  Earlier sketch in SATA 218
Wight, James Alfred
  See Herriot, James
Wignell, Edel 1936- 69

Wijnberg, Ellen 85
Wijngaard, Juan 1951- 230
Wikland, Ilon 1930- 93
  Brief entry 32
Wikler, Madeline 1943- 114
Wilber, Donald N(ewton) 1907-1997 35
Wilbur, C. Keith 1923- 27
Wilbur, Frances 1921- 107
Wilbur, Helen L. 1948- 204
Wilbur, Richard 1921- 108
  Earlier sketch in SATA 9
Wilbur, Richard Purdy
  See Wilbur, Richard
Wilburn, Kathy 1948- 68
Wilcox, Charlotte 1948- 72
Wilcox, Leah 1975(?)- 207
Wilcox, R(uth) Turner 1888-1970 36
Wilcox, Roger
  See Collins, Paul
Wild, Jocelyn 1941- 46
Wild, Kate 1954- 192
Wild, Margaret 1948- 197
  Earlier sketch in SATA 151
Wild, Robin (Evans) 1936- 46
Wild, Robyn 1947- 117
Wilde, D. Gunther
  See Hurwood, Bernhardt J.
Wilde, Oscar 1854(?)-1900 24
  See also CLR 114
Wilde, Oscar Fingal O'Flahertie Willis
  See Wilde, Oscar
Wilder, Buck
  See Smith, Tim(othy R.)
Wilder, Laura Elizabeth Ingalls
  See Wilder, Laura Ingalls
Wilder, Laura Ingalls 1867-1957 100
  Earlier sketches in SATA 15, 29
  See also CLR 111
Wildish, Lee 231
Wildsmith, Brian 1930- 124
  Earlier sketches in SATA 16, 69
  See also CLR 52
  See also SAAS 5
Wiles, Deborah 171
Wilhelm, Doug 1952- 190
Wilhelm, Hans 1945- 196
  Autobiography Feature 196
  Earlier sketches in SATA 58, 135
  See also CLR 46
  See also SAAS 21
Wilkie, Katharine E(lliott) 1904-1980 31
Wilkin, Eloise 1904-1987 49
  Obituary 54
Wilkins, Ebony Joy 234
Wilkins, Frances 1923- 14
Wilkins, Kim 147
Wilkins, Marilyn (Ruth) 1926- 30
Wilkins, Marne
  See Wilkins, Marilyn (Ruth)
Wilkins, Mary Huiskamp 1926- 2
  See also CLR 42
Wilkins, Mary Huiskamp Calhoun
  See Wilkins, Mary Huiskamp
Wilkins, Rose 180
Wilkinson, (Thomas) Barry 1923- 50
  Brief entry 32
Wilkinson, Beth 1925- 80
Wilkinson, Brenda 1946- 91
  Earlier sketch in SATA 14
  See also CLR 20
Wilkinson, (John) Burke 1913-2000 4
Wilkinson, Carole 1950- 210
Wilkinson, Sylvia 1940- 56
  Brief entry 39
Wilkon, Jozef 1930- 133
  Earlier sketches in SATA 31, 71
Wilkowski, Sue 193
Wilks, Michael Thomas 1947- 44
  See Wilks, Mike
Wilks, Mike 224
  See Wilks, Michael Thomas

Will
  See Lipkind, William
Willard, Barbara (Mary) 1909-1994 .... *74*
  Earlier sketch in SATA *17*
  See also CLR *2*
  See also SAAS *5*
Willard, Elizabeth Kimmel
  See Kimmel, Elizabeth Cody
Willard, Mildred Wilds 1911-1978 .... *14*
Willard, Nancy 1936- *191*
  Brief entry *30*
  Earlier sketches in SATA *37, 71, 127*
  See also CLR *5*
Willcox, Isobel 1907-1996 .... *42*
Willems, Mo *228*
  Earlier sketches in SATA *154, 180*
  See also CLR *114*
Willett, Edward 1959- *115*
Willett, Edward C.
  See Willett, Edward
Willey, Bee *184*
Willey, Margaret 1950- *226*
  Earlier sketch in SATA *86*
Willey, Robert
  See Ley, Willy
Willhoite, Michael A. 1946- *71*
William, Kate
  See Armstrong, Jennifer
Williams, Alex 1969- *209*
Williams, Arlene *171*
Williams, Barbara 1925- *107*
  Earlier sketch in SATA *11*
  See also CLR *48*
  See also SAAS *16*
Williams, Barbara 1937- *62*
Williams, Beryl
  See Epstein, Beryl
Williams, Brian (Peter) 1943- *54*
Williams, Carol Lynch 1959- *212*
  Earlier sketch in SATA *110*
Williams, Charles
  See Collier, James Lincoln
Williams, Clyde C. 1881-1974 .... *8*
  Obituary *27*
Williams, Coe
  See Harrison, C(hester) William
Williams, Colleen Madonna Flood 1963- .. *156*
Williams, Cynthia G. 1958- *123*
Williams, Dar 1967- *168*
Williams, Donna Reilly 1945- *83*
Williams, Dorothy
  See Williams, Marcia
Williams, Dorothy Snowden
  See Williams, Dar
Williams, Eric (Ernest) 1911-1983 .... *14*
  Obituary *38*
Williams, Ferelith Eccles
  See Eccles Williams, Ferelith
Williams, Frances B.
  See Browin, Frances Williams
Williams, Garth (Montgomery) 1912-1996 .. *66*
  Obituary *90*
  Earlier sketch in SATA *18*
  See also CLR *57*
  See also SAAS *7*
Williams, Guy R(ichard) 1920- *11*
Williams, Hawley
  See Heyliger, William
Williams, Helen 1948- *77*
Williams, J. R.
  See Williams, Jeanne
Williams, J. Walker
  See Wodehouse, P. G.
Williams, Jay 1914-1978 .... *41*
  Obituary *24*
  Earlier sketch in SATA *3*
  See also CLR *8*
Williams, Jeanne 1930- *5*
Williams, Jenny 1939- *60*
Williams, Karen Lynn 1952- *224*
  Earlier sketches in SATA *66, 99*

Williams, Kathryn 1981- *222*
Williams, Katie 1978- *235*
Williams, Kit 1946(?)- *44*
  See also CLR *4*
Williams, L. E.
  See Williams, Laura E.
Williams, Laura E.
  See Williams, Laura Ellen
Williams, Laura Ellen *180*
Williams, Leslie 1941- *42*
Williams, Linda 1948- *59*
Williams, Louise Bonino 1904(?)-1984
  Obituary *39*
Williams, Lynn
  See Hale, Arlene
Williams, Maiya 1962- *230*
Williams, Marcia 1945- *159*
  Earlier sketches in SATA *71, 97*
Williams, Marcia Dorothy
  See Williams, Marcia
Williams, Margery
  See Bianco, Margery Williams
Williams, Mark
  See Arthur, Robert, (Jr.)
Williams, Mark London 1959- *140*
Williams, Maureen 1951- *12*
Williams, Michael
  See St. John, Wylly Folk
Williams, Patrick J.
  See Griffin, W. E. B.
Williams, Paulette Linda
  See Shange, Ntozake
Williams, Pete
  See Faulknor, Cliff(ord Vernon)
Williams, Richard Treat
  See Williams, Treat
Williams, S. P.
  See Hart, Virginia
Williams, Sam *177*
  Earlier sketch in SATA *124*
Williams, Selma R(uth) 1925- *14*
Williams, Sherley Anne 1944-1999 .... *78*
  Obituary *116*
Williams, Sheron 1955- *77*
Williams, Shirley
  See Williams, Sherley Anne
Williams, Slim
  See Williams, Clyde C.
Williams, Sophy 1965- *135*
Williams, Sue 1948-2007 .... *208*
Williams, Susan
  See Beckhorn, Susan Williams
Williams, Suzanne
  See Williams, Suzanne Morgan
Williams, Suzanne 1953- *202*
  Earlier sketch in SATA *71*
Williams, Suzanne M.
  See Williams, Suzanne Morgan
Williams, Suzanne Morgan 1949- *207*
Williams, Treat 1951- *234*
Williams, Ursula Moray
  See Moray Williams, Ursula
Williams, Vera B(aker) 1927- *102*
  Brief entry *33*
  Earlier sketch in SATA *53*
  See also CLR *9*
Williams-Andriani, Renee 1963- *98*
Williams-Ellis, (Mary) Amabel (Nassau
  Strachey) 1894-1984 .... *29*
  Obituary *41*
Williams-Garcia, Rita 1957- *160*
  Earlier sketch in SATA *98*
  See also CLR *36*
Williamson, Gwyneth 1965- *109*
Williamson, Henry (William) 1895-1977 ..... *37*
  Obituary *30*
Williamson, Joanne S(mall) 1926- *122*
  Earlier sketch in SATA *3*
Williamson, Kate T. 1979- *215*
Williamson, Melanie *196*

Willis, Charles
  See Clarke, Arthur C.
Willis, Connie 1945- *110*
  See also CLR *66*
Willis, Cynthia Chapman *215*
Willis, Jeanne 1959- *237*
  Earlier sketches in SATA *61, 123, 195*
Willis, Jeanne Mary
  See Willis, Jeanne
Willis, Meredith Sue 1946- *101*
Willis, Nancy Carol 1952- *139*
  Earlier sketch in SATA *93*
Willis, Paul J. 1955- *113*
Willms, Russ *95*
Willner-Pardo, Gina 1957- *235*
Willoughby, Lee Davis
  See Avallone, Michael (Angelo, Jr.)
  and Brandner, Gary (Phil)
  and Deming, Richard
  and DeAndrea, William L(ouis)
  and Laymon, Richard (Carl)
  and Streib, Dan(iel Thomas)
  and Toombs, John
  and Webb, Jean Francis (III)
Willson, Robina Beckles
  See Beckles Willson, Robina
Willson, Sarah
  See Albee, Sarah
Wilma, Dana
  See Faralla, Dana
Wilsdorf, Anne 1954- *191*
Wilson, Anne 1974- *224*
Wilson, April *80*
Wilson, Barbara Ker
  See Ker Wilson, Barbara
Wilson, Beth P(ierre) *8*
Wilson, Budge 1927- *55*
  Brief entry *51*
Wilson, Carletta 1951- *81*
Wilson, Carter 1941- *6*
Wilson, Charles Morrow 1905-1977 .... *30*
Wilson, Christopher B. 1910(?)-1985
  Obituary *46*
Wilson, Darryl B(abe) 1939- *90*
Wilson, Diane Lee *172*
Wilson, Dirk
  See Pohl, Frederik
Wilson, Dorothy Clarke 1904-2003 .... *16*
Wilson, Edward A(rthur) 1886-1970 .... *38*
Wilson, Ellen (Janet Cameron) (?)-1976 .... *9*
  Obituary *26*
Wilson, Eric (H.) 1940- *34*
  Brief entry *32*
Wilson, Erica *51*
Wilson, Forrest 1918- *27*
Wilson, Gahan 1930- *35*
  Brief entry *27*
Wilson, Gina 1943- *85*
  Brief entry *34*
  Earlier sketch in SATA *36*
Wilson, (Leslie) Granville 1912- *14*
Wilson, Hazel (Hutchins) 1898-1992 .... *3*
  Obituary *73*
Wilson, J(erry) M. 1964- *121*
Wilson, Jacqueline 1945- *199*
  Brief entry *52*
  Earlier sketches in SATA *61, 102, 153*
Wilson, John 1922- *22*
Wilson, John 1951- *227*
  Earlier sketch in SATA *182*
Wilson, John Alexander
  See Wilson, John
Wilson, Johnniece Marshall 1944- *75*
Wilson, Jonathan 1950- *181*
Wilson, Joyce M. *84*
  Earlier sketch in SATA *21*
  See also SAAS *24*
Wilson, Karma *221*
  Earlier sketch in SATA *174*
Wilson, Leslie 1952- *166*
Wilson, Linda Miller 1936- *116*

Wilson, Lionel 1924-2003 33
    Brief entry 31
    Obituary 144
Wilson, Marjorie
    See Wilson, Budge
Wilson, Martin 1973- 205
Wilson, Maurice (Charles John) 1914- 46
Wilson, Nancy Hope 1947- 138
    Earlier sketch in SATA *81*
Wilson, Nathan D.
    See Wilson, N.D.
Wilson, N.D. 1978- 194
Wilson, Nick
    See Ellis, Edward S.
Wilson, Phil 1948- 181
Wilson, Ron(ald William) 1941- 38
Wilson, Sarah 1934- 208
    Earlier sketches in SATA *50, 142*
Wilson, Tom 1931-2011 33
    Brief entry 30
Wilson, Troy 1970- 169
Wilson, Walt(er N.) 1939- 14
Wilson-Max, Ken 1965- 170
    Earlier sketch in SATA *93*
Wilton, Elizabeth 1937- 14
Wilton, Hal
    See Pepper, Frank S.
Wilwerding, Walter Joseph 1891-1966 9
Wimmer, Mike 1961- 194
    Earlier sketch in SATA *70*
Winborn, Marsha (Lynn) 1947- 75
Winch, John 1944- 165
    Earlier sketch in SATA *117*
Winchester, James H(ugh) 1917-1985 30
    Obituary 45
Winchester, Stanley
    See Youd, Samuel
Windawi, Thura al- 1983(?)- 165
Winders, Gertrude Hecker -1987 3
Windham, Basil
    See Wodehouse, P. G.
Windham, Kathryn T. 1918-2011 14
Windham, Kathryn Tucker
    See Windham, Kathryn T.
Windham, Sophie 184
Windling, Terri 1958- 233
    Earlier sketch in SATA *151*
Windrow, Martin
    See Windrow, Martin Clive
Windrow, Martin C.
    See Windrow, Martin Clive
Windrow, Martin Clive 1944- 68
Windsor, Claire
    See Hamerstrom, Frances
Windsor, Linda 1950- 124
Windsor, Patricia 1938- 78
    Earlier sketch in SATA *30*
    See also SAAS *19*
Wineman-Marcus, Irene 1952- 81
Winer, Yvonne 1934- 120
Winerip, Michael 175
Winfield, Arthur M.
    See Stratemeyer, Edward L.
Winfield, Edna
    See Stratemeyer, Edward L.
Winfield, Julia
    See Armstrong, Jennifer
Wing, Natasha 1960- 200
    Earlier sketch in SATA *82*
Wingerter, Linda S. 1973(?)- 207
Winget, Susan 211
Winick, Judd 1970- 124
Winks, Robin William 1930-2003 61
Winn, Alison
    See Wharmby, Margot
Winn, Chris 1952- 42
Winn, Janet Bruce 1928- 43
Winn, Marie 1936(?)- 38
Winnick, Karen B. 1946- 211
Winnick, Karen B(eth) B(inkoff) 1946- 51
Winn-Lederer, Ilene 198

Winslow, Barbara 1947- 91
Winstead, Rosie 180
Winston, Clara 1921-1983 54
    Obituary 39
Winston, Richard 1917-1979 54
Winston, Sherri 1964(?)- 201
Winter, Janet 1926- 126
Winter, Jeanette 1939- 184
    Earlier sketch in SATA *151*
Winter, Jonah 1962- 225
    Earlier sketch in SATA *179*
Winter, Milo (Kendall) 1888-1956 21
Winter, Paula Cecelia 1929- 48
Winter, R. R.
    See Winterbotham, R(ussell) R(obert)
Winter, Susan 182
Winterbotham, R(ussell) R(obert)
    1904-1971 10
Winterbotham, Russ
    See Winterbotham, R(ussell) R(obert)
Winterfeld, Henry 1901-1990 55
Winters, J. C.
    See Cross, Gilbert B.
Winters, Jon
    See Cross, Gilbert B.
Winters, Katherine
    See Winters, Kay
Winters, Kay 1936- 153
    Earlier sketch in SATA *103*
Winters, Nina 1944- 62
Winters, Paul A. 1965- 106
Winterson, Jeanette 1959- 190
Winterton, Gayle
    See Adams, William Taylor
Winthrop, Elizabeth 1948- 164
    Autobiography Feature 116
    Earlier sketches in SATA *8, 76*
    See also CLR *89*
Winton, Ian (Kenneth) 1960- 76
Winton, Tim 1960- 98
Wintz-Litty, Julie
    See Litty, Julie
Wirt, Ann
    See Benson, Mildred
Wirt, Mildred A.
    See Benson, Mildred
Wirtenberg, Patricia Z. 1932-2007 10
Wirtenberg, Patricia Zarrella
    See Wirtenberg, Patricia Z.
Wirth, Beverly 1938- 63
Wirths, Claudine (Turner) G(ibson)
    1926-2000 104
    Earlier sketch in SATA *64*
Wise, Bill 1958- 191
Wise, Lenny
    See Wise, Leonard
Wise, Leonard 1940- 167
Wise, Leonard A.
    See Wise, Leonard
Wise, Leonard Allan
    See Wise, Leonard
Wise, William 1923- 163
    Earlier sketch in SATA *4*
Wise, Winifred E. 2
Wiseman, Ann (Sayre) 1926- 31
Wiseman, B(ernard) 1922-1995 4
Wiseman, David 1916- 43
    Brief entry 40
Wiseman, Eva 1947- 210
Wishinsky, Frieda 1948- 166
    Earlier sketches in SATA *70, 112*
Wisler, G(ary) Clifton 1950- 103
    Brief entry 46
    Earlier sketch in SATA *58*
Wismer, Donald (Richard) 1946- 59
Wisner, Bill
    See Wisner, William L.
Wisner, William L. 1914(?)-1983 42
Wisnewski, Andrea 234
Wisnewski, David 1953-2002
    See Wisniewski, David

Wisniewski, David 1953-2002 95
    Obituary 139
    See also CLR *51*
Wister, Owen 1860-1938 62
Witham, (Phillip) Ross 1917- 37
Withers, Carl A. 1900-1970 14
Withers, Pam 1956- 182
Withrow, Sarah 1966- 199
    Earlier sketch in SATA *124*
Witt, Dick 1948- 80
Witt, Shirley Hill 1934- 17
Wittanen, Etolin 1907- 55
Wittels, Harriet Joan 1938- 31
Wittenstein, Vicki Oransky 1954- 228
Wittig, Susan
    See Albert, Susan Wittig
Wittlinger, Ellen 1948- 189
    Autobiography Feature 128
    Earlier sketches in SATA *83, 122*
Wittman, Sally (Anne Christensen) 1941- 30
Witty, Paul 1898-1976 50
    Obituary 30
Wodehouse, P. G. 1881-1975 22
Wodehouse, Pelham Grenville
    See Wodehouse, P. G.
Wodge, Dreary
    See Gorey, Edward (St. John)
Woelfle, Gretchen 1945- 145
Wohlberg, Meg 1905-1990 41
    Obituary 66
Wohlrabe, Raymond A. 1900-1977 4
Wohnoutka, Mike 230
    Earlier sketch in SATA *195*
Wojciechowska, Maia (Teresa) 1927-2002 ... 83
    Autobiography Feature 104
    Obituary 134
    Earlier sketches in SATA *1, 28*
    See also CLR *1*
    See also SAAS *1*
Wojciechowski, Susan 126
    Earlier sketch in SATA *78*
Wojnarowski, Adrian 1970- 190
Wojtowycz, David 1969- 236
Wojtusik, Elizabeth 208
Wolcott, Patty 1929- 14
Wold, Allen L. 1943- 64
Wold, Jo Anne 1938- 30
Woldin, Beth Weiner 1955- 34
Wolf, Allan 1963- 192
Wolf, Bernard 1930- 102
    Brief entry 37
Wolf, Erica (Van Varick) 1978- 156
Wolf, Gita 1956- 101
Wolf, J. M.
    See Wolf, Joan M.
Wolf, Janet 1957- 78
Wolf, Joan M. 1966- 193
Wolf, Sallie 1950- 205
    Earlier sketch in SATA *80*
Wolfe, Art 1952- 76
Wolfe, Burton H. 1932- 5
Wolfe, Frances 216
Wolfe, Gene 1931- 165
    Earlier sketch in SATA *118*
Wolfe, Gene Rodman
    See Wolfe, Gene
Wolfe, Gillian 199
Wolfe, Louis 1905-1985 8
    Obituary 133
Wolfe, Rinna (Evelyn) 1925- 38
Wolfenden, George
    See Beardmore, George
Wolfer, Dianne 1961- 167
    Autobiography Feature 117
    Earlier sketch in SATA *104*
Wolff, Alexander (Nikolaus) 1957- 137
    Earlier sketch in SATA *63*
Wolff, Ashley 1956- 203
    Earlier sketches in SATA *50, 81, 155*
Wolff, Diane 1945- 27

Wolff, Ferida 1946- *164*
Earlier sketch in SATA *79*
Wolff, Jason 1972- *213*
Wolff, Jennifer Ashley
See Wolff, Ashley
Wolff, Nancy *202*
Wolff, Robert Jay 1905-1977 .... *10*
Wolff, Sonia
See Levitin, Sonia
Wolff, Virginia Euwer 1937- *137*
Earlier sketch in SATA *78*
See also CLR *62*
Wolfhard, Steve *235*
Wolfman, Judy 1933- *138*
Wolfson, Evelyn 1937- *62*
Wolitzer, Hilma 1930- *31*
Wolkoff, Judie (Edwards) *93*
Brief entry *37*
Wolkstein, Diane 1942- *138*
Earlier sketches in SATA *7, 82*
Wollheim, Donald A(llen) 1914-1990
Obituary *69*
Wolny, P.
See Janeczko, Paul B(ryan)
Wolters, Richard A. 1920-1993 .... *35*
Wondriska, William 1931- *6*
Wong, Jade Snow 1922-2006 .... *112*
Obituary *175*
Wong, Janet S. 1962- *210*
Earlier sketches in SATA *98, 148*
See also CLR *94*
Wong, Marissa Lopez *226*
Wong, Nicole *214*
Woo, Howie 1974- *207*
Wood, Addie Robinson
See Wiggin, Eric E.
Wood, Anne (Savage) 1937- *64*
Wood, Audrey *198*
Brief entry *44*
Earlier sketches in SATA *50, 81, 139*
See also CLR *26*
Wood, Catherine
See Etchison, Birdie L(ee)
Wood, David 1944- *212*
Earlier sketch in SATA *87*
Wood, Don 1945- *50*
Brief entry *44*
See also CLR *26*
Wood, Douglas 1951- *234*
Earlier sketches in SATA *81, 132, 180*
Wood, Douglas Eric
See Wood, Douglas
Wood, Edgar A(llardyce) 1907-1998 .... *14*
Wood, Esther
See Brady, Esther Wood
Wood, Frances Elizabeth *34*
Wood, Frances M. 1951- *97*
Wood, Jacqueline
See Wood, Jakki
Wood, Jakki 1957- *211*
Wood, James Playsted 1905- *1*
Wood, Jenny 1955- *88*
Wood, John Norris 1930- *85*
Wood, June Rae 1946- *120*
Earlier sketch in SATA *79*
See also CLR *82*
Wood, Kerry
See Wood, Edgar A(llardyce)
Wood, Kim Marie *134*
Wood, Laura N.
See Roper, Laura (Newbold) Wood
Wood, Linda C(arol) 1945- *59*
Wood, Marcia 1956- *80*
Wood, Marcia Mae
See Wood, Marcia
Wood, Nancy
See Wood, Nancy C.
Wood, Nancy C. 1936- *178*
Earlier sketch in SATA *6*
Wood, Nuria
See Nobisso, Josephine

Wood, Owen 1929- *64*
Wood, Phyllis Anderson 1923- *33*
Brief entry *30*
Wood, Richard 1949- *110*
Wood, Tim(othy William Russell) 1946- *88*
Wood, Wallace 1927-1981
Obituary *33*
Woodard, Carol 1929- *14*
Woodburn, John Henry 1914- *11*
Woodbury, David Oakes 1896-1981 .... *62*
Woodford, Peggy 1937- *25*
Woodhouse, Barbara (Blackburn)
1910-1988 .... *63*
Woodhull, Ann Love *194*
Wooding, Chris 1977- *166*
Wooding, Sharon
See Wooding, Sharon L(ouise)
Wooding, Sharon L(ouise) 1943- *66*
Woodman, Allen 1954- *76*
Woodrich, Mary Neville 1915- *2*
Woodruff, Elvira 1951- *211*
Earlier sketches in SATA *70, 106, 162*
Woodruff, Joan Leslie 1953- *104*
Woodruff, Liza 1971(?)- *182*
Woodruff, Marian
See Goudge, Eileen
Woodruff, Noah 1977- *86*
Woods, George A(llan) 1926-1988 .... *30*
Obituary *57*
Woods, Geraldine 1948- *111*
Brief entry *42*
Earlier sketch in SATA *56*
Woods, Harold 1945- *56*
Brief entry *42*
Woods, Lawrence
See Lowndes, Robert A(ugustine) W(ard)
Woods, Margaret 1921- *2*
Woods, Nat
See Stratemeyer, Edward L.
Woods, Titania
See Weatherly, Lee
Woodson, Jack
See Woodson, John Waddie Jr.
Woodson, Jacqueline 1964- *189*
Earlier sketches in SATA *94, 139*
See also CLR *49*
Woodson, Jacqueline Amanda
See Woodson, Jacqueline
Woodson, John Waddie Jr. 1913- *10*
Woodtor, Dee
See Woodtor, Delores Parmer
Woodtor, Dee Parmer 1945(?)-2002
See Woodtor, Delores Parmer
Woodtor, Delores Parmer 1945-2002 .... *93*
Wood-Trost, Lucille
See Trost, Lucille W(ood)
Woodward, (Landon) Cleveland 1900-1986 . *10*
Obituary *48*
Woodworth, Chris 1957- *168*
Woodworth, Viki 1952- *127*
Woody, Regina Jones 1894-1983 .... *3*
Woodyadd, Charlotte
See Hough, Charlotte
Woog, Adam 1953- *125*
Earlier sketch in SATA *84*
Wooldridge, Connie Nordhielm 1950- *143*
Earlier sketch in SATA *92*
Wooldridge, Frosty 1947- *140*
Wooldridge, Rhoda 1906-1988 .... *22*
Wooley, Susan Frelick 1945- *113*
Woolf, Paula 1950- *104*
Woolfe, Angela 1976- *169*
Woolley, Catherine 1904-2005 .... *3*
Obituary *166*
Woolman, Steven 1969-2004 .... *163*
Earlier sketch in SATA *90*
Woolsey, Janette 1904-1989 .... *3*
Obituary *131*
Worcester, Donald E(mmet) 1915- *18*
Word, Reagan 1944- *103*

Work, Virginia 1946- *57*
Brief entry *45*
Worline, Bonnie Bess 1914- *14*
Wormell, Christopher 1955- *154*
Earlier sketch in SATA *103*
Wormell, Mary 1959- *96*
Wormser, Richard 1933- *106*
Autobiography Feature *118*
See also SAAS *26*
Wormser, Sophie 1897-1979 .... *22*
Worth, Richard
See Wiggin, Eric E.
Worth, Richard 1945- *59*
Brief entry *46*
Worth, Valerie 1933-1994 .... *81*
Earlier sketches in SATA *8, 70*
See also CLR *21*
Worthington, Leonie 1956- *200*
Wortis, Avi
See Avi
Wortis, Edward Irving
See Avi
Wosmek, Frances 1917- *29*
Woychuk, Denis 1953- *71*
Wrede, Patricia C(ollins) 1953- *146*
Earlier sketch in SATA *67*
Wriggins, Sally Hovey 1922- *17*
Wright, Alexandra 1979- *103*
Wright, Betty Ren 1927- *109*
Brief entry *48*
Earlier sketch in SATA *63*
Wright, Cliff 1963- *168*
Earlier sketch in SATA *76*
Wright, Courtni
See Wright, Courtni C(rump)
Wright, Courtni C(rump) 1950- *84*
Wright, Courtni Crump
See Wright, Courtni C(rump)
Wright, Dare 1914(?)-2001 .... *21*
Obituary *124*
Wright, David K. 1943- *112*
Earlier sketch in SATA *73*
Wright, Elinor
See Lyon, Elinor
Wright, Enid Meadowcroft (LaMonte)
1898-1966 .... *3*
Wright, Esmond 1915-2003 .... *10*
Wright, Frances Fitzpatrick 1897-1982 .... *10*
Wright, J. B.
See Barkan, Joanne
Wright, Johanna *220*
Wright, Judith 1915-2000 .... *14*
Obituary *121*
Wright, Judith Arundell
See Wright, Judith
Wright, Katrina
See Gater, Dilys
Wright, Kenneth
See del Rey, Lester
Wright, Kit 1944- *87*
Wright, Leslie B(ailey) 1959- *91*
Wright, Maureen 1961- *233*
Wright, Michael 1954- *198*
Wright, Nancy Means *38*
Wright, R(obert) H(amilton) 1906- *6*
Wright, Rachel *220*
Earlier sketch in SATA *134*
Wright, Simeon 1942- *232*
Wright, Susan Kimmel 1950- *97*
Wrightfrierson
See Wright-Frierson, Virginia (Marguerite)
Wright-Frierson, Virginia (Marguerite)
1949- *110*
Earlier sketch in SATA *58*
Wrightson, Alice Patricia
See Wrightson, Patricia
Wrightson, Patricia 1921-2010 .... *112*
Obituary *215*
Earlier sketches in SATA *8, 66*
See also CLR *154*
See also SAAS *4*

Wroble, Lisa A. 1963- *134*
Wrongo, I.B.
  See Katz, Alan
Wronker, Lili
  See Wronker, Lili Cassel
Wronker, Lili Cassel 1924- *10*
Wryde, Dogear
  See Gorey, Edward (St. John)
Wu, Donald *212*
Wu, Elizabeth
  See Wu, Liz
Wu, Liz *184*
Wu, Norbert 1961- *155*
  Earlier sketch in SATA *101*
Wulf, Linda Press *205*
Wulffson, Don 1943- *155*
  Earlier sketches in SATA *32, 88*
Wulffson, Don L.
  See Wulffson, Don
Wummer, Amy 1955- *201*
Wunderli, Stephen 1958- *79*
Wunsch, Josephine (McLean) 1914- *64*
Wunsch, Marjory 1942- *220*
  Earlier sketch in SATA *82*
Wuorio, Eva-Lis 1918- *34*
  Brief entry *28*
Wurts, Janny 1953- *98*
Wyatt, B. D.
  See Robinson, Spider
Wyatt, David 1968- *185*
Wyatt, Jane
  See Bradbury, Bianca (Ryley)
Wyatt, Melissa 1963- *177*
Wyatt, Valerie *209*
Wyeth, Betsy James 1921- *41*
Wyeth, N(ewell) C(onvers) 1882-1945 .... *17*
  See also CLR *106*
Wyler, Rose 1909-2000 .... *18*
  Obituary *121*
Wylie, Betty Jane *48*
Wylie, Laura
  See Matthews, Patricia
Wylie, Laurie
  See Matthews, Patricia
Wyllie, Stephen *86*
Wyman, Andrea *75*
Wyman, Carolyn 1956- *83*
Wymer, Norman (George) 1911- *25*
Wynard, Talbot
  See Hamilton, Charles (Harold St. John)
Wyndham, John
  See Harris, John (Wyndham Parkes Lucas)
  Beynon
Wyndham, Lee
  See Hyndman, Jane Andrews Lee
Wyndham, Robert
  See Hyndman, Robert Utley
Wynne, Patricia J. *210*
Wynne-Jones, Tim 1948- *186*
  Autobiography Feature *136*
  Earlier sketches in SATA *67, 96, 136*
  See also CLR *58*
Wynne-Jones, Timothy
  See Wynne-Jones, Tim
Wynter, Edward (John) 1914- *14*
Wynyard, Talbot
  See Hamilton, Charles (Harold St. John)
Wyshynski, Sue *233*
Wyss, Johann David Von 1743-1818 .... *29*
  Brief entry *27*
  See also CLR *92*
Wyss, Thelma Hatch 1934- *202*
  Earlier sketches in SATA *10, 140*

X

Xavier, Father
  See Hurwood, Bernhardt J.
Xuan, YongSheng 1952- *226*
  Autobiography Feature *226*
  Earlier sketch in SATA *116*

Y

Yaccarino, Dan *192*
  Earlier sketch in SATA *141*
Yadin, (Rav-Aloof) Yigael 1917-1984 .... *55*
Yaffe, Alan
  See Yorinks, Arthur
Yagher, Kevin 1962- *143*
Yakovetic, (Joseph Sandy) 1952- *59*
Yakovetic, Joe
  See Yakovetic, (Joseph Sandy)
Yamada, Utako 1963- *188*
Yamaguchi, Marianne (Illenberger) 1936- *7*
Yamaka, Sara 1978- *92*
Yamanaka, Lois-Ann 1961- *166*
Yamasaki, Katie *206*
Yancey, Diane 1951- *138*
  Earlier sketch in SATA *81*
Yancey, Richard
  See Yancey, Rick
Yancey, Rick *193*
Yang, Belle 1960- *170*
Yang, James 1960- *190*
Yang, Jay 1941- *12*
Yang, Mingyi 1943- *72*
Yanok, Johnny *236*
Yarbrough, Camille 1938- *79*
  See also CLR *29*
Yarbrough, Ira 1910(?)-1983
  Obituary *35*
Yaroslava
  See Mills, Yaroslava Surmach
Yarrow, Peter 1938- *195*
Yashima, Taro
  See Iwamatsu, Jun Atsushi
Yates, Elizabeth 1905-2001 .... *68*
  Obituary *128*
  Earlier sketch in SATA *4*
  See also SAAS *6*
Yates, Janelle K(aye) 1957- *77*
Yates, John 1939- *74*
Yates, Kelly 1971- *208*
Yates, Louise 1983(?)- *218*
Yates, Philip 1956- *212*
  Earlier sketches in SATA *92, 149*
Yates, Raymond F(rancis) 1895-1966 .... *31*
Yaukey, Grace S(ydenstricker) 1899-1994 ... *80*
  Earlier sketch in SATA *5*
Yayo 1961- *226*
Yazzie, Johnson 1946- *205*
Ye, Ting-xing 1952- *106*
Yeahpau, Thomas M. 1975- *187*
Yeakley, Marjory Hall 1908- *21*
Yeates, Thomas 1955- *230*
Yeatman, Linda 1938- *42*
Yeatts, Tabatha 1970- *215*
Yee, Brenda Shannon *133*
Yee, Lisa 1959- *218*
  Earlier sketch in SATA *160*
Yee, Paul 1956- *211*
  Earlier sketches in SATA *67, 96, 143*
  See also CLR *44*
Yee, Tammy *206*
Yee, Wong Herbert 1953- *172*
  Earlier sketches in SATA *78, 115*
Yee, Ying S.
  See Lee, Y.S.
Yeh, Chun-Chan 1914- *79*
Ye Junjian
  See Yeh, Chun-Chan

Yelchin, Eugene 1956- *232*
  Earlier sketch in SATA *196*
Yenawine, Philip 1942- *85*
Yensid, Retlaw
  See Disney, Walt(er Elias)
Yeo, Wilma (Lethem) 1918-1994 .... *81*
  Earlier sketch in SATA *24*
Yeoman, John 1934- *80*
  Earlier sketch in SATA *28*
  See also CLR *46*
Yep, Kathleen S. *203*
Yep, Laurence 1948- *213*
  Earlier sketches in SATA *7, 69, 123, 176*
  See also CLR *132*
Yep, Laurence Michael
  See Yep, Laurence
Yepsen, Roger B(ennet), Jr. 1947- *59*
Yerian, Cameron John *21*
Yerian, Margaret A. *21*
Yerxa, Leo 1947- *181*
Yetska
  See Ironside, Jetske
Yezerski, Thomas F. 1969- *190*
Yin *194*
Ylvisaker, Anne 1965(?)- *172*
Yoder, Carolyn P. 1953- *149*
Yoder, Carolyn Patricia
  See Yoder, Carolyn P.
Yoder, Dorothy Meenen 1921- *96*
Yoder, Dot
  See Yoder, Dorothy Meenen
Yoder, Walter D. 1933- *88*
Yohalem, Eve *219*
Yolen, Jane 1939- *230*
  Autobiography Feature *111*
  Earlier sketches in SATA *4, 40, 75, 112, 158,
  194*
  See also CLR *149*
  See also SAAS *1*
Yolen, Jane Hyatt
  See Yolen, Jane
Yonezu, Yusuke *196*
Yonge, Charlotte 1823-1901 .... *17*
Yonge, Charlotte Mary
  See Yonge, Charlotte
Yoo, Paula 1969(?)- *174*
Yoo, Taeeun *191*
Yoon, Salina 1972- *204*
Yorinks, Adrienne 1956- *171*
Yorinks, Arthur 1953- *200*
  Earlier sketches in SATA *33, 49, 85, 144*
  See also CLR *20*
York, Alison
  See Nicole, Christopher
York, Andrew
  See Nicole, Christopher
York, Carol Beach 1928- *77*
  Earlier sketch in SATA *6*
York, Rebecca
  See Buckholtz, Eileen (Garber)
  and Glick, Ruth
York, Simon
  See Heinlein, Robert A.
Yoshida, Toshi 1911- *77*
Yoshikawa, Sachiko *181*
Yost, Edna 1889-1971
  Obituary *26*
Youd, C. S.
  See Youd, Samuel
Youd, Samuel 1922- *135*
  Brief entry *30*
  Earlier sketch in SATA *47*
  See also CLR *2*
  See also SAAS *6*
Youme
  See Landowne, Youme
Young, Amy L. *185*
Young, Anne Mortimer
  See Mortimer, Anne

Young, Bob
  See Young, Robert W(illiam)
  and Young, James Robert
Young, Carol 1945- *102*
Young, Catherine
  See Olds, Helen Diehl
Young, Clarence
  See Garis, Howard R.
  and Stratemeyer, Edward L.
Young, Collier
  See Bloch, Robert (Albert)
Young, Dan 1952- *126*
Young, Dianne 1959- *88*
Young, Dorothea Bennett 1924- *31*
Young, Ed 1931- *211*
  Earlier sketches in SATA *10, 74, 122, 173*
  See also CLR *27*
Young, Ed Tse-chun
  See Young, Ed
Young, Edward
  See Reinfeld, Fred
Young, E.L. 1973- *219*
Young, Elaine L.
  See Schulte, Elaine L(ouise)
Young, Emma L.
  See Young, E.L.
Young, James
  See Graham, Ian
Young, Jan
  See Young, Janet Randall
Young, Janet 1957- *188*
Young, Janet Randall 1919-1994 .... *3*
Young, Janet Ruth
  See Young, Janet
Young, Jeff C. 1948- *132*
Young, John
  See Macintosh, Brownie
Young, Judy 1956- *207*
  Earlier sketch in SATA *155*
Young, Judy (Elaine) Dockrey 1949- *72*
Young, Karen Romano 1959- *237*
  Earlier sketches in SATA *116, 168*
Young, Ken 1956- *86*
Young, Lois Horton 1911-1981 .... *26*
Young, Louisa *161*
Young, Louise B. 1919- *64*
Young, Margaret B. 1922-2009 .... *2*
Young, Margaret Buckner
  See Young, Margaret B.
Young, Mary 1940- *89*
Young, Miriam 1913-1974 .... *7*
Young, Ned *233*
Young, Noela 1930- *89*
Young, (Rodney Lee) Patrick (Jr.) 1937- *22*
Young, Percy M(arshall) 1912-2004 .... *31*
  Obituary *154*
Young, Richard Alan 1946- *72*
Young, Robert W(illiam) 1916-1969 .... *3*
Young, Ross B. 1955- *150*
Young, Ruth 1946- *67*
Young, Sara
  See Pennypacker, Sara
Young, Scott A. 1918-2005 .... *5*
Young, Scott Alexander
  See Young, Scott A.
Young, Selina 1971-2006 .... *201*
Young, Vivien
  See Gater, Dilys
Younger, Barbara 1954- *108*
Youngs, Betty 1934-1985 .... *53*
  Obituary *42*
Younkin, Paula 1942- *77*
Yount, Lisa (Ann) 1944- *124*
  Earlier sketch in SATA *74*
Yourgrau, Barry *179*
Yuditskaya, Tatyana 1964- *75*
Yue, Stephanie 1984- *231*
Yum, Hyewon *211*
Yumoto, Kazumi 1959- *153*

Z

Zach, Cheryl (Byrd) 1947- *98*
  Brief entry *51*
  Earlier sketch in SATA *58*
  See also SAAS *24*
Zacharias, Gary L. 1946- *153*
Zadoff, Allen 1967- *224*
Zaffo, George J. (?)-1984 .... *42*
Zagarenski, Pamela 1969(?)- *183*
Zagwyn, Deborah Turney 1953- *138*
  Earlier sketch in SATA *78*
Zahares, Wade *193*
Zahedi, Morteza 1978- *233*
Zahidi, Murtiza
  See Zahedi, Morteza
Zahler, Diane *228*
Zahn, Timothy 1951- *156*
  Earlier sketch in SATA *91*
Zaid, Barry 1938- *51*
Zaidenberg, Arthur 1908(?)-1990 .... *34*
  Obituary *66*
Zakanitch, Robert Rahway 1935- *231*
Zakanitch, Robert S.
  See Zakanitch, Robert Rahway
Zalben, Jane Breskin 1950- *170*
  Earlier sketches in SATA *7, 79, 120*
  See also CLR *84*
Zallinger, Jean (Day) 1918- *115*
  Earlier sketches in SATA *14, 80*
Zallinger, Peter Franz 1943- *49*
Zambreno, Mary Frances 1954- *140*
  Earlier sketch in SATA *75*
Zanderbergen, George
  See May, Julian
Zappa, Ahmet 1974- *180*
Zappa, Ahmet Emuukha Rodan
  See Zappa, Ahmet
Zappitello, Beth *237*
Zappler, Lisbeth 1930- *10*
Zarchy, Harry 1912-1987 .... *34*
Zarin, Cynthia 1959- *192*
  Earlier sketch in SATA *108*
Zaring, Jane (Thomas) 1936- *40*
Zarins, Joyce Audy
  See dos Santos, Joyce Audy
Zaslavsky, Claudia 1917- *36*
Zaugg, Sandra L. 1938- *118*
Zaugg, Sandy
  See Zaugg, Sandra L.
Zaunders, Bo 1939- *137*
Zawadzki, Marek 1958- *97*
Zebra, A.
  See Scoltock, Jack
Zebrowski, George 1945- *67*
Zebrowski, George T.
  See Zebrowski, George
Zecca, Katherine *207*
Zeck, Gerald Anthony 1939- *40*
Zeck, Gerry
  See Zeck, Gerald Anthony
Zed, Dr.
  See Penrose, Gordon
Zei, Alki 1925- *24*
  See also CLR *6*
Zeier, Joan T(heresa) 1931- *81*
Zeinert, Karen 1942-2002 .... *137*
  Earlier sketch in SATA *79*
Zeises, Lara M. 1976- *184*
  Earlier sketch in SATA *145*
Zelazny, Roger 1937-1995 .... *57*
  Brief entry *39*
Zelazny, Roger Joseph
  See Zelazny, Roger
Zeldis, Malcah 1931- *146*
  Earlier sketch in SATA *86*
Zelinsky, Paul O. 1953- *154*
  Brief entry *33*
  Earlier sketches in SATA *49, 102*
  See also CLR *55*

Zellan, Audrey Penn
  See Penn, Audrey
Zemach, Harve
  See Fischtrom, Harvey
Zemach, Kaethe 1958- *149*
  Brief entry *39*
  Earlier sketch in SATA *49*
Zemach, Margot 1931-1989 .... *70*
  Obituary *59*
  Earlier sketch in SATA *21*
Zemach-Bersin, Kaethe
  See Zemach, Kaethe
Zeman, Ludmila 1947- *153*
Zepeda, Gwendolyn 1971- *206*
Zephaniah, Benjamin 1958- *189*
  Earlier sketches in SATA *86, 140*
Zephaniah, Benjamin Obadiah Iqbal
  See Zephaniah, Benjamin
Zephaniah, Benjamin Pbadiah Iqubal
  See Zephaniah, Benjamin
Zerman, Melvyn Bernard 1930-2010 .... *46*
Zettner, Pat 1940- *70*
Zevin, Gabrielle 1977- *176*
Zhang, Christopher Zhong-Yuan 1954- *91*
Zhang, Song Nan 1942- *170*
  Earlier sketch in SATA *85*
Ziefert, Harriet 1941- *205*
  Earlier sketches in SATA *101, 154*
Ziegler, Jack (Denmore) 1942- *60*
Ziemienski, Dennis (Theodore) 1947- *10*
Ziliox, Marc
  See Fichter, George S.
Zillah
  See Macdonald, Zillah K(atherine)
Zim, Herbert S(pencer) 1909-1994 .... *30*
  Obituary *85*
  Earlier sketch in SATA *1*
  See also CLR *2*
  See also SAAS *2*
Zim, Sonia Bleeker 1909-1971 .... *2*
  Obituary *26*
Zima, Gordon 1920- *90*
Zimelman, Nathan 1921- *65*
  Brief entry *37*
Zimmer, Dirk 1943- *147*
  Earlier sketch in SATA *65*
Zimmer, Tracie Vaughn *169*
Zimmerman, Andrea 1950- *192*
  Earlier sketch in SATA *123*
Zimmerman, Andrea Griffing
  See Zimmerman, Andrea
Zimmerman, H. Werner 1951- *101*
Zimmerman, Heinz Werner
  See Zimmerman, H. Werner
Zimmerman, Naoma 1914-2004 .... *10*
Zimmermann, Arnold E. 1909- *58*
Zimmermann, Karl 1943- *211*
Zimmermann, Karl R.
  See Zimmermann, Karl
Zimmett, Debbie
  See Becker, Deborah Zimmett
Zimmy
  See Stratemeyer, Edward L.
Zimnik, Reiner 1930- *36*
  See also CLR *3*
Zindel, Bonnie 1943- *34*
Zindel, Lizabeth *187*
Zindel, Paul 1936-2003 .... *102*
  Obituary *142*
  Earlier sketches in SATA *16, 58*
  See also CLR *85*
Ziner, Feenie
  See Ziner, Florence
Ziner, Florence 1921- *5*
Zingara, Professor
  See Leeming, Joseph
Zinger, Yitskhok
  See Singer, Isaac Bashevis
Zink, Michelle 1969- *220*
Zion, Eugene 1913-1975 .... *18*

Zion, Gene
  See Zion, Eugene
Zobel, Allia
  See Zobel Nolan, Allia
Zobel Nolan, Allia *218*
Zoehfeld, Kathleen Weidner 1954- *193*
Zohorsky, Janet R. 1958- *148*
Zolkower, Edie Stoltz *171*
Zolkowski, Cathy (A.) 1969- *121*
Zollars, Jaime *191*
Zolotow, Charlotte 1915- *138*
  Earlier sketches in SATA *1, 35, 78*
  See also CLR *77*
Zolotow, Charlotte Gertrude Shapiro
  See Zolotow, Charlotte
Zolotow, Ellen
  See Dragonwagon, Crescent
Zonderman, Jon 1957- *92*

Zonia, Dhimitri 1921- *20*
Zonta, Pat 1951- *143*
Zubrowski, Bernard 1939- *90*
  Earlier sketch in SATA *35*
Zubrowski, Bernie
  See Zubrowski, Bernard
Zucker, Jonny *228*
Zucker, Miriam S.
  See Reichert, Miriam Zucker
Zuckerman, Amy *217*
Zuckerman, Andrew 1977- *224*
Zuckerman, Linda *190*
Zudeck, Darryl 1961- *61*
Zug, Mark *204*
Zulkey, Claire 1979- *225*
Zupa, G. Anthony
  See Zeck, Gerald Anthony

Zupancic, Lilijana Praprotnik
  See Prap, Lila
Zurbo, Matt(hew) 1967- *98*
Zurhorst, Charles (Stewart, Jr.) 1913-1989 .. *12*
Zurlo, Tony 1941- *145*
Zuromskis, Diane
  See Stanley, Diane
Zuromskis, Diane Stanley
  See Stanley, Diane
Zusak, Markus 1975- *149*
Zwahlen, Diana 1947- *88*
Zweifel, Frances W. 1931- *14*
Zwerger, Lisbeth 1954- *194*
  Earlier sketches in SATA *66, 130*
  See also CLR *46*
  See also SAAS *13*
Zwinger, Ann (H.) 1925- *46*
Zymet, Cathy Alter 1965- *121*